THE MACARTHUR NEW TESTAMENT COMMENTARY

INDEX

John MacArthur

MOODY PUBLISHERS/CHICAGO

Library of Congress Cataloging-in-Publication Data

Names: MacArthur, John, 1939- author.
Title: The MacArthur New Testament commentary. Index / John MacArthur.
Description: Chicago : Moody Publishers, 2016.
Identifiers: LCCN 2016022331 (print) | LCCN 2016023434 (ebook) | ISBN 9780802414618 | ISBN 9780802494535 ()
Subjects: LCSH: Bible--Commentaries--Indexes. | MacArthur, John, 1939- MacArthur New Testament commentary--Indexes.
Classification: LCC Z7772.L1 M28 2016 BS491.3 (print) | LCC Z7772.L1 (ebook) | DDC 225.7--dc23
LC record available at https://lccn.loc.gov/2016022331

Moody Publishers
820 N. LaSalle Boulevard
Chicago, IL 60610

1 3 5 7 9 10 8 6 4 2

Printed in the United States of America

Contents

HOW TO READ THE SCRIPTURE INDEX

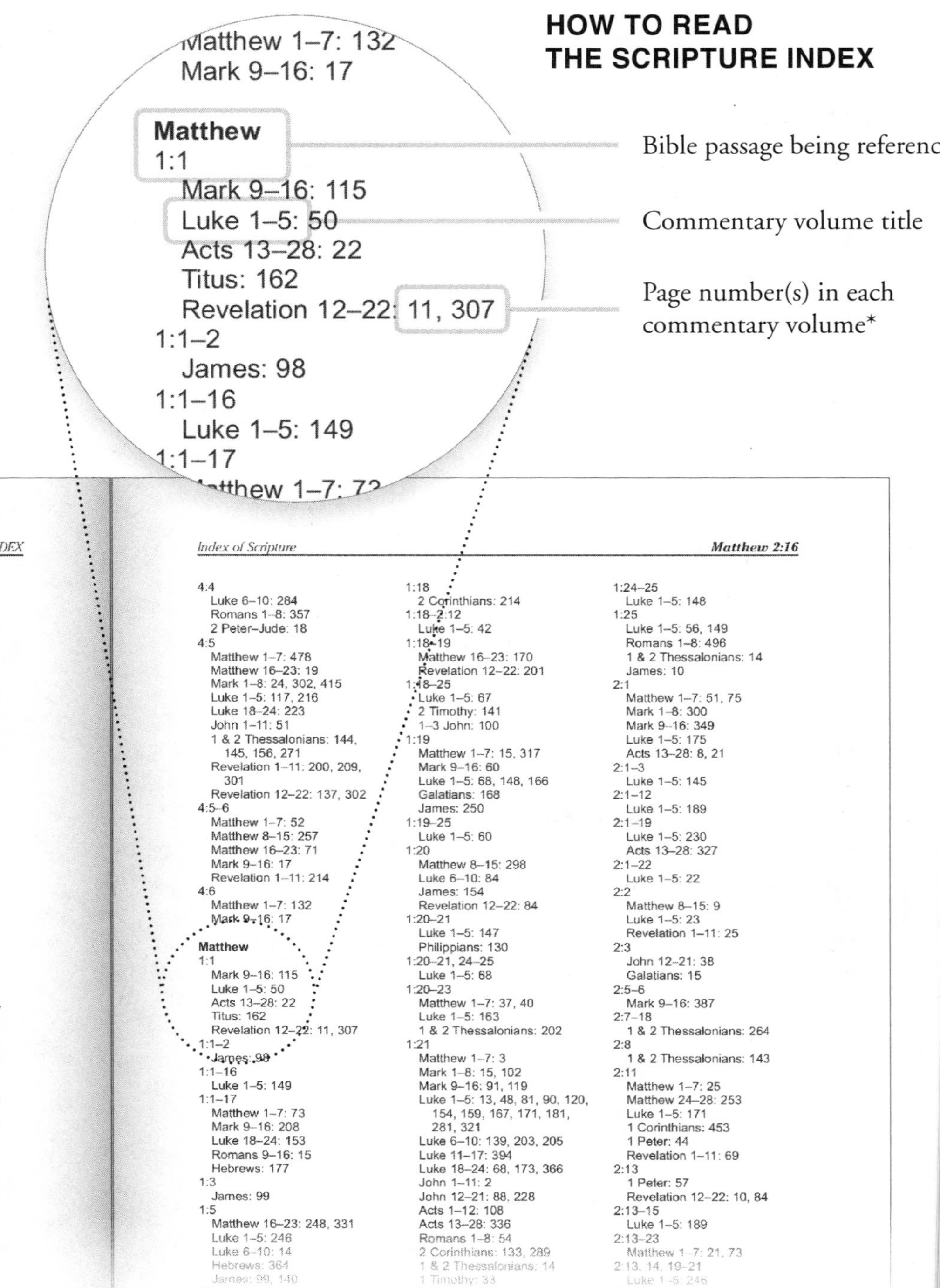

*Over the lifetime of each commentary volume there have been multiple reprints that may affect page number accuracy. Page numbers in this index reflect the most recent printings.

Preface

It continues to be a rewarding, divine communion for me to preach expositionally through the New Testament. My goal is always to have deep fellowship with the Lord in the understanding of His Word and out of that experience to explain to His people what a passage means. In the words of Nehemiah 8:8, I strive "to give the sense" of it so they may truly hear God speak and, in so doing, may respond to Him.

Obviously, God's people need to understand Him, which demands knowing His Word of Truth (2 Tim. 2:15) and allowing that Word to dwell in them richly (Col. 3:16). The dominant thrust of my ministry, therefore, is to help make God's living Word alive to His people. It is a refreshing adventure.

You are now holding in your hands a complete, combined index of all thirty–three volumes of the New Testament commentary series. It synthesizes the existing indexes in the back of each volume, allowing you to trace across the entire set any mention of a particular Scripture passage, Greek or Hebrew word, or subject. From there you

can corroborate your findings to fit your needs. Please note that because some commentaries were printed decades ago, and have gone through numerous reprints since then, page numbers in the index may not match exactly to your copy. We have made every effort to make this index as up–to–date as possible.

My prayer is that the users of this index are strengthened by God in their study. May the Holy Spirit speak clearly to you in His Word, which holds the power of eternal life, and may His revelation penetrate your mind and heart to bring about greater obedience and faithfulness—to the glory of our great God.

Indexes

Many of the following terms have been grouped together by lexical form even though another form of the same word may appear in the text.

Index of Greek Words and Phrases

abba
Luke 11–17: 12
abussos
Luke 6–10: 222
1 Peter: 210
Revelation 1–11: 257
Revelation 12–22: 234
adelphos
Luke 6–10: 202
1 & 2 Thessalonians: 212
adēmoneō
Mark 9–16: 299
Philippians: 205
adiakritos
James: 179
adialeiptōs
2 Timothy: 6
adikeō
2 Corinthians: 237
2 Peter–Jude: 99
adikia
Romans 1–8: 66
adō
Ephesians: 259
adokimos
Romans 1–8: 108
2 Timothy: 121
Titus: 68
adolos
1 Peter: 99
aetos
Revelation 12–22: 32
agalliaō
Matthew 1–7: 231
Luke 1–5: 79
Acts 1–12: 89
1 Peter: 41, 252
agalliasis
Acts 1–12: 89
agamos
1 Corinthians: 162, 184
aganakteō
Luke 11–17: 202
2 Corinthians: 267
aganaktēsis
2 Corinthians: 267
agapaō
Matthew 16–23: 339
Mark 9–16: 201
Luke 6–10: 353
John 1–11: 188
John 12–21: 172, 227, 401
1 Corinthians: 115
Colossians and Philemon: 168–169
1 & 2 Thessalonians: 118
1 Peter: 47, 90, 193
2 Peter–Jude: 152

1–3 John: 148, 217
agapē
Matthew 1–7: 345, 347
Matthew 16–23: 336
John 12–21: 286
Romans 9–16: 359
1 Corinthians: 329–30, 332, 334, 337–38, 488
2 Corinthians: 58, 229, 286
Galatians: 165
Ephesians: 14, 108, 109, 127, 197, 209
Philippians: 41, 42, 107, 108
Colossians and Philemon: 213
1 & 2 Thessalonians: 17, 90, 118, 173
1 Timothy: 18, 263
2 Timothy: 18, 94, 130
Titus: 152
James: 192
1 Peter: 241
2 Peter–Jude: 42
1–3 John: 115, 165
agapētos
Matthew 1–7: 81
Mark 1–8: 37
Colossians and Philemon: 211, 220
1 Peter: 249
1–3 John: 165, 244
agathoergeō
1 Timothy: 283
agathos
Luke 18–24: 36
1 Corinthians: 83
Galatians: 168, 182, 191
Ephesians: 186
1 Timothy: 18, 82, 116
agathōsunē
Ephesians: 209
agchō
2 Peter–Jude: 155
agnoeō
1 Corinthians: 282
agnōsia
1 Peter: 150
agō
Romans 1–8: 430
agōn
Colossians and Philemon: 84
1 & 2 Thessalonians: 36
1 Timothy: 265
2 Timothy: 192
agōnia
Luke 18–24: 306
1 Peter: 150
agōnizomai
Matthew 1–7: 455
Matthew 8–15: 474
Luke 11–17: 219
Romans 9–16: 351
Colossians and Philemon: 81–82, 196–97
1 Timothy: 166, 265
2 Timothy: 192
agora
Matthew 8–15: 260
Luke 6–10: 164
Acts 13–28: 103
Ephesians: 18
1 Timothy: 221
agorazō
Luke 1–5: 96
Ephesians: 18
2 Peter–Jude: 73
Revelation 1–11: 172
agoreuō
Galatians: 125
aichmalōtizō
2 Corinthians: 330
aichmalotōs
Colossians and Philemon: 194
aidōs
1 Timothy: 81
aiōn
Matthew 24–28: 126
John 12–21: 253
2 Corinthians: 132
Galatians: 6
1 & 2 Thessalonians: 244
aiōnos
1 Corinthians: 60
airō
Matthew 16–23: 49
1–3 John: 124
aischrokerdēs
Titus: 39
aischros
Titus: 39
aischunē
2 Corinthians: 126
aischunō
1 Peter: 255
aisthēsis
Philippians: 46
aiteō
Luke 18–24: 294
James: 190
akantha
Luke 6–10: 189
akarpos
2 Peter–Jude: 43
akatastasia
James: 175, 176
akatastatos
James: 158
akatharsia
Romans 1–8: 102
2 Corinthians: 436
Galatians: 161
Ephesians: 200
Colossians and Philemon: 138
1 & 2 Thessalonians: 37, 38
akeraios
Philippians: 182
akoloutheō
Matthew 1–7: 116
Mark 1–8: 428
Luke 1–5: 331
Luke 6–10: 315
John 1–11: 57, 335
akouō
Romans 1–8: 138
Philippians: 158
1–3 John: 16

akrasia
Matthew 16–23: 386
akratēs
2 Timothy: 115
akratesteron
Ephesians: 236
akribōs
Ephesians: 219
1 & 2 Thessalonians: 143
akroatēs
Romans 1–8: 138
James: 80
akrogōniaios
1 Peter: 121
alalos
Mark 1–8: 380
alazōn
2 Timothy: 112
alazoneia
James: 234
aleiphō
James: 277
alētheia
2 Corinthians: 477
Ephesians: 349
1–3 John: 215
alētheuō
Ephesians: 159
alēthinos
John 1–11: 32, 244
John 12–21: 144
1–3 John: 210
Revelation 1–11: 119
alēthōs
Matthew 8–15: 159
Luke 6–10: 60
John 1–11: 72
Romans 9–16: 24
alla
1 Corinthians: 143
2 Corinthians: 126
Philippians: 126
1 & 2 Thessalonians: 35
2 Peter–Jude: 65
allēgoreō
Galatians: 122, 125
allēlouia
Revelation 12–22: 196
allos
Luke 18–24: 84
John 12–21: 112, 113
Galatians: 14, 125
Revelation 1–11: 217, 240, 278
Revelation 12–22: 58, 178, 180
allotriepiskopos
1 Peter: 254–55
alogos
2 Peter–Jude: 175
amachos
1 Timothy: 111
amarantos
1 Peter: 35
ameleō
1 Timothy: 178
amemptos
Philippians: 181, 182
amemptōs
1 & 2 Thessalonians: 207
amēn
Matthew 1–7: 261
Matthew 8–15: 104, 255
Luke 18–24: 244
John 1–11: 102, 191, 196, 236, 243, 359–60, 381–82, 425
ametakinētos
1 Corinthians: 447
amiantos
James: 89
1 Peter: 35
amōmos
Ephesians: 14
Philippians: 182
Colossians and Philemon: 65
2 Peter–Jude: 212
amphiblēstron
Matthew 1–7: 115
Matthew 8–15: 394
anaballō
Acts 13–28: 309
anablepsis
Mark 1–8: 408
anachōreō
Matthew 1–7: 105
anachusis
1 Peter: 229
anadeiknumi
Luke 6–10: 325
anagennaō
1 Peter: 91
anaginōskō
2 Corinthians: 36
anakainoō
Colossians and Philemon: 150
anakrazō
Mark 1–8: 59
anakrinō
Acts 13–28: 121
1 Corinthians: 100, 201
analambanō
Luke 6–10: 310
analēmpsis
Luke 6–10: 310
analogia
1 Corinthians: 303
analuō
Philippians: 78
analusis
Philippians: 79
2 Timothy: 190
ananeoō
Ephesians: 177
ananēphō
2 Timothy: 102
anankē
1 Corinthians: 179
anapauō
Matthew 8–15: 275
1 Corinthians: 483
2 Corinthians: 269
Colossians and Philemon: 215
1 Peter: 253

anapherō
1 Peter: 114, 170
anaskeuazō
Acts 13–28: 72
anastasis
Acts 13–28: 131
Revelation 12–22: 238
anastrephō
1 Timothy: 135
anathema
1 Corinthians: 284, 488
Galatians: 17
anathematizō
Mark 9–16: 338
anatithēmi
Galatians: 35
anatolē
Luke 1–5: 122
anatrephō
2 Timothy: 81
anazēteō
Acts 1–12: 314
anazōpureō
2 Timothy: 15
andrapodon
James: 12
anechō
2 Timothy: 181
anegklētos
Colossians and Philemon: 65
1 Timothy: 129
aneklalētō
1 Peter: 47
anēkō
Ephesians: 282
anendektos
Luke 11–17: 377
anengklētos
1 Timothy: 103
Titus: 22
anepilēmptos
1 Timothy: 103
Titus: 23
anepsios
Luke 6–10: 202
anesis
1 & 2 Thessalonians: 246
anexomai
Colossians and Philemon: 156
angelos
2 Corinthians: 401
Revelation 1–11: 47
anistēmi
Luke 1–5: 331
Galatians: 49
anochē
Romans 1–8: 119
anoētos
Galatians: 63
Titus: 147
anoia
Luke 6–10: 10
anomia
Matthew 1–7: 391
Luke 11–17: 38
2 Corinthians: 248
1 & 2 Thessalonians: 272
1 Timothy: 21
anosios
2 Timothy: 114
anōthen
John 1–11: 130
antapodidōmi
1 & 2 Thessalonians: 83, 241
antechō
Titus: 45
anthistēmi
Matthew 1–7: 332
James: 204
anthrōpinēs hēmeras
1 Corinthians: 100
anthrōpinos
1 Corinthians: 228
anthrōpos
John 1–11: 31
Titus: 151
1 Peter: 180
anti
Matthew 16–23: 245, 246
1 & 2 Thessalonians: 264
1–3 John: 94
antichristos
1 & 2 Thessalonians: 264
1–3 John: 94
antidikos
1 Peter: 281
antilegō
Luke 1–5: 184
Acts 13–28: 36
Titus: 100
antilēmpsis
1 Corinthians: 324
antilogia
Titus: 101
antilutron
Matthew 16–23: 245
antitassō
Acts 13–28: 149
antithesis
1 Timothy: 292
antitossomai
James: 199
antitupos
1 Peter: 217
anudros
2 Peter–Jude: 180
anupokritos
2 Timothy: 8
1 Peter: 90
anupotaktos
Titus: 31
apagō
Luke 18–24: 367
1 Corinthians: 283
apaideutos
2 Timothy: 97
apairō
Matthew 8–15: 69
Mark 1–8: 130
apallotrioō
Colossians and Philemon: 60

aparchē
Matthew 1–7: 116
Romans 9–16: 113, 364
aparneomai
Matthew 16–23: 47
Mark 1–8: 425
apataō
1 & 2 Thessalonians: 270
apatēs
Colossians and Philemon: 100
Apatouria
Galatians: 104
apechō
1 & 2 Thessalonians: 199
apeirastos
James: 47
apeitheō
Acts 13–28: 45
Romans 9–16: 90, 352
apeithēs
Luke 1–5: 40
apekdechomai
Romans 1–8: 453
1 Corinthians: 20
Philippians: 261
aphelotēs
Acts 1–12: 89
aphesis
Luke 1–5: 272
Colossians and Philemon: 42
aphiēmi
Matthew 1–7: 397
Matthew 8–15: 51
Matthew 24–28: 272
1 Corinthians: 165
Ephesians: 18, 22
1–3 John: 39
aphistēmi
1 Timothy: 147
aphōnos
1 Corinthians: 284
aphorizō
Romans 1–8: 8
aphormē
Romans 1–8: 371
Galatians: 146
1 Timothy: 213
aphrōn
Luke 11–17: 99, 134
1 Peter: 150
aphrosunē
Mark 1–8: 358
2 Corinthians: 386
aphtharsia
1 Timothy: 277
aphtharton
1 Peter: 35
aphthoria
Titus: 94
apisteō
2 Timothy: 66
apo
Romans 1–8: 452
Ephesians: 79
Titus: 62
James: 46, 50
apo tou nun
John 1–11: 330
apodeiknumi
Acts 1–12: 59
apodidōmi
Matthew 16–23: 321
1 Peter: 189
apodiorizō
2 Peter–Jude: 199
apodokimazō
1 Peter: 105
apogenomenoi
1 Peter: 171
apokalupsis
Romans 1–8: 453
Galatians: 24
1 & 2 Thessalonians: 233
1 Peter: 46, 63
Revelation 1–11: 3, 14, 15
apokaluptō
Romans 1–8: 63
apokaradokia
Romans 1–8: 452
Philippians: 75
apokatallassō
Ephesians: 79
Colossians and Philemon: 56
apokathistanō
Luke 1–5: 132
apokeimai
Colossians and Philemon: 19
apokoptō
Galatians: 142
Philippians: 219
apokrina
2 Corinthians: 26
apokrinomai
Acts 1–12: 104
apokruphos
Colossians and Philemon: 91
apōleia
Matthew 1–7: 457
1 & 2 Thessalonians: 273
1 Timothy: 256
2 Peter–Jude: 71, 76
apollumi
Matthew 8–15: 222
Matthew 16–23: 121
Luke 1–5: 286
Luke 18–24: 75
Romans 1–8: 137
Romans 9–16: 294
2 Corinthians: 143
James: 225
Revelation 1–11: 264
apologia
Acts 1–12: 200
2 Corinthians: 267
Philippians: 31
2 Timothy: 212
1 Peter: 201
apoluō
Matthew 1–7: 18, 315
Acts 13–28: 7
apolutrōsis
Romans 1–8: 208

Colossians and Philemon: 41–42
apopsuchō
Luke 18–24: 234
aporeō
Luke 18–24: 234
2 Corinthians: 143
Galatians: 120
aporia
Luke 18–24: 234
apospaō
Acts 13–28: 226, 235
apostasia
1 & 2 Thessalonians: 271
1–3 John: 98
apostellō
Acts 13–28: 47, 335
2 Corinthians: 409
1 Timothy: 3
2 Timothy: 2
apostēreō
1 Timothy: 244
apostolos
Matthew 8–15: 120
Luke 6–10: 17
Acts 13–28: 47, 335
Romans 1–8: 7, 21, 22
1 Corinthians: 3, 4, 323
2 Corinthians: 409
Galatians: 2
Ephesians: 1, 141
Philippians: 203, 204
1 Timothy: 3
2 Timothy: 2
Titus: 4
apostrephō
2 Timothy: 183
aposunagōgos
Matthew 1–7: 123
John 1–11: 404
apotassō
Luke 11–17: 285
apōtheō
Romans 9–16: 95
1 Timothy: 54
apothēsaurizō
1 Timothy: 285
apothnēskō
Romans 1–8: 317
Colossians and Philemon: 130
apotithēmi
Ephesians: 183
Colossians and Philemon: 143
James: 74
1 Peter: 97
apotomia
Romans 9–16: 117
apotomos
Titus: 62
apotrepō
2 Timothy: 118
aproskopos
1 Corinthians: 249
Philippians: 51, 52
apsinthos
Revelation 1–11: 249
ara
Romans 1–8: 189
archaios
Romans 1–8: 323
archē
John 1–11: 15–20
Romans 1–8: 516
Ephesians: 48
Philippians: 122
Colossians and Philemon: 51
Revelation 1–11: 134
archēgos
Acts 1–12: 110, 169
archisunagōgos
Matthew 8–15: 76
Luke 1–5: 267
Luke 11–17: 199
architektōn
1 Corinthians: 79
architelōnēs
Luke 18–24: 72
archōn
Matthew 8–15: 76
1 Corinthians: 60
Ephesians: 56
aretē
1 Peter: 133
2 Peter–Jude: 40
argos
Matthew 8–15: 320
2 Peter–Jude: 43
argurion
Matthew 24–28: 322
arguros
Luke 11–17: 345
arketos
1 Peter: 228
arneomai
Luke 6–10: 270
2 Peter–Jude: 72
arnion
Revelation 1–11: 167
arnos
Revelation 1–11: 167
arrabōn
Galatians: 66
Ephesians: 36
Colossians and Philemon: 39–40
arrōstos
Matthew 8–15: 428
arsenokoitais
1 Timothy: 22
arti
Galatians: 17
artigennēta
1 Peter: 98
artios
2 Timothy: 162
aschēmōn
1 Corinthians: 320
asebeia
Romans 1–8: 66
Titus: 116
asebēs
2 Peter–Jude: 161

aselgeia
Mark 1–8: 358
Romans 9–16: 267
2 Corinthians: 436
Galatians: 161
Ephesians: 170
1 Peter: 228
2 Peter–Jude: 77, 90–92, 161
asōtia
Ephesians: 242
Titus: 31
1 Peter: 229
aspazomai
1–3 John: 238
asphalēs
Philippians: 216
asphalōs
Acts 1–12: 68
assarion
Matthew 8–15: 223
astēr
Matthew 1–7: 29
Revelation 1–11: 206, 248
astheneia
Luke 11–17: 200
astheneō
Philippians: 205
James: 276, 277
asthenēs
1 & 2 Thessalonians: 179
astorgos
Ephesians: 292
2 Timothy: 114
asunetos
Ephesians: 90
ataktos
1 & 2 Thessalonians: 177
ataktōs
1 & 2 Thessalonians: 304, 308
atenizō
Acts 1–12: 100
Acts 13–28: 279
athanasia
1 Timothy: 277
atheos
Ephesians: 74
athesmos
2 Peter–Jude: 91, 136
atheteō
2 Peter–Jude: 173
athleō
Philippians: 91
2 Timothy: 46
atomos
1 Corinthians: 443
atopos
1 & 2 Thessalonians: 295
auchmēros
2 Peter–Jude: 63
autarkeia
2 Corinthians: 316
1 Timothy: 251
2 Peter–Jude: 25
authadēs
Titus: 35
2 Peter–Jude: 97
authairetos
2 Corinthians: 281
authentein
1 Timothy: 87
autos
Matthew 1–7: 161, 174, 197, 207
Luke 6–10: 126
Ephesians: 76, 91
1 & 2 Thessalonians: 87, 313
2 Timothy: 108
1 Peter: 170
auxanō
1 Peter: 100
2 Peter–Jude: 137
auxēsis
Ephesians: 161
axioō
1 Timothy: 220
axios
Matthew 1–7: 65
Ephesians: 119
Revelation 1–11: 158

ballō
Matthew 8–15: 345
baptistēs
Matthew 1–7: 51
baptizō
Matthew 1–7: 75, 79
Acts 1–12: 259
Romans 1–8: 320
1 Corinthians: 311
1 Peter: 217
barbaroi
Acts 13–28: 360
barēo
Luke 18–24: 256
baros
Galatians: 180
basanismos
Revelation 12–22: 185
basanizō
2 Peter–Jude: 91
basileia
Matthew 1–7: x, 426
Matthew 16–23: 59
basileion
1 Peter: 125
basileuō
Matthew 1–7: x
basileus
Matthew 1–7: x
2 Timothy: 63
basilikos
John 1–11: 166
baskainō
Galatians: 64
bastazō
Romans 9–16: 307
bathmos
1 Timothy: 131
bathos
Romans 1–8: 517
battalogeō
Matthew 1–7: 368

bdelugma
Matthew 24–28: 34
Mark 9–16: 244
Titus: 67, 68
bdeluktos
Titus: 67
bdelussō
Romans 1–8: 156
bebaioō
Colossians and Philemon: 93
bebaios
2 Peter–Jude: 44
bebaiōsis
Philippians: 31
bebēlos
1 Timothy: 163, 292
Beliar
2 Corinthians: 250
bēma
Acts 13–28: 317
Romans 9–16: 284
1 Corinthians: 79, 321
2 Corinthians: 177
1 & 2 Thessalonians: 74
2 Timothy: 28, 48
Bethesda
John 1–11: 173
biazō
Matthew 8–15: 256, 474
biblaridion
Revelation 1–11: 281
biblion
Revelation 1–11: 163, 281
biblos
Matthew 1–7: 3
bioō
1 Peter: 227
bios
Luke 11–17: 133
John 1–11: 21
Revelation 12–22: 62
blasphēmeō
Titus: 88, 143
1 Peter: 229
2 Peter–Jude: 98, 174
blasphēmia
Mark 1–8: 358
Ephesians: 190
Colossians and Philemon: 144
blasphēmos
2 Timothy: 113
blepō
Matthew 1–7: 302
Matthew 24–28: 17
Philippians: 217
Colossians and Philemon: 99
boōntos
Matthew 1–7: 57
boskō
John 12–21: 402
Acts 13–28: 224
1 Peter: 265
boulē
Romans 1–8: 496
1 Corinthians: 102
boulēma
1 Peter: 228
boulomai
Acts 1–12: 62
Acts 13–28: 329
1 Timothy: 78, 212, 255
James: 59
brabeuō
John 12–21: 128
Colossians and Philemon: 158
bradunō
2 Peter–Jude: 122
brechō
Luke 6–10: 173
brephē
1 Peter: 98
brephos
Mark 9–16: 64
Luke 18–24: 25
brōsis
Matthew 1–7: 411
buthizō
1 Timothy: 256

catharsis
2 Peter–Jude: 44
chairō
Matthew 24–28: 313
Acts 13–28: 72
2 Corinthians: 483
Philippians: 10, 194
James: 3, 13
1 Peter: 41, 252
1–3 John: 236
chalepos
2 Timothy: 107
chara
Galatians: 5, 166
Philippians: 10
charactēr
Colossians and Philemon: 45
charagma
Revelation 12–22: 63
charassō
Revelation 12–22: 63
charis
1 Corinthians: 11, 12, 19
2 Corinthians: 42, 284, 402
Ephesians: 2, 20, 135
Philippians: 95
Colossians and Philemon: 160
2 Timothy: 15
1 Peter: 182
2 Peter–Jude: 24
charisma
Romans 1–8: 302
1 Corinthians: 19, 290
Ephesians: 135
1 Timothy: 179
2 Timothy: 15
1 Peter: 243
charizō
Luke 6–10: 175
Romans 1–8: 506
Galatians: 85
Philippians: 95, 143

Colossians and Philemon: 157
cheirographos
Colossians and Philemon: 112
chēra
1 Corinthians: 162
1 Timothy: 196
chiliarchos
John 12–21: 315
Acts 13–28: 260
chitōn
2 Peter–Jude: 203–4
chlōros
Revelation 1–11: 183
cholē
Acts 1–12: 246
choregōs
2 Peter–Jude: 39–40
chōreō
Matthew 16–23: 17
John 1–11: 368
chōris
1 Corinthians: 109
chōrizō
Matthew 1–7: 318
Matthew 16–23: 167
1 Corinthians: 165, 167
chortazō
Matthew 1–7: 183
Matthew 8–15: 430
Mark 1–8: 320, 387
Luke 6–10: 97, 255
chrēmatismos
Romans 9–16: 100
chrēsis
Romans 1–8: 105
chrēsteuomai
1 Corinthians: 339
chrēstos
Ephesians: 209
chrēstotēs
Romans 1–8: 187
Galatians: 168
Titus: 151
chriō
2 Corinthians: 45
James: 277
chrisma
2 Corinthians: 45
1–3 John: 102
Christos
Matthew 1–7: 3
Mark 1–8: 13, 416
Luke 6–10: 262
Ephesians: 209
1 & 2 Thessalonians: 264
1–3 John: 94
chronos
Matthew 24–28: 143
Mark 1–8: 48
Romans 9–16: 258
Ephesians: 221
1 & 2 Thessalonians: 142
2 Timothy: 107
1 Peter: 83
Revelation 1–11: 23
chrusodaktulios
James: 102
corinthiazesthai
1 Corinthians: viii

daimonizomai
Matthew 8–15: 41
Luke 1–5: 283
Luke 6–10: 219
dakruō
John 1–11: 466–67
daneion
Matthew 16–23: 150
dapanaō
2 Corinthians: 426
James: 190
de
2 Corinthians: 276
1 & 2 Thessalonians: 267
1 Timothy: 102, 250, 261
James: 264
1 Peter: 187
dechomai
Matthew 16–23: 103
James: 74
dedōrēmenēs
2 Peter–Jude: 27
deēsis
Romans 9–16: 57
Ephesians: 379
Philippians: 21
1 Timothy: 201
2 Timothy: 6
1 Peter: 194
dei
John 1–11: 141, 393
1 Corinthians: 268
Ephesians: 240
deilia
2 Timothy: 17
deilos
Matthew 8–15: 34
Mark 1–8: 233
deipneō
Revelation 1–11: 140
deipnon
John 12–21: 3
1 Corinthians: 269
deka
Matthew 8–15: 477
Mark 1–8: 374
dektos
Acts 1–12: 301
deleazō
James: 49
2 Peter–Jude: 101
dēloō
1 Peter: 55
deō
Acts 13–28: 217
deomai
2 Corinthians: 284
derō
Mark 9–16: 166
Luke 18–24: 122

desmon
Mark 1–8: 378
Philippians: 60
despotēs
Acts 1–12: 140, 141
1 Timothy: 231
2 Timothy: 91
Titus: 99
1 Peter: 159
2 Peter–Jude: 72, 162
Revelation 1–11: 195
dia
Ephesians: 140
Titus: 20
Revelation 1–11: 124
diaballō
Luke 11–17: 335
diabolos
Matthew 1–7: 86
Luke 1–5: 255
John 1–11: 273
1 Timothy: 130
2 Timothy: 115
Titus: 77
James: 205
1 Peter: 281
1–3 John: 126
Revelation 12–22: 19, 235
diacheirizō
Acts 1–12: 169
diadēma
Revelation 1–11: 178, 179
Revelation 12–22: 7, 113, 217
diagō
Titus: 149
diagonguzō
Luke 18–24: 73
diaireseis
1 Corinthians: 290
diakatelegchomai
Acts 13–28: 163
diakōluō
Matthew 1–7: 76
diakoneō
Matthew 24–28: 284
Mark 1–8: 46
Acts 1–12: 183
1 Corinthians: 480
2 Corinthians: 82
1 Timothy: 124, 125
diakonia
Acts 1–12: 183
1 Corinthians: 480
2 Corinthians: 201
1 Timothy: 28, 124, 125
diakonion
1 Timothy: 125
diakonissa
1 Timothy: 130
diakonos
Matthew 16–23: 241
Mark 9–16: 109
John 1–11: 80
Acts 1–12: 182, 183
Romans 1–8: 5
Romans 9–16: 360
1 Corinthians: 74, 97, 480
Ephesians: 93
Colossians and Philemon: 193
1 & 2 Thessalonians: 78
1 Timothy: 124, 125, 130, 158
dialcos
1 Corinthians: vii
dialegomai
Luke 1–5: 193
Acts 13–28: 120, 173, 203
2 Timothy: 97
dialogismos
Mark 1–8: 357
Philippians: 180
diamarturomai
Acts 13–28: 216
Colossians and Philemon: 184
2 Timothy: 71, 167
diamenō
Galatians: 40
dianoia
Ephesians: 57
diapleō
Mark 1–8: 408
diapriō
Acts 1–12: 170, 219
diaskorpizō
Luke 11–17: 310
diaspora
1 Peter: 15
diastellomai
Mark 1–8: 379, 403
diastrephō
Matthew 16–23: 77
Acts 13–28: 226
Philippians: 184
diatarassomai
Luke 1–5: 47
diatassō
Galatians: 87
diathēkē
Galatians: 83
diatribō
John 1–11: 125
dichazō
Matthew 8–15: 231
dichotomeō
Matthew 24–28: 79
didachē
Matthew 1–7: 125
Acts 1–12: 50
2 Timothy: 179
didaktikos
1 Timothy: 108
2 Timothy: 99
didaskalein
1 Timothy: 16
didaskaleō
1 Timothy: 238
didaskalia
1 Timothy: 176, 220
2 Timothy: 128, 154
Titus: 48
didaskalos
Matthew 8–15: 21
Matthew 16–23: 188

Luke 1–5: 193
Luke 6–10: 235
Ephesians: 143
Titus: 21
James: 146

didaskō
Matthew 1–7: 124
1 Timothy: 86

didōmi
John 1–11: 244
2 Timothy: 17
Revelation 1–11: 241

didrachma
Matthew 16–23: 86, 89

diegeirō
2 Peter–Jude: 51

dierchomai
Acts 1–12: 232

dikaioō
Romans 1–8: 208
Galatians: 56
Ephesians: 17
1 Timothy: 140
James: 137, 138

dikaiōs
Acts 1–12: 109
Ephesians: 312
Philippians: 30, 290
Titus: 41, 42
2 Peter–Jude: 50

dikaiosunē
Matthew 1–7: 354
Galatians: 56
1 Timothy: 262
2 Timothy: 200

Dikē
Acts 13–28: 362

dilogos
1 Timothy: 127

diōgmos
2 Timothy: 131

diōkō
Matthew 1–7: 224
Romans 9–16: 50
1 Corinthians: 371
2 Corinthians: 143
2 Timothy: 131
Revelation 12–22: 29

dipsuchos
James: 210

dogma
Colossians and Philemon: 112

dokeō
John 1–11: 40
1–3 John: 8

dokimazō
Romans 1–8: 153
2 Corinthians: 277, 307, 460
Galatians: 181
Ephesians: 210
Philippians: 47
1 & 2 Thessalonians: 38, 199
1 Timothy: 129
1–3 John: 154

dokimē
Romans 1–8: 282
2 Corinthians: 277
Philippians: 198

dokimion
James: 26
1 Peter: 43

dokimos
Romans 9–16: 298, 366
1 Corinthians: 269
2 Timothy: 75

dokos
Luke 6–10: 115

dolioō
Romans 1–8: 188

doloō
2 Corinthians: 128

dolos
Mark 1–8: 358
Acts 13–28: 10
2 Corinthians: 427
1 & 2 Thessalonians: 38
1 Peter: 98

doma
Ephesians: 138

dōrea
Acts 1–12: 75
Ephesians: 135
1 Peter: 243

dōreomai
2 Peter–Jude: 30

dōron
Matthew 8–15: 454

doulagōgeō
1 Corinthians: 215

doulē
Luke 1–5: 60, 80

douleuō
Luke 11–17: 321, 339
John 12–21: 160
Acts 13–28: 210
Romans 1–8: 363
Philippians: 199
1 & 2 Thessalonians: 27

douloō
1 Corinthians: 212
Titus: 78

doulos
Matthew 8–15: 12
Matthew 16–23: 242
Matthew 24–28: 99
Mark 9–16: 109
Luke 1–5: 159
Luke 6–10: 125
Luke 11–17: 386
John 1–11: 80
John 12–21: 160
Acts 13–28: 210
Romans 1–8: 4, 5
1 Corinthians: 74
Ephesians: 323
Philippians: 13, 129
Colossians and Philemon: 24, 196
1 Timothy: 158, 230, 231
2 Timothy: 98
Titus: 3, 96
James: 12
2 Peter–Jude: 19, 149–50

Revelation 1–11: 18
doxa
Philippians: 111, 311
Colossians and Philemon: 33
2 Peter–Jude: 60, 98, 174
doxazō
Matthew 1–7: 247
Luke 11–17: 15
Romans 1–8: 83
1 & 2 Thessalonians: 294
1 Peter: 47
dromos
2 Timothy: 194
dunamai
Colossians and Philemon: 33
dunamis
Matthew 16–23: 286
Mark 9–16: 152
Luke 18–24: 112
Acts 1–12: 19, 60, 234
Acts 13–28: 30, 161
Romans 1–8: 51, 517
1 Corinthians: 302
2 Corinthians: 280
Galatians: 69
Ephesians: 46, 48
2 Timothy: 17
dunastēs
1 Timothy: 276
dunateō
2 Corinthians: 315
dunatos
Acts 13–28: 161
2 Timothy: 27
duskolōs
Matthew 16–23: 198
dusnōetos
2 Peter–Jude: 135

echidna
Matthew 1–7: 63
Matthew 16–23: 387, 388
echō
Philippians: 186
Colossians and Philemon: 212
echthra
Ephesians: 78
echthros
Colossians and Philemon: 60
egeirō
Matthew 8–15: 255
Mark 9–16: 401
eggizō
1 Peter: 235
egkomboomai
1 Peter: 277
egkrateia
2 Peter–Jude: 41
egō
Matthew 1–7: 302, 344
Matthew 24–28: 194, 346
John 1–11: 51, 246, 348
John 12–21: 172
2 Timothy: 25
1–3 John: 217
Revelation 1–11: 50
Revelation 12–22: 296
ei
Romans 1–8: 502
1 Corinthians: 203
Philippians: 103, 104
1–3 John: 236
eikōn
Colossians and Philemon: 45
eilē
2 Corinthians: 34, 74
eilikrineia
2 Corinthians: 34, 74
eilikrinēs
Philippians: 49, 51
eimi
John 1–11: 16, 20, 246, 348, 356
eirēnē
John 12–21: 122
1 Corinthians: 7
Galatians: 167
Ephesians: 2
Colossians and Philemon: 158
1 & 2 Thessalonians: 204
2 Timothy: 94
1 Peter: 193
2 Peter–Jude: 24, 132
eis
Matthew 24–28: 345
Acts 1–12: 74
Romans 1–8: 347
Colossians and Philemon: 17
1 & 2 Thessalonians: 81
eis touto gar
1 Timothy: 165–66
eisdechomai
2 Corinthians: 255
eita
John 1–11: 200
1 Corinthians: 419
ek
John 1–11: 272
John 12–21: 330
1 & 2 Thessalonians: 13
Revelation 1–11: 124, 125
ekballō
Matthew 1–7: 85
Matthew 8–15: 400
Mark 1–8: 42
ekdapanaō
2 Corinthians: 426
ekdikeo
Luke 18–24: 7
ekdikēsis
1 & 2 Thessalonians: 236
ekdotos
Acts 1–12: 62
ekkathairō
2 Timothy: 88
ekklēsia
Matthew 16–23: 32, 133, 134
Acts 1–12: 38
1 Corinthians: 267
1 & 2 Thessalonians: 13
James: 102
ekklinatō
1 Peter: 192

ekklinō
Romans 1–8: 185
ekkoptō
Romans 9–16: 117
eklegō
Ephesians: 11
ekleipō
Matthew 24–28: 268
eklektos
Romans 9–16: 368
1 Peter: 16, 105
1–3 John: 216, 217
eklogēn charitos
Romans 9–16: 101
ekluō
Mark 1–8: 386
Galatians: 190
ekpalai
2 Peter–Jude: 83
ekpiptō
Galatians: 135
ekplēssō
Matthew 1–7: 487
Mark 1–8: 62, 274, 380
Luke 1–5: 282
Luke 6–10: 294
ekporneuō
2 Peter–Jude: 166
ekstasia
1 Corinthians: 280
ekstasis
Mark 9–16: 403, 416
Acts 13–28: 269
ekstrephō
Titus: 166
ekteleō
Luke 11–17: 286
ektenēs
Acts 1–12: 323
1 Peter: 241
ektenōs
Acts 1–12: 323
Philippians: 45
1 Peter: 90
ekthambeō
Mark 9–16: 401
ektrepō
1 Timothy: 292
2 Timothy: 183
eleēmōn
Matthew 1–7: 189
eleēmosunē
Matthew 1–7: 355
eleeō
Matthew 16–23: 75
1 Timothy: 29
elegmos
2 Timothy: 157–59, 177
elenchō
Matthew 16–23: 128
Ephesians: 212
1 Timothy: 222
Titus: 132
2 Peter–Jude: 189
eleos
Luke 1–5: 120
Titus: 154
elpis
1 & 2 Thessalonians: 19
Titus: 119
elpisate
1 Peter: 62
elpizō
1 Timothy: 200
emauton
1 Corinthians: 212
embrimaomai
Matthew 8–15: 93
John 1–11: 466, 472
empaiktēs
2 Peter–Jude: 146
empaizō
Matthew 1–7: 43
emphutos
James: 75
empiptō
1 Timothy: 255
emplekō
2 Timothy: 44
emporeuomai
2 Peter–Jude: 78
emporos
Matthew 8–15: 383
en
Luke 11–17: 404
Romans 9–16: 377
1 Corinthians: 312
Ephesians: 175
Colossians and Philemon: 17
1 & 2 Thessalonians: 189
1 Peter: 279
Revelation 1–11: 124
enarchomai
Philippians: 26
endeigma
1 & 2 Thessalonians: 229
endeiknumi
Titus: 102
endeixis
Philippians: 93
endunō
2 Timothy: 119
enduō
Ephesians: 337
Colossians and Philemon: 155
energeia
Ephesians: 46
Colossians and Philemon: 109
1 & 2 Thessalonians: 282
energēma
1 Corinthians: 292
energeō
Galatians: 41
Ephesians: 31
Philippians: 167, 172
James: 280
energēs
Colossians and Philemon: 213
engus
Philippians: 276
enkakeō
2 Corinthians: 125

Galatians: 190
enkaleō
Titus: 22
enkataleipo
2 Timothy: 206
enkoptō
Romans 9–16: 342
enkrateia
Galatians: 169
Ephesians: 200
enoikeō
Colossians and Philemon: 159
enorkizō
1 & 2 Thessalonians: 215
entellō
Acts 1–12: 13
enthusiasmos
1 Corinthians: 280
entimos
Luke 6–10: 125
1 Peter: 105, 121
entolē
1–3 John: 57
Revelation 12–22: 34
entos
Luke 11–17: 404
entrepō
Luke 18–24: 5
epagōnizomai
2 Peter–Jude: 155
epaischunomai
Mark 1–8: 432
epakoloutheō
1 Timothy: 209
epangellō
1 Timothy: 82
epanorthōsis
2 Timothy: 160
eparkeō
1 Timothy: 209
epechō
Philippians: 186
epeita
John 1–11: 200
James: 178
epekteinō
Philippians: 247
eperōtēma
1 Peter: 218
ephebos
Galatians: 104
ephistēmi
Acts 1–12: 129
2 Timothy: 175, 190
epi
Matthew 1–7: 63
John 1–11: 154
Philippians: 28
Colossians and Philemon: 17, 28
Titus: 20
epiblepō
Luke 6–10: 291
epichorēgeō
Galatians: 69
2 Peter–Jude: 39
epichorēgia
Philippians: 74
epidiorthoō
Titus: 20
epieikeia
2 Corinthians: 324
epieikēs
Philippians: 276
1 Timothy: 111
Titus: 143
James: 178
1 Peter: 159
epiginōskō
1 Corinthians: 484
2 Corinthians: 36
epignōsis
Romans 9–16: 59, 60
Ephesians: 157
Colossians and Philemon: 28, 32, 150, 214
2 Timothy: 102, 120
Titus: 7
2 Peter–Jude: 24, 28
epikaleō
Acts 13–28: 269
1 Peter: 68
epilambanomai
Luke 11–17: 260
epilusis
2 Timothy: 144
2 Peter–Jude: 65
epimelomai
1 Timothy: 117
epimenō
Romans 1–8: 316
epiorkeō
Matthew 1–7: 321
epiphainō
Titus: 107
epiphaneia
1 Timothy: 267
2 Timothy: 24, 170
Titus: 119
epiplēssō
1 Timothy: 186
epipotheō
2 Timothy: 7
1 Peter: 98
epiripto
1 Peter: 280
episkeptomai
Acts 1–12: 181
James: 89
episkiazō
Luke 1–5: 57
episkopeō
Ephesians: 143
Titus: 34
1 Peter: 267
episkopos
Ephesians: 144, 145, 147
1 & 2 Thessalonians: 167
1 Timothy: xii, 98
Titus: 21, 34
1 Peter: 174, 263, 267

epispaomai
1 Corinthians: 172
epistatēs
Luke 1–5: 305, 307
Luke 11–17: 391
epistēmōn
James: 168
epistērizō
Acts 13–28: 55
epistrephō
Luke 6–10: 272
Acts 1–12: 114, 282
Acts 13–28: 337
1 & 2 Thessalonians: 27
James: 289, 290
1 Peter: 173
epitagē
1 Timothy: 5
Titus: 125
epitamaō
Mark 1–8: 417
epitassō
Titus: 126
epiteleō
2 Corinthians: 257
Philippians: 28
epithumeō
Matthew 1–7: 302
2 Corinthians: 172
1 Timothy: 95
James: 188
1 Peter: 57
epithumia
Romans 1–8: 101
Galatians: 153
Ephesians: 57
1 & 2 Thessalonians: 109
1 Timothy: 256
James: 50, 52
1 Peter: 73, 227, 229
2 Peter–Jude: 31
1–3 John: 87
epitimaō
Matthew 16–23: 39
Mark 9–16: 65
Luke 1–5: 292
Luke 6–10: 263
Luke 11–17: 379
Luke 18–24: 26
epitimia
Luke 18–24: 26
2 Corinthians: 56
epitrepō
1 Timothy: 86
epizēteō
Matthew 8–15: 299
Luke 11–17: 144
Romans 9–16: 102
epoikodomeō
Colossians and Philemon: 93
epoptai
2 Peter–Jude: 59
erchomai
Matthew 1–7: 380
1 Peter: 104
2 Peter–Jude: 112
Revelation 1–11: 28, 230
erēmos
Mark 1–8: 78
Luke 6–10: 254
Revelation 12–22: 163
erethizō
Colossians and Philemon: 171
ergasia
Ephesians: 171
ergazomai
Galatians: 191
1 & 2 Thessalonians: 308
ergon
Ephesians: 285
1 & 2 Thessalonians: 15, 17
Revelation 12–22: 104
eris
Romans 9–16: 267
2 Corinthians: 434
Philippians: 65
eritheia
Romans 1–8: 133
2 Corinthians: 435
Philippians: 67, 110
James: 171
erōs (non bib.)
Matthew 1–7: 345
Matthew 16–23: 339
1 Corinthians: 370
Ephesians: 127
2 Timothy: 18
erōtaō
John 1–11: 166
1 & 2 Thessalonians: 268
errizōmenoi
Colossians and Philemon: 92–93
ethnos
Matthew 1–7: 106, 425
Matthew 16–23: 299
Matthew 24–28: 116
1 Corinthians: 283
Ephesians: 165
1 Peter: 129, 140
Revelation 12–22: 285
eti
John 1–11: 158
Revelation 12–22: 298
etropophorēsen
Acts 13–28: 19
euangelion
Matthew 8–15: 105
Mark 1–8: 12, 13, 14, 27
Romans 1–8: xi, 9
Ephesians: 142
Colossians and Philemon: 12
1 & 2 Thessalonians: 81
2 Timothy: 185
Revelation 12–22: 86
euangelistēs
Ephesians: 142
2 Timothy: 185
euangelizō
Luke 1–5: 29, 157
Luke 6–10: 180
Acts 1–12: 232
Ephesians: 79, 139, 142

1 & 2 Thessalonians: 81
2 Timothy: 185
1 Peter: 93, 209
euarestos
2 Corinthians: 173
Titus: 99
eucharisteō
Matthew 24–28: 151
Mark 9–16: 290
Luke 18–24: 281
1 Corinthians: 272
Philippians: 19
euchomai
Matthew 24–28: 168
euchrēstos
2 Timothy: 91
eudokeō
Matthew 1–7: 81
Luke 11–17: 146
2 Corinthians: 406
eudokia
Luke 6–10: 343
Philippians: 66, 173
1 & 2 Thessalonians: 257
eudoō
1–3 John: 245
eulabēs
Luke 1–5: 176
eulogeō
Luke 11–17: 15
Ephesians: 7
eulogētos
2 Corinthians: 18
eumetadotos
1 Timothy: 283
euphēmos
Philippians: 290
eurēka
1–3 John: 151, 152
euros
Acts 13–28: 349
euschēmonōs
1 Corinthians: 395
eusebeia
1 Timothy: 139, 164, 240, 251, 262
James: 88
2 Peter–Jude: 28, 41–42
eusplagchnos
1 Peter: 188
euthumeō
James: 276
euthus
Mark 1–8: 33, 63
eutrapelia
Ephesians: 201
exagorazō
Galatians: 78, 108
Ephesians: 18, 222
exaireō
Galatians: 6
exaiteō
Luke 18–24: 294
exaleiphō
Acts 1–12: 117
Colossians and Philemon: 112
exangellō
1 Peter: 133
exapataō
1 & 2 Thessalonians: 270
exaporeō
2 Corinthians: 143
exēcheō
1 & 2 Thessalonians: 26
exegeirō
Romans 9–16: 33
exēgeomai
John 1–11: 46
exelkō
James: 49
existēmi
Matthew 8–15: 306
Mark 1–8: 266, 332
Luke 6–10: 237
2 Corinthians: 188
exodos
2 Peter–Jude: 52
exomologeō
Matthew 1–7: 58
Philippians: 144, 146
exorkistēs
Acts 13–28: 176
exousia
Matthew 1–7: 488
Matthew 8–15: 127
Matthew 16–23: 286
Matthew 24–28: 338
Mark 1–8: 61, 287
Mark 9–16: 152
1 Corinthians: 259
Ephesians: 48
Colossians and Philemon: 40
exousiazō
Matthew 16–23: 239
1 Corinthians: 157
exoutheneō
Romans 9–16: 278
1 & 2 Thessalonians: 196

gangraina
2 Timothy: 79
gar
John 1–11: 165
2 Corinthians: 354
Galatians: 22
gē
Matthew 24–28: 268
Mark 9–16: 376
John 1–11: 130
gegennētai
1–3 John: 177
gehenna
Matthew 1–7: 296
Matthew 16–23: 380, 388
James: 157
2 Peter–Jude: 85, 186
Revelation 12–22: 255
genea
Matthew 24–28: 64
Luke 6–10: 163
Luke 11–17: 82

genesis
Matthew 1–7: 3
gennaō
1–3 John: 165
gennēma
Matthew 1–7: 63, 296
genoito
Romans 1–8: 72, 316 ,367
Romans 9–16: 31, 96
Galatians: 204
geōrgos
John 12–21: 145
ginomai
Matthew 1–7: 263, 348
John 1–11: 16, 20, 31, 39
2 Corinthians: 196
James: 79
1 Peter: 197
2 Peter–Jude: 64–65
Revelation 12–22: 151
ginōskō
Romans 1–8: 384
2 Corinthians: 36
Philippians: 235
James: 25
1–3 John: 55, 75, 114, 143
Revelation 1–11: 59
gleukos
Ephesians: 235, 236
glōssa
Acts 1–12: 42
1 Corinthians: 331
Philippians: 146
glōssēi/glōssais, lalein
1 Corinthians: 370
gnēsios
1 Timothy: 6
Titus: 14
gnōmē
1 Corinthians: 179
gnōrizō
Galatians: 23
Philippians: 78
2 Peter–Jude: 58
gnōsis
Matthew 8–15: 348
Romans 9–16: 59
Philippians: 235
Colossians and Philemon: 7
Titus: 80
2 Peter–Jude: 24, 28
1–3 John: 8
Revelation 1–11: 134
goēs
2 Timothy: 133
gogguzō
John 1–11: 251
gongusmos
Philippians: 179
grammateus
Matthew 1–7: 276
Matthew 8–15: 399
graphē
Acts 13–28: 161
2 Timothy: 145, 146
2 Peter–Jude: 136
graphō
Galatians: 195
2 Peter–Jude: 136
grēgoreō
1 Corinthians: 472
1 & 2 Thessalonians: 160
1 Peter: 280
gumnazō
1 Timothy: 164
2 Peter–Jude: 101
gunē
Romans 1–8: 105

hadrotēs
2 Corinthians: 306
hagiasmos
1 & 2 Thessalonians: 103
1 Peter: 21
hagiazō
Matthew 1–7: 378
Luke 11–17: 15
1 Corinthians: 5, 6
1 & 2 Thessalonians: 202
2 Timothy: 90
1 Peter: 200
hagios
Acts 1–12: 109
Romans 1–8: 29
1 Corinthians: 5
Philippians: 14, 310
Colossians and Philemon: 14, 39, 65
Titus: 41
James: 177
1 Peter: 129
hagiotēs
2 Corinthians: 34
hagneia
1 Timothy: 175
hagnos
2 Corinthians: 266
Philippians: 290
1 Timothy: 225
Titus: 85
James: 177
hagnotēs
2 Corinthians: 228
hairesis
2 Peter–Jude: 71–72
hairetikos
Titus: 164
hairetizō
Matthew 8–15: 297
halusis
Philippians: 60
hamartanō
Matthew 16–23: 126
John 1–11: 330
1–3 John: 45, 205
hamartia
Matthew 1–7: 391
Luke 11–17: 38
John 12–21: 197
Ephesians: 54
James: 113
hamartōlos
Matthew 8–15: 62

Luke 6–10: 107
James: 208, 209
hapax
1 Peter: 207
2 Peter–Jude: 156
haplōs
James: 36
haplotēs
1 Corinthians: 286
2 Corinthians: 279
haplous
Matthew 1–7: 413, 414
haptō
2 Corinthians: 255
harpagē
Matthew 16–23: 385
Luke 11–17: 99
harpagmos
Philippians: 125
harpax
Matthew 1–7: 464
harpazō
2 Corinthians: 395
1 & 2 Thessalonians: 134
2 Peter–Jude: 203
hē
Ephesians: 135
heautou
2 Corinthians: 257
Philippians: 161
Titus: 120
hēdeōs
2 Corinthians: 426
hēdonē
2 Timothy: 116
Titus: 149
hēdonōn
James: 186
hedraiōma
1 Timothy: 136
hedraios
1 Corinthians: 447
hēgemōn
Matthew 1–7: 33
hēgeomai
Philippians: 226
1 Timothy: 231
James: 21
hēgnikotes
1 Peter: 89
hekastos
Ephesians: 134
hēkō
1–3 John: 210
helkos
Revelation 12–22: 139
helkuō
Ephesians: 10
hēsuchazō
1 & 2 Thessalonians: 119
hēsuchia
1 Timothy: 85, 86
hetairos
Matthew 16–23: 212
Matthew 24–28: 187
heterodidaskaleō
1 Timothy: 16, 238
heteros
Luke 18–24: 84
John 12–21: 112, 113
1 Timothy: 16, 238
Revelation 1–11: 279
Revelation 12–22: 178
heterozugeō
2 Corinthians: 246
hetoimasia
Ephesians: 354
hetoimazō
2 Timothy: 92
hēttēma
1 Corinthians: 139
hiatros
Luke 1–5: 12
hieron
Luke 1–5: 180
hieroprepēs
1 Timothy: 127
Titus: 77
hieros
Mark 9–16: 136
Luke 18–24: 104, 105
hieros grammata
2 Timothy: 138, 144
hikanoō
Ephesians: 43
Colossians and Philemon: 37, 39
hikanos
1 Corinthians: 274
hilaros
2 Corinthians: 315
hilaskomai
1–3 John: 46
hilasmos
1–3 John: 46, 167
hilastērion
Romans 1–8: 209
1–3 John: 46, 47
himatia
James: 244
hina
Ephesians: 96, 106
Philippians: 81, 144, 181
2 Timothy: 61
Titus: 78
histēmi
Romans 1–8: 277
Ephesians: 338
2 Peter–Jude: 211
ho
Matthew 8–15: 240
Matthew 24–28: 280
John 1–11: 19, 31
hoian
Matthew 1–7: 222
holoklēros
1 & 2 Thessalonians: 206
James: 32
holos
1 & 2 Thessalonians: 205
homeiromai
1 & 2 Thessalonians: 46

homoiōma
Philippians: 130, 131
homoios
1 Peter: 276
homologeō
Luke 11–17: 120
Romans 9–16: 76
Philippians: 146
1 Timothy: 139
1–3 John: 39, 157
homoousios
John 1–11: 38
homophrones
1 Peter: 187
hoplizō
1 Peter: 224
hoplon
1 Peter: 224
hopōs
Matthew 16–23: 392
horaō
Matthew 16–23: 12
Matthew 24–28: 225
Luke 11–17: 132
1 Timothy: 141
James: 154
Revelation 1–11: 215, 278
horizō
Acts 1–12: 62
Romans 1–8: 15, 496
horkos
Matthew 1–7: 321
hormaō
Acts 1–12: 223
hormē
Acts 13–28: 47
hos
2 Corinthians: 201
1 Timothy: 139, 140
Titus: 120
1 Peter: 170
hosiōs
Titus: 41, 42
hosiotēs
Ephesians: 178
hōste
2 Corinthians: 195
Philippians: 156
hotan
James: 24
hous
1–3 John: 217
houtos
Matthew 1–7: 374
Mark 9–16: 66
John 1–11: 272
Ephesians: 61
2 Peter–Jude: 21
1–3 John: 191
hubris
Philippians: 112
hubristēs
1 Timothy: 29
hubrizō
1 & 2 Thessalonians: 35
hudōr
1 Peter: 217
hugiainō
1 Timothy: 22, 240
2 Timothy: 181
Titus: 48, 71, 74, 95
huion theou
Matthew 24–28: 280
huios
Matthew 1–7: 217
Luke 11–17: 322
Galatians: 109
1 Timothy: 6
huiothesia
Galatians: 109
Ephesians: 18
humeis
Matthew 24–28: 62
hupagō
Luke 6–10: 328
hupakōes
1 Peter: 66
hupakouō
Romans 9–16: 84
Ephesians: 280, 311
Philippians: 158
Colossians and Philemon: 170
hupantēsis
Matthew 24–28: 86
huparchō
Acts 1–12: 221
Philippians: 122
2 Peter–Jude: 43
huper
John 1–11: 432
1 Corinthians: 425
2 Corinthians: 190
Philippians: 140
1 & 2 Thessalonians: 164
1 Timothy: 31
James: 199
huperauxanō
1 & 2 Thessalonians: 225
huperbolē
2 Corinthians: 156
huperechō
Philippians: 113, 234
huperēphania
Mark 1–8: 358
huperēphanos
James: 199
hupēretēs
Romans 1–8: 5
1 Corinthians: 96, 97
hupernikaō
Romans 1–8: 514
1–3 John: 174
huperperissos
Mark 1–8: 380
huperphanos
2 Timothy: 112
huperpleonazō
1 Timothy: 31
huperupsoō
Philippians: 140

hupo
Romans 1–8: 180
Philippians: 122, 158
James: 46, 50
hupoballō
Acts 1–12: 193
hupogrammon
1 Peter: 167
hupokrisis
1 Peter: 98
hupokritēs
Matthew 1–7: 354
Matthew 16–23: 375
Luke 11–17: 112
2 Timothy: 8
hupomenō
1 Corinthians: 355
James: 259
hupomimnēskō
Titus: 140
hupomonē
Romans 1–8: 282
2 Corinthians: 226, 227, 421
Colossians and Philemon: 34
1 & 2 Thessalonians: 19, 229, 298
1 Timothy: 264
2 Timothy: 130
James: 26, 253
2 Peter–Jude: 41
Revelation 1–11: 40, 59
hupōpiazō
Luke 18–24: 6
1 Corinthians: 149, 215
hupostellō
Acts 13–28: 213
Galatians: 51
hupotagē
1 Timothy: 85, 116
hupotassō
Ephesians: 276, 280, 282, 285
Philippians: 263
Colossians and Philemon: 168
Titus: 99
James: 204
1 Peter: 145, 159, 177, 220, 276
hupotithemi
1 Timothy: 159
hupotupōsis
1 Timothy: 33
2 Timothy: 30
hupsēlophroneō
1 Timothy: 281
hupsistos
Luke 1–5: 49
hupsōma
Romans 1–8: 517
hupsoō
Luke 11–17: 15
Philippians: 140
1 Peter: 279
hustereō
Romans 1–8: 208

iama
1 Corinthians: 300
iaomai
Matthew 8–15: 81
Mark 1–8: 261
Mark 9–16: 117
Luke 11–17: 394
James: 279
iaspis
Revelation 12–22: 279
ichnos
1 Peter: 167
ichthus
Matthew 8–15: 222
idios
1 Timothy: 231
idiōtēs
1 Corinthians: 377, 384
2 Corinthians: 358
idou
Matthew 24–28: 346
Luke 6–10: 230, 352
Luke 11–17: 404
James: 154
Revelation 1–11: 28
Iēsous
Mark 1–8: 15
iōta
Matthew 1–7: 262
iris
Revelation 1–11: 280
ischuō
Philippians: 303
ischus
Ephesians: 47
isopsuchos
Philippians: 197
isos
Philippians: 125, 197
isotimon
2 Peter–Jude: 20

kagō
Revelation 12–22: 296
kai
Romans 1–8: 496
Ephesians: 3, 143
Colossians and Philemon: 14
Revelation 12–22: 294, 296
kai eidon
Revelation 12–22: 233, 234, 247, 262, 285
kai idou
Mark 9–16: 77
Luke 6–10: 172
Luke 11–17: 200
Luke 18–24: 420
kai nun
1–3 John: 229
kainos
John 1–11: 123
2 Corinthians: 97, 196
Ephesians: 78, 178
2 Peter–Jude: 131
1–3 John: 64, 229
Revelation 1–11: 91
Revelation 12–22: 263
kairos
Matthew 8–15: 283, 416

Matthew 24–28: 143
Mark 1–8: 48
Acts 1–12: 20, 118
Romans 1–8: 322
Romans 9–16: 258, 259
1 Corinthians: 182
Galatians: 191
Ephesians: 221
1 & 2 Thessalonians: 142
2 Timothy: 107, 180, 190
1 Peter: 256, 279
1–3 John: 64
Revelation 1–11: 23, 319
kakalalias
1 Peter: 98
kakia
Ephesians: 190
Colossians and Philemon: 144
Titus: 149
James: 74, 103
1 Peter: 97, 151
kakoō
Acts 13–28: 45
kakopatheia
James: 258
kakopatheō
2 Timothy: 184
James: 275
kakopoios
1 Peter: 140, 254
kakōs
1 Corinthians: 267
2 Corinthians: 178
James: 190, 258
1 Peter: 189
1–3 John: 133
Revelation 12–22: 139
kalamos
Revelation 1–11: 293
kalaphileō
Luke 6–10: 173
kaleō
Matthew 8–15: 66, 120
1 & 2 Thessalonians: 13
1 Peter: 131, 180
2 Peter–Jude: 150
kalodidaskalos
Titus: 78
kalōs
Matthew 1–7: 246
Mark 1–8: 380
Luke 6–10: 104
John 1–11: 431–32, 444
Galatians: 182, 191
Ephesians: 209
Philippians: 306
1 & 2 Thessalonians: 199
1 Timothy: 21, 43, 98, 116, 158, 219, 265
2 Timothy: 193
Titus: 94
James: 235
1 Peter: 139
kamēlos
Matthew 16–23: 19
kamptō
Philippians: 144
kananaios
Matthew 8–15: 170
kanōn
Galatians: 210
kaos
Galatians: 206
kapēleuō
2 Corinthians: 74
kapēlos
2 Corinthians: 74
kardia
Matthew 1–7: 202
Ephesians: 45
karphos
Matthew 1–7: 435
Luke 6–10: 115
kata
Matthew 16–23: 238, 239
Galatians: 88
Ephesians: 79, 106
Philippians: 248
1 Timothy: 221
kata bathous
2 Corinthians: 279
kata mesēmbrian
Acts 1–12: 253
katabainō
Luke 6–10: 209
kataballō
2 Corinthians: 143
katadikazō
James: 249
katadouloō
2 Corinthians: 372
Galatians: 39
katadunasteuō
James: 110
kataischunō
1 Peter: 121
katakauchaomai
James: 171
kataklusmos
Matthew 24–28: 74
2 Peter–Jude: 88
katakrima
Romans 1–8: 399
1 Corinthians: 274
katakrisis
2 Corinthians: 238–39
katakurieuō
Matthew 16–23: 238
1 Peter: 269
katalaleō
2 Corinthians: 435
James: 221
1 Peter: 204
katalalia
2 Corinthians: 435
James: 221
katalalos
James: 221
katalambanō
John 1–11: 23
kataleipō, kataphroneō
Matthew 16–23: 8

katallagē
2 Corinthians: 200
katallassō
2 Corinthians: 200
Ephesians: 18
Colossians and Philemon: 56
kataluma
Luke 1–5: 149
kataluō
Matthew 1–7: 269
Romans 9–16: 299
katangellō
Philippians: 69
Colossians and Philemon: 79
katanoeō
James: 84
katanussō
Acts 1–12: 71
katapherō
Acts 13–28: 204
kataphroneō
Romans 1–8: 118
1 Timothy: 233
katapinō
2 Corinthians: 58
katargeō
Romans 1–8: 325
1 Corinthians: 359, 365
Galatians: 135
Ephesians: 78
1 & 2 Thessalonians: 281
2 Timothy: 24
katarizō
1 Corinthians: 28
katartisis
2 Corinthians: 478, 483
katartismos
Ephesians: 152
katartizō
2 Corinthians: 478, 483
Galatians: 179
Ephesians: 153
kataskēnoō
Luke 11–17: 209
Acts 1–12: 66
katastolē
1 Timothy: 79
katastrēniaō
1 Timothy: 211
katastrōnnumi
1 Corinthians: 221
katastrophē
2 Timothy: 74
2 Peter–Jude: 89
katatemnō
Philippians: 219
katathematizō
Matthew 24–28: 218
katatomē
Galatians: 47
Philippians: 219, 220
katēcheō
Acts 13–28: 250
Romans 1–8: 153
katechō
Philippians: 186
1 & 2 Thessalonians: 277
katēgoria
1 Timothy: 221
katergazomai
Philippians: 156, 161
1 Peter: 228
katesthiō
Luke 18–24: 166
kateuthunō
1 & 2 Thessalonians: 297
kathairesis
2 Corinthians: 479, 483
kathairō
2 Timothy: 88
katharismos
2 Peter–Jude: 43–44
katharizō
Matthew 8–15: 82
Luke 11–17: 394
katharos
Matthew 1–7: 204
1 & 2 Thessalonians: 37
James: 89
Revelation 12–22: 203
katharsia
Galatians: 161
kathedra
Matthew 16–23: 357
katheudō
1 & 2 Thessalonians: 159
kathistēmi
Romans 1–8: 307
James: 193
katho
1 Peter: 251
katioō
James: 244
katischuō
Matthew 16–23: 32
katoikeō
Matthew 8–15: 337
Luke 11–17: 76
Ephesians: 106
Colossians and Philemon: 103
2 Peter–Jude: 131
katoikētērion
Ephesians: 83
kauchaomai
Romans 1–8: 279
2 Corinthians: 32
Galatians: 205
Philippians: 187, 222
James: 39, 234
kauchēma
1 Corinthians: 209
2 Corinthians: 32, 187
kauchēsis
2 Corinthians: 32, 240
kaustēriazō
1 Timothy: 151
keimai
Philippians: 67
keleusma
1 & 2 Thessalonians: 134
kenodoxia
Philippians: 111

kenon
1 & 2 Thessalonians: 81
kenoō
Philippians: 126
kenos
1 Corinthians: 411
Philippians: 111
1 & 2 Thessalonians: 34
kēnsos
Matthew 16–23: 318
keraia
Matthew 1–7: 262
kerdainō
Matthew 16–23: 132
kerdos
Philippians: 226
Titus: 39
kērugma
Matthew 1–7: 124
Acts 1–12: 50
Titus: 12, 13
2 Peter–Jude: 29
kērugmatos
1 Corinthians: 45
kērussō
Matthew 1–7: 52, 108, 124
Matthew 8–15: 105
Mark 1–8: 286
Luke 6–10: 180, 242
Acts 1–12: 50, 233
Ephesians: 139
2 Timothy: 171
1 Peter: 209
klaiō
John 1–11: 466–67
James: 242
Revelation 1–11: 165
kleptō
Mark 1–8: 357
Ephesians: 186
klērō
Ephesians: 29, 30
klērōn
1 Peter: 270
klēronomeō
Matthew 1–7: 174
klēronomia
Luke 11–17: 308
1 Peter: 34–35
klēsis
Ephesians: 119
1 Peter: 131
klētos
1 Peter: 131
2 Peter–Jude: 150
klibanos
Matthew 1–7: 424
klinariōn
Acts 1–12: 164
klopē
Mark 1–8: 357
koilia
Philippians: 258
koimaō
1 & 2 Thessalonians: 125
koinē
Luke 1–5: 11
koinōneō
Galatians: 182
1 Timothy: 225
koinōnia
Acts 1–12: 84
Romans 9–16: 346, 347
1 Corinthians: 22, 237, 451
Philippians: 22, 23, 105
Colossians and Philemon: 213
1 Timothy: 284
1 Peter: 251
1–3 John: 18
koinōnikos
1 Timothy: 284
koinōnos
2 Corinthians: 307
Colossians and Philemon: 224
1 Peter: 266
2 Peter–Jude: 30
koinoō
Matthew 8–15: 456
Mark 1–8: 350
koitē
Romans 9–16: 266, 267
kollaō
Luke 11–17: 311
Revelation 12–22: 182
koloboō
Matthew 24–28: 45
Mark 9–16: 249
komē
1 Corinthians: 262
komizō
2 Corinthians: 178
1 Peter: 48
kōmos
Romans 9–16: 266
1 Peter: 229
kophinos
Matthew 8–15: 480
Mark 1–8: 389
kōphos
Matthew 8–15: 95
Luke 1–5: 90
kopiaō
Matthew 8–15: 275
Romans 9–16: 364
1 Corinthians: 111
Colossians and Philemon: 81
1 & 2 Thessalonians: 168
1 Timothy: 100, 166, 220
2 Timothy: 48
Titus: 44
kopos
1 Corinthians: 460
2 Corinthians: 228, 388
1 & 2 Thessalonians: 17
Revelation 1–11: 59
Revelation 12–22: 104
koptō
Revelation 1–11: 34
korban
Matthew 8–15: 454, 455

Korinthia korē
Acts 13–28: 146
2 Corinthians: 35
Korinthiastēs
Acts 13–28: 146
2 Corinthians: 35
korinthiazesthai
1 Corinthians: x
korinthiazomai
Acts 13–28: 146
2 Corinthians: 35
kosmeō
1 Timothy: 78
Titus: 103
Revelation 12–22: 265
kosmiōs
1 Timothy: 79, 107
kosmos
John 1–11: 33, 56, 130, 346–47
John 12–21: 171
1 Corinthians: 91
Galatians: 206, 207
Ephesians: 55
1 Timothy: 79, 107
James: 92, 156, 193
Revelation 12–22: 265
krabattōn
Acts 1–12: 164
kradzō
Mark 9–16: 115
kraipalē
Luke 18–24: 256
kranion
Matthew 24–28: 253
krataioō
1 Corinthians: 475
krateō
Revelation 1–11: 104, 216
kratos
Ephesians: 47
Colossians and Philemon: 33
1 Peter: 288
kraugazō
Matthew 8–15: 299
John 1–11: 474
kraugē
Ephesians: 190
krazō
Matthew 8–15: 89
Matthew 16–23: 249
Romans 9–16: 47
James: 246
Revelation 1–11: 195
krima
1 Corinthians: 274
James: 150
1 Peter: 256
Revelation 12–22: 87
krinō
Matthew 1–7: 432
Romans 9–16: 278, 290
2 Corinthians: 34, 74
2 Timothy: 169
James: 222
krisis
James: 271
Revelation 12–22: 87
kritēs
James: 225
ktisis
Colossians and Philemon: 47
1 Peter: 149
kubernēsis
1 Corinthians: 324
kubia
Ephesians: 158
kullos
Matthew 8–15: 477, 481
kunarion
Mark 1–8: 369
Philippians: 217
kuōn
Philippians: 217
kurios
Matthew 1–7: 414
Matthew 16–23: 347
Luke 1–5: 159, 307
John 1–11: 245
John 12–21: 160
Romans 9–16: 74
1 Corinthians: 286–87
Philippians: 144
2 Peter–Jude: 162, 173
1–3 John: 216
Revelation 1–11: 195, 230, 311
kuriotēs
Ephesians: 48
2 Peter–Jude: 92–93, 173
kuroō
2 Corinthians: 58

lagchanō
2 Peter–Jude: 20
lailaps
Mark 1–8: 229
Luke 6–10: 209
lalein glōssēi/glōssais
1 Corinthians: 370
laleō
Ephesians: 258
Titus: 70, 132
lambanō
John 1–11: 34–35
Acts 13–28: 164
Romans 9–16: 318
Philippians: 244
2 Peter–Jude: 43
lampas
Matthew 24–28: 86
Revelation 1–11: 248
lampros
James: 102
Revelation 12–22: 188, 203
lanthanō
2 Peter–Jude: 118
laos
Luke 6–10: 87
latreuō
Romans 1–8: 36
Philippians: 221
2 Timothy: 4, 5
Revelation 1–11: 232

legō
Matthew 1–7: 344
Luke 18–24: 434
Ephesians: 201
James: 46
leitourgeō
Acts 13–28: 5
Romans 9–16: 347
leitourgia
2 Corinthians: 318
Philippians: 192
leitourgos
Romans 9–16: 332
Philippians: 204
lepra
Luke 1–5: 313
lepros
Matthew 8–15: 5
Mark 1–8: 86
lepta
Luke 18–24: 169
lēstēs
Matthew 24–28: 257
Mark 9–16: 315, 367
lēthē
2 Peter–Jude: 43
leukos
Revelation 1–11: 46, 225
lian
Matthew 1–7: 44
limos
Luke 18–24: 205
lithos
1 Peter: 104
logikos
1 Peter: 99
logios
Acts 13–28: 161
Romans 1–8: 168, 169
logismos
2 Corinthians: 328
1 Peter: 148
logizomai
Romans 1–8: 116, 237, 333, 449
1 Corinthians: 347
2 Corinthians: 86
Philippians: 285
logō aletheias
James: 62
logomacheō
2 Timothy: 72
logomachia
1 Timothy: 242
logos
Matthew 1–7: 76, 326
Luke 1–5: 205
John 1–11: 16–18
Romans 1–8: 168
1 Corinthians: 40, 298
2 Corinthians: 206, 285
Ephesians: 370
Philippians: 311
1 Timothy: 220
2 Timothy: 157
Titus: 45, 95
1 Peter: 201
loidoreō
Acts 13–28: 281, 282
1 Corinthians: 112
loidoria
1 Peter: 190
loidoroumenon
1 Peter: 168
loimos
Luke 18–24: 205
loipos
1 & 2 Thessalonians: 293
1 Timothy: 223
2 Timothy: 198
luchnos
Matthew 24–28: 86
John 1–11: 31, 210
luō
Matthew 1–7: 269
lupē
2 Corinthians: 315
lupeō
Matthew 16–23: 121
Mark 9–16: 287
Romans 9–16: 293
lutron
Matthew 16–23: 245
Mark 9–16: 109
lutroō
Ephesians: 18
Titus: 121
1 Peter: 72
lutrōsis
Luke 1–5: 96
Romans 1–8: 208

machaira
John 12–21: 311
2 Corinthians: 262
2 Timothy: 157, 158
Revelation 1–11: 180
machē
2 Corinthians: 262
machomai
John 1–11: 259
magos
Matthew 1–7: 28
Acts 13–28: 8
magueō
Matthew 1–7: 28
mainomai
1 Corinthians: 384
makarios
Matthew 1–7: 141, 142, 144, 157
Luke 6–10: 95
1 Timothy: 275
James: 41
1 Peter: 198
Revelation 12–22: 93
makarismos
Galatians: 116
Makedonas
Acts 13–28: 186
makros
Luke 18–24: 9
James: 253

makrothumeō
Luke 18–24: 9
1 Corinthians: 338
1 & 2 Thessalonians: 179
2 Timothy: 178
James: 253
2 Peter–Jude: 122
makrothumia
Romans 1–8: 119
2 Corinthians: 228
Galatians: 167
Ephesians: 126
Colossians and Philemon: 34, 156
1 Timothy: 33
2 Timothy: 130
James: 258
Revelation 1–11: 59
malakos
Luke 6–10: 154
malista
2 Corinthians: 204
1 Timothy: 168, 220
mallon
Philippians: 58
manthanō
Matthew 8–15: 277
Matthew 24–28: 62
Mark 9–16: 258
Ephesians: 173
Philippians: 291
1 Timothy: 82
2 Timothy: 134
maranatha
2 Peter–Jude: 110, 129
martur
2 Timothy: 13
martureō
Luke 6–10: 49
John 1–11: 31, 50
2 Corinthians: 280
marturēs
Acts 1–12: 21
marturia
John 1–11: 31, 50
1 Corinthians: 15
1 Timothy: 119
marturion
Mark 9–16: 237
1 Corinthians: 15, 54
marturomai
Galatians: 134
1 & 2 Thessalonians: 52
martus
1 Peter: 266
1–3 John: 190
Revelation 1–11: 87, 298
mastigos
Mark 1–8: 261
mastix
Mark 1–8: 163
mataios
1 Corinthians: 90
mataiotēs
Romans 1–8: 454
Ephesians: 168
mathētēs
Matthew 8–15: 32, 120, 133, 277
Mark 1–8: 118, 161, 228, 402
Luke 6–10: 15, 208
Luke 11–17: 116, 279
John 1–11: 268, 357
Acts 1–12: 283
Acts 13–28: 164
Philippians: 291
2 Timothy: 134
mathēteuō
Matthew 24–28: 340
mathētria
Acts 1–12: 283
mē
Matthew 1–7: 324
Mark 9–16: 167
Luke 1–5: 111
Romans 1–8: 172, 316, 367
Romans 9–16: 31, 96
Galatians: 204
1 & 2 Thessalonians: 270
1 Timothy: 111
1 Peter: 189
mēdeis
2 Corinthians: 226
Philippians: 109
1 & 2 Thessalonians: 270
megaleiotēs
Matthew 16–23: 78
2 Peter–Jude: 60
megalunō
Luke 1–5: 79
megas
Matthew 16–23: 239
Mark 1–8: 229
Luke 1–5: 48, 292
Luke 6–10: 209, 211
2 Peter–Jude: 30
Revelation 12–22: 3, 138
megistan
Revelation 1–11: 207
mēketi hamartane
John 1–11: 330
meletaō
1 Timothy: 180
mellō
Matthew 24–28: 18
mempsimoiros
2 Peter–Jude: 190
menō
John 12–21: 142
1–3 John: 103, 111, 148, 219, 235
mēpote
Luke 18–24: 255
merimnaō
Philippians: 197
mesoō
John 1–11: 288
Revelation 12
meta
John 1–11: 220
Colossians and Philemon: 34
metamelomai
Matthew 24–28: 226
Luke 6–10: 272

metamorphoō
Matthew 16–23: 63
Mark 9–16: 5
2 Corinthians: 116
metanoeō
Matthew 1–7: 53, 109
Matthew 24–28: 226
Mark 1–8: 49
Luke 6–10: 272
Acts 1–12: 73, 246
Revelation 1–11: 89
metanoia
Mark 1–8: 21
Acts 13–28: 216, 337
Romans 1–8: 120
Colossians and Philemon: 16
2 Timothy: 101
metastrephō
Galatians: 15
metatithēmi
Galatians: 13
methē
Romans 9–16: 266
methistemi
Colossians and Philemon: 41
methodia
Ephesians: 158, 338
methuskō
John 1–11: 82
mēti ara
2 Corinthians: 42
metochē
2 Corinthians: 248
miainō
2 Peter–Jude: 172–73
miasma
2 Peter–Jude: 106
miasmos
2 Peter–Jude: 92
mikros
Matthew 1–7: 458
Matthew 8–15: 167
Luke 6–10: 69
milion
Matthew 1–7: 334
mimeomai
1 & 2 Thessalonians: 23, 305
mimētēs
Ephesians: 194
mogilalos
Mark 1–8: 381
moichaō
Matthew 1–7: 302
moicheia
Mark 1–8: 357
molis
1 Peter: 257
molos
1 Peter: 257
molunō
Revelation 1–11: 113
molusmos
2 Corinthians: 257
monogenēs
Luke 1–5: 149, 196
John 1–11: 42
Colossians and Philemon: 46
monoō
1 Timothy: 200
monos
Philippians: 84
mōria
1 Corinthians: 40, 88
mōrologia
Ephesians: 201
mōros
Matthew 1–7: 295
1 Corinthians: 88
Ephesians: 201
2 Timothy: 97
Titus: 161
morphē
Philippians: 122, 129, 131
morphoō
Galatians: 120
morphōsis
Romans 1–8: 155
2 Timothy: 117
muktērizō
Galatians: 186
mulos onikos
Matthew 16–23: 104
murias
Matthew 16–23: 148
Acts 13–28: 249
murioi
1 Corinthians: 378
murious
1 Corinthians: 116
mustērion
Mark 1–8: 197
Romans 9–16: 386
1 Corinthians: 61, 98
Ephesians: ix
Colossians and Philemon: 78
1 & 2 Thessalonians: 278
muthos
1 Timothy: 163
2 Peter–Jude: 58
mythos
2 Corinthians: 206

nai
Revelation 1–11: 34
Revelation 12–22: 104
naos
Matthew 24–28: 227, 273
Luke 1–5: 180
Luke 18–24: 105
Revelation 1–11: 293
Revelation 12–22: 132
nekroō
Colossians and Philemon: 136
nekrōsis
2 Corinthians: 144
nemō
Titus: 34
neophutos
1 Timothy: 117
neos
Romans 1–8: 322

neotēs
1 Timothy: 173
nēphalios
1 Timothy: 105, 106
Titus: 74
nēphō
2 Timothy: 183
1 Peter: 280
nēpios
Matthew 8–15: 271
Galatians: 104
Ephesians: 158
nēsteia
Matthew 1–7: 400
nikaō
1–3 John: 174
noēma
2 Corinthians: 132
noeō
1 Timothy: 21
2 Timothy: 49
James: 84
nomikos
Luke 6–10: 352
nomizō
Acts 13–28: 53
nomos
Romans 1–8: 201, 202
Titus: 34
1–3 John: 57
nomothetēs
James: 225
nophizō
Titus: 101
nothos
1 Timothy: 6
nous
Romans 1–8: 416
1 Corinthians: 65
1 & 2 Thessalonians: 269
nouthesia
1 Corinthians: 226
Ephesians: 319
noutheteō
Acts 13–28: 228
Romans 9–16: 328
1 Corinthians: 114
Colossians and Philemon: 79
1 & 2 Thessalonians: 170, 177
nun
John 1–11: 330

ō
1 Timothy: 261
ochlos
Mark 1–8: 415
Luke 6–10: 260
ochurōma
2 Corinthians: 328
ōdinas
Acts 1–12: 65
oida
Mark 1–8: 30
Romans 1–8: 115, 194
2 Corinthians: 195
Philippians: 72
1 & 2 Thessalonians: 20, 106
1 Timothy: 135
2 Timothy: 27
1–3 John: 114, 124
Revelation 1–11: 59
oikeō
Romans 1–8: 420
Ephesians: 106
oiketēs
1 Peter: 159
oikodespoteō
1 Timothy: 213
oikodomē
1 Corinthians: 385
Ephesians: 156
oikodomeō
1 Corinthians: 245
oikonomia
Ephesians: 89, 95
Colossians and Philemon: 72
oikonomos
1 Corinthians: 98
Titus: 34
oikos
Ephesians: 285
1 Timothy: 135
Titus: 34
oikourgos
Ephesians: 285
oiktirmos
Philippians: 105
Colossians and Philemon: 155
oinophlugia
1 Peter: 229
oinos
Matthew 8–15: 261
Ephesians: 236, 237, 238, 240
Titus: 36
olethros
1 Corinthians: 126
1 & 2 Thessalonians: 150, 245
1 Timothy: 256
oligopsuchos
1 & 2 Thessalonians: 178
ololuzō
James: 243
omnumi
Matthew 24–28: 218
omnuō
Mark 9–16: 338
onar
Matthew 1–7: 21
oneidizō
Matthew 1–7: 224
1 Peter: 253
oninēmi
Colossians and Philemon: 227
onomazō
1 Corinthians: 131
opheilēma
Matthew 1–7: 391
opheilō
Romans 9–16: 307
1 & 2 Thessalonians: 225
ōphelimos
2 Timothy: 152

ophis
Matthew 16–23: 387
ophthalmos
Mark 1–8: 358
opse de sabbatōn
Matthew 24–28: 306
opsōnion
2 Corinthians: 366
oregō
2 Corinthians: 172
1 Timothy: 95
orgē
Romans 1–8: 60, 133
Ephesians: 190
Colossians and Philemon: 143
1 & 2 Thessalonians: 29, 163
orgilos
Titus: 36
orgizō
Matthew 1–7: 294
Ephesians: 184
orthoō
Titus: 20
orthopodeō
Galatians: 54
orthōs
Mark 1–8: 378
Mark 9–16: 177
Galatians: 54
Titus: 20
orthotomeō
2 Timothy: 76
ostrakinos
2 Corinthians: 140
ou
John 1–11: 248, 282
1 & 2 Thessalonians: 151
James: 161
ouai
Matthew 1–7: 144
Matthew 16–23: 375
Luke 6–10: 95
2 Peter–Jude: 176
oude
Galatians: 24
ouketi
Romans 1–8: 386, 399
oun
John 1–11: 165, 166
oupō
John 1–11: 282, 283
ousias
Luke 11–17: 308

paidagōgos
1 Corinthians: 116
Galatians: 95, 96, 98, 105
paideia
Matthew 16–23: 179
Mark 9–16: 64
Ephesians: 319
2 Timothy: 161
1–3 John: 74
paideuō
1 Timothy: 55
2 Timothy: 100
Titus: 113
James: 271
paidion
Matthew 16–23: 95
2 Timothy: 161
pais
Matthew 8–15: 12, 297
Luke 6–10: 125
Acts 1–12: 106
Acts 13–28: 204
Ephesians: 319
palaios
Romans 1–8: 323
palē
Ephesians: 340
Philippians: 241
palingenesia
Matthew 16–23: 204
Titus: 154
pandocheion
Luke 1–5: 149
panourgia
2 Corinthians: 127
Ephesians: 158
panourgos
2 Corinthians: 427
panti
1 & 2 Thessalonians: 189
pantokratōr
Revelation 1–11: 315
para
Matthew 8–15: 345
Mark 1–8: 194
John 12–21: 354
Titus: 36
1–3 John: 219
parabasis
Matthew 1–7: 391
Luke 11–17: 38
Galatians: 86
parabatēs
James: 113
parabolē
Matthew 8–15: 345
Mark 1–8: 194
Luke 6–10: 114, 187
paraboleuomai
1 Corinthians: 485
Philippians: 207
paradechomai
1 Timothy: 221
paradidōmi
Matthew 24–28: 23, 147
Mark 9–16: 34, 235, 286
Romans 1–8: 99, 347
1 Corinthians: 126
2 Corinthians: 145
paradosis
1 Corinthians: 252
Colossians and Philemon: 101
paraginomai
Matthew 1–7: 51, 75
paragō
1–3 John: 90
paraiteomai
1 Timothy: 162, 210

Titus: 164
parakaleō
Matthew 1–7: 161
Mark 1–8: 376
1 Corinthians: 25
2 Corinthians: 58, 223, 402, 484
Ephesians: 118, 148
Colossians and Philemon: 85–86
1 & 2 Thessalonians: 51, 95, 177
1 Timothy: 15, 186
2 Timothy: 178
Titus: 48, 91, 132
1 Peter: 137, 263
2 Peter–Jude: 155
paraklēsis
Philippians: 104
paraklētos
John 12–21: 112, 113
1 Corinthians: 25
Philippians: 104
1 & 2 Thessalonians: 51
1 Timothy: 186
Titus: 48
1–3 John: 46
parakoloutheō
2 Timothy: 127
parakuptō
James: 85
1 Peter: 58
paralambanō
Philippians: 292
1 & 2 Thessalonians: 57
paralogizomai
James: 83
paralutikos
Matthew 8–15: 50
paramutheomai
1 & 2 Thessalonians: 51, 178
paramuthion
Philippians: 104
parangelia
1 & 2 Thessalonians: 98
1 Timothy: 41
parangellō
Matthew 8–15: 185
Luke 6–10: 263
1 Corinthians: 267
1 Timothy: 15
paraphroneō
2 Corinthians: 386
paraphronia
2 Peter–Jude: 103
paraptōma
Matthew 1–7: 391
Luke 11–17: 38
Romans 1–8: 302
Galatians: 177, 178
Ephesians: 54
paratēreō
Luke 6–10: 7
parathēkē
1 Timothy: 291
2 Timothy: 41
paratithēmi
1 Timothy: 43
2 Timothy: 41
1 Peter: 258
pardidōmi
1 Peter: 168
2 Peter–Jude: 85–86
pareisdunō
2 Peter–Jude: 71, 158–59
pareispherō
2 Peter–Jude: 39
parelēluthōs chronos
1 Peter: 228
parembolē
Revelation 12–22: 242
parepidēmos
1 Peter: 15, 137
paresis
Romans 1–8: 218
paristēmi
1 Corinthians: 195
2 Timothy: 75
paroikos
1 Peter: 137
paroimia
John 1–11: 429
John 12–21: 224
paroinos
Ephesians: 237, 240
Titus: 36, 37
parorgismos
Ephesians: 184
parousia
Matthew 16–23: 52
Matthew 24–28: 10
1 & 2 Thessalonians: 74, 91, 128, 207, 233, 268
James: 253, 257, 258
2 Peter–Jude: 10, 59, 129
paroxunō
Acts 13–28: 82, 130
1 Corinthians: 345
parrēsia
John 1–11: 302–3
2 Corinthians: 108, 240
1 Timothy: 131
1–3 John: 113, 145, 170, 203
parrēsiazomai
Acts 13–28: 172
parthenos
Matthew 1–7: 20
Luke 1–5: 44, 56
1 Corinthians: 162
pas
John 1–11: 246, 249
2 Corinthians: 315
paschō
Galatians: 68
1 Peter: 198
patēr
Matthew 1–7: 376
Luke 11–17: 12
John 1–11: 17–18
Ephesians: 316
Colossians and Philemon: 171
pathēma
Romans 1–8: 449
pathos
Colossians and Philemon: 139
1 & 2 Thessalonians: 109

James: 258
Paulos
Titus: 2
pauō
1 Corinthians: 359
peirasmos
Matthew 1–7: 87, 395
Luke 6–10: 192
1 Corinthians: 227
James: 25, 45, 48
2 Peter–Jude: 92
peirazō
Matthew 1–7: 87, 88
Mark 1–8: 42, 43
2 Corinthians: 460
peitharcheō
Acts 1–12: 169
peithō
John 12–21: 159
Acts 13–28: 173
2 Corinthians: 185
Philippians: 26
Colossians and Philemon: 15
1–3 John: 144
pelekizō
Revelation 12–22: 237
penēs
Luke 1–5: 270
Revelation 1–11: 76
penichros
Matthew 1–7: 145
Luke 18–24: 169
pentheō
Matthew 1–7: 157, 161
2 Corinthians: 437
peran
Matthew 16–23: 163
peri de
1 & 2 Thessalonians: 142
periagō
Matthew 1–7: 122
1 Corinthians: 201
periergazomai
1 & 2 Thessalonians: 120, 308
periergos
1 Timothy: 212
periistēmi
Titus: 161
perilupos
Matthew 24–28: 172
peripateō
Romans 1–8: 410
Galatians: 152
periphroneō
Titus: 133
peripiptō
James: 25
peripoiēsis
1 Peter: 130
perisseia
2 Corinthians: 278
James: 74
perisseuēte
1 & 2 Thessalonians: 95
perisseuma
Matthew 8–15: 319
perisseuō
Luke 11–17: 133
1 Corinthians: 447
2 Corinthians: 279
Philippians: 44
Colossians and Philemon: 93
perissos
John 1–11: 431
peritithēmi
1 Corinthians: 320
peritomē
Philippians: 220
perpereuomai
1 Corinthians: 341
petra
Matthew 1–7: 482, 483
Matthew 16–23: 28
1 Corinthians: 220
petros
Matthew 16–23: 28
Luke 6–10: 25
John 1–11: 67
1 Corinthians: 220
phainomai
James: 199
phaneroō
2 Corinthians: 176
1 Timothy: 140
1 Peter: 82, 270
1–3 John: 17, 124
phanerōsis
1 Corinthians: 293
phantasia
Acts 13–28: 329
phantasma
Matthew 8–15: 440
Mark 1–8: 330
pharmakeia
Matthew 24–28: 27
Galatians: 161, 162
Revelation 12–22: 191
pharmakos
Revelation 1–11: 273
Revelation 12–22: 273, 309
phaulos
1 Corinthians: 83
2 Corinthians: 178
James: 103, 176
pheidomai
2 Corinthians: 445
pherō
1 Peter: 63
pheugō
Matthew 1–7: 40
Matthew 24–28: 41
Mark 9–16: 246
1 Timothy: 261
2 Timothy: 92
phialas
Revelation 12–22: 132
philadelphia
1 & 2 Thessalonians: 117
1 Peter: 90
philadelphos
1 Peter: 188

philagathos
Titus: 40
philandros
Titus: 83
philanthrōpia
Titus: 151, 152
philarguria
1 Timothy: 257
philarguros
Luke 11–17: 344
philautos
2 Timothy: 108
philēdonos
2 Timothy: 116
phileō
Matthew 16–23: 339
Matthew 24–28: 186
Mark 9–16: 201
Luke 11–17: 345
John 1–11: 188, 454
John 12–21: 172, 227, 401, 402
1 Corinthians: 488
Colossians and Philemon: 95
2 Timothy: 108
Titus: 151
James: 192
1 Peter: 188
philia
Matthew 1–7: 345
1 Corinthians: 115, 329
Ephesians: 127, 197
James: 192
philoprōteuō
1–3 John: 256
philos
Matthew 24–28: 187
Luke 11–17: 53
2 Corinthians: 172
2 Timothy: 18, 116
Titus: 40
James: 192
1–3 John: 256
philosophia
1 Corinthians: 36
Colossians and Philemon: 95, 100
philotimeomai
2 Corinthians: 172
1 & 2 Thessalonians: 119
philoxenos
1 Timothy: 107
Titus: 40
phimoō
Matthew 16–23: 336
1 Peter: 150
phlogizō
James: 157
phobeō
Matthew 8–15: 55
Matthew 24–28: 279
Mark 1–8: 248
Mark 9–16: 403, 416
Luke 6–10: 223
2 Corinthians: 434
phobos
Mark 1–8: 106
Luke 1–5: 325
Luke 6–10: 223
Acts 1–12: 86
2 Corinthians: 262
Philippians: 160
2 Timothy: 17
1 Peter: 178
phoneuō
James: 189, 249
phonos
Mark 1–8: 357
phortia
Luke 11–17: 104
phortion
Galatians: 181, 182
phōs
John 1–11: 31, 210
phōsphoros
2 Peter–Jude: 64
phōstēr
Philippians: 185
Revelation 12–22: 279
phrēn
Titus: 41
phrissō
James: 132
phronēma
Romans 1–8: 417, 419
phroneō
Romans 1–8: 416
Philippians: 30, 31, 106, 109, 249
Colossians and Philemon: 129
phronēsis
Luke 1–5: 40
Ephesians: 25
phronimos
Luke 11–17: 162
phronimōs
Luke 11–17: 337
phroureō
Philippians: 284
phtheirō
2 Corinthians: 237
phthonos
Philippians: 64
1 Peter: 98
phthora
Galatians: 188
2 Peter–Jude: 31
phulakē
1 Peter: 210
phulaktēria
Matthew 16–23: 364
phulassō
Luke 11–17: 132
John 12–21: 278
Ephesians: 367
1 Timothy: 291
2 Timothy: 27
2 Peter–Jude: 208
phusioō
1 Corinthians: 108, 119
phusis
1 Corinthians: 262
pikrainō
Colossians and Philemon: 169

pikria
Acts 1–12: 246
Romans 1–8: 189
Ephesians: 190
pikros
James: 171
pinakidion
Luke 1–5: 90
piptō
Romans 9–16: 117
1 Corinthians: 358
pisteuō
John 1–11: 95, 162
John 12–21: 99, 159
Acts 13–28: 164
Romans 1–8: 55
2 Timothy: 27
1–3 John: 177
pistis
2 Corinthians: 460
Galatians: 168
Ephesians: 61
Colossians and Philemon: 15
1 & 2 Thessalonians: 229
1 Timothy: 211
2 Timothy: 93, 129
2 Peter–Jude: 21
Revelation 1–11: 99
pistos
Luke 11–17: 162
2 Timothy: 41
Titus: 30, 102
planaō
Matthew 16–23: 332
Mark 9–16: 190
Galatians: 185
Titus: 148
James: 285, 286
Revelation 12–22: 19, 61
planē
James: 286
planos
1 Timothy: 149
1–3 John: 231
plastos
2 Peter–Jude: 78–79
plateia
Matthew 1–7: 365
plēgē
Revelation 12–22: 123
plēn
Luke 6–10: 99
Ephesians: 305
Philippians: 250
pleonazō
1 Timothy: 31
2 Peter–Jude: 43
pleonekteō
2 Corinthians: 237
pleonexia
Mark 1–8: 357
Luke 11–17: 132
Ephesians: 172
Colossians and Philemon: 139
2 Peter–Jude: 78
plērēs
Luke 1–5: 254
Acts 1–12: 189
plērōma
Ephesians: 49
Colossians and Philemon: 52, 103, 104
plēroō
Matthew 1–7: 45
2 Corinthians: 318
Ephesians: 111, 248, 250
Colossians and Philemon: 28, 103, 104
1 & 2 Thessalonians: 257
plērophoreō
Luke 1–5: 13
Colossians and Philemon: 197
2 Timothy: 186
plēssō
Revelation 1–11: 250
plēthunō
1 Peter: 25
2 Peter–Jude: 154
plousios
Luke 18–24: 169
Ephesians: 58
Colossians and Philemon: 159
ploutos
2 Corinthians: 279
pneuma
John 12–21: 114
1 Corinthians: 312, 376
Ephesians: 44
1 & 2 Thessalonians: 206
1 Peter: 209
Revelation 12–22: 62
pneumatikos
1 Corinthians: 282
Ephesians: 8, 135
poiēma
Ephesians: 63
poieō
Matthew 8–15: 316
Matthew 16–23: 359
Acts 1–12: 190
2 Timothy: 185
James: 80
2 Peter–Jude: 44
1–3 John: 181
Revelation 12–22: 60
poikilos
James: 25
1 Peter: 43
poimainō
Matthew 1–7: 33
John 12–21: 402
Acts 13–28: 224
Ephesians: 144
Titus: 21
1 Peter: 265
2 Peter–Jude: 180
Revelation 1–11: 233
Revelation 12–22: 11
poimēn
Ephesians: 143, 145
1 & 2 Thessalonians: 167
Titus: 21
1 Peter: 263

poimnion
1 Peter: 267
polis
Matthew 8–15: 477
Mark 1–8: 374
Philippians: 84
politeuma
Philippians: 260
politeuomai
Philippians: 84, 85
pollē epithumia
1 & 2 Thessalonians: 70
polus
2 Corinthians: 277
polusplagchnos
James: 261
polutelēs
Ephesians: 283
ponēria
Mark 1–8: 358
Luke 11–17: 99
ponēros
Matthew 1–7: 414
Mark 1–8: 358
2 Corinthians: 178
Ephesians: 359
1 & 2 Thessalonians: 295
2 Timothy: 133
James: 103, 235
1–3 John: 132
Revelation 12–22: 139
poreuomai
1 Peter: 209, 228
2 Peter–Jude: 112
porneia
Matthew 1–7: 317
Matthew 16–23: 171
Mark 1–8: 357
Romans 9–16: 266
1 Corinthians: viii, 123
2 Corinthians: 436
Galatians: 161
Ephesians: 200, 273
Colossians and Philemon: 138
1 & 2 Thessalonians: 104
Revelation 1–11: 274
porneuō
Revelation 12–22: 162
pornos
Revelation 12–22: 309
pōroō
2 Corinthians: 110
pōrōsis
Ephesians: 169
potapos
2 Peter–Jude: 128, 152
1–3 John: 114, 115
potos
1 Peter: 229
pous
Galatians: 54
pragma
Romans 9–16: 361
James: 176
praitōrion
Philippians: 61
praos
Matthew 1–7: 170
praotēs
Ephesians: 124, 126
prasiai
Matthew 8–15: 430
prassō
Galatians: 162
Philippians: 291
praupathia
1 Timothy: 264
praus
2 Timothy: 100
Titus: 144, 145
prautēs
2 Corinthians: 324
Galatians: 169
Colossians and Philemon: 156
2 Timothy: 99, 100
Titus: 144, 145
James: 75, 169
praxeis
Acts 13–28: 177
prepō
Titus: 70
presbeuō
2 Corinthians: 206
presbus
2 Corinthians: 206
presbuterion
1 Peter: 263
presbuteros
Ephesians: 144, 145, 146
1 & 2 Thessalonians: 167
1 Timothy: xii, 186
Titus: 21
1–3 John: 215
Revelation 1–11: 149
presbutēs
Colossians and Philemon: 221
Titus: 73
proagō
1 Timothy: 43
1–3 John: 235
proaireō
2 Corinthians: 315
proaitiaomai
Romans 1–8: 180
proamartanō
2 Corinthians: 437
probatikos
John 1–11: 173
proeuangelizōmai
Ephesians: 142
proginōskō
Acts 1–12: 63
Romans 1–8: 496
Romans 9–16: 99
1 Peter: 20, 82
prognōsis
Acts 1–12: 63
1 Peter: 19–20
prographō
Galatians: 65
2 Peter–Jude: 160

prōi
John 12–21: 325
proistēmi
Ephesians: 147
1 & 2 Thessalonians: 169
1 Timothy: 219
prokopē
Philippians: 59, 81
1 Timothy: 181
prokoptō
Luke 1–5: 197
Galatians: 27
prolambanō
Galatians: 177
promarturomai
1 Peter: 55
pronoeō
1 Timothy: 202
pronoia
Romans 9–16: 269
proorizō
Acts 1–12: 141
Romans 1–8: 497
propempō
Romans 9–16: 344
prophasis
1 & 2 Thessalonians: 41
prophēteia
1 & 2 Thessalonians: 196
2 Timothy: 144
prophēteuō
Luke 1–5: 96
1 Corinthians: 303
1 & 2 Thessalonians: 196
pros
Matthew 1–7: 302
Matthew 8–15: 120
John 1–11: 17–18, 45–46
Romans 9–16: 274
1 Peter: 104
prosagō
1 Peter: 207
prosagōgē
Romans 1–8: 276
Ephesians: 80
prosdechomai
Philippians: 206
Titus: 119
2 Peter–Jude: 201
prosechō
Matthew 1–7: 353
Ephesians: 240
1 Timothy: 127, 149, 175
proserchomai
1 Timothy: 239
1 Peter: 104
proseuchē
Ephesians: 379
1 Timothy: 201
proseuchomai
Matthew 24–28: 168
1 & 2 Thessalonians: 186, 293
proskairos
2 Corinthians: 157
proskaleō
Matthew 8–15: 120
James: 277
proskartereō
Ephesians: 381
Colossians and Philemon: 179
proskollaō
Ephesians: 302
proskopē
2 Corinthians: 226
proskuneō
Matthew 8–15: 8, 42, 76, 77, 473
Mark 1–8: 243, 368
Luke 1–5: 315
proslambanō
Romans 9–16: 274, 318
prosmenō
1 Timothy: 15
prosōpolēmpsia
James: 98
prosōpolēmpteō
James: 98
prosōpolēmptēs
Romans 1–8: 135
James: 98
prosphilēs
Philippians: 290
prostassō
Acts 1–12: 299
prostatis
Romans 9–16: 361
prōteuō
1–3 John: 256
prothumia
2 Corinthians: 301
prothumōs
1 Peter: 269
prōtos
Matthew 8–15: 136, 137
Luke 6–10: 25
Acts 13–28: 338
2 Corinthians: 284
1 Timothy: 198
1–3 John: 256
prōtostatēs
Acts 13–28: 304
prōtotokos
Luke 1–5: 149, 196
Colossians and Philemon: 46–47, 51–52
1–3 John: 117
Revelation 1–11: 25, 134
proxenos
1–3 John: 242
psallō
Ephesians: 259
James: 276
psēlaphaō
1–3 John: 17
pseudadelphos
Galatians: 38
pseudapostoloi
2 Corinthians: 370
pseudodidaskaloi
2 Peter–Jude: 7
pseudos
1 & 2 Thessalonians: 282
psuchē
Matthew 1–7: 419

Philippians: 89, 197
1 & 2 Thessalonians: 206
James: 287
1 Peter: 209
psuchikos
2 Peter–Jude: 199
ptōcheia
2 Corinthians: 279
Revelation 1–11: 76
ptōchos
Matthew 1–7: 145
Luke 1–5: 270
Luke 6–10: 95
Luke 11–17: 361
Luke 18–24: 169
2 Corinthians: 279
ptōēsis
1 Peter: 181
ptōssō
Luke 6–10: 95
pturō
Philippians: 93
puroō
2 Corinthians: 392
purōsis
1 Peter: 249

rhadiourgia
Acts 13–28: 10
rhēma
Luke 1–5: 205
2 Corinthians: 447
Ephesians: 370, 371
2 Timothy: 157
1 Peter: 93
rhipē
1 Corinthians: 443
rhiptō
Matthew 8–15: 112, 477
rhoizēdon
2 Peter–Jude: 124
Revelation 12–22: 250
rhomphaia
Ephesians: 360, 370
rhumē
Matthew 1–7: 365
rhuomai
Romans 1–8: 392
rhuparia
James: 74
ruomai
Colossians and Philemon: 40

sabbaton
Matthew 8–15: 280
sagēnē
Matthew 8–15: 394
sainō
1 & 2 Thessalonians: 79
saleuō
1 & 2 Thessalonians: 269
sapros
Ephesians: 187
sarkinos
1 Corinthians: 70
2 Peter–Jude: 172
sarx
John 1–11: 39, 105, 260
Galatians: 155, 156
Ephesians: 57
2 Peter–Jude: 172
satanas
Revelation 12–22: 235
schēma
1 Corinthians: 181
Philippians: 122, 131
schisma
1 Corinthians: 27, 268
schizo
Mark 1–8: 34
Sebastos
Acts 13–28: 329
sebomai
1 Timothy: 126
seismos
Matthew 8–15: 33
Mark 1–8: 230
Luke 6–10: 209
Revelation 1–11: 204
selēniazō
Matthew 1–7: 127
sēmeion
Acts 1–12: 61
Revelation 12–22: 3
semnos
Philippians: 290
1 Timothy: 126, 127
Titus: 74
sēpō
James: 244
Sicarii
Acts 13–28: 303
sikarios
Acts 13–28: 263
sikera
Ephesians: 235, 240
skandalizō
Matthew 1–7: 304
Matthew 8–15: 134, 246, 359, 412
Matthew 16–23: 104
Matthew 24–28: 159
Mark 1–8: 203, 278
Mark 9–16: 44, 296
John 1–11: 270
John 12–21: 190
skandalon
Matthew 16–23: 42
Luke 11–17: 377
skenē
Revelation 12–22: 266
skēnōma
2 Peter–Jude: 51
skēnoō
John 1–11: 41
2 Corinthians: 162
skēnopoios
Acts 13–28: 148
skeuos
1 & 2 Thessalonians: 106, 107
2 Timothy: 87
sklēros
John 1–11: 269

sklērotēses
Romans 1–8: 120
sklērunō
Acts 13–28: 173
Romans 9–16: 35
skoliois
Acts 1–12: 76
Philippians: 183, 184
1 Peter: 160
skolops
2 Corinthians: 400
skopeō
Luke 11–17: 90
Romans 9–16: 372
Galatians: 179
Philippians: 255
skopos
Philippians: 248
skubalon
Philippians: 236
skullō
Matthew 8–15: 112
Luke 6–10: 127
sōma
John 1–11: 260
sophia
1 Corinthians: 37, 298
Ephesians: 25
Colossians and Philemon: 30, 95
sophia logou
1 Corinthians: 37
sophizō
2 Peter–Jude: 58
sophos
1 Corinthians: 80
James: 168
sōphrōn
Titus: 41
sōphroneō
2 Timothy: 19
1 Peter: 240
sōphronismos
2 Timothy: 19
sōphronizō
Titus: 78
sōphronōs
Titus: 117
sōphrosunēs
1 Timothy: 81
sōtēr
2 Corinthians: 204
1 Timothy: 168
sōtēria
Romans 1–8: 54
Philippians: 73
1 Peter: 37
sōzō
Matthew 8–15: 82
Matthew 16–23: 252
Mark 1–8: 261
Mark 9–16: 117
Luke 6–10: 234
Luke 11–17: 394
Acts 1–12: 135
Romans 9–16: 83
2 Corinthians: 204
1 Timothy: 89, 168
Titus: 41, 153
James: 290
spatalaō
1 Timothy: 201
James: 247
spendō
Philippians: 191
sperma
Matthew 8–15: 369
Romans 9–16: 48
Galatians: 84
spermologos
Acts 13–28: 131
sphazō
1–3 John: 133
sphragis
2 Timothy: 81
Revelation 1–11: 217
sphragizō
2 Corinthians: 45
spiloō
2 Peter–Jude: 204
splanchna
Matthew 8–15: 109
Luke 1–5: 120
Philippians: 105
Colossians and Philemon: 155, 215, 222
splanchnizomai
Matthew 8–15: 427, 478
Mark 1–8: 316, 385
splanchnon
Luke 6–10: 327
Ephesians: 45
Philippians: 32
spoudazō
Ephesians: 128
Philippians: 102
2 Timothy: 74
2 Peter–Jude: 44
spoudē
2 Corinthians: 285
2 Peter–Jude: 39, 44, 155
spuris
Matthew 8–15: 480
Mark 1–8: 389
stadia
Revelation 12–22: 117
stegō
1 Corinthians: 204, 352
stēkō
Philippians: 86, 267
1 & 2 Thessalonians: 82
stellō
1 & 2 Thessalonians: 304
stenazō
Romans 1–8: 457
James: 257
stenochōreō
2 Corinthians: 143, 236
stenochōria
Romans 1–8: 134, 511
2 Corinthians: 227
stenos
Matthew 1–7: 455

stephanos
Philippians: 269
2 Timothy: 47, 199, 200
Revelation 1–11: 78, 149, 178, 179, 262
Revelation 12–22: 5, 113
stereōma
Colossians and Philemon: 91–92
stereos
1 Peter: 285
stērigmos
2 Peter–Jude: 136
stērizō
Luke 6–10: 310
Romans 9–16: 383
James: 255
2 Peter–Jude: 50
sthenos
Philippians: 205
stoicheion
Galatians: 105
Colossians and Philemon: 102
2 Peter–Jude: 124
Revelation 12–22: 250
stoicheō
Philippians: 250
stolē
Revelation 1–11: 196, 225
storgē
Matthew 1–7: 345
2 Timothy: 114
stratēgos
Acts 1–12: 128
Acts 13–28: 103
strateuma
Matthew 16–23: 308
strateuomai
2 Corinthians: 328
stratiōtēs
Philippians: 203
strephō
Matthew 16–23: 98
su
Matthew 8–15: 141
1 Timothy: 261
sulagōgeō
Colossians and Philemon: 99
sulaō
2 Corinthians: 366
sumbainō
1 Peter: 250
sumbasileuō
2 Timothy: 63
sumbibazō
Colossians and Philemon: 87
summorphos
Philippians: 263
sumpatheis
1 Peter: 188
sumpherō
1 Corinthians: 147, 293
sumphōneō
Matthew 16–23: 138
sumphōnēsis
2 Corinthians: 250
sumplēroō
Luke 6–10: 310
sumpsuchos
Philippians: 108
sun
Philippians: 91, 203
2 Timothy: 43
sunagō
Luke 11–17: 309
sunagōgē
Matthew 16–23: 134
James: 102
sunagōnizomai
Romans 9–16: 351
sunanamignumi
1 Corinthians: 130
1 & 2 Thessalonians: 309
sunarmologeō
Ephesians: 83
sunarpazō
Acts 1–12: 194
sunathleō
Philippians: 91, 272
sunbibazō
Acts 13–28: 188
sunchairō
Philippians: 194, 195
sundoulos
Colossians and Philemon: 24, 193
sunechō
2 Corinthians: 190
Philippians: 78
sunechomai
Luke 11–17: 171
sunedrion
Matthew 24–28: 198
Acts 13–28: 278
suneidēsis
Romans 1–8: 141
2 Corinthians: 30
1 Peter: 202
sunergeō
Romans 1–8: 473
2 Corinthians: 221
sunergos
2 Corinthians: 307
Philippians: 203
Colossians and Philemon: 211
1 & 2 Thessalonians: 78
sunesis
Ephesians: 90
Colossians and Philemon: 30, 90
suneuōcheomai
2 Peter–Jude: 100
sungenis
Luke 1–5: 58
sungnōmē
1 Corinthians: 158
suniēmi
Matthew 8–15: 399
sunistanō
2 Corinthians: 80
sunkakopatheō
2 Timothy: 21, 43
sunkleiō
Galatians: 88
sunkoinōneō
Ephesians: 211

sunkoinōnos
1 Corinthians: 213
sunochē
Luke 18–24: 234
sunoikeō
1 Peter: 181
sunteleia
Matthew 24–28: 11
sunthlibo
Mark 1–8: 260
suntribō
Luke 6–10: 291
suntrimma
Romans 1–8: 191
suntrophos
Acts 13–28: 4
sunzaō
Romans 1–8: 327
suschēmatizō
Philippians: 131
sustratiōtēs
Philippians: 203
suzaō
Romans 1–8: 327
suzēteō
Acts 1–12: 193
suzētētēs
1 Corinthians: 43
suzugos
Philippians: 272

ta kata eme
Philippians: 58
tacheōs
Galatians: 12
tachinos
2 Peter–Jude: 76
tachion
1 Timothy: 134
tachos
Revelation 1–11: 20, 21
tachu
Romans 9–16: 377
Revelation 1–11: 306
tagma
John 1–11: 199–200
talaipōria
James: 243
tameion
Matthew 1–7: 366
tapeinoō
Matthew 16–23: 98
Philippians: 132
James: 213
tapeinophrones
1 Peter: 188
tapeinophrosunē
Ephesians: 120
Philippians: 112
Colossians and Philemon: 120, 156
1 Peter: 277
tapeinos
2 Corinthians: 262, 325
Philippians: 112
tarassō
John 1–11: 466
John 12–21: 38, 98
Acts 13–28: 72
Galatians: 15
tassō
Acts 13–28: 39
1 Corinthians: 479–80
taxis
Colossians and Philemon: 91–92
tē kuriakē hēmera
Revelation 1–11: 41
tē pistei
1 Peter: 285
teinō
Philippians: 247
teknion
Galatians: 120
1–3 John: 73, 74
teknogoneō
1 Timothy: 213
teknon
Matthew 1–7: 217
Matthew 8–15: 51
Luke 11–17: 322
Ephesians: 311
Colossians and Philemon: 170
1 Timothy: 6
Titus: 14, 30
teknotropheō
1 Timothy: 208
tektōn
Matthew 1–7: 15
Matthew 8–15: 410
Mark 1–8: 276
teleioō
Philippians: 244
teleios
Matthew 1–7: 350
1 Corinthians: 60, 365
Ephesians: 158
Colossians and Philemon: 197
James: 32, 151
teleō
John 12–21: 356
Philippians: 28
telēs
1 & 2 Thessalonians: 205
telōnēs
Matthew 1–7: xi
telos
John 12–21: 63
1 Corinthians: 419
2 Corinthians: 36
1 Peter: 187, 235
tennō
Titus: 62
tephroō
2 Peter–Jude: 89
tēreō
Matthew 16–23: 359
John 12–21: 263, 278
Ephesians: 367
1 Timothy: 225
2 Timothy: 197
James: 91
1 Peter: 36
2 Peter–Jude: 153

1–3 John: 57, 181
Revelation 1–11: 125
Revelation 12–22: 294
tēreō ek
Revelation 1–11: 124, 125
tēs
Galatians: 41
thambeō
Matthew 16–23: 221
thanatoō
Romans 1–8: 360
thanatos
2 Corinthians: 144
Revelation 1–11: 184
tharreō
2 Corinthians: 270, 326
tharseō
Matthew 8–15: 51
Mark 1–8: 331
thaumazō
Matthew 8–15: 36, 100, 478
Mark 1–8: 250, 375
Mark 9–16: 348
Luke 1–5: 163
Luke 6–10: 294
Galatians: 12
1–3 John: 134
theaomai
Matthew 1–7: 354
1–3 John: 16
theios
John 1–11: 18–19
thelēma
Ephesians: 57
1 Timothy: 5
thelō
Philippians: 171
thēlus
Romans 1–8: 105
themelios
1 Timothy: 285
theodidaktos
1 & 2 Thessalonians: 118
theopneustos
2 Timothy: 142
theōreō
Matthew 8–15: 440
Acts 13–28: 249
theos
Matthew 24–28: 280
John 1–11: 18–19, 45
1 Corinthians: 372
1 Timothy: 139
theosebeia
1 Timothy: 82
therapeia
Revelation 12–22: 287
therapeuō
Matthew 8–15: 81
Mark 1–8: 261
thērion
Acts 13–28: 362
Revelation 12–22: 41
thēsaurizō
Matthew 1–7: 409
thēsauros
Matthew 1–7: 409
Matthew 8–15: 319
thesis
Galatians: 109
thlibō
2 Corinthians: 143
1 Timothy: 209
thlipsis
Romans 1–8: 134, 281, 511
1 Corinthians: 181
2 Corinthians: 21–22, 227, 277
Colossians and Philemon: 76
1 & 2 Thessalonians: 25, 244
Revelation 1–11: 71
thorubeō
Acts 13–28: 204
thorubos
Acts 13–28: 194
thrēskos
James: 88
throeō
1 & 2 Thessalonians: 269
thumoō
Matthew 1–7: 44
thumos
Luke 18–24: 9
Romans 1–8: 60, 134
2 Corinthians: 435
Ephesians: 190
Colossians and Philemon: 143–44
James: 253
Revelation 12–22: 23, 90, 123
thureos
Ephesians: 358, 359
thusia
Philippians: 192
timaō
Mark 9–16: 65
Ephesians: 312
1 Timothy: 197
timē
2 Corinthians: 172
1 Timothy: 218
Titus: 39
2 Peter–Jude: 60
timios
2 Peter–Jude: 30
tis
Romans 1–8: 510
tithēmi
Luke 1–5: 132
John 12–21: 163
1 Corinthians: 322
2 Corinthians: 205
to
Acts 13–28: 363
Philippians: 106, 109
1 Peter: 187
toioutos
Mark 9–16: 66
tolmaō
Matthew 8–15: 51
Mark 9–16: 390
1 Corinthians: 137
2 Corinthians: 326

2 Peter–Jude: 97
ton
John 1–11: 17–18, 45
tou
Luke 1–5: 248
John 1–11: 330
Ephesians: 368
Colossians and Philemon: 38, 41
Titus: 120
trapeza
Acts 1–12: 179
trechō
Luke 11–17: 315
1 & 2 Thessalonians: 294
trephō
James: 248
tribous
Matthew 1–7: 57
tromos
Mark 9–16: 403, 416
Philippians: 160
truphaō
James: 247
tunchanō
2 Timothy: 61
tuphoō
1 Timothy: 118, 241
2 Timothy: 116
tupos
Romans 1–8: 347
1 & 2 Thessalonians: 26
1 Timothy: 173
Titus: 92, 93
tuptō
Acts 13–28: 281

xenizō
1 Peter: 220, 249
xenos
Titus: 40
1 Peter: 249
1–3 John: 242
xērainō
Mark 1–8: 152
xulon
1 Peter: 7

zaō
Revelation 1–11: 152
Revelation 12–22: 238
zēloō
1 Corinthians: 325, 340
James: 189
zēlos
Romans 9–16: 267
2 Corinthians: 435
zēlōtēs
Matthew 8–15: 170
Luke 6–10: 70
1 Peter: 197
zēmia
Philippians: 226
zēteō
Luke 11–17: 144
Philippians: 198
Colossians and Philemon: 128
zētēsis
1 Timothy: 242
2 Timothy: 97
zētountes
1 & 2 Thessalonians: 41
zizanion
Matthew 8–15: 367
zōē
Luke 11–17: 133
John 1–11: 21–22
Revelation 12–22: 62
zōēn
1 Peter: 193
zōgreō
Luke 1–5: 309
zōogoneō
1 Timothy: 266

Index of Latin Words

assensus
John 1–11: 356

crurifragium
Luke 18–24: 399
John 12–21: 363

fiducia
John 1–11: 356

notitia
John 1–11: 356

patria potestas
1 Peter: 176

potestas
1 Peter: 176

Tartarus
1 Peter: 210–11
Revelation 1–11: 257

Latin Words

Index of Hebrew/Aramaic Words

Abba
Mark 9–16: 301
Abba (Aram.)
Matthew 1–7: 376
Ephesians: 15
ʼadāmā
1 Corinthians: 238
adonai
John 12–21: 262
ʼādonay
Matthew 16–23: 347, 348
1 Corinthians: 286
aheb
Matthew 16–23: 339
ʿalmâ
Matthew 1–7: 20
ʼānâ
Matthew 8–15: 68

bar (Aram.)
Matthew 8–15: 158
basar
Mark 1–8: 13
betûlâ
Matthew 1–7: 20
brm
Titus: 64
brshth
Titus: 64

Corban
Mark 1–8: 346

dābaq
Matthew 16–23: 165

`ebed
John 12–21: 160
Romans 1–8: 4, 5
El Elyon
Matthew 1–7: 377
Elohim
Matthew 1–7: 377
Ephphatha (Aram.)
Mark 1–8: 377

gabbai
Mark 1–8: 115
gannâ
Matthew 8–15: 170

halal
Revelation 12–22: 196
hārâ
Romans 1–8: 65
hārôn
Romans 1–8: 65
hēmâh
Romans 1–8: 65
hesed
Matthew 1–7: 190
hôbā' (Aram.)
Matthew 1–7: 392

hûg
Galatians: 184
huppah
Matthew 1–7: 16

illem
Mark 1–8: 381

Jehovah–Jireh
Matthew 1–7: 377
Mark 1–8: 313
Jehovah–Shalom
Matthew 1–7: 377
Jehovah–Tsidkenu
Matthew 1–7: 377

kiddushin
Matthew 1–7: 16
kinnor
Mark 1–8: 50
kôkāb
Matthew 1–7: 29

leb
Matthew 8–15: 169

mārâ
Matthew 1–7: 295
mashiach
Mark 1–8: 416
māshîah
Matthew 1–7: 3
mishkān
Matthew 1–7: 21
mohar
Matthew 1–7: 16
mokhes
Mark 1–8: 115
Luke 1–5: 330, 331

na'arâ
Matthew 1–7: 20
nābāʼ
1 Corinthians: 303
nachash
Revelation 12–22: 7
nāzîr
Ephesians: 239
nēser
Matthew 1–7: 47

qāhāl (Aram.)
Matthew 16–23: 32
qâtsaph
Romans 1–8: 65
qodesh
Philippians: 14

rosh hakeneseth
Matthew 8–15: 76

sab
Ephesians: 145

satan
Revelation 12–22: 235
shabbāt
Matthew 8–15: 280
Mark 1–8: 139
shad
Matthew 8–15: 168
Shaddai
Matthew 16–23: 364
shākan
Matthew 1–7: 21
shalom
Matthew 1–7: 211
shālôm
Matthew 8–15: 195
1 Corinthians: 7
Ephesians: 3
shēkār
Ephesians: 235, 239
shekinah
Matthew 1–7: 21
Mark 9–16: 13
Shema
Mark 1–8: 343
sheol
Matthew 16–23: 32
Revelation 12–22: 252
shiqquwts
Mark 9–16: 244

tamim
Titus: 26
tannin
Revelation 12–22: 7
tephillin
Matthew 16–23: 364
teshûqâ
Ephesians: 281
Tîrôsh
Ephesians: 235
tow`ebah
Mark 9–16: 244
t'shûqâ
Titus: 80
tummah
Titus: 26
tzaraath
Mark 1–8: 86

yada
Philippians: 145, 235
Yah
Revelation 12–22: 196
Yahweh
Matthew 16–23: 348
Mark 1–8: 19, 225
yasha
Romans 9–16: 83
yayin
Ephesians: 235, 236, 237, 239
Yeshua
Mark 1–8: 15
yhwh
1 Corinthians: 286–87
YHWH
Matthew 16–23: 96
Philippians: 145

zā'am
Romans 1–8: 65
zaqēn
Ephesians: 145

Index of Scripture

Genesis
1:1
Luke 6–10: 142
Luke 11–17: 17
John 1–11: 16, 20, 22
Acts 13–28: 137
2 Corinthians: 290
1 & 2 Thessalonians: 302
1 Timothy: 271
Revelation 1–11: 158, 285
1:2
Luke 1–5: 57
John 12–21: 114
2 Corinthians: 113
1 & 2 Thessalonians: 51
1:3
Mark 1–8: 378
John 12–21: 309
2 Corinthians: 134
1:5
1 Timothy: 242
1:8
1 Timothy: 242
1:9–10
Mark 1–8: 232
1:11–12
2 Corinthians: 317
1 Peter: 92
1:13
1 Timothy: 242
1:14
Revelation 12–22: 279
1:14–19
Revelation 12–22: 144
1:16
Revelation 12–22: 279
1:19
1 Timothy: 242
1:20
Mark 1–8: 378
Revelation 12–22: 262
1:21
Revelation 12–22: 6, 141
1:23
1 Timothy: 242
1:26
Matthew 8–15: 29, 349
Hebrews: 24
1 Peter: 152
2 Peter–Jude: 98
1:26–27
Mark 1–8: 154
Colossians and Philemon: 45
1 & 2 Thessalonians: 209
1–3 John: 88
1:26–30
Romans 1–8: 292
1:26–31
Hebrews: 54
Revelation 12–22: 64
1:27
Matthew 16–23: 165
1 Corinthians: 142, 258
1:27–28
Matthew 16–23: 161
1:28
Matthew 1–7: 132
Matthew 24–28: 342
Mark 9–16: 56
1 Corinthians: 155, 156
Hebrews: 430
Revelation 1–11: 320
1:28–29
1 Timothy: 154
1:30
2 Peter–Jude: 99
1:31
Mark 1–8: 70
John 1–11: 20
1 Corinthians: 438
Colossians and Philemon: 57
1 Timothy: 36, 154, 242
1–2
Matthew 16–23: 169
Luke 18–24: 396
1 Corinthians: 38
2
Hebrews: 101
2:2
Mark 1–8: 137
Luke 6–10: 3
2:2–3
John 12–21: 202
2:3
Matthew 8–15: 280
1 & 2 Thessalonians: 202
2:7
John 12–21: 382
1 Corinthians: 238, 258, 438, 439
James: 287
Revelation 1–11: 304
2:9
1 Corinthians: 438
Revelation 1–11: 65
Revelation 12–22: 286
2:9–23
1 Corinthians: 259
2:10–14
Revelation 12–22: 146
2:14
Hebrews: 327
Revelation 1–11: 269
2:15
1 & 2 Thessalonians: 303
1 Timothy: 228
Revelation 1–11: 244
2:15–17
Romans 1–8: 292
2:16–17
Romans 1–8: 2, 122
Hebrews: 55
2:17
Luke 1–5: 27
Romans 1–8: 294
Romans 9–16: 223
Hebrews: 58
1 Peter: 50
Revelation 12–22: 287
2:18
1 Corinthians: 155, 156
1 & 2 Thessalonians: 43
1 Timothy: 88
Hebrews: 430
2:18–24
1 Timothy: 154
2:20
1 Corinthians: 259
2:21–22
1 Corinthians: 258
2:24
Matthew 1–7: 311
Matthew 16–23: 165
Mark 9–16: 55
Romans 1–8: 294
1 Corinthians: 165
3
Luke 18–24: 49
1–3 John: 87, 94
3:1
Matthew 1–7: 90
Luke 1–5: 255, 256
2 Corinthians: 356
Philippians: 52
1 Peter: 285
Revelation 12–22: 7
3:1–5
Luke 1–5: 217
3:1–6
James: 220
1 Peter: 214
2 Peter–Jude: 157
Revelation 12–22: 235
3:1–7
Romans 1–8: 2
Romans 9–16: 223
Galatians: 204
1 Timothy: 88
1 Peter: 209, 280
1–3 John: 89
3:1–13
Matthew 1–7: 64
1 Peter: 284
3:1–24
John 12–21: 202
3:1ff.
Revelation 12–22: 6, 19
3:2–5
Revelation 12–22: 19
3:2–6
Revelation 12–22: 54
3:4
John 12–21: 361
Romans 1–8: 294
2 Corinthians: 356
Revelation 12–22: 20, 246
3:4–5
Matthew 1–7: 96
3:5
2 Corinthians: 356
1 Timothy: 38

James: 173
3:6–8
John 1–11: 342
3:6–13
Luke 1–5: 58
3:7
Mark 1–8: 243
Luke 6–10: 220
3:8
Matthew 16–23: 69
Romans 1–8: 83
3:8–9
Luke 18–24: 68
3:9
Matthew 24–28: 331
Luke 18–24: 440
3:12
Matthew 1–7: 95
Philippians: 176
James: 145, 158
3:12–13
James: 46
3:13
1 & 2 Thessalonians: 266
1 Timothy: 83
3:13–15
2 Peter–Jude: 83
3:14
Revelation 12–22: 7
3:14–15
1 & 2 Thessalonians: 264
3:15
Matthew 1–7: ix, 17, 113
Matthew 8–15: 88, 268
Matthew 24–28: 266
Mark 1–8: 43, 147, 421
Mark 9–16: 266
Luke 1–5: 42, 55, 174, 288
Luke 6–10: 82, 205, 340
Luke 11–17: 371, 411
Luke 18–24: 307, 425, 455
John 1–11: 136
John 12–21: 82, 240
Acts 1–12: 38
Acts 13–28: 21, 291
Galatians: 84
1 & 2 Thessalonians: 88
Hebrews: 296
1 Peter: 209–10, 215
2 Peter–Jude: 188
1–3 John: 189
Revelation 1–11: 254
Revelation 12–22: 6, 11, 15, 211, 302
3:16
Matthew 1–7: 311
Matthew 16–23: 161
John 12–21: 217
Romans 1–8: 457
Romans 9–16: 225
1 Corinthians: 392
1 Timothy: 90
Titus: 79
Hebrews: 56
3:16–17
1 Corinthians: 258
3:16–19
Matthew 16–23: 161
1 Peter: 43
3:17
Matthew 1–7: 90, 311
3:17–19
Mark 1–8: 70
Luke 18–24: 286
Romans 1–8: 454
1 & 2 Thessalonians: 303
Hebrews: 56
1 Peter: 159
3:18
Matthew 24–28: 249
3:19
1 & 2 Thessalonians: 306
3:21
Luke 1–5: 321
Luke 18–24: 383, 424
3:22
1 Corinthians: 438
1–3 John: 184
Revelation 1–11: 65
3:22–23
Hebrews: 56
3:22–24
Revelation 12–22: 286
3:23–24
John 1–11: 342
3:24
Revelation 1–11: 153, 238
4
1 Peter: 214
4:1
Philippians: 235
Hebrews: 296
4:1–15
2 Peter–Jude: 176–77
4:2–4
2 Corinthians: 281
4:2b–8
1–3 John: 132
4:3–5
Hebrews: 298
1–3 John: 132
4:3–7
Galatians: 204
4:5–8
Matthew 1–7: 352
4:7
Matthew 16–23: 161
Romans 1–8: 389
Titus: 80
James: 198
4:8
Matthew 1–7: 289
4:9, 13
Matthew 1–7: 290
4:10
Romans 9–16: 226
Hebrews: 303
James: 246
4:11–12
Hebrews: 303
4:13–14
Philippians: 176
4:16
Hebrews: 300
4:17
Romans 1–8: 496
Philippians: 235
4:19
1 Peter: 213
4:21–22
Hebrews: 297
4:23–24
Matthew 1–7: 330
1–3 John: 252
4:24
Matthew 16–23: 145
4:25
Philippians: 235
4:26
Romans 1–8: 90
1 & 2 Thessalonians: 260
5
Mark 9–16: 67
Luke 1–5: 244
Luke 11–17: 369
1 Peter: 214
5:5
John 12–21: 47
2 Corinthians: 210
5:8
2 Corinthians: 210
5:11
2 Corinthians: 210
5:14
2 Corinthians: 210
5:17
2 Corinthians: 210
5:20
2 Corinthians: 210
5:21–24
Hebrews: 306, 310
2 Peter–Jude: 188
5:24
Luke 1–5: 35
Luke 18–24: 453
Hebrews: 314
2 Peter–Jude: 188
Revelation 12–22: 250, 262
5:27
2 Corinthians: 210
5:29
Hebrews: 322
5:31
2 Corinthians: 210
5:32
Hebrews: 319
6
Luke 1–5: 286
Hebrews: 56
1 Peter: 211–12
6:1–2
Mark 1–8: 63
6:1–4
Luke 6–10: 222
1 Peter: 211–12
2 Peter–Jude: 86, 164
Revelation 1–11: 254, 258
Revelation 12–22: 8

Scripture

6:1–13
1–3 John: 94
6:2
Hebrews: 322
6:3
Matthew 16–23: 288, 308
Luke 11–17: 177, 221, 417
Luke 18–24: 117
2 Corinthians: 115, 225
1 & 2 Thessalonians: 65, 279, 285
Hebrews: 103, 322, 323
1 Peter: 133, 216
Revelation 1–11: 190, 268
Revelation 12–22: 303
6:4
1 Peter: 214
6:5
Matthew 1–7: 203, 238
Mark 1–8: 357
Luke 11–17: 416
Luke 18–24: 20
Hebrews: 322
James: 198
1 Peter: 31–32, 74, 151, 217
1–3 John: 45, 86
6:5–6
1 & 2 Thessalonians: 65
6:5–7
Luke 1–5: 27
1 Peter: 213
6:5–8
Revelation 12–22: 120
6:5–13
2 Peter–Jude: 87
6:6
Hebrews: 322
6:6–7
1–3 John: 47
6:8
Hebrews: 320
1 Peter: 52
6:9
Philippians: 155
2 Timothy: 172
Hebrews: 318, 319, 320, 324
James: 250
6:9–8:22
1 Peter: 216
6:11–13
1 Peter: 213
2 Peter–Jude: 165
6:13–14
Hebrews: 318
6:18
Hebrews: 320
6–7
Romans 1–8: 61
6–8
2 Peter–Jude: 184
Revelation 12–22: 122
7:10–12
Luke 11–17: 417
7:10–24
2 Peter–Jude: 88
7:13
Luke 11–17: 218
7:19–20
2 Peter–Jude: 88
8:20
Matthew 24–28: 152
Luke 18–24: 424
2 Corinthians: 281
8:20–21
Philippians: 307
8:21
Mark 9–16: 67
Luke 18–24: 27
2 Corinthians: 210
James: 198
1 Peter: 31
9:3
1 Timothy: 154
9:4
Acts 13–28: 71
9:5–6
1 Peter: 149
Revelation 12–22: 51
9:6
Matthew 1–7: 290, 292
Matthew 24–28: 190
Luke 18–24: 316
Romans 9–16: 225, 226
9:6b
1 Peter: 152
9:8–11
1 Peter: 133
9:9–17
Luke 1–5: 95
9:12–16
Revelation 1–11: 280
9:13–17
Revelation 1–11: 148
9:15
Hebrews: 324
9:16
2 Corinthians: 87
Hebrews: 320
9:20–21
Luke 6–10: 20
Hebrews: 320
9:20–27
John 1–11: 79
1 Timothy: 106
9:21
Luke 18–24: 256
9:26
Matthew 24–28: 232
Luke 1–5: 96
9:26–27
Mark 9–16: 64
9:29
2 Corinthians: 210
10
Luke 1–5: 244
10:2
Revelation 12–22: 241
10:9
Revelation 12–22: 90, 158
10:9–10
1 Corinthians: 279
10:10–11
Matthew 1–7: 5
10:10–12
Revelation 12–22: 158
10:19
Mark 1–8: 365
11
Luke 1–5: 244
11:1–4
Revelation 12–22: 90
11:1–9
Romans 1–8: 61
1–3 John: 94, 253
Revelation 1–11: 310
Revelation 12–22: 157
11:2–4
1–3 John: 89
11:3–4
Revelation 12–22: 182
11:4
1 Corinthians: 279
11:5
Matthew 1–7: 432
11:5–9
Revelation 12–22: 90
11:7–8
1 Corinthians: 279
11:8
Revelation 12–22: 158
11:15–17
2 Corinthians: 384–85
11:26
Romans 1–8: 260
11:28
Romans 1–8: 260
11:29
1 Peter: 213
11:30
Luke 1–5: 106
11:31
Luke 1–5: 105, 106
Acts 1–12: 203
Romans 1–8: 235, 260
11:32
Acts 1–12: 203
Romans 1–8: 236
12
Luke 1–5: 106, 107
Luke 11–17: 248
12:1
Luke 1–5: 106, 127
Galatians: 101
12:1–2
Romans 1–8: 260
Revelation 12–22: 5
12:1–3
Luke 1–5: 83, 106
Luke 11–17: 415
John 1–11: 383
2 Corinthians: 385
Hebrews: 162
Revelation 1–11: 223
12:1–4
Acts 1–12: 203
Romans 1–8: 251

12:1–7
James: 137
12:1ff.
Acts 1–12: 58
12:2
Luke 1–5: 106
12:2–3
Matthew 16–23: 307
Luke 1–5: 106, 127
Acts 13–28: 21
Romans 1–8: 236
Romans 9–16: 93
Galatians: 72
12:3
Matthew 1–7: 113
Matthew 8–15: 90, 187, 299
Matthew 16–23: 102, 379
Matthew 24–28: 332
Mark 9–16: 42
Luke 1–5: 106
Luke 18–24: 269
Acts 13–28: 363
Romans 1–8: 148, 154, 171, 254
Romans 9–16: 83, 89, 107, 110, 115, 388
Galatians: 105
Ephesians: 90, 91, 308
1 & 2 Thessalonians: 242
2 Timothy: 144
Hebrews: 213
James: 33
12:4
Romans 1–8: 236, 260
12:4–5
Luke 1–5: 106
12:6–7
Acts 1–12: 206
12:7
Luke 1–5: 106, 174
Acts 1–12: 204
Romans 1–8: 236
1 Corinthians: 219
12:8
Romans 1–8: 236
12:10
Luke 11–17: 310
Romans 1–8: 260
12:10–17
Romans 1–8: 236
12:11–19
Matthew 1–7: 6
12:11–20
Revelation 12–22: 68
12:12
Luke 6–10: 21
Hebrews: 356
12:13
2 Corinthians: 139
Hebrews: 340
12:14–20
Romans 1–8: 260
12:15–17
Romans 9–16: 14
12:19
James: 138
1 Peter: 213
13
Luke 1–5: 107
13:1–11
John 1–11: 424
13:2
Luke 11–17: 128
Romans 1–8: 261
2 Corinthians: 272
13:5–9
Matthew 1–7: 172
Romans 1–8: 260
13:5–13
2 Peter–Jude: 90
13:12
2 Peter–Jude: 88
13:13
James: 208, 286
13:14–15
Galatians: 101
Revelation 12–22: 239
13:14–16
Romans 9–16: 93
13:15
Acts 1–12: 204
13:16
Romans 1–8: 254
13–15
Luke 1–5: 217
14
Hebrews: 172, 173
14:8
2 Peter–Jude: 88
14:13
2 Corinthians: 385
14:14
Luke 1–5: 176
14:18
Matthew 16–23: 38
Romans 9–16: 138
Hebrews: 123, 175
1–3 John: 242
14:18–20
Luke 1–5: 49
1 Corinthians: 205, 454
1 Peter: 126
14:19
Mark 1–8: 244
Acts 13–28: 138
14:20
2 Corinthians: 281
14:22
Hebrews: 175
14:22–24
Matthew 1–7: 321
15
Luke 1–5: 106, 107
Hebrews: 165
15:1
John 1–11: 16
Romans 1–8: 260
1 & 2 Thessalonians: 294
Revelation 1–11: 50
15:1–3
Romans 1–8: 265
15:1–21
John 1–11: 383
15:1,4–7
Galatians: 83
15:1a
Galatians: 124
15:2, 5–6
Galatians: 73
15:4
1 & 2 Thessalonians: 294
15:5
Romans 1–8: 254, 260
Romans 9–16: 93, 145
2 Corinthians: 395
Revelation 12–22: 262
15:5–6
Romans 1–8: 263
15:6
Matthew 1–7: 68, 280
Luke 1–5: 21, 24, 176
Luke 11–17: 84, 370
Luke 18–24: 13
Romans 1–8: 233, 236, 251, 260, 270
Galatians: 73, 101
Colossians and Philemon: 107
James: 34, 137, 139, 197
2 Peter–Jude: 90
15:7
Luke 1–5: 107
Acts 1–12: 203
Romans 1–8: 235
15:8
Luke 1–5: 107
15:8–21
Romans 9–16: 93, 131
15:9–10
Matthew 24–28: 152
15:9–17
Luke 1–5: 108
15:9–18
1 Peter: 24
15:10
Mark 9–16: 291
15:12
Luke 18–24: 389
15:13
Acts 1–12: 204
15:14
Acts 1–12: 204
15:14–15
Luke 1–5: 127
15:16
1 & 2 Thessalonians: 65
Hebrews: 363
15:17
Luke 1–5: 127
15:18
Luke 1–5: 107
Acts 1–12: 204
Revelation 1–11: 269
Revelation 12–22: 146, 239
15:18–21
Luke 1–5: 108
Romans 1–8: 254

16:1–3
Romans 9–16: 22
16:1, 14
Hebrews: 332
16:1–6
2 Peter–Jude: 90
16:1–15
Romans 1–8: 236
16:2
Romans 1–8: 261
16:2–4
Romans 1–8: 251
16:3
Luke 1–5: 108
16:4
Ephesians: 294
16:7–13
Luke 6–10: 143
1 Timothy: 83
16:7–14
John 1–11: 41
16:11
Luke 1–5: 108
16:16
Romans 1–8: 251
17
Luke 1–5: 107, 108
17:1
Revelation 1–11: 156
Revelation 12–22: 130
17:1–8
John 1–11: 383
James: 33
17:2
Luke 1–5: 108
1 & 2 Thessalonians: 62
17:3
Revelation 1–11: 158, 228
17:4
Luke 1–5: 108
17:5
Luke 1–5: 108
Romans 1–8: 254, 258
17:5–8
Romans 1–8: 262
17:5, 23
Luke 1–5: 89
17:7
Luke 1–5: 109, 128
2 Corinthians: 88
Ephesians: 73
17:7–8
Luke 18–24: 246
Revelation 12–22: 272
17:8
Acts 1–12: 204
Galatians: 101
17:9–10
Galatians: 132
17:9–14
Luke 1–5: 89, 167
17:10
Galatians: 73
17:10–12
Romans 1–8: 159
Philippians: 228
17:10–14
Romans 1–8: 249
Colossians and Philemon: 106
17:11
Philippians: 218
17:12
Philippians: 218
17:13
Luke 1–5: 109
17:14
Philippians: 218
17:15–19
Luke 1–5: 174
17:15–21
Luke 1–5: 109
17:17
2 Corinthians: 16
Hebrews: 332
17:18
Luke 18–24: 2
Romans 1–8: 262
Romans 9–16: 22
17:19
Luke 1–5: 90, 109
Romans 1–8: 262
2 Corinthians: 16
17:19–21
James: 33
17:19, 21
Romans 9–16: 22, 23, 25
17:21
Romans 1–8: 262
17:23–25
Romans 1–8: 251
18
Ephesians: 106
18:1
Hebrews: 427
18:1–2
1 Peter: 213
18:1–8
Luke 11–17: 54
Luke 18–24: 436
Revelation 12–22: 287
18:1–15
Luke 1–5: 59
18:2
Luke 18–24: 411
Acts 1–12: 22
18:3
Hebrews: 427
18:4
Luke 6–10: 176
18:6
Matthew 8–15: 372
18:8
1 Peter: 213
18:9–15
Luke 1–5: 106
18:10
2 Corinthians: 16
18:10, 14
Luke 1–5: 174
Romans 9–16: 25
18:10–14
James: 33
18:10–19
2 Corinthians: 88
18:11–14
Romans 1–8: 264
18:12
Romans 1–8: 265
2 Corinthians: 16
Hebrews: 332
1 Peter: 50
18:14
2 Corinthians: 16
1 & 2 Thessalonians: 161
18:15
Acts 1–12: 216
18:16–19:29
2 Peter–Jude: 77, 165–66
18:18
Romans 1–8: 254
18:19
Acts 13–28: 161
2 Peter–Jude: 102
18:20
1 Corinthians: 142
James: 246
18:21
Matthew 1–7: 433
18:22–33
Romans 1–8: 293
18:23–32
Ephesians: 103
18:23–33
2 Peter–Jude: 90
18:25
Luke 1–5: 273
Luke 11–17: 41
John 1–11: 14, 92
John 12–21: 324
Romans 1–8: 173
Romans 9–16: 31
1 & 2 Thessalonians: 240
1–3 John: 39, 43
Revelation 12–22: 143
18:27
Matthew 16–23: 231
Mark 1–8: 234
Mark 9–16: 102
Luke 1–5: 307
Luke 6–10: 213
1 Corinthians: 106
18:32
Matthew 1–7: 242
18–19
Romans 1–8: 61
1 Peter: 215
19:1
Ephesians: 107
Hebrews: 427
1 Peter: 211, 213, 220
Revelation 1–11: 258
19:1–8
2 Peter–Jude: 90
19:1–22
John 12–21: 40
19:1–29
Revelation 12–22: 122

19:4–5
1 Corinthians: 142
1 Peter: 211
Revelation 1–11: 258
19:4–11
2 Peter–Jude: 89
19:5
1 Peter: 213
19:8
Luke 11–17: 54
Philippians: 235
1 Peter: 20
19:11
Matthew 8–15: 265
Matthew 24–28: 195
Romans 1–8: 105
James: 189
1–3 John: 67
19:12–13
Revelation 12–22: 181
19:13
James: 246
1 Peter: 194
19:14
2 Peter–Jude: 90
19:16
Luke 11–17: 218, 417
19:17
Luke 11–17: 418
2 Peter–Jude: 90
19:17, 26
1–3 John: 88
19:24
Matthew 1–7: 70
Matthew 8–15: 196
Luke 1–5: 27
1–3 John: 162
Revelation 1–11: 245
Revelation 12–22: 61, 242
19:24–25
Matthew 24–28: 111
Luke 18–24: 396
Ephesians: 294
2 Peter–Jude: 89
Revelation 12–22: 91
19:24–28
Revelation 1–11: 271
19:28
Revelation 1–11: 259
Revelation 12–22: 187, 199
20:1–18
Matthew 1–7: 6
Revelation 12–22: 68
20:2
2 Corinthians: 139
Hebrews: 340, 356
James: 138
20:2–3
1 Peter: 213
20:6
1 Corinthians: 155
20:7
Luke 11–17: 2
20:10
Hebrews: 340
20:17
John 12–21: 233
20:22
Hebrews: 340
21:1–2
Luke 1–5: 174
21:1–3
Luke 1–5: 109
21:1–8
Luke 1–5: 106
21:2
Hebrews: 332
21:6
Luke 1–5: 88
21:12
Matthew 8–15: 90
Luke 1–5: 196
2 Corinthians: 16
21:23–24
Matthew 1–7: 321
21:25–31
James: 266
Revelation 1–11: 284
21:33
Luke 1–5: 71
21:34
Luke 1–5: 109
22
Luke 1–5: 107, 109
Luke 18–24: 50
22:1–2
2 Corinthians: 15–16
22:1–13
Matthew 1–7: 6
Romans 1–8: 505
22:1–14
Matthew 24–28: 266
22:1–18
Luke 1-5: 76
22:1–19
1 Peter: 43
22:2
Matthew 16–23: 38
Mark 9–16: 132
Luke 1–5: 109
Romans 9–16: 145
James: 33
22:3
James: 138
22:5
John 1–11: 194
James: 138
22:6
John 12–21: 348
22:7–9
Matthew 16–23: 231
22:8
Romans 1–8: 254
1 Corinthians: 402
James: 34
22:9
John 12–21: 315
22:9–12
James: 137
22:11–12
Luke 1–5: 109
22:11–13
Romans 1–8: 237
22:12
Luke 1–5: 157
James: 34
22:13
Matthew 8–15: 439
2 Corinthians: 281
22:14
Matthew 1–7: 420
Matthew 16–23: 222
Mark 1–8: 313
Luke 18–24: 50
1 Corinthians: 402
22:16–17
Matthew 1–7: 321
22:16–18
Hebrews: 196
James: 269
Revelation 1–11: 284
22:17
Romans 9–16: 145
Hebrews: 163
Revelation 12–22: 241, 262
22:17–18
Romans 1–8: 255
22:18
Matthew 24–28: 232
Luke 1–5: 174
Luke 18–24: 446
John 12–21: 279
Romans 1–8: 254
Ephesians: 91
23
Acts 1–12: 204
23:2
Matthew 1–7: 155
23:3–11
Romans 1–8: 237
23:4
1 Peter: 15
23:9–20
Hebrews: 330
23:16–20
Romans 1–8: 260
23:19
John 1–11: 472
24
1 Corinthians: 341
24:1–4, 10
Matthew 1–7: 321
24:2
Matthew 8–15: 297
24:2–4
James: 266
24:3
Revelation 12–22: 145
24:12
Luke 18–24: 2
24:12–14
Luke 11–17: 6
Luke 18–24: 17
John 12–21: 233
24:14
James: 12

24:16
Philippians: 235
24:43
Matthew 1–7: 20
24:53
1 Timothy: 79
24:67
Colossians and Philemon: 169
25:1
1 Peter: 213
25:1–2
Romans 9–16: 22
25:7
Romans 1–8: 260
25:8–10
2 Peter–Jude: 114
25:9
Luke 6–10: 319
25:21
Luke 11–17: 2
Hebrews: 340
25:21–23
Luke 1–5: 69
25:23
Hebrews: 340
25:26
Luke 1–5: 89
25:30–33
Luke 6–10: 21
25:33
Hebrews: 340
26
Luke 1–5: 107
26:3–4
Hebrews: 339
26:3–5
Ephesians: 73
26:4
Ephesians: 91
26:4–5
Romans 1–8: 232
26:7
Luke 6–10: 21
26:8
1 Corinthians: 222
26:12
Luke 6–10: 189
26:12–14
John 1–11: 424
26:13
Luke 11–17: 128
2 Corinthians: 272
26:14
James: 198
26:24
Luke 1–5: 157
Luke 18–24: 147
Romans 1–8: 5
James: 12
26:24–25
Hebrews: 340
26:26–31
James: 266
Revelation 1–11: 284
26:31
Matthew 1–7: 321
27:7
2 Timothy: 71
Hebrews: 340
27:28, 37
Luke 1–5: 36
27:43
John 1–11: 142
28
Luke 1–5: 107
28:12
Matthew 1–7: 37
1 Peter: 220
28:13
Matthew 16–23: 333
28:13–15
Ephesians: 73
28:14
Mark 1–8: 362
Ephesians: 91
28:16–17
Hebrews: 341
28:20–21
Hebrews: 341
28:20–22
1 Corinthians: 454
28:22
2 Corinthians: 281
29:9
Luke 11–17: 296
29:13
Luke 6–10: 176
29:20–23
John 1–11: 78
29:24
1 Timothy: 229
29:31
Luke 11–17: 283
John 12–21: 28
29:32–33
Ephesians: 310
29:32–35:18
Revelation 1–11: 220
29:33
Luke 1–5: 176
30:1
Matthew 1–7: 45
James: 198
30:1–2, 23
Luke 1–5: 25
30:2
Luke 1–5: 71
30:22–23
Luke 1–5: 59
30:43
Luke 11–17: 128
2 Corinthians: 272
31
James: 159
31:1
James: 218
31:5
Hebrews: 341
31:11
Matthew 1–7: 37
31:38
John 1–11: 142
31:39
Luke 11–17: 297
31:44–53
Matthew 1–7: 321
32:5
Luke 11–17: 367
32:10
Matthew 16–23: 231
1 Corinthians: 106
Hebrews: 434
32:24
Romans 9–16: 351
32:24–26
Hebrews: 341
32:24–30
Ephesians: 103
32:26
Matthew 8–15: 474
32:28
Romans 9–16: 13
33:5
Luke 1–5: 25
33:10
1 & 2 Thessalonians: 71
34:3
Ephesians: 294
34:25
Luke 1–5: 176
35
Luke 1–5: 107
35:11
Revelation 12–22: 130
35:16
Matthew 1–7: 25
35:19
Matthew 1–7: 25
Luke 1–5: 147
35:22
Philippians: 267
35:28–29
2 Peter–Jude: 114
37:5ff.
Acts 1–12: 205
37:9–11
Revelation 12–22: 5
37:15
James: 285
37:25
Matthew 1–7: 36
37:29
Mark 9–16: 328
37:34
Matthew 1–7: 157
Revelation 1–11: 299
38:6–10
Luke 18–24: 145
38:8
Luke 1–5: 247
38:8–10
Matthew 16–23: 331
38:11
1 Timothy: 194
38:13–18
Ephesians: 294
39:1 (LXX)
Acts 1–12: 254

39:2–3
Mark 9–16: 387
Luke 18–24: 398
39:2–4
1 Peter: 150
39:5
Acts 13–28: 351
39:7
Mark 9–16: 44
39:7–10
1 & 2 Thessalonians: 105
39:7–12
Ephesians: 294
Revelation 12–22: 181
39:10
1 Corinthians: 148
39:12
1 Corinthians: 148
39:14
2 Corinthians: 385
39:17
2 Corinthians: 385
39:23
Acts 13–28: 351
40:15
2 Corinthians: 385
40:20
Luke 1–5: 140
41:9
1–3 John: 38
41:10, 38
Matthew 8–15: 297
41:12
2 Corinthians: 385
41:34
2 Corinthians: 282
41:34–35
1 Corinthians: 454
41:36, 48–49
Romans 9–16: 231
41:37–41
1 Peter: 150
41:38–39
Romans 1–8: 432
41:39–44
Luke 6–10: 14
41:42
Revelation 1–11: 217
Revelation 12–22: 203
41:46
Luke 1–5: 248
42:8–21
1 Peter: 204
42:18
Luke 1–5: 157
42:21
1 Peter: 204
43:9
Hebrews: 197
43:11
Matthew 1–7: 36
43:29
1 Peter: 52
43:32
1 & 2 Thessalonians: 306
43:33
Luke 1–5: 149
44:16
1–3 John: 38
44:30
Matthew 1–7: 218
44:33
Hebrews: 197
45:1–15
2 Corinthians: 54–55
45:2
Matthew 1–7: 172
45:4ff.
1 Timothy: 188
45:5–8
Acts 13–28: 101
45:5, 8
Matthew 1–7: 172
45:7
Luke 6–10: 14
45:7–8
Acts 13–28: 320
45:8
Philippians: 60
45:9
Luke 6–10: 14
45:9–11
1 Timothy: 199
45:22
James: 244
45:26
Luke 6–10: 14
46:8
Revelation 1–11: 220
46:26–27
Acts 1–12: 205
46:26ff.
1 Timothy: 199
46:27
Acts 1–12: 205
46:32
John 1–11: 424
47:3
John 1–11: 424
47:9
2 Corinthians: 162
47:24
2 Corinthians: 282
47:26
Romans 9–16: 231
48:3
Revelation 12–22: 130
48:8–20
Matthew 24–28: 121
48:11
1 & 2 Thessalonians: 71
48:15
Acts 13–28: 307
48:18
1 Peter: 219
48:19
Hebrews: 341
48:21–22
Hebrews: 342
49:3
Hebrews: 30
49:3–4
Titus: 29
49:3–27
Revelation 1–11: 220
49:4
Philippians: 267
49:5–7
1 Peter: 108
49:8
John 1–11: 152
49:8–10
Revelation 1–11: 166
49:10
Matthew 1–7: ix
Matthew 8–15: 90
Matthew 24–28: 232
Luke 1–5: 42
Luke 18–24: 189, 442
John 1–11: 398
Acts 1–12: 58
Hebrews: 191
Revelation 12–22: 11, 211
49:13
Mark 1–8: 365
49:28
Mark 9–16: 64
49:29–50:13
Luke 6–10: 319
49:31
Romans 1–8: 237
49:33
2 Peter–Jude: 114
50:13
Acts 1–12: 206
50:13–14
Romans 1–8: 237
50:15–21
2 Corinthians: 55
50:15ff.
1 Timothy: 188
50:19–20
Matthew 1–7: 172
1 Peter: 206
50:19–21
Matthew 1–7: 397
Matthew 16–23: 142, 231
50:20
Matthew 1–7: 88
Matthew 24–28: 290
Mark 9–16: 288, 316, 374
Luke 6–10: 14
John 1–11: 484
John 12–21: 24
Acts 1–12: 111, 142
Acts 13–28: 101
Romans 1–8: 477
Romans 9–16: 343
2 Corinthians: 400
Philippians: 60, 298
Colossians and Philemon: 223
1 & 2 Thessalonians: 185, 189
James: 21
50:20–21
1 Peter: 190
50:24
Hebrews: 342

50:25
Hebrews: 342

Exodus
1
1 & 2 Thessalonians: 264
1:5
Acts 1–12: 205
1:8
Acts 1–12: 209
Acts 13–28: 19
1:8–9
Revelation 12–22: 9
1:13–14
Acts 1–12: 209
1:15–2:10
Revelation 12–22: 9
1:15–17
Acts 1–12: 138
1:15–22
Acts 1–12: 209
1:16
2 Corinthians: 385
1:17, 20
Romans 9–16: 214
1:19
2 Corinthians: 385
1:22
Acts 1–12: 209
2:1–6
Acts 1–12: 209
2:1–10
Romans 1–8: 435
2:6
2 Corinthians: 385
2:7
2 Corinthians: 385
2:7–9
Acts 1–12: 209
2:8
Matthew 1–7: 20
2:11–12
2 Corinthians: 139
2:11–25
James: 18
2:14
Acts 1–12: 210
2:15
Acts 1–12: 210
Hebrews: 355
2:20
1–3 John: 242
2:22
Acts 1–12: 210
1 Peter: 15
3:1
Luke 1–5: 155
Luke 11–17: 296
John 1–11: 424
3:1–10
1 Peter: 54
3:1ff.
Acts 1–12: 210
3:2
John 1–11: 41
1 & 2 Thessalonians: 235
3:2–3
Luke 18–24: 396
3:2–10
1 Peter: 140
3:5
Acts 1–12: 210
3:6
Matthew 1–7: 263
Matthew 16–23: 333
Mark 9–16: 192
Luke 6–10: 138
Luke 18–24: 147
Acts 1–12: 105, 210
1 Corinthians: 423
2 Corinthians: 18, 393
3:7
Matthew 8–15: 439
John 1–11: 33
Acts 1–12: 210
3:10
John 1–11: 33
Acts 1–12: 210
3:11
Matthew 1–7: 173
Matthew 16–23: 231
Luke 1–5: 64
1 Corinthians: 106
3:13–14
John 12–21: 77
3:13–15
Philippians: 145
3:14
Mark 9–16: 210, 211
John 1–11: 22, 348
John 12–21: 138, 228
Romans 1–8: 149
Revelation 1–11: 50
3:14–15
Luke 1–5: 159
1 Corinthians: 222
3:15
Acts 13–28: 307
2 Corinthians: 18, 393
3:15–16
Matthew 16–23: 333
Luke 18–24: 147
Acts 1–12: 105
3:16
2 Corinthians: 18, 393
3:19–20
1 Peter: 279
4:1
Luke 1–5: 64
4:1–9
2 Corinthians: 415
4:5
Luke 18–24: 147
2 Corinthians: 393
4:10
Matthew 1–7: 173
Luke 6–10: 45
Romans 9–16: 170
2 Corinthians: 139
Ephesians: 125
4:10–12
Matthew 1–7: 461
2 Timothy: 149
Titus: 73
4:10–16
1 Timothy: 42
4:11
John 1–11: 454
4:14–15
Romans 9–16: 170
4:14–16
2 Timothy: 149
4:15
Matthew 16–23: 333
4:16
John 1–11: 445
4:21
John 1–11: 163, 416
John 12–21: 54
Romans 9–16: 103
1 & 2 Thessalonians: 284
4:22
Luke 1–5: 196
Romans 9–16: 13
1 & 2 Thessalonians: 62
4:24–26
Romans 1–8: 159
4:25
Luke 1–5: 89
4:31
Hebrews: 357
5:2
Luke 1–5: 82
2 Peter–Jude: 24, 73
5:22–23
Philippians: 177
5–12
Ephesians: 125
6:3
Revelation 12–22: 130
6:6
Acts 13–28: 19
6:6–7
Matthew 24–28: 141
2 Corinthians: 416
6:7
John 1–11: 33
Revelation 12–22: 272
6:8
James: 269
6:9
Hebrews: 357
7:3
John 1–11: 163
1 & 2 Thessalonians: 284
7:9
Revelation 12–22: 7
7:11
1 & 2 Thessalonians: 71
7:11–12
Matthew 16–23: 354
Mark 1–8: 398
Revelation 12–22: 60
7:11, 22
Romans 1–8: 93
7:13, 14, 22
John 12–21: 54

7:14–17:7
2 Peter–Jude: 163
7:15
Revelation 12–22: 7
7:16
Romans 1–8: 350
7:17–21
Revelation 1–11: 301
7:20
Revelation 1–11: 249
7:20–21
Revelation 1–11: 248
7:20–24
Revelation 12–22: 140, 142
7:21
Revelation 1–11: 248
7:22
Matthew 16–23: 354
Acts 13–28: 177
Revelation 12–22: 60
7:24
Revelation 1–11: 248
7–11
Matthew 16–23: 5
7–12
Revelation 12–22: 138
8:5
Revelation 12–22: 147
8:7
Matthew 16–23: 354
Romans 1–8: 93
8:8–9
Revelation 12–22: 140
8:15
Luke 6–10: 190
John 1–11: 163, 416
Acts 1–12: 220
Romans 9–16: 103
1 & 2 Thessalonians: 284
Revelation 1–11: 316
8:19
Mark 1–8: 240
Luke 11–17: 66
Acts 1–12: 220
Revelation 1–11: 316
8:22ff.
Revelation 1–11: 260
8:32
Mark 1–8: 399
John 1–11: 163, 416
Acts 1–12: 220
1 & 2 Thessalonians: 284
Revelation 1–11: 316
9:4ff.
Revelation 1–11: 260
9:7
Acts 1–12: 220
Revelation 1–11: 316
9:9–11 (LXX)
Revelation 12–22: 139
9:12
Mark 1–8: 399
John 1–11: 163
Romans 9–16: 103
1 & 2 Thessalonians: 284
9:13–25
Revelation 1–11: 245
9:16
Romans 9–16: 33
1 Corinthians: 244
9:23
Revelation 1–11: 282
9:23–24
Revelation 12–22: 153
9:25
Revelation 1–11: 246
9:27
Matthew 1–7: 66
9:33
Acts 1–12: 313
9:34
John 1–11: 163
Acts 1–12: 220
1 & 2 Thessalonians: 284
Revelation 1–11: 316
9:34–35
Matthew 16–23: 390
10:1
John 1–11: 163, 416
Acts 1–12: 220
1 & 2 Thessalonians: 284
Revelation 1–11: 316
10:4–5
Revelation 1–11: 259, 262
10:12–15
Revelation 1–11: 262
10:12–20
Revelation 1–11: 259
10:14–15
Matthew 24–28: 268
10:20
John 1–11: 163, 416
Romans 9–16: 103
1 & 2 Thessalonians: 284
10:21–22
Mark 9–16: 376
Luke 18–24: 389
Revelation 1–11: 205, 250
10:21–23
Revelation 12–22: 145
10:21–29
Revelation 12–22: 145
10:25
2 Corinthians: 281
10:27
John 1–11: 163, 416
1 & 2 Thessalonians: 284
10:29
1 & 2 Thessalonians: 71
11:5
Hebrews: 357
11:10
John 1–11: 163, 416
Acts 1–12: 220
1 & 2 Thessalonians: 284
Revelation 1–11: 316
12
Luke 18–24: 425
2 Peter–Jude: 163
12:1–13
Luke 18–24: 50
1 Peter: 72
12:1–14
1 Corinthians: 266
12:1–36
John 1–11: 55
12:1–51
Luke 1–5: 191
12:2–6
Matthew 16–23: 257
Matthew 24–28: 140
Mark 9–16: 124
Luke 18–24: 93
12:3
1 Timothy: 83
12:3–6
Revelation 1–11: 167
12:5
Matthew 1–7: 80
Mark 1–8: 37
2 Corinthians: 214
12:5–7
Matthew 16–23: 222
12:6
Matthew 24–28: 141, 145
Luke 18–24: 273
12:7
John 12–21: 62
Hebrews: 357
12:8–10
Matthew 24–28: 141
12:11
Matthew 24–28: 146
Mark 1–8: 289
Mark 9–16: 285
Luke 11–17: 158
Ephesians: 349
1 Peter: 64
12:14–15
Matthew 24–28: 140
12:15, 18–19
Matthew 8–15: 372
12:21
Ephesians: 145, 146
12:21–23
Luke 18–24: 50
12:22–23
Mark 9–16: 268
12:23
Luke 18–24: 265
1 Corinthians: 128, 225
12:26–27
Luke 1–5: 192
12:29
Matthew 24–28: 89
12:39
1 Corinthians: 128
12:40
Acts 1–12: 204
12:46
Matthew 16–23: 222
Matthew 24–28: 151
Mark 9–16: 290, 388
Luke 18–24: 282, 400
13:1–2
Luke 1–5: 169-170
1 & 2 Thessalonians: 202

13:1–10
Matthew 16–23: 364
13:3
1 Corinthians: 129
13:3–10
2 Peter–Jude: 48
13:3–16
1 Peter: 279
13:5
James: 269
13:7
1 Corinthians: 129
13:9
Matthew 16–23: 363
13:11
James: 269
13:11–15
Luke 1–5: 170
13:11–16
Matthew 16–23: 364
13:12
Romans 1–8: 8
13:16
Matthew 16–23: 363
13:19
Hebrews: 342
13:21
Matthew 1–7: 29
Matthew 16–23: 67
Luke 6–10: 286
1 Corinthians: 219
1 & 2 Thessalonians: 194
Revelation 12–22: 279
13:21–22
John 1–11: 451
1–3 John: 23
Revelation 1–11: 32
13:26
Matthew 8–15: 65
14
Romans 1–8: 61
14:3
James: 285
14:4
Luke 18–24: 398
John 1–11: 163, 416, 450
1 & 2 Thessalonians: 284
14:8
John 1–11: 163, 416
1 & 2 Thessalonians: 284
14:9ff.
Revelation 1–11: 271
14:11
Hebrews: 358
14:13–14
Philippians: 154
Hebrews: 358
14:15–16
Philippians: 154
14:16
1 Corinthians: 220
14:17
1 Corinthians: 244
14:17–18
John 1–11: 450
14:20
Matthew 1–7: 30
14:31
James: 12
15:1–6
Romans 9–16: 34
15:1–18
Ephesians: 257
Philippians: 177
Revelation 1–11: 312
Revelation 12–22: 129
15:1–21
Luke 1–5: 82, 94
Ephesians: 265
15:1, 21
Luke 1–5: 94
15:3
Revelation 12–22: 216
15:6
Luke 1–5: 91
Romans 1–8: 53
1 Peter: 219
15:7
Romans 1–8: 65
15:11
Acts 1–12: 45
Romans 9–16: 61, 62
1 & 2 Thessalonians: 209
1 Timothy: 278
2 Peter–Jude: 29
1–3 John: 25, 39, 45, 81
Revelation 1–11: 155
Revelation 12–22: 47
15:11–12
1 Peter: 288
15:12
Revelation 12–22: 33
15:14–15
Romans 9–16: 34
15:20
Luke 1–5: 185
1 Timothy: 84
15:20–21
Ephesians: 257
15:23–27
Philippians: 177
15:25
Revelation 1–11: 249
16:1–3
Luke 11–17: 240
16:2–8
Philippians: 177
16:4
2 Corinthians: 59
James: 17
1 Peter: 43
16:10
John 1–11: 451
Romans 9–16: 14
Revelation 1–11: 32
16:12ff.
Revelation 12–22: 32
16:13–15
Luke 18–24: 396
16:14ff.
Revelation 1–11: 90
16:15
1 Corinthians: 220
16:23
John 1–11: 14
16:23–29
2 Corinthians: 281
16:29
John 1–11: 14
16:33
Revelation 1–11: 90
17:1–2
Hebrews: 89
17:1–7
Philippians: 177
17:2
Luke 6–10: 53
17:4
James: 258
17:6
1 Corinthians: 220
17:7
Hebrews: 90
17:8–13
Colossians and Philemon: 190
18:5–12
Luke 6–10: 329
18:9
Luke 6–10: 339
Philippians: 275
18:14ff.
Acts 1–12: 280
18:16
Romans 1–8: 356
18:20–21
Ephesians: 146
18:21
Luke 1–5: 157
1 Peter: 68
18:21–22
James: 249
19:3–20:17
1 Peter: 24
19:5
John 1–11: 398
2 Corinthians: 289
1 Peter: 130
19:5–6
John 1–11: 152
Romans 9–16: 83, 89
2 Corinthians: 385
Philippians: 229
1 & 2 Thessalonians: 202
1 Peter: 67
19:6
Matthew 1–7: 113, 116
Matthew 8–15: 350
Matthew 16–23: 379
Mark 1–8: 362
Romans 1–8: 167
Romans 9–16: 13, 79, 107, 209, 388
Ephesians: 308
2 Timothy: 42
Hebrews: 166, 214
1 Peter: 129

19:7–9
Ephesians: 145
19:9
Romans 1–8: 276
19:9–15
1 Corinthians: 158
19:10
Hebrews: 411
19:10–11
Luke 11–17: 231
19:12
Luke 11–17: 5
1 & 2 Thessalonians: 202
Hebrews: 411
19:15
Hebrews: 411
19:16
Luke 18–24: 389
Revelation 1–11: 32, 42, 151
19:16–18
Hebrews: 411
Revelation 12–22: 133
19:16–19
1 & 2 Thessalonians: 134
Revelation 1–11: 242
19:16, 19
John 12–21: 40
19:18
Matthew 24–28: 274, 308
Mark 9–16: 379
Luke 18–24: 390
1 & 2 Thessalonians: 235
Revelation 1–11: 204
Revelation 12–22: 279
19:20–21
Romans 1–8: 276
19:21–22
Hebrews: 411
19:22
James: 206
19:23
1 & 2 Thessalonians: 202
19:24
Galatians: 87
19–31
Romans 9–16: 14
20
2 Peter–Jude: 49
20:1
Matthew 1–7: 253
20:1–17
Mark 1–8: 137
20:2–6
Matthew 1–7: 253
20:3
Mark 9–16: 179
Luke 1–5: 79
Acts 13–28: 71
1 Corinthians: 223
James: 223
20:3–5
Romans 1–8: 91
20:3–11
Matthew 16–23: 190
Ephesians: 178
20:3, 23
Luke 1–5: 74
20:4
Matthew 16–23: 320
Mark 9–16: 180
Luke 18–24: 135
1 Corinthians: 234
James: 223
Revelation 1–11: 282
20:4–6
Mark 9–16: 202
20:4, 6
Matthew 1–7: 148
20:5–6
Romans 1–8: 482
20:6
Matthew 16–23: 340
20:7
Matthew 8–15: 448
Luke 1–5: 323
James: 223, 268, 271
20:8
Matthew 24–28: 292
Acts 13–28: 202
James: 223
20:8–11
Matthew 24–28: 307
Mark 1–8: 150
Luke 6–10: 3, 6
Luke 11–17: 15
20:9
Luke 11–17: 130
2 Corinthians: 273
1 & 2 Thessalonians: 302
20:9–11
Matthew 8–15: 281
20:10
Luke 18–24: 403
1 Timothy: 230
20:11
Matthew 16–23: 23
1 Timothy: 242
Revelation 1–11: 158, 282, 285
20:12
Matthew 8–15: 454
Mark 1–8: 345
Luke 11–17: 283
Ephesians: 312
Colossians and Philemon: 170
1 Timothy: 22, 189, 197, 198
James: 223
20:12–16
Matthew 16–23: 190
20:12–17
Ephesians: 178
20:12, 16
Romans 9–16: 251
20:12, 17
Matthew 1–7: 148
20:13
Matthew 1–7: 290, 292
Matthew 24–28: 222
2 Corinthians: 50
1 Timothy: 22
James: 223
20:13–14
James: 114
20:13–17
Mark 1–8: 357
20:14
Matthew 1–7: 300
Matthew 16–23: 167
Mark 9–16: 55
1 & 2 Thessalonians: 105, 180
James: 223
20:14, 17
Matthew 1–7: 312
20:15
Luke 11–17: 130, 333
2 Corinthians: 272
James: 223
20:16
Mark 9–16: 321
1 & 2 Thessalonians: 180
1 Timothy: 22
James: 223
20:17
Matthew 1–7: 312
Mark 9–16: 55
James: 223
20:18–19
Luke 1–5: 307
Luke 6–10: 213
Hebrews: 411
20:19
2 Corinthians: 97
Hebrews: 212
20:20
Hebrews: 411
20:21
Revelation 1–11: 32
21:2
Ephesians: 324
1 Timothy: 229
Revelation 12–22: 64
21:2–6
1 Corinthians: 211
Galatians: 148
21:5–6
Romans 1–8: 5
Ephesians: 324
Philippians: 13
1 Timothy: 229
Revelation 1–11: 19
21:7
1 Timothy: 229
21:15
Titus: 73, 76
21:15–17
Colossians and Philemon: 170
21:15, 17
Ephesians: 312
1 Timothy: 22
21:16
Ephesians: 323
1 Timothy: 22
21:17
Matthew 8–15: 454
Mark 1–8: 345
1 Timothy: 187

21:20
1 Timothy: 230
21:22–25
Luke 1–5: 37
21:23–24
Revelation 12–22: 183
21:24
Matthew 1–7: 329
Romans 9–16: 201
21:26–27
Ephesians: 324
1 Timothy: 230
21:28–32
1 Timothy: 83
21:32
Mark 9–16: 276, 309
Luke 18–24: 271
22:1
Luke 18–24: 74
22:4
Revelation 12–22: 184
22:7
Revelation 12–22: 184
22:9
Revelation 12–22: 184
22:10–11
James: 267
22:16–17
Matthew 16–23: 166
22:21
1 Peter: 15
22:22
Mark 9–16: 219
Luke 1–5: 275
Luke 18–24: 5, 166
James: 90
22:22–24
1 Timothy: 194
22:24
Romans 1–8: 273
22:25
Luke 11–17: 130
Romans 9–16: 245
2 Corinthians: 272
22:26–27
Matthew 1–7: 334
1 Peter: 52
22:28
Luke 11–17: 230
Acts 13–28: 282
James: 98
22:31
Luke 11–17: 362
2 Corinthians: 443
Philippians: 217
Revelation 12–22: 308
23:4
James: 285
23:4–5
Matthew 1–7: 338
Luke 6–10: 357
23:7
Mark 1–8: 96
Luke 11–17: 37
23:16
Acts 1–12: 39
23:17
Luke 1–5: 191
23:19
James: 63
23:20
Revelation 12–22: 296
23:20, 23
Luke 1–5: 29
23:31
Revelation 1–11: 269
24:1–2
Mark 9–16: 198
24:1–8
Romans 1–8: 347
24:3–4
John 1–11: 16
24:3–8
1 Peter: 23
24:4–8
Luke 1–5: 115
24:6–8
Hebrews: 236
24:7
2 Timothy: 155
24:7–8
2 Corinthians: 88
24:8
Matthew 24–28: 152
Luke 18–24: 284
24:9–10
John 12–21: 105
24:10
Revelation 12–22: 124
24:15–18
Revelation 1–11: 32
24:16
1 & 2 Thessalonians: 137
24:16–17
Luke 1–5: 156
John 1–11: 451
Romans 9–16: 14
24:17
Matthew 1–7: 29, 70
Luke 1–5: 156
Revelation 12–22: 279
25:1–2
1 Corinthians: 455
2 Corinthians: 282
25:8
Acts 1–12: 214
25:9
Acts 1–12: 214
25:10–22
1–3 John: 47
25:16
Revelation 12–22: 132
25:17
Hebrews: 223
25:18
Matthew 24–28: 311
25:21
Revelation 12–22: 132
25:22
Romans 9–16: 14
Hebrews: 223
Revelation 1–11: 321
Revelation 12–22: 132
25:30
Mark 1–8: 144
Luke 6–10: 5
25:31–40
Revelation 1–11: 43
25:40
Acts 1–12: 214
25–40
Hebrews: 221
26:33–34
Revelation 1–11: 321
Revelation 12–22: 132
28:1
Hebrews: 120
1 Peter: 108
28:4
Revelation 1–11: 44
28:15
Revelation 1–11: 91
28:17–20
Revelation 1–11: 147
Revelation 12–22: 282
28:30
Revelation 1–11: 91
28:35
Romans 1–8: 276
28:41
Acts 13–28: 5
2 Corinthians: 45
28:41ff.
1 & 2 Thessalonians: 202
28–29
1 Peter: 108
29:8–9, 44
Luke 1–5: 23
29:9
Luke 1–5: 24
29:10
1 Timothy: 224
29:15
1 Timothy: 224
29:17
Matthew 24–28: 79
29:18
Philippians: 307
29:19
1 Timothy: 224
29:31–33
1 Peter: 207
29:36
1 Peter: 207
29:38–42
John 1–11: 55
29:40
Ephesians: 234
29:42–43
Romans 9–16: 14
29:43
Mark 9–16: 3
29:43–46
Romans 9–16: 15
29:45
Philippians: 170
Revelation 12–22: 272

30:1–10
Revelation 1–11: 267
30:3
Revelation 1–11: 240
30:6
Revelation 1–11: 240
Revelation 12–22: 132
30:7–8
Luke 1–5: 26
Revelation 1–11: 240
Revelation 12–22: 116
30:11–16
Matthew 16–23: 86
1 Peter: 76–77
30:13
1 Peter: 76
30:13–14
John 1–11: 90
30:14
Romans 9–16: 232
30:15
1 Peter: 76
30:18–21
James: 207
30:22–33
Mark 1–8: 295
30:23
Matthew 24–28: 253
Mark 9–16: 364
30:23–25
1 Peter: 111
30:29
1 Peter: 111
30:34–38
1 Peter: 113
31:2–3
Luke 1–5: 180
2 Corinthians: 114
31:3
Ephesians: 246
31:6
2 Corinthians: 114
31:12–17
Mark 1–8: 137
31:16–17
Acts 13–28: 202
31:18
2 Corinthians: 83, 98
32
Luke 1–5: 115
1 Timothy: 147
32:1
Acts 1–12: 213
32:1–4
1 Corinthians: 234
32:1–5
Hebrews: 356
32:1–6
Matthew 1–7: 147
Romans 1–8: 92
32:1–9, 19–20, 25
1–3 John: 89
32:1–24
Luke 6–10: 21
32:2–6
Romans 9–16: 32
32:4
1 Corinthians: 222
32:6
1 Corinthians: 222
32:7–8
Luke 1–5: 74
32:7–9
1 Corinthians: 234
32:9
Acts 1–12: 215
1–3 John: 56
32:11–13
Luke 18–24: 2
Ephesians: 103
32:15–16
2 Corinthians: 83, 100
32:19–29, 30–32
Ephesians: 125
32:23
Acts 1–12: 213
32:28
Mark 1–8: 270
Acts 1–12: 213
Romans 9–16: 32
1 Corinthians: 222
32:30–31
Romans 9–16: 32
32:32
Matthew 1–7: 113
Romans 9–16: 12
2 Corinthians: 111, 477
Philippians: 273
32:32–33
Acts 13–28: 39
32:33
Revelation 1–11: 115
33:1–3
Romans 9–16: 32
33:5
Acts 1–12: 215
33:7
Hebrews: 441
33:9
Hebrews: 441
Revelation 1–11: 32
33:11
Matthew 1–7: 181
Mark 9–16: 198
Romans 9–16: 32
Philippians: 167
33:12–13
Romans 9–16: 32
33:13
Luke 11–17: 6
33:15
Hebrews: 247
33:17
Matthew 1–7: 181
1 Peter: 20
33:17–23
1 & 2 Thessalonians: 71
33:18
Matthew 1–7: 181, 208
Luke 11–17: 16
Romans 9–16: 124
33:18–19
Matthew 16–23: 55
Acts 1–12: 203
James: 261
Revelation 12–22: 279
33:18–23
John 1–11: 451
33:19
Matthew 1–7: 181
Luke 11–17: 236, 369
Romans 1–8: 83
Romans 9–16: 31, 32
2 Corinthians: 102
1 & 2 Thessalonians: 260
1 Peter: 32, 52
33:19–20
1 Timothy: 278
33:19–21
Mark 1–8: 235
33:20
2 Corinthians: 109
Hebrews: xvi
Revelation 1–11: 33, 281
Revelation 12–22: 288
33:20–34:7
Romans 1–8: 84
33:22–34:5
Luke 1–5: 156
34:5
Revelation 1–11: 32
34:5–7
Matthew 1–7: 377
34:6
Luke 1–5: 153
Luke 6–10: 365
Luke 11–17: 183, 235
Luke 18–24: 188
John 12–21: 96
1 & 2 Thessalonians: 180
James: 253, 261
1 Peter: 32, 45, 52
2 Peter–Jude: 25
34:6–7
Matthew 8–15: 304, 469
Matthew 24–28: 212
Mark 1–8: 97
Luke 1–5: 321
Luke 6–10: 136
Luke 11–17: 369, 380
Luke 18–24: 263
Colossians and Philemon: 201
34:7
Luke 1–5: 206
34:10
2 Corinthians: 416
34:12–16
2 Peter–Jude: 103
34:14
Revelation 12–22: 296
34:17
Acts 13–28: 71
34:21
Matthew 8–15: 283
34:22–23
Luke 1–5: 191
Acts 1–12: 39

34:27–35
Acts 1–12: 196
34:28
Mark 1–8: 44
John 1–11: 16
34:29
Matthew 24–28: 309
2 Corinthians: 101
Hebrews: 74
34:29–30
Mark 9–16: 15
Revelation 12–22: 279
34:29–35
1–3 John: 23
Revelation 1–11: 281
34:29, 35
Luke 1–5: 156
34:30
Matthew 1–7: 29
2 Corinthians: 101–2, 109
34:32
2 Corinthians: 102
34:33–35
1 Corinthians: 258
2 Corinthians: 102, 109
34:34
2 Corinthians: 112
34:35
Mark 9–16: 15
Revelation 12–22: 279
35–40
Hebrews: 82
35:21
Matthew 1–7: 412
35:29
2 Corinthians: 385
35:30–31
2 Corinthians: 114
35:31
Ephesians: 246
35:34
2 Corinthians: 114
36:1
2 Corinthians: 114
36:6
1 Corinthians: 455
38:8
1 Timothy: 83
38:21
Revelation 12–22: 132
39:10–13
Revelation 12–22: 282
40
Hebrews: 82
40:5
Revelation 1–11: 194
Revelation 12–22: 116
40:13–15
Luke 1–5: 24
1 Peter: 111
40:20
Revelation 12–22: 132
40:34
Romans 1–8: 84
Romans 9–16: 14
1 & 2 Thessalonians: 137
James: 97
Revelation 12–22: 279
40:34–35
Luke 1–5: 156
John 1–11: 41, 451
Revelation 12–22: 133
40:34–38
Revelation 1–11: 32
40:36–38
Romans 1–8: 84

Leviticus
1:1–17
Ephesians: 198
1:3
Matthew 1–7: 80
Mark 1–8: 37
1:3–17
John 12–21: 35
1–3 John: 47
1:4
Hebrews: 140
1:4–5
1 Peter: 207
1:5
James: 107
1–3 John: 133
1:9
Philippians: 307
1:9, 13, 17
Ephesians: 199
1:10
James: 107
1:13
Philippians: 307
1:14
James: 107
1:17
Philippians: 307
2
Hebrews: 122
2:1–16
Ephesians: 198
2:2, 9, 12
Ephesians: 199
2:2, 15–16
Matthew 1–7: 36
2:13
Matthew 1–7: 241
Mark 9–16: 48
Luke 11–17: 288
3:1–17
Ephesians: 198
3:3
Matthew 8–15: 9
3:5, 16
Ephesians: 199
3:8
Hebrews: 140
3:13
Hebrews: 140
3:17
Acts 13–28: 71
4:1–5:13
1–3 John: 47
4:1–26, 32–35
Ephesians: 199
4:15
1 Timothy: 224
4:27–31
Ephesians: 198
5:1–19
Ephesians: 199
5:3
Mark 1–8: 90
Luke 1–5: 315
5:4–6
Matthew 1–7: 323
5:5–7
John 1–11: 55
5:6–7
Colossians and Philemon: 64
Hebrews: 237
5:7
Ephesians: 238
5:11
Ephesians: 238
Colossians and Philemon: 64
Hebrews: 237
5:14–6:7
1–3 John: 47
5:19
James: 224
6:2
James: 225
6:8–13
1–3 John: 47
6:24–30
1–3 John: 47
7:1–10
1–3 John: 47
7:26
Acts 13–28: 71
8
1 Peter: 112
8:6
1 Peter: 110
8:6–36
1 Peter: 109–10
8:7–9
1 Peter: 111
8:8
Revelation 1–11: 91
8:12
1 Peter: 111
8:14–29
1 Peter: 110
8:30
1 Peter: 111
8:33
1 Peter: 112
8:34
1 Peter: 207
8–9
1 Peter: 108
9:2–4
1 Peter: 112
9:22
Luke 18–24: 452
9:22–23
1 Peter: 112

9:23
Luke 6–10: 280
Romans 9–16: 14
9:23–29
John 1–11: 451
9:24
Hebrews: 302
Revelation 1–11: 228
10:1–2
Revelation 12–22: 61
10:1–3
1 Peter: 112
10:1–7
Mark 9–16: 132
Luke 1–5: 29
10:2
Revelation 1–11: 302
Revelation 12–22: 242
10:3
James: 150, 206
10:9
Ephesians: 238
1 Timothy: 106
Titus: 37
10:9–11
1 Peter: 113
11
Acts 1–12: 295
11:1–47
Mark 1–8: 352
11:3
John 1–11: 81
11:4
Matthew 16–23: 385
11:4–8
Matthew 1–7: 61
11:7
Mark 1–8: 247
Luke 18–24: 226
2 Peter–Jude: 108
11:10
Revelation 12–22: 147
11:12
Matthew 1–7: 445
11:13–15
Luke 11–17: 140
11:22
Mark 1–8: 24
11:41
Revelation 12–22: 147
11:42
Matthew 16–23: 385
11:43–45
1 Peter: 67
11:44
Matthew 1–7: 279
Romans 1–8: 333
2 Corinthians: 443
Titus: 71
Hebrews: 254
1 Peter: 67
11:44–45
Luke 11–17: 347
11:45
Luke 18–24: 12
2 Corinthians: 443
12:1–5
Luke 1–5: 169
12:2–3
Colossians and Philemon: 106
12:3
Luke 1–5: 89, 167
Philippians: 218, 228
12:6
Luke 1–5: 171
12:6–8
Matthew 1–7: 25
2 Corinthians: 292
12:8
Luke 1–5: 171
13
Mark 1–8: 87
13–14
Luke 1–5: 313
Luke 11–17: 389
13:12–17
Mark 1–8: 87
13:45–46
Mark 1–8: 87
Mark 9–16: 273
Luke 1–5: 313, 314
Luke 11–17: 391
14
Mark 1–8: 91
14:1–20
Luke 1–5: 316
14:1–32
Luke 11–17: 392
14:2–32
Matthew 8–15: 296
14:10
Luke 1–5: 316
15:1–3
Luke 11–17: 258
15:19
Luke 1–5: 169
15:19–27
Luke 6–10: 232
15:25–27
Matthew 8–15: 80
Mark 1–8: 258
16:2
1 Peter: 108
16:2–16
1 Peter: 207
Revelation 1–11: 321
16:4
James: 207
Revelation 1–11: 44
16:5
Hebrews: 226
16:8–10
2 Peter–Jude: 20
16:8ff.
Acts 1–12: 35
16:12–13
Luke 1–5: 26
1 Peter: 113
16:13
Revelation 12–22: 132
16:14
1 Corinthians: 353
16:15–17
1–3 John: 49
16:29
Matthew 1–7: 400
16:29–31
Mark 1–8: 128
Luke 18–24: 18
16:29–34
1 Peter: 108
16:29, 31
Matthew 8–15: 68
Luke 1–5: 339
16:33
Romans 9–16: 295
17:7
Luke 1–5: 280
John 12–21: 175
1 Timothy: 146
17:11
Luke 18–24: 284
1 Corinthians: 238
Hebrews: 237
1 Peter: 80, 207
17:12–14
Acts 13–28: 71
17:14
Matthew 24–28: 153
18
Matthew 1–7: 316
18:2, 4–6
1 Peter: 67
18:3
1 Timothy: 114
18:3–4
Ephesians: 309
18:5
Luke 6–10: 354
Romans 9–16: 69
18:7–8
1 Corinthians: 123
18:9–18
1 Timothy: 189
18:16
Mark 1–8: 304
18:16–19
Mark 1–8: 243
18:21
Luke 1–5: 153
1 Peter: 67
Revelation 12–22: 10
18:22
2 Peter–Jude: 86, 166
18:22–29
Luke 18–24: 224
18:24
Ephesians: 309
18:29
1 Corinthians: 123
18:30
1 Peter: 67
19:1–2
1 Peter: 67
19:2
John 12–21: 254
2 Corinthians: 443
James: 48

1 Peter: 67, 129
1–3 John: 45
19:2, 37
1–3 John: 114
19:3
Luke 11–17: 308
John 1–11: 14
1 Peter: 67
19:5
Philippians: 307
19:9–10
2 Corinthians: 282
James: 107
19:10
Romans 9–16: 232
19:10, 12, 14, 16
1 Peter: 67
19:12
Matthew 1–7: 321, 323
James: 268
19:13
Matthew 16–23: 210
Luke 11–17: 312
James: 246
19:14
Mark 1–8: 407
19:15
James: 94, 97, 249
19:16
James: 218
19:16–17
Matthew 16–23: 129
19:17
Matthew 1–7: 432
1 Timothy: 188
19:18
Matthew 1–7: 340
Matthew 8–15: 285
Matthew 16–23: 190, 201
Luke 1–5: 220
Luke 11–17: 361
Romans 1–8: 370
Philippians: 41
1 & 2 Thessalonians: 180
Titus: 127
James: 112
1 Peter: 67, 189
1–3 John: 61, 131, 229
19:20
Mark 9–16: 55
19:26
Acts 13–28: 71
19:28
1 Peter: 67
Revelation 1–11: 34
19:30–32
1 Peter: 67
19:32
1 Timothy: 186
Titus: 73
James: 97
19:34
Luke 6–10: 357
1 Peter: 67
19:36–37
1 Peter: 67
20:2–5
Luke 1–5: 153
20:7
2 Corinthians: 443
20:7–8
1 Peter: 67
20:9
Colossians and Philemon: 170
20:10
Matthew 1–7: 302, 310, 317
Matthew 16–23: 167
Luke 1–5: 60
20:10–14
Matthew 1–7: 312, 317
20:17–19
1 Timothy: 189
20:21
Mark 1–8: 304
Luke 1–5: 231
20:24
2 Corinthians: 254–55
1 Peter: 67
20:25–26
Acts 1–12: 295
20:26
John 1–11: 152
Romans 1–8: 8
2 Corinthians: 254–55, 257, 443
1 Peter: 67, 129
21:5
Philippians: 219
21:6–8
1 Peter: 67
21:7
Matthew 16–23: 168
21:7, 14
Matthew 1–7: 314
Luke 1–5: 24
21:10
Luke 18–24: 325
21:10–11
Luke 6–10: 320
21:12
1 Peter: 67
21:14
Matthew 16–23: 168
21:15
1 Peter: 67
21:17–23
Luke 1–5: 24
21:18
Mark 1–8: 407
21:23
1 Peter: 67
22:2
1 Peter: 67
22:16
1 Peter: 67
22:29
Philippians: 307
22:32–33
1 Peter: 67
23
Acts 1–12: 39
23:3
Matthew 16–23: 23
23:10
1 Corinthians: 416
23:10–11
James: 63
23:15
Acts 1–12: 40
23:15ff.
Acts 1–12: 40
23:17
Matthew 8–15: 374
23:18
Philippians: 192
23:20
Acts 1–12: 40
23:22
1 Peter: 67
23:24
1 & 2 Thessalonians: 134
23:26–27
1 Peter: 207
23:27–32
Matthew 24–28: 139
23:33–43
Mark 9–16: 268
23:33–44
Matthew 16–23: 66
23:37
Philippians: 192
23:40
John 12–21: 15
Revelation 1–11: 226
24:8–9
Mark 1–8: 145
24:9
Mark 1–8: 144
Luke 6–10: 6
24:10–16
Mark 1–8: 104
Luke 1–5: 323
24:14
Acts 1–12: 223
24:14–16
Luke 11–17: 239
2 Corinthians: 389
Hebrews: 46
24:16
Matthew 8–15: 311
Matthew 24–28: 207
Luke 18–24: 155, 337, 380
Acts 1–12: 193, 223
24:19–20
Revelation 12–22: 183
24:20
Matthew 1–7: 329
24:23
2 Corinthians: 389
25:3
Revelation 12–22: 65
25:8–13
James: 107
25:10
Luke 1–5: 146
Ephesians: 324

25:17
1 Peter: 68
25:25
Luke 1–5: 244
James: 102, 108
25:32–33
Acts 1–12: 151
25:35
Matthew 1–7: 355
25:35–36
Romans 9–16: 245
25:35–37
James: 102, 107
25:36–37
2 Corinthians: 272
25:39
James: 102, 108
25:39–41, 46
Ephesians: 324
25:39ff.
1 Timothy: 229
25:44
Ephesians: 324
25:44–46
1 Timothy: 229
25:46
1 Timothy: 229
26:3
1 & 2 Thessalonians: 315
26:6
Matthew 1–7: 213
1 & 2 Thessalonians: 315
26:11–12
2 Corinthians: 253
Revelation 1–11: 233
Revelation 12–22: 266
26:12
John 1–11: 33
Revelation 12–22: 272
26:21
James: 225
26:26
Revelation 1–11: 182
26:27
Matthew 8–15: 52
26:33–39
Revelation 12–22: 293
26:41
Philippians: 218
26:42
Luke 1–5: 83
26:46
1–3 John: 45
27:13
Luke 18–24: 423
27:27
Luke 18–24: 423
27:30
Matthew 16–23: 383
Romans 9–16: 231
1 Corinthians: 454
27:30–32
2 Corinthians: 282
27:30–33
Luke 11–17: 101

Numbers
1:5–15
Revelation 1–11: 220
1:23
Luke 1–5: 176
1:50
Revelation 12–22: 132
1:50–51
2 Peter–Jude: 178
1:53
Revelation 12–22: 132
2
Revelation 12–22: 281
2:3–31
Revelation 1–11: 220
3:3
Luke 1–5: 24
2 Corinthians: 45
3:6–8
2 Peter–Jude: 178
3:6–10
John 1–11: 50
3:12–13
Luke 1–5: 170
3:16
1 & 2 Thessalonians: 294
3:41, 44, 45
Luke 1–5: 170
4:3, 35, 39, 43, 47
Luke 1–5: 248
4:5
Revelation 12–22: 132
4:5–6
Luke 1–5: 75
4:30
Matthew 1–7: 75
5:2
Matthew 8–15: 6
Mark 1–8: 87
Luke 1–5: 276
5:2–3
Luke 11–17: 390
5:6–7
Luke 18–24: 74
5:6–8
Colossians and Philemon: 224
5:14–15
Luke 1–5: 23
5:19–22
James: 267
5:22
Revelation 1–11: 133
6:1–4
1 Timothy: 225
6:2
1 Timothy: 83
6:2–4
Luke 6–10: 154
Ephesians: 239
Titus: 38
6:2–5
Acts 13–28: 159
6:2ff.
James: 268
6:3
1 Timothy: 106

6:5–7
Ephesians: 239
6:9–12
Acts 13–28: 252
6:12
Acts 13–28: 252
6:13–21
Acts 13–28: 159
6:14
Philippians: 182
6:14ff.
Acts 13–28: 253
6:18
Acts 13–28: 252
6:23–27
Luke 1–5: 29
6:26
Philippians: 284
1 & 2 Thessalonians: 314
7:89
Revelation 1–11: 321
Revelation 12–22: 132
8:10
Acts 13–28: 7
1 Timothy: 224
8:11–14
Romans 1–8: 8
8:14–16
Hebrews: 174
8:24
Matthew 1–7: 75
8:24–25
Hebrews: 174
9:6
John 1–11: 485
9:12
Mark 9–16: 388
Luke 18–24: 274
John 12–21: 62
9:17
Matthew 16–23: 67
10:2
1 & 2 Thessalonians: 134
Revelation 1–11: 239
10:9
Luke 1–5: 154
1 & 2 Thessalonians: 134
10:10
1 & 2 Thessalonians: 134
Revelation 1–11: 239
10:11
Revelation 12–22: 132
10:34
Revelation 1–11: 32
10:35
Philippians: 221
11:1
Revelation 1–11: 302
Revelation 12–22: 124
11:1–3
Luke 11–17: 240
11:1–14:38
2 Peter–Jude: 163
11:5
Acts 1–12: 212

11:10
Mark 1–8: 156
11:11–15
Acts 13–28: 144
11:12
1 & 2 Thessalonians: 45
11:16
Acts 13–28: 278
Ephesians: 145
11:16–17
John 1–11: 101
Ephesians: 146
Colossians and Philemon: 191
11:17
Luke 1–5: 239
2 Corinthians: 114
11:20
James: 226
11:23
Luke 1–5: 91
11:25
Luke 1–5: 180
2 Corinthians: 114
1 Peter: 263
1–3 John: 215
11:28–29
1 Corinthians: 107
11:29
James: 147
12
Matthew 1–7: 37, 171, 173
12:1–2
2 Corinthians: 454
12:1–10
Romans 1–8: 61
12:3
Mark 9–16: 102
Luke 11–17: 376
Ephesians: 125
Philippians: 112
James: 169
12:7
Matthew 16–23: 337
John 12–21: 160
Romans 1–8: 5
12:7–8
Hebrews: 79
12:8
1–3 John: 237
12:13
John 12–21: 234
12:14
Luke 18–24: 338
13:30
Matthew 16–23: 74
Acts 13–28: 234
Philippians: 177
13:30–33
1 Peter: 214
13:31–33
Philippians: 177
13:32
Mark 1–8: 270
13:32–33
Hebrews: 356
14:1–38
Luke 11–17: 240
14:2
Philippians: 177
14:3–4
Philippians: 177
14:7–9
Acts 13–28: 234
14:10
John 1–11: 451
Philippians: 177
14:11
Philippians: 178
14:13–19
Luke 11–17: 2
Ephesians: 103
14:18
Mark 1–8: 96
Luke 1–5: 206, 321
Acts 1–12: 117
1 & 2 Thessalonians: 180
James: 261
14:19
1 Timothy: 58
14:21
James: 269
14:22–23
Philippians: 178
Hebrews: 91
14:24
James: 12
14:26–38
2 Peter–Jude: 163–64
14:28
James: 269
14:28–29
Philippians: 178
14:34–37
Philippians: 178
15:3
Philippians: 307
15:5
Ephesians: 234
15:19–21
Romans 9–16: 113
15:20
Romans 1–8: 8
15:22–29
1 Timothy: 30
15:22–31
Acts 1–12: 111
15:25
1 Peter: 207
15:28
Hebrews: 121
15:30
Hebrews: 121
15:30–31
1 Timothy: 31
15:30–36
Hebrews: 47
15:35
Matthew 24–28: 253
Mark 9–16: 362
15:35–36
2 Corinthians: 389
15:36
John 12–21: 348
15:37–41
Matthew 1–7: 362–63
Matthew 16–23: 338
Mark 1–8: 259
Luke 6–10: 233
Romans 1–8: 370
15:38
Matthew 8–15: 80
15:38–40
Matthew 16–23: 365
Luke 18–24: 164
15:40
2 Corinthians: 443
16
Hebrews: 110, 120
2 Peter–Jude: 178
16:1–40
1 Peter: 108
16:3
2 Corinthians: 454
16:3, 13
Romans 9–16: 220
16:5
2 Timothy: 82
16:19
John 1–11: 451
16:25–32
Romans 1–8: 120
16:26, 32
2 Timothy: 82
16:28–33
Revelation 12–22: 33
16:32–33, 35
Matthew 1–7: 70
16:32–35
1 Corinthians: 225
16:35
Revelation 1–11: 302
Revelation 12–22: 124
16:41
1 Corinthians: 225
16:42
John 1–11: 451
18:2–4
John 1–11: 50
18:3
2 Peter–Jude: 178
18:7
Luke 1–5: 23, 24
18:8–24
1 Corinthians: 205
18:15–16
Luke 1–5: 170
18:19
Luke 11–17: 288
18:20
Acts 1–12: 151
18:20–24
1 Peter: 34
18:21
1 Corinthians: 454
2 Corinthians: 282
18:21–24
Romans 9–16: 231

18:24
Acts 1–12: 151
18:26
1 Corinthians: 455
18:28
Matthew 16–23: 329
19:2
Philippians: 182
19:11
Mark 1–8: 242
Mark 9–16: 364
19:11–22
Luke 11–17: 102
19:11, 14, 16
John 12–21: 326
19:16
Matthew 16–23: 386
John 1–11: 472
19:17–19
Mark 1–8: 354
John 1–11: 105
20
Luke 18–24: 425
20:2–5
Luke 6–10: 53
20:3
2 Corinthians: 454
20:6
Mark 9–16: 3
Luke 6–10: 53
20:7–8
Luke 6–10: 53
20:7–12
John 1–11: 342
20:8–12
1 Corinthians: 221
20:10
2 Corinthians: 454
20:10–12
Luke 6–10: 21
20:12
Luke 6–10: 54
Luke 11–17: 15
20:14–21
Luke 1–5: 22
20:23–29
Hebrews: 198
21
Acts 13–28: 24
21:1–3
Acts 1–12: 320
21:4–9
1 Peter: 33
21:5
1 Corinthians: 224
21:6
John 12–21: 349
1 Corinthians: 225
21:8
Hebrews: 172
21:8–9
Mark 9–16: 267
21:17–18
Revelation 12–22: 127
21:21–31
Acts 1–12: 320
21:29
Revelation 1–11: 251
21:33–35
Acts 1–12: 320
21:34
John 12–21: 98
22
1 Corinthians: 208
22:1–6
2 Peter–Jude: 102
22:16–34
1 Corinthians: 332
22:22–35
2 Peter–Jude: 103
22:23
Revelation 1–11: 89
22:28–30
Luke 18–24: 396
22:34
Matthew 1–7: 66
22–24
Luke 11–17: 129
2 Corinthians: 272
2 Peter–Jude: 102, 177–78
Revelation 12–22: 56, 57
23
Matthew 1–7: 480
23:10
Matthew 1–7: 194
23:19
Luke 1–5: 87
Luke 11–17: 154
Romans 9–16: 130
1 & 2 Thessalonians: 161, 319
Revelation 1–11: 30, 196
Revelation 12–22: 211
24
2 Corinthians: 282
24:7
2 Peter–Jude: 64
Revelation 12–22: 241
24:17
Acts 13–28: 22
1 Peter: 56
1–3 John: 189
Revelation 12–22: 307
24:19
Romans 9–16: 33
25
Revelation 1–11: 88
25:1–2
1 Corinthians: 223
25:1–9
Ephesians: 203
25:1–18
2 Peter–Jude: 103
25:4–5
Revelation 1–11: 88
25:7–13
1 Peter: 113
25:9
1 Corinthians: 223
Revelation 1–11: 88
25:10–13
Luke 1–5: 95
2 Corinthians: 87
25:13
Luke 1–5: 113
26:4–51
Revelation 1–11: 220
26:53–55
Luke 1–5: 244
26:53–56
1 Peter: 34
26:55ff.
Acts 1–12: 35
26:59
Luke 1–5: 59
26:65
John 12–21: 309
27:1–11
Luke 11–17: 131
27:7–11
1 Peter: 34
27:16–17
John 1–11: 424
27:17
Mark 1–8: 317
27:18
2 Corinthians: 114
27:18–23
Acts 13–28: 7
1 Timothy: 224
27:21
John 1–11: 484
Revelation 1–11: 91
28:9–10
Matthew 8–15: 286
Mark 1–8: 145
28:11–14
Colossians and Philemon: 118
29:5–6
Revelation 12–22: 5
30:2
Matthew 1–7: 321, 323
Matthew 8–15: 454
James: 268
30:9
1 Timothy: 211
31:7–35
1 Timothy: 229
31:8
Luke 11–17: 129
1 Corinthians: 332
2 Corinthians: 272
2 Peter–Jude: 103
Revelation 12–22: 56
31:9–20
2 Peter–Jude: 103
31:16
1 Corinthians: 332
Revelation 1–11: 88
31:17–18
Philippians: 235
31:18
1 Peter: 20
31:22–23
1 Peter: 43
31:35
Philippians: 235
1 Peter: 20

32:23
Matthew 24–28: 110
Galatians: 187
1–3 John: 201
33:52
Mark 1–8: 366
34:2
1 Peter: 34
34:11
Mark 1–8: 50, 228
Luke 1–5: 302
Luke 6–10: 208
John 12–21: 390
35
Hebrews: 168
35:25
Luke 1–5: 203
35:28
Mark 9–16: 336
35:30–31
Matthew 1–7: 292
35:33
Romans 9–16: 226
36:1–12
1 Timothy: 83
36:5
1 & 2 Thessalonians: 294

Deuteronomy

1:1
1 Timothy: 83
1:7
Revelation 1–11: 269
Revelation 12–22: 146
1:9–18
Ephesians: 145
1:10
Revelation 12–22: 262
1:11
Philippians: 283
1:13–17
Ephesians: 146
1:17
James: 94, 113
Revelation 1–11: 320
1:28
Hebrews: 362
1:29–30
Hebrews: 362
1:31
Acts 13–28: 19
1:33
Matthew 16–23: 67
1:34
Romans 1–8: 65
1:39
Luke 18–24: 28
2:7
Acts 13–28: 19
2:15
Acts 1–12: 313
2:30
Luke 18–24: 398
3:20
1 Peter: 34
3:24
Luke 1–5: 59
3:28
1 Peter: 34
4:2
Mark 9–16: 261
Luke 18–24: 250
John 12–21: 207
Ephesians: 369
1 Timothy: 288
Revelation 12–22: 309
4:5–8
Romans 9–16: 14
4:5, 14
2 Timothy: 156
4:9
1 & 2 Thessalonians: 50
4:10
Mark 9–16: 143
4:13
Luke 1–5: 95
1 & 2 Thessalonians: 62
4:13–14
Matthew 1–7: 255
4:14–18
Luke 1–5: 74
4:14–19
1 Corinthians: 235
4:19
Revelation 12–22: 262
4:24
Matthew 1–7: 70
1 & 2 Thessalonians: 235
Revelation 1–11: 148
4:27
John 1–11: 152
1 Peter: 129
4:28
Revelation 1–11: 273
4:29
Mark 9–16: 75
Hebrews: 262
4:30–31
Revelation 1–11: 31
4:31
Mark 1–8: 96, 386
Romans 9–16: 198
4:33
1 & 2 Thessalonians: 235
4:34
Acts 13–28: 19
4:35
Acts 13–28: 135
2 Corinthians: 488
Ephesians: 131
1 Timothy: 33, 71, 275
1 Peter: 200
4:37
Luke 11–17: 245
John 1–11: 398
2 Corinthians: 315
Revelation 1–11: 130
4:39
2 Corinthians: 488
1 Timothy: 33, 71, 275
Revelation 12–22: 262
5:1–22
2 Peter–Jude: 49
5:4
1 & 2 Thessalonians: 235
5:5
John 1–11: 16
2 Corinthians: 97
1 & 2 Thessalonians: 294
Hebrews: 212
5:7
Acts 13–28: 71
5:11
1 & 2 Thessalonians: 260
5:12–15
Mark 1–8: 137
5:15
Acts 13–28: 19
5:16
1 Timothy: 189
5:17, 18
James: 114
5:24
Luke 1–5: 156
5:24–26
1 & 2 Thessalonians: 235
5:26
Revelation 1–11: 217, 315
5:29
1 Peter: 68
5:32
Mark 9–16: 200–201
5:33
Mark 9–16: 200–201
Galatians: 88
6:1–2
Mark 9–16: 201
6:1–9
Romans 1–8: 356
6:2
Mark 9–16: 201
6:3
John 1–11: 398
6:4
Mark 9–16: 200
Romans 1–8: 226
2 Corinthians: 488
Ephesians: 131, 308
1 Timothy: 33, 71, 275
1–3 John: 162
6:4–5
Mark 1–8: 338
Romans 9–16: 70
James: 131
6:4–7
Matthew 16–23: 183
1 Timothy: 83
6:4–9
Matthew 1–7: 362
Matthew 16–23: 338, 364
Romans 1–8: 370
2 Peter–Jude: 48
6:4ff.
Acts 13–28: 17
6:5
Matthew 1–7: 340, 453
Matthew 16–23: 190, 201, 339

Matthew 24–28: 101
Mark 1–8: 356
John 12–21: 89
Romans 1–8: 370
1 Corinthians: 377
Philippians: 41
James: 39, 112
1 Peter: 275
1–3 John: 61, 229
6:5–6
Ephesians: 308
6:6
Hebrews: 215
6:6–9
1 & 2 Thessalonians: 198
6:7
Ephesians: 308
1 & 2 Thessalonians: 108
6:8
Matthew 16–23: 363
Ephesians: 308
6:8–9
Matthew 16–23: 183
Hebrews: 215
6:9
Matthew 16–23: 339
Romans 1–8: 370
Ephesians: 308
6:12
Matthew 16–23: 183
2 Peter–Jude: 48
6:13
Matthew 1–7: 322
Luke 1–5: 259, 307
James: 268
1 Peter: 68
Revelation 12–22: 200
6:14
Matthew 16–23: 183
6:16
Mark 1–8: 401
Luke 1–5: 260
6:17–18
2 Corinthians: 443
6:24
1 Peter: 68
7:1
Acts 13–28: 19
7:1–3
Mark 9–16: 59
7:2
Matthew 8–15: 468
7:3
Matthew 1–7: 8
7:6
John 1–11: 152
2 Corinthians: 443
1 Peter: 16
Revelation 12–22: 5
7:6–7
1 Peter: 130
7:6–8
Luke 11–17: 245
John 1–11: 398
John 12–21: 20
Romans 9–16: 100
1 Peter: 67
7:6–9
1 Peter: 124
7:7
1 & 2 Thessalonians: 286
7:7–8
Luke 1–5: 128
Luke 6–10: 45
John 1–11: 204
Romans 1–8: 488, 499
1 Corinthians: 14
Galatians: 28
1 & 2 Thessalonians: 20
Hebrews: 71, 165
James: 107
1–3 John: 81, 115
Revelation 1–11: 130
Revelation 12–22: 204
7:7–9
Romans 9–16: 70
7:9
Luke 1–5: 174
1 & 2 Thessalonians: 296
1 Peter: 63
7:9–10
Mark 9–16: 203
7:10
Mark 1–8: 96
Philippians: 221
7:13
Luke 1–5: 36, 71
7:18
2 Peter–Jude: 48
7:19
Acts 13–28: 19
7:25
Luke 18–24: 225
Romans 1–8: 157
1 Timothy: 255
8:1–18
Matthew 1–7: 91
8:1–20
1–3 John: 153
8:2
Acts 13–28: 19
2 Corinthians: 13, 59
1 Peter: 43–44
2 Peter–Jude: 48
8:3
Matthew 1–7: 91
Luke 1–5: 257
1 Corinthians: 63
1 & 2 Thessalonians: 196
2 Timothy: 150
1 Peter: 42, 100
1–3 John: 90
8:4
Acts 13–28: 19
8:6
James: 167
Revelation 12–22: 200
8:8
Matthew 16–23: 277
8:11–14
Mark 9–16: 101
Luke 11–17: 130
2 Corinthians: 272
8:11–18
1 Timothy: 248
8:14
2 Corinthians: 272
8:15
Mark 1–8: 44
8:15–16
Romans 1–8: 474
8:16
2 Corinthians: 59
8:17–18
Luke 11–17: 333
8:18
Luke 11–17: 128
2 Corinthians: 272
1 Timothy: 280
James: 240
8:18–20
2 Peter–Jude: 48
9:3
Matthew 1–7: 70
1 & 2 Thessalonians: 235
Revelation 12–22: 124
9:4
Luke 1–5: 21
9:4–5
Romans 9–16: 70
9:10
John 1–11: 16
9:24
Luke 11–17: 20
9:29
Acts 13–28: 19
2 Corinthians: 315
10:9
Acts 1–12: 151
10:12
Mark 1–8: 354
James: 19, 167
1 Peter: 68
Revelation 12–22: 200
10:12–13
Mark 1–8: 353
Luke 1–5: 309
1–3 John: 28
10:12–13, 16
Matthew 8–15: 458
10:14
2 Corinthians: 289
10:14–15
Romans 1–8: 167
10:15
John 1–11: 152, 398
Romans 9–16: 70
10:16
Matthew 8–15: 459
Luke 1–5: 167
John 1–11: 34
2 Corinthians: 110
Philippians: 219
Colossians and Philemon: 107
10:17
John 1–11: 14
Acts 1–12: 300
Philippians: 315

1 Timothy: 276
James: 94
Revelation 1–11: 3
Revelation 12–22: 171, 221, 251
10:18
Luke 18–24: 166
10:19
1 & 2 Thessalonians: 90
1–3 John: 242
10:20
Matthew 16–23: 165
Revelation 12–22: 200
10:22
Acts 1–12: 205
11:4
Revelation 1–11: 271
11:11
2 Corinthians: 395
11:13
Mark 1–8: 338, 354
Mark 9–16: 202
Romans 1–8: 370
Galatians: 148
Philippians: 31
1 Peter: 124
1–3 John: 183
11:13–21
Matthew 1–7: 362
Matthew 16–23: 338, 364
Romans 1–8: 370
11:18
Matthew 16–23: 363
11:20
Matthew 16–23: 339
Romans 1–8: 370
11:22
Matthew 16–23: 165
11:24
Revelation 1–11: 269
Revelation 12–22: 146
11:26–28
Acts 13–28: 358
11:28
James: 285
12:9
1 Peter: 34
12:10–11
2 Corinthians: 282
12:10–19
Romans 9–16: 232
12:11
Matthew 16–23: 383
12:16
Acts 13–28: 71
12:17
Matthew 16–23: 383
12:17–18
2 Corinthians: 282
12:18
1 & 2 Thessalonians: 184
12:20
John 1–11: 398
12:23
Acts 13–28: 71
12:31
Luke 11–17: 374
12:32
Ephesians: 369
Revelation 12–22: 310
13:1–3
2 Corinthians: 334
13:1–5
1 Timothy: 14
2 Peter–Jude: 68, 172
Revelation 12–22: 54
13:3
Luke 11–17: 48
2 Corinthians: 59–60
James: 19
13:3–4
James: 17
13:4
Matthew 16–23: 165
Luke 1–5: 308
1 Peter: 153
1–3 John: 181
Revelation 12–22: 200
13:5
Mark 9–16: 216
Luke 6–10: 112
Luke 11–17: 255
13:6
Romans 9–16: 222
13:6–11
1 Timothy: 223
13:12–15
Acts 1–12: 321
13:12–18
1 Timothy: 150
13:13
2 Corinthians: 250
Hebrews: 270
14:1
Revelation 1–11: 34
14:2
John 1–11: 152
Romans 1–8: 167
Romans 9–16: 70
1 Peter: 16, 130
Revelation 12–22: 5
14:7–8
Matthew 1–7: 61
14:8
Mark 1–8: 247
14:23
James: 167
14:28–29
Matthew 16–23: 383
1 Corinthians: 455
2 Corinthians: 282
James: 90
14:29
Luke 1–5: 275
Acts 1–12: 178
Romans 9–16: 232
1 Timothy: 214
15:1–2
James: 107
15:4–6
Luke 11–17: 129
15:6
John 1–11: 398
15:7–8
Matthew 1–7: 195
15:7–10
Romans 9–16: 245
15:7–11
James: 94
15:9
Matthew 1–7: 195
15:9–11
James: 246
15:10
2 Corinthians: 316–17
15:10–11
2 Corinthians: 316–17
15:12–17
1 Timothy: 229
15:13–14
Matthew 1–7: 355
Ephesians: 324
15:15–16
Romans 9–16: 70
15:23
Acts 13–28: 71
16:2–7
1 Peter: 73
16:3
Luke 18–24: 282
16:9–15
1 Timothy: 83
16:10
Matthew 1–7: 358
16:11
Acts 1–12: 178
16:11, 14
Luke 1–5: 275
16:16
Luke 1–5: 191
Luke 18–24: 265
16:18
Ephesians: 145
16:18–20
Matthew 24–28: 199
Mark 9–16: 320
Luke 18–24: 330
16:19
James: 94, 113
17:1
Matthew 1–7: 80
Mark 1–8: 37
17:3
Acts 1–12: 213
17:6
Mark 9–16: 4
Luke 1–5: 165
Luke 18–24: 330
Revelation 1–11: 298
17:7
Matthew 24–28: 199
Acts 1–12: 224
17:8–12
Acts 13–28: 282
17:8–13
James: 249

17:12–13
1 Timothy: 223
17:13
Romans 9–16: 222
17:14–15
1 Peter: 145
17:16
2 Corinthians: 447
17:19
James: 167
17:19–20
1 & 2 Thessalonians: 89
18:4
James: 63
18:9
1 Timothy: 114
18:9–14
Matthew 24–28: 2
18:15
Mark 1–8: 302
Acts 1–12: 121, 211
Romans 1–8: 12
1 Peter: 56
Revelation 1–11: 301
18:15–18
Luke 1–5: 42, 175
Luke 6–10: 139
John 1–11: 52
18:15–19
Luke 6–10: 143
18:16
1 & 2 Thessalonians: 235
18:18
Revelation 1–11: 301
18:18–22
Luke 18–24: 422, 425
18:19
Acts 1–12: 122
18:20
Revelation 12–22: 56
18:20–22
2 Peter–Jude: 68
19
Matthew 1–7: 330
Hebrews: 168
19:8
John 1–11: 398
19:12
Ephesians: 145
19:13
Romans 9–16: 222
19:15
Matthew 8–15: 184
Matthew 16–23: 62, 133
Mark 1–8: 286
Mark 9–16: 400
Luke 1–5: 165
Luke 6–10: 325
Luke 18–24: 330, 351, 411, 412
2 Corinthians: 447
1 Timothy: 222
Revelation 1–11: 298
19:16–19
Matthew 24–28: 199
Mark 9–16: 321
Luke 18–24: 330
19:16–20
1 Timothy: 223
James: 249
19:18–20
Acts 1–12: 246
19:20
Matthew 1–7: 329
19:21
Matthew 1–7: 329
Romans 9–16: 222
Revelation 12–22: 183
20:1
Revelation 1–11: 271
20:4
Luke 1–5: 153
20:10–14
1 Timothy: 229
20:17
James: 268
21:1–9
Luke 18–24: 360
21:15–17
Luke 1–5: 149
Luke 11–17: 131, 283
21:17
Luke 11–17: 308
21:18–21
2 Corinthians: 452
Hebrews: 395
21:22–23
Mark 9–16: 387
Luke 18–24: 399
John 12–21: 363
Acts 1–12: 155
Revelation 1–11: 303
21:23
Matthew 1–7: 169
Matthew 24–28: 228, 253, 292
Mark 9–16: 368
Luke 18–24: 382
Acts 1–12: 169
1 Corinthians: 285
Philippians: 135
1 Peter: 224
22:1
James: 285
22:1–4
Matthew 1–7: 338
22:5
Luke 18–24: 224
1 Corinthians: 142
22:10
2 Corinthians: 246
22:12
Mark 1–8: 259
Luke 6–10: 233
22:13–21
Luke 1–5: 60
22:14
Matthew 1–7: 313
22:19
Matthew 1–7: 20, 313
Matthew 16–23: 168
22:22
Matthew 1–7: 302
Luke 11–17: 351
22:22–24
Matthew 1–7: 310
Matthew 16–23: 167
22:23–24
Matthew 1–7: 17
22:28–29
Matthew 1–7: 313, 315
22:29
Matthew 16–23: 168
23:1
Acts 1–12: 254
23:4–5
2 Peter–Jude: 103
23:13–14
Matthew 1–7: 310
23:14
Mark 9–16: 58
Luke 1–5: 154
23:15–16
Ephesians: 324
1 Timothy: 230
23:18
Philippians: 217
Revelation 12–22: 309
23:21
Matthew 1–7: 321
23:24–25
Matthew 8–15: 283
23:25
Mark 1–8: 142
Luke 6–10: 5
24
Matthew 1–7: 310
Ephesians: 273
24:1–4
Matthew 1–7: 309–11, 313–16
Matthew 16–23: 168, 169
Mark 9–16: 57
Luke 11–17: 351, 352
Romans 1–8: 122
24:5
Luke 11–17: 272
24:7
1 Timothy: 22
24:14–15
Luke 11–17: 312
James: 246
24:14, 15
1 Timothy: 221
24:15
Matthew 16–23: 210
James: 247
24:17
Luke 18–24: 5
24:17–21
Luke 1–5: 275
24:19–21
Acts 1–12: 178
25:1–3
2 Corinthians: 389
25:2
Romans 9–16: 222
25:3
Matthew 8–15: 204
Acts 1–12: 173

Romans 9–16: 222
25:4
John 12–21: 200
1 Corinthians: 203
1 Timothy: 220
2 Timothy: 146
25:5–6
Matthew 16–23: 330
Mark 9–16: 188
Luke 18–24: 144–45
25:5–7
Luke 1–5: 247
25:5–10
1 Timothy: 194
25:7–8
1–3 John: 215
25:9
Mark 9–16: 330
Luke 18–24: 338
25:13–16
Luke 18–24: 224
26:1
1 Peter: 34
26:1–11
Revelation 12–22: 79
26:7
Acts 13–28: 307
26:8
Acts 13–28: 19
26:11
Philippians: 275
26:12
Acts 1–12: 178
26:15
1 Peter: 35
26:16
Mark 1–8: 338
Philippians: 31
26:18
John 1–11: 398
1 Peter: 130
26:18–19
John 1–11: 152
Titus: 123
27–28
Romans 1–8: 70
Romans 9–16: 14
27:1
Ephesians: 145
27:3
John 1–11: 398
27:11–26
Luke 1–5: 116
27:12–13
Revelation 1–11: 220
27:15
Revelation 1–11: 273
27:16
Luke 6–10: 161
27:18
James: 285
27:19
Luke 18–24: 6
1 Timothy: 194, 214
James: 90
27:22
1 Timothy: 189
27:25
Matthew 24–28: 227
27:26
Romans 1–8: 366, 367
Galatians: 135
Hebrews: 413
28:1
1 & 2 Thessalonians: 66
28:1–3
Matthew 1–7: 408
28:1–6
Matthew 16–23: 279
28:1–14
Luke 1–5: 115
28:1ff.
Acts 13–28: 358
28:9
James: 269
28:9–10
John 1–11: 152
28:15
1 & 2 Thessalonians: 66
28:15–19
Matthew 16–23: 279
28:15–22
Romans 1–8: 366
28:15–68
Matthew 16–23: 402
Mark 9–16: 135
Luke 1–5: 116
2 Peter–Jude: 184
Revelation 12–22: 25
28:15ff.
1 Timothy: 147
28:27
Revelation 12–22: 139
28:35
Revelation 12–22: 139
28:38
Revelation 1–11: 259, 262
28:49
1 Corinthians: 382
Revelation 1–11: 251
28:58
2 Peter–Jude: 29
1–3 John: 73
28:64
1 Peter: 129
29:1
Luke 1–5: 118
29:4
Romans 9–16: 103
Revelation 12–22: 304
29:5
Acts 13–28: 19
29:13
Revelation 12–22: 272
29:14–15
1 & 2 Thessalonians: 62
29:18
Revelation 1–11: 249
29:18–19
Hebrews: 407
29:18–21
Revelation 1–11: 220
29:19
1 & 2 Thessalonians: 315
29:20
Hebrews: 407
1–3 John: 81
29:23
2 Peter–Jude: 88
29:29
Matthew 1–7: 382
Luke 1–5: 47
John 1–11: 471
Acts 1–12: 20
Romans 9–16: 136
1 Corinthians: 27, 65
2 Corinthians: 396
Colossians and Philemon: 78
1 & 2 Thessalonians: 204
Revelation 1–11: 284
30:1–3
Luke 1–5: 118
30:1–5
Revelation 12–22: 229
30:2
Mark 1–8: 354
30:3
Luke 11–17: 237
30:5
John 1–11: 152
30:6
Luke 1–5: 119, 167
Romans 1–8: 252
Philippians: 219
Colossians and Philemon: 107
30:8–10
Luke 1–5: 25
30:9
Luke 6–10: 338
30:9–10
Romans 9–16: 70
30:14
Romans 9–16: 72
30:17
James: 285
30:19
Hebrews: 346
30:19–20
Matthew 1–7: 450
James: 202
31:6
2 Corinthians: 21
31:7
1 Peter: 34
31:7–8
1 & 2 Thessalonians: 50
31:8
2 Corinthians: 21
Hebrews: 163
31:9
Ephesians: 145
31:16
Matthew 16–23: 329
31:19–22
Revelation 12–22: 127

31:23
1 & 2 Thessalonians: 50
31:27
Luke 11–17: 20
31:28
Ephesians: 145
31:29
Revelation 1–11: 273
32:1–44
Revelation 12–22: 127
32:3–4
1 Peter: 105
32:4
Luke 1–5: 174
Romans 1–8: 217
1 Peter: 200
Revelation 12–22: 123, 130, 246
32:5
Mark 9–16: 26
Philippians: 183
32:5–6
2 Peter–Jude: 73
32:6
Luke 11–17: 11
1 Peter: 30
32:8
Mark 1–8: 244
Luke 1–5: 49
Acts 13–28: 140
32:9
John 1–11: 152, 398
32:9–11
Luke 11–17: 237
Revelation 12–22: 31
32:9–14
Ephesians: 72
32:15
1 Peter: 52
32:17
Luke 1–5: 280
John 12–21: 175
1 Corinthians: 240
2 Corinthians: 251, 467
1 Timothy: 146
1–3 John: 153
Revelation 1–11: 273
32:20
Mark 1–8: 400
32:21
Romans 9–16: 89
1 Corinthians: 241
32:21–22
Romans 1–8: 274
32:22
Luke 11–17: 170
Ephesians: 139
32:24
Revelation 1–11: 182
32:29
James: 165
32:33
Romans 1–8: 340
32:35
Matthew 1–7: 330
Romans 9–16: 202
1 Corinthians: 21
1 & 2 Thessalonians: 111, 180, 236, 241
2 Timothy: 211
Revelation 1–11: 188
32:35–36
1 Peter: 189
32:39
Matthew 16–23: 329
Luke 18–24: 287
John 1–11: 348
Romans 1–8: 53
2 Corinthians: 488
Ephesians: 131
1 Timothy: 275
James: 225, 237
32:40
James: 269
Revelation 1–11: 284
32:41
Matthew 16–23: 340
1–3 John: 81
Revelation 1–11: 188
32:42–43
Revelation 12–22: 198
32:43
1 Peter: 53
Revelation 1–11: 188
Revelation 12–22: 195
33:1
1 Timothy: 259
33:2
1 & 2 Thessalonians: 234
Hebrews: 46
1 Peter: 219
Revelation 1–11: 227
33:6–25
Revelation 1–11: 220
33:8
Revelation 1–11: 91
33:10
1 Peter: 113
33:26
2 Corinthians: 404
33:27
Romans 1–8: 474, 518
33:27–29
Ephesians: 72
33:29
Luke 1–5: 154, 167
34:5
Mark 1–8: 36
2 Peter–Jude: 18
34:5–6
Revelation 1–11: 301, 305
Revelation 12–22: 17
34:6
Luke 6–10: 283
Revelation 12–22: 17
34:9
1 Timothy: 224
34:10
Mark 1–8: 298
Mark 9–16: 198

Joshua
1:1–2
2 Timothy: 188
1:2
Titus: 3
1:4
Revelation 1–11: 269
Revelation 12–22: 146
1:5
Matthew 8–15: 441
Acts 13–28: 150
1:5–9
1 & 2 Thessalonians: 50
1:6–7
2 Timothy: 36
1:6–9
Philippians: 277
1:7
1 Peter: 199
1:7–8
2 Timothy: 156
1:8
Luke 1–5: 25, 76
1 & 2 Thessalonians: 198
1 Timothy: 137
2 Timothy: 152
James: 82
1 Peter: 99
1–3 John: 76
1:8–9
1 & 2 Thessalonians: 58
1:9
Acts 13–28: 150
2 Corinthians: 404
1 Peter: 199
2:1–21
Matthew 1–7: 8
2:9–11
Romans 9–16: 35
2:9–12
James: 141
2:10–12
Matthew 8–15: 52
2:11
Hebrews: 364
2:12–20
James: 266
2:15
2 Corinthians: 393
2:19
Acts 13–28: 149
3:4
Acts 1–12: 28
3:10
Matthew 1–7: 342
1 Timothy: 136
Revelation 1–11: 51, 217, 315
3:14–17
Luke 18–24: 396
3:14ff.
Acts 1–12: 214
4:16
Revelation 12–22: 132
4:23–24
Luke 1–5: 92

4:24
Acts 1–12: 313
1 Peter: 68
5:2
Romans 1–8: 252
5:13–15
John 1–11: 41
Acts 1–12: 22
5:14
Revelation 1–11: 158, 228
6:3–5
Hebrews: 362
6:8
Hebrews: 362
6:17–18
Galatians: 9
6:22–25
Matthew 1–7: 8
6:26
James: 267
7:1
Mark 1–8: 156
7:1–25
Luke 11–17: 129
2 Corinthians: 272
7:1–26
Romans 1–8: 294
1 Timothy: 256
7:6
Matthew 16–23: 231
Revelation 12–22: 189
7:7
Acts 13–28: 145
7:14
Acts 1–12: 35
2 Peter–Jude: 20
7:19
Romans 1–8: 219
1 Corinthians: 244
7:19–25
Revelation 12–22: 144
7:20
Matthew 1–7: 66
Romans 1–8: 75
7:20–25
Romans 1–8: 63
7:21
James: 244
7:24–25
2 Corinthians: 389
7:25
Mark 9–16: 347
8:8
1 & 2 Thessalonians: 294
8:20–21
Revelation 12–22: 187
8:29
Acts 1–12: 320
8:31
Luke 6–10: 284
9:3–14
James: 268
9:3–27
Luke 6–10: 21
9:4
Mark 1–8: 133
9:13
Mark 1–8: 133
9:15
Matthew 1–7: 322
James: 268
9:16
James: 268
9:20
Matthew 1–7: 323
10:12–13
Matthew 24–28: 268
2 Timothy: 150
10:12–14
John 12–21: 234
10:23–26
Luke 1–5: 82
10:24
Matthew 16–23: 348
10:24–25
Acts 1–12: 67
10:24–26
Mark 9–16: 209
Luke 18–24: 154
10:25
1 Peter: 199
11:4
Revelation 1–11: 271
Revelation 12–22: 241
11:8
Mark 1–8: 365
11:18–20
Romans 9–16: 36
11:23
1 Peter: 34
12:3
Mark 1–8: 228
Luke 1–5: 302
Luke 6–10: 208
12:7–24
Acts 1–12: 320
13:7–22:34
Revelation 1–11: 220
13:22
Revelation 12–22: 56
13:27
Mark 1–8: 50, 228
Luke 1–5: 302
John 12–21: 390
13:32–33
1 Peter: 34
13:33
1 Peter: 38
14
Matthew 1–7: 415
14:1
1 Peter: 34
14:1ff.
Acts 13–28: 20
15:8
Mark 9–16: 48
16:10
1 Timothy: 230
18:1
Acts 1–12: 214
20
Hebrews: 168
21:43–45
Luke 11–17: 248
21:45
Luke 1–5: 87, 174
22:5
Matthew 16–23: 165
Mark 1–8: 338, 354
1–3 John: 231
22:20
1–3 John: 88
22:22
1 & 2 Thessalonians: 272
23:5
John 1–11: 398
23:8
Matthew 16–23: 165
23:9
Acts 1–12: 214
23:11–13
2 Peter–Jude: 103
23:14
Luke 1–5: 28
Acts 1–12: 31
Romans 9–16: 92
23:16
Romans 1–8: 274
24:2
Luke 1–5: 105
Luke 6–10: 14
Romans 1–8: 90, 235, 260
2 Corinthians: 384
Hebrews: 327
24:9–10
Revelation 12–22: 56
24:13–15
Matthew 1–7: 450
24:14
1 Peter: 192
Revelation 12–22: 200
24:15
Luke 1–5: 116
Hebrews: 346
24:16
Luke 1–5: 116
24:18
Acts 1–12: 214
24:20
Luke 1–5: 116
24:21,24
Luke 1–5: 116
24:22–24
1 Peter: 200
24:23
Matthew 8–15: 458
Galatians: 148
24:24
1 Peter: 124
24:29
Romans 1–8: 5
Titus: 3
James: 12
2 Peter–Jude: 18
24:32
John 1–11: 142
Acts 1–12: 206

Judges
1:6–7
Matthew 1–7: 434
1:16
Luke 18–24: 59
1:21
Philippians: 230
1:28
1 Timothy: 230
2:1–4
John 1–11: 41
2:7
Luke 1–5: 116
John 1–11: 204
2:7–11
Mark 1–8: 270
2:10
1 & 2 Thessalonians: 108, 242
2 Peter–Jude: 24
2:10–11
Mark 1–8: 400
2:10–12
John 1–11: 204
2:10–15
Luke 1–5: 116
2:13
Mark 1–8: 366
2:17
John 1–11: 204
Revelation 12–22: 165
2:18
Luke 1–5: 154
2:22
Acts 13–28: 162
3:9
2 Corinthians: 204
1 Timothy: 168
3:9–10
2 Corinthians: 114
4–5
Luke 18–24: 203
Revelation 12–22: 150
4:4
Luke 1–5: 185
1 Timothy: 84
4:4–5:31
1 Timothy: 83
4:4–14
Acts 13–28: 234
4:8
Hebrews: 365
4:9
Hebrews: 365
4:15
Hebrews: 365
4:22
Matthew 8–15: 112
5:1
Ephesians: 257
5:1–31
Luke 1–5: 94
1 Peter: 115
Revelation 12–22: 128
5:3
Luke 1–5: 94
Revelation 1–11: 171
5:11
Revelation 12–22: 130
5:19
Revelation 12–22: 150
5:24
Luke 1–5: 71
5:30
James: 244
6:1–6
Luke 6–10: 38
6:8
1 Timothy: 260
6:11–24
John 1–11: 41
6:12
Luke 1–5: 47
6:14
1 Timothy: 168
6:15
1 Corinthians: 106
6:15–16
Matthew 1–7: 151
6:16–23
Luke 1–5: 64
6:19
Matthew 8–15: 372
6:21
Hebrews: 302
6:22
Acts 1–12: 294
6:22–23
Luke 1–5: 27
6:23
Luke 1–5: 157
Revelation 1–11: 50
6:24
Matthew 1–7: 214
John 12–21: 125
1 & 2 Thessalonians: 313
6:33
Revelation 12–22: 150
6:34
Luke 1–5: 239
2 Corinthians: 114
Galatians: 99
1 & 2 Thessalonians: 134
6:36–40
Luke 1–5: 65
6:37–40
Luke 18–24: 396
7
Revelation 12–22: 150
7:2
Luke 6–10: 38
Ephesians: 355
7:3
Luke 6–10: 38
Hebrews: 356
7:6–8
Luke 6–10: 38
7:12
Luke 6–10: 38
Hebrews: 364
Revelation 12–22: 241
7:16
Revelation 1–11: 151
7:16–22
Hebrews: 364
7:16–25
Luke 6–10: 38
7:20
Acts 1–12: 26
Revelation 1–11: 151
7:22
Ephesians: 355
8:23
Luke 18–24: 363
8:26
Revelation 1–11: 44
Revelation 12–22: 164
8:27
Revelation 12–22: 165
8:33
John 1–11: 204
Revelation 12–22: 165
8:34
Luke 1–5: 154
9:1–6
1–3 John: 253
9:7–15
Mark 9–16: 258
9:10–11
Matthew 24–28: 61
Luke 18–24: 243
9:23
Mark 1–8: 246
10:6
Mark 1–8: 366
10:13
Romans 1–8: 99
1 & 2 Thessalonians: 285
10:16
John 1–11: 205
11:12
John 1–11: 79
11:29
2 Corinthians: 114
11:29–32
Hebrews: 366
11:30–31
Matthew 1–7: 322
11:30–36
James: 268
13:2–22
Luke 6–10: 143
13:2–23
1 Peter: 140
13:3
1 Timothy: 83
13:3–5
Ephesians: 239
13:3–23
John 1–11: 41
13:4
Ephesians: 239
13:5
Hebrews: 366
13:6
1 Timothy: 260
13:7
Matthew 8–15: 253

13:15
1–3 John: 242
13:20
Acts 1–12: 294
Revelation 1–11: 228
13:22
Mark 1–8: 234
Luke 1–5: 307
Luke 6–10: 213
Revelation 1–11: 49
13:25
2 Corinthians: 114
Ephesians: 247
Hebrews: 365
14:3
Philippians: 218
14:5
2 Corinthians: 390
14:6
2 Corinthians: 114
14:8–9
Mark 1–8: 24
14:10
John 1–11: 78
14:12
James: 244
14:19
2 Corinthians: 114
Hebrews: 365
15:14
2 Corinthians: 114
Hebrews: 365
15:15–16
Matthew 24–28: 289
15:15–20
Luke 6–10: 38
15:18
Philippians: 218
16:4–6
Luke 11–17: 129
2 Corinthians: 272
16:16
Revelation 1–11: 112
16:17
Matthew 8–15: 253
Luke 1–5: 37
Acts 13–28: 159, 252
16:20
Ephesians: 247
Revelation 1–11: 112
16:27–30
Luke 11–17: 129
2 Corinthians: 272
16:28
Hebrews: 365
17:6
Romans 9–16: 177
1 Corinthians: 381
Galatians: 143
18
Revelation 1–11: 220
19:20
John 12–21: 122
19:21
Luke 6–10: 176
19:22
2 Corinthians: 250
1 & 2 Thessalonians: 158
20:1
Matthew 16–23: 18
Mark 1–8: 414
20:26
Mark 1–8: 128
Luke 1–5: 339
21:1–13
James: 159
21:2–3
Luke 18–24: 17
21:11–12
Philippians: 235
21:12
1 Peter: 20
21:16
Ephesians: 145
21:25
Matthew 1–7: 267
Romans 9–16: 177
1 Corinthians: 381

Ruth

1:1
Luke 11–17: 310
1:6
Luke 6–10: 138
1 Peter: 140
1:14
Matthew 16–23: 165
1:16
1 Timothy: 194
1:16–17
2 Corinthians: 239
1:20
Romans 1–8: 476
1:22
Matthew 1–7: 25
2:1
Mark 9–16: 189
Luke 11–17: 128, 367
Luke 18–24: 145
2 Corinthians: 272
2:4
Matthew 1–7: 25
2:9
1 Corinthians: 155
3:11
1 Peter: 180
3:12
1 Timothy: 194
4:1–6
Luke 1–5: 244
4:1–10
Matthew 16–23: 331
1 Timothy: 194
4:1–11
Luke 6–10: 135
4:1–13
Mark 9–16: 189
Luke 18–24: 145
4:10
Luke 1–5: 247
4:10–13
John 1–11: 78
4:11
Matthew 1–7: 25
4:14
Luke 1–5: 96
4:17
Luke 1–5: 89

1 Samuel

1:1
Mark 9–16: 389
Luke 18–24: 401
John 12–21: 365
1:1–2:10
Luke 1–5: 60
1:2–11
Luke 18–24: 371
1:2, 5
Luke 1–5: 54
1:4–11
Luke 1–5: 25
1:6
Luke 1–5: 59
1:7, 10–16
Luke 1–5: 185
1:9–20
Matthew 16–23: 271
1:10–12
Luke 11–17: 2
1:11
Matthew 8–15: 253
Luke 1–5: 77
Acts 13–28: 159, 252
Ephesians: 239
1:13
Luke 18–24: 18
1:15
Ephesians: 239
1:17
John 12–21: 234
1:19
Philippians: 235
1:19–2:10
Luke 1–5: 31
1:21–22, 23
Ephesians: 287
2:1
Philippians: 275
Revelation 1–11: 168
Revelation 12–22: 42, 194
2:1–10
Luke 1–5: 77, 94
2:2
2 Corinthians: 488
1 Timothy: 275, 278
1–3 John: 25, 45
Revelation 1–11: 155
Revelation 12–22: 130
2:6–8
Luke 18–24: 287
2:6–9
Mark 9–16: 386
Luke 18–24: 397
2:7
1 Timothy: 247, 280

Hebrews: 434
2:10
Mark 1–8: 15, 416
Luke 1–5: 97
Revelation 1–11: 168, 282
Revelation 12–22: 42
2:12
Matthew 1–7: 408
2 Corinthians: 250
1 & 2 Thessalonians: 158, 242
2 Peter–Jude: 24
2:12–25
Matthew 16–23: 183
2:13–17,22
Matthew 1–7: 408
2:14
2 Corinthians: 385
2:18
Hebrews: 366
2:26
1 Peter: 45
2:27
Mark 1–8: 36
1 Timothy: 260
2:29
John 1–11: 33
2:30
John 12–21: 30
1 & 2 Thessalonians: 260
Hebrews: 335
2–4
1 Corinthians: 114
3
1 Peter: 54
3:2–21
1 Peter: 140
3:3
Revelation 1–11: 321
3:7
1 & 2 Thessalonians: 294
3:18
Acts 13–28: 241
3:20
Acts 1–12: 122
3:21
John 1–11: 17
1 & 2 Thessalonians: 294
3:35
James: 267
4–5
2 Corinthians: 252
4–6
Romans 1–8: 75
4:1–2
2 Corinthians: 252
4:3
Ephesians: 145
4:3–5
2 Corinthians: 252
4:4
Revelation 1–11: 153
Revelation 12–22: 132
4:6
2 Corinthians: 385
4:7–8
Revelation 1–11: 251
4:9
2 Corinthians: 385
4:10–11
2 Corinthians: 252
4:12
Revelation 12–22: 189
4:21
Matthew 16–23: 402
Luke 11–17: 242
Ephesians: 336
1 & 2 Thessalonians: 62
4:21–22
Mark 1–8: 281
5:1–2
2 Corinthians: 252
5:3
2 Corinthians: 252
5:6
Acts 1–12: 313
5:6, 9
Luke 1–5: 92
6:6
1 & 2 Thessalonians: 284
Revelation 1–11: 316
6:7
Luke 11–17: 34
6:20
Revelation 1–11: 156
7:3
Mark 1–8: 338
7:3–5
1 Timothy: 58
7:5–9
Luke 18–24: 2
7:6
Mark 1–8: 128
Luke 1–5: 339
7:10
Revelation 1–11: 282
7:13
Acts 1–12: 313
8:4–6
Mark 1–8: 298
8:5
Acts 13–28: 20
8:7
Luke 11–17: 11
Luke 18–24: 363
Acts 13–28: 20
9:2
1 Timothy: 53, 124
9:6ff.
1 Timothy: 260
9:21
Philippians: 230
10:5
Revelation 1–11: 170
10:6
2 Corinthians: 114
10:8
Luke 1–5: 75
10:9
Matthew 1–7: 203
10:10
Matthew 1–7: 480
2 Corinthians: 114
10:20
Acts 1–12: 35
10:21
Philippians: 230
10:22
1 Timothy: 53
10:23
1 Timothy: 53
10:24
1 Peter: 145
10:26
2 Timothy: 204
10:27
1 Timothy: 53
11:3
Ephesians: 145
11:6
2 Corinthians: 114
11:7
1 Timothy: 53
11:12–13
1 Timothy: 53
12:7
Revelation 12–22: 130
12:12
Matthew 1–7: 125
12:14
1 Peter: 68
Revelation 12–22: 200
12:19–23
1 & 2 Thessalonians: 255
12:20
Mark 1–8: 338, 354
12:22
John 12–21: 99
Romans 9–16: 96
Galatians: 28
12:23
Acts 13–28: 162
Ephesians: 383
1 Timothy: 59
2 Peter–Jude: 102
12:24
Luke 1–5: 309
Revelation 12–22: 200
13:1
Acts 13–28: 20
13:1–2
Acts 13–28: 20
13:3
2 Corinthians: 385
1 & 2 Thessalonians: 134
Revelation 1–11: 239
13:5
Luke 6–10: 38
Revelation 1–11: 271
Revelation 12–22: 241
13:6
Luke 6–10: 39
13:7
Luke 6–10: 39
13:7–14
Luke 6–10: 38
13:8–9
1 Timothy: 53

13:8–14
1 Peter: 108
13:9, 14
Matthew 1–7: 203
13:12
Luke 1–5: 75
13:14
Luke 6–10: 21
Acts 1–12: 122
Romans 1–8: 388
Romans 9–16: 355
2 Corinthians: 12, 139
Philippians: 36
1 Timothy: 94, 124
Titus: 29
James: 145
Revelation 12–22: 68
13:19
2 Corinthians: 385
13:19–22
Luke 6–10: 38
14:6
Philippians: 218
14:11
Luke 6–10: 39
2 Corinthians: 385
14:13–14
Luke 6–10: 39
14:15
Luke 6–10: 39
14:20–23
Luke 6–10: 39
14:21
2 Corinthians: 385
14:24
Matthew 1–7: 322
James: 268
14:24–30
1 Timothy: 53
14:25–26
Mark 1–8: 24
14:30
James: 268
14:34
Acts 13–28: 71
14:37–45
1 Timothy: 53
14:38–43
2 Peter–Jude: 20
14:41ff.
Acts 1–12: 35
14:44
Acts 13–28: 291
14:45
Luke 18–24: 217
Acts 13–28: 355
14:45–46
Luke 6–10: 39
15
Luke 1–5: 147
15:1
2 Corinthians: 45
15:1ff.
Acts 13–28: 20
15:2–28
1 Timothy: 53
15:3–19
Matthew 1–7: 203
15:3, 9
Matthew 1–7: 192
15:10ff.
John 1–11: 17
15:11
1 Timothy: 147
Hebrews: 270
15:16–19
Luke 11–17: 230
15:22
Matthew 1–7: 298
Romans 1–8: 424
Romans 9–16: 145
Hebrews: 251
1 Peter: 113, 161
15:22b
1–3 John: 182
15:23, 28
Matthew 1–7: 203
15:24
Matthew 1–7: 66
15:24–25
Acts 13–28: 216
15:28
Acts 1–12: 122
Romans 1–8: 424
15:29
John 1–11: 450
1 & 2 Thessalonians: 319
Titus: 11
1–3 John: 198
Revelation 1–11: 196
15:30
Matthew 1–7: 164
15:33
Mark 9–16: 46
15:35
Romans 9–16: 10
16
Acts 13–28: 288
16:1–13
2 Corinthians: 45
16:4
Ephesians: 145
16:5
1 & 2 Thessalonians: 202
16:6–7
Matthew 8–15: 458
16:7
Matthew 1–7: 135, 279, 292, 299
Matthew 8–15: 53
Mark 1–8: 104, 121, 338, 352
Luke 1–5: 323
Luke 11–17: 100, 348
John 1–11: 366
Romans 1–8: 116, 468
2 Corinthians: 40, 176
Philippians: 213
1 & 2 Thessalonians: 91, 230
1 Timothy: 53, 123
James: 225
16:11
John 1–11: 424
16:11–13
Luke 1–5: 155
16:12
1 Timothy: 53
16:12–13
1 & 2 Thessalonians: 202
16:13
Matthew 1–7: 75
Acts 1–12: 122
2 Corinthians: 114
1 Timothy: 53
1 Peter: 111
16:14
Mark 1–8: 246
2 Corinthians: 114
Ephesians: 247
1 Timothy: 53
16:14–16
1 Timothy: 53
16:14–18
Acts 13–28: 289
16:21
Acts 13–28: 289
16:23
Ephesians: 263
17:12
Luke 1–5: 147
17:12,15
Matthew 1–7: 25
17:17–51
Acts 13–28: 289
17:26
Ephesians: 71
Philippians: 218
1 Timothy: 136, 167
Revelation 1–11: 51, 217, 315
17:28
John 1–11: 424
17:32–37
Acts 13–28: 234
17:34
John 1–11: 424
17:34–35
Luke 11–17: 297
17:43
Luke 11–17: 362
Philippians: 217
Revelation 12–22: 308
17:45
James: 247
17:46
Hebrews: 366
17:52
Acts 13–28: 289
18:4
Revelation 1–11: 44
18:5
Acts 13–28: 289
18:6–9
Acts 13–28: 289
18:6–11
1 Peter: 156
18:10–11
Acts 13–28: 289
Revelation 12–22: 10

18:17
Acts 13–28: 289
18:21
Acts 13–28: 289
18:30
Acts 13–28: 289
19:1–7
Acts 13–28: 289
19:1ff.
Acts 13–28: 289
19:9–10
1 Peter: 156
19:11–17
Acts 13–28: 289
19:18–24
Acts 13–28: 289
19:23
James: 267
20:6
Luke 1–5: 147
20:12–17
James: 267
Revelation 1–11: 284
20:16
Matthew 1–7: 321
20:17
1 Corinthians: 341
1–3 John: 63
21:1–6
Luke 6–10: 5
21:4
Matthew 8–15: 285
21:4–6
Mark 1–8: 144
21:10–22:1
Acts 13–28: 20
21:13
Matthew 1–7: 203
21:14–15
Philippians: 277
22:1
Philippians: 277
22:3
Revelation 1–11: 168
22:3–4
James: 219
22:9–19
1 Timothy: 53
James: 159
22:11–18
Mark 1–8: 144
22:32
1 Timothy: 275
23:14
Acts 13–28: 289
23:24–28
Acts 13–28: 289
24:1–7
Ephesians: 125
24:2–12
1 Peter: 156–57
24:2ff.
Acts 13–28: 289
24:3–7
Matthew 1–7: 339
24:4
Revelation 1–11: 44
24:5
1 Timothy: 222
24:5–6
Matthew 1–7: 173
24:6
Matthew 16–23: 142
24:9
James: 219
24:12
Matthew 16–23: 142
24:14
Philippians: 217
Revelation 12–22: 308
24:21–22
James: 267
25:25
Luke 18–24: 256
25:32–33
Matthew 16–23: 143
25:40ff.
2 Corinthians: 409
25:40–42
Luke 6–10: 17
26:2ff.
Acts 13–28: 289
26:6–12
1 Peter: 157
26:11
Matthew 16–23: 142
26:21
Ephesians: 220
28:1–2
Acts 13–28: 289
28:3–25
Matthew 24–28: 2
28:4ff.
1 Timothy: 53
28:14
Revelation 1–11: 44
28:17
Acts 1–12: 122
28:24
Luke 11–17: 317
29:1
2 Corinthians: 385
29:1–11
Acts 13–28: 289
29:3
2 Corinthians: 385
30:26
Ephesians: 145
31:4
Philippians: 218
31:9
Mark 1–8: 12
31:10
Mark 1–8: 366
31:13
Luke 1–5: 339

2 Samuel
1:1–16
1 Timothy: 222
1:1ff.
Acts 13–28: 289
1:2
Revelation 12–22: 189
1:6
Revelation 1–11: 271
1:12
Mark 1–8: 128
Luke 1–5: 339
1:16
Acts 13–28: 149
1:20
Philippians: 218
1:24
Revelation 12–22: 163
2:4
2 Corinthians: 45
2:8–3:21
Matthew 8–15: 217
2:8–9
Acts 13–28: 289
3:8
Revelation 12–22: 308
3:18
Luke 1–5: 98, 154
John 1–11: 33
1 Timothy: 168
James: 12
2 Peter–Jude: 18
3:31
Revelation 1–11: 299
3:32
John 1–11: 465
3:35
Acts 13–28: 291
4:10
Mark 1–8: 12
4:11
James: 250
5:2
John 1–11: 424
5:4
Luke 1–5: 248
5:5–9
Matthew 16–23: 38
5:7
1 Peter: 120
5:7–9
Luke 1–5: 147
6:2
Revelation 1–11: 153
Revelation 12–22: 132
6:3
Luke 1–5: 75
6:3–4, 6–7
Luke 1–5: 30
6:5
Revelation 1–11: 170
Revelation 12–22: 75, 125
6:6–7
1 Peter: 108
6:9
Revelation 1–11: 156
6:15
1 & 2 Thessalonians: 134

7
Luke 1–5: 128
Luke 11–17: 401
Luke 18–24: 442
Acts 1–12: 214
Acts 13–28: 22
7:1–17
Luke 1–5: 35
7:4ff.
John 1–11: 17
7:5
Romans 1–8: 5
7:8
John 1–11: 424
7:8–16
Romans 9–16: 14
7:11–15
James: 269
7:11–16
Acts 1–12: 66
7:12
Luke 1–5: 45, 128
7:12–13
Matthew 16–23: 345
Luke 1–5: 128, 174
7:12–14
Mark 9–16: 208
Luke 1–5: 100
Luke 18–24: 60, 152–53
7:12–14a, 16
Matthew 8–15: 90
7:12–16
Matthew 1–7: 2
Matthew 8–15: 306
Mark 1–8: 180
2 Corinthians: 88
Revelation 1–11: 311
Revelation 12–22: 11, 229, 307
7:12–17
Luke 11–17: 248
7:13
Matthew 24–28: 232
Acts 1–12: 58
Revelation 12–22: 211
7:13, 16
Luke 1–5: 100
7:14
2 Corinthians: 255
Galatians: 108
1 Timothy: 184
Hebrews: 27, 28
7:15–16
Matthew 16–23: 345
7:16
Matthew 1–7: ix
Luke 1–5: 174
7:18–29
Luke 11–17: 2
John 12–21: 234
7:22
Matthew 16–23: 36
2 Corinthians: 488
1 Timothy: 275
7:24
Revelation 12–22: 272
7:28
Matthew 16–23: 36
Luke 18–24: 188
1 & 2 Thessalonians: 319
8:2
Revelation 1–11: 293
8:4
Revelation 1–11: 271
8:17
Matthew 1–7: 62
9:1–13
Romans 1–8: 436
9:8
Philippians: 217
Revelation 12–22: 308
9:9–10
1 Timothy: 230
10
James: 159, 219
10:3
James: 220
10:4
2 Corinthians: 409
10:6
2 Corinthians: 409
10:12
1 Peter: 199
10:12–13
1 & 2 Thessalonians: 50
11
2 Corinthians: 139
11:1–4
Luke 6–10: 21
Acts 13–28: 20
11:1–15
Romans 1–8: 189
11:1–17
Revelation 12–22: 69
11:1–27
Matthew 1–7: 8
11:3
James: 189
11:14–15
Luke 6–10: 21
11:27
1 Corinthians: 148
12
Acts 1–12: 144
12:5–7
Matthew 16–23: 297
12:9
Luke 11–17: 381
Acts 13–28: 20
2 Corinthians: 51
James: 225
Revelation 12–22: 69
12:9–11
Titus: 88
12:10
Hebrews: 386
12:10–11
1 Corinthians: 148
12:11
Romans 9–16: 33
12:13
Mark 9–16: 59, 69
Luke 18–24: 29
Romans 9–16: 145
1 Corinthians: 148
2 Corinthians: 468
12:14
1 Corinthians: 148
Titus: 89
12:14, 24
Matthew 1–7: 8
12:16
Matthew 1–7: 402
Luke 1–5: 185, 339
Luke 18–24: 2
12:21
Luke 18–24: 29
12:23
Matthew 8–15: 271
Matthew 16–23: 181
Luke 6–10: 351
Luke 18–24: 29
1 Corinthians: 427
12:26–29
James: 220
12:30
Revelation 12–22: 217
13:2
Matthew 1–7: 154
13:22–33
Luke 18–24: 29
13:28–29
1 Timothy: 106
14:11
Acts 13–28: 355
14:14
John 12–21: 360
14:17
1 & 2 Thessalonians: 199
14:33–15:6
Romans 1–8: 340
14:33–15:12
1–3 John: 85
15:5
2 Corinthians: 486
15:7–10
Matthew 1–7: 352
15:10
1 & 2 Thessalonians: 134
Revelation 1–11: 309
15:10–13
John 12–21: 72
15:15
Philippians: 14
15:23
John 12–21: 305
15:31
John 12–21: 73
15:32
Revelation 12–22: 189
15–17
Matthew 8–15: 349
James: 189
16:3
James: 218
16:5–10
Matthew 1–7: 339

16:5–12
Matthew 1–7: 173
16:5–14
Ephesians: 125
16:9
Philippians: 217
Revelation 12–22: 308
16:10
John 1–11: 79
16:15–17:3
Mark 9–16: 287
17:14
Luke 18–24: 398
18:5
1 Peter: 190
18:9–14
John 1–11: 366
18:9–15
1–3 John: 254
18:20–27
Mark 1–8: 12
18:33
Matthew 1–7: 342
18:33–19:4
Matthew 1–7: 154
Luke 18–24: 29
19:5–6
Matthew 1–7: 155
19:13
Acts 13–28: 291
19:22
John 1–11: 79
19:22–23
Matthew 16–23: 143
19:25–27
James: 218
20:1
1 & 2 Thessalonians: 134
20:1ff.
Acts 13–28: 289
20:2
Matthew 16–23: 165
20:9
2 Corinthians: 486
21:1
Luke 11–17: 310
21:7
James: 267
22:1,4
Luke 1–5: 154
22:2–3
Ephesians: 112
22:3
Luke 1–5: 77, 153
1 Timothy: 69
1 Peter: 280
Revelation 12–22: 42
22:8
Matthew 24–28: 274
22:11
Revelation 1–11: 153
Revelation 12–22: 31, 132
22:14
Mark 1–8: 244
Luke 1–5: 49
Revelation 1–11: 282
22:17
Revelation 12–22: 33
22:26
Matthew 1–7: 197
22:32
2 Corinthians: 488
22:48
Romans 9–16: 202
Revelation 12–22: 198
22:50
Romans 9–16: 324
1 Peter: 53
Revelation 12–22: 194
22:51
Mark 1–8: 15, 416
23:1
Luke 6–10: 21
2 Corinthians: 12, 139
23:1–2
Luke 11–17: 351
23:2
John 12–21: 207
23:5
Luke 1–5: 99
2 Corinthians: 88
23:6
1 & 2 Thessalonians: 158
23:34
James: 189
24:1
James: 48
24:10
2 Corinthians: 468
Ephesians: 220
1 Peter: 204
24:11
John 1–11: 17
24:14
2 Corinthians: 19
24:15–16
1 Corinthians: 225
24:16–17
Revelation 1–11: 215
24:17
Luke 18–24: 2
24:24
Matthew 1–7: 358
John 12–21: 5
1 Corinthians: 455

1 Kings

1:5
1–3 John: 254
1:32
Matthew 1–7: 62
1:32–40
Luke 18–24: 94
1:33
Mark 9–16: 126
1:34
1 & 2 Thessalonians: 134
Revelation 1–11: 239
1:38
Luke 18–24: 94
1:39
2 Corinthians: 45
1 & 2 Thessalonians: 134
Revelation 1–11: 239, 309
1:41
1 & 2 Thessalonians: 134
1:52
Luke 18–24: 217
Acts 13–28: 355
2:4
Luke 1–5: 174
Philippians: 31
2:10
John 1–11: 456
2:23
Acts 13–28: 291
2:27
John 1–11: 17
2:28–34
Luke 11–17: 108
2:33
Matthew 1–7: 213
2:37
Acts 13–28: 149
3:3
Matthew 1–7: 37
1 Timothy: 115
3:5–6
James: 164
3:6
Romans 9–16: 132
3:8
Revelation 12–22: 5
3:9
1 & 2 Thessalonians: 199
3:9–12
James: 164
3:16–27
1 Corinthians: 340
4:20
Revelation 12–22: 241
4:29–31
James: 164
5:1
2 Corinthians: 45
5:11
Acts 1–12: 326
5:12
James: 164
6:7
1 Peter: 121
6:11
1 & 2 Thessalonians: 294
6:11–13
John 1–11: 17
6:13
John 1–11: 33
6:23–28
Revelation 1–11: 154
7:13–14
2 Corinthians: 114
7:40
Revelation 1–11: 171
7:45
Revelation 1–11: 171
7:50
Revelation 1–11: 171, 240
Revelation 12–22: 133

8
Luke 18–24: 107
8:1
1 Peter: 120
8:10
1 & 2 Thessalonians: 137
8:10–11
Luke 1–5: 156
John 1–11: 41, 451
1 Peter: 107
Revelation 12–22: 133, 279
8:10–12
Revelation 1–11: 32
8:11
Romans 1–8: 84
Romans 9–16: 14
James: 97
1 Peter: 253
8:15
Acts 1–12: 31
8:20
Acts 1–12: 31
8:22
1 Timothy: 75
8:22–53
Luke 11–17: 2
8:23
Matthew 8–15: 458
2 Corinthians: 488
1 Timothy: 275
8:24
Acts 1–12: 31
8:24–25
Luke 1–5: 174
8:27
Acts 1–12: 215
Acts 13–28: 138
1 Peter: 200
8:28–30
Matthew 16–23: 270
8:29
Mark 9–16: 138
Luke 18–24: 107
8:30
Luke 18–24: 107
2 Corinthians: 395
Revelation 12–22: 262
8:33–34
Luke 18–24: 107
8:35
2 Corinthians: 395
8:35–36
Luke 18–24: 107
8:36
1 Peter: 34
8:37
Revelation 1–11: 262
8:38
1–3 John: 85
8:38–39a
Luke 18–24: 107
8:39
Matthew 1–7: 283
Matthew 8–15: 53
Mark 1–8: 104, 338, 352
Luke 1–5: 323
Romans 1–8: 468
James: 225
8:41–43
Luke 18–24: 446
8:42
Luke 18–24: 107
8:43
Acts 13–28: 135
8:46
Mark 9–16: 202
Luke 1–5: 179
Luke 11–17: 37, 181
Luke 18–24: 13
Acts 13–28: 26
2 Corinthians: 12, 210, 213
1 & 2 Thessalonians: 286
Revelation 12–22: 69, 80
8:54
Luke 18–24: 17
8:55–56
Romans 9–16: 92
8:56
Luke 1–5: 28, 87, 174
Luke 18–24: 189
8:56–61
Philippians: 154
8:60
2 Corinthians: 488
1 Timothy: 275
8:61
Mark 1–8: 352
2 Corinthians: 352
8:61–62
Luke 18–24: 107
8:66
Luke 1–5: 98
9:1–5
2 Corinthians: 183
9:5
Luke 1–5: 174
9:6–7
Luke 11–17: 243
10:1–9
Revelation 12–22: 236
10:1–13
Matthew 8–15: 331
10:14
Matthew 16–23: 148
10:22
Romans 9–16: 344
10:23
Luke 11–17: 128
2 Corinthians: 272
10:23–24
James: 164
10:27
Matthew 1–7: 143
11:1–2
2 Corinthians: 256
11:1–8
Matthew 1–7: 6
11:1–11
2 Corinthians: 256
11:4
Luke 18–24: 286
John 1–11: 342
2 Corinthians: 256, 352
11:5–8
2 Corinthians: 256
11:9–11
2 Corinthians: 256
11:26ff.
Luke 6–10: 74
11:29–39
Acts 13–28: 241
11:43
John 1–11: 456
12:4, 14
Romans 9–16: 231
12:15
John 12–21: 24
12:22
1 Timothy: 260
12:24
1 & 2 Thessalonians: 294
13:1–26
1 Timothy: 267
13:1ff.
1 Timothy: 260
13:24
2 Corinthians: 390
14:11
Philippians: 217
2 Peter–Jude: 108
Revelation 12–22: 308
14:22–24
Revelation 12–22: 165
15:1–3
2 Corinthians: 352
15:5
Titus: 29
15:11
1 Timothy: 115
15:12
Luke 1–5: 74
15:14
2 Corinthians: 352
15:25–26
Romans 1–8: 61
16:1–2
1 Timothy: 115
16:1–4
John 1–11: 17
16:4
Philippians: 217
Revelation 12–22: 308
16:9
Luke 18–24: 256
16:18–19
1 Timothy: 115
16:24
Acts 1–12: 232
16:25–26
1 Timothy: 115
16:30
Acts 13–28: 114
16:30–31
1 Timothy: 115
Revelation 1–11: 100
16:31
Matthew 16–23: 105
Luke 1–5: 276

16:33
Luke 1–5: 275
17–19
Mark 9–16: 6
17:1
Luke 1–5: 39
Acts 13–28: 114
Revelation 1–11: 300
17:1–6
Revelation 12–22: 32
17:2–4
John 1–11: 17
17:8
John 1–11: 17
17:8–16
John 1–11: 83
1 Timothy: 200
17:8–23
Hebrews: 367
17:9
Matthew 8–15: 467
Mark 1–8: 365
17:11
James: 280
17:17–23
Revelation 1–11: 25
17:17–24
Luke 18–24: 396
2 Corinthians: 415
17:18
Luke 1–5: 276
1 Timothy: 260
17:21
Luke 11–17: 2
Acts 13–28: 204
17:22
1 Corinthians: 416
17:24
1 Timothy: 260
18:1
John 1–11: 17
18:1–2
Luke 11–17: 310
18:4
Mark 1–8: 298
18:12
Luke 1–5: 239
Acts 1–12: 259
18:16–46
Matthew 1–7: 86
18:17
Matthew 1–7: 217
Acts 13–28: 114
2 Corinthians: 220
James: 258
18:17–18
Luke 1–5: 38
18:17–40
Luke 6–10: 38
18:17ff.
Revelation 12–22: 57
18:18
Luke 11–17: 230
John 1–11: 51
18:20–40
1–3 John: 153
18:20ff.
Acts 13–28: 145
18:21
Matthew 1–7: 450
John 1–11: 51
Hebrews: 346, 403
James: 38
18:25–29
Philippians: 314
18:26
Luke 1–5: 152
18:26–29
Matthew 1–7: 364, 368
18:27
Luke 1–5: 152
2 Corinthians: 213
18:27–19:18
Ephesians: 361
18:28
Matthew 1–7: 204
Luke 1–5: 152
2 Corinthians: 213
Philippians: 219
Revelation 1–11: 34
18:29
Luke 1–5: 152
18:36
Acts 1–12: 105
2 Corinthians: 18
18:36–38
2 Corinthians: 415
18:38
Hebrews: 302
Revelation 12–22: 61
18:38–40
Philippians: 34
18:39
Revelation 1–11: 228
18:44–45
Luke 11–17: 175
18:46
Luke 11–17: 158
1 Peter: 64
19:1–2
James: 259
19:1–3
Luke 6–10: 21
2 Corinthians: 139
19:1–4
Matthew 1–7: 86
19:1–10
Mark 9–16: 18
19:3
James: 280
19:3–4
Philippians: 34
19:4
Acts 13–28: 145
Colossians and Philemon: 73
19:5
1 Peter: 57
19:8
Mark 1–8: 44
19:9
John 1–11: 17
19:9–10
Luke 11–17: 7
19:9–14
James: 280
19:9–18
Romans 9–16: 100
19:10
1 & 2 Thessalonians: 62
19:10, 18
Romans 9–16: 100
19:11
Matthew 24–28: 274, 308
19:11–12
Revelation 1–11: 204
19:16
2 Corinthians: 45
20:7
Ephesians: 145
20:16–34
Ephesians: 231
20:36
2 Corinthians: 390
20:42
Ephesians: 223
21:1–13
James: 159
21:1–16
Luke 6–10: 54
21:6–16
Ephesians: 35
21:10
1 & 2 Thessalonians: 158
21:13
James: 218
21:17–19
John 1–11: 17
21:17–22
Luke 11–17: 230
21:17–24
John 1–11: 51
21:17–29
Luke 1–5: 39
21:19
2 Peter–Jude: 107
Revelation 12–22: 308
21:20
James: 258
21:23–24
Philippians: 217
2 Peter–Jude: 108
Revelation 12–22: 308
21:25
Acts 13–28: 114
21:27
Matthew 1–7: 403
Mark 1–8: 128
Luke 1–5: 339
Luke 6–10: 334
22:1–28
2 Peter–Jude: 69
22:10
Revelation 1–11: 44
22:10–28
Revelation 12–22: 56
22:17
Mark 1–8: 317

22:19
Revelation 1–11: 147
22:19–22
Revelation 12–22: 147
22:19–23
Mark 1–8: 246
1 & 2 Thessalonians: 285
22:22
1 & 2 Thessalonians: 71
22:24
Matthew 16–23: 298
Mark 9–16: 168
22:38
Revelation 12–22: 308

2 Kings
1:2
Mark 1–8: 181
Romans 1–8: 95
1:8
Matthew 1–7: 57
Mark 1–8: 23
John 1–11: 51
1:9–12
Luke 6–10: 42
Revelation 12–22: 61
1:9, 11
Titus: 40
1:10
2 Corinthians: 415
Revelation 1–11: 300
Revelation 12–22: 242
1:12
2 Corinthians: 415
Revelation 1–11: 300
Revelation 12–22: 242
2:11
Matthew 16–23: 69
Luke 6–10: 283
Luke 18–24: 396
John 1–11: 51
Revelation 1–11: 305
Revelation 12–22: 250, 262
2:11–12
2 Peter–Jude: 188
Revelation 1–11: 301
2:12–15
2 Timothy: 188
2:16
Luke 1–5: 239
Acts 1–12: 259
2:23
Luke 11–17: 344
2:24
2 Corinthians: 390
3:1–3
1 Timothy: 115
3:3
Matthew 16–23: 105
3:15
Revelation 1–11: 171
3:24
2 Corinthians: 385
4:1
1 Timothy: 229
4:1–7
John 1–11: 83
4:7ff.
1 Timothy: 260
4:8
1–3 John: 242
4:13
Philippians: 299
4:18–37
Hebrews: 367
4:29
Luke 11–17: 158
1 Peter: 64
4:32–36
Revelation 1–11: 25
4:33
Luke 11–17: 2
4:34
Acts 13–28: 204
4:34–36
1 Corinthians: 416
5:1
Luke 1–5: 276
5:5
James: 244
5:15–27
Hebrews: 433
5:22
James: 244
5:25–27
Luke 1–5: 314
Luke 11–17: 389
6:15–17
Hebrews: 37
6:22
1 & 2 Thessalonians: 181
6:25–29
Luke 11–17: 310
6:30
Revelation 1–11: 299
6:31
Acts 13–28: 291
7:1
1 & 2 Thessalonians: 294
7:3
Mark 1–8: 88
Luke 1–5: 314
Luke 11–17: 390
7:3–4
Luke 1–5: 276
7:9
Mark 1–8: 12
8:1
Revelation 1–11: 182
8:13
Philippians: 217
Revelation 12–22: 308
9:1
1 Peter: 64
9:7
Revelation 1–11: 320
9:13
Matthew 16–23: 260
Luke 18–24: 95
Revelation 1–11: 309
9:30–37
Revelation 1–11: 101
10:16
Luke 6–10: 42
10:29
1 Timothy: 115
10:31
Luke 6–10: 42
1 Timothy: 115
11:1–2
John 1–11: 24
11:12
Revelation 1–11: 309
11:14
Revelation 1–11: 309
11:15
Acts 13–28: 260
12:13
Revelation 12–22: 133
12:13–14
Revelation 1–11: 171
13:1–2
1 Timothy: 115
13:5
2 Corinthians: 204
1 Timothy: 168
13:6
1 Timothy: 115
13:10–11
1 Timothy: 115
13:20–21
Revelation 1–11: 25
13:23
Matthew 8–15: 476
Mark 1–8: 386
Luke 11–17: 236
14:7
Luke 1–5: 22
14:8–14
Luke 11–17: 375
14:18–20
Luke 6–10: 74
14:23–24
1 Timothy: 115
14:25
Luke 11–17: 85
15:8–9
1 Timothy: 115
15:17–18
1 Timothy: 115
15:23–24
1 Timothy: 115
15:27–28
1 Timothy: 115
15:29
Matthew 1–7: 107
15:30
John 12–21: 73
16:3
Luke 18–24: 224
2 Corinthians: 213
Revelation 12–22: 10
16:10–16
Philippians: 192
17
1 Corinthians: 42

17:1–6
Acts 1–12: 233
17:6
Acts 1–12: 233
17:6–12
Luke 1–5: 74
17:7–17
Luke 11–17: 240–41
17:7–18
Acts 13–28: 71
17:7–23
Revelation 12–22: 26
17:13
Acts 1–12: 114
Acts 13–28: 374
1 & 2 Thessalonians: 64
17:13–15
Revelation 1–11: 290
17:13–16
Romans 1–8: 92
17:14
Luke 6–10: 191
John 1–11: 34
2 Corinthians: 110
17:16
Acts 1–12: 213
17:22
Matthew 16–23: 105
1 Timothy: 115
17:23–24
John 1–11: 144
17:24ff.
Acts 1–12: 233
17:25
2 Corinthians: 390
17:29–31
John 1–11: 144
17:33
Acts 1–12: 233
17:36
Acts 13–28: 19
17:38
2 Peter–Jude: 48
17:39
Luke 1–5: 154
Revelation 12–22: 200
18–19
Romans 1–8: 61
18:1–3
1 Timothy: 115
18:9–12
Acts 1–12: 233
18:14
2 Timothy: 151
19:1
Revelation 1–11: 299
19:4
1 Timothy: 167
2 Peter–Jude: 98
Revelation 1–11: 217, 315
19:15
2 Corinthians: 488
1 Timothy: 275
19:15–19
Luke 11–17: 2
19:16
1 Timothy: 167
Revelation 1–11: 315
19:18
Revelation 1–11: 273
19:19
2 Corinthians: 488
1 Timothy: 275
19:22
1–3 John: 81
Revelation 1–11: 118
19:35
Matthew 8–15: 44
Matthew 24–28: 191
Mark 1–8: 246
Mark 9–16: 314
Luke 18–24: 316, 396
Acts 1–12: 320
Revelation 1–11: 215
20:1–6
John 12–21: 234
1 & 2 Thessalonians: 255
20:2–3
Luke 1–5: 65
20:3
Mark 1–8: 338, 352
20:5
John 1–11: 33
20:12–17
1 & 2 Thessalonians: 256
20:20
Luke 11–17: 187
21:1–9
2 Corinthians: 251
Revelation 12–22: 165
21:2
Matthew 16–23: 18
21:3
Acts 1–12: 213
21:6
Matthew 24–28: 2
21:10–15
2 Corinthians: 252
21:13
Revelation 1–11: 293
21:16
Luke 11–17: 231
21:22
Acts 13–28: 162
22:1–2
1 Timothy: 115
22:11–13
2 Timothy: 156
22:13
Matthew 8–15: 263
Romans 1–8: 65
22:14
Luke 1–5: 185
1 Timothy: 84
22:17
1 & 2 Thessalonians: 66
Revelation 1–11: 273
22:19
1 Timothy: 124
22:24
Luke 18–24: 124
23:1
Ephesians: 145
23:2
Revelation 1–11: 320
23:4–12
John 12–21: 305
23:10
Matthew 16–23: 380
Mark 9–16: 48
Luke 1–5: 153
2 Corinthians: 213
James: 157
Revelation 12–22: 255
23:35
Romans 9–16: 231
1 Peter: 44
25:15
Revelation 1–11: 240
Revelation 12–22: 133
25:23
Mark 1–8: 20

1 Chronicles
1–9
Luke 1–5: 244
2:1–8:40
Revelation 1–11: 220
3:15
Mark 1–8: 20
3:17–18
Luke 1–5: 249
3:19
Luke 1–5: 249
5:1
Luke 1–5: 149
Acts 1–12: 205
Philippians: 267
Revelation 1–11: 220
5:20
Luke 11–17: 2
5:25
Revelation 12–22: 165
5:26
Luke 18–24: 398
6:39
1 Peter: 219
6:49
1 Peter: 207
11:2
John 1–11: 33
11:3
1 & 2 Thessalonians: 294
11:7
Luke 1–5: 147
12:17
Acts 13–28: 307
12:18
2 Corinthians: 114
12:32
Acts 1–12: 182
Romans 9–16: 258
1 Timothy: 106
13:8
Revelation 12–22: 75, 125
15:2
2 Peter–Jude: 178

15:16
Revelation 1–11: 170
Revelation 12–22: 75, 125
15:20
Revelation 1–11: 170
15:27
Revelation 12–22: 203
15:28
Revelation 1–11: 170
Revelation 12–22: 75, 125
16:5
Revelation 1–11: 170
16:6
Revelation 1–11: 239
16:9
Revelation 12–22: 194
16:12
2 Peter–Jude: 48
16:18
1 Peter: 34
16:23
1 Peter: 51
16:23–24
Matthew 24–28: 332
16:23–24, 28–29
Romans 9–16: 125
16:27
Luke 11–17: 292
1 Peter: 40
16:34
Revelation 12–22: 194
16:35
Luke 1–5: 167
Revelation 12–22: 194
16:41
Revelation 12–22: 194
16:42
Revelation 1–11: 239
17:6
John 1–11: 424
17:11–14
James: 269
17:20
Revelation 1–11: 155
18:3
Revelation 1–11: 269
21
1 Peter: 77
21:1
James: 48
Revelation 1–11: 254
21:1–8
Ephesians: 347
21:7
Revelation 1–11: 254
21:12
Revelation 1–11: 184
21:16
Acts 1–12: 294
Revelation 1–11: 299
21:24
2 Corinthians: 280
21:26
Hebrews: 302
Revelation 12–22: 61
22:8
Matthew 1–7: 6
Hebrews: 386
23:3
Luke 1–5: 248
23:14
1 Timothy: 259
23:24
Matthew 1–7: 75
24:4–5
Revelation 1–11: 149–50
24:4–19
Luke 1–5: 24
24:7–18
Revelation 1–11: 149–50
25
Revelation 1–11: 150
25:1
Revelation 1–11: 171
25:3
Revelation 1–11: 171
25:6
Revelation 1–11: 171
25:8–31
2 Peter–Jude: 20
28:4–5
Galatians: 28
28:9
Matthew 1–7: 283
Matthew 8–15: 53
Mark 1–8: 104–5, 338, 352
Mark 9–16: 75
Luke 1–5: 323
Luke 11–17: 348
Acts 13–28: 135
Romans 1–8: 143
2 Corinthians: 352
1 & 2 Thessalonians: 91
1 Timothy: 124
Hebrews: 310
James: 206
Revelation 1–11: 102
28:10
1 Peter: 199
28:17
Revelation 1–11: 171
Revelation 12–22: 133
28:20
1 Peter: 199
29:1
Philippians: 36
29:1–9
2 Corinthians: 282
29:1–17
1 Timothy: 283
29:2–6, 9
Matthew 1–7: 412
29:3
James: 244
29:4
Matthew 16–23: 148
29:7
Matthew 16–23: 148
29:8
Luke 18–24: 177
29:10
James: 160
29:10–14
2 Peter–Jude: 25
29:10–16
Mark 9–16: 102
29:11
Matthew 1–7: 397, 420
Matthew 8–15: 349
Luke 1–5: 259
1 & 2 Thessalonians: 302
Revelation 12–22: 197
29:11–12
Matthew 16–23: 231
Matthew 24–28: 288
Luke 18–24: 287
Acts 1–12: 15
Revelation 1–11: 156
29:12
Matthew 1–7: 420
Luke 1–5: 26
1 Timothy: 247, 280
29:14
1 Peter: 74–75
29:15
2 Corinthians: 162
Revelation 12–22: 261
29:17
Philippians: 36
1 Peter: 40
29:17–18
1 Peter: 74
29:18
Acts 1–12: 105
Acts 13–28: 307
2 Corinthians: 18
29:19
John 12–21: 234
2 Corinthians: 352
29:20
James: 160

2 Chronicles
1:11
John 1–11: 33
1:11–12
Luke 11–17: 367
2:6
Acts 13–28: 138
3:1
Mark 9–16: 132
4:22
Revelation 1–11: 171
5:7
Revelation 1–11: 321
5:12
Revelation 1–11: 170
5:12–13
Ephesians: 262
Revelation 1–11: 239
Revelation 12–22: 75, 125
5:12–14
Luke 1–5: 94
5:13
1 Peter: 107
Revelation 1–11: 171

6:1–42
Matthew 1–7: 366
6:14
2 Corinthians: 488
1 Timothy: 275
6:18
Acts 13–28: 138
6:30
1 & 2 Thessalonians: 91
6:36
James: 151
7:1
Hebrews: 302
Revelation 12–22: 61
7:1–3
Luke 1–5: 156
7:2–3
1 Peter: 107
7:10
Philippians: 275
7:13
Revelation 1–11: 259, 262
7:14
Luke 1–5: 219
Luke 11–17: 6
James: 214
7:16
1 & 2 Thessalonians: 202
9:3–4
1 Peter: 186
9:26
Revelation 1–11: 269
11:2–4
John 1–11: 17
11:16
Matthew 8–15: 458
13:5
Matthew 1–7: 241
Luke 11–17: 288
13:7
2 Corinthians: 250
13:12
Revelation 1–11: 239
15:1
Luke 1–5: 239
15:1–2
1 & 2 Thessalonians: 64
James: 206
15:2
Romans 1–8: 99
1 & 2 Thessalonians: 285
15:3
1 & 2 Thessalonians: 319
15:14
James: 267
16:9
Matthew 1–7: 283
19:2
Philippians: 221
19:3
1 Timothy: 124
19:6–7
Luke 18–24: 4
19:7
Acts 1–12: 300
Philippians: 315
James: 94
20:1–12
Ephesians: 266
20:3
Matthew 1–7: 402
Mark 1–8: 128
Luke 1–5: 339
20:6
Matthew 24–28: 288
Luke 1–5: 259
Acts 13–28: 307
20:7
Luke 11–17: 363
John 12–21: 161
James: 140, 197
Revelation 12–22: 68
20:9
Revelation 1–11: 184
20:12
Acts 13–28: 119
20:14
2 Corinthians: 114
20:15
Ephesians: 342, 355
20:18
Revelation 1–11: 228
20:20
1 Peter: 47
20:20–21
Romans 9–16: 61
20:20–22
Ephesians: 266
20:21
Acts 13–28: 119
Revelation 12–22: 194
20:22
Acts 13–28: 119
20:22–24
Ephesians: 355
21:3
Luke 1–5: 149
21:11
James: 191
Revelation 12–22: 165
21:13
James: 191
21:17
Revelation 12–22: 10
21–22
1 & 2 Thessalonians: 264
22:10–12
1 Peter: 210
Revelation 12–22: 10
23:3
1 Peter: 210
23:12–21
1 Peter: 210
24:18
1 & 2 Thessalonians: 66
24:19
1 & 2 Thessalonians: 64
24:20
Romans 1–8: 99
2 Corinthians: 114
1 & 2 Thessalonians: 285
24:20–21
Matthew 16–23: 394
Mark 1–8: 298
1 & 2 Thessalonians: 62
24:20–22
Matthew 16–23: 298
Luke 11–17: 108, 231
Acts 1–12: 225
1 & 2 Thessalonians: 64
25:2
1 Timothy: 145
25:7
1 Timothy: 260
25:14
1 Timothy: 146
25:14–15
Hebrews: 270
25:27
1 Timothy: 146
Hebrews: 270
26:4–5
Matthew 1–7: 173
26:15
Acts 13–28: 358
26:16
Matthew 1–7: 173
26:16–21
Luke 1–5: 30
1 Peter: 108
26:16–23
Luke 1–5: 314
Luke 11–17: 389
26:17–21
Mark 1–8: 89
26:21
Matthew 1–7: 173
28:3
Matthew 1–7: 296
Mark 9–16: 48
Revelation 12–22: 10
29:1–2
1 Timothy: 115
29:5
Philippians: 169
29:11
Luke 1–5: 26
Philippians: 169
Revelation 1–11: 240
Revelation 12–22: 116
29:19
1 & 2 Thessalonians: 272
29:20
Philippians: 169
29:25
Revelation 1–11: 170
29:27
Revelation 12–22: 128
29:30
Matthew 8–15: 376
29:36
Philippians: 169
30:1
Philippians: 169
30:1–11
Revelation 1–11: 220

30:6
Luke 1–5: 185
Acts 1–12: 105
2 Corinthians: 18
30:8
2 Corinthians: 110
30:8–9
Philippians: 170
30:9
John 12–21: 46
James: 261
30:11
Luke 1–5: 185
30:12
Philippians: 170
30:16
1 Timothy: 259
31:10
2 Peter–Jude: 25
31:17
Matthew 1–7: 75
32:19
Revelation 1–11: 273
32:21
1 Corinthians: 225
Revelation 12–22: 296
32:25
2 Peter–Jude: 97
32:26
Matthew 16–23: 231
32:31
2 Corinthians: 13
James: 17
33:12
Matthew 16–23: 231
33:12–13
Romans 1–8: 477
34:1–2
1 Timothy: 115
34:1–9
Revelation 1–11: 220
34:14–33
Romans 1–8: 169
34:25
Revelation 1–11: 273
34:27
Matthew 16–23: 231
35:11
1 Peter: 113
35:22
Luke 18–24: 203
Revelation 12–22: 150
36:13–15
Matthew 8–15: 476
36:14–16
Acts 13–28: 71
36:15–16
Luke 11–17: 236
Revelation 1–11: 290
36:16
1 & 2 Thessalonians: 64, 66
36:22–23
Luke 6–10: 135
Acts 1–12: 44

Ezra
1
2 Timothy: 151
1:1
Luke 18–24: 398
1 & 2 Thessalonians: 294
1:5
Philippians: 171
2:36–38
Luke 1–5: 24
2:61–62
Matthew 1–7: 2
Luke 1–5: 244
3:2
Luke 1–5: 249
1 Timothy: 259
3:7
Acts 1–12: 326
3:8
Matthew 1–7: 75
3:11
Revelation 12–22: 194
3:12
Mark 9–16: 132
1 Peter: 40
4:1–2
John 1–11: 144
4:1–3
John 1–11: 379
Acts 1–12: 233
4:3
John 1–11: 144
4:7–16
James: 218
4:8
Matthew 1–7: 276
4:17–24
James: 218
5:2
Acts 1–12: 214
5:5
John 1–11: 101
5:9
John 1–11: 101
5:11
Luke 6–10: 343
5:11–12
Revelation 12–22: 145
5:12
Acts 1–12: 214
6:7–8
John 1–11: 101
6:9
Mark 9–16: 48
6:9–10
Luke 11–17: 288
6:14
John 1–11: 101
7:9
Acts 1–12: 313
7:10
Mark 1–8: 61
Acts 13–28: 122
1 Timothy: 124
Titus: 49
1 Peter: 112
1–3 John: 57
7:21–26
Luke 1–5: 146
7:25
James: 166
7:27
Luke 1–5: 96
Acts 13–28: 307
Philippians: 171
7:28
Luke 1–5: 92
8:15
Matthew 8–15: 116
8:18
Acts 1–12: 313
8:20
1 Timothy: 230
8:21
Matthew 1–7: 402
Mark 1–8: 128
8:21, 23
Luke 1–5: 339
8:22–23
Matthew 1–7: 402
8:23
Mark 1–8: 128
Luke 1–5: 185
8:27
1 Peter: 44
8:31
Luke 1–5: 154
9:1–2
Mark 9–16: 59
9:5–15
Luke 11–17: 2
9:6
Matthew 16–23: 148
Luke 11–17: 313
9:11
Revelation 1–11: 320
9:12
2 Peter–Jude: 103
9:13
1–3 John: 27
10:3
Matthew 16–23: 169
10:3–5
Matthew 1–7: 314
10:5
James: 267
10:6
Matthew 1–7: 403
10:8
John 1–11: 101
10:14
Ephesians: 145

Nehemiah
1:1–6:15
James: 78
1:2–3
Luke 11–17: 51
1:4
Mark 1–8: 128
Luke 1–5: 185, 339
Luke 11–17: 51

Acts 13–28: 5
1:4–5
Revelation 12–22: 145
1:4–11
Luke 11–17: 2
John 12–21: 234
1:5
Mark 9–16: 203
John 12–21: 400
1:10
2 Corinthians: 315
1:11
Philippians: 221
2:4
Colossians and Philemon: 27
2:6
John 12–21: 15
2:7
2 Corinthians: 80
2:8
Acts 1–12: 313
2:13
Matthew 8–15: 116
2:18
Acts 1–12: 313
2:19
1 & 2 Thessalonians: 209
3:3
Luke 18–24: 436
4:1–3
John 1–11: 144
5:1–8
1 Timothy: 229
5:4
Romans 9–16: 231
5:7
Luke 11–17: 333
2 Corinthians: 272
5:10
2 Corinthians: 272
6:5–7
James: 218–19
6:10–12
Revelation 12–22: 56
6:14
Luke 1–5: 185
1 Timothy: 84
Revelation 12–22: 56
7:2
Luke 1–5: 157
7:67
1 Timothy: 83
8:1–3
2 Timothy: 140
James: 78
1 Peter: 100
8:1–8
Philippians: 231
1 Timothy: 176
8:3
2 Peter–Jude: 82
8:4–8
1 Peter: 263
8:5–6
James: 78
8:5–8
Matthew 1–7: 412
8:6
1 Timothy: 75
Revelation 1–11: 133
8:8
Matthew 1–7: 286
Mark 1–8: 342
2 Corinthians: viii
Colossians and Philemon: vi
James: 78
1 Peter: vii
2 Peter–Jude: vii
8:10
Luke 1–5: 93
Galatians: 166
1 & 2 Thessalonians: 184, 185
1 Peter: 40
8:15–17
Revelation 1–11: 226
9–10
Matthew 1–7: 412
9:1
Mark 1–8: 128
Luke 1–5: 339
Luke 6–10: 334
9:1–3
James: 79
9:2–3
2 Timothy: 140
9:4
Revelation 1–11: 173
9:5
1 Peter: 263
9:5–38
Matthew 1–7: 366
9:5ff.
Acts 1–12: 203
9:6
2 Corinthians: 488
1 Timothy: 271, 275
1 Peter: 58
9:6–7
Luke 1–5: 306
9:7
Acts 1–12: 203
9:8
1 Timothy: 123
9:10
2 Corinthians: 416
9:12
John 1–11: 334
9:13
Ephesians: 312
9:14
Acts 13–28: 202
9:16–19
Acts 13–28: 19
9:17
Matthew 1–7: 393
Mark 1–8: 97, 386
Luke 1–5: 153, 206, 321
Luke 6–10: 365
Romans 9–16: 198
2 Corinthians: 50
James: 261
2 Peter–Jude: 73
9:17–38
Luke 11–17: 236
9:19
John 1–11: 334
9:21
Acts 13–28: 19
9:26
Luke 11–17: 106
1 Timothy: 147
James: 258
1 Peter: 227
9:26–27, 31, 32
Romans 9–16: 97
9:26–32
Luke 11–17: 248
9:27
Luke 18–24: 2
2 Corinthians: 204
1 Timothy: 168
9:28–29
1 & 2 Thessalonians: 209–10
9:29
Luke 6–10: 191, 354
John 1–11: 34
2 Corinthians: 110
9:30
Mark 9–16: 159
Luke 18–24: 117
2 Corinthians: 114
Revelation 12–22: 303
9:33
Mark 1–8: 97
9:38
James: 79
10:28–29
2 Timothy: 140
James: 79
10:28–30
James: 267
10:29
Matthew 1–7: 321
10:32
Matthew 16–23: 86
10:32–33
2 Corinthians: 282
10:33
Revelation 12–22: 5
11:1
Revelation 12–22: 264
11:3
2 Corinthians: 385
12:1
Luke 1–5: 249
12:24
1 Timothy: 260
12:27
Revelation 12–22: 75, 125
12:31, 38
Ephesians: 257
12:36
1 Timothy: 260
12:46
Revelation 1–11: 171
13:1–2
Revelation 12–22: 56

13:18
1 & 2 Thessalonians: 66
13:26
Titus: 29

Esther
2:5
Philippians: 230
2:5–11
Romans 1–8: 435
2:21–23
Luke 6–10: 74
3
1 & 2 Thessalonians: 264
3–9
Revelation 12–22: 10
3:1–4:3
1 Peter: 210
3:5
1–3 John: 254
3:8
James: 219
3:10
Revelation 1–11: 217
4–9
1 & 2 Thessalonians: 264
4:1
Luke 6–10: 334
4:1–3
Mark 1–8: 128
Luke 1–5: 339
4:3
Luke 6–10: 334
4:14
Luke 18–24: 398
Romans 9–16: 25
Philippians: 298
4:16
Matthew 1–7: 402
Matthew 24–28: 299
5:1
Matthew 24–28: 299
Revelation 1–11: 44
5:1–2
Hebrews: 115
7:7–10
1 Corinthians: 90
7:10
Matthew 1–7: 434
1–3 John: 254
8:2
Revelation 1–11: 217
8:8
Revelation 1–11: 217
8:15
Revelation 12–22: 164, 203
9:16–19
Matthew 24–28: 139

Job
1
Matthew 1–7: 126
2 Corinthians: 400
Revelation 12–22: 8, 16
1:1
Matthew 1–7: 157, 339
Luke 1–5: 25
Hebrews: 388
1:1–5
1 Timothy: 48
1:3
Luke 11–17: 128
2 Corinthians: 272
1:5
1 & 2 Thessalonians: 202
1:6
Luke 1–5: 280
1 Timothy: 37
1 Peter: 212
Revelation 1–11: 257
Revelation 12–22: 8
1:6–2:7
1–3 John: 94
1:6–2:10
1 Peter: 44
1:6–12
Luke 18–24: 294
2 Corinthians: 13
1 Timothy: 49
1 Peter: 281
1:8
Romans 1–8: 507
Romans 9–16: 313
1 Corinthians: 228
James: 12
1:8–11
Romans 1–8: 506–7
1:9
Luke 1–5: 157
1:9–11
Mark 1–8: 246
1:11
1 Corinthians: 228
Revelation 12–22: 21
1:12
Mark 9–16: 277
Luke 18–24: 270
Hebrews: 388
2 Peter–Jude: 82
Revelation 12–22: 241
1:13–22
1 Timothy: 49
1:20
Mark 9–16: 328
1:21
John 1–11: 460
Romans 1–8: 476
Ephesians: 267
1 Timothy: 248, 252
James: 260
1:22
James: 260
Revelation 1–11: 78
1–2
John 1–11: 454
1 Peter: 209
2
2 Corinthians: 400
Revelation 12–22: 8, 16
2:1
Luke 1–5: 280
1 Peter: 212
Revelation 12–22: 8
2:1–7
2 Corinthians: 13
1 Peter: 281
2:3
2 Corinthians: 183
1 & 2 Thessalonians: 121
Titus: 26
2:5
Revelation 12–22: 21
2:6
Mark 9–16: 277
Luke 18–24: 270
1 & 2 Thessalonians: 72
Hebrews: 388
Revelation 12–22: 241
2:7
Luke 11–17: 201
Revelation 12–22: 139
2:8
1 & 2 Thessalonians: 71
2:9
Romans 9–16: 31
2 Corinthians: 183
Titus: 26
1 Peter: 249
Revelation 1–11: 254
2:10
Hebrews: 388
James: 260
Revelation 1–11: 78
2:12
Revelation 12–22: 189
3:1–11
James: 260
3:1ff.
Acts 13–28: 145
3:11–17
Mark 9–16: 69
Luke 18–24: 28–29
3:17–19
1 Peter: 93
3:19
Revelation 1–11: 320
4:4–10
Mark 1–8: 288
4:6
2 Corinthians: 183
4:7
Matthew 8–15: 50
Luke 11–17: 183
4:7–9
Luke 1–5: 314
Luke 11–17: 389
Galatians: 116
4:8
Galatians: 187
Revelation 12–22: 122
4:18
Matthew 8–15: 297
5:6–7
1 Peter: 42
5:7
Matthew 8–15: 52
Luke 11–17: 180
Luke 18–24: 286

John 12–21: 96
Romans 1–8: 340, 396
2 Corinthians: 12, 149
Philippians: 56
James: 16, 252
5:8–11
James: 32
5:9
Romans 1–8: 53
5:11
Matthew 1–7: 170
Romans 9–16: 33
5:12
Luke 18–24: 397
5:17
2 Corinthians: 443
1 Timothy: 184
1 Peter: 42, 250
5:17–24
1 & 2 Thessalonians: 315
5:19
1 Corinthians: 229
6:10
Revelation 1–11: 118
7:6
John 12–21: 212
Ephesians: 73
James: 233
7:6–7
2 Peter–Jude: 51
7:9
James: 233
7:11–16
James: 260
7:12
Revelation 12–22: 6
8:1–6
Galatians: 116
8:3
Revelation 12–22: 131
8:5
1 & 2 Thessalonians: 87
8:9
James: 233
8:13
Matthew 1–7: 353
Luke 11–17: 13
Romans 9–16: 313
1 Peter: 33
8:19
1 Peter: 40
2 Peter–Jude: 102
9:2
Luke 18–24: 13
Acts 13–28: 26
Romans 1–8: 197
9:3–20
Romans 1–8: 198
9:4
Luke 1–5: 59
Romans 1–8: 53
James: 166
9:7–8
Mark 9–16: 376
9:16ff.
Acts 13–28: 145
9:19
Revelation 1–11: 156
9:25–26
James: 233
2 Peter–Jude: 51
9:33
1 Timothy: 71
10:14
Mark 1–8: 96
10:15
Revelation 1–11: 251
11:7–9
1 Corinthians: 363
11:13–20
Galatians: 116
12:6
Revelation 1–11: 276
12:7
Revelation 12–22: 262
12:9–10
James: 237
12:10
Romans 1–8: 119
12:12
Titus: 72
13:11
Revelation 1–11: 156
13:13
2 Corinthians: 13–14
13:15
Matthew 16–23: 74
2 Corinthians: 107
Ephesians: 361
1 Timothy: 50
James: 24, 260
1 Peter: 63
1–3 John: 179
Revelation 1–11: 78
Revelation 12–22: 49
13:16
Philippians: 72
13:23
2 Corinthians: 460
1–3 John: 56
13:24
Luke 11–17: 180
2 Corinthians: 12
13:28
James: 244
14:1
Matthew 8–15: 255
Luke 11–17: 180
Luke 18–24: 286
John 12–21: 96
2 Corinthians: 12
Philippians: 56
James: 16
1–3 John: 200
14:1–2
John 1–11: 460
John 12–21: 360
James: 233
1 Peter: 93
2 Peter–Jude: 51
14:4
1 Peter: 88
14:14
Matthew 24–28: 304
John 1–11: 193
15:14
Matthew 8–15: 255
Luke 1–5: 58, 179
John 12–21: 123
Romans 1–8: 296
15:14–16
Revelation 12–22: 80
15:15
Revelation 12–22: 263
15:34
Matthew 1–7: 353
Matthew 16–23: 320
16:2
2 Corinthians: 13
16:2ff.
James: 260
16:15
Revelation 1–11: 299
Revelation 12–22: 42
17:9
1 & 2 Thessalonians: 20
2 Timothy: 161
James: 29
17:15
John 12–21: 212
18:14
Mark 1–8: 252
John 1–11: 460, 474
John 12–21: 361
18:21
1 & 2 Thessalonians: 242
19:2
James: 155
19:6–11
2 Corinthians: 13
19:10
John 12–21: 212
19:20
Matthew 16–23: 165
19:21
2 Corinthians: 13
19:25
Luke 11–17: 370, 393
19:25–26
Matthew 24–28: 304
Philippians: 73
Hebrews: 334
1 Peter: 42
1–3 John: 108
19:25–27
Mark 9–16: 185
Luke 18–24: 142
John 1–11: 194, 463
Acts 13–28: 307
James: 260
19:26
1 Corinthians: 408, 432
1 Timothy: 272
Hebrews: 140
19:26–27
Mark 9–16: 15
Luke 6–10: 351
Acts 13–28: 371

Philippians: 80
20:5
Hebrews: 352
21:7
John 1–11: 365
Revelation 1–11: 276
21:7–15
Hebrews: 351
21:13
John 1–11: 364
Hebrews: 352
21:14–15
Romans 1–8: 108
21:20
Revelation 12–22: 91
21:27
1 Corinthians: 354
21:30
Revelation 12–22: 122, 175
21:34
2 Corinthians: 13
22:2–3
Acts 13–28: 139
22:9
Luke 18–24: 6
22:12
Revelation 12–22: 262
22:29
2 Corinthians: 377
1 Peter: 278
23:10
Luke 11–17: 47
Romans 1–8: 479
James: 24
1 Peter: 43, 250
23:12
Ephesians: 110
1 & 2 Thessalonians: 198
1 Timothy: 293
1 Peter: 95, 100
Revelation 1–11: 122
23:13
Matthew 24–28: 288
Mark 9–16: 386
24:2–4
James: 242
24:3
Luke 18–24: 6
24:13–17
Romans 9–16: 264
25:4
Luke 1–5: 46
Acts 13–28: 26
Romans 1–8: 198
Galatians: 55
26:2–3, 7–8, 11, 13–14
Ephesians: 112
26:6
Ephesians: 139
Revelation 1–11: 264
26:7
Luke 1–5: 252
26:7–8, 10
Galatians: 184
26:12
Revelation 12–22: 41
26:14
Mark 1–8: 332
Luke 6–10: 280
1 Corinthians: 363
27:1–6
1 Peter: 44
27:5
2 Corinthians: 183
27:5–6
Titus: 26
27:6
1 Peter: 204
27:13–17
James: 244
27:20
Revelation 12–22: 33
28
Colossians and Philemon: 29
28:1, 3–4, 6–7, 10–11
Matthew 8–15: 385
28:12
James: 166
28:12–13, 21, 23, 28
Matthew 8–15: 385
28:12–22
James: 36
28:15–16
1 Peter: 44
28:22
Revelation 1–11: 264
28:23
James: 36
28:28
Luke 1–5: 157
2 Corinthians: 186, 257
James: 166
29:15
Mark 1–8: 407
30:1
2 Peter–Jude: 108
30:20–21
1 Peter: 279
31:1
1 Timothy: 190
31:1, 7–8
Matthew 1–7: 304
31:4
Mark 1–8: 329
31:4–6
2 Corinthians: 460
31:6
2 Corinthians: 183
31:9–11
Matthew 1–7: 302
31:12
Revelation 1–11: 264
31:24–25
Luke 11–17: 130
Hebrews: 433
31:24–28
Luke 11–17: 333
1 Corinthians: 233
2 Corinthians: 272
31:28
Hebrews: 433
31:29–30
Matthew 1–7: 338
31:31–32
Matthew 1–7: 338
31:32
1–3 John: 243
31:38
James: 246
32:4
1 Timothy: 186
32:6
1 Timothy: 186
32:18–20
Matthew 8–15: 319
32:21–22
1 & 2 Thessalonians: 41
33:4
Luke 1–5: 57
2 Corinthians: 114
33:13
John 1–11: 471
33:14–16
Matthew 1–7: 37
33:26
Romans 1–8: 240
34:14–15
Ephesians: 172
34:19
Acts 1–12: 300
Philippians: 315
James: 97
Revelation 12–22: 251
34:22
Luke 11–17: 117
34:24
Luke 1–5: 82
34:32
2 Timothy: 155
35:12
Matthew 8–15: 321
Mark 9–16: 100
Acts 1–12: 241
36:3
1 Peter: 169
36:3–4
1–3 John: 76
36:5–6
Mark 1–8: 288
36:13
Matthew 1–7: 353
37:5
Revelation 1–11: 284
37:23
Luke 1–5: 91
1 & 2 Thessalonians: 241
37:23–24
Revelation 12–22: 246
38:1–41
1 Peter: 288
38:3
Luke 11–17: 158
38:7
1 Corinthians: 259
1 Timothy: 38
1 Peter: 58, 212
Revelation 1–11: 171, 256

Revelation 12–22: 8
38:22–23
Revelation 1–11: 245
38:41
Matthew 1–7: 422
Luke 11–17: 141
1 Corinthians: 203
James: 285
38–39
1 Timothy: 50
Hebrews: 307
39:19–25
Revelation 1–11: 178
40:2
John 1–11: 471
40:4
Mark 9–16: 102
41:11
Romans 9–16: 136
2 Corinthians: 289
42:1–2
1 Peter: 19
42:1–6
John 12–21: 282
1 & 2 Thessalonians: 226
1 Timothy: 50
1 Peter: 44
42:2
Luke 11–17: 51, 398
1 & 2 Thessalonians: 89, 141, 254, 278, 288
Revelation 12–22: 185
42:2–6
2 Corinthians: 14
42:3
Hebrews: 388
42:5
Matthew 1–7: 208
Hebrews: 389
42:5–6
Matthew 1–7: 157
Matthew 8–15: 36
Mark 1–8: 234
Luke 1–5: 307
Romans 1–8: 477
Hebrews: 388
James: 17
Revelation 1–11: 49
42:6
Matthew 16–23: 148
Luke 11–17: 369
Ephesians: 124
42:7–8
Romans 1–8: 507
42:8–10
Luke 18–24: 2
42:10
Hebrews: 388
42:10–17
James: 261
1 Peter: 44
42:12–17
Matthew 1–7: 410

Psalms
1
2 Peter–Jude: 179
1:1
Acts 1–12: 275
James: 208, 286
1:1, 2
1–3 John: 39, 57
1:1–2
Luke 1–5: 171
Romans 9–16: 186
1 & 2 Thessalonians: 198
Revelation 12–22: 93
1:1–3
Luke 6–10: 147
John 12–21: 149
Philippians: 274
1:1–6
1 & 2 Thessalonians: 210
1:2
Luke 1–5: 76
Romans 1–8: 223, 390
Ephesians: 110
1 & 2 Thessalonians: 108
James: 69
1 Peter: 95
1–3 John: 75
Revelation 12–22: 310
1:2–3
Matthew 8–15: 361
1 & 2 Thessalonians: 58
1:2–4
Matthew 1–7: 454
1:3–4
Matthew 8–15: 98
1:4
Luke 1–5: 223
Ephesians: 6
1:5
James: 208, 286
1:6
Matthew 1–7: 457
2
Luke 11–17: 210
Revelation 1–11: 31
2:1
Revelation 1–11: 316
2:1–2
Matthew 24–28: 232
Acts 1–12: 140
2:1–3
Luke 18–24: 52
Revelation 12–22: 148
2:1–6
Mark 1–8: 156
2:1–12
Mark 1–8: 147
2:2
Matthew 16–23: 205
Mark 9–16: 197
Luke 1–5: 98
Luke 18–24: 351
Hebrews: 35
2:2–4
Revelation 12–22: 175
2:2–6
Revelation 1–11: 157
2:3
Acts 13–28: 168
2:4
Matthew 24–28: 250
2:5
Revelation 1–11: 316
2:5, 12
Romans 1–8: 60
2:6
Matthew 8–15: 309
Luke 1–5: 211
Luke 18–24: 89
2:6–7
Hebrews: 11
2:6–8
Matthew 1–7: ix–x
Acts 13–28: 114
Revelation 1–11: 25
Revelation 12–22: 239
2:6–9
Luke 1–5: 42, 175
Luke 11–17: 154, 207
1 Peter: 53
Revelation 1–11: 29, 312
Revelation 12–22: 71, 211
2:6–12
John 1–11: 381
Revelation 1–11: 170
Revelation 12–22: 229
2:7
Mark 1–8: 36
Luke 1–5: 175, 240
Luke 18–24: 189
Acts 13–28: 25
Galatians: 108
Hebrews: 27, 29, 123
2:7–8
Luke 11–17: 21
2:7–9
Revelation 1–11: 105
Revelation 12–22: 11
2:8
Matthew 1–7: 96
Luke 1–5: 258
Philippians: 141
1 Peter: 147
Revelation 12–22: 21
2:8–9
Matthew 16–23: 205
Mark 9–16: 257
Luke 18–24: 238
1 & 2 Thessalonians: 246
Hebrews: 11
Revelation 12–22: 219
2:9
Luke 1–5: 50
John 12–21: 18
Revelation 1–11: 233, 277
Revelation 12–22: 198, 236, 239, 240
2:10–11
James: 165
2:11
Luke 1–5: 309

2 Corinthians: 484
1 & 2 Thessalonians: 184
2:12
Acts 1–12: 58
Acts 13–28: 27
1 Timothy: 275
Revelation 1–11: 316
Revelation 12–22: 94, 118
3:7
Matthew 1–7: 342
Revelation 1–11: 319
3:8
Luke 11–17: 371
1 Peter: 50, 52
4:1
Luke 18–24: 61
1 & 2 Thessalonians: 187
4:3
1 & 2 Thessalonians: 103
4:4
Luke 1–5: 76
4:7
1 Peter: 40, 47
4:7–8
Philippians: 10, 69
4:8
Romans 1–8: 518
5:2
Galatians: 180
1 & 2 Thessalonians: 87
1 Peter: 194
5:3
Luke 11–17: 7
5:4
1 Timothy: 278
5:4–5
Luke 11–17: 374
Revelation 1–11: 195
5:5
Romans 9–16: 63
5:9
Romans 1–8: 188
1 & 2 Thessalonians: 41
James: 145
5:10
James: 288
5:11
1 & 2 Thessalonians: 81, 184
1 Peter: 40
6:8
Luke 11–17: 222
6:32
1–3 John: 35
7
Revelation 1–11: 188
7:1–5
Acts 13–28: 118
7:2
1 Peter: 281
7:4–5
Matthew 1–7: 339
7:6
Revelation 1–11: 319
7:8
2 Corinthians: 184
7:9
Luke 6–10: 200
Romans 9–16: 31
Revelation 1–11: 102
7:10
Luke 1–5: 167
Acts 13–28: 118
7:11
Matthew 1–7: 294
Matthew 16–23: 192
Acts 13–28: 120
Romans 1–8: 65, 68
Romans 9–16: 63
2 Corinthians: 12
1–3 John: 39, 43
Revelation 1–11: 199
Revelation 12–22: 120
7:17
Matthew 1–7: 377
Luke 1–5: 49, 93
Luke 11–17: 5
Hebrews: 443
Revelation 1–11: 171
Revelation 12–22: 194
8
Hebrews: 53
2 Peter–Jude: 179
8:1
James: 145
2 Peter–Jude: 29
8:2
Matthew 16–23: 273
8:3
2 Corinthians: 395
1 Peter: 71, 288
Revelation 12–22: 262
8:3–4
1–3 John: 88
8:4–6
1 & 2 Thessalonians: 209
8:6
Ephesians: 49
9:1
Luke 11–17: 6
Revelation 12–22: 194
9:2
1 Peter: 40
Revelation 1–11: 171
9:3–4
Matthew 8–15: 245
9:4, 8
Romans 1–8: 115
9:7–8
Revelation 12–22: 175, 247
9:9
Matthew 8–15: 439
9:10
Matthew 1–7: 377
John 12–21: 99, 261
Acts 13–28: 135
1 & 2 Thessalonians: 194
1 Peter: 280
1–3 John: 74
9:14
Philippians: 216
1 Peter: 51
Revelation 12–22: 194
9:17
1 & 2 Thessalonians: 242
1–3 John: 86
9:18
Matthew 8–15: 191
Luke 6–10: 243
9:20
1 Peter: 147
10:1
Matthew 8–15: 34
2 Corinthians: 12
10:1–5
Revelation 1–11: 276
10:2
Matthew 8–15: 191
10:3
2 Corinthians: 309
10:4
Mark 9–16: 75
Luke 11–17: 375
Acts 1–12: 241
10:7
Matthew 8–15: 321
Romans 1–8: 189
10:9–10
1 Peter: 281
10:16
Matthew 1–7: 55
Acts 1–12: 15
10:17
Matthew 16–23: 231
Mark 9–16: 102
Luke 6–10: 299
James: 214
1 Peter: 112
11:4
Revelation 1–11: 146
11:6
Mark 9–16: 302
Luke 18–24: 304
Revelation 1–11: 245
Revelation 12–22: 91
11:7
1 Peter: 169
12:3
Acts 1–12: 241
Acts 13–28: 306
1 & 2 Thessalonians: 41
12:4
Colossians and Philemon: 187
1–3 John: 85
12:5
Matthew 8–15: 191
12:6
Matthew 24–28: 68
13:1
1–3 John: 179
Revelation 1–11: 196
13:3
John 1–11: 456
13:5
Philippians: 216, 275
1 Peter: 63, 280
Revelation 12–22: 194

14
Romans 1–8: 346
James: 57
14:1
Matthew 1–7: 295
Matthew 8–15: 357
Mark 9–16: 202
Luke 11–17: 134, 342
Acts 13–28: 134
Romans 1–8: 68, 88
James: 226
14:1–3
Matthew 1–7: 476
2 Corinthians: 12, 210
James: 57
1 Peter: 19
14:2
Romans 1–8: 183, 184
James: 196
Revelation 12–22: 262
14:3
Romans 1–8: 185
1–3 John: 86
14:6
Matthew 8–15: 191
15
2 Corinthians: 478–79
15:1–2
2 Corinthians: 184
Titus: 26
15:1–4
Matthew 16–23: 116
James: 268
15:1, 4
Matthew 1–7: 322
15:3
James: 218
15:5
2 Corinthians: 272
16
Matthew 16–23: 37
Luke 18–24: 430
Acts 13–28: 25, 120
16:3
Revelation 1–11: 320
16:5
Galatians: 101
16:5–6
1 Peter: 38
16:8
Matthew 1–7: 378, 415
Luke 1–5: 79
Luke 11–17: 16
Romans 1–8: 185, 213
Ephesians: 118
16:8–9
1 & 2 Thessalonians: 184
16:8–11
Matthew 16–23: 181
Luke 18–24: 442
Acts 1–12: 65
1 Corinthians: 402
1 & 2 Thessalonians: 185
Hebrews: 124
16:9–10
Matthew 16–23: 327
16:9–11
Mark 9–16: 185
Luke 18–24: 142
16:10
Matthew 16–23: 222, 227
Matthew 24–28: 232
Mark 1–8: 419
Mark 9–16: 94
Luke 18–24: 189
John 1–11: 14, 463
John 12–21: 368
Acts 1–12: 109
Acts 13–28: 338
Ephesians: 139
1 Timothy: 272
1 Peter: 53
16:10–11
Philippians: 80
16:11
John 12–21: 296
Acts 1–12: 66
Ephesians: 230
Philippians: 10, 216, 263
1 & 2 Thessalonians: 184
Hebrews: 247
1 Peter: 40
1–3 John: 20
Revelation 12–22: 260
17
Matthew 1–7: 190
17:1
Luke 11–17: 52
17:3
2 Corinthians: 460
James: 8
17:4
2 Peter–Jude: 63
17:7
Luke 1–5: 153
17:8
Revelation 12–22: 31
17:12
1 Peter: 281
17:15
Luke 18–24: 29
John 12–21: 300
Ephesians: 112
Philippians: 80
1 Timothy: 257
18
2 Peter–Jude: 179
18:1
John 12–21: 400
18:1–3
Matthew 16–23: 340
18:2
Matthew 8–15: 439
Luke 6–10: 120
Revelation 1–11: 168
Revelation 12–22: 42
18:6
Luke 11–17: 5
Luke 18–24: 2
18:7
Matthew 24–28: 274
Luke 18–24: 390
18:10
Revelation 12–22: 31
18:12
Mark 9–16: 376
18:13
Mark 1–8: 244
Revelation 1–11: 282
18:16
Revelation 12–22: 33
18:20
James: 208
18:27
Matthew 16–23: 231
18:30
Luke 18–24: 418
Ephesians: 359
1 & 2 Thessalonians: 294
18:31
2 Corinthians: 488
1 Timothy: 275
18:32
2 Peter–Jude: 30
18:46
1 Timothy: 5
18:49
1 Peter: 53
19:1
John 1–11: 450
Acts 13–28: 133
Romans 1–8: 79, 84
Romans 9–16: 124
Ephesians: 15, 96
2 Peter–Jude: 29
1–3 John: 73
19:1–2
Revelation 1–11: 255
19:1–3
Romans 9–16: 87
19:1–4
Colossians and Philemon: 48
Revelation 12–22: 88
19:1–6
Acts 13–28: 51
1–3 John: 82
19:4
Romans 9–16: 87
19:7
Luke 1–5: 86
1 & 2 Thessalonians: 198
1 Timothy: 21
2 Timothy: 142
James: 145
1–3 John: 85
19:7–8
Luke 1–5: 24
Ephesians: 369
1 & 2 Thessalonians: 89
James: 69
19:7–9
James: 85
1 Peter: 27
19:7–10
Romans 1–8: 357
19:7–11
John 12–21: 199–200
Romans 1–8: 374

2 Corinthians: 90
1 & 2 Thessalonians: 108, 185, 198
1–3 John: 124
19:7–13
2 Timothy: 153
19:7–14
1 & 2 Thessalonians: 194
19:7b
2 Peter–Jude: 57
19:8
Ephesians: 312
1 & 2 Thessalonians: 198, 297
James: 145
1–3 John: 14
19:9
Matthew 24–28: 68
2 Corinthians: 186, 257
Philippians: 289
1 Peter: 68
Revelation 12–22: 131, 143
19:9–10
1 Peter: 95
19:10
2 Corinthians: 102
1 Peter: 44
Revelation 1–11: 287
19:11
1 & 2 Thessalonians: 89
19:14
Matthew 1–7: 203
20:1
1 & 2 Thessalonians: 187
20:6
Mark 9–16: 209
20:7
Matthew 1–7: 377
John 12–21: 261
2 Corinthians: 348
Philippians: 222
21:1
Philippians: 275
1 Peter: 51
21:1–2
Acts 13–28: 358
21:2–3
1 & 2 Thessalonians: 258
21:6
1 & 2 Thessalonians: 184
22
Matthew 16–23: 37
Luke 1–5: 131, 136, 260
Luke 18–24: 289, 342, 377, 425
Acts 1–12: 64, 65, 111
Acts 13–28: 24, 120, 211, 338
1 Corinthians: 402
1 & 2 Thessalonians: 144
Hebrews: 235
1 Peter: 53
22:1
Matthew 16–23: 222
Matthew 24–28: 232
Mark 9–16: 96
Luke 11–17: 180
Acts 13–28: 24
2 Corinthians: 12
22:1–18
Mark 1–8: 191
Mark 9–16: 267
22:1–31
Mark 1–8: 147
22:3
Luke 11–17: 6
1–3 John: 25
Revelation 12–22: 130
22:6–8
Luke 11–17: 232
Luke 18–24: 50–51
John 1–11: 438
John 12–21: 35
22:7–8
Matthew 24–28: 259
Luke 11–17: 344
Luke 18–24: 382
22:7–8, 14–18
1–3 John: 194
22:11
James: 16
22:12
2 Timothy: 14
22:13–21
1 Peter: 281
22:14–17
Luke 18–24: 51
22:14–18
John 12–21: 35
22:16
Matthew 16–23: 222
Matthew 24–28: 118
Philippians: 217
22:17
Acts 13–28: 24
22:18
Matthew 16–23: 222
Mark 9–16: 366
Luke 18–24: 383
John 12–21: 279, 351
Acts 13–28: 24
22:22
John 12–21: 261
22:23
2 Corinthians: 186
1 Peter: 200
Revelation 12–22: 200
22:25
Revelation 12–22: 200
22:26
Luke 1–5: 164
22:27
John 12–21: 22
22:27–28
1 Peter: 56
22:28
Luke 1–5: 259
1 & 2 Thessalonians: 254
1 Peter: 147
23
Matthew 1–7: 33, 161
Luke 11–17: 299
Ephesians: 63, 259
1 & 2 Thessalonians: 44
1 Peter: 261
2 Peter–Jude: 179
Revelation 1–11: 233
23:1
Luke 1–5: 155
Luke 11–17: 141
John 1–11: 14
John 12–21: 142
Philippians: 168, 169
1 Peter: 174, 270
23:1, 2
1–3 John: 146
23:1, 5
Matthew 1–7: 184
23:2
1 Peter: 262
23:3
Philippians: 169
1–3 John: 107
23:4
Matthew 8–15: 439
John 12–21: 96
Romans 1–8: 516
Philippians: 169
1 Peter: 280
23:5
Luke 6–10: 173
James: 278
23:6
John 12–21: 299
Galatians: 168
Philippians: 169
24:1
Matthew 1–7: 420
John 12–21: 142
Acts 13–28: 138
1 Corinthians: 247
2 Corinthians: 289
Revelation 1–11: 315
24:3
1 Timothy: 18
24:3–4
Matthew 1–7: 205
Luke 1–5: 77
James: 209
24:4
Romans 9–16: 147
1 Timothy: 18
24:7–10
John 1–11: 450
24:8
Revelation 12–22: 216
24:8–10
Luke 11–17: 397
24:10
Matthew 1–7: viii
John 1–11: 14
25:1–2
John 12–21: 98
25:2
2 Timothy: 13
25:4
1 & 2 Thessalonians: 194
25:4–5
Romans 1–8: 431

25:5
Luke 1–5: 153
1 Timothy: 5
25:6
Romans 1–8: 27
25:8
1 Peter: 274
25:8–9
Acts 13–28: 162
25:9
Matthew 1–7: 171
Luke 6–10: 299
Romans 1–8: 431
1 Peter: 277
25:10
Romans 1–8: 473
1 & 2 Thessalonians: 96
2 Peter–Jude: 82
25:12
Luke 11–17: 14
25:14
Ephesians: ix
Colossians and Philemon: 78
1 Peter: 68
Revelation 12–22: 200
25:21
2 Corinthians: 184
26:1
2 Corinthians: 184
1 & 2 Thessalonians: 121
26:1–2
James: 8
26:2
Matthew 1–7: 203
2 Corinthians: 460
Colossians and Philemon: 86
26:7
Acts 1–12: 45
Revelation 12–22: 194
26:8
1 & 2 Thessalonians: 62
26:11
2 Corinthians: 184
27:1
Matthew 16–23: 11
John 1–11: 14, 334
Romans 1–8: 503
Ephesians: 205, 210
1 & 2 Thessalonians: 187
Hebrews: 356
1 Peter: 52, 200
1–3 John: 23
27:1–3
Acts 13–28: 118
27:4
Matthew 16–23: 271
Luke 18–24: 107
1 & 2 Thessalonians: 187
Hebrews: 334
27:7
Luke 11–17: 52
27:8
Matthew 1–7: 203
1 & 2 Thessalonians: 97
James: 207
27:9
1 Timothy: 5
27:13
Galatians: 168
27:14
1 Corinthians: 476
Philippians: 277
28:2
Luke 18–24: 17
28:7
1 & 2 Thessalonians: 184, 185
29
2 Peter–Jude: 179
29:1
1 Peter: 212
Revelation 12–22: 8
29:1–2
Romans 1–8: 83
1 Corinthians: 244
29:2
Luke 11–17: 15
Philippians: 221
29:3
John 1–11: 450
Acts 1–12: 203
29:10
Matthew 8–15: 349
Luke 1–5: 61
Luke 11–17: 399
Acts 1–12: 15
29:11
Matthew 1–7: 213
John 12–21: 122
Philippians: 284
1 & 2 Thessalonians: 314
30:4
Luke 1–5: 93, 164
Romans 9–16: 62
Colossians and Philemon: 36
Revelation 12–22: 194
30:5
James: 261
1 Peter: 42
30:7
Revelation 12–22: 169
31
1 Peter: 259–60
31:1
1 Peter: 169
31:5
Luke 1–5: 303
Acts 13–28: 24
Romans 9–16: 92
Philippians: 290
1 & 2 Thessalonians: 319
2 Peter–Jude: 82
31:13
James: 219
31:14
1 Peter: 63
31:23
Matthew 16–23: 231, 340
Luke 1–5: 79
Acts 13–28: 118
Romans 1–8: 483
31:24
2 Corinthians: 107
32
Luke 1–5: 206
Acts 13–28: 20, 26
Romans 1–8: 242
32:1
Luke 11–17: 41, 369
Luke 18–24: 13
Acts 13–28: 109
2 Corinthians: 216
Colossians and Philemon: 110
James: 290
32:1–2
Matthew 1–7: 158, 201
Luke 1–5: 24
Romans 1–8: 203
2 Corinthians: 90, 205
1–3 John: 73
Revelation 12–22: 94
32:1–2, 5
Luke 1–5: 206–7
32:1–2a
1–3 John: 35
32:3
Matthew 1–7: 66
32:3–5
Matthew 1–7: 158
John 12–21: 129
32:5
Luke 6–10: 354
Luke 11–17: 313
John 1–11: 417
2 Corinthians: 31, 217, 468
1 & 2 Thessalonians: 97, 188
James: 279
1–3 John: 30
32:6
Revelation 12–22: 33
32:8
2 Peter–Jude: 30
32:8–9
1 Peter: 274
32:10
1 Timothy: 257
32:11
Philippians: 216
1 & 2 Thessalonians: 184
1 Peter: 40
33
2 Peter–Jude: 179
33:1
Luke 1–5: 164
Ephesians: 256
Philippians: 216, 221
33:1–3
Revelation 12–22: 75
33:2
Revelation 1–11: 170
Revelation 12–22: 75, 125
33:3
Revelation 1–11: 171, 173
33:4
Luke 1–5: 174
Luke 18–24: 418

33:5
Romans 1–8: 119
1 Peter: 45
33:6
John 1–11: 17
Revelation 1–11: 285
33:8
1 Peter: 68
33:8–9
Romans 1–8: 53
33:9
Revelation 1–11: 156
33:10
Luke 18–24: 397
33:11
Luke 11–17: 398
Hebrews: 166
33:12
Acts 13–28: 129
Revelation 12–22: 5
33:13–14
2 Corinthians: 395
33:17
Revelation 1–11: 271
33:18
2 Corinthians: 107
1 Peter: 33, 286
Revelation 12–22: 200
33:18–19
Luke 11–17: 35
33:21
Romans 1–8: 287
Philippians: 216
33:22
2 Corinthians: 107
34
Luke 11–17: 145
34:1
Luke 1–5: 164
34:2
Luke 1–5: 77
2 Corinthians: 349
Philippians: 222
34:3
Matthew 1–7: 378
Romans 1–8: 287
1–3 John: 106
34:7
Revelation 12–22: 200
34:8
1 & 2 Thessalonians: 96
1 Timothy: 275
Hebrews: 145
34:8–10
Luke 11–17: 145
34:9
1 Peter: 68, 200
Revelation 1–11: 320
Revelation 12–22: 200
34:10
Matthew 1–7: 184
Luke 1–5: 82
Luke 11–17: 141
34:11
2 Corinthians: 257
34:13
James: 145
34:14
John 12–21: 127
1 & 2 Thessalonians: 199
34:15
Luke 6–10: 365
Luke 11–17: 145
34:17–19
Revelation 1–11: 213
34:18
Matthew 1–7: 146
Matthew 16–23: 48
Luke 1–5: 271
Luke 6–10: 96
Philippians: 277
34:19
Luke 11–17: 145
2 Timothy: 132
1 Peter: 43
34:20
Matthew 24–28: 293
Mark 9–16: 94, 290, 388
John 12–21: 364
Acts 13–28: 24
35
Revelation 1–11: 188
35:1–8
Revelation 1–11: 319
35:9
Philippians: 216, 275
Revelation 12–22: 194
35:10
Matthew 8–15: 191
Revelation 12–22: 47
35:12–15
Matthew 1–7: 339
35:13
Matthew 1–7: 402
Luke 1–5: 185
Acts 13–28: 5
35:16
Acts 1–12: 219
35:17
1 Peter: 281
Revelation 1–11: 196
35:28
James: 145
36:1
Romans 1–8: 192
36:1–3
Romans 1–8: 188
36:1, 4
Romans 9–16: 269
36:5
Luke 1–5: 174
Romans 1–8: 272
1 & 2 Thessalonians: 296
36:6
1 Timothy: 271
36:7
Matthew 16–23: 401
Romans 1–8: 27
1 Peter: 280
1–3 John: 36
Revelation 12–22: 31
36:9
Matthew 1–7: 244
Luke 11–17: 88
John 1–11: 23, 334
Acts 1–12: 110
1 Timothy: 277
37
Luke 1–5: 258
37:1–5
1 & 2 Thessalonians: 88
37:2
Luke 11–17: 145
37:3
1 Peter: 197
37:3–4
Hebrews: 160
37:3–4, 10–11
Matthew 1–7: 389
37:3–5
Luke 11–17: 145
James: 232
37:4
Matthew 8–15: 185
Acts 1–12: 298
Acts 13–28: 358
Philippians: 221
1 & 2 Thessalonians: 258
James: 236
1 Peter: 40
1–3 John: 204
37:5
2 Corinthians: 345
1 & 2 Thessalonians: 195
1 Peter: 280
37:7–11
James: 33
37:9
Luke 11–17: 145
37:10
Matthew 1–7: 174
37:11
Matthew 1–7: 174
Luke 11–17: 145
Philippians: 112
1 Peter: 278
37:12
Acts 1–12: 171, 219
37:14
Acts 1–12: 171
37:16
1 & 2 Thessalonians: 97
Hebrews: 354
37:18–19
Luke 11–17: 35
37:21
Luke 11–17: 130
2 Corinthians: 272
1 & 2 Thessalonians: 309
37:21, 26
Romans 9–16: 245
37:23–24
2 Corinthians: 150
37:23–34
Revelation 12–22: 96
37:24
1 Peter: 36, 279

37:25
Matthew 1–7: 389
Luke 1–5: 257
Luke 11–17: 35, 141, 145
2 Corinthians: 279
37:26
1 & 2 Thessalonians: 309
37:27
1 & 2 Thessalonians: 199
37:28
2 Corinthians: 21
1 & 2 Thessalonians: 189
1 Timothy: 271
James: 28
37:30–31
2 Corinthians: 37
37:32
Acts 1–12: 171
37:39
1 Peter: 89
37:39–40
Revelation 12–22: 70
38
Acts 13–28: 20, 26
1–3 John: 35
38:1–4
Romans 1–8: 392
38:1–8
1–3 John: 142
38:4
Romans 1–8: 459
38:9–10
Romans 1–8: 459
38:12
1 & 2 Thessalonians: 209
38:15
2 Corinthians: 107
38:18
1–3 John: 36
39:1
James: 145, 153
39:4
Matthew 1–7: 161
1 Peter: 93
39:4–5
James: 237
39:5
2 Peter–Jude: 51
39:6
James: 244
39:7
2 Corinthians: 107
1 Peter: 33
40
Revelation 1–11: 188
40:1–2
James: 26
40:3
Romans 1–8: 322
Ephesians: 257
Revelation 1–11: 171
Revelation 12–22: 75
40:4
1 Timothy: 275
Revelation 12–22: 94
40:5
Acts 1–12: 45
1 Corinthians: 363
40:6–8
Hebrews: 253
40:7
Luke 6–10: 142
Luke 18–24: 425
40:7–8
Luke 1–5: 43
40:8
Luke 1–5: 167, 171
Luke 18–24: 304
James: 229
1 Peter: 91, 95
40:9
Mark 1–8: 12
40:9–10
Acts 13–28: 214
2 Timothy: 10
40:10
Luke 1–5: 174
1 & 2 Thessalonians: 296
40:16
Philippians: 216, 275
1 Peter: 51
41:1
Luke 6–10: 308
1 & 2 Thessalonians: 309
James: 102, 107
Revelation 12–22: 94
41:2
James: 28
41:4
Luke 18–24: 61
41:7–8
James: 218
41:9
Matthew 8–15: 174
Matthew 16–23: 226
Matthew 24–28: 191, 232
Mark 9–16: 96, 277, 286, 315, 317
Luke 6–10: 79
Luke 18–24: 53, 271, 289, 442
John 12–21: 34, 76
Acts 13–28: 22
1–3 John: 189
41:11
1 Peter: 45
41:12
2 Corinthians: 184
41:13
Romans 9–16: 381
42
2 Peter–Jude: 179
42:1
Matthew 1–7: 208
Philippians: 221
1 & 2 Thessalonians: 96
2 Timothy: 162
James: 43, 65, 206
42:1–2
Romans 1–8: 223, 483
2 Corinthians: 170
1 & 2 Thessalonians: 187
Revelation 12–22: 260, 271
42:1–3
Matthew 1–7: 156
42:2
1 Timothy: 136, 167
Revelation 1–11: 217, 315
42:5
Romans 9–16: 313
2 Corinthians: 107
Philippians: 17
1 & 2 Thessalonians: 315
42:7
1 Peter: 43
42:8
2 Peter–Jude: 25
42:11
2 Corinthians: 107
Philippians: 17
1 & 2 Thessalonians: 315
Hebrews: 391
43:3
John 1–11: 334
43:3–4
1 Peter: 40
43:4
Romans 1–8: 287
Philippians: 221
43:5
2 Corinthians: 107
Philippians: 17
1 & 2 Thessalonians: 315
Hebrews: 443
44:1–4
1 & 2 Thessalonians: 188
44:3
John 1–11: 334
Acts 13–28: 19
44:8
Revelation 12–22: 194
44:18
1 Timothy: 150
44:21
Luke 11–17: 181
1 & 2 Thessalonians: 91
Revelation 12–22: 253
44:24
2 Corinthians: 12
44:26
Revelation 1–11: 319
45:3–5
Revelation 12–22: 216
45:6
Acts 1–12: 15
45:7
Romans 1–8: 60
45:8
Mark 9–16: 364
45:13
Matthew 1–7: 279
45:14
James: 244
46
2 Peter–Jude: 179
46:1
1 & 2 Thessalonians: 316

46:1–3
Matthew 8–15: 35
Romans 1–8: 503
46:10
1 Peter: 147
46:11
Romans 1–8: 503
47:2
1 & 2 Thessalonians: 254
47:7
1 & 2 Thessalonians: 254
47:8
1 & 2 Thessalonians: 209
1 Peter: 147
Revelation 1–11: 147, 155
48:2
1 Peter: 120
Revelation 12–22: 71
48:6
John 12–21: 217
48:10
Romans 9–16: 31
1–3 John: 25
48:11
Revelation 12–22: 195
49:15
Matthew 16–23: 327
Matthew 24–28: 304
Mark 9–16: 185
Luke 18–24: 142
Philippians: 80
1 Timothy: 272
50:2
Hebrews: 413
50:3
Revelation 12–22: 124
50:6
Romans 1–8: 173
50:7
John 1–11: 33
50:9–12
Acts 13–28: 139
50:10–12
1 Timothy: 282
Revelation 1–11: 173
50:12
2 Corinthians: 289
50:14
Matthew 16–23: 382
Colossians and Philemon: 36
50:15
Luke 11–17: 5
2 Corinthians: 120
50:16–20
Romans 1–8: 156
50:16–21
Romans 9–16: 63
50:19–20
James: 218
50:21
Luke 11–17: 10
John 1–11: 76
Revelation 1–11: 187
50:23
Luke 1–5: 77
1 Corinthians: 244
1 Peter: 288
51
Luke 11–17: 39, 41, 381
Acts 13–28: 20, 26
1 Corinthians: 148
2 Corinthians: 57
1–3 John: 35
51:1
Matthew 1–7: 66, 190
Matthew 8–15: 469
Luke 11–17: 236
Luke 18–24: 61
51:1–3
Romans 1–8: 383
51:1–4
Romans 1–8: 224
51:1–9
1–3 John: 38
51:1–14
Romans 1–8: 242
51:1–17
1–3 John: 88
51:1, 3
Matthew 1–7: 147
1–3 John: 30
51:2
Luke 11–17: 2
John 12–21: 67
51:3
Matthew 1–7: 161, 164
Hebrews: 250, 352
51:3–4
Matthew 1–7: 157
51:4
Matthew 16–23: 148
Mark 1–8: 104
Luke 1–5: 323
Luke 11–17: 37, 43, 381
Romans 1–8: 157, 172
2 Corinthians: 51
Colossians and Philemon: 218
James: 225
1 Peter: 226
Revelation 1–11: 189
51:5
Matthew 1–7: 239
Matthew 8–15: 318
Mark 1–8: 350
Mark 9–16: 67
Luke 1–5: 58, 169
Luke 11–17: 37
Luke 18–24: 27
Romans 1–8: 296, 395
2 Corinthians: 210
Philippians: 50, 218
51:6
Matthew 1–7: 292, 326
51:6, 10
Matthew 1–7: 203
51:7
James: 177
Revelation 1–11: 231
Revelation 12–22: 308
51:9
Luke 1–5: 207
Acts 1–12: 117
51:9–10
Mark 1–8: 354
51:10
Matthew 1–7: 150, 207
Philippians: 31
1 Timothy: 18
James: 177, 209
51:10, 12–13
Matthew 1–7: 436
51:10, 13
Matthew 1–7: 67
51:11
2 Corinthians: 114
Ephesians: 247
51:12
John 12–21: 151
Romans 1–8: 380
2 Corinthians: 57
Galatians: 189
Ephesians: 353
Philippians: 32, 188, 216
1 & 2 Thessalonians: 25
1 Peter: 40
51:13
Matthew 16–23: 98
James: 208, 286
51:14
2 Corinthians: 57
51:17
Matthew 1–7: 146
Matthew 16–23: 48
Luke 1–5: 271, 308
Luke 6–10: 128, 299
Romans 9–16: 145
2 Corinthians: 112, 438
Hebrews: 251
51:18
1 Peter: 120
51:19
Philippians: 307
52:1
Romans 1–8: 119
1 Peter: 120
52:1–5
James: 221
52:2–4
James: 155
52:4
James: 145
52:7
2 Corinthians: 272
53
Matthew 1–7: 295
53:1
Romans 1–8: 88
Colossians and Philemon: 85
53:1–3
Matthew 1–7: 476
2 Corinthians: 12, 210
1 Peter: 19
53:3
Romans 1–8: 183
54:6
Revelation 12–22: 194
55
Revelation 1–11: 188

55:1–2
Luke 11–17: 52
55:4
Mark 1–8: 253
John 12–21: 361
55:6–8
Matthew 1–7: 153
55:12–14
Matthew 24–28: 147, 191
Mark 9–16: 286
Luke 18–24: 271
John 12–21: 76
1 Peter: 279
55:12–15
Acts 1–12: 33
55:13
Philippians: 197
55:17
Acts 1–12: 98
55:17, 19
Ephesians: 379
55:21
James: 157
55:22
Mark 1–8: 233
Philippians: 33
James: 261
1 Peter: 279–80
56:1–13
Acts 13–28: 290
56:3
John 12–21: 99
Romans 1–8: 518
56:4
1 Timothy: 271
56:8
Romans 9–16: 198
56:11
1 Timothy: 271
Revelation 1–11: 77
56:12
Matthew 16–23: 382
57
Matthew 1–7: 203
57:1
Revelation 12–22: 31
57:1–3
Philippians: 277
57:2
1 Peter: 279
57:4
James: 155
57:5
2 Peter–Jude: 29
57:7
Romans 1–8: 425
Philippians: 31, 277
57:10
2 Peter–Jude: 82
58
Revelation 1–11: 188
58:3
Luke 18–24: 27
Romans 1–8: 296
2 Corinthians: 210
Philippians: 218
1 Peter: 88
58:3–4
Matthew 1–7: 326
58:6
1 Peter: 281
58:10
1 & 2 Thessalonians: 236
58:10–11
Revelation 12–22: 195, 198
58:11
Matthew 8–15: 245
Romans 1–8: 173
Hebrews: 310
59
2 Peter–Jude: 179
Revelation 1–11: 188
59:7
James: 157
59:13
Acts 1–12: 15
61:1
Luke 11–17: 52
61:4
Revelation 12–22: 31
61:8
Matthew 16–23: 382
Revelation 1–11: 171
62:5
Romans 9–16: 313
2 Corinthians: 107
62:8
Mark 9–16: 147
Luke 11–17: 7
62:10
Hebrews: 433
62:11
Matthew 8–15: 30
Luke 1–5: 91, 306
Romans 1–8: 79
Romans 9–16: 218
Philippians: 283
62:12
Matthew 16–23: 52
2 Timothy: 199
63:1
Matthew 1–7: 181
63:1–2
Matthew 8–15: 30
1 & 2 Thessalonians: 96, 187
James: 207
63:1–3
Romans 1–8: 483
63:1–5
1 Timothy: 252
63:1–8
Matthew 16–23: 340
63:2
Luke 6–10: 97
63:3
2 Corinthians: 17
63:3–7
James: 20
63:4
1 Timothy: 75
63:5
Luke 11–17: 8
63:6
Luke 1–5: 76
63:7
Revelation 12–22: 31
63:9
Ephesians: 139
63:9, 10
Ephesians: 139
63:11
Titus: 54
64:1–10
James: 159
64:3
James: 157
64:3–4
Romans 1–8: 190
64:5
1 Peter: 229
64:7–9
Revelation 1–11: 188
65:2
Luke 11–17: 2
65:3
Luke 1–5: 207, 321
Acts 1–12: 117
65:4
Luke 18–24: 107
1 Timothy: 275
1 Peter: 26
Revelation 12–22: 94
65:5
1 Peter: 63
65:5–7
Mark 1–8: 231
Luke 6–10: 210
65:6
Matthew 8–15: 30
65:9
1 Peter: 140
65:13
James: 246
66:1
Ephesians: 258
Revelation 1–11: 227
66:3
2 Corinthians: 315
66:3, 5
1 Peter: 134
66:4
Revelation 12–22: 131
66:7
1 Peter: 147, 288
2 Peter–Jude: 213
66:8–9
1 Timothy: 271
66:12
1 Peter: 43
66:16
Luke 1–5: 157
66:18
Matthew 1–7: 298, 394
Luke 11–17: 2, 45, 382
John 12–21: 150
1 Timothy: 75
James: 280
1–3 John: 204

66:20
1 & 2 Thessalonians: 185
67:1
Revelation 1–11: 223
67:1–7
Mark 1–8: 362
67:2
Revelation 1–11: 223
67:7
Revelation 1–11: 223
68
2 Peter–Jude: 179
68:1–2
Revelation 1–11: 319
68:2
2 Timothy: 72
68:3
1 & 2 Thessalonians: 184
1 Peter: 47
68:5
Luke 18–24: 6
1 Timothy: 194
James: 90
68:7–8
2 Timothy: 71
68:8
Revelation 1–11: 204
68:10
James: 102, 107
68:17
1 & 2 Thessalonians: 234
Hebrews: 46
68:18
2 Corinthians: 293
Ephesians: 137
68:21
1 & 2 Thessalonians: 236
James: 195
68:25
Matthew 1–7: 20
68:35
Matthew 1–7: 142
69
Revelation 1–11: 188
69:1–2
Revelation 12–22: 33
69:4
Acts 13–28: 24
69:9
Matthew 16–23: 340
Mark 9–16: 138
Luke 11–17: 413
Romans 1–8: 484
Romans 9–16: 310
1 Corinthians: 350
2 Corinthians: 264
Ephesians: 184
Philippians: 137
1 & 2 Thessalonians: 144
Hebrews: 354
69:10
Mark 1–8: 128
Luke 1–5: 339
69:13
Matthew 24–28: 96
69:13–14
Revelation 12–22: 33
69:20
Matthew 24–28: 293
69:21
Luke 18–24: 52
Acts 13–28: 24
69:22–23
Romans 9–16: 104
69:22–24
Matthew 1–7: 342
69:25
Acts 1–12: 33
69:27
1 & 2 Thessalonians: 237
69:28
Acts 13–28: 39
Philippians: 273
Revelation 1–11: 115
69:34
Revelation 1–11: 173, 282
70:4
Philippians: 216
71:5
2 Corinthians: 27, 107
Ephesians: 73
71:14
2 Corinthians: 107
71:15–16
1 & 2 Thessalonians: 96
2 Timothy: 10
71:17
Titus: 72
1 Peter: 134
71:19
Romans 9–16: 31
1–3 John: 25
71:22
Revelation 1–11: 118, 170
Revelation 12–22: 75, 125
71:23
Philippians: 275
1 & 2 Thessalonians: 185
1 Peter: 51
72
Matthew 8–15: 230
Ephesians: 91
2 Peter–Jude: 179
72:4
James: 102, 107
72:7
Luke 11–17: 169
72:8
Matthew 8–15: 370
72:8–17
1 Peter: 56
72:9
James: 195
72:11
1 Peter: 147
72:12
James: 102, 107
72:18
Matthew 1–7: 142
72:18–19
Romans 9–16: 382
72:19
Luke 11–17: 15
John 1–11: 450
73:1
Matthew 1–7: 203
1 Timothy: 18
73:3–12
1 Timothy: 280
73:3–13
Luke 1–5: 257–58
73:12–13
Hebrews: 351
73:13
1 Corinthians: 411
73:22
Matthew 16–23: 2
73:23–26
1 Peter: 38
73:24
Matthew 16–23: 327
Matthew 24–28: 304
Mark 9–16: 185
Luke 18–24: 142
1 & 2 Thessalonians: 52
73:25
Romans 1–8: 223, 444, 483
2 Corinthians: 170, 432
Philippians: 221
Hebrews: 415
James: 43
Revelation 12–22: 266
73:25–26
Revelation 12–22: 260
73:27
Matthew 8–15: 328
James: 191
73:28
Philippians: 277
James: 206
1 Peter: 134
74:1
John 1–11: 424
74:10
Matthew 16–23: 56
74:10–11
Revelation 1–11: 276
74:13
Revelation 12–22: 6
74:13–14
Revelation 12–22: 41
75:1
Philippians: 277
Colossians and Philemon: 36, 182
Revelation 12–22: 194
75:4–5
Revelation 12–22: 42
75:6–7
Luke 11–17: 264
75:7
Luke 6–10: 63
75:8
Revelation 12–22: 91
75:10
Revelation 1–11: 168

76:6–7
Romans 1–8: 60
76:6–8
1 Peter: 194
76:8–9
Revelation 1–11: 238
76:9
Luke 6–10: 299
76:10
John 1–11: 484
John 12–21: 77, 335
Acts 1–12: 141
Acts 13–28: 100, 190
77:1–10
Mark 9–16: 143
77:11
Acts 1–12: 45
77:11–20
Mark 9–16: 143
77:12
1 Peter: 134
77:14
1 Peter: 134
77:19
Romans 9–16: 135
77:20
John 1–11: 424
Acts 13–28: 224
78
Acts 1–12: 203
1 Timothy: 147
78:4
Acts 1–12: 45
78:5
Revelation 12–22: 132
78:5–7
Romans 1–8: 267
78:7
2 Peter–Jude: 48
78:11
2 Peter–Jude: 48
78:14
1–3 John: 23
78:19–22
John 1–11: 399
78:32
John 1–11: 399
78:34
1 Peter: 43
78:35
Acts 13–28: 97
78:38
Luke 11–17: 236
78:38–39
Romans 1–8: 218
78:40
Revelation 1–11: 131
78:40–41
Philippians: 178
78:41
Revelation 1–11: 118
78:42
2 Peter–Jude: 48
78:43–44
Revelation 12–22: 142
78:45
Revelation 12–22: 147
78:46
Revelation 1–11: 262
78:49
Revelation 1–11: 215
78:49–51
Romans 1–8: 60
78:52
John 1–11: 424
Acts 13–28: 224
78:55
1 Peter: 34
78:59
1 & 2 Thessalonians: 66
78:65
Luke 1–5: 36
78:68
Revelation 12–22: 242
78:70
2 Peter–Jude: 18
78:70–72
John 1–11: 424
78:72
Matthew 1–7: 203
2 Corinthians: 183
79:5–6
Romans 9–16: 82
79:6
1 & 2 Thessalonians: 108
79:10
Revelation 1–11: 188
Revelation 12–22: 198
79:11
Matthew 8–15: 30
Romans 1–8: 53, 79
2 Corinthians: 315
79:12
1 & 2 Thessalonians: 237
79:13
John 1–11: 424
80:1
John 1–11: 424
Acts 13–28: 224
Revelation 1–11: 153, 233
Revelation 12–22: 132
80:8–16
Luke 18–24: 123
81:3
Revelation 1–11: 239
Revelation 12–22: 5
81:10
James: 37
81:11
Revelation 12–22: 247
81:11–12
Romans 1–8: 98
1 & 2 Thessalonians: 280
81:15
Philippians: 221
82:5
Matthew 16–23: 2
Luke 1–5: 122, 272
82:6
John 1–11: 445
83:1–2
Revelation 1–11: 276
83:18
1 Peter: 147
84
Ephesians: 259
84:1–2
1 & 2 Thessalonians: 187
84:2
Philippians: 221
1 Timothy: 136, 167
James: 207
Revelation 1–11: 51, 217, 315
84:2–4
Romans 1–8: 483
84:4
Revelation 12–22: 94
84:5
Revelation 12–22: 94
84:11
Mark 9–16: 147
Luke 11–17: 57
Philippians: 275
1 & 2 Thessalonians: 320
1 Peter: 52
2 Peter–Jude: 24–25
84:12
1 Timothy: 275
85:2
Acts 1–12: 117
James: 290
85:8
1 & 2 Thessalonians: 314
2 Peter–Jude: 24
85:9
Revelation 1–11: 320
Revelation 12–22: 200
85:10
Matthew 1–7: 192, 211
John 12–21: 124
Romans 1–8: 219
1 & 2 Thessalonians: 314
Hebrews: 177
86:5
Matthew 8–15: 304
Luke 1–5: 207, 322
Luke 11–17: 37
Acts 1–12: 117
Romans 9–16: 132
Colossians and Philemon: 111
86:8–10
Revelation 1–11: 155
86:9
Revelation 12–22: 130
86:10
2 Corinthians: 488
1 Timothy: 275
86:11
Luke 1–5: 76
Philippians: 247
86:15
Mark 1–8: 96
Luke 1–5: 120
2 Corinthians: 19
Galatians: 167
1 & 2 Thessalonians: 180, 319

Titus: 152
James: 253, 261
87:2
Revelation 12–22: 242
88:11
Revelation 1–11: 264
88:14
1–3 John: 179
89
Matthew 16–23: 345
Luke 1–5: 99, 128
89:1–2
1 & 2 Thessalonians: 296
89:3
Matthew 8–15: 306
Mark 1–8: 180
89:3–4
Luke 1–5: 174
Luke 18–24: 153
James: 269
89:3, 49
Matthew 1–7: 321
89:5
Acts 1–12: 45
Revelation 12–22: 194
89:5–7
1 & 2 Thessalonians: 234
89:6
1 Peter: 212
Revelation 12–22: 8
89:6–8
Revelation 1–11: 155
89:8
Luke 1–5: 174
Romans 1–8: 53
1 & 2 Thessalonians: 296
89:9–10
Revelation 12–22: 41
89:10
Acts 13–28: 19
89:13
Luke 1–5: 60
Acts 13–28: 19
Romans 1–8: 53
1 Peter: 288
89:16
1 & 2 Thessalonians: 185
89:17
Revelation 1–11: 168
Revelation 12–22: 42
89:20
2 Corinthians: 45
Philippians: 29
89:21
Acts 13–28: 19
89:24
1 & 2 Thessalonians: 296
Revelation 1–11: 168
Revelation 12–22: 42
89:26
Matthew 1--7: 375
89:27
Philippians: 141
Colossians and Philemon: 46
Hebrews: 11
Revelation 1–11: 25, 134
89:29
1 Peter: 35
89:30–32
Hebrews: 387
1 Peter: 43
89:31–37
Romans 9–16: 96
89:33
Philippians: 29
1 & 2 Thessalonians: 296
89:33–34
Hebrews: 387
89:35–37
Luke 18–24: 153
89:47a
2 Peter–Jude: 51
89:48
John 12–21: 360
89:52
Romans 9–16: 382
90
2 Peter–Jude: 179
90:1
1 Timothy: 259
90:2
1 Timothy: 277
1 Peter: 200
1–3 John: 76
Revelation 1–11: 158
90:4
Revelation 12–22: 203
90:5–6
2 Peter–Jude: 51
90:7–9
Romans 1–8: 60
90:8
Matthew 24–28: 110
Galatians: 187
90:10
John 1–11: 460
James: 233
2 Peter–Jude: 51
90:11
Romans 1–8: 74
Revelation 1–11: 157
90:12
Colossians and Philemon: 186
90:14
1 & 2 Thessalonians: 258
91
2 Peter–Jude: 179
91:1, 4, 11
Romans 9–16: 280
91:3–4
1 & 2 Thessalonians: 189
91:3–10
Revelation 1–11: 213
91:4
Luke 1–5: 174
Revelation 12–22: 31
91:5–16
Revelation 12–22: 73
91:11
Revelation 12–22: 296
91:11–12
Matthew 1–7: 93
Luke 1–5: 260
1 Peter: 57
91:11–14
1 Timothy: 271
91:15
Romans 1–8: 475
92:1
Luke 1–5: 93
Colossians and Philemon: 36
92:1–4
Revelation 1–11: 170
92:2
1 & 2 Thessalonians: 296
92:4
Philippians: 221
92:5
Philippians: 288
92:5–6
Matthew 16–23: 35
92:8
Romans 9–16: 236
92:10
Revelation 12–22: 42
92:14
Titus: 73
92:15
1 Peter: 200
93:1
2 Peter–Jude: 29
93:1–2
Romans 9–16: 236
93:2
Revelation 1–11: 158
93:5
2 Peter–Jude: 57
94:1
1 & 2 Thessalonians: 180
94:1–2
Revelation 1–11: 188
Revelation 12–22: 198
94:1–10
Revelation 12–22: 127
94:2
Romans 1–8: 173
94:3–4
Revelation 1–11: 276
94:10
Romans 9–16: 237
1 Corinthians: 192
94:14
Romans 9–16: 96
94:21–23
Revelation 12–22: 127
94:23
Revelation 1–11: 188
95
2 Corinthians: 463
95:1
Philippians: 221
95:1–6
2 Peter–Jude: 137
95:3
1 & 2 Thessalonians: 254
95:6
Mark 9–16: 148
2 Corinthians: 345

95:6–8
Matthew 24–28: 96
95:7
John 1–11: 424
95:7–8
Revelation 12–22: 298
95:7–9, 11
Matthew 8–15: 276
95:7–11
Acts 13–28: 19, 32
Hebrews: 87
95:10
Romans 9–16: 56
96:1
Revelation 1–11: 171
96:1–2
Ephesians: 257
Revelation 12–22: 75
96:2
1 Peter: 51, 288
96:3
Acts 1–12: 45
96:3–5
Romans 9–16: 237
96:5
Revelation 1–11: 273
96:8
Luke 11–17: 16
96:10
Matthew 1–7: 129
1 Peter: 147
96:11–13
Revelation 12–22: 195
96:13
Romans 1–8: 115
Revelation 12–22: 120, 175
97
2 Peter–Jude: 179
97:3
Revelation 12–22: 124
97:7
Hebrews: 29
97:10
Matthew 16–23: 340
Romans 9–16: 185
1 & 2 Thessalonians: 199
James: 28
2 Peter–Jude: 90
1–3 John: 36, 39
97:11
1 Peter: 47
97:12
Colossians and Philemon: 36
Revelation 12–22: 194
98
2 Peter–Jude: 179
98:1
Revelation 1–11: 171
98:1–2
Revelation 12–22: 75
98:2
1–3 John: 25
98:3
Luke 1–5: 83
Revelation 1–11: 223
98:4
Philippians: 221
Revelation 1–11: 173
98:8
James: 246
98:9
Romans 9–16: 237
1 Peter: 169
Revelation 12–22: 120
99:1
Revelation 12–22: 132
99:3
Luke 1–5: 77
99:5
Revelation 12–22: 130
99:8
2 Corinthians: 50
99:9
1 Peter: 200
Revelation 12–22: 130
100:1
Revelation 1–11: 227
100:1–3
Mark 1–8: 362
100:2
1 & 2 Thessalonians: 184
100:3
John 1–11: 424
John 12–21: 267
100:3a
1 Peter: 152
100:4
Luke 1–5: 164
Ephesians: 264
100:5
Luke 1–5: 174
101:2
2 Corinthians: 184
Titus: 26
101:4
Romans 9–16: 185
101:5
James: 218
101:6
2 Corinthians: 184
Titus: 27
102
Hebrews: 35
1–3 John: 35
102:1–2
Luke 11–17: 52
102:11
James: 233
102:13
Luke 11–17: 237
102:15
Luke 11–17: 16
102:21
1 Peter: 120
102:24–27
Revelation 1–11: 158
102:25
John 1–11: 20
1 Peter: 288
Revelation 1–11: 285
102:25–26
Matthew 1–7: 262
Luke 11–17: 351
Revelation 12–22: 249, 263
102:26–27
1 Peter: 52
103:1
Luke 1–5: 76
103:2
Philippians: 34
2 Peter–Jude: 48
103:3
Matthew 8–15: 304
103:6
John 12–21: 301
Revelation 12–22: 130
103:8
Luke 1–5: 153
John 12–21: 46, 233
2 Corinthians: 19
James: 261
103:8–12
Mark 1–8: 96
103:10–12
Luke 11–17: 369–70
103:11
Matthew 1–7: 194
1 Peter: 68
2 Peter–Jude: 25
Revelation 1–11: 320
Revelation 12–22: 200
103:12
Matthew 8–15: 52
Mark 1–8: 103
Luke 1–5: 207, 322
2 Corinthians: 31, 200, 216
Ephesians: 23
Philippians: 35
Colossians and Philemon: 42
James: 290
103:13
Matthew 1–7: 375
2 Corinthians: 19
James: 261
Revelation 12–22: 200
103:14–16
1 Corinthians: 436
103:15
1 Peter: 93
103:17
Luke 1–5: 82
2 Corinthians: 19
Revelation 12–22: 200
103:19
Matthew 1–7: 380
Matthew 8–15: 349
Mark 9–16: 386
Luke 11–17: 10, 24
Acts 13–28: 138
2 Corinthians: 312
1 & 2 Thessalonians: 254
1 Peter: 288
Revelation 1–11: 146
Revelation 12–22: 229
103:20
Matthew 1–7: 384

Matthew 8–15: 44
Mark 1–8: 247
Revelation 1–11: 228
103.8
Luke 18–24: 8
104
2 Peter–Jude: 179
104:1
2 Peter–Jude: 29
104:1–2
Luke 1–5: 156
1 Timothy: 277
104:2
John 1–11: 334
Revelation 12–22: 267, 279
104:3
Matthew 24–28: 55
Mark 9–16: 256
Luke 18–24: 231
Revelation 12–22: 31
104:14
1 & 2 Thessalonians: 302
104:14–15
John 1–11: 79
Acts 13–28: 139
104:15
Ephesians: 234
1 Timothy: 105
104:21
1 Peter: 281
104:23
1 & 2 Thessalonians: 303
104:24
James: 166
1 Peter: 45, 134
104:24–30
Luke 1–5: 306
104:27
Luke 11–17: 141
104:28
1 & 2 Thessalonians: 258
104:30
2 Corinthians: 114
104:31
1 Peter: 245
104:33
Revelation 1–11: 171
104:35
Revelation 12–22: 196
104.30
Luke 1–5: 57
105
Romans 9–16: 35
105:1
Romans 9–16: 82
105:1–5
2 Peter–Jude: 137
105:2
Luke 1–5: 93
Revelation 12–22: 194
105:5
Mark 9–16: 143
105:8–10
Romans 9–16: 96
105:11
1 Peter: 34
105:15
1 Timothy: 222
105:16
Revelation 1–11: 182
105:26
2 Peter–Jude: 18
105:32
Revelation 1–11: 245
105:34
Revelation 1–11: 259, 262
105:43
Luke 11–17: 292
1 Peter: 16
106
Matthew 1–7: 357
Romans 9–16: 35
106:1
Revelation 12–22: 194
106:3
Revelation 12–22: 94
106:4
1 Peter: 45, 140
106:5
Revelation 12–22: 5
106:7
2 Peter–Jude: 48
106:8
Romans 1–8: 54
106:10
Luke 1–5: 100, 154
106:13
2 Peter–Jude: 48
106:17–18
Revelation 1–11: 302
106:19–20
1–3 John: 88
106:21
Luke 1–5: 153, 167
Luke 18–24: 68
2 Corinthians: 199
1 Timothy: 69
Revelation 1–11: 222
106:24
John 1–11: 399
106:24–25
Philippians: 178
1 Peter: 227
106:28–29
1 Corinthians: 236
106:36–37
1 Timothy: 146
106:37
Luke 1–5: 280
1 Corinthians: 240
Revelation 1–11: 273
106:37–38
Revelation 12–22: 10
106:44–45
Romans 9–16: 96
106:47
Revelation 12–22: 194
106:48
Romans 9–16: 382
Revelation 12–22: 200
107
Matthew 1–7: 184
1 Peter: 76
2 Peter–Jude: 179
107:1
Revelation 12–22: 194
107:8
Acts 1–12: 45
Romans 1–8: 119
2 Peter–Jude: 25
Revelation 12–22: 194
107:9
1 & 2 Thessalonians: 258
1 Timothy: 252
Revelation 12–22: 305
107:10–16
1 & 2 Thessalonians: 154
107:10, 14
Luke 1–5: 122
107:11
1 Peter: 227
107:15
Revelation 12–22: 194
107:16
Matthew 16–23: 139
107:21
Acts 1–12: 45
Revelation 12–22: 194
107:21–22
Colossians and Philemon: 36
107:22
1 Peter: 134
107:23–30
Matthew 8–15: 35
107:23–31
Mark 1–8: 231–32
107:31
Revelation 12–22: 194
107:41
Ephesians: xi
108:3
Hebrews: 443
108:4
Mark 1–8: 96
1 Peter: 32
2 Peter–Jude: 82
108:5
John 1–11: 450
109
Revelation 1–11: 188
109:3
Matthew 8–15: 321
James: 218
109:8
Acts 1–12: 33
109:12
1 & 2 Thessalonians: 237
109:14–16
Matthew 1–7: 193
109:18
Romans 9–16: 264
109:25
Acts 13–28: 24
110
Mark 9–16: 209, 217
Luke 1–5: 99
Luke 18–24: 154
Hebrews: 166, 172

110:1
Matthew 16–23: 222, 347
Mark 1–8: 148
Mark 9–16: 328
Luke 1–5: 175
Luke 18–24: 339
John 12–21: 135
Romans 1–8: 508
1 Corinthians: 287
Colossians and Philemon: 130
Hebrews: 36, 175
110:2
Revelation 12–22: 152
110:3
Philippians: 171
1 & 2 Thessalonians: 208
1 Peter: 26
110:4
Matthew 1–7: 321
Matthew 16–23: 348
Luke 1–5: 175
Acts 13–28: 22
Hebrews: 123, 173, 175, 185, 191, 196
110:6
Revelation 12–22: 120
111:4
Luke 6–10: 137
Acts 1–12: 45
Titus: 152
James: 261
111:5
1 Peter: 63
111:6–7
1 Peter: 134
111:7
2 Peter–Jude: 57
111:9
Revelation 1–11: 155
Revelation 12–22: 130
111:10
Luke 1–5: 157, 309
2 Corinthians: 186, 257
Philippians: 160
1 Peter: 68, 200
Revelation 12–22: 87
112:1
1 Timothy: 275
Revelation 12–22: 94
112:4
James: 261
112:9
1 & 2 Thessalonians: 309
Revelation 12–22: 42
113
Luke 18–24: 280, 282
113:1–6
2 Peter–Jude: 137
113:4
John 1–11: 450
1 Peter: 147, 245
113:5
Revelation 12–22: 47
113:7
James: 107
113:9
Matthew 24–28: 284
Luke 1–5: 25
113–118
Matthew 16–23: 261
Luke 18–24: 280
1 Corinthians: 271
Revelation 12–22: 197
114
Luke 18–24: 280
2 Peter–Jude: 179
115:1
Luke 11–17: 15
Romans 1–8: 129, 212
2 Corinthians: 349
1 & 2 Thessalonians: 287
1 Peter: 26
115:1–8
Revelation 1–11: 273
115:3
Matthew 24–28: 288
Luke 18–24: 287
Acts 1–12: 31
1 Peter: 19
Revelation 1–11: 156
115:4–7
1 Corinthians: 193–94
115:4–8
Mark 1–8: 367
115:5
Revelation 12–22: 62
115:5–7
Revelation 1–11: 273
115:11
1 Peter: 68
115:13
1 Peter: 68
Revelation 1–11: 320
115:15
Revelation 1–11: 285
115–118
Luke 18–24: 280
116:1
1 & 2 Thessalonians: 185
116:2
1 & 2 Thessalonians: 194
116:4–5
Romans 9–16: 82
116:5
Luke 6–10: 136–37
Romans 9–16: 31
James: 261
1 Peter: 52
116:6
James: 28
116:10
2 Corinthians: 146
116:12
1 Corinthians: 424
116:13
Revelation 12–22: 133
116:15
Romans 1–8: 516
Hebrews: 314, 337
Revelation 12–22: 104
116:17
1 & 2 Thessalonians: 185
117:1
Romans 9–16: 324
1 Peter: 53
117:2
2 Peter–Jude: 82
118
Mark 9–16: 292
Luke 18–24: 127
118:1
Revelation 12–22: 194
118:4
1 Peter: 68
118:6
1 Timothy: 271
1 Peter: 199
118:17
1 Peter: 134
118:21
1 & 2 Thessalonians: 185
118:22
Matthew 16–23: 296
Luke 18–24: 442
John 12–21: 279
Acts 1–12: 135
Acts 13–28: 119
Ephesians: 82
1 Peter: 53, 123
118:26
Luke 11–17: 246
Luke 18–24: 95
118:27
John 12–21: 315
118:29
Revelation 12–22: 194
119
Matthew 1–7: 204
Romans 1–8: 390–91
Romans 9–16: 243
2 Timothy: 152
1 Peter: 95–96
119:1
Romans 1–8: 356
James: 66
1–3 John: 28
119:1–2
Romans 1–8: 373
119:1–8
1 & 2 Thessalonians: 198
119:2
Mark 9–16: 75
Revelation 12–22: 94
119:4
Romans 1–8: 356
119:5
Luke 11–17: 6
Romans 1–8: 356
119:5–6
Romans 1–8: 426
119:7
1 Peter: 27
2 Peter–Jude: 90
119:9
1 & 2 Thessalonians: 89, 198
2 Timothy: 93

119:9–11
  2 Timothy: 160
  James: 53
119:10
  Mark 9–16: 75
  James: 66
119:11
  Matthew 1–7: 91, 396
  Mark 1–8: 359
  Romans 1–8: 356, 376, 381, 426, 480
  Romans 9–16: 151
  2 Corinthians: 37
  Philippians: 31
  1 & 2 Thessalonians: 108, 198
  1 Timothy: 103, 137
  James: 69
119:12
  Romans 1–8: 356
119:14
  1 & 2 Thessalonians: 185
  James: 66
  1–3 John: 183
119:14–16
  1 Peter: 27
119:15, 23, 48, 78, 97, 99, 148
  Luke 1–5: 76
119:16
  Romans 1–8: 356
  2 Peter–Jude: 48
  1–3 John: 183
119:18
  Matthew 8–15: 354
  Matthew 16–23: 11
  Luke 11–17: 91
  1 Corinthians: 64
119:19
  2 Corinthians: 162
  1 Peter: 15
  Revelation 12–22: 261
119:20
  Matthew 1–7: 185
119:24
  1 & 2 Thessalonians: 58
  1–3 John: 183
119:29, 163
  Matthew 1–7: 322
119:33
  Matthew 16–23: 11
119:34
  Romans 1–8: 356
  Philippians: 289
  1–3 John: 45
119:35
  Romans 1–8: 432
119:36
  Matthew 16–23: 11
  Philippians: 31, 171
119:37–38
  Matthew 1–7: 304
119:42
  John 12–21: 200
119:43
  Luke 18–24: 418
119:46
  2 Timothy: 10
  1 Peter: 134, 200
119:49
  2 Corinthians: 107
119:49, 116, 166
  Romans 9–16: 313
119:50
  Matthew 8–15: 241
119:59
  James: 8
119:63
  Acts 1–12: 275
  1 Peter: 200
119:66
  1–3 John: 57
119:67
  Romans 1–8: 479
  1 & 2 Thessalonians: 227
119:67–69
  2 Peter–Jude: 90
119:68
  Romans 1–8: 119
119:70
  Revelation 12–22: 310
119:70, 77, 92, 174
  Luke 1–5: 171
119:71
  Romans 1–8: 479
  1 & 2 Thessalonians: 227
  1 Peter: 43
119:72
  Matthew 16–23: 340
  Romans 1–8: 484
119:73
  Matthew 16–23: 11
119:75
  Romans 1–8: 479
  1 & 2 Thessalonians: 227, 296
  Revelation 12–22: 143
119:75, 128
  Ephesians: 312
119:77
  2 Peter–Jude: 90
  Revelation 12–22: 310
119:81
  1–3 John: 107
119:89
  2 Peter–Jude: 57
119:90
  Luke 1–5: 174
  1 & 2 Thessalonians: 296
119:92
  Revelation 12–22: 310
119:93
  1 & 2 Thessalonians: 89
119:96
  Matthew 1–7: 338
119:97
  Matthew 1–7: 180
  Matthew 16–23: 340
  Romans 1–8: 356, 364, 412
  2 Corinthians: 84, 102, 115
  Colossians and Philemon: 32
  1 & 2 Thessalonians: 108
  1 Timothy: 293
  Hebrews: 34
  1–3 John: 206
  Revelation 12–22: 310
119:97–104
  1 Peter: 96
119:97–106
  2 Corinthians: 129
119:99
  1 & 2 Thessalonians: 89
119:99–100, 104–105
  2 Timothy: 159
119:100
  1 Peter: 276
119:103
  Matthew 1–7: 265
  Matthew 16–23: 340
  2 Corinthians: 102
  1–3 John: 184
119:104
  1–3 John: 81
119:105
  Matthew 1–7: 244
  Mark 1–8: 213, 410
  Luke 1–5: 37
  John 1–11: 23, 334
  Romans 1–8: 381
  Ephesians: 213, 370
  1 & 2 Thessalonians: 89, 97, 108, 198
  1 Peter: 290
  2 Peter–Jude: 96
  1–3 John: 14
119:105, 130
  1–3 John: 24
119:106
  2 Corinthians: 38
  2 Peter–Jude: 90
119:111
  1 & 2 Thessalonians: 185
  James: 69
119:113
  2 Corinthians: 102, 115, 129
  Revelation 12–22: 310
119:116
  1 & 2 Thessalonians: 198
119:119
  2 Corinthians: 129
119:121
  2 Peter–Jude: 90
119:123
  2 Peter–Jude: 90
119:127
  2 Corinthians: 129
119:130
  John 1–11: 334
  Ephesians: 205
  Colossians and Philemon: 39
  1 & 2 Thessalonians: 89, 195
119:133
  Romans 1–8: 432
119:136
  Matthew 1–7: 165
  Romans 9–16: 10
119:137, 142
  Romans 9–16: 31
119:140
  Luke 18–24: 418

119:142
John 12–21: 222
119:142, 160
Luke 1–5: 77
119:147
1 & 2 Thessalonians: 58
119:150
1–3 John: 128
119:151
Philippians: 277, 289
119:153
2 Peter–Jude: 48
119:155
James: 67
119:160
Romans 1–8: 356
119:161
2 Corinthians: 129
1 Timothy: 288
119:162
2 Corinthians: 129
1 & 2 Thessalonians: 185
119:163
Matthew 1–7: 326
2 Corinthians: 102, 115
Revelation 12–22: 310
119:165
Matthew 16–23: 340
Romans 1–8: 356, 483
2 Corinthians: 90, 102
Hebrews: 396
119:166
2 Corinthians: 107
119:167
Revelation 12–22: 310
119:172
Romans 1–8: 356
1 Peter: 169
119:174
2 Corinthians: 129
Revelation 12–22: 310
119:176
Matthew 1–7: 204
120:2
Matthew 1–7: 322
120:5
Revelation 1–11: 251
121:1–8
2 Peter–Jude: 25
122:4
Revelation 12–22: 194
124
2 Peter–Jude: 179
124:2–5
Revelation 12–22: 33
124:8
Revelation 1–11: 285
125:1
John 12–21: 99
Philippians: 277
125:4
1 Peter: 197
126:5
Philippians: 188
126:5–6
Matthew 1–7: 165
126:6
Acts 13–28: 212
127:3
Matthew 16–23: 182
Luke 1–5: 25, 71
1 Timothy: 213
127:3–5
Ephesians: 310
127:5
1 Timothy: 213
128:1
John 12–21: 69
1 Timothy: 275
130
1–3 John: 35
130:1–5
Romans 1–8: 392
130:3–4
Luke 1–5: 24, 207, 322
Acts 1–12: 117
2 Corinthians: 216
Colossians and Philemon: 110
130:5
Romans 9–16: 313
2 Corinthians: 107
131:1–2
James: 32
1 Peter: 278
131:2
Matthew 1–7: 150
131:3
2 Corinthians: 107
132
Luke 1–5: 99, 128
132:2
Matthew 1–7: 321
132:6
Matthew 1–7: 25
132:8
Revelation 1–11: 321
132:11–12
James: 269
Revelation 12–22: 307
132:13–14
Hebrews: 176, 413
132:16
1 & 2 Thessalonians: 184
2 Peter–Jude: 30
132:17
Luke 1–5: 98
133:1
Romans 9–16: 303
1 Corinthians: 30
2 Corinthians: 269
Hebrews: 424
133:3
Hebrews: 414
134:2
Luke 18–24: 452
1 Timothy: 75
134:3
Revelation 1–11: 285
135
2 Peter–Jude: 179
135:4
Romans 1–8: 167
1 Peter: 16
135:6
Matthew 24–28: 288
1 Peter: 19
135:15
Revelation 1–11: 273
135:15–17
Revelation 1–11: 273
Revelation 12–22: 62
136
Romans 9–16: 35
136:1
Romans 9–16: 132
136:1–3
1 & 2 Thessalonians: 189
136:2, 3
1 Timothy: 276
136:12
Acts 13–28: 19
1 Peter: 288
136:23
Luke 1–5: 77
136:26
Revelation 12–22: 145, 194
137
Revelation 1–11: 188
137:1–4
Revelation 1–11: 269
Revelation 12–22: 74
137:5–6
Matthew 16–23: 38
137:7
Luke 1–5: 22
137:8
Revelation 12–22: 183
137:9
1 & 2 Thessalonians: 237
138:2
Luke 1–5: 303
Luke 6–10: 307
Romans 1–8: 484
1 & 2 Thessalonians: 96
1 Timothy: 146, 288
138:5
John 1–11: 450
1 Peter: 245
2 Peter–Jude: 29
138:6
Matthew 8–15: 270
Matthew 16–23: 231
Mark 9–16: 100
Philippians: 112
138:8
1 & 2 Thessalonians: 258
1 Peter: 279
139
Revelation 1–11: 188
139:1–3
Romans 1–8: 144
139:1–5
1 & 2 Thessalonians: 185
139:1–6
1 Corinthians: 363
139:1–12
Acts 13–28: 138

139:3
Philippians: 170
139:6
Romans 9–16: 135
139:7
Mark 1–8: 329
139:7–8
Revelation 12–22: 92
139:7–12
Luke 11–17: 14
1 & 2 Thessalonians: 316
Revelation 1–11: 208
139:8
Mark 9–16: 185
Luke 11–17: 364
Luke 18–24: 142
139:8–10
Matthew 8–15: 439
139:9–10
Mark 1–8: 329
139:13–14
Matthew 16–23: 182
139:14
Revelation 12–22: 130, 194
139:15
Ephesians: 139
139:21–22
1 & 2 Thessalonians: 237
139:22–24
Matthew 1–7: 343
139:23–24
Luke 1–5: 76
Romans 1–8: 425
2 Corinthians: 35, 460
Colossians and Philemon: 86
James: 8
1–3 John: 36
140
Matthew 1–7: 295
140:3
Romans 1–8: 189
James: 145
140:7
1 Timothy: 271
140:11
James: 218
140:12
Matthew 8–15: 191
140:13
Revelation 12–22: 194
141:2
1 Timothy: 75
Revelation 1–11: 171, 194
Revelation 12–22: 116
141:3
Matthew 8–15: 321
Ephesians: 187
Colossians and Philemon: 187
James: 158
141:8
Luke 11–17: 47
143
1–3 John: 35
143:1
Luke 11–17: 52
1 & 2 Thessalonians: 87
143:2
Mark 9–16: 67
Luke 18–24: 13
2 Corinthians: 12
1 & 2 Thessalonians: 286
Revelation 12–22: 80
143:5
Mark 9–16: 144
143:6
James: 207
143:10
Luke 18–24: 304
Romans 1–8: 431
Romans 9–16: 351
1 & 2 Thessalonians: 195
James: 229
144
Revelation 1–11: 188
144:7
Revelation 12–22: 33
144:9
Revelation 1–11: 170, 171
Revelation 12–22: 75, 125
144:9–10
Revelation 12–22: 75
144:15
Acts 13–28: 129
Hebrews: 166
145:3
1 Peter: 200
145:4
1 Peter: 134
145:5
1 Peter: 200
2 Peter–Jude: 29
145:8
Mark 1–8: 96
Luke 1–5: 120
Romans 9–16: 31
James: 261
145:8–9
Matthew 8–15: 91
1 Timothy: 69
145:9
Romans 1–8: 119
1 & 2 Thessalonians: 189
145:11–12
1–3 John: 18
145:13
Matthew 1–7: 55, 380
Acts 1–12: 15
145:15–16
Matthew 1–7: 348
145:16
1 & 2 Thessalonians: 258
145:17
1 & 2 Thessalonians: 209
145:18
Luke 11–17: 5
Philippians: 277
James: 206
145:19
Acts 13–28: 358
146:2
Revelation 1–11: 171
146:5
2 Corinthians: 107
Ephesians: 73
146:5–6
Acts 13–28: 137
Revelation 1–11: 285
146:9
1 Timothy: 194
147
2 Peter–Jude: 179
147:9
1 Corinthians: 203
147:11
Revelation 1–11: 320
147:15
1 & 2 Thessalonians: 294
147:15–19
2 Timothy: 149
147:19
1 & 2 Thessalonians: 62
147:19–20
Romans 1–8: 152
Philippians: 229
147:20
Ephesians: 72
148
Romans 1–8: 84
2 Peter–Jude: 137, 179
148:2
Ephesians: 96
1 Peter: 58
148:7
Revelation 12–22: 6
148:13
John 1–11: 450
1 Peter: 288
149
Matthew 1–7: 175
149:1
Revelation 1–11: 171
Revelation 12–22: 75
149:2
Luke 18–24: 363
149:4
2 Corinthians: 241
149:7–9
Matthew 1–7: 175
150
Romans 9–16: 382
2 Peter–Jude: 137
150:3
Revelation 1–11: 170
Revelation 12–22: 75, 125
150:6
Revelation 1–11: 173

Proverbs
1:7
Matthew 8–15: 357
Luke 1–5: 157
Romans 1–8: 108
2 Corinthians: 186, 257
Philippians: 160
Revelation 12–22: 87
1:8
Ephesians: 313

Colossians and Philemon: 170
1 Timothy: 189
1:9
1 & 2 Thessalonians: 73
1:10
Mark 9–16: 44
1:10–17
1 Peter: 285
1:20–23
John 1–11: 291
1:20–33
John 1–11: 291
1:22
Luke 6–10: 188
1:23
1 & 2 Thessalonians: 194
1:23–31
1 & 2 Thessalonians: 280
1:24–33
John 1–11: 291–92
1:31–33
Galatians: 187
1:32–33
Matthew 1–7: 69
1:33
1 Peter: 181
2:1–6
Philippians: 289
2:2–5
James: 36
2:3
1 & 2 Thessalonians: 199
2 Peter–Jude: 194
2:3–22
Matthew 1–7: 69
2:5
2 Peter–Jude: 24
2:6–8
2 Peter–Jude: 30
2:7
2 Corinthians: 184
2:13
Luke 1–5: 122
1–3 John: 62
2:13–15
Philippians: 183
2:14
Matthew 1–7: 159
2:16
1 Timothy: 190
3:1
Ephesians: 313
3:3
Luke 6–10: 307
3:4
2 Corinthians: 307
3:5
Ephesians: 347
Philippians: 31
3:5–6
Romans 1–8: 431
1 & 2 Thessalonians: 88, 195
James: 232
1 Peter: 280
3:5–7
James: 35
3:7
1 & 2 Thessalonians: 199
3:7–8
1 Timothy: 165
3:9
1 Timothy: 218
3:9–10
Matthew 1–7: 413
1 Corinthians: 455
2 Corinthians: 313
Philippians: 308
3:11–12
Matthew 16–23: 125
2 Corinthians: 443, 446
Hebrews: 389
1 Peter: 250
3:12
1 Corinthians: 119
Hebrews: 394
Revelation 1–11: 3
3:17
James: 35
3:18
Revelation 12–22: 287
3:19
James: 166
3:27
2 Corinthians: 272
Philippians: 24
1 Peter: 197
3:32
Ephesians: ix
Colossians and Philemon: 78
3:33–35
Matthew 1–7: 69
3:34
Luke 1–5: 47
Luke 6–10: 300
1 & 2 Thessalonians: 320
2 Timothy: 113
1 Peter: 26, 278
3:35
1 & 2 Thessalonians: 52
4:1–4
Ephesians: 313
1 Timothy: 186
4:5–6
James: 166
4:7
James: 163
4:14–15
1 Peter: 285
4:17
Ephesians: 242
4:18
Ephesians: 214
1 & 2 Thessalonians: 19
Titus: 73
1 Peter: 279
4:19
Matthew 16–23: 2
Mark 1–8: 396
Luke 1–5: 122
John 1–11: 23
4:20–22
Hebrews: 44
4:23
Matthew 1–7: 135, 202
Matthew 16–23: 339
Mark 9–16: 47, 201
Romans 9–16: 76
2 Corinthians: 38
Ephesians: 262
Philippians: 31, 290
Colossians and Philemon: 86
1 & 2 Thessalonians: 91
James: 82, 171
1 Peter: 91
Revelation 1–11: 65
4:25–27
Philippians: 247
2 Timothy: 194
Hebrews: 402
5:3
1 Corinthians: 147
1 Timothy: 190
5:3–4
Matthew 8–15: 321
5:4
Revelation 1–11: 249
5:4–6
1 Corinthians: 147
5:8
1 Corinthians: 148
1 Timothy: 190
5:9–11
1 Corinthians: 148
5:18–19
Matthew 1–7: 301
Matthew 16–23: 173
1 Corinthians: 147, 156
1 Peter: 181
5:22
Acts 1–12: 246
1 & 2 Thessalonians: 284
6:1–5
Luke 11–17: 130
6:6–8
Matthew 1–7: 410
Luke 11–17: 140
2 Corinthians: 273
6:6–12
Luke 6–10: 106
6:12
Matthew 8–15: 321
Mark 1–8: 352
6:16–17
Matthew 1–7: 326
Galatians: 181
1 Timothy: 173
James: 200
Revelation 12–22: 185
6:16–17a
1 Peter: 278
6:16–19
Matthew 1–7: 291
Luke 11–17: 374
Acts 1–12: 241
Romans 9–16: 187
James: 221
1 Peter: 192
1–3 John: 81

6:17
James: 145
6:18
Mark 1–8: 356
6:19
James: 218
6:20
Colossians and Philemon: 170
1 Timothy: 83, 189
6:23
Mark 1–8: 213
John 1–11: 23
Ephesians: 213
1 & 2 Thessalonians: 89, 97
1 Timothy: 185
2 Timothy: 160
1 Peter: 192
2 Peter–Jude: 62
1–3 John: 24, 155, 210
6:24
1 Timothy: 190
6:25
1 Timothy: 190
6:27–29
Titus: 28
6:29
1 Corinthians: 155
6:30–31
Titus: 28
6:32–33
1 Timothy: 105
Titus: 28
6:33
1 Timothy: 223
7:1–3
Ephesians: 314
7:6–23
Mark 9–16: 44
7:7–12
1 Timothy: 190
7:10
Revelation 12–22: 164
7:13
1 Corinthians: 487
1 Timothy: 190
7:17
Mark 9–16: 364
7:25–27
1 Timothy: 190
8
James: 166
8:13
Matthew 16–23: 230
Mark 9–16: 100
Acts 1–12: 241
Romans 1–8: 186
Romans 9–16: 185
1 Corinthians: 343
2 Corinthians: 186, 257
1 & 2 Thessalonians: 199
1 Peter: 278
2 Peter–Jude: 90
1–3 John: 39, 81
8:15
Acts 13–28: 220
8:17
Hebrews: 310
8:32
Revelation 12–22: 94
8:34
Ephesians: 359, 369
1 & 2 Thessalonians: 198
Revelation 12–22: 94
8:35
1 Peter: 45
8:36
Matthew 16–23: 340
9:10
Matthew 16–23: 68
Luke 1–5: 157, 309
Romans 1–8: 192
Romans 9–16: 185
2 Corinthians: 186, 257
Philippians: 160
Colossians and Philemon: 186
1 Timothy: 223
James: 176
1 Peter: 68
Revelation 12–22: 87
9:17–18
1 Corinthians: 148
10:1
2 Corinthians: 447
Ephesians: 314
10:4
Luke 11–17: 131
10:5
Matthew 24–28: 96
2 Corinthians: 447
10:12
1 Corinthians: 352
Ephesians: 127
1 & 2 Thessalonians: 173
10:18
James: 218
1 Peter: 192
10:22
James: 240
10:24
Acts 13–28: 358
10:26
1 & 2 Thessalonians: 303
10:28
1 Peter: 33, 286
1–3 John: 106
10:29
Acts 13–28: 162
10:31–32
Romans 1–8: 187
11:1
Luke 18–24: 224
11:2
Mark 9–16: 32, 298
1 Corinthians: 343
Ephesians: 121
Philippians: 112
11:3
2 Corinthians: 184
11:4
James: 245
Revelation 1–11: 207
11:9
James: 218
11:11
Matthew 8–15: 321
11:13
1 & 2 Thessalonians: 180
1 Timothy: 212
11:14
Romans 9–16: 136
11:17
Matthew 1–7: 193
Luke 6–10: 308
11:18
1 & 2 Thessalonians: 111
2 Peter–Jude: 102
11:20
Luke 11–17: 343
Philippians: 36
11:23
1 Peter: 197
11:24
Luke 11–17: 131
1 Corinthians: 455
11:24–25
2 Corinthians: 313
Philippians: 307
1 Timothy: 249
11:25
Matthew 1–7: 358
11:28
2 Corinthians: 272
1 Timothy: 249, 282
11:30
Matthew 1–7: 113
Matthew 16–23: 132
1 Corinthians: 211
Philippians: 53
James: 290
Revelation 12–22: 287
11:31
Luke 6–10: 172
James: 286
1 Peter: 257
12:5
1 Corinthians: 324
12:10
Matthew 1–7: 193
12:17
1 Peter: 192
12:19
1 Peter: 192
12:22
Matthew 8–15: 321
Luke 18–24: 224
1 Timothy: 173
1 Peter: 192
12:27
1 & 2 Thessalonians: 303
13:2–3
1 & 2 Thessalonians: 180
13:4
2 Peter–Jude: 51
13:6
James: 286
13:10
1 Corinthians: 343

13:12
2 Corinthians: 262
Revelation 12–22: 287
13:13
Luke 18–24: 418
13:16
Mark 1–8: 358
13:18
1 Timothy: 185
13:20
2 Timothy: 88
13:21
Matthew 24–28: 110
13:22
John 12–21: 110
James: 286
13:24
Matthew 16–23: 125
Ephesians: 319
1 & 2 Thessalonians: 50
1 Timothy: 117
Hebrews: 394
14:12
Matthew 1–7: 455
Matthew 16–23: 35
Romans 1–8: 186
1 Corinthians: 42
Hebrews: 299
James: 288
14:15
1 & 2 Thessalonians: 199
14:16
1 & 2 Thessalonians: 199
14:21
Romans 9–16: 177
14:22
James: 285
14:23
Matthew 1–7: 410
Luke 11–17: 131, 332
2 Corinthians: 273
14:26
1 Peter: 200
14:26–27
1 Peter: 68
14:28
Acts 13–28: 220
14:31
Romans 9–16: 178
14:33
1 & 2 Thessalonians: 199
14:35
1 Peter: 150
15:1
John 1–11: 380
1 & 2 Thessalonians: 180
15:2
Matthew 8–15: 321
Romans 1–8: 187
15:3
Matthew 8–15: 440
Mark 1–8: 328
15:4
1 & 2 Thessalonians: 180
Revelation 12–22: 287
15:5
Luke 6–10: 161
15:8
Mark 9–16: 216
Luke 11–17: 2
Philippians: 36
James: 280
15:8–9
Luke 18–24: 224
15:9
Luke 11–17: 343
1–3 John: 85, 128
15:11
James: 225
Revelation 1–11: 264
15:14
1 Peter: 275
15:18
James: 253
15:19
1 & 2 Thessalonians: 303
1 Peter: 280
15:23
Ephesians: 188
15:25
Luke 18–24: 6, 166
15:28
Romans 1–8: 187
James: 155
15:31
1 Timothy: 185
15:32
1 Timothy: 185
15:33
Matthew 16–23: 231
Luke 1–5: 157
2 Corinthians: 257
Ephesians: 122
1 Peter: 68
16
Matthew 1–7: 148, 283
16:3
2 Corinthians: 345
1 & 2 Thessalonians: 195
16:4
Luke 18–24: 287
16:5
Matthew 16–23: 230
Luke 1–5: 79
Luke 6–10: 305
Luke 11–17: 264, 375
Acts 1–12: 241
James: 200
1–3 John: 251
16:6
Romans 1–8: 193
2 Corinthians: 257
16:9
Matthew 24–28: 290
Luke 6–10: 134
Romans 9–16: 343
Philippians: 298
16:10
Acts 13–28: 220
16:12
Acts 13–28: 220
16:16
James: 166
16:18
Mark 9–16: 298
Luke 18–24: 322
Acts 1–12: 241
1 Corinthians: 226, 343
Ephesians: 121
1 Timothy: 118
James: 200
Revelation 12–22: 1
16:18–19
1–3 John: 88
16:19
Philippians: 112
16:20
John 12–21: 69
16:21
1 & 2 Thessalonians: 199
16:26
1 & 2 Thessalonians: 307
16:27
James: 155
16:28
1 Timothy: 212
James: 218
16:31
1 Timothy: 186
1 Peter: 276
16:32
Ephesians: 125
James: 253
16:33
Acts 1–12: 35
1 & 2 Thessalonians: 254
2 Peter–Jude: 20
17:3
2 Corinthians: 12
1 Peter: 43, 249
17:5
Matthew 1–7: 339
Romans 9–16: 197
James: 102, 107
17:9
James: 218
17:15
Luke 11–17: 37
17:17
2 Corinthians: 21
1 & 2 Thessalonians: 168
17:20
James: 145
17:21
2 Corinthians: 447
Ephesians: 314
17:22
Matthew 1–7: 159
Ephesians: 230
17:25
2 Corinthians: 447
17:28
James: 69
18:2
Mark 1–8: 358
18:2, 6
2 Timothy: 96

18:8
James: 218
18:9
Romans 9–16: 190
18:13
Matthew 1–7: 432
1 & 2 Thessalonians: 180
18:15
1 Peter: 275
18:18
Acts 1–12: 35
2 Peter–Jude: 20
18:21
1 & 2 Thessalonians: 180
18:22
Matthew 16–23: 173
18:23
1 Timothy: 281
18:24
2 Corinthians: 21
19:1
2 Corinthians: 184
1 Peter: 190
19:2
Colossians and Philemon: 29
19:3
James: 47
2 Peter–Jude: 73
19:11
Matthew 1–7: 394
Matthew 16–23: 143
19:13
Ephesians: 314
19:14
Matthew 16–23: 173
19:15
2 Corinthians: 273
19:17
Luke 6–10: 96
Romans 9–16: 245
2 Corinthians: 313
Philippians: 307
19:18
Matthew 16–23: 125
19:21
Matthew 24–28: 290
Mark 9–16: 272
John 1–11: 484
Romans 9–16: 343
Philippians: 298
1 & 2 Thessalonians: 178, 189
Revelation 12–22: 185
19:23
1 Peter: 68
19:25
1 Timothy: 185
19:26
Luke 6–10: 161
Ephesians: 314
20:1
Luke 1–5: 36
Ephesians: 231, 235, 242
1 Timothy: 106
20:4
Luke 11–17: 141
20:6
2 Corinthians: 352
20:7
2 Corinthians: 184
20:8
Acts 13–28: 220
20:9
Mark 9–16: 67
Luke 1–5: 179
Luke 11–17: 37
Luke 18–24: 13
2 Corinthians: 12, 210
1 & 2 Thessalonians: 286
James: 151
1 Peter: 26
1–3 John: 57
Revelation 12–22: 69, 80
20:12
1–3 John: 88
20:13
2 Corinthians: 273
20:19
1 & 2 Thessalonians: 41, 180
1 Timothy: 212
James: 218
20:22
1 & 2 Thessalonians: 180
1 Peter: 189
Revelation 12–22: 184
20:26
Acts 13–28: 220
20:28
Acts 13–28: 220
2 Corinthians: 352
20:29
1 Timothy: 186
1 Peter: 89, 276
21:1
Mark 9–16: 386
Luke 1–5: 146
Luke 6–10: 134
Philippians: 171
21:2
Philippians: 213
1 & 2 Thessalonians: 91
21:3
Mark 1–8: 121
Luke 1–5: 333
21:4
Matthew 16–23: 230
Luke 6–10: 305
Acts 1–12: 241
Ephesians: 121
1–3 John: 251
21:5
Luke 11–17: 131
21:8
Philippians: 183
21:10
James: 198
21:13
James: 102, 107
21:17
Luke 11–17: 131
2 Corinthians: 273
21:20
Luke 11–17: 130, 332
2 Corinthians: 273
21:21
2 Corinthians: 352
21:30
Matthew 24–28: 288
Acts 1–12: 319
2 Corinthians: 22
21:31
Revelation 1–11: 178, 271
22:1
James: 217
22:3
1 & 2 Thessalonians: 199
22:4
Mark 9–16: 40
Ephesians: 122
1 Peter: 278
22:6
Matthew 16–23: 182
Luke 18–24: 31
Galatians: 187
Ephesians: 319
22:9
Philippians: 307
22:14
1 Timothy: 190
22:15
Mark 9–16: 67
1 Timothy: 117
22:17
1 Peter: 275
22:21
1–3 John: 14
22:24–25
1 Timothy: 114
23:4
Matthew 1–7: 408
23:4–5
Matthew 1–7: 144
Luke 11–17: 129
John 1–11: 364
2 Corinthians: 272, 313
1 Timothy: 282
James: 245
23:5
Hebrews: 434
23:7
Matthew 1–7: 202, 299
Philippians: 285
1 Peter: 275
1–3 John: 56
23:13–14
1 Timothy: 117
23:17
Luke 11–17: 119
2 Corinthians: 257
23:18
Luke 11–17: 13
23:19
Colossians and Philemon: 86
23:19–21
Ephesians: 231
23:21
2 Corinthians: 273

23:22
1 Timothy: 189
23:23
Luke 6–10: 2
23:24
Ephesians: 310
23:27–28
Ephesians: 231
23:29–31
Ephesians: 231
23:29–35
1 Timothy: 106
23:32–33
Ephesians: 231
23:35
Ephesians: 231
24:3–4
Matthew 1–7: 410
24:8
Romans 9–16: 269
24:9
1–3 John: 85
24:12
1 & 2 Thessalonians: 91
2 Timothy: 199
1–3 John: 144
Revelation 1–11: 102
24:21
1 Peter: 178
Revelation 12–22: 87
24:23
James: 94, 97
24:26
Ephesians: 188
24:28
1 & 2 Thessalonians: 180
24:29
Matthew 1–7: 330, 339
Luke 6–10: 106
1 Peter: 189
24:30–31
2 Peter–Jude: 51
24:30–34
2 Corinthians: 273
1 & 2 Thessalonians: 303
25:6–7
Luke 11–17: 262
25:11
Ephesians: 188
25:12
Ephesians: 188
25:14
1–3 John: 88
25:21
Matthew 1–7: 330, 339
Revelation 1–11: 189
25:21– 22
Romans 9–16: 203
1 & 2 Thessalonians: 181
25:25
1 Corinthians: 483
25:28
Matthew 1–7: 171
26:4
2 Corinthians: 187
26:5
2 Corinthians: 346
26:12
1 & 2 Thessalonians: 195
26:20
Matthew 8–15: 321
1 Timothy: 212
James: 155, 218
26:21
James: 155
26:22
James: 218
26:28
Matthew 8–15: 321
Acts 13–28: 306
James: 145
27:1
James: 232
27:2
2 Corinthians: 187, 345, 408
Ephesians: 122
1 & 2 Thessalonians: 228
27:4
1 Corinthians: 341
27:6
Acts 1–12: 161
1 Corinthians: 132
2 Corinthians: 48, 239
1 & 2 Thessalonians: 168
27:7
Matthew 1–7: 184
27:8
1 Corinthians: 324
27:9
1 & 2 Thessalonians: 168
27:17
Colossians and Philemon: 191
1 & 2 Thessalonians: 168
27:20
Revelation 1–11: 264
27:23–24
Luke 11–17: 130, 332
2 Corinthians: 273
27:23–27
John 12–21: 110
1 & 2 Thessalonians: 120
27:24
John 1–11: 364
1 Timothy: 252
28:6
2 Corinthians: 184
28:8
2 Corinthians: 272
28:9
Luke 11–17: 2, 343
James: 280
28:11
1 Timothy: 281
28:13
Matthew 1–7: 393
John 1–11: 417
Romans 1–8: 223
2 Corinthians: 31, 438, 468
1 & 2 Thessalonians: 188
Hebrews: 250
James: 279
1–3 John: 30, 36, 206
28:14
Luke 6–10: 191
Philippians: 160
Revelation 12–22: 133
28:18
Philippians: 183
28:19
Matthew 1–7: 410
Luke 11–17: 131
2 Corinthians: 273
28:20
Acts 13–28: 366
28:21
James: 94, 97
28:22
Matthew 1–7: 414
28:23
1 & 2 Thessalonians: 41
James: 145
28:24
Ephesians: 314
28:25
Mark 9–16: 32
Luke 11–17: 375
28:27
2 Corinthians: 313
Philippians: 307
1 & 2 Thessalonians: 309
James: 102, 107
29:1
Hebrews: 94
29:4
Acts 13–28: 220
29:5
Acts 13–28: 306
29:7
James: 102
29:9
2 Corinthians: 187
29:12
1 Timothy: 114
29:14
Acts 13–28: 220
29:15
Luke 6–10: 161
2 Corinthians: 447
1 Timothy: 117, 185
Hebrews: 394
29:20
James: 69
29:23
Mark 9–16: 100
1 Peter: 278
Revelation 12–22: 185
29:25
Matthew 8–15: 416
Acts 13–28: 210, 213
1 Peter: 199
29:27
John 12–21: 171
30:4
Mark 1–8: 148
Hebrews: 27
30:5–6
Ephesians: 359, 369

1 & 2 Thessalonians: 198
Revelation 12–22: 310
30:7–9
Luke 11–17: 33
30:8–9
Luke 11–17: 129
1 Timothy: 251
30:9
2 Corinthians: 272
30:12
Matthew 1–7: 487
30:15
Colossians and Philemon: 35
1 Timothy: 250
Hebrews: 425
30:17
Colossians and Philemon: 170
1 Timothy: 187
30:19
Matthew 1–7: 20
30:25
2 Corinthians: 273
30:27
Revelation 1–11: 263
31:4
Acts 13–28: 220
1 Timothy: 106, 225
31:4–5
Ephesians: 239
Titus: 38
31:6
Luke 1–5: 37
John 1–11: 79
Ephesians: 234
31:6–7
Ephesians: 239
31:9
James: 102, 107
31:10, 22
Ephesians: 283
31:10–31
Ephesians: 287
1 Timothy: 209
1 Peter: 180
31:18
Matthew 1–7: 246
31:20
Acts 1–12: 283
James: 102
31:22
1 Timothy: 79

Ecclesiastes
1:1
James: 164
1:2
John 1–11: 342
Philippians: 1
1:2–3
Matthew 1–7: 143
1 Corinthians: 428
1:3
1 & 2 Thessalonians: 301
1:9
1 & 2 Thessalonians: 140
1:12–16
1 Peter: 186
1:14
1–3 John: 86
1:16
James: 164
1:16–18
James: 165
2:1–11
James: 165
2:3
Luke 1–5: 36
2:3–11
1 Peter: 186
2:4–9
James: 164
2:4–10
James: 248
2:11
1 & 2 Thessalonians: 301
James: 248
2:12–16
James: 165
2:14
Luke 1–5: 122
John 1–11: 332
2:17
Luke 18–24: 286
James: 16
1 Peter: 186
2:17–23
James: 165
2:18
1 & 2 Thessalonians: 301
2:18–19
Luke 11–17: 135
2:22
1 & 2 Thessalonians: 301
2:22–23
Luke 18–24: 286
2:23
Philippians: 56
James: 16
2:24
1 & 2 Thessalonians: 302
2:24–25
James: 165
2:26
Ephesians: 168
1 Peter: 47
3:2
John 12–21: 360
3:4
Luke 1–5: 340
Ephesians: 230
3:9
1 & 2 Thessalonians: 301
3:11
Matthew 24–28: 318
Luke 6–10: 351
Luke 18–24: 140
3:13
1 & 2 Thessalonians: 302
3:20
1 Corinthians: 436
4:1–3
1 Peter: 186
4:2–3
James: 165
4:4
1 & 2 Thessalonians: 301
4:8
1 & 2 Thessalonians: 301
4:9–12
Luke 6–10: 325
Colossians and Philemon: 191
5
1 Peter: 190
5:7
Luke 1–5: 157
5:10
Luke 11–17: 129, 133
2 Corinthians: 272
1 Timothy: 252
Hebrews: 432
5:10–11
James: 244
5:11
1 Timothy: 253
5:13
James: 244
5:15
1 Timothy: 252
5:15–16
1 & 2 Thessalonians: 302
5:16
1 & 2 Thessalonians: 301
5:18–20
1 Timothy: 282
5:19–20
1 & 2 Thessalonians: 302
6:7
1 & 2 Thessalonians: 302
7:1
James: 217
Revelation 12–22: 261
7:6
Philippians: 32
7:20
Mark 9–16: 202
Luke 1–5: 58, 179
Luke 11–17: 37
Luke 18–24: 13, 27
2 Corinthians: 12
1 & 2 Thessalonians: 286
James: 91
1 Peter: 131
1–3 John: 45
Revelation 12–22: 69, 80
8:8
John 1–11: 460
8:11
John 12–21: 49
Romans 9–16: 222, 224
8:12
Luke 1–5: 157
Revelation 1–11: 320
8:17
James: 165
9:1
Ephesians: 217

9:3
Romans 1–8: 102
1 Peter: 31
9:8
Luke 6–10: 173
9:10
Romans 9–16: 190
Ephesians: 328
9:17
Matthew 8–15: 300
10:1–3
Mark 1–8: 358
10:16
Revelation 1–11: 251
11:1, 6
Matthew 24–28: 96
11:9
Matthew 8–15: 220
Titus: 95
12:1
1 Timothy: 271
Titus: 95
12:1–3
Titus: 72
12:1–7
2 Corinthians: 153
12:5
2 Corinthians: 155
12:10–11
Ephesians: 188
12:13
Luke 1–5: 62, 157
Romans 1–8: 356
1 Peter: 153
1–3 John: 182
12:14
Luke 6–10: 200
Luke 11–17: 117
Hebrews: 140
Revelation 12–22: 253

Song of Solomon
1
Matthew 1–7: 20
1:10
1 Peter: 179
1:10–11
1 Timothy: 79
2:3–4
Ephesians: 274
2:10–11, 16
Ephesians: 274
2:15
Luke 6–10: 318
Luke 11–17: 230
Romans 9–16: 197
3:6–7
Matthew 1–7: 36
3:11
John 1–11: 78
4:9
1 Timothy: 79
4:11
1 Corinthians: 487
1 Peter: 179
5:4
Philippians: 32
5:16
Ephesians: 274
6
Matthew 1–7: 20
7:1
1 Peter: 179

Isaiah
1
Matthew 1–7: 239
2 Peter–Jude: 184
1:1–16
Luke 18–24: 381
1:2
Ephesians: 369
1 & 2 Thessalonians: 198
James: 225
1:2–3
Romans 1–8: 333
1:2–4
Romans 9–16: 56
1:3
John 1–11: 33
1:4–5
Luke 1–5: 219
1:4–6
1–3 John: 86
1:6
James: 278
1:9
Romans 9–16: 48
1:10
Luke 6–10: 198
John 12–21: 200
1 & 2 Thessalonians: 294
1:11
Matthew 1–7: 297, 353
Mark 1–8: 339
John 1–11: 55
Hebrews: 251
1:11–16
Luke 11–17: 342
1:11–17
Mark 1–8: 155
Luke 1–5: 333
Luke 6–10: 8–9
1:11–20
Luke 1–5: 75
1:13–14
Hebrews: 251
Revelation 12–22: 5
1:13–15
Matthew 1–7: 353
Matthew 8–15: 448
1:15
1 Timothy: 75
1:15–16
James: 208
1:15–18
Hebrews: 251
1:16
2 Corinthians: 257
1:16–17
Matthew 1–7: 66, 297
1:16–18
Matthew 1–7: 353
1:17
Luke 18–24: 6
1 Timothy: 194
1:18
Matthew 24–28: 249
Luke 1–5: 207, 322
Ephesians: 299
Philippians: 286, 287
Colossians and Philemon: 110
James: 231
1 Peter: 274
Revelation 1–11: 231
Revelation 12–22: 163, 308
1:18–19
1 & 2 Thessalonians: 97
1:21
Revelation 12–22: 161
1:23
Luke 11–17: 230
1:28
James: 209
2:2
Luke 1–5: 211
Acts 1–12: 15, 53
2 Timothy: 107
Revelation 12–22: 169
2:2–3
Luke 18–24: 446
Revelation 1–11: 312
2:2–4
Luke 11–17: 224
Hebrews: 60
Revelation 1–11: 214
Revelation 12–22: 229
2:3
Romans 1–8: 56
Romans 9–16: 347
1 Peter: 120
Revelation 12–22: 152
2:4
Hebrews: 57
2:8
Revelation 1–11: 273
2:10–11
Revelation 1–11: 209
2:11
Ephesians: 121
2:11–12
Mark 9–16: 100
2:12
Matthew 1–7: 478
Mark 9–16: 32
Luke 1–5: 216
Luke 11–17: 376
1 & 2 Thessalonians: 144
2:17
Mark 9–16: 100
2:17–21
Revelation 1–11: 208
2:19–21
Revelation 1–11: 209
2:20–21
James: 245

3:1
Revelation 1–11: 182
3:9
Luke 11–17: 101
Revelation 1–11: 251
3:10–11
Romans 1–8: 127
3:11
Matthew 24–28: 110
3:12
1 Corinthians: 254
3:14–15
James: 102, 107, 240
Revelation 12–22: 191
3:15
Matthew 8–15: 191
3:16–24
1 Peter: 179
3:16ff.
Revelation 12–22: 185
4:3
1 Peter: 120
4:4
John 1–11: 105
4:4–5
Matthew 16–23: 67
4:5
Revelation 12–22: 279
4:6–7
James: 40
5
2 Peter–Jude: 184
5:1
Ephesians: 235
5:1–2
Mark 9–16: 167
Luke 11–17: 190
5:1–4
Revelation 1–11: 131
5:1–6
Matthew 8–15: 313
5:1–7
Matthew 16–23: 280, 402
Mark 9–16: 134–135
Luke 11–17: 242
John 1–11: 205
John 12–21: 143–44
5:2
Romans 9–16: 13
5:3–4
Luke 11–17: 190
5:4
Mark 9–16: 168
Romans 1–8: 168
Galatians: 117
5:7
Mark 9–16: 167
Luke 18–24: 123
5:8
Revelation 12–22: 191
5:8–10
James: 240
5:11
Ephesians: 231
5:13
Romans 9–16: 56
5:20
Luke 6–10: 298
John 1–11: 23
1 Corinthians: 349
2 Corinthians: 249
Ephesians: 206
2 Timothy: 115
1–3 John: 25
5:28
Revelation 1–11: 271
5:30
Matthew 24–28: 268
6
Matthew 24–28: 280
1 Peter: 54
Revelation 1–11: 146
6:1
Matthew 1–7: 151
Luke 18–24: 260
Philippians: 171
Revelation 1–11: 44, 147
6:1–3
Acts 1–12: 222
6:1–4
John 12–21: 105
Revelation 12–22: 133
6:1–5
Matthew 1–7: 114
Luke 1–5: 157
John 1–11: 451
6:1–10
Luke 1–5: 49
6:1, 3, 5
Ephesians: 124
6:1, 5
Matthew 8–15: 37, 46
6:2
Revelation 1–11: 154, 238
6:2–7
Matthew 24–28: 71
6:3
Matthew 16–23: 55
Luke 18–24: 157
John 1–11: 450
John 12–21: 291
Romans 9–16: 124
James: 48
1 Peter: 58
2 Peter–Jude: 29
1–3 John: 25
Revelation 1–11: 118, 155
Revelation 12–22: 65, 130
6:5
Matthew 1–7: 164
Matthew 16–23: 69, 231
Mark 1–8: 235
Mark 9–16: 211
Luke 1–5: 157, 308
Luke 6–10: 21, 271
Romans 1–8: 383
Romans 9–16: 63
2 Corinthians: 139, 345
Philippians: 171
Titus: 54
James: 145, 213
1 Peter: 167
1–3 John: 38
Revelation 1–11: 49, 156
6:5–9
Luke 1–5: 308
6:6
Revelation 1–11: 240
6:8
Matthew 24–28: 336
Romans 1–8: 40
2 Timothy: 181
1–3 John: 162
6:8–11
Luke 1–5: 309
1 Timothy: 42
6:8–13
Mark 1–8: 205
6:9
Matthew 16–23: 94
6:9–10
Matthew 1–7: 436
Matthew 16–23: 252, 263
Mark 1–8: 198
John 12–21: 41
Acts 13–28: 374
1 & 2 Thessalonians: 284
2 Timothy: 181
6:9–12
Ephesians: 126
6:9–13
Romans 9–16: 101
6:10
John 1–11: 14
6:11
1 Peter: 54
7:14
Matthew 1–7: x, 17, 19, 20
Matthew 8–15: 329
Matthew 24–28: 232
Mark 1–8: 147
Luke 1–5: 43, 48, 55, 174
Luke 6–10: 207
Luke 18–24: 189, 442
Acts 1–12: 104
Acts 13–28: 21
1 & 2 Thessalonians: 144
1–3 John: 189
Revelation 12–22: 11, 293
7:15–16
Matthew 1–7: 20
7:17
Revelation 1–11: 220
8:3
Luke 1–5: 185
1 Timothy: 84
8:9–10
Luke 18–24: 398
8:12
1 Peter: 123
8:12b–13
1 Peter: 199
8:13
1 Peter: 200
8:13–15
Luke 1–5: 183
8:14
Acts 1–12: 148

Acts 13–28: 119
1 Peter: 53
8:14–15
Luke 18–24: 128
1 Peter: 123
8:19
John 1–11: 474
Revelation 1–11: 14
8:19–20
2 Timothy: 159
8:19–31
2 Peter–Jude: 83
8:20
Matthew 1–7: 471
8:22
James: 16
9:1
Matthew 1–7: 106
Luke 1–5: 44
1 Peter: 7
2 Peter–Jude: 11
9:1–2
Mark 1–8: 29
Luke 1–5: 182
Hebrews: 142
9:1–7
Mark 1–8: 15
9:2
Luke 1–5: 20, 122, 158
John 1–11: 411
1 & 2 Thessalonians: 154
9:6
Matthew 1–7: 213
Matthew 8–15: 230
Mark 1–8: 148, 224
Luke 1–5: 175
Luke 11–17: 18, 169
John 1–11: 14, 465
Acts 1–12: 53, 104
Acts 13–28: 21
2 Corinthians: 319
Ephesians: 79
Philippians: 263
1 & 2 Thessalonians: 313
Revelation 12–22: 11, 194
9:6–7
Matthew 1–7: x
Matthew 8–15: 306
Matthew 24–28: 3, 118
Mark 1–8: 180, 191
Luke 11–17: 154, 401
Luke 18–24: 190
1 & 2 Thessalonians: 154
1 Peter: 53, 55
Revelation 1–11: 29, 31
Revelation 12–22: 197
9:7
Matthew 24–28: 115
Luke 1–5: 100, 174
John 12–21: 43
Acts 1–12: 53
Romans 1–8: 14
1 Peter: 125
Revelation 12–22: 211
9:13–17
2 Peter–Jude: 83
9:14–16
Acts 13–28: 220
9:15
James: 285
Revelation 12–22: 56
9:15–16
Matthew 1–7: 270
9:19
Romans 1–8: 61
10:1–2
Romans 9–16: 238
10:1–3
James: 107
10:1–4
James: 240
10:3
1 Peter: 140
10:5
Romans 9–16: 45
10:5–7
Luke 1–5: 146
10:12
1 Peter: 120
10:12–15
Acts 13–28: 140
10:20
Matthew 24–28: 32
10:20–21
John 1–11: 14
10:20–22
Revelation 1–11: 291
10:21–22
Matthew 24–28: 32
10:22
Matthew 16–23: 402
Romans 9–16: 6, 47
10:23
Romans 9–16: 48
11
Matthew 1–7: 47, 69
11:1
Acts 13–28: 22
Revelation 1–11: 167
11:1–2
Matthew 24–28: 3
Luke 18–24: 189
11:1–5
1 Peter: 53
Revelation 1–11: 31
11:1–9
Romans 9–16: 111
11:1–10
Revelation 12–22: 229
11:2
Mark 1–8: 35
1 & 2 Thessalonians: 51, 196
Revelation 1–11: 25, 108, 151
11:3–5
Revelation 12–22: 239
11:4
Luke 18–24: 238
1 & 2 Thessalonians: 281
Revelation 12–22: 239
11:5
Romans 1–8: 272
11:6
Luke 6–10: 206
Hebrews: 60
Revelation 12–22: 228
11:6–7
Matthew 1–7: 144
11:6–8
Revelation 1–11: 277
11:6–9
Matthew 24–28: 56
John 1–11: 21
Philippians: 263
Colossians and Philemon: 57
11:6–10
Acts 1–12: 119
11:6–12
Acts 1–12: 15
11:7–9
Revelation 12–22: 239
11:8–9
Hebrews: 60
11:9
Matthew 8–15: 476
Luke 1–5: 211
1 Corinthians: 365
Revelation 1–11: 277
Revelation 12–22: 239
11:9–12
Revelation 12–22: 71
11:10
John 12–21: 22
Romans 9–16: 324
Ephesians: 91
1 Peter: 53
Revelation 1–11: 167, 223
11:11
Revelation 1–11: 291
11:11–12
Romans 9–16: 6
Revelation 1–11: 31
11:12
Revelation 12–22: 241
11:12, 13
James: 13
11:35
Hebrews: 52
12:1–6
Revelation 12–22: 229
12:2
Titus: 109
12:3
Revelation 12–22: 286
12:3–4
Revelation 12–22: 239
13:1
Matthew 24–28: 52
13:1–14:27
Revelation 12–22: 167, 293
13:6
Luke 1–5: 216
1 & 2 Thessalonians: 144
James: 243
Revelation 1–11: 157, 200
13:6–9
Revelation 12–22: 121

13:6–12
Matthew 24–28: 52
13:6–13
Luke 18–24: 232
13:6–22
2 Corinthians: 37
Philippians: 28
Revelation 1–11: 200
13:6ff.
Acts 1–12: 54
13:8
Luke 18–24: 234
13:9
Romans 1–8: 70
1 & 2 Thessalonians: 144, 145
James: 209
Revelation 1–11: 200
13:9–10
Luke 18–24: 207
Revelation 1–11: 205, 250
13:9–13
Mark 9–16: 254
Revelation 1–11: 209
13:10
1 & 2 Thessalonians: 146
Revelation 1–11: 205
Revelation 12–22: 145, 262
13:10–11
Matthew 24–28: 269
13:11
Romans 9–16: 238
13:11–13
Revelation 12–22: 109
13:13
Hebrews: 417
13:13–16
Matthew 24–28: 52
13:17
Matthew 24–28: 52
13:18
Luke 1–5: 71
13:19
Luke 11–17: 375
13:19–22
Revelation 12–22: 177, 191
13:20
2 Timothy: 151
13:21
Revelation 12–22: 167
13–14
2 Timothy: 151
13–23
2 Peter–Jude: 184
14:4–6, 11
Romans 9–16: 238
14:4, 12
Romans 9–16: 219
14:12
Luke 1–5: 255
Luke 6–10: 341
Titus: 147
2 Peter–Jude: 165
Revelation 12–22: 19
14:12–14
Luke 1–5: 280
1 Timothy: 37, 118
Revelation 12–22: 16, 169
14:12–15
Romans 1–8: 136
2 Peter–Jude: 164
Revelation 1–11: 256
Revelation 12–22: 2, 8
14:12–16
1 Peter: 281
14:12–17
Mark 1–8: 64
Ephesians: 338
Philippians: 109
14:12–23
Ephesians: 121
14:12ff.
Acts 13–28: 291
14:13
Luke 1–5: 255
1 Corinthians: 68–9
14:13–14
Matthew 1–7: 177
Romans 1–8: 1
1 & 2 Thessalonians: 274
James: 224, 231, 235
14:14
Luke 1–5: 49, 259
Revelation 12–22: 19, 47
14:15
Matthew 1–7: 177
14:22–23
Revelation 12–22: 177, 191
14:24
Matthew 1–7: 385
Hebrews: 166
1 Peter: 19
14:24–27
1 Peter: 279
14:27
Luke 11–17: 398
Revelation 12–22: 185
15:3
James: 243
16:7
James: 243
16:11
Philippians: 32
17:8
Revelation 1–11: 273
17:10–11
Matthew 8–15: 114
17:10a
2 Peter–Jude: 48
17:12
Revelation 12–22: 41
18:6
Revelation 12–22: 222
19:1
Matthew 24–28: 55
Luke 18–24: 231
19:12
1 Corinthians: 43
19:14
1 Corinthians: 43
19:16
Luke 1–5: 92
19:22
Romans 1–8: 101
20:2
Revelation 1–11: 299
20:2–6
Acts 13–28: 241
20:3
Romans 1–8: 5
James: 12
21:1–10
2 Timothy: 151
21:9
Revelation 12–22: 179
22:12
James: 212
22:12–13
Matthew 1–7: 159
22:13
1 Corinthians: 428
22:22
Revelation 1–11: 119
23:1
James: 243
23:1–18
Mark 1–8: 315
23:1ff.
Revelation 12–22: 293
23:9
Matthew 16–23: 231
23:15–17
Revelation 12–22: 161
23:17
1 Peter: 140
24:1–6
Luke 18–24: 232–33
24:2
Matthew 16–23: 373
24:4–6
Revelation 12–22: 144
24:5
Revelation 12–22: 263
24:14
1 Peter: 288
24:17–23
Revelation 1–11: 317
24:18–23
Luke 18–24: 233
24:19–20
Revelation 12–22: 152
24:21–22
Revelation 12–22: 235
24:21–23
Mark 1–8: 240
Revelation 12–22: 109
24:23
Colossians and Philemon: 57
1 Peter: 120
Revelation 1–11: 149
Revelation 12–22: 71, 145, 152, 229, 242
25:1
Acts 1–12: 45
Revelation 12–22: 194
25:4
James: 102

25:6
John 1–11: 80
25:6–9
Luke 6–10: 251
Luke 11–17: 269
25:6–10
Revelation 12–22: 205
25:8
Matthew 24–28: 232
1 Corinthians: 445
2 Timothy: 24
Revelation 1–11: 233
Revelation 12–22: 269
25:9
1 Peter: 51
26:1–4
Revelation 12–22: 205
26:3
Luke 1–5: 62
Acts 13–28: 129
Philippians: 284
1 & 2 Thessalonians: 314
26:3–4
Matthew 1–7: 427
26:4
Luke 6–10: 120
Romans 1–8: 53
1 Peter: 280
26:9
Matthew 1–7: 185
26:11
2 Corinthians: 465
26:12
1 & 2 Thessalonians: 314
2 Peter–Jude: 24
26:17–18
Revelation 12–22: 5
26:19
Matthew 24–28: 304
Luke 6–10: 148
Luke 18–24: 142
Acts 13–28: 307, 371
1 Timothy: 272
Revelation 12–22: 205
26:20–21
Revelation 1–11: 317
27:1
Revelation 12–22: 6, 41
27:9
Romans 9–16: 130
27:11
1 Timothy: 271
28:2
Revelation 1–11: 245
28:7
1 Timothy: 110
28:7–8
Ephesians: 232
28:9–10
1 Corinthians: 382
28:12
1 Corinthians: 382
28:14–17
2 Peter–Jude: 83
28:16
Acts 1–12: 148
Acts 13–28: 119
Romans 9–16: 51, 79
Ephesians: 82, 83
1 Peter: 53
28:17
Revelation 1–11: 293
29
Mark 1–8: 345
29:6
Matthew 24–28: 274
Revelation 1–11: 204, 282
29:10
Romans 9–16: 103
29:13
Matthew 1–7: 254
Matthew 8–15: 455
Mark 1–8: 344
Luke 1–5: 21, 78, 217
Luke 11–17: 295, 342
Romans 9–16: 252
Galatians: 46
Philippians: 215, 222
1 & 2 Thessalonians: 209, 288
James: 206, 284
29:14
1 Corinthians: 41
29:16
Philippians: 178
29:18
Matthew 8–15: 191, 309
Mark 1–8: 410
Luke 1–5: 175
John 1–11: 411
1 Corinthians: 365
29:18–19
Matthew 1–7: 128
1 Peter: 55
29:19
1 & 2 Thessalonians: 184
29:24
1–3 John: 14
30:9
Luke 11–17: 20
30:9–10
Matthew 1–7: 460
Matthew 16–23: 358
30:15
1 & 2 Thessalonians: 119
30:18
Luke 1–5: 88
Luke 11–17: 236
2 Corinthians: 446
1 & 2 Thessalonians: 258
James: 261
30:19
1 Peter: 120
30:20–21
1 & 2 Thessalonians: 108
30:21
Romans 1–8: 431
30:22
Romans 1–8: 340
30:23–24
Matthew 8–15: 48
Romans 1–8: 457
Revelation 12–22: 239
30:26
Matthew 8–15: 75
Colossians and Philemon: 58
30:27–33
Revelation 1–11: 318
30:33
1 & 2 Thessalonians: 281
2 Peter–Jude: 166
Revelation 12–22: 255
32:1
Philippians: 263
32:7
James: 218
32:11–12
1 & 2 Thessalonians: 184
32:14–15
Mark 1–8: 381
32:15
John 1–11: 105
John 12–21: 381
32:15–20
Revelation 12–22: 229
32:17
1 & 2 Thessalonians: 119, 314
Hebrews: 177
James: 181
Revelation 12–22: 239
33:5
John 1–11: 450
33:13–16
Luke 11–17: 146
33:14
Titus: 26
33:15
Titus: 26
33:16
Matthew 1–7: 90
33:17–22
Mark 1–8: 191
33:18
1 Corinthians: 43
33:22
Luke 6–10: 157
Luke 18–24: 363
James: 225
33:24
Matthew 8–15: 48
Luke 6–10: 253
Revelation 12–22: 239
34:1–3
Revelation 1–11: 188
34:1–4
Revelation 1–11: 176
34:1–5
Matthew 24–28: 53
34:4
Revelation 1–11: 209
34:5–8
James: 249
34:8
Luke 1–5: 216
Luke 18–24: 223
1 & 2 Thessalonians: 144
Revelation 1–11: 188, 209
34:10
Revelation 1–11: 259

Revelation 12–22: 187, 199
34:11
Revelation 12–22: 179
35:1
Romans 1–8: 453
Revelation 1–11: 277
Revelation 12–22: 152
35:1–2
Hebrews: 60, 402
Revelation 12–22: 229, 239
35:1–2, 7
Matthew 8–15: 48
35:1–7
Romans 1–8: 457
35:1–10
Acts 1–12: 119
35:3–4
Hebrews: 402
35:4
Revelation 1–11: 189
35:5
Matthew 8–15: 246
Mark 1–8: 410
35:5–6
Matthew 1–7: 129
Matthew 8–15: 75, 191, 309
Matthew 24–28: 232
Revelation 12–22: 239
35:5, 6
John 12–21: 279
35:6
Acts 1–12: 102
35:7
Revelation 12–22: 239
35:8–10
Mark 1–8: 381
35:10
1 & 2 Thessalonians: 184
1 Peter: 40, 51
37:16
2 Corinthians: 488
1 Timothy: 275
Revelation 1–11: 153, 285
Revelation 12–22: 132
37:19
Revelation 1–11: 273
37:20
2 Corinthians: 488
1 Timothy: 275
37:36
1 Corinthians: 42
37:36–38
1 Corinthians: 227
37:38
Acts 1–12: 320
38:1–20
Acts 13–28: 145
38:12
2 Corinthians: 162
38:17
Luke 1–5: 207, 322
Luke 11–17: 39
2 Corinthians: 50, 200, 216
40
Mark 1–8: 18
Luke 1–5: 210, 211
40:1
Luke 1–5: 178
2 Corinthians: 20
40:1–2
Matthew 8–15: 48
Luke 11–17: 401
Luke 18–24: 381
Revelation 12–22: 184
40:3
Matthew 1–7: 74
Mark 1–8: 16, 17, 18
Luke 1–5: 21, 175
Luke 6–10: 154
John 12–21: 279
40:3–4
Mark 9–16: 17
Luke 1–5: 245
Luke 11–17: 220
40:3–5
Luke 1–5: 210
Luke 6–10: 155
Acts 13–28: 22
40:4
Revelation 12–22: 153
40:4–5
Matthew 1–7: 57
40:5
Luke 6–10: 280
1 & 2 Thessalonians: 195
Titus: 107
40:6
1 Peter: 92
40:6–8
John 12–21: 360
James: 41, 63, 233
40:6–11, 28–31
Luke 1–5: 211
40:8
Luke 18–24: 250
John 1–11: 14
2 Corinthians: 417
1 Peter: 92
2 Peter–Jude: 49
40:9
Mark 1–8: 13
40:9–11
Mark 1–8: 18
40:10
Luke 1–5: 178
Acts 13–28: 19
40:11
Luke 1–5: 155
Luke 6–10: 231
Acts 13–28: 224
2 Timothy: 58
Revelation 1–11: 233
40:12–13
2 Corinthians: 114
40:13
Romans 9–16: 136
40:15
Acts 1–12: 319
Revelation 12–22: 175
40:17
Acts 1–12: 319
Revelation 12–22: 175
40:18
Revelation 12–22: 47
40:19–20
Revelation 1–11: 273
40:21–26
Revelation 12–22: 88
40:22
Romans 1–8: 503
Galatians: 184
40:25
Revelation 12–22: 47
40:25–31
1 Timothy: 276
40:26
Romans 1–8: 503
Revelation 1–11: 158
40:28
John 1–11: 20
Acts 13–28: 137
Romans 1–8: 503
1 Timothy: 271, 277
Revelation 1–11: 156, 158
40:28–31
2 Corinthians: 154
40:29–31
Acts 13–28: 153
Ephesians: 362
Philippians: 303
40:31
2 Peter–Jude: 30
Revelation 12–22: 31
40–66
Mark 1–8: 13
Luke 1–5: 166
41:4
John 1–11: 348
Revelation 1–11: 50, 68
Revelation 12–22: 306
41:8
Luke 6–10: 14
John 12–21: 161
Romans 1–8: 232
James: 140, 197
Revelation 12–22: 68
41:8–10, 13
Luke 1–5: 211
41:10
Acts 13–28: 150
2 Corinthians: 21
James: 20
2 Peter–Jude: 30
41:13–14
2 Peter–Jude: 30
41:14
John 1–11: 14
41:17
Matthew 8–15: 191
Mark 1–8: 288
Luke 6–10: 243
41:21–23
Luke 18–24: 221
41:22–23
John 12–21: 138
42
Hebrews: 166

42:1
Matthew 8–15: 293
Mark 1–8: 35, 37
Acts 1–12: 106
Acts 13–28: 38
1–3 John: 193
42:1–2
Mark 9–16: 348
42:1–4
Acts 1–12: 107
42:3
Mark 1–8: 268
Philippians: 105
42:3–4
Mark 1–8: 191
42:5
John 1–11: 20
Revelation 1–11: 285
42:5–7
Luke 1–5: 271
42:6
Matthew 16–23: 11
Luke 1–5: 158, 182
John 1–11: 484
Acts 1–12: 250
Acts 13–28: 38, 338
Romans 1–8: 154
Romans 9–16: 388
Ephesians: 69
Philippians: 185
1 Peter: 56
42:6–7
Luke 1–5: 122
42:6–12
Mark 1–8: 363
42:7
Matthew 8–15: 191
Luke 1–5: 272
John 1–11: 411
42:8
Luke 1–5: 49, 79
Luke 11–17: 15
John 1–11: 14, 450
John 12–21: 249
Philippians: 222
1 & 2 Thessalonians: 260
2 Peter–Jude: 29
Revelation 12–22: 87, 172, 185
42:9
John 12–21: 137
42:10
Revelation 1–11: 171
Revelation 12–22: 75
42:12
1 Peter: 288
2 Peter–Jude: 29
42:13
James: 195
42:19
Acts 1–12: 106
42:21
Romans 1–8: 357
43:1
1 Timothy: 271
43:1–2
2 Corinthians: 404
43:1–7
Revelation 12–22: 98
43:1, 5
Luke 1–5: 157
43:3
Luke 1–5: 168
2 Corinthians: 199
1 Timothy: 69
2 Peter–Jude: 23
Revelation 1–11: 222
43:3, 11
Luke 1–5: 153
43:8
John 1–11: 409
43:10
John 1–11: 348
2 Corinthians: 488
1 Timothy: 33, 71, 275
1 Peter: 200
43:10–13
1–3 John: 190
43:11
Luke 1–5: 77, 153, 168, 229
Luke 18–24: 68
John 1–11: 14
1 Timothy: 69
2 Peter–Jude: 23
Revelation 1–11: 222
43:13
Luke 1–5: 79
Romans 1–8: 53
1 & 2 Thessalonians: 141, 162
1 Timothy: 275
Revelation 1–11: 119
Revelation 12–22: 153, 175, 186
43:15
1 Timothy: 271
Revelation 1–11: 118
43:17
Revelation 1–11: 178
43:20
Romans 9–16: 124
Revelation 12–22: 5
43:21
Romans 1–8: 167
Romans 9–16: 126
Hebrews: 165
1 Peter: 124, 288
43:25
Matthew 8–15: 53
Mark 1–8: 96
Luke 1–5: 207, 322
John 1–11: 348
Acts 1–12: 117
2 Corinthians: 50, 216
1–3 John: 57
Revelation 12–22: 182
44:1–5
Romans 1–8: 171
44:2
Luke 1–5: 157
44:3
John 1–11: 105
Acts 1–12: 75
44:6
John 1–11: 14
2 Corinthians: 488
1 Timothy: 33, 71, 275
Revelation 1–11: 3, 50, 68
Revelation 12–22: 271, 306
44:6–7
Luke 18–24: 221
44:7
Revelation 1–11: 14
44:8
2 Corinthians: 488
1 Timothy: 275
44:8–20
Revelation 1–11: 273
44:9–17
Romans 1–8: 91
44:17
1 Corinthians: 235
44:20
Romans 1–8: 103
44:21–22
Matthew 8–15: 48
44:22
Luke 1–5: 207, 322
Acts 1–12: 117
2 Corinthians: 50, 216
44:23
Ephesians: 139
44:28
2 Timothy: 151
44:28–45:5
Mark 9–16: 387
Luke 18–24: 398
45:1–4
Luke 1–5: 146
45:1–14
2 Timothy: 151
45:4
Mark 9–16: 249
45:4–5
1 & 2 Thessalonians: 108
45:5
Mark 1–8: 362
Romans 1–8: 212, 226
1 Timothy: 33, 71, 275
45:5–6
2 Corinthians: 488
45:6
1 Timothy: 33, 71, 275
45:7
Mark 1–8: 246
45:8
Romans 1–8: 200
45:9
Philippians: 178
James: 226
45:14
Ephesians: 131
Revelation 1–11: 123
45:15
Luke 1–5: 153
2 Corinthians: 12, 199
2 Peter–Jude: 23
Revelation 1–11: 222

45:15, 17
Luke 1–5: 168
45:17
Luke 11–17: 217
Revelation 12–22: 98
45:18
John 1–11: 20, 348
Acts 13–28: 137
45:20–21
Luke 18–24: 222
45:20–24
1 Peter: 53
45:20–25
1 & 2 Thessalonians: 240
45:21
Luke 1–5: 153, 168
2 Corinthians: 488
1 Timothy: 33, 71, 275
Titus: 109
2 Peter–Jude: 23
Revelation 1–11: 14, 222
45:21–23
Romans 1–8: 212
45:22
Matthew 8–15: 268
Luke 1–5: 168
Luke 18–24: 446
John 12–21: 22
Romans 1–8: 28
2 Corinthians: 112, 202
1 Timothy: 33, 69, 71, 275
1 Peter: 52
2 Peter–Jude: 28, 151
1–3 John: 39
Revelation 1–11: 224
Revelation 12–22: 305
45:22–23
Philippians: 145
45:23
Luke 18–24: 157
Romans 9–16: 285
Philippians: 146
45:24
Romans 9–16: 67
45:25
Luke 1–5: 181
46:3–4
Romans 9–16: 13
46:4
John 1–11: 348
46:5
Revelation 12–22: 47
46:5–10
Luke 18–24: 222
46:7
Revelation 12–22: 62
46:8–10
Mark 9–16: 143
Luke 11–17: 399
46:9
2 Corinthians: 488
Ephesians: 131
1 Timothy: 33, 71, 275
46:9–10
Matthew 24–28: 288
Luke 18–24: 287
1 Timothy: 73
1 Peter: 19
Revelation 1–11: 14
46:9–11
Romans 1–8: 488
1 & 2 Thessalonians: 254
Revelation 1–11: 119
46:10
Mark 9–16: 261
Acts 1–12: 31
1 & 2 Thessalonians: 141, 278
1 Timothy: 70
1 Peter: 279
Revelation 1–11: 156
Revelation 12–22: 175, 186
46:11
1 Timothy: 276
46:13
Luke 1–5: 181
Hebrews: 413
47:5
Revelation 12–22: 167
47:7
Revelation 12–22: 185
47:7–10
James: 234
47:8
Revelation 12–22: 185
47:9
Revelation 12–22: 185
47:12–15
2 Peter–Jude: 160
48:1
Luke 1–5: 78, 217
Luke 11–17: 342
48:8
Mark 9–16: 67
2 Corinthians: 210
48:11
John 1–11: 14, 450
Romans 1–8: 129
Philippians: 222
2 Peter–Jude: 29
Revelation 12–22: 87
48:12
Revelation 1–11: 50, 68
Revelation 12–22: 271, 306
48:13
1 Peter: 279, 288
48:16–17
Romans 1–8: 431
48:17
John 1–11: 14
48:18
Revelation 1–11: 131
48:20
Revelation 12–22: 181
48:22
Matthew 1–7: 212
John 12–21: 126
Ephesians: 128
Philippians: 284
1 & 2 Thessalonians: 314
49–57
Hebrews: 166
49:1
Acts 1–12: 295
Galatians: 28
49:1–2
1 Peter: 20
49:4
1 Corinthians: 411
49:5–7
Acts 1–12: 106
49:6
Matthew 8–15: 350
Matthew 16–23: 379
Matthew 24–28: 332
Mark 1–8: 363
Luke 1–5: 182
Luke 18–24: 446–47
John 1–11: 32, 484
Acts 13–28: 38, 338
Romans 9–16: 107, 323, 388
Ephesians: 69, 91, 205
Philippians: 185
49:6–9
Luke 1–5: 158
49:7
John 1–11: 438
1 & 2 Thessalonians: 296
1–3 John: 39
49:8
Luke 1–5: 273
2 Corinthians: 225
49:8–13
Luke 1–5: 178
49:10
Revelation 1–11: 233
49:13
2 Corinthians: 17, 20, 263
49:14–16
Luke 1–5: 211
Revelation 12–22: 98
49:18
James: 269
49:23
Revelation 1–11: 123
49:24–25
Mark 1–8: 182–83
49:26
Luke 1–5: 153, 168
2 Corinthians: 199
Revelation 1–11: 222
50:1
Matthew 1–7: 313
Matthew 8–15: 328
Matthew 16–23: 169
Mark 9–16: 60
Revelation 12–22: 4
50:2b
Luke 1–5: 306
50:4
Ephesians: 188
50:6
Matthew 1–7: 333
Matthew 24–28: 232
Mark 9–16: 361
Luke 1–5: 175
John 1–11: 438

50:7
1 Peter: 122
50:7–9
John 1–11: 302
50:8
1 & 2 Thessalonians: 89
50:9
James: 244
51:1–2
Romans 9–16: 114
Hebrews: 327
51:1–3,12
Luke 1–5: 211
51:2
Luke 6–10: 14
51:3
2 Corinthians: 20
Revelation 1–11: 277
51:3, 12
Luke 1–5: 178
51:4
Luke 1–5: 158
51:4–5
Luke 1–5: 182
51:5
Matthew 1–7: 182
51:6
Revelation 12–22: 98, 249
Matthew 1–7: 262
51:7
Matthew 8–15: 458
Mark 1–8: 354
51:8
James: 244
51:9
Matthew 8–15: 34
Acts 13–28: 19
Revelation 12–22: 6
51:12
Matthew 8–15: 241
2 Corinthians: 17
51:13–15
2 Peter–Jude: 48
51:13a
2 Peter–Jude: 48
51:17
Matthew 16–23: 390
Mark 9–16: 106
Revelation 12–22: 91
51:22
Revelation 12–22: 91
52
2 Corinthians: 254
52:1
Revelation 12–22: 264
52:2
1 Peter: 120
52:3
1 Peter: 77
52:5
Romans 1–8: 158
Romans 9–16: 323
Philippians: 185
1 Timothy: 232
52:7
Mark 1–8: 13
Acts 1–12: 50
Romans 9–16: 84
Ephesians: 354
52:9
Luke 1–5: 178, 211
2 Corinthians: 17, 20
52:10
Luke 1–5: 182
Romans 9–16: 84
Revelation 1–11: 224
52:11
2 Timothy: 89
52:13–53:12
Mark 1–8: 13, 147, 191
Mark 9–16: 90
Luke 18–24: 46–47
John 12–21: 34
Acts 1–12: 106
52:15
Romans 9–16: 337
53
Matthew 16–23: 37
Luke 1–5: 104, 131, 136, 153, 260
Luke 6–10: 285
Luke 11–17: 232, 329
Luke 18–24: 51, 92, 289, 316, 425
Acts 1–12: 53, 64, 111
Acts 13–28: 120, 211, 338
1 Corinthians: 402
2 Corinthians: 213, 325
Philippians: 238
Hebrews: 235
1 Peter: 53, 173
53:1
John 12–21: 53
Romans 9–16: 84
53:1–11a
Luke 18–24: 96
53:1–12
Mark 9–16: 230
Luke 11–17: 246
53:2
Matthew 1–7: 47
53:2–3
Matthew 1–7: 169
53:2–8
Matthew 16–23: 225
53:2–9
1–3 John: 194–95
53:3
Matthew 1–7: 48, 94, 161
Matthew 8–15: 110
Matthew 16–23: 273
Matthew 24–28: 166
Mark 9–16: 294, 347
Luke 6–10: 228, 327
Luke 18–24: 53, 110, 299
John 1–11: 438, 467
John 12–21: 240
Acts 1–12: 104, 111
Acts 13–28: 24, 145
Galatians: 166
Philippians: 131
1 Peter: 1
Revelation 12–22: 212, 279
53:3–4
Revelation 12–22: 269
53:3–5
Mark 9–16: 378
53:3–5, 7, 10–11
Matthew 24–28: 191
53:3–12
Mark 1–8: 419–20
53:3, 5–6
Matthew 24–28: 256
53:4
Mark 1–8: 77
Luke 18–24: 382
2 Timothy: 58
53:4–5
Matthew 16–23: 246
Romans 1–8: 239
1 Corinthians: 353
Hebrews: 252–53
1 Peter: 53, 56, 170
53:4–6
Luke 1–5: 153, 175
Romans 1–8: 505
2 Corinthians: 191, 215
1 & 2 Thessalonians: 247
1 Peter: 206
1–3 John: 168
53:4–6, 8, 10–12
Luke 1–5: 122
53:4–8
Romans 1–8: 409
53:4–10
Luke 6–10: 264
53:5
Matthew 8–15: 19, 75
Matthew 24–28: 267, 270
Mark 9–16: 344
Luke 18–24: 283, 377, 390
Romans 9–16: 86
1 & 2 Thessalonians: 204
1 Peter: 88, 172
2 Peter–Jude: 75
Revelation 12–22: 270
53:5–6
Revelation 12–22: 253
53:5–10
1–3 John: 48
53:5–12
Luke 18–24: 174–75
53:6
Matthew 1–7: 447
Luke 1–5: 58
Luke 11–17: 40
Romans 1–8: 185, 493
Philippians: 129
Titus: 112
1 Peter: 173, 262
53:6, 10
John 12–21: 304
53:7
Matthew 24–28: 238
Mark 9–16: 326
Luke 18–24: 350
John 1–11: 55
John 12–21: 340

1 Peter: 168
Revelation 1–11: 168
53:7–8
Acts 1–12: 257
53:7–10
Revelation 12–22: 293
53:8
Luke 1–5: 153, 340
53:8–12
Matthew 24–28: 118
1 Peter: 206
53:9
Matthew 24–28: 291, 294
Mark 9–16: 94
Luke 1–5: 167
Luke 18–24: 55
John 12–21: 279, 324, 365
Acts 13–28: 24
2 Corinthians: 478
1 Peter: 166–67
53:10
Matthew 16–23: 226
Mark 1–8: 37
Mark 9–16: 370
Luke 1–5: 168
Luke 6–10: 295
Luke 11–17: 146, 234
Luke 18–24: 269, 288
John 12–21: 335
Romans 1–8: 505
1 Peter: 224
53:10–11
Mark 9–16: 374
1–3 John: 30
53:10–12
Mark 1–8: 5, 425
Mark 9–16: 269, 305, 308
Luke 1–5: 153–54
53:11
Luke 18–24: 13
Acts 1–12: 303
Acts 13–28: 268
Romans 1–8: 5
Romans 9–16: 387
1 & 2 Thessalonians: 163
1 Peter: 170, 206
1–3 John: 39, 48
53:11–12
2 Corinthians: 191
53:12
Matthew 1–7: 78
Matthew 16–23: 226
Mark 1–8: 32
Mark 9–16: 368
Luke 18–24: 298, 384
John 12–21: 279, 351
Romans 1–8: 334, 509
1 & 2 Thessalonians: 234, 247
1 Timothy: 75
1 Peter: 166
54:1–3
Ephesians: 91
1 Peter: 122
54:3
Luke 11–17: 210
54:4–5
1 Peter: 122
54:4–8
Luke 1–5: 211
54:5
Revelation 1–11: 118
54:5–6
Revelation 12–22: 203, 206
54:7–8
1 Peter: 42
54:10
Matthew 24–28: 118
Luke 1–5: 123
Luke 11–17: 249
Hebrews: 393
1 Peter: 122
54:11
Luke 1–5: 178
54:17
Acts 13–28: 150
55:1
Matthew 8–15: 390
Matthew 24–28: 91
Luke 6–10: 347
Luke 11–17: 218
John 1–11: 105
John 12–21: 258
Acts 1–12: 245
2 Corinthians: 202, 213
Ephesians: 234
1 Timothy: 69
Revelation 1–11: 138
Revelation 12–22: 271, 305
55:1–2
2 Corinthians: 90
1 Peter: 52
55:1–9
Luke 18–24: 381
55:1, 3
Matthew 8–15: 268
55:2
1 Timothy: 252
55:3
Luke 18–24: 127
Acts 13–28: 25
55:6
Matthew 24–28: 96
Mark 9–16: 74
Luke 11–17: 178, 191
Romans 1–8: 28
2 Peter–Jude: 151
55:6–7
Luke 1–5: 177, 207
Luke 18–24: 239
Acts 1–12: 257, 293
Romans 1–8: 170
2 Corinthians: 90
Ephesians: 176, 214
Philippians: 173
1 & 2 Thessalonians: 240
James: 202, 210
1 Peter: 52
1–3 John: 35
55:7
Matthew 1–7: 163
Luke 1–5: 322
Luke 11–17: 369
2 Corinthians: 433
Colossians and Philemon: 110
55:8–9
Matthew 16–23: 35
Mark 1–8: 421
Luke 1–5: 82
1 Peter: 14
55:9
1 & 2 Thessalonians: 204
55:10
2 Corinthians: 317, 395
55:10–11
2 Corinthians: 480
2 Timothy: 148
1 Peter: 96–97
2 Peter–Jude: 57
55:11
Luke 6–10: 133
Acts 1–12: 31
Romans 9–16: 21
2 Corinthians: 74
Ephesians: 369
Philippians: 68
1 & 2 Thessalonians: 58, 198
1 Peter: 279
55:12
Luke 11–17: 169
Romans 1–8: 453
1 & 2 Thessalonians: 184
James: 246
56:3–5
Acts 1–12: 255
56:6
Romans 1–8: 482
1 & 2 Thessalonians: 17
56:6–7
Luke 11–17: 217
56:6–8
John 1–11: 484
56:7
Matthew 16–23: 270
Mark 9–16: 138
Luke 18–24: 17, 106
Philippians: 307
1 & 2 Thessalonians: 184
56:9–12
1 Timothy: 110
56:10–12
Luke 6–10: 244
Luke 11–17: 102
56:11
Matthew 8–15: 193
Luke 6–10: 112
Luke 11–17: 254
Acts 13–28: 230
Romans 1–8: 156
Titus: 40
57:15
Matthew 1–7: 151
Matthew 8–15: 272, 458
Luke 1–5: 80, 308
Luke 6–10: 299, 345
John 1–11: 450
2 Corinthians: 112, 438
1 & 2 Thessalonians: 209

James: 214
1 Peter: 278
Revelation 1–11: 158
Revelation 12–22: 130
57:18
Luke 1–5: 178, 211
57:19
Luke 11–17: 169
1 & 2 Thessalonians: 314
57:20
Revelation 12–22: 41
57:20–21
2 Peter–Jude: 181
57:21
Matthew 8–15: 52
1 & 2 Thessalonians: 314
Hebrews: 404
58:1–4
Philippians: 215
58:2
Matthew 1–7: 357
58:3
Hebrews: 444
58:3–4
Mark 1–8: 128
58:6
Luke 1–5: 270
58:6–7
Hebrews: 444
58:6–14
Mark 1–8: 156
Luke 6–10: 9
58:7
1 & 2 Thessalonians: 309
58:11
1 Timothy: 252
59:1
Luke 1–5: 168
59:1–2
Matthew 1–7: 205
2 Corinthians: 446
59:1–3
Romans 1–8: 188
59:2
Luke 1–5: 209
Luke 11–17: 37
Romans 1–8: 417
2 Corinthians: 200, 205
Colossians and Philemon: 61
James: 208
59:3
James: 145
59:9–10
Luke 1–5: 122
59:12
James: 288
59:16
Luke 1–5: 122
59:17
1 & 2 Thessalonians: 161
59:17–18
Revelation 1–11: 188
59:18
Revelation 12–22: 176
59:19
2 Peter–Jude: 29
59:20
Luke 1–5: 122
59:21
Luke 1–5: 122
1 & 2 Thessalonians: 112
60:1
Ephesians: 213
60:1–3
Luke 1–5: 158, 182
Luke 18–24: 447
Ephesians: 91
1 Peter: 56
60:1–5
Luke 1–5: 122
60:1–62:7
Mark 1–8: 192
60:3
Ephesians: 69
Revelation 12–22: 73
60:10–14
Revelation 1–11: 31
60:10–18
Revelation 12–22: 229
60:11–12
1 Peter: 56
60:14
Revelation 1–11: 123
60:16
Luke 1–5: 153, 168
2 Corinthians: 199
2 Peter–Jude: 23
Revelation 1–11: 222
60:19
Ephesians: 205
1–3 John: 165
Revelation 12–22: 279
60:19–20
Luke 1–5: 123
Colossians and Philemon: 58
1–3 John: 23
60:21
Revelation 12–22: 239
61:1
Matthew 1–7: 80
Matthew 8–15: 246
Mark 1–8: 15, 35
Luke 1–5: 155
61:1–2
Matthew 1–7: 69
Matthew 16–23: 366
Mark 1–8: 13, 272
Luke 1–5: 178, 270, 274, 282
Luke 18–24: 336
John 1–11: 32
61:1–3
Matthew 8–15: 241
Luke 11–17: 58
61:2
Luke 1–5: 211, 216
1 & 2 Thessalonians: 144
Revelation 1–11: 188
61:2–3
Matthew 1–7: 161
Luke 6–10: 97
61:3
Revelation 12–22: 239
61:4–6
1 Peter: 132
61:7
Revelation 12–22: 239
61:8
Revelation 1–11: 61
61:10
Matthew 16–23: 312
Luke 1–5: 25, 35, 342
Luke 6–10: 192
Luke 18–24: 383
Romans 9–16: 257
2 Corinthians: 103, 205
Philippians: 275
1 & 2 Thessalonians: 185
1 Timothy: 79
1 Peter: 40
2 Peter–Jude: 23
Revelation 1–11: 139
Revelation 12–22: 150
62:1–2
Ephesians: 69
62:4–5
Mark 1–8: 130
Luke 1–5: 340
62:5
Luke 11–17: 292
Revelation 12–22: 203
62:8
Acts 13–28: 19
62:11
Luke 18–24: 94
62:12
1 Peter: 129
63:1
Revelation 12–22: 117, 150
63:1–3
Revelation 12–22: 220
63:1–4
Luke 18–24: 238
63:1–6
Revelation 12–22: 109, 217
63:1, 8
Luke 1–5: 168
63:3
Revelation 12–22: 117
63:4
Luke 1–5: 216, 273
1 & 2 Thessalonians: 144
Revelation 1–11: 188
63:7
Matthew 1–7: 190
Romans 1–8: 28
63:7–9
Ephesians: 72
1 & 2 Thessalonians: 180
63:8
2 Corinthians: 199, 205
1 Timothy: 169
Revelation 1–11: 222
63:8–9
Luke 1–5: 153
63:8–10
2 Corinthians: 204–5
1 Timothy: 168

63:9
Luke 1–5: 121, 154
Hebrews: 393
1 Peter: 31
63:10
Matthew 16–23: 288
Luke 11–17: 20
Luke 18–24: 117
John 12–21: 51
1 & 2 Thessalonians: 194
1 Timothy: 169
Revelation 1–11: 131
Revelation 12–22: 303
63:11
Acts 13–28: 224
63:15
Philippians: 32
63:16
Matthew 1–7: 354, 375
John 1–11: 14
Philippians: 166
1 Peter: 30
64:1
Mark 1–8: 34
64:1–2
Revelation 12–22: 211
64:4
1 Corinthians: 61
64:6
Matthew 1–7: 476
Matthew 8–15: 390
Matthew 16–23: 214
Mark 1–8: 110, 132, 348
Luke 1–5: 21, 315
Luke 11–17: 71
Luke 18–24: 13, 146
Acts 1–12: 240
Romans 1–8: 199, 340, 409
Romans 9–16: 67
1 Corinthians: 13
2 Corinthians: 211
Ephesians: 352
Philippians: 213, 236
Hebrews: 68, 357, 404, 410
Revelation 1–11: 113, 138, 139, 231
Revelation 12–22: 308
64:6–8
Romans 9–16: 38
64:7
Romans 9–16: 351
64:8
Philippians: 166
1 Peter: 30
65:1
Romans 9–16: 89
65:1–2
1 Peter: 53
65:2
1 Corinthians: 236
65:5
Luke 11–17: 113
65:16
Luke 1–5: 303
Luke 18–24: 188
Philippians: 290
1 & 2 Thessalonians: 319
1–3 John: 214
Revelation 1–11: 133
65:17
Matthew 16–23: 204
Luke 6–10: 228
Luke 11–17: 151
Romans 1–8: 452
1 Corinthians: 61
Revelation 1–11: 320
Revelation 12–22: 249, 263
65:17–19
Luke 1–5: 49
65:17–25
Revelation 12–22: 4
65:20
Mark 1–8: 381
Revelation 1–11: 277
Revelation 12–22: 239
65:20–22
Revelation 12–22: 229
65:20–23
Luke 18–24: 249
Revelation 12–22: 62, 70, 285
65:23
Revelation 12–22: 72
65:25
John 1–11: 21
Colossians and Philemon: 57
66:1
Mark 9–16: 32
Luke 6–10: 343
Acts 1–12: 215
Revelation 1–11: 146
66:2
Matthew 1–7: 146
Matthew 16–23: 231
Mark 1–8: 342
Luke 1–5: 271, 308
Luke 6–10: 271, 299
2 Corinthians: 112, 438
1 Timothy: 288
James: 200
1 Peter: 278
66:2–3
Matthew 8–15: 449
66:6
Revelation 12–22: 138
66:7–9
Revelation 12–22: 5
66:10–13
Luke 1–5: 179
66:10–22
Matthew 16–23: 403
66:12–13
Luke 1–5: 211
1 Peter: 56
66:13
2 Corinthians: 17, 20
66:15
Revelation 12–22: 124
66:15–16
1 & 2 Thessalonians: 236
2 Peter–Jude: 116
Revelation 12–22: 219
66:16
1 & 2 Thessalonians: 235
66:22
Matthew 16–23: 204
Matthew 24–28: 118
Revelation 1–11: 320
Revelation 12–22: 263
66:23
Revelation 12–22: 131
66:24
Luke 11–17: 365
James: 157, 288
Revelation 12–22: 92, 224, 256

Jeremiah

1:1–2
Luke 1–5: 205
1:2
John 1–11: 17, 49
1:4
1 & 2 Thessalonians: 294
2 Peter–Jude: 65
1:4–5
Luke 1–5: 38
1 Peter: 54
1:5
Matthew 8–15: 184
Luke 6–10: 45
Acts 1–12: 295
Romans 1–8: 496
1 Corinthians: 209
Galatians: 28
1 & 2 Thessalonians: 103, 202
1 Peter: 20
1:5–19
Ephesians: 126
1:9
Matthew 1–7: 255
2 Timothy: 149
1 Peter: 55
1:11
Revelation 1–11: 229
1:13
Revelation 1–11: 229
1:16
Revelation 1–11: 273
1:17
Luke 11–17: 158
1 Peter: 64
1:17–19
Acts 13–28: 150
1:18
Hebrews: 446
2–9
2 Peter–Jude: 184
2:2
Mark 1–8: 130
Luke 1–5: 340
2:2–13
Revelation 1–11: 62
2:8
2 Corinthians: 334
1 & 2 Thessalonians: 242
Revelation 12–22: 56

2:11
John 1–11: 33
2:13
John 12–21: 108, 223
Colossians and Philemon: 124
2:19
1 & 2 Thessalonians: 272
2:21
Luke 18–24: 123
John 12–21: 143
2:22
1 Peter: 32, 50
2:32
1 Peter: 179
3:1
Matthew 1–7: 313
Revelation 12–22: 4
3:3
Revelation 12–22: 165
3:6
Revelation 12–22: 165
3:6–8
Matthew 16–23: 169
3:6–10
Matthew 8–15: 328
3:8
Matthew 1–7: 317
Matthew 16–23: 164
Mark 9–16: 60
Ephesians: 302
James: 191
3:8–9
Revelation 12–22: 165
3:10
Hebrews: 262
3:14–18
Revelation 12–22: 229
3:15
John 1–11: 424
3:17
Revelation 12–22: 242
3:19
1 Peter: 30
3:20
John 1–11: 205
Revelation 12–22: 4
4:3–4
Romans 1–8: 252
4:4
Luke 1–5: 167
Philippians: 218
Colossians and Philemon: 107
1 & 2 Thessalonians: 66
4:13
Revelation 1–11: 251
4:14
James: 210
4:22
Romans 1–8: 108
1 Peter: 274
4:31
Revelation 12–22: 5
5:4–5
Acts 13–28: 162
5:5–6
James: 288
5:11–12
John 1–11: 205
5:15
1 Corinthians: 382
5:21
Matthew 16–23: 2
Luke 1–5: 272
Luke 6–10: 114
John 1–11: 410
Hebrews: 413
Revelation 12–22: 304
5:25
Romans 1–8: 380
1 Peter: 162
5:27–29
James: 242
5:30–31
Matthew 1–7: 462
2 Timothy: 182
2 Peter–Jude: 69
5:31
Matthew 1–7: 471
Matthew 16–23: 373
Luke 18–24: 160
Acts 13–28: 220
2 Corinthians: 334
2 Peter–Jude: 103
6:1
1 & 2 Thessalonians: 149
6:10
Revelation 12–22: 304
6:13
Luke 11–17: 345
Acts 13–28: 230
1 Peter: 269
6:13–15
2 Peter–Jude: 69
6:14
Matthew 1–7: 471
Mark 9–16: 216
John 12–21: 126
Romans 1–8: 191
1 & 2 Thessalonians: 149, 314
Revelation 1–11: 179, 201
6:15
Luke 6–10: 277
6:20
Matthew 8–15: 331
6:23
Revelation 1–11: 178, 271
6:28
James: 218
6:30
Romans 1–8: 108
7:3–7
Romans 1–8: 152
7:4
Luke 11–17: 342–43
7:5–7
James: 90
7:6
Luke 18–24: 5
7:8–11
Luke 11–17: 343
7:9–10
Matthew 1–7: 297
7:11
Matthew 16–23: 271
Mark 9–16: 139
Luke 18–24: 108
7:12–16
1 Timothy: 59
7:16
Luke 11–17: 343
7:16–20
Luke 1–5: 61
7:18
Philippians: 192
7:20
Romans 1–8: 61
7:23
Revelation 12–22: 272
7:24
1 Peter: 74
7:25
Titus: 3
Revelation 1–11: 320
7:25–26
Acts 13–28: 374
Revelation 1–11: 130
7:26
John 1–11: 34
2 Corinthians: 110
7:27
1 Timothy: 43
7:31
Luke 11–17: 118
7:31–32
Revelation 12–22: 255
7:33
Revelation 12–22: 222
8:1–2
2 Peter–Jude: 99
8:2
Acts 1–12: 213
8:4–5
Acts 1–12: 114
8:7
Matthew 24–28: 96
8:9
1 Corinthians: 42
8:10
Acts 13–28: 230
8:11
1 & 2 Thessalonians: 149, 314
Revelation 1–11: 179, 201
8:11–12
Matthew 1–7: 212
8:18
1 Corinthians: 332
8:21
1 Corinthians: 332
9:1
Matthew 1–7: 156, 165
Mark 1–8: 299
Romans 9–16: 10
1 Corinthians: 332
2 Timothy: 52
Hebrews: 446
9:1–3
Romans 9–16: 198

9:1–6
1 & 2 Thessalonians: 174
9:2–3
Hebrews: 446
9:3
Matthew 1–7: 326
1 & 2 Thessalonians: 108, 242
9:3–5
Romans 1–8: 189
9:4
James: 218
9:5
1–3 John: 214
9:6
1 & 2 Thessalonians: 242
9:6–9
2 Peter–Jude: 83
9:8
Matthew 8–15: 321
9:14
1 Peter: 74
9:15
Revelation 1–11: 249
9:23–24
Romans 9–16: 31, 61
2 Corinthians: 32, 349
Philippians: 222
1 & 2 Thessalonians: 96
9:24
Matthew 1–7: 190
Acts 13–28: 135
1 Peter: 169
9:24–26
Romans 1–8: 253
9:25–26
Romans 1–8: 160
9:26
Philippians: 218
10:3–5
Revelation 1–11: 273
10:5
Revelation 12–22: 62
10:7
James: 167
Revelation 12–22: 130
10:10
Matthew 24–28: 274
John 1–11: 102
Colossians and Philemon: 61
1 & 2 Thessalonians: 319
1 Timothy: 136
Revelation 1–11: 217, 315
10:10–12
Revelation 1–11: 158
10:12
Luke 6–10: 206
Acts 13–28: 137
Romans 1–8: 53
James: 167
10:23
Matthew 24–28: 291
John 12–21: 24
Romans 1–8: 431
Romans 9–16: 343
Philippians: 298
1 & 2 Thessalonians: 195
10:25
1 & 2 Thessalonians: 108, 242
11:4
Luke 6–10: 198
Revelation 12–22: 272
11:7
Mark 9–16: 159
Luke 18–24: 117
11:8
1 Peter: 74
11:11
Luke 18–24: 117
11:16–17
Romans 9–16: 115
11:18
1 & 2 Thessalonians: 237
11:19–20
Matthew 1–7: 353
11:20
1 & 2 Thessalonians: 237
Revelation 1–11: 102
11:21
1 & 2 Thessalonians: 237
11:22–23
1 & 2 Thessalonians: 237
12:1
Hebrews: 351
12:1–3
Revelation 1–11: 277
12:1, 3
2 Timothy: 52
12:2
Luke 1–5: 21, 78, 217
James: 284
12:4, 5
2 Timothy: 52
12:10
Matthew 16–23: 373
12:16
Matthew 1–7: 322
13:1–11
Acts 13–28: 241
13:10
1 Peter: 74
13:11
Romans 9–16: 125
13:15–16
Romans 1–8: 85
13:15–17
Romans 9–16: 11
13:16
Luke 11–17: 238
Romans 9–16: 125
13:17
Matthew 8–15: 427
Matthew 16–23: 400
Acts 13–28: 224
13:21
Revelation 12–22: 5
13:23
Matthew 1–7: 392
Matthew 8–15: 52
Matthew 16–23: 201
Mark 9–16: 85
Luke 1–5: 179
Luke 11–17: 72
Luke 18–24: 13
Acts 13–28: 90
Romans 1–8: 52, 340
James: 59
1 Peter: 32
1–3 John: 86
13:25
Romans 1–8: 103
13:27
Matthew 8–15: 328
14:8
Luke 1–5: 153, 168
Romans 9–16: 313
Ephesians: 73
14:10–11
1 Timothy: 59
14:12
Revelation 1–11: 184
14:13
Mark 9–16: 216
Luke 6–10: 113
Luke 11–17: 255
14:13–14
1 & 2 Thessalonians: 149
Revelation 1–11: 179
14:13–15
Revelation 12–22: 56
14:14
Matthew 16–23: 357
Luke 18–24: 160
2 Corinthians: 334
2 Timothy: 105
Titus: 58
2 Peter–Jude: 64
14:14–15
2 Peter–Jude: 83
14:14ff.
1 Timothy: 14
14:15
Luke 6–10: 112
2 Peter–Jude: 99
15:15
Revelation 12–22: 198
15:16
Matthew 1–7: 184, 265
Ephesians: 110, 361
Philippians: 10
1 & 2 Thessalonians: 185, 198
2 Timothy: 149
Hebrews: 145
1–3 John: 238
Revelation 1–11: 287
15:19
2 Timothy: 89
16:4
Revelation 1–11: 182
16:6
Revelation 1–11: 320
16:12
1 Peter: 74
16:14–15
1 Peter: 132
16:17
Mark 1–8: 329
16:18
Mark 9–16: 244

Revelation 12–22: 184
17:7
1 Peter: 53
1–3 John: 109
17:9
Matthew 1–7: 212, 239
Matthew 8–15: 318
Mark 9–16: 67
Luke 1–5: 114, 179
Luke 6–10: 302
Luke 18–24: 13
John 1–11: 352
Romans 1–8: 101, 296
2 Corinthians: 12, 115, 174
Galatians: 186
Colossians and Philemon: 85
Titus: 147
James: 50, 198
1 Peter: 32
1–3 John: 29, 47
17:9–10
Matthew 1–7: 203
1 Peter: 32
17:10
Matthew 1–7: 284
Mark 1–8: 105, 356
Luke 1–5: 323
Romans 1–8: 127, 144
Revelation 1–11: 102
17:13
Ephesians: 73
17:18
Revelation 12–22: 184
17:19
1 Peter: 31
17:23
John 1–11: 34
2 Corinthians: 110
18:3–6
Romans 9–16: 38
18:6
Philippians: 178
Revelation 1–11: 119
18:12
Matthew 1–7: 162
1 Peter: 50, 74
18:16
Mark 9–16: 368
18:18
James: 259
18:19–23
1 & 2 Thessalonians: 238
19:2–6
Revelation 12–22: 256
19:3–7
Romans 1–8: 70
19:3–9
1 & 2 Thessalonians: 238
19:4–5
Mark 9–16: 68
Luke 18–24: 28
19:6
Matthew 1–7: 296
Revelation 12–22: 255
19:9
Matthew 8–15: 52
19:13
Acts 1–12: 213
19:15
2 Corinthians: 110
20:1–2
James: 259
20:9
1 Corinthians: 209
2 Corinthians: 349
Colossians and Philemon: 70
1 Timothy: 42
2 Timothy: 176
James: 258
20:12
Revelation 1–11: 102
Revelation 12–22: 198
20:13
Luke 1–5: 94
20:18
Luke 11–17: 180
2 Corinthians: 12
21:5
Acts 1–12: 322
Acts 13–28: 19
21:8
Matthew 1–7: 450
22:3
Luke 18–24: 166
22:13
James: 246
22:13–17
Romans 9–16: 239
22:21
John 12–21: 48
1 Peter: 227
22:24
James: 269
22:24–30
Luke 1–5: 247
22:30
Matthew 1–7: 3
23:1–2
Mark 1–8: 288
John 1–11: 426
23:1–4
1 Peter: 265
23:1ff.
1 Timothy: 14
23:2
2 Corinthians: 392
23:2–3
Acts 13–28: 224
23:2, 21, 32
Titus: 58
23:3
Matthew 16–23: 402
Luke 11–17: 218
Romans 9–16: 6
23:4
John 1–11: 424
1 Corinthians: 365
23:5
Matthew 8–15: 309, 329
Luke 1–5: 43, 97, 174
Luke 11–17: 154, 401
Luke 18–24: 190
Acts 13–28: 22
Revelation 1–11: 25
Revelation 12–22: 197
23:5–6
Matthew 16–23: 346, 403
Matthew 24–28: 3
Mark 1–8: 148
Luke 11–17: 249
Revelation 1–11: 167
Revelation 12–22: 229
23:5–8
Revelation 1–11: 29, 31
23:6
John 1–11: 14
23:11
Revelation 12–22: 56
23:13
Revelation 12–22: 56
23:13–14
Titus: 58
23:13–17
Luke 18–24: 160
23:14
Galatians: 11
2 Timothy: 105, 106
Revelation 12–22: 56
23:14–16
2 Peter–Jude: 69
23:15
Revelation 1–11: 249
Revelation 12–22: 56
23:16
2 Timothy: 105
Revelation 12–22: 54
23:16–25
2 Peter–Jude: 65
23:17
1 Peter: 74
23:18
Hebrews: 10
23:20
Acts 1–12: 53
23:21
Matthew 16–23: 357
Acts 1–12: 27
Romans 1–8: 7
2 Peter–Jude: 69
23:21–22
Luke 18–24: 161
Revelation 12–22: 55
23:21, 32
Ephesians: 94
23:22
Hebrews: 10
23:24
1 Peter: 288
23:25–27
2 Peter–Jude: 69
23:25–32
Luke 18–24: 161
2 Peter–Jude: 172
Revelation 12–22: 55
23:28
1 Peter: 55
23:30–33
Revelation 1–11: 31

23:32
Matthew 16–23: 357
Acts 1–12: 27
2 Corinthians: 345
Titus: 68
2 Peter–Jude: 64
23:36
Revelation 1–11: 217
24:1–10
Matthew 24–28: 61
Luke 18–24: 243
24:5
Romans 1–8: 477
24:5–7
Romans 1–8: 474
24:7
Acts 13–28: 135
2 Corinthians: 253
Hebrews: 262
James: 61
Revelation 12–22: 266, 272
24:10
Revelation 1–11: 184
25:1–6
Revelation 1–11: 291
25:4
Revelation 1–11: 130
25:4–5
1 & 2 Thessalonians: 64
25:6
1 Corinthians: 241
25:6–7
Revelation 1–11: 273
25:9
1 Corinthians: 241
25:14
Revelation 1–11: 273
25:15
Matthew 16–23: 390
Revelation 12–22: 91
25:15–17
Luke 18–24: 304
25:30
Revelation 1–11: 282
26:8
James: 259
26:18
1 Peter: 120
26:20–23
Mark 1–8: 298
Luke 11–17: 231
26:23
1 & 2 Thessalonians: 62
27:5
Acts 13–28: 19
Romans 1–8: 53
27:14–16
Revelation 12–22: 55
27:22
1 Peter: 140
28
Revelation 12–22: 56
28:1–17
2 Peter–Jude: 69
28:15–17
2 Peter–Jude: 68
29:4–14
1 Peter: 145–46
29:7
Romans 9–16: 214
29:8–9
Revelation 12–22: 55
29:10
Luke 1–5: 96
1 Peter: 140
29:11
Matthew 1–7: 214
2 Corinthians: 107
29:11–13
James: 36
29:13
Matthew 1–7: 30, 455
Matthew 16–23: 144, 250
Mark 1–8: 338
Luke 6–10: 269
Luke 18–24: 75
Acts 1–12: 254, 293
Acts 13–28: 97
Romans 1–8: 67, 81, 142, 184
Romans 9–16: 88, 135
Philippians: 31
Hebrews: 310
James: 206
29:13–14
Matthew 16–23: 11
29:19
Acts 13–28: 374
Revelation 1–11: 130
29:21
2 Corinthians: 334–35
2 Peter–Jude: 68
29:21–22
Revelation 12–22: 56
29:21–23
Revelation 12–22: 56
29:24–32
Revelation 12–22: 56
29:31
Acts 1–12: 27
29:32
2 Peter–Jude: 68
30:1–8
Luke 18–24: 227
30:3
Revelation 12–22: 229
30:5–8
Revelation 12–22: 239
30:5–9
Matthew 24–28: 32
30:7
Matthew 16–23: 402
Revelation 1–11: 124, 176
Revelation 12–22: 27
30:10–11
Romans 9–16: 97
30:17
Luke 6–10: 253
30:22
Revelation 12–22: 266, 272
31
Luke 1–5: 129
Luke 11–17: 401
John 12–21: 25
Hebrews: 212
31:1
Revelation 12–22: 266
31:3
Romans 1–8: 28
Ephesians: 302
1–3 John: 39
31:9
1 Peter: 30
31:10
Acts 13–28: 224
Romans 9–16: 97
31:12
John 1–11: 79–80
31:13
Luke 1–5: 179
31:14
Matthew 1–7: 184
31:15
Matthew 1–7: 45
31:16
Matthew 1–7: 45
31:17
John 12–21: 212
2 Corinthians: 107
31:20
Luke 1–5: 83
Philippians: 32
31:22
Matthew 1–7: 16
31:31
Matthew 1–7: 252
Luke 1–5: 129
31:31, 33
Romans 9–16: 387
31:31–33
Matthew 16–23: 170
Romans 1–8: 129
Romans 9–16: 94
31:31–34
Luke 1–5: 119, 177, 200
Luke 11–17: 369
Luke 18–24: 269, 284
John 1–11: 105
John 12–21: 89
Acts 1–12: 195
Romans 9–16: 14, 129
2 Corinthians: 88, 104
Hebrews: 187, 256
James: 59
1 Peter: 89
1–3 John: 56
Revelation 12–22: 86
31:32
Luke 1–5: 119
Revelation 12–22: 203
31:32–33
Luke 1–5: 129
31:33
Mark 1–8: 26, 358
Luke 1–5: 119
2 Corinthians: 83, 90
Ephesians: 73
1–3 John: 45
Revelation 12–22: 266

31:33–34
Luke 1–5: 129
31:34
Matthew 8–15: 52
Mark 1–8: 103
Luke 1–5: 120, 206, 322
Acts 1–12: 303
Acts 13–28: 135
2 Corinthians: 50, 97–98
Ephesians: 299
1 & 2 Thessalonians: 96
1–3 John: 39
Revelation 12–22: 182
31:35
Luke 1–5: 129
31:35–36
Matthew 24–28: 118
31:35–37
Luke 11–17: 249
Luke 18–24: 245–46
Revelation 1–11: 31
Revelation 12–22: 4
31:35–40
Revelation 12–22: 229
32:2
James: 259
Revelation 1–11: 163
32:6–7
Revelation 1–11: 163
32:9–15
Revelation 1–11: 163
32:15
Revelation 1–11: 163
32:17
Acts 13–28: 19, 137
2 Corinthians: 315
1 & 2 Thessalonians: 161
1 Peter: 19
Revelation 1–11: 158, 285
32:17–25
John 12–21: 234
32:17, 27
Luke 1–5: 59
32:19
1 & 2 Thessalonians: 241
32:20
2 Corinthians: 416
32:21
Acts 13–28: 19
32:24–25
Revelation 1–11: 163
32:27
1 & 2 Thessalonians: 161
32:30
Revelation 1–11: 273
32:35
Mark 9--16: 48
Luke 1–5: 153
2 Corinthians: 213
32:37, 41
Luke 11–17: 292
32:38
Romans 1–8: 277
Romans 9–16: 129
Revelation 12–22: 266
32:38–39
Romans 9–16: 304
32:40
Romans 1–8: 277
1 & 2 Thessalonians: 19
Revelation 12–22: 101
32:41
Luke 6–10: 338
Luke 18–24: 69
32:42
Romans 9–16: 21
33:8
Luke 1–5: 206
33:11
Revelation 12–22: 194
33:14–16
Hebrews: 6
33:14–18
Revelation 12–22: 229
33:14–21
Mark 1–8: 192
33:15
Luke 1–5: 211
33:15–17
Revelation 1–11: 167
33:17–22
Luke 18–24: 246
33:19–26
1 & 2 Thessalonians: 66
33:20
Matthew 24–28: 118
33:20–26
Revelation 12–22: 4
33:21–22
Luke 1–5: 98
33:25–26
Revelation 1–11: 31
33:26
Luke 1–5: 121
34:1–3
Romans 9–16: 238
34:12–22
Romans 9–16: 238
34:14
2 Corinthians: 385
34:18–19
1 Peter: 24
35:1–19
Ephesians: 240
35:4
1 Timothy: 260
35:14b
1 Peter: 227
35:15
Acts 13–28: 374
Revelation 1–11: 130
37:11
Acts 13–28: 114
37:13–16
Mark 9–16: 168
James: 259
38:1–6
James: 259
38:2–3
Acts 13–28: 115
38:2–4
2 Corinthians: 220
38:4
Acts 13–28: 115
38:9
Mark 9–16: 168
Luke 18–24: 124
39:3
Matthew 1–7: 27
40:1
Matthew 1–7: 45
40:8
Mark 1–8: 20
42:1–43:7
Romans 1–8: 199
42:19–22
Luke 11–17: 115
43:1–4
James: 259
44:4
Acts 13–28: 374
2 Peter–Jude: 18
Revelation 1–11: 61
44:4–5
Luke 11–17: 374
1 Timothy: 185
Revelation 1–11: 130
44:4–6
Revelation 1–11: 290
44:8
Revelation 1–11: 273
44:13
Revelation 1–11: 184
44:15–17
Romans 1–8: 340
44:15–19
James: 259
Revelation 12–22: 159
44:16–19
Luke 1–5: 61
44:17–19
Matthew 1–7: 5
44:20–27
Revelation 12–22: 160
44:22
1 Peter: 133
45:5
2 Corinthians: 172
46–51
2 Peter–Jude: 184
46:8
Revelation 12–22: 33
46:10
Revelation 1–11: 189
46:18
James: 269
46:21
James: 248
46:27–28
Luke 1–5: 157
46:28
Revelation 1–11: 31
Revelation 12–22: 4
47:2
Revelation 12–22: 33

48:11
James: 33
48:20
James: 243
48:25
Revelation 1–11: 168
Revelation 12–22: 42
48:35–37
2 Corinthians: 192
49:11
1 Timothy: 200
49:19
Revelation 12–22: 47
49:36
Revelation 1–11: 216
49:39
Acts 1–12: 53
50:8
Revelation 12–22: 167, 181
50:13
Revelation 12–22: 177, 191
50:14–15
Revelation 12–22: 183
50:15
Revelation 12–22: 167
50:19
James: 13
50:20
Luke 1–5: 206
50:26–27
James: 249
50:29
Revelation 12–22: 183
50:31–32
Ephesians: 121
50:38
Acts 13–28: 186
50:39
Revelation 12–22: 177, 191
50–51
Revelation 12–22: 167, 293
51:6
Revelation 12–22: 167, 181
51:7
Revelation 12–22: 162, 164, 167, 184
51:8
Revelation 12–22: 167
51:9
Revelation 12–22: 167, 182
51:12
1 Peter: 279
51:13
Revelation 12–22: 161, 167
51:15
Revelation 1–11: 285
51:24
Revelation 12–22: 167, 183
51:25
Revelation 12–22: 169
51:27
Revelation 1–11: 263
51:34
Revelation 12–22: 6
51:36
Revelation 12–22: 198
51:37
Revelation 12–22: 177, 191
51:40
James: 249
51:45
Revelation 12–22: 167, 181
51:56
Revelation 12–22: 183
51:61–64
Revelation 12–22: 190
51:63–64
Revelation 12–22: 167
52:18–19
Revelation 1–11: 240
52:19
Revelation 1–11: 171

Lamentations

1:12
Matthew 1–7: 34
1:15
Revelation 12–22: 117
1:18
Romans 1–8: 63
1:20
Philippians: 32
2:9
1 & 2 Thessalonians: 64
2:10
Revelation 12–22: 189
2:11
Philippians: 32
2:14
Luke 6–10: 113
Luke 11–17: 255
1 & 2 Thessalonians: 149
1 Timothy: 14
2 Peter–Jude: 104
Revelation 12–22: 56
2:15
Mark 9–16: 368
2:19
Mark 9–16: 148
3:21–23
2 Corinthians: 26
3:22
Matthew 1–7: 191
Matthew 8–15: 476
Mark 1–8: 386
Luke 6–10: 137
Romans 9–16: 198
Galatians: 169
Titus: 152
1 Peter: 32, 132
3:22–23
Matthew 1–7: 427
Matthew 8–15: 91
Luke 11–17: 236
James: 261
1 Peter: 101
2 Peter–Jude: 25
3:23
Luke 1–5: 174
Romans 1–8: 272
1 & 2 Thessalonians: 296
3:24
Romans 1–8: 444
2 Corinthians: 107
1 Peter: 38
3:30
2 Corinthians: 381
3:31–33
Hebrews: 392
3:35, 38
Luke 1–5: 49
3:37–38
Luke 18–24: 287
3:38
Mark 1–8: 244, 246
3:39
Philippians: 179
3:40
2 Corinthians: 460
James: 8
3:57
Luke 1–5: 157
4:5
Revelation 12–22: 164
4:7
Ephesians: 239
4:16
1 Peter: 194
4:21
Mark 9–16: 302
Luke 18–24: 304
5:15–16
James: 213
5:18
Luke 6–10: 318
5:19
John 1–11: 102

Ezekiel

1
Revelation 1–11: 144
1:1
Luke 1–5: 238, 248
Revelation 1–11: 145
1:1–19
Matthew 1–7: 79
1:3
Luke 1–5: 205
John 1–11: 17, 49
1:4–25
Revelation 1–11: 153
Revelation 12–22: 132
1:6
Revelation 1–11: 154
1:12
Revelation 1–11: 152
1:13
Revelation 1–11: 151
1:17
Revelation 1–11: 152
1:18
Revelation 1–11: 154
1:22
Revelation 1–11: 152
Revelation 12–22: 124
1:26
Revelation 1–11: 152

1:26–28
Acts 1–12: 222
1–3 John: 144
Revelation 1–11: 147
1:27–28
Luke 1–5: 156
1:28
Mark 1–8: 235
Mark 9–16: 3, 14
Luke 1–5: 157, 287, 308
Luke 6–10: 280
Revelation 1–11: 49, 148, 158, 228
Revelation 12–22: 296
2:2
Revelation 1–11: 41
2:3–6
1 Timothy: 185
2:3, 7
2 Timothy: 150
2:4–5
1 Timothy: 43
2:5
Luke 11–17: 20
2:6
Mark 9–16: 168
Luke 18–24: 124
2:7
1 Peter: 55
2:7–8
1 Timothy: 42
2:9–3:3
Revelation 1–11: 287
2:9–10
Revelation 1–11: 164
3:1–3
Revelation 1–11: 287
3:5–9
Acts 13–28: 241
3:7
1 Timothy: 43
3:10
2 Timothy: 150
3:12
Acts 1–12: 259
Revelation 1–11: 41, 42
3:14
Acts 1–12: 259
Revelation 1–11: 41
3:17–18
James: 72
3:17–19
James: 148
3:17–21
1 Timothy: 160
3:19
1 & 2 Thessalonians: 64
3:23
Luke 1–5: 157
Revelation 1–11: 49, 158, 228
3:26
Matthew 1–7: 136
3:26–27
Titus: 54
4–5
Acts 13–28: 241
4:9
Luke 11–17: 34
4:16–17
Revelation 1–11: 182
5:11
James: 269
5:16
Revelation 1–11: 182
6:8
Matthew 16–23: 402
6:9
John 1–11: 205
1–3 John: 85
Revelation 1–11: 131
6:11
Revelation 1–11: 184
7:19
Romans 1–8: 61
James: 245
7:20
Luke 18–24: 225
7:23–24
Romans 9–16: 226
8
2 Corinthians: 252
8:1
Luke 1–5: 267
Luke 11–17: 199
8:3
Acts 1–12: 259
2 Corinthians: 252
8:4
2 Corinthians: 252
8:4–18
Romans 1–8: 84
8:6
2 Corinthians: 252–53
8:11–12
2 Corinthians: 253
8:13–14
Matthew 1–7: 5
8:14
2 Corinthians: 253
Revelation 12–22: 160
8:16
2 Corinthians: 253
8:18
2 Corinthians: 253
8–11
1 & 2 Thessalonians: 66
9:3
Mark 9–16: 132
Luke 1–5: 156
9:3–6
Revelation 1–11: 218
9:4
Matthew 1–7: 165
9:4–6
Revelation 1–11: 261
9:8
Luke 18–24: 2, 17
Revelation 1–11: 49
10:2
Revelation 1–11: 240
10:4
Revelation 12–22: 279
10:4, 18, 19
Luke 1–5: 156
10:12
Revelation 1–11: 154
10:15
Revelation 1–11: 153, 178
Revelation 12–22: 132
10:18–19
Acts 1–12: 23
11:5
Mark 1–8: 105
Luke 1–5: 323
2 Corinthians: 114
11:18–20
John 1–11: 105
11:19
Luke 1–5: 222
Romans 9–16: 387
1 & 2 Thessalonians: 193
11:19–20
2 Corinthians: 83
Hebrews: 215
11:20
John 1–11: 33
Revelation 12–22: 272
11:22–23
Luke 1–5: 156
Romans 1–8: 84
11:23
Matthew 24–28: 8
11:24
John 12–21: 114
12:2
Revelation 12–22: 304
13:1–7
2 Peter–Jude: 69
13:1–10
Luke 18–24: 161
13:1ff.
1 Timothy: 14
13:2–3
Revelation 12–22: 56
13:3
Matthew 16–23: 354
2 Peter–Jude: 65
Revelation 1–11: 251
13:4
Luke 6–10: 318
13:5
Luke 1–5: 216
1 & 2 Thessalonians: 144
Revelation 1–11: 200
13:5–16
Revelation 1–11: 204
13:8–9
2 Peter–Jude: 83
13:9
Luke 6–10: 100
13:9–10
2 Peter–Jude: 104
13:10
1 & 2 Thessalonians: 314
13:10–16
Acts 13–28: 281
1 & 2 Thessalonians: 149

13:15–19
2 Peter–Jude: 69
13:17
Revelation 12–22: 56
13:19
Matthew 8–15: 180
14:3
1 Corinthians: 223
14:6
Acts 1–12: 114
14:11
James: 285
14:12–21
Revelation 1–11: 184
14:13
Revelation 1–11: 182
14:16
James: 269
14:18
James: 269
14:20
James: 269
14:22–23
Luke 1–5: 179
16
Revelation 12–22: 162
16:1–5
Luke 1–5: 160
16:4–14
Matthew 16–23: 307
Ephesians: 72
16:7–14
Revelation 12–22: 203
16:8–15
Revelation 1–11: 63
16:10
James: 244
16:13
James: 244
16:18
James: 244
16:20
Revelation 12–22: 10
16:20–21
Luke 18–24: 25
16:21
Mark 9–16: 68
2 Corinthians: 213
16:23
Revelation 1–11: 251
16:30
John 1–11: 205
16:30–31
Revelation 12–22: 165
16:32
Matthew 16–23: 169
James: 191
16:32–35
Revelation 12–22: 4
16:36
Revelation 12–22: 165
16:48
James: 269
16:49
1 Timothy: 201
16:59
1 Peter: 129
16:60
2 Corinthians: 88
16:60–63
Luke 1–5: 206
17:16
James: 269
17:19
James: 269
17:23
Mark 1–8: 221
17:24
Luke 6–10: 63
18:2–4
Matthew 16–23: 208
18:3
James: 269
18:4
Luke 1–5: 27
Luke 11–17: 369
2 Corinthians: 202, 204, 210
1 Timothy: 168
Hebrews: 63, 138, 234
James: 287
18:12
Matthew 8–15: 191
18:13
Acts 13–28: 149
18:20
2 Corinthians: 210
James: 287
18:23
Matthew 8–15: 396
Mark 9–16: 207
John 12–21: 48
2 Corinthians: 73
Colossians and Philemon: 111
1 Timothy: 69
1 Peter: 32
Revelation 12–22: 196
18:28
James: 8
18:30–32
Luke 1–5: 207
Luke 11–17: 369
2 Corinthians: 192
Revelation 1–11: 139
18:31
Luke 11–17: 320
Romans 1–8: 322
James: 210
18:32
Romans 9–16: 42
2 Corinthians: 73, 204
1 Timothy: 69, 168
Hebrews: 392
1 Peter: 32
Revelation 12–22: 196
20:3
James: 269
20:11
Luke 6–10: 354
20:12
Acts 13–28: 202
20:30
John 1–11: 205
20:30–33
Revelation 12–22: 165
20:31
James: 269
20:33
James: 269
20:33–34
Acts 13–28: 19
20:33–38
Luke 11–17: 249
Luke 18–24: 194
Romans 9–16: 128
1 Peter: 279
20:33–44
2 Peter–Jude: 184
20:34
2 Corinthians: 255
20:37–38
John 1–11: 425
20:38
1 Timothy: 147
Revelation 12–22: 28
21:12
James: 243
22:12
Romans 1–8: 156
22:25
Mark 1–8: 288
2 Corinthians: 335
1 Peter: 281
Revelation 12–22: 56
22:26–28
Acts 13–28: 220
22:27
Luke 11–17: 230
22:28
2 Corinthians: 335
22:30
1 Timothy: 94
23
Revelation 12–22: 162
23:6
Revelation 12–22: 164
23:23–24
Revelation 1–11: 271
23:31–33
Luke 18–24: 304
23:37
2 Corinthians: 213
24:15–18
James: 259
25–32
2 Peter–Jude: 184
25:12–14
Luke 1–5: 22
26:1–21
2 Timothy: 151
26:13
Ephesians: 260
26:16
James: 244
26–28
Mark 1–8: 315
1 & 2 Thessalonians: 239

27:3
Revelation 12–22: 185
27:12–24
Revelation 12–22: 188
27:16
James: 244
27:17
Acts 1–12: 326
27:22
1 Peter: 44
27:24
James: 244
27:30
Revelation 12–22: 189
28:1–5
1 Timothy: 281
28:1–10
Ephesians: 338
1 Timothy: 37
28:1–19
1 Timothy: 37
1 Peter: 281
28:2
Revelation 12–22: 185
28:3–4
Matthew 8–15: 44
28:11–15
Matthew 8–15: 264
Luke 1–5: 255
Revelation 1–11: 279
28:11–19
Ephesians: 121
1 Timothy: 36, 37, 118
Revelation 12–22: 16
28:12
1 Timothy: 37, 118
28:12–14
Romans 9–16: 219
28:12–16
Luke 1–5: 280
Revelation 1–11: 256
28:12–17
1–3 John: 126
Revelation 12–22: 2, 8
28:12–19
Mark 1–8: 64
28:12ff.
Acts 13–28: 291
28:13
1 Timothy: 37
28:13–14
1 Timothy: 38
28:14
2 Corinthians: 482
Ephesians: 339
1 Timothy: 37, 118
Revelation 1–11: 154
Revelation 12–22: 2, 235
28:15
Luke 1–5: 255
1 Timothy: 37
28:16
1 Timothy: 37, 118
Revelation 1–11: 154
28:17
1 Timothy: 37
28:25
James: 12
29:1–5
Revelation 12–22: 7
29:3
Revelation 12–22: 6
29:6
Revelation 1–11: 293
29:18
2 Timothy: 151
30:2–19
Revelation 1–11: 200
30:2ff.
Acts 1–12: 54
30:3
Luke 1–5: 216
1 & 2 Thessalonians: 144
Revelation 1–11: 200
Revelation 12–22: 121
30:10–26
2 Timothy: 151
31:3–6
Matthew 8–15: 371
Mark 1–8: 220
Luke 11–17: 212
32:2
Revelation 12–22: 6
32:7–8
Mark 9–16: 376
Revelation 1–11: 209, 250
33:2–5
Acts 13–28: 149
33:3
Revelation 1–11: 239
33:4
Acts 13–28: 149
33:7–9
Acts 13–28: 214, 221
James: 148
33:11
Luke 18–24: 151, 258
Romans 1–8: 28, 81
2 Corinthians: 73, 192
Colossians and Philemon: 111
1 Timothy: 63, 68, 69
Hebrews: 86
James: 269
2 Peter–Jude: 151
Revelation 1–11: 139
Revelation 12–22: 196
33:17–20
1 & 2 Thessalonians: 241
33:18–19
Matthew 1–7: 65
33:19
Luke 1–5: 207, 219
33:22
Matthew 1–7: 136
33:25
Acts 13–28: 71
33:27
James: 269
33:30–32
1 Timothy: 43
33:31
Luke 1–5: 78, 267
2 Timothy: 118
33:31–32
Luke 1–5: 217
Luke 11–17: 114
2 Timothy: 182
34:1–10
Mark 1–8: 150, 166, 339
34:2–4
Matthew 8–15: 113
34:2–5
Matthew 16–23: 362
34:2–6
2 Corinthians: 392
34:2–10
Mark 1–8: 356
John 1–11: 426–27
34:2–16
1 Peter: 265
34:2ff.
Acts 13–28: 224
34:5
Mark 1–8: 317
34:8
James: 269
34:11
Luke 18–24: 68
34:11–25
Mark 1–8: 150
34:11–31
Matthew 16–23: 7
34:12–16
John 1–11: 424
34:16
Luke 6–10: 253
2 Corinthians: 199
34:23
Revelation 1–11: 233
34:23–24
Luke 1–5: 211
1 Peter: 174
Revelation 12–22: 229
34:24
Revelation 12–22: 272
34:25
Matthew 1–7: 213
Luke 11–17: 169
34:26
Acts 1–12: 118
35:6
James: 269
35:11
James: 269
35:15
Luke 1–5: 22
36
Matthew 8–15: 48
Acts 1–12: 20
36:16–38
Revelation 12–22: 229
36:17, 19–20
Titus: 89
36:17–20
Romans 1–8: 158
36:22–36
Luke 18–24: 194–95

36:23
1 Corinthians: 248
36:24–27
Mark 1–8: 354
Luke 1–5: 130
Luke 11–17: 415
John 1–11: 105
2 Corinthians: 115
36:25
Luke 1–5: 120
John 1–11: 54
Hebrews: 140
36:25–26
Matthew 1–7: 71, 200
Mark 1–8: 26
James: 59
36:25–27
Mark 1–8: 358, 429
Luke 11–17: 58
Luke 18–24: 269, 284
Acts 1–12: 17
1 Corinthians: 68
James: 62, 210
1 Peter: 89
Revelation 12–22: 86
36:25–31
1 Peter: 129
36:25–35
Revelation 12–22: 212
36:26
Luke 1–5: 119, 222
Luke 11–17: 105
Romans 1–8: 120, 322
Philippians: 242
36:26–27
Matthew 8–15: 455
Luke 1–5: 180
2 Corinthians: 83
Hebrews: 215
36:27
Luke 1–5: 120, 223
Luke 18–24: 448
Acts 1–12: 75
1 & 2 Thessalonians: 108, 112, 118, 193, 195
36:28
Revelation 12–22: 272
36:32
Luke 1–5: 130
36:33
John 1–11: 54
36:34–35
Revelation 1–11: 277
36:37
John 1–11: 54
36:37, 38
Luke 1–5: 130
36–37
Revelation 1–11: 31
37
Luke 11–17: 155
James: 13
37:1–14
Mark 9–16: 184
1 Corinthians: 408
37:1ff.
Revelation 12–22: 212
37:9–14
John 12–21: 382
37:9ff.
Acts 1–12: 40
37:11–14
1 & 2 Thessalonians: 193
37:14
Luke 1–5: 223
Luke 18–24: 448
Acts 1–12: 75
37:15–22
James: 12
37:15–28
Revelation 12–22: 229
37:16–17, 19
Romans 9–16: 304
37:20–22
1 Peter: 132
37:21–25
Matthew 16–23: 346
37:21–28
Revelation 12–22: 4
37:23
John 1–11: 54
Revelation 12–22: 272
37:24
1 Peter: 174
37:25
John 12–21: 43
37:26
Luke 1–5: 200
Luke 11–17: 169
Romans 9–16: 14
2 Corinthians: 88
37:27
2 Corinthians: 253
Revelation 1–11: 233
Revelation 12–22: 266, 272
37:28
1 & 2 Thessalonians: 89, 202
38
Matthew 16–23: 7
38:2
1 & 2 Thessalonians: 264
38:2–6
Matthew 24–28: 35
38:4
Revelation 1–11: 271
38:12
Revelation 12–22: 242
38:15
Revelation 1–11: 271
38:16
Acts 1–12: 53
38:16–23
Revelation 1–11: 318–19
38:17
Revelation 1–11: 320
38:19
Revelation 1–11: 204
38:19–23
Luke 18–24: 234
38:20
Revelation 12–22: 262
38:22
Luke 1–5: 223
Revelation 1–11: 245
38–39
Revelation 12–22: 211, 241
39:1–4
Revelation 12–22: 219
39:4
Revelation 12–22: 241
39:12
Revelation 12–22: 222
39:17
Revelation 12–22: 241
39:17–19
James: 249
39:17–20
Revelation 12–22: 219, 222, 241
39:25
Luke 1–5: 83, 121
James: 261
39:29
Luke 18–24: 448
40:3–43:17
Revelation 1–11: 293
40:3ff.
Revelation 12–22: 281
40:5
Romans 9–16: 119
40–48
Revelation 1–11: 31, 232, 294
43:2
Luke 1–5: 156
Acts 1–12: 40
Revelation 1–11: 47
Revelation 12–22: 75
43:3
Revelation 1–11: 49, 158
43:7
Revelation 12–22: 242
43:9
James: 206
43:23–24
Luke 11–17: 288
44:3
Acts 1–12: 118
44:4
Revelation 1–11: 49, 158
44:7
Philippians: 219
44:9
Philippians: 219
44:10
1 Corinthians: 236
44:13
James: 206
44:22
Luke 1–5: 24
45:18–25
Mark 9–16: 291
45:21
Luke 18–24: 281
46:13
2 Corinthians: 214
48
Revelation 12–22: 281

48:1–2
Revelation 1–11: 220
48:31–34
Revelation 1–11: 220
48:32
Revelation 1–11: 220
48:35
Hebrews: 331
Revelation 12–22: 266

Daniel
1:8–16
Luke 1–5: 35
1:8, 12–13
Romans 9–16: 215
1:12–15
Romans 9–16: 215
1:17
James: 165
1:18–21
1 Peter: 150
1–2
Hebrews: 356
2
Matthew 16–23: 7
2:1ff.
Acts 13–28: 8
2:18
Revelation 12–22: 145
2:19
Revelation 12–22: 145
2:19–20
Luke 1–5: 96
2:20
2 Corinthians: 393
2:20–21
Matthew 1–7: 420
2:20–23
James: 166
2:21
Luke 1–5: 259
1 & 2 Thessalonians: 142
2:22
Luke 11–17: 88
2:23
Acts 13–28: 307
2:24
Matthew 1–7: 27
2:28
Revelation 12–22: 262
2:32–35
Matthew 16–23: 300
2:34
Luke 18–24: 127
Revelation 12–22: 43
2:34–35
Revelation 1–11: 313
2:35
Revelation 12–22: 169, 239
2:36ff.
Acts 13–28: 140
2:37
Revelation 12–22: 145
2:41–44
Revelation 12–22: 42
2:44
Matthew 1–7: 55
Matthew 24–28: 3
Acts 1–12: 15
1 Peter: 55
Revelation 12–22: 4, 145
2:44–45
Luke 1–5: 211
Revelation 1–11: 313
Revelation 12–22: 229
2:45
Romans 9–16: 51
Revelation 12–22: 43
2:47
1 Timothy: 276
2:48
Matthew 1–7: 27
3
Revelation 12–22: 61
3:6
Revelation 12–22: 62
3:16–18
Acts 13–28: 234
Romans 1–8: 266
3:16–18, 27
Romans 9–16: 215
3:17
2 Timothy: 132
Hebrews: 369
3:17–18
Matthew 8–15: 9
Matthew 16–23: 74
3:18
Hebrews: 369
3:24–27
Titus: 108
3:25
John 1–11: 41
3:26
Mark 1–8: 244
3:28
Revelation 12–22: 296
4
Romans 1–8: 61
4:3
Matthew 1–7: 55
4:10–12
Matthew 8–15: 371
Mark 1–8: 220
Luke 11–17: 211
4:17
John 1–11: 102
Acts 13–28: 320
Revelation 12–22: 47
4:17, 25
Luke 1–5: 259
4:19–29, 33–34
Romans 9–16: 125
4:20–22
Mark 1–8: 220
4:25
John 1–11: 102
Revelation 12–22: 47
4:25, 27
Romans 9–16: 238
4:25, 32
Romans 1–8: 93
4:27
Luke 6–10: 308
1 Timothy: 187
4:29–30
Matthew 1–7: 178
4:30
2 Corinthians: 378
1–3 John: 254
4:30–32
Romans 9–16: 236
4:31–32
Matthew 1–7: 178
Romans 1–8: 93
4:31–33
1–3 John: 254–55
4:32
John 1–11: 102
Revelation 12–22: 47
4:33
Romans 9–16: 125
4:34
Luke 11–17: 399
Acts 1–12: 15
Romans 1–8: 93
Romans 9–16: 125, 237
Revelation 1–11: 157
4:34–35
Matthew 24–28: 288
Acts 13–28: 138
4:35
Luke 1–5: 306
Revelation 1–11: 119, 156
Revelation 12–22: 186
4:37
Matthew 16–23: 231
Luke 1–5: 61
Luke 11–17: 264
Romans 1–8: 93
Revelation 12–22: 130
5
Romans 1–8: 61
Ephesians: 231
5:1–29
Romans 1–8: 94
5:1–30
Revelation 12–22: 180
5:3–6, 25
Matthew 1–7: 143
5:7
Revelation 12–22: 164
5:14
James: 165
5:16
Revelation 12–22: 164
5:18
Acts 13–28: 97
5:18–28
Galatians: 184
5:20
Luke 1–5: 82
2 Corinthians: 378
1 & 2 Thessalonians: 195
5:22–23
2 Corinthians: 378

5:23
Revelation 1–11: 273
5:26
Luke 11–17: 22
5:27
Revelation 1–11: 112
5:29
Revelation 12–22: 164
5:30
Revelation 12–22: 185
6:1–23
1 Peter: 36
6:1ff.
James: 259
6:4–9
Matthew 1–7: 27
6:4–10
Acts 1–12: 138
6:7, 21, 23
Romans 9–16: 215
6:10
Matthew 1–7: 363
Matthew 16–23: 74
Acts 13–28: 234
Ephesians: 266
1 & 2 Thessalonians: 189
6:16–23
Luke 18–24: 396
2 Timothy: 213
6:17
Romans 1–8: 461
Revelation 1–11: 217
6:19–22
Titus: 108
6:20
James: 12
Revelation 1–11: 217
6:21–23
Romans 1–8: 476
6:22
Revelation 12–22: 296
6:25–28
Romans 1–8: 140
6:26
Matthew 1–7: 229
Acts 1–12: 15
7
Matthew 16–23: 7
7:2
Revelation 1–11: 216
7:3–7
Revelation 12–22: 43
7:7
Revelation 12–22: 42, 44
7:8
1 & 2 Thessalonians: 146, 264, 266
Revelation 12–22: 37, 168
7:9
2 Corinthians: 442
Revelation 1–11: 3, 46
7:9–10
Matthew 16–23: 54
Luke 6–10: 277
Revelation 1–11: 147
Revelation 12–22: 247, 252
7:9–14
Mark 1–8: 432–33
7:10
Hebrews: 23, 415
Revelation 1–11: 172, 228
7:11
Revelation 12–22: 47
7:13
Matthew 1–7: x
Matthew 16–23: 19
Mark 1–8: 418
Mark 9–16: 18
Luke 18–24: 49, 75, 231, 289
John 12–21: 43
Acts 1–12: 23
2 Peter–Jude: 189
Revelation 1–11: 32, 43
Revelation 12–22: 112, 113
7:13–14
Matthew 16–23: 205
Matthew 24–28: 55, 339
Mark 1–8: 105, 146, 148
Mark 9–16: 96, 328
Luke 1–5: 258
Luke 6–10: 260
Luke 11–17: 412
Luke 18–24: 190, 338–39
1 & 2 Thessalonians: 254
1 Peter: 55
Revelation 1–11: 29, 168, 313
Revelation 12–22: 62, 112
7:14
2 Corinthians: 442
7:14, 27
Luke 1–5: 49
7:15
2 Corinthians: 442
Revelation 1–11: 147
7:15–16
Luke 1–5: 27
7:16–24
Revelation 12–22: 42
7:18
Luke 6–10: 206, 351
Luke 18–24: 43
Hebrews: 55
1 Peter: 133
2 Peter–Jude: 201
Revelation 1–11: 29, 313, 320
7:20
Revelation 12–22: 47, 168
7:21
1 & 2 Thessalonians: 266
Revelation 12–22: 37
7:22
2 Peter–Jude: 189
Revelation 1–11: 313
Revelation 12–22: 37
7:23
1 & 2 Thessalonians: 266
Revelation 12–22: 37, 42, 168
7:23–25
Revelation 12–22: 7
7:24
Matthew 24–28: 19
1 & 2 Thessalonians: 264
Revelation 12–22: 37, 42
7:24–27
Matthew 8–15: 48
7:25
Matthew 24–28: 44, 70, 114
Luke 11–17: 157
1 & 2 Thessalonians: 142, 266, 267
Revelation 12–22: 32, 37, 41, 47, 48, 49, 163
7:26
1 & 2 Thessalonians: 266, 280
7:27
Matthew 16–23: 205
Luke 6–10: 206
Romans 9–16: 6
1 & 2 Thessalonians: 266
Hebrews: 55
Revelation 1–11: 313
7–8
1–3 John: 96
8:9
1 & 2 Thessalonians: 264
8:9–14
John 1–11: 439
8:11
Revelation 12–22: 38
8:15–17
Matthew 16–23: 69
Revelation 12–22: 84
8:15–18
Mark 9–16: 401
Luke 1–5: 157
Luke 18–24: 411
8:16–17
1 Peter: 57
8:17
Revelation 1–11: 49
Revelation 12–22: 296
8:23
Matthew 24–28: 18
Mark 9–16: 232
1 & 2 Thessalonians: 65, 266
8:23–25
Matthew 8–15: 48
John 1–11: 439
Revelation 12–22: 37
8:24
1 & 2 Thessalonians: 266
Revelation 1–11: 181
8:24–25
Revelation 12–22: 41
8:25
1 & 2 Thessalonians: 266
Revelation 12–22: 168
8:26
Revelation 1–11: 283
Revelation 12–22: 297
9
1 Timothy: 39
9:2
John 1–11: 17
1 & 2 Thessalonians: 255, 294
9:2–3
Matthew 1–7: 403

9:3
Mark 1–8: 128
Luke 1–5: 185, 339
Luke 6–10: 334
Luke 11–17: 7
Acts 13–28: 5
Revelation 1–11: 299
9:3–19
John 12–21: 234
1 & 2 Thessalonians: 255
9:4
John 12–21: 400
1–3 John: 231
9:4–19
1 & 2 Thessalonians: 187
9:6
James: 258
Revelation 1–11: 320
9:8
1 Peter: 162
9:9
Matthew 8–15: 304
Luke 1–5: 24, 207
2 Corinthians: 50
9:13–19
Luke 18–24: 2
9:16
Revelation 12–22: 130
9:17–19
1 Timothy: 59
9:18
Matthew 8–15: 91
9:19
1 & 2 Thessalonians: 260
9:20
Luke 18–24: 2
1–3 John: 38
9:20–27
Revelation 1–11: 31
9:21–22
Revelation 12–22: 84
9:21–23
1 Peter: 57
9:24
Matthew 24–28: 34, 56
Revelation 12–22: 48, 264
9:24–26
Luke 18–24: 91, 225, 425
1 Peter: 55
9:24–27
Mark 1–8: 147
Luke 11–17: 156
1 & 2 Thessalonians: 142, 266
Revelation 1–11: 179, 294
Revelation 12–22: 4
9:25
Matthew 16–23: 259
Matthew 24–28: 35, 66
John 12–21: 15
9:25–26
Mark 1–8: 15
Luke 1–5: 43, 159
John 12–21: 34
9:25–27
Revelation 1–11: 124
9:26
Matthew 24–28: 35
1 & 2 Thessalonians: 264
Revelation 12–22: 38
9:26–27
Ephesians: 339
Revelation 12–22: 38
9:27
Matthew 24–28: 16, 19, 33, 34, 35, 70, 114
Mark 9–16: 231, 243, 244, 253
Luke 18–24: 225
Romans 9–16: 119
1 & 2 Thessalonians: 146, 265, 266, 274, 281
Revelation 1–11: 178, 191, 192, 230, 231, 294, 295
Revelation 12–22: 28, 49, 58
10
Hebrews: 53
10:4–9
Acts 1–12: 294
10:5–6
John 1–11: 41
Revelation 1–11: 280
10:5–6, 11–13
Romans 9–16: 219
10:6
Revelation 1–11: 97
10:7–9, 16–17
Luke 1–5: 157
10:8–9
Matthew 8–15: 37
Revelation 1–11: 49
10:9
Mark 1–8: 235
10:11
1 Peter: 57
10:12
2 Corinthians: 377
1 Peter: 277
Revelation 12–22: 17
10:12–13
1 Timothy: 39
Revelation 12–22: 16, 85
10:12, 19
Luke 1–5: 27, 157
10:13
Matthew 8–15: 44
Luke 6–10: 222
Ephesians: 332, 341
1 Peter: 57, 209, 282
2 Peter–Jude: 98
Revelation 1–11: 269, 280
Revelation 12–22: 17, 234
10:13–11:1
Acts 13–28: 9
10:13, 21
Luke 1–5: 29
10:16
Luke 18–24: 411
10:20
Luke 6–10: 222
Revelation 1–11: 269
Revelation 12–22: 17
10:21
1 & 2 Thessalonians: 277
1 Peter: 282
2 Peter–Jude: 62
Revelation 12–22: 234
11:21
Matthew 24–28: 34
Revelation 12–22: 168
11:21–35
John 1–11: 439
11:24
Luke 18–24: 225
11:26
Revelation 12–22: 33
11:30
Luke 18–24: 226
11:31
Matthew 24–28: 34
Mark 9–16: 133, 244
Luke 18–24: 225, 242
1 & 2 Thessalonians: 146
Revelation 1–11: 181, 192
Revelation 12–22: 28, 32, 40, 49, 58, 61
11:32
Acts 13–28: 129
11:36
Matthew 24–28: 18
2 Corinthians: 345
1 & 2 Thessalonians: 264, 267
Revelation 12–22: 47, 59, 163
11:36–12:3
Matthew 8–15: 48
11:36–37
Revelation 12–22: 37
11:36–45
John 1–11: 427
1 & 2 Thessalonians: 146, 147
Revelation 1–11: 181
Revelation 12–22: 38–39, 41
11:37
1 & 2 Thessalonians: 267
11:40
Matthew 24–28: 19
Revelation 1–11: 271
11:40–41
Revelation 12–22: 12
11:40–45
Matthew 24–28: 34
11:41
Matthew 24–28: 19
Revelation 12–22: 32
11:41–45
Matthew 24–28: 19–20
11:45
1 & 2 Thessalonians: 267, 280
Revelation 12–22: 117
12:1
Matthew 1–7: 45
Matthew 24–28: 32
Luke 6–10: 342
Luke 18–24: 223
Acts 13–28: 39
Philippians: 273
1 Peter: 282

Revelation 12–22: 17, 234, 255
12:1–2
Matthew 24–28: 16
Mark 9–16: 6, 15
Revelation 12–22: 219
12:1–3
1 & 2 Thessalonians: 249
Revelation 1–11: 31
12:1–11
Revelation 12–22: 28
12:2
Matthew 16–23: 85, 327
Matthew 24–28: 304
Mark 9–16: 185, 396
Luke 11–17: 365
Luke 18–24: 142, 388, 407
John 1–11: 456, 463
Acts 13–28: 307, 371
1 Corinthians: 366, 408, 418
Philippians: 262
1 Timothy: 272
James: 288
1 Peter: 209, 256
1–3 John: 197
Revelation 12–22: 28, 92, 205, 242, 250
12:3
Matthew 1–7: 113, 182
Matthew 8–15: 379
Romans 1–8: 450
2 Corinthians: 148
Philippians: 185
Titus: 105
Revelation 1–11: 105
Revelation 12–22: 307
12:4–10
Revelation 12–22: 297
12:6–7
1 Peter: 57
12:7
Matthew 24–28: 44, 70, 114
Luke 18–24: 227
1 & 2 Thessalonians: 142
Revelation 1–11: 284
Revelation 12–22: 17, 32
12:9
Revelation 1–11: 283
12:11
Matthew 24–28: 34, 36, 70, 114
Luke 18–24: 225
1 & 2 Thessalonians: 142, 146
Revelation 1–11: 181, 192, 295
Revelation 12–22: 28, 32, 49, 58, 61
12:11–12
Revelation 1–11: 297
12:12
Matthew 24–28: 36, 70, 114
Luke 18–24: 228
1 & 2 Thessalonians: 142

Hosea
1:1
Luke 1–5: 205
John 1–11: 17
1:2
Romans 9–16: 44
James: 191, 259
1:3–4, 6, 8–9
Romans 9–16: 45
1:4, 6, 9
Luke 1–5: 90
1:6–10
1 Peter: 132
1:7
Revelation 1–11: 271
1:10
Romans 9–16: 47
Ephesians: 91
1 Peter: 53, 132
Revelation 1–11: 51, 217
2:2
Revelation 12–22: 4
2:14–23
Revelation 1–11: 31
Revelation 12–22: 27
2:14, 19
Romans 9–16: 45
2:16
Revelation 12–22: 203
2:16–20
Mark 1–8: 130
Luke 1–5: 340
2:19
Luke 11–17: 250
Revelation 12–22: 203
2:20
2 Peter–Jude: 24
2:23
Romans 9–16: 44
1 Peter: 53
3
Matthew 1–7: 42
3:4–5
Luke 11–17: 249
Revelation 1–11: 31
Revelation 12–22: 229
3:5
Luke 1–5: 211
Acts 1–12: 53
4:1
1 & 2 Thessalonians: 242, 294
4:6
John 1–11: 33
Acts 1–12: 83
Romans 1–8: 55, 333
Romans 9–16: 56
1 Corinthians: 192
Ephesians: 154
Colossians and Philemon: 29
1 & 2 Thessalonians: 242
1 Peter: 274
4:9
Acts 13–28: 3, 220
1 Timothy: 91, 114, 216
4:11
Luke 1–5: 36

4:17
Matthew 8–15: 462
Matthew 16–23: 288
John 1–11: 418
Acts 1–12: 213
Romans 1–8: 98
1 & 2 Thessalonians: 280
Revelation 1–11: 220
Revelation 12–22: 122, 298
5:4
1 & 2 Thessalonians: 242
2 Peter–Jude: 24
5:5
2 Corinthians: 378
5:6
2 Corinthians: 225
6:1–2
Matthew 16–23: 327
6:2
Matthew 24–28: 232, 304
1 Corinthians: 402
6:3
Colossians and Philemon: 29
James: 167
6:4
2 Corinthians: 353
Galatians: 118
6:5
1 & 2 Thessalonians: 281
6:6
Matthew 8–15: 65
Luke 1–5: 333
2 Corinthians: 353
Philippians: 313
1 & 2 Thessalonians: 96
7:3–7
Luke 11–17: 230
7:13
Revelation 1–11: 251
8:1
Luke 11–17: 20
Revelation 1–11: 251
8:7
Galatians: 187
8:7–14
2 Peter–Jude: 48
9:1
Matthew 8–15: 328
9:4
Philippians: 192
9:7
Mark 9–16: 216
Luke 11–17: 254
Luke 18–24: 99
9:7–9
2 Peter–Jude: 160
9:10
Matthew 24–28: 61
Mark 9–16: 258
Luke 18–24: 243
9:17
1 Peter: 129
10:8
Revelation 1–11: 208, 209
10:12
2 Corinthians: 317

Galatians: 187
10:12–13
2 Peter–Jude: 99
11:1
Matthew 1–7: 42
Matthew 16–23: 307
Romans 1–8: 119
Romans 9–16: 13
Hebrews: 354
11:1–4
Galatians: 118
11:3–4
Matthew 1–7: 42
Romans 1–8: 119
11:7
Romans 1–8: 119
11:8–9
Philippians: 173
11:10
Revelation 1–11: 282
11:12
Luke 1–5: 174
12:7
2 Corinthians: 272
12:10
1 Peter: 51
13:4
Luke 1–5: 153, 168
2 Corinthians: 199
Revelation 1–11: 222
13:6
Mark 9–16: 101
13:14
John 1–11: 194
1 Corinthians: 445
1 Timothy: 272
2 Timothy: 24
13:15
Revelation 1–11: 216
13:16
Matthew 24–28: 43
14:1–2
Matthew 1–7: 65
Galatians: 118
14:1–3
Revelation 1–11: 65
14:2
John 12–21: 149
14:3
Revelation 1–11: 273
14:4
Romans 1–8: 475
Revelation 12–22: 206
14:4–5
Ephesians: 303
14:4–7
Revelation 1–11: 31
14:8
Galatians: 164
14:9
Ephesians: 312
Revelation 12–22: 130

Joel
1:1
Luke 1–5: 205
John 1–11: 17
1:1–2:11
Revelation 12–22: 110
1:1–7
Revelation 1–11: 259
1:4–7
Matthew 24–28: 61
1:4–12
Revelation 1–11: 200
1:5
Ephesians: 242
1:6
Revelation 1–11: 263
1:6–7
Luke 18–24: 243
1:8
Matthew 1–7: 20
1:10
Ephesians: 235
1:13–14
Mark 1–8: 128
Luke 1–5: 339
1:15
Luke 1–5: 216
Luke 11–17: 403
Acts 1–12: 54
2 Corinthians: 37
Philippians: 28
1 & 2 Thessalonians: 144, 145
Revelation 1–11: 200
Revelation 12–22: 121
2
Matthew 1–7: 478
Acts 1–12: 20
2:1
Matthew 24–28: 53
Luke 1–5: 216
1 & 2 Thessalonians: 144, 145
2:1–2
Luke 18–24: 233, 389
Revelation 1–11: 203, 309
2:1–5
Revelation 1–11: 259
2:1–11
Acts 1–12: 54
2:1–17
Revelation 1–11: 200
2:1, 11
Luke 1–5: 216
2:1ff.
Revelation 1–11: 262
2:2
Matthew 24–28: 269
1 & 2 Thessalonians: 158
Revelation 12–22: 145
2:4
Revelation 1–11: 271
2:4–5
Revelation 1–11: 262, 263
2:10
Matthew 24–28: 308
Revelation 1–11: 203, 204, 205, 250
2:10–11
Matthew 24–28: 53
Mark 9–16: 255
2:11
2 Corinthians: 37
Philippians: 28
1 & 2 Thessalonians: 144, 145
Revelation 1–11: 200
2:12
Mark 1–8: 128
2:12–13
Mark 1–8: 339
Luke 11–17: 71
2:12–14, 16
1 Corinthians: 158
2:12, 15
Luke 1–5: 339
2:13
Matthew 8–15: 91
Mark 1–8: 96, 386
Luke 1–5: 40, 153
Luke 6–10: 137
Luke 11–17: 236
Romans 9–16: 198
James: 261
2:15
Mark 1–8: 128
2:18–3:21
Revelation 12–22: 110
2:20
1 Corinthians: 362
2:21–27
Luke 6–10: 206
1 Corinthians: 362
Revelation 12–22: 239
2:23
1 Corinthians: 362
2:23–24
1 & 2 Thessalonians: 184
2:24–27
1 Corinthians: 362
2:25
Acts 1–12: 121
Revelation 1–11: 259
2:26
Acts 1–12: 118
2:27
2 Corinthians: 488
1 Timothy: 275
2:28
Matthew 1–7: 71
Mark 1–8: 26
1 Corinthians: 362, 364
Ephesians: 145
2:28–29
Luke 18–24: 448
John 1–11: 105
Acts 1–12: 67, 75
Ephesians: 91
2:28–32
Matthew 16–23: 59
Luke 18–24: 442
Acts 1–12: 53
1 Corinthians: 362
2 Peter–Jude: 171
Revelation 1–11: 200, 224
Revelation 12–22: 137

2:30
Revelation 1–11: 209, 245, 259
2:30–31
Matthew 24–28: 53
Acts 1–12: 121
1 & 2 Thessalonians: 146
Revelation 1–11: 250
2:31
Matthew 8–15: 327
Mark 9–16: 255
Luke 18–24: 207
1 & 2 Thessalonians: 144, 271
Revelation 1–11: 203, 205
2:32
Romans 9–16: 82
1 Corinthians: 287
2 Timothy: 94, 173
Revelation 12–22: 71
3:1–2
Luke 1–5: 220
Luke 18–24: 233
Revelation 1–11: 31
Revelation 12–22: 211
3:1–14
1 & 2 Thessalonians: 145
3:2
John 1–11: 33
Revelation 12–22: 120, 148
3:2–14
1 & 2 Thessalonians: 146
3:3
Ephesians: 242
3:4
Luke 6–10: 87
3:8
Matthew 8–15: 331
3:9–13
Revelation 12–22: 148
3:9–17
Luke 18–24: 193
Revelation 1–11: 31
3:11–14
Matthew 8–15: 114
3:12
Revelation 12–22: 120
3:12–13
Revelation 12–22: 110
3:12–14
Matthew 24–28: 116
Luke 1–5: 220
Luke 6–10: 327
Revelation 12–22: 211, 220
3:12–16
2 Peter–Jude: 184
3:12–21
Revelation 12–22: 219
3:13
Revelation 12–22: 117
3:14
Luke 1–5: 216
Acts 1–12: 54
1 & 2 Thessalonians: 144, 271
3:14–15
Revelation 12–22: 145
3:14–16
Acts 1–12: 121
3:15
1 & 2 Thessalonians: 146
Revelation 1–11: 250
3:16
Revelation 1–11: 203, 282
Revelation 12–22: 150
3:16–17
Matthew 24–28: 116
3:18
John 1–11: 80
3:18–21
Revelation 1–11: 31
3:20–21
Revelation 12–22: 198

Amos
1:2
1 Peter: 120
Revelation 1–11: 282
1:3
Luke 11–17: 380
1:3–13
Matthew 16–23: 145
1:9
Matthew 8–15: 264
1:9–10
Mark 1–8: 315
1:11–12
Luke 1–5: 22
Romans 9–16: 26
2:2
Luke 6–10: 75
2:4
Romans 9–16: 239
2:6
Matthew 8–15: 180
Mark 1–8: 288
2:6–7
James: 107
2:11
Ephesians: 239
2:12
Ephesians: 239
3:2
Matthew 16–23: 307
Mark 9–16: 132
John 1–11: 152, 398
John 12–21: 20, 56
Romans 1–8: 134, 168, 170, 496
2 Corinthians: 385
Ephesians: 68, 72
Philippians: 229, 235
1 Peter: 20
3:3
2 Corinthians: 250
Hebrews: 311
James: 197
3:6
Luke 6–10: 135
Luke 18–24: 287
3:7
Ephesians: ix
Titus: 3
Hebrews: 10
1 Peter: 51
2 Peter–Jude: 18
Revelation 1–11: 320
3:7–8
1 Peter: 55
3:8
Revelation 1–11: 282
3:11–12
Romans 9–16: 48
4:1
Mark 1–8: 288
James: 107
Revelation 12–22: 191
4:1–3
James: 241
4:2
Luke 18–24: 99
4:4–5
Matthew 1–7: 353
Hebrews: 251
4:11
2 Peter–Jude: 203
4:12
Revelation 12–22: 121
5:4
Mark 9–16: 74
Luke 18–24: 75
5:7
Revelation 1–11: 249
5:10–15
Luke 18–24: 4–5
5:11
Matthew 8–15: 191
Revelation 12–22: 191
5:11–12
James: 107
5:12
James: 250
5:15
James: 250
5:18
Luke 1–5: 216
1 & 2 Thessalonians: 144, 158
Revelation 1–11: 200
5:18–20
Acts 1–12: 54
Revelation 1–11: 200
5:20
Matthew 24–28: 269
Luke 18–24: 389
1 & 2 Thessalonians: 144, 158
Revelation 1–11: 200
5:21
Revelation 1–11: 61
5:21–23
Luke 11–17: 342, 374
5:21–24
Matthew 1–7: 353
Matthew 8–15: 66, 449
Mark 1–8: 121, 339, 354
Luke 1–5: 79, 333
5:21–25
Hebrews: 251
5:21–27
Luke 1–5: 75

5:23
Colossians and Philemon: 160
5:23–24
Ephesians: 260
5:24
Matthew 8–15: 301
5:25–26
Acts 13–28: 19
5:25–27
Acts 1–12: 213
6:1
Hebrews: 373
Revelation 1–11: 251
6:12
Philippians: 53
Revelation 1–11: 249
7:1
Revelation 1–11: 262
7:7–9
Revelation 1–11: 293
7:8
Revelation 1–11: 229
7:10
2 Corinthians: 220
7:10–11
Acts 13–28: 115
7:10–13
Luke 18–24: 124
James: 259
7:12
Acts 13–28: 115
1 & 2 Thessalonians: 306
7:15
John 1–11: 33
7:16
John 12–21: 200
7:17
Revelation 1–11: 293
8:2
Revelation 1–11: 229
8:3
James: 243
8:4–6
Revelation 12–22: 191
8:4–10
James: 241
8:5
Luke 11–17: 333
Romans 1–8: 156
2 Corinthians: 272
8:5–6
Matthew 8–15: 191
8:9
Revelation 1–11: 250
8:10
Ephesians: 260
8:11
Luke 11–17: 413
Acts 13–28: 15
Titus: 13
8:14
Revelation 1–11: 220
9:2
Luke 11–17: 364
9:2–3
Revelation 1–11: 208
9:8
Revelation 12–22: 4
9:8–15
Revelation 1–11: 31
9:10
James: 209
9:11
Matthew 16–23: 346
Mark 9–16: 208
Luke 18–24: 153
Romans 9–16: 119
9:11–12
Luke 18–24: 192
Acts 13–28: 69
9:11–15
Revelation 12–22: 229
9:11ff.
Ephesians: 91
9:13–14
John 1–11: 80

Obadiah
1–14
Luke 1–5: 216
1 & 2 Thessalonians: 145
1–21
Luke 1–5: 22
1:13
John 1–11: 33
3
2 Corinthians: 378
10
Romans 9–16: 26
11–14
Revelation 1–11: 200
15
Luke 1–5: 216
Luke 18–24: 223
Acts 1–12: 54
1 & 2 Thessalonians: 144
15–21
Luke 1–5: 216
1 & 2 Thessalonians: 145
17
Revelation 1–11: 31
21
1 Timothy: 168
Revelation 1–11: 31

Jonah
1–3
Luke 11–17: 224
1:1
Luke 1–5: 205
John 1–11: 17
1:1–2
Luke 6–10: 21
Luke 11–17: 85
1 Timothy: 42
1:2
Romans 9–16: 239
1:3
Romans 9–16: 344
1:7
2 Peter–Jude: 20
1:9
2 Corinthians: 385
Revelation 12–22: 145
1:15–17
Luke 6–10: 21
Luke 18–24: 396
1:17
Matthew 8–15: 329
2:1–2
1 & 2 Thessalonians: 187
2:1–9
Luke 11–17: 2, 7
2:7
James: 275
2:9
Ephesians: 266
1 & 2 Thessalonians: 89
1 Peter: 52, 124
2 Peter–Jude: 28, 202
3:1
John 1–11: 49
3:1–3
Luke 6–10: 21
3:4
Matthew 8–15: 331
Luke 11–17: 87
2 Timothy: 172
3:4–10
Luke 11–17: 369
3:5
Matthew 8–15: 264
Romans 9–16: 80
3:5–6
Matthew 8–15: 330
3:5, 7
Matthew 1–7: 403
3:10
Matthew 1–7: 66
Luke 1–5: 219
3:10–4:4
Acts 1–12: 290
3–4
Luke 11–17: 183
4:1–2
Romans 9–16: 80
Ephesians: 69
4:1–3
Mark 1–8: 363
Luke 6–10: 21
Acts 1–12: 250
Acts 13–28: 36
4:1–9
Philippians: 68
4:1–11
1 Timothy: 60
4:2
Matthew 16–23: 379
Luke 1–5: 153
Luke 6–10: 137
John 1–11: 155
John 12–21: 46
Romans 1–8: 148, 227
Romans 9–16: 198
James: 261
1 Peter: 52

4:11
Luke 18–24: 28

Micah

1:1
Luke 1–5: 205
John 1–11: 17
1:3–4
2 Peter–Jude: 116
2:1
Revelation 1–11: 251
2:1–5
James: 242
2:2
2 Corinthians: 309
2:8
James: 225
2:12
Acts 13–28: 224
2:12–13
Luke 11–17: 210
3:2
Matthew 1–7: 208
3:2–3
2 Corinthians: 424
3:5
Mark 1–8: 288
Mark 9–16: 217
Luke 6–10: 112, 244
Luke 11–17: 131, 345
Luke 18–24: 166
2 Corinthians: 424
1 & 2 Thessalonians: 149
Revelation 1–11: 201
3:5–7
2 Corinthians: 335
2 Peter–Jude: 68
3:8
Luke 1–5: 180, 239
Romans 1–8: 427
3:11
Acts 13–28: 230
James: 249
1 Peter: 269
Revelation 12–22: 56
3:11–12
Romans 1–8: 149
3:12
1 Peter: 120
4:1
Acts 1–12: 53
Romans 9–16: 119
4:1–2
Luke 18–24: 127
4:1–3
Revelation 1–11: 314
4:1–5
Revelation 1–11: 214
4:1–8
Luke 11–17: 210
Revelation 1–11: 31
Revelation 12–22: 229
4:2
Revelation 12–22: 239
4:3
Luke 11–17: 154
Luke 18–24: 190
4:7
Revelation 12–22: 152, 242
4:8
Luke 18–24: 371
Revelation 1–11: 31
4:10
Revelation 12–22: 5
4:12
Matthew 16–23: 2
4:13
Luke 1–5: 97
Revelation 1–11: 168
Revelation 12–22: 42
5
Matthew 1–7: 25, 33
5:1–4
Hebrews: 6
5:2
Matthew 8–15: 329
Matthew 16–23: 346
Matthew 24–28: 118, 232
Mark 1–8: 29, 148
Luke 1–5: 142, 147, 148, 174
Luke 11–17: 210, 226
Luke 18–24: 153, 189, 442
John 1–11: 14, 398, 465
Acts 13–28: 21
2 Corinthians: 290
Colossians and Philemon: 47–48
1 Timothy: 277
Hebrews: 378
Revelation 1–11: 158
Revelation 12–22: 11, 293
5:2–4
Matthew 8–15: 198
5:3
Revelation 12–22: 5
5:4
Acts 13–28: 224
5:13
Revelation 1–11: 273
5:15
Luke 18–24: 223
Revelation 1–11: 189
6:3
John 1–11: 33
6:5
Revelation 12–22: 130
6:6–7
Romans 1–8: 240
6:6–8
Matthew 1–7: 353
6:7
1 Peter: 26
6:8
Matthew 16–23: 384
Luke 1–5: 333
2 Corinthians: 376
1 Peter: 277
1–3 John: 28
6:9
Luke 1–5: 157
6:11
2 Corinthians: 272
7:3
James: 249
7:6
Matthew 8–15: 230
Luke 11–17: 173
7:7
1 Timothy: 5
7:14
John 1–11: 424
Acts 13–28: 224
7:14–20
Revelation 1–11: 31
7:18
Matthew 24–28: 212
Luke 1–5: 322
Luke 6–10: 314
Romans 1–8: 475
2 Corinthians: 50
Colossians and Philemon: 110–11
1 Peter: 32
1–3 John: 23
Revelation 12–22: 47
7:18–19
Matthew 8–15: 53, 304
Luke 1–5: 24, 177
Luke 11–17: 39, 370
2 Corinthians: 19–20, 31
Ephesians: 23
1 Peter: 203
1–3 John: 35
7:19
Matthew 8–15: 52
Mark 1–8: 103, 386
Luke 1–5: 207, 322
Luke 11–17: 42, 236
2 Corinthians: 50, 200, 216
Ephesians: 299
Colossians and Philemon: 42
James: 290

Nahum

1
Matthew 1–7: 479
1:2
Romans 9–16: 202
Colossians and Philemon: 61
1 & 2 Thessalonians: 180
James: 195, 196
Revelation 1–11: 189
1:2–3
Romans 1–8: 70
1:3
Luke 1–5: 91
Luke 11–17: 37
Romans 1–8: 79
2 Corinthians: 315
1:5
Luke 18–24: 390
1:6
2 Peter–Jude: 189
Revelation 1–11: 157, 209
1:7
1 Peter: 84, 120, 153, 280
1:8
James: 195

1:15–3:19
2 Timothy: 151
2:3–4
Revelation 1–11: 151
2:13
Revelation 1–11: 259
3:1
Romans 9–16: 80
Revelation 1–11: 251
Revelation 12–22: 161
3:2–3
Revelation 1–11: 271
3:4
Revelation 12–22: 161
3:15
Revelation 1–11: 259

Habakkuk
1:2
Romans 1–8: 297
1 Peter: 54
1:2–4
Philippians: 33, 277
1:5
Acts 13–28: 27
1:5–11
2 Corinthians: 14
Philippians: 278
1:6
Romans 9–16: 33
1:8
Revelation 1–11: 251
1:12
1 Timothy: 277
Revelation 1–11: 158
Revelation 12–22: 130
1:12–13
2 Corinthians: 14–15
Philippians: 278
1:13
Matthew 24–28: 173, 270
Luke 1–5: 240
Luke 11–17: 41, 369
John 12–21: 291
Romans 1–8: 63, 217, 297
Romans 9–16: 39
2 Corinthians: 215
Colossians and Philemon: 61
James: 48
Revelation 1–11: 155, 195, 277
Revelation 12–22: 131, 216
1:16
1 Corinthians: 233
2:4
Luke 1–5: 24
Luke 11–17: 347, 370
Luke 18–24: 13
Romans 1–8: 57, 232, 367
2 Corinthians: 377
Ephesians: 358
Philippians: 278
Hebrews: 286
2:6
Revelation 1–11: 251
2:11
James: 246
2:11–12
Luke 18–24: 98
2:14
Mark 9–16: 3
1 Peter: 245
Revelation 1–11: 287
2:15–16
Ephesians: 242
2:16
Matthew 16–23: 390
Luke 18–24: 304
2:18–19
Revelation 12–22: 62
2:20
Revelation 1–11: 238
3:2
1 Peter: 31
Revelation 1–11: 212
Revelation 12–22: 133
3:3
Revelation 1–11: 118
3:3–4
Luke 1–5: 156
John 1–11: 334
1 Peter: 253
Revelation 12–22: 279
3:14
Matthew 8–15: 191
3:15
Mark 1–8: 332
3:17–18
Philippians: 33
1 & 2 Thessalonians: 184
James: 17
1 Peter: 40
3:17–19
Romans 1–8: 297
Philippians: 279
3:18
Philippians: 275
1 Timothy: 5

Zephaniah
1:1
Luke 1–5: 205
John 1–11: 17
1:3
Revelation 1–11: 248
1:4
1 Peter: 279
1:4–6
2 Peter–Jude: 73, 160
1:7
Luke 1–5: 216
Luke 18–24: 223
1 & 2 Thessalonians: 144
Revelation 1–11: 238
1:7–14
Luke 1–5: 216
1 & 2 Thessalonians: 145
1:7, 14
Luke 1–5: 216
1:10
Luke 18–24: 436
1:14
1 & 2 Thessalonians: 144
2 Peter–Jude: 64
Revelation 1–11: 209
1:14–15
Matthew 24–28: 269
Luke 18–24: 389
1:14–16
Revelation 1–11: 239
1:14–18
Luke 18–24: 234
Acts 1–12: 54
2 Peter–Jude: 116
Revelation 1–11: 200
Revelation 12–22: 121–22, 224
1:15
1 & 2 Thessalonians: 158
Revelation 1–11: 204
Revelation 12–22: 145
1:18
Luke 1–5: 223
1 Timothy: 257
James: 243, 245
Revelation 1–11: 207
2
Matthew 1–7: 175
2:1–3
1–3 John: 166
2:5
Revelation 1–11: 251
2:8
John 1–11: 33
2:9
James: 269
2:13
1 Peter: 279
2:15
Revelation 12–22: 185
3:1–8
2 Peter–Jude: 83
3:8
Luke 1–5: 220
Revelation 1–11: 31
Revelation 12–22: 123
3:8–20
1 & 2 Thessalonians: 145
3:9
Romans 9–16: 304
3:11–13
Luke 1–5: 49
3:13
Revelation 12–22: 80
3:14
Luke 18–24: 371
3:14–17
Luke 11–17: 293
3:14–20
Revelation 1–11: 31
Revelation 12–22: 229
3:16
1 Peter: 120
3:17
Luke 6–10: 338
2 Corinthians: 241
1–3 John: 23

Haggai
1:1
Luke 1–5: 205, 249
John 1–11: 17, 49
1:1–11
Luke 11–17: 141
1:5
Romans 1–8: 425
2 Corinthians: 461
James: 8
1:7
Romans 1–8: 425
2 Corinthians: 461
James: 8
1:11
Revelation 1–11: 182
2:6
Hebrews: 417
Revelation 12–22: 152
2:6–7
Matthew 24–28: 53
Mark 9–16: 255
Luke 18–24: 234
2:8
Luke 11–17: 333
2:9
Romans 9–16: 119
Revelation 1–11: 294
2:14
Revelation 1–11: 273
2:17
Revelation 1–11: 245
2:22–23
Matthew 24–28: 20

Zechariah
1:1
Matthew 16–23: 394
Luke 11–17: 108
John 1–11: 17, 49
1:3
James: 206
1:6
Revelation 1–11: 320
1:9
Luke 1–5: 27
1:11–21
John 1–11: 41
1:16
1 & 2 Thessalonians: 134
1:17
Luke 1–5: 179
1 Peter: 120
2:1–5
Romans 9–16: 119
Revelation 1–11: 293
2:3
Luke 1–5: 27
2:8
Matthew 1–7: 218
Matthew 16–23: 31, 105
Mark 9–16: 42
Romans 9–16: 127
Revelation 12–22: 126
2:10
Revelation 12–22: 266
2:10–11
Revelation 1–11: 233
2:10–12
Luke 11–17: 211
2:10–13
1 Peter: 55
2:13
Revelation 1–11: 238
3:1
2 Corinthians: 408
Ephesians: 338
1 Peter: 209, 281
1–3 John: 43, 126
Revelation 1–11: 254
Revelation 12–22: 21
3:1–2
Matthew 8–15: 48
Romans 1–8: 507
3:1–5
Luke 18–24: 294
3:1–10
Revelation 1–11: 300
3:2
2 Timothy: 79
2 Peter–Jude: 174, 203
Revelation 12–22: 18
3:3
Revelation 1–11: 231
Revelation 12–22: 308
3:3–4
1–3 John: 85
Revelation 1–11: 139
3:3–5
2 Peter–Jude: 175
3:8–10
Revelation 1–11: 300
3:9–10
Matthew 16–23: 277
4:1
Luke 1–5: 27
4:1–3
Romans 9–16: 121
4:1–10
Revelation 1–11: 25, 108, 151
4:1–14
Revelation 1–11: 299
4:2
Revelation 1–11: 43, 229
4:4–6
Romans 9–16: 121
4:5
Revelation 1–11: 229
4:6
Romans 1–8: 427
Colossians and Philemon: 136
1 & 2 Thessalonians: 195, 204, 259
2 Timothy: 18
Revelation 1–11: 300
4:7–10
Romans 9–16: 121
4:10
Mark 1–8: 329
4:11–14
Romans 9–16: 121
6:12–13
Romans 9–16: 119
Hebrews: 166
Revelation 1–11: 294
6:13
Hebrews: 175
7:5, 9–10
Matthew 1–7: 404
7:9
Luke 6–10: 308
7:10
Luke 18–24: 166
7:12
Luke 1–5: 180
Revelation 1–11: 130
7:14
1 Peter: 129
8:1–8
Luke 18–24: 127
8:1–13
Revelation 12–22: 4
8:3
Revelation 1–11: 233
8:7–8
John 1–11: 33
8:8
Revelation 1–11: 233
Revelation 12–22: 266, 272
8:12
Matthew 16–23: 402
8:16
Ephesians: 183
1 Peter: 192
8:17
Luke 11–17: 374
Titus: 58
Revelation 1–11: 61
8:20–23
Luke 11–17: 211
Acts 13–28: 69
Revelation 1–11: 214
8:22–23
Luke 11–17: 217
8:23
Revelation 12–22: 73
9
2 Peter–Jude: 184
9:9
Matthew 8–15: 309
Matthew 16–23: 222, 259
Matthew 24–28: 118
Mark 9–16: 126, 259
Luke 1–5: 43
Luke 6–10: 61
Luke 18–24: 52, 89, 93, 371
John 12–21: 61
Acts 13–28: 22
2 Corinthians: 325
Philippians: 112
1 & 2 Thessalonians: 184
Titus: 144
Hebrews: 6
1 Peter: 125
1–3 John: 30, 66
Revelation 1–11: 25
Revelation 12–22: 215

9:10
Revelation 1–11: 178
9:14–16
1 & 2 Thessalonians: 134
9:16
Hebrews: 6
10:2
1 Timothy: 14
10:3
Acts 13–28: 224
1 Peter: 140
Revelation 1–11: 178
11:2
James: 243
11:12
Matthew 16–23: 222
Matthew 24–28: 118, 232
Mark 9–16: 168, 316
Luke 18–24: 124, 271
Acts 13–28: 22
11:12–13
Matthew 8–15: 175, 181
Mark 1–8: 419
Mark 9–16: 277
Luke 18–24: 189, 271, 425
John 12–21: 34
11:15–17
1 & 2 Thessalonians: 264
11:16
Matthew 1–7: 462
Matthew 8–15: 295
Romans 9–16: 33
2 Corinthians: 392
11:16–17
John 1–11: 427
2 Timothy: 105
1–3 John: 96
11:17
2 Peter–Jude: 176
12:1
Acts 13–28: 137
12:1–9
Luke 18–24: 223
12:2
Luke 18–24: 304
2 Peter–Jude: 184
12:3–9
Revelation 12–22: 211
12:8–9
Mark 9–16: 247
Luke 18–24: 177
12:8–10
Matthew 16–23: 403
12:8–14
Romans 9–16: 119
12:9
2 Peter–Jude: 184
12:9–10
Luke 11–17: 250
12:10
Matthew 8–15: 343
Matthew 16–23: 222
Matthew 24–28: 118, 262, 267
Mark 1–8: 191
Mark 9–16: 18, 140, 374, 389
Luke 1–5: 101, 110, 120, 131, 136
Luke 6–10: 135
Luke 11–17: 155, 177, 246, 410
Luke 18–24: 51, 96, 98, 177–78, 189, 289, 298, 377, 400, 442
John 1–11: 14
John 12–21: 31, 34, 132, 279, 364
Acts 1–12: 72, 111
Acts 13–28: 24, 375
Romans 1–8: 171
Romans 9–16: 6, 110, 118
1 Corinthians: 158
2 Corinthians: 98
1 & 2 Thessalonians: 66
1 Peter: 55, 282
Revelation 1–11: 7, 33, 123, 194
Revelation 12–22: 27, 79
12:10–11
Matthew 24–28: 54
Mark 9–16: 258
12:10–13:1
Mark 1–8: 148
Acts 1–12: 120, 205
Revelation 1–11: 215, 219, 293, 294
Revelation 12–22: 4, 11
12:10–14
Luke 18–24: 371
Revelation 12–22: 70
12:10–14:9
Acts 1–12: 121
12:10ff.
Revelation 1–11: 223
12:11–12
Matthew 16–23: 404
12:12
1 Corinthians: 158
12–14
Luke 1–5: 131
13:1
Luke 1–5: 131
Luke 11–17: 250, 411
Luke 18–24: 99, 178
John 1–11: 54, 105
John 12–21: 31, 34
Acts 1–12: 72, 303
Romans 9–16: 110
1 Peter: 282
Revelation 1–11: 33
Revelation 12–22: 70
13:1–2
Matthew 16–23: 404
Romans 9–16: 119
13:1, 8
Luke 1–5: 211
13:2–6
Matthew 24–28: 160
13:3
Matthew 8–15: 209
13:4
Matthew 1–7: 465
2 Corinthians: 335
2 Timothy: 105
13:7
Matthew 16–23: 222
Mark 9–16: 94, 296, 316
Luke 1–5: 340
Luke 18–24: 52, 295, 316
2 Corinthians: 423
1 Peter: 55, 270
13:8
1 & 2 Thessalonians: 265
13:8–9
Matthew 24–28: 41, 50
Mark 9–16: 246
Romans 1–8: 479
Revelation 1–11: 215, 219, 293, 295, 297
Revelation 12–22: 4, 28, 62
13:8–14:2
Matthew 24–28: 32–33
13:9
Matthew 16–23: 43
Matthew 24–28: 14, 41
1 Peter: 43
Revelation 12–22: 70
13–14
Revelation 1–11: 31
14
Acts 1–12: 205
14:1
Matthew 24–28: 3
Luke 1–5: 216
Luke 18–24: 223
1 & 2 Thessalonians: 144
Revelation 1–11: 200
Revelation 12–22: 137
14:1–3
Luke 18–24: 203
Revelation 12–22: 150
14:1–4
Revelation 12–22: 117
14:1–5
Revelation 1–11: 295
14:1–11
Matthew 16–23: 403
Luke 18–24: 223
14:1–13
Revelation 12–22: 226
14:1ff.
Acts 1–12: 120
14:2
Luke 18–24: 178
14:2–3
Matthew 24–28: 20
Mark 9–16: 232
Revelation 12–22: 148
14:3
Matthew 16–23: 404
14:3–4
Revelation 12–22: 211
14:4
Matthew 16–23: 69
Matthew 24–28: 115
Luke 1–5: 101
Luke 11–17: 156
Luke 18–24: 221, 223, 452

Acts 1–12: 23, 28
Revelation 12–22: 71, 152, 212, 242, 302
14:4–8
Philippians: 263
14:4–9
Luke 11–17: 154, 415
1 Peter: 282
Revelation 1–11: 29
14:4–10
Revelation 12–22: 152
14:5
Revelation 12–22: 224
14:5b–7
John 1–11: 334
14:6–7
Matthew 24–28: 55
Mark 9–16: 254
Luke 18–24: 231
14:8
Matthew 16–23: 38
Matthew 24–28: 3, 57
Revelation 12–22: 152
14:8–9
Matthew 8–15: 343
Matthew 16–23: 404
14:9
Matthew 16–23: 66
Luke 1–5: 131
Acts 1–12: 15
Romans 9–16: 304
Philippians: 263
Revelation 1–11: 314
14:9–11
Hebrews: 52
Revelation 12–22: 229, 242
14:9, 11, 16
Romans 9–16: 110
14:10
Revelation 12–22: 152
14:10–11
Matthew 16–23: 38
14:11
Matthew 24–28: 3
14:12
Revelation 12–22: 140
14:16
Matthew 16–23: 66
Revelation 12–22: 131, 239
14:16–17
1 Peter: 55
14:16–19
Mark 9–16: 7
Luke 6–10: 285
Revelation 12–22: 240
14:16–21
Luke 1–5: 49
Luke 6–10: 85
1 Peter: 282
14:20
Revelation 1–11: 171
Revelation 12–22: 133
14:20–21
John 1–11: 91

Malachi
1:1
John 1–11: 17
John 12–21: 200
1 & 2 Thessalonians: 294
1:2–3
Luke 11–17: 283
Romans 9–16: 26
1:6
Luke 11–17: 14
Colossians and Philemon: 181
1 Peter: 30
1:6–7
Matthew 8–15: 449
1:6–8
1–3 John: 26
1:8
Romans 9–16: 147
1:14
1 & 2 Thessalonians: 254
2
1 Peter: 108
2:1–3
1 Peter: 113
2:1–4
1–3 John: 27
2:6–7
1 Peter: 113
2:7
Luke 1–5: 23
2:9
James: 94
2:10
Matthew 1–7: 375
1 Peter: 30
2:11
John 1–11: 205
2:13–16
Matthew 1–7: 312
2:14–16
Matthew 16–23: 162, 166
2:16
Matthew 1–7: 318
Mark 9–16: 52, 53
1 Corinthians: 165
Ephesians: 302
1 Timothy: 105
Titus: 28
2:17
Romans 1–8: 217
2 Peter–Jude: 112
3
Matthew 1–7: 253
3:1
Mark 1–8: 16, 17, 18
Mark 9–16: 7, 17
Luke 1–5: 21, 38, 117, 160, 175, 200, 245
Luke 6–10: 156, 285
John 1–11: 51, 136
Acts 13–28: 22
Romans 9–16: 119
3:1–3
John 1–11: 91
1 Peter: 250
3:2
Revelation 1–11: 157
Revelation 12–22: 302
3:2–3
1 & 2 Thessalonians: 194
3:2–6
2 Peter–Jude: 184
3:5
1 & 2 Thessalonians: 156
James: 242, 246
3:6
Matthew 16–23: 162
Romans 9–16: 31
Galatians: 169
James: 55
3:8
Luke 11–17: 130
2 Corinthians: 272, 282
3:8–9
Romans 1–8: 156
3:8–10
1 Corinthians: 455
3:8, 10
Romans 9–16: 232
3:10
Ephesians: 359
3:16
Romans 9–16: 101
Revelation 12–22: 255
3:16–4:2
Revelation 1–11: 214, 280, 309
3:16–4:3
2 Peter–Jude: 91–92
3:16–17
Philippians: 167, 273
Hebrews: 154
Revelation 1–11: 104, 113, 278
Revelation 12–22: 69, 149
3:16–18
Matthew 24–28: 76
Ephesians: 302
1 & 2 Thessalonians: 156
3:17
Ephesians: 30
1 Peter: 130
Revelation 1–11: 148
4:1
Matthew 1–7: 70
Matthew 16–23: 231
2 Corinthians: 377–78
Ephesians: 121
Revelation 1–11: 200, 281
Revelation 12–22: 137
4:1–2
Revelation 1–11: 189
4:1–3
2 Peter–Jude: 116
4:1–4
Revelation 1–11: 29
4:2
Matthew 8–15: 75
Luke 1–5: 20, 122, 200
Hebrews: 154
4:4
Luke 6–10: 284

Romans 1–8: 357
2 Peter–Jude: 18
4:5
Matthew 1–7: 478
Matthew 16–23: 19
Mark 1–8: 24, 302, 415
Luke 1–5: 117, 216
Luke 18–24: 223
John 1–11: 51
1 & 2 Thessalonians: 144, 145, 156, 271
Revelation 1–11: 200, 209, 301
Revelation 12–22: 137, 302
4:5–6
Matthew 1–7: 52
Matthew 8–15: 257
Matthew 16–23: 71
Mark 9–16: 17
Revelation 1–11: 214
4:6
Matthew 1–7: 132
Mark 9–16: 17

Matthew
1:1
Mark 9–16: 115
Luke 1–5: 50
Acts 13–28: 22
Titus: 162
Revelation 12–22: 11, 307
1:1–2
James: 98
1:1–16
Luke 1–5: 149
1:1–17
Matthew 1–7: 73
Mark 9–16: 208
Luke 18–24: 153
Romans 9–16: 15
Hebrews: 177
1:3
James: 99
1:5
Matthew 16–23: 248, 331
Luke 1–5: 246
Luke 6–10: 14
Hebrews: 364
James: 99, 140
1:5–7
James: 989
1:6
Matthew 16–23: 346
Mark 9–16: 116
Romans 1–8: 14
1:10
James: 98
1:11
Luke 1–5: 247
1:16
Matthew 1–7: 15
Romans 1–8: 14
1:16, 18, 19, 20, 24
Luke 1–5: 246
1:18
2 Corinthians: 214
1:18–2:12
Luke 1–5: 42
1:18–19
Matthew 16–23: 170
Revelation 12–22: 201
1:18–25
Luke 1–5: 67
2 Timothy: 141
1–3 John: 100
1:19
Matthew 1–7: 15, 317
Mark 9–16: 60
Luke 1–5: 68, 148, 166
Galatians: 168
James: 250
1:19–25
Luke 1–5: 60
1:20
Matthew 8–15: 298
Luke 6–10: 84
James: 154
Revelation 12–22: 84
1:20–21
Luke 1–5: 147
Philippians: 130
1:20–21, 24–25
Luke 1–5: 68
1:20–23
Matthew 1–7: 37, 40
Luke 1–5: 163
1 & 2 Thessalonians: 202
1:21
Matthew 1–7: 3
Mark 1–8: 15, 102
Mark 9–16: 91, 119
Luke 1–5: 13, 48, 81, 90, 120, 154, 159, 167, 171, 181, 281, 321
Luke 6–10: 139, 203, 205
Luke 11–17: 394
Luke 18–24: 68, 173, 366
John 1–11: 2
John 12–21: 88, 228
Acts 1–12: 108
Acts 13–28: 336
Romans 1–8: 54
2 Corinthians: 133, 289
1 & 2 Thessalonians: 14
1 Timothy: 33
Hebrews: 416
James: 225, 290
1 Peter: 171, 191
2 Peter–Jude: 23
1–3 John: 30, 206
1:22–23
Luke 1–5: 174
1:23
Matthew 1–7: x, 76
Matthew 24–28: 232
Mark 1–8: 175
Luke 1–5: 48, 49, 55, 56, 234
Luke 6–10: 144
Luke 18–24: 355
James: 154
1:24–25
Luke 1–5: 148
1:25
Luke 1–5: 56, 149
Romans 1–8: 496
1 & 2 Thessalonians: 14
James: 10
2:1
Matthew 1–7: 51, 75
Mark 1–8: 300
Mark 9–16: 349
Luke 1–5: 175
Acts 13–28: 8, 21
2:1–3
Luke 1–5: 145
2:1–12
Luke 1–5: 189
2:1–19
Luke 1–5: 230
Acts 13–28: 327
2:1–22
Luke 1–5: 22
2:2
Matthew 8–15: 9
Luke 1–5: 23
Revelation 1–11: 25
2:3
John 12–21: 38
Galatians: 15
2:5–6
Mark 9–16: 387
2:7–18
1 & 2 Thessalonians: 264
2:8
1 & 2 Thessalonians: 143
2:11
Matthew 1–7: 25
Matthew 24–28: 253
Luke 1–5: 171
1 Corinthians: 453
1 Peter: 44
Revelation 1–11: 69
2:13
1 Peter: 57
Revelation 12–22: 10, 84
2:13–15
Luke 1–5: 189
2:13–23
Matthew 1–7: 21, 73
2:13, 14, 19–21
Luke 1–5: 246
2:13, 17, 23
Matthew 1–7: 19
2:13, 19–20, 22
Matthew 1–7: 37
2:15
Acts 1–12: 320
Hebrews: 354
2:16
Matthew 1–7: 26, 32
Mark 1–8: 300
Luke 11–17: 194
Luke 18–24: 266
John 1–11: 24
John 12–21: 363
Acts 1–12: 320
Romans 9–16: 209
Revelation 12–22: 10

2:16–18
Luke 1–5: 23, 189
1 Peter: 210
2:19
Mark 1–8: 300
Revelation 12–22: 84
2:19–23
Luke 1–5: 189
2:22
Matthew 8–15: 417
Mark 1–8: 300
2:23
Mark 1–8: 273
Luke 18–24: 60
3
Matthew 1–7: 53, 59, 74, 76, 79, 105
3:1
Luke 1–5: 86, 204
Luke 6–10: 154
John 1–11: 29
Revelation 1–11: 291
Revelation 12–22: 32
3:1–2
Matthew 8–15: 187
Luke 6–10: 158
Acts 1–12: 114
Ephesians: 11
2 Timothy: 172
3:1–3
Luke 1–5: 175
3:1–5
John 12–21: 74
3:1–6
Luke 1–5: 39
3:1–10
Matthew 1–7: 125
3:1–12
Matthew 1–7: 73
John 1–11: 29
3:2
Matthew 8–15: 275, 418
Matthew 16–23: 96, 193
Mark 1–8: 303
Mark 9–16: 227
Luke 1–5: 117
Luke 6–10: 272, 324
Luke 11–17: 188, 250, 274
John 1–11: 49, 51
Acts 1–12: 73
Romans 1–8: 147
Ephesians: x, 174
1 & 2 Thessalonians: 297
2 Timothy: 177
Hebrews: 138
Revelation 1–11: 139
3:2, 6, 11
Matthew 1–7: 75
3:2, 8, 11
Titus: 116
3:3
Mark 1–8: 17
Luke 1–5: 117
John 1–11: 29
3:4
Matthew 8–15: 253, 261
Luke 1–5: 34
Luke 6–10: 14, 165
3:5
Matthew 8–15: 418
Mark 1–8: 304
Luke 1–5: 205, 214
John 1–11: 49
3:5–6
Matthew 16–23: 291
Luke 1–5: 205
Luke 6–10: 162
3:5–8
Matthew 16–23: 377
3:6
Matthew 16–23: 287
Matthew 24–28: 343
Luke 1–5: 205, 209
3:6–8
Acts 1–12: 115
3:7
Matthew 8–15: 420
Matthew 16–23: 3, 388
Mark 1–8: 22, 127, 305
Luke 1–5: 217
Luke 6–10: 152
Luke 11–17: 190
Romans 1–8: 189
2 Corinthians: 188
1 & 2 Thessalonians: 66, 163
3:7–8
Mark 1–8: 21, 31
Romans 1–8: 70
Philippians: 210
3:7–9
Matthew 16–23: 291
Romans 1–8: 150
James: 120
3:7–10
Matthew 8–15: 252
Mark 9–16: 157–58
Luke 1–5: 87, 117
John 1–11: 50
3:7–11
Luke 1–5: 38
3:7–12
Luke 1–5: 205, 210
3:8
Matthew 16–23: 299
Mark 1–8: 212
John 12–21: 23, 86, 148
Acts 13–28: 337
2 Corinthians: 266
Colossians and Philemon: 222
1 & 2 Thessalonians: 97
James: 8
Revelation 1–11: 139
3:8–9
Mark 1–8: 21
3:9
Romans 1–8: 161
Galatians: 123
3:9–10
Acts 1–12: 70
3:10
Ephesians: 209
2 Timothy: 193
2 Peter–Jude: 181
3:10–12
John 1–11: 51
Revelation 12–22: 256
3:11
Matthew 8–15: 240
Matthew 16–23: 232
1 Corinthians: 311, 312
Ephesians: 122
3:11–12
Matthew 8–15: 245
Acts 1–12: 41
Romans 1–8: 71
Revelation 12–22: 137
3:11, 14
Matthew 8–15: 251
3:12
Matthew 24–28: 62
Mark 1–8: 22
Luke 11–17: 365, 366
1 & 2 Thessalonians: 163, 235, 239
James: 245
Revelation 12–22: 92
3:13
Matthew 1–7: 51
3:13–17
Mark 1–8: 28, 127
Luke 1–5: 57
Acts 1–12: 302
1 Corinthians: 266
1 & 2 Thessalonians: 202
3:14
Matthew 8–15: 328
Mark 1–8: 30
Luke 1–5: 236
1 Corinthians: 106
3:15
Matthew 24–28: 143
Mark 1–8: 31
Luke 1–5: 167, 197, 237
John 12–21: 254
1–3 John: 193
3:16
Matthew 8–15: 298
3:16–17
Romans 1–8: 17
1–3 John: 163
3:17
Matthew 1–7: 84
Matthew 8–15: 297, 340
Matthew 16–23: 68
Matthew 24–28: 194
Luke 11–17: 120
Luke 18–24: 422
John 12–21: 40, 135, 181, 254, 292
Romans 9–16: 74
1 Corinthians: 287
2 Corinthians: 214
Ephesians: 19, 123
Philippians: 128, 130, 150
1 Timothy: 140
Hebrews: 279
4:1
Matthew 8–15: 313

Mark 1–8: 42
Acts 1–12: 13
1 Corinthians: 228
Ephesians: 250
1 Timothy: 130
James: 46, 48
Revelation 1–11: 310
4:1–10
Romans 1–8: 480
Hebrews: 378, 450
4:1–11
Luke 18–24: 300
John 1–11: 24
Galatians: 167
Philippians: 130
1 & 2 Thessalonians: 198, 265, 298
1 Timothy: 50
Titus: 55
1 Peter: 166, 210, 226, 282
Revelation 1–11: 255
Revelation 12–22: 10
4:2
Mark 1–8: 44, 229
Mark 9–16: 133
Luke 6–10: 128
2 Corinthians: 293
4:3
Matthew 1–7: 86
4:3–4
Mark 1–8: 44
Philippians: 125
4:3–9
Ephesians: 359
4:3–10
Matthew 24–28: 169
Ephesians: 338
1 & 2 Thessalonians: 71
4:4
Mark 1–8: 16
Romans 1–8: 181
1 Corinthians: 63
1 & 2 Thessalonians: 194, 196
2 Timothy: 150
1 Peter: 192
1–3 John: 72
4:4–11
1 & 2 Thessalonians: 91
4:4, 7, 10
Matthew 1–7: 264
Ephesians: 370
4:5
Revelation 12–22: 264
4:5–6
John 12–21: 13
4:5–7
Mark 1–8: 45
4:6
Ephesians: 338
2 Timothy: 118
4:6–7
Romans 1–8: 181
4:8
Luke 1–5: 258
4:8–9
Matthew 8–15: 438
Matthew 24–28: 339
Mark 1–8: 327
4:8–10
Mark 1–8: 44
4:9
Revelation 12–22: 15
4:10
Matthew 8–15: 76
Matthew 16–23: 41
Mark 1–8: 256
Mark 9–16: 211
Luke 1–5: 74, 261
Luke 18–24: 157
John 1–11: 15
Romans 1–8: 181
Philippians: 222
Colossians and Philemon: 120
1 Timothy: 280
1 Peter: 200
Revelation 1–11: 170
Revelation 12–22: 87, 207, 296
4:11
Mark 9–16: 304
Luke 1–5: 257
Luke 18–24: 305
James: 205
1 Peter: 57–58, 220
4:12
Matthew 8–15: 68, 418
Mark 1–8: 47, 304
Luke 1–5: 39, 228
John 1–11: 3
4:12–16
Luke 1–5: 182
1 & 2 Thessalonians: 155
2 Peter–Jude: 62
4:12–17
Matthew 1–7: 103, 122
4:13
Mark 1–8: 60
Mark 9–16: 36
Luke 1–5: 282, 331
Luke 6–10: 25, 123, 126
4:13–18:35
Luke 1–5: 265
4:15
James: 4
4:15–16
Matthew 24–28: 312
4:16
Acts 13–28: 336
Hebrews: 142
4:17
Matthew 8–15: 105
Matthew 16–23: 96, 285
Mark 9–16: 42
Luke 1–5: 281, 341
Luke 6–10: 84, 88, 94, 158, 180, 181, 272
Luke 11–17: 23, 24, 188, 216, 402
John 12–21: 183
Acts 1–12: 48, 73, 114
Acts 13–28: 216
Romans 1–8: 147
Ephesians: x, 11, 174
1 & 2 Thessalonians: 297
2 Timothy: 177
Titus: 116
Hebrews: 138
1–3 John: 38
Revelation 1–11: 139, 291
4:18
Matthew 8–15: 60
Luke 1–5: 292, 304
Luke 6–10: 25, 39, 40
1 Peter: 4
2 Peter–Jude: 2
4:18–19
Matthew 8–15: 146, 394
4:18–21
Matthew 8–15: 136
4:18–22
Matthew 1–7: 122
Luke 1–5: 291, 304
John 1–11: 2, 8, 58
4:19
Matthew 24–28: 341
Luke 6–10: 40
John 12–21: 391, 401
Philippians: 253
1 & 2 Thessalonians: 97
2 Peter–Jude: 3
4:20–22
Matthew 8–15: 328
4:21
Matthew 24–28: 285
Luke 6–10: 40
2 Corinthians: 478, 483
4:22
Luke 6–10: 40
4:23
Matthew 8–15: 104, 238
Matthew 24–28: 339
Mark 1–8: 271
Mark 9–16: 119
Luke 1–5: 293
Luke 6–10: 294
Luke 11–17: 217, 387
Luke 18–24: 64, 113
John 12–21: 331
Acts 1–12: 15
2 Corinthians: 347
Colossians and Philemon: 12
James: 147
1–3 John: 16
Revelation 12–22: 86
4:23–24
Matthew 8–15: 4
Mark 1–8: 84
John 1–11: 218
1 Peter: 32
1–3 John: 17
Revelation 1–11: 263
4:23–25
Matthew 8–15: 246
4:24
Matthew 16–23: 78
Matthew 24–28: 339
Mark 1–8: 63, 101, 242, 274
Mark 9–16: 118

Luke 1–5: 283, 293
Luke 18–24: 63
Acts 1–12: 234
4:24–25
Matthew 8–15: 467, 477
4:25
Luke 6–10: 41
2 Peter–Jude: 11
5:1
Matthew 8–15: 32
Luke 1–5: 304
Luke 6–10: 86
Acts 13–28: 92
5:1–7:27
1–3 John: 64
5:1–11
Luke 18–24: 444
5:1–12
Luke 1–5: 206
5:2–7
2 Corinthians: 102
5:3
Matthew 8–15: 51, 270, 358
Matthew 16–23: 48, 97
Mark 1–8: 369
Luke 1–5: 270, 315, 341
Luke 6–10: 318
John 12–21: 108
Acts 1–12: 242
Romans 1–8: 224
2 Corinthians: 112, 294, 344, 468
Ephesians: 44, 122
Philippians: 112, 124
James: 40, 106, 179, 200, 213
5:3–4
Luke 18–24: 387
5:3–4, 6
Matthew 1–7: 455
5:3–5
Luke 11–17: 264
1 Peter: 277
5:3–6
Matthew 8–15: 474
Luke 11–17: 83
5:3–11
2 Corinthians: 208
Ephesians: 230
5:3–12
Matthew 1–7: 132, 136
Matthew 8–15: 27
Matthew 16–23: 149
James: 9
Revelation 1–11: 22
Revelation 12–22: 95
5:4
John 12–21: 120
2 Corinthians: 20, 468
James: 212, 243
1–3 John: 73
Revelation 1–11: 139
5:5
Matthew 1–7: 97
1 Corinthians: 92
2 Corinthians: 468
Ephesians: 124
Philippians: 112
Titus: 145
James: 40, 75, 169, 179
2 Peter–Jude: 49
5:6
Matthew 1–7: 479
Matthew 8–15: 195, 430
Mark 1–8: 320, 321
Acts 1–12: 301
Romans 1–8: 390
1 Corinthians: 109
2 Corinthians: 469
Philippians: 245
2 Timothy: 200
James: 179
Revelation 1–11: 139
Revelation 12–22: 271, 305
5:7
Matthew 1–7: 394
Matthew 16–23: 156
Mark 1–8: 121
Luke 1–5: 333
Colossians and Philemon: 202
James: 117, 179
5:8
Matthew 8–15: 464
Mark 1–8: 339
John 12–21: 239, 300
Philippians: 31, 263
1 Timothy: 278
James: 177
Revelation 12–22: 260, 266, 267, 288
5:9
John 1–11: 18
John 12–21: 43
Ephesians: 79
Philippians: 273
James: 178
1 Peter: 193
5:10
Matthew 16–23: 237
Luke 18–24: 297
Romans 1–8: 281
5:10–11
Matthew 8–15: 203
James: 23
5:10–12
Matthew 1–7: 145
Acts 1–12: 166
Romans 1–8: 281, 447, 511
Philippians: 180
1 & 2 Thessalonians: 97, 178, 184, 298
James: 179, 252
1 Peter: 199, 252
5:11
John 12–21: 174
Romans 1–8: 281
1 & 2 Thessalonians: 199
James: 37
1 Peter: 7
5:11–12
Matthew 16–23: 237
Luke 11–17: 239
1 & 2 Thessalonians: 79
2 Timothy: 198
5:12
Romans 1–8: 281
2 Corinthians: 349
Philippians: 248, 260
1 & 2 Thessalonians: 52, 185
1 Peter: 41
Revelation 1–11: 319
Revelation 12–22: 260
5:13
Mark 9–16: 49
John 12–21: 156
Ephesians: 172
2 Peter–Jude: 196
5:13–14
Matthew 1–7: 231
Luke 11–17: 73
Acts 13–28: 180
Colossians and Philemon: 164–65
1 & 2 Thessalonians: 277
5:13–16
Matthew 8–15: 345
1 Corinthians: 131
Hebrews: 372, 404
James: 9
5:14
Luke 11–17: 77
Ephesians: 208–209
Philippians: 185
1 & 2 Thessalonians: 157
1 Timothy: 228
James: 200
1–3 John: 2
5:14–16
Matthew 1–7: 145
Mark 1–8: 213
Luke 6–10: 199
Romans 1–8: 154
1 Peter: 153
5:15–16
Matthew 1–7: 231
1 Peter: 160
5:16
Matthew 1–7: 349, 378
Luke 11–17: 16
Acts 13–28: 129
1 Corinthians: 15
Philippians: 166, 185, 186, 314
1 & 2 Thessalonians: 121, 248, 260
Titus: 31, 89, 96, 118, 123
Hebrews: 421
James: 120
1 Peter: 31, 136, 140
1–3 John: 68, 171
5:17
Matthew 8–15: 281
Matthew 16–23: 23, 259
Matthew 24–28: 143
Luke 6–10: 71
Luke 11–17: 170
John 12–21: 283
Acts 13–28: 53
Romans 1–8: 228, 406

Romans 9–16: 323
2 Corinthians: 415
Hebrews: 4
5:17–18
Matthew 16–23: 337
Mark 9–16: 192, 199
Romans 1–8: 13
Romans 9–16: 67
2 Corinthians: 417
2 Timothy: 145
1–3 John: 57
5:17–19
Matthew 8–15: 70
Mark 1–8: 132
Luke 1–5: 341
Luke 11–17: 391
Romans 1–8: 358
Romans 9–16: 253
5:17–20
Galatians: 123
James: 9, 86
5:17–48
Luke 11–17: 351
5:18
Mark 9–16: 260
Luke 6–10: 93, 333
Luke 11–17: 351
Luke 18–24: 244
John 12–21: 204, 283
1 & 2 Thessalonians: 198
2 Peter–Jude: 49, 57
Revelation 1–11: 133
Revelation 12–22: 249
5:18–19
James: 114
5:18, 26
Matthew 1–7: 321
5:19
James: 114
5:19–20
1 Peter: 127
5:20
Matthew 1–7: 134, 139, 145, 148, 452, 481
Matthew 8–15: 63, 334, 452, 455
Matthew 16–23: 171, 312, 355, 358
Mark 1–8: 347
Luke 1–5: 206, 319
Luke 11–17: 43, 84, 103, 256
Luke 18–24: 16
Romans 1–8: 370, 410
Romans 9–16: 66, 127
2 Corinthians: 468, 469
Ephesians: 352
5:20–22
Romans 1–8: 114
5:20–48
Mark 9–16: 80
5:20, 22, 28, 48
Galatians: 95
5:21
Matthew 8–15: 53
Romans 1–8: 12
James: 249
5:21–6:18
Matthew 1–7: 253
5:21–22
Luke 11–17: 381
John 1–11: 170
Romans 1–8: 228, 370
2 Corinthians: 50, 469
Ephesians: 185
Colossians and Philemon: 218
James: 223
1–3 John: 67, 134
5:21–22, 27–28
Romans 9–16: 251
5:21–30
1 Corinthians: 213
5:21–37
Matthew 8–15: 463
Mark 1–8: 358
5:21–47
Luke 1–5: 206
Luke 18–24: 12
5:21–48
Matthew 16–23: 359
Mark 1–8: 339
Mark 9–16: 92
Hebrews: 188
James: 9
5:22
Matthew 8–15: 396
Matthew 16–23: 191
Mark 9–16: 47
Luke 11–17: 99, 118, 356
Romans 1–8: 71
2 Corinthians: 465
Galatians: 56, 77
Colossians and Philemon: 144
1 & 2 Thessalonians: 180
James: 157, 288
1 Peter: 210
2 Peter–Jude: 186
Revelation 1–11: 257
Revelation 12–22: 256
5:22, 27–28
Matthew 1–7: 277
5:22, 29
Matthew 1–7: 70
5:23–24
Matthew 1–7: 216
Luke 11–17: 45
John 12–21: 90
2 Corinthians: 52, 57
1 & 2 Thessalonians: 110
5:24
Ephesians: 347
5:25
Luke 18–24: 4
Romans 1–8: 99
5:27
Romans 1–8: 12
5:27–28
Mark 1–8: 150
John 1–11: 170
Romans 1–8: 114, 228, 370
2 Corinthians: 469
1 & 2 Thessalonians: 105
5:28
Matthew 16–23: 167, 191
Mark 9–16: 55
Luke 11–17: 412
Romans 1–8: 156
Galatians: 56
Colossians and Philemon: 138–39
Titus: 28
5:29
1 Corinthians: 417
1 & 2 Thessalonians: 173
Hebrews: 276
James: 245
Revelation 12–22: 256
5:29–30
Matthew 1–7: 216
Mark 9–16: 44, 47
Romans 1–8: 71, 423
Colossians and Philemon: 136
James: 288
1–3 John: 40
5:30
Revelation 12–22: 256
5:31–32
Mark 9–16: 54
Luke 11–17: 352
Romans 1–8: 360, 370
1 Corinthians: 165
Ephesians: 302
1 Timothy: 105, 212
5:31–34
John 1–11: 170
5:32
Matthew 16–23: 106, 164, 171
Romans 1–8: 156
1 Corinthians: 165
1 & 2 Thessalonians: 111
Titus: 28
5:33
Mark 1–8: 307
Romans 1–8: 12
5:33–36
James: 264
5:33–37
Romans 1–8: 370
2 Corinthians: 43, 469
Hebrews: 167
James: 269
5:34
Revelation 12–22: 262
5:34–35
Matthew 16–23: 191
Revelation 1–11: 284
5:34–37
Matthew 16–23: 382
5:35
Titus: 121
5:37
James: 161, 270
5:38
Romans 1–8: 12
Revelation 12–22: 183
5:38–39
John 1–11: 170

5:38–42
Matthew 8–15: 149
2 Corinthians: 469
5:38–45a
1 Peter: 189
5:38–48
1 & 2 Thessalonians: 236
5:39
1 Corinthians: 338
5:39–40
1 Corinthians: 140
5:39–41
1 Corinthians: 213
5:39–42
James: 250
5:40
Luke 6–10: 106
5:40–41
1 Corinthians: 339
5:41
Matthew 24–28: 235
Luke 18–24: 368
5:42
Matthew 1–7: 146
Romans 9–16: 246
5:43
Matthew 1–7: 188
Luke 6–10: 103
Romans 1–8: 12
Titus: 127
5:43–44
John 1–11: 170
Ephesians: 127
1 & 2 Thessalonians: 181
1 Timothy: 67
Hebrews: 426
2 Peter–Jude: 196
5:43–46
Philippians: 42
5:43–47
Mark 9–16: 203
5:43–48
James: 91
5:44
Luke 18–24: 3
John 12–21: 64, 267
Romans 9–16: 247
2 Corinthians: 229
1 & 2 Thessalonians: 17, 90
1 Peter: 192
1–3 John: 67
5:44–45
Matthew 1–7: 216
Luke 11–17: 43, 380
1 Corinthians: 329
2 Corinthians: 50, 52
Colossians and Philemon: 220
1–3 John: 244
5:44–45, 48
Matthew 1–7: 394
5:44–47
Matthew 1–7: 188
5:45
Mark 1–8: 313
Luke 6–10: 93, 108, 251
Luke 11–17: 395
John 12–21: 267
Acts 1–12: 116
Acts 13–28: 140
2 Corinthians: 192, 204
Ephesians: 29, 172
Philippians: 166, 314
1 Timothy: 67, 168
1 Peter: 31
1–3 John: 166
5:46
Matthew 1–7: 188
Romans 1–8: 285
Ephesians: 199
Titus: 83
Hebrews: 426
5:48
Matthew 1–7: 138, 148, 205, 280
Matthew 8–15: 130
Mark 9–16: 79
Luke 1–5: 206
Luke 6–10: 24
Luke 11–17: 38
Acts 13–28: 310
Romans 1–8: 147, 182, 370, 410
Romans 9–16: 63
1 Corinthians: 26, 364
2 Corinthians: 257
Galatians: 77, 205
Ephesians: 54, 194
Philippians: 47, 166, 213, 314
1 & 2 Thessalonians: 203
Titus: 43, 123
James: 115
Revelation 1–11: 45, 54
Revelation 12–22: 253
5–7
Luke 1–5: 217
1–3 John: 16
6
Matthew 8–15: 164
6:1
Matthew 16–23: 363
Galatians: 196
Philippians: 166, 314
1 Peter: 31
6:1–2
Luke 11–17: 348
6:1–5
Mark 9–16: 37, 38
Luke 1–5: 319
Luke 11–17: 256
Luke 18–24: 113
6:1–6
Acts 1–12: 153
6:1–18
Luke 1–5: 206
Luke 18–24: 19
1 & 2 Thessalonians: 96
James: 9
6:2
Matthew 1–7: 482
Matthew 8–15: 68
Luke 6–10: 162
Luke 11–17: 113, 125, 175, 195
Luke 18–24: 132
Romans 9–16: 175
2 Corinthians: 182
James: 180
Revelation 1–11: 133
6:2–3
Luke 11–17: 333
1 & 2 Thessalonians: 308
6:2–4
Luke 11–17: 334
James: 246
6:2–6
Mark 1–8: 128
6:2–6, 16–18
Luke 1–5: 339
6:2, 5, 16
Matthew 1–7: 321–22, 340
Luke 1–5: 24, 337
6:3
1 Corinthians: 335
6:3–4
Acts 1–12: 150
6:4
Romans 1–8: 144
6:4, 6, 18
2 Timothy: 199
6:5
Mark 9–16: 148, 219
Luke 11–17: 4, 113, 125
Luke 18–24: 17
2 Corinthians: 182
James: 180, 192
6:5–6
1 & 2 Thessalonians: 186
6:5–18
Matthew 1–7: 278
6:6
Luke 11–17: 4, 6, 118
Romans 1–8: 144
6:7
Matthew 16–23: 278
Mark 9–16: 220
Luke 11–17: 4, 5
1 Corinthians: 372
Ephesians: 380
6:8
Matthew 1–7: 91
Luke 11–17: 11
2 Timothy: 27
6:9
Matthew 1–7: 367
John 12–21: 39, 297
Philippians: 166
1 Peter: 31
1–3 John: 163
6:9–10
Mark 9–16: 144
1 Corinthians: 26
1 & 2 Thessalonians: 187, 252
Revelation 1–11: 286
6:9–13
Mark 9–16: 142
Luke 11–17: 3
John 12–21: 244

6:10
Matthew 1–7: 381
Matthew 8–15: 349, 436
Mark 1–8: 79
Luke 1–5: 260
Luke 18–24: 7, 304
John 12–21: 299
Acts 13–28: 241
1 & 2 Thessalonians: 213, 255
James: 230
Revelation 1–11: 308, 315
6:11
Matthew 8–15: 479
Mark 1–8: 388
1 & 2 Thessalonians: 187
6:12
Matthew 1–7: 479
Matthew 16–23: 157
Luke 11–17: 38, 42
Colossians and Philemon: 202
1 & 2 Thessalonians: 97
6:12, 14–15
Ephesians: 24
6:13
Matthew 1–7: 331
Matthew 16–23: 108
Matthew 24–28: 176
Luke 18–24: 302
Romans 9–16: 382
1 Corinthians: 228, 229
Galatians: 156
Philippians: 161
1 & 2 Thessalonians: 187
James: 25, 48
6:14
James: 96
6:14–15
Matthew 1–7: 188, 197
Matthew 16–23: 155
Mark 9–16: 148
Luke 11–17: 382
Romans 9–16: 248
2 Corinthians: 52, 57
Philippians: 35
Colossians and Philemon: 202, 208–9, 219
1–3 John: 35
6:15
Matthew 8–15: 66
6:16
Luke 11–17: 113, 125
2 Corinthians: 182
Galatians: 211
James: 180
6:16–17
Philippians: 114
1 Timothy: 152
6:16–18
Luke 1–5: 341
Acts 1–12: 153
Acts 13–28: 5
Colossians and Philemon: 123
6:17
Acts 13–28: 5
James: 277
6:18
Luke 11–17: 348
Romans 1–8: 144
6:19–20
Matthew 1–7: 231
Luke 11–17: 135
2 Corinthians: 232
Philippians: 307
1 Timothy: 253
James: 244
6:19–21
Mark 1–8: 204
Luke 11–17: 139, 147
Romans 1–8: 446
2 Corinthians: 178
1 Timothy: 282
James: 240
1 Peter: 36
6:19–34
James: 9
6:20
1 Corinthians: 450
2 Corinthians: 278
Philippians: 260
2 Timothy: 198
6:20–21
John 12–21: 296
6:21
Matthew 16–23: 200
Mark 9–16: 83
1 Corinthians: 236
1 Timothy: 247
James: 242
6:22–23
Matthew 16–23: 252
1–3 John: 28
6:23
John 1–11: 419
6:24
Matthew 1–7: 204, 444
Mark 1–8: 116, 204
Mark 9–16: 81
Luke 11–17: 139, 148, 340
Acts 13–28: 230
Romans 1–8: 133, 223, 344
Romans 9–16: 85
1 Corinthians: 240
2 Corinthians: 373
Philippians: 14, 199
2 Timothy: 45
Titus: 45
James: 39, 197, 210, 240, 242
6:24–33
1 Timothy: 254
6:25
Luke 11–17: 138
6:25–28
Philippians: 197
6:25–33
Luke 11–17: 33
6:25–34
Matthew 16–23: 79
Luke 11–17: 119, 130
Luke 18–24: 257
2 Corinthians: 280
Philippians: 33, 280, 287
1 & 2 Thessalonians: 252
6:25, 32–33
Matthew 1–7: 391
6:26
Luke 11–17: 140
1 Corinthians: 203
6:26–30
Luke 6–10: 365
6:27
Luke 11–17: 142
1 Peter: 92
6:28–29
1 Peter: 93
6:28–30
Matthew 1–7: 92
6:28–33
Philippians: 275
6:30
Matthew 8–15: 224
Mark 1–8: 233
Mark 9–16: 26
Luke 6–10: 129, 144, 211
Luke 11–17: 143
John 12–21: 135
1 Peter: 93
6:31–33
Matthew 16–23: 13
Mark 1–8: 290, 391
Luke 1–5: 257
6:32
Matthew 8–15: 440
1 Corinthians: 183
6:33
Matthew 1–7: 92, 96, 201
Luke 11–17: 146
Romans 1–8: 185, 212, 390
1 Corinthians: 140
2 Corinthians: 277
Philippians: 221
Colossians and Philemon: 128
1 & 2 Thessalonians: 194, 213, 229
1 Timothy: 249
2 Timothy: 194
Hebrews: 310
1 Peter: 35, 65
6:33–34
1 & 2 Thessalonians: 184
6:34
John 12–21: 96
7:1
Matthew 16–23: 124
Galatians: 178
7:1–3
Luke 6–10: 314
Romans 1–8: 114
7:1–5
Romans 9–16: 290
James: 222
7:1–12
James: 9
7:3–5
Matthew 16–23: 131
7:4–5
Luke 11–17: 113

7:5
Galatians: 181
Philippians: 50
James: 180
7:6
Matthew 1–7: 439
Matthew 8–15: 383, 413
Matthew 16–23: 34
Mark 1–8: 281
Luke 6–10: 246, 286, 331
Acts 13–28: 149
7:7
Matthew 16–23: 282
Mark 1–8: 371
1 Peter: 194
7:7–8
Mark 9–16: 28
Luke 11–17: 13, 34
7:7–11
Mark 9–16: 146
James: 37, 55, 206
7:8
Romans 1–8: 184
7:9
Luke 11–17: 56
Ephesians: 359
7:11
Matthew 1–7: 97, 376
Luke 11–17: 57
1 & 2 Thessalonians: 172
7:12
Acts 13–28: 372
Romans 9–16: 253
2 Corinthians: 415
Philippians: 43
Hebrews: 427
7:13
Matthew 1–7: 477
Luke 1–5: 206
Acts 1–12: 70
Ephesians: 174
Philippians: 217
James: 9
7:13–14
Matthew 1–7: 451, 471
Matthew 8–15: 256
Mark 1–8: 193
Luke 1–5: 210
Luke 6–10: 268
Luke 11–17: 25, 95, 220
Luke 18–24: 34, 230
John 12–21: 152, 252, 399
Acts 1–12: 136, 238
Romans 1–8: 25
1 Corinthians: 400
2 Corinthians: 192, 202
1 Peter: 127
2 Peter–Jude: 195
Revelation 1–11: 230
7:13–15
Luke 11–17: 254, 377
7:14
Matthew 8–15: 387, 482
Matthew 16–23: 198
Luke 6–10: 186, 324
Luke 11–17: 281
John 12–21: 173
2 Corinthians: 129–30
James: 177
7:15
Matthew 1–7: 353, 431
Matthew 8–15: 200, 295
Luke 6–10: 98, 116
Luke 11–17: 95
Luke 18–24: 162, 171
John 1–11: 20
Acts 1–12: 94
Acts 13–28: 226
2 Corinthians: 335
Philippians: 92, 217, 256
Colossians and Philemon: 99
1 Timothy: 14
2 Timothy: 105
2 Peter–Jude: 2, 170
1–3 John: 2, 152, 153, 231
Revelation 1–11: 60
Revelation 12–22: 55, 58
7:15–16
Romans 9–16: 374
Ephesians: 210
7:15–17
Titus: 8
1–3 John: 155
7:15–20
Mark 1–8: 136
Mark 9–16: 218
Luke 6–10: 3, 191
Luke 18–24: 202
1 Timothy: 45, 240
James: 9
2 Peter–Jude: 148
1–3 John: 29
7:16
Matthew 16–23: 57
Acts 13–28: 337
Romans 1–8: 128
2 Corinthians: 340
Titus: 67
James: 161
Revelation 1–11: 103, 136
7:16–17
Matthew 16–23: 312
James: 82
7:16–18
Galatians: 164
James: 124
7:16–20
Mark 1–8: 206
Mark 9–16: 135
Galatians: 174
James: 121
2 Peter–Jude: 15
7:17–18
1–3 John: 28, 112
7:17–18, 21–23
1–3 John: 25
7:17–20
2 Peter–Jude: 181
7:18
Matthew 1–7: 479
Matthew 16–23: 278
James: 161
7:19
Luke 1–5: 219, 223
Ephesians: 209
James: 133, 288
2 Peter–Jude: 186
Revelation 12–22: 256
7:19–20
James: 139
7:20
Acts 13–28: 337
Romans 1–8: 128
2 Corinthians: 340
James: 161
7:21
Matthew 1–7: 378
Matthew 8–15: 410
Matthew 16–23: 50, 57, 97
Mark 1–8: 187
Luke 6–10: 119, 275
Luke 11–17: 11, 25, 281
John 12–21: 239, 404
Romans 1–8: 90
Romans 9–16: 242
2 Corinthians: 470
1 & 2 Thessalonians: 98
2 Timothy: 52
James: 120, 229
1 Peter: 31, 127, 227
1–3 John: 57
Revelation 1–11: 137
7:21–22
Luke 11–17: 121
James: 81
7:21–23
Matthew 1–7: 232
Matthew 8–15: 340
Matthew 16–23: 312
Mark 1–8: 434
Mark 9–16: 39
Luke 6–10: 289, 304
Luke 11–17: 94, 282
Luke 18–24: 371
Acts 1–12: 297
Romans 1–8: 222
1 Corinthians: 120
Philippians: 144, 148, 210
1 & 2 Thessalonians: 209
Hebrews: 136, 260, 407
James: 8, 130, 142, 175, 283
2 Peter–Jude: 28
1–3 John: 64, 123
7:21–27
James: 10
7:22
Matthew 16–23: 23
Luke 11–17: 221
1 & 2 Thessalonians: 282
Revelation 12–22: 255
7:22–23
Matthew 1–7: 458
Matthew 16–23: 58, 311
Matthew 24–28: 90
Luke 11–17: 357
Acts 1–12: 96
Romans 1–8: 147
Romans 9–16: 261

1 Corinthians: 400
Philippians: 215
Colossians and Philemon: 66
Hebrews: 100, 282
1 Peter: 20
Revelation 1–11: 136
7:22–27
Romans 1–8: 26
2 Corinthians: 470
Philippians: 148
7:23
Matthew 24–28: 25, 108, 122
Luke 1–5: 214
Luke 11–17: 121, 222
Luke 18–24: 85
John 12–21: 159
Acts 1–12: 238
Romans 1–8: 496–97
2 Corinthians: 249, 460
1 & 2 Thessalonians: 243, 245
James: 286
Revelation 12–22: 92, 255
7:23–24
James: 177
7:24
Luke 11–17: 77
Revelation 12–22: 304
7:24–25
Matthew 1–7: 483
7:24–27
Matthew 8–15: 99
Romans 1–8: 139
1 Corinthians: 81, 400
2 Corinthians: 465
1 Peter: 24, 227
7:26–27
Matthew 8–15: 358
Luke 1–5: 206
Romans 1–8: 147
7:28
Matthew 1–7: 125
Mark 1–8: 332
Mark 9–16: 174
Luke 6–10: 122
Luke 11–17: 81
7:28–29
Matthew 1–7: 122, 136
Matthew 8–15: 2, 313
Mark 1–8: 61
Luke 1–5: 225, 274
Luke 6–10: 16, 88
Luke 11–17: 176
Luke 18–24: 112, 157, 339, 422
John 1–11: 170
John 12–21: 49, 175
Acts 1–12: 136
Titus: 126
1 Peter: 165
7:29
Matthew 1–7: 108
Matthew 8–15: 20, 437
Matthew 16–23: 286, 357
Mark 1–8: 152
Mark 9–16: 152
Luke 1–5: 303
John 12–21: 251
2 Corinthians: 123
8:1–4
Mark 1–8: 85
8:2
Mark 1–8: 89
Luke 1–5: 314, 315
8:2–3
John 1–11: 218
John 12–21: 13
8:4
Mark 1–8: 267, 379
Luke 6–10: 238
Luke 18–24: 321
8:5
Luke 6–10: 207
8:5–13
Matthew 16–23: 252
Mark 1–8: 163
Luke 1–5: 292
Romans 9–16: 209
8:5–16
John 1–11: 218
8:5ff.
Acts 13–28: 346
8:6
Luke 6–10: 126
Revelation 1–11: 263
8:9
Philippians: 203
1 Timothy: 230
8:10
Mark 1–8: 370
8:10–12
Matthew 1–7: 69
8:11
Luke 11–17: 23
John 12–21: 205
Hebrews: 416
Revelation 12–22: 204
8:11–12
Luke 6–10: 100, 129
Luke 11–17: 223, 367
Acts 1–12: 221
Romans 9–16: 107
Revelation 12–22: 202
8:12
Matthew 16–23: 10
Matthew 24–28: 228, 269
Luke 1–5: 216
Luke 6–10: 292
Luke 11–17: 223
Luke 18–24: 389
John 1–11: 419
Acts 1–12: 124
Romans 1–8: 71, 397
2 Corinthians: 203, 249
Ephesians: 208
1 & 2 Thessalonians: 157, 164, 245
1 Timothy: 167
James: 288
2 Peter–Jude: 105
Revelation 12–22: 185, 189, 242, 256
8:13
Luke 1–5: 292
Luke 18–24: 63
Acts 1–12: 101
8:14–17
1 Peter: 165
8:15
Luke 1–5: 292
8:16
Matthew 16–23: 78
Mark 1–8: 75
Luke 1–5: 283
Acts 1–12: 234
8:16–17
Mark 1–8: 226
1 Corinthians: 300
1 Peter: 172
8:17
Matthew 1–7: 19
Mark 1–8: 77
Luke 18–24: 298
Revelation 12–22: 270
8:18–22
Luke 6–10: 316
John 1–11: 335
8:19–20
Romans 1–8: 51
8:19–22
Matthew 16–23: 97, 194
8:20
Matthew 1–7: 50, 74, 146
Mark 1–8: 224
1 Corinthians: 111
Philippians: 124
Hebrews: 450
Revelation 12–22: 112, 113
8:21
Luke 6–10: 317
8:21–22
Mark 1–8: 118
Romans 1–8: 51
Ephesians: 53
8:22
John 1–11: 419
2 Corinthians: 131
Philippians: 253
8:23–24
Luke 1–5: 303
Luke 18–24: 155
8:24
Mark 1–8: 230
Luke 6–10: 210
Revelation 1–11: 204
8:25
Matthew 16–23: 252
Luke 6–10: 20
Luke 18–24: 320
1 Timothy: 89
8:26
Matthew 16–23: 21, 23, 79
Mark 9–16: 26, 146
Luke 6–10: 20, 182
Luke 11–17: 384
Acts 1–12: 10
1 & 2 Thessalonians: 180

8:28
Mark 1–8: 241, 243
Luke 6–10: 219
Acts 1–12: 234
2 Timothy: 107
Revelation 1–11: 263
8:28–32
1–3 John: 17
8:28–34
Mark 1–8: 240
8:29
Mark 1–8: 244
Luke 1–5: 195, 256, 286
Luke 6–10: 221
Acts 13–28: 170
2 Corinthians: 467
Hebrews: 277
8:29–31
James: 132
8:32
Matthew 16–23: 78
Matthew 24–28: 339
Luke 6–10: 219
Acts 1–12: 223
8:33
Mark 1–8: 247, 249
Luke 6–10: 219
8:34
Luke 6–10: 223
9:1
Matthew 1–7: 106
Luke 1–5: 317
9:1–8
Matthew 1–7: 488
Mark 1–8: 101
9:2
Mark 1–8: 331
Acts 1–12: 74
Philippians: 131
Hebrews: 137
9:2–6
Matthew 16–23: 286
9:2–7
John 1–11: 218
9:2–8
Mark 1–8: 5
9:3
Luke 6–10: 317
Luke 18–24: 54, 380
9:4
Matthew 1–7: 202
9:5–6
Hebrews: 137
9:5–13
1 Peter: 32
9:6
John 1–11: 470
2 Corinthians: 123
Philippians: 131
1 & 2 Thessalonians: 172
Revelation 12–22: 112
9:6–8
Luke 18–24: 112
9:8
Mark 1–8: 107
Luke 1–5: 325
John 12–21: 241
9:9
Mark 1–8: 60, 114
Luke 1–5: 331
Luke 6–10: 65
Philippians: 253
9:9–10
Matthew 1–7: xi
9:9–13
Luke 18–24: 320
9:10
Luke 1–5: 332
Luke 6–10: 66
9:10–11
Matthew 1–7: xi
Luke 11–17: 257
Luke 18–24: 72
2 Corinthians: 245
9:10–13
Luke 1–5: 156
Luke 6–10: 172
Romans 9–16: 320
9:11
Matthew 1–7: 341
Luke 6–10: 166
Luke 11–17: 194
9:11–12
Romans 9–16: 66
9:12
Luke 1–5: 12
9:13
Matthew 1–7: 9
Mark 1–8: 120
Luke 1–5: 333
Luke 11–17: 170, 320
1 Corinthians: 143
Philippians: 192
1 Timothy: 33
James: 209, 286, 287
9:14
Mark 1–8: 126
Luke 1–5: 319, 338
Luke 6–10: 145
Acts 13–28: 164
1 Peter: 54
9:14–15
Matthew 1–7: 402
Philippians: 114
1 Timothy: 152
9:14–17
Mark 1–8: 125
9:15
Mark 1–8: 130
Luke 1–5: 340
Luke 6–10: 166
Revelation 12–22: 202
9:16
Luke 1–5: 341
1 Corinthians: 27
9:17
Ephesians: 236
9:18
Mark 1–8: 256
Luke 6–10: 235
Revelation 12–22: 238
9:19–22
Acts 1–12: 280
9:20
Matthew 16–23: 365
Mark 9–16: 219
Luke 18–24: 164
9:20–22
Matthew 1–7: 119
John 1–11: 218
9:21
Luke 6–10: 233
Acts 13–28: 175
9:21–22
Mark 1–8: 261
2 Corinthians: 204
1 Timothy: 89, 168
9:22
Mark 1–8: 331
9:23
Mark 1–8: 263
Acts 13–28: 204
1 & 2 Thessalonians: 184
9:23–25
Revelation 1–11: 25
9:26
Luke 6–10: 237
9:27
Matthew 16–23: 346
Luke 11–17: 391
Luke 18–24: 153
Philippians: 206
1 Peter: 31
Revelation 1–11: 167, 195
9:27–30
John 1–11: 218
9:27–34
John 1–11: 171
9:32
Mark 1–8: 242
Luke 6–10: 219
9:32–33
Luke 11–17: 194
9:32–34
Acts 1–12: 234
9:33
Matthew 16–23: 78
Mark 1–8: 67, 177
Mark 9–16: 25
Luke 1–5: 287
Luke 11–17: 62
9:34
Luke 1–5: 50
Luke 11–17: 206
John 1–11: 479
9:35
Matthew 1–7: 128
Matthew 16–23: 285
Matthew 24–28: 339
Luke 1–5: 293
Luke 18–24: 113
John 1–11: 218
Acts 1–12: 15
2 Corinthians: 347
James: 147
9:36
Matthew 1–7: 136

Matthew 16–23: 362
Mark 1–8: 77, 265, 377
Mark 9–16: 116
Luke 6–10: 231
Acts 13–28: 3, 220
2 Corinthians: 123
1 & 2 Thessalonians: 167
1 Peter: 173, 262
9:37–38
Matthew 24–28: 62
1 & 2 Thessalonians: 188
1 Timothy: 57
9:38
1 Corinthians: 117
10:1
Matthew 1–7: 115
Matthew 24–28: 339
Mark 1–8: 118, 168, 182
Luke 1–5: 282
Luke 11–17: 75
John 12–21: 251
Acts 1–12: 96
Romans 1–8: 7
1 Corinthians: 300
2 Corinthians: 413
1 & 2 Thessalonians: 88
2 Peter–Jude: 19
Revelation 12–22: 147
10:1–5
Luke 6–10: 18
10:2
Luke 6–10: 25, 39
2 Corinthians: 409
1 Peter: 14
10:2–4
Mark 1–8: 169
Luke 6–10: 16
John 1–11: 3
John 12–21: 274
Acts 1–12: 51
1 Peter: 4
2 Peter–Jude: 2
10:3
Matthew 24–28: 285
Luke 1–5: 331
Luke 6–10: 71
Acts 1–12: 28
10:4
Luke 18–24: 271
John 12–21: 73
2 Peter–Jude: 2
10:4–7
Philippians: 215
10:5
Luke 18–24: 445
John 1–11: 3
John 12–21: 26
10:5–6
Luke 6–10: 179, 242
Acts 13–28: 36
10:5–7
Revelation 1–11: 291
10:5–42
1–3 John: 16
10:6
Matthew 24–28: 342
Luke 11–17: 347
10:6–8
Matthew 16–23: 76
10:6–15
Mark 1–8: 314
10:7
Luke 6–10: 324
Acts 1–12: 15, 49
10:7–8
Matthew 1–7: 128
10:8
Luke 6–10: 244
Acts 13–28: 171
2 Corinthians: 413
Philippians: 205
James: 276
10:8–9
Mark 1–8: 292
10:9
Luke 6–10: 245
10:9–13
2 Corinthians: 292
10:10
Mark 1–8: 290
10:11–15
Mark 1–8: 293
10:14
Matthew 1–7: 439
Acts 1–12: 291
Philippians: 206
10:14–15
Romans 1–8: 71
2 Peter–Jude: 89
Revelation 12–22: 254
10:15
Luke 6–10: 246
Revelation 12–22: 108
10:16
Acts 13–28: 226
Romans 9–16: 217, 376
Philippians: 182
2 Peter–Jude: 204
10:16–17
Mark 9–16: 234
10:16–18
Luke 6–10: 329
10:16–18, 21–22
2 Timothy: 180
10:16–22
Luke 6–10: 319
10:16–24
2 Corinthians: 144
10:16–25
Mark 1–8: 294–95
2 Corinthians: 387
10:16–38
Mark 1–8: 285
10:17
Mark 1–8: 279
Luke 1–5: 268
Luke 18–24: 208, 214
Romans 1–8: 99
2 Corinthians: 389
Hebrews: 394
10:18–22
Romans 9–16: 217
10:19
Romans 1–8: 99
Philippians: 197
10:19–20
Philippians: 74
2 Timothy: 17
10:20
Acts 1–12: 17
1 Peter: 31
10:21
Luke 11–17: 174
Romans 1–8: 99
10:21–22
2 Timothy: 116
10:22
Matthew 24–28: 28
Luke 18–24: 215, 217
John 12–21: 30
2 Corinthians: 25
Philippians: 96
1 Timothy: 89, 181
1 Peter: 7, 279
Revelation 1–11: 79, 122, 126
Revelation 12–22: 100
10:22–24
2 Timothy: 56
10:23
Acts 13–28: 47
2 Peter–Jude: 111
10:24
Acts 13–28: 210
Romans 9–16: 319
2 Corinthians: 220
Philippians: 129
Colossians and Philemon: 75
10:24–25
Matthew 24–28: 25
Mark 1–8: 427
John 12–21: 173
Romans 1–8: 447
Philippians: 96, 144
1 & 2 Thessalonians: 79
1 Peter: 198
10:24–38
Mark 1–8: 167
10:25
Matthew 16–23: 19
Mark 1–8: 181, 184
Romans 1–8: 95
Philippians: 197
10:26
Mark 1–8: 214
Revelation 1–11: 46
10:27
Luke 6–10: 200
10:28
Luke 1–5: 157, 271
Luke 11–17: 366
Romans 1–8: 71, 137
Romans 9–16: 294
1 Corinthians: 417
Titus: 108
Hebrews: 98
James: 225, 245, 288
1–3 John: 45

Revelation 12–22: 87, 92, 120, 255, 256
10:29
Luke 1–5: 304
Philippians: 314
10:29–31
1 Timothy: 271
10:32
Acts 13–28: 268
James: 140
1 Peter: 31
1–3 John: 185
Revelation 1–11: 79, 116
10:32–33
Matthew 16–23: 97
Matthew 24–28: 26
Luke 1–5: 206, 236
Acts 1–12: 73
10:32–39
Acts 1–12: 163
10:32, 33
2 Timothy: 12
10:33
2 Timothy: 65
10:34
Matthew 1–7: 211
Luke 11–17: 173
Acts 13–28: 53
10:34–36
Matthew 16–23: 49
Luke 6–10: 136, 266–67
Luke 11–17: 283
Acts 13–28: 30
10:34–37
John 1–11: 229
10:35–36
Mark 1–8: 279
10:37
Luke 11–17: 284
John 12–21: 227
Romans 1–8: 223
Philippians: 222
1 & 2 Thessalonians: 284
James: 192
10:37–38
Matthew 16–23: 233
Revelation 1–11: 54
10:37–39
Matthew 16–23: 46, 198
Mark 1–8: 424
Luke 6–10: 267
John 12–21: 28
Romans 1–8: 512
2 Timothy: 13
10:38
Matthew 24–28: 26, 285, 341
Mark 9–16: 42
1 Timothy: 265
2 Timothy: 212
10:38–39
Matthew 16–23: 95, 97
John 12–21: 403
2 Timothy: 52
1 Peter: 225, 249
Revelation 12–22: 23
10:39
Matthew 16–23: 100
James: 204
10:40
Matthew 24–28: 124, 232
Luke 1–5: 297
Romans 9–16: 318
10:40–42
Acts 13–28: 363
10:41
James: 250
1–3 John: 249
Revelation 1–11: 320
10:41–42
Revelation 1–11: 319
11:1
Luke 1–5: 281
Acts 1–12: 48
11:1–3
Matthew 16–23: 21
1 Peter: 54–55
11:1–5
John 12–21: 320
11:1–6
Acts 1–12: 61
11:2
Mark 1–8: 28
Acts 13–28: 164
11:2–3
Revelation 1–11: 28
11:2–5
John 1–11: 58, 170
11:2–6
Luke 1–5: 66
11:3–5
Matthew 1–7: 264
11:4–5
Matthew 1–7: 128
Matthew 16–23: 272
11:4–6
Matthew 24–28: 123
11:5
Mark 9–16: 15, 115, 118
Luke 1–5: 175, 293
Luke 18–24: 60, 63
11:7
1 & 2 Thessalonians: 269
1–3 John: 16
11:8
Luke 1–5: 205
11:10
Mark 1–8: 17
11:11
Matthew 1–7: 12, 50, 51, 60, 76, 133
Matthew 16–23: 232, 291
Mark 1–8: 18
Luke 1–5: 25, 54, 66, 214, 222, 228
Luke 6–10: 14
Luke 11–17: 349
John 1–11: 30, 48
John 12–21: 314
Acts 13–28: 22
1 Corinthians: 51
Ephesians: 240
Hebrews: 350
Revelation 12–22: 204
11:12
Acts 13–28: 55
1 & 2 Thessalonians: 134
11:12–14
Mark 1–8: 24
11:13–14
Mark 1–8: 302
Mark 9–16: 377
Luke 1–5: 39
11:14
Matthew 1–7: 52
Matthew 16–23: 71
Mark 9–16: 19
Luke 6–10: 155
Revelation 1–11: 301
11:15
Luke 11–17: 289
Revelation 12–22: 51
11:16–19
Mark 9–16: 64
Luke 18–24: 26
2 Peter–Jude: 196
11:18
Mark 1–8: 242
Luke 1–5: 283
2 Corinthians: 188
James: 219
11:19
Matthew 1–7: xi, 227
Mark 1–8: 126, 137
Luke 1–5: 156
Luke 6–10: 167
1 Corinthians: 298
2 Corinthians: 188
James: 219
1–3 John: 191
11:20
Luke 11–17: 188, 202
1 & 2 Thessalonians: 282
11:20–21
John 12–21: 183
11:20–22
1 & 2 Thessalonians: 239
11:20–23
Romans 1–8: 138
11:20–24
Matthew 1–7: 54
Mark 1–8: 280, 409
Luke 18–24: 175
Hebrews: 47
1 Peter: 140
11:20–30
John 1–11: 171
11:21
Mark 1–8: 370
1 & 2 Thessalonians: 282
Revelation 1–11: 251
11:21–24
Mark 1–8: 163
Acts 1–12: 115
2 Peter–Jude: 186
Revelation 12–22: 254
11:22
Revelation 12–22: 108

11:22–23
James: 37
11:23
Mark 1–8: 68
Mark 9–16: 211
Acts 1–12: 66
1 & 2 Thessalonians: 282
2 Peter–Jude: 89–90
11:23–24
Matthew 1–7: 106
11:24
1 & 2 Thessalonians: 239
Revelation 12–22: 108
11:25
Matthew 1–7: 438
Luke 1–5: 61
Luke 11–17: 10
Acts 1–12: 104
1 Corinthians: 18, 50
Ephesians: 25
Colossians and Philemon: 36
11:25–26
John 1–11: 473
11:25–27
1 Peter: 31
11:25–30
1 & 2 Thessalonians: 83
11:27
Matthew 1–7: 82
Matthew 16–23: 24
Mark 1–8: 36, 224
Mark 9–16: 152
Luke 1–5: 229
Luke 11–17: 219
Luke 18–24: 112
John 1–11: 14
John 12–21: 65, 118, 225, 302
1 Timothy: 5
1 Peter: 30
11:28
Matthew 1–7: 162
Matthew 16–23: 23
Mark 1–8: 321
Luke 6–10: 347, 348
Luke 18–24: 65
Romans 1–8: 28
1 Corinthians: 483
2 Corinthians: 202
1 Peter: 106
2 Peter–Jude: 28
Revelation 12–22: 305, 307
11:28–29
Matthew 16–23: 401
Galatians: 168
1 & 2 Thessalonians: 246
James: 202
1 Peter: 104
11:28–30
Matthew 16–23: 362
Mark 1–8: 140
Luke 1–5: 163, 273
Luke 6–10: 4, 231, 238, 256
Luke 11–17: 67, 87, 105
2 Corinthians: 192
Ephesians: 11
1 Timothy: 230
1–3 John: 183
11:28, 29
Romans 9–16: 319
11:29
Mark 9–16: 33
John 12–21: 18
Acts 13–28: 246
1 Corinthians: 106, 115
2 Corinthians: 345
Galatians: 169
Ephesians: 121, 124, 173
Philippians: 112, 119, 124
Titus: 144
Hebrews: 77, 425
James: 169
1 Peter: 189, 278
11:29–30
Matthew 1–7: 456
Philippians: 96
Colossians and Philemon: 156
James: 100
11:30
1 Corinthians: 339
Galatians: 182
James: 87
12:1
Mark 1–8: 141
Luke 6–10: 188
Luke 11–17: 82
12:1–14
Mark 1–8: 151
Luke 11–17: 197
John 1–11: 171
12:3
Luke 18–24: 424
12:5–6
Mark 1–8: 145
12:6
Matthew 16–23: 88
12:7
Mark 1–8: 146
Luke 6–10: 6, 7
Luke 11–17: 259
12:8
Matthew 16–23: 23
John 1–11: 14
Acts 1–12: 104
12:9–13
John 1–11: 218
12:10–12
Mark 1–8: 154
12:11
Luke 11–17: 203
12:14
Matthew 24–28: 260
Luke 6–10: 10
12:14–15
John 12–21: 14
12:15
Mark 1–8: 158
Luke 1–5: 293
Luke 18–24: 63
John 1–11: 218
12:16
Mark 1–8: 379
Luke 18–24: 321
12:17
Matthew 1–7: 19
12:18
Luke 6–10: 225
Luke 18–24: 422
Acts 1–12: 13, 106
Philippians: 156
12:18–20
Philippians: 105
12:18–21
Acts 1–12: 107
12:19–20
2 Peter–Jude: 62
12:20
Matthew 16–23: 119
12:21
Luke 6–10: 225
12:22
Matthew 16–23: 78
Matthew 24–28: 339
Mark 1–8: 182
John 1–11: 171
12:22–23
Mark 1–8: 180
12:22–24
Mark 1–8: 111
12:22–28
Acts 1–12: 234
12:22–30
Luke 11–17: 61
12:23
Matthew 16–23: 347
Mark 9–16: 208
Luke 18–24: 60, 96, 153
Philippians: 184
Revelation 1–11: 167
12:24
Matthew 16–23: 4, 19, 273, 286, 343
Matthew 24–28: 73, 261
Mark 1–8: 66, 67, 84, 125, 149, 180, 359
Luke 1–5: 275, 296
Luke 11–17: 61, 81, 259
John 1–11: 479
John 12–21: 52
Romans 9–16: 74
2 Corinthians: 189
Philippians: 214
1 & 2 Thessalonians: 64
Revelation 1–11: 310
12:24–32
Romans 1–8: 17
12:24ff.
Acts 1–12: 46
12:25
Mark 1–8: 182
John 12–21: 216
12:25–26
Mark 1–8: 84
Acts 13–28: 176
12:25–32
Luke 18–24: 118
12:26
Revelation 1–11: 310

12:26–28
Mark 1–8: 175
12:27
Acts 13–28: 176
12:28
Matthew 1–7: 80, 128
Mark 1–8: 239
Acts 1–12: 13
1–3 John: 195
12:28–32
Philippians: 156
12:30
Mark 1–8: 175
Luke 6–10: 335
John 12–21: 343
Acts 13–28: 40, 320
Romans 1–8: 482
James: 210
1–3 John: 197
Revelation 12–22: 2
12:31
Luke 11–17: 123
Revelation 12–22: 303
12:31–32
Luke 1–5: 240
Luke 11–17: 62
Luke 18–24: 384
John 12–21: 175
Acts 13–28: 149
2 Corinthians: 189
Ephesians: 189
Philippians: 214
1–3 John: 205
12:32
Mark 1–8: 183
2 Corinthians: 132
Hebrews: 241
12:33
Luke 6–10: 117
2 Timothy: 193
12:34
Matthew 1–7: 63
Mark 1–8: 352
Luke 1–5: 78, 217
Luke 6–10: 292
Luke 11–17: 82
Luke 18–24: 20
Romans 1–8: 189
2 Corinthians: 235
Ephesians: 187
Colossians and Philemon: 177
James: 88, 265
1 Peter: 192
12:34–35
Matthew 1–7: 471
Romans 1–8: 187
Colossians and Philemon: 86
James: 82
12:34–37
1 Timothy: 173
12:35
Ephesians: 54
1 & 2 Thessalonians: 91, 199
1–3 John: 169
12:35–36
Colossians and Philemon: 144
12:36
1 & 2 Thessalonians: 74
2 Peter–Jude: 184
Revelation 12–22: 108
12:36–37
Romans 1–8: 71
James: 144
12:37
Colossians and Philemon: 177
James: 88
Revelation 12–22: 253
12:38
Matthew 16–23: 281
Luke 1–5: 291, 319
Luke 6–10: 353
Luke 11–17: 368, 403
Acts 1–12: 104
12:38–39
Matthew 16–23: 80
12:38–40
Matthew 24–28: 299
John 12–21: 373
1 Corinthians: 46
12:38–41
Matthew 1–7: 54
12:38–42
Luke 6–10: 148
12:39
Matthew 1–7: 94
Mark 1–8: 281
Luke 6–10: 292
Luke 11–17: 238, 368
Luke 18–24: 246
Acts 1–12: 76
Philippians: 184
James: 191, 192
12:39–40
Matthew 24–28: 74
Mark 1–8: 400
Luke 11–17: 85
John 12–21: 213
1 Corinthians: 402
12:40
Matthew 16–23: 37
Matthew 24–28: 292, 299
Mark 9–16: 391
Luke 18–24: 396, 402
John 12–21: 132
Ephesians: 139
12:41
Matthew 1–7: 124
John 12–21: 183
Acts 1–12: 75
2 Timothy: 172
Titus: 13
Revelation 12–22: 236
12:41–42
Revelation 12–22: 108
12:43
Luke 1–5: 282
12:43–45
Mark 1–8: 245
Luke 1–5: 284
Luke 6–10: 222
Luke 11–17: 74
Romans 1–8: 222
12:44
Luke 11–17: 75
12:45
Acts 1–12: 76
Philippians: 184
12:46
Matthew 1–7: 22
12:46–47
Mark 1–8: 277
Luke 1–5: 149
James: 10
12:46–50
Luke 1–5: 80
12:47–50
James: 4
12:48–50
Luke 1–5: 184
12:50
Matthew 1–7: 376
John 1–11: 356
Romans 1–8: 493
13
Luke 11–17: 207
Romans 1–8: 465
13:1
Luke 1–5: 304
13:1–9
Hebrews: 271
13:1–23
1 Corinthians: 400
1–3 John: 140
13:1–52
Mark 1–8: 113, 194
13:1ff.
Acts 1–12: 15
13:2
Luke 1–5: 304
Luke 6–10: 187
John 1–11: 170
Acts 13–28: 92
13:2–9
Matthew 1–7: 61
13:3–7
John 12–21: 85
13:3–8
Colossians and Philemon: 22
13:3–9
Acts 1–12: 80
Philippians: 210
13:3–23
Matthew 1–7: 55
Romans 1–8: 226
1–3 John: 80
13:3–33
1–3 John: 16
13:3–52
Mark 1–8: 221
13:5–6
Matthew 24–28: 188
2 Timothy: 180, 206
13:5–7
1 Peter: 43
13:5–7, 20–22
1–3 John: 178
13:7, 22
2 Timothy: 206

13:8
Matthew 16–23: 278
Luke 6–10: 189
James: 75
13:8, 23
1–3 John: 178
13:8, 48
2 Timothy: 193
13:9
Matthew 24–28: 23
Revelation 12–22: 51
13:10
Mark 1–8: 197
John 12–21: 224
13:10–11
Matthew 16–23: 15
Luke 11–17: 216
2 Timothy: 148
13:10–11,13
Matthew 24–28: 61
13:10–13
Mark 9–16: 171
Luke 11–17: 264
13:11
Matthew 16–23: 2
Mark 9–16: 103
Luke 18–24: 125
John 12–21: 162
1 Corinthians: 372
2 Corinthians: 109
Ephesians: ix–x
James: 66
Revelation 1–11: 19, 286
13:11–12
Mark 1–8: 182
Philippians: 44
13:11–13
1 & 2 Thessalonians: 284
13:11–15
John 12–21: 225
13:11–16
Luke 11–17: 403
13:11–17
Luke 18–24: 126
13:11, 13
Matthew 1–7: 438
13:12–13
Luke 6–10: 190
13:13
Revelation 1–11: 19
13:13–15
Matthew 16–23: 7
Luke 11–17: 90, 304
13:14
1 & 2 Thessalonians: 197
13:14–15
Acts 13–28: 374
Romans 9–16: 101
1 & 2 Thessalonians: 284
13:16
James: 66
13:16–17
Luke 18–24: 56
1–3 John: 17
13:17
Luke 11–17: 412
1 Peter: 54
13:18–23
2 Corinthians: 464
Philippians: 210
Hebrews: 271
James: 67
13:19
Mark 1–8: 200, 201
Acts 1–12: 252
2 Corinthians: 206
Ephesians: 371
Philippians: 286
1 & 2 Thessalonians: 71, 166, 296
2 Timothy: 133
1–3 John: 83
Revelation 12–22: 16
13:19–22
Colossians and Philemon: 185
13:20–21
Matthew 1–7: 223, 485
Matthew 16–23: 50
Acts 1–12: 174
Acts 13–28: 55
Galatians: 199
Ephesians: 371
1 & 2 Thessalonians: 80, 226, 248
2 Timothy: 206
Hebrews: 281
Revelation 12–22: 273
13:20–22
Luke 11–17: 287
John 12–21: 152
2 Peter–Jude: 72
13:20–23
James: 285
13:21
Luke 6–10: 192
Acts 1–12: 80
13:21–22
John 1–11: 229
13:22
Matthew 1–7: 144
Matthew 16–23: 51
Luke 6–10: 194
2 Corinthians: 279
Ephesians: 371
2 Timothy: 44
James: 195, 242, 244
13:23
Luke 6–10: 195
John 12–21: 149
Ephesians: 371
1 & 2 Thessalonians: 81
James: 75, 121
1 Peter: 274
13:24–30
Matthew 1–7: 55
Luke 6–10: 120, 314
Luke 11–17: 420
Luke 18–24: 243
Acts 1–12: 238
Galatians: 34
Philippians: 32
1 & 2 Thessalonians: 137
2 Timothy: 87
James: 185, 201, 285
1–3 John: 22
13:24–30, 36–43
Matthew 1–7: 120
13:24–43
Hebrews: 152
Revelation 1–11: 192
13:25
Matthew 1–7: 353
13:25–30
2 Corinthians: 459, 467
13:30
Matthew 24–28: 62
1 & 2 Thessalonians: 235
Revelation 12–22: 111
13:31–32
Luke 6–10: 187
Colossians and Philemon: 22
13:32
Matthew 16–23: 80
Luke 11–17: 208, 209
13:33
1 Corinthians: 128
13:34
Mark 1–8: 194
Luke 6–10: 187
13:34–35
Mark 1–8: 198
Ephesians: ix
13:34–43
1 Corinthians: 400
13:34–50
Luke 18–24: 247
1 & 2 Thessalonians: 135
13:35
Matthew 1–7: 19
James: 92
Revelation 12–22: 50
13:36–42
2 Corinthians: 459, 467
2 Peter–Jude: 72
13:36–43
Matthew 1–7: 72
Luke 18–24: 192
Acts 1–12: 239
Philippians: 32
James: 185
13:37
Mark 1–8: 200
Luke 6–10: 190
13:37–39
Revelation 12–22: 16
13:37–42
Revelation 12–22: 123
13:37–43
James: 285
13:38
Luke 1–5: 196
1 & 2 Thessalonians: 296
James: 235
2 Peter–Jude: 196
1–3 John: 28
13:38–39
Revelation 1–11: 255

13:38–42
Hebrews: 277
13:39
Matthew 24–28: 11
2 Corinthians: 132
Revelation 12–22: 115
13:39–41
Revelation 1–11: 238
13:39–42
Luke 11–17: 120
1 Peter: 57
Revelation 1–11: 215
Revelation 12–22: 111
13:40
2 Corinthians: 132
James: 287
Revelation 12–22: 114, 256
13:40–42
1 & 2 Thessalonians: 163, 235
James: 288
2 Peter–Jude: 185–86
Revelation 12–22: 225
13:40–43
Revelation 1–11: 154
13:40–50
Acts 1–12: 19
Revelation 12–22: 176
13:41
1 Peter: 123, 220
1–3 John: 67
Revelation 12–22: 215
13:41–42
Acts 1–12: 221
2 Corinthians: 203, 249
1 & 2 Thessalonians: 234
1 Timothy: 167
James: 247
Revelation 12–22: 84, 132, 211
13:41–43
Romans 1–8: 126
13:41, 49
Matthew 24–28: 57
13:42
Mark 9–16: 48
Romans 1–8: 137
1 & 2 Thessalonians: 245
James: 245, 287
2 Peter–Jude: 105
1–3 John: 48
Revelation 12–22: 185, 189, 224, 242, 256
13:42, 50
Luke 1–5: 216
13:43
1 Corinthians: 440
1 Peter: 31
Revelation 1–11: 48, 105
Revelation 12–22: 51
13:44
Luke 18–24: 42, 84
2 Corinthians: 137, 140
Philippians: 227
13:44–46
Matthew 1–7: 381, 455
Matthew 16–23: 193
Matthew 24–28: 91
Mark 1–8: 425, 430
Luke 6–10: 181, 194
Luke 11–17: 26, 140, 281
Romans 1–8: 241, 354
James: 122
13:45–46
Philippians: 227
13:46
Luke 18–24: 42
2 Corinthians: 138
13:47–50
Matthew 1–7: 72
1 Corinthians: 400
1 & 2 Thessalonians: 137
James: 285
2 Peter–Jude: 72
13:48
John 12–21: 152
13:49
Matthew 24–28: 11
Luke 1–5: 176
2 Corinthians: 132
Revelation 1–11: 154
Revelation 12–22: 115
13:49–50
John 12–21: 152
2 Corinthians: 203
1 & 2 Thessalonians: 234
1 Timothy: 167
Hebrews: 277
Revelation 1–11: 215, 238
Revelation 12–22: 84, 132
13:50
Acts 1–12: 221
Romans 1–8: 137
1 & 2 Thessalonians: 163, 245
James: 245, 287
Revelation 12–22: 185, 189, 242, 256
13:54
1 Corinthians: 298
2 Corinthians: 123
13:54–56
Matthew 1–7: 4
Luke 1–5: 248
13:54–57
Luke 1–5: 80
1 Peter: 123
13:54–58
Mark 1–8: 271
John 1–11: 171, 478
13:55
Matthew 1–7: 15
Mark 1–8: 276
Luke 1–5: 248
Luke 6–10: 25, 202
Acts 1–12: 325
2 Corinthians: 455
James: 10
1 Peter: 4
2 Peter–Jude: 2, 18
13:55–56
Matthew 1–7: 22
Mark 1–8: 178
Luke 1–5: 149, 183
13:57
John 1–11: 3
13:58
Luke 1–5: 276
14:1–2
Matthew 16–23: 19
Mark 1–8: 162
Luke 11–17: 229
14:1–10
Luke 1–5: 39
14:2
Luke 1–5: 232
2 Corinthians: 123
14:3
John 1–11: 3
Acts 13–28: 217
14:3–4
Matthew 1–7: 104
Matthew 16–23: 168
Luke 1–5: 34
14:3–5
Matthew 16–23: 287
14:3–11
Luke 18–24: 349
14:3–12
Matthew 16–23: 164
Luke 11–17: 107, 349
14:5
Mark 1–8: 305
Luke 1–5: 231
Luke 11–17: 228
14:6
Luke 1–5: 140
14:6–10
Luke 1–5: 87
14:6–11
Matthew 1–7: 104
14:7
Luke 1–5: 232
14:7–9
James: 268
14:9
Luke 1–5: 230
14:9–10
Luke 11–17: 229
14:10
Luke 1–5: 232
James: 259
14:12
Mark 1–8: 309
Luke 6–10: 49
14:13–14
Mark 1–8: 280
14:13–21
Mark 1–8: 177
14:13–22
Mark 1–8: 312
14:14
Matthew 1–7: 136
Mark 1–8: 317
Luke 6–10: 89
Luke 11–17: 388
John 1–11: 218
John 12–21: 264
2 Corinthians: 123
1 Peter: 32

14:14–21
Luke 6–10: 16
14:15
Matthew 1–7: 117
Mark 1–8: 318, 328
14:19
Matthew 1–7: 366
Mark 9–16: 289
Luke 11–17: 3
14:21
Mark 1–8: 313, 321
Luke 6–10: 57
14:22
John 1–11: 2
14:22–33
Luke 1–5: 303
14:23
Mark 1–8: 78, 327, 414
Luke 11–17: 3
Luke 18–24: 320
John 12–21: 265
Acts 1–12: 285
1 & 2 Thessalonians: 186
14:24
Mark 1–8: 330
14:25
Mark 1–8: 329
Luke 18–24: 58
14:25–32
Luke 6–10: 16
14:25–34
Luke 6–10: 29
14:26
Matthew 24–28: 279
Mark 1–8: 107
Luke 1–5: 325
Luke 6–10: 29
John 12–21: 78
Galatians: 15
Philippians: 160
Revelation 1–11: 195
14:27
Luke 1–5: 157
Luke 6–10: 29
Revelation 1–11: 50
14:27–31
Ephesians: 252
14:28
Luke 6–10: 29
Luke 18–24: 321
14:28–31
Mark 1–8: 331
14:29
Mark 1–8: 333
Mark 9–16: 146
Luke 6–10: 29
14:30
Mark 1–8: 330
Luke 6–10: 29
Revelation 1–11: 195
14:31
Matthew 16–23: 21, 79
Matthew 24–28: 214
Mark 1–8: 404
Luke 6–10: 20, 29
Luke 11–17: 260
Luke 18–24: 321
Acts 1–12: 10
14:33
Matthew 24–28: 281, 337
Mark 1–8: 234, 325, 332, 374, 391, 413
Mark 9–16: 227
Luke 1–5: 195
Luke 6–10: 213, 258
Luke 18–24: 157
John 1–11: 14–15
John 12–21: 251
15:1–2
Matthew 16–23: 37
Luke 11–17: 98
15:1–6
1 Timothy: 197
Titus: 126
15:1–9
Matthew 16–23: 355
John 1–11: 479
Philippians: 111, 231
James: 192
15:2
Matthew 16–23: 3
Ephesians: 146
1 & 2 Thessalonians: 306
15:2–6
Luke 1–5: 318
1 Corinthians: 252
15:2–9
Mark 1–8: 100
15:3
Mark 1–8: 140
1 & 2 Thessalonians: 288
15:3–6
Mark 1–8: 132
Luke 1–5: 319, 341
Romans 1–8: 371
Ephesians: 313
15:5
Mark 1–8: 346
15:6
Matthew 1–7: 254, 430
Matthew 16–23: 359
Mark 1–8: 139, 142
Romans 1–8: 12
Galatians: 24
1 & 2 Thessalonians: 288
2 Timothy: 101
15:6–8
James: 89
15:7
Matthew 1–7: 61
Luke 1–5: 319
Luke 11–17: 96
Acts 1–12: 153
2 Corinthians: 182
Philippians: 50
15:7–8
Titus: 93
15:7–9
Luke 1–5: 78, 341
15:8–9
Romans 9–16: 56
15:9
Matthew 1–7: 147
Mark 1–8: 128, 139
Acts 13–28: 157
Galatians: 138
15:11
Matthew 16–23: 12
Titus: 66
15:12
Matthew 16–23: 3
15:12–14
Mark 1–8: 355–56
15:13
2 Peter–Jude: 181
15:14
Matthew 16–23: 4, 6, 381
Mark 1–8: 166
Mark 9–16: 115
Luke 1–5: 319, 333
Luke 6–10: 162, 179
Luke 11–17: 89, 256, 347
John 1–11: 410
John 12–21: 53
Acts 1–12: 223
Acts 13–28: 220
1 & 2 Thessalonians: 285
Hebrews: 137
Revelation 1–11: 139
Revelation 12–22: 298
15:15
Mark 1–8: 356
Luke 6–10: 28
15:15–16
Luke 6–10: 182
15:15–20
Titus: 66
15:16
Luke 6–10: 19
15:16–20
1 & 2 Thessalonians: 91
15:18
Romans 1–8: 187
15:18–19
Ephesians: 54
James: 50
1 Peter: 167
15:18–20
1–3 John: 85
15:19
Matthew 1–7: 290
Mark 1–8: 357
Romans 1–8: 295
Romans 9–16: 251
1 & 2 Thessalonians: 105, 199
James: 144, 171, 210, 218
15:19–20
Romans 1–8: 101
Titus: 147–48
15:20
James: 218
15:21
Mark 1–8: 365
15:22
Matthew 16–23: 249
Luke 18–24: 153
Philippians: 206

Revelation 1–11: 167, 195
15:22–23
James: 246
15:24
Mark 9–16: 226
Luke 6–10: 179
Luke 18–24: 175, 445
Acts 13–28: 36
Romans 1–8: 55
Colossians and Philemon: 77
15:26–27
Luke 11–17: 362
Philippians: 217
15:27
Mark 9–16: 102
15:28
Matthew 16–23: 98
15:29
Mark 1–8: 384
15:29–31
Mark 1–8: 375
15:29–39
Matthew 8–15: 404
15:30
Mark 1–8: 84
John 1–11: 218
1 Peter: 32
15:31
Luke 1–5: 325
15:32
Matthew 1–7: 136
Mark 1–8: 77
Luke 6–10: 326
John 12–21: 213
2 Corinthians: 123
15:32–38
Luke 6–10: 16
15:32–39
Matthew 16–23: 3, 13
15:36
Luke 11–17: 3
John 12–21: 235
15:38
Mark 1–8: 390
15:39
Mark 1–8: 390
16:1
Luke 1–5: 291
16:1–3
Matthew 24–28: 73
Romans 9–16: 258
Philippians: 286
16:1–4
John 1–11: 171
2 Peter–Jude: 195
16:1–5
Mark 1–8: 400
16:1–12
James: 110
16:4
Matthew 24–28: 73
Mark 1–8: 99, 401
Acts 1–12: 76
James: 191, 192
16:6
Matthew 1–7: 62
Matthew 16–23: 286
Mark 9–16: 226, 270
Luke 11–17: 116, 213
Luke 18–24: 320
Colossians and Philemon: 99
16:6–12
Matthew 16–23: 355
16:6,1 2
Galatians: 140
16:8
Matthew 16–23: 21, 79
Luke 6–10: 20, 211
Acts 1–12: 10
1 & 2 Thessalonians: 180
16:8–11
Luke 18–24: 320
16:9–11
Luke 6–10: 19
16:12
Mark 1–8: 405
1 & 2 Thessalonians: 208
16:13
Matthew 16–23: 27, 62
Luke 6–10: 146, 259
Luke 18–24: 321
16:13–14
Matthew 8–15: 243
16:14
Matthew 16–23: 71
John 1–11: 26, 52
16:15
Mark 1–8: 415
Mark 9–16: 205
Luke 1–5: 234
John 12–21: 137
16:15–16
Matthew 8–15: 138
16:15–17
Ephesians: 252
16:16
Matthew 16–23: 36, 46, 77
Mark 1–8: 15, 175, 423
Mark 9–16: 2, 334
Luke 6–10: 30, 64, 69, 132
Luke 18–24: 126
John 12–21: 36, 92, 264, 385
James: 160
Revelation 1–11: 51, 217, 315
16:16–17
Matthew 8–15: 43, 139
Matthew 24–28: 281
Luke 6–10: 30, 31
John 12–21: 210
1 Timothy: 275
16:16–18
Matthew 1–7: 483
Luke 1–5: 292
16:16, 21–22
Matthew 8–15: 244
16:16, 22
Matthew 24–28: 162
Galatians: 51
16:17
Luke 6–10: 25, 31, 262
Luke 18–24: 321
Colossians and Philemon: 16
1 Peter: 4
2 Peter–Jude: 2
16:17–19
Luke 6–10: 30–31
Luke 18–24: 126
16:18
Matthew 8–15: 138, 139, 375
Matthew 16–23: 41
Matthew 24–28: 315
Mark 1–8: 72, 219
1 Corinthians: 278
2 Corinthians: 70, 412, 430, 440
Ephesians: 96, 151, 343
1 & 2 Thessalonians: 165, 302
1 Timothy: 91, 216
2 Timothy: 121
Revelation 1–11: 48, 86
16:18–19
Matthew 16–23: 29
1 & 2 Thessalonians: 83
16:19
Matthew 16–23: 381
John 12–21: 382
Revelation 1–11: 119
16:20–23
Mark 1–8: 417
16:21
Matthew 16–23: 50, 62, 85
Matthew 24–28: 213, 250, 299
Mark 9–16: 91, 401
Luke 6–10: 31
Luke 18–24: 411
John 1–11: 171
John 12–21: 92
1 Peter: 2
16:21–22
Luke 1–5: 340
Luke 18–24: 369
Acts 13–28: 120
16:21–23
Matthew 8–15: 124, 140
John 1–11: 24
Acts 1–12: 153
1 & 2 Thessalonians: 265
16:21–24
Matthew 16–23: 33
16:21–25
Matthew 16–23: 56
16:21, 24–25
2 Timothy: 52
16:22
Matthew 1–7: 76
Matthew 16–23: 66
Mark 1–8: 420
Luke 6–10: 31
Luke 18–24: 321
John 12–21: 66
1 Corinthians: 41
16:22–23
Luke 18–24: 270, 295
Ephesians: 252
Philippians: 133
16:23
Matthew 16–23: 95
Matthew 24–28: 171

Mark 1–8: 420
Luke 1–5: 261
Luke 6–10: 30, 31
Luke 18–24: 321
1 Corinthians: 41
16:24
Matthew 8–15: 24, 25, 256, 391
Matthew 16–23: 43
Mark 9–16: 42
Luke 6–10: 315
Luke 11–17: 284
John 12–21: 404
Romans 1–8: 224
Philippians: 253
2 Timothy: 45, 212
Hebrews: 335
Revelation 12–22: 78
16:24–25
Matthew 1–7: 453
Luke 18–24: 34
Acts 13–28: 55
Romans 1–8: 353
James: 203
16:24–26
Matthew 16–23: 95
1 Peter: 249
Revelation 1–11: 99
16:24–27
Luke 6–10: 266
1–3 John: 66
16:24–28
Mark 1–8: 424
16:25
Matthew 1–7: 113
Matthew 8–15: 99
16:25–26
Philippians: 227
16:26
Romans 9–16: 140
James: 245
16:27
Matthew 8–15: 379
Matthew 16–23: 64, 214
Luke 11–17: 117
John 12–21: 241
Romans 1–8: 127
1 Corinthians: 287
1 & 2 Thessalonians: 92, 234
2 Timothy: 199
Titus: 119
James: 247
1 Peter: 31
Revelation 1–11: 28, 103, 215, 238
Revelation 12–22: 215, 254
16:27–28
Matthew 8–15: 386
Matthew 16–23: 62
16:28
Matthew 8–15: 105
2 Peter–Jude: 60
Revelation 12–22: 302
16–23
2 Peter–Jude: 61
17:1
Mark 9–16: 105
Luke 6–10: 39, 47, 281
John 1–11: 8
Acts 1–12: 98
2 Peter–Jude: 4
1–3 John: 6
17:1–2
Luke 1–5: 157
Luke 18–24: 237
John 1–11: 452
2 Corinthians: 113
17:1–5
Luke 1–5: 240
17:1–6
Luke 1–5: 308
17:1–8
Luke 1–5: 49
Titus: 120
17:1–13
2 Peter–Jude: 61
17:2
Matthew 1–7: 29
Matthew 8–15: 88
Matthew 16–23: 74
Matthew 24–28: 57
Mark 9–16: 5
Romans 1–8: 84
Romans 9–16: 124, 150
1 Peter: 245
Revelation 1–11: 113, 226
Revelation 12–22: 279
17:3
Mark 1–8: 44
Philippians: 79
1 & 2 Thessalonians: 126
Revelation 1–11: 301
17:4
Matthew 8–15: 442
Mark 9–16: 7
Luke 6–10: 285
Acts 1–12: 104
17:5
Matthew 24–28: 194
Mark 1–8: 36, 186
Luke 1–5: 57, 235
Luke 6–10: 286
Luke 18–24: 124
John 12–21: 40
Romans 9–16: 74
1 Corinthians: 287
2 Corinthians: 214
Philippians: 130, 150, 158
1 & 2 Thessalonians: 137
Revelation 1–11: 47
Revelation 12–22: 112
17:5–6
Luke 1–5: 157
17:6
Matthew 24–28: 279
Mark 9–16: 8
Luke 6–10: 286
Revelation 1–11: 49, 158, 228
Revelation 12–22: 296
17:7
Luke 1–5: 157
Revelation 1–11: 50
17:9
Mark 1–8: 418
Acts 1–12: 13
17:10–13
Luke 1–5: 39
John 1–11: 51
17:11–13
Matthew 1–7: 52
17:12
1 Peter: 2
17:13
Mark 9–16: 18
17:14–18
Acts 13–28: 169
17:14–20
Mark 9–16: 23
17:14–21
Luke 6–10: 289
17:15
Matthew 1–7: 127
Luke 6–10: 290, 291
17:16
Matthew 8–15: 125
17:16, 19
Matthew 8–15: 40
17:17
Luke 6–10: 254
Acts 1–12: 76
Philippians: 184
17:18
Mark 9–16: 29
17:19
Luke 6–10: 20
17:19–20
Luke 6–10: 235
17:20
Matthew 8–15: 370
Matthew 16–23: 85, 282
Mark 1–8: 220
Luke 11–17: 385
1 Corinthians: 299, 334
17:21
Matthew 8–15: 44
Acts 13–28: 5
17:22
Mark 9–16: 35
2 Corinthians: 145
17:22–23
Matthew 24–28: 213
Luke 18–24: 120
17:23
Matthew 24–28: 299
Mark 9–16: 35
17:24
Matthew 16–23: 62
17:24–25
1 Peter: 4
2 Peter–Jude: 3
17:24–27
Matthew 8–15: 140, 394
Luke 1–5: 237
Luke 18–24: 71
John 1–11: 90
Romans 9–16: 233
1 Corinthians: 455

2 Corinthians: 283
Titus: 142
17:25
Luke 6–10: 33
John 12–21: 401
17:25–27
Matthew 1–7: 78
17:26
Luke 6–10: 33
17:27
Mark 9–16: 95
Luke 1–5: 305
Luke 6–10: 34
Luke 18–24: 53
Romans 1–8: 17
18
Matthew 1–7: 149, 356, 453
Matthew 16–23: 143
1 Corinthians: 125
2 Corinthians: 442
1 Timothy: 47
1 Peter: 270
18:1–4
Matthew 1–7: 381
Matthew 16–23: 29
Mark 9–16: 49
18:1–5
Luke 18–24: 292
18:1, 6–7
Romans 9–16: 275
18:2–4
Matthew 1–7: 175
Acts 1–12: 242
18:3
Matthew 8–15: 105, 271
Matthew 24–28: 98
Luke 18–24: 31
James: 289
18:3–4
Matthew 1–7: 148
Ephesians: 122
18:3–5
Matthew 16–23: 180
Matthew 24–28: 124
18:3, 6, 10, 14
Romans 9–16: 294
18:4
Matthew 16–23: 113
Luke 1–5: 47
2 Corinthians: 345
18:5
Romans 9–16: 322
1 Corinthians: 311
Philippians: 206
18:5–10
Romans 9–16: 361
18:5–14
1 Peter: 270
18:6
Matthew 8–15: 300
Matthew 16–23: 114
Luke 6–10: 303
Romans 9–16: 320
Galatians: 141
Philippians: 51
James: 222
18:6–7
Romans 9–16: 275
1 & 2 Thessalonians: 110
18:6–10
1 & 2 Thessalonians: 180, 242
Revelation 1–11: 101
Revelation 12–22: 126
18:6–14
1 Corinthians: 192
18:7
1 Corinthians: 268
2 Corinthians: 227
18:7–9
Luke 11–17: 378
18:8
Matthew 8–15: 477
Colossians and Philemon: 136
1 & 2 Thessalonians: 163, 245
Revelation 12–22: 92
18:8–9
1 & 2 Thessalonians: 173
James: 288
Revelation 12–22: 256
18:8–10
Romans 9–16: 276
James: 222
18:9
Revelation 12–22: 256
18:10
Matthew 16–23: 114
Matthew 24–28: 71
Luke 11–17: 300, 363
Luke 18–24: 306
1 Corinthians: 259, 320
Revelation 1–11: 149
Revelation 12–22: 84
18:10, 14
Ephesians: 97
18:11
Matthew 8–15: 340
Romans 1–8: 54
James: 290
18:12–13
James: 285
18:14
Matthew 16–23: 114
2 Corinthians: 442
Galatians: 179
18:15
2 Corinthians: 447
1 Timothy: 188
18:15–17
Matthew 1–7: 216, 331, 431
Matthew 16–23: 33
Luke 11–17: 379
Romans 9–16: 272
1 Corinthians: 125
2 Corinthians: 441, 443
Galatians: 176
Ephesians: 212
1 Timothy: 54
Titus: 133
James: 96, 221
Revelation 1–11: 46, 94
18:15–18
2 Corinthians: 56
1 & 2 Thessalonians: 166, 176
1 Timothy: 185
Revelation 1–11: 87
18:15–19
1 Corinthians: 78
18:15–20
Acts 1–12: 161
1 Corinthians: 115
1 Peter: 69–70
18:15ff.
1 Timothy: 170
Revelation 1–11: 59
18:16
Luke 1–5: 165
2 Corinthians: 447
1 Timothy: 222
1–3 John: 190
Revelation 1–11: 298
18:17
Matthew 1–7: xi
Mark 1–8: 114
Luke 1–5: 329
Luke 11–17: 378
2 Corinthians: 447
1 & 2 Thessalonians: 304, 310
1 Timothy: 223
18:18–20
1 Corinthians: 126
1 Timothy: 223
18:20
Matthew 16–23: 349
John 1–11: 14
Revelation 1–11: 43
18:21
Matthew 1–7: 117
Luke 6–10: 28
Luke 11–17: 380
2 Corinthians: 54
18:21–22
Matthew 1–7: 197
1 Corinthians: 140
Colossians and Philemon: 228
1 Timothy: 224
1–3 John: 171
18:21–35
Matthew 1–7: 397
2 Corinthians: 51
Ephesians: 190
1 & 2 Thessalonians: 180
18:22
2 Corinthians: 54
Ephesians: 195
18:23
Philippians: 306
18:23–27
Romans 1–8: 399
18:23–34
1 Peter: 230
18:23–35
Matthew 1–7: 197
Matthew 8–15: 66
Mark 9–16: 149
Luke 1–5: 271
Luke 11–17: 43, 381
Ephesians: 58
Colossians and Philemon: 111

18:25
Luke 11–17: 44
18:26
Luke 11–17: 44, 312
James: 253
18:27
Matthew 8–15: 111
Luke 11–17: 44
2 Corinthians: 205
18:27–34
Philippians: 144
18:28
Luke 11–17: 44
18:29
James: 253
18:30
Luke 11–17: 44
18:31
Luke 11–17: 381
2 Corinthians: 51
Colossians and Philemon: 219
18:32–34
2 Corinthians: 51
18:34
Luke 11–17: 382
Romans 1–8: 99
2 Corinthians: 51
18:35
2 Corinthians: 57
Philippians: 31
19
Matthew 1–7: 310, 312, 313, 316, 317
19:2
Matthew 8–15: 4
Mark 9–16: 53
John 1–11: 218
19:3
Matthew 16–23: 171
19:3–12
Matthew 16–23: 178
Luke 18–24: 25
Romans 1–8: 360, 370
19:4
Mark 1–8: 144
Mark 9–16: 55
Luke 6–10: 5
19:4–10
Ephesians: 302
19:5–6
1 Corinthians: 165
19:6
Ephesians: 303
19:7–9
Ephesians: 303
1 Timothy: 212
19:8
Romans 1–8: 120
19:8–9
1 Corinthians: 165
19:9
Romans 1–8: 156
1 Corinthians: 167
1 & 2 Thessalonians: 111
1 Timothy: 105
19:10
Mark 9–16: 60
1 Corinthians: 186
19:11
James: 66
19:12
1 Corinthians: 159
Colossians and Philemon: 136
19:13
Matthew 1–7: 117
Luke 11–17: 3
John 12–21: 235
19:13–14
Luke 6–10: 231
Galatians: 168
19:13–15
Luke 18–24: 25
19:14
Luke 18–24: 31
19:15
1 Timothy: 224
19:16
Mark 9–16: 76, 199
Romans 1–8: 198
2 Corinthians: 468
Philippians: 213
1 & 2 Thessalonians: 245
19:16, 22
2 Corinthians: 468
19:16–17
James: 109
19:16–21
John 12–21: 85
19:16–22
Matthew 8–15: 25
Mark 1–8: 367
Romans 1–8: 221, 407
Romans 9–16: 74
2 Corinthians: 470
Ephesians: 176
1 & 2 Thessalonians: 295
Revelation 1–11: 137
19:16–30
Luke 18–24: 35
19:17
Mark 9–16: 80
Ephesians: 7
19:18
James: 249
19:19
Matthew 1–7: 338
19:20
Romans 1–8: 369
Romans 9–16: 69
Philippians: 213, 240
19:21
Matthew 1–7: 409
Luke 11–17: 128, 147
1 Corinthians: 453
2 Corinthians: 278
Philippians: 253
James: 108
1 Peter: 239
Revelation 12–22: 78, 260
19:21–22
Philippians: 148
James: 242
19:21–26
Philippians: 214
19:22
Mark 9–16: 77
Luke 11–17: 128
Luke 18–24: 40
John 1–11: 6
Romans 1–8: 513
19:23
Luke 18–24: 40
19:23–24
James: 109
19:25
Matthew 1–7: 280
Luke 18–24: 13
James: 290
19:26
Matthew 1–7: 280, 350
Matthew 8–15: 157
Luke 1–5: 59
Hebrews: 333
1 Peter: 288
2 Peter–Jude: 26
Revelation 1–11: 156
19:27
Matthew 8–15: 138
Mark 9–16: 103
Luke 6–10: 28, 320
Luke 18–24: 42
John 12–21: 98, 107, 265, 404
2 Corinthians: 414
Ephesians: 39
1 Timothy: 248
19:27–28
Luke 18–24: 294
19:27–29
Acts 13–28: 55
Hebrews: 434
19:27–30
1 Corinthians: 74
19:28
Matthew 1–7: 433
Matthew 8–15: 127, 136, 148, 158, 168, 476
Matthew 24–28: 118
Mark 9–16: 86
Luke 18–24: 43
Acts 1–12: 31, 34, 121
Acts 13–28: 301, 333
Romans 1–8: 456
1 Corinthians: 110, 138
2 Corinthians: 414
2 Timothy: 64
James: 12, 64
Revelation 1–11: 31, 141, 149, 220
Revelation 12–22: 228, 237
19:28–30
James: 109
19:29
Luke 11–17: 94, 174
Colossians and Philemon: 38
1 & 2 Thessalonians: 245
19:30
1 Corinthians: 321

19:30–20:16
Mark 9–16: 87
20:1–16
1 Corinthians: 74, 340
2 Timothy: 200
James: 246
20:1ff.
1 Timothy: 229
20:10
Acts 13–28: 53
20:11
Philippians: 179
20:13–14
Luke 11–17: 312
20:13–16
James: 99
20:15
1 Corinthians: 340
20:16
Luke 1–5: 40
20:17–19
Mark 9–16: 91
Luke 18–24: 52
2 Corinthians: 412
20:18
Matthew 24–28: 260
20:18–19
Matthew 16–23: 266
Matthew 24–28: 213, 250
Luke 18–24: 342
2 Corinthians: 145
20:19
Matthew 1–7: 43
Matthew 24–28: 299
John 12–21: 334
20:20
Matthew 8–15: 77
20:20–21
Matthew 8–15: 124
Matthew 16–23: 29, 95, 365
Luke 6–10: 20
1–3 John: 255
20:20–23
1 Corinthians: 321
2 Corinthians: 155–56
James: 260
1 Peter: 252
20:20–28
Luke 6–10: 35
20:21
Mark 9–16: 105
20:21–22
Matthew 8–15: 149
John 12–21: 275
20:22
Mark 9–16: 295
20:22–23
1 Corinthians: 311
20:23
Matthew 8–15: 151
Mark 9–16: 107
Luke 6–10: 43
Acts 1–12: 321
20:24
Luke 6–10: 43
2 Corinthians: 267
20:25
2 Corinthians: 342
20:25–28
Luke 6–10: 43
Philippians: 121
Titus: 36
1 Peter: 269
1–3 John: 255
20:26–27
Luke 18–24: 292
20:26–28
1 Corinthians: 482
2 Corinthians: 343
1 & 2 Thessalonians: 97
20:27
1 Corinthians: 321
20:28
Matthew 8–15: 82
Matthew 16–23: 37, 368
Matthew 24–28: 270
Luke 1–5: 150
Luke 18–24: 173, 293
John 12–21: 28, 42, 43, 66, 133, 228
Acts 1–12: 107
1 Corinthians: 385
Philippians: 128, 129
1 Peter: 52, 171
2 Peter–Jude: 30
20:29
Luke 18–24: 59
20:30
Matthew 16–23: 346
Luke 18–24: 60
20:30–31
Revelation 1–11: 167, 195
20:34
Mark 9–16: 117
Luke 18–24: 62, 64
2 Corinthians: 123
21:1
John 12–21: 17
21:1–5
2 Peter–Jude: 62
21:2
Luke 18–24: 93
Acts 13–28: 217
21:4
Matthew 1–7: 19
21:4–5
Luke 18–24: 94
21:5
Matthew 1–7: 170
John 12–21: 17
Philippians: 112
2 Timothy: 98, 100
Titus: 144
James: 169
Revelation 1–11: 25
21:8–9
Matthew 8–15: 101
21:9
Matthew 8–15: 90, 306
Matthew 16–23: 250, 296, 403
Matthew 24–28: 7, 133, 207
Mark 1–8: 367
Mark 9–16: 115, 127, 208
Luke 1–5: 247
Luke 18–24: 95, 153
John 1–11: 26
2 Corinthians: 468
James: 246
Revelation 1–11: 167
21:9–16
Galatians: 123
21:10
Acts 13–28: 260
21:11
Luke 1–5: 269
Acts 1–12: 59
21:11–12
1 Corinthians: 346
21:12
Matthew 1–7: 331
Mark 9–16: 137
Acts 1–12: 179
Ephesians: 185
21:12–13
Matthew 1–7: 62, 294, 408
Matthew 8–15: 149
Matthew 24–28: 132
Mark 1–8: 156
Luke 1–5: 204
Romans 1–8: 63
Romans 9–16: 233
James: 73
Revelation 1–11: 209
21:12–16
John 1–11: 91
21:13
Matthew 16–23: 284, 402
Mark 1–8: 137
Luke 18–24: 17
John 1–11: 90
Romans 1–8: 156
Ephesians: 125
21:14
Matthew 8–15: 4
Mark 1–8: 84
Mark 9–16: 112, 139
Luke 18–24: 108
21:15
Matthew 8–15: 89
Matthew 16–23: 3
Mark 9–16: 66
Luke 18–24: 109
2 Corinthians: 267
Revelation 1–11: 167
21:15–16
Mark 9–16: 64
21:16
Matthew 16–23: 374
Mark 1–8: 225
Luke 18–24: 25
21:17
John 12–21: 306
21:18
Mark 1–8: 229
2 Corinthians: 293
21:19
Mark 9–16: 134
Luke 6–10: 122

Revelation 1–11: 108
21:21–22
James: 38
21:23
Matthew 16–23: 374
21:23–27
Matthew 1–7: 488
Matthew 16–23: 274
21:25
Mark 9–16: 18
21:26
Matthew 1–7: 57, 105
Luke 6–10: 152
21:28–31
Matthew 8–15: 99
Acts 1–12: 115
21:28–32
Acts 1–12: 297
21:31
Luke 1–5: 329
Luke 6–10: 292
Revelation 1–11: 137
21:31–32
Matthew 1–7: xi
Luke 1–5: 220
Luke 11–17: 395
1 Corinthians: 13
21:33
Luke 18–24: 121
John 12–21: 145
Romans 9–16: 89
21:33–39
Matthew 16–23: 401
2 Corinthians: 387
21:33–41
Acts 13–28: 374
21:33–43
John 12–21: 144
Acts 13–28: 156
21:33–44
Hebrews: 13
21:33–46
Acts 1–12: 211
1 & 2 Thessalonians: 63
21:34–41
Romans 9–16: 89
21:35
Mark 9–16: 166
21:37–43
1 Peter: 140
21:38
Luke 11–17: 308
John 12–21: 110
21:41
Luke 18–24: 123
21:42
Luke 6–10: 5
Ephesians: 82
1 Peter: 120
21:42–44
Luke 1–5: 183
21:43
Matthew 1–7: 257
Luke 18–24: 125
Romans 9–16: 107, 115
21:43–44
Mark 9–16: 170
21:45
Matthew 16–23: 284
Matthew 24–28: 298
21:46
Mark 9–16: 196
Luke 18–24: 132
22:1
Acts 1–12: 104
22:1–9
Acts 13–28: 156
Romans 1–8: 168
22:1–10
Matthew 8–15: 67
Matthew 24–28: 342
22:1–14
Matthew 1–7: 381
Matthew 24–28: 113
Luke 11–17: 250, 270
Romans 9–16: 107
Revelation 12–22: 202
22:2
2 Peter–Jude: 26
22:2–4
Luke 11–17: 159, 317
22:2–6
2 Corinthians: 387
22:5
Matthew 8–15: 263
22:8
Revelation 1–11: 18
22:9–10
Matthew 24–28: 87
James: 99
22:11–13
Matthew 24–28: 87, 108
22:12
Matthew 16–23: 336
22:13
Matthew 8–15: 397
Matthew 16–23: 10
Matthew 24–28: 269
Mark 9–16: 48
John 1–11: 419
Acts 1–12: 221
2 Corinthians: 203, 249
1 & 2 Thessalonians: 164, 245
1 Timothy: 167
Hebrews: 48
James: 288
2 Peter–Jude: 105
Revelation 12–22: 185, 189, 242, 256
22:14
Matthew 1–7: 458
John 12–21: 267
Romans 1–8: 485
1 & 2 Thessalonians: 256, 287
1 Timothy: 63, 68, 72
Revelation 1–11: 230
Revelation 12–22: 171
22:15
Mark 9–16: 175
Luke 18–24: 131
22:15–16, 23, 34–35
Matthew 1–7: 62
22:15–17
Romans 9–16: 233
22:15–21
1 Corinthians: 455
2 Corinthians: 283
Titus: 141
22:16
Luke 1–5: 23
Luke 18–24: 133
2 Timothy: 156
James: 97
22:16–17
Titus: 141
22:17
Matthew 8–15: 60
Matthew 16–23: 336
22:17–21
Luke 1–5: 220
22:18
Matthew 1–7: 61
Mark 9–16: 179
Acts 1–12: 153
2 Corinthians: 182
Titus: 93
James: 180
22:18–21
Romans 9–16: 234
22:19–21
Luke 11–17: 113
Romans 1–8: 157
22:21
Matthew 8–15: 201
Matthew 24–28: 235
John 1–11: 483
John 12–21: 329
Romans 9–16: 210, 211
Colossians and Philemon: 77
22:21–22
Matthew 8–15: 20
22:22
Mark 9–16: 182
22:23
Matthew 16–23: 336
John 1–11: 482
John 12–21: 9
Acts 13–28: 334
22:23–32
1 Corinthians: 423
James: 110
22:23–33
Acts 13–28: 284
22:28–30
Hebrews: 23
22:29
Matthew 1–7: 263
Luke 18–24: 146, 424
Acts 13–28: 23
Romans 1–8: 52
Romans 9–16: 55
James: 285
22:29–30
Titus: 55
22:30
Matthew 1–7: 263
Matthew 24–28: 66

Romans 1–8: 298
1 Corinthians: 181
22:31
Luke 6–10: 5
22:31–32
Matthew 1–7: 263
22:32
Acts 1–12: 105
1 Corinthians: 436
2 Corinthians: 393
22:33
Luke 18–24: 148
22:34
Titus: 55
22:34–40
Luke 11–17: 361
Romans 1–8: 370
1–3 John: 62, 64
22:34–45
Luke 18–24: 148
22:35
Matthew 8–15: 326
Mark 9–16: 197, 218
Luke 1–5: 319
22:35–36, 37, 39, 46
Titus: 55
22:36
Matthew 1–7: 200
22:36–40
Galatians: 148
Philippians: 41
22:37
John 12–21: 400
Romans 9–16: 139
1 Corinthians: 377
Philippians: 31, 289
1 & 2 Thessalonians: 162
James: 53, 207
1 Peter: 275
22:37–38
Luke 1–5: 220
Revelation 1–11: 54
22:37–39
Matthew 1–7: 269
Matthew 16–23: 201
Romans 9–16: 251
Ephesians: 109
1 & 2 Thessalonians: 117
1 Timothy: 263
2 Timothy: 109
James: 112
1 Peter: 193
22:37–40
Romans 1–8: 407
Romans 9–16: 184
Ephesians: 77
Philippians: 44
1 & 2 Thessalonians: 81
James: 111, 224
1–3 John: 229
22:37, 39
1 Timothy: 18
22:38
Luke 11–17: 73
James: 19
22:38–40
James: 111
22:39
Matthew 1–7: 338, 446
Colossians and Philemon: 218
James: 19, 131
22:40
Mark 9–16: 203
2 Corinthians: 415
22:41–42
Luke 18–24: 152
22:41–45
Luke 18–24: 339
22:42
Matthew 1–7: 14
Matthew 8–15: 90
Mark 9–16: 207
Luke 18–24: 152
Revelation 1–11: 167
22:44
Acts 1–12: 222
22:46
Matthew 16–23: 355
Luke 18–24: 148, 155
23
Matthew 1–7: 144, 278, 443
Mark 1–8: 112
Luke 11–17: 71, 114
2 Corinthians: 182
23:1–3
Luke 1–5: 204
1 Timothy: 114
23:1–7
Luke 18–24: 268
23:1–12
Luke 18–24: 165
Romans 9–16: 55
23:1–33
Luke 1–5: 200
Luke 6–10: 94
23:1–36
Matthew 1–7: 105
Mark 9–16: 152, 178, 271, 311
Luke 6–10: 3
Luke 18–24: 169, 369
23:1–39
Mark 1–8: 202
Mark 9–16: 308
23:1ff.
Luke 1–5: 166
23:2
Matthew 16–23: 337
Luke 11–17: 104
Luke 18–24: 163
James: 146
23:2–3
Luke 1–5: 319
Acts 1–12: 12
Romans 9–16: 210
23:2–4
Acts 13–28: 26
2 Corinthians: 392
Galatians: 200
23:2–36
Matthew 16–23: 3
23:2, 13, 14, 15, 23, 25, 27, 29
Luke 1–5: 319
23:3
Matthew 16–23: 290
Romans 1–8: 156
2 Corinthians: 182
Titus: 93
23:4
Matthew 8–15: 113, 275
Matthew 16–23: 341
Matthew 24–28: 227
Mark 1–8: 151
Luke 1–5: 206, 319
Luke 6–10: 4
Luke 11–17: 202
Luke 18–24: 132, 344
Acts 13–28: 68
Philippians: 237
James: 123
23:4–7
Philippians: 121
23:5
Matthew 8–15: 80
Matthew 16–23: 338
Mark 1–8: 259
Luke 1–5: 337
Luke 6–10: 300
Luke 11–17: 113
23:5–7
Matthew 1–7: 60
Mark 9–16: 37
Luke 1–5: 21, 341
Luke 11–17: 385
Luke 18–24: 113
1 Timothy: 19
James: 146
1–3 John: 255
23:6
Matthew 16–23: 236
Luke 6–10: 8, 43
Luke 11–17: 101, 113, 262
James: 103
23:6–7
Mark 9–16: 197
Luke 18–24: 132
1 Corinthians: 128
23:7
Mark 9–16: 219
Luke 11–17: 101, 113
Luke 18–24: 164
23:8–12
Luke 11–17: 102
Philippians: 122, 316
23:9
Philippians: 166
1 Peter: 31
23:11
Luke 6–10: 24
2 Corinthians: 345
Philippians: 130
23:11–12
Matthew 16–23: 99
1 Timothy: 118
23:12
Matthew 1–7: 149
Luke 11–17: 264

John 12–21: 29
Philippians: 138
James: 200, 214
23:13
Matthew 1–7: 64, 278
Mark 1–8: 339
Mark 9–16: 220
Luke 6–10: 127
Luke 11–17: 254, 347
Galatians: 119
Titus: 93
23:13–15
Luke 6–10: 116
23:13–15, 23, 25 ,27
Matthew 8–15: 160
23:13–16
2 Corinthians: 182
23:13, 23, 25
Matthew 1–7: 61
23:13–30
Matthew 8–15: 461
1 & 2 Thessalonians: 62
23:13–33
1 Corinthians: 128
23:13–36
Mark 1–8: 350, 432
Acts 1–12: 153
Galatians: 138
1 & 2 Thessalonians: 239
2 Peter–Jude: 69–70
23:14
Matthew 1–7: 278
Romans 1–8: 156
23:15
Matthew 8–15: 317, 337, 462
Matthew 16–23: 11
Mark 1–8: 136, 345, 356
Mark 9–16: 220
Luke 1–5: 195, 319
Luke 6–10: 114, 162
Luke 11–17: 99, 112, 280
Luke 18–24: 132, 159
Romans 1–8: 154
Galatians: 197
Revelation 12–22: 256
23:16
Mark 9–16: 220
Acts 1–12: 223
James: 271
Revelation 12–22: 298
23:16–17
John 1–11: 410
Revelation 1–11: 139
23:16–22
James: 264, 270
Revelation 1–11: 284
23:16, 18
Matthew 1–7: 325
23:17, 19–20
Matthew 1–7: 325
23:19
John 1–11: 410
Revelation 1–11: 139
23:21–22
Matthew 1–7: 325
23:23
Matthew 1–7: 63, 205, 269, 278
Matthew 8–15: 65, 317, 397
Matthew 16–23: 359
Mark 9–16: 199, 221
Luke 1–5: 319
Luke 18–24: 19
John 1–11: 100
2 Corinthians: 182, 283
2 Timothy: 94
James: 114
23:23–25
1 & 2 Thessalonians: 209
23:24
John 1–11: 410
Acts 1–12: 223
2 Corinthians: 58
Revelation 1–11: 139
Revelation 12–22: 298
23:24–28
Romans 1–8: 154
23:25
Matthew 1–7: 277
Mark 1–8: 355
Luke 11–17: 73
2 Corinthians: 183
2 Timothy: 115, 117
23:25–26
Matthew 1–7: 205
23:25–28
Matthew 16–23: 360
Mark 9–16: 202
Luke 1–5: 337
Luke 11–17: 99
23:25–31
Matthew 1–7: 277
23:25–33
Matthew 8–15: 335
23:26
Luke 11–17: 404
John 1–11: 410
Revelation 1–11: 139
23:27
Matthew 1–7: 353
Matthew 16–23: 14, 191
Mark 1–8: 149, 339, 403
Mark 9–16: 221
Luke 6–10: 162
Luke 18–24: 164
Acts 13–28: 281
Romans 1–8: 117
2 Corinthians: 126, 183
Ephesians: 200
23:27–28
Matthew 8–15: 325
Mark 1–8: 244, 354
Luke 1–5: 21
2 Corinthians: 187–88, 249
Philippians: 213
1 & 2 Thessalonians: 209
James: 180
23:28
Matthew 1–7: 61
Luke 6–10: 116
Luke 11–17: 320
23:29
2 Corinthians: 183
23:29–30
Mark 9–16: 221
Luke 11–17: 106
23:29–31
Matthew 16–23: 298
23:29–36
Mark 1–8: 299
23:29–39
Mark 9–16: 168
23:30
Acts 1–12: 216
23:30–35
Colossians and Philemon: 63
23:31
Mark 9–16: 169
James: 249, 258
23:31–35
1 & 2 Thessalonians: 62
23:32
Matthew 16–23: 390
Luke 11–17: 108
1 & 2 Thessalonians: 65
23:33
Matthew 1–7: 64
Luke 1–5: 217
Luke 11–17: 71
2 Corinthians: 183
James: 288
Revelation 12–22: 256
23:34
Acts 1–12: 171
2 Corinthians: 389
Hebrews: 394
Revelation 12–22: 29
23:34–36
John 12–21: 406
23:35
Matthew 16–23: 403
Luke 11–17: 108
James: 249
23:35–38
1 & 2 Thessalonians: 64
23:37
Matthew 1–7: 112, 156
Matthew 8–15: 110, 179
Matthew 16–23: 375
Acts 1–12: 122, 171
Romans 9–16: 90, 320
2 Corinthians: 192
1 & 2 Thessalonians: 283
1 Timothy: 70
Hebrews: 41
James: 258
23:37–38
Mark 1–8: 157, 310
Mark 9–16: 158
Acts 13–28: 156
23:37–39
Matthew 16–23: 289
Luke 18–24: 175
1 & 2 Thessalonians: 83, 174
1 Peter: 32
23:38
Matthew 24–28: 9, 10

John 1–11: 91
23:39
Matthew 16–23: 397
Matthew 24–28: 10
Luke 1–5: 101
Luke 11–17: 173
Acts 1–12: 121
24
Luke 18–24: 190, 252
Acts 1–12: 19
1 Corinthians: 180, 419
Revelation 1–11: 286
24:1–2
Luke 18–24: 446
24:2
Matthew 1–7: 253
24:3
Matthew 16–23: 6
Mark 9–16: 230, 242, 255
Luke 18–24: 175, 176, 178, 242, 452
2 Corinthians: 132
1 & 2 Thessalonians: 74
James: 253
Revelation 1–11: 286
24:3–5, 24
Matthew 1–7: 460
24:4
1 & 2 Thessalonians: 270
24:4–5
2 Corinthians: 335
Philippians: 256
2 Peter–Jude: 70
24:4–7
Revelation 1–11: 177
24:4–10
Revelation 1–11: 178
24:4–12
1 Timothy: 148
24:4–33
1 & 2 Thessalonians: 143
24:5
1 & 2 Thessalonians: 146, 148
Revelation 12–22: 61
24:5–26
James: 254
24:6
1 Corinthians: 268
James: 184
24:6–7
Matthew 16–23: 6
1 & 2 Thessalonians: 147
Revelation 1–11: 180
24:6–8
Revelation 1–11: 176
24:7
Matthew 24–28: 308
1 & 2 Thessalonians: 147
Revelation 1–11: 182, 184, 204
Revelation 12–22: 34, 152
24:7–8
Matthew 1–7: 157
24:8
John 12–21: 214
1 & 2 Thessalonians: 146
Revelation 1–11: 177, 180, 191
24:9
John 12–21: 174
2 Corinthians: 145
1 & 2 Thessalonians: 148
1 Peter: 7
Revelation 1–11: 177, 181, 192
24:9–10
Hebrews: 274
24:9–12
Luke 18–24: 227
24:9–14
John 12–21: 171
24:10
Hebrews: 271
24:10–12
Revelation 1–11: 192
24:11
Luke 18–24: 202
Acts 1–12: 94
1 & 2 Thessalonians: 148
1 Timothy: 14
Hebrews: 274
2 Peter–Jude: 70
Revelation 12–22: 56, 61
24:11–12
Matthew 16–23: 6
1 & 2 Thessalonians: 272
2 Timothy: 106
24:11–12, 24
2 Timothy: 106
24:12
Luke 18–24: 217
1 & 2 Thessalonians: 272
1 Timothy: 148
Hebrews: 425
24:12–13
Mark 1–8: 228
24:13
Luke 6–10: 192
Luke 18–24: 259
Romans 9–16: 312
2 Corinthians: 13
Philippians: 163
1 & 2 Thessalonians: 19, 207
1 Timothy: 181
James: 28
1 Peter: 279
2 Peter–Jude: 27
1–3 John: 111
Revelation 1–11: 79, 99, 126, 193
Revelation 12–22: 23, 100, 238, 273
24:13–22
Revelation 1–11: 231
24:14
John 12–21: 24
Romans 9–16: 88
Colossians and Philemon: 21
1 & 2 Thessalonians: 148, 277
Revelation 1–11: 193, 224, 272, 292
Revelation 12–22: 86
24:15
Luke 18–24: 224, 230
John 12–21: 204
1 & 2 Thessalonians: 146, 267, 273, 274
Titus: 68
Revelation 1–11: 181, 192, 294, 295
Revelation 12–22: 32, 40, 49, 58, 61
24:15–16
Revelation 12–22: 28, 32, 39
24:15–18
Luke 11–17: 418
24:15–20
Revelation 1–11: 296
24:15–21
Revelation 12–22: 12
24:15–22
Revelation 12–22: 29–30
24:15–25
1–3 John: 97
24:15–31
1 & 2 Thessalonians: 266
James: 174
24:16–22
Revelation 1–11: 194
24:21
Matthew 8–15: 198
Matthew 16–23: 402
Matthew 24–28: 16, 31
Mark 9–16: 248
Luke 11–17: 416
1 & 2 Thessalonians: 267
Revelation 1–11: 2, 191, 203, 230, 231, 266, 292
Revelation 12–22: 2, 12, 27, 32, 96
24:21–22
Matthew 1–7: 45
Revelation 12–22: 3, 108
24:22
Acts 13–28: 38
1 & 2 Thessalonians: 20, 287
1 Timothy: 89
1–3 John: 217
Revelation 12–22: 30, 96
24:22–24
1 Peter: 17
24:23–24
Matthew 24–28: 18
24:24
Matthew 1–7: 94, 461, 463, 468, 480
Matthew 16–23: 354
Acts 1–12: 94
Acts 13–28: 38
Romans 1–8: 468
Romans 9–16: 374
Galatians: 10, 185
Ephesians: 339
1 & 2 Thessalonians: 20, 148, 149, 233, 272, 282, 287
1 Timothy: 14
2 Timothy: 68, 121
Titus: 148

2 Peter–Jude: 70
1–3 John: 15, 232
Revelation 12–22: 50, 61, 169
24:27
Matthew 24–28: 10
Luke 11–17: 154
1 & 2 Thessalonians: 74
1 Timothy: 273
James: 253
Revelation 1–11: 15
Revelation 12–22: 112, 211, 279, 302
24:27–28
Revelation 12–22: 222
24:27–30
James: 254
24:27–31
Revelation 12–22: 214
24:28
Revelation 12–22: 32
24:29
Matthew 24–28: 16
Romans 1–8: 85
1 & 2 Thessalonians: 269
Revelation 1–11: 177, 203, 205
Revelation 12–22: 221
24:29–30
Matthew 16–23: 5
Matthew 24–28: 16, 70
Luke 11–17: 414
Luke 18–24: 195
Acts 1–12: 55
1 Timothy: 273
Revelation 12–22: 213
24:29–31
Matthew 16–23: 55
Matthew 24–28: 115
Luke 11–17: 411
2 Peter–Jude: 111
24:29–44
1 & 2 Thessalonians: 135
24:29–25:46
Acts 1–12: 53
24:30
Matthew 16–23: 64
Matthew 24–28: 89, 339
Luke 1–5: 10, 157
Luke 11–17: 155
Luke 18–24: 236
Acts 1–12: 23
Romans 1–8: 85
Romans 9–16: 261
1 & 2 Thessalonians: 231, 233
Revelation 1–11: 32, 279, 280
Revelation 12–22: 112, 113, 211, 279
24:30–31
1 Corinthians: 419
Revelation 12–22: 171
24:31
Matthew 8–15: 379
Mark 9–16: 257
Acts 13–28: 38
1 & 2 Thessalonians: 20, 136, 234, 235, 287
James: 254
Revelation 1–11: 216
Revelation 12–22: 84
24:32–35
Matthew 24–28: 16
24:33
Luke 18–24: 238
24:34
Matthew 24–28: 16, 71, 88
Luke 11–17: 151, 152
24:35
Matthew 1–7: 262
John 1–11: 14
2 Corinthians: 417
2 Timothy: 150
1–3 John: 160
Revelation 12–22: 249
24:36
Luke 1–5: 305
Luke 11–17: 157, 417
Luke 18–24: 228
1 Corinthians: 418
2 Corinthians: 19
Philippians: 128
1 & 2 Thessalonians: 123, 131, 142
Revelation 1–11: 201, 270
24:37
Matthew 24–28: 10
1 & 2 Thessalonians: 74
James: 253
24:37–39
1 & 2 Thessalonians: 149
Hebrews: 324
Revelation 1–11: 203
24:37–41
Luke 11–17: 419
1 & 2 Thessalonians: 137
24:37–42
Luke 18–24: 254
24:37–44
Revelation 12–22: 211
24:37ff.
Revelation 1–11: 177
24:38
Luke 6–10: 165
24:38–39
Matthew 1–7: 263
24:38, 40–41
Matthew 8–15: 396
24:39
Matthew 24–28: 10
1 & 2 Thessalonians: 74
James: 253
24:39–41
James: 254
24:40–41
Matthew 24–28: 88
24:42
1 Corinthians: 418, 473
Revelation 1–11: 21, 28, 201
24:42–43
Revelation 12–22: 149
24:42–44
Luke 11–17: 157
1 Peter: 238
24:43
1 & 2 Thessalonians: 143, 159
Revelation 1–11: 114
24:44
Luke 18–24: 197, 255
Acts 1–12: 40
1 Corinthians: 418
1 & 2 Thessalonians: 142
Revelation 1–11: 28
24:44–46
James: 177
24:44–51
Luke 11–17: 162
24:45
Luke 18–24: 255
24:45–46
1 Corinthians: 100
24:45–51
Luke 11–17: 114, 154
1 & 2 Thessalonians: 132
2 Peter–Jude: 85
24:46
2 Peter–Jude: 150
24:48–49
Luke 18–24: 255
24:50
1 Corinthians: 418
1 & 2 Thessalonians: 142
Revelation 1–11: 201
24:50–51
James: 180
2 Peter–Jude: 185–86
24:51
Luke 11–17: 164
Luke 18–24: 255
Acts 1–12: 153, 221
2 Corinthians: 203
1 & 2 Thessalonians: 245
1 Timothy: 167
Revelation 12–22: 185, 189, 242, 256
24:64
Acts 1–12: 222
24–25
Luke 11–17: 154
James: 254
Revelation 1–11: 28
25
Luke 18–24: 190
1 Corinthians: 419
Revelation 1–11: 286
25:1ff.
Acts 1–12: 19
25:1–12
Matthew 1–7: 474
Luke 6–10: 164
Luke 11–17: 159, 276
John 12–21: 152
Acts 13–28: 301
25:1–13
Matthew 1–7: 478
Luke 1–5: 45
Romans 1–8: 222
Philippians: 215
1 & 2 Thessalonians: 74, 132

Revelation 12–22: 150, 202, 298
25:1–30
1 Corinthians: 400
25:5
Luke 18–24: 79
25:6
James: 154
25:8
1 & 2 Thessalonians: 194
25:11–12
1 Corinthians: 400
25:13
Luke 18–24: 252
1 Corinthians: 418
1 & 2 Thessalonians: 132, 142
Revelation 1–11: 28, 201
25:14–29
Luke 11–17: 339
25:14–30
Luke 18–24: 80
Romans 9–16: 246
1 Corinthians: 464
2 Peter–Jude: 85
Revelation 12–22: 299
25:15
2 Corinthians: 280
25:19
Luke 18–24: 79
Philippians: 306
25:21
Matthew 16–23: 58, 243
Luke 11–17: 147, 293
Acts 1–12: 226
Acts 13–28: 218
Romans 1–8: 131, 445
Romans 9–16: 192
1 Corinthians: 78
2 Corinthians: 350
Ephesians: 327
Philippians: 36, 128, 263
1 & 2 Thessalonians: 73
1 Timothy: 165
2 Timothy: 45, 75, 163, 202
Titus: 10, 30
Hebrews: 380
James: 113, 258
Revelation 1–11: 305
25:21–34
Acts 1–12: 20
25:23
Acts 1–12: 232
1 Corinthians: 78, 464
Philippians: 36, 128
1 & 2 Thessalonians: 73
Titus: 30
James: 113, 258
1 Peter: 271
25:24
Luke 11–17: 310
25:24–30
John 12–21: 152
25:27
Luke 11–17: 130
2 Corinthians: 273
25:29
2 Timothy: 200
25:30
Matthew 16–23: 10
Matthew 24–28: 269
John 1–11: 419
Acts 1–12: 221
2 Corinthians: 203, 249
Philippians: 94
1 & 2 Thessalonians: 164, 245
1 Timothy: 167
Revelation 12–22: 185, 189, 242, 256
25:31
Matthew 16–23: 64
Matthew 24–28: 57
Luke 1–5: 184
Luke 6–10: 281
Luke 18–24: 190, 238
1 & 2 Thessalonians: 231, 234
1 Timothy: 273
James: 247
1 Peter: 220
2 Peter–Jude: 111
Revelation 1–11: 215, 238, 279
Revelation 12–22: 84, 211, 212, 219
25:31–32
2 Corinthians: 177
25:31–33
2 Timothy: 169
1 Peter: 230
2 Peter–Jude: 184
25:31–36
Revelation 12–22: 70
25:31–40
Matthew 16–23: 104
Revelation 12–22: 30, 62
25:31–41
James: 128
25:31–46
Matthew 16–23: 52
Mark 9–16: 247
Luke 11–17: 156
Luke 18–24: 82, 193, 221, 223
1 Corinthians: 311
1 & 2 Thessalonians: 136, 249
2 Timothy: 87
Hebrews: 141
Revelation 1–11: 31, 297
Revelation 12–22: 70, 87, 211, 215, 219
25:31ff.
Acts 13–28: 307, 363
Revelation 1–11: 154, 214
25:32–33, 41–46
Matthew 1–7: 474
25:32–46
Matthew 24–28: 75
25:34
Matthew 1–7: 97
Matthew 8–15: 229
Luke 11–17: 23
Luke 18–24: 238
John 12–21: 301
Romans 1–8: 444
Ephesians: 14
Philippians: 273
1 & 2 Thessalonians: 163, 278
1 Peter: 31, 37
1–3 John: 107
Revelation 1–11: 214
Revelation 12–22: 50
25:34–36
Matthew 24–28: 135
25:34–40
Acts 13–28: 210
1 Corinthians: 480
Revelation 1–11: 319
25:34–46
Mark 9–16: 44
25:35–36
James: 89
25:35–36, 40
Romans 9–16: 247
25:35–40
Romans 9–16: 361
1 & 2 Thessalonians: 117
25:36
James: 276
25:37–39
1 Peter: 235
25:37–40
1 Peter: 278
25:39
James: 276
25:40
Hebrews: 427
James: 113
25:41
Matthew 8–15: 229, 349, 379, 396
Mark 1–8: 58, 64, 244
Luke 1–5: 219, 281, 286
Luke 6–10: 221, 290
Romans 9–16: 40
1 Corinthians: 417
2 Corinthians: 192, 202, 203, 210
Philippians: 94
Colossians and Philemon: 59
1 & 2 Thessalonians: 163, 239, 245
1 Timothy: 167
Hebrews: 48
James: 157, 245, 287, 288
1 Peter: 215, 227
2 Peter–Jude: 105
1–3 John: 36
Revelation 12–22: 18, 20, 92, 131, 211, 224, 225, 234, 242, 255, 256
25:41–45
Matthew 1–7: 193
Luke 6–10: 303
Revelation 12–22: 126
25:41–46
Matthew 16–23: 108
1 Peter: 227, 230
1–3 John: 25
Revelation 1–11: 214

Revelation 12–22: 233
25:41, 46
Luke 1–5: 216
25:45
Hebrews: 427
James: 128
25:46
Matthew 1–7: 72
Matthew 8–15: 222, 398
Matthew 24–28: 116
Luke 6–10: 352
1 Corinthians: 417
2 Corinthians: 202, 203, 210
Philippians: 258
Colossians and Philemon: 59
1 & 2 Thessalonians: 163, 239, 245
1 Timothy: 167
James: 225, 287, 288
Revelation 12–22: 92, 242
26:2
Matthew 24–28: 168
2 Corinthians: 145
26:3–4
Luke 18–24: 267
26:3–5
Luke 18–24: 91
26:3–16
Luke 18–24: 312
26:4
Mark 1–8: 359
26:4–5
John 12–21: 306
26:5
Luke 18–24: 120, 269
26:6
Luke 6–10: 78
John 12–21: 3
1 Peter: 4
2 Peter–Jude: 2, 18
1–3 John: 243
26:6–13
Luke 6–10: 171
Luke 18–24: 93
John 1–11: 3, 453
26:7
John 12–21: 5
26:8
2 Corinthians: 267
26:8–9
John 12–21: 7, 75
26:12
John 12–21: 8
26:14
Matthew 8–15: 206
Luke 18–24: 272, 311, 433
1 Peter: 47
26:14–16
Matthew 8–15: 179
Matthew 24–28: 185
Luke 11–17: 129
2 Corinthians: 272
26:14, 47
Matthew 24–28: 182
26:16
1 Peter: 47
26:17–19
Mark 9–16: 279
26:18
Mark 9–16: 268
Luke 18–24: 273
Romans 9–16: 259
26:20
John 1–11: 6
John 12–21: 317
26:21, 24
Matthew 24–28: 195
26:22
Matthew 8–15: 176
Mark 9–16: 287
Luke 18–24: 290
26:24
Mark 9–16: 35, 163
Luke 11–17: 129, 168
Luke 18–24: 275
John 12–21: 6, 64, 77, 153
Acts 1–12: 32
Acts 13–28: 301
2 Corinthians: 212
2 Timothy: 80
26:25
Luke 11–17: 279
Luke 18–24: 312
John 12–21: 79
26:26
Luke 18–24: 282
26:26–27
Mark 1–8: 79
Luke 11–17: 3
26:26–28
1 Peter: 206
26:27
1 Corinthians: 237
26:27–28
1 Peter: 24
26:28
Matthew 8–15: 105
Luke 1–5: 154, 272, 321, 328
Luke 11–17: 40
Luke 18–24: 284
John 12–21: 133
Acts 1–12: 75, 303
Acts 13–28: 336
2 Corinthians: 97, 98
Ephesians: 21, 22
Colossians and Philemon: 110
Hebrews: 237
1 Peter: 171
1–3 John: 73
Revelation 1–11: 232
Revelation 12–22: 308
26:29
Matthew 8–15: 294
1 Corinthians: 273
26:30
1 Corinthians: 272
Ephesians: 257
26:30–31
Luke 18–24: 323
26:30–35
Luke 18–24: 294
26:31
Matthew 24–28: 168, 193
Luke 1–5: 340
John 12–21: 177, 191
Ephesians: 384
26:31–32
Luke 6–10: 31
26:31–35, 69–75
Matthew 8–15: 140
26:32
Matthew 24–28: 312
Luke 18–24: 295
26:33
Matthew 24–28: 212
Mark 9–16: 107
Luke 6–10: 31
John 12–21: 93, 400
26:33–35
Mark 1–8: 170
26:33, 35
Matthew 8–15: 21
26:33, 69–75
Matthew 8–15: 141
26:34
Matthew 16–23: 47
26:35
Luke 6–10: 31
26:36
Luke 18–24: 300, 302
John 12–21: 306
26:36–42
1 & 2 Thessalonians: 85
26:36–44
Luke 11–17: 3
26:36–46
2 Peter–Jude: 51
26:37
Mark 9–16: 210
26:37–38
Luke 11–17: 268
Philippians: 205
26:38
Matthew 16–23: 339
Luke 18–24: 306
Philippians: 128
James: 16
26:38–46
1 & 2 Thessalonians: 186
26:39
Matthew 1–7: 396
Matthew 16–23: 237, 259
Matthew 24–28: 173, 254
Mark 9–16: 106
Luke 11–17: 27
Luke 18–24: 303
John 1–11: 473
Romans 1–8: 307
Romans 9–16: 310
2 Corinthians: 156
Philippians: 133
Hebrews: 378
1 Peter: 31
26:39–44
Matthew 1–7: 369
Luke 11–17: 51
Philippians: 127

26:39–45
Luke 18–24: 303
26:39, 42
Matthew 1–7: 91, 95
Romans 9–16: 242
Ephesians: 174
26:40–41
Colossians and Philemon: 182
26:40–41, 43, 45
Matthew 24–28: 213
26:40–45
Matthew 16–23: 62
Luke 18–24: 324
26:40, 45
Matthew 1–7: 117
26:41
Matthew 24–28: 168
Luke 1–5: 261
Luke 11–17: 2, 30
John 12–21: 93
1 Corinthians: 437
2 Corinthians: 37, 481
Ephesians: 381
Philippians: 205, 266
1 & 2 Thessalonians: 91, 195
James: 25, 51
1 Peter: 281
1–3 John: 37
26:42
Matthew 16–23: 259
John 1–11: 473
Romans 1–8: 307
26:43
Luke 18–24: 256
26:45
Matthew 1–7: 104
Mark 9–16: 268
2 Corinthians: 269
26:47
Luke 18–24: 311
Ephesians: 368
26:48
Luke 6–10: 80
2 Corinthians: 486
26:49
Luke 18–24: 314
John 12–21: 308
1 & 2 Thessalonians: 215
26:50
Luke 18–24: 314
John 12–21: 81
26:50–53
1 Peter: 150
26:51
Matthew 24–28: 213
26:52
Luke 18–24: 316
John 12–21: 311
Romans 9–16: 221, 225, 373
1–3 John: 134
Revelation 12–22: 51
26:52–53
Matthew 8–15: 294
Matthew 24–28: 214
26:52–54
Mark 9–16: 335, 347
26:53
Matthew 1–7: 98, 172
Matthew 8–15: 437
Matthew 16–23: 274
John 12–21: 39
Ephesians: 125
Philippians: 125
2 Timothy: 100
Titus: 145
26:54
Matthew 1–7: 19
Mark 9–16: 314
Luke 18–24: 290, 316
26:55–56
John 12–21: 191
26:56
Matthew 16–23: 238
Matthew 24–28: 157
Mark 9–16: 107, 296
Luke 6–10: 29, 240
Luke 11–17: 30
Luke 18–24: 53
John 12–21: 230, 317, 376
26:56, 58
2 Timothy: 11
26:57
Matthew 24–28: 131, 214
Luke 18–24: 367
26:57–58
Matthew 24–28: 215
Mark 9–16: 336
26:57–60
James: 159
26:57–68
1 Peter: 168
26:58
John 1–11: 2
John 12–21: 317
26:58–75
Luke 11–17: 30
26:59
Mark 9–16: 325
Luke 18–24: 335
James: 219
26:59–61
Luke 11–17: 110
Acts 1–12: 193
26:59–68
1 & 2 Thessalonians: 298
26:60
Matthew 1–7: 461
Mark 9–16: 325
Luke 18–24: 335
26:61
Matthew 1–7: 253
Matthew 24–28: 259
26:62–63
Luke 18–24: 51
26:63
Matthew 16–23: 288
Matthew 24–28: 280
Mark 9–16: 327
Luke 18–24: 336
Revelation 1–11: 51
26:63–64
Matthew 1–7: 322
Luke 18–24: 336
John 12–21: 12
Acts 1–12: 223
2 Corinthians: 43
James: 269
Revelation 1–11: 32
26:63–66
Matthew 24–28: 223, 233
Luke 1–5: 195
26:64
John 12–21: 135
Acts 1–12: 23
1 Corinthians: 287
Revelation 1–11: 28
Revelation 12–22: 112, 211
26:64–65
John 1–11: 484
26:65
Luke 1–5: 323
Luke 18–24: 337, 380
Acts 13–28: 50
26:67
Luke 18–24: 338
1 Peter: 252
Revelation 12–22: 212
26:67–68
Matthew 1–7: 225, 333
26:68
Matthew 24–28: 249
Mark 9–16: 330, 360
26:69–70
Acts 1–12: 10
26:69–74
Matthew 1–7: 322
Luke 6–10: 32
2 Corinthians: 139
26:69–75
Luke 6–10: 20
1 & 2 Thessalonians: 226
Revelation 12–22: 69
26:70
Luke 18–24: 326
26:70–74, 75
2 Timothy: 11
26:71
Mark 9–16: 338
26:72
Mark 9–16: 338
Luke 18–24: 326
26:73
Matthew 1–7: 106
Mark 9–16: 338
26:74
Matthew 24–28: 162
Luke 18–24: 327
Ephesians: 187
26:74–75
James: 160
26:75
Matthew 1–7: 322
Matthew 16–23: 340
Mark 9–16: 339
Romans 1–8: 484
2 Timothy: 65
James: 242

27:1
John 12–21: 325
27:1–2
Matthew 24–28: 234
Mark 9–16: 35
27:2
Acts 13–28: 217
27:3
Luke 6–10: 81
John 12–21: 85
Acts 13–28: 216
Ephesians: 145
27:3–4
Matthew 8–15: 181
Luke 18–24: 343
27:3–5
Mark 9–16: 313
2 Corinthians: 266, 467
1 Timothy: 256
1–3 John: 40
27:3–8
Acts 1–12: 33
27:3–10
Luke 18–24: 271
27:4
Matthew 1–7: 66
27:5
Luke 18–24: 344
John 12–21: 381
Acts 1–12: 33
27:6
Matthew 8–15: 181
1 & 2 Thessalonians: 172
1 Timothy: 218
27:6–10
Luke 18–24: 344
27:7–8
Matthew 8–15: 181
27:9
1 & 2 Thessalonians: 172
1 Timothy: 197, 218
27:11
Matthew 24–28: 113
John 12–21: 16
2 Corinthians: 289
Colossians and Philemon: 41
1 Timothy: 267
27:11–14
1 Peter: 168
27:12
Luke 18–24: 346
1 Peter: 252
27:12–14
2 Corinthians: 447
27:14
Matthew 8–15: 20
27:15
Luke 18–24: 358
27:15–26
John 12–21: 315
27:17–18
Matthew 24–28: 113
27:18
Luke 1–5: 320
Luke 18–24: 345, 356
Philippians: 64
27:19
Matthew 24–28: 279
Mark 9–16: 348, 353, 361
Luke 18–24: 347, 359
John 12–21: 337
Acts 1–12: 108, 109
Acts 13–28: 317
2 Corinthians: 177
27:20
Luke 18–24: 422
John 12–21: 337
27:20–21
Matthew 24–28: 209
27:20–23
Mark 1–8: 181
Luke 18–24: 382
27:20–25
John 1–11: 137
1 & 2 Thessalonians: 63
27:21–22
Matthew 16–23: 300
27:22
Matthew 16–23: 350
Mark 9–16: 96, 171
Luke 18–24: 53, 342, 360
John 12–21: 337, 343
27:22–23
Acts 1–12: 62
1–3 John: 191
27:22–25
2 Corinthians: 468
27:23
Mark 9–16: 171
James: 247
27:24
Mark 9–16: 348, 354
Luke 11–17: 227
Luke 18–24: 360
Acts 13–28: 194
27:24–25
Colossians and Philemon: 63
27:25
Luke 18–24: 392
John 12–21: 334
Acts 1–12: 168
Acts 13–28: 149
27:26
Luke 6–10: 295
Luke 18–24: 358, 361
2 Corinthians: 145
27:26–30
Matthew 16–23: 225
27:26–31
1 Peter: 168
27:27
Philippians: 6, 61
27:27–30
Luke 18–24: 383
27:27–31
Luke 11–17: 227
Revelation 12–22: 212
27:29
Mark 1–8: 203
John 12–21: 338
2 Timothy: 199
27:29–31
Matthew 1–7: 295
1 Peter: 252
27:30
Acts 13–28: 281
27:31
John 12–21: 348
27:32
John 12–21: 338
1 Peter: 4
2 Peter–Jude: 2, 18
27:34
Luke 18–24: 379, 383
John 12–21: 356
Acts 13–28: 24
27:35
2 Corinthians: 455
27:37
John 12–21: 352
27:38
1 Peter: 166
27:39
Acts 13–28: 24
27:39–40
Luke 18–24: 382
John 1–11: 91
John 12–21: 9
27:39–43
John 12–21: 350
27:39–44
1 Peter: 252
27:40
Matthew 1–7: 91
1 Timothy: 89
2 Timothy: 212
27:40, 43
Luke 1–5: 195
27:41
Matthew 1–7: 43
Mark 9–16: 156
Luke 6–10: 317
Luke 18–24: 114
Ephesians: 145
27:42
Matthew 24–28: 321
John 12–21: 217
1 Timothy: 89
27:42–43
Matthew 1–7: 169
27:43
Hebrews: 379
27:44
Luke 18–24: 384
27:45
Mark 9–16: 386
1–3 John: 194
Revelation 1–11: 205
27:46
Matthew 1–7: xii, 376
Matthew 24–28: 144, 174
Mark 1–8: 94
Mark 9–16: 93, 377
Luke 1–5: 238, 258
Luke 6–10: 338
Luke 11–17: 3, 181
Luke 18–24: 50, 53

John 12–21: 78, 230, 255, 350
Acts 13–28: 24
Romans 9–16: 314
2 Corinthians: 12, 215
Ephesians: 199
Philippians: 128
1 Peter: 30, 209
27:49
1 Timothy: 89
27:50
Matthew 16–23: 249
Matthew 24–28: 144
John 12–21: 356
1 Peter: 224
27:50–51
Hebrews: 217
27:51
Matthew 1–7: 257
Matthew 24–28: 308
Luke 1–5: 171
Luke 18–24: 390
John 12–21: 226
Romans 1–8: 276
Revelation 1–11: 204
27:51–54
Revelation 12–22: 152
27:52
Mark 1–8: 264
1 & 2 Thessalonians: 125
Revelation 1–11: 320
27:52–53
Luke 18–24: 390
27:53
Revelation 12–22: 264
27:54
Matthew 1–7: xii
Mark 1–8: 412
Mark 9–16: 381
Luke 1–5: 195
Luke 18–24: 385, 391
John 12–21: 351
Acts 13–28: 346
Revelation 1–11: 204
27:55
Luke 1–5: 13
27:55–56
Matthew 1–7: xii
Matthew 24–28: 307
Luke 6–10: 43
John 1–11: 8
1–3 John: 6
27:56
Matthew 16–23: 236
Luke 6–10: 183
John 1–11: 7, 457
1–3 John: 6
27:57
Mark 9–16: 391
Luke 11–17: 128
Luke 18–24: 402
John 12–21: 366
27:57–58
Matthew 8–15: 33
27:57–60
Luke 18–24: 51
27:60
Mark 9–16: 392
John 12–21: 367
27:61
Matthew 24–28: 307
John 12–21: 355
27:62–63
John 1–11: 26
27:62–64
Matthew 24–28: 260
Luke 18–24: 403
27:62–66
Mark 9–16: 393, 399
Luke 18–24: 410
Ephesians: 35
27:63
Luke 18–24: 266
Revelation 12–22: 238
27:66
2 Corinthians: 45
Revelation 1–11: 217
28:1
Mark 9–16: 398
Luke 18–24: 409
28:2
1 Timothy: 141
28:2–4
Matthew 8–15: 55
Luke 1–5: 157
28:2–5
Acts 1–12: 294
28:3
Revelation 1–11: 113, 226
28:3–4
Hebrews: 23
28:4
Matthew 24–28: 297
Luke 18–24: 410
28:4,8
Luke 1–5: 325
28:5–7
John 12–21: 368
28:5, 10
Luke 1–5: 157
28:7
Matthew 24–28: 161
Mark 9–16: 297
Luke 6–10: 27
2 Peter–Jude: 3
28:8
Mark 9–16: 403
Luke 18–24: 412
28:8–10
Mark 9–16: 403, 404
Luke 18–24: 433
28:9
Luke 18–24: 157
John 1–11: 14–15
John 12–21: 379
1 Corinthians: 403
2 Corinthians: 483
28:9–10
Luke 18–24: 412
28:10
Mark 9–16: 340
Luke 6–10: 32
Revelation 1–11: 50
28:10, 16
John 12–21: 389
28:11–14
Matthew 24–28: 301
Mark 9–16: 394
Luke 11–17: 202
28:11–15
Matthew 1–7: xii
Matthew 8–15: 330
Matthew 16–23: 8
Mark 9–16: 369
Luke 11–17: 84, 86, 371
Luke 18–24: 403
John 12–21: 217, 369, 375
Acts 1–12: 137
28:12
Philippians: 203
28:13
1 & 2 Thessalonians: 125
28:16
Luke 18–24: 451
John 12–21: 390
28:16–17
Luke 11–17: 207
28:17
Luke 18–24: 421
Philippians: 131
28:18
Matthew 1–7: xii, 488
Matthew 8–15: 437
Matthew 24–28: 72, 232
Mark 1–8: 56
Mark 9–16: 211
Luke 6–10: 295, 345
Luke 18–24: 111
John 1–11: 14
1 Corinthians: 253, 287, 420
2 Corinthians: 290
Philippians: 140
1 & 2 Thessalonians: 254
Revelation 12–22: 21
28:18–19
Matthew 1–7: 109, 118
Matthew 8–15: 273
Matthew 16–23: 358
Mark 1–8: 250
2 Peter–Jude: 29
28:18–20
Matthew 8–15: 49
Mark 1–8: 53, 201, 312
Mark 9–16: 297
Philippians: 168
1 & 2 Thessalonians: 111, 195, 318
28:19
Matthew 1–7: 114
Matthew 8–15: 468
Matthew 16–23: 309
Matthew 24–28: 312
Mark 1–8: 168, 374
Luke 6–10: 200
Luke 11–17: 72, 216
Luke 18–24: 126, 258
John 12–21: 118
Acts 13–28: 78

Romans 9–16: 81
1 Corinthians: 117, 266, 311, 425
2 Corinthians: 202, 208
Ephesians: 69, 131
2 Timothy: 42, 61
1–3 John: 162
28:19–20
Matthew 8–15: 105, 127
Mark 1–8: 284
Luke 1–5: 31, 158, 182, 342
Luke 6–10: 103, 159, 225, 242
John 12–21: 284, 377, 381
Acts 1–12: 13, 21, 159, 290, 309
Acts 13–28: 80
Romans 9–16: 87, 154, 173, 216
1 Corinthians: 460, 463
2 Corinthians: 201, 245, 257
Ephesians: 39
Philippians: 25, 158, 185
1 & 2 Thessalonians: 32, 47, 97
1 Timothy: 138, 142
2 Timothy: 194
James: 148, 289
2 Peter–Jude: 19
1–3 John: 57
28:20
Matthew 1–7: 118
Matthew 8–15: 217
Matthew 24–28: 11, 232
Luke 18–24: 448, 453
John 1–11: 14
John 12–21: 215
Acts 13–28: 150
Romans 1–8: 24, 320
2 Corinthians: 132
1 & 2 Thessalonians: 297, 316
Hebrews: 241
Revelation 1–11: 43

Mark
1:1
Mark 1–8: 1, 4, 27, 47, 56, 71, 136, 160, 175, 332
Mark 9–16: 367, 394, 404
Luke 1–5: 194
John 1–11: 2
Acts 1–12: 104
Revelation 12–22: 86
1:1–8
Mark 1–8: 11
1:1–13
Mark 1–8: 7
1:2
Mark 1–8: 191
1:2–3
Mark 1–8: 16, 160
John 1–11: 29
1:2–8
Mark 1–8: 27, 40, 41, 56
1:2–11
Mark 1–8: 176
1:3
Mark 1–8: 33
1:4
Mark 1–8: 29, 287
Revelation 12–22: 32
1:4–5
Mark 1–8: 23
1:4–6
Mark 1–8: 19
1:4–8
Mark 1–8: 28
1:5
Mark 1–8: 127
Luke 1–5: 205
Luke 6–10: 152
1:6
Mark 1–8: 23
Mark 9–16: 18
Hebrews: 350
1:7
Mark 1–8: 31, 126
1:7–8
Mark 1–8: 25, 191
John 1–11: 29
1:8
Mark 1–8: 136
1:9
Mark 1–8: 271
1:9–11
Mark 1–8: 27, 28, 40, 41, 126
1:10
Mark 1–8: 35
1:10–11
Mark 1–8: 33
1:11
Mark 1–8: 5, 19, 36
1:12
Matthew 1–7: 85
Mark 1–8: 183
Mark 9–16: 417
Luke 1–5: 254
Acts 1–12: 13
Ephesians: 250
1:12–13
Mark 1–8: 41, 56
1:12–20
Mark 1–8: 39, 40, 41, 57
1:13
Matthew 1–7: 87, 89
Mark 1–8: 239
John 12–21: 139
1 Peter: 280
1:14
Mark 1–8: 167, 200, 213, 286
Luke 1–5: 228, 335
Luke 6–10: 7
John 12–21: 320
Acts 1–12: 48
Romans 1–8: 99
1 & 2 Thessalonians: 35
Revelation 12–22: 86
1:14–15
Matthew 1–7: 381, 454
Mark 1–8: 46, 80, 238, 369
Luke 11–17: 199, 205
1 Peter: 32
1:14–20
Mark 1–8: 98
1:14–9:50
Luke 1–5: 265
1:15
Matthew 1–7: 54
Matthew 8–15: 351
Mark 1–8: 5, 84, 317
Luke 6–10: 93
Luke 11–17: 165, 285
Acts 1–12: 15
Acts 13–28: 173
Romans 9–16: 259
Philippians: 223
1 & 2 Thessalonians: 287, 297
1–3 John: 37
1:16
Luke 6–10: 39
1:16–20
Mark 1–8: 7, 50, 56, 71, 72, 116, 161, 165
Luke 1–5: 291, 292, 304
1:17–20
Mark 1–8: 5
1:18
Mark 1–8: 160
1:19–20
Mark 1–8: 52
John 12–21: 318
1:20
Matthew 8–15: 149
Mark 1–8: 56, 160
Luke 6–10: 41, 184
John 1–11: 7
Hebrews: 137
1–3 John: 6
1:21
Mark 9–16: 36
Luke 1–5: 269
Luke 6–10: 39
1 Peter: 4
2 Peter–Jude: 2
1:21–22
Mark 1–8: 59
1:21–28
Mark 1–8: 55, 56, 57, 59, 70, 256
1:22
Matthew 1–7: 286
Matthew 16–23: 286
Mark 1–8: 51, 71, 152, 274
John 12–21: 251
1:23
Mark 1–8: 59, 66
Luke 1–5: 283
Acts 1–12: 234
Revelation 12–22: 147
1:23–24
Mark 1–8: 63
1:23–25
Luke 1–5: 281
1:23–26
Mark 1–8: 280
Luke 11–17: 201
1:23–27
Mark 1–8: 63

1–3 John: 17
Revelation 1–11: 260
1:24
Mark 1–8: 136, 164, 271
Luke 1–5: 234
Acts 1–12: 66
2 Corinthians: 468
Philippians: 310
Revelation 1–11: 118
1:24–27
Mark 1–8: 5
1:25
Matthew 16–23: 336
Mark 1–8: 98, 232, 267
Mark 9–16: 65
Luke 6–10: 263
1:25–26
Mark 1–8: 136
Mark 9–16: 29
1:25–28
Mark 1–8: 65
1:25, 34
Luke 1–5: 287
1:26
Mark 1–8: 371
Acts 1–12: 234
1:27
Matthew 8–15: 40, 437
Mark 1–8: 72, 98, 157, 239
Mark 9–16: 153
Luke 1–5: 303
Titus: 125
1:28
Matthew 8–15: 246
Mark 1–8: 274
1:29
Matthew 8–15: 146
Mark 1–8: 33, 99
Mark 9–16: 36
Luke 1–5: 292
Luke 6–10: 26, 39
1 Peter: 4
2 Peter–Jude: 2, 3
1:29–30
Matthew 8–15: 138
1:29–34
Mark 1–8: 70, 71, 136
1:29–39
Mark 1–8: 69–70, 71, 81
1:30
Matthew 8–15: 16
Luke 6–10: 26
1:31
Matthew 8–15: 16
Mark 1–8: 98
Luke 1–5: 292
1:32
Mark 1–8: 177, 242
1:32–33
1 Peter: 4
2 Peter–Jude: 2
1:32–34
Luke 6–10: 294
Acts 13–28: 169
1:33
Luke 1–5: 295
1:33–34
Mark 1–8: 99
1:34
Mark 1–8: 66, 98
Luke 1–5: 256, 283, 286
John 1–11: 23
Acts 13–28: 97
1 Peter: 32
1:35
Mark 1–8: 78, 414
Luke 1–5: 238, 296
Luke 11–17: 3
John 12–21: 235
1 & 2 Thessalonians: 186
1:36–39
Mark 1–8: 71, 79
1:38
Mark 1–8: 84, 98, 200, 213
Luke 1–5: 282, 304
Luke 6–10: 235
Revelation 1–11: 291
1:38–39
Mark 1–8: 92
Acts 1–12: 48
1:39
Mark 1–8: 67
Luke 1–5: 297, 317
John 12–21: 13
1:40
Mark 1–8: 86
Luke 11–17: 237
1:40–41
Matthew 8–15: 111
1:40–44
Mark 1–8: 163
1:40–45
Mark 1–8: 83, 85, 101, 267, 379
Mark 9–16: 15
1:41
Matthew 8–15: 75
Mark 1–8: 77, 265
Mark 9–16: 116
Luke 1–5: 315
Luke 6–10: 231, 326
2 Corinthians: 123
1:41–44
Mark 1–8: 86, 89–90
1:42
Mark 1–8: 98
1:45
Matthew 8–15: 11
Mark 1–8: 85, 86, 92, 98, 161
Luke 1–5: 316
1–8
Mark 1–8: 15
2:1
Matthew 8–15: 49
Mark 1–8: 60
2:1–2
Mark 1–8: 98
2:1–3:6
Mark 1–8: 7
2:1–12
Mark 1–8: 96, 98, 112
2:2
Mark 1–8: 93
Luke 1–5: 318, 320
2:3–4
Matthew 8–15: 50
Mark 1–8: 101
2:3–12
Mark 1–8: 5
1 Peter: 32
2:4
Mark 1–8: 177
Luke 1–5: 320
2:5
Mark 1–8: 102
2:5, 9
1–3 John: 17
2:5–10
Matthew 24–28: 232
Mark 1–8: 175
2:5–11
Mark 1–8: 225
2:5–12
Mark 1–8: 160
2:6–7
Mark 9–16: 154
Luke 6–10: 317
2:6–11
Mark 1–8: 103–4
2:7
Mark 1–8: 202
Mark 9–16: 211
John 1–11: 14
2:8
Luke 1–5: 323
2:10
Mark 1–8: 125
John 1–11: 2, 14
John 12–21: 251
1 & 2 Thessalonians: 172
Revelation 12–22: 112
2:12
Matthew 8–15: 55
Mark 1–8: 76, 106
Luke 1–5: 294, 325
John 12–21: 106
2:13
Mark 1–8: 93, 161
Luke 1–5: 329
2:13–14
Mark 1–8: 113
Luke 1–5: 330
2:13–16
Matthew 1–7: xi
2:13–17
Mark 1–8: 109, 125, 136, 190
2:14
Matthew 1–7: xi
Matthew 8–15: 60
Mark 1–8: 52, 119, 160
2:14–15
Mark 1–8: 165, 171
2:15
Mark 1–8: 117
2:16
Matthew 1–7: 189
Matthew 16–23: 3

Mark 1–8: 118
Luke 1–5: 319
Luke 6–10: 107
Luke 11–17: 257
2:17
Mark 1–8: 120, 137
Luke 1–5: 12
James: 209
1 Peter: 108–9
2:18
Mark 1–8: 126
Luke 1–5: 338
Acts 13–28: 164
2:18–22
Mark 1–8: 123, 124
2:19–20
Mark 1–8: 129
Mark 9–16: 91
Luke 1–5: 340
Revelation 12–22: 202
2:21–22
Mark 1–8: 131
2:23–28
Mark 1–8: 5, 135, 136, 138, 141, 151, 195
2:24
Mark 1–8: 142
2:25–26
Mark 1–8: 143
2:27
Luke 6–10: 6
2:27–28
Mark 1–8: 145
2:28
Mark 1–8: 154, 224
Revelation 12–22: 112
3:1–2
Mark 1–8: 152
Luke 1–5: 269
3:1–6
Mark 1–8: 147, 151, 226
3:2
Matthew 24–28: 261
Luke 6–10: 7
Luke 11–17: 258
John 1–11: 49
3:3–5
Mark 1–8: 153–54
3:4
Matthew 8–15: 289
3:4–6
Mark 1–8: 17
3:5
Matthew 8–15: 289
Mark 9–16: 210, 226
Luke 6–10: 10
Luke 11–17: 260, 268
Luke 18–24: 155, 299
Romans 1–8: 120
Ephesians: 184
3:6
Matthew 1–7: 222
Matthew 8–15: 306
Matthew 16–23: 3
Mark 1–8: 57, 157, 161, 165, 180, 255, 271, 306, 341
Luke 6–10: 10
3:7
Mark 1–8: 113
3:7–8
Mark 1–8: 93
3:7–9
Mark 1–8: 160
3:7–10
Mark 1–8: 181
3:7–12
Mark 1–8: 177
3:7–13
Mark 1–8: 301
3:7–19
Mark 1–8: 159–60
3:8
Matthew 8–15: 299, 467
3:9
Mark 1–8: 228
Luke 1–5: 302
3:10
Mark 1–8: 407
Luke 1–5: 292
Luke 6–10: 294
3:10–12
Mark 1–8: 163
3:11
Mark 1–8: 15, 57, 165, 182, 239
Luke 1–5: 256, 281, 286
Acts 1–12: 234
3:11, 30
Luke 1–5: 282
3:12
Luke 1–5: 287
3:13
1 Corinthians: 323
2 Peter–Jude: 19
3:13–15
Matthew 1–7: 115
3:13–17
Mark 1–8: 284
3:13–19
Mark 1–8: 165, 176
2 Corinthians: 307
1 & 2 Thessalonians: 173, 202
3:14
Matthew 8–15: 126
Luke 6–10: 17
2 Corinthians: 413
3:14–15
Revelation 12–22: 40
3:14–19
John 1–11: 3
3:15
Acts 13–28: 97
2 Corinthians: 413
3:16
Luke 18–24: 295, 433
1 Peter: 14
3:16–17
Luke 6–10: 42
3:16–19
Matthew 8–15: 136
Mark 1–8: 169
Luke 6–10: 16
1 Peter: 4
2 Peter–Jude: 2
3:17
Matthew 8–15: 149
Matthew 16–23: 236
Matthew 24–28: 285
Mark 1–8: 4, 52
Mark 9–16: 104
Luke 1–5: 195
Luke 6–10: 42, 313
1 & 2 Thessalonians: 158
1–3 John: 6
3:17–18
1 Corinthians: 404
3:18
Matthew 8–15: 155, 161
Acts 1–12: 28
3:18–19
Mark 1–8: 161
3:19
Luke 6–10: 75
3:20
Mark 1–8: 181, 314
3:20–21
Mark 1–8: 176
3:20–35
Mark 1–8: 173–74, 176
3:21
Matthew 8–15: 339
Mark 1–8: 194, 266
Luke 6–10: 203, 237
Acts 13–28: 339
James: 10
1–3 John: 191
3:21–22
Mark 1–8: 28
3:22
Matthew 8–15: 218
Mark 1–8: 57, 162, 192, 194, 198, 202, 214, 255, 340, 341, 375, 399
Luke 1–5: 283, 296
Luke 6–10: 317
Luke 11–17: 194
Revelation 1–11: 310
3:22–30
Mark 1–8: 179, 275
3:28
Luke 18–24: 244
3:28–30
Mark 1–8: 199
1–3 John: 195
3:31–32
Acts 1–12: 29
3:31–35
Mark 1–8: 185
Luke 6–10: 202
James: 10
3:32
Mark 1–8: 194
3:33–35
John 12–21: 159
Acts 1–12: 29
3:35
Luke 11–17: 27
Romans 9–16: 242

James: 229
1 Peter: 201
4:1
Mark 1–8: 113, 162
Luke 1–5: 302
4:1–9
Mark 1–8: 193
4:1–20
Mark 1–8: 189–90
4:1–32
John 12–21: 27
4:1–34
Mark 1–8: 7, 211
4:2–20
Mark 1–8: 217
4:3–20
Mark 1–8: 211
4:8
Luke 6–10: 189
4:9
1 Peter: 137
Revelation 12–22: 51
4:9–13
Mark 1–8: 196–97
4:10
Luke 18–24: 433
4:10–13
Mark 1–8: 193
Luke 6–10: 182
4:11
Romans 9–16: 387
4:11–12
Mark 1–8: 214, 404
Luke 6–10: 188
4:12
Mark 1–8: 397
Luke 1–5: 39
Romans 9–16: 101
1 & 2 Thessalonians: 284
4:13
Luke 6–10: 19
Luke 18–24: 320
4:13–20
Revelation 1–11: 79
4:14–20
Mark 1–8: 193, 200
4:14–30
Mark 1–8: 47
4:15
Mark 1–8: 201, 211, 275
2 Corinthians: 408
4:16–17
Mark 1–8: 202, 211, 428
Luke 6–10: 319
Acts 13–28: 55
Revelation 12–22: 101
4:16–19
Mark 1–8: 228
4:18–19
Matthew 16–23: 200
Mark 1–8: 203, 211
Luke 18–24: 256
4:19
Luke 11–17: 130
2 Corinthians: 272
4:20
Mark 1–8: 205, 211
Luke 6–10: 195
4:21
Mark 1–8: 250
1 Peter: 160
4:21–23
Mark 1–8: 212
4:21–34
Mark 1–8: 209–10
4:23
Luke 11–17: 289
Revelation 12–22: 51
4:24
James: 66
4:24–25
Mark 1–8: 215
4:26–28
Romans 1–8: 226
4:26–29
Mark 1–8: 217
2 Corinthians: 222
1–3 John: 16
4:30–34
Mark 1–8: 219
4:31
Mark 1–8: 73
4:35
Luke 6–10: 207
4:35–36
Mark 1–8: 227
4:35–41
Mark 1–8: 223, 226, 254
4:35–5:43
Mark 1–8: 7
4:36
Matthew 8–15: 32, 41
John 12–21: 112
4:37
Matthew 8–15: 33
Luke 6–10: 209
4:37–38
Mark 1–8: 229
4:37–41
Mark 1–8: 328
4:37–41a
Mark 9–16: 302
4:38
Matthew 8–15: 33, 34
Mark 1–8: 51, 231
Luke 6–10: 210, 251
2 Corinthians: 293
4:38–39
Romans 1–8: 17
4:38–40
Hebrews: 356
4:38–41
Matthew 8–15: 46
4:39
Matthew 8–15: 36
Matthew 16–23: 336
Mark 1–8: 5
Luke 1–5: 292
Luke 6–10: 211
4:39–40
Mark 1–8: 232
4:40
Matthew 8–15: 125
Mark 1–8: 74, 75, 248
4:41
Mark 1–8: 107, 234, 250, 330
Luke 1–5: 157, 325
5:1
Matthew 8–15: 41
Mark 1–8: 227, 241
5:1–7
Mark 1–8: 240
Luke 1–5: 281
5:1–13
Acts 13–28: 170
5:1–20
Mark 1–8: 227, 237, 240, 255, 374
5:2
Luke 1–5: 283
5:2, 8, 13
Luke 1–5: 282
5:3–4
Acts 13–28: 176
5:4
Matthew 8–15: 44
5:4–5
Matthew 8–15: 42
5:5
Matthew 8–15: 41, 89
Luke 6–10: 220
5:7
Matthew 16–23: 78
Mark 1–8: 15, 57
Acts 1–12: 234
Romans 1–8: 205
James: 132
5:8
Luke 1–5: 283
5:8–16
Mark 1–8: 244–45
5:9
Matthew 8–15: 42
Mark 1–8: 4
5:13
Matthew 8–15: 43
Mark 1–8: 5
Acts 1–12: 223
5:14–15
Matthew 8–15: 46
5:16
Acts 13–28: 102
5:17
Acts 13–28: 102
5:17–20
Mark 1–8: 249
5:18
Matthew 8–15: 46
5:19
Matthew 1–7: 119
Mark 1–8: 101
2 Corinthians: 123
1 Peter: 31
5:19–20
Mark 1–8: 379
5:20
Luke 6–10: 41, 57

John 12–21: 26
2 Peter–Jude: 11
5:21
Mark 1–8: 113
Luke 6–10: 229
5:21–24
Mark 1–8: 254
5:21–34
Matthew 1–7: 119
5:21–43
Mark 1–8: 251–52
5:22
Matthew 8–15: 105
Luke 1–5: 267
Luke 11–17: 199
5:22–24
Luke 18–24: 64
5:22–24, 35–43
Luke 1–5: 293
5:23
Matthew 8–15: 77
Mark 1–8: 407
2 Corinthians: 204
1 Timothy: 168
Revelation 12–22: 238
5:24
Matthew 8–15: 79
5:25–32
Philippians: 315
5:25–34
Mark 1–8: 258
Luke 1–5: 292
1 Timothy: 85
5:26
Matthew 8–15: 80, 192
Luke 1–5: 12
5:28–29
Mark 1–8: 334
5:29
Matthew 8–15: 81
Mark 1–8: 5
Luke 1–5: 293
Luke 18–24: 63
Acts 1–12: 101
5:30
2 Peter–Jude: 26
5:31
Luke 6–10: 234
5:33
Luke 1–5: 157
5:34–36
Mark 9–16: 28
5:35
Matthew 8–15: 77
5:35–40
Mark 1–8: 262
5:35–43
Mark 1–8: 288
5:37
Matthew 16–23: 62
Mark 9–16: 4
Luke 6–10: 39
John 1–11: 8
Acts 1–12: 98
1–3 John: 6
5:38
Acts 13–28: 204
5:38–39
1 & 2 Thessalonians: 184
James: 242
5:38–40
Mark 9–16: 363
5:38–43
John 12–21: 251
5:40
Luke 6–10: 236
Acts 1–12: 284
5:40–41
Matthew 8–15: 85
5:41–42
Matthew 24–28: 339
5:42
Mark 1–8: 74
5:43
Mark 1–8: 91
Mark 9–16: 15
6:1–6
Mark 1–8: 269, 293, 364
6:2
Mark 1–8: 273
Luke 1–5: 269
Luke 6–10: 250
1 Corinthians: 298
2 Corinthians: 415
6:3
Matthew 1–7: 22
Matthew 8–15: 411
Mark 1–8: 172
Luke 1–5: 50, 248
Acts 1–12: 28
2 Corinthians: 292, 455
James: 10
6:3a
Mark 1–8: 275
6:3b–4
Mark 1–8: 277
6:4
John 1–11: 3
James: 10
6:5
Matthew 8–15: 412
Luke 1–5: 315
6:5–6
Mark 1–8: 57, 279
6:6
Matthew 8–15: 20
Mark 1–8: 270
Luke 1–5: 276
Luke 6–10: 123, 240
6:7
Matthew 8–15: 121, 135, 198
Mark 9–16: 169
Luke 6–10: 325
2 Corinthians: 413
6:7–11
Matthew 1–7: 118
6:7–12
Revelation 1–11: 291
6:7–13
Mark 1–8: 7, 76, 214, 283, 314, 339
6:7b
Mark 1–8: 287
6:8–9
Mark 1–8: 289
6:10
Mark 1–8: 291
6:11
Mark 1–8: 292
Acts 1–12: 291
6:12
Matthew 1–7: 54
Luke 11–17: 216, 313
John 12–21: 183
1 & 2 Thessalonians: 297
1–3 John: 121
Revelation 1–11: 139
6:12–13
Mark 1–8: 294
Mark 9–16: 169
6:13
Matthew 16–23: 76
Mark 9–16: 30
2 Corinthians: 413
James: 278
6:14–15
Mark 1–8: 301
6:14–16
Mark 1–8: 314
Luke 11–17: 229
6:14–29
Mark 1–8: 297–98
Mark 9–16: 349
Luke 1–5: 34
Acts 13–28: 327
6:14, 22
Luke 1–5: 230
6:15
Mark 1–8: 278
6:17
Mark 1–8: 178
John 1–11: 3
6:17–18
Mark 9–16: 54
Luke 6–10: 145
Luke 11–17: 228
6:19
Luke 1–5: 231
Luke 11–17: 228
6:20
Matthew 8–15: 420
Luke 18–24: 234
John 1–11: 29
Hebrews: 145
6:21
2 Corinthians: 284
6:21–29
Mark 1–8: 306
6:23
Matthew 8–15: 421
Matthew 16–23: 236
6:25
Matthew 8–15: 421
Romans 9–16: 177
6:27
Mark 1–8: 4
Titus: 125

6:30–32
Mark 1–8: 313, 339
6:30–44
Mark 1–8: 311–12, 313
6:31
Matthew 8–15: 423
Mark 1–8: 318
Luke 6–10: 251
2 Corinthians: 269
1 Peter: 253
6:31–32
Luke 1–5: 303
6:33
Matthew 8–15: 426
Luke 6–10: 252
6:33–34
Mark 1–8: 316, 324, 405
6:33–44
Mark 1–8: 326, 351
6:34
Mark 1–8: 5
Luke 11–17: 298
1 & 2 Thessalonians: 167
1 Peter: 262
6:35
Mark 1–8: 326, 403
6:35–44
Mark 1–8: 317–18, 389
6:38–44
Philippians: 125
6:39
Luke 6–10: 254
Revelation 1–11: 183
6:40
Matthew 8–15: 430, 432, 480
6:41
Mark 1–8: 388
6:41–44
Mark 1–8: 407
6:42
Mark 1–8: 387
6:45
Luke 18–24: 320
John 1–11: 2
6:45–46
Mark 1–8: 325
6:45–56
Mark 1–8: 324
6:45–8:26
Mark 1–8: 6
Luke 1–5: 13
Luke 6–10: 259
6:46
1 & 2 Thessalonians: 186
6:47
Luke 18–24: 320
6:47–52
Mark 1–8: 327–28
6:48
Matthew 8–15: 439, 440
Mark 1–8: 4
6:50
Matthew 8–15: 441
6:51
Matthew 8–15: 445
Mark 1–8: 333
6:52
Matthew 8–15: 445
Mark 1–8: 325
Luke 6–10: 30
6:53–56
Mark 1–8: 333
6:56
Matthew 8–15: 457
Mark 1–8: 164, 351
Philippians: 205
James: 276
7:1
Luke 1–5: 319
Luke 11–17: 103
7:1–5
Mark 1–8: 340
7:1–13
Mark 1–8: 5, 337–38, 340, 391
7:3
Luke 11–17: 104
7:3, 5
Ephesians: 146
7:5
Colossians and Philemon: 101
1–3 John: 246
7:5–9
Titus: 64
7:6
Mark 1–8: 16
7:6–7
Matthew 1–7: 353
Luke 1–5: 21, 75
7:6–9
Mark 1–8: 343
7:6–13
Mark 1–8: 166
7:7–8
Matthew 1–7: 278
7:8–9
Mark 9–16: 92
Colossians and Philemon: 101
1 & 2 Thessalonians: 288
7:8–13
Luke 1–5: 318
Luke 11–17: 255
7:9–13
Luke 18–24: 170
7:10
1 Timothy: 242
7:10–13
Matthew 1–7: 190
Mark 1–8: 345
7:11
Mark 1–8: 4
7:13
Romans 9–16: 56
1 & 2 Thessalonians: 288
Titus: 45, 95
7:14–15
Mark 1–8: 74
7:14–16
Mark 1–8: 351
7:14–19
Colossians and Philemon: 118
7:14–23
Mark 1–8: 349, 350
Acts 1–12: 296
1–3 John: 87
7:15
Matthew 8–15: 458
Romans 9–16: 292
1 Corinthians: 195
7:17
Matthew 8–15: 461
7:17–23
Mark 1–8: 355
7:18
Luke 18–24: 320
7:18–19
Luke 6–10: 331
7:19
Matthew 8–15: 458
Galatians: 58
7:20–22
Mark 9–16: 32
7:20–23
Mark 9–16: 47
Galatians: 160
Philippians: 285
James: 156
1–3 John: 26
7:21–22
Mark 9–16: 106
2 Corinthians: 309
Colossians and Philemon: 138–39
1 & 2 Thessalonians: 105
2 Timothy: 113
7:21–23
Matthew 1–7: 212
1 Peter: 31
7:23
1 & 2 Thessalonians: 199
7:24
Mark 1–8: 285, 364
7:24b
Matthew 8–15: 467
7:24–30
Mark 1–8: 361, 364
Luke 18–24: 58
7:24–31
Luke 6–10: 87
7:24–8:10
Mark 1–8: 414
7:24–9:50
Mark 1–8: 8
7:25
Luke 1–5: 282, 283
Luke 6–10: 220
7:25–26
Mark 1–8: 366
7:26
Matthew 8–15: 469
7:27
Mark 1–8: 368
7:28
Mark 1–8: 369
7:29
Mark 1–8: 5

7:29–30
Mark 1–8: 371
7:31
Matthew 8–15: 476
Mark 1–8: 384
Luke 6–10: 41
2 Peter–Jude: 11
7:31–37
Mark 1–8: 373, 375
7:31–8:9
Mark 1–8: 250
7:32
Mark 1–8: 375
7:32–37
Mark 1–8: 408
7:32, 37
Luke 1–5: 90
7:33–35
Mark 1–8: 376–77
7:34
Mark 9–16: 294
Luke 18–24: 299
James: 257
7:36
Mark 1–8: 91
7:36–37
Mark 1–8: 378
7:37
Mark 1–8: 398
8:1–3
Mark 1–8: 385
8:1–8
Luke 6–10: 250
8:1–9
Philippians: 125
8:1–10
Mark 1–8: 177, 379, 383–84, 405
8:6
Ephesians: 268
8:6–9
Mark 1–8: 388
8:9
Luke 6–10: 86
8:10
Matthew 16–23: 3
Mark 1–8: 390
Luke 1–5: 303
8:10–12
Mark 1–8: 8
8:11–12
Mark 1–8: 397
8:11–13
Mark 1–8: 409
8:11–26
Mark 1–8: 396, 397
8:13–21
Mark 1–8: 401–2
8:14
Matthew 16–23: 12
8:14–21
Mark 1–8: 418
8:17
Mark 1–8: 57
Mark 9–16: 23
Luke 6–10: 19
8:18
Revelation 12–22: 304
8:18–20
Mark 1–8: 389
8:22
Mark 1–8: 376
8:22–25
Luke 1–5: 293
8:22–26
Matthew 8–15: 10
Mark 1–8: 163, 406–7
8:23
Mark 1–8: 377
8:26
Mark 1–8: 91, 379
8:27
Matthew 16–23: 18
Mark 9–16: 5
Luke 6–10: 259
8:27–30
Mark 1–8: 413–14
8:27–33
Mark 1–8: 411
8:29
Mark 1–8: 4, 165, 192, 413
Luke 6–10: 262
John 12–21: 264
8:31
Matthew 24–28: 260
Mark 9–16: 2, 91, 268, 383
Luke 18–24: 265, 304, 409
John 12–21: 7, 213
1 Corinthians: 398
1 Peter: 2
Revelation 12–22: 112
8:31–32
Mark 9–16: 13
8:31–33
Mark 1–8: 417
Hebrews: 252
8:32
Mark 9–16: 2
Romans 9–16: 318
8:32–33
Revelation 1–11: 255
8:33
Mark 9–16: 2
8:34
Matthew 16–23: 47
Mark 1–8: 51, 425
Philippians: 96
Hebrews: 368
James: 142
8:34–38
Mark 1–8: 5, 99, 423, 428
Luke 6–10: 266
8:35
John 12–21: 174
Revelation 12–22: 273
8:35–37
Mark 1–8: 430
8:36
Luke 11–17: 358
1 Timothy: 253
Revelation 12–22: 189
8:36–37
Acts 13–28: 184
2 Timothy: 13
James: 287
8:38
Mark 1–8: 431
Luke 11–17: 238
Acts 1–12: 76
Philippians: 310
1 & 2 Thessalonians: 234
2 Timothy: 12
James: 191, 192, 247
2 Peter–Jude: 111
Revelation 1–11: 28
9
Matthew 1–7: 127
9:1
Revelation 1–11: 133
9:1–3
Matthew 8–15: 31
9:1–8
Matthew 16–23: 60
Mark 9–16: 1
9:1–10
Mark 1–8: 8
Luke 6–10: 50
9:2
Mark 1–8: 170
Mark 9–16: 299
Acts 1–12: 98
9:2–3
Mark 9–16: 4
9:3
Revelation 1–11: 113, 226
9:4–5
Mark 9–16: 5
9:5
Hebrews: 189
9:5–6
Mark 9–16: 7
9:7
Mark 1–8: 5, 15
Luke 1–5: 57
9:7–8
Mark 9–16: 8
Hebrews: 189
9:9
Mark 9–16: 25
John 12–21: 132
Revelation 12–22: 112
9:9–10
Mark 9–16: 14
John 12–21: 205, 224
9:9–13
Mark 9–16: 11
9:10
Matthew 24–28: 300
9:11–12
Mark 9–16: 16
9:12
Acts 1–12: 121
1 Peter: 2
9:13
Mark 1–8: 16
Mark 9–16: 18

9:14
Luke 6–10: 290
9:14–15
Matthew 16–23: 75
9:14–18a
Mark 9–16: 24
9:14–29
Mark 9–16: 21–22
Luke 6–10: 289
9:17
Matthew 16–23: 76
Mark 1–8: 381
9:17–22
Matthew 8–15: 41
9:18b–19
Mark 9–16: 26
9:19
Luke 11–17: 239
Acts 1–12: 76
9:20
Revelation 1–11: 260
9:20–22
Revelation 1–11: 263
9:20–24
Mark 9–16: 27
9:21
Matthew 16–23: 75
9:22
Mark 9–16: 146
Luke 6–10: 290, 293
9:23
Hebrews: 333
9:24
Matthew 8–15: 36, 239
Matthew 16–23: 77
Mark 9–16: 115
Luke 6–10: 235
Acts 1–12: 189
Hebrews: 90
Revelation 1–11: 195
9:25
Mark 1–8: 5
Luke 1–5: 90, 282
9:25–27
Mark 1–8: 66
Mark 9–16: 29
9:26
Matthew 16–23: 78
James: 246
Revelation 1–11: 260
9:27
Matthew 16–23: 78
9:28
Matthew 16–23: 78
9:28–29
Mark 9–16: 29
9:29
Matthew 8–15: 44
Matthew 16–23: 81
Mark 1–8: 182
Luke 6–10: 292
9:30
Mark 1–8: 401
9:30–32
Mark 9–16: 33
9:30–41
Mark 9–16: 31–32
9:30–50
Romans 9–16: 275
9:31
Luke 18–24: 265, 409
John 12–21: 7, 224
9:31–32
Mark 1–8: 131
Mark 9–16: 13
Luke 1–5: 340
John 12–21: 92
9:32
Matthew 16–23: 85, 95
Luke 6–10: 19
9:33
Luke 6–10: 300
9:33–34
Matthew 8–15: 124
Matthew 16–23: 94, 238
Luke 6–10: 20, 42
9:33–37
Mark 9–16: 103
9:33–41
Mark 9–16: 35–36
9:34
Mark 9–16: 36
9:35
Mark 9–16: 37
Luke 6–10: 35
Luke 18–24: 433
9:35–37
1 Corinthians: 110
9:36
Matthew 8–15: 125
Matthew 16–23: 96
Luke 6–10: 302
9:36–37
Mark 9–16: 38
9:37
Matthew 24–28: 232
Mark 9–16: 43
Luke 1–5: 297
Luke 6–10: 335
Luke 18–24: 355
9:38
Matthew 8–15: 151
9:38–40
Matthew 1–7: 480
Mark 9–16: 39
9:40
Mark 1–8: 175
9:41
Mark 9–16: 40
Revelation 1–11: 319
9:42
Mark 9–16: 42
1 & 2 Thessalonians: 239
9:42–50
Mark 9–16: 41
9:43
Matthew 8–15: 397
Mark 9–16: 46
2 Corinthians: 465
Philippians: 219
Revelation 12–22: 92, 242, 256
9:43–44
Matthew 8–15: 115
Matthew 24–28: 228
Hebrews: 48
James: 157
Revelation 12–22: 242
9:43–48
James: 245
Revelation 12–22: 225
9:43–49
James: 287
1–3 John: 91
9:43, 45, 47
Romans 9–16: 127
9:43, 47
Matthew 1–7: 70
9:44
Matthew 8–15: 379, 397
Titus: 108
Revelation 12–22: 256
9:45
Mark 9–16: 46
Philippians: 219
Revelation 12–22: 256
9:47
Revelation 12–22: 256
9:47–48
Matthew 1–7: 487
Mark 9–16: 46
9:48
Luke 1–5: 216
Luke 11–17: 365
1 & 2 Thessalonians: 194
Revelation 12–22: 92, 199, 224, 242
9:50
John 12–21: 125
9–16
Mark 1–8: 15
10
Matthew 1–7: 316
10:1
Matthew 16–23: 163
Luke 11–17: 227
10:1–12
Mark 9–16: 51
10:1–52
Mark 1–8: 8
10:2
Mark 9–16: 54
10:2–12
Luke 18–24: 25
10:3–4
Mark 9–16: 57
10:5
Mark 9–16: 58
10:6
Luke 6–10: 92
John 12–21: 204
10:6–9
Mark 9–16: 54
10:10
Matthew 16–23: 172

10:10–12
Mark 9–16: 58
10:11–12
Matthew 1–7: 315
Romans 1–8: 370
10:13
Matthew 16–23: 178
10:13–16
Mark 9–16: 63
Luke 18–24: 25
10:14
Matthew 16–23: 180
Mark 9–16: 65
Luke 18–24: 26
2 Corinthians: 267
10:15
Mark 9–16: 70
Luke 18–24: 31
10:16
Matthew 16–23: 181
10:17
Matthew 16–23: 187, 188
Mark 9–16: 76
Luke 6–10: 267
Luke 18–24: 36
1 & 2 Thessalonians: 245
10:17–22
Mark 9–16: 76
Luke 11–17: 219
John 1–11: 26
Hebrews: 408
2 Peter–Jude: 105
10:17–27
Mark 1–8: 424
10:17–31
Mark 9–16: 73–74
10:18
1 & 2 Thessalonians: 258
10:18–19
Mark 9–16: 78
10:19
James: 249
10:20
Matthew 16–23: 191
Mark 1–8: 111
Mark 9–16: 80
Luke 1–5: 328
John 1–11: 103
10:21
Matthew 16–23: 46, 194
Luke 1–5: 331
1 Corinthians: 453
2 Corinthians: 192
1–3 John: 244
Revelation 1–11: 139
10:21–22
Mark 1–8: 116
Mark 9–16: 80–81
10:22
Mark 9–16: 77, 204
Luke 1–5: 331
Luke 6–10: 269
10:23
Matthew 16–23: 198
Luke 11–17: 357
10:23–24
Luke 18–24: 41
10:23–27
Mark 9–16: 82
10:23–31
Mark 9–16: 82
10:24
Matthew 16–23: 201
John 1–11: 104
Acts 1–12: 104
10:25
Mark 1–8: 204
10:28
John 12–21: 274
10:29–30
Matthew 1–7: 229
Philippians: 96
10:29–31
Revelation 1–11: 319
10:30
Matthew 16–23: 205
1 & 2 Thessalonians: 245
1 Peter: 162
1–3 John: 96, 202
10:32
Matthew 16–23: 221
Mark 1–8: 410
Mark 9–16: 76, 92
10:32–33
Mark 9–16: 163
10:32–34
Mark 9–16: 89
Luke 18–24: 52, 266, 305
John 12–21: 35
10:33–34
Mark 9–16: 13, 95, 330
Luke 18–24: 409
John 12–21: 328
10:35
Matthew 16–23: 236
10:35–37
Matthew 16–23: 29
Mark 9–16: 104
10:35–42
Mark 9–16: 104
10:35–45
Mark 9–16: 99, 100
10:37
Mark 1–8: 325
Luke 6–10: 43
10:38
Matthew 1–7: 78
Mark 1–8: 33
Luke 11–17: 171
10:38–40
Mark 9–16: 106
10:39
John 1–11: 7
10:41
Mark 9–16: 66
2 Corinthians: 267
10:41–42
Mark 9–16: 107
10:42–44
1 Timothy: 96
10:43–45
Mark 9–16: 108
Acts 13–28: 344
10:44
1 Corinthians: 212
10:45
Mark 1–8: 5, 192, 324
Luke 1–5: 40
Luke 18–24: 94, 366
John 12–21: 36, 40
Acts 13–28: 361
1 Corinthians: 291
Titus: 121
1 Peter: 170
10:46
Matthew 16–23: 249
Luke 18–24: 60, 64
Acts 1–12: 99
10:46–48
Mark 9–16: 113
10:46–52
Mark 1–8: 163
Mark 9–16: 111
10:47
Acts 1–12: 59
Philippians: 206
10:49
Mark 1–8: 331
10:49–50
Matthew 16–23: 251
Luke 18–24: 62
10:49–52
Mark 9–16: 116
10:51
Matthew 16–23: 251
10:52
Matthew 8–15: 82
Matthew 16–23: 252
Mark 1–8: 261
11:1
Matthew 16–23: 257
11:1–10
Mark 9–16: 227
11:1–11
Mark 9–16: 121–22
11:1–16:20
Mark 1–8: 9
11:1b–7
Mark 9–16: 124
11:2
Matthew 16–23: 259
11:5–6
Matthew 16–23: 258
11:7–10
Mark 9–16: 256
11:8–10
Mark 9–16: 271, 310, 352, 390
11:9
Mark 9–16: 170
John 12–21: 15
11:9–10
Mark 9–16: 271
11:10
Mark 9–16: 115
Luke 18–24: 96

11:11
Matthew 16–23: 265, 276
Mark 9–16: 128
Luke 18–24: 102, 433
11:11–12
Luke 18–24: 452
11:12–14
Mark 9–16: 133, 258
11:12–21
Mark 9–16: 131, 132
11:13
Matthew 16–23: 277
Luke 1–5: 305
11:14
Matthew 16–23: 276
Mark 1–8: 5
Acts 1–12: 104
11:15–17
Matthew 24–28: 203
11:15–18
Mark 9–16: 311, 323
John 1–11: 91
Titus: 126
11:15–19
Mark 9–16: 226
11:15–21
Mark 9–16: 135–36
11:16
Matthew 16–23: 269
John 1–11: 91
11:17
Matthew 1–7: 264
Matthew 16–23: 270
Ephesians: 77
11:18
Matthew 24–28: 203
Luke 18–24: 109
11:20
Matthew 16–23: 276, 278, 280
Mark 9–16: 142
11:20–12:44
Mark 1–8: 9
11:21
Matthew 8–15: 138
Matthew 16–23: 277
11:22–25
Mark 9–16: 141, 144
11:23
Mark 9–16: 145
11:24
1 & 2 Thessalonians: 186
11:25
Mark 9–16: 148
Luke 6–10: 110
Luke 11–17: 380
Luke 18–24: 303
1 Peter: 31
11:27
Matthew 16–23: 284
Luke 18–24: 113
11:27–28
Mark 9–16: 154–155
Titus: 126
11:27–33
Mark 9–16: 151
11:28
Mark 1–8: 38
Mark 9–16: 206
11:29–33
Mark 1–8: 38
Titus: 126
11:33b
Mark 9–16: 158
11:53
Mark 1–8: 106
12:1–9
Mark 9–16: 164–65
12:1–11
Mark 1–8: 299
12:1–12
Mark 9–16: 161–62
12:1, 2, 7, 9
John 12–21: 145
12:2–5
Matthew 16–23: 295
12:5
Matthew 16–23: 295
12:7
Luke 11–17: 308
12:10
Mark 1–8: 144
Luke 6–10: 5
Luke 18–24: 424
12:10–11
Mark 9–16: 167
Acts 1–12: 135
12:13
Mark 9–16: 175
Luke 1–5: 23
Luke 18–24: 131
12:13–17
Mark 9–16: 173, 196
12:13–33
Mark 9–16: 206
12:14a
Mark 9–16: 177
12:14b–17
Mark 9–16: 178
12:15
Mark 1–8: 4
Luke 11–17: 113
12:18–27
Mark 9–16: 183–84
Luke 18–24: 151
12:19–23
Mark 9–16: 188
12:24
Romans 1–8: 169
2 Peter–Jude: 197
12:24–27
Mark 9–16: 189
12:26
Matthew 1–7: 263
1 Timothy: 242
12:28
Matthew 16–23: 336, 337
12:28–30
Luke 6–10: 181
12:28–31
Mark 1–8: 137
Luke 1–5: 115
Luke 6–10: 353
12:28–34
Mark 9–16: 195
Luke 18–24: 151
12:28a
Mark 9–16: 197
12:29–30
Mark 1–8: 347
2 Peter–Jude: 48
1–3 John: 166
12:30
Matthew 16–23: 339
Revelation 1–11: 63
12:30–31
Mark 9–16: 275
2 Corinthians: 84
12:31
Matthew 1–7: 338
12:32
Matthew 16–23: 349
12:32–33
Matthew 1–7: 340
2 Peter–Jude: 48
12:32–34
Matthew 16–23: 342
Mark 9–16: 204
12:34
Matthew 16–23: 349
Mark 9–16: 206
Luke 18–24: 150
12:35
Matthew 16–23: 345
Mark 9–16: 127, 206
Luke 18–24: 96, 152
Revelation 1–11: 167
12:35–37
Mark 9–16: 205
Revelation 12–22: 307
12:36
Matthew 16–23: 348
Luke 18–24: 154
12:36–37
Mark 9–16: 209
12:37
Matthew 16–23: 350
1 Corinthians: 119
James: 99
12:38
Luke 11–17: 101
12:38–40
Matthew 8–15: 191
Mark 1–8: 5
Hebrews: 48
2 Peter–Jude: 69–70
Revelation 12–22: 254
12:38–44
Mark 9–16: 215
12:38a
Mark 9–16: 217
12:38b–40a
Mark 9–16: 218
12:39
Luke 6–10: 8
12:40
Matthew 1–7: 363
Matthew 16–23: 374

12:41
Luke 18–24: 169
12:41–44
Matthew 1–7: 358
Mark 9–16: 221
Acts 1–12: 284
1 Corinthians: 452
1 Timothy: 194
12:42
2 Corinthians: 279
12:42–44
Luke 11–17: 361
2 Corinthians: 280
James: 100, 244
12:43–44
1–3 John: 136
12:44
2 Corinthians: 279
13
Luke 18–24: 191, 252
James: 254
13:1
Matthew 24–28: 8
13:1–2
Mark 9–16: 228
13:1–3
Mark 9–16: 291
13:1–13
Mark 9–16: 225–26, 228
13:3
Matthew 24–28: 9
Luke 18–24: 242
John 1–11: 8
Acts 1–12: 98
1–3 John: 6
13:3–4
Luke 6–10: 28
13:4
Matthew 8–15: 138
13:4–6
Mark 9–16: 229
13:5
1 & 2 Thessalonians: 270
13:5–37
Mark 9–16: 227, 252
13:6
1–3 John: 94
Revelation 12–22: 36, 61
13:6–37
Mark 9–16: 363
13:7–8
Mark 9–16: 232
Revelation 1–11: 180
13:9
Acts 13–28: 222
13:9–12
Mark 9–16: 234
13:11
Luke 18–24: 214
Philippians: 74
13:12
Matthew 8–15: 209
Matthew 24–28: 26
13:13
1 Peter: 7
13:13b
Mark 9–16: 237
13:14b–18
Mark 9–16: 246
13:14–20
Revelation 1–11: 231
13:14–23
Mark 9–16: 241, 259
13:16–19
Acts 1–12: 51
13:19
John 1–11: 20
1–3 John: 94
13:19–23
Mark 9–16: 248
13:20
Matthew 16–23: 252
Mark 9–16: 239
Acts 13–28: 268
1 & 2 Thessalonians: 287
1 Peter: 17
13:21–22
1–3 John: 94
Revelation 12–22: 36
13:22
Acts 1–12: 96
1 & 2 Thessalonians: 287
2 Timothy: 121
Revelation 12–22: 56, 61, 147
13:24
Luke 18–24: 230
Revelation 1–11: 251
Revelation 12–22: 145
13:24–25
Revelation 1–11: 205
13:24–27
Mark 9–16: 250, 253
13:24–37
Mark 9–16: 251–52
13:26
Revelation 1–11: 280
13:26–27
John 12–21: 251
1 & 2 Thessalonians: 133
13:27
1 & 2 Thessalonians: 287
13:28
James: 25
13:28–30
Mark 9–16: 258
13:31
Mark 9–16: 260
Luke 1–5: 79
13:32
Matthew 24–28: 63
Mark 1–8: 15
Luke 11–17: 153
Luke 18–24: 244
Acts 1–12: 20
1 Timothy: 274
Hebrews: 23
Revelation 1–11: 17
13:32–37
Mark 9–16: 261
13:33
Ephesians: 381
13:33–37
Luke 18–24: 80, 197
Acts 1–12: 20
Revelation 12–22: 298
13:34
Revelation 1–11: 18
13:35
Mark 1–8: 4
13:35–37
2 Peter–Jude: 51
13:36
Luke 1–5: 160
14:1
Luke 11–17: 274, 329
Luke 18–24: 120
John 12–21: 139
14:1a
Mark 9–16: 267
14:1–2
John 1–11: 2
14:1–16
Mark 9–16: 265–66
14:1–72
Mark 1–8: 9
14:3
Luke 6–10: 25
John 12–21: 3, 5, 7
Ephesians: 283
14:3–5
Matthew 24–28: 134
14:3–9
Mark 9–16: 272
John 1–11: 3, 453
14:4
Matthew 24–28: 135
Mark 9–16: 66
2 Corinthians: 267
14:4–5
John 12–21: 7
14:5
Matthew 8–15: 93
14:7
John 12–21: 8
14:9
John 12–21: 5
14:10
Luke 18–24: 311
14:10–11
Mark 9–16: 276
Luke 6–10: 79
John 12–21: 8
14:10, 20, 43
Matthew 24–28: 182
14:11
John 12–21: 81
14:12
Mark 1–8: 4
14:12–16
Mark 9–16: 277–78
Luke 18–24: 274
14:13
Matthew 24–28: 142
Romans 9–16: 307
14:14–15
Matthew 24–28: 142

14:15
Matthew 24–28: 143
14:17–18
John 1–11: 6
14:17–20
John 12–21: 79
14:17–21
Mark 9–16: 284
14:17–26
Mark 9–16: 283
14:19
John 12–21: 79
14:20–21
Mark 9–16: 312
14:21
Mark 9–16: 313
1 & 2 Thessalonians: 239
14:22–25
1 Peter: 248
14:22–26
Mark 9–16: 289
14:23
Matthew 24–28: 151
14:25
Luke 11–17: 23
14:26
Mark 9–16: 309
14:26–31
Luke 18–24: 294
14:27
Mark 9–16: 334
1 Peter: 44
14:27–31
Mark 9–16: 295
14:27–42
Mark 9–16: 293–94, 295
14:28
John 12–21: 389
14:29
Mark 9–16: 333
14:29–31, 66–72
Galatians: 51
14:30
Mark 9–16: 339
14:30–31
Mark 1–8: 425
14:31
Matthew 24–28: 213
Mark 9–16: 339
Luke 18–24: 302, 324
2 Corinthians: 239
14:32–34
Mark 9–16: 299
14:33
Matthew 16–23: 62
Mark 9–16: 105
Luke 6–10: 39, 282
Luke 18–24: 302, 303
John 1–11: 8
Acts 1–12: 98
1–3 John: 6
14:33–34
Philippians: 205
14:34
Luke 18–24: 300, 306
14:35–36
Mark 9–16: 300
14:36
Matthew 24–28: 174
Mark 1–8: 327
Luke 1–5: 290
Luke 18–24: 304
Romans 1–8: 437
Hebrews: 253, 450
1 Peter: 31
14:37
Matthew 8–15: 139
2 Peter–Jude: 3
14:37–38
Luke 6–10: 27
14:37–41a
Mark 9–16: 334
14:38
Matthew 1–7: 89
Mark 9–16: 332
1 Corinthians: 229, 472, 473
James: 37
14:41
Luke 18–24: 307
2 Corinthians: 269
14:41b–42
Mark 9–16: 304
14:43
Mark 9–16: 309
Luke 18–24: 114, 268, 311, 313
John 12–21: 6
14:43–52
Mark 9–16: 307
14:44
Matthew 8–15: 179
Luke 18–24: 314
John 12–21: 308
1 Corinthians: 283
14:44–46
Mark 9–16: 312
14:47
Mark 9–16: 313
14:48
Acts 1–12: 104
14:48–49
Mark 9–16: 315
14:50
Matthew 8–15: 125
Mark 1–8: 220
Mark 9–16: 393, 400
Luke 1–5: 340
Luke 6–10: 20
Luke 18–24: 403
14:50–52
1 Peter: 44
14:53
Luke 18–24: 330, 335
14:53–54
Mark 9–16: 323
14:53–65
Mark 9–16: 308, 319–20
Acts 13–28: 278
14:54
Matthew 24–28: 215
John 1–11: 2
14:55–59
Mark 9–16: 325
14:55–65
Mark 9–16: 344
14:56
Matthew 24–28: 205
Luke 18–24: 325
14:56, 59
John 12–21: 351
14:57–58
Acts 13–28: 259
14:58
Matthew 24–28: 205
Mark 9–16: 367
Luke 18–24: 335
John 1–11: 2
2 Corinthians: 163
14:58–59
Matthew 24–28: 206
14:60–61a
Mark 9–16: 326
14:61
2 Corinthians: 393
14:61–62
Mark 1–8: 5, 175, 224
14:61–65
1 & 2 Thessalonians: 63
14:61b–65
Mark 9–16: 327
14:62
Matthew 24–28: 207
Mark 1–8: 433
Mark 9–16: 333
Luke 18–24: 191, 336
Acts 1–12: 240
Revelation 1–11: 280
14:64
Matthew 24–28: 209
14:64–65
Mark 9–16: 360
14:65
Matthew 24–28: 210
Luke 1–5: 175
Luke 18–24: 338, 350
1 Peter: 168
14:66–67
John 12–21: 319
14:66–72
Mark 1–8: 416
Mark 9–16: 331, 403
John 12–21: 231
14:66–72a
Mark 9–16: 335
14:67
Acts 1–12: 59
14:68
Matthew 24–28: 216
Luke 18–24: 326
14:71
Matthew 8–15: 311
14:72
Matthew 24–28: 218
Luke 18–24: 327
James: 212
14:72b
Mark 9–16: 339

15:1
Matthew 24–28: 184, 223
15:1–5
Mark 9–16: 322
15:1–15
Mark 9–16: 343–44
15:1b–5
Mark 9–16: 345
15:6
Luke 18–24: 358
15:6–15
Mark 9–16: 350
15:7
Mark 9–16: 310
Luke 18–24: 313
John 12–21: 337
15:8
Matthew 24–28: 240
15:10
Acts 1–12: 205
Philippians: 64
15:11
John 12–21: 337
15:11–14
1 & 2 Thessalonians: 63
15:12
Mark 9–16: 355
Luke 18–24: 360
15:13–14
Matthew 16–23: 249
Mark 9–16: 174
15:15
Mark 9–16: 97, 364
Luke 18–24: 361
15:16
1 Corinthians: 283
Philippians: 6, 61
15:16–20
Mark 9–16: 359
15:16–32
Mark 9–16: 357–58
15:17
Matthew 24–28: 249
15:19
Luke 18–24: 361
15:19–20
Matthew 1–7: 225
15:20
Matthew 1–7: 43
15:21
Matthew 24–28: 244, 252
Mark 1–8: 4
Luke 6–10: 25
Luke 18–24: 368
Acts 13–28: 4
Romans 9–16: 368
15:21–25
Mark 9–16: 362
15:22
Mark 1–8: 4
15:22, 34
Luke 1–5: 290
15:23
Matthew 1–7: 36
Matthew 24–28: 201, 253
15:24
John 12–21: 349
2 Corinthians: 455
15:25
Matthew 24–28: 267
15:26–32
Mark 9–16: 366–67
15:29
John 1–11: 2
15:32
Luke 18–24: 370, 384
15:33–38
Mark 9–16: 375
15:33–41
Mark 9–16: 373, 374
15:34
Matthew 24–28: 269
Luke 18–24: 390
2 Corinthians: 19
15:37
Matthew 8–15: 89
John 12–21: 356
15:37–39
Hebrews: 217
15:38
Matthew 1–7: 272
Mark 1–8: 34
Luke 18–24: 282
15:39
Matthew 24–28: 279
Mark 1–8: 15
Mark 9–16: 370, 380
Luke 6–10: 124, 248
Luke 18–24: 368
1–3 John: 194
15:40
Matthew 16–23: 236
Matthew 24–28: 285
Mark 9–16: 105, 390
Luke 6–10: 43, 69
John 1–11: 7–8
1–3 John: 6
15:40–41
Mark 9–16: 382
Luke 1–5: 13
15:42
Matthew 24–28: 145, 300
15:42–47
Mark 9–16: 385, 386, 389
15:43
Matthew 24–28: 294, 295
Luke 18–24: 401
John 12–21: 366
Acts 13–28: 278
15:43–45
Matthew 24–28: 273
John 12–21: 357
15:44–45
Matthew 24–28: 295
Luke 18–24: 399, 402, 430, 431
John 12–21: 364, 366, 374
15:47
Matthew 24–28: 296, 297
Luke 6–10: 183
Luke 18–24: 432
16:1
Matthew 24–28: 307
John 12–21: 354
James: 277–78
16:1–8
Mark 1–8: 9, 253
Mark 9–16: 395
16:2
Matthew 24–28: 300
Mark 9–16: 398
Luke 18–24: 409
John 12–21: 368
16:3
Matthew 24–28: 308
Luke 18–24: 410
16:4–5
Matthew 24–28: 297
16:5
John 12–21: 378
Acts 1–12: 22
Revelation 1–11: 113, 226
16:5–7
Matthew 24–28: 297
John 12–21: 368
16:6
Matthew 24–28: 310
Philippians: 140
16:7
John 12–21: 389
16:8
Mark 9–16: 412
16:9
1 Corinthians: 403
1 Timothy: 85
16:9–10
Mark 9–16: 413
16:9–14
1 Peter: 225
16:9–20
Mark 9–16: 407–8, 415
16:10
Matthew 1–7: 157
16:10–13
John 12–21: 385
16:11
Matthew 24–28: 313
Mark 9–16: 413
16:12
1 Corinthians: 403
16:12–13
Mark 9–16: 414
16:14
Matthew 8–15: 125
Mark 9–16: 414
1 Corinthians: 403
16:15
Matthew 8–15: 105, 374
Mark 1–8: 362
Mark 9–16: 414
Acts 1–12: 49
Acts 13–28: 52
Romans 9–16: 211, 216
Ephesians: 69
1 & 2 Thessalonians: 97
1 Timothy: 72
James: 203

1–3 John: 166
16:16
Matthew 24–28: 343
Mark 9–16: 414
Romans 1–8: 396
Titus: 113
16:17
Mark 9–16: 415
16:17–18
1 Corinthians: 281
16:19
Acts 1–12: 67
16:19–20
Mark 1–8: 5
Mark 9–16: 415
16:20
Acts 1–12: 86
Romans 9–16: 168, 336
2 Peter–Jude: 19

Luke
1
Matthew 1–7: 50
1:1–3a
Luke 1–5: 11
1:1–4
Luke 1–5: 9
Acts 1–12: 207
1–3 John: 18
1:2
1 Corinthians: 97
1:2–3
Luke 1–5: 3
1:3
Mark 1–8: 4, 6
Luke 1–5: 336
Acts 1–12: 5
1 & 2 Thessalonians: 143
1:3–4
Mark 1–8: 12
1:3b–4
Luke 1–5: 15
1:4
Luke 1–5: 4, 336
1–3 John: 14
1:5
Luke 1–5: 59, 142, 175, 230
Luke 18–24: 401
Acts 13–28: 327
1:5–6
2 Corinthians: 110
1:5–14, 18–25
Luke 1–5: 19
1:5a
Luke 1–5: 22
1:5b–7
Luke 1–5: 23
1:6
Luke 1–5: 172, 176
Romans 1–8: 410
Philippians: 181, 233
1–3 John: 128
1:6–7
Matthew 1–7: 51
1:7
Luke 1–5: 204
Luke 18–24: 371
John 1–11: 29, 48
1:7, 24
Luke 1–5: 54
1:8–10
Luke 1–5: 26
1 Peter: 117
Revelation 1–11: 241, 293
1:8–17
John 1–11: 29
1:9–10
Revelation 1–11: 171
1:9, 21, 22
Luke 1–5: 180
1:10
Revelation 1–11: 194
Revelation 12–22: 116
1:11
Matthew 1–7: 51
1:11–13
Acts 1–12: 294
1:11–14
Luke 1–5: 27
1:11–19
Revelation 12–22: 84
1:11–20
Matthew 1–7: 40
1:12
Matthew 8–15: 55
Mark 1–8: 107
John 12–21: 98
Galatians: 15
1:12, 26–30
Luke 1–5: 157
1:12, 30, 65
Luke 1–5: 5
1:12, 65
Luke 1–5: 325
1:13
Matthew 1–7: 18
Philippians: 21
2 Timothy: 6
1:13–15
Matthew 1–7: 51
1:13–17
1 Corinthians: 209
Galatians: 28
1 & 2 Thessalonians: 202
1:13–17, 76
Luke 1–5: 227
1:14, 44, 47, 58
Luke 1–5: 4
1:15
Matthew 1–7: 58
Matthew 8–15: 253, 298, 418
Luke 1–5: 35, 180
Luke 6–10: 146, 153, 154, 165
Acts 13–28: 159, 252
Ephesians: 235, 239, 240, 315
1:15–16
Matthew 1–7: 51
Hebrews: 350
1:15–17
Mark 1–8: 23–24
Luke 1–5: 33
Titus: 38, 106
1:15, 35, 41, 67
Luke 1–5: 5
1:16
Matthew 1–7: 58
Luke 1–5: 28
1 & 2 Thessalonians: 27
James: 289
1:16–17
Matthew 8–15: 256
Acts 1–12: 114
Acts 13–28: 162, 337
1:16,17b
Luke 1–5: 39
1:17
Matthew 1–7: 51, 52, 75
Matthew 8–15: 257, 418
Matthew 16–23: 71
Mark 1–8: 302
Luke 1–5: 105, 175, 245
Luke 6–10: 155
John 1–11: 29
1 & 2 Thessalonians: 145
James: 289
Revelation 1–11: 301
1:17a
Luke 1–5: 38
1:18
Titus: 73
1:18–25
Luke 1–5: 28
1:19
Luke 1–5: 157
2 Timothy: 71
1 Peter: 57
Revelation 1–11: 238
1:21, 63
Luke 1–5: 163
1:24–25
Luke 18–24: 371
1:26
Matthew 1–7: 74
Luke 1–5: 43
1:26–27
Revelation 12–22: 84
1:26–33
Luke 1–5: 41
1:26–35
Philippians: 130
1 Peter: 58, 198–99
1:26–38
Matthew 1–7: 15, 40
Luke 1–5: 163
2 Timothy: 141
1:26–2:20
Luke 1–5: 42
1:26–2:38
Matthew 8–15: 339
1:27
Luke 1–5: 44
Romans 1–8: 14
1:27, 30–56
Luke 1–5: 246
1:28
Matthew 1–7: 5
1 Peter: 57

1:28–30
Luke 1–5: 45
1:30
Luke 1–5: 27
Acts 1–12: 294
1:30–35
Philippians: 130
1:31
1–3 John: 16
1:31–33
Matthew 24–28: 115
Mark 1–8: 178
Luke 1–5: 48
Luke 11–17: 247
Acts 1–12: 58
1 & 2 Thessalonians: 202
Revelation 1–11: 314
Revelation 12–22: 232
1:31–35
Luke 1–5: 141
1:32
Matthew 16–23: 250
Titus: 121
Hebrews: 27, 28
Revelation 12–22: 237
1:32–33
Matthew 8–15: 90
Luke 1–5: 159, 174
Luke 11–17: 400
Luke 18–24: 61
2 Timothy: 57
1:32, 35
Matthew 1–7: 76
Galatians: 108
1:33
Mark 9–16: 122
Luke 1–5: 249
Acts 1–12: 53
1 Corinthians: 420
1 Peter: 125
1:34
Matthew 1–7: 15, 16
Luke 1–5: 56
1:34–35
Luke 1–5: 175
1:34–38
Luke 1–5: 53
1:35
Matthew 24–28: 280
Mark 1–8: 35, 183
Luke 1–5: 57, 189, 194, 239
Luke 18–24: 431
John 12–21: 374
Romans 1–8: 427
2 Corinthians: 214
Hebrews: 28
1 Peter: 206
1–3 John: 195
Revelation 1–11: 118
1:36
Matthew 1–7: 15
Luke 1–5: 58
John 1–11: 29
John 12–21: 318
1:37
Luke 1–5: 59
1:38
Matthew 1–7: 5
Luke 1–5: 47, 60
1:39
Romans 9–16: 177
1:39–40
Luke 1–5: 67
1:39–45
Matthew 1–7: 40
Luke 1–5: 63
1:39–56
Matthew 1–7: 75
1:41
Luke 1–5: 180
1:41–45
Luke 1–5: 4, 94, 181, 186
Luke 6–10: 85
1:41a, 44
Luke 1–5: 68
1:41b–43, 45
Luke 1–5: 69, 70
1:42
Acts 1–12: 29
1 Peter: 190, 198
1:43
Matthew 1–7: 75
1:44
Mark 1–8: 30
1:45
Matthew 1–7: 15
1:46–48
Matthew 1–7: 5
1:46–48a
Luke 1–5: 78
1:46–50
Acts 1–12: 29
1:46–55
Matthew 1–7: 15, 16
Luke 1–5: 4, 73, 181, 186
1:46b, 47b
Luke 1–5: 81
1:46ff.
1 Timothy: 85
1:47
Matthew 1–7: 5
Matthew 8–15: 410
Luke 1–5: 153, 166, 168
2 Corinthians: 199
Philippians: 216
1 Peter: 41
Revelation 1–11: 222
1:47, 49
Matthew 1–7: 15
1:48
Matthew 8–15: 410
1:48b–55
Luke 1–5: 81
1:49
Philippians: 310
1:49–50, 52–53
Matthew 8–15: 98
1:49–51
1 Peter: 279
1:50
Luke 1–5: 121
Revelation 1–11: 320
Revelation 12–22: 200
1:51
Matthew 16–23: 231
Revelation 12–22: 185
1:52
Mark 9–16: 102
Luke 1–5: 155
1:53
Matthew 1–7: 182
1:54
Luke 1–5: 121
1:56–58
Luke 1–5: 87
1:56–66
Luke 1–5: 85
1:58
Philippians: 194
1:59
Luke 1–5: 167
1:59–63
Luke 1–5: 88
1:63
Luke 1–5: 95
1:64
Luke 1–5: 164
1:64–66
Luke 1–5: 91
1:65
Mark 1–8: 107
1:67
Luke 1–5: 131, 180
1:67–71
Luke 1–5: 93, 105
1:67–75
Luke 1–5: 117
1:67–79
Luke 1–5: 4, 94, 181, 186
Luke 11–17: 349
Acts 1–12: 18
1:67, 76
Matthew 1–7: 51
1:68
Luke 1–5: 158
Luke 6–10: 138
Hebrews: 54
James: 89
1 Peter: 140
1:68–69
Matthew 8–15: 90
Luke 1–5: 189
1:68–69, 77
Luke 1–5: 153
1:69
Luke 1–5: 181
1:69b
Luke 1–5: 97
1:70
Luke 1–5: 98
1 Peter: 56
Revelation 12–22: 293
1:71
Luke 1–5: 100
2 Corinthians: 204
1 Timothy: 168
1:72
Luke 1–5: 121

1:72–73
Luke 18–24: 246
1:72–75
Luke 1–5: 103
Luke 18–24: 194
1:72a
Luke 1–5: 105
1:72b–73
Luke 1–5: 106
1:73
Luke 6–10: 14
James: 269
Revelation 1–11: 284
1:74–75
Luke 1–5: 109
1:75
Ephesians: 178
1:76
Luke 1–5: 200
1:76–77
Luke 1–5: 207
1:76–79
Romans 9–16: 132
1 & 2 Thessalonians: 154
1:76–80
Luke 1–5: 113
1:77
Luke 1–5: 118
Acts 13–28: 336
1:77–78
1–3 John: 39
1:78
Luke 11–17: 88
2 Corinthians: 20
Philippians: 32
Hebrews: 54
James: 89, 261
1 Peter: 31, 140
1:78–79
Matthew 8–15: 231
Luke 1–5: 189
Romans 1–8: 200
Philippians: 185
1:78a
Luke 1–5: 120
1:78b–79
Luke 1–5: 121
1:79
Matthew 1–7: 244
Luke 11–17: 169
1 & 2 Thessalonians: 204
1:80
Matthew 1–7: 51, 75
Mark 1–8: 20, 30
Luke 1–5: 141, 200, 236
Luke 6–10: 14
2
Matthew 1–7: 2, 25
2:1
Luke 1–5: 201
Philippians: 3, 61
2:1–2
1 Peter: 149
2:1–3
Luke 1–5: 142
2:1–4
Matthew 16–23: 318
Luke 11–17: 52
Luke 18–24: 398
2:1–7
Luke 1–5: 139
2:1–11
Luke 1–5: 266
2:4
Matthew 8–15: 90
Luke 1–5: 158
2:4–5
Matthew 1–7: 47
Luke 1–5: 146
2:4, 11
Matthew 1–7: 25
2:5, 16, 19, 34
Luke 1–5: 246
2:6–7
Luke 1–5: 148
2:7
Mark 1–8: 277
Luke 1–5: 160
2 Corinthians: 292
James: 10
1–3 John: 242
2:8–10a
Luke 1–5: 155
2:8–14
Matthew 1–7: 40
2:8–20
Luke 1–5: 151, 152, 175
2:9
Matthew 1–7: 29
Matthew 8–15: 55
Matthew 24–28: 267
Mark 1–8: 107
Luke 1–5: 160, 325
2 Timothy: 175
Revelation 12–22: 279
2:9–10
Luke 1–5: 5
Acts 1–12: 294
2:9–11
Philippians: 130
2:9–13
Revelation 12–22: 84
2:10
Luke 1–5: 4, 27
Ephesians: 142, 230
1 & 2 Thessalonians: 185
1 Peter: 40
1–3 John: 19
2:10–11
Philippians: 10
1 & 2 Thessalonians: 184
2:10–11, 27–32, 34, 38
Luke 1–5: 189
2:10–14
1 Peter: 57–58
2:10–15
Mark 9–16: 401
2:10b
Luke 1–5: 158
2:11
Luke 1–5: 152, 153, 181
Acts 1–12: 104
Philippians: 147
1–3 John: 30
Revelation 1–11: 222
2:11–12
Luke 1–5: 158
2:13–14
Luke 1–5: 5, 94, 160, 186
Romans 9–16: 382
Revelation 1–11: 171
2:13–14, 38
Luke 1–5: 181
2:14
Luke 11–17: 169
Ephesians: 79
1 & 2 Thessalonians: 204
2:14, 20
John 12–21: 241
2:15
Philippians: 78
1 Peter: 220
2:15–16
1 Peter: 165
2:15–21
Luke 1–5: 162
2:18, 33
Luke 1–5: 193
2:19, 51
Luke 1–5: 92
2:21
Luke 1–5: 48, 166
2:21–24
Luke 1–5: 149, 165
2:21–27
Matthew 1–7: 25
2:21–38
Luke 1–5: 166
1 Corinthians: 163
2 Timothy: 141
2:22
Hebrews: 74
2:22–24
Luke 1–5: 168, 180, 189
2:22–33
Matthew 1–7: 21
2:22–38
Luke 1–5: 191
2:22, 23, 24, 27, 39
Luke 1–5: 166
2:23
Luke 1–5: 171
2:24
Matthew 1–7: 25
2 Corinthians: 292
2:25
Luke 1–5: 155, 175
Luke 6–10: 40, 330
Luke 18–24: 401
Acts 1–12: 231
2:25–27
Luke 1–5: 5
2:25–32
Luke 1–5: 5
1–3 John: 17
2:25–35
Luke 1–5: 176
John 1–11: 79

2:25–38
Matthew 1–7: 40
Matthew 8–15: 160, 328
Luke 1–5: 173, 174, 189
2:25, 38
Luke 1–5: 200
2:25a
Luke 1–5: 176
2:25b
Luke 1–5: 177
2:25c–27
Luke 1–5: 179
2:26
Matthew 1–7: 168
2:26, 29
Luke 1–5: 176
2:26, 30–32
Matthew 8–15: 98
2:28–30
Titus: 107
2:28–33
Luke 1–5: 181
2:29
Acts 1–12: 140
Revelation 12–22: 200, 293
2:29–32
1 & 2 Thessalonians: 196
2:29–35
1 & 2 Thessalonians: 202
2:30
Luke 1–5: 153
2:30–32
Matthew 1–7: 103
Luke 1–5: 158
Romans 1–8: 200
2:32
Matthew 1–7: 108
1 Peter: 140
1–3 John: 62
Revelation 1–11: 3, 15
2:33
Luke 1–5: 163
2:34
Matthew 1–7: 69, 94
Matthew 16–23: 5
Luke 1–5: 51
Luke 11–17: 194
Philippians: 67
Revelation 12–22: 238
2:34–35
Matthew 16–23: 223
Luke 1–5: 164, 183
2:35
Luke 1–5: 196
1 Peter: 198
2:36
Luke 1–5: 94, 245
2 Corinthians: 110
2:36–37
Luke 18–24: 401
1 Timothy: 201
2:36–38
Luke 1–5: 184
John 1–11: 79
2:36–39
1 Timothy: 85
2:37
Luke 11–17: 2
Acts 13–28: 5
1 Timothy: 147
Titus: 77
Revelation 1–11: 232
2:38
Luke 1–5: 96, 105, 155, 175
1 & 2 Thessalonians: 196
Titus: 77
Revelation 12–22: 194
2:38–39
Luke 1–5: 189
2:39
Luke 1–5: 171
2:39–52
Matthew 1–7: 51
Luke 1–5: 187, 188
2:40
Matthew 1–7: 75
Mark 1–8: 271
Luke 1–5: 190
2:40–51
Philippians: 130
2:41–42
Matthew 16–23: 272
2:41–51
Luke 1–5: 183, 191, 199
2:42–52
Matthew 1–7: 22
2:44
Luke 1–5: 192
Acts 13–28: 53
2:45–47
1 Peter: 165
2:46–47
Mark 1–8: 178
2:49
Matthew 1–7: 77
Matthew 16–23: 88, 220
Luke 1–5: 184, 191
Romans 1–8: 307
Ephesians: 278
Philippians: 119
2:50
Mark 1–8: 402
2:51
Luke 1–5: 200
James: 204
1 Peter: 177
2:51–52
Ephesians: 314
2:52
Matthew 8–15: 298
Matthew 24–28: 72
Luke 1–5: 197
Luke 18–24: 155
John 1–11: 79
Philippians: 130
1 Peter: 166
2 Peter–Jude: 30
3
Matthew 1–7: 15, 60, 468
Luke 1–5: 123
3:1
Luke 1–5: 22, 143
Luke 6–10: 247
Luke 18–24: 342
Acts 1–12: 321
Acts 13–28: 327
1 Peter: 149
3:1–2a
Luke 1–5: 201
3:1–6
Matthew 1–7: 454
Luke 1–5: 199
3:1–18
Matthew 1–7: 59
Luke 18–24: 116
3:2
Matthew 16–23: 284
John 1–11: 49, 483
Acts 13–28: 278, 280
3:2b–3a
Luke 1–5: 204
3:3
Luke 1–5: 4, 117
1–3 John: 192
3:3–9
Luke 11–17: 313
3:3b
Luke 1–5: 205
3:4–5
Luke 1–5: 215
Luke 11–17: 220
3:4–6
Luke 1–5: 210
3:4–14
1–3 John: 38
3:5–6
1 & 2 Thessalonians: 196
3:6
Titus: 107
3:7
Luke 6–10: 152
Revelation 12–22: 137
3:7–17
Luke 1–5: 210, 213, 214
3:7a
Luke 1–5: 215
3:7b
Luke 1–5: 217
3:8
Mark 1–8: 21
Luke 6–10: 117, 165, 351
Acts 13–28: 216
2 Corinthians: 266
3:8, 11
Romans 9–16: 175
3:8a, 9–14
Luke 1–5: 218
3:8b
Luke 1–5: 221
3:9
Luke 6–10: 148, 165
Revelation 12–22: 256
3:10
Romans 1–8: 198
3:11
Matthew 1–7: 65, 468
Mark 1–8: 106

3:11–14
Matthew 1–7: 60
3:12
Matthew 16–23: 291
Luke 1–5: 193
Luke 18–24: 17, 71
3:12–13
Mark 1–8: 114
Luke 1–5: 330
3:13
Matthew 1–7: 65, 468
3:14
Matthew 1–7: 65
Luke 6–10: 105
Philippians: 296
3:15
Matthew 8–15: 252
Luke 1–5: 92
John 1–11: 50
3:15–17
Luke 1–5: 222
3:15–20
Luke 1–5: 15
3:16
John 1–11: 30
3:16–17
Revelation 12–22: 256
3:16, 22
Luke 1–5: 5
3:17
Matthew 1–7: 70
Luke 6–10: 148, 165
John 12–21: 152
Romans 9–16: 373
Revelation 12–22: 92, 225
3:18
Matthew 1–7: 60
Luke 1–5: 157, 228
Luke 6–10: 7
3:18–20
Luke 1–5: 225
3:19
Luke 1–5: 230
3:19–20
Matthew 1–7: 104
2 Timothy: 177
3:20
Mark 1–8: 127
Luke 1–5: 202, 338
Luke 6–10: 247
John 1–11: 3
3:21
Matthew 1–7: 75
Mark 1–8: 28, 33, 78
Luke 1–5: 5, 238, 317
Luke 11–17: 2
John 12–21: 235
3:21–22
Luke 1–5: 233
Acts 1–12: 17, 302
3:22
Luke 1–5: 190, 305, 320
Acts 1–12: 13, 41
Hebrews: 28
3:22a
Luke 1–5: 238
3:22b
Luke 1–5: 240
3:23
Matthew 1–7: 3, 15, 18, 74
Luke 1–5: 197, 201
Romans 1–8: 14
3:23–38
Matthew 1–7: 3
Mark 9–16: 208
Luke 1–5: 243–44
Luke 18–24: 153
Romans 9–16: 15
Hebrews: 177
3:23a
Luke 1–5: 248
3:23b
Luke 1–5: 248
3:27
Luke 1–5: 249
3:30
Luke 1–5: 176
3:31
Romans 1–8: 14
3:31–32
James: 98
3:32
Acts 13–28: 22
3:34
James: 98
4:1
Matthew 1–7: 86
Mark 1–8: 183
Luke 1–5: 320
Acts 1–12: 13, 17
Ephesians: 250
Philippians: 156
4:1–2
Luke 1–5: 254
4:1–12
Romans 1–8: 480
1 Peter: 282
4:1–13
Mark 1–8: 239
Luke 1–5: 251, 312
Luke 11–17: 194
Luke 18–24: 300
John 1–11: 49
1–3 John: 89
4:1, 14, 18
Luke 1–5: 5
4:2
Matthew 1–7: 87, 89
Ephesians: 332
4:3–4
Mark 1–8: 44
Luke 1–5: 256
4:3–12
Luke 1–5: 255–56
4:3, 9
Luke 1–5: 195
4:5–6
John 12–21: 42
Revelation 12–22: 212
4:5–8
Mark 1–8: 44
Luke 1–5: 258
Revelation 1–11: 310
4:6
Luke 18–24: 195
Romans 9–16: 219
4:8
Luke 1–5: 307
4:9–12
Mark 1–8: 45
Luke 1–5: 259–60
4:13
Matthew 1–7: 97
Matthew 8–15: 437
Mark 1–8: 46
Matthew 16–23: 41
Luke 1–5: 261
1 Timothy: 147
4:14
Mark 1–8: 42, 61, 274
Luke 6–10: 126
Acts 1–12: 13
Philippians: 156
2 Peter–Jude: 26
4:14–15
Luke 1–5: 264
Luke 6–10: 7
4:14–30
Luke 1–5: 263–64, 285, 328
4:14, 16
Matthew 1–7: 106
4:14a, 16
Matthew 8–15: 407
4:15
Luke 6–10: 2
4:15–21
Matthew 8–15: 104
James: 147
4:16
Mark 1–8: 60
Luke 11–17: 198
4:16–21
Matthew 1–7: 264
Matthew 8–15: 104
Matthew 16–23: 366
Luke 1–5: 268–69
Acts 1–12: 48
1 Peter: 53
2 Peter–Jude: 62
4:16–29
Mark 1–8: 178
4:16–30
Matthew 24–28: 130
Luke 6–10: 240
Luke 11–17: 194
4:16–31
Mark 1–8: 60
John 1–11: 478
4:16ff.
1 Timothy: 176
4:17–18
John 1–11: 32
4:17–21
2 Corinthians: 110
4:17–22
Matthew 8–15: 407
4:18
Matthew 16–23: 114, 199

Mark 1–8: 42, 111, 149, 418
Luke 1–5: 328
Luke 6–10: 7
Luke 11–17: 83, 176, 226
Luke 18–24: 60, 267
Acts 1–12: 13
2 Corinthians: 45, 347
Philippians: 156
4:18–19
Matthew 8–15: 298
Matthew 24–28: 124
Acts 1–12: 18
Acts 13–28: 15
Romans 9–16: 178
4:18–21
Matthew 16–23: 23
Matthew 24–28: 14, 207
Mark 1–8: 276
Mark 9–16: 328
Luke 6–10: 7
4:18, 43
Luke 1–5: 157
4:20
Luke 1–5: 304
Acts 13–28: 92
4:21
Mark 1–8: 272
Luke 1–5: 155
Luke 18–24: 336
4:22
Matthew 1–7: 106, 125
Luke 1–5: 163, 193
Luke 6–10: 122
2 Corinthians: 123
Ephesians: 188
4:22, 32, 36
Luke 1–5: 193
4:23
Matthew 8–15: 412
Mark 1–8: 73, 272
Luke 1–5: 12
4:23–27
Matthew 1–7: 106
4:23–30
Matthew 1–7: 106
4:24
Matthew 8–15: 412
Mark 1–8: 278
John 1–11: 3
Revelation 1–11: 133
4:25
James: 280
Revelation 1–11: 302
4:25–26
Mark 1–8: 365
4:25–30
John 1–11: 154
4:27–28
Luke 11–17: 51
4:28–29
Romans 1–8: 134
1–3 John: 134
4:28–30
Mark 9–16: 316
Luke 1–5: 184, 273–74
Luke 11–17: 176, 200
John 12–21: 363
Ephesians: 188
1 & 2 Thessalonians: 264, 295
Revelation 12–22: 10
4:29
Mark 1–8: 273
Luke 6–10: 318
1 Timothy: 39
4:29–31
Matthew 8–15: 49
4:30
John 12–21: 51
4:31
Luke 1–5: 267
Luke 6–10: 7, 25
James: 147
4:31–34a
Luke 1–5: 281
4:31–35
Mark 1–8: 153
4:31–36
Mark 1–8: 226
4:31–37
Luke 1–5: 279
4:32
Matthew 1–7: 126
Matthew 8–15: 31
Mark 1–8: 152
Luke 6–10: 86
John 12–21: 49
4:33
Mark 1–8: 242
Acts 1–12: 234
4:33–35
Luke 11–17: 61
Acts 13–28: 170
4:33–35, 41
Luke 1–5: 312
4:34
Luke 6–10: 217, 221
John 1–11: 23
Acts 1–12: 66, 109
Philippians: 310
4:34b
Luke 1–5: 285
4:34c
Luke 1–5: 286
4:35
Mark 1–8: 67
4:35–37
Luke 1–5: 287
4:36
Luke 18–24: 112
1 Corinthians: 302
2 Corinthians: 123
4:37
Mark 1–8: 116
Luke 1–5: 331
4:38
Matthew 8–15: 16
Mark 1–8: 73
Luke 6–10: 25, 26
1 Peter: 4
2 Peter–Jude: 2–3
4:38–39
Luke 6–10: 25
Luke 18–24: 63
4:38–40
Luke 1–5: 291, 312
4:38–44
Luke 1–5: 289, 301
4:39
Matthew 8–15: 16
Mark 1–8: 73
Luke 1–5: 91
Acts 1–12: 183
1 Timothy: 124
4:40
Luke 1–5: 315
Philippians: 205
James: 276
4:41
Matthew 8–15: 43
Mark 1–8: 63, 64
Luke 1–5: 195, 295
Luke 6–10: 238
Acts 1–12: 97, 234
Acts 13–28: 97
Philippians: 48
James: 132
4:42
Mark 1–8: 78, 79, 80
Luke 1–5: 317
Luke 6–10: 2
4:42–44
Luke 1–5: 296
4:43
Matthew 1–7: 380
Luke 1–5: 281–82, 304
Luke 6–10: 242
Luke 11–17: 23
Luke 18–24: 73
Acts 1–12: 15, 48
Acts 13–28: 15
4:44
Luke 6–10: 7
5:1
Matthew 1–7: 105
Luke 1–5: 205
Luke 6–10: 208
Luke 18–24: 360
John 12–21: 390
5:1–3
Mark 1–8: 177
Luke 1–5: 301
1 Peter: 4–5
5:1–8
2 Peter–Jude: 2–3
5:1–11
Matthew 1–7: 114
Luke 1–5: 299–300, 312
Luke 6–10: 40
5:3
Matthew 8–15: 138
Luke 6–10: 26
5:4
Matthew 8–15: 138–39
5:4–6
John 12–21: 107
1–3 John: 17
5:4–6a
Luke 1–5: 304

5:4–9
Luke 6–10: 16, 207
5:5
Luke 6–10: 26
Luke 11–17: 391
2 Corinthians: 388
5:6–11
Luke 6–10: 18
5:6b–7
Luke 1–5: 305
5:7
Luke 1–5: 306
2 Corinthians: 248
Hebrews: 144
5:8
Matthew 1–7: 147, 164
Matthew 8–15: 37, 46, 59
Matthew 16–23: 232
Luke 1–5: 71, 157
Luke 6–10: 127, 271
Luke 11–17: 394
Romans 9–16: 63
1 Corinthians: 106
2 Corinthians: 139, 344–45
Ephesians: 124
James: 214
1–3 John: 38, 144
5:8–10a
Luke 1–5: 307
5:8–11
Luke 6–10: 16
5:9
Luke 1–5: 193
5:10
Matthew 8–15: 138
Luke 1–5: 157, 292
Luke 6–10: 26, 41, 47
Acts 1–12: 98
1 Peter: 4
2 Peter–Jude: 3
5:10, 26
Luke 1–5: 5
5:10b–11
Luke 1–5: 308
5:11
Matthew 1–7: 114
Matthew 8–15: 125
Luke 6–10: 40, 64
Luke 18–24: 320
Hebrews: 356
5:11, 27–28
John 12–21: 404
5:12
Mark 1–8: 86
Luke 1–5: 293
Luke 18–24: 63
2 Corinthians: 284
5:12–13
Luke 11–17: 390
5:12–16
Luke 1–5: 312–13
5:12–26
Luke 1–5: 311–12
5:12b
Luke 1–5: 313
5:12c
Luke 1–5: 314
5:13
Mark 9–16: 118
Luke 1–5: 293
Luke 18–24: 63
Acts 1–12: 101
5:13–16
Luke 1–5: 315
5:14
Matthew 8–15: 185–86
5:15
Matthew 8–15: 246
Mark 1–8: 85
Luke 1–5: 320
Luke 6–10: 2, 7
Luke 11–17: 388
5:16
Mark 1–8: 414
Luke 1–5: 5, 238
Luke 6–10: 15
1 & 2 Thessalonians: 186
5:17
Mark 1–8: 98, 99, 100
Mark 9–16: 197
Luke 1–5: 332
Luke 6–10: 2, 7, 15
Luke 11–17: 103
Acts 1–12: 18
Philippians: 156
2 Peter–Jude: 26
5:17–19
Luke 1–5: 318
Luke 6–10: 232
5:17–26
Mark 1–8: 101
Luke 1–5: 317, 329, 338
Luke 6–10: 7
5:18
Mark 1–8: 101
5:18–26
Mark 1–8: 5
5:19
Matthew 8–15: 50
5:20
Luke 1–5: 321, 331
Luke 18–24: 64
1–3 John: 106
5:20–25
Luke 1–5: 4
5:21
Mark 9–16: 152
Luke 6–10: 15, 171, 353
Luke 11–17: 37, 80
Luke 18–24: 112
John 1–11: 479
1 Corinthians: 354
2 Corinthians: 288
5:21–24
Luke 1–5: 323
5:21, 30
Luke 1–5: 319
5:22
Luke 6–10: 8, 175
John 12–21: 216
5:23
Luke 6–10: 5
5:24
Luke 6–10: 7
John 12–21: 251
5:25
Mark 1–8: 106
5:25–26
Luke 1–5: 164, 324
5:26
Luke 6–10: 2
1 Corinthians: 354
Ephesians: 250
5:27
Luke 6–10: 65
Luke 18–24: 72
5:27–28
Luke 1–5: 309
Luke 6–10: 16, 18
5:27–29
Luke 1–5: 329
Luke 6–10: 170
Luke 11–17: 83
5:27–32
Luke 1–5: 327
Luke 18–24: 71
5:28
Matthew 8–15: 61
Mark 1–8: 116
5:29
Mark 1–8: 117
Luke 6–10: 66
5:29–32
Luke 11–17: 80
5:30
Matthew 1–7: xi
Mark 1–8: 114, 119
Luke 1–5: 329
Luke 6–10: 15, 65
Philippians: 179
5:30–31
Romans 9–16: 321
5:30–32
Luke 1–5: 332, 338
5:31
Luke 1–5: 12
5:31–32
Luke 18–24: 174
John 12–21: 260
5:32
Mark 1–8: 80, 120
Luke 1–5: 155, 341
Luke 6–10: 2, 181
Luke 11–17: 71, 123, 280
John 12–21: 183
Acts 13–28: 216
Romans 1–8: 239
Philippians: 223
1 Timothy: 21
James: 209
5:33
Mark 1–8: 126
Luke 1–5: 185, 338
Luke 11–17: 4
Acts 13–28: 5, 164
Philippians: 21

2 Timothy: 6
5:33–35
Acts 13–28: 5
5:33–39
Mark 1–8: 125
Luke 1–5: 335
5:34–35
Mark 1–8: 130
Luke 1–5: 340
Luke 18–24: 47
Revelation 12–22: 202
5:36–39
Luke 1–5: 341
Luke 6–10: 3
5:39
Mark 1–8: 132, 133
5:42
Luke 1–5: 301
5:44
Luke 1–5: 301
6:1
Mark 1–8: 141
6:1–5
Luke 6–10: 3
6:1–11
Luke 6–10: 1
6:2
Luke 6–10: 15
6:5
Luke 11–17: 80, 197, 259
Luke 18–24: 106
6:6
Mark 1–8: 152
6:6–11
Luke 11–17: 80, 258
6:7
Matthew 1–7: 222
Luke 1–5: 319
Luke 6–10: 15, 317
6:8
Mark 1–8: 153
John 12–21: 216
6:11
Matthew 8–15: 289
Mark 1–8: 157
Luke 1–5: 325
Luke 6–10: 15
Ephesians: 250
6:12
Matthew 8–15: 122
Mark 1–8: 167, 327
Luke 1–5: 5
Luke 6–10: 15
6:12–13
Luke 6–10: 13
Luke 11–17: 3
Acts 1–12: 285
1 & 2 Thessalonians: 44
6:12–16
Luke 11–17: 383
John 12–21: 74
1 & 2 Thessalonians: 202
6:13
Matthew 1–7: 116
Acts 1–12: 26
Acts 13–28: 268
2 Corinthians: 410
1 Timothy: 4
2 Peter–Jude: 19
6:13–16
Matthew 24–28: 99
Mark 1–8: 169
John 1–11: 3
1 Peter: 4
2 Peter–Jude: 2
6:13a
Luke 6–10: 15
6:13b
Luke 6–10: 17
6:14
Matthew 8–15: 155
1 Peter: 14
6:14–16
Matthew 8–15: 136
Acts 1–12: 51
6:14a
Luke 6–10: 23
6:14b
Luke 6–10: 39
6:14b, c
Luke 6–10: 37
6:14c
Luke 6–10: 41
6:14d
Luke 6–10: 45
6:14e, f
Luke 6–10: 53
6:15
Matthew 8–15: 161, 170
Luke 1–5: 331
Luke 6–10: 25
6:15–16a
Luke 6–10: 63
6:16
Luke 1–5: 226
John 12–21: 6, 73, 118
6:16–20
Mark 1–8: 303
6:16b
Luke 6–10: 73
6:17–19
Luke 6–10: 83
1 Peter: 32
6:18
1 Corinthians: 302
6:19
Mark 1–8: 84
Mark 9–16: 118
Luke 1–5: 293
Luke 18–24: 63
6:20
Matthew 1–7: 145
Luke 11–17: 205
6:20–26
Matthew 8–15: 98
Luke 6–10: 91
6:21
Matthew 1–7: 181
James: 213
6:22
Mark 1–8: 224
John 12–21: 30, 174
James: 23
1 Peter: 198
Revelation 12–22: 112
6:22–23
1 & 2 Thessalonians: 184
1 Peter: 251
6:23
Luke 1–5: 4
2 Corinthians: 349, 484
Philippians: 248
6:24–25
James: 243
6:25
Matthew 1–7: 154
James: 213
6:26
Matthew 1–7: 222
2 Corinthians: 230
6:27
Matthew 8–15: 202
6:27–30, 32–33
Romans 9–16: 196
6:27–38
Luke 6–10: 101
1 & 2 Thessalonians: 181
6:32–35
1 Peter: 158
6:33
Ephesians: 55
6:35
Romans 9–16: 246
2 Corinthians: 257
Ephesians: 190
Colossians and Philemon: 36, 155
Titus: 87, 151
6:36
Matthew 1–7: 194
Mark 1–8: 121
Luke 1–5: 120, 333
Luke 11–17: 45
6:37
Luke 1–5: 4
6:38
Matthew 1–7: 358
Matthew 8–15: 482, 483
1 Corinthians: 455
2 Corinthians: 273, 278, 299
Philippians: 307
1 Timothy: 249
James: 244
6:39
Luke 11–17: 105
Revelation 1–11: 139
Revelation 12–22: 298
6:39–49
Luke 6–10: 111–12
6:40
Matthew 8–15: 126, 217
John 12–21: 69
1 Corinthians: 482
1 Timothy: 91
6:41–42
Luke 6–10: 115
6:43
John 12–21: 148–49

6:43–45
James: 265
6:45
Mark 1–8: 352
Luke 1–5: 114
Luke 6–10: 302
Luke 18–24: 20
1 Corinthians: 453
1 Peter: 167
6:46
Matthew 1–7: 478
Matthew 8–15: 410
Luke 6–10: 289
Luke 11–17: 25
John 12–21: 68, 111
Romans 1–8: 483
1 Corinthians: 286
2 Corinthians: 470
Galatians: 153
James: 83, 286
2 Peter–Jude: 28
Revelation 12–22: 103
6:46–49
Philippians: 148
James: 82, 129
6:47
Luke 6–10: 364
Revelation 12–22: 304
6:47–49
Matthew 24–28: 91
7:1
Luke 6–10: 87
7:1–10
Luke 1–5: 15
Luke 6–10: 121
7:2
Matthew 8–15: 12
7:2–5
Matthew 8–15: 12
7:3
Matthew 8–15: 13
7:5
Luke 1–5: 282
7:7–8
Matthew 8–15: 156
7:8
Luke 11–17: 120
7:9
Mark 1–8: 270
Luke 1–5: 163
7:11–15
Mark 1–8: 253
Luke 1–5: 293
Luke 18–24: 64
John 12–21: 13
Acts 1–12: 284
Revelation 1–11: 25
7:11–16
Luke 6–10: 164
7:11–17
Mark 1–8: 226
Luke 6–10: 131
1 Timothy: 195
7:12
Luke 1–5: 149
Luke 18–24: 3
7:12–15
Luke 6–10: 326
John 12–21: 213
1–3 John: 17
7:13
Mark 1–8: 385
Luke 6–10: 89, 231
Luke 11–17: 237
2 Corinthians: 123
James: 242
Revelation 1–11: 165
7:14
Luke 1–5: 315
Luke 6–10: 186
7:15
1 Corinthians: 416
7:16
Matthew 8–15: 55
Mark 1–8: 107, 175
Luke 1–5: 5, 158, 164, 325
Acts 1–12: 86
Titus: 121
James: 89
1 Peter: 140
7:18
Matthew 8–15: 239
1 Peter: 54
7:18–19
Acts 13–28: 164
7:18–20
Luke 6–10: 145
7:18–23
John 1–11: 29
7:18–24
Luke 11–17: 4
7:19
Matthew 8–15: 240
Luke 1–5: 338
7:19–20
Luke 1–5: 223
Revelation 1–11: 28
7:19–22
John 1–11: 58
7:20–23
Acts 1–12: 61
7:21
Matthew 8–15: 296
7:22
Mark 1–8: 85
Luke 1–5: 157
Luke 6–10: 7
John 1–11: 470
7:24
Revelation 1–11: 47
7:24–25
Luke 6–10: 153
7:25
1 Peter: 125
7:27
Mark 1–8: 17
7:28–30
Mark 9–16: 157
7:29–34
Luke 18–24: 71
7:30
Matthew 16–23: 3
Luke 1–5: 319
7:32
Luke 6–10: 164
Luke 18–24: 371
7:33
Luke 6–10: 157
7:34
Mark 1–8: 111, 137, 370
Luke 1–5: 329
Luke 6–10: 172
John 12–21: 324
2 Corinthians: 245
Revelation 12–22: 112
7:35
1 Corinthians: 298
James: 138
7:36
Luke 1–5: 332
1–3 John: 243
7:36–40
1 Peter: 4
7:36–45
Romans 9–16: 370
7:36–47
1 Corinthians: 344
Ephesians: 196
7:36–50
Luke 1–5: 16
Luke 6–10: 25, 183
Luke 11–17: 257, 344
2 Peter–Jude: 2
7:37
James: 209, 286
7:37–38
Luke 1–5: 156
Luke 6–10: 172
7:37–50
Matthew 16–23: 74
John 12–21: 355
Acts 1–12: 74
7:38
James: 242
7:38, 45
Matthew 24–28: 187
7:39
Matthew 1–7: 61
Mark 1–8: 99, 111
James: 286
7:41–50
Luke 1–5: 4
7:42–43, 47
Matthew 8–15: 165
7:45
2 Corinthians: 486
7:46
James: 277, 278
7:47
Matthew 1–7: 156
Romans 1–8: 483
Philippians: 131
7:48
Luke 1–5: 321
1–3 John: 17
7:50
Mark 1–8: 261
Luke 6–10: 234

7–17
Luke 1–5: 228
8:1
Luke 1–5: 157
Luke 11–17: 205
Luke 18–24: 433
Acts 1–12: 48
8:1–3
Luke 1–5: 13
2 Corinthians: 292
8:2
Matthew 24–28: 285
Mark 9–16: 413
8:2–3
Matthew 24–28: 284
Mark 9–16: 383
Luke 18–24: 370
1 Timothy: 85
8:3
Luke 11–17: 207
8:4–5
Mark 1–8: 387
8:4–15
2 Timothy: 140
8:5
Matthew 8–15: 346
Mark 1–8: 195
8:6
Mark 1–8: 196
8:6–7
Luke 6–10: 157
8:8
Mark 1–8: 355
Revelation 12–22: 51
8:9–18
Luke 18–24: 175
8:10
Luke 11–17: 289
Luke 18–24: 98
Romans 9–16: 101
1 & 2 Thessalonians: 284
8:11
Mark 1–8: 200
8:12
Luke 6–10: 198
Ephesians: 339
James: 290
Revelation 1–11: 255
8:13
Philippians: 206
Colossians and Philemon: 66
1 Timothy: 147
Hebrews: 275
James: 16
8:13–14
2 Corinthians: 467
1–3 John: 37
8:14
Luke 6–10: 320
James: 187
8:15
Hebrews: 266
James: 16
Revelation 1–11: 79
8:16
Matthew 8–15: 220
Luke 6–10: 199
8:17
Revelation 12–22: 253
8:18
James: 66
8:19–21
Luke 1–5: 197
Luke 6–10: 202
James: 10
8:21
Luke 11–17: 77, 346
Revelation 12–22: 304
8:22–25
Luke 6–10: 205
8:23
Mark 1–8: 229, 230
8:24
Luke 1–5: 292
8:25
Mark 1–8: 248
Luke 1–5: 163
Luke 6–10: 223
Titus: 125
James: 214
8:25, 37, 50
Luke 1–5: 5
8:25, 56
Luke 1–5: 193
8:26
Matthew 8–15: 41
Mark 1–8: 241
8:26–39
Mark 1–8: 240
8:27
Mark 1–8: 242
Luke 1–5: 283
8:27–28
Luke 18–24: 411
8:27–29
Matthew 8–15: 42
8:28
Luke 1–5: 285, 286
8:29
Mark 1–8: 243
Acts 1–12: 194
8:30
Mark 1–8: 245
Luke 1–5: 283
8:31
Mark 1–8: 57, 244, 245
2 Corinthians: 467
1 Peter: 211
Revelation 12–22: 41, 168, 234
8:32
Matthew 8–15: 44
8:35
Matthew 8–15: 45
8:36
Mark 1–8: 242
2 Corinthians: 204
1 Timothy: 168
8:37
Matthew 8–15: 55
Luke 6–10: 229
Luke 11–17: 171
8:40
Mark 1–8: 255
8:42
Luke 1–5: 149
8:43
Matthew 8–15: 80, 81
Mark 1–8: 259
Luke 1–5: 12
8:44
Luke 1–5: 91
8:45
Mark 1–8: 260
Luke 6–10: 29
Philippians: 78
8:45–46
Luke 1–5: 305
8:45–48
Luke 6–10: 234
8:46
Matthew 8–15: 81
8:47
Mark 1–8: 261
8:48
Mark 1–8: 261
8:49–50
Luke 6–10: 235
8:50
Mark 1–8: 263
2 Corinthians: 204
1 Timothy: 168
8:51
Mark 1–8: 263
Acts 1–12: 98
8:51–52
Luke 18–24: 370
8:52
Mark 1–8: 264
James: 242
Revelation 1–11: 166
8:53
Mark 1–8: 265
8:54–55
Luke 6–10: 236
8:55
Matthew 8–15: 85
Mark 1–8: 266
8:56
Luke 6–10: 237
9:1
Matthew 8–15: 40
Mark 1–8: 65
Mark 9–16: 159
Luke 1–5: 294
Luke 6–10: 16
1 Corinthians: 302
2 Corinthians: 413
9:1–2
Luke 18–24: 125
9:1–6
Mark 1–8: 214
Luke 6–10: 301
9:2
Mark 1–8: 286
Acts 1–12: 15
2 Corinthians: 413

9:3
Mark 1–8: 289
9:3–4
Luke 18–24: 297
9:4
Luke 6–10: 331
9:5
Acts 1–12: 291
Acts 13–28: 149
9:5–9
Luke 6–10: 246
9:6
Luke 1–5: 157
Luke 18–24: 125
9:6–7
Luke 1–5: 43
9:7
Matthew 16–23: 317
9:7–8
Matthew 8–15: 418
9:7–9
Mark 1–8: 302
Luke 18–24: 349–50
9:9
Matthew 8–15: 418, 422
Mark 1–8: 303
Luke 1–5: 202
Luke 6–10: 247, 257
Luke 11–17: 229
Luke 18–24: 350
9:10
Mark 1–8: 315
Luke 6–10: 251
John 12–21: 228
9:10–17
Mark 1–8: 312
9:11
Matthew 8–15: 429
Mark 1–8: 316
9:17
Luke 11–17: 133
9:18
Matthew 16–23: 18
Luke 1–5: 238
Luke 11–17: 3
1 & 2 Thessalonians: 186
9:18–22
Luke 6–10: 257
9:18, 28–29
Luke 1–5: 5
9:19
Matthew 16–23: 20
9:20
Mark 1–8: 413, 415
Luke 6–10: 257
John 12–21: 264
9:21
Mark 1–8: 379
9:21–22
Luke 18–24: 48
9:22
Mark 9–16: 270
Luke 11–17: 414
Luke 18–24: 114, 263, 366, 441
1 Peter: 2
Revelation 12–22: 112
9:22–23
Luke 1–5: 15
9:23
Mark 9–16: 14, 42
Luke 6–10: 268, 315, 319, 350
Luke 11–17: 25, 140, 219, 278, 281, 350
John 1–11: 99
Acts 1–12: 297
2 Corinthians: 145
Philippians: 252
Colossians and Philemon: 136
1 & 2 Thessalonians: 248
1 Peter: 225, 239
1–3 John: 41, 60
9:23–24
Mark 9–16: 155
Luke 6–10: 321
Luke 11–17: 25, 120
Luke 18–24: 39
1 Peter: 112
9:23–25
Mark 1–8: 203
Luke 1–5: 309
Luke 11–17: 419
Luke 18–24: 35
2 Peter–Jude: 205
9:23–26
Luke 6–10: 265
Luke 11–17: 161
1 Peter: 127
1–3 John: 38
9:23, 49, 57, 59, 61
Luke 1–5: 309
9:23, 57–62
1–3 John: 149
9:24
1 Timothy: 272
9:24–25
Luke 6–10: 276
Luke 18–24: 42
9:26
Matthew 1–7: 222
Luke 6–10: 277, 281
Philippians: 310
Revelation 1–11: 28
9:27
2 Peter–Jude: 60
9:27–36
Matthew 16–23: 60
Mark 9–16: 3
2 Peter–Jude: 29
9:28
Mark 9–16: 4
Acts 1–12: 98
9:28–29
Luke 11–17: 3
1 & 2 Thessalonians: 186
9:28–32
Luke 1–5: 156
9:28,32
Matthew 24–28: 175
9:29
Luke 6–10: 282
Luke 18–24: 421
9:30–32
2 Peter–Jude: 61
9:31
Matthew 16–23: 64, 65, 67
9:31–32
Philippians: 127
9:32
Matthew 16–23: 62, 63
Mark 9–16: 5, 6
9:32–33
Luke 6–10: 284
9:33
Matthew 16–23: 66, 67
Mark 9–16: 7
9:34
Luke 1–5: 5, 57
9:34–36
Luke 6–10: 285
9:35
Mark 9–16: 8
John 12–21: 331
9:37–39
Luke 6–10: 289
9:38
Matthew 16–23: 75
Luke 1–5: 149
2 Corinthians: 284
9:39
Matthew 16–23: 76
Mark 1–8: 63
James: 246
9:40–42a
Luke 6–10: 291
9:41
Mark 9–16: 26
Acts 1–12: 76
9:42
Luke 1–5: 283
1 Corinthians: 302
9:43
Matthew 8–15: 101
Matthew 16–23: 78
Luke 1–5: 163, 193
2 Peter–Jude: 60
9:43–48
Romans 9–16: 275
9:43c–44
Luke 6–10: 295
9:44
Mark 9–16: 34, 35
Luke 6–10: 309
Luke 18–24: 48
Hebrews: 44
9:44–45
Mark 9–16: 95
Luke 1–5: 196
Luke 18–24: 49
9:45
Mark 9–16: 35, 227
Luke 6–10: 19
9:46
Matthew 16–23: 94
Luke 6–10: 35
9:46–48
Luke 6–10: 20

9:47
Luke 6–10: 302
9:48
Luke 18–24: 444
9:49
2 Corinthians: 139
9:49–50
Luke 6–10: 304
9:51
Matthew 8–15: 467
Matthew 16–23: 85, 221
Mark 1–8: 364
Luke 6–10: 42, 133, 240, 297, 309
Luke 18–24: 48, 58, 92
James: 255
9:51–56
Mark 9–16: 104
9:51–19:27
Luke 6–10: 362
Luke 11–17: 217
9:52
Luke 6–10: 42
Revelation 1–11: 47
9:52–53
Acts 1–12: 233
9:52–54
Matthew 8–15: 149
9:52–56
Luke 6–10: 311
9:53
Luke 6–10: 42
9:54
Matthew 8–15: 376, 377
Mark 1–8: 52, 170
Luke 1–5: 223
Luke 6–10: 42
2 Corinthians: 139
Revelation 12–22: 242
9:54–56
Romans 9–16: 373
9:55–56
Matthew 8–15: 149
Luke 6–10: 42
9:56
Matthew 16–23: 119
Galatians: 179
James: 290
9:57
Luke 6–10: 209, 267
9:57–58
Luke 6–10: 317
9:57–62
Matthew 1–7: 485
Matthew 8–15: 231
Matthew 24–28: 26
Mark 1–8: 228
Luke 6–10: 315
John 1–11: 99
Acts 1–12: 162, 297
Acts 13–28: 301
Romans 1–8: 513
Romans 9–16: 74
2 Timothy: 44
9:58
Luke 1–5: 150, 258
2 Corinthians: 291–92
Hebrews: 12
9:59
Luke 6–10: 209
9:59–62
Matthew 8–15: 216
Mark 9–16: 86
9:60
Acts 13–28: 15
Titus: 13
Revelation 1–11: 111
9:61
Luke 6–10: 209
9:61–62
Matthew 8–15: 32, 390
Luke 6–10: 320
9:62
Luke 6–10: 209
Philippians: 247
10
James: 289
10:1
1 Corinthians: 300
10:1–3
Luke 18–24: 125
10:1–9
Luke 1–5: 294
10:1–16
Matthew 8–15: 268
Luke 6–10: 323–24
10:2
John 12–21: 163
10:4–7
1–3 John: 243
10:5–6
Ephesians: 80
10:5–11
Luke 6–10: 330
10:7
Luke 6–10: 184
1 Corinthians: 205
1 Timothy: 220
2 Timothy: 146
Titus: 39
10:9
Luke 11–17: 23
10:9, 17
Matthew 24–28: 339
10:10–12
Luke 6–10: 313
Acts 13–28: 40
10:10–16
Luke 6–10: 332
10:12–15
Luke 6–10: 333
10:13
Luke 6–10: 252
10:13–14
Mark 1–8: 409
10:15
Mark 1–8: 68
10:16
Matthew 16–23: 103, 119
Luke 11–17: 122
1–3 John: 158
10:17
Mark 1–8: 285
Luke 6–10: 304
Luke 18–24: 125
Acts 13–28: 171
1 Peter: 177
10:17–24
Luke 6–10: 337
10:18
Matthew 8–15: 310
Luke 1–5: 280
Ephesians: 338
1 Timothy: 38
1–3 John: 126
Revelation 1–11: 162, 256
Revelation 12–22: 1, 19
10:20
Matthew 16–23: 47
Philippians: 216, 260, 273
1 & 2 Thessalonians: 184, 185
Hebrews: 415
1 Peter: 17, 26, 177
1–3 John: 90
Revelation 12–22: 255
10:21
Luke 1–5: 5
Luke 11–17: 3
1 Peter: 41, 278
1–3 John: 158
10:21–22
Luke 1–5: 194
1 Peter: 31
10:22
Luke 11–17: 116
1 Peter: 30
10:23–24
John 12–21: 161
10:25
Matthew 8–15: 326
Mark 1–8: 100
Luke 1–5: 319
Luke 6–10: 352
1 & 2 Thessalonians: 245
10:25–26
2 Timothy: 140
10:25–28
Romans 1–8: 371
10:25–37
Luke 6–10: 349–50
Luke 11–17: 198
Romans 9–16: 248, 251
1 Corinthians: 451
Colossians and Philemon: 156
10:26
Luke 6–10: 5
10:26–27
Matthew 1–7: 340
10:26–28
Luke 6–10: 353
10:27
Matthew 1–7: 338
10:29, 36–37
Matthew 1–7: 344
10:30
Luke 11–17: 358
2 Corinthians: 228

James: 25
10:30–32
Luke 11–17: 361
10:30–34
Philippians: 104
10:30–35
Philippians: 43
James: 128
10:30–37
Matthew 1–7: 338
James: 112, 179
10:32
Luke 1–5: 245
10:33
Mark 1–8: 77
10:33–35
1 Corinthians: 487
10:34
Luke 1–5: 149
Ephesians: 234
James: 278
10:34–35
1 Timothy: 117
10:35
Philippians: 104
10:38
2 Corinthians: 292
1–3 John: 243
10:38–40
Luke 1–5: 332
10:38–42
Luke 6–10: 361
John 12–21: 3
1 Corinthians: 260
1 Timothy: 85
10:39
Mark 9–16: 273
Luke 6–10: 364
10:40
Acts 1–12: 183
2 Corinthians: 201
1 Timothy: 124
10:40–42
Luke 6–10: 365
10:41
Matthew 16–23: 400
Luke 18–24: 390
Acts 1–12: 268
Philippians: 197
10:41–42
1–3 John: 213
10:42
Matthew 24–28: 135
Mark 9–16: 275
11:1
Matthew 1–7: 366, 374
Luke 1–5: 5
Acts 13–28: 164
11:1–2
1 & 2 Thessalonians: 186
11:1–2a
Luke 11–17: 1
11:1–2d
Luke 11–17: 19
11:1–4
Luke 11–17: 8, 51
11:1b
Luke 11–17: 3
11:2
Luke 18–24: 304
11:2b
Luke 11–17: 5
11:2b, c
Luke 11–17: 9
11:3
Luke 11–17: 31, 32
11:3–4
Luke 11–17: 31
11:4
Luke 1–5: 4
Luke 11–17: 379
1–3 John: 34
11:4a
Luke 11–17: 36
11:4b
Luke 11–17: 46
11:5–8
Matthew 16–23: 282
Luke 11–17: 8, 53
11:5–10
Mark 9–16: 30
Ephesians: 103
Colossians and Philemon: 180
1 & 2 Thessalonians: 186
11:5–13
Luke 11–17: 49
11:8
Matthew 16–23: 80
Luke 11–17: 273
11:9
Ephesians: 381
11:9–10
Luke 11–17: 8, 55
11:9–13
1 & 2 Thessalonians: 187
11:10
Romans 9–16: 352
Hebrews: 310
11:11–12
Luke 11–17: 55
11:11–13
Luke 11–17: 8
11:12
Matthew 1–7: 445
11:13
Luke 1–5: 5
Luke 11–17: 56
Acts 1–12: 17
Galatians: 69
Ephesians: 55
James: 55
11:14
Mark 1–8: 182
Luke 1–5: 193
Luke 6–10: 260
11:14–23
Luke 11–17: 59
11:14, 38
Luke 1–5: 163
11:15
Matthew 8–15: 40
Mark 1–8: 106, 181, 184
Luke 11–17: 81, 115, 123
John 1–11: 479
Ephesians: 339
11:15, 53
Luke 1–5: 325
11:16
Luke 11–17: 81
11:17
Luke 6–10: 8
11:17–18
Luke 11–17: 64
11:17–22
Mark 1–8: 239
11:17–23
Luke 11–17: 63
11:19
Luke 6–10: 166
Luke 11–17: 65
11:19–20
Luke 1–5: 193
11:20
Matthew 8–15: 40
Luke 11–17: 206, 208
John 1–11: 470
11:20–22
Luke 6–10: 218
11:20–23
Luke 11–17: 66
11:21
John 12–21: 278
11:21–22
1 & 2 Thessalonians: 88
11:23
Mark 1–8: 175
Luke 11–17: 60, 74
John 1–11: 478
John 12–21: 10, 155, 180
1–3 John: 209
11:24–26
Luke 11–17: 75
2 Timothy: 93
2 Peter–Jude: 180
11:24–28
Luke 11–17: 69
11:27
Mark 1–8: 186
Luke 1–5: 71
11:27–28
Luke 1–5: 197
Luke 11–17: 76
Acts 1–12: 29
11:28
Luke 1–5: 62
John 12–21: 69
Acts 13–28: 358
Ephesians: 370
1 & 2 Thessalonians: 89, 198
1 Timothy: 137
1–3 John: 142, 182
Revelation 1–11: 22
Revelation 12–22: 304
11:29
Luke 6–10: 179
Luke 11–17: 61, 63, 81
Acts 1–12: 76

11:29–32
Luke 11–17: 82
11:29–33a
Mark 9–16: 156
11:29–36
Luke 11–17: 79, 80
11:29a
Luke 11–17: 82
11:29b–30
Luke 11–17: 85
11:31
Luke 1–5: 100
11:31–32
Luke 11–17: 86
11:33
Luke 11–17: 88
11:33–36
Luke 11–17: 87
11:34
Luke 11–17: 89
11:35
Luke 11–17: 90
11:36
Luke 11–17: 90
1 & 2 Thessalonians: 205
11:37
Luke 1–5: 332
11:37–38
Luke 11–17: 80
11:37–41
Titus: 65
11:37–54
Luke 11–17: 94
11:38
Luke 11–17: 98
11:38–39
Luke 1–5: 319
11:38–44
Luke 11–17: 97
11:39
Luke 11–17: 83, 345
11:39–40
Luke 11–17: 256
11:39–41
Matthew 1–7: 135
11:39–44
Mark 1–8: 351
11:39–52
Luke 1–5: 341
2 Peter–Jude: 69–70
11:40–41
Luke 11–17: 99
11:42
Luke 11–17: 100
Luke 18–24: 19
11:43
Luke 6–10: 8
Luke 11–17: 262
11:43–44
Luke 11–17: 101
11:44
Matthew 1–7: 353
Luke 18–24: 164
2 Peter–Jude: 187
11:45–54
Luke 11–17: 103
11:45, 46, 52
Luke 1–5: 319
11:46
Mark 1–8: 140
Luke 6–10: 4
Luke 11–17: 104
Acts 1–12: 117
Acts 13–28: 26, 68
Philippians: 237
11:47–51
Luke 11–17: 105
Acts 1–12: 215
11:50
Revelation 12–22: 50
11:52
Matthew 16–23: 377, 381
11:52–54
Luke 11–17: 108
11:53
Luke 1–5: 319
11:53–54
Mark 9–16: 24
Luke 11–17: 116
12
Matthew 1–7: 353
Luke 11–17: 157
12:1
Matthew 8–15: 373
Matthew 16–23: 14
Mark 9–16: 226
Luke 6–10: 16, 260
Luke 11–17: 189, 377
2 Corinthians: 182
James: 180
12:1–2
Mark 1–8: 214
12:1–12
Luke 11–17: 111, 112
12:1–13:9
Luke 11–17: 139, 282
12:2–7
Luke 11–17: 117
12:4–5
Luke 18–24: 386
1 Peter: 199
12:5
Luke 11–17: 273
1 Peter: 168
Revelation 1–11: 202
Revelation 12–22: 85, 256
12:8
Revelation 12–22: 112
12:8–9
Mark 1–8: 225
Luke 11–17: 119–20
12:10
Luke 1–5: 4
12:10–12
Luke 11–17: 121
12:10, 12
Luke 1–5: 5
12:11
John 1–11: 15
12:11–12
Luke 18–24: 214
Acts 1–12: 133, 221
12:12
Acts 1–12: 17
Philippians: 74
12:13–21
Luke 11–17: 127, 139
12:14
Luke 18–24: 4
12:15
Matthew 1–7: 143
Luke 11–17: 132
2 Corinthians: 279
Ephesians: 172
Hebrews: 433
12:15–21
1 Timothy: 253
12:16–20
Matthew 24–28: 71
Luke 11–17: 133
John 12–21: 361
12:16–21
Matthew 1–7: 178
Mark 1–8: 431
Mark 9–16: 83
1 Timothy: 282
James: 232, 244
Revelation 12–22: 192
12:18
Matthew 1–7: 411
12:18–19
2 Corinthians: 317
12:18–21
Matthew 16–23: 200
12:19
Luke 11–17: 361
2 Corinthians: 269
James: 244
12:19–20
Ephesians: 264
12:20
Luke 11–17: 100, 221, 338
John 1–11: 460
12:21
Luke 11–17: 135
James: 250
12:22–23
Luke 11–17: 139
12:22–34
Luke 11–17: 137–38
Acts 13–28: 290
12:24
Luke 11–17: 140, 143
12:25–26
Luke 11–17: 141
12:27–29
Luke 11–17: 142
12:28
Mark 1–8: 233
Mark 9–16: 30
Acts 1–12: 10
1 & 2 Thessalonians: 180
12:30
Hebrews: 434
1 Peter: 31
12:30–31
Luke 11–17: 143

12:32
Matthew 1–7: 151, 458
Luke 1–5: 157
Luke 6–10: 348
Luke 11–17: 218
John 12–21: 61
Philippians: 173
Colossians and Philemon: 41
1 & 2 Thessalonians: 248
Hebrews: 98
1 Peter: 31
Revelation 1–11: 121
12:32–34
Luke 11–17: 146
12:33
Acts 13–28: 340
2 Corinthians: 232, 278
1 Peter: 35
12:34
Luke 11–17: 128
2 Corinthians: 272
Revelation 12–22: 261
12:35
Ephesians: 349
1 Peter: 65
12:35–37
Matthew 24–28: 78
1 Peter: 46, 238
12:35–40
Matthew 24–28: 77
Luke 11–17: 157–58
Luke 18–24: 191
Revelation 1–11: 23, 201
Revelation 12–22: 268, 288
12:35–48
Luke 11–17: 149–50
12:35a
Luke 11–17: 158
12:35b
Luke 11–17: 158
12:36–38
Luke 11–17: 159
12:36–40
Acts 1–12: 19
12:37
Luke 6–10: 97
Luke 11–17: 386
12:39
Revelation 1–11: 114
12:39–40
Luke 11–17: 160
12:40
Luke 11–17: 157, 221
Luke 18–24: 252
Revelation 1–11: 28
12:41
Luke 6–10: 28
Luke 11–17: 184
12:41–48
Luke 11–17: 161–62, 173
James: 236
12:42–44
Luke 11–17: 162
12:42–47
Philippians: 144
12:45–46
1 & 2 Thessalonians: 161
12:45–48
Luke 11–17: 163
12:46–48
2 Peter–Jude: 186
12:47
Hebrews: 48
James: 236
12:47–48
Matthew 8–15: 398
Mark 9–16: 288
Luke 6–10: 333
John 12–21: 224
Romans 1–8: 137
Philippians: 214
1 & 2 Thessalonians: 243
Hebrews: 278
James: 289
Revelation 12–22: 225, 254
12:48
Matthew 1–7: 434
1 Corinthians: 332
2 Corinthians: 228
Galatians: 110
Ephesians: 240
1 Timothy: 267
1 Peter: 61
2 Peter–Jude: 85
Revelation 12–22: 123
12:49–50
Luke 11–17: 170
12:49–59
Luke 11–17: 167–68, 168
12:49, 51–52
Matthew 8–15: 230
12:50
Matthew 1–7: 78
Mark 1–8: 32
Mark 9–16: 91, 106
Luke 18–24: 47
12:51
Luke 1–5: 183
John 1–11: 481
John 12–21: 2
12:51–53
Luke 11–17: 172–73
Colossians and Philemon: 170–71
Revelation 1–11: 72
12:54–56
Luke 11–17: 175
12:54–57
Luke 11–17: 113
12:54–59
Luke 11–17: 174, 283
12:56
2 Corinthians: 182
Philippians: 47, 50
12:57
Philippians: 286
12:57–59
Luke 11–17: 177
13
Matthew 1–7: 127
13:1
Matthew 24–28: 238
Luke 1–5: 202
Luke 18–24: 351, 357
John 1–11: 483
13:1–3a
Luke 11–17: 184
13:1–5
Luke 6–10: 94
Luke 11–17: 165, 184
John 12–21: 383
Romans 1–8: 123, 193
1 & 2 Thessalonians: 241
13:1–9
Luke 11–17: 179, 221
13:2
Mark 1–8: 163
13:2–5
Luke 1–5: 193
13:3
Luke 11–17: 221
Romans 9–16: 294
2 Corinthians: 131
Philippians: 223
Revelation 1–11: 139
13:3b
Luke 11–17: 187
13:3, 5
Mark 9–16: 42
13:4
John 1–11: 5
13:4–5a
Luke 11–17: 187
13:5
2 Corinthians: 131
Philippians: 223
Revelation 1–11: 139
13:6–9
Matthew 16–23: 278
Luke 11–17: 188–89
John 12–21: 48
13:10
Luke 11–17: 198
13:10–16
Revelation 12–22: 16
13:10–17
Mark 1–8: 153
Luke 11–17: 193–94
13:10, 22
Luke 1–5: 267
13:11
Mark 1–8: 63
13:11–13
Luke 11–17: 113, 200
1 Timothy: 85
13:13
Luke 1–5: 164, 315, 324
13:14
Mark 9–16: 66
Luke 1–5: 267
2 Corinthians: 267
13:14–17
Luke 11–17: 201
13:15
Luke 11–17: 260
2 Corinthians: 182

Philippians: 50
13:15–16
Matthew 8–15: 149
Luke 11–17: 114
13:17
Mark 1–8: 106
Luke 1–5: 4, 325
Luke 11–17: 260
13:18–19
Luke 11–17: 208
13:18–21
Luke 11–17: 205
Luke 18–24: 201
13:19
Luke 11–17: 384
13:20–21
Luke 11–17: 212
13:21
Mark 1–8: 403
13:22–30
Luke 11–17: 315
13:23
Mark 1–8: 193
Mark 9–16: 14
Luke 6–10: 269
13:23–24
Matthew 1–7: 455
John 12–21: 53
2 Corinthians: 192, 202
1–3 John: 38
13:23b–24
Luke 11–17: 218
13:24
Matthew 1–7: 474
Luke 11–17: 255
Luke 18–24: 258
John 12–21: 103
2 Timothy: 192
13:24–25
Revelation 12–22: 298
13:24–27
Matthew 1–7: 458
Luke 18–24: 239
13:24–28
Luke 1–5: 221
Luke 11–17: 282
13:25–28
Matthew 24–28: 92
13:25a
Luke 11–17: 220
13:25b–27
Luke 11–17: 222
13:26–27
Hebrews: 100
13:27
Luke 18–24: 85
1 & 2 Thessalonians: 245
13:28
Luke 1–5: 216
Luke 6–10: 100
Acts 1–12: 221
1 & 2 Thessalonians: 245
1 Timothy: 167
Revelation 12–22: 204, 242, 256
13:28–29
Luke 11–17: 23
13:28–30
Luke 11–17: 160, 223
13:31
Matthew 16–23: 317
Mark 1–8: 303
Luke 6–10: 248
Luke 18–24: 351
13:31–32
Mark 1–8: 285
13:31–33
Mark 9–16: 349
Luke 11–17: 225
Luke 18–24: 350
Acts 13–28: 327
13:31–35
Luke 1–5: 184
13:31a
Luke 11–17: 227
13:31b
Luke 11–17: 228
13:32
Matthew 8–15: 422
Mark 9–16: 400
Luke 18–24: 47
13:32–33
Mark 9–16: 91
Luke 11–17: 229
13:33
Matthew 16–23: 38, 259, 317
Luke 6–10: 133, 179
13:34
Matthew 1–7: 385
Matthew 16–23: 194
Mark 9–16: 26
Luke 11–17: 237–38
Acts 1–12: 268
1 Corinthians: 20
Galatians: 117
Hebrews: 447
Revelation 1–11: 132
13:34–35
Luke 11–17: 190, 235, 280
Luke 18–24: 47, 98, 175, 371
13:35
Luke 1–5: 110
Luke 11–17: 274
Luke 18–24: 446
13:35a
Luke 11–17: 241
13:35b
Luke 11–17: 244
14:1
Luke 1–5: 332
Luke 6–10: 7
1–3 John: 243
14:1a
Luke 11–17: 257
14:1b–2
Luke 11–17: 258
14:1–2
Acts 1–12: 99
14:1–12
Luke 6–10: 145
14:1–14
Luke 11–17: 253, 254
14:3
Luke 1–5: 319
Acts 1–12: 104
14:3–6
Luke 11–17: 259
14:4
1 & 2 Thessalonians: 119
14:7
Luke 11–17: 376
14:7–10
Luke 11–17: 261
14:7–11
Mark 9–16: 219
14:11
Luke 1–5: 47, 80
Luke 6–10: 63
Luke 11–17: 264
Philippians: 138
1 Peter: 279
Revelation 12–22: 185
14:12
1 Timothy: 107
14:12–14
Luke 11–17: 261
Romans 9–16: 194, 199
1 & 2 Thessalonians: 309
Titus: 40
14:13
2 Corinthians: 279
14:13–14
Ephesians: 187
14:13, 21
2 Corinthians: 279
14:14
1 Corinthians: 416
Revelation 12–22: 238
14:15
1 & 2 Thessalonians: 306
14:15–23
Luke 1–5: 15
14:15–24
Luke 11–17: 250, 267–68
14:16
2 Corinthians: 291
14:16–17
Luke 11–17: 270
14:16–24
John 1–11: 154
14:18–20
Luke 11–17: 271
14:19
Philippians: 47
14:21–23
Luke 11–17: 272
14:21–24
Romans 9–16: 90
14:24
Luke 11–17: 273
14:25
Luke 1–5: 302
14:25–27
Luke 11–17: 282
1–3 John: 38

14:25–33
Philippians: 148
14:25–35
Luke 11–17: 277–78
2 Corinthians: 469–70
14:26
Matthew 1–7: 456
Mark 9–16: 42
Luke 6–10: 268, 321
Luke 11–17: 25, 219, 419
Romans 1–8: 55
Colossians and Philemon: 171
James: 17, 19
1–3 John: 66
14:26–33
John 12–21: 29, 398
Acts 1–12: 73
Romans 1–8: 353
14:26–35
Acts 13–28: 55
14:27
Matthew 24–28: 341
Luke 11–17: 25
2 Corinthians: 25
James: 204
14:27–28
Mark 1–8: 424
14:27–33
1 Peter: 128
14:27–35
John 1–11: 228–29
14:28
Matthew 1–7: 453
14:28–32
Luke 6–10: 269
Luke 11–17: 286
14:28–33
Matthew 8–15: 391
John 12–21: 194
14:28, 31
Matthew 1–7: 456
14:28, 31, 33
Romans 9–16: 343
14:31
Ephesians: 348
14:33
Matthew 16–23: 185, 195
Luke 11–17: 25, 147, 219, 282
14:34
Mark 9–16: 49
14:34–35
Luke 11–17: 288
14:35
Mark 9–16: 49
Revelation 12–22: 51
15
Matthew 1–7: x, 376
Luke 11–17: 329
Luke 18–24: 68
1 Peter: 39
15:1–2
Mark 1–8: 106, 149
Luke 1–5: 156, 325
Luke 11–17: 257, 305, 350
15:1–3
Luke 11–17: 335
15:1–10
Luke 11–17: 291–92
15:1–32
Luke 1–5: 4
15:2
Matthew 8–15: 66
Luke 1–5: 319
Philippians: 206
15:3–7
Matthew 16–23: 120
Luke 11–17: 295–96
Romans 9–16: 319
1 Peter: 261
15:3–32
Luke 11–17: 350
15:4–7
1 Peter: 39
15:5–6
Philippians: 317
15:5–10, 22–32
Luke 1–5: 4
15:6
Philippians: 195
15:7
Mark 1–8: 121
Luke 1–5: 334
Luke 6–10: 341
Luke 11–17: 273, 321
Luke 18–24: 151
Acts 13–28: 249
Galatians: 118
Philippians: 35, 223
James: 286, 287, 289
1 Peter: 58
Revelation 1–11: 139, 228
15:7, 10
John 12–21: 255
15:7, 10, 20–27
Luke 1–5: 88
15:8–10
Luke 11–17: 299
1 Peter: 39
15:9
Philippians: 195, 317
15:10
Matthew 16–23: 214
Luke 1–5: 161
Luke 6–10: 341
Acts 13–28: 249
Ephesians: 97
Philippians: 35, 223
Hebrews: 23
James: 286, 287
1 Peter: 58, 220
Revelation 1–11: 139, 228
Revelation 12–22: 75
15:11–12
Luke 11–17: 307
15:11–19
Luke 11–17: 306–7
15:11–24
Matthew 16–23: 151
15:11–32
Luke 1–5: 16, 168
Luke 11–17: 301, 303–4
Luke 18–24: 73
2 Corinthians: 50
Colossians and Philemon: 201–2
1 Peter: 39
2 Peter–Jude: 134
1–3 John: 16
15:13
Luke 11–17: 335
Ephesians: 242
James: 190, 247
15:13–16
Luke 11–17: 309
15:17–19
Luke 11–17: 311–12
Luke 18–24: 387
15:17–21
Romans 1–8: 224
15:17–24
2 Peter–Jude: 26
15:18
1–3 John: 38
15:18–19
James: 214
15:20
Matthew 24–28: 187
15:20–24
Luke 11–17: 313–14
15:20–32
Luke 11–17: 43
15:21
1–3 John: 27
15:22
Luke 11–17: 316
15:22–24
James: 206, 214
15:23–24
Luke 11–17: 317
15:24
Revelation 1–11: 111
15:25–30
Luke 11–17: 83, 318–19
15:25–32
Luke 11–17: 318
15:27
2 Timothy: 181
15:29
Philippians: 199
15:31–32
Luke 11–17: 322
15:32
Acts 13–28: 249
Revelation 1–11: 111
16:1
Luke 11–17: 328
16:1–8
Luke 11–17: 334
2 Peter–Jude: 85
16:1–13
Luke 11–17: 331–32
16:1ff.
1 Timothy: 229
16:2
Philippians: 306
16:3
Mark 9–16: 115

16:8
Luke 1–5: 196
Luke 18–24: 146
2 Corinthians: 132
1 & 2 Thessalonians: 158
16:9
Matthew 1–7: 413
2 Corinthians: 319
1 & 2 Thessalonians: 73, 244
1 Timothy: 249, 285
16:9–13
Luke 11–17: 337–38
16:10
Matthew 1–7: 358
1 Corinthians: 452, 464
2 Corinthians: 279
16:10–11
1 Corinthians: 454
16:11–12
Matthew 1–7: 359
16:13
John 12–21: 401
Titus: 45
James: 239
1–3 John: 85
16:14
Matthew 1–7: 407
Luke 11–17: 131, 298, 328, 335, 358
16:14–15
Galatians: 196
16:14–18
Luke 11–17: 341
16:14a
Luke 11–17: 344
16:15
Matthew 1–7: 278, 430
Mark 1–8: 355
Luke 1–5: 21, 337, 341
Luke 11–17: 376
16:15a
Luke 11–17: 346
16:15b
Luke 11–17: 348
16:15c
Luke 11–17: 348
16:16
Luke 1–5: 157
Luke 6–10: 269
Luke 11–17: 25, 281, 349
Acts 13–28: 372
16:17
Matthew 24–28: 68
2 Timothy: 145
Revelation 12–22: 249
16:17–18
Luke 11–17: 350
16:19–21
Luke 11–17: 360
Acts 1–12: 99
16:19–25
James: 243
16:19–26
Luke 11–17: 359
16:19–31
Mark 1–8: 264
Mark 9–16: 84
Luke 11–17: 355–56
Acts 1–12: 225
1 & 2 Thessalonians: 126
16:20
Matthew 1–7: 145
2 Corinthians: 279
16:20–31
Matthew 16–23: 202
16:21
Revelation 12–22: 139
16:22
Luke 11–17: 362
16:22–26
2 Peter–Jude: 186
16:23
1 Corinthians: 417
Revelation 12–22: 91, 224, 252
16:23–24
Luke 6–10: 334
James: 245
Revelation 12–22: 185, 242
16:23–26
Luke 11–17: 363
16:24
Matthew 1–7: 79
16:24–26
Luke 1–5: 221
16:25
Luke 6–10: 99
Philippians: 263
16:25–26
Matthew 1–7: 69
16:26
Matthew 24–28: 322
1 & 2 Thessalonians: 245
16:28
Revelation 12–22: 185
16:29
Romans 1–8: 169
16:30–31
Matthew 24–28: 261
Acts 1–12: 115
16:31
Matthew 8–15: 330, 410
Matthew 16–23: 5
Hebrews: 90
Revelation 1–11: 305
Revelation 12–22: 153
17:1–2
Luke 11–17: 377
17:1–10
Luke 11–17: 373, 374
17:3
Matthew 16–23: 144
Acts 1–12: 161
2 Corinthians: 59
1 Timothy: 188
17:3–4
Matthew 1–7: 397
Luke 1–5: 4
Luke 11–17: 378
Colossians and Philemon: 228
1 & 2 Thessalonians: 180
17:4
Matthew 16–23: 145
Luke 6–10: 272
Luke 11–17: 44
17:5
Matthew 8–15: 36
John 12–21: 137
17:5–6
Mark 9–16: 146
Luke 11–17: 383
17:7–10
Luke 11–17: 385
1 Timothy: 42, 231
17:8
Acts 1–12: 183
1 Timothy: 124
Revelation 1–11: 140
17:10
Matthew 1–7: 360, 486
Matthew 16–23: 243
Matthew 24–28: 103
1 Corinthians: 97
Philippians: 47, 130, 174
17:11–14
Luke 11–17: 390
17:11–19
Matthew 8–15: 295, 337
Mark 1–8: 163, 280
Luke 11–17: 387
Luke 18–24: 58
17:11–37
Mark 9–16: 34
17:11–19:28
John 1–11: 485
17:12
Luke 1–5: 314
17:12–13
Philippians: 206
17:12–19
Matthew 16–23: 252
17:14
Mark 9–16: 118
Luke 1–5: 293
Luke 18–24: 63
Acts 1–12: 101
17:15
Luke 1–5: 164, 324
17:15–19
Luke 11–17: 392
17:16
Mark 1–8: 366
17:17–19
Mark 1–8: 75
17:18–19
Ephesians: 264
Revelation 1–11: 305
17:19
Mark 1–8: 261
Luke 6–10: 234
17:20
Luke 18–24: 35
17:20–21
Matthew 8–15: 244, 370, 386
Luke 11–17: 209, 397
17:20–37
Acts 1–12: 19

17:20–18:8
Luke 18–24: 13
17:20a
Luke 11–17: 401
17:20b–21
Luke 11–17: 403
17:20ff.
Acts 1–12: 15
17:21
Matthew 1–7: 380
Mark 1–8: 48
Luke 11–17: 23
1 & 2 Thessalonians: 52
17:21–42
1 Peter: 121
17:22
Luke 11–17: 412
Luke 18–24: 7, 188
17:22–37
Luke 11–17: 407–8
17:23–24
Luke 11–17: 413
17:24
Luke 18–24: 188
17:25
Luke 1–5: 15
Luke 18–24: 366
John 12–21: 132
1 Peter: 2
17:26–28, 30
Matthew 8–15: 263
17:26–30
Luke 11–17: 415–16
Luke 18–24: 258
17:28–29
Luke 18–24: 254
17:28–32
2 Peter–Jude: 89
17:29
Matthew 1–7: 263
Revelation 12–22: 91, 225
17:31–33
Luke 11–17: 418
17:32
John 12–21: 205
17:34–36
Luke 11–17: 419
17:37
Luke 11–17: 402, 420
Revelation 12–22: 32, 222
18
Luke 6–10: 310
18:1
Matthew 1–7: 383
Matthew 16–23: 80
Luke 11–17: 2, 29
Luke 18–24: 7
Acts 1–12: 85
Ephesians: 361, 377
Philippians: 38
18:1–8
Matthew 16–23: 282
Mark 1–8: 368
Luke 18–24: 1, 14
Ephesians: 103
Colossians and Philemon: 179–80
1 & 2 Thessalonians: 186
18:1ff.
1 Timothy: 194
18:2–5
Luke 11–17: 29
Luke 18–24: 3
18:2–7
Matthew 1–7: 369
18:6–8a
Luke 18–24: 8
18:7
Acts 13–28: 38
1 & 2 Thessalonians: 20, 287
1 Peter: 17
Revelation 1–11: 54
18:7–8
Ephesians: 381
Revelation 1–11: 195
18:8
Luke 1–5: 50
18:8b
Luke 18–24: 9
18:9
Luke 11–17: 263
Luke 18–24: 14
Romans 1–8: 201, 367
2 Timothy: 112
18:9–11
Luke 11–17: 370
18:9–14
Matthew 1–7: 147
Mark 1–8: 121, 126, 149, 354
Mark 9–16: 77
Luke 18–24: 11, 24, 35
Acts 1–12: 242
Romans 9–16: 321
1 Corinthians: 13
2 Corinthians: 99
Galatians: 196
18:10–13
Luke 18–24: 17, 71
18:10–14
Matthew 8–15: 67, 91
1 & 2 Thessalonians: 209
Hebrews: 240
18:11
Matthew 1–7: 164, 293, 340, 464
Matthew 16–23: 278
Mark 9–16: 220
Luke 1–5: 329
Luke 18–24: 303
2 Corinthians: 345
Hebrews: 300
18:11–12
Matthew 8–15: 335
Luke 1–5: 337
Luke 11–17: 263, 375
Romans 1–8: 369
2 Corinthians: 345
Ephesians: 264
Philippians: 138
1 & 2 Thessalonians: 195
1–3 John: 88
18:11–13
Luke 1–5: 143
18:11–14
Matthew 1–7: 430
2 Corinthians: 112
2 Timothy: 112–13
18:12
Matthew 1–7: 401
Matthew 8–15: 68
Mark 1–8: 128
Luke 1–5: 339
18:13
Matthew 1–7: 453
Matthew 8–15: 58, 164
Matthew 16–23: 149
Mark 1–8: 367
Mark 9–16: 85, 202
Luke 1–5: 271, 307, 322
Luke 6–10: 127, 355
Luke 11–17: 39, 395
Luke 18–24: 17, 386
John 12–21: 239
Romans 1–8: 221, 373
2 Corinthians: 88
James: 209, 211, 286
1–3 John: 38, 46, 53, 143
18:13–14
Mark 1–8: 103
Luke 1–5: 4, 156, 329
Acts 1–12: 74
Ephesians: 124
James: 200, 287
1 Peter: 278
1–3 John: 31, 35, 66
18:14
Matthew 16–23: 48
Mark 1–8: 426
Luke 1–5: 16, 322, 334
Luke 11–17: 263
Luke 18–24: 24
Ephesians: 264
Philippians: 138
1–3 John: 53
18:14a
Luke 18–24: 21
18:14b
Luke 18–24: 21
18:15
Matthew 16–23: 178
18:15–17
Mark 9–16: 63
Luke 18–24: 23
18:15a
Luke 18–24: 24
18:15b
Luke 18–24: 26
18:16
Mark 9–16: 66
Luke 18–24: 24, 26
18:17
Matthew 16–23: 182
Luke 18–24: 24, 31
18:18
Matthew 1–7: 201
Matthew 16–23: 188
Mark 9–16: 64

1 & 2 Thessalonians: 245
18:18–19
Luke 18–24: 35
18:18–23
Matthew 24–28: 341
Luke 11–17: 285
Acts 13–28: 108
18:18–25
Luke 6–10: 194
18:18–27
Luke 11–17: 83
John 1–11: 335
John 12–21: 184
Acts 1–12: 73, 74
18:18–30
Luke 18–24: 33–34
18:19
Luke 1–5: 46
18:20
James: 249
18:20–23
Luke 18–24: 37
18:21
Matthew 1–7: 201, 453
Luke 11–17: 321
Romans 1–8: 114
2 Corinthians: 112
James: 197
18:22
Matthew 1–7: 453
Matthew 8–15: 390
Luke 11–17: 140
18:22, 28, 43
Luke 1–5: 309
18:23
Matthew 1–7: 66, 201, 453
Mark 9–16: 64
18:24
Matthew 16–23: 198
Luke 1–5: 155
18:24–30
Luke 18–24: 40
18:25
Luke 1–5: 271
18:27
John 12–21: 184
18:28
Luke 6–10: 184
18:28–30
Luke 6–10: 19
18:29–30
Matthew 1–7: 390
18:30
2 Corinthians: 132
1 & 2 Thessalonians: 245
18:31
Matthew 16–23: 221
Mark 9–16: 92
Luke 1–5: 133
Luke 18–24: 48, 441
John 12–21: 204
18:31–33
Matthew 1–7: 94
Luke 18–24: 263
18:31–34
Matthew 8–15: 124
Mark 9–16: 2, 91
Luke 1–5: 15
Luke 18–24: 45
John 12–21: 35, 206
18:32
Luke 18–24: 338
1 Timothy: 29
18:32–33
Luke 1–5: 133
18:32–33a
Luke 18–24: 52
18:33
Luke 18–24: 120
18:33b
Luke 18–24: 55
18:34
Luke 1–5: 196
Luke 6–10: 19
Luke 18–24: 55
18:35
Matthew 16–23: 248, 249
18:35–39
Luke 18–24: 59
18:35–43
Luke 18–24: 57, 79, 90
18:39
Mark 9–16: 116
Philippians: 206
18:40–43a
Luke 18–24: 61
18:43
Luke 1–5: 91, 164, 324
18:43b
Luke 18–24: 64
19:1
Luke 18–24: 48
19:1–2
Matthew 16–23: 249
19:1–4
Luke 18–24: 69
19:1–10
Mark 9–16: 112
Luke 1–5: 16, 220
Luke 18–24: 67, 90
John 1–11: 479
Romans 9–16: 209
Galatians: 138
19:2–9
Mark 9–16: 123
19:5–6
1–3 John: 74
19:5–7
Luke 18–24: 72
1–3 John: 243
19:5–9
Matthew 16–23: 194
19:7
Luke 6–10: 166, 172
19:8
Matthew 8–15: 63
Luke 1–5: 220
Luke 11–17: 128
2 Corinthians: 283
James: 125
19:8–9
James: 108
19:8–10
Luke 18–24: 74
1–3 John: 40
19:9
Luke 11–17: 128, 203
Revelation 1–11: 311
19:10
Matthew 1–7: 112
Matthew 8–15: 67, 70, 156, 267
Matthew 16–23: 119
Matthew 24–28: 333
Mark 1–8: 80, 112, 238, 267, 321, 324, 380
Mark 9–16: 119
Luke 1–5: 4, 13, 15, 48, 81, 154, 159, 281, 332
Luke 6–10: 42, 92, 171, 223, 313
Luke 11–17: 87, 170, 280, 295, 320
Luke 18–24: 173
John 1–11: 483
John 12–21: 155, 253, 292
Acts 1–12: 159
1 Corinthians: 170, 460
Ephesians: 120
Philippians: 209, 253
1 Timothy: 33
Titus: 106, 141
Hebrews: 3
James: 225, 289, 290
1–3 John: 17, 30
Revelation 12–22: 108, 157
19:11
Matthew 24–28: 9, 14
Mark 9–16: 227
Luke 11–17: 402
Luke 18–24: 48, 297
1 & 2 Thessalonians: 117
19:11–27
Matthew 24–28: 97
Mark 9–16: 253
Luke 18–24: 77–78
Revelation 1–11: 30
19:12–13
1 & 2 Thessalonians: 117
19:12–14
Romans 9–16: 95
19:12–19
Matthew 24–28: 104
19:12–27
2 Peter–Jude: 85
19:14
Matthew 8–15: 20, 352
Matthew 16–23: 262, 276
Luke 18–24: 81
19:15–19
Luke 18–24: 82
19:20–26
Luke 18–24: 83
19:22
Matthew 8–15: 321
19:23
Acts 1–12: 179

19:26
Luke 11–17: 273
19:27
Luke 6–10: 297
Luke 18–24: 81
19:28–35
Luke 18–24: 92
19:28–44
Luke 18–24: 87–88
19:29
Matthew 16–23: 257
19:30
Matthew 16–23: 259
19:30–34
Mark 9–16: 95
Luke 18–24: 53
19:31
Mark 9–16: 125
19:33
Matthew 16–23: 258
19:33–35
Luke 18–24: 301
19:35
Matthew 16–23: 260
1 Peter: 280
19:36–38
Luke 18–24: 94–95
19:37
Mark 9–16: 127
Luke 11–17: 393
2 Corinthians: 415
19:37–38
Romans 9–16: 382
19:38
1 & 2 Thessalonians: 204
Revelation 1–11: 25
19:39
Matthew 16–23: 296
19:39–44
Luke 18–24: 97
19:40
Matthew 16–23: 273
19:41
Matthew 1–7: 165
Matthew 8–15: 396
Matthew 24–28: 167
Mark 1–8: 399
Luke 11–17: 268
Luke 18–24: 128, 300
Revelation 1–11: 165
19:41–42
Matthew 1–7: 439
Matthew 8–15: 110
Matthew 16–23: 375, 400
Luke 18–24: 117
19:41–44
Matthew 1–7: 45
Matthew 16–23: 289
Matthew 24–28: 111
Mark 9–16: 128
Luke 6–10: 139
Luke 11–17: 177, 238
Luke 18–24: 151
John 12–21: 17, 406
Acts 1–12: 120
Romans 9–16: 198
1 Corinthians: 332
2 Corinthians: 192
19:42
Matthew 8–15: 427
Matthew 16–23: 2
19:43
Luke 11–17: 171
Philippians: 78
19:44
1 Corinthians: 382
1 Peter: 140
19:45a
Luke 18–24: 103
19:45b
Luke 18–24: 106
19:45–46
Luke 18–24: 369
19:45–48
Luke 18–24: 101, 143
19:46
Luke 18–24: 106
19:47
Matthew 16–23: 285
Mark 1–8: 106
Mark 9–16: 139
Luke 1–5: 158, 184, 325
Luke 18–24: 113, 143
2 Corinthians: 284
19:47–48
Mark 1–8: 274
Luke 18–24: 115, 265, 382
19:47a
Luke 18–24: 108
19:47b–48
Luke 18–24: 109
19:48
Matthew 16–23: 269, 285
Mark 1–8: 62, 152, 176
20
Luke 18–24: 113
20:1
Matthew 16–23: 284
Mark 9–16: 155
Luke 1–5: 157, 282
Luke 6–10: 7
Luke 18–24: 143
Acts 1–12: 48
Ephesians: 142
2 Timothy: 175
20:1–8
Luke 18–24: 111
20:1b–2
Luke 18–24: 114
20:3–4
Luke 6–10: 5
20:3–7
Luke 18–24: 115
20:6
Mark 9–16: 158
Luke 1–5: 222
20:8
Luke 18–24: 116
20:9–15
Luke 18–24: 366
20:9–16
Luke 11–17: 232
20:9–16a
Luke 18–24: 121
20:9–18
Mark 1–8: 299
Luke 18–24: 119–20
20:9–19
1 & 2 Thessalonians: 239
20:14–20
Luke 1–5: 184
20:16
Mark 9–16: 167
Romans 9–16: 96
20:16b
Luke 18–24: 123
20:17
Luke 18–24: 127
20:18
Mark 9–16: 171
Luke 18–24: 128
20:19
Mark 9–16: 347
Luke 18–24: 115, 128, 143
20:19–26
Luke 18–24: 129, 144
20:19a
Luke 18–24: 131
20:19b
Luke 18–24: 131
20:20
Matthew 16–23: 317, 318
Mark 9–16: 175
Luke 6–10: 7
Luke 11–17: 115
Luke 18–24: 132
John 1–11: 15–16
20:21
Mark 9–16: 177
Luke 18–24: 133
1 & 2 Thessalonians: 172
20:21–25
Luke 18–24: 345
20:22–25
Luke 18–24: 134
20:23
Mark 9–16: 179
2 Corinthians: 127
Ephesians: 158
20:24
Luke 6–10: 5
20:25
Luke 18–24: 71
20:26
Luke 1–5: 163, 193
Luke 11–17: 260
Luke 18–24: 136
20:27
Luke 18–24: 142
20:27–40
Luke 18–24: 139–40, 151
20:28–33
Luke 18–24: 144
20:34
Mark 9–16: 191
2 Corinthians: 132
20:34–36
1 Corinthians: 438

20:34–38
Luke 18–24: 145
20:36
Matthew 16–23: 332
Luke 1–5: 196
John 12–21: 156
Hebrews: 58
20:37
Matthew 16–23: 333
20:39
Matthew 16–23: 334, 349
20:39–40
Luke 18–24: 147
20:40
Luke 18–24: 162, 175
20:41
Luke 18–24: 151
20:41–44
Luke 1–5: 193
Luke 18–24: 149
20:42–44
Luke 18–24: 153
20:45
Mark 9–16: 217
20:45–47
Luke 11–17: 353
20:45–21:4
Luke 18–24: 159
20:46
Luke 6–10: 8
Luke 11–17: 262
20:46a
Luke 18–24: 163
20:46b–47a
Luke 18–24: 164
20:46–47
Luke 1–5: 341
Luke 11–17: 385
20:47
Matthew 16–23: 374
Luke 18–24: 167
2 Corinthians: 392
1 Timothy: 194
1–3 John: 255
20:47b
Luke 18–24: 166
21
Mark 9–16: 230
James: 254
21:1–4
Luke 11–17: 339
Luke 18–24: 167
2 Corinthians: 279
21:2
Matthew 1–7: 145
21:5–6
Luke 18–24: 176, 390
21:5–7
Luke 18–24: 173
21:5–36
Luke 18–24: 167, 191, 292
Acts 1–12: 19
21:6
Luke 18–24: 99
21:7
Luke 18–24: 178, 246
21:7–33
Luke 18–24: 252
21:7–36
Luke 18–24: 281
21:8
Matthew 24–28: 18
Luke 11–17: 414
Luke 18–24: 185, 201
1 & 2 Thessalonians: 270
James: 285
21:8–19
Luke 18–24: 199–200
21:8–24
John 12–21: 230–31
21:8–36
Mark 9–16: 243
21:9
James: 176
Revelation 1–11: 180
21:9–11
Luke 18–24: 202
21:11
Matthew 16–23: 5
Matthew 24–28: 21
Mark 9–16: 233
Revelation 1–11: 203, 206, 248
21:12
1 Peter: 16
21:12–13
Luke 11–17: 124
21:12–19
Luke 18–24: 208
21:15
Acts 1–12: 137
21:18
Acts 13–28: 355
21:19
Luke 11–17: 124
21:20
Matthew 24–28: 33
Luke 18–24: 242
21:20–24
Luke 18–24: 219, 222
21:22
Matthew 16–23: 394
1 & 2 Thessalonians: 239
Revelation 1–11: 189
21:23
Luke 1–5: 158
Luke 18–24: 372
21:24
Acts 13–28: 140
1 & 2 Thessalonians: 142
Revelation 1–11: 296
21:25
Matthew 16–23: 5
1 & 2 Thessalonians: 146
Revelation 1–11: 205, 251
Revelation 12–22: 145
21:25–26
Matthew 24–28: 51
Mark 9–16: 255
Revelation 1–11: 203
21:25–28
Luke 18–24: 229
21:25a
Luke 18–24: 230
21:25b
Luke 18–24: 234
21:26
Matthew 8–15: 56
Philippians: 160
Revelation 1–11: 202
21:26a
Luke 18–24: 234
21:27
Luke 6–10: 281
Luke 18–24: 236
Revelation 1–11: 280
21:28
Matthew 24–28: 56
Luke 18–24: 238
21:29
Mark 9–16: 259
21:29–30
Luke 18–24: 243
21:29–33
Luke 18–24: 241
21:31
Matthew 24–28: 63
21:31–32
Luke 18–24: 243
21:33
Luke 18–24: 249
Revelation 1–11: 196
Revelation 12–22: 249, 263, 270
21:34
Luke 18–24: 114, 255
Acts 13–28: 222
21:34a
Luke 18–24: 253
21:34–36
Matthew 24–28: 93
Mark 9–16: 263
Luke 18–24: 251
Revelation 1–11: 28
21:35
Luke 18–24: 258
21:36
Luke 6–10: 281
Luke 18–24: 259
Ephesians: 103, 379
21:36a
Luke 18–24: 253
21:37
John 12–21: 306
21:37–38
Mark 9–16: 171
Luke 18–24: 113
1 & 2 Thessalonians: 186
21:37–22:1
Luke 18–24: 264
21:37–22:13
Luke 18–24: 261–62
22:2
Matthew 8–15: 179
Luke 18–24: 115, 268, 317
John 12–21: 14
22:3
Matthew 24–28: 186, 225

Luke 18–24: 289, 310
John 12–21: 6, 80
2 Corinthians: 408
1 Peter: 282
Revelation 1–11: 255
Revelation 12–22: 40
22:3a
Luke 18–24: 269
22:3–5
Luke 18–24: 120
22:3b–6
Luke 18–24: 270
22:4
Matthew 24–28: 184
22:4–5
Luke 18–24: 289
22:6
Matthew 24–28: 136, 185
Mark 9–16: 276
Luke 18–24: 289
22:7–13
Luke 18–24: 272
22:8
Matthew 24–28: 142
Mark 9–16: 125, 278
John 1–11: 7
Acts 1–12: 98
22:8–12
Luke 1–5: 305
22:10
Matthew 24–28: 142
Mark 9–16: 95
22:11
Luke 1–5: 149
22:11–12
Luke 18–24: 301
22:14
Luke 1–5: 332
John 1–11: 6
John 12–21: 317
22:14–18
Luke 18–24: 279
22:14–20
Luke 18–24: 277
22:15
Matthew 24–28: 143
Mark 9–16: 279, 285
Luke 18–24: 280
Galatians: 154
1 Peter: 2
1–3 John: 87
22:16
Luke 18–24: 264
Revelation 1–11: 140
22:18
Luke 18–24: 281
22:19
Matthew 24–28: 152
1 Corinthians: 237
Ephesians: 268
1 & 2 Thessalonians: 97
22:19–20
Luke 18–24: 282
1 Corinthians: 266
22:20
Matthew 24–28: 142, 152
Mark 9–16: 279
Luke 1–5: 117
John 1–11: 17
1 Corinthians: 266, 271
2 Corinthians: 115
Revelation 1–11: 140
22:21–22
Matthew 8–15: 175
Romans 9–16: 103
22:21–23
Luke 18–24: 288
22:21–38
Luke 18–24: 285–86
1 Corinthians: 272
22:22
Matthew 24–28: 131
Mark 9–16: 269
Luke 6–10: 77
Luke 18–24: 267
John 12–21: 76–77, 335
Acts 1–12: 32, 63
2 Corinthians: 212
22:23
Matthew 24–28: 148
John 12–21: 79
22:23–24
Matthew 8–15: 176
22:24
Matthew 16–23: 95, 215, 238
Matthew 24–28: 146
Mark 9–16: 36, 49, 107
Luke 6–10: 20, 35, 43
Luke 18–24: 213, 280
1 Corinthians: 330
Ephesians: 198
Philippians: 120
Titus: 24
1 Peter: 90
1–3 John: 71
22:24–27
Galatians: 147
1 Peter: 278
22:24–30
Luke 18–24: 291
22:25–26
Matthew 24–28: 146
Titus: 24
22:27
Matthew 16–23: 244
John 12–21: 69, 393
Acts 1–12: 183
Philippians: 129
2 Peter–Jude: 30
1–3 John: 66
22:28
Mark 1–8: 45
Luke 1–5: 261
22:28–30
James: 23
22:29
John 12–21: 239, 311
1 Peter: 31
22:29–30
Matthew 8–15: 105
Luke 6–10: 16
Luke 11–17: 224
1 Peter: 125
1–3 John: 186
Revelation 1–11: 140, 141
22:30
Acts 13–28: 333
Revelation 1–11: 149, 220
22:31
Matthew 16–23: 400
Matthew 24–28: 162
Mark 1–8: 246
Luke 6–10: 27, 35, 342
John 12–21: 401
Acts 1–12: 268
2 Corinthians: 408
1 & 2 Thessalonians: 226, 255
1 Timothy: 39
1 Peter: 5
2 Peter–Jude: 3
1–3 John: 207
22:31–32
Mark 9–16: 333
Luke 6–10: 20
Luke 18–24: 323
John 12–21: 282
Romans 1–8: 467, 507
2 Corinthians: 17, 23
Ephesians: 336
1 & 2 Thessalonians: 71
James: 20, 27
1–3 John: 112
Revelation 1–11: 78, 255
22:31–33
1 Timothy: 52
22:31–34
Mark 9–16: 298
1 Peter: 283
2 Peter–Jude: 50
22:32
Matthew 1–7: 437
Matthew 8–15: 438
Matthew 24–28: 218
Mark 1–8: 327
Mark 9–16: 339
Luke 6–10: 35
Luke 18–24: 2, 302, 328
1 & 2 Thessalonians: 226, 255
22:32–34
Matthew 24–28: 162
22:32, 40–46
Luke 1–5: 5
22:32b–34
Luke 18–24: 295
22:33
Matthew 8–15: 125
John 12–21: 93
1 Timothy: 52
22:33–34, 54–62
1 Corinthians: 227
22:34
Matthew 8–15: 125
Revelation 1–11: 255
22:35
Luke 6–10: 245, 329
22:35–37
Mark 1–8: 290

22:35–38
Luke 18–24: 297
22:36
Matthew 24–28: 189
Luke 18–24: 315
22:37
Mark 9–16: 387
Luke 18–24: 73
Romans 1–8: 334
22:38
Matthew 24–28: 189
Mark 9–16: 313
22:39–46
Luke 18–24: 299, 452
22:39–53
1 & 2 Thessalonians: 298
22:40
Matthew 24–28: 168
Luke 18–24: 301, 324
22:41
Matthew 24–28: 173
Luke 18–24: 302
Acts 13–28: 235
1 & 2 Thessalonians: 186
22:41–44
Mark 1–8: 327
22:42
Luke 1–5: 260
Luke 11–17: 172
Luke 18–24: 91, 303
John 12–21: 254
Acts 13–28: 241
2 Peter–Jude: 17–18
1–3 John: 204
22:42–44
Matthew 16–23: 41
22:43
Mark 9–16: 304
1 Peter: 58
22:43–46
Luke 18–24: 305
22:44
Matthew 24–28: 172
Luke 1–5: 2, 253
Luke 18–24: 379
John 12–21: 275
Acts 1–12: 323
Ephesians: 332
Philippians: 128, 205
22:45
Matthew 16–23: 62
Matthew 24–28: 175
Mark 9–16: 5, 303
1 & 2 Thessalonians: 125
22:47
Matthew 24–28: 182
Mark 9–16: 310
John 12–21: 82
22:47a
Luke 18–24: 311
22:47b–48
Luke 18–24: 314
22:47–48
Mark 9–16: 96, 312
Luke 18–24: 53
1 Peter: 47
22:47–53
Luke 18–24: 309
22:48
Matthew 24–28: 187
22:49
Matthew 24–28: 189
Luke 6–10: 29
22:49–51
Luke 18–24: 315
22:50
Mark 9–16: 314
22:50–51
Mark 1–8: 74
22:51
Matthew 24–28: 192
Luke 1–5: 315
Luke 6–10: 29
John 12–21: 311
22:52
Matthew 24–28: 183, 184
Mark 9–16: 310
John 12–21: 307
Ephesians: 145
22:52–53
Luke 18–24: 316
22:53
Matthew 24–28: 172
Mark 1–8: 45
Mark 9–16: 164
Luke 1–5: 122
Acts 13–28: 320
2 Corinthians: 249
Ephesians: 207
1 & 2 Thessalonians: 157
22:54
Mark 9–16: 322, 335
22:54–55
John 1–11: 2
22:54–61
Revelation 1–11: 255
22:54–62
Luke 18–24: 296, 319, 322–23
1 Peter:47
2 Peter–Jude: 50
22:57
Matthew 24–28: 215
Mark 9–16: 337
22:58
Matthew 24–28: 217
Mark 9–16: 338
22:59
Matthew 24–28: 217
22:60
Matthew 24–28: 218
22:61
Matthew 24–28: 217, 218, 225
Luke 6–10: 32
John 12–21: 322
22:62
Luke 6–10: 32
Revelation 1–11: 165, 255
22:63
Matthew 1–7: 43
Luke 11–17: 171
Luke 18–24: 54
22:63–65
1 Peter: 168
22:63–71
Luke 18–24: 329, 337
22:64
Matthew 24–28: 209
22:64–65
Acts 13–28: 149
22:65
Matthew 24–28: 210
Mark 9–16: 156, 329
Luke 11–17: 195
1 & 2 Thessalonians: 209
22:66
Matthew 24–28: 198, 223
Luke 1–5: 158
Luke 18–24: 114
22:66–71
Mark 9–16: 345
22:67–69
Luke 18–24: 117
22:69
Matthew 8–15: 377
Acts 1–12: 67, 222
23:1–2
Mark 9–16: 182
23:1–12
Luke 18–24: 341–42
23:2
Matthew 24–28: 235
Mark 9–16: 329, 367
Luke 18–24: 137, 344
John 12–21: 329, 332
Philippians: 184
23:2, 5
Matthew 1–7: 217
23:2, 35
Galatians: 24
23:3
Luke 18–24: 346
Revelation 1–11: 25
23:4
Matthew 16–23: 20
Mark 9–16: 348, 367
Luke 18–24: 335, 347
Acts 1–12: 108
2 Corinthians: 214
23:4, 14–16, 20, 22–25
Matthew 8–15: 421
23:5
Matthew 24–28: 237
Mark 9–16: 349
Luke 1–5: 267
Luke 18–24: 347
2 Corinthians: 220
23:5–7
Matthew 24–28: 239
23:5, 14
Luke 1–5: 158
23:6–7
Luke 18–24: 348
John 12–21: 340
23:6–11
Mark 1–8: 309
23:6–12
Mark 9–16: 308

23:7
Luke 6–10: 248
John 12–21: 336
23:7–12
Luke 1–5: 202, 232
Acts 13–28: 327
23:8
Matthew 8–15: 419
Matthew 24–28: 239
Mark 1–8: 162
23:8–9
Mark 1–8: 281
Luke 18–24: 336
23:8–9, 11
Matthew 8–15: 422
23:8–12
Mark 9–16: 350
Luke 18–24: 348
23:9–10
Matthew 24–28: 239
23:11
Matthew 1–7: 43
Matthew 24–28: 239
Luke 18–24: 16, 54
James: 103
23:13
Matthew 24–28: 241
Luke 11–17: 233
Luke 18–24: 366
23:13–15
Matthew 24–28: 240
Luke 18–24: 355
23:13–22
Acts 1–12: 108
23:13–24
Luke 1–5: 50
23:13–25
Luke 18–24: 353–54
23:14
2 Corinthians: 214
23:14–15
Luke 18–24: 350
23:16
Matthew 24–28: 244
Luke 18–24: 358
Acts 1–12: 108
1 Timothy: 55
Revelation 1–11: 139
23:16, 22
John 12–21: 337
23:17–19
Luke 18–24: 358
23:18
Acts 13–28: 261, 267
23:18–23
Luke 18–24: 98
23:19
Luke 18–24: 372
John 12–21: 337
23:20–23
Luke 18–24: 359
23:20–25
1 & 2 Thessalonians: 63
23:21
Luke 6–10: 230
Luke 18–24: 109
23:22
Acts 1–12: 108
2 Corinthians: 214
1 Timothy: 55
Revelation 1–11: 139
23:24
2 Timothy: 213
23:24–25
Luke 18–24: 361
23:25
Matthew 24–28: 241
23:26
John 12–21: 348
Acts 1–12: 193
23:26–32
Luke 18–24: 365
23:26a
Luke 18–24: 367
23:26b
Luke 18–24: 368
23:27–31
Matthew 24–28: 251
23:27a
Luke 18–24: 369
23:27b–31
Luke 18–24: 370
23:30
Revelation 1–11: 208
23:32
Luke 18–24: 372
23:33
Matthew 8–15: 297
Matthew 24–28: 253
John 12–21: 349
23:33–49
Luke 18–24: 375–76
23:34
Matthew 1–7: 196, 333
Matthew 8–15: 304, 378
Matthew 16–23: 142
Matthew 24–28: 267, 281
Mark 9–16: 94, 375
Luke 6–10: 105, 110
John 1–11: 473
John 12–21: 267
Acts 1–12: 111
Romans 9–16: 58, 196, 320
1 Corinthians: 338
2 Corinthians: 52
Colossians and Philemon: 226, 235
1 Timothy: 31, 67, 75
1 Peter: 31
Revelation 1–11: 190
23:34a
Luke 18–24: 384
23:34b–39
Luke 18–24: 382
23:34–39
Luke 18–24: 381
23:34, 46
John 12–21: 235
23:35
Matthew 16–23: 252
Mark 9–16: 97
Acts 13–28: 24
23:35–37
Luke 18–24: 54
23:35–39
Mark 9–16: 93
Luke 18–24: 51
23:36–37
Matthew 24–28: 256
23:38
John 12–21: 352
23:39–43
Mark 9–16: 370
Luke 18–24: 373
John 12–21: 352
23:40–43
Luke 18–24: 385
23:41
Luke 6–10: 146
John 12–21: 324
2 Corinthians: 214
1 & 2 Thessalonians: 295
1 Peter: 168
1–3 John: 27
23:42–43
Matthew 24–28: 262
Romans 1–8: 17
23:43
Matthew 1–7: 133, 196
Matthew 24–28: 267
John 12–21: 100
Acts 1–12: 225
2 Corinthians: 395
Philippians: 79
1 & 2 Thessalonians: 126
Revelation 1–11: 65
Revelation 12–22: 262
23:44–45
Acts 1–12: 55
23:44–46
Luke 18–24: 388
Hebrews: 217
23:45
Matthew 24–28: 268
Luke 18–24: 295
Hebrews: 415
23:46
Matthew 24–28: 272
Luke 1–5: 2, 236
John 1–11: 473
John 12–21: 357
Acts 1–12: 224
Acts 13–28: 24
Hebrews: 379
1 Peter: 168
23:47
Matthew 24–28: 280, 281
Mark 9–16: 381
Luke 1–5: 164
Luke 18–24: 401
Acts 1–12: 109
2 Corinthians: 214
23:47–49
Luke 18–24: 391
23:48
Matthew 24–28: 282
Luke 18–24: 20, 370, 389

23:49, 55
Luke 1–5: 13
23:50
John 12–21: 366
23:50–51
Matthew 24–28: 209, 294
Mark 9–16: 329
23:50–56
Luke 18–24: 395, 400
23:51
Matthew 24–28: 294
Mark 9–16: 390
23:55
Luke 6–10: 183
1–3 John: 16
23:55–56
Luke 18–24: 409
23:55–24:1
John 12–21: 366
23:56
Mark 9–16: 393
1 & 2 Thessalonians: 119
23:56–24:1
Matthew 24–28: 296
24:1
Matthew 24–28: 300, 307
24:1–3
Luke 18–24: 409, 430
24:1–7
John 12–21: 378
24:1–12
Luke 18–24: 405–6
1 Peter: 53
24:4
Luke 18–24: 234, 421
John 12–21: 378
24:4–7
Luke 18–24: 409, 410
John 12–21: 368
1 Timothy: 141
24:5–7
Matthew 24–28: 311
Luke 18–24: 266
24:6
Matthew 1–7: 144
24:6–7
John 1–11: 470
John 12–21: 37, 366
24:6–8
Luke 18–24: 441
24:8
Matthew 24–28: 310
24:8–10
Luke 18–24: 411
24:9–11
John 12–21: 385
24:10
Matthew 24–28: 307
Mark 1–8: 172
24:10–11
Mark 9–16: 404, 413
24:11
Matthew 24–28: 324
Acts 1–12: 10
24:11–12
Luke 18–24: 413
24:12
Luke 6–10: 122
John 12–21: 369
James: 85
1 Peter: 41
24:12, 41
Luke 1–5: 163
24:13–16
Romans 1–8: 464
24:13–24
Luke 18–24: 419–20
24:13–31
John 12–21: 375
24:13–32
Luke 18–24: 417–18, 432, 433
24:13–35
Mark 9–16: 414
24:15
Matthew 24–28: 312
1 Corinthians: 403, 434
24:17
1 Peter: 41
24:17–21
John 12–21: 216
24:19
Luke 18–24: 60
Acts 1–12: 59
24:19–24
Matthew 8–15: 244
24:20
John 12–21: 334
24:21
Luke 1–5: 96
Luke 18–24: 79
Acts 1–12: 19
1 & 2 Thessalonians: 117
24:21–24
Matthew 8–15: 163
24:23
Revelation 12–22: 238
24:23–25
Luke 18–24: 414
24:25
Matthew 1–7: 295
Mark 9–16: 94
Luke 1–5: 133
Luke 6–10: 142
Romans 1–8: 12
2 Corinthians: 110
Galatians: 63
Philippians: 31
James: 171
24:25–26
Matthew 16–23: 223
Mark 9–16: 163
Luke 18–24: 52, 264, 266
John 12–21: 36, 385
Acts 13–28: 120
1 Peter: 166
24:25–27
Matthew 16–23: 259
Luke 1–5: 43
Luke 18–24: 47, 56
John 1–11: 136
John 12–21: 28
Acts 1–12: 122, 255
Acts 13–28: 121
1 Corinthians: 401
1 Peter: 55
24:25–27, 44–47
Luke 1–5: 175
1–3 John: 189
24:25, 26, 44
Luke 1–5: 15
24:25, 27
Matthew 8–15: 242
24:26
John 12–21: 140
1 Peter: 2
24:27
Luke 1–5: 282
Luke 11–17: 109
Acts 13–28: 149, 307
Romans 1–8: 12
Colossians and Philemon: 43–44
2 Timothy: 145
24:27, 32
Romans 9–16: 173
24:28–32
Luke 18–24: 425–26
24:29–30
1–3 John: 243
24:30
Luke 1–5: 332
Luke 11–17: 3
John 12–21: 235
Romans 1–8: 464
24:30–31
Romans 1–8: 464
24:31
1 Corinthians: 403, 434
24:31–32
Ephesians: 45
24:31–39
1 Corinthians: 403
24:32
Matthew 16–23: 16
Luke 18–24: 443
1 Peter: 41
24:33–34
2 Peter–Jude: 59
24:33–35
Luke 18–24: 433
24:33–43
Luke 18–24: 429
24:34
Matthew 24–28: 312
John 12–21: 376, 401
1 Corinthians: 403
24:36
1 Corinthians: 403, 434
24:36–37
Luke 18–24: 434
24:36–40
Mark 9–16: 414
24:38–43
Luke 18–24: 435
24:39
John 12–21: 380
Acts 1–12: 14
1 Peter: 208

1–3 John: 17, 23
24:39–43
1 Corinthians: 410
24:41
Luke 1–5: 193
24:41–43
John 12–21: 381
Acts 1–12: 14
24:42–43
Revelation 12–22: 287
24:44
Luke 1–5: 10, 233
Luke 6–10: 71
John 12–21: 22
Acts 13–28: 307
2 Corinthians: 44
1 Timothy: 242
24:44–45
Luke 18–24: 441
John 1–11: 136
Romans 1–8: 432
24:44–49
Luke 18–24: 439
24:44–53
Luke 1–5: 17
24:45
Matthew 8–15: 354
Luke 6–10: 19
1 Corinthians: 65
2 Corinthians: 132
24:45–48
Luke 1–5: 14
24:46
Luke 18–24: 443
Acts 1–12: 65
1 Peter: 2
24:46–47
1 Timothy: 138
1 Peter: 52
24:47
Mark 1–8: 21, 426
Luke 1–5: 4, 182, 321
Luke 11–17: 188
John 12–21: 184
Acts 1–12: 75, 123
Acts 13–28: 36, 52, 217, 336
2 Corinthians: 202–3
Philippians: 223
James: 203
24:47b
Luke 18–24: 444
24:47c
Luke 18–24: 445
24:48
Luke 18–24: 447
24:49
Luke 18–24: 448, 451
John 12–21: 185
Acts 1–12: 16, 17, 27
24:50
Acts 1–12: 22, 28
24:50–51
Luke 1–5: 238
Luke 11–17: 3
Luke 18–24: 451
24:50–53
Luke 18–24: 449
24:51–53
Mark 9–16: 415
24:52
Mark 9–16: 129
Luke 1–5: 4
2 Corinthians: 484
1 & 2 Thessalonians: 184
24:52–53
Luke 1–5: 164
Luke 18–24: 453
1 Peter: 41
24:53
Acts 1–12: 28

John

1:1
Mark 1–8: 36, 175
Mark 9–16: 96, 262
Luke 1–5: 54
Luke 18–24: 237
John 1–11: 3, 9, 22, 46, 86
John 12–21: 301, 302
Acts 1–12: 104
2 Corinthians: 19, 488
Galatians: 108
Ephesians: 278
Hebrews: 35
1–3 John: 4, 100
Revelation 1–11: 7
Revelation 12–22: 218
1:1, 2
1–3 John: 163
1:1–2
Mark 1–8: 224
John 1–11: 15–20
John 12–21: 225, 255
Philippians: 123
Colossians and Philemon: 48
1–3 John: 157, 191
1:1–3
Mark 1–8: 146, 254, 378, 412
Hebrews: 28
1:1–4
John 1–11: 82
1–3 John: 17, 23
1:1–4, 14
Titus: 45
1:1–5
John 1–11: 13–24
1:1–13
1–3 John: 24
1:1, 14
Matthew 24–28: 71
1:1–18
John 1–11: 1, 10, 15, 38
1:2–3
Romans 1–8: 16
Philippians: 129
1:3
Matthew 24–28: 232
Mark 1–8: 163, 232, 313, 330, 389
Mark 9–16: 211
Luke 1–5: 304
Luke 6–10: 255
Luke 18–24: 81
John 1–11: 16–17, 20–21
2 Corinthians: 290
Colossians and Philemon: 47
Hebrews: 14, 70, 81
Revelation 1–11: 134
1:3–5
2 Peter–Jude: 29
1:4
John 12–21: 102
Acts 1–12: 110, 167
1 & 2 Thessalonians: 157
Revelation 1–11: 51
1:4–5
Matthew 1–7: 101
John 1–11: 21
Acts 13–28: 336
Philippians: 185
1–3 John: 28
1:4, 9
Matthew 24–28: 267
1:5
Luke 1–5: 184
John 1–11: 48
John 12–21: 276
2 Corinthians: 249
1 & 2 Thessalonians: 157
1:6
Luke 1–5: 38
John 1–11: 18
1:6–8
Luke 1–5: 222
John 1–11: 28, 49
1:6–13
John 1–11: 25–36
1:7
Luke 1–5: 234
1:7–8
Matthew 8–15: 152
1:7–9
Acts 13–28: 336
1:8–9
Matthew 1–7: 101
1:9
Matthew 1–7: 240, 245
Matthew 8–15: 351
Mark 1–8: 410
Luke 1–5: 21, 122
Luke 11–17: 88
John 12–21: 144, 174
Romans 1–8: 78, 200
Romans 9–16: 88, 265
Ephesians: 74, 205
1 & 2 Thessalonians: 157
1 Timothy: 32
2 Peter–Jude: 82
1–3 John: 23
1:9–11
Matthew 8–15: 387
Matthew 16–23: 2, 251
John 1–11: 24, 31–34
1:9–13
Luke 1–5: 183
1:10
Luke 1–5: 150

John 1–11: 16
2 Corinthians: 290
1 & 2 Thessalonians: 233
1:10–11
Matthew 8–15: 169, 290
Luke 18–24: 99, 189
John 1–11: 438
Philippians: 131
1 Peter: 1
1:11
Matthew 8–15: 20, 343
Matthew 16–23: 226, 280, 401
Matthew 24–28: 85
Mark 1–8: 148, 191, 419, 432
Mark 9–16: 226
Luke 1–5: 50, 258
Luke 11–17: 176, 194, 242
Luke 18–24: 53, 80, 366
John 1–11: 50
John 12–21: 52, 276, 280
Acts 1–12: 108, 211
Acts 13–28: 31, 37
Romans 9–16: 94
1–3 John: 50, 191
1:11–13
Mark 9–16: 85
Luke 18–24: 42
Romans 1–8: 241
1:12
Matthew 1–7: 375
Matthew 8–15: 175, 343
Matthew 16–23: 286
Mark 1–8: 186, 261, 402
Mark 9–16: 153
Luke 1–5: 241
Luke 6–10: 234, 288
Luke 11–17: 12, 147
Luke 18–24: 112
John 1–11: 16, 22, 48, 162, 478
John 12–21: 267, 287
Acts 1–12: 74, 104
Romans 1–8: 52
2 Corinthians: 89, 207, 216
Galatians: 98
Ephesians: 194
Philippians: 26, 95, 123, 181, 212
1 & 2 Thessalonians: 287
Hebrews: 163, 393
1 Peter: 106
2 Peter–Jude: 30
1–3 John: 4, 115, 177
Revelation 12–22: 272
1:12–13
Mark 1–8: 358
John 1–11: 18, 34–35, 412
Acts 1–12: 293
Romans 1–8: 488
Galatians: 7
1 & 2 Thessalonians: 89, 193
James: 59
1 Peter: 25, 33, 50, 92
2 Peter–Jude: 29
1:13
John 1–11: 49
Acts 13–28: 90
Romans 1–8: 495, 499
Philippians: 181
1:13–17
John 1–11: 48
1:14
Matthew 1–7: 378
Matthew 8–15: 78
Matthew 16–23: 64, 350
Matthew 24–28: 331
Mark 1–8: 224, 412
Mark 9–16: 3
Luke 1–5: 54, 58, 140, 190, 254
Luke 6–10: 61, 143, 286
John 1–11: 9, 13, 16, 39–43, 46, 82, 451–52
John 12–21: 300
Romans 1–8: 16, 84, 362
Romans 9–16: 53, 124, 314
2 Corinthians: 113, 128, 133 162, 188
Philippians: 123
1 & 2 Thessalonians: 216, 319
1 Timothy: 140
Hebrews: 28
1 Peter: 45, 52
2 Peter–Jude: 29, 82
1–3 John: 157
Revelation 1–11: 233
Revelation 12–22: 218, 279
1:14–18
John 1–11: 37–38
1:14, 16
Titus: 107
1:14, 16–18, 37–51
1–3 John: 18
1:14, 17
Luke 1–5: 28, 303
1:14, 18
Luke 1–5: 196
Galatians: 108
1:15
Luke 1–5: 38, 70
John 1–11: 30–31, 49, 209
1:15–16
John 1–11: 44
1 Peter: 114
1:16
Mark 1–8: 212
Luke 6–10: 201
Colossians and Philemon: 52, 104
2 Peter–Jude: 24–25
1:16–20
Mark 1–8: 167
1:17
Matthew 16–23: 192
Luke 1–5: 336
John 1–11: 46
2 Corinthians: 188, 461
1 & 2 Thessalonians: 216, 283, 319, 320
1 Timothy: 27
Titus: 115
2 Peter–Jude: 82
1:17–18
John 1–11: 45–46
1:18
Matthew 8–15: 274
Luke 6–10: 217
John 1–11: 46, 48
John 12–21: 103, 277, 283
Acts 13–28: 132
Hebrews: 307
Revelation 12–22: 267, 288
1:19
John 1–11: 251
1:19–20
Matthew 1–7: 52
Luke 1–5: 222
1:19–22
Acts 13–28: 30
1:19–23
John 1–11: 209
Acts 13–28: 23
1:19–25
Matthew 16–23: 291
1:19–27
Luke 1–5: 34
1:19–37
John 1–11: 47–58
1:19–4:42
Matthew 1–7: 103
1:20
John 1–11: 48
1:21
Matthew 1–7: 52
Matthew 8–15: 257
Matthew 16–23: 72
Mark 9–16: 18
Luke 1–5: 39
Luke 6–10: 155
John 1–11: 5
Acts 1–12: 122
Revelation 1–11: 301
1:23
Matthew 1–7: 52
Mark 1–8: 17
John 1–11: 31, 209
1:25
John 1–11: 5
Acts 1–12: 122
1:25–27
John 1–11: 209
1:26–27
1 Corinthians: 106
1:26–29
Luke 18–24: 116
1:27
Matthew 1–7: 103
Luke 1–5: 223
1 Corinthians: 343
1:28
Matthew 1–7: 75
Mark 1–8: 29
Luke 1–5: 205
John 1–11: 5, 453
1:29
Matthew 1–7: 75, 76, 103
Matthew 16–23: 223, 287
Matthew 24–28: 128, 131, 152

Mark 1–8: 30, 126, 425
Mark 9–16: 284
Luke 1–5: 13, 87, 120, 154, 192, 215
Luke 11–17: 17, 206
Luke 18–24: 52, 93, 174, 263, 279
John 1–11: 30–31, 77, 244, 287
John 12–21: 231, 240, 346
Acts 13–28: 23, 162
Romans 9–16: 260, 294
2 Corinthians: 133, 202, 214
Ephesians: 198
2 Timothy: 142, 172
Titus: 112
Hebrews: 172
1 Peter: 50, 55, 170, 206, 226
1–3 John: 4, 35, 124
Revelation 1–11: 167, 168
1:29–34
Mark 1–8: 28, 30
John 1–11: 55–77, 209
1:29, 36
Luke 1–5: 338
1:29, 41
1–3 John: 17
1:31
Luke 1–5: 236
John 1–11: 209
1:32
Mark 1–8: 34
John 1–11: 31
1:32–33
Luke 1–5: 238
1:32–34
Luke 1–5: 57
1–3 John: 193
1:33
Matthew 1–7: 80
Mark 1–8: 30, 32
Acts 1–12: 18
1:34
Matthew 1–7: 103
Matthew 16–23: 21, 287
Luke 1–5: 194
John 1–11: 2, 31
1:35
Luke 1–5: 303
John 1–11: 6
Acts 13–28: 164
1:35–37
Matthew 1–7: 103
Mark 1–8: 309
John 1–11: 57–58
1:35–40
John 1–11: 8
1–3 John: 6
1:35–42
Mark 1–8: 50
Luke 1–5: 292
Luke 6–10: 17
John 1–11: 2, 10
1:35–51
Mark 1–8: 161, 284
Luke 6–10: 18
1:36
Mark 1–8: 50
Luke 6–10: 40
Luke 18–24: 93
John 1–11: 31
Acts 13–28: 23
Revelation 1–11: 168
1:36–37
Matthew 8–15: 146
Mark 1–8: 126
1:37
Luke 1–5: 338
John 1–11: 8
1:37–39
Luke 6–10: 40
1:37–40
Matthew 1–7: 103
1:37–42
Matthew 8–15: 146
1:38
Mark 9–16: 197
Luke 11–17: 103
Luke 18–24: 163
1:38–42
John 1–11: 63–69
1:38, 49
Luke 1–5: 319
1:38–51
John 1–11: 59–74
1:39
John 1–11: 6
1:40
Luke 6–10: 39
1:40–42
Matthew 8–15: 136
Mark 1–8: 50
1 Peter: 4
2 Peter–Jude: 2
1:41
Matthew 16–23: 20
Luke 6–10: 40
John 1–11: 9, 49
Acts 1–12: 112
1:41–42
Mark 1–8: 170
Luke 1–5: 303
1–3 John: 18
1:42
Mark 1–8: 72, 170
Luke 6–10: 25, 40
John 1–11: 29
John 12–21: 401
1 Peter: 4
2 Peter–Jude: 2, 18
1:43
Matthew 8–15: 156
Luke 6–10: 56, 59, 315
1:43–49
1–3 John: 100
1:43–51
John 1–11: 69–74, 77
1:44
Matthew 8–15: 146
Mark 1–8: 72
Luke 1–5: 282, 292
Luke 6–10: 25, 39
John 1–11: 49
John 12–21: 26
James: 99
1 Peter: 4
2 Peter–Jude: 2
1:44–45
Mark 1–8: 407
1:45
Matthew 1–7: 48
Matthew 8–15: 159
Mark 1–8: 171
Luke 1–5: 269
Luke 6–10: 251
Luke 11–17: 350
John 1–11: 287
John 12–21: 353
Acts 13–28: 307
1:45–46
Acts 1–12: 44
1:45–48
Luke 18–24: 73
1:45–51
Luke 6–10: 59
1:46
Matthew 1–7: 47
Matthew 8–15: 370
Mark 1–8: 64, 220
Luke 1–5: 80
Luke 6–10: 250
Acts 1–12: 59, 129, 195
Acts 13–28: 304
1:47
Matthew 1–7: 47
Mark 1–8: 171
Romans 9–16: 24
Philippians: 127
1:47c
Matthew 8–15: 159
1:47–48
Luke 1–5: 305
Luke 18–24: 93
1:48
Matthew 8–15: 160
Matthew 16–23: 277
Luke 11–17: 189
Philippians: 127
1:49
Matthew 16–23: 20
Mark 1–8: 412
Luke 1–5: 58, 194, 305
Luke 6–10: 147
Luke 18–24: 163
John 1–11: 287, 464
1 Peter: 125
Revelation 1–11: 25
1:50
Matthew 8–15: 160
1:51
Matthew 1–7: 322
John 1–11: 2, 236, 359, 413
John 12–21: 27
Revelation 1–11: 133
2
Luke 18–24: 130
1–3 John: 63

2:1–2
John 1–11: 77
2:1–10
Luke 6–10: 164
Luke 18–24: 58
John 1–11: 5, 10
2:1–11
Matthew 1–7: 103
Matthew 8–15: 156
Mark 9–16: 112
Luke 1–5: 45, 183
John 1–11: 1, 10, 75–84, 470
2:3–5
John 1–11: 78
2:3–6
1–3 John: 142
2:4
Luke 1–5: 80, 184
John 12–21: 27
2 Corinthians: 347
Colossians and Philemon: 77
2:5
Acts 1–12: 183
1 Timothy: 124
2:5, 9
Romans 9–16: 360
2:6
John 1–11: 6
2:6–10
John 1–11: 81–82
Ephesians: 234
1–3 John: 17
2:6–11
Matthew 16–23: 23
2:9
Acts 1–12: 183
2:10
Ephesians: 238
2:11
Mark 1–8: 178
Luke 1–5: 36
John 1–11: 6, 82–83, 230, 452
John 12–21: 241
1 Corinthians: 301
James: 11
Revelation 12–22: 60
2:12
Luke 1–5: 149
Luke 6–10: 202
John 1–11: 3
James: 10
2:12–17
John 1–11: 89–92
2:12–25
Matthew 1–7: 103
John 1–11: 85–96
2:13
John 1–11: 439, 485
2:13–16
Matthew 16–23: 38, 131
Mark 9–16: 136, 271, 311
Luke 1–5: 204
Luke 18–24: 310
2:13–17
Matthew 24–28: 203
Mark 9–16: 324
Luke 11–17: 226
Luke 18–24: 120, 420
2 Corinthians: 264
Revelation 1–11: 209
2:13–18
Mark 9–16: 152
2:13–20
Mark 9–16: 174
2:13–22
Mark 9–16: 226
Luke 6–10: 241
2:14
Luke 1–5: 203
Luke 18–24: 334
John 1–11: 86
2:14–15
Matthew 1–7: 172
2:14–16
Matthew 1–7: 384, 408
Matthew 16–23: 267
Matthew 24–28: 132
Luke 1–5: 320
Romans 1–8: 63
Romans 9–16: 233
James: 73
2:14–17
Matthew 1–7: 294
2:15
Matthew 1–7: 331
Ephesians: 185
2:15–21
John 12–21: 206
2:16
Matthew 16–23: 88
Luke 18–24: 106
John 1–11: 86
2:17
Matthew 1–7: 342
John 1–11: 6
1 & 2 Thessalonians: 144
2:18
Luke 11–17: 195
Luke 18–24: 115
2 Corinthians: 454
2:18–20
John 1–11: 251
2:18–22
Luke 18–24: 430
John 1–11: 92–94
John 12–21: 373
Acts 1–12: 65
2:19
Matthew 16–23: 37
Luke 18–24: 335
John 1–11: 2, 470
John 12–21: 224
Acts 1–12: 195
2 Corinthians: 163
2:19–20
Matthew 24–28: 205
2:19–21
Mark 9–16: 297
John 12–21: 138
Philippians: 238
2:20
Mark 9–16: 133
Luke 1–5: 201
John 1–11: 5, 438
2:21
John 1–11: 470
Acts 1–12: 195
2 Corinthians: 163
2:22
John 1–11: 6
John 12–21: 214
2:23
Luke 6–10: 163
Luke 18–24: 58
John 1–11: 480
Revelation 12–22: 60
2:23–24
Mark 1–8: 103
Romans 9–16: 74
Hebrews: 266
2:23–25
Matthew 8–15: 22
Mark 1–8: 161
Luke 6–10: 87
Luke 18–24: 34
John 1–11: 94–96, 99
Acts 1–12: 243
James: 120
2:24
Mark 1–8: 57, 271, 272
2:24–25
Matthew 1–7: 104
Mark 1–8: 80, 93, 192, 415
Mark 9–16: 95, 368
Luke 6–10: 61
Luke 18–24: 53
2:25
Matthew 8–15: 53
Matthew 16–23: 319, 349
Matthew 24–28: 72
Mark 1–8: 77, 105
Mark 9–16: 78, 179
Luke 1–5: 305, 323
Luke 6–10: 302
Luke 11–17: 64, 348
Philippians: 127
2–3
John 1–11: 1
3:1
Matthew 16–23: 356
John 1–11: 482
Acts 13–28: 284
3:1–2
Mark 9–16: 119
3:1–3
Luke 18–24: 36
John 1–11: 99–103
3:1–8
Mark 9–16: 74
3:1–10
John 1–11: 97–107
3:1–15
1 Peter: 33
3:1–21
Matthew 1–7: 103
Luke 18–24: 402
John 1–11: 1, 10

3:1ff.
Acts 1–12: 257
3:2
Matthew 1–7: 201
Matthew 8–15: 32, 135, 409
Mark 1–8: 169, 256
Mark 9–16: 77, 78
Luke 1–5: 319
Luke 18–24: 163
John 1–11: 9, 18, 100
Acts 1–12: 60, 61, 95
2 Corinthians: 415
3:2–3
James: 120
3:2–8
James: 60
3:3
Luke 6–10: 48
Luke 11–17: 403
Luke 18–24: 244
John 1–11: 236, 359
Romans 1–8: 296
2 Corinthians: 115, 243
Galatians: 126, 209
2 Peter–Jude: 31
Revelation 1–11: 133
3:3–4
Luke 18–24: 37
3:3–6
Philippians: 181
3:3–7
Luke 6–10: 270
3:3–8
Mark 1–8: 186, 217, 358
1 Corinthians: 143
1 & 2 Thessalonians: 279, 287
James: 62
1 Peter: 21
2 Peter–Jude: 29
1–3 John: 127
3:3–12
Matthew 8–15: 272
3:3, 5
Matthew 1–7: 322
3:3ff.
Acts 1–12: 15
3:4
Romans 9–16: 242
3:4–8
John 1–11: 103–6
3:4–10
Matthew 1–7: 479
2 Corinthians: 248
3:5
Luke 6–10: 117
John 1–11: 4, 236, 359
Acts 1–12: 273
Romans 1–8: 404
Romans 9–16: 127
2 Corinthians: 89, 115
Ephesians: 189
Titus: 14, 154
Hebrews: 140
Revelation 1–11: 133
3:5–6
Mark 1–8: 26, 354
3:5–7
1–3 John: 4
3:5–8
Mark 1–8: 218
John 12–21: 209
1–3 John: 19
3:6
Romans 1–8: 419
1 Corinthians: 117
1 & 2 Thessalonians: 51, 193
3:7
2 Corinthians: 243
1 Peter: 32
1–3 John: 114
3:7–8
Luke 11–17: 123
3:8
Luke 18–24: 73
Acts 1–12: 40
1 & 2 Thessalonians: 193
1 Peter: 92
3:9–10
John 1–11: 106–7
3:10
Mark 1–8: 144
3:11
John 1–11: 359
Revelation 1–11: 133
3:11–12
John 1–11: 111–12
3:11–13
John 1–11: 347
3:11–13, 32–34
John 12–21: 111
3:11–21
John 1–11: 109–19
3:13
Matthew 24–28: 72
Luke 1–5: 194
3:13–17
John 1–11: 113–17
3:14
Matthew 1–7: 263
Mark 9–16: 163
Luke 6–10: 310
John 12–21: 36, 204
Acts 13–28: 24
1 Corinthians: 268
Galatians: 192
Hebrews: 172
3:14–16
Matthew 8–15: 274
1 Peter: 217
3:14–17
Acts 1–12: 303
Acts 13–28: 336
1 Peter: 50
3:14–18
1–3 John: 48
3:15
Luke 1–5: 328
Luke 11–17: 12
1 & 2 Thessalonians: 245
3:15–16
Mark 9–16: 68
John 1–11: 9, 22, 382, 478
Romans 9–16: 295
Ephesians: 198
1 & 2 Thessalonians: 287
2 Peter–Jude: 27
1–3 John: 4
Revelation 12–22: 305
3:15–17
John 1–11: 27
3:15–18
Mark 9–16: 330
Revelation 1–11: 54
3:16
Matthew 1–7: 346
Matthew 8–15: 175
Matthew 16–23: 339
Matthew 24–28: 332
Mark 1–8: 97
Luke 1–5: 159, 168
Luke 6–10: 51
John 1–11: 2, 382
John 12–21: 63, 227
Acts 1–12: 74
Romans 1–8: 20, 26, 61, 268, 283, 504
Romans 9–16: 11, 76, 84, 94, 294, 311
1 Corinthians: 329
2 Corinthians: 202, 207, 212, 314
Galatians: 7
Ephesians: 135, 195
Philippians: 40
Colossians and Philemon: 60
1 & 2 Thessalonians: 245
1 Timothy: 142
2 Timothy: 94
Titus: 16, 110, 152
Hebrews: 199, 310, 392
1 Peter: 170
1–3 John: 4, 82, 166
Revelation 1–11: 139, 242
Revelation 12–22: 49, 98, 194
3:16–17
Matthew 1–7: 112
Romans 1–8: 21, 487
Romans 9–16: 86
2 Corinthians: 319
Philippians: 41, 119, 166
Titus: 14, 151, 153
3:16–18
Luke 18–24: 215
2 Corinthians: 216
Galatians: 210
Titus: 113
3:16, 18
Luke 1–5: 196
2 Timothy: 61, 66
3:16–21
Philippians: 94
3:17
John 1–11: 244
Romans 1–8: 398
1 Timothy: 32
Hebrews: 207
James: 290
1–3 John: 23

3:17–21
1 Peter: 32
3:18
Mark 1–8: 270, 397
Mark 9–16: 414
Luke 18–24: 373
John 1–11: 478
Acts 13–28: 37, 278
Romans 1–8: 499
Romans 9–16: 36, 86
2 Corinthians: 89, 207
1 & 2 Thessalonians: 163
Revelation 1–11: 242
Revelation 12–22: 251
3:18–20
Matthew 8–15: 409
Mark 1–8: 275
Revelation 1–11: 139
3:18–21
John 1–11: 118–19
3:19
Matthew 1–7: 392
Matthew 8–15: 290, 309
Matthew 16–23: 2
Mark 1–8: 249
Luke 1–5: 122, 184, 208, 272
Luke 6–10: 191, 224
Luke 11–17: 372
Acts 1–12: 62, 108, 168
Acts 13–28: 124
Romans 1–8: 68
1 Corinthians: 284
2 Corinthians: 131–32, 249
Philippians: 186
1 & 2 Thessalonians: 155, 199
1 Timothy: 32
2 Timothy: 117
1 Peter: 50
1–3 John: 23
Revelation 1–11: 102
Revelation 12–22: 92, 240
3:19–20
Matthew 1–7: 208
Matthew 8–15: 20
Matthew 16–23: 252
Luke 1–5: 272
Luke 11–17: 89
John 1–11: 162
John 12–21: 52
Romans 1–8: 67, 86, 109, 398
Colossians and Philemon: 60
1 & 2 Thessalonians: 22, 157, 283
James: 58, 59
1 Peter: 131
1–3 John: 86
Revelation 1–11: 242
3:19–21
Matthew 1–7: 102
Matthew 16–23: 4
John 1–11: 15, 442
Acts 13–28: 336
Romans 1–8: 340
Ephesians: 208
3:20
2 Timothy: 158
1–3 John: 14
3:21
John 1–11: 18
1 & 2 Thessalonians: 157
1–3 John: 14
3:22
Luke 6–10: 76
3:22–24
Mark 1–8: 303
3:22–36
Matthew 1–7: 103
Luke 1–5: 228
John 1–11: 121–22
3:23
Matthew 1–7: 79
Mark 1–8: 20
John 1–11: 58
3:23, 26
Luke 1–5: 205
3:24
Mark 1–8: 47
John 1–11: 3
3:25
John 1–11: 30
Acts 13–28: 164
3:25–30
Luke 18–24: 116
John 1–11: 51, 126
3:26
Matthew 8–15: 152
Luke 1–5: 234
3:26–30
John 1–11: 30
3:27
2 Peter–Jude: 28
3:27–30
John 1–11: 58
3:28–29
Revelation 12–22: 202
3:28–30
Luke 1–5: 338
3:28, 30
Matthew 8–15: 68
3:29
Mark 1–8: 130
Luke 1–5: 69, 340
Revelation 12–22: 204
3:30
Matthew 1–7: 58, 71, 103
Matthew 8–15: 239, 250, 418
Mark 1–8: 25, 127
Luke 11–17: 349
1 Corinthians: 343
Ephesians: 122, 252
3:31
John 1–11: 130
Revelation 1–11: 28
3:31–36
John 1–11: 129–33
3:32
John 1–11: 130–31, 438
3:33
John 1–11: 131
2 Corinthians: 45
2 Peter–Jude: 82
3:34
Matthew 1–7: 80, 108
John 1–11: 131–32
John 12–21: 105
1 Corinthians: 313
Ephesians: 248
3:35
Matthew 8–15: 152
Luke 6–10: 50
John 1–11: 132–33
1 Peter: 31
3:35–36
John 12–21: 252
3:36
Matthew 8–15: 409
Luke 1–5: 10, 40, 166, 183
Luke 11–17: 165, 274
Luke 18–24: 128, 151
John 1–11: 9, 22, 27, 478
John 12–21: 159, 184
Acts 13–28: 45
Romans 1–8: 61, 71
2 Corinthians: 89, 207
Colossians and Philemon: 61
1 & 2 Thessalonians: 66, 163, 245, 287
1 Peter: 32
1–3 John: 100
Revelation 1–11: 54
Revelation 12–22: 49, 98, 137
4:1
John 1–11: 325
4:1–2
Matthew 1–7: 79
4:1–3
John 1–11: 438
4:1–6
John 1–11: 140–42
4:1–26
John 1–11: 135–50
Philippians: 220
4:1–42
Matthew 1–7: 103
4:1, 3
Matthew 1–7: 105
4:2
1 Corinthians: 32
4:3
Mark 1–8: 412
4:3–42
Mark 1–8: 40
4:4
Luke 6–10: 133
4:4–42
Mark 1–8: 47
4:4ff.
Acts 1–12: 233
4:5–6
Mark 9–16: 210
Luke 18–24: 155
4:5–42
Matthew 8–15: 388
John 1–11: 2
4:5ff.
Acts 1–12: 257

4:6
Matthew 8–15: 275
Mark 9–16: 134
Luke 6–10: 128
John 1–11: 6
2 Corinthians: 388
4:7
Mark 1–8: 229
Mark 9–16: 134
Luke 6–10: 208
John 12–21: 135
2 Corinthians: 293
4:7–15
John 1–11: 142–46
4:7–26
Galatians: 138
4:7–42
Matthew 1–7: 119
Matthew 8–15: 187
4:7, 16
1–3 John: 23
4:8
1–3 John: 23
4:9
Luke 6–10: 42
Luke 11–17: 393
Luke 18–24: 59
John 1–11: 5
Acts 1–12: 233, 299
4:10
Philippians: 95
Hebrews: 143
4:13–14
Luke 18–24: 215
Revelation 12–22: 271, 286
4:14
Matthew 1–7: 184
Mark 1–8: 124
John 1–11: 9, 382
Romans 1–8: 20
Ephesians: 135
1 & 2 Thessalonians: 245
Hebrews: 143
Revelation 12–22: 305
4:15
John 1–11: 156
4:16–18
Matthew 16–23: 224
4:16–19
John 1–11: 146–47
4:18
Matthew 1–7: 213
Mark 9–16: 95
4:19
Luke 18–24: 422
John 1–11: 156
4:20–24
Matthew 8–15: 9
Acts 1–12: 233
1 Timothy: 83
4:20–26
John 1–11: 148–50
4:21–22
Matthew 1–7: 213
4:21–24
Matthew 8–15: 76
Mark 1–8: 256
1 Timothy: 33
Hebrews: 189
4:22
Matthew 8–15: 187, 468
Matthew 24–28: 41
Mark 1–8: 368
Luke 1–5: 107, 158
Romans 1–8: 55
Romans 9–16: 58, 111, 347
1 & 2 Thessalonians: 172
Hebrews: 164, 214
4:22–26
Romans 9–16: 3, 15
4:23
Matthew 8–15: 481
Romans 9–16: 138
Philippians: 313
Hebrews: 76
Revelation 12–22: 207, 268, 284
4:23–24
Mark 1–8: 391
Mark 9–16: 136
Luke 1–5: 76
Luke 18–24: 104
Romans 1–8: 33
James: 207
4:24
Matthew 8–15: 455
Luke 1–5: 78
1 Corinthians: 235
Philippians: 287, 313
1 & 2 Thessalonians: 194
1–3 John: 23
4:25
Acts 1–12: 112, 233
Hebrews: 6
4:25–26
Matthew 8–15: 5
Matthew 16–23: 351
Matthew 24–28: 207
Luke 1–5: 71
Luke 11–17: 393
John 1–11: 9, 25
John 12–21: 12
1 Timothy: 85
4:25–29, 40–42
Matthew 8–15: 147
4:26
Matthew 8–15: 299
Mark 1–8: 363
Luke 1–5: 233
John 1–11: 14, 156, 414
1–3 John: 23
4:27
John 1–11: 5–6, 154
4:27–42
John 1–11: 151–52
4:28
John 1–11: 81
4:28–29
Matthew 1–7: 119
4:28–30
John 1–11: 156
4:29
John 1–11: 31
4:30
John 1–11: 158
4:31–34
John 1–11: 157
4:31–38
John 1–11: 157
4:34
Matthew 1–7: 91
Matthew 8–15: 294, 313
Matthew 16–23: 259
Matthew 24–28: 72
Mark 1–8: 35, 183, 327
Mark 9–16: 109, 262, 269, 302, 316
Luke 1–5: 194, 257, 297
Luke 11–17: 27, 231
Luke 18–24: 264
John 1–11: 474
John 12–21: 28
Romans 1–8: 307
Romans 9–16: 242, 310
1 Corinthians: 254
Ephesians: 174, 227, 250, 285
Hebrews: 450
James: 230
1 Peter: 168
1–3 John: 171, 193
4:35
2 Corinthians: 225
James: 154
4:35–38
John 1–11: 158
4:36
1 & 2 Thessalonians: 245
4:39
John 1–11: 287
4:39–42
Matthew 16–23: 351
Luke 6–10: 170
John 1–11: 159, 244
4:40
John 1–11: 6
1–3 John: 243
4:41
John 1–11: 287
4:42
Luke 1–5: 154
Luke 18–24: 174
John 1–11: 9
2 Corinthians: 202
1 Timothy: 142
4:43
John 1–11: 6
4:43–45
John 1–11: 164
4:43–54
John 1–11: 161–62
4:44
Luke 1–5: 275
Luke 18–24: 338
John 1–11: 3
4:46
James: 276

4:46–47
John 1–11: 167
4:46–49
John 1–11: 165
4:46–53
John 1–11: 455
1–3 John: 17
4:46–54
John 1–11: 470
4:48
John 1–11: 164
4:50–54
John 1–11: 167
4:52
John 1–11: 6
4:52–53
John 1–11: 167
4:53
Luke 1–5: 40
John 1–11: 287
4:54
John 1–11: 230
5:1
John 1–11: 439
5:1–9
Mark 1–8: 153
5:1–9a
John 1–11: 172
5:1–15
John 1–11: 2
5:1–16
John 1–11: 169–70
5:1–17
John 1–11: 230, 470
5:1–18
John 1–11: 10
5:2
John 1–11: 5
5:3
Philippians: 205
5:5–9
1–3 John: 17
5:7
Luke 1–5: 27
5:8–9
Mark 9–16: 118
Luke 1–5: 293
5:9
Acts 1–12: 101
5:9b–16
John 1–11: 175
5:9–18
Mark 1–8: 138
5:10
John 1–11: 251
5:13
Mark 1–8: 280
1–3 John: 141
5:15–16
John 1–11: 251
5:16
Acts 1–12: 170
1 Peter: 282
5:16–18
Matthew 16–23: 38
John 1–11: 438
5:16–21
Matthew 8–15: 3
5:17
Matthew 16–23: 216
Matthew 24–28: 291
Luke 1–5: 195
Luke 11–17: 11
John 12–21: 239
5:17–18
Matthew 1–7: 82
Matthew 24–28: 207
Mark 1–8: 36
Mark 9–16: 78
Luke 18–24: 37
John 1–11: 185
John 12–21: 136
2 Corinthians: 19
Philippians: 125
1 Timothy: 5
5:17–19
John 12–21: 278
5:17–20
Acts 1–12: 61
5:17–23
1 Peter: 31
5:17–24
John 1–11: 181
5:17–47
John 1–11: 478
5:18
Matthew 1–7: 13
Matthew 8–15: 273
Matthew 16–23: 287
Matthew 24–28: 130, 174
Mark 1–8: 104, 165, 225
Mark 9–16: 14, 206, 269, 301
Luke 1–5: 195, 323
Luke 11–17: 11, 227
Luke 18–24: 120
John 1–11: 14, 251
John 12–21: 104, 106
Romans 9–16: 314
Galatians: 24
Philippians: 130
Hebrews: 33
Revelation 1–11: 96
5:18–47
Matthew 1–7: 13
5:18,30
Romans 9–16: 310
5:19
Matthew 16–23: 131
Mark 9–16: 153–54
Luke 18–24: 301
John 1–11: 359
John 12–21: 136
Acts 1–12: 104
Hebrews: 69
Revelation 1–11: 133
5:19–20
John 1–11: 187
5:19, 30
Matthew 8–15: 122
5:19–30
Matthew 8–15: 313
Mark 1–8: 183
5:20
Matthew 8–15: 152
Mark 1–8: 5, 37
Mark 9–16: 77
2 Timothy: 108
James: 192
5:21
Matthew 8–15: 75
Matthew 16–23: 286
John 1–11: 14, 188, 463–64
1 Peter: 18
5:21–29
Acts 1–12: 303
Hebrews: 141
5:22
Matthew 1–7: 433
Matthew 8–15: 437
Matthew 16–23: 52, 299
Matthew 24–28: 112, 315, 339
Mark 1–8: 431
Mark 9–16: 153, 328
Luke 6–10: 328
Luke 11–17: 132
Luke 18–24: 97, 112
John 1–11: 189
John 12–21: 342
2 Corinthians: 177
Philippians: 142
2 Timothy: 168
James: 271
Revelation 1–11: 105
Revelation 12–22: 113, 215, 249
5:22–23
Philippians: 142
5:22–27
Acts 13–28: 142
1 Peter: 230
5:22–29
Luke 18–24: 363
5:22–30
Luke 18–24: 342
5:22, 27, 30
John 12–21: 53
5:23
Matthew 1–7: 82
Matthew 24–28: 232
Mark 9–16: 181
Luke 6–10: 303
Luke 11–17: 120, 122
Luke 18–24: 157, 355
John 12–21: 118, 175
Acts 13–28: 307
2 Corinthians: 290
Philippians: 150
2 Peter–Jude: 138
1–3 John: 100, 157
Revelation 12–22: 87
5:23–24
John 1–11: 190, 474
5:24
Luke 1–5: 302
Luke 6–10: 95, 176
Luke 11–17: 178, 280
Luke 18–24: 215

John 1–11: 9, 28, 157, 236, 359, 382, 478
2 Corinthians: 207, 210
1 & 2 Thessalonians: 163, 164, 198, 245, 287
1 Timothy: 293
2 Timothy: 150
James: 271
2 Peter–Jude: 27
1–3 John: 19, 33, 72, 133
Revelation 1–11: 54
Revelation 12–22: 49, 99, 251, 304
5:24, 30, 36, 37
Luke 1–5: 297
5:24, 38, 40
Titus: 111
5:25
John 1–11: 196, 359
1 & 2 Thessalonians: 134
1–3 John: 4
Revelation 1–11: 319
5:25b
John 1–11: 198
5:25–26
John 1–11: 195–96
5:25–29
Luke 11–17: 154
John 1–11: 193, 463–64
Philippians: 142
5:26
Matthew 16–23: 286
John 1–11: 21, 197
Acts 1–12: 110
1 Timothy: 277
1–3 John: 17
Revelation 1–11: 51
5:26–27
Revelation 12–22: 249
5:26–27, 36–38
1 Corinthians: 287
5:27
Matthew 16–23: 286
Mark 9–16: 153
Acts 1–12: 104
1 Corinthians: 420
2 Corinthians: 177
James: 271
Revelation 1–11: 105
Revelation 12–22: 112, 113, 215
5:27–29
Matthew 24–28: 339
John 1–11: 198
5:28–29
Luke 6–10: 237
Luke 11–17: 264
Luke 18–24: 406
Acts 1–12: 70
Acts 13–28: 307, 334
Romans 1–8: 127
James: 125
Revelation 1–11: 47, 319
Revelation 12–22: 108, 272
5:28a
John 1–11: 199
5:28b–29a
John 1–11: 200
5:29
Matthew 8–15: 396
Matthew 16–23: 52
Romans 1–8: 492
1 Corinthians: 416, 418
1 & 2 Thessalonians: 163, 239
James: 176, 271
Revelation 12–22: 99, 238, 248, 250
5:30
Matthew 1–7: 91, 95, 360
Matthew 16–23: 131, 259
Matthew 24–28: 72
Mark 1–8: 32
Mark 9–16: 154
Luke 1–5: 194
John 1–11: 157, 474
John 12–21: 278
Acts 1–12: 61
Romans 1–8: 307
Romans 9–16: 242, 340
1 Corinthians: 254
2 Corinthians: 347
Galatians: 7
Ephesians: 174, 278
Philippians: 119, 127
Colossians and Philemon: 77
Hebrews: 378
James: 230, 271
1 Peter: 206
5:30–47
John 1–11: 203–4
5:31–32
Revelation 1–11: 7
5:31–32, 36–37
Matthew 8–15: 297
5:32
Mark 1–8: 36
John 1–11: 212
5:32–36
Luke 18–24: 116
5:32–37
Acts 1–12: 59
5:33
Mark 1–8: 126
Luke 1–5: 234
John 1–11: 31
5:33–35
John 1–11: 209
5:34
James: 290
5:35
Luke 1–5: 175
Luke 6–10: 157
John 1–11: 31
5:36
Matthew 8–15: 152, 317
Mark 1–8: 106, 163, 275, 288, 400
Mark 9–16: 158, 206, 369
Luke 1–5: 233
Luke 11–17: 89, 388
John 1–11: 31, 157, 211, 470
John 12–21: 181
Acts 1–12: 61
2 Corinthians: 415
1 Peter: 134
5:36–37
John 1–11: 347
John 12–21: 106
5:36–38
John 1–11: 474
5:37
John 1–11: 31
John 12–21: 241
5:37–38
Luke 18–24: 151
John 1–11: 212
5:37–39
1 Corinthians: 63
5:37–39, 46
2 Timothy: 140–41
5:37–40
James: 67
5:38
John 1–11: 27
5:38–40
Matthew 8–15: 20
1 & 2 Thessalonians: 283
5:39
Matthew 8–15: 356
Matthew 16–23: 29
Luke 1–5: 10, 175, 233
Luke 18–24: 425
John 1–11: 31, 34
John 12–21: 181
Acts 1–12: 122, 216, 255
Acts 13–28: 23, 121, 149, 307
Romans 1–8: 169, 204
1 Corinthians: 81
2 Corinthians: 110
Colossians and Philemon: 44
1 & 2 Thessalonians: 108, 194, 195, 245
2 Timothy: 141
Hebrews: 100
1–3 John: 189
5:39–40
Mark 1–8: 148
John 1–11: 9
Hebrews: 41
James: 192, 199
1–3 John: 17, 190
5:39–47
John 1–11: 213–16
5:40
Matthew 1–7: 385
Matthew 16–23: 312
Luke 1–5: 163
Acts 13–28: 37
2 Peter–Jude: 21
Revelation 12–22: 247
5:42
1 Peter: 88
1–3 John: 23
5:43
Luke 11–17: 170
John 1–11: 27
John 12–21: 16

5:44
Luke 11–17: 262, 376
Philippians: 313
5:45–47
1 Corinthians: 64
5:46
Acts 1–12: 216, 255
Acts 13–28: 121, 149, 307
2 Corinthians: 110
Hebrews: 82
6
Acts 1–12: 61
6:1
Matthew 1–7: 105
Mark 1–8: 50
Luke 1–5: 302
Luke 6–10: 208
6:1–4
John 1–11: 219
6:1–13
Luke 6–10: 193
6:1–14
Matthew 16–23: 13
John 1–11: 470
6:1–15
Mark 1–8: 312
John 1–11: 10, 217–18
6:2
Matthew 8–15: 426
Mark 1–8: 316
Luke 6–10: 252
John 1–11: 9, 57
John 12–21: 23
Revelation 12–22: 60
6:4
Matthew 8–15: 426
Luke 6–10: 255
John 1–11: 5, 485
6:5
Matthew 8–15: 156, 428
Mark 1–8: 171
Luke 6–10: 40, 254
2 Corinthians: 15
6:5–6
James: 18
6:5–7
Mark 1–8: 319
6:5–9
Matthew 8–15: 146
John 1–11: 221
6:6
2 Corinthians: 15
2 Timothy: 27
6:6, 11
Matthew 8–15: 430
6:7
Luke 6–10: 40
6:7–9
2 Corinthians: 15
6:8
Luke 6–10: 39
6:8–9
Matthew 8–15: 429
Mark 1–8: 319
6:9
Luke 6–10: 40
John 1–11: 6
6:10
Mark 1–8: 385
6:10–13
John 1–11: 223
6:11
Mark 1–8: 79
Colossians and Philemon: 36
6:14
Mark 1–8: 278, 321
John 1–11: 9, 52
Acts 1–12: 61, 122, 211
1 Timothy: 32
Revelation 1–11: 28, 301
6:14–15
Matthew 1–7: 94
Mark 1–8: 91, 324, 417
Mark 9–16: 123
Luke 1–5: 118
Luke 6–10: 237, 260, 263
Luke 11–17: 218, 394
Luke 18–24: 90, 103
John 1–11: 5, 26, 225, 243
John 12–21: 16, 50
Hebrews: 267
6:14–15a
Matthew 8–15: 436
6:15
Matthew 1–7: 133
Matthew 8–15: 296, 312, 426, 431, 466, 467
Matthew 16–23: 62, 70, 266
Matthew 24–28: 235
Mark 1–8: 78, 158, 340, 379
Mark 9–16: 311
Luke 18–24: 320
John 1–11: 2, 150, 483
1 & 2 Thessalonians: 186
Revelation 1–11: 167
6:15–21
John 1–11: 470
6:15, 26
Matthew 8–15: 243
6:16–19
John 1–11: 231
6:16–21
John 1–11: 230
6:16–29
John 1–11: 227–28
6:17
Mark 1–8: 326
6:18
Mark 1–8: 328
Luke 18–24: 320
6:19
Matthew 8–15: 438
Mark 1–8: 329
John 1–11: 6
6:20–21
John 1–11: 233
6:21
Matthew 8–15: 445, 449
Mark 1–8: 332, 333
6:22–24
Mark 1–8: 327
John 1–11: 235
6:22–25
Luke 6–10: 256
6:22–29
John 1–11: 234
6:22–71
John 1–11: 2, 11
6:24
Mark 1–8: 334
6:25
Luke 1–5: 319
6:25–29
John 1–11: 236
6:26
Matthew 8–15: 94, 133
Mark 1–8: 99
John 1–11: 359
6:26–27
Luke 6–10: 252
6:26–58
Mark 1–8: 334
6:26–71
Matthew 8–15: 457
6:27
Matthew 8–15: 133
John 1–11: 9, 382
2 Corinthians: 45
Ephesians: 131
1 & 2 Thessalonians: 245
Revelation 1–11: 217
Revelation 12–22: 112
6:27–28
Romans 1–8: 198
6:28
Matthew 1–7: 201
Mark 9–16: 78
Luke 18–24: 37
6:28–29
Matthew 16–23: 188
6:28, 34
Matthew 8–15: 433
6:29
Matthew 8–15: 339
John 1–11: 34, 162, 243, 474, 478
Hebrews: 125
1–3 John: 19, 91
6:30
Matthew 1–7: 95
2 Corinthians: 454
6:30–33
John 1–11: 242
6:30–50
John 1–11: 239–40
6:31, 58
Matthew 1–7: 263
6:32
John 1–11: 359
John 12–21: 144
1 Peter: 31
6:33
Luke 6–10: 366
John 1–11: 9, 347
6:33–35, 48–51
Matthew 8–15: 450
6:34–40
John 1–11: 244–45

6:35
Matthew 1–7: 184
Matthew 8–15: 267, 274
Mark 1–8: 321, 384
Luke 18–24: 216, 283
John 1–11: 9, 150, 463, 470, 478
John 12–21: 102, 143
Ephesians: 135
1 Peter: 104
1–3 John: 4
Revelation 12–22: 305
6:35–40
Galatians: 153
2 Peter–Jude: 27
6:35, 37
Titus: 111
6:36
John 1–11: 27
6:36–47
John 1–11: 35
6:37
Matthew 8–15: 26, 79, 274, 356, 468
Matthew 16–23: 31, 216
Mark 1–8: 99, 122, 167, 262, 367, 371
Mark 9–16: 119, 238, 250
Luke 1–5: 120
Luke 11–17: 178
Luke 18–24: 65
John 1–11: 22, 27
Acts 1–12: 267, 293
Acts 13–28: 93
Romans 1–8: 20, 185, 207, 278, 442, 495
Romans 9–16: 37, 42, 321
2 Corinthians: 216
Philippians: 29, 30
1 & 2 Thessalonians: 20, 193, 208, 286
2 Timothy: 121
Titus: 108
Hebrews: 201, 320
1 Peter: 31, 104
2 Peter–Jude: 29
Revelation 12–22: 73, 307
6:37–40
John 12–21: 310
2 Corinthians: 168
2 Timothy: 82
1 Peter: 23
2 Peter–Jude: 207
1–3 John: 17
Revelation 12–22: 99
6:37–40, 44
2 Timothy: 23
6:37–44
Mark 1–8: 218
2 Peter–Jude: 153
6:37, 39
John 12–21: 247
Ephesians: 365
Titus: 111
6:37, 39–40
Titus: 122
6:37, 40
Matthew 1–7: 458
John 12–21: 273
Titus: 11
6:37, 44
Luke 1–5: 163
6:37–45
1 Peter: 17
6:38
Matthew 1–7: 91
Matthew 8–15: 294
Matthew 16–23: 131, 286
Matthew 24–28: 72
Mark 9–16: 154
Luke 1–5: 194
Luke 6–10: 92
Luke 11–17: 170
John 1–11: 157, 347
John 12–21: 241
Acts 1–12: 107
Romans 1–8: 307
Romans 9–16: 242, 310
1 Corinthians: 254
2 Corinthians: 347
Galatians: 7
Ephesians: 174
Philippians: 127
1–3 John: 60
6:38–39
John 1–11: 474
6:38, 39, 44, 57
Luke 1–5: 297
6:38, 42
Luke 1–5: 194
6:39
Matthew 16–23: 216
John 1–11: 22
Romans 1–8: 20
Philippians: 29
Hebrews: 83
James: 27
1–3 John: 44, 166
Revelation 1–11: 77
6:39–40
Luke 1–5: 194
John 1–11: 461, 463
Romans 1–8: 442
Philippians: 261
1 & 2 Thessalonians: 286
1–3 John: 109
6:40
Mark 1–8: 192
Mark 9–16: 238
John 1–11: 9, 22, 28, 382, 478
2 Corinthians: 207
Philippians: 168
1 & 2 Thessalonians: 245, 287
6:40, 47
Luke 1–5: 328
6:41
John 1–11: 150
Colossians and Philemon: 119
6:41–43
John 1–11: 438
6:41–50
John 1–11: 251
6:42
Mark 1–8: 277
Philippians: 131
6:44
Matthew 16–23: 193, 203
Mark 1–8: 99, 205, 370, 416
Mark 9–16: 74
Luke 1–5: 120
Luke 6–10: 56
Luke 11–17: 219
John 1–11: 22, 70, 157, 247, 412, 463, 474
John 12–21: 162, 196, 269, 288
Acts 1–12: 252, 267
Acts 13–28: 93, 268
Romans 1–8: 185, 346, 495
Romans 9–16: 36
1 Corinthians: 409
2 Corinthians: 131
Ephesians: 119
Philippians: 23, 27, 151, 168
Colossians and Philemon: 16
1 & 2 Thessalonians: 20, 193, 256, 286
Hebrews: 103, 142, 266
James: 60, 206
1 Peter: 17, 26, 31, 104
2 Peter–Jude: 207
Revelation 12–22: 99, 156, 171, 305
6:44–45
1 & 2 Thessalonians: 208
2 Peter–Jude: 29
6:44, 65
Matthew 8–15: 156
6:45
Mark 1–8: 16
Ephesians: 173
James: 67
6:46
Revelation 12–22: 267, 288
6:47
John 1–11: 22, 28, 236, 359, 382, 478
2 Corinthians: 207
Colossians and Philemon: 16
1 & 2 Thessalonians: 245, 287
Revelation 1–11: 54
6:47–48
John 1–11: 9
6:48
John 1–11: 150
Acts 1–12: 143
6:48–51
2 Peter–Jude: 30–31
Revelation 1–11: 91
6:51
Matthew 16–23: 23
Mark 1–8: 384
John 1–11: 150, 257
Romans 1–8: 407
Romans 9–16: 295
2 Corinthians: 191, 202
Hebrews: 144

6:51–59
John 1–11: 255
6:52
John 1–11: 259
6:53
Philippians: 179
6:53–54
Colossians and Philemon: 63
6:53–58
Hebrews: 440
1 Peter: 127
1–3 John: 103–4
6:53–59
John 1–11: 260–63
6:53–65
Luke 6–10: 16, 30
6:53–66
Matthew 8–15: 215
6:53, 60, 66
Matthew 8–15: 32
6:54
John 1–11: 382, 463
1 & 2 Thessalonians: 245
6:55–58
Galatians: 198
6:56
2 Corinthians: 466
6:57
John 1–11: 157, 474
6:58
2 Peter–Jude: 10
6:59
Mark 1–8: 334
Luke 6–10: 180
Luke 11–17: 199
6:60
Luke 11–17: 279
1 Peter: 127
6:60, 66
Galatians: 198
6:60–66
Matthew 8–15: 466
Luke 6–10: 315
John 1–11: 268
1 & 2 Thessalonians: 295
6:60–69
Mark 1–8: 163
6:60–71
John 1–11: 265
6:61
Matthew 8–15: 134
Philippians: 179
6:62
John 12–21: 65
Acts 1–12: 13
Revelation 12–22: 112
6:63
John 1–11: 9, 382
Philippians: 186, 223
2 Timothy: 150
6:64
Matthew 8–15: 174
Mark 1–8: 367
Mark 9–16: 276
Luke 1–5: 305
Luke 6–10: 76
Luke 18–24: 271
Acts 1–12: 32
6:64–65
1 & 2 Thessalonians: 208
2 Peter–Jude: 29
6:64–70
John 12–21: 210
6:65
Mark 1–8: 205
John 1–11: 22, 247
Acts 13–28: 38
Romans 1–8: 346, 486
2 Corinthians: 216
2 Timothy: 61
Hebrews: 103
James: 206
1 Peter: 104
6:66
Matthew 8–15: 174, 276
Matthew 16–23: 11
Mark 1–8: 99, 118, 161, 176, 192, 228, 271, 313, 320, 322, 325, 364
Luke 6–10: 16, 230
John 1–11: 438
Acts 13–28: 164
Colossians and Philemon: 66
1 Timothy: 147
2 Timothy: 66
6:66–68
Matthew 8–15: 139
Philippians: 186
6:66–69
Matthew 1–7: 450
Luke 18–24: 293, 321
John 12–21: 137
6:67
Mark 1–8: 200
Luke 6–10: 30
Luke 18–24: 433
John 1–11: 3
6:67–69
Matthew 16–23: 11
6:67–71
John 1–11: 272
6:68
Matthew 1–7: 265
Matthew 8–15: 473
John 1–11: 9, 382
1 & 2 Thessalonians: 245
6:68–69
Matthew 16–23: 21, 204
6:69
John 1–11: 464
Acts 1–12: 66, 109, 303
Acts 13–28: 336
Philippians: 311
Revelation 1–11: 118
6:70
Matthew 8–15: 52, 175
Matthew 24–28: 149, 226
Mark 1–8: 172
Luke 6–10: 16
John 12–21: 68, 77
6:70–71
Luke 18–24: 271, 289
John 1–11: 3
Acts 1–12: 32
Romans 9–16: 35
2 Corinthians: 410
Philippians: 215
1 Timothy: 146
Revelation 12–22: 45
6:71
Matthew 24–28: 182
Luke 6–10: 25
Luke 18–24: 272, 273
John 1–11: 5
John 12–21: 6, 73
1 Peter: 4
7:1
Luke 18–24: 267
John 1–11: 251, 278, 438
John 12–21: 7
7:1–5
1 & 2 Thessalonians: 295
7:1–9
John 1–11: 278
7:1–13
John 1–11: 275
1 Peter: 282
7:1–19
Matthew 16–23: 38
7:2
John 1–11: 5, 300, 439
7:2–5
John 1–11: 280
James: 10
7:3–5
John 1–11: 300
7:3, 5, 10
Luke 1–5: 149
7:5
Matthew 8–15: 339, 412
Mark 1–8: 178
Luke 6–10: 203
Acts 1–12: 29
1 Corinthians: 404
Philippians: 127, 132
James: 3
7:6–9
John 1–11: 281
7:7
Mark 9–16: 237
2 Corinthians: 2, 481
Philippians: 221
James: 92
7:8
Mark 1–8: 161
John 1–11: 485
7:10
Mark 1–8: 277
John 1–11: 300, 439
7:10–13
John 1–11: 283
7:12
Luke 18–24: 422
John 1–11: 25–26
2 Corinthians: 230
7:13
Mark 1–8: 202

7:14
Luke 6–10: 230
John 1–11: 300
7:14–24
John 1–11: 285
7:15
Matthew 8–15: 20, 408
Luke 6–10: 60
John 1–11: 5, 7
1 Peter: 8
7:15–16
Mark 1–8: 274
John 1–11: 289
Acts 1–12: 136
7:15–18
John 1–11: 301
7:16
Matthew 16–23: 131
Luke 1–5: 303
John 1–11: 157, 474
John 12–21: 111
7:16–17
Titus: 127
7:17
John 1–11: 290, 442
Acts 1–12: 255, 293
Acts 13–28: 121
Romans 1–8: 142
Ephesians: 220
Colossians and Philemon: 29
James: 229
7:18
Matthew 1–7: 470
John 1–11: 292, 474
John 12–21: 241, 290
1 & 2 Thessalonians: 319
Hebrews: 80
7:19
John 1–11: 301
7:19–20
John 1–11: 294
7:20
Mark 1–8: 242
Luke 1–5: 280, 283
John 1–11: 27, 301, 438, 478
2 Corinthians: 188
Philippians: 132
7:21–24
John 1–11: 295–96, 301
7:22
2 Peter–Jude: 10
7:24
Matthew 1–7: 430
Philippians: 127
James: 95
7:25
Matthew 24–28: 130
Luke 18–24: 267
7:25–29
John 1–11: 301
7:25–36
John 1–11: 299–300
7:26–27
Matthew 1–7: 4
John 1–11: 5, 438
7:27
Luke 1–5: 274
Philippians: 132
7:28
John 12–21: 175
1 & 2 Thessalonians: 242, 319
2 Peter–Jude: 82
7:28–29
John 1–11: 474
Philippians: 127
7:28–49
Luke 11–17: 80
7:30
Matthew 1–7: 104
Mark 1–8: 161
Luke 1–5: 276
Luke 6–10: 179
Luke 18–24: 264
John 1–11: 456, 485
John 12–21: 2
Acts 13–28: 320
2 Corinthians: 347
Revelation 12–22: 10
7:30–32
John 1–11: 305
7:30–52
John 1–11: 438
7:31
John 1–11: 5, 9, 435
2 Corinthians: 415
7:32
Matthew 24–28: 183
John 1–11: 325
Acts 1–12: 170
1 Peter: 282
7:33
Luke 6–10: 68
Luke 11–17: 191
John 1–11: 474
John 12–21: 50, 135, 229
Revelation 1–11: 197
7:33–34
John 1–11: 343
7:33–36
John 1–11: 307–8
7:34
John 12–21: 29
1 & 2 Thessalonians: 130
7:35
John 1–11: 5, 343
1 Peter: 15
7:37
Luke 1–5: 163
John 1–11: 439
Romans 1–8: 28
Romans 9–16: 320
2 Peter–Jude: 28
Revelation 12–22: 305
7:37–38
John 1–11: 2
1 Peter: 104
Revelation 12–22: 271
7:37–39
John 1–11: 311–12
Acts 1–12: 38
1 Corinthians: 312
2 Corinthians: 116
7:37–52
John 1–11: 309–20, 322
7:38
John 1–11: 478
Romans 1–8: 284
Ephesians: 135
2 Timothy: 145
Revelation 12–22: 286
7:38–39
1 Corinthians: 152
7:39
Luke 18–24: 454
John 12–21: 107
Acts 1–12: 17, 67
Ephesians: 138
7:40
Acts 1–12: 122
Revelation 1–11: 301
7:40–41
Matthew 1–7: 4
7:40–41a
John 1–11: 316
7:40–42
John 1–11: 5
7:40–44
1 & 2 Thessalonians: 295
7:40–52
John 1–11: 316
7:41
Matthew 1–7: 107
Mark 1–8: 64
Luke 6–10: 180
Acts 1–12: 129
Acts 13–28: 304
James: 99
7:41b–44
John 1–11: 317
7:42
Matthew 1–7: 4, 33
Matthew 8–15: 90
Matthew 16–23: 250
2 Timothy: 145
Hebrews: 27
7:43
Luke 11–17: 173
1 Corinthians: 27
7:44–45
Matthew 16–23: 38
7:44–46
Matthew 24–28: 130, 183
7:45–46
John 1–11: 300
7:45–49
John 1–11: 318
7:45–52
John 1–11: 325
7:46
Matthew 1–7: 122
Matthew 8–15: 20
Mark 1–8: 332
Mark 9–16: 212
Luke 1–5: 225, 274, 302
Luke 6–10: 16, 163
Luke 18–24: 339, 422
John 12–21: 49, 106, 175

Acts 1–12: 136
7:48
Luke 1–5: 155
Romans 9–16: 88
7:48–49
Matthew 1–7: 341
7:49
Matthew 1–7: 61
Mark 1–8: 99
Luke 1–5: 318
Luke 6–10: 156
Luke 11–17: 96, 102, 202, 256
Luke 18–24: 18, 132
John 1–11: 319
2 Corinthians: 195
7:50
Acts 13–28: 278
7:50–52
John 1–11: 319
7:51–52
Matthew 1–7: 107
7:52
Mark 1–8: 64
Luke 11–17: 187
Luke 18–24: 125
Acts 1–12: 44, 129
Acts 13–28: 304
James: 99
7:53–8:1
Matthew 8–15: 22
Philippians: 124
7:53–8:2
John 1–11: 324
7:53–8:11
John 1–11: 321
7:55–56
Revelation 1–11: 145
7–11
Mark 9–16: 34
Luke 6–10: 309
8:1–2
1 & 2 Thessalonians: 186
8:2
Luke 1–5: 304
John 1–11: 329
8:3
Luke 1–5: 319
Luke 6–10: 353
8:3–8
John 1–11: 325
8:3–11
Galatians: 138, 178
8:4–5
Matthew 1–7: 302
8:7
Matthew 1–7: 317
Matthew 24–28: 199
Romans 1–8: 316
8:7–9
Romans 1–8: 406
8:7–11
Matthew 1–7: 189
8:9a
John 1–11: 329
8:9b–11
John 1–11: 329
8:11
1 Corinthians: 10
Philippians: 144
8:12
Matthew 1–7: 102, 108
Matthew 16–23: 11
Matthew 24–28: 267
Mark 1–8: 150
Mark 9–16: 211
Luke 1–5: 122, 204, 272
Luke 6–10: 114
Luke 11–17: 81, 88, 91
John 1–11: 14, 15, 23, 57, 150, 333, 359, 463, 478
Acts 1–12: 104
Acts 13–28: 336
Romans 9–16: 76
2 Corinthians: 112–13, 249
Ephesians: 205, 208
Colossians and Philemon: 21
1 & 2 Thessalonians: 155, 157, 164
Hebrews: 15
1–3 John: 23, 28, 36, 60, 66
Revelation 12–22: 307
8:12–21
John 1–11: 331
8:13
Luke 11–17: 80, 377
John 1–11: 325, 336
8:13–59
John 1–11: 438
8:14
John 1–11: 347
8:14–19
John 1–11: 337
8:15
Matthew 1–7: 430
8:16
John 1–11: 474
8:16, 18, 26, 29, 42
Luke 1–5: 297
8:17
Acts 1–12: 22
2 Corinthians: 447
Revelation 1–11: 298
8:18
Mark 1–8: 36
John 1–11: 31
Acts 1–12: 59
8:18–19, 28–29, 38, 49
Luke 1–5: 194
8:19
Matthew 24–28: 232
Luke 18–24: 355
John 12–21: 193
Romans 9–16: 55
8:19, 42
Matthew 8–15: 234
8:20
Matthew 1–7: 102, 104
Luke 1–5: 276
John 1–11: 5, 333, 456, 485
John 12–21: 2, 27
Romans 9–16: 24
2 Corinthians: 347
Revelation 12–22: 10
8:21
Matthew 8–15: 67
Luke 11–17: 191
John 1–11: 339
1 Corinthians: 412
Hebrews: 19
James: 287
8:21–24
Revelation 1–11: 230
8:22
John 1–11: 343
8:22–30
John 1–11: 341
8:23
Mark 1–8: 225
John 1–11: 9, 346
John 12–21: 139
2 Timothy: 77
James: 92, 121
8:24
Mark 1–8: 270
Luke 1–5: 10, 51, 160, 183, 315
Luke 6–10: 132
Luke 18–24: 151, 315
John 1–11: 2, 14, 24, 348, 385, 478
John 12–21: 2, 138
Acts 13–28: 37
Romans 9–16: 36
2 Corinthians: 19, 202, 203, 207, 249
1 & 2 Thessalonians: 283
1 Timothy: 7, 167
Titus: 108
James: 121, 287
1–3 John: 94
Revelation 12–22: 247
8:24, 28, 58
1–3 John: 23
8:25–30
John 1–11: 349
8:25, 27–29
Romans 9–16: 311
8:26
Luke 6–10: 362
8:28
Matthew 8–15: 122
Mark 9–16: 154
John 1–11: 14
Acts 1–12: 61
Titus: 127
Hebrews: 79
Revelation 12–22: 112
8:29
Hebrews: 80
1–3 John: 60
8:30
John 1–11: 34, 162, 354
James: 121
8:30–31
Acts 1–12: 297
8:31
Matthew 1–7: 475, 478
Matthew 16–23: 50

Matthew 24–28: 25, 340
Mark 1–8: 118, 187, 203, 205
John 12–21: 146, 160, 269
Acts 1–12: 80, 314
Acts 13–28: 33, 55
Romans 1–8: 205, 241, 347
Romans 9–16: 117
1 Corinthians: 400
2 Corinthians: 467
Galatians: 136, 189
Philippians: 148
Colossians and Philemon: 66
1 & 2 Thessalonians: 20
1 Timothy: 8, 181, 293
2 Timothy: 77
Hebrews: 83, 93, 266, 301
James: 28, 66, 78, 286
1 Peter: 36
2 Peter–Jude: 27
1–3 John: 219
Revelation 1–11: 79
Revelation 12–22: 101, 102, 273
8:31a
John 1–11: 354
8:31b
John 1–11: 356
8:31–32
Luke 1–5: 303
John 1–11: 354
John 12–21: 210
Romans 1–8: 149, 514
Romans 9–16: 53, 85
1 Corinthians: 52, 189
1 & 2 Thessalonians: 58, 194
James: 116
1 Peter: 95
8:31–33
Matthew 1–7: 168
Romans 9–16: 210
Galatians: 74
8:31–36
Mark 1–8: 137
John 1–11: 351
8:32
Mark 1–8: 211
Luke 1–5: 336
Acts 13–28: 90
1 & 2 Thessalonians: 157
2 Peter–Jude: 24
1–3 John: 4, 14
8:32a
John 1–11: 358
8:32b
John 1–11: 358
8:32–40
Romans 9–16: 24
8:33
Matthew 24–28: 2
Luke 1–5: 221, 274
Romans 1–8: 149
Philippians: 199
8:33–34
John 1–11: 359
8:33–44
Galatians: 124
8:33–59
Luke 11–17: 269
8:34
Luke 1–5: 96, 271
John 1–11: 355
Acts 13–28: 168, 320
Romans 1–8: 149, 341
Galatians: 143
1 Peter: 229
8:34–36
James: 85
8:34, 37
Romans 9–16: 85
8:35
Hebrews: 82
8:35–36
John 1–11: 360–61
8:36
Mark 1–8: 58
Galatians: 126
8:37
Luke 11–17: 176
Luke 18–24: 120
James: 68
8:37–38
John 1–11: 367
8:37–40
Luke 1–5: 209
8:37–47
John 1–11: 363–64, 378
8:37, 39, 40, 44
Galatians: 74
8:38
Matthew 1–7: 108
John 1–11: 355
Hebrews: 79
8:39
Luke 1–5: 221
Hebrews: 100
8:39–40
Matthew 1–7: 69
8:39–42, 44
Romans 9–16: 86
8:39–44
1–3 John: 73
8:40
Luke 18–24: 120
John 1–11: 350
8:40–42
Romans 1–8: 149
8:41
Luke 1–5: 56
John 1–11: 355
Romans 1–8: 396
1 & 2 Thessalonians: 104
James: 219
8:41a
John 1–11: 389
8:41–44
Matthew 8–15: 152
8:41b–47
John 1–11: 370–71
8:42
Mark 9–16: 203
Luke 11–17: 96, 122
John 1–11: 355
John 12–21: 84, 383
1 & 2 Thessalonians: 81
1 Peter: 123
Revelation 1–11: 54
8:42–44
Matthew 8–15: 15
1–3 John: 28
8:43
John 1–11: 442
John 12–21: 41
James: 68
8:43–45
Acts 13–28: 94
8:43–47
Luke 6–10: 364
Romans 9–16: 24
8:44
Matthew 1–7: 64, 290, 319, 375
Matthew 8–15: 52, 290, 377
Matthew 16–23: 41, 355, 372, 381
Matthew 24–28: 46, 262
Mark 1–8: 166, 202
Mark 9–16: 154, 216
Luke 1–5: 196, 255
Luke 6–10: 93
Luke 11–17: 66, 95, 144
Luke 18–24: 29, 132, 313
John 1–11: 355, 378
John 12–21: 52, 175
Acts 13–28: 169, 251
Romans 1–8: 103, 149, 255, 273, 296, 340, 382, 396
Romans 9–16: 226
1 Corinthians: 304, 417
2 Corinthians: 132, 230, 250, 408, 482
Galatians: 10, 97, 186
Ephesians: 182, 207, 338, 346
Philippians: 52
Colossians and Philemon: 145
1 & 2 Thessalonians: 71
1 Timothy: 14
2 Timothy: 68, 76, 117
Titus: 11, 77, 148
Hebrews: 160
James: 58, 205, 263, 272
1 Peter: 282, 285
2 Peter–Jude: 67
1–3 John: 4
Revelation 1–11: 71, 255
Revelation 12–22: 6, 14, 20, 40, 42, 54, 156, 235, 246
8:44a
1–3 John: 132
8:44–45
Mark 1–8: 62
8:45
John 1–11: 27
Romans 1–8: 86
Romans 9–16: 54
8:45–46
Luke 1–5: 303
Revelation 12–22: 215

8:45–47
1 & 2 Thessalonians: 283
8:46
Matthew 8–15: 20, 310
Mark 9–16: 174
Luke 1–5: 58, 167, 253
Luke 6–10: 174
Luke 11–17: 176
John 1–11: 25, 88
John 12–21: 324
1 Peter: 166, 168
1–3 John: 48
8:47
Matthew 1–7: 265
Ephesians: 369
1 Timothy: 10
James: 68
1–3 John: 159
8:48
Luke 6–10: 312
Luke 11–17: 80
John 1–11: 27, 251, 479
Acts 1–12: 233
Acts 13–28: 339
2 Corinthians: 188
Philippians: 132
James: 219
8:48–51
John 1–11: 378
8:48–59
John 1–11: 375
1 & 2 Thessalonians: 295
8:48, 49, 52
Luke 1–5: 283
8:49–50
Matthew 1–7: 360
8:51
John 1–11: 359
1–3 John: 4
8:52
John 1–11: 27, 251, 479
Acts 13–28: 339
2 Corinthians: 188
8:52–58
John 1–11: 382
8:54
John 12–21: 241
Hebrews: 123
1 Peter: 31
8:54–55
Romans 9–16: 55
1 & 2 Thessalonians: 242
8:56
Matthew 24–28: 153
Luke 6–10: 14
Romans 1–8: 149, 235, 255, 267
Romans 9–16: 7
Galatians: 75
2 Timothy: 142
Hebrews: 348, 354
James: 140
8:58
Matthew 24–28: 207
Mark 1–8: 138
Luke 18–24: 156
John 1–11: 9, 14, 24–25, 359, 478
Romans 1–8: 149
2 Corinthians: 19, 290
Philippians: 123, 130
Colossians and Philemon: 45, 48
1 Timothy: 140
8:58–59
Matthew 24–28: 194
Luke 1–5: 323
Luke 11–17: 80
Revelation 1–11: 50
8:59
Matthew 1–7: 189
Luke 1–5: 276
John 1–11: 455
Acts 1–12: 170
Romans 1–8: 150
1 Peter: 282
8:59a
John 1–11: 384
8:59b
John 1–11: 384–85
9:1
John 1–11: 390
9:1–2
Matthew 8–15: 50
Mark 1–8: 376
Mark 9–16: 115
Philippians: 65
9:1–3
Matthew 1–7: 126
Mark 9–16: 27
Luke 1–5: 25, 314
Luke 11–17: 389
9:1–7
1–3 John: 17
9:1–12
John 1–11: 387–96
9:1–14
Mark 1–8: 153
9:1–38
Matthew 8–15: 388
9:1–41
Mark 1–8: 163
John 1–11: 10, 470, 483
9:2
Matthew 16–23: 271
Mark 1–8: 163
Luke 1–5: 320
Luke 11–17: 363
John 1–11: 5
Romans 1–8: 180
Galatians: 116
9:2–3
Matthew 8–15: 413
1 Corinthians: 126
9:2–5
John 1–11: 391–94
9:4
Matthew 8–15: 314
John 1–11: 456
Acts 1–12: 23
Romans 9–16: 190
2 Corinthians: 225
Colossians and Philemon: 186
2 Timothy: 163
9:5
Matthew 1–7: 102, 240
Luke 1–5: 122, 272
John 1–11: 15
Acts 13–28: 336
1 & 2 Thessalonians: 164
Hebrews: 223
1–3 John: 23
9:6
Mark 1–8: 377, 408
Luke 18–24: 62
9:6–7
Matthew 8–15: 10
John 1–11: 394–95
9:6–41
Matthew 8–15: 414
9:7
Luke 11–17: 187
John 1–11: 5
9:8
Mark 9–16: 115
Luke 18–24: 60
9:8–12
John 1–11: 395–96
9:9
1 Corinthians: 45
9:9–10, 21–23
1 Corinthians: 93
9:13–16
John 1–11: 325, 401
9:13–34
John 1–11: 397–408, 412
9:15–16
Luke 11–17: 257
9:16
Matthew 16–23: 378
Luke 11–17: 198, 259
John 1–11: 9, 18, 438, 480–48
9:17–24
John 1–11: 402–3
9:20
Matthew 16–23: 378
9:20–22
Luke 6–10: 262
9:21–22
John 1–11: 412
9:22
Matthew 16–23: 378
John 12–21: 54
Acts 1–12: 73
Ephesians: 116
9:24
Luke 18–24: 54
John 1–11: 438
9:25–30
John 1–11: 404–5
9:28
Mark 9–16: 97
Luke 18–24: 54
Acts 13–28: 281
9:29
John 1–11: 438
9:30, 32–33
Matthew 8–15: 20

9:30–33
Matthew 1–7: 122
Matthew 8–15: 190
Matthew 16–23: 378
9:31–33
Matthew 16–23: 288
9:31–34
John 1–11: 406
9:32
Luke 1–5: 294
9:33–34
Romans 1–8: 180
9:35
John 1–11: 412
9:35–37
Mark 1–8: 224
1–3 John: 100
9:35–38
John 1–11: 412–15, 479
Philippians: 144
9:35–41
John 1–11: 409
9:36
John 1–11: 413
9:37–38a
John 1–11: 414
9:38
Luke 18–24: 157
John 1–11: 14
Philippians: 131
9:38b
John 1–11: 414
9:39
Luke 11–17: 171
John 1–11: 377, 416
2 Corinthians: 177
9:39–41
John 1–11: 415, 483
Romans 9–16: 55
1–3 John: 4
9:40
John 1–11: 377, 417
9:40–41
John 1–11: 325, 438
9:41a
John 1–11: 417
9:41b
John 1–11: 418
10:1
Matthew 16–23: 358
John 1–11: 359
10:1, 5
Matthew 8–15: 113
10:1–5
1 Peter: 267
10:1–6
John 1–11: 425
10:1–10
John 1–11: 424
10:1–14
Matthew 1–7: 479
10:1–16
1 & 2 Thessalonians: 108
10:1–21
John 1–11: 421–22
10:1–39
John 1–11: 2
10:1ff.
Acts 13–28: 224
10:2
1 Peter: 270
10:2–5
1 & 2 Thessalonians: 83
10:3
1 Corinthians: 436
10:3–5
Mark 9–16: 232
Revelation 12–22: 61
10:4
1 & 2 Thessalonians: 172, 195
10:4–5
1–3 John: 101
10:4–5, 14
Galatians: 141
10:6
Luke 1–5: 196
10:7
John 1–11: 150, 359, 463, 478
Revelation 1–11: 119
10:7–8
Acts 1–12: 135
10:7–9
Romans 1–8: 353
10:7–10
John 1–11: 430
10:8
Luke 6–10: 162
Luke 11–17: 254
10:9
Matthew 1–7: 452
Matthew 16–23: 23
Luke 18–24: 283
John 1–11: 150, 478
John 12–21: 320
Titus: 110
James: 290
Revelation 1–11: 119
10:10
Matthew 16–23: 358
Luke 11–17: 170
John 1–11: 9, 342
John 12–21: 280
2 Timothy: 3
James: 62
2 Peter–Jude: 25, 30
10:11
Mark 1–8: 131, 317
Luke 11–17: 296, 298
Luke 18–24: 51
John 1–11: 150, 463, 478
John 12–21: 89
Acts 1–12: 104, 211
2 Corinthians: 203, 213
1 & 2 Thessalonians: 164
1 Peter: 171, 174, 206, 267, 270
1–3 John: 4, 49
10:11–13
John 1–11: 431–32
2 Corinthians: 342
10:11–15
Matthew 8–15: 199
10:11–16
John 1–11: 431
1 & 2 Thessalonians: 83
10:11, 14
Luke 1–5: 155
Titus: 24
10:11ff.
Revelation 1–11: 233
10:12
John 1–11: 425
1 Peter: 270
10:12–13
Luke 11–17: 296
10:13
John 1–11: 431
10:14
John 1–11: 14, 150, 463, 478
Acts 1–12: 211
Romans 1–8: 496
Philippians: 29, 235
1 Peter: 21, 174
Revelation 12–22: 61
10:14–15
John 1–11: 432–33
10:14–18
1 Peter: 171
10:15
Matthew 16–23: 85
1 Peter: 170, 206
10:16
John 1–11: 426, 433
Acts 1–12: 300
Romans 9–16: 304
2 Corinthians: 82
Ephesians: 138
1 Peter: 17, 21, 270
10:17
Matthew 16–23: 85
Philippians: 133
10:17–18
Matthew 1–7: 105
Matthew 16–23: 37, 269
Matthew 24–28: 174
Mark 9–16: 162, 316
Luke 18–24: 91, 266, 278, 391
John 1–11: 434
John 12–21: 251
Acts 1–12: 62
Romans 9–16: 311
Galatians: 60
Philippians: 238
Colossians and Philemon: 62
1 Timothy: 71–72
1 Peter: 170
1–3 John: 60
10:18
Matthew 8–15: 426
Matthew 16–23: 85, 286
Matthew 24–28: 130, 272, 309, 310, 339
Mark 9–16: 153
John 1–11: 453
John 12–21: 81, 335
2 Corinthians: 213

Philippians: 134
Hebrews: 65
10:19–21
Matthew 1–7: 122
John 1–11: 435, 481
10:20
Mark 1–8: 184, 214
John 1–11: 438, 478–79
Acts 13–28: 339
2 Corinthians: 188
10:21
Mark 1–8: 175, 242
Luke 1–5: 283
10:22–24
John 1–11: 438–39
10:22–39
John 1–11: 452
1 & 2 Thessalonians: 295
10:22–42
John 1–11: 437–38
10:23
Mark 9–16: 155
John 1–11: 5
Acts 1–12: 102
10:23ff.
Acts 1–12: 161
10:24
John 1–11: 377
10:24–25
Matthew 8–15: 244
10:24–29
1 Peter: 171
10:25
Luke 6–10: 49
Luke 11–17: 63, 176, 259
Luke 18–24: 339, 396
John 1–11: 31, 354
Acts 1–12: 95
2 Corinthians: 415
1 Peter: 134
10:25–26
John 1–11: 27
10:25, 30
Matthew 8–15: 3
10:25–31
John 1–11: 441
10:26
Matthew 8–15: 244
10:26–27
James: 68
1 Peter: 270
10:26–28
1 Peter: 21
10:27
Matthew 1–7: 246
John 1–11: 57
John 12–21: 160
2 Corinthians: 82, 338
Ephesians: 157
Revelation 1–11: 54
Revelation 12–22: 78
10:27–28
Matthew 24–28: 47
Romans 9–16: 280
Philippians: 29
1 & 2 Thessalonians: 83, 108
2 Timothy: 58, 82
2 Peter–Jude: 153
10:27–29
Mark 9–16: 250
Luke 18–24: 216
John 1–11: 426
Acts 1–12: 267
Romans 1–8: 336
1 & 2 Thessalonians: 178, 286
Titus: 123
Hebrews: 146
2 Peter–Jude: 208
1–3 John: 101, 103, 112
Revelation 12–22: 49, 100
10:27–30
Revelation 12–22: 61
10:28
John 1–11: 9, 382
Romans 1–8: 468, 508
Colossians and Philemon: 131
1 & 2 Thessalonians: 245
Titus: 108
James: 62
1 Peter: 36, 191
10:28–29
Mark 9–16: 250
Galatians: 141
Ephesians: 365
Philippians: 33, 164
1 & 2 Thessalonians: 134
2 Timothy: 29
James: 27
2 Peter–Jude: 27, 207
1–3 John: 19
Revelation 1–11: 77
Revelation 12–22: 14, 73
10:28–30
John 1–11: 24
10:29
Matthew 1–7: 376
10:29–33
Matthew 1–7: 82
10:30
Mark 1–8: 175, 181
Luke 1–5: 49
Luke 18–24: 155
John 1–11: 9, 478
Romans 9–16: 311
2 Corinthians: 19
Galatians: 7, 24
Ephesians: 278
Philippians: 125, 127
1 Timothy: 5
Hebrews: 33, 279
1 Peter: 30
2 Peter–Jude: 26
10:30–31
Matthew 8–15: 273
10:30–33
Colossians and Philemon: 45
10:30, 38
1–3 John: 157
10:31
Matthew 16–23: 287
Luke 11–17: 176
Acts 1–12: 170
10:31–36
Acts 1–12: 275
10:32–33
John 1–11: 444
10:33
Mark 1–8: 104, 370
Mark 9–16: 97
Luke 1–5: 323
Luke 18–24: 380
John 1–11: 89
Philippians: 130, 132
Hebrews: 33
10:34–36
Titus: 45
10:34–38
John 1–11: 445
10:35
Matthew 1–7: 263
Matthew 24–28: 68
Mark 9–16: 18, 261
John 12–21: 204
2 Timothy: 145
10:35b
2 Peter–Jude: 57
10:36
Luke 1–5: 195
Acts 1–12: 194
1 & 2 Thessalonians: 202
1 Peter: 31
10:37
John 1–11: 355
Hebrews: 80
10:37–38
Matthew 8–15: 409
Matthew 24–28: 208
Mark 1–8: 106, 275
Acts 1–12: 95
10:37–39
Acts 1–12: 61
10:38
Matthew 8–15: 4
Mark 1–8: 77, 85, 163
John 12–21: 55
Philippians: 125
Hebrews: 49
10:39
Luke 1–5: 276
1–3 John: 134
10:39–42
John 1–11: 446
10:40
Luke 1–5: 205
John 1–11: 453
10:40–42
Luke 11–17: 227
10:41
Matthew 1–7: 126
Luke 18–24: 116
10:41–42
John 1–11: 455
10:42
John 1–11: 479, 480
11
Luke 6–10: 67
1 Peter: 254

11:1
Luke 6–10: 363
Luke 18–24: 93, 452
John 1–11: 3, 5
11:1–2
John 1–11: 452–53
11:1–16
John 1–11: 449–50, 471
11:1–44
1 Peter: 165
11:1–45
Luke 11–17: 190
11:1–46
John 1–11: 2
11:2
John 1–11: 3
James: 278
11:2–3
Philippians: 205
11:3
James: 192
11:3–6
John 1–11: 453–55
11:4
John 1–11: 478
John 12–21: 241
11:5
Mark 9–16: 210
John 1–11: 438
11:7–16
John 1–11: 455
11:8
John 1–11: 457
1 Peter: 282
11:9
1 & 2 Thessalonians: 164
11:9–10
John 1–11: 485
11:11
Matthew 8–15: 85
Mark 1–8: 264
1 Corinthians: 274
1 & 2 Thessalonians: 125
2 Peter–Jude: 114
11:11–12
Acts 1–12: 226
11:11–14
Luke 6–10: 236
Philippians: 79
11:12
John 1–11: 457
2 Corinthians: 204
1 Timothy: 168
11:12–15
Mark 1–8: 264
11:14
Revelation 1–11: 301
11:14–44
Mark 9–16: 119
Luke 1–5: 293
Luke 18–24: 64
11:15
Matthew 8–15: 161
John 1–11: 450, 452
11:16
Matthew 8–15: 60, 178
Matthew 16–23: 37, 221
Mark 1–8: 171
Luke 6–10: 67
Luke 18–24: 49
11:17
John 1–11: 6
11:17–19
John 1–11: 461
11:17–36
John 1–11: 459–60, 471
11:17–44
John 1–11: 5
11:18
Luke 6–10: 67
Luke 18–24: 92
John 1–11: 5
11:19
1 & 2 Thessalonians: 51
11:19–20
John 1–11: 465–66
11:20–27
John 1–11: 462–65
11:21
Matthew 8–15: 78
Mark 1–8: 262
John 1–11: 466, 472
11:24
Matthew 16–23: 85
Acts 13–28: 334
11:24–27
1 & 2 Thessalonians: 178
1–3 John: 17
11:25
Matthew 8–15: 86
Matthew 24–28: 161, 306
Mark 1–8: 71
Luke 18–24: 58, 90
John 1–11: 150, 470, 478
Acts 1–12: 61, 65, 110, 167
1 Corinthians: 398, 409
Hebrews: 140
2 Peter–Jude: 30
1–3 John: 4
Revelation 1–11: 52
Revelation 12–22: 238
11:25–26
Mark 1–8: 253
Luke 18–24: 147
John 1–11: 461, 471, 478
Romans 1–8: 336
Hebrews: 67
1 Peter: 34
1–3 John: 17
Revelation 1–11: 69
11:25–44
John 1–11: 14
11:27
Luke 1–5: 195
1 Timothy: 32
Revelation 1–11: 28
11:28–36
John 1–11: 465
11:30–44
Revelation 1–11: 25
11:31
John 1–11: 57
1 & 2 Thessalonians: 51
James: 242
11:31–33
John 1–11: 479
11:32
Mark 1–8: 262, 366
11:32–45
Mark 9–16: 273
11:33
Mark 9–16: 300
Luke 6–10: 327
John 12–21: 38
Romans 1–8: 478
1 & 2 Thessalonians: 126
James: 16, 242
11:33–35
Galatians: 165
11:33–38
Matthew 8–15: 74
11:33–44
1 & 2 Thessalonians: 83
11:33, 35
Matthew 8–15: 109
11:34
Mark 1–8: 90
11:35
Matthew 1–7: 156
Matthew 8–15: 427
Matthew 24–28: 166, 170
Luke 11–17: 268
Luke 18–24: 300
John 1–11: 466–67
Romans 9–16: 198
1 & 2 Thessalonians: 126
Hebrews: 450
11:36
Matthew 8–15: 20
11:36–37
John 1–11: 481
11:37
John 1–11: 471–72
11:37–44
John 1–11: 469
11:38–39
John 1–11: 471–72
11:38–44
Revelation 1–11: 301
11:38–45
1–3 John: 17
11:39
Matthew 24–28: 308
John 1–11: 6
1 Corinthians: 436
11:40
John 1–11: 471, 472, 478
11:41
Luke 18–24: 17
Ephesians: 268
Colossians and Philemon: 36
11:41–42
Mark 1–8: 79
Luke 1–5: 238
Luke 11–17: 3
John 1–11: 473
Ephesians: 265
1 & 2 Thessalonians: 85

11:43
Luke 6–10: 137
1 & 2 Thessalonians: 134
11:43–44
Matthew 24–28: 339
Mark 1–8: 74
Luke 6–10: 237
John 1–11: 474
11:44
Luke 18–24: 431
John 12–21: 374
Romans 1–8: 331
1 Corinthians: 416
11:45
Luke 18–24: 120
John 1–11: 479
11:45–52
1–3 John: 50
11:45–57
John 1–11: 471, 477–78
11:46
John 1–11: 480
11:46–53
John 1–11: 325
Acts 1–12: 61
11:46–54
John 1–11: 480–81
11:46–57
John 1–11: 438
11:47
Mark 9–16: 119
Luke 1–5: 275, 293, 320
Luke 11–17: 62
Luke 18–24: 64
John 1–11: 10, 441
2 Corinthians: 415
11:47–48
Acts 1–12: 129
1 Peter: 282
11:47–50
Matthew 16–23: 330
Mark 9–16: 123, 186
Luke 11–17: 233
Luke 18–24: 90, 268
John 1–11: 50
11:47–52
Mark 9–16: 271
John 1–11: 482
11:47–53
Mark 1–8: 271, 279, 403
Luke 11–17: 81
Luke 18–24: 342
John 1–11: 2
11:49–50
Luke 1–5: 203
Luke 18–24: 120
Acts 1–12: 129
11:49–51
Matthew 16–23: 261
11:49–52
Mark 9–16: 327
11:50
Matthew 24–28: 132
John 12–21: 10
11:50–52
John 1–11: 433
Revelation 1–11: 224
11:51–52
Luke 1–5: 203
Ephesians: 138
11:52
1–3 John: 50
11:53
Luke 11–17: 94, 274
Luke 18–24: 334
John 1–11: 452
John 12–21: 9
1 Peter: 282
11:54
Luke 11–17: 390
Revelation 12–22: 32
11:55
John 1–11: 5
11:55–57
John 1–11: 485
11:57
Matthew 16–23: 260
John 1–11: 325
John 12–21: 3
Acts 1–12: 170
1 Peter: 282
12:1
Mark 9–16: 272
Luke 18–24: 93
12:1–3
Matthew 16–23: 257
Matthew 24–28: 134
Luke 6–10: 25
12:1–8
Luke 6–10: 171, 184
12:1–11
John 12–21: 1–10, 14
12:2
Mark 9–16: 273
Luke 11–17: 96
Acts 1–12: 183
1 Timothy: 124
12:3
Matthew 24–28: 134
John 1–11: 6
James: 209, 278
12:3–6
2 Corinthians: 292
12:3–8
Matthew 16–23: 257
12:4–6
Mark 9–16: 274
1 Timothy: 128
12:4–8
John 12–21: 6
12:5
Matthew 8–15: 176
John 12–21: 74
12:5–6
Luke 11–17: 344
Acts 1–12: 32
12:6
Matthew 24–28: 186, 188
Luke 18–24: 271
James: 108
12:7
Matthew 16–23: 37
12:9
Matthew 16–23: 257
Mark 9–16: 124
Luke 18–24: 93
12:10–11
Luke 11–17: 371
12:12
Matthew 16–23: 257
Luke 18–24: 93
12:12–13
Luke 18–24: 95
12:12–15
Philippians: 120
1 Peter: 125
1–3 John: 100
12:12–16
John 12–21: 11–18
12:12–19
Matthew 16–23: 62, 70
12:13
Matthew 16–23: 260
Mark 9–16: 127
John 1–11: 6
John 12–21: 9
Revelation 1–11: 226
12:13, 17–18
Matthew 1–7: 94
12:14
Mark 1–8: 16
Mark 9–16: 125
12:16
Matthew 16–23: 260
Mark 1–8: 267, 380
Luke 1–5: 196
Luke 6–10: 19
Luke 18–24: 95
John 1–11: 6
John 12–21: 119, 206
12:17–18
Acts 1–12: 61
12:17–26
John 12–21: 19–31
12:18
John 1–11: 10
12:19
John 1–11: 325, 482
12:20
Luke 6–10: 41
12:20–21
Matthew 8–15: 155
12:20–22
Matthew 8–15: 147
Mark 1–8: 171
12:21
Mark 1–8: 315, 326
Luke 6–10: 41
12:21–22
John 1–11: 3
12:22
Luke 6–10: 41
12:23
Matthew 1–7: 104
Mark 1–8: 161
John 1–11: 485
12:24
Luke 18–24: 55, 304

John 1–11: 359
John 12–21: 97
1 Corinthians: 433
12:24–25
Matthew 16–23: 46
12:25
Mark 9–16: 42
Luke 11–17: 219, 284
1 Corinthians: 433
1 & 2 Thessalonians: 245
James: 142
1 Peter: 137
12:26
Matthew 16–23: 50
Mark 9–16: 42
Luke 6–10: 315
Luke 11–17: 125
John 1–11: 57
1 Corinthians: 480
1 & 2 Thessalonians: 260
1 Timothy: 124
12:27
Matthew 16–23: 86
Mark 9–16: 91
Luke 11–17: 15
Luke 18–24: 47
John 1–11: 466
John 12–21: 78, 346
Hebrews: 124
James: 16
12:27–34
John 12–21: 33
12:27, 47
John 12–21: 228
12:28
Matthew 16–23: 68
Mark 1–8: 36
Luke 1–5: 238
Luke 11–17: 3
John 1–11: 473
John 12–21: 290
1 Corinthians: 15
1 Peter: 31
12:28–30
Revelation 1–11: 282
12:29
Acts 1–12: 267
Acts 13–28: 267
12:31
Matthew 1–7: 86
Matthew 8–15: 29, 349
Luke 1–5: 259, 280
Luke 6–10: 340
Luke 11–17: 95, 155
Luke 18–24: 195
John 12–21: 171
Romans 1–8: 396, 408
Romans 9–16: 219
2 Corinthians: 132
Ephesians: 338
Hebrews: 52
1–3 John: 83, 126
Revelation 1–11: 32, 168, 310
Revelation 12–22: 2, 14, 15, 212
12:31–33
James: 205
12:32
Matthew 24–28: 282
Mark 9–16: 302
Luke 18–24: 342
Ephesians: 119
12:32–33
1 Peter: 52
12:34
Luke 6–10: 261
John 1–11: 5
12:35
Mark 9–16: 158
Luke 11–17: 176
John 1–11: 456
2 Corinthians: 249
1 & 2 Thessalonians: 155
1–3 John: 4, 36, 230
Revelation 1–11: 197
12:35–36
Matthew 24–28: 97
John 1–11: 15
Ephesians: 170
12:35–40
Mark 1–8: 221–22
Hebrews: 143
12:35–50
John 12–21: 45–46
12:36
Luke 1–5: 196
Luke 6–10: 261
Luke 11–17: 337
John 1–11: 34
Acts 13–28: 336
1 & 2 Thessalonians: 158
1–3 John: 23
12:36, 37, 42
John 1–11: 14
12:37
Matthew 1–7: 94
Mark 1–8: 107, 176
Luke 1–5: 275, 325
Luke 6–10: 88
Luke 11–17: 86, 418
John 12–21: 377
Acts 13–28: 375
2 Corinthians: 415
12:37–38
Romans 9–16: 86
12:37–40
Matthew 8–15: 271
Luke 6–10: 261
Luke 11–17: 164
John 1–11: 438
12:37–41
John 12–21: 13
12:37, 39–40
Ephesians: 169
12:38–40
Revelation 1–11: 272
12:39–40
Acts 13–28: 374, 375
12:40
Luke 1–5: 272
John 1–11: 14
John 12–21: 41
Romans 9–16: 101
1 & 2 Thessalonians: 284
James: 279
Revelation 1–11: 139
12:40–41
John 1–11: 14
12:41
Luke 1–5: 49
12:42
Mark 1–8: 202
John 1–11: 14, 26, 325
12:42–43
Mark 1–8: 192
Luke 18–24: 401
Ephesians: 116
1 & 2 Thessalonians: 284
Hebrews: xiii
12:43
Matthew 1–7: 123
Luke 1–5: 341
12:44
Matthew 24–28: 232
Luke 18–24: 355
John 1–11: 34, 162
12:44–50
Matthew 1–7: 122
12:44, 45, 49
Luke 1–5: 297
12:45
John 12–21: 262
2 Peter–Jude: 26
12:46
Luke 1–5: 122, 272
Luke 11–17: 170
John 1–11: 15
John 12–21: 276
Acts 13–28: 336
2 Corinthians: 134, 249
1 & 2 Thessalonians: 155, 164
1 Timothy: 32
1–3 John: 23
12:46–47
1 Timothy: 32
12:47
Luke 6–10: 313
Luke 18–24: 174
12:48–50
2 Timothy: 145
12:49
Matthew 1–7: 108
Matthew 24–28: 129, 175
Mark 9–16: 154
Philippians: 119
Hebrews: 79
12:49–50
Luke 1–5: 303
2 Timothy: 150
12:49–53
John 1–11: 482
12:50
John 1–11: 9
1 & 2 Thessalonians: 245
13:1
Mark 1–8: 231
Luke 18–24: 292

John 12–21: 226, 280
Acts 1–12: 13
Romans 1–8: 510
1 Corinthians: 329
2 Corinthians: 314
Hebrews: 450
1–3 John: 64, 230
13:1b
1–3 John: 167
13:1, 4–5
Colossians and Philemon: 19
13:1–5
Luke 11–17: 160
13:1–7
Acts 1–12: 107
13:1, 12
John 12–21: 260
13:1–15
Luke 6–10: 20
John 1–11: 2
John 12–21: 393
13:1–17
John 12–21: 59–69, 75
1–3 John: 65
13:1–16:33
Titus: 165
13:1, 34
John 12–21: 179
13:2
Matthew 24–28: 226
Mark 9–16: 164
Luke 18–24: 270, 289
John 1–11: 5
1 & 2 Thessalonians: 273
13:3
Mark 9–16: 152
Acts 1–12: 13
Philippians: 120
13:3–5
Luke 18–24: 280
13:3–10
1–3 John: 35
13:3–11
1 Peter: 277
13:3–15
Mark 9–16: 33
2 Corinthians: 345
13:3–17
Luke 18–24: 293
1 & 2 Thessalonians: 83
1 Peter: 277
13:3–20
Mark 9–16: 286
13:3ff.
Acts 13–28: 361
13:4–5
Matthew 16–23: 244, 368
Matthew 24–28: 146
Philippians: 120
13:4, 5, 12–17
Titus: 24
13:5–9
Matthew 8–15: 123
13:5–11
Matthew 1–7: 393
13:5–15
Matthew 1–7: 71
Matthew 8–15: 125
13:5–17
1 Timothy: 208
13:5–20
Mark 9–16: 287
13:6
Luke 11–17: 41
13:6–10
Mark 9–16: 148
Luke 6–10: 35
13:8
1 Peter: 110
13:9
Matthew 8–15: 443
Luke 6–10: 35
13:10
Matthew 16–23: 156
John 12–21: 75, 282
Ephesians: 300
13:10–11
Matthew 8–15: 178
Luke 6–10: 79
13:12–16
Ephesians: 198
13:12–17
Matthew 16–23: 244, 368
Philippians: 120
1–3 John: 16
13:13
John 12–21: 260
Acts 1–12: 104
Philippians: 147
13:13–16
Philippians: 43
13:13–17
James: 130
13:14
Ephesians: 298
13:14–17
Philippians: 129
13:15
Matthew 24–28: 146
Acts 13–28: 208
13:16
John 1–11: 359
13:17
James: 237
13:18
Matthew 8–15: 174, 178
Matthew 24–28: 148
Luke 6–10: 16, 77, 79
Acts 13–28: 268
1 Peter: 17
13:18–30
John 12–21: 71–72
13:19
John 1–11: 14
13:20
Mark 9–16: 43
Luke 6–10: 17, 335
2 Corinthians: 409
Hebrews: 445
13:20–21
1 Peter: 270
13:21
John 1–11: 466
John 12–21: 74
James: 16
13:21–30
1–3 John: 90
13:22
Matthew 24–28: 147
Mark 9–16: 276
Luke 18–24: 234
13:22–23
John 1–11: 7
13:23
Matthew 8–15: 152
13:23–24
John 1–11: 7
13:23, 25
1–3 John: 17
13:24
Luke 18–24: 290
John 1–11: 6
13:24–26
Matthew 24–28: 150
13:24–30
Mark 9–16: 287–88
13:25–26
Matthew 8–15: 176
13:26
Matthew 1–7: 79
Matthew 8–15: 378
John 1–11: 5
13:26–27
John 12–21: 236
13:27
Matthew 8–15: 175, 177, 179
Matthew 16–23: 390
Matthew 24–28: 150, 171
Luke 1–5: 261
2 Corinthians: 408
1 Timothy: 53
13:27–29
2 Corinthians: 292
13:27–30
Mark 9–16: 278
Luke 18–24: 290
13:27–31
1–3 John: 111
13:28
John 1–11: 6
13:28–29
Luke 18–24: 291
13:29
Matthew 1–7: 355
Matthew 8–15: 176
13:30
Matthew 24–28: 185
Luke 18–24: 312
John 1–11: 6
13:31–32
Philippians: 150
13:31–38
John 12–21: 83
13:33
John 12–21: 97
1–3 John: 73

13:33–35
1–3 John: 130
13:34
Matthew 1–7: 345, 448
Galatians: 180
Ephesians: 77, 107, 298
Philippians: 43
James: 111
1 Peter: 93, 190
13:34–35
Luke 6–10: 102
John 12–21: 292
Romans 9–16: 247, 273
1 Corinthians: 330
2 Corinthians: 58, 308, 487
Ephesians: 162, 198
Philippians: 89
Colossians and Philemon: 18
1 & 2 Thessalonians: 81, 89, 117, 118, 227
1 Timothy: 184
Hebrews: 154
James: 91, 185
1 Peter: 153, 188, 193
1–3 John: 68
13:35
Matthew 1–7: 348
Matthew 24–28: 124, 330
Acts 1–12: 90, 147
Acts 13–28: 96, 109
Romans 9–16: 184, 188, 371
1 & 2 Thessalonians: 17
1 Timothy: 18, 202
Titus: 165
Hebrews: 406, 424
1–3 John: 172
13:36–37
John 12–21: 400
13:36–38
John 12–21: 260
13:37
Mark 9–16: 107
13:37–38
1–3 John: 136
13:38
John 12–21: 275
13–16
Mark 9–16: 285
Luke 18–24: 310
John 1–11: 2
13–17
Matthew 24–28: 193
Mark 9–16: 279
Luke 18–24: 292
2 Corinthians: 412
14
Luke 18–24: 192
14–17
Luke 18–24: 452
14:1
Matthew 24–28: 232
John 1–11: 34, 162, 478
Acts 13–28: 72
Galatians: 167
14:1–3
Mark 9–16: 257
Luke 11–17: 156, 417
Luke 18–24: 228, 247, 454
John 12–21: 61
Philippians: 33, 263
1 & 2 Thessalonians: 124, 130, 164, 248, 274, 302
Titus: 120
James: 110, 256
1 Peter: 16
2 Peter–Jude: 30
Revelation 1–11: 32
Revelation 12–22: 213, 265, 266, 276
14:1–4
Matthew 8–15: 162
Philippians: 130
1 Timothy: 273
1–3 John: 65
Revelation 1–11: 124, 150
14:1–6
1 & 2 Thessalonians: 92
Revelation 12–22: 15
14:1–14
John 12–21: 95–96
14:2
Matthew 16–23: 215
Matthew 24–28: 315
Luke 11–17: 154
Philippians: 140
1 & 2 Thessalonians: 52
14:2–3
Matthew 1–7: 457
Romans 1–8: 505
Ephesians: 247
Philippians: 261
Revelation 1–11: 30, 145
Revelation 12–22: 202, 212, 262
14:3
Luke 11–17: 156
Luke 18–24: 191
John 12–21: 299
1 Corinthians: 444
1 & 2 Thessalonians: 135
Revelation 12–22: 212, 304
14:5
Matthew 16–23: 21
14:6
Matthew 1–7: 280, 452
Matthew 8–15: 58, 105
Matthew 16–23: 280, 299
Mark 1–8: 63, 97, 103, 124, 321, 362
Mark 9–16: 77
Luke 1–5: 120, 183, 303, 322, 336, 342
Luke 6–10: 58, 118
Luke 11–17: 122
Luke 18–24: 151
John 1–11: 9, 150, 463, 478
John 12–21: 252
Acts 1–12: 110, 135, 167, 266
Acts 13–28: 108, 183
Romans 1–8: 34, 103, 185, 347, 353
Romans 9–16: 53
1 Corinthians: 52
2 Corinthians: 89, 123, 128, 188, 207
Galatians: 97
Philippians: 92
1 & 2 Thessalonians: 283, 319
2 Timothy: 3
Hebrews: 138, 186, 200
2 Peter–Jude: 24
1–3 John: 177
Revelation 1–11: 51, 119, 133
14:6–11
Matthew 1–7: 82
14:6–13
1 Peter: 30
14:6, 17
Ephesians: 183
2 Timothy: 67
14:7
Matthew 24–28: 232
14:7–9
Luke 6–10: 132
14:7–10
2 Peter–Jude: 30
14:8
Matthew 8–15: 158
14:8–11
1–3 John: 17
14:9
Matthew 8–15: 14, 244
Matthew 16–23: 401
Matthew 24–28: 232
Luke 11–17: 400
Luke 18–24: 355
2 Corinthians: 19, 123
Philippians: 125
Colossians and Philemon: 45
1 Timothy: 140
2 Peter–Jude: 50
14:10
Mark 9–16: 154
Acts 1–12: 61
14:10–11
Matthew 8–15: 3
John 1–11: 470
14:10–12
Acts 1–12: 87
14:11
Matthew 1–7: 128
Matthew 8–15: 4
John 1–11: 354
Acts 1–12: 95
2 Corinthians: 415
Ephesians: 278
14:12
John 1–11: 478
Ephesians: 138, 247
14:12–14
Ephesians: 112
14:12–18
Luke 18–24: 298
14:13
Matthew 1–7: 364, 372
Luke 11–17: 10
Acts 13–28: 229
1 Corinthians: 244

Ephesians: 381
Philippians: 150
1 & 2 Thessalonians: 187
14:13–14
Matthew 16–23: 281
Mark 1–8: 225
Mark 9–16: 142, 147
John 12–21: 178, 393
Acts 1–12: 30, 85, 104
Ephesians: 247
Colossians and Philemon: 130
Titus: 128
James: 36, 278
1 Peter: 114, 183
1–3 John: 145
14:14–17
2 Peter–Jude: 201
14:15
Matthew 16–23: 340
Mark 1–8: 187, 205, 347
Luke 11–17: 25, 77
John 1–11: 356
John 12–21: 269, 400
Acts 1–12: 297
Acts 13–28: 337
2 Corinthians: 470
Philippians: 46
1 Timothy: 8
Titus: 84
James: 43
1 Peter: 193
1–3 John: 57, 73, 182, 230
Revelation 12–22: 34, 294
14:15–26
John 12–21: 109–10
14:15, 21
Matthew 8–15: 152–53
14:15, 21, 23
Luke 1–5: 166
John 12–21: 146
14:16
Matthew 1–7: 161
Matthew 8–15: 126
John 1–11: 314
Acts 1–12: 17
Romans 1–8: 506
Romans 9–16: 139
1 Corinthians: 25
2 Corinthians: 120
Philippians: 104
1 & 2 Thessalonians: 194
1 Timothy: 186
Hebrews: 92
James: 28
1–3 John: 46, 163
14:16–17
Matthew 1–7: 71
Mark 1–8: 26
Luke 18–24: 448
1 Corinthians: 152
2 Corinthians: 115
Ephesians: 246
Philippians: 74, 170
1 & 2 Thessalonians: 51, 112, 118
2 Timothy: 30
1–3 John: 66
14:16–18
1 & 2 Thessalonians: 316
14:16–21
Acts 1–12: 18
14:16, 18, 23
1–3 John: 162
14:16, 26
Ephesians: 189
Titus: 48
1–3 John: 46
14:17
Luke 1–5: 179, 336
Luke 11–17: 154
John 12–21: 104
Acts 1–12: 17
Philippians: 124
1 & 2 Thessalonians: 193, 319
Hebrews: 215
James: 59
2 Peter–Jude: 13
Revelation 1–11: 54
Revelation 12–22: 211
14:18
Revelation 1–11: 44
14:19
Matthew 16–23: 33
Matthew 24–28: 306
Luke 18–24: 407
John 1–11: 461
Acts 1–12: 64, 65
1 Corinthians: 311, 413
1 & 2 Thessalonians: 128
2 Timothy: 57, 58
Hebrews: 66, 70
1 Peter: 34
Revelation 1–11: 52
14:20
John 1–11: 314
2 Corinthians: 145, 466
Ephesians: 247
14:21
Matthew 1–7: 376
Matthew 8–15: 169
Matthew 16–23: 340
Luke 11–17: 25
John 1–11: 356–57
Acts 1–12: 297
Acts 13–28: 337
Romans 1–8: 347, 485
1 Corinthians: 192
Philippians: 46
1 Timothy: 8
2 Timothy: 94
Titus: 84
James: 121
1 Peter: 47, 88, 123
1–3 John: 58, 182
Revelation 1–11: 54
Revelation 12–22: 34, 103, 294
14:21–24
James: 66
14:21, 23
John 12–21: 225
Romans 9–16: 250
14:22
Luke 6–10: 72
14:23
Luke 11–17: 25
Acts 1–12: 297
Romans 1–8: 347
1 Corinthians: 92
Philippians: 46
1 & 2 Thessalonians: 224
1 Timothy: 8
James: 83
1 Peter: 31, 193
Revelation 1–11: 44, 54
Revelation 12–22: 294, 310
14:23–24
Matthew 8–15: 169
Matthew 16–23: 340
Luke 6–10: 275
John 1–11: 357
2 Corinthians: 470
Philippians: 148
1 Peter: 123
1–3 John: 182
Revelation 1–11: 122
14:23–26
Matthew 24–28: 345
14:23–34
1–3 John: 58
14:24
Luke 11–17: 25
Romans 1–8: 347
James: 83
14:25–26
Romans 1–8: 432
Galatians: 20
Ephesians: 91
1–3 John: 65
14:26
Matthew 8–15: 134
Matthew 16–23: 15
Mark 1–8: 6, 168, 406
Luke 6–10: 30
Luke 11–17: 57
Luke 18–24: 126
John 1–11: 17, 314
John 12–21: 114, 283
Acts 1–12: 17, 104
1 Corinthians: 25, 63
2 Corinthians: 120, 413
Ephesians: 158, 189
1 & 2 Thessalonians: 51, 108, 118, 166, 278
1 Timothy: 4, 186
2 Timothy: 145
Hebrews: 216
1 Peter: 267
2 Peter–Jude: 9, 19, 30
Revelation 1–11: 30
14:27
Matthew 1–7: 138
Matthew 8–15: 24, 232
Luke 1–5: 123
Luke 6–10: 238
Luke 11–17: 169
John 12–21: 121, 252
Romans 1–8: 484

1 Corinthians: 7
Galatians: 167
Ephesians: 79, 247, 364
Philippians: 34, 284
1 & 2 Thessalonians: 204, 314, 316
2 Peter–Jude: 24
1–3 John: 65
14:28
Romans 1–8: 215
2 Corinthians: 19
14:28–31
John 12–21: 131
14:30
Matthew 1–7: 86
Matthew 8–15: 29
Matthew 24–28: 172
Luke 1–5: 280
Romans 9–16: 219
1 Corinthians: 21
2 Corinthians: 132
Hebrews: 52, 202
James: 92
Revelation 1–11: 32, 310
Revelation 12–22: 14, 212
14:31
Mark 1–8: 85
Luke 6–10: 50
Hebrews: 252
1–3 John: 60
15
Romans 1–8: 465
15:1
Luke 18–24: 283
John 1–11: 150, 463, 478
15:1–2
Romans 1–8: 362, 364
2 Timothy: 160
15:1–3
1 & 2 Thessalonians: 208
15:1–4
Acts 1–12: 80
15:1–6
Acts 13–28: 33
15:1–11
Matthew 8–15: 387
John 12–21: 141, 253
1–3 John: 65
15:1, 5
John 12–21: 102
15:2
Luke 6–10: 195
Revelation 1–11: 46
15:2–5
Matthew 8–15: 362
15:2, 6
Matthew 8–15: 350
15:3
John 12–21: 282
Ephesians: 153
15:4–5
Acts 1–12: 282
2 Corinthians: 222
Philippians: 54, 165
Colossians and Philemon: 32, 121
1 & 2 Thessalonians: 96, 208
1–3 John: 59, 69
15:4–10
Mark 1–8: 212
Ephesians: 362
15:4–11
1 Peter: 107
15:5
Matthew 1–7: 118
Matthew 8–15: 211
Matthew 16–23: 103, 278, 299
Matthew 24–28: 152
Luke 18–24: 283
John 1–11: 150, 463, 478
John 12–21: 116, 237
Romans 1–8: 387
1 Corinthians: 310
1 & 2 Thessalonians: 16
1 Timothy: 183
15:5–6
Romans 9–16: 117
James: 121
15:5–8
Mark 1–8: 205
15:6
Matthew 1–7: 70
Matthew 24–28: 188
Luke 1–5: 223
Luke 11–17: 288, 356
John 12–21: 82
Romans 1–8: 186
Revelation 12–22: 101, 256
15:7
Mark 9–16: 147
Galatians: 189
1 & 2 Thessalonians: 258
James: 66, 67
15:7–10
1–3 John: 146
15:7–11
John 12–21: 393
15:7–15
1 Corinthians: 312
15:8
Matthew 1–7: 454
John 1–11: 451
Romans 9–16: 183
1 Corinthians: 244
Galatians: 164
Philippians: 54
Colossians and Philemon: 31
James: 121
15:8, 10
Matthew 1–7: 469
15:9
1 Corinthians: 330
1 Peter: 31
15:9–10
James: 43
15:9–11
2 Peter–Jude: 201
15:10
John 1–11: 357
John 12–21: 252
Acts 1–12: 297
Romans 1–8: 347
2 Corinthians: 470
Ephesians: 278
Philippians: 46, 119
1 Peter: 168
1–3 John: 23, 58
Revelation 12–22: 34, 294
15:10–11
John 12–21: 219
15:10, 14
Luke 1–5: 166
15:11
Luke 6–10: 352
John 12–21: 179, 252
Acts 1–12: 102, 259
2 Corinthians: 484
Ephesians: 247
Philippians: 10, 187, 216
1 & 2 Thessalonians: 185
1 Peter: 48
1–3 John: 19, 20, 238
15:12
1 Peter: 153, 190
Revelation 12–22: 34
15:12–13
Luke 6–10: 35
15:12–16
John 12–21: 155
15:13
Matthew 16–23: 245
Mark 1–8: 393
John 12–21: 86
Acts 13–28: 193
Romans 9–16: 249
2 Corinthians: 238
Galatians: 165
Ephesians: 108
Philippians: 134
1 Timothy: 174
2 Timothy: 18
1–3 John: 115, 168
15:13–14
Revelation 1–11: 122
15:13–19
James: 192
15:14
Luke 6–10: 275
Luke 11–17: 25
Acts 1–12: 297
Romans 1–8: 483
Philippians: 148
James: 83, 140
1–3 John: 182
Revelation 1–11: 54
Revelation 12–22: 103
15:14–17
1 & 2 Thessalonians: 98
15:15
Matthew 24–28: 72
Luke 6–10: 362
Philippians: 78, 124
1 Peter: 152
15:15–17
1 Peter: 267
15:16
Matthew 1–7: 116
Matthew 8–15: 121

Mark 9–16: 147
Luke 1–5: 38
Luke 6–10: 16, 24, 195
John 1–11: 35, 70
John 12–21: 76, 92, 237, 393–94
Acts 1–12: 13, 26, 295
Acts 13–28: 268
Romans 1–8: 45
Romans 9–16: 36
Ephesians: 119
Philippians: 23
1 & 2 Thessalonians: 20, 258
Titus: 6
James: 60, 121
1 Peter: 17–19, 124
15:17
Luke 6–10: 35, 104
15:17–20
Acts 1–12: 166
15:17–25
John 12–21: 165
15:18
Luke 18–24: 215
Colossians and Philemon: 75
1 Peter: 88, 249
1–3 John: 83
15:18–19
Matthew 8–15: 218
Luke 11–17: 281
John 12–21: 123
1 Peter: 162
1–3 John: 134
15:18–20
Mark 9–16: 237
Luke 11–17: 195
Acts 1–12: 127
2 Corinthians: 25, 220
15:18–21
Matthew 1–7: 228
Matthew 8–15: 126, 205
Romans 1–8: 449
2 Corinthians: 144, 387, 421–22
1 & 2 Thessalonians: 178
2 Timothy: 133
15:18–25
Acts 13–28: 319
15:19
John 12–21: 100, 155, 180
Acts 13–28: 268
2 Corinthians: 2, 481
Philippians: 25
James: 200
1 Peter: 137
1–3 John: 4
Revelation 1–11: 82
15:19–20
Matthew 1–7: 456
Philippians: 25
15:20
Matthew 8–15: 211, 324
Acts 1–12: 230
Romans 1–8: 281
1 Corinthians: 65
Philippians: 56, 180
Colossians and Philemon: 185
1 & 2 Thessalonians: 97, 213
2 Timothy: 53
Hebrews: 368
James: 16, 23, 34, 252
2 Peter–Jude: 48
15:20–21
1 Peter: 251
15:23
Matthew 8–15: 325
Matthew 24–28: 232
15:23–24
Philippians: 221
15:24
Matthew 8–15: 3
Luke 11–17: 81, 84
John 1–11: 354
15:24–25
Acts 1–12: 62
15:25
Matthew 1–7: 114
Luke 18–24: 81
Acts 1–12: 268
Acts 13–28: 24
Titus: 45
15:26
Luke 1–5: 234, 336
Luke 11–17: 123
John 1–11: 17, 31
John 12–21: 119
Acts 1–12: 17, 18
1 Corinthians: 25, 152, 287
2 Corinthians: 120
Ephesians: 189
Philippians: 74
1 & 2 Thessalonians: 51, 194, 278, 319
1 Timothy: 186
2 Peter–Jude: 13
Revelation 1–11: 30
Revelation 12–22: 211, 303
15:26–27
John 1–11: 314
John 12–21: 177
Ephesians: 91
15:27
John 1–11: 31
16
Matthew 1–7: 114
16:1–2
Romans 9–16: 81
2 Timothy: 180
16:1–4
Luke 6–10: 329
2 Corinthians: 387
16:1–4, 22, 32–33
Matthew 8–15: 126
16:1–11
John 12–21: 187
16:2
Matthew 1–7: 456
Matthew 8–15: 23
Luke 6–10: 104, 105
John 12–21: 167
Acts 1–12: 127, 230
Acts 13–28: 292
1 Corinthians: 179
2 Corinthians: 275
1 & 2 Thessalonians: 242
16:2–3
Mark 9–16: 234
Philippians: 96
16:3
John 12–21: 176
16:5–11
1 Peter: 267
16:6
Ephesians: 250
16:7
Luke 18–24: 454
John 1–11: 315
John 12–21: 218
Acts 1–12: 17, 18, 27
Romans 9–16: 54
1 Corinthians: 25
2 Corinthians: 120
Ephesians: 189
Philippians: 140
1 & 2 Thessalonians: 194
1 Timothy: 186
1–3 John: 46
16:7–11
Acts 1–12: 170
16:8
Matthew 16–23: 148
Luke 1–5: 208
Luke 6–10: 195
Luke 11–17: 39, 58, 123
Luke 18–24: 444
2 Corinthians: 115
1 & 2 Thessalonians: 279, 302
Titus: 116
Revelation 1–11: 139, 168
Revelation 12–22: 303
16:8–9
Matthew 16–23: 193
John 1–11: 162
Acts 1–12: 72
Romans 1–8: 81
Titus: 113
16:8–11
Matthew 16–23: 97
Mark 1–8: 205
Acts 1–12: 301
Acts 13–28: 335
Ephesians: 189
Hebrews: 280
Revelation 12–22: 303
16:9
Matthew 8–15: 324
John 1–11: 34
Acts 1–12: 268, 273
Acts 13–28: 373
16:11
Matthew 1–7: 86
Mark 1–8: 238
Luke 1–5: 280
Romans 9–16: 219
2 Corinthians: 132
Ephesians: 339
Revelation 1–11: 32, 168, 310
Revelation 12–22: 2, 14, 212

16:12
John 12–21: 205
16:12–14
2 Timothy: 146
16:12–15
Matthew 16–23: 15
John 12–21: 199, 283
16:13
Luke 1–5: 336
Luke 11–17: 57
Romans 9–16: 54
2 Corinthians: 413–14
Galatians: 69
Ephesians: 189
1 & 2 Thessalonians: 118, 278, 319
1 Timothy: 149
2 Peter–Jude: 13, 19, 30
1–3 John: 28, 42, 102, 160
Revelation 1–11: 30
Revelation 12–22: 211
16:13–14
Luke 1–5: 234
Luke 6–10: 30
John 1–11: 314
Ephesians: 158
16:13–15
Matthew 1–7: 118
Mark 1–8: 187
Philippians: 130
16:14
Ephesians: 189
Hebrews: 378
Revelation 12–22: 304
16:14–15
1 & 2 Thessalonians: 195
16:15
Luke 1–5: 71
16:16
John 12–21: 50
16:16–21
Luke 6–10: 250
16:16–24
John 12–21: 211–19
16:17
John 12–21: 381
16:20
Philippians: 188
1 Peter: 41
16:20–21
James: 23
16:20–22
Mark 1–8: 130
1 & 2 Thessalonians: 184
16:20, 21–22
Galatians: 166
16:21
Luke 1–5: 169
16:22
Matthew 1–7: 456
2 Corinthians: 484
Philippians: 188, 216
16:22, 23
1–3 John: 19
16:23
Mark 9–16: 147
1 Peter: 31
16:23–24
1 & 2 Thessalonians: 87
1–3 John: 204
16:24
Mark 9–16: 147
Acts 1–12: 102
2 Corinthians: 57
Galatians: 166
1 & 2 Thessalonians: 185
1–3 John: 20
16:25–33
John 12–21: 221–32
16:26
Mark 9–16: 147
16:27
2 Timothy: 108
James: 192
1 Peter: 123
16:28
Luke 11–17: 170
Acts 1–12: 13
1 Timothy: 32
1–3 John: 191
16:30
Luke 1–5: 305
John 1–11: 14
1 & 2 Thessalonians: 185
16:32
John 12–21: 275
16:33
Matthew 1–7: 214
Acts 13–28: 55
Romans 1–8: 134, 484
2 Corinthians: 120, 149, 398
Ephesians: 80, 364
Philippians: 56, 252, 265
Colossians and Philemon: 185
1 & 2 Thessalonians: 79, 314
2 Timothy: 21, 54
James: 16, 34, 252
1 Peter: 42
2 Peter–Jude: 24
1–3 John: 159, 174
17
Luke 1–5: 238
John 1–11: 2
1 Corinthians: 372
2 Peter–Jude: 208
17:1
Matthew 1–7: 104
John 1–11: 473
John 12–21: 233–44
1 Corinthians: 15
Philippians: 125, 126, 150
1 Peter: 30–31
17:1b–5
John 12–21: 245–56
17:1–5
Matthew 1–7: 82
John 12–21: 40
1 Timothy: 5
17:1–6
Acts 1–12: 22
17:1–26
Philippians: 130
1 & 2 Thessalonians: 186
17:2
Matthew 16–23: 286
Matthew 24–28: 339
Mark 9–16: 152, 154
Acts 1–12: 267
2 Corinthians: 123
Galatians: 156
Philippians: 125, 164
1 & 2 Thessalonians: 245
Revelation 12–22: 21
17:2–3
John 1–11: 9
Philippians: 24
17:2–4, 6
John 12–21: 291
17:3
Luke 18–24: 36
Acts 13–28: 129, 135
Ephesians: 380
Philippians: 235, 313
1 & 2 Thessalonians: 242, 245, 319
2 Timothy: 2
James: 206
1–3 John: 4, 28, 203
17:3–4
Matthew 24–28: 333
17:4
Luke 6–10: 178
Acts 1–12: 10
Romans 1–8: 214
Romans 9–16: 341
1 Corinthians: 464
Ephesians: 285
Hebrews: 81
17:4–5
1 Corinthians: 15
Philippians: 150
Hebrews: 80, 109, 380
17:5
Matthew 8–15: 438
Matthew 24–28: 271
Mark 1–8: 225
Mark 9–16: 5
Luke 11–17: 172
Luke 18–24: 302, 305
John 1–11: 14, 17, 473
John 12–21: 87
Romans 1–8: 16
Romans 9–16: 310
2 Corinthians: 290, 292
Philippians: 123, 125, 126, 141
1 Timothy: 140
Hebrews: 225
1 Peter: 30
1–3 John: 163
Revelation 1–11: 170
17:6
Matthew 1–7: 377
Matthew 8–15: 122
Luke 11–17: 16
Acts 1–12: 267
1 Timothy: 69
James: 66

1 Peter: 17–18
17:6–10
John 12–21: 257
17:6–12
John 1–11: 35
17:6–26
Matthew 8–15: 438
Mark 1–8: 327
Luke 18–24: 298
1 & 2 Thessalonians: 83
17:6, 11, 15–16
Galatians: 208
17:7–8
Matthew 1–7: 109
17:8
Luke 6–10: 363
John 1–11: 478
17:8, 18, 21, 23, 25
Luke 1–5: 297
17:9
Acts 1–12: 267
2 Corinthians: 203
1 & 2 Thessalonians: 20
1 Timothy: 68
1 Peter: 17
17:9–10
1 Peter: 21
17:9–24
1 & 2 Thessalonians: 85
17:11
Luke 18–24: 216
John 1–11: 473
Acts 1–12: 267
Romans 9–16: 305
1 Corinthians: 25
Philippians: 127, 311
1 Timothy: 5
2 Peter–Jude: 153
1–3 John: 208
17:11–12, 15
2 Timothy: 197
17:11–19
John 12–21: 271
17:11–26
Luke 6–10: 20
17:11, 14–18
Galatians: 6
17:11, 16
Romans 9–16: 211
17:11, 21–23
Ephesians: 66, 128, 347
17:12
Matthew 8–15: 175
Matthew 24–28: 149
Luke 1–5: 195
Luke 6–10: 81
John 12–21: 266
Acts 1–12: 32
Philippians: 164, 215
1 & 2 Thessalonians: 273
1 Timothy: 73
James: 26, 27
1 Peter: 17–18
Revelation 12–22: 45
17:13
Acts 1–12: 13, 259
2 Corinthians: 57, 484
Philippians: 216
1–3 John: 20, 238
17:14
Acts 1–12: 101
2 Corinthians: 481
Philippians: 184
1 Timothy: 138
James: 193, 200
17:14–16
Matthew 8–15: 374
17:14–18
Matthew 1–7: 231
17:15
Matthew 1–7: 396
Luke 1–5: 255
Luke 11–17: 47
1 Corinthians: 131
2 Corinthians: 112
Philippians: 184
1 & 2 Thessalonians: 296
James: 235
2 Peter–Jude: 153
Revelation 1–11: 125, 310
17:15–16
Hebrews: 450
1–3 John: 135
17:15–16, 18
Matthew 1–7: 236
17:15–18
Matthew 1–7: 301, 418
Romans 1–8: 225
Hebrews: 442
17:16
Philippians: 184
James: 200
17:17
Luke 1–5: 77, 87
Luke 6–10: 186
Luke 18–24: 418
John 12–21: 207, 222
Romans 9–16: 54, 92
2 Corinthians: 477
Ephesians: 183, 369
Philippians: 289
1 & 2 Thessalonians: 58, 89, 103, 166, 198, 202, 208, 287
2 Timothy: 67, 76, 120
Titus: 8, 12
James: 66
1 Peter: 274
2 Peter–Jude: 24
1–3 John: 28, 42, 107, 142, 143
17:17–18
Philippians: 184
17:17, 19
Luke 1–5: 336
17:18
Matthew 24–28: 333
1 Corinthians: 131
James: 200
17:19
1 & 2 Thessalonians: 103, 202
Hebrews: 279
2 Peter–Jude: 50
17:19–26
1–3 John: 76
17:20
John 1–11: 34, 162
2 Peter–Jude: 20
17:20–21
John 1–11: 478
Romans 9–16: 273
1 Peter: 21
17:20–23
John 12–21: 285
2 Corinthians: 186
Ephesians: 92–93
Colossians and Philemon: 87
1 Peter: 188
17:21
Mark 1–8: 181
John 1–11: 473
Acts 1–12: 90, 147, 290
Romans 1–8: 402
2 Corinthians: 269
Philippians: 101, 127, 138
1 Timothy: 68
Hebrews: 406
James: 185, 206
17:21–22
1 Corinthians: 32
Philippians: 89, 125
1 Timothy: 5
17:21–23
Romans 9–16: 315
1 Corinthians: 25
Galatians: 58
17:21–24
Romans 1–8: 517
17:22
John 12–21: 249
Romans 1–8: 280, 445
1 Corinthians: 91
Philippians: 139
17:22–23
Philippians: 170
17:22–26
2 Peter–Jude: 152
17:23
Philippians: 41, 184
1 & 2 Thessalonians: 97
1 Timothy: 68
17:24
Luke 11–17: 408
John 1–11: 46, 382
John 12–21: 100
Acts 1–12: 267
Philippians: 123, 125, 126, 164
2 Timothy: 24
Titus: 11
1 Peter: 17–28
Revelation 12–22: 266, 279
17:24–25
John 1–11: 473
17:24–26
John 12–21: 295, 297, 299, 300, 302

17:25
John 12–21: 176
Titus: 41
1 Peter: 168
17:26
2 Timothy: 94, 130
18
John 1–11: 4
18:1–11
John 12–21: 303
18:2
Matthew 24–28: 167
Mark 9–16: 299, 309
Luke 6–10: 80
Luke 18–24: 300, 301
John 12–21: 81
18:3
Matthew 8–15: 180
Matthew 24–28: 183, 184, 191, 260
Mark 9–16: 310
John 1–11: 6, 325
18:3–11
Ephesians: 252
18:4–6
Matthew 24–28: 194
Mark 9–16: 314
18:4–9
1 Corinthians: 229
18:5
Matthew 24–28: 192
Acts 1–12: 59
1–3 John: 23
18:5–6
John 1–11: 14
18:6
Matthew 8–15: 294
Matthew 24–28: 189, 214
Ephesians: 355
18:7
Acts 1–12: 59
18:7–8
Matthew 24–28: 195
18:7–9
James: 26
18:8
Matthew 8–15: 110
Mark 9–16: 316
John 1–11: 14
18:9
Philippians: 164
James: 27
18:10
Matthew 8–15: 138
Matthew 24–28: 189
Mark 9–16: 334
Luke 6–10: 29
Luke 18–24: 315
Philippians: 219
18:10–11
Matthew 8–15: 141
1 Corinthians: 41
1 Peter: 150
18:11
Matthew 24–28: 192, 254
Luke 6–10: 29, 34
Luke 18–24: 305
2 Corinthians: 212
18:12
Mark 9–16: 317
Luke 18–24: 313
John 1–11: 6
18:12–13
Mark 9–16: 323
Luke 18–24: 333
18:12–27
John 12–21: 313–14
18:13
Matthew 24–28: 144, 202, 214
18:13–23
Mark 9–16: 137
Luke 18–24: 105
18:13–24
Mark 9–16: 335
18:15
Mark 1–8: 51
Luke 18–24: 325
John 1–11: 57
18:15–16
Matthew 24–28: 215
Mark 9–16: 324
18:15–17
Mark 1–8: 2
Mark 9–16: 337
18:15–18
Acts 1–12: 136
18:15–27
Ephesians: 252
18:15ff.
Acts 1–12: 98
18:16
Matthew 24–28: 215
18:17
Mark 9–16: 337
Luke 18–24: 326
John 12–21: 288
Hebrews: 356
18:19
Matthew 24–28: 203
Luke 18–24: 324, 334
18:19–24
Mark 9–16: 323
18:20
Luke 6–10: 180
18:20–21
Matthew 24–28: 203
18:21
Luke 18–24: 336
18:22
Matthew 24–28: 204
18:23
Matthew 24–28: 204
Acts 13–28: 281
18:24
Mark 9–16: 336
Luke 18–24: 335
18:25
Hebrews: 356
18:26
Matthew 24–28: 218
Luke 18–24: 327
Philippians: 219
18:27
Hebrews: 356
18:28
Matthew 24–28: 224, 234
Luke 18–24: 345, 399
John 1–11: 5
John 12–21: 62
Acts 1–12: 299
Philippians: 6, 61
18:28–38
John 12–21: 323–32
18:28–19:11
1 Peter: 168
18:29
Matthew 24–28: 234
18:29–32
Mark 9–16: 346
18:30
Matthew 24–28: 234
Mark 9–16: 35
18:31
Matthew 24–28: 201, 224, 233, 235
Mark 1–8: 158
Luke 18–24: 52
John 1–11: 2, 482
Acts 1–12: 223
Acts 13–28: 279
2 Corinthians: 389
18:32
Matthew 24–28: 235
18:33
Philippians: 6, 61
18:33–37
Matthew 24–28: 278
1 Timothy: 272
18:33–38
1 & 2 Thessalonians: 298
18:33–19:16
Mark 9–16: 322
18:34
Luke 18–24: 346
18:34–36
Matthew 24–28: 236
18:34–37
1 Peter: 168
18:35
Luke 18–24: 346
18:36
Matthew 1–7: 133
Matthew 8–15: 105, 386, 431
Matthew 16–23: 34, 240, 261
Matthew 24–28: 189
Luke 11–17: 207
Luke 18–24: 315, 346
Romans 9–16: 351
1 Corinthians: 170
Philippians: 260
Colossians and Philemon: 125
1 Peter: 148
Revelation 1–11: 167
18:36–37
1 Peter: 125
18:37
Matthew 1–7: 2
Luke 1–5: 336

Luke 11–17: 170
Romans 9–16: 53
2 Corinthians: 289
1 Timothy: 32
1–3 John: 4, 58
Revelation 1–11: 25
Revelation 12–22: 304
18:37–38
Matthew 24–28: 236
18:38
Matthew 24–28: 237
Mark 9–16: 97
Luke 1–5: 202
Luke 11–17: 185
Luke 18–24: 347, 355
Acts 1–12: 108
Ephesians: 175
1 Timothy: 287
18:38–39
Mark 9–16: 348
18:39–19:16
John 12–21: 333–34
18:40
Matthew 16–23: 262
Matthew 24–28: 241
19:1
Luke 18–24: 361
Acts 13–28: 272
19:1–11
1 & 2 Thessalonians: 298
19:1–16
Luke 11–17: 63
19:1–18
Acts 1–12: 224
19:2
Matthew 24–28: 249
Luke 6–10: 189
Philippians: 203
19:3
Matthew 24–28: 250
Luke 18–24: 361
19:4
Matthew 24–28: 184
Luke 18–24: 361
Acts 1–12: 108
19:4–5
Mark 9–16: 361
19:4–8
Matthew 24–28: 250
19:6
Luke 18–24: 361
Acts 1–12: 108
19:7
Matthew 24–28: 280
Mark 1–8: 104
Mark 9–16: 367
Luke 1–5: 195, 323
Luke 18–24: 337, 362
19:7–9
Luke 18–24: 347
19:9
Luke 18–24: 336, 362
Philippians: 6, 61
19:10
Luke 18–24: 266, 342
19:10–11
Matthew 24–28: 130
Acts 1–12: 62
Acts 13–28: 320
19:10–12
Matthew 24–28: 251
19:10, 16, 18
John 12–21: 334
19:11
Matthew 16–23: 37, 269
Luke 18–24: 362
Hebrews: 278
19:12
Matthew 16–23: 224
Mark 1–8: 158
Mark 9–16: 315
Luke 18–24: 362
Acts 13–28: 124
19:12–16
Luke 1–5: 50
1 & 2 Thessalonians: 63
19:13
Acts 13–28: 317
2 Corinthians: 177
19:13–16
Matthew 24–28: 251
19:14
Matthew 24–28: 144, 241
Mark 1–8: 181
Mark 9–16: 366
Luke 18–24: 356, 363
John 1–11: 6
John 12–21: 62
19:15
Luke 18–24: 363
John 1–11: 486
Acts 13–28: 261, 267
Romans 9–16: 94
2 Corinthians: 220
19:17
Mark 9–16: 362
19:17–30
John 12–21: 345–57
19:19
Luke 18–24: 383
Acts 1–12: 59
1 Peter: 125
19:19–20
Matthew 24–28: 257
19:20
Mark 9–16: 367
19:21
Mark 9–16: 353
19:21–22
Matthew 24–28: 257
19:23
Luke 18–24: 383
John 1–11: 6
Philippians: 203
19:23–24
Matthew 24–28: 256
Acts 13–28: 24
19:23–25
Mark 9–16: 365–66
19:25
Matthew 1–7: 15
Matthew 8–15: 168
Matthew 16–23: 236
Matthew 24–28: 285
Mark 9–16: 105, 382
Luke 1–5: 184
Luke 6–10: 43
John 1–11: 8
1–3 John: 6
19:25–27
Matthew 24–28: 283
Luke 1–5: 80, 164
Luke 18–24: 393
19:25–30
2 Peter–Jude: 59
19:26
Matthew 1–7: 22
Matthew 8–15: 152
Matthew 24–28: 285
Luke 18–24: 392
19:26–27
Matthew 1–7: 196
Matthew 8–15: 110, 339
Matthew 24–28: 267
Mark 1–8: 186
Mark 9–16: 390
Ephesians: 286
1 Timothy: 202
19:28
Mark 1–8: 229
Mark 9–16: 377
Luke 6–10: 128
Luke 18–24: 391
2 Corinthians: 293
19:28–29
Matthew 24–28: 271
19:30
Matthew 16–23: 220
Matthew 24–28: 272
Mark 9–16: 378
Luke 11–17: 172
Luke 18–24: 391, 454
John 12–21: 380
Romans 9–16: 341
Colossians and Philemon: 62
Hebrews: 379
1 Peter: 235
Revelation 12–22: 151, 270
19:30–37
1 Peter: 171
19:31
Matthew 24–28: 292
Mark 9–16: 388, 391
19:31–32
Luke 18–24: 380
19:31–37
1 Peter: 208
19:31–20:10
John 12–21: 359–60
19:32–33
Mark 9–16: 388
19:33
John 12–21: 374
Acts 13–28: 24
1 Corinthians: 272
19:34
Matthew 24–28: 293

Luke 18–24: 380, 431
Acts 13–28: 24
Colossians and Philemon: 62
19:35
Luke 1–5: 234
John 1–11: 31, 478
2 Peter–Jude: 13
Revelation 1–11: 22
19:35–37
1–3 John: 18
19:36
Matthew 24–28: 151, 293
Luke 18–24: 282
1 Corinthians: 238, 272
19:37
Matthew 24–28: 293
John 1–11: 14
Revelation 1–11: 7
19:38
Matthew 24–28: 295
Mark 9–16: 207, 390
John 12–21: 318
19:38–40
John 12–21: 8
James: 101
19:38–42
Luke 18–24: 430
19:39
Matthew 1–7: 36
Matthew 16–23: 356
Matthew 24–28: 253
Mark 1–8: 100
Revelation 1–11: 69
19:39–40
Matthew 24–28: 296
Mark 9–16: 392
19:40
Luke 18–24: 402
John 1–11: 5
19:41
Mark 9–16: 392
19:42
Matthew 24–28: 296
20:1
Matthew 16–23: 285
Matthew 24–28: 300, 307, 309
Mark 9–16: 413
Luke 18–24: 409
20:1–2
Luke 18–24: 412
20:1–10
Mark 1–8: 253
20:1–18
Luke 6–10: 183
20:1–29
John 1–11: 10
20:2
Matthew 8–15: 152
Matthew 24–28: 312
Mark 9–16: 399
2 Timothy: 108
1–3 John: 216
20:2–10
Mark 9–16: 340
20:2ff.
Acts 1–12: 98
20:3–4
Matthew 24–28: 309
20:3–8
Luke 18–24: 430
20:4
Matthew 8–15: 138
20:4–6
Luke 6–10: 29
20:5
James: 85
20:5–10, 11–16, 18
Matthew 24–28: 313
20:6
Luke 18–24: 414
John 1–11: 57
20:6–7
Matthew 24–28: 310
Mark 9–16: 400
20:7
John 1–11: 6
20:9
Matthew 8–15: 163
Matthew 24–28: 300
John 1–11: 6
John 12–21: 376
20:10
Mark 9–16: 403
20:11
Luke 18–24: 412
James: 85, 242
1 Peter: 58
20:11–17
Matthew 24–28: 297
Luke 18–24: 433
20:11–18
John 12–21: 376
1 Timothy: 85
20:11–31
John 12–21: 372–86
20:12
Matthew 24–28: 311
Luke 18–24: 413
Revelation 1–11: 149
20:14
Luke 18–24: 413
20:14–15
Luke 18–24: 421
20:14–16
Romans 1–8: 464
1 Corinthians: 403
20:15
Luke 18–24: 435
John 12–21: 375
20:17
Luke 11–17: 12
Luke 18–24: 413
Acts 1–12: 13
Romans 1–8: 464
2 Corinthians: 19, 393
Philippians: 140
1 Peter: 31
20:17–18
Mark 9–16: 413
20:18
Mark 9–16: 403
20:19
Matthew 24–28: 312
Mark 9–16: 393, 399
Luke 18–24: 403
John 12–21: 376
Acts 1–12: 10, 14, 28
Romans 1–8: 464
1 Corinthians: 403, 434
Philippians: 262
1 & 2 Thessalonians: 314
20:19–20
1 Corinthians: 403, 453
20:20
Luke 6–10: 68
Romans 1–8: 464
1 Peter: 208
20:21
Matthew 24–28: 333
Ephesians: 278
1 & 2 Thessalonians: 314
20:22
Matthew 16–23: 358
Acts 1–12: 11, 17, 18
1 Corinthians: 152
20:23
Matthew 16–23: 33, 137
20:24
Luke 6–10: 68
Luke 18–24: 433, 435
20:24–25
Luke 6–10: 144
20:24–28
John 1–11: 457
20:24–29
Mark 1–8: 171
20:25
Matthew 8–15: 137, 163
Matthew 24–28: 254
Luke 6–10: 66
John 12–21: 275
2 Corinthians: 488
Titus: 93
1 Peter: 58
20:26
Matthew 24–28: 312, 335
Mark 9–16: 404
Romans 1–8: 464
1 Corinthians: 453
1 & 2 Thessalonians: 314
20:26–27
Matthew 8–15: 163
20:27
Matthew 24–28: 293
Luke 6–10: 69
John 12–21: 249
Romans 1–8: 464
20:28
Matthew 24–28: 337
Luke 1–5: 71
Luke 6–10: 132
Luke 18–24: 155
John 1–11: 9, 14, 24
John 12–21: 104
1 Corinthians: 287
2 Corinthians: 19
Ephesians: 131

Philippians: 125, 147
20:29
Luke 1–5: 63
John 1–11: 14
Acts 1–12: 16
Acts 13–28: 132
Romans 1–8: 242
Hebrews: 287, 360, 370
Revelation 12–22: 95
20:30
John 1–11: 10, 77
Acts 1–12: 14
20:30–31
Matthew 1–7: 121
Matthew 16–23: 349
Luke 1–5: 14
Luke 6–10: 20
John 1–11: vii
Acts 1–12: 115
1 Corinthians: 301
2 Peter–Jude: 24, 29
1–3 John: 16, 18
20:31
Luke 1–5: 195, 265, 290
Luke 6–10: 258
Luke 18–24: 404
John 1–11: 9, 15, 22, 44, 464, 478
Acts 13–28: 108
Romans 9–16: 76
1 & 2 Thessalonians: 89
2 Timothy: 152
1–3 John: 4, 9, 147, 202
21
Luke 6–10: 35, 36
21:1
Matthew 24–28: 312
Mark 1–8: 50
Luke 1–5: 302
1 Corinthians: 403
21:1–3
Luke 1–5: 331
21:1–4
1 Corinthians: 404
21:1–6
Luke 1–5: 305
21:1–14
John 12–21: 387–88
21:1–17
Matthew 24–28: 335
21:1–25
John 12–21: 376
21:2
Luke 6–10: 60, 67
John 1–11: 6
21:2–3
Matthew 8–15: 155
Luke 1–5: 303
21:3
Luke 1–5: 304
Luke 6–10: 27, 32
Galatians: 51
1 Peter: 5
2 Peter–Jude: 3
21:4–7
Luke 6–10: 32
21:4–11
Mark 1–8: 226
21:5–11
Luke 6–10: 16
21:6
Luke 18–24: 432
21:6–11
John 1–11: 10
21:7
John 1–11: 6–7
21:7, 20
Matthew 8–15: 152
21:8
Mark 1–8: 51
John 1–11: 6
21:9
Luke 6–10: 32
21:9–13
Luke 18–24: 432
21:11
John 1–11: 6
21:12
John 1–11: 6
21:15–17
Matthew 8–15: 139
Matthew 24–28: 219
Mark 1–8: 2
Mark 9–16: 340
Luke 6–10: 27, 32
Luke 18–24: 328
John 1–11: 29
John 12–21: 93
Acts 13–28: 224
Ephesians: 333
2 Timothy: 11, 65
Hebrews: 155
1 Peter: 5, 193, 265–66
2 Peter–Jude: 3
Revelation 1–11: 54
21:15–18
Matthew 8–15: 443
21:15–19
Matthew 8–15: 140
Luke 18–24: 296
John 1–11: 2
21:15–22
Matthew 16–23: 136
Romans 9–16: 247
1 Peter: 47, 283
21:15–23
Revelation 1–11: 255
21:15–25
John 12–21: 397–98
21:16
Matthew 1–7: 33
1 Peter: 7
21:17
Matthew 8–15: 152
Mark 9–16: 334
Luke 1–5: 305
John 1–11: 14
Romans 9–16: 293
1 & 2 Thessalonians: 291
21:18
Luke 6–10: 33, 36
John 12–21: 27
Acts 1–12: 323
2 Peter–Jude: 4–5, 10
21:18–19
Matthew 8–15: 141
1 & 2 Thessalonians: 226
2 Timothy: 65
1 Peter: 225
2 Peter–Jude: 52
21:19
Luke 6–10: 33, 36
21:19–22
Matthew 8–15: 70
21:20
John 1–11: 6, 57
1–3 John: 17
21:20–22
Luke 6–10: 28
21:21
Matthew 8–15: 138
21:22
2 Timothy: 195
21:22–23
John 1–11: 9
21:24
John 1–11: 7
2 Peter–Jude: 24
1–3 John: 18
Revelation 1–11: 22
21:24–25
Luke 1–5: 14
1–3 John: 16
21:25
Matthew 1–7: 47
Mark 1–8: 84
Mark 9–16: 212
Luke 6–10: 259
Luke 18–24: 157, 396
John 1–11: 77
John 12–21: 205
Acts 13–28: 230
2 Timothy: 39
James: 92

Acts

1
Matthew 1–7: 32, 71, 244, 380
Luke 1–5: 131
1:1
Luke 1–5: 1, 3, 16
Luke 18–24: 454
Acts 13–28: 208
1:1–2
Luke 1–5: 131
2 Timothy: 39
1:1–3
2 Corinthians: 412
1–3 John: 18
1:2
Matthew 8–15: 313
Luke 6–10: 310
Acts 1–12: 13, 22
Acts 13–28: 268
1:2–3
Matthew 1–7: 125
1:2–9
1 Peter: 53

2 Peter–Jude: 19
1:3
Matthew 8–15: 124, 270
Matthew 16–23: 15, 285
Matthew 24–28: 336
Mark 1–8: 317, 405
Mark 9–16: 16
Luke 1–5: 131
Luke 6–10: 19
Luke 11–17: 23, 206, 404
Luke 18–24: 43, 113
John 12–21: 218, 379
Acts 1–12: 60
1 Corinthians: 404, 460
1 Peter: 2
Revelation 12–22: 238
1:4
Matthew 8–15: 117
Luke 18–24: 454
Acts 1–12: 27
Galatians: 69
1:4–5
Luke 18–24: 443
Acts 1–12: 41
1 & 2 Thessalonians: 194
1:4–8
1–3 John: 148
1:4–11
Mark 9–16: 404
1:5
Mark 1–8: 26
Acts 1–12: 38, 40, 311
1 Corinthians: 312
1:6
Matthew 8–15: 243
Matthew 16–23: 215
Matthew 24–28: 10
Luke 1–5: 100, 132, 181
Luke 6–10: 71, 76, 146
Luke 18–24: 79, 186, 297
John 12–21: 18, 105
Acts 1–12: 121
Acts 13–28: 333
1 & 2 Thessalonians: 117, 142
Revelation 1–11: 286
1:6–7
Mark 9–16: 227
Revelation 1–11: 31
1:6–11
1 & 2 Thessalonians: 44
1:7
Matthew 24–28: 72
Mark 9–16: 262
Luke 1–5: 132
Acts 1–12: 118
1 & 2 Thessalonians: 132, 142
1 Timothy: 274
Revelation 1–11: 21, 201
1:7–8
Romans 9–16: 261
1:8
Matthew 8–15: 121, 126, 135, 187, 468, 482
Mark 1–8: 214, 284, 374, 384
Mark 9–16: 267, 299
Luke 1–5: 234
Luke 6–10: 18, 20, 90, 240
Luke 11–17: 58
Luke 18–24: 447
John 12–21: 178, 179, 275, 288, 377, 381
Acts 1–12: 6, 38, 123–24, 147, 159, 164, 177, 190, 229, 233, 304, 309, 312, 316
Acts 13–28: 368
Romans 1–8: 427, 438, 474
Romans 9–16: 58, 81
1 Corinthians: 15, 16, 117, 152
2 Corinthians: 202–3
Ephesians: 47, 69, 113, 138
Philippians: 75, 105, 168, 170
Colossians and Philemon: 23, 33
1 & 2 Thessalonians: 22, 166, 195, 316, 317–18
1 Timothy: 142
2 Timothy: 30, 39, 61
1 Peter: 134
1:8–11
1 Timothy: 267
1:9
Luke 18–24: 231
Acts 1–12: 13
Philippians: 140
1 & 2 Thessalonians: 137
Revelation 1–11: 32
Revelation 12–22: 112, 262
1:9–10
1 Timothy: 142
1:9–11
Mark 9–16: 256
Luke 18–24: 223
John 12–21: 88
Acts 1–12: 67
1 & 2 Thessalonians: 28, 133, 233
James: 256
1 Peter: 220
2 Peter–Jude: 59
Revelation 1–11: 145
Revelation 12–22: 214
1:10
Mark 9–16: 400
Acts 1–12: 100
Revelation 1–11: 113, 149
1:10–11
Luke 18–24: 453
1 Timothy: 141
1 Peter: 58
1:10–12
1 Peter: 7
1:11
Matthew 24–28: 47, 54, 116
Luke 11–17: 152, 153
Luke 18–24: 196, 245, 455
Acts 1–12: 13, 22
Romans 9–16: 261
1 Corinthians: 439, 444
Galatians: 169
Philippians: 260, 261
1 & 2 Thessalonians: 231
1 Timothy: 273
1:12
John 12–21: 2
1:12–14
Mark 9–16: 149
1:12–15
1 Corinthians: 260
1:12–17
1 Peter: 266
1:13
Matthew 8–15: 136, 155, 161, 170
Matthew 24–28: 285
Mark 1–8: 169
Mark 9–16: 382
Luke 6–10: 16
John 1–11: 8
John 12–21: 274
Acts 1–12: 39, 51, 141
James: 11
1 Peter: 4, 14
2 Peter–Jude: 2, 18
1:13–14
1 Timothy: 85
1:13–15
Acts 1–12: 139
1:14
Matthew 8–15: 339, 412
Mark 1–8: 179, 277
Luke 1–5: 80, 149
Luke 6–10: 202
Luke 11–17: 2, 7
John 1–11: 28
John 12–21: 355
Acts 1–12: 85
Acts 13–28: 229
Romans 9–16: 192
1 & 2 Thessalonians: 186
1 Peter: 10
1–3 John: 18
1:15
Matthew 8–15: 370
Mark 1–8: 192
Luke 11–17: 404
John 12–21: 107
Acts 1–12: 39
1:15–16
1 Peter: 255–56
1:15–17
Matthew 8–15: 142
1:15–20
2 Corinthians: 411
1:15–26
Mark 1–8: 172
Luke 18–24: 294
1 Peter: 5
2 Peter–Jude: 3
1:16
John 12–21: 200
1:16–26
2 Peter–Jude: 20
1:17
1 Peter: 7
2 Peter–Jude: 5

1:18
Matthew 8–15: 109
Luke 1–5: 120
Ephesians: 45
Philippians: 32
1 Peter: 10
1:18–19
1 & 2 Thessalonians: 274
1:19
Luke 1–5: 2
1:20
Mark 1–8: 16
1:20–21
1 Peter: 7
1:21–22
Matthew 8–15: 175
Luke 1–5: 14, 248
John 12–21: 185
Acts 13–28: 335
1 Corinthians: 201
2 Corinthians: 307
Galatians: 20
1 Timothy: 4
1:21–26
1 Corinthians: 2
2 Corinthians: 411
Philippians: 204
2 Timothy: 39
1:22
Luke 18–24: 436
Acts 1–12: 13, 22
1 Corinthians: 2, 403
Galatians: 2
2 Peter–Jude: 19
1:22–24
1 Corinthians: 323
1:23
Matthew 8–15: 400
Acts 13–28: 72
1:23–26
Luke 6–10: 16, 241
1:24
Luke 6–10: 325
Luke 11–17: 2
Acts 1–12: 85
Acts 13–28: 229
Romans 1–8: 468
1:24–25
1 & 2 Thessalonians: 86
1:25
Luke 6–10: 78
John 12–21: 7
2 Corinthians: 272
1:26
Matthew 8–15: 136
Matthew 16–23: 205
Mark 1–8: 169
Luke 18–24: 398
1 Corinthians: 323
2 Corinthians: 409
Ephesians: 2, 141
1–2
Mark 1–8: 170
2
Matthew 24–28: 139
Acts 13–28: 165
2:1–4
Matthew 1–7: 71
Mark 1–8: 26
Acts 1–12: 273
Acts 13–28: 166
1 & 2 Thessalonians: 44
2:1–13
Luke 11–17: 195
Ephesians: x
2:1–41
Luke 18–24: 192
2:2
Luke 1–5: 160
2:2–4
Matthew 16–23: 59
Ephesians: 246
1 & 2 Thessalonians: 194
2:3
Matthew 1–7: 71
2:3–4
Luke 18–24: 397
1 Corinthians: 281
2:4
Matthew 8–15: 121
Mark 9–16: 412, 415
Luke 1–5: 254
Acts 1–12: 51, 133, 169, 253, 273
1 Corinthians: 361
1 Peter: 7
2:4–47
John 12–21: 217
2:4, 7–12, 37–38
Romans 9–16: 305
2:5
Luke 1–5: 176
Acts 1–12: 231
2:5–11
James: 13
2:6
1 Corinthians: 376
2:7
Luke 1–5: 163
James: 99
1 Peter: 7
2:7–11
1 Corinthians: 382
2:9
1 Peter: 9, 15
2:9–10
1 Peter: 10
2:10
Luke 18–24: 368
2:11
1 Corinthians: 383, 384
Titus: 59
James: 158
2:13
John 12–21: 114
Acts 1–12: 52
Acts 13–28: 276
Ephesians: 235, 246
Revelation 1–11: 72
2:14
Matthew 8–15: 139
Acts 1–12: 59, 253, 273
1 Corinthians: 2
Ephesians: 148
2:14–36
Luke 18–24: 442
1 Corinthians: 398
1 Peter: 266
2:14–40
Mark 9–16: 340
Luke 6–10: 29, 31
John 1–11: 240
John 12–21: 403
1 Peter: 5
2 Peter–Jude: 3
2:14–41
Ephesians: 253
2:14–42
John 12–21: 288
2:14ff.
Acts 13–28: 16, 95
Revelation 1–11: 255, 291
2:15–36
Mark 1–8: 170
2:16
Matthew 16–23: 59
2:16–17
Matthew 8–15: 88
2 Timothy: 107
James: 245
2:16–21
Acts 1–12: 58
2:17
Matthew 16–23: 59
1 Corinthians: 152, 362, 364
Ephesians: x, 145
2:17–21
Matthew 16–23: 59
1 Corinthians: 362
1 & 2 Thessalonians: 196
Revelation 1–11: 224
2:19
Matthew 16–23: 5
2:19–20
1 & 2 Thessalonians: 150
2:20
2 Corinthians: 37
Philippians: 28
1 & 2 Thessalonians: 144
2 Peter–Jude: 5
Revelation 1–11: 200, 205
Revelation 12–22: 145
2:20–21
Matthew 24–28: 75
2:21
Luke 11–17: 394
James: 290
2:21–36
2 Peter–Jude: 23
2:22
Matthew 24–28: 342
Luke 6–10: 250
Luke 11–17: 329
Luke 18–24: 58
John 12–21: 181
Acts 1–12: 100, 102
Acts 13–28: 174
1 Corinthians: 302

2 Corinthians: 214
Hebrews: 49
1 Peter: 105–6, 134
2 Peter–Jude: 30
2:22–23
Matthew 16–23: 39, 85
Mark 9–16: 354
Luke 11–17: 233
Luke 18–24: 317, 360
John 1–11: 34
1 Corinthians: 410
1 & 2 Thessalonians: 62, 64
Revelation 1–11: 33
2:22–24
Mark 1–8: 421
Luke 1–5: 15
Acts 13–28: 101
1 & 2 Thessalonians: 202, 265
2:22–24, 40–41
2 Timothy: 12
2:22–32
Luke 18–24: 436
2:22–36
John 12–21: 230
2:22ff.
Acts 1–12: 2
2:23
Matthew 16–23: 65
Matthew 24–28: 131, 148, 186, 241
Mark 9–16: 35, 112, 154, 163, 269, 280, 288
Luke 6–10: 77, 263
Luke 11–17: 234
Luke 18–24: 52, 58, 110, 267, 275, 288, 289, 342, 398
John 12–21: 68, 304, 334, 335
Acts 1–12: 32, 111, 168
Acts 13–28: 320
Romans 1–8: 496, 497
Romans 9–16: 99
2 Corinthians: 212, 455
Titus: 155
1 Peter: 7, 20, 224, 279
2:23a
Mark 9–16: 344
2:23–24
Matthew 24–28: 305
John 12–21: 37
Acts 1–12: 134, 169
1 Corinthians: 41
2:23–32
John 12–21: 195
2:24
Matthew 16–23: 33
Mark 9–16: 401
Luke 18–24: 411
Acts 1–12: 34, 72, 147
Acts 13–28: 24
2 Corinthians: 147, 455
1 & 2 Thessalonians: 28
Revelation 12–22: 11
2:24–32
Mark 1–8: 253
2:25–28
Matthew 16–23: 181
1 & 2 Thessalonians: 196
2:25–31
1 Corinthians: 402
2:26
1 Peter: 41
2:27
John 1–11: 14
Acts 1–12: 104
Philippians: 311
Titus: 42
2:28–32
Matthew 16–23: 59
2:29
Hebrews: 75
2:29–30
Matthew 8–15: 90
2:30
James: 269
Revelation 1–11: 284
2:31
Acts 1–12: 72
2:31–32
1 Corinthians: 410
2:32
Mark 9–16: 12
Acts 1–12: 34, 72, 147
Acts 13–28: 24
2 Corinthians: 147, 455
Philippians: 140
1 & 2 Thessalonians: 28
Hebrews: 191
1 Peter: 7, 105
2:32–33
1 Corinthians: 312
2:32–36
Luke 1–5: 175
2:33
Mark 9–16: 328
Luke 18–24: 80, 307, 453
John 12–21: 381
Acts 1–12: 17, 107
1 Corinthians: 152
Ephesians: 138
1 & 2 Thessalonians: 234
1 Peter: 7
2 Peter–Jude: 30
2:33–35
Luke 18–24: 339
2:34
Acts 1–12: 222
2:34–35
1 & 2 Thessalonians: 196
2:34–36
1 Corinthians: 287
2:36
Matthew 24–28: 339
Luke 18–24: 410
Acts 1–12: 168, 169
Romans 1–8: 25
1 Corinthians: 382
Philippians: 147
1 & 2 Thessalonians: 62, 64
Hebrews: 12
2:36–37
Acts 13–28: 216
2:36–38
Mark 9–16: 358
2:36–41
Matthew 24–28: 282
2:37
Luke 11–17: 336
Acts 1–12: 112
Romans 1–8: 198
1 Corinthians: 380
2:37–38
Mark 9–16: 370
2 Timothy: 178
Titus: 116
2:37–38, 41
Matthew 24–28: 263
2:37–39
1–3 John: 53
2:37–47
1 Corinthians: 380
2:38
Matthew 1–7: 54, 109
Matthew 8–15: 58, 275
Matthew 24–28: 344
Luke 1–5: 272, 321
Luke 6–10: 84
Luke 18–24: 444, 445
John 12–21: 184
Acts 1–12: 103, 114, 243, 259, 303
1 Corinthians: 152
Ephesians: 174
Philippians: 92
1 & 2 Thessalonians: 297
Hebrews: 139
1–3 John: 36, 39
Revelation 1–11: 139
2:38–39
Acts 13–28: 108
1 & 2 Thessalonians: 118
Titus: 155
1 Peter: 57
1–3 John: 41
2:38–40
Ephesians: 176
2:39
Matthew 8–15: 120
Matthew 16–23: 31
Acts 1–12: 303
Romans 9–16: 15
Ephesians: 175
2:40
Romans 1–8: 54
Ephesians: 174
Philippians: 184
James: 290
2:41
Matthew 16–23: 355
Matthew 24–28: 344
Mark 1–8: 168, 220
Luke 11–17: 177
Acts 1–12: 159, 176
Acts 13–28: 85, 95, 216
Romans 9–16: 101
1 Corinthians: 294
2 Corinthians: 274
1 Timothy: 142

2:41–47
Philippians: 105
2:42
Matthew 8–15: 134
Matthew 16–23: 28
Mark 1–8: 168
Mark 9–16: 170
Luke 1–5: 14
Luke 6–10: 18, 241
John 12–21: 288
Acts 1–12: 14, 311
Acts 13–28: 229, 240, 248
Romans 1–8: 347
Romans 9–16: 172, 192
1 Corinthians: 2, 266, 403
2 Corinthians: 412
Galatians: 21
Ephesians: 142, 379
Philippians: 102, 291
Colossians and Philemon: 12
1 & 2 Thessalonians: 82, 186
1 Timothy: 4, 10, 43, 82, 176
Titus: 48
1 Peter: 6
1–3 John: 15, 37
2:42, 44
Romans 9–16: 193
2:42–46
1 Corinthians: 486
2:42, 46–47
Titus: 32
2:42–47
Matthew 1–7: 113
1 & 2 Thessalonians: 175
2:43
Matthew 8–15: 55
Mark 1–8: 107
Mark 9–16: 415
Luke 1–5: 325
Acts 1–12: 96, 233
2 Corinthians: 416, 417
Philippians: 160
2:44
1 Corinthians: 268
Philippians: 102
2:44–45
Romans 9–16: 176
1 Corinthians: 450, 453
2 Corinthians: 275
James: 101
2:44–46
Acts 1–12: 149
Philippians: 89
1 & 2 Thessalonians: 97
2:44–47
1–3 John: 18
2:45
Matthew 1–7: 413
Galatians: 42
James: 127
2:46
Acts 1–12: 98
Acts 13–28: 157
1 Corinthians: 486
Philippians: 102
2:46–47
1 Corinthians: 25
2:47
Luke 1–5: 77
Acts 1–12: 148, 159
Acts 13–28: 85
Titus: 153
James: 290
3
Luke 1–5: 133
3:1
Acts 1–12: 88, 130, 293
Acts 13–28: 157
3:1–7
Ephesians: 253
3:1–8
Luke 18–24: 445
2 Corinthians: 413
3:1–9
1 Peter: 5
3:1–10
Mark 1–8: 76
Acts 1–12: 86, 98, 164
3:1–11
Luke 6–10: 51
John 1–11: 7, 8
Acts 1–12: 97
3:1–4:12
1 Corinthians: 81
3:2
Luke 1–5: 294
Luke 18–24: 60
Acts 1–12: 139
3:2–8
Matthew 8–15: 127
Luke 1–5: 294
3:6
Acts 1–12: 59, 104, 105, 281
3:8
Acts 1–12: 282
3:10
Luke 18–24: 104
2 Peter–Jude: 5
3:11
John 1–11: 440
3:11ff.
Acts 1–12: 161
3:12
Matthew 16–23: 29
Luke 1–5: 163
1 Timothy: 164
2 Peter–Jude: 5
3:12–15
Luke 11–17: 414–15
3:12–26
Luke 6–10: 29
John 12–21: 403
Acts 13–28: 276
1 Corinthians: 398
1 Peter: 5, 266
2 Peter–Jude: 3
3:12ff.
Acts 1–12: 2
Acts 13–28: 95
Revelation 1–11: 291
3:13
Mark 9–16: 35
John 12–21: 87
Acts 1–12: 104
Acts 13–28: 307
2 Corinthians: 145, 393
James: 12
3:13–14
Luke 6–10: 270
3:13–14, 17
Romans 9–16: 56
3:13–15
Mark 1–8: 191
Luke 1–5: 133
John 1–11: 34
John 12–21: 334
Acts 1–12: 169
1 Corinthians: 41
2 Timothy: 65
3:14
Matthew 24–28: 232
Luke 11–17: 242
Luke 18–24: 355
John 1–11: 14
Acts 1–12: 216
Acts 13–28: 268
2 Corinthians: 214
Philippians: 311
1–3 John: 102
Revelation 1–11: 119
3:14–15
Mark 9–16: 374
Luke 11–17: 245
Acts 1–12: 65, 134
Hebrews: 98
Revelation 1–11: 33
3:15
Luke 18–24: 447
Acts 1–12: 34, 59, 147, 168, 169
Acts 13–28: 24
Romans 9–16: 95
2 Corinthians: 147, 455
1 & 2 Thessalonians: 28
Hebrews: 66
3:16
Acts 1–12: 104
Acts 13–28: 320
Ephesians: 61
1 & 2 Thessalonians: 172
2 Peter–Jude: 21
3:17
1 Timothy: 31
3:18
Mark 1–8: 191
Mark 9–16: 11, 163
Luke 1–5: 133
Luke 11–17: 371
Luke 18–24: 275
John 12–21: 246, 335
2 Corinthians: 212, 214
1 Peter: 2, 7
3:19
Matthew 8–15: 58, 275
Matthew 16–23: 98
Mark 1–8: 21, 287

Luke 18–24: 43
Acts 1–12: 73, 74, 282
Acts 13–28: 336
1 Corinthians: 347
Ephesians: 174
Philippians: 223
1 & 2 Thessalonians: 297
2 Timothy: 71
James: 289
1–3 John: 36
Revelation 1–11: 139
Revelation 12–22: 228
3:19–21
Luke 1–5: 133
Luke 11–17: 415
1 & 2 Thessalonians: 246
3:20–21
Revelation 1–11: 145
3:20–22
Luke 1–5: 175
3:21
Matthew 16–23: 204, 259
1 Peter: 235
Revelation 12–22: 228
3:22
Luke 1–5: 42
Luke 18–24: 422, 425
1 Peter: 7, 58
3:22–23
John 1–11: 52
3:22–24
Acts 13–28: 333
3:25
Luke 1–5: 174
3:25–26
Matthew 8–15: 472
Hebrews: 98
3:25–27
Luke 1–5: 133
3:26
Matthew 1–7: 44
Matthew 16–23: 98
Luke 1–5: 208
Acts 1–12: 106
Acts 13–28: 36
2 Corinthians: 455
1 Timothy: 63
4
Acts 1–12: 280
Acts 13–28: 31
4:1
Matthew 1–7: 62
2 Timothy: 175
4:1–2
Matthew 16–23: 330
Mark 1–8: 398
1 Corinthians: 409
4:1–3
Mark 9–16: 187
Luke 11–17: 107
Acts 1–12: 168
James: 110
1 Peter: 2
4:1–4
Acts 1–12: 166
4:1–21
1 & 2 Thessalonians: 295
4:1–22
Ephesians: 253
1 & 2 Thessalonians: 65
4:1–31
Acts 1–12: 178
Acts 13–28: 180, 319
Philippians: 265
4:2
Luke 18–24: 407
Acts 1–12: 48
Acts 13–28: 276
4:2–3
Revelation 1–11: 72
4:3
Acts 1–12: 321
Acts 13–28: 276
1 & 2 Thessalonians: 213
4:3–4
1 Peter: 10
4:4
Acts 1–12: 145, 159, 176, 177, 178, 313
Acts 13–28: 85
Romans 9–16: 101
2 Corinthians: 274
4:5
1 Peter: 7
4:5–7
Acts 1–12: 168
4:5–12
1 Peter: 2
4:5–22
Acts 13–28: 278
4:6
Luke 1–5: 203
Acts 1–12: 166
Acts 13–28: 278
4:7ff.
Acts 1–12: 46
4:8
Acts 1–12: 41, 42, 141, 253, 273
Acts 13–28: 279
Ephesians: 146, 251
4:8–12
Luke 1–5: 70
Luke 6–10: 29
1 Peter: 266
4:8–20
1 Peter: 5
2 Peter–Jude: 3
4:8ff.
Acts 1–12: 220
4:9
2 Corinthians: 204
1 Timothy: 168
4:10
Matthew 24–28: 305
Luke 18–24: 422
John 1–11: 34
John 12–21: 334
Acts 1–12: 59, 104, 169
Acts 13–28: 24
2 Corinthians: 147, 455
1 & 2 Thessalonians: 64
1 Peter: 106
4:10–11
Matthew 8–15: 142
Luke 18–24: 128
Acts 1–12: 168
4:10–12
Matthew 16–23: 297
Philippians: 92
2 Timothy: 152
4:10ff.
Acts 1–12: 2
4:11
Mark 9–16: 170
Luke 18–24: 16
Acts 1–12: 68
Ephesians: 82
1 Peter: 7, 106, 120
4:11–12
1 & 2 Thessalonians: 165
4:12
Matthew 1–7: 452
Matthew 8–15: 340
Mark 1–8: 80, 103, 124, 253, 382, 412
Luke 1–5: 10, 51, 120, 154, 181, 183, 214, 229, 315, 322, 336, 342
Luke 6–10: 58, 118, 139
Luke 18–24: 151, 444
John 1–11: 14
John 12–21: 10, 232
Acts 1–12: 104, 294
Acts 13–28: 52, 108, 142
Romans 1–8: 352
2 Corinthians: 89, 123, 200–201, 207, 217, 465
Galatians: 142
Ephesians: 29, 130
1 Timothy: 71
2 Timothy: 61
Hebrews: 62, 139, 200, 234, 299
1 Peter: 26
2 Peter–Jude: 23
1–3 John: 100, 102, 210
Revelation 1–11: 54, 119
4:13
Matthew 8–15: 126, 409
Mark 9–16: 236
Luke 1–5: 163
Luke 6–10: 14, 30, 180
Luke 18–24: 125, 214
John 1–11: 7
Acts 1–12: 98
2 Corinthians: 85
1 Timothy: 131
1 Peter: 7, 8
4:13–18
2 Peter–Jude: 151
4:13–21
John 1–11: 8
1 Peter: 44
4:16
1 Peter: 7

4:16–17
Matthew 16–23: 378
4:18
Matthew 8–15: 186
Acts 13–28: 276
Romans 9–16: 216
Revelation 1–11: 72
4:18–20
Luke 6–10: 36
Titus: 142
4:19
Luke 1–5: 35
Luke 18–24: 136
John 1–11: 7
Acts 1–12: 98
4:19–20
Matthew 16–23: 90
Luke 6–10: 29
Acts 13–28: 46, 276
Romans 9–16: 216
Ephesians: 312
2 Timothy: 12
4:20
Acts 1–12: 147, 275
1 Peter: 134
4:23–31
Acts 1–12: 323
Acts 13–28: 229
1 & 2 Thessalonians: 187
4:24
Matthew 1–7: 366
4:24–28
Luke 18–24: 363–64
4:24–30
1 & 2 Thessalonians: 85, 86, 176
4:24–31
Acts 1–12: 85
4:25
Luke 18–24: 154
4:25–26
1 & 2 Thessalonians: 196
4:25–27
Luke 18–24: 351
4:25–28
Mark 9–16: 197
4:26
Revelation 1–11: 310
4:26–28
Matthew 16–23: 336
4:27
Luke 11–17: 234
Acts 1–12: 106
2 Corinthians: 45
Philippians: 311
4:27–28
Mark 1–8: 166
Mark 9–16: 344, 368
Luke 18–24: 288
John 12–21: 246
Acts 1–12: 62
Romans 1–8: 497
Philippians: 298
1 Peter: 206
4:29
Luke 11–17: 386
John 12–21: 267
Acts 13–28: 46, 172
1 Corinthians: 16
2 Corinthians: 85
Revelation 12–22: 200, 293
4:29–31
Acts 13–28: 45
4:30
Acts 1–12: 106, 233
2 Corinthians: 416
Philippians: 311
4:31
Luke 1–5: 70
John 1–11: 302
Acts 1–12: 41, 42, 253, 256, 273
1 Corinthians: 16
1 & 2 Thessalonians: 269
4:32
Acts 1–12: 153
1 Corinthians: 30
2 Corinthians: 275
Philippians: 89
James: 185
4:32–35
Acts 1–12: 139
James: 127–28
4:32–37
Acts 13–28: 199, 234
4:32, 34–35
Romans 9–16: 305
4:33
Luke 1–5: 234
1 Corinthians: 456
2 Corinthians: 413
2 Peter–Jude: 24
4:34
Acts 1–12: 88
1 Corinthians: 450
2 Corinthians: 275
1 Timothy: 218
4:34–35
Acts 1–12: 316
1 Timothy: 283
4:34–37
James: 101
4:35
Matthew 16–23: 124
1 Corinthians: 453
4:35–37
Acts 13–28: 248
4:36
Luke 1–5: 245
Acts 1–12: 277
Acts 13–28: 4, 7, 82
Philippians: 272
1 & 2 Thessalonians: 158
2 Timothy: 209
4:36–37
Acts 1–12: 314
2 Corinthians: 312
4:37
1 Corinthians: 453
2 Corinthians: 305
5
Acts 1–12: 280
Acts 13–28: 31
5:1–2
Luke 11–17: 129
2 Corinthians: 272
5:1–4
Titus: 102
5:1–6
1 & 2 Thessalonians: 176
5:1–10
Matthew 1–7: 126, 352
Matthew 16–23: 147
Romans 1–8: 120
Romans 9–16: 176
1 & 2 Thessalonians: 72
Hebrews: 433
5:1–11
Matthew 1–7: 92
Matthew 16–23: 124, 383
Luke 11–17: 114
Acts 1–12: 146, 160, 178
Romans 1–8: 193
1 Corinthians: 127, 274
2 Corinthians: 442
Philippians: 215
1 & 2 Thessalonians: 71
1 Peter: 5
2 Peter–Jude: 3
1–3 John: 205
Revelation 1–11: 46, 94, 125
Revelation 12–22: 16
5:2
Acts 13–28: 248
1 Corinthians: 453
5:2–3
1 & 2 Thessalonians: 172
5:3
Matthew 1–7: 410
Matthew 8–15: 53
John 12–21: 113
1 Corinthians: 240
2 Corinthians: 408, 488
Ephesians: 189, 250
1–3 John: 126, 155
Revelation 1–11: 255
Revelation 12–22: 235
5:3–4
2 Corinthians: 113
Ephesians: 131
1 & 2 Thessalonians: 194
5:3–4, 9
Matthew 8–15: 54
5:3–5
1 Corinthians: 224
5:4
Acts 1–12: 88
5:5
Luke 11–17: 129
Acts 1–12: 86, 162
2 Corinthians: 272
5:5–6
John 1–11: 462
5:5–10
Ephesians: 315
5:5, 11
Matthew 8–15: 56

5:5–11
1 Timothy: 223
Revelation 1–11: 255
5:6
Acts 1–12: 283
5:9
Ephesians: 189
5:9–10
1 Corinthians: 224
5:10
John 1–11: 461
Acts 1–12: 283
2 Corinthians: 272
5:11
Acts 1–12: 86, 162
Romans 1–8: 477
5:12
John 1–11: 440
Acts 1–12: 86
2 Corinthians: 416, 417
5:12–14
Acts 1–12: 190
5:12–16
John 12–21: 106
Acts 1–12: 233, 284
1 Peter: 5
5:13
Acts 1–12: 176, 188
5:13–14
Acts 1–12: 82
5:14
John 12–21: 156
Acts 1–12: 92, 130, 159, 177, 178, 313
Acts 13–28: 85, 108
5:14–16
Luke 18–24: 397
5:15
Acts 13–28: 175
5:15–16
Acts 1–12: 86, 97
5:16
Luke 1–5: 283, 294
Acts 1–12: 177, 229
Acts 13–28: 171
2 Corinthians: 417
Revelation 12–22: 147
5:17
Acts 13–28: 36, 65
2 Peter–Jude: 72
5:17–18
Acts 1–12: 46
Acts 13–28: 276
1 & 2 Thessalonians: 65
James: 110
1 Peter: 2
2 Peter–Jude: 151
Revelation 1–11: 72
5:17–29
1 Peter: 44
5:17–41
Acts 1–12: 178
Philippians: 265
1 & 2 Thessalonians: 295
5:17–42
Luke 11–17: 195
Acts 13–28: 180, 319
5:17ff.
Acts 1–12: 324
5:18
Luke 18–24: 208, 209
Acts 1–12: 168, 321
1 & 2 Thessalonians: 213
Hebrews: 140
5:18–41
Luke 11–17: 107
5:19
Acts 1–12: 321
Revelation 12–22: 296
5:19–20
Acts 13–28: 276
5:19–25
Acts 13–28: 104
1 Peter: 2
5:20
Philippians: 187
5:21
Matthew 24–28: 198
Acts 13–28: 276
5:21ff.
Acts 13–28: 278
5:24
Acts 13–28: 278
5:24–26
Acts 13–28: 279
5:25–33
1 & 2 Thessalonians: 65
5:26
Acts 1–12: 194
5:26–28
2 Peter–Jude: 151
5:26–40
1 Peter: 2
5:27–29
Luke 6–10: 36
5:27ff.
Acts 1–12: 220
5:28
Matthew 16–23: 355
Matthew 24–28: 244
Luke 18–24: 360
Acts 1–12: 169, 177
Acts 13–28: 276
Revelation 1–11: 72
5:28–29
Matthew 16–23: 322
Romans 9–16: 216
5:29
Mark 1–8: 305
Acts 1–12: 138
Acts 13–28: 337
1 Corinthians: 268
1 Timothy: 234
5:29–32
Mark 1–8: 170
Luke 6–10: 29
5:30
Luke 18–24: 444
John 1–11: 34
Acts 1–12: 34, 59, 147
Acts 13–28: 24, 307
2 Corinthians: 147, 455
Philippians: 140
1 & 2 Thessalonians: 64
1 Peter: 7, 106
5:30–31
1 Corinthians: 413
5:30–32
John 12–21: 182
1 & 2 Thessalonians: 28
5:31
Matthew 1–7: 67
Matthew 8–15: 58
Mark 1–8: 21
Luke 1–5: 153, 208, 214, 321
Acts 1–12: 67, 73, 74, 75, 107, 117
Acts 13–28: 336
2 Corinthians: 133, 266
Ephesians: 174
Philippians: 140, 223
Hebrews: 66
1 Peter: 219
2 Peter–Jude: 23
Revelation 12–22: 214
5:31–32
Luke 1–5: 234
1 Peter: 24, 134
5:32
Matthew 16–23: 50
Luke 1–5: 76, 166
John 12–21: 182
5:33–40
2 Peter–Jude: 151
5:34
2 Corinthians: 157
5:34–40
Luke 1–5: 318
Luke 11–17: 97
John 1–11: 100
5:37
Matthew 16–23: 319
Luke 1–5: 145
Luke 6–10: 70
1 Timothy: 147
2 Peter–Jude: 149
5:39
John 12–21: 24
Acts 1–12: 322
James: 226
5:40
Luke 18–24: 208
Acts 1–12: 46, 104
Acts 13–28: 276, 279
2 Corinthians: 389
Revelation 1–11: 72
5:40–41
Philippians: 194
1 & 2 Thessalonians: 65
1 Peter: 44, 198
5:41
Mark 9–16: 238
Luke 6–10: 99
Luke 11–17: 182
Acts 1–12: 140
Acts 13–28: 74
2 Corinthians: 15, 25, 278
Ephesians: 266

Philippians: 97, 193, 275
Colossians and Philemon: 75
1 & 2 Thessalonians: 25, 97, 184, 189
2 Timothy: 22
Hebrews: 354
1 Peter: 7, 44

5:42
Luke 1–5: 157
John 1–11: 240
Acts 1–12: 48
Acts 13–28: 95, 276
1 Corinthians: 486
Titus: 13

6:1
Luke 6–10: 56
John 1–11: 230
Acts 1–12: 174, 313
1 Corinthians: 486
2 Corinthians: 201, 312, 385
Philippians: 230
1 Timothy: 125
James: 4

6:1–2
John 1–11: 230, 357

6:1, 4
James: 101

6:1–6
Acts 1–12: 280
1 & 2 Thessalonians: 202

6:1ff.
Acts 1–12: 149, 284

6:2
Luke 18–24: 434
1 Corinthians: 480

6:2–3
1 Corinthians: 456

6:2–4
1 Corinthians: 480

6:2, 4
Ephesians: 154
Titus: 50

6:2–5
1 Corinthians: 465

6:2–6
Acts 13–28: 248

6:3
Acts 1–12: 221
Acts 13–28: 3
Ephesians: 219, 287
James: 168
1 Peter: 255–56

6:3–4
Romans 9–16: 172
1 Timothy: 16

6:3–6
1 & 2 Thessalonians: 173

6:3–8
Acts 1–12: 253

6:4
John 12–21: 242
Acts 13–28: 5, 149, 197, 229
Romans 9–16: 192
1 Corinthians: 4, 480
Ephesians: 1, 153, 154
Philippians: 39
1 & 2 Thessalonians: 86, 92, 187, 212, 253, 291
1 Timothy: 125
Titus: 46
James: 277

6:4–5
Ephesians: 251

6:5
Matthew 8–15: 155
Luke 6–10: 59
Acts 1–12: 41, 42, 182, 203, 221, 232, 273
Acts 13–28: 71
Ephesians: 250
2 Timothy: 185
1 Peter: 143

6:5–6
Acts 13–28: 239

6:6
Acts 13–28: 229
1 Timothy: 224
Hebrews: 140

6:7
Matthew 24–28: 263
Mark 9–16: 207, 370
Luke 1–5: 166
Luke 18–24: 385
John 1–11: 230, 357
John 12–21: 111
Acts 1–12: 130, 159, 297, 313
Acts 13–28: 85, 178
Romans 9–16: 84
1 Corinthians: 304
1 & 2 Thessalonians: 197

6:8
Luke 1–5: 294
Acts 1–12: 233, 273
1 Corinthians: 302
2 Corinthians: 417
1 Timothy: 126

6:8–10
Acts 13–28: 163

6:8–14
1 Peter: 143–44
1–3 John: 133

6:8–15
Acts 1–12: 200

6:8–7:60
James: 159

6:8–8:40
1 Corinthians: 465

6:9
Mark 9–16: 25
Luke 18–24: 102, 368
Acts 1–12: 188, 264

6:9–10
Acts 13–28: 276

6:9–15
Acts 13–28: 180, 319

6:9ff.
Revelation 1–11: 72

6:10
1 Corinthians: 298
James: 168

6:11
Acts 13–28: 276

6:11–14
Acts 13–28: 259

6:12
Acts 1–12: 129
2 Timothy: 175

6:12–14
Matthew 24–28: 201

6:12–15
Matthew 24–28: 235
Mark 9–16: 346
Acts 13–28: 277

6:12–7:56
1 Peter: 2

6:12ff.
Acts 1–12: 230
Acts 13–28: 278

6:13
Luke 1–5: 323
Acts 13–28: 259
Galatians: 142

6:13–14
John 1–11: 92, 482
Acts 1–12: 193

6:14
Acts 13–28: 304

6:15
Acts 1–12: 203
1 Peter: 144

7
Acts 13–28: 31

7:1
1 Peter: 144

7:1–50
Acts 13–28: 277

7:1–51
Acts 1–12: 189

7:1–53
Mark 9–16: 236

7:1–56
John 1–11: 240
Revelation 1–11: 291

7:1ff.
Acts 1–12: 2

7:2
Luke 1–5: 105
Acts 13–28: 264, 279
Romans 9–16: 124

7:2–5
Hebrews: 326

7:2–53
1 & 2 Thessalonians: 196
1 Peter: 144

7:2ff.
Acts 1–12: 257

7:3
Luke 1–5: 106

7:5
Acts 1–12: 208

7:6
1 Corinthians: 212

7:7
Philippians: 199

7:8
Philippians: 218

7:10
1 Peter: 149

7:13
Philippians: 78
7:16
1 & 2 Thessalonians: 172
7:19
Mark 9–16: 65
7:20
Hebrews: 348
7:22
Hebrews: 349
7:23
Luke 6–10: 14
7:24
1 & 2 Thessalonians: 236
7:25
Acts 13–28: 53
2 Corinthians: 204
1 Timothy: 168
Hebrews: 349
7:29
1 Peter: 15
7:30
Luke 6–10: 14
7:31
Luke 1–5: 163
7:32
Acts 1–12: 105
7:34
Romans 1–8: 457
7:36
2 Corinthians: 415
7:37
John 1–11: 52
7:38
Matthew 16–23: 32
Romans 1–8: 168, 358
Hebrews: 46
Revelation 12–22: 84
7:38–42
Romans 1–8: 99
1 & 2 Thessalonians: 285
7:41
Philippians: 192
Revelation 1–11: 273
7:43
Matthew 8–15: 9
7:44
Revelation 12–22: 132
7:48
Luke 1–5: 49
7:48–50
Hebrews: 229
7:51
John 12–21: 48
Acts 1–12: 189
2 Corinthians: 110, 464
Ephesians: 189
Colossians and Philemon: 107
1 & 2 Thessalonians: 194, 279
James: 226
Revelation 12–22: 303
7:51–52
Luke 18–24: 124
7:51–53
Mark 1–8: 270, 299
Acts 1–12: 195
Acts 13–28: 277
Hebrews: 25
7:52
Mark 1–8: 298
John 12–21: 334
Acts 1–12: 189
Acts 13–28: 268
James: 258
7:53
Luke 11–17: 400
Romans 1–8: 117, 358
2 Corinthians: 461
1 & 2 Thessalonians: 234
Hebrews: 46
Revelation 1–11: 21
Revelation 12–22: 84, 296
7:54
Acts 1–12: 170
Acts 13–28: 186
7:54–60
Matthew 24–28: 201, 235
John 12–21: 232
Acts 1–12: 188
Acts 13–28: 277
1 Peter: 169
Revelation 1–11: 72
7:54–8:1
1 Peter: 144
7:54–8:3
1 & 2 Thessalonians: 295
7:54–8:4
1 & 2 Thessalonians: 60
7:55
Luke 1–5: 238
John 12–21: 297
Acts 1–12: 41, 42, 203, 253
Ephesians: 251
Hebrews: 208, 292
Revelation 12–22: 262
7:55–56
Acts 1–12: 67, 189
Philippians: 141
1 & 2 Thessalonians: 234
1 Peter: 200, 219, 254
Revelation 12–22: 214
7:56
Matthew 1–7: 79
Matthew 8–15: 377
1 & 2 Thessalonians: 133
Revelation 1–11: 17, 145
7:57–60
1 Peter: 2, 198
7:58
Acts 1–12: 188, 193
Acts 13–28: 334
Ephesians: 183
Colossians and Philemon: 71
1 Timothy: 173
7:58–60
Matthew 16–23: 391
Luke 1–5: 226
Luke 11–17: 107
John 12–21: 328
Acts 1–12: 46
7:59
Mark 1–8: 225
Acts 1–12: 190
1 & 2 Thessalonians: 87
7:59–60
Luke 6–10: 110
John 1–11: 15
Acts 1–12: 189
Philippians: 79
1 Timothy: 60
1 Peter: 254
7:59–8:1
1 Corinthians: 426
7:60
Matthew 1–7: 196, 397
Matthew 16–23: 142
Mark 1–8: 264
Acts 1–12: 190
Romans 9–16: 58, 196
1 Corinthians: 274, 338, 355
Colossians and Philemon: 226
1 & 2 Thessalonians: 85, 125
1 Timothy: 67
2 Timothy: 213
Revelation 1–11: 190, 195
8
Acts 13–28: 165
8:1
Luke 11–17: 107, 240
Acts 1–12: 183, 188, 193, 277
Acts 13–28: 101, 277
2 Corinthians: 275
1 Timothy: 3, 29
James: 73
8:1–2
Acts 1–12: 281
James: 252
8:1–3
Acts 1–12: 265
Acts 13–28: 333
Romans 9–16: 98
1 Corinthians: 450
2 Corinthians: 386
1 & 2 Thessalonians: 166
8:1–4
Matthew 1–7: 113
Matthew 16–23: 391
John 12–21: 166
Acts 13–28: 47, 180, 319, 346
James: 274
1 Peter: 2
8:1, 3
Romans 9–16: 8
8:1ff.
Revelation 1–11: 72
8:2
Luke 1–5: 176
Acts 1–12: 188, 224
8:3
Luke 18–24: 208
Acts 13–28: 103, 277
Romans 1–8: 99
Galatians: 26
Philippians: 231
1 Timothy: 3, 29
8:3–4
1 Peter: 198

8:4
John 1–11: 240
Acts 1–12: 48, 312
Acts 13–28: 277
Ephesians: 142
Philippians: 231
1 & 2 Thessalonians: 59
8:4–5
Acts 13–28: 16, 95
8:4–13, 26–40
Matthew 8–15: 155
8:4–25
Acts 1–12: 183
8:4–40
Ephesians: 142
8:4, 12, 25, 35, 40
Luke 1–5: 157
8:5
Acts 1–12: 48, 312
Acts 13–28: 239
8:5–7
1 Corinthians: 300
8:5–17
Matthew 1–7: 71
8:5ff.
1 Timothy: 126
8:6–7
Luke 1–5: 294
Acts 1–12: 190
8:6–8
Luke 6–10: 314
8:7
Luke 1–5: 283
Acts 1–12: 97
Acts 13–28: 171
1 Corinthians: 302
8:9
Matthew 1–7: 28
1 Timothy: 241
James: 133
2 Peter–Jude: 18
8:9–11
Acts 13–28: 8
1 & 2 Thessalonians: 38
Revelation 12–22: 60
8:9–13
Philippians: 211
8:9–24
Luke 6–10: 25
Philippians: 256
1 & 2 Thessalonians: 71
1 Peter: 4
2 Peter–Jude: 2
8:9ff.
Acts 13–28: 96
8:12
Luke 6–10: 181
John 1–11: 240
Acts 1–12: 48, 75, 104
Acts 13–28: 16, 108
James: 133
Revelation 1–11: 291
8:13
Acts 1–12: 74, 87
Philippians: 211
James: 133
8:13, 18–23
Luke 1–5: 214
8:14
John 1–11: 7, 8
Acts 1–12: 98
Philippians: 206
1 & 2 Thessalonians: 57, 294
8:14–15
Luke 18–24: 3
8:14–16
Acts 1–12: 17
8:14–17
Acts 1–12: 273
Acts 13–28: 165
8:14–19
Acts 1–12: 42, 304
8:14–24
Philippians: 211
8:17
Acts 1–12: 253
1 Corinthians: 313
Hebrews: 140
8:17–18
Acts 1–12: 142
1 Timothy: 224
8:18–20
Matthew 8–15: 192
8:18–22
James: 133
8:18–23
1 Timothy: 245
8:18, 24
Romans 9–16: 162
8:20
Acts 13–28: 53
1 Peter: 5, 243
2 Peter–Jude: 4
8:20–22
Matthew 8–15: 54
8:20–23
1 Timothy: 256
8:21–22
Hebrews: 262
8:21–23
Acts 1–12: 74
Philippians: 213
8:22
Acts 1–12: 73
Revelation 1–11: 139
8:23
Ephesians: 190
8:25
Acts 1–12: 48, 312
1 & 2 Thessalonians: 294
8:26
Matthew 8–15: 79
Revelation 12–22: 84
8:26–29
1 & 2 Thessalonians: 195
8:26–35
Luke 18–24: 442
8:26–38
2 Timothy: 185
James: 101
8:26–39
Matthew 8–15: 389
Romans 1–8: 81
2 Timothy: 141
8:26–40
Acts 1–12: 183, 290
8:26ff.
Acts 1–12: 2
Acts 13–28: 239
8:27
2 Corinthians: 312
8:29
Acts 1–12: 2
8:30–31
2 Corinthians: 91
8:32
Revelation 1–11: 168
8:32–34
Matthew 24–28: 131
8:33
James: 271
8:34–39
Acts 1–12: 75
8:35
John 1–11: 240
Acts 1–12: 48
Colossians and Philemon: 44
Revelation 1–11: 291
8:37
Philippians: 31
James: 171
8:38
Matthew 24–28: 344
8:39
1 & 2 Thessalonians: 135
8:40
John 1–11: 240
Acts 1–12: 48, 232, 312
Acts 13–28: 239
Revelation 1–11: 291
9:1
Mark 1–8: 150
John 1–11: 230, 357
Acts 13–28: 334
Romans 9–16: 7
1 Corinthians: 2
1 Timothy: 29
9:1–2
Matthew 8–15: 206
Matthew 16–23: 391
Acts 13–28: 333
Romans 9–16: 8, 98
Galatians: 26
Philippians: 232
Colossians and Philemon: 71
1 Timothy: 3
2 Timothy: 131
1 Peter: 2
9:1–6
1 Corinthians: 97
Philippians: 65
9:1–8
1 Corinthians: 405
Ephesians: xii
9:1–9
John 12–21: 376
Philippians: 226

9:1–16
Galatians: 24
9:1–18
Romans 1–8: 368
1 & 2 Thessalonians: 39
1 Timothy: 3
9:1–19
2 Corinthians: 150
1 & 2 Thessalonians: 60
9:1ff.
Acts 1–12: 231
Acts 13–28: 107, 257, 266
9:2
John 12–21: 103
Acts 13–28: 173, 183, 217, 265, 307
Romans 1–8: 185
2 Corinthians: 80
1 Peter: 256
2 Peter–Jude: 77
9:2, 20
Luke 1–5: 267
9:3
Matthew 1–7: 29
Luke 1–5: 160
1–3 John: 23
9:3–6
1 Corinthians: 3, 209
Galatians: 29
9:3–12
2 Corinthians: 395
9:3–18
1 Peter: 2
9:4
Matthew 16–23: 31, 103, 400
Mark 9–16: 43
Luke 1–5: 157
Luke 11–17: 239
Galatians: 211
Revelation 1–11: 158
9:4–5
1 Corinthians: 201
1 Timothy: 29
9:4, 8
Matthew 8–15: 37
9:5
Galatians: 27, 209
9:7
Acts 13–28: 267
9:10
Acts 1–12: 312
9:11
John 12–21: 235
1 & 2 Thessalonians: 86
9:11–12
Acts 13–28: 267
9:12
Acts 13–28: 150
9:13
John 12–21: 156
Philippians: 15
1 Timothy: 29
1 Peter: 256
Revelation 1–11: 320
9:13–14
Acts 13–28: 268
9:14
Luke 18–24: 445
9:15
Matthew 1–7: 113
Acts 13–28: 267, 268, 270
Romans 1–8: 26, 46
Romans 9–16: 10, 78
1 Corinthians: 80, 200, 209
2 Corinthians: 307, 410
Ephesians: xii, 88
Philippians: 67
1 & 2 Thessalonians: 39, 107
1 Timothy: 4
2 Timothy: 25
9:15–16
Acts 13–28: 56
2 Corinthians: 387
Philippians: 96
9:15–18
1 & 2 Thessalonians: 89
9:16
Luke 6–10: 98
John 12–21: 174, 192
Acts 1–12: 230
Acts 13–28: 212
Romans 9–16: 341
1 & 2 Thessalonians: 79
1 Peter: 2, 7
9:17
Acts 1–12: 41, 42, 267
Acts 13–28: 7, 267
1 Corinthians: 3
Ephesians: 251
1 Timothy: 224
9:18
Matthew 24–28: 344
9:19
John 1–11: 230, 357
9:19–22
James: 150
9:20
Matthew 8–15: 104, 187
Mark 1–8: 61
Luke 1–5: 195
Acts 1–12: 48
Acts 13–28: 15, 212
Romans 9–16: 3, 58
2 Corinthians: 150, 390
1 & 2 Thessalonians: 61
9:20–22
Acts 13–28: 337
9:20–23
Acts 13–28: 31
Revelation 1–11: 72
9:20–25
John 12–21: 166
Acts 13–28: 269
Philippians: 2
1 Peter: 2
9:20, 23, 30
Romans 9–16: 353
9:21
Acts 13–28: 314
Philippians: 232
9:22
Acts 1–12: 2
Acts 13–28: 163, 314
2 Corinthians: 150
1 & 2 Thessalonians: 61, 318
9:22–23
Acts 1–12: 171
9:22–24
Luke 6–10: 54
9:22–25
Philippians: 300
1 Timothy: 3
9:23
Acts 13–28: 212, 277, 293, 314, 319
2 Corinthians: 22, 388
2 Timothy: 131
9:23–24
Luke 18–24: 209
1 Corinthians: 479
2 Corinthians: 143, 393
9:23–25
2 Corinthians: 150
Galatians: 31
1 & 2 Thessalonians: 82, 293
9:24
Acts 13–28: 314
2 Corinthians: 231
9:25
Matthew 8–15: 480
Acts 13–28: 187
2 Corinthians: 392, 393
9:26
John 1–11: 230
Acts 1–12: 230
1 Corinthians: 3
2 Corinthians: 393
Galatians: 31
1 Timothy: 29
9:26–27
Acts 1–12: 150
9:26–29
Acts 13–28: 337
9:27
Acts 1–12: 104, 267, 314
Acts 13–28: 4, 267
Romans 9–16: 329
Galatians: 52
9:27–28
John 1–11: 302
Acts 13–28: 46
9:28–29
Acts 13–28: 270
2 Corinthians: 143
9:29
Acts 13–28: 293
2 Corinthians: 231, 388, 390
Philippians: 230
9:30
Acts 1–12: 314
Acts 13–28: 72, 187, 270
2 Corinthians: 395
1 Peter: 255–56
9:31
Matthew 8–15: 56
John 12–21: 97
Acts 1–12: 130, 159, 313
Acts 13–28: 85

2 Corinthians: 23, 257
Philippians: 160
Colossians and Philemon: 22
1 & 2 Thessalonians: 166
1 Timothy: 223
9:32
Acts 1–12: 232
Philippians: 15
9:32–35
Acts 1–12: 86
9:33–34
Luke 1–5: 294
9:33–36
Acts 1–12: 97
9:34
Luke 1–5: 294
9:34–41
2 Corinthians: 413
9:35
Acts 1–12: 114, 313
Acts 13–28: 337
1 & 2 Thessalonians: 27
James: 289
9:35–36
Acts 1–12: 312
9:36
John 1–11: 230
Acts 1–12: 97
1 Timothy: 209
9:36–41
1 Timothy: 195
9:36–42
Acts 13–28: 53
9:37
Philippians: 205
James: 276
9:38
John 1–11: 230, 357
9:39
James: 242
9:40
Matthew 8–15: 85
1 & 2 Thessalonians: 86
9:40–41
Luke 18–24: 397
9:40–42
Acts 1–12: 86
9:41
Revelation 12–22: 238
9:42
Acts 1–12: 303, 313
9:43
Luke 6–10: 25
1 Peter: 4
2 Peter–Jude: 2, 18
1–3 John: 243
10
Matthew 8–15: 142, 188, 389
Acts 13–28: 156, 165
Romans 9–16: 209, 247
Galatians: 58
Ephesians: 70, 91
10:1–2
Matthew 1–7: 28
Acts 1–12: 254
2 Corinthians: 312
10:1–33
Matthew 8–15: 460
10:1–34
Matthew 8–15: 477
10:1–35
Matthew 1–7: 67
10:1–48
Matthew 24–28: 342
Luke 6–10: 31
Acts 1–12: 253, 310
2 Peter–Jude: 21–22
10:1–11:18
1 Peter: 5
2 Peter–Jude: 4
10:1ff.
Acts 13–28: 346
10:2
Matthew 8–15: 12
Matthew 16–23: 380
Acts 13–28: 93
Romans 1–8: 82, 192
Ephesians: 379
10:2, 7
Matthew 16–23: 380
10:7
Philippians: 203
10:9
1 & 2 Thessalonians: 86, 186
10:9–15
1 Timothy: 154
10:9–16
Luke 18–24: 445
Acts 13–28: 71, 157
Ephesians: 68
Colossians and Philemon: 118
10:9–48
Galatians: 40
10:9ff.
Revelation 1–11: 41
10:10
Acts 13–28: 270
10:10–16, 28
1 Corinthians: 195
10:10–17
Titus: 66
10:12–13, 15
Romans 9–16: 291–92
10:13–15
Acts 13–28: 65
10:14
Matthew 8–15: 463
10:15
Mark 1–8: 357
Hebrews: 438
10:15–16, 28
Romans 9–16: 278
10:19–20
Matthew 8–15: 239
10:20–48
Titus: 67
10:22
Matthew 16–23: 380
Luke 1–5: 176
Luke 6–10: 57
John 12–21: 24–25
Philippians: 310
James: 167, 250
10:23
1 Corinthians: 486
10:24ff.
Acts 1–12: 312
10:25
Matthew 1–7: 35
10:25–26
Luke 18–24: 157
John 1–11: 15
Acts 1–12: 281
Romans 9–16: 126
10:27–48
1 Corinthians: 486
10:28
Mark 1–8: 387
Luke 1–5: 143, 181
John 12–21: 21
Ephesians: 69
10:28, 34
Romans 9–16: 292
10:30
James: 103
Revelation 12–22: 203
10:32
Luke 6–10: 27
10:34
Matthew 8–15: 84
Romans 1–8: 136
Galatians: 50
Philippians: 315
James: 98
1 Peter: 7
10:34–35
Matthew 16–23: 116
Romans 9–16: 321
10:34–48
Luke 1–5: 15
Luke 6–10: 311
Acts 1–12: 75
10:35
Matthew 16–23: 380
Galatians: 100
James: 95
10:36
Matthew 1–7: 215
Mark 1–8: 369
Luke 1–5: 157, 161
Ephesians: 80
Philippians: 147
1 & 2 Thessalonians: 204, 314
10:37–38
Luke 1–5: 248
10:37–43
1 Timothy: 138
10:38
Matthew 8–15: 298, 313
Mark 1–8: 35, 183, 416
Luke 1–5: 265, 269
Luke 18–24: 60
Acts 1–12: 59
Romans 1–8: 427
2 Corinthians: 45, 415
Philippians: 156
Hebrews: 35
Revelation 12–22: 16

10:38–39
John 1–11: 34
1 Peter: 106
10:38–40
Luke 18–24: 407
10:39
2 Corinthians: 411
1 & 2 Thessalonians: 64
1 Peter: 7
10:39–40
Acts 1–12: 65, 134
10:39–42
Acts 1–12: 26
10:40
Matthew 24–28: 305
Luke 18–24: 436
Acts 1–12: 34, 59, 147
Acts 13–28: 24
2 Corinthians: 147
10:40–41
2 Corinthians: 411
10:41
2 Corinthians: 410
Revelation 12–22: 287
10:42
Mark 9–16: 354
Acts 1–12: 48
Acts 13–28: 195
2 Corinthians: 177, 413
Philippians: 142
James: 257
1 Peter: 7
Revelation 1–11: 195
Revelation 12–22: 113, 215, 249
10:42–43
Luke 1–5: 120
10:43
Matthew 8–15: 274
Mark 1–8: 102–3, 124
Mark 9–16: 148
Luke 1–5: 86, 321
Luke 6–10: 85, 186
Luke 18–24: 444
Acts 1–12: 75, 104, 117
Acts 13–28: 67, 108, 336
2 Corinthians: 52
Colossians and Philemon: 110
1 & 2 Thessalonians: 287
1–3 John: 73
Revelation 1–11: 54
10:44
Matthew 1–7: 71
Acts 13–28: 109
Romans 1–8: 82
1 & 2 Thessalonians: 185
10:44–45
Acts 13–28: 67
1 Corinthians: 313
Galatians: 67
10:44–46
Acts 1–12: 142, 273
1 Corinthians: 383
10:44–47
Acts 1–12: 42
10:44–48
Matthew 1–7: 71
Luke 6–10: 124
Acts 1–12: 17, 74
Acts 13–28: 66, 269
10:45
Acts 1–12: 310
Philippians: 218
10:46
Acts 1–12: 104
10:47
Acts 1–12: 75
Acts 13–28: 269
10:48
Matthew 24–28: 344
Acts 1–12: 308
Romans 1–8: 82
11
Acts 13–28: 156
11:1–2
Philippians: 26–27
11:1–3
Luke 18–24: 445
2 Corinthians: 318
11:1–18
Mark 1–8: 362
11:2
John 1–11: 439
Acts 1–12: 230
Philippians: 218
11:2–3
Acts 1–12: 299
Acts 13–28: 157
2 Corinthians: 87
11:3
Luke 1–5: 143, 181
John 12–21: 21
Philippians: 218
11:4
Acts 13–28: 248
11:4–17
2 Peter–Jude: 21–22
11:4–18
2 Corinthians: 318
11:5
Luke 11–17: 2
Acts 13–28: 270
11:12
Acts 1–12: 298
11:14
John 1–11: 168
Acts 1–12: 301, 304
Acts 13–28: 109
James: 290
11:15
Acts 13–28: 166
11:15–17
Acts 1–12: 41
1 Corinthians: 313
2 Peter–Jude: 20
11:15–18
1 Peter: 21
11:16
Matthew 1–7: 71
John 1–11: 168
1 & 2 Thessalonians: 294
11:17
Acts 1–12: 303, 304
Acts 13–28: 108, 164, 166
Titus: 67
11:17–18
Acts 13–28: 67, 166
Hebrews: 139
11:18
Matthew 1–7: 67
Mark 1–8: 21
Luke 1–5: 208, 218
Luke 6–10: 272
Acts 1–12: 73, 301
Acts 13–28: 249, 375
2 Corinthians: 131, 266
Philippians: 27, 223
Colossians and Philemon: 16, 23
1 & 2 Thessalonians: 287
1–3 John: 36, 53
Revelation 1–11: 139, 140
11:19
Acts 13–28: 237, 239
Romans 1–8: 134
James: 73, 252
1 Peter: 2
11:19–20
Acts 1–12: 231
Acts 13–28: 2
11:19–21
Acts 13–28: 101
11:20
Luke 1–5: 157
Luke 18–24: 369
John 1–11: 240
Acts 1–12: 48
11:20–26
Galatians: 32
11:21
Matthew 16–23: 98
Acts 1–12: 114, 159, 282, 285
Acts 13–28: 2, 108, 337
1 & 2 Thessalonians: 27
11:21–23
Revelation 12–22: 194
11:21–28
1 Corinthians: 323
Ephesians: 141
11:22
Acts 1–12: 230
Acts 13–28: 4
11:22–24
Acts 1–12: 150
11:22,24
Ephesians: 251
11:23
Philippians: 266
Revelation 12–22: 100
11:24
Luke 1–5: 254
Acts 1–12: 151, 159, 182, 313
Acts 13–28: 2, 7
11:25–26
Acts 1–12: 278
Acts 13–28: 4
2 Corinthians: 389

11:26
Luke 11–17: 279
John 1–11: 230, 357
Acts 13–28: 2
Romans 9–16: 19, 256
2 Corinthians: 124
1 Peter: 256
11:27–28
Romans 9–16: 171
11:27–29
2 Corinthians: 275
11:27–30
Acts 13–28: 2
Galatians: 34
1 & 2 Thessalonians: 196, 213
11:28
Acts 13–28: 3, 199, 240–41
1 Corinthians: 322
Ephesians: 140
11:29
John 1–11: 230
1 Corinthians: 480
11:29–30
Acts 1–12: 183
1 Corinthians: 451
Galatians: 43
Ephesians: 146
James: 102
11:30
Acts 1–12: 150, 328
Acts 13–28: 4, 248
Philippians: 15
1 Timothy: 125
12
Acts 13–28: 31
12:1
Luke 1–5: 230
12:1–2
Luke 1–5: 225
Luke 6–10: 43
Luke 11–17: 107
12:1–3
Matthew 8–15: 150, 206
Acts 13–28: 277
Revelation 1–11: 72
12:1–4
Mark 1–8: 300
1 & 2 Thessalonians: 60, 295
1 Peter: 198
12:1–11
1 Peter: 2
12:1–19
Luke 11–17: 195
12:1–23
Acts 13–28: 327
12:2
Matthew 16–23: 64, 238, 391
Mark 9–16: 107
John 1–11: 6
Acts 13–28: 248
Ephesians: 368
James: 3
12:3–11
Luke 18–24: 296
John 12–21: 166
Acts 1–12: 166
12:5
Luke 11–17: 29
Luke 18–24: 3
John 12–21: 272
Acts 13–28: 229
1 Peter: 90
Revelation 1–11: 125
12:6
Acts 13–28: 217, 261
Philippians: 203
1 & 2 Thessalonians: 125
12:6–11
Acts 13–28: 104
2 Corinthians: 418
12:7
Romans 9–16: 377
2 Timothy: 175
12:7–11
Acts 13–28: 277
1 Peter: 57
Revelation 12–22: 84, 296
12:7ff.
Acts 13–28: 107
12:9
Luke 18–24: 435
12:10
1 Timothy: 147
12:11–16
1 & 2 Thessalonians: 187
12:12
Matthew 8–15: 60
Mark 1–8: 1, 2
Acts 1–12: 28, 149, 151
Acts 13–28: 7, 229
1 Corinthians: 260
1 Peter: 290
12:12–15
Matthew 16–23: 118
Ephesians: 379
12:12–16
Luke 1–5: 28
Luke 18–24: 436
12:17
Luke 18–24: 192
Acts 1–12: 29
Acts 13–28: 17, 70, 248, 264, 277
Titus: 163
James: 3, 11
1 Peter: 255
12:19
Luke 18–24: 367
Acts 13–28: 107, 355
1 Corinthians: 283
12:21
2 Corinthians: 177
12:21–23
Luke 11–17: 186
12:22
Acts 13–28: 52
1–3 John: 255
12:22–23
Romans 1–8: 85
Romans 9–16: 125
12:23
Ephesians: 54
12:24
Acts 1–12: 130
Acts 13–28: 178
12:24–25
Galatians: 34
12:25
Mark 1–8: 1
Acts 1–12: 316
Acts 13–28: 7
1 Peter: 290
13:1
Luke 1–5: 176
Luke 18–24: 369
Acts 1–12: 150
Acts 13–28: 15
1 Corinthians: 323, 324, 332
2 Corinthians: 473
Ephesians: xii, 141, 146
Titus: 27
13:1–3
Acts 13–28: 44
Romans 9–16: 378
2 Corinthians: 395
Galatians: 3
1 & 2 Thessalonians: 167, 173, 202
1 Peter: 51
13:1–4
1 & 2 Thessalonians: 89
13:1ff.
Acts 1–12: 316
1 Timothy: 3
13:2
Matthew 8–15: 120
Acts 1–12: 2
Acts 13–28: 2, 229
Romans 1–8: 8
2 Corinthians: 229
Galatians: 35
Ephesians: 189, 285
Philippians: 67
1 Timothy: 100, 180
Titus: 34
13:2, 3
Titus: 22
13:2–3
Matthew 1–7: 403
Mark 1–8: 130
Luke 1–5: 341
Romans 9–16: 334, 344
13:2–3, 14
Romans 9–16: 355
13:2–4
Acts 13–28: 56
1 & 2 Thessalonians: 166
13:2ff.
Acts 1–12: 150
13:3
Luke 1–5: 185
Acts 1–12: 184
1 Timothy: 224
13:4
Acts 13–28: 2
2 Corinthians: 389
13:4–5
1 Peter: 290

13:4–12
Romans 9–16: 209
13:5
Matthew 8–15: 104, 187
Mark 1–8: 1, 61
Acts 1–12: 48, 328
Acts 13–28: 195
Colossians and Philemon: 195
1 & 2 Thessalonians: 294
James: 147
13:5, 14
Romans 9–16: 3
13:6
Acts 1–12: 232, 241
Acts 13–28: 176, 212, 319
Revelation 1–11: 72
13:6–8
Acts 13–28: 31, 277
2 Corinthians: 390
13:6–10
James: 195
13:6–12
1 Corinthians: 302
Revelation 12–22: 56
13:6ff.
Acts 13–28: 96, 117
13:7
James: 101
13:7–10
Galatians: 10
13:8
1 & 2 Thessalonians: 71
1–3 John: 15
13:8–11
Luke 18–24: 397
Philippians: 256
13:9
Acts 1–12: 41, 42, 133, 142
Acts 13–28: 2
2 Corinthians: 229
Ephesians: xii, 251
1 Timothy: 3
13:9–11
1 & 2 Thessalonians: 168
13:10
Philippians: 184
Revelation 12–22: 16
13:11
2 Corinthians: 453
13:12
Acts 13–28: 108
James: 101
13:13
Acts 1–12: 328
Acts 13–28: 194
2 Corinthians: 389
Colossians and Philemon: 195, 230
2 Timothy: 209
1 Peter: 290
13:14
Acts 1–12: 272
Acts 13–28: 56
Romans 9–16: 58
1 Corinthians: 453
2 Corinthians: 389, 390
13:14–15
Luke 1–5: 267
James: 147
13:14–14:23
Galatians: xi
13:14ff.
Acts 1–12: 2
13:15
Acts 13–28: 372
Hebrews: 453
13:15ff.
Acts 13–28: 95
Revelation 1–11: 291
13:16
Acts 13–28: 264
13:16–41
Acts 13–28: 149
13:16ff.
Acts 13–28: 120, 372
13:21
Philippians: 230
13:22
2 Corinthians: 12
Colossians and Philemon: 41
1 Timothy: 124
Titus: 29
Hebrews: 366
Revelation 12–22: 68–69
13:22–23
Luke 1–5: 35, 174
13:22, 36
Romans 9–16: 355
13:23
Luke 1–5: 153
13:23–33
Acts 13–28: 333
13:25
2 Timothy: 194
13:26
2 Corinthians: 206
Philippians: 187
13:26–29
1–3 John: 190
13:27
John 12–21: 335
Acts 1–12: 111
2 Corinthians: 111, 147
13:27–28
Luke 1–5: 50
13:27–29
Mark 9–16: 164
John 1–11: 34
Acts 1–12: 62
13:27–30
Luke 18–24: 407
Acts 1–12: 65, 134
13:30
Acts 1–12: 34, 59, 147
2 Corinthians: 147, 455
13:30–37
Acts 13–28: 338
13:30, 37
Matthew 24–28: 305
13:31
John 12–21: 182
13:32
Luke 1–5: 157
Acts 1–12: 48
Acts 13–28: 195
2 Peter–Jude: 10
13:32–33
Romans 9–16: 75
13:32–34
Romans 9–16: 15
13:32–35
2 Timothy: 144
13:33
Acts 1–12: 34, 59, 147
2 Corinthians: 147, 455
Hebrews: 29
James: 276
13:33–35
1 & 2 Thessalonians: 28
13:33–39
Philippians: 140
13:34
Acts 1–12: 34, 59, 147
Titus: 30
13:35
Philippians: 311
13:36
1 & 2 Thessalonians: 125
13:37
Acts 1–12: 34, 59, 147
2 Corinthians: 455
13:38
Luke 1–5: 321
Acts 1–12: 75
Acts 13–28: 336
2 Corinthians: 133
Hebrews: 75
13:38–39
Mark 1–8: 97
Acts 1–12: 303
Acts 13–28: 68, 108
Romans 1–8: 406
Romans 9–16: 8
Ephesians: 22
Colossians and Philemon: 110–11
2 Peter–Jude: 23
1–3 John: 30
13:39
Acts 1–12: 303
Acts 13–28: 336
Romans 1–8: 207
Galatians: 65
Philippians: 237
Hebrews: 74
2 Peter–Jude: 20
1–3 John: 36
Revelation 12–22: 49
13:40–50
1 & 2 Thessalonians: 61
13:41
Luke 1–5: 163
13:42
Acts 13–28: 55
13:43
Acts 1–12: 314
Philippians: 163

1 & 2 Thessalonians: 207
1 Timothy: 181
13:43–45
Titus: 101
13:44
1 & 2 Thessalonians: 57, 294
13:44–49
1 & 2 Thessalonians: 294
13:44–52
Acts 13–28: 180
13:45
Matthew 16–23: 391
Acts 13–28: 117, 212, 277, 319
2 Corinthians: 150, 228, 390
2 Timothy: 131
Revelation 1–11: 72
13:45, 50
Galatians: 115
13:46
John 12–21: 20
Acts 13–28: 46
Romans 9–16: 86, 329
1 Corinthians: 56
1 & 2 Thessalonians: 245, 294
13:46–47
Acts 13–28: 375
Romans 9–16: 108, 388
Ephesians: 91
13:46–48
1 & 2 Thessalonians: 20
Titus: 6
13:46–49
1 Peter: 18
13:47
Matthew 8–15: 187
Acts 13–28: 336
Romans 9–16: 323
1 & 2 Thessalonians: 164
13:48
John 12–21: 162, 258
Acts 1–12: 252, 293
Acts 13–28: 94, 108, 151
1 Corinthians: 479
Galatians: 116
Ephesians: 12
Philippians: 27
1 & 2 Thessalonians: 193, 245, 294
1 Peter: 124
1–3 John: 171
13:48–49
Matthew 16–23: 31
13:49
1 & 2 Thessalonians: 294
13:50
Matthew 16–23: 380, 391
Acts 13–28: 44, 73, 117
Romans 9–16: 353
2 Corinthians: 150, 159, 284, 393
1 & 2 Thessalonians: 213, 293
1 Peter: 198
13:50–51
Mark 1–8: 293
Luke 6–10: 246
13:51
Matthew 8–15: 196
Acts 1–12: 291
Acts 13–28: 149
13:52
John 1–11: 230, 357
Acts 1–12: 259
Ephesians: 251
14:1
Acts 1–12: 272, 313
Acts 13–28: 108
Romans 9–16: 3, 58
James: 147
14:1–7
1 & 2 Thessalonians: 61
14:1–13
1 Peter: 15
14:1–20
1 & 2 Thessalonians: 82
14:2
Acts 13–28: 31, 117, 212, 277, 319
Romans 9–16: 353
2 Corinthians: 390, 393
Revelation 1–11: 72
14:3
John 1–11: 302
Acts 1–12: 233
Romans 9–16: 329
1 Corinthians: 302
2 Corinthians: 150, 416
Hebrews: 50
14:3–5
2 Corinthians: 388
14:4
Acts 13–28: 373
1 Corinthians: 323
2 Corinthians: 409
14:4–6
2 Corinthians: 151
1 & 2 Thessalonians: 293, 295
14:5–6
John 12–21: 166
Acts 13–28: 117
2 Corinthians: 143
Philippians: 2
1 Peter: 2–3
14:6–23
Philippians: 195
1 Timothy: 7
14:6ff.
Acts 13–28: 83, 362
14:7
John 1–11: 240
Acts 1–12: 48
Acts 13–28: 195
14:7, 15, 21
Luke 1–5: 157–58
14:8
Luke 1–5: 294
14:8–10
Acts 13–28: 83
2 Corinthians: 413
Philippians: 38
14:8–10, 19
2 Timothy: 132
14:8–18
1 Corinthians: 108
14:8–19
Acts 13–28: 180
14:9
Acts 1–12: 110
14:11
Luke 18–24: 362
14:11–12, 14–15
Romans 9–16: 126
14:11–13
Matthew 1–7: 35
14:11–15
Acts 1–12: 298
14:11–18
Acts 13–28: 83
14:12
2 Corinthians: 86
14:14
Romans 1–8: 22
Philippians: 204
1 Timothy: 4
14:14–17
Revelation 12–22: 89
14:15
Luke 6–10: 201
John 1–11: 240
Acts 1–12: 48, 114, 282
Acts 13–28: 195, 337
James: 289
Revelation 1–11: 51, 285
14:15–17
Romans 1–8: 78
1–3 John: 226
14:16
Romans 1–8: 99
1 & 2 Thessalonians: 285
Revelation 12–22: 175
14:16–17
John 12–21: 47
14:17
Romans 1–8: 79
2 Corinthians: 204
1 Timothy: 168
14:19
Acts 13–28: 31, 83, 117, 212, 277, 319
Romans 9–16: 353
2 Corinthians: 22, 143, 228, 231, 389–90
Galatians: 22, 115, 116, 210
Philippians: 301
Revelation 1–11: 72
14:19–20
Acts 1–12: 230
Acts 13–28: 73
2 Corinthians: 151
1 & 2 Thessalonians: 61
1 Peter: 3
14:19–22
1 Peter: 257
14:20–22
John 1–11: 357
14:21
John 1–11: 240
Acts 1–12: 48, 313

Acts 13–28: 195
14:21–22
Romans 9–16: 174
Philippians: 81
1 & 2 Thessalonians: 79
14:21–23
Titus: 21
14:22
Mark 9–16: 8, 86
John 12–21: 171, 193
Acts 1–12: 314
Acts 13–28: 211
Romans 1–8: 134
2 Corinthians: 120, 149, 227
Ephesians: 148
Philippians: 163, 245, 252, 265, 266
Colossians and Philemon: 185
1 & 2 Thessalonians: 89, 166, 207, 229, 248
1 Timothy: 181, 265
James: 252
1 Peter: 42
1–3 John: 15
Revelation 1–11: 68
Revelation 12–22: 100
14:23
Matthew 1–7: 403
Mark 1–8: 130
Luke 1–5: 185, 341
Acts 1–12: 182, 303
Acts 13–28: 5, 221, 229, 248
Ephesians: 1, 147
Philippians: 15
1 & 2 Thessalonians: 167
1 Timothy: xii, 93, 100, 125, 224
Titus: 22
Hebrews: 444
14:24
Acts 1–12: 232
14:24–27
Luke 1–5: 15
14:25
Acts 13–28: 16
14:25–26
2 Corinthians: 389
14:26–15:4
Galatians: 32
14:27
Acts 13–28: 63, 248, 375
Romans 9–16: 334
1 Corinthians: 465
2 Corinthians: 67
Colossians and Philemon: 183
1 Peter: 89
14:28
John 1–11: 357
15
Luke 1–5: 134
Acts 1–12: 150
Acts 13–28: 156, 202, 250
1 Corinthians: 403
Galatians: 35
Ephesians: 70
James: 5, 11
15:1
Mark 1–8: 110
Acts 13–28: 250
1 Corinthians: 188
Philippians: 218, 228
15:1–2
Romans 1–8: 313
Galatians: 35
15:1–6
Romans 9–16: 129
15:1–11
Mark 9–16: 238
15:1–21
Luke 18–24: 445
15:1–29
Romans 1–8: 503
15:1, 5
Galatians: 133
15:2
John 1–11: 439
Acts 13–28: 248
1 Corinthians: 29
Philippians: 15
1 Timothy: 93, 125
15:2, 4, 6, 22, 23
Ephesians: 146
15:2ff.
1 & 2 Thessalonians: 167
15:3
Acts 1–12: 232
Romans 9–16: 344
2 Corinthians: 484
Philippians: 317
1 & 2 Thessalonians: 185
15:4
Acts 1–12: 230
Acts 13–28: 248
Philippians: 15
1 Timothy: 93, 125
15:5
Matthew 8–15: 186
Mark 1–8: 100, 110
Mark 9–16: 199
Luke 6–10: 11
Acts 1–12: 310
Acts 13–28: 284
Romans 1–8: 249, 313
Romans 9–16: 275, 296
15:5–11
2 Peter–Jude: 22
15:5, 10–11
Titus: 163
15:5, 10, 12–20, 22–23
Titus: 59
15:6
Acts 13–28: 248
Philippians: 15
1 Timothy: 93, 125
15:6–21
2 Peter–Jude: 135
15:6–30
1 Corinthians: 29
15:7
2 Corinthians: 206
Ephesians: 88
15:7–8
Acts 1–12: 306
Galatians: 67
15:7–9
1 Peter: 21
15:7–12
1 Peter: 5
2 Peter–Jude: 4
15:8
1 & 2 Thessalonians: 118
15:8–9
Mark 1–8: 359
Acts 1–12: 42
15:8–11
Galatians: 50
15:9
John 12–21: 84
Acts 1–12: 303
Acts 13–28: 336
2 Corinthians: 257
15:9–11
Romans 1–8: 313–14
15:10
Matthew 8–15: 275
Mark 1–8: 140
Mark 9–16: 199
Luke 1–5: 206, 273, 319
Luke 6–10: 4
Luke 11–17: 104
John 1–11: 230, 357
Acts 13–28: 26, 65
Romans 1–8: 366
Romans 9–16: 308
2 Corinthians: 94
Philippians: 237
15:10–11
Galatians: 56
15:11
Acts 13–28: 108
Philippians: 23
1 & 2 Thessalonians: 320
1 Peter: 220
15:12
Luke 1–5: 294
Acts 1–12: 190, 233
Acts 13–28: 248
Romans 9–16: 334
2 Corinthians: 416
Galatians: 36
15:12–18
Romans 9–16: 129
15:12–19
Luke 1–5: 15
15:12–29
Romans 1–8: 314
15:13
Mark 1–8: 277
1 Peter: 255
15:13–17
Galatians: 75
15:13–18
Luke 1–5: 134
15:13–21
1 Corinthians: 404
15:13–22
Matthew 8–15: 338

15:13–35
Mark 1–8: 179
15:13ff.
Acts 1–12: 29
15:14
Luke 1–5: 176
James: 3, 89
1 Peter: 8, 17
2 Peter–Jude: 4
15:14–15
James: 64
15:14–18
Acts 13–28: 375
Ephesians: 138
15:16–17
Romans 1–8: 184
15:19
Matthew 16–23: 98
Acts 1–12: 114, 282
Acts 13–28: 337
1 Corinthians: 188
Galatians: 50
James: 3
15:19–29
Romans 1–8: 248
15:20
1 Corinthians: 188
1 & 2 Thessalonians: 104, 105
15:21
2 Corinthians: 111
1 Timothy: 176
15:22
Acts 13–28: 248
2 Corinthians: 43
Ephesians: 148
1 & 2 Thessalonians: 222
15:22–23
1 Timothy: 93, 125
15:22–24
Galatians: 41
15:22–29
1 & 2 Thessalonians: 167
15:22ff.
1 Timothy: 98
15:23
Acts 1–12: 278
Acts 13–28: 248
Philippians: 15
James: 3
15:23–29
1 & 2 Thessalonians: 196
15:24
2 Corinthians: 80, 337, 348
Galatians: 16, 37
Titus: 161
James: 3
15:25
James: 3
15:26
Acts 1–12: 104
15:27
1 & 2 Thessalonians: 222
15:28
Acts 1–12: 2
2 Corinthians: 348
15:28–29
Colossians and Philemon: 118
Revelation 1–11: 94
15:29
Romans 9–16: 296
1 Corinthians: 188
1 & 2 Thessalonians: 104
Revelation 1–11: 89
15:31
1 Corinthians: 29
15:32
Acts 13–28: 55, 83, 241
Romans 9–16: 171
1 & 2 Thessalonians: 79, 222
15:35
Luke 1–5: 158
John 1–11: 240
Acts 1–12: 48
Acts 13–28: 4, 195
Romans 9–16: 173
15:35–36
Acts 13–28: 160
1 & 2 Thessalonians: 294
15:36
1 Corinthians: 462
15:36–39
Colossians and Philemon: 230
2 Timothy: 209
15:36–40
Acts 1–12: 328
Acts 13–28: 10
15:36–41
Acts 1–12: 150
1 Peter: 290
15:37
Mark 1–8: 1
15:37–39
Acts 13–28: 237, 254
1 Corinthians: 468
Colossians and Philemon: 195
15:37–40
Galatians: 52
15:38
Acts 13–28: 10
Romans 9–16: 364
15:39
Mark 1–8: 1
Acts 13–28: 130
Romans 9–16: 364
15:39–40
2 Corinthians: 43–44
15:39–41
Mark 1–8: 1
15:40
Acts 13–28: 72
1 & 2 Thessalonians: 13, 223
1 Peter: 289
2 Peter–Jude: 135
15:41
Acts 1–12: 232
Acts 13–28: 55, 145
1 & 2 Thessalonians: 79
16:1
Acts 13–28: 48, 54, 201
2 Corinthians: 17, 44
1 & 2 Thessalonians: 223
1 Timothy: 6
16:1–3
Acts 13–28: 251
Romans 1–8: 166
Galatians: 38, 133, 141
1 & 2 Thessalonians: 13, 78, 222, 223
1 Timothy: 180
2 Timothy: 41
16:1–5
Galatians: xii
1 & 2 Thessalonians: 167
1 Peter: 15
16:2
Philippians: 197
1 Timothy: 8
2 Timothy: 8
16:3
Romans 1–8: 252
Philippians: 196
1 Timothy: 9
2 Timothy: 8
16:4
Acts 13–28: 72, 83, 248
1 Corinthians: 323
Ephesians: 146
1 Timothy: 125
16:5
Acts 1–12: 130, 313
1–3 John: 15
16:6
Acts 1–12: 232
16:6–7
Acts 13–28: 237
1 Corinthians: 463
2 Corinthians: 158, 229
Ephesians: 189
16:6–8
Acts 13–28: 91
16:6–10
Romans 9–16: 340
2 Corinthians: 87
1 & 2 Thessalonians: 4, 118, 293
16:7
Luke 1–5: 239
Romans 9–16: 342
1 Corinthians: 119
Titus: 2
1 Peter: 9, 16
16:7–8
Revelation 1–11: 84
16:7–10
Philippians: 19
16:8–11
2 Corinthians: 67
16:9
Acts 13–28: 91
Colossians and Philemon: 183
16:9–10
Acts 13–28: 150, 237
1 Corinthians: 463
2 Corinthians: 394
Philippians: 4
16:10
Matthew 8–15: 120

Luke 1–5: 157–58
Acts 1–12: 48
Acts 13–28: 91, 195
Colossians and Philemon: 183
16:10–17
Luke 1–5: 3
Acts 1–12: 2
16:11
Acts 13–28: 201
Romans 9–16: 378
2 Corinthians: 389
16:11–12
Acts 13–28: 201
16:11–15
1 & 2 Thessalonians: 294
16:11–17:13
1 Corinthians: 203
16:11–18:1
1 Corinthians: viii
16:12
2 Corinthians: 284
Philippians: 3, 84, 317
16:12–40
Philippians: 196
1 & 2 Thessalonians: 118
16:13
Romans 9–16: 3, 58, 332
Philippians: 3, 271, 272
1 & 2 Thessalonians: 3
16:13–15
Philippians: 4, 19
16:14
Matthew 1–7: 28
Matthew 16–23: 380
Romans 1–8: 82
2 Corinthians: 131
Philippians: 26, 158, 272
Colossians and Philemon: 23
1 & 2 Thessalonians: 193
2 Timothy: 138
James: 101
2 Peter–Jude: 29, 151
1–3 John: 149
Revelation 1–11: 97
16:14–15
Matthew 8–15: 389
2 Corinthians: 312
1–3 John: 243
16:15
John 1–11: 168
Acts 1–12: 306
Philippians: 272
Titus: 30
16:16–17
1 Corinthians: 305
Philippians: 272
16:16–18
Mark 1–8: 63, 76
Luke 1–5: 283, 287, 296
Acts 1–12: 97
2 Corinthians: 413
Philippians: 20
16:16–19
Mark 1–8: 66
16:16–24
2 Corinthians: 151
1 & 2 Thessalonians: 34, 295
16:16–34
1 & 2 Thessalonians: 82, 293
16:16–40
Acts 13–28: 116, 180
2 Corinthians: 262, 390
Philippians: 2, 97
1 Peter: 3
16:17
Mark 1–8: 244
Romans 1–8: 185, 205
2 Peter–Jude: 77
Revelation 12–22: 200, 293
16:18
Mark 9–16: 415
Acts 13–28: 171
Philippians: 272
16:18–21
1 Peter: 140
16:19
Luke 11–17: 260
Acts 13–28: 72
1 & 2 Thessalonians: 118
16:19–21
Philippians: 272
16:19–22
Luke 18–24: 209
16:19–23
Philippians: 20
16:19–34
1 & 2 Thessalonians: 223
16:20
2 Corinthians: 220
16:20–24
1 Peter: 198
16:21
Philippians: 317
16:22
2 Corinthians: 153
16:22–23
Acts 13–28: 186
2 Corinthians: 228, 389
16:22–24
Acts 13–28: 146
1 Corinthians: 56
Philippians: 272, 301
16:22–25
1 & 2 Thessalonians: 25
16:23
1 & 2 Thessalonians: 213
Revelation 12–22: 123
16:23–24
Mark 9–16: 235
2 Corinthians: 388
16:23ff.
Acts 1–12: 166
Acts 13–28: 257
16:24
2 Corinthians: 153, 228
16:24–25
Ephesians: 262
James: 22
16:25
Luke 1–5: 164
Acts 13–28: 72, 229
Romans 9–16: 212
Ephesians: 257
Philippians: 20
Colossians and Philemon: 34, 74
1 & 2 Thessalonians: 118
1 Peter: 289
Revelation 1–11: 171
16:25–26
Philippians: 65
16:25–34
Acts 1–12: 253
Philippians: 4, 272
16:26
1 & 2 Thessalonians: 269
Revelation 1–11: 204
16:26–34
Philippians: 20
16:27
Acts 1–12: 326
Acts 13–28: 53, 355
16:28–34
1 & 2 Thessalonians: 294
16:29
Acts 13–28: 72
1 & 2 Thessalonians: 118
16:30
Acts 1–12: 72
Romans 1–8: 198
16:30–32
Acts 13–28: 95
16:31
Mark 9–16: 78, 371
Luke 1–5: 328
John 1–11: 22
John 12–21: 258
Acts 1–12: 74, 303
Acts 13–28: 268, 336
2 Corinthians: 89, 217
Philippians: 24, 151
1 & 2 Thessalonians: 287
James: 203, 290
1–3 John: 41, 73, 147, 226
Revelation 12–22: 49
16:31–33
Acts 1–12: 75
16:31–34
John 1–11: 168
16:32
1 & 2 Thessalonians: 294
16:32–33
Philippians: 158
16:33
Acts 13–28: 95
Revelation 12–22: 123
16:34
1 & 2 Thessalonians: 184
1 Peter: 41
1–3 John: 243
Revelation 12–22: 194
16:35–39
Philippians: 272
16:37
Acts 13–28: 83
2 Corinthians: 389
1 & 2 Thessalonians: 222

16:37–38
Acts 1–12: 108
16:37–40
1 & 2 Thessalonians: 295
16:39–40
Acts 13–28: 145
16:40
Luke 11–17: 360
1 Corinthians: 260
Philippians: 20, 272
16–18
1 & 2 Thessalonians: 7
17:1
Acts 1–12: 272
Acts 13–28: 200
1 & 2 Thessalonians: 3
17:1–2
Luke 18–24: 9
Acts 1–12: 230
Romans 9–16: 3
17:1–4
1 Corinthians: 80
1 & 2 Thessalonians: 24, 56, 60, 295
17:1–9
Acts 13–28: 180, 319
1 & 2 Thessalonians: 223, 293
17:1–10
1 & 2 Thessalonians: 68, 82
17:1–13
Philippians: 297
17:1–15
1 & 2 Thessalonians: 78
17:2
Luke 1–5: 193
Acts 1–12: 188
Acts 13–28: 196
1 Corinthians: 453, 479
1 & 2 Thessalonians: 5
2 Timothy: 97
17:2–3
Acts 1–12: 200
1 & 2 Thessalonians: 56
Hebrews: 62
17:2–4
1 & 2 Thessalonians: 97
17:3
Mark 9–16: 12
Acts 1–12: 48
Acts 13–28: 195
1 Peter: 2
17:4
Matthew 16–23: 380
Acts 1–12: 50
Acts 13–28: 72, 145
2 Corinthians: 185, 284, 312
1 & 2 Thessalonians: 13, 57, 222, 223
James: 101
17:4–5
Acts 13–28: 373
2 Corinthians: 388
17:5
Mark 9–16: 156
Luke 18–24: 114, 209
Acts 13–28: 31
2 Corinthians: 228, 390
17:5–6
1 & 2 Thessalonians: 35
17:5–7
1–3 John: 243
17:5–8
2 Corinthians: 277, 390
1 & 2 Thessalonians: 60
17:5–9
2 Corinthians: 388
Philippians: 2
1 & 2 Thessalonians: 3, 295
1 Peter: 3, 198
17:5–10
Romans 9–16: 378
2 Corinthians: 151
Philippians: 301
1 & 2 Thessalonians: 24, 222
17:5ff.
Acts 13–28: 212, 277
Revelation 1–11: 72
17:6
Luke 1–5: 144
Luke 6–10: 24
John 12–21: 24, 120
Acts 1–12: 21, 174
2 Corinthians: 160, 220
Ephesians: 251
1 & 2 Thessalonians: 4
17:7
Mark 9–16: 129
Luke 1–5: 143
Acts 1–12: 15
Acts 13–28: 304
1 & 2 Thessalonians: 5, 35, 306
17:8
1 & 2 Thessalonians: 5
17:9
1 & 2 Thessalonians: 72
17:10
Acts 1–12: 272
Acts 13–28: 72, 145, 187
1 Corinthians: 56
1 & 2 Thessalonians: 60, 64, 223
17:10–11
Acts 13–28: 32
1 & 2 Thessalonians: 197
17:10–12
Acts 13–28: 95
Romans 9–16: 379
17:10–14
1 & 2 Thessalonians: 118
17:11
Matthew 8–15: 105, 243
Luke 6–10: 49, 144
Acts 1–12: 83
1 Corinthians: 304, 381
Philippians: 158, 206, 285
1 & 2 Thessalonians: 108, 195, 199
2 Timothy: 97, 122, 159
James: 75
1 Peter: 274
1–3 John: 154, 160
17:11–12
1 & 2 Thessalonians: 294
2 Timothy: 141
17:12
Acts 1–12: 313
Acts 13–28: 108, 145
17:13
Acts 1–12: 48
Acts 13–28: 31, 195, 212, 277, 319
2 Corinthians: 151, 390, 393
Philippians: 301
1 & 2 Thessalonians: 269
2 Timothy: 132
Revelation 1–11: 72
17:13–14
John 12–21: 166
1 Corinthians: 56
Philippians: 2
1 Peter: 3
17:13–15
1 Timothy: 6
17:14
Acts 13–28: 72, 145, 187
Philippians: 199
1 & 2 Thessalonians: 77, 118, 223, 293
17:14–15
2 Corinthians: 389
17:14–18:18
Philippians: 297
17:15
Acts 13–28: 72, 148
1 & 2 Thessalonians: 6, 77
1 Timothy: 6
Revelation 1–11: 21
17:16
2 Corinthians: 194
Philippians: 287
17:16–17
Romans 9–16: 373
17:16–34
Luke 11–17: 196
Acts 13–28: 180
Philippians: 2
1 & 2 Thessalonians: 293
17:17
Matthew 16–23: 380
Luke 1–5: 267
James: 167
17:18
Mark 9–16: 12
Luke 1–5: 158
1 Corinthians: 111
1 Peter: 3
17:18–21
1 Corinthians: 40
17:18–34
Philippians: 301
17:19–32
Acts 13–28: 145
17:21
1 Corinthians: 46
2 Timothy: 182
17:22–23
Ephesians: 74

17:22–26
Revelation 1–11: 285
17:22–31
Acts 13–28: 51
Revelation 12–22: 89
17:23
1 Corinthians: 45, 372
Philippians: 287
1 & 2 Thessalonians: 108
1–3 John: 226
17:23–28
Romans 1–8: 78
James: 207
17:24
Luke 1–5: 61
Luke 6–10: 343
Hebrews: 229
17:24–26
Romans 9–16: 220
17:24–31
Philippians: 287
17:25
Matthew 16–23: 148
2 Corinthians: 204
1 Timothy: 168
17:26
Luke 1–5: 259
Luke 11–17: 22
17:26–27
Romans 1–8: 142
17:28
Matthew 1–7: 375
John 1–11: 22
1 Timothy: 271
17:29
Acts 13–28: 53
1 Corinthians: 234
17:30
Luke 11–17: 219
John 12–21: 47
Acts 1–12: 72, 73, 115
Acts 13–28: 52, 173, 217
Philippians: 223
1 & 2 Thessalonians: 244, 297
1 Timothy: 63, 170
James: 202
1–3 John: 39
Revelation 1–11: 139
17:30–31
Luke 1–5: 322
Acts 1–12: 116, 303
Acts 13–28: 45
Romans 1–8: 218
1 & 2 Thessalonians: 65
Hebrews: 188, 278
1–3 John: 166
Revelation 1–11: 190
17:31
Mark 9–16: 396
Luke 6–10: 332
Luke 11–17: 250
Luke 18–24: 407
Acts 1–12: 53
Acts 13–28: 373
2 Corinthians: 177
1 & 2 Thessalonians: 28, 234, 302
Revelation 1–11: 195, 319
Revelation 12–22: 113, 120, 176, 215, 249
17:32
Acts 13–28: 32, 301
1 Corinthians: 40, 56, 408
2 Timothy: 80
17:34
1 Corinthians: 478
18:1
2 Corinthians: 4
1 & 2 Thessalonians: 7
18:1–3
Romans 9–16: 363
James: 101
1–3 John: 243
18:1–8
2 Corinthians: 408
18:1–10
2 Corinthians: 300
18:1–11
1 Corinthians: 201
18:1–17
2 Corinthians: 23
Titus: 147
18:2
Acts 1–12: 45
Acts 13–28: 103
2 Corinthians: 4
1 Peter: 15
18:2–3
Ephesians: 284
18:2, 4, 18–19, 24, 26
2 Timothy: 214
18:3
Matthew 16–23: 3
1 Corinthians: 204
2 Corinthians: 4, 162, 390
1 & 2 Thessalonians: 169
2 Timothy: 76
18:4
Matthew 8–15: 104, 187
Mark 1–8: 61
Acts 1–12: 50, 272
Acts 13–28: 120
2 Corinthians: 185
18:4–6
1 & 2 Thessalonians: 294
18:4–7
1 Corinthians: 80
1 & 2 Thessalonians: 5
18:4, 19
Luke 1–5: 267
2 Timothy: 97
18:5
Acts 1–12: 2
Acts 13–28: 72, 182
2 Corinthians: 4, 18, 44
Philippians: 196, 306
1 & 2 Thessalonians: 6, 7, 8, 77, 223
1 Timothy: 6
18:5–6
Acts 1–12: 230
2 Corinthians: 151
18:5–7
1 & 2 Thessalonians: 78
18:5–17
Acts 13–28: 181, 319
18:6
Matthew 1–7: 439
Acts 13–28: 31, 36, 212, 277, 375
Romans 9–16: 108, 111
2 Corinthians: 390
Revelation 1–11: 72
18:6–8
Acts 13–28: 373
18:7
Matthew 16–23: 380
Romans 9–16: 379
1–3 John: 243
18:7–8
James: 101
18:8
Matthew 24–28: 344
Luke 1–5: 267
Luke 11–17: 199
John 1–11: 168
Acts 13–28: 108, 109, 200
1 Corinthians: viii, 4, 32
2 Corinthians: 4
18:9
John 12–21: 98, 376
Acts 13–28: 284, 290
18:9–10
Acts 13–28: 335
1 Corinthians: 201, 405
2 Corinthians: 394–95, 412
1 & 2 Thessalonians: 318
1 Timothy: 4
18:9–11
Philippians: 65
1 & 2 Thessalonians: 293
18:10
John 12–21: 263
Ephesians: 138
18:11
1 Corinthians: ix, 56, 118
2 Corinthians: 35, 66, 80, 94, 185, 234, 300, 408, 476
18:12
Acts 13–28: 317
Romans 9–16: 353
2 Corinthians: 177
Philippians: 301
1 & 2 Thessalonians: 8
18:12–13
Acts 13–28: 212, 277
2 Corinthians: 4
Revelation 1–11: 72
18:12–15
Luke 18–24: 210
Acts 13–28: 157
18:12–16
Acts 13–28: 304, 328
2 Corinthians: 390, 393
Revelation 1–11: 39
18:12–17
John 12–21: 166

Acts 13–28: 200
1 Corinthians: 4
2 Corinthians: 3, 228
Philippians: 2
1 & 2 Thessalonians: 8, 61, 295
1 Peter: 3
18:12–22
1 Corinthians: ix
18:12ff.
Acts 1–12: 6
Acts 13–28: 317
18:13
Mark 9–16: 176
2 Corinthians: 159
18:14–15
Acts 13–28: 158, 187
18:14–16
2 Corinthians: 4
18:16
2 Corinthians: 177
18:17
Acts 13–28: 200
2 Corinthians: 177
18:18
Luke 11–17: 285
Acts 13–28: 157, 251, 254
Romans 9–16: 359
1 Corinthians: 212
2 Corinthians: 4, 8, 300, 389, 476
James: 267
1 Peter: 15
Revelation 1–11: 284
18:18–19
1 Corinthians: 486
Revelation 1–11: 56
18:19
Acts 13–28: 120
18:19–21
Acts 13–28: 172
Revelation 1–11: 56
18:21
Acts 13–28: 163
James: 237
18:21–22
2 Corinthians: 389
18:22
2 Corinthians: 8
18:23
John 1–11: 230, 357
Acts 1–12: 232
Acts 13–28: 55, 164, 181
1 & 2 Thessalonians: 79
1 Peter: 15
18:24
Acts 1–12: 257
Acts 13–28: 122
Titus: 49
18:24–25
Romans 9–16: 173
Titus: 167
18:24–26
Romans 9–16: 364
1 Corinthians: 260, 486
Revelation 1–11: 56
18:24–28
Acts 1–12: 2
1 Corinthians: 469
18:24–19:1
1 Corinthians: ix
18:25
Romans 9–16: 191
1 & 2 Thessalonians: 143
18:25–26
2 Peter–Jude: 77
18:26
Luke 1–5: 16
Acts 1–12: 266
Romans 9–16: 318
1 Timothy: 87
18:26–27
Titus: 168
18:27
John 1–11: 230, 357
Romans 9–16: 361
2 Corinthians: 80
1 & 2 Thessalonians: 320
19:1
Acts 1–12: 232
Acts 13–28: 162
2 Corinthians: 8
19:1–3
Matthew 8–15: 68
Acts 13–28: 23
19:1–5
Matthew 24–28: 344
Luke 1–5: 16
John 1–11: 30
19:1–6
Galatians: 67
19:1–7
Matthew 1–7: 71
Mark 1–8: 127
Luke 1–5: 338
Acts 1–12: 17, 42
1 Corinthians: 466
Revelation 1–11: 56
19:3–4
Mark 1–8: 21
19:4
Matthew 1–7: 71
Mark 1–8: 22
Acts 1–12: 303
19:5
Revelation 1–11: 56
19:6
Acts 1–12: 142
19:8
Matthew 8–15: 187
Mark 1–8: 61
Luke 1–5: 267
Luke 11–17: 405
John 1–11: 302
Acts 1–12: 50, 273
Acts 13–28: 46, 215
Romans 9–16: 3, 329
1 Corinthians: 56
2 Corinthians: 8, 185
19:8–9
Acts 13–28: 120, 157, 319, 373
Ephesians: 332
19:8–10
Acts 13–28: 375
1 Corinthians: 466
1 & 2 Thessalonians: 61
19:9
John 1–11: 230, 357
Acts 1–12: 266
Acts 13–28: 31, 183, 212, 265, 277, 307
Romans 1–8: 185
2 Corinthians: 390
Philippians: 2
1 Peter: 3
2 Peter–Jude: 77
Revelation 1–11: 72
19:10
Luke 1–5: 14
Acts 13–28: 215
2 Corinthians: 8
1 & 2 Thessalonians: 294
1 Peter: 9, 15
1–3 John: 30
Revelation 1–11: 55, 56, 69, 84, 97, 109, 120, 134
19:10–11
Ephesians: 332
19:11
2 Corinthians: 416
19:11–12
Luke 11–17: 65
Luke 18–24: 397
Acts 1–12: 97
2 Corinthians: 413
Philippians: 38
Revelation 1–11: 56
19:11–19
1 Corinthians: 466
19:12
Philippians: 205
19:13–14
Matthew 1–7: 480
Matthew 8–15: 309
Luke 1–5: 284
1 Corinthians: 466
19:13–15
Titus: 128
19:13–16
Matthew 8–15: 40
Mark 1–8: 63, 65, 239
Mark 9–16: 39
Luke 11–17: 65
Acts 1–12: 234
Ephesians: 332
Revelation 1–11: 56–57
19:13–41
1 & 2 Thessalonians: 82, 293
19:14–16
1 Corinthians: 302
19:15
Matthew 16–23: 78
Luke 1–5: 283
James: 132
19:16
Matthew 8–15: 44
Philippians: 303

19:16–17
Titus: 129
19:17
Mark 1–8: 107
Luke 1–5: 325
Acts 1–12: 86
Revelation 1–11: 57
19:17–19
1 Corinthians: 466
19:17–20
Ephesians: 332
19:18–19
Acts 13–28: 184
James: 126
Revelation 1–11: 57
19:18–20
1 & 2 Thessalonians: 294
19:19
1 & 2 Thessalonians: 172
1 Peter: 140
19:20
Acts 1–12: 130
Acts 13–28: 183, 184
1 Corinthians: 466
Philippians: 303
1 & 2 Thessalonians: 294
19:21
Acts 1–12: 232
Acts 13–28: 195, 237, 359
2 Corinthians: 348
19:21–22
Philippians: 199
19:21–41
Acts 13–28: 314
Philippians: 2
1 Peter: 3
19:22
Romans 9–16: 379
1 Corinthians: 467
2 Corinthians: 18
Philippians: 196
1 & 2 Thessalonians: 78, 223
1 Timothy: 6
2 Timothy: 214
19:23
Acts 1–12: 266
Acts 13–28: 173, 265, 307
Romans 1–8: 185
2 Corinthians: 151
1 Peter: 279
2 Peter–Jude: 77
19:23–24
1 Corinthians: 428
19:23–27
Luke 18–24: 211
John 12–21: 168
2 Corinthians: 159–60
19:23–28
1–3 John: 214
19:23–40
Ephesians: 332
19:23–41
2 Corinthians: 66, 388, 390
Ephesians: 83
Philippians: 62
1–3 John: 210, 260
Revelation 1–11: 57
19:23ff.
Acts 13–28: 102
Revelation 1–11: 39
19:24
2 Timothy: 211
Revelation 1–11: 58
19:24–27
1 Peter: 140
19:24–28
Ephesians: 166
19:24–29
Matthew 8–15: 204
19:24–34
Matthew 1–7: 368
19:26
1 Corinthians: 193
2 Corinthians: 185
1 Peter: 9
19:26–28
Romans 1–8: 134
19:27
Luke 1–5: 144
Revelation 1–11: 58
19:28
1 Timothy: 139
19:29
Acts 1–12: 194, 223
Acts 13–28: 47, 346
2 Corinthians: 228
Philippians: 7, 315
1 & 2 Thessalonians: 4
Revelation 1–11: 57
19:31
Acts 1–12: 6
19:32
Matthew 16–23: 32
Acts 13–28: 261
James: 102, 246
19:33
Acts 13–28: 17, 264
19:34
James: 246
19:35
Revelation 1–11: 58
19:35–41
Romans 1–8: 140
19:37
Acts 1–12: 6
Acts 13–28: 317
Romans 1–8: 157
19:38–39
Romans 9–16: 225
19:39
James: 102
19:41
Matthew 16–23: 32
James: 102
20:1
John 1–11: 230, 357
2 Corinthians: 479
20:1–2
2 Corinthians: 484
20:1–6
2 Timothy: 214
20:2
Acts 1–12: 232
2 Corinthians: 479
20:2–3
2 Corinthians: 479
20:2–4
2 Corinthians: 309
20:3
John 12–21: 166
Acts 13–28: 31, 205, 212, 277, 293, 319
Romans 1–8: 35
2 Corinthians: 22, 143, 151, 231, 390
Philippians: 2, 301
1 Peter: 3
Revelation 1–11: 72
20:3–4
Philippians: 199
20:3, 19
Romans 9–16: 353
20:4
Acts 13–28: 123, 186, 346
Philippians: 196, 315
Colossians and Philemon: 192
1 & 2 Thessalonians: 4
1 Timothy: 6
2 Timothy: 210
Titus: 167
20:4–5
1 & 2 Thessalonians: 78
20:4–6
Ephesians: 384
20:5–21:18
Luke 1–5: 3
20:6
Acts 13–28: 91
20:6–12
2 Corinthians: 67
20:7
Matthew 1–7: 326
Matthew 8–15: 287
Mark 1–8: 141
Luke 18–24: 409
1 Corinthians: 453
Colossians and Philemon: 118
20:9–10
2 Timothy: 215
20:9–12
Luke 1–5: 294
Philippians: 38
20:15
Acts 13–28: 221
20:15–17
Revelation 1–11: 41
20:16
Acts 13–28: 200, 236
20:17
Acts 1–12: 182
Acts 13–28: 221, 248
Ephesians: 143, 147
1 & 2 Thessalonians: 167
1 Timothy: 93, 125, 218
20:17–20
Luke 6–10: 159

20:17–24
Acts 13–28: 221
20:17–38
Revelation 1–11: 56
20:17, 28
Titus: 21
20:17ff.
1 Timothy: 92
20:18
1 & 2 Thessalonians: 305
20:18–19
Philippians: 2, 113
20:18–20
1 & 2 Thessalonians: 169
20:18–21
Acts 1–12: 180
2 Timothy: 129
20:18, 20–21, 27
2 Timothy: 156
20:19
Matthew 16–23: 232
Acts 13–28: 293
1 Corinthians: 97, 106, 333
2 Corinthians: 345, 346, 390
Philippians: 112, 199, 257
1 & 2 Thessalonians: 184
20:19–20
Acts 13–28: 5
20:20
1 Corinthians: 245
2 Corinthians: 235
Philippians: 292
1 Timothy: 266
20:20–21, 27
1 Corinthians: 98
20:20–24
Ephesians: 88
20:21
Matthew 1–7: 454
Matthew 8–15: 470
Luke 1–5: 234
Acts 1–12: 73, 114
Romans 9–16: 87
1 Corinthians: 15
Ephesians: 174, 176
Philippians: 223
1 & 2 Thessalonians: 20, 27
Hebrews: 138
1–3 John: 19
Revelation 1–11: 139
20:22
Acts 13–28: 237
20:22–23
Acts 13–28: 237, 254, 273
Romans 1–8: 47
Philippians: 2
1 Peter: 3
20:22–24
Luke 6–10: 274
Acts 13–28: 116
Romans 9–16: 341, 353
1 Timothy: 272
20:23
Acts 13–28: 234, 238
2 Corinthians: 227
20:23–24
2 Timothy: 195
20:24
Matthew 1–7: 426
Matthew 8–15: 222
Luke 1–5: 328
Acts 13–28: 187, 237
Romans 1–8: 47
2 Corinthians: 125, 193, 227, 228
Galatians: 190
Ephesians: 223
Philippians: 13, 58, 76, 200, 242
Colossians and Philemon: 76
1 & 2 Thessalonians: 294, 320
1 Timothy: 42
2 Timothy: 25, 45, 53, 194
Titus: 4
2 Peter–Jude: 52
1–3 John: 176
Revelation 12–22: 23, 86
20:25
Acts 1–12: 16, 48
Acts 13–28: 195
Revelation 12–22: 229
20:26–27
2 Timothy: 129
James: 148, 151
20:26–28
James: 72
20:26, 31
2 Timothy: 158
20:27
Matthew 1–7: 270
Matthew 24–28: 345
Acts 13–28: 184
1 Corinthians: 56, 464
2 Corinthians: 235, 360
Colossians and Philemon: 76
1 & 2 Thessalonians: 111, 141
1 Timothy: 266
2 Timothy: 172
Hebrews: 131
1–3 John: 214
Revelation 12–22: 297
20:27–28
1 & 2 Thessalonians: 292
20:27–32
Romans 9–16: 374
1 Timothy: 239
20:28
Matthew 1–7: 33
Matthew 16–23: 31
John 12–21: 163, 402
Acts 13–28: 206
Romans 9–16: 283
1 Corinthians: 26
2 Corinthians: 18, 440, 473
Ephesians: 144, 148
Philippians: 15
Colossians and Philemon: 84
1 & 2 Thessalonians: 59, 165, 166, 167
1 Timothy: 93, 98, 135, 218, 262
Titus: 22, 34, 35, 121
James: 89
1 Peter: 130
1–3 John: 37, 153
Revelation 1–11: 43, 232
Revelation 12–22: 79, 308
20:28–29
Matthew 8–15: 113
John 1–11: 425
20:28–30
Matthew 1–7: 270
Romans 1–8: 504
Galatians: 11, 34
Philippians: 92
2 Timothy: 69
20:28–31
Philippians: 257
1 & 2 Thessalonians: 32
2 Timothy: 166
Revelation 1–11: 60
20:28–32
1 Timothy: 40
2 Peter–Jude: 79, 96
20:29
Matthew 8–15: 200, 204–5
Matthew 16–23: 354
Luke 6–10: 55
Luke 18–24: 171
John 1–11: 20
Acts 1–12: 94
2 Corinthians: 336
Philippians: 217
2 Peter–Jude: 2
1–3 John: 2, 232, 237
20:29–30
Luke 11–17: 255
Acts 13–28: 62
Ephesians: 148, 333
Philippians: 86
1 & 2 Thessalonians: 80, 136
1 Timothy: 7, 14, 92, 148
2 Timothy: 94, 105, 123, 154
Titus: 51, 57
Hebrews: 436
1–3 John: 15
Revelation 1–11: 100
20:29–31
Matthew 1–7: 461
Acts 13–28: 195
Colossians and Philemon: 99
2 Peter–Jude: 148
20:29–32
1 & 2 Thessalonians: 76
1 Timothy: 159
20:30
Luke 11–17: 110
Acts 13–28: 235
2 Corinthians: 485
Galatians: xi, 11
Philippians: 184
1 Timothy: 16
Revelation 1–11: 48
20:30–31
Ephesians: 158
20:31
Matthew 1–7: 156

Acts 13–28: 81, 174, 184, 258
1 Corinthians: 116
2 Corinthians: 228
Philippians: 7, 216, 257
Colossians and Philemon: 79
1 & 2 Thessalonians: 170, 177, 178
1 Timothy: 92, 201, 289
Revelation 1–11: 56
20:31–32
Acts 13–28: 55
20:32
Mark 9–16: 22
Luke 6–10: 366
Luke 18–24: 250
Acts 13–28: 56, 75, 336
Romans 1–8: 475
1 Corinthians: 245
2 Corinthians: 394
Galatians: 101
Ephesians: 156
Colossians and Philemon: 40, 93
1 & 2 Thessalonians: 58, 89, 103, 104, 108, 170, 202, 320
2 Timothy: 160
Titus: 8, 12, 46
Hebrews: 436
1 Peter: 35, 129
20:33
1 Timothy: 111, 245
James: 244
20:33–34
Romans 1–8: 34
1 & 2 Thessalonians: 41
20:33–35
1 Corinthians: 209
Ephesians: 187
1 & 2 Thessalonians: 293
1 Timothy: 261
1 Peter: 268
20:34
Matthew 1–7: 146
1 Corinthians: 204
2 Corinthians: 228, 390
Philippians: 300
1 & 2 Thessalonians: 305, 306
20:34–35
2 Corinthians: 388
20:35
Matthew 1–7: 47
Luke 11–17: 130
Acts 1–12: 151
Romans 9–16: 172, 276
1 Corinthians: 324
2 Corinthians: 273, 278
Philippians: 307
1 & 2 Thessalonians: 131, 309
Titus: 93
James: 276
2 Peter–Jude: 48
20:36
1 & 2 Thessalonians: 86
20:36–38
Romans 9–16: 370
Philippians: 7
1 & 2 Thessalonians: 69
2 Timothy: 7
20:37
Matthew 24–28: 187
Mark 9–16: 312
20:37–38
1 & 2 Thessalonians: 184
20:38
Matthew 1–7: 156
Acts 13–28: 238, 247
21:1–8
Romans 9–16: 378
21:4
John 1–11: 357
Acts 13–28: 254, 273
21:5
Acts 13–28: 247
Romans 9–16: 344
1 & 2 Thessalonians: 86
21:8
Luke 6–10: 59
Acts 1–12: 182, 183, 232
Ephesians: 142
Philippians: 7
1 Timothy: 126
2 Timothy: 185
1–3 John: 243
21:8–11
Acts 1–12: 54
21:9
Luke 1–5: 185
Acts 1–12: 260
1 Corinthians: 256
1 Timothy: 85
21:10–11
Matthew 8–15: 221
Acts 13–28: 3, 218, 261
Romans 9–16: 171, 353
1 Corinthians: 322
Ephesians: 140
1 Timothy: 43
21:10–13
Acts 13–28: 273
21:11
Acts 13–28: 217, 254
1 & 2 Thessalonians: 131
21:11–13
2 Timothy: 176
21:12
John 1–11: 439
Acts 13–28: 238
21:13
Luke 6–10: 274
Acts 1–12: 104
Acts 13–28: 218, 273, 332
Romans 9–16: 356
Ephesians: 127
Philippians: 76
21:13–14
Romans 1–8: 40
21:14
1 & 2 Thessalonians: 119, 213
21:15
John 1–11: 439
Acts 13–28: 247
21:16
John 1–11: 357
Acts 13–28: 247
1–3 John: 243
21:17
Acts 1–12: 230
21:17–18
James: 11
21:17–20
Galatians: 41
21:17, 19–20
Romans 9–16: 354
21:18
Acts 13–28: 345
Titus: 163
21:20–26
Romans 1–8: 357
1 Corinthians: 212
21:20ff.
Acts 13–28: 290
21:21
Acts 13–28: 258
1 & 2 Thessalonians: 272
Hebrews: 271
21:21–24
Romans 1–8: 166
21:23–26
Galatians: 115
21:23–27
Acts 13–28: 306
21:24–26
Romans 1–8: 166
21:25
1 & 2 Thessalonians: 104
21:26
Acts 1–12: 88
Acts 13–28: 157
21:26–30
Philippians: 301
21:27
1 & 2 Thessalonians: 82
21:27–28
Mark 1–8: 104
Luke 1–5: 323
21:27–29
Romans 9–16: 81
21:27–30
Romans 1–8: 357
21:27b–31
Acts 13–28: 186
21:27–32
2 Corinthians: 151, 390
Ephesians: 77
21:27–33
Acts 13–28: 314
21:27–36
Philippians: 2
1 & 2 Thessalonians: 82
1 Peter: 3
21:27–28:16
Ephesians: 87
21:27ff.
Acts 13–28: 31, 212, 258, 277, 290, 319, 338, 369
Revelation 1–11: 72

21:28
Matthew 24–28: 36
John 1–11: 92, 482
Acts 1–12: 230
Acts 13–28: 265, 271, 304
Romans 1–8: 165
Romans 9–16: 81
2 Corinthians: 100
21:28–29
Revelation 1–11: 295
21:28–36
Romans 1–8: 314
21:29
Acts 13–28: 53, 201
2 Timothy: 215
21:30
2 Corinthians: 228
21:30–31
2 Corinthians: 22
21:30–32
2 Corinthians: 153, 388
21:30–39
John 12–21: 122
21:31–33
Luke 18–24: 209
21:31–35
Philippians: 301
21:32
Acts 13–28: 281
21:33–28:31
Philippians: 57
21:34
Acts 13–28: 194, 271
Revelation 12–22: 242
21:35
Romans 9–16: 308
21:36
Acts 13–28: 267
21:37
2 Corinthians: 385
Revelation 12–22: 242
21:37–22:21
Acts 13–28: 314
21:38
Luke 1–5: 166
21:39
Acts 1–12: 193, 264
21:40
Acts 13–28: 17
2 Corinthians: 385
Philippians: 230
22:1
Acts 1–12: 200
Acts 13–28: 273
2 Corinthians: 267
22:1–16
Acts 1–12: 264
22:3
Acts 1–12: 172, 193, 264
Acts 13–28: 92, 333, 347
Romans 1–8: 369, 392
Romans 9–16: 54, 59
2 Corinthians: 157, 385
Ephesians: xi
Philippians: 230
Colossians and Philemon: 70
22:3–5
Acts 1–12: 232
22:3–16
2 Corinthians: 112
22:3–21
2 Timothy: 25
22:3, 29
Matthew 1–7: 226
22:4
John 12–21: 192
Acts 1–12: 231, 266
Acts 13–28: 183
Colossians and Philemon: 71
2 Timothy: 131
2 Peter–Jude: 77
22:4–5
Ephesians: xi
Philippians: 232
22:5
Matthew 24–28: 198
Mark 9–16: 321
Acts 1–12: 231
2 Corinthians: 80, 386
22:6
Acts 1–12: 267
22:7
Matthew 8–15: 206
22:7–8
1 Timothy: 29
22:9
Acts 1–12: 267
Acts 13–28: 93
22:10
Acts 1–12: 72, 270
Romans 1–8: 198
Colossians and Philemon: 72
22:11–15
1 Corinthians: 3
22:12
Luke 1–5: 176–77
Acts 1–12: 271
22:14
Acts 1–12: 216, 267
Acts 13–28: 267
Romans 9–16: 356
1 Timothy: 27
22:14–15
Acts 1–12: 273
Romans 1–8: 6
1 Timothy: 3
22:15
Acts 13–28: 270, 332
1 Peter: 266
22:16
Acts 1–12: 274
Romans 1–8: 321
22:17–18
Acts 13–28: 150
1 Corinthians: 201
Philippians: 65
1 Timothy: 4
22:17–21
Acts 1–12: 278
Acts 13–28: 284, 290, 335
2 Corinthians: 412
Revelation 1–11: 41
22:18
Romans 9–16: 377
1 Corinthians: 15
22:19
Matthew 8–15: 204
22:19–20
Acts 1–12: 232
22:20
Acts 1–12: 226
22:21
Acts 13–28: 277
Romans 1–8: 26
Romans 9–16: 111
2 Corinthians: 347
Ephesians: 88
22:21–22
Acts 1–12: 299
22:21–23
Matthew 8–15: 299
Acts 13–28: 338
22:22
Acts 13–28: 261
2 Peter–Jude: 77
22:22–23
2 Corinthians: 228
22:24
Revelation 12–22: 242
22:24–29
2 Corinthians: 388
22:25–28
1 Timothy: 3
22:25–29
Acts 1–12: 108
22:28
Acts 1–12: 264
Acts 13–28: 296
22:29
Acts 13–28: 277
22:30
Acts 1–12: 224
22:30–23:11
Acts 13–28: 314
22:30ff.
Acts 1–12: 230
Acts 13–28: 258, 369
23
2 Corinthians: 326
23:1
Acts 13–28: 238
Romans 1–8: 141
Romans 9–16: 9, 282
2 Corinthians: 31, 40, 185
Galatians: xii
Philippians: 18, 52, 73
1 Timothy: 151
James: 91
23:1–5
Matthew 1–7: 328
Matthew 24–28: 204
1 Corinthians: 346
1 Peter: 190
23:1–10
Acts 13–28: 308
23:2
John 12–21: 321
Titus: 125

23:2–3
Luke 18–24: 334
23:3
Matthew 8–15: 202
Philippians: 254
James: 160, 252
23:3–5
James: 98
23:4–5
James: 252
23:5
Philippians: 254
James: 160
23:6
Matthew 24–28: 184, 305
Luke 11–17: 100
Acts 1–12: 264
Acts 13–28: 278, 370
Romans 9–16: 8
Philippians: 231
23:6–8
Matthew 1–7: 62
Matthew 16–23: 329
Luke 1–5: 319
Luke 11–17: 256
23:6–9
Matthew 16–23: 4
23:6–10
Mark 9–16: 311
23:8
Matthew 1–7: 33
Matthew 16–23: 14
Luke 1–5: 166, 319
Luke 18–24: 143
John 1–11: 482
Acts 1–12: 129
Acts 13–28: 64
23:8ff.
Acts 13–28: 65
23:9
Luke 1–5: 319
James: 226
23:10
Acts 13–28: 278
Romans 1–8: 140
2 Corinthians: 228, 388
Revelation 12–22: 242
23:11
Mark 1–8: 331
Acts 13–28: 150, 290, 335, 340, 362
Romans 9–16: 353
1 Corinthians: 15, 405
2 Corinthians: 394–95, 412
Philippians: 65
1 & 2 Thessalonians: 293
1 Timothy: 4
23:12
2 Corinthians: 143, 231
23:12–13
2 Corinthians: 22
23:12–15
Matthew 24–28: 235
23:12–21
2 Corinthians: 388
23:12–22
2 Corinthians: 151, 390
23:12–33
Acts 13–28: 314
23:12–35
Philippians: 2
23:12–24:9
1 Peter: 3
23:12ff.
Acts 13–28: 31, 212, 319, 338
Revelation 1–11: 72
23:16
Revelation 12–22: 242
23:17–35
Romans 1–8: 140
23:18
2 Corinthians: 388
23:26
Luke 1–5: 16
Acts 13–28: 72, 260
James: 3
23:27
2 Timothy: 175
23:28–29
Acts 13–28: 370
23:29
Acts 13–28: 304, 309, 310
23:32
Revelation 12–22: 242
23:35
Luke 18–24: 209
2 Corinthians: 388
Philippians: 6, 61
Colossians and Philemon: 4
24
2 Corinthians: 326
24:1–27
Acts 13–28: 314
24:1ff.
Acts 13–28: 258, 369
24:3
Luke 1–5: 16
Acts 1–12: 5
24:4
2 Corinthians: 324
24:5
Matthew 1–7: 48
Acts 13–28: 115
2 Corinthians: 157, 220
2 Peter–Jude: 72
24:5–6
Acts 13–28: 317, 370
24:6
John 1–11: 92
Acts 1–12: 230
24:11
John 1–11: 439
24:14
Acts 1–12: 266
Acts 13–28: 173, 183, 265
Romans 1–8: 186
1 Timothy: 137
2 Timothy: 5
2 Peter–Jude: 65–66, 72
24:14–15
Acts 13–28: 333, 370–71
24:15
Luke 11–17: 264
Romans 1–8: 492
Revelation 12–22: 238, 250
24:15, 21
Matthew 24–28: 305
24:16
Acts 13–28: 238, 279, 280
Romans 1–8: 141
Romans 9–16: 292
1 Corinthians: 189
2 Corinthians: 31, 40, 185
Philippians: 18, 51, 52, 73
1 Timothy: 18, 45, 151
James: 91
24:17
Acts 13–28: 248
1 Corinthians: 450
Galatians: 43
24:21
Acts 13–28: 283
James: 246
Revelation 1–11: 319
24:22
Acts 1–12: 266
Acts 13–28: 173, 183, 265
24:22–27
Acts 13–28: 326, 370
24:23–27
2 Corinthians: 228
24:24
1 Timothy: 4
24:24–25
Ephesians: 200
24:25
Luke 18–24: 239
Romans 1–8: 71
2 Corinthians: 468
1 & 2 Thessalonians: 163
2 Timothy: 97
James: 197
24:26
Colossians and Philemon: 4
24:27
Luke 1–5: 13
Acts 13–28: 199, 240, 303
2 Corinthians: 388
Philippians: 59
25
2 Corinthians: 326
25:1
John 1–11: 439
25:1–12
Acts 13–28: 258, 369
25:2
2 Corinthians: 284
25:2–3
2 Corinthians: 390
25:2–5
Acts 13–28: 338
25:3
Acts 13–28: 327, 328
2 Corinthians: 231
25:4
Revelation 1–11: 21, 125

25:4–5
Acts 13–28: 328
25:5
1 & 2 Thessalonians: 295
25:6
Acts 13–28: 328
2 Corinthians: 177
25:7
Acts 1–12: 60
25:8
Acts 1–12: 230
Acts 13–28: 306
25:9
John 1–11: 439
Acts 13–28: 326, 328
Colossians and Philemon: 4
25:10
Acts 13–28: 317, 328
2 Corinthians: 177
25:10–11
Philippians: 2
1 Peter: 3
25:11
Matthew 24–28: 190
Acts 13–28: 325, 328
Romans 9–16: 224, 226
2 Corinthians: 326
Philippians: 67
Colossians and Philemon: 4
25:11–12
Philippians: 6, 296
25:12
Luke 6–10: 54
25:13
Acts 13–28: 327
25:13ff.
Acts 13–28: 258, 369
25:14–21
1 Timothy: xi
25:16
Acts 1–12: 108, 200
Acts 13–28: 308, 376
2 Corinthians: 267
25:17
Acts 13–28: 317
2 Corinthians: 177
25:18–19
Acts 13–28: 370
25:19
1 & 2 Thessalonians: 232
25:20
Luke 18–24: 234
25:21
Philippians: 296
25:21–27
Luke 6–10: 54
25:23
Acts 13–28: 327
25:23–27
Luke 18–24: 348
25:23ff.
Acts 1–12: 273
25:25
Acts 1–12: 6
26
2 Corinthians: 326
26:1
Acts 13–28: 17
26:1–32
Luke 18–24: 209
26:2–23
2 Timothy: 25
26:3
Acts 13–28: 327
Ephesians: 118
26:4
2 Corinthians: 385
Philippians: 230
26:4–5
Romans 9–16: 59
2 Corinthians: 230
26:4–18
Acts 1–12: 264
Acts 13–28: 266
26:5
Luke 6–10: 270
Galatians: 24
Philippians: 231
James: 88
2 Peter–Jude: 72
26:6
Acts 13–28: 371
26:7
Acts 1–12: 323
James: 12
1 Peter: 90
26:8
Matthew 24–28: 305
1 Corinthians: 432
26:9
Luke 1–5: 269
John 12–21: 167
Acts 1–12: 59
26:9–11
John 12–21: 192
Acts 1–12: 265
2 Corinthians: 195
Philippians: 232
Colossians and Philemon: 71
1 Timothy: 3
1 Peter: 198
26:9ff.
Acts 1–12: 232
26:10
Luke 11–17: 107
Acts 1–12: 231
Acts 13–28: 279
1 Timothy: 29
Revelation 1–11: 320
26:11
Luke 11–17: 275
Acts 1–12: 231
1 Corinthians: 285
Galatians: 27
1 Timothy: 29
Revelation 12–22: 29
26:12–18
Colossians and Philemon: 71
26:13
Matthew 1–7: 29
Acts 1–12: 267
Acts 13–28: 267
26:13–14
Revelation 1–11: 49
26:13–18
1 Corinthians: 209
26:14
Acts 1–12: 267, 269
Acts 13–28: 267
Romans 1–8: 368
2 Corinthians: 385
26:14–15
1 Timothy: 29
26:15
2 Corinthians: 196
26:15–17
Galatians: 29
26:15–18
2 Corinthians: 17, 347
26:15–20
Acts 13–28: 15
26:16
Luke 18–24: 447
John 12–21: 182
Acts 1–12: 267
Acts 13–28: 267
2 Corinthians: 78, 125, 410
Ephesians: 94
1 Timothy: 27
26:16–18
Matthew 24–28: 343
Romans 1–8: 6
1 Corinthians: 33
1 Timothy: 3
26:17–18
Romans 9–16: 111
26:18
Matthew 16–23: 98
Luke 1–5: 272, 321
Luke 6–10: 199
Luke 11–17: 77, 281
John 12–21: 82, 172
Acts 1–12: 75, 114, 282
1 Corinthians: 6
2 Corinthians: 132, 244, 249
Colossians and Philemon: 39, 111
1 & 2 Thessalonians: 27, 103, 104, 155, 202
James: 289
1 Peter: 35, 37, 130
Revelation 1–11: 125, 139
26:19
1 Corinthians: 209
1 & 2 Thessalonians: 294
1 Timothy: 31, 42, 270
26:19–20
Acts 1–12: 114
26:19–22
Romans 1–8: 166
26:20
Matthew 1–7: 54, 65
Matthew 16–23: 98
Luke 1–5: 218
Acts 1–12: 73, 74, 114, 282
Acts 13–28: 216
2 Corinthians: 266
Ephesians: 174

Philippians: 223
1 & 2 Thessalonians: 27, 244, 297
Hebrews: 138
James: 8, 289
Revelation 1–11: 139
26:21
Acts 1–12: 169
26:22
Revelation 1–11: 320
26:22–23
Acts 13–28: 38
1 Corinthians: 402
Galatians: 76
26:23
Luke 1–5: 181
Luke 6–10: 199
John 12–21: 37
Acts 13–28: 336
Hebrews: 138
1 Peter: 2
26:24
Luke 6–10: 46
Acts 13–28: 328
2 Corinthians: 86, 189
1 Peter: 8
26:24–32
1 & 2 Thessalonians: 293
26:25
Luke 1–5: 16
Acts 1–12: 5
2 Corinthians: 189
1 Timothy: 81
26:26
Acts 1–12: 39
26:28
Acts 13–28: 332
Romans 9–16: 256
2 Corinthians: 185
1 Peter: 256
26:29
Hebrews: 394
26:30
Acts 13–28: 327
26:30–32
Acts 13–28: 258
26:31–32
Acts 13–28: 370
26:32
Acts 1–12: 6
Philippians: 296
1 Timothy: xi
27
2 Corinthians: 151, 389
27:1
Luke 6–10: 124
27:1–28:16
Luke 1–5: 3
27:1–28:28
1 Peter: 3
27:2
Acts 13–28: 186
Philippians: 315
1 & 2 Thessalonians: 4
27:3
Acts 1–12: 6
Acts 13–28: 365
Titus: 151
27:10
Luke 11–17: 104
27:11
1 Corinthians: 324
27:14–26
1 & 2 Thessalonians: 82
27:15
2 Peter–Jude: 65
27:17
2 Peter–Jude: 65
27:20
Luke 18–24: 360
27:21–25
Romans 1–8: 266
27:21–26
1 & 2 Thessalonians: 168
27:22
Acts 13–28: 359
27:22–24
1 Corinthians: 300
27:22–25
Romans 1–8: 37
27:22–26
1 & 2 Thessalonians: 293
Titus: 152
27:23
Luke 18–24: 136
Acts 13–28: 210
Philippians: 19
27:23–24
Acts 13–28: 150, 365
2 Corinthians: 395
Revelation 12–22: 84
27:24
Acts 13–28: 362
2 Corinthians: 326
Philippians: 296
27:25
Matthew 8–15: 441
27:26
Acts 13–28: 359
27:26–44
1 & 2 Thessalonians: 293
27:32
Philippians: 219
27:34
2 Corinthians: 204
1 Timothy: 168
27:35
Revelation 12–22: 194
27:37
Acts 13–28: 236
James: 153
27:41
James: 25
27:42
Acts 1–12: 326
Acts 13–28: 107
28:1–2
Acts 13–28: 365
28:1–10
1 & 2 Thessalonians: 293
28:2
Romans 9–16: 274, 318
Titus: 152
28:2, 6
Ephesians: 55
28:3
Matthew 16–23: 388
Luke 18–24: 397
28:3–4
Galatians: 116
28:3–5
Matthew 1–7: 64
Mark 9–16: 415
28:3, 6
Matthew 8–15: 317
28:4
Mark 1–8: 164
28:6
Matthew 16–23: 388
1 & 2 Thessalonians: 295
28:7
Acts 13–28: 365
2 Corinthians: 284
1–3 John: 243
28:8
Luke 1–5: 294
Luke 11–17: 2
Acts 1–12: 97
1 Corinthians: 360
2 Corinthians: 413
Philippians: 205
1 & 2 Thessalonians: 86
28:9
Luke 1–5: 294
28:10
Acts 13–28: 365
Romans 1–8: 140
28:14
Acts 13–28: 365
28:14–31
Philippians: 5
28:15
Acts 13–28: 365
Romans 9–16: 355
28:16
2 Corinthians: 228
Philippians: 5, 18, 57, 190, 196, 203, 269, 296
28:16, 30
Colossians and Philemon: 74
28:16–31
2 Corinthians: 388
28:17
Acts 1–12: 230
2 Corinthians: 284
28:17–28
Acts 13–28: 258
28:17–31
Philippians: 57
28:19
Philippians: 296
28:20
Ephesians: 73
Philippians: 60, 269
28:22
2 Peter–Jude: 72
28:22, 25–28
Romans 9–16: 108

28:23
Acts 1–12: 2, 180
Acts 13–28: 173
1 Corinthians: 486
Philippians: 18, 196
28:23–24
Acts 1–12: 51
2 Corinthians: 185
28:23–28
2 Corinthians: 390
28:23–31
Colossians and Philemon: 4
28:24
1 & 2 Thessalonians: 57
28:25–26
Acts 1–12: 220
28:26–27
John 12–21: 41
1 & 2 Thessalonians: 284
28:27
James: 279
28:30
2 Corinthians: 228
Philippians: 5, 18, 57, 60, 269, 296
2 Timothy: 207
28:30–31
Acts 1–12: 180
Acts 13–28: 257
Philippians: 61, 190, 196, 202
28:31
Acts 1–12: 48, 130
Acts 13–28: 173, 195, 221
Philippians: 5
1–3 John: 203

Romans
1:1
Matthew 16–23: 242
Mark 1–8: 47
Luke 1–5: 335
John 12–21: 4
Acts 13–28: 47, 210
Romans 1–8: 3, 267
Romans 9–16: 98, 191
1 Corinthians: 74, 290, 323
2 Corinthians: 17, 134, 410
Ephesians: 2
Philippians: 13, 91, 204
1 & 2 Thessalonians: 21, 35
1 Timothy: 230
Hebrews: 371
James: 12, 204
2 Peter–Jude: 18
Revelation 12–22: 200, 293
1:1–4
Matthew 16–23: 68
1 Corinthians: 410
1:1–5
Romans 9–16: 2, 157
1:1–18
Romans 1–8: 201
1:1, 5
Romans 9–16: 331
1:2–4
Matthew 16–23: 350
1:3
Matthew 8–15: 90
Mark 9–16: 210
Luke 1–5: 45, 106, 174
Luke 18–24: 155
Philippians: 77
1 Timothy: 140
1–3 John: 16
Revelation 1–11: 167
Revelation 12–22: 11, 307
1:3–4
1 & 2 Thessalonians: 28
Hebrews: 29
1:4
Mark 1–8: 35, 183, 253
Luke 1–5: 58, 195
Luke 18–24: 430
John 1–11: 470
John 12–21: 372
Acts 13–28: 24
Romans 9–16: 75
Philippians: 140
1 Timothy: 141
2 Peter–Jude: 26
1:4–5
Romans 9–16: 322
1:4–6
Romans 9–16: 84
1:5
Matthew 16–23: 50
Luke 1–5: 166
Acts 1–12: 169, 297
Acts 13–28: 47, 73
Romans 1–8: 46
Romans 9–16: 335
2 Corinthians: 208, 347, 410
Ephesians: 10, 39
Philippians: 158
1 & 2 Thessalonians: 244
1 Timothy: 27
Hebrews: 125, 155
1 Peter: 22, 90, 182
1–3 John: 182, 248
Revelation 1–11: 54
1:6
John 12–21: 156
1 & 2 Thessalonians: 256
1:6–7
Luke 18–24: 68
1 & 2 Thessalonians: 287
2 Peter–Jude: 29
1:7
Matthew 1–7: 81
Matthew 8–15: 145
Mark 1–8: 37
John 12–21: 125, 142
Romans 9–16: 141
2 Corinthians: 257, 487
Ephesians: 19
Philippians: 16, 310
1 & 2 Thessalonians: 87, 203, 204, 216, 224, 256
1 Peter: 25, 31
Revelation 1–11: 24, 320
1:7–8
Acts 13–28: 147
1:7–12
1 & 2 Thessalonians: 69
1:8
Romans 1–8: 25
Romans 9–16: 376
Colossians and Philemon: 21
1 & 2 Thessalonians: 57
Revelation 12–22: 194
1:8–10
John 12–21: 235
Hebrews: 155
1:8–12
1 & 2 Thessalonians: 83, 86
1:9
Luke 1–5: 76
Romans 9–16: 191
Philippians: 39
1:9–10
Acts 1–12: 180
Acts 13–28: 229
Romans 9–16: 9
Philippians: 57
1 & 2 Thessalonians: 253, 293
2 Timothy: 6
1:9–11
Acts 13–28: 285
1:9–12
1 & 2 Thessalonians: 166
1:10
Luke 11–17: 2
Romans 9–16: 355
Philippians: 57
1 & 2 Thessalonians: 213
James: 237
1–3 John: 245
1:10–11
Romans 1–8: 38
1:10–13
Romans 9–16: 345
1:11
Acts 13–28: 181, 359
Romans 9–16: 175
1 & 2 Thessalonians: 79
1:11–12
1 Corinthians: 319
1:12
Romans 1–8: 475
1:13
Mark 1–8: 213
Romans 9–16: 2
1 Corinthians: 191, 282
2 Corinthians: 25, 194
Philippians: 53, 57, 58, 78
Colossians and Philemon: 31
1 & 2 Thessalonians: 125
Revelation 1–11: 55
1:13–14, 16
Romans 9–16: 323
1:14
Acts 13–28: 215
Ephesians: 66
Philippians: 58
1:14–15
Acts 1–12: 147
1:14–16
Matthew 1–7: 113

Philippians: 200
1 Peter: 268
1:15
Acts 13–28: 359
Romans 1–8: 38
2 Corinthians: 146
Philippians: 57
1:15–16
2 Corinthians: 198
1:15–17
1 & 2 Thessalonians: 294
1:16
Matthew 1–7: 44
Matthew 8–15: 175, 227, 468
Matthew 16–23: 19
Matthew 24–28: 157, 342
Mark 1–8: 110, 363, 368
Luke 1–5: 158, 328
Luke 6–10: 24, 58, 242
Luke 11–17: 73, 244, 275
John 12–21: 382
Acts 1–12: 124, 229, 257, 302
Acts 13–28: 23, 30, 36, 215, 369
Romans 1–8: 228
Romans 9–16: 3, 58, 79, 81, 94, 111, 385
1 Corinthians: 80
2 Corinthians: 90, 123, 127, 229
Ephesians: 47
Philippians: 58
Colossians and Philemon: 13, 21, 184
1 & 2 Thessalonians: 287, 288
Hebrews: 104
James: 75, 225
1 Peter: 51
1–3 John: 228
Revelation 1–11: 54, 55
1:16–17
Romans 1–8: 201, 307, 411
2 Corinthians: 126
1 Peter: 57
1:17
Luke 1–5: 176
Romans 1–8: 240
Ephesians: 358
1–3 John: 35
1:18
Matthew 8–15: 209
Matthew 16–23: 148
Matthew 24–28: 110
Romans 1–8: 273
Philippians: 64
Colossians and Philemon: 141
1 & 2 Thessalonians: 163
2 Timothy: 183
Titus: 116
James: 188
1 Peter: 32
2 Peter–Jude: 113
Revelation 1–11: 264
Revelation 12–22: 108
1:18–19
Romans 9–16: 223, 384
James: 188
1:18–20
Acts 13–28: 51
Romans 1–8: 113, 341
Romans 9–16: 71, 87
1 Corinthians: 44
1 & 2 Thessalonians: 242
Hebrews: 199
Revelation 12–22: 89, 240
1:18–21
John 1–11: 24, 32, 39
Romans 1–8: 146, 378
Romans 9–16: 60, 62, 125
Galatians: 92
Philippians: 34
1 & 2 Thessalonians: 243
1:18, 21, 28–32
Titus: 146
1:18–23
Matthew 8–15: 97
Luke 1–5: 74
Luke 11–17: 95
Acts 1–12: 328
Acts 13–28: 134
Romans 9–16: 243
1 Corinthians: 42
1:18–24
Colossians and Philemon: 61
1:18–25
1 & 2 Thessalonians: 279
1:18–32
Luke 11–17: 74, 163
Romans 1–8: 140
1 Timothy: 69
1 Peter: 228
Revelation 1–11: 273
Revelation 12–22: 49, 298
1:18–3:20
Romans 1–8: 201
1:18ff.
Acts 1–12: 301
Acts 13–28: 141
1:19
Acts 13–28: 133
2 Corinthians: 43
1:19–20
Matthew 16–23: 26
Romans 1–8: 68, 114
Ephesians: ix, 74
1 & 2 Thessalonians: 285
2 Timothy: 13
Titus: 129
1–3 John: 228
1:19–21
James: 26
1:19–21, 25
Galatians: 111
1:20
Matthew 8–15: 30
Acts 1–12: 255
Acts 13–28: 52
Romans 1–8: 113, 137, 183, 218, 455
2 Corinthians: 123
Revelation 12–22: 91, 254
1:20–21
Matthew 16–23: 2
1:21
Luke 11–17: 90
Romans 1–8: 340
1 Corinthians: 233
2 Corinthians: 257, 468
Ephesians: 54, 74, 90, 168, 269
1 & 2 Thessalonians: 189, 285
Titus: 130
James: 188
Revelation 12–22: 87, 156
1:21–22
Colossians and Philemon: 36, 97
1:21–22, 24
Ephesians: 169
1:21–23
1 Corinthians: 232
James: 236
1:21–32
1 & 2 Thessalonians: 210
1:22
1 Timothy: 242
1:22–32
1–3 John: 228
1:23
Acts 13–28: 130
1:23–24, 26–30
Romans 9–16: 384–85
1:24
Matthew 16–23: 8
Mark 1–8: 397, 401
Luke 11–17: 221, 242
Acts 1–12: 213
James: 188
Revelation 12–22: 77, 122
1:24–27
1 & 2 Thessalonians: 108
1:24–28
1 & 2 Thessalonians: 109, 285
1:24–32
1 & 2 Thessalonians: 104
1–3 John: 228
1:25
Matthew 16–23: 381
Luke 11–17: 133
John 1–11: 20
1 Corinthians: 39
2 Corinthians: 44, 393
1 Timothy: 271
Revelation 1–11: 247
1:26
Matthew 16–23: 8
Acts 1–12: 213
1 & 2 Thessalonians: 109
James: 188
Revelation 12–22: 77, 122
1:28
Matthew 16–23: 8, 390
Acts 1–12: 213
1 Corinthians: 233
Philippians: 85, 286
1 & 2 Thessalonians: 108
1 Timothy: 243

Titus: 147
James: 188
1 Peter: 275
Revelation 12–22: 77, 122
1:28–29
2 Corinthians: 309
1:28–31
Matthew 1–7: 291
2 Corinthians: 434
1:28–32
Mark 1–8: 397
Revelation 12–22: 272
1:28, 32
2 Timothy: 121
1:29
2 Corinthians: 434–35
Ephesians: 172
Philippians: 64
Revelation 12–22: 309
1:29–30
1 & 2 Thessalonians: 199
1:29–31
Matthew 1–7: 193
Romans 1–8: 115
1:30
Matthew 16–23: 230
Mark 9–16: 101
Philippians: 112, 221
1 Timothy: 29
2 Timothy: 57
James: 199, 218, 221, 226
1:32
Matthew 16–23: 390
Romans 1–8: 114, 115, 146, 378
Ephesians: 297
1 & 2 Thessalonians: 256
1:32–2:1
1 Corinthians: 233
2
Hebrews: 74
2:1
Revelation 12–22: 91
2:1–2
Matthew 1–7: 434
2:1–3
Acts 13–28: 361
Romans 1–8: 481
2:1–10
Revelation 1–11: 316
2:1–16
Romans 1–8: 147
2:1ff.
Acts 1–12: 301
2:2
1 & 2 Thessalonians: 104
2:3–4
2 Timothy: 179
2:4
Matthew 8–15: 470
Luke 1–5: 154
Luke 6–10: 109
Luke 11–17: 13
Luke 18–24: 9
John 12–21: 80
Acts 1–12: 116
1 Corinthians: 339
Galatians: 167
Ephesians: 95, 190
Philippians: 223
Colossians and Philemon: 155
Titus: 110, 151
James: 253
2 Peter–Jude: 28
Revelation 1–11: 54, 139
Revelation 12–22: 144
2:4–5
Mark 1–8: 97
Luke 6–10: 256
2:4–11
1 & 2 Thessalonians: 56
2:5
Luke 6–10: 302, 332
Romans 1–8: 126
Colossians and Philemon: 141
1 & 2 Thessalonians: 163, 233
Titus: 110
James: 288
Revelation 12–22: 143, 248
2:5–6
1 & 2 Thessalonians: 65
Hebrews: 352
James: 245
Revelation 12–22: 108
2:5–8
Matthew 16–23: 52
2:5–9
Revelation 12–22: 211
2:5, 8
Luke 1–5: 215
2:6
Luke 1–5: 218
Romans 1–8: 397
Revelation 1–11: 103
2:6–7
1 & 2 Thessalonians: 16
1 Peter: 45
2:6–8
Revelation 1–11: 136
Revelation 12–22: 101
2:6–10
Matthew 16–23: 57
James: 125
2:6–11
James: 116
2:7
Matthew 8–15: 210
Luke 6–10: 352
2 Corinthians: 227
Philippians: 163
1 & 2 Thessalonians: 19, 245
1 Timothy: 181
2:8
Luke 1–5: 336
John 12–21: 56
Acts 13–28: 45
Romans 1–8: 397
Romans 9–16: 85
1 & 2 Thessalonians: 163
Revelation 12–22: 49
2:9
Matthew 24–28: 110
2:9–10
Galatians: 187
2:9–11
Matthew 16–23: 208
James: 95
2:10
Romans 9–16: 3
1 & 2 Thessalonians: 315
1 Peter: 45
2:11
Acts 1–12: 300
Romans 9–16: 199, 321
Ephesians: 74
Philippians: 315
James: 97
Revelation 12–22: 251
2:11–12
Acts 13–28: 361
2:11–12, 28–29
Romans 9–16: 385
2:11–15
Romans 1–8: 194, 203, 227
2:12
Romans 9–16: 294
2 Corinthians: 131
Revelation 12–22: 254
2:13–15
Acts 13–28: 52
2:13–16
James: 125
2:14
2 Corinthians: 30
1 Peter: 140, 202
2:14–15
Acts 13–28: 140, 280, 360
Romans 1–8: 146
Romans 9–16: 112, 223
1 Corinthians: 446
Galatians: 92
1 & 2 Thessalonians: 243
1 Timothy: 18, 45, 128, 151
James: 188
Revelation 12–22: 254
2:14–16
1–3 John: 25
2:15
Acts 13–28: 362
Romans 1–8: 113, 184, 368
Ephesians: 74, 77
1 Peter: 218
2:16
Mark 9–16: 354
Luke 6–10: 200
Luke 11–17: 117
Philippians: 142
1 & 2 Thessalonians: 234
Revelation 1–11: 195
Revelation 12–22: 215, 249, 253
2:17
Romans 1–8: 222
Philippians: 222
2:17–18
John 1–11: 367
2:17–19, 21, 23–24
Titus: 89

2:17–20
Acts 1–12: 65
Romans 9–16: 54
Philippians: 185
2:17–21
Matthew 16–23: 376
Hebrews: 131
2:17–25
Romans 1–8: 179
2:17–29
Romans 1–8: 167
1–3 John: 71
2:17–3:20
1 Corinthians: 14
2:17ff.
Acts 1–12: 201
2:19
Revelation 1–11: 139
2:19–20
Matthew 16–23: 381
Luke 11–17: 174
2:19–21
Matthew 1–7: 245
2:20
Luke 11–17: 100
2:21
Philippians: 185
2:21–22
Matthew 1–7: 245
2:23
Philippians: 222
2:23–24
Romans 1–8: 222
Philippians: 185
1 Timothy: 119, 232
2:23–29
Luke 6–10: 355
John 1–11: 367
2:24
Luke 6–10: 127
Romans 9–16: 323
2 Corinthians: 186, 225
1 & 2 Thessalonians: 257
2:25
Colossians and Philemon: 107
Hebrews: 100
2:25–29
Romans 1–8: 248
Philippians: 219
2:27
Acts 13–28: 360
2:27–28
2 Corinthians: 99
2:28
Colossians and Philemon: 107
2:28–29
Mark 1–8: 353
Luke 1–5: 177, 206, 221
Luke 18–24: 74
Romans 1–8: 253
Romans 9–16: 4, 22
Galatians: 48, 74, 128, 210
Ephesians: 71
Hebrews: xix
2 Peter–Jude: 48
1–3 John: 193
Revelation 1–11: 76, 123
2:29
Matthew 8–15: 159
Luke 6–10: 330
Luke 11–17: 100
Colossians and Philemon: 107
1 & 2 Thessalonians: 193
Hebrews: 100
1 Peter: 45
3:1
Romans 1–8: 271
3:1–2
Matthew 1–7: 68
Matthew 8–15: 14
Philippians: 229
Hebrews: 133
1 Peter: 129
3:1–3
Luke 1–5: 100
3:1–4
Luke 1–5: 134
1 & 2 Thessalonians: 56
3:2
Matthew 1–7: 292, 362
Matthew 16–23: 376
Luke 1–5: 106
Romans 1–8: 114, 358
Romans 9–16: 14, 60, 66
1 Corinthians: 339
Philippians: 220
2 Timothy: 42, 144
3:3
Luke 1–5: 174
Acts 13–28: 23
Romans 1–8: 325
1 & 2 Thessalonians: 229
2 Timothy: 93, 130
3:3–4
Matthew 1–7: 13
3:4
Mark 1–8: 16
Romans 1–8: 115, 228, 316, 367
Ephesians: 18
1 & 2 Thessalonians: 319
James: 137
3:4, 6, 31
Romans 9–16: 96
3:5
Romans 1–8: 271
1 & 2 Thessalonians: 163, 236
Revelation 12–22: 137
3:5–6
Romans 1–8: 314
3:6
Romans 1–8: 228, 316, 367
Revelation 1–11: 195
3:7
2 Peter–Jude: 13
3:7–9
Acts 13–28: 23
3:8
Romans 1–8: 271, 314
James: 219
3:9
Romans 1–8: 271
1 Corinthians: 14
3:9–10
1–3 John: 44
3:9–10, 12, 23
Matthew 8–15: 318
3:9–18
Romans 1–8: 397
1 Peter: 92
1–3 John: 228
3:9–23
Romans 1–8: 187
3:10
Luke 6–10: 108
Luke 11–17: 37
Luke 18–24: 146
2 Corinthians: 12, 210, 211, 398
Ephesians: 18
3:10–11, 23
Ephesians: 297
3:10–12
Matthew 8–15: 59
Mark 9–16: 67, 74
Luke 1–5: 179
Luke 11–17: 72
Acts 1–12: 267
Romans 1–8: 346
Titus: 114
James: 57
3:10–18
Luke 1–5: 114–15
John 12–21: 196
Acts 1–12: 301
2 Corinthians: 115
Titus: 148
James: 288
3:10–23
1–3 John: 29
3:10, 20
Romans 9–16: 385
3:10, 23
Luke 1–5: 159
3:11
Acts 13–28: 93
James: 196
Revelation 12–22: 156
3:12
Matthew 1–7: 447, 476
Acts 1–12: 70
3:13–14
Matthew 8–15: 319
Titus: 54
James: 145
3:13–18
James: 58
3:16
James: 211, 243
3:17
Luke 1–5: 123
John 12–21: 126
3:18
Luke 18–24: 386
Titus: 114
3:19
Romans 1–8: 228
Romans 9–16: 134

1 Timothy: 21
1 Peter: 230
3:19–20
Matthew 16–23: 201
Romans 1–8: 358
Philippians: 237
1 Timothy: 21, 89
3:20
Matthew 1–7: 451
Matthew 16–23: 359
Mark 9–16: 78
Luke 1–5: 21, 113–14, 319
Luke 11–17: 347
Acts 1–12: 70
Romans 1–8: 229, 360, 368
2 Corinthians: 89, 99, 100
Philippians: 167, 213
1 Timothy: 21
Hebrews: 306
2 Peter–Jude: 24
1–3 John: 259
3:20–21
1 & 2 Thessalonians: 15
3:20–22
Acts 13–28: 26
Romans 9–16: 68
Philippians: 78
3:20–25
Acts 13–28: 108
3:20–30
1 & 2 Thessalonians: 258
3:20
Galatians: 78
3:21
Luke 11–17: 349, 371
Acts 13–28: 23, 372
Romans 1–8: 240
3:21–22
Matthew 1–7: 68, 280
Romans 1–8: 195
Romans 9–16: 4, 79
2 Corinthians: 89, 103
Ephesians: 2
3:21–23
1 & 2 Thessalonians: 208
3:21–24
Romans 1–8: 57
Romans 9–16: 134, 206
Philippians: 155
Revelation 12–22: 203
3:21–25
1 & 2 Thessalonians: 203
3:21–26
Mark 1–8: 122
Romans 1–8: 420
1–3 John: 70
3:21–28
Acts 13–28: 336
3:21–30
Acts 1–12: 74
3:21–5:2
Romans 1–8: 304
3:22
Luke 11–17: 83
John 12–21: 105
Romans 1–8: 307
Romans 9–16: 257
2 Corinthians: 191, 217
Hebrews: 324
3:22–23
1 Corinthians: 14
3:22–30
Revelation 12–22: 49
3:22, 24
Titus: 5
1–3 John: 36
3:23
Matthew 8–15: 52
Matthew 16–23: 217
Mark 1–8: 96, 252, 350
Mark 9–16: 332
Luke 1–5: 10, 114, 179
Luke 11–17: 37, 181
John 12–21: 123
Acts 1–12: 70
Romans 1–8: 183, 395, 442
1 Corinthians: 446
2 Corinthians: 12, 191, 210, 214
Ephesians: 54
Philippians: 206, 237
James: 151
1–3 John: 45
Revelation 12–22: 253
3:23–24
2 Corinthians: 52
3:24
Luke 1–5: 40, 46, 47, 96
John 12–21: 133
Romans 1–8: 21, 140
2 Corinthians: 213, 217
Philippians: 318
Colossians and Philemon: 42, 111
1 & 2 Thessalonians: 163, 216, 320
1 Timothy: 27
James: 137
1 Peter: 32, 182
2 Peter–Jude: 24, 25
1–3 John: 44
Revelation 12–22: 305
3:24–25
2 Corinthians: 104, 106, 190
Galatians: 206
Ephesians: 21
1 & 2 Thessalonians: 15
Hebrews: 4, 161, 234–35, 326
Revelation 12–22: 308
3:24–26
2 Corinthians: 192
3:25
Luke 1–5: 10
Luke 11–17: 172
John 12–21: 47, 250, 356
1 & 2 Thessalonians: 180
1–3 John: 37, 46, 192
Revelation 1–11: 232
3:25–26
John 12–21: 346
1 Corinthians: 353
2 Corinthians: 191
3:26
Mark 1–8: 103
Luke 1–5: 10, 322
Luke 11–17: 178
Luke 18–24: 267
Romans 9–16: 259
1 Corinthians: 144
2 Corinthians: 196, 205, 211, 217
1 & 2 Thessalonians: 128, 163, 247
Titus: 41
1–3 John: 44
3:27
2 Corinthians: 32, 240
Philippians: 222
3:27–28
John 12–21: 172
3:28
Luke 1–5: 63, 114, 319
Acts 13–28: 26, 64, 268
Romans 1–8: 140, 202, 307
2 Corinthians: 192, 207, 217
Philippians: 78
1 & 2 Thessalonians: 208
1 Timothy: 21
James: 137
3:28–30
Romans 9–16: 4
3:29
Romans 1–8: 271
Romans 9–16: 323
Revelation 1–11: 224
3:29–30
Acts 1–12: 300
3:30
Romans 1–8: 233, 234
2 Corinthians: 192, 207
1 & 2 Thessalonians: 89
3:31
Romans 1–8: 316, 325, 358, 363, 367
4
Acts 1–12: 204
4:1
Romans 1–8: 271
Galatians: 155
4:1–3
Matthew 1–7: 68
Romans 1–8: 228
1 Peter: 89
4:1–5
Philippians: 78
4:1–5, 11
Romans 9–16: 5
4:1–8
Romans 1–8: 247, 263
4:1–11
Romans 9–16: 50
4:1–12
Matthew 8–15: 459
Mark 1–8: 353
4:1–13
Romans 1–8: 308
4:1–16
John 1–11: 31

4:1–24
1–3 John: 35
4:1–25
James: 137
4:2
Matthew 1–7: 280
Romans 1–8: 220
2 Corinthians: 187
4:2–3
Acts 1–12: 70
4:2–5
James: 139
4:3
Matthew 1–7: 275
Luke 11–17: 40
Acts 13–28: 196
Romans 1–8: 256, 270
Romans 9–16: 70
1 Corinthians: 425
James: 34
4:3–5
Philippians: 156
4:3–11
Galatians: 101
4:3, 9, 21–22
Luke 1–5: 21
4:4
1 Corinthians: 12
1 & 2 Thessalonians: 15
4:4–5
Galatians: 5
1 & 2 Thessalonians: 208, 258
4:5
Matthew 1–7: 206
Mark 1–8: 122
Luke 1–5: 315, 328
Luke 11–17: 316
Acts 1–12: 74
Acts 13–28: 336
Romans 1–8: 204, 307, 314
Romans 9–16: 257
1 Corinthians: 53
2 Corinthians: 192, 207
Ephesians: 210
Philippians: 23
Titus: 5
Hebrews: 161, 320
Revelation 1–11: 54
Revelation 12–22: 49, 203
4:5–6
Mark 1–8: 110
4:6
Luke 1–5: 328
Romans 1–8: 203
4:6–8
1–3 John: 36, 41
4:6–9
1 Timothy: 275
4:6, 11
2 Timothy: 201
4:6, 11, 22–24
Ephesians: 352
4:7
Acts 1–12: 75
Acts 13–28: 109
2 Corinthians: 248
1 Timothy: 275
Hebrews: 137
4:7–8
Acts 13–28: 336
Revelation 12–22: 22, 94
4:7–12
Galatians: 73
4:8
1 Corinthians: 347
2 Corinthians: 205
4:9–12
Ephesians: 71
4:9–17
Romans 1–8: 263
4:10
Matthew 1–7: 280
4:11
Matthew 1–7: 280
Romans 1–8: 235, 444
Romans 9–16: 14, 27, 70, 115
1 Corinthians: 219
Galatians: 74
Ephesians: 10
Colossians and Philemon: 107
Hebrews: 161
James: 34, 140
4:11–12
Luke 1–5: 105, 110
4:11, 16
Ephesians: 284
4:13
Romans 1–8: 204, 240, 271, 307
Romans 9–16: 70
4:14
Romans 1–8: 325
Philippians: 126
4:15
Romans 1–8: 140, 203, 368
Romans 9–16: 69
1 Corinthians: 445
1 & 2 Thessalonians: 163
1–3 John: 123
4:16
Luke 6–10: 14
1 & 2 Thessalonians: 216
James: 34
4:16–20
1 Peter: 63
4:17
Matthew 8–15: 481
Romans 1–8: 263
4:18–21
1 Peter: 286
4:19
Luke 1–5: 54
James: 276
4:20
Matthew 8–15: 474
Mark 1–8: 371
Romans 1–8: 204
1 Corinthians: 244, 300
Ephesians: 126
Revelation 1–11: 305
4:21
Ephesians: 28
4:22–24
Philippians: 15
4:22–25
1 Corinthians: 144, 146
4:23
Ephesians: 18
4:24
Romans 9–16: 75
2 Corinthians: 207
4:24–25
Mark 9–16: 401
1 Corinthians: 413
4:25
Matthew 24–28: 270
Mark 1–8: 382
Mark 9–16: 376, 396
Luke 1–5: 10
Luke 18–24: 55, 406, 407, 443
John 1–11: 96
John 12–21: 372
Acts 1–12: 64
Romans 1–8: 100, 508
2 Corinthians: 38, 89, 145, 216
1 & 2 Thessalonians: 128
Revelation 12–22: 50
5:1
Luke 1–5: 123, 161
Luke 6–10: 186, 331
John 12–21: 380
Acts 13–28: 108, 336
Romans 1–8: 204
2 Corinthians: 192, 207
Ephesians: 355
Philippians: 243, 283
Colossians and Philemon: 158
1 & 2 Thessalonians: 15, 163, 204, 258, 314
Hebrews: 176
James: 115, 137
1 Peter: 25
1–3 John: 36, 44, 52
Revelation 1–11: 242
5:1–2
Romans 1–8: 304
1 & 2 Thessalonians: 18, 90, 185, 208
1 Peter: 34, 289
2 Peter–Jude: 24
1–3 John: 106
5:1–3
1 Corinthians: 12
5:1–4
1 & 2 Thessalonians: 25
5:1–5
1–3 John: 118
5:1, 10–11
1–3 John: 46
5:2
2 Corinthians: 47
Galatians: 13
Ephesians: 135
Philippians: 222, 283, 318
1 & 2 Thessalonians: 73, 184
1 Timothy: 28
James: 234

1 Peter: 33, 42
5:2–5
Romans 9–16: 192
5:2, 3, 11
Galatians: 205
5:3
2 Corinthians: 227, 421
1 & 2 Thessalonians: 194
James: 234
1 Peter: 42–43
5:3–4
2 Corinthians: 15
Philippians: 40
James: 19
5:3–5
2 Corinthians: 15, 27
Philippians: 97
1 & 2 Thessalonians: 118
5:5
Matthew 1–7: 345, 447–48
Matthew 16–23: 341
Luke 6–10: 48
Luke 11–17: 58
Luke 18–24: 36
John 12–21: 89, 302
Acts 1–12: 226
Romans 1–8: 28, 482
Romans 9–16: 249
1 Corinthians: 330
Galatians: 165
Ephesians: 8, 43, 109, 194
Philippians: 32, 41, 42, 104
1 & 2 Thessalonians: 193, 228
1 Timothy: 202, 264
2 Timothy: 18, 102, 202
Hebrews: 423
1 Peter: 26, 33, 89, 90, 286
1–3 John: 36, 81, 130, 230
5:5, 8
1–3 John: 23
5:6
Luke 1–5: 168
Luke 11–17: 38
Romans 1–8: 52, 373
Philippians: 133
James: 115
1 Peter: 221
5:6–8
Luke 18–24: 288
5:6–10
2 Corinthians: 191
Ephesians: 355
5:6–11
Mark 1–8: 112, 131
Colossians and Philemon: 61–62
5:7
Galatians: 168
5:7–8
Ephesians: 297
5:8
Luke 6–10: 107
John 12–21: 39, 225, 227
Romans 9–16: 320
2 Corinthians: 212
Galatians: 165
Ephesians: 120
1 & 2 Thessalonians: 164
2 Timothy: 94
James: 103, 115, 209, 225, 286, 287
1 Peter: 19, 170, 193
1–3 John: 48, 71
5:8–9
Romans 1–8: 215
Galatians: 205
1 & 2 Thessalonians: 163
1 Peter: 191
5:8–10
Matthew 1–7: 346
Mark 9–16: 238
John 12–21: 37, 298
Romans 9–16: 110
Ephesians: 79
Philippians: 27
5:8–11
1 Peter: 206
2 Peter–Jude: 209
5:8, 10
Ephesians: 190
5:9
Mark 1–8: 96
Luke 11–17: 217
John 12–21: 132
Romans 1–8: 55
2 Corinthians: 190
Colossians and Philemon: 61, 64, 142
1 & 2 Thessalonians: 163
James: 137
1 Peter: 48
1–3 John: 37
Revelation 1–11: 232
Revelation 12–22: 238, 256, 308
5:9–10
James: 290
5:9–11
2 Corinthians: 199
5:10
Matthew 1–7: 215
Matthew 8–15: 311
Matthew 16–23: 192
Luke 1–5: 161
John 12–21: 310
Acts 1–12: 302
Romans 1–8: 273, 277, 408, 495
Romans 9–16: 131
1 Corinthians: 329
2 Corinthians: 212
Galatians: 97, 155
Ephesians: 18, 365
Philippians: 85
Colossians and Philemon: 62, 64
2 Timothy: 22
Titus: 146
Hebrews: 147, 261
James: 196, 225
Revelation 1–11: 232
5:10–11
James: 115
5:11
2 Corinthians: 200
Philippians: 187, 222
1 & 2 Thessalonians: 184, 185
James: 234
1 Peter: 40
5:12
Matthew 1–7: 476
Mark 1–8: 77, 252, 350
Luke 1–5: 58
Romans 1–8: 372
1 Corinthians: 445
1–3 John: 45, 109
Revelation 1–11: 254
Revelation 12–22: 120
5:12–19
Philippians: 133
5:12–21
Mark 9–16: 67
Luke 18–24: 27
Romans 1–8: 343
2 Corinthians: 210
Colossians and Philemon: 149
1 Timothy: 89
5:13
Romans 1–8: 140, 368, 372
2 Corinthians: 100
5:15
Romans 1–8: 306
2 Corinthians: 279
1 & 2 Thessalonians: 320
1 Peter: 182, 220
2 Peter–Jude: 25, 30
5:15–16
1 Corinthians: 290
5:15, 18, 20
Titus: 112
5:17
Matthew 1–7: 280
1 Corinthians: 445
2 Corinthians: 278
2 Timothy: 64
1 Peter: 182
5:17–18
Romans 1–8: 396
5:18
Matthew 1–7: 273
John 12–21: 123
Acts 1–12: 70
Ephesians: 18
5:18–19
Romans 1–8: 14
5:18–21
Ephesians: 337
5:19
Mark 1–8: 96, 348, 350
Mark 9–16: 369
Luke 1–5: 58
John 12–21: 43
1 Corinthians: 417, 439, 446
2 Corinthians: 192, 248
James: 209
Revelation 12–22: 203

5:20
Matthew 1–7: 393
Matthew 16–23: 217
Romans 1–8: 277, 314, 317, 358
1 Corinthians: 143
2 Corinthians: 99, 100, 101
Ephesians: 25
Colossians and Philemon: 111
1 Timothy: 29, 31
Hebrews: 238
5:20–21
2 Peter–Jude: 25
5:20–6:1–2
Romans 1–8: 174
5:21
Matthew 1–7: 281
John 12–21: 252
1 Corinthians: 439
1 & 2 Thessalonians: 245
Titus: 117
5:32
Romans 1–8: 114–15
5–6
Hebrews: 249
6
Ephesians: 202
6:1
Acts 13–28: 23
Romans 1–8: 363
1 Corinthians: 146
Hebrews: 238
6:1, 2
Titus: 19
6:1–2
Colossians and Philemon: 143
6:1–2, 11–13
Ephesians: 353
6:1–4
John 12–21: 38
2 Corinthians: 192
6:1–10
1 Corinthians: 220
6:1–11
Philippians: 15
6:1–13
Matthew 16–23: 187
6:1–14
Galatians: 59
6:1–22
1 & 2 Thessalonians: 287
6:2
Romans 1–8: 367
2 Corinthians: 113
6:2–8
Ephesians: 176
6:2, 15
Romans 9–16: 96
6:3
Ephesians: 29
6:3–4
Matthew 24–28: 343
1 Corinthians: 425
Philippians: 311
Colossians and Philemon: 109, 127
1 & 2 Thessalonians: 23
1 Peter: 92, 218
6:3–5
Romans 1–8: 401
1 Corinthians: 312
Galatians: 98
1–3 John: 19
6:3–7
Romans 1–8: 361
6:3–11
1 Peter: 171
6:3–14
1 Peter: 89
6:4
Matthew 1–7: 79
Matthew 24–28: 310
Luke 18–24: 408
John 12–21: 186
Ephesians: 59, 164, 182
1 & 2 Thessalonians: 52, 158
Hebrews: 310
James: 60
1–3 John: 36, 127
6:4–5
Matthew 1–7: 206
Acts 1–12: 64, 117
2 Corinthians: 193
Ephesians: 29
Philippians: 239
6:4–5, 7–8
2 Timothy: 63
6:4–6
Acts 1–12: 41
Ephesians: 275
6:4–7
1–3 John: 125
6:4–11
2 Corinthians: 456
6:5–6
Romans 1–8: 462
6:5–11
Hebrews: 58
6:6
Colossians and Philemon: 108, 135, 148
1 & 2 Thessalonians: 208
1 Peter: 73, 92
6:6–7
Galatians: 208
6:6–18
2 Corinthians: 442
6:6, 16–20
Luke 1–5: 271
6:7
2 Corinthians: 113
6:8
2 Corinthians: 193
Ephesians: 59
6:8–12
1 Peter: 227–28
6:9
Matthew 16–23: 33
Luke 18–24: 411
1 Corinthians: 444
Revelation 1–11: 51, 69
6:10–11
2 Corinthians: 193
6:10–12
1 Peter: 48
6:11
1 & 2 Thessalonians: 59, 224
6:11–12
Matthew 16–23: 153
6:11–13
Romans 9–16: 330
Galatians: 153
Ephesians: 59
Colossians and Philemon: 137
1–3 John: 128
6:11–17
1–3 John: 29
6:11–19
Colossians and Philemon: 127
6:12
Matthew 1–7: 272
Ephesians: 178
1 & 2 Thessalonians: 109
6:12, 13
Romans 9–16: 144
6:12–13
Romans 1–8: 462
1 & 2 Thessalonians: 205
James: 188
6:12–14
Titus: 116
1–3 John: 41
Revelation 12–22: 101
6:13
Ephesians: 178, 179, 210
1 Peter: 115
6:13, 19
2 Timothy: 201
6:14
Matthew 1–7: 272
Luke 1–5: 88
Romans 1–8: 358
1 Corinthians: 146, 149, 446
2 Corinthians: 113
Galatians: 97
6:14–17
Romans 1–8: 462
6:14, 18–22
Ephesians: 365
6:15
Matthew 1–7: 272
Acts 13–28: 23
Romans 1–8: 316, 363, 367
6:15–18
1–3 John: 42
6:16
Acts 13–28: 320, 337
2 Corinthians: 486
1 & 2 Thessalonians: 172
Titus: 121
1 Peter: 90
2 Peter–Jude: 105
1–3 John: 206
6:16–17
Romans 9–16: 85
6:16–18
Matthew 1–7: 385

Acts 13–28: 90
1 & 2 Thessalonians: 16, 27
James: 86
1–3 John: 123, 144
6:16–22
Matthew 1–7: 415
Ephesians: 275
James: 205
1 Peter: 152, 172
6:16, 17
Ephesians: 57
6:17
Matthew 24–28: 346
Mark 1–8: 359
John 12–21: 159
Acts 13–28: 168
Romans 1–8: 206
Romans 9–16: 335
1 Corinthians: 283
Philippians: 158, 216
1 Timothy: 18
1 Peter: 90
Revelation 12–22: 194
6:17–18
Mark 1–8: 359, 427
Romans 1–8: 306
Romans 9–16: 182
1 Peter: 22, 92
1–3 John: 125
6:17–18, 22
Romans 9–16: 283
6:17–19
Galatians: 129
6:17–22
Titus: 122
1–3 John: 207
6:18
Matthew 16–23: 245
Romans 1–8: 278
1 Corinthians: 212
Galatians: 39
Ephesians: 18
1 Peter: 48
6:18–22
Colossians and Philemon: 55
6:19
Romans 1–8: 326
1 Corinthians: 129
2 Corinthians: 248, 481
Philippians: 77, 161
1 & 2 Thessalonians: 204
2 Timothy: 91
Titus: 115, 149
6:21
2 Corinthians: 267
Ephesians: 297
6:21–22
1 & 2 Thessalonians: 16
6:22
Romans 1–8: 45
1 Corinthians: 174
Galatians: 148
1 & 2 Thessalonians: 103, 208, 245
Titus: 3
1 Peter: 22
6:23
Matthew 1–7: 476
Matthew 16–23: 188
Mark 1–8: 252
Mark 9–16: 67
Romans 1–8: 328, 360
1 Corinthians: 11, 290, 413, 446
2 Corinthians: 99, 191, 204, 213
Galatians: 94, 165, 188, 205
Ephesians: 18, 52
Philippians: 206, 310
1 & 2 Thessalonians: 245
1 Timothy: 168
Titus: 108
Hebrews: 58, 63, 138
James: 53, 288
1 Peter: 50, 191, 206
1–3 John: 30, 44
7
Matthew 1–7: 273
7:1–2, 4
Galatians: 59
7:1–3
Titus: 27
7:1–6
2 Corinthians: 113
7:2
Acts 13–28: 217
Romans 1–8: 325
1 Corinthians: 167
7:2–3
1 Peter: 177
7:3
1 Corinthians: 167
1 Timothy: 212
7:4
Colossians and Philemon: 31
7:4–6
1 Peter: 218
7:5
Romans 9–16: 142
Galatians: 155
Philippians: 77
1 Peter: 228
1–3 John: 87
7:5–6
Romans 1–8: 367
7:6
Romans 1–8: 372
1 Corinthians: 146, 446
2 Corinthians: 99
Galatians: 39
Philippians: 13, 199
7:7
Acts 13–28: 23
Romans 1–8: 140, 316
2 Corinthians: 99–100
7:7, 9
Galatians: 93
7:7–11
Luke 18–24: 39
Romans 1–8: 257
Philippians: 233
7:7–13
Mark 9–16: 79
7:8
Mark 1–8: 150
2 Corinthians: 100
7:8–11
Luke 1–5: 115
Galatians: 157
7:9
2 Corinthians: 101
Galatians: 88
1 Timothy: 31
7:9–10
1–3 John: 142
7:9–11
Matthew 1–7: 273
Luke 6–10: 298
2 Corinthians: 90, 99, 101
Hebrews: 412
7:9–13
Philippians: 237
7:10
Galatians: 77
7:10–11
Romans 1–8: 406
7:11
Hebrews: 93
7:12
Matthew 1–7: 273
Matthew 8–15: 459
Mark 9–16: 78
Luke 1–5: 24, 121, 341
Acts 13–28: 158, 265
Romans 1–8: 256, 308, 338, 358, 381, 410
2 Corinthians: 89, 99
Galatians: 87
1 Timothy: 21
7:13
Matthew 16–23: 148
Acts 13–28: 23
Romans 1–8: 316, 367
7:14
Acts 13–28: 158
2 Corinthians: 101, 163
Ephesians: 18
7:14–15, 19
Romans 9–16: 241
7:14–15, 19–21
Romans 9–16: 185
7:14–23
2 Corinthians: 126
1 Peter: 138
7:14–24
Revelation 12–22: 68
7:14–25
Matthew 1–7: 394, 475
Galatians: 171
Ephesians: 164, 249
Philippians: 243
Colossians and Philemon: 149
1 & 2 Thessalonians: 32, 159, 258
1 Timothy: 36, 262
Hebrews: 329
James: 92

1 Peter: 22, 93
1–3 John: 30, 122, 144, 145
7:14ff.
Acts 13–28: 281
Philippians: 160
7:15
Matthew 1–7: 160
Matthew 16–23: 340
Romans 1–8: 332
1 Corinthians: 68
2 Peter–Jude: 48
7:15–19
James: 81
7:15–20
1–3 John: 36
7:15–22
James: 178
7:15–23
Colossians and Philemon: 108
7:15–24
Luke 6–10: 299
7:15–25
Matthew 1–7: 204
Matthew 24–28: 177
1 Corinthians: 141
Ephesians: 183
James: 197
1–3 John: 39
7:15, 21, 25
Matthew 1–7: 204
7:16
Mark 1–8: 132
Romans 1–8: 224
1 & 2 Thessalonians: 199
2 Timothy: 193
7:17
2 Corinthians: 163
7:17–18
Ephesians: 164
7:17–24
1–3 John: 109
7:17, 18, 20, 23
Ephesians: 178–79
7:17, 19–22, 25
Matthew 1–7: 206
7:18
Matthew 1–7: 147, 157
Matthew 8–15: 130
Matthew 16–23: 47
Luke 6–10: 269, 271
Romans 1–8: 332, 338, 383
2 Corinthians: 481
Galatians: 188, 209
Philippians: 77, 168, 180, 223, 238
1 & 2 Thessalonians: 107, 195
James: 158, 188
7:18–19
Matthew 1–7: 160
James: 92
2 Peter–Jude: 48
7:18–19, 21–23
Galatians: 155
7:18–20
1 & 2 Thessalonians: 16
7:18–24
1–3 John: 37
7:18–25
Luke 18–24: 301
James: 50
7:19
Matthew 8–15: 52
1 Corinthians: 68
7:20
2 Corinthians: 163
7:21
Matthew 1–7: 160
2 Corinthians: 163
7:21–22
Romans 9–16: 243
7:21–25
Philippians: 44–45
1 & 2 Thessalonians: 208
1–3 John: 57
7:22
Matthew 1–7: 180
Matthew 16–23: 359
Romans 1–8: 417
Romans 9–16: 244
Philippians: 242
James: 230
1 Peter: 95
7:22–23
Romans 1–8: 338
Romans 9–16: 142
1 Corinthians: 68
Ephesians: 105
7:22–24
Galatians: 156
7:23
Romans 9–16: 351
Ephesians: 253
James: 188
7:23–25
Revelation 12–22: 194
7:23, 25
Luke 1–5: 115
7:24
Matthew 1–7: 184
Luke 18–24: 260
2 Corinthians: 125, 163, 345, 468
Galatians: 89
Philippians: 172, 240, 262, 266
James: 211
1–3 John: 39
7:24–25
Matthew 1–7: 160
Romans 1–8: 338
7:25
Matthew 1–7: 160, 273
Galatians: 77
Philippians: 199, 223
8
Matthew 1–7: 78, 273, 392
8:1
Acts 1–12: 117
1 Corinthians: 79, 102, 274
2 Corinthians: 45, 140, 177, 196
Galatians: 94
Ephesians: 365
Philippians: 243, 311
1 & 2 Thessalonians: 59, 163, 164, 224, 308
Hebrews: 141, 249, 385
James: 258
1 Peter: 48, 256
1–3 John: 144
Revelation 1–11: 242
Revelation 12–22: 19, 22, 154, 251, 269
8:1–2
Luke 1–5: 120
Ephesians: 23
1 Peter: 22
1–3 John: 29
8:1–3
Matthew 16–23: 245
Galatians: 206
8:1–4
Romans 9–16: 244
8:1, 28–35, 37–39
1–3 John: 33–34
8:2
Matthew 16–23: 33
Acts 13–28: 90
2 Corinthians: 89, 99, 102, 113, 140
Galatians: 39, 88, 156
Titus: 154
James: 265
1 Peter: 21, 91
8:3
Matthew 16–23: 67
Mark 1–8: 110
Luke 6–10: 356
2 Corinthians: 165, 292
Philippians: 131, 205
Colossians and Philemon: 64
1 & 2 Thessalonians: 164
James: 276
1 Peter: 224
Revelation 1–11: 167
8:3–4
Matthew 1–7: 259
Romans 1–8: 229
Galatians: 108, 158
8:3–9
1 & 2 Thessalonians: 193
8:4
Romans 1–8: 373
Philippians: 223
1 & 2 Thessalonians: 257
2 Timothy: 201
Hebrews: 313
James: 81, 86
1–3 John: 28, 36
Revelation 1–11: 54
8:4–5
Matthew 1–7: 281
Philippians: 107
8:4–11
1 Corinthians: 54
8:4–14
1 Corinthians: 72

8:5
Philippians: 77, 286, 288
Colossians and Philemon: 90
8:5–6
Ephesians: 105
Revelation 12–22: 261
8:5–8
Ephesians: 275
1 & 2 Thessalonians: 107
1 Peter: 275
8:5–9
Luke 1–5: 76
1 Peter: 137
8:5–11
Matthew 1–7: 206
8:6
Acts 13–28: 129
Philippians: 223, 286, 288
8:6–7
Ephesians: 249
8:6–8
Ephesians: 249
8:6–9
James: 196
8:7
Matthew 8–15: 356
Matthew 16–23: 42
John 12–21: 174
Romans 1–8: 133, 223, 273, 390, 495
Romans 9–16: 131
Galatians: 210
Ephesians: 120
Philippians: 221, 286
1 & 2 Thessalonians: 209
1 Timothy: 243
2 Timothy: 14
James: 225
1 Peter: 177
Revelation 12–22: 240
8:7–8
Romans 9–16: 50
2 Corinthians: 481
Colossians and Philemon: 61
1 Peter: 31, 92
1–3 John: 85, 227
8:8
Luke 6–10: 347
Luke 11–17: 77, 83, 105
Romans 9–16: 140
Philippians: 223
8:8–9
Matthew 8–15: 297
Ephesians: 105
8:9
Matthew 16–23: 50
Luke 1–5: 180
Luke 11–17: 57
Luke 18–24: 448
John 12–21: 115, 215, 278, 382
Acts 1–12: 18, 38, 169, 245, 304
Acts 13–28: 67, 164
Romans 1–8: 362
Romans 9–16: 330
1 Corinthians: 70, 152, 282, 313
2 Corinthians: 45, 114, 168, 482, 489
Galatians: 66, 152
Ephesians: 34, 38, 44, 247, 249
Philippians: 74, 124, 220, 243
1 & 2 Thessalonians: 14, 51, 112, 193, 203
2 Timothy: 31
James: 59
1 Peter: 55
2 Peter–Jude: 30
1–3 John: 103, 162
Revelation 1–11: 54
Revelation 12–22: 171
8:9–10
Philippians: 170
8:9–11
2 Corinthians: 466
8:9–13
2 Peter–Jude: 30
8:9, 11
Ephesians: 106
8:10
Romans 1–8: 373, 391
1 & 2 Thessalonians: 206
8:11
Matthew 24–28: 310
Mark 1–8: 267
2 Corinthians: 147
Philippians: 124, 243
1 & 2 Thessalonians: 14, 118, 193
1–3 John: 29
Revelation 1–11: 54
8:11–15
2 Peter–Jude: 31
8:11, 13
Romans 9–16: 144
8:12–13
2 Corinthians: 482
8:12–14,26
Galatians: 156
8:12–15
1 Peter: 137
8:13
Mark 9–16: 46, 332
1 Corinthians: 149
Ephesians: 105, 275
Philippians: 223
Colossians and Philemon: 135, 137
1 & 2 Thessalonians: 107, 195, 205, 208
1–3 John: 36, 206
8:14
Romans 1–8: 284
Galatians: 158
1 & 2 Thessalonians: 193
Hebrews: 393
1–3 John: 149
Revelation 1–11: 54
8:14–15
John 12–21: 379
James: 86
8:14–16
Matthew 1–7: 475
Galatians: 109
1–3 John: 54
8:14–17
Matthew 8–15: 15
Mark 1–8: 186, 198, 210
Romans 9–16: 314
Revelation 12–22: 272
8:14–18
1–3 John: 116
8:14–27
1 & 2 Thessalonians: 185
8:15
Matthew 16–23: 68
Mark 9–16: 301
Luke 1–5: 157
John 12–21: 298
2 Corinthians: 113
Ephesians: 15, 81
Philippians: 124, 181, 314
1 Peter: 31
1–3 John: 42
8:15–16
1 & 2 Thessalonians: 51, 194
Hebrews: 393
8:15–17
Ephesians: 80
1 & 2 Thessalonians: 193
8:16
Acts 1–12: 304
2 Corinthians: 466
Galatians: 66, 98
Ephesians: 247
1 & 2 Thessalonians: 113
2 Peter–Jude: 209
1–3 John: 52, 115
8:16–17
Matthew 16–23: 215
Matthew 24–28: 122
Romans 1–8: 255, 284
2 Corinthians: 107
Ephesians: 10, 34
Colossians and Philemon: 39
1 & 2 Thessalonians: 74
2 Timothy: 62
Titus: 156
Hebrews: 12
1 Peter: 21, 38
2 Peter–Jude: 25
Revelation 1–11: 54
8:16–18
James: 40
8:17
Matthew 1–7: 97, 217
Matthew 16–23: 113
Matthew 24–28: 79
Luke 11–17: 147
Luke 18–24: 250
Acts 1–12: 166
1 Corinthians: 91
2 Corinthians: 25, 294
Galatians: 68, 101, 110
Ephesians: viii, 82
Philippians: 95, 245

1 & 2 Thessalonians: 91
Hebrews: 68, 415
1 Peter: 206
8:17–18
Matthew 1–7: 150
2 Corinthians: 155
Colossians and Philemon: 75
1 & 2 Thessalonians: 92
Hebrews: 414
1 Peter: 3, 42
8:18
Matthew 16–23: 234
Matthew 24–28: 59
Romans 1–8: 282, 393
1 Corinthians: 61
2 Corinthians: 147, 161, 227
Ephesians: 98
Colossians and Philemon: 20
1 & 2 Thessalonians: 52, 185, 247
1 Timothy: 274, 277
2 Timothy: 26, 132
Hebrews: 355, 368
James: 24, 252, 254
1 Peter: 42, 46, 251, 286
8:18–19
Philippians: 29
1 & 2 Thessalonians: 248
8:18–21
Luke 11–17: 213
8:18–22
Luke 11–17: 156
8:18–23
Luke 18–24: 242
8:18–24
2 Corinthians: 163
8:18–25
1 Corinthians: 68
2 Corinthians: 71
James: 19
8:18, 21
Galatians: 137
8:18, 23
Titus: 10
8:19
Matthew 8–15: 220
2 Corinthians: 165
Philippians: 261
Colossians and Philemon: 131
1 Timothy: 273
Revelation 1–11: 3, 15
8:19–20
1 & 2 Thessalonians: 73
8:19–21
Luke 11–17: 404
John 1–11: 21
Revelation 1–11: 320
Revelation 12–22: 204
8:19–22
Matthew 24–28: 53, 266
Hebrews: 57
James: 64
Revelation 1–11: 159, 163, 173
Revelation 12–22: 21
8:19, 22–23
Matthew 1–7: 160
8:19, 23
1–3 John: 30
8:20
Matthew 8–15: 52
Mark 1–8: 70
Romans 1–8: 340, 396
Colossians and Philemon: 57
8:20–22
Luke 18–24: 220
1 Peter: 35
8:21
Matthew 24–28: 59
Romans 1–8: 131, 282
Romans 9–16: 111
1 Corinthians: 146
2 Corinthians: 163
Ephesians: 18
Colossians and Philemon: 58
8:21–22
Matthew 8–15: 377
Matthew 24–28: 119
8:22
Matthew 24–28: 249
Luke 18–24: 208
Romans 1–8: 340, 396
Colossians and Philemon: 57
Hebrews: 14
1 Peter: 35
8:22–23
Romans 1–8: 337
2 Corinthians: 154
Titus: 119
8:22–24
Ephesians: 164
8:22–25
Mark 1–8: 78
1 Peter: 172
1–3 John: 106
8:23
Matthew 1–7: 281
Matthew 16–23: 68
Matthew 24–28: 59
Mark 1–8: 71
Romans 1–8: 282, 393, 419
Romans 9–16: 144, 260, 269
1 Corinthians: 41, 70
2 Corinthians: 161, 163, 167
Galatians: 188
Ephesians: 34, 179
Philippians: 29, 180, 181, 240, 243, 261, 262, 314
Colossians and Philemon: 108, 137, 138, 145, 149
1 & 2 Thessalonians: 107, 132, 162
James: 257
1 Peter: 85, 138
1–3 John: 203
Revelation 12–22: 272
8:23–24
Ephesians: 366
8:23–25
2 Corinthians: 107
8:24
1 & 2 Thessalonians: 18
1 Timothy: 167
8:24–25
Romans 9–16: 192
8:25
Luke 1–5: 64
2 Corinthians: 227
Philippians: 261
8:26
Matthew 1–7: 372
John 12–21: 113, 178
Acts 1–12: 304
Ephesians: 158, 189, 247, 383
Philippians: 75, 105, 141
1 & 2 Thessalonians: 186
1 Timothy: 62
8:26–27
John 12–21: 208
Romans 1–8: 472
Philippians: 245
1–3 John: 163
8:26–30
John 12–21: 209
8:27
Ephesians: 189
1 & 2 Thessalonians: 87
Revelation 1–11: 320
8:28
Matthew 24–28: 301
Mark 1–8: 235, 246
Mark 9–16: 288
Luke 11–17: 183, 234
John 12–21: 231
Acts 13–28: 100, 105
Romans 1–8: 336
1 Corinthians: 70, 91, 92
2 Corinthians: 471
Galatians: 167
Ephesians: 7, 267
Philippians: 33, 72, 124, 171, 283, 298
Colossians and Philemon: 183, 223
1 & 2 Thessalonians: 17, 172, 189, 256
Titus: 75
Hebrews: 434
James: 21, 232, 261
1 Peter: 204, 279
1–3 John: 166
8:28–29
1 & 2 Thessalonians: 178, 201
Revelation 1–11: 77
8:28–30
2 Corinthians: 71, 167–68
Galatians: 140
Philippians: 164
1 & 2 Thessalonians: 184, 185, 208
James: 110
1 Peter: 18, 51, 122
1–3 John: 164
Revelation 12–22: 99
8:28–39
Revelation 1–11: 116

8:28, 29
Ephesians: 13
8:29
Matthew 1–7: 139
Matthew 16–23: 24, 37
Matthew 24–28: 122
Luke 1–5: 196
John 12–21: 249, 257, 284, 379
Romans 1–8: 280
Romans 9–16: 368
2 Corinthians: 124, 168
Galatians: 120
Ephesians: 29, 46, 63, 92, 130, 157, 194, 274
Philippians: 28, 124, 172, 246, 253, 263
Colossians and Philemon: 45, 46, 151
1 & 2 Thessalonians: 288
2 Timothy: 57, 61
Hebrews: 397, 415
James: 202, 206
1 Peter: 23
1–3 John: 28
8:29–30
John 12–21: 247, 277
Acts 1–12: 141
Romans 1–8: 279
Romans 9–16: 100, 130
1 Corinthians: 399
2 Corinthians: 107
Philippians: 15, 23, 27, 173
1 & 2 Thessalonians: 286
2 Timothy: 82
Titus: 10, 111
Hebrews: 167
James: 61
1 Peter: 17–19
2 Peter–Jude: 28
8:29–39
Revelation 12–22: 14
8:29ff.
Acts 1–12: 252
8:30
Mark 9–16: 239
Luke 18–24: 216, 250
Romans 1–8: 28, 131
1 Corinthians: 22
Galatians: 13, 135
Ephesians: 119, 366
Philippians: 124
1 & 2 Thessalonians: 89, 91, 203, 256, 288
1 Timothy: 265
8:30–39
1 Peter: 279
8:31
Revelation 1–11: 51
8:31–34
Romans 1–8: 278
1 Corinthians: 79
James: 258
Revelation 12–22: 19
8:31–35
1 Peter: 122
8:31, 37–39
Ephesians: 356
8:31–39
2 Corinthians: 21
Philippians: 169
Colossians and Philemon: 131–32
1 Peter: 36, 286
2 Peter–Jude: 153
1–3 John: 108–9, 208–9
Revelation 12–22: 74
8:32
Luke 1–5: 168
Luke 6–10: 295
Romans 1–8: 100
2 Corinthians: 145, 213, 232
1 Peter: 206
2 Peter–Jude: 18, 25
1–3 John: 44
8:33
Acts 13–28: 38
1 Corinthians: 146
Colossians and Philemon: 55, 65
1 & 2 Thessalonians: 20, 89, 287
Revelation 1–11: 54
8:33–34
Matthew 1–7: 392
Luke 1–5: 24
Acts 13–28: 336
1 & 2 Thessalonians: 163
1–3 John: 44
Revelation 1–11: 45
8:33–34, 38–39
Romans 9–16: 280
8:33–39
1–3 John: 37
8:34
Luke 18–24: 307, 453
John 12–21: 88, 140, 213, 273
Acts 1–12: 67
2 Corinthians: 177
Philippians: 141
1 & 2 Thessalonians: 234, 302
Hebrews: 20
Revelation 1–11: 242
Revelation 12–22: 214
8:35
Hebrews: 146
1 Peter: 193
2 Peter–Jude: 18
8:35–39
John 12–21: 280, 310
2 Corinthians: 152, 168, 189–90
1 & 2 Thessalonians: 226, 288
2 Timothy: 28, 54
1 Peter: 16
1–3 John: 19
Revelation 1–11: 26
8:35, 37–39
Matthew 8–15: 210
8:36
John 12–21: 174
2 Corinthians: 144
8:37
Luke 1–5: 285
2 Corinthians: 71
Ephesians: 265
Revelation 12–22: 51, 68
8:37–39
1 Corinthians: 92
Colossians and Philemon: 113
1 Peter: 122
8:38
Mark 1–8: 250
John 1–11: 16
1 & 2 Thessalonians: 134
8:38–39
Mark 1–8: 234
Mark 9–16: 239
Luke 6–10: 212
John 12–21: 92, 232
Romans 1–8: 275
Romans 9–16: 2, 11
2 Corinthians: 391
Ephesians: 365
Philippians: 29, 276
1 & 2 Thessalonians: 178
Hebrews: 146
2 Peter–Jude: 18, 153, 210
1–3 John: 54
Revelation 12–22: 23, 49
8:39
Romans 1–8: 20
1 Peter: 193
1–3 John: 23, 36
9
Romans 9–16: 57
9:1
Matthew 1–7: 324
Acts 13–28: 149
1 Corinthians: 479
2 Corinthians: 43
1 & 2 Thessalonians: 319
1 Timothy: 151
James: 267
1–3 John: 142
9:1–3
Acts 13–28: 117, 273, 314, 369
Romans 9–16: 20, 128
1 Corinthians: 333
2 Corinthians: 194, 476–77
Ephesians: 118
Hebrews: 40
Revelation 1–11: 288
9:1–4
2 Corinthians: 158
Philippians: 42
9:1–5
Acts 13–28: 259
Romans 9–16: 7, 20
1 & 2 Thessalonians: 64
9:2
2 Corinthians: 231
Philippians: 257
9:2–3
Acts 13–28: 211
1 Corinthians: 479
Philippians: 39

9:3
Matthew 1–7: 113
Luke 1–5: 177
Acts 13–28: 216
Romans 9–16: 108
1 Corinthians: 212
Philippians: 77, 191
1 Timothy: 68
Hebrews: 260
9:3–4
Matthew 24–28: 91
Romans 9–16: 111
2 Corinthians: 111
Hebrews: 423
9:3–5
Acts 1–12: 123
Romans 1–8: 167
Philippians: 229
9:4
Luke 1–5: 106
John 12–21: 191
Romans 1–8: 114
Romans 9–16: 66, 92
2 Corinthians: 385
Ephesians: 73
Hebrews: 166
9:4–5
Matthew 1–7: 68
Matthew 16–23: 376
Mark 1–8: 369
Luke 1–5: 96
Luke 11–17: 190, 274, 400
Acts 1–12: 201
Romans 9–16: 5, 21
2 Corinthians: 211, 385
1 & 2 Thessalonians: 62
Revelation 1–11: 130
9:5
Luke 1–5: 106
John 1–11: 7, 14
2 Corinthians: 19, 44, 393, 488
Philippians: 150
Hebrews: 33
2 Peter–Jude: 10, 23, 114
Revelation 1–11: 254
Revelation 12–22: 11
9:6
Luke 1–5: 126
Acts 1–12: 70
Romans 1–8: 161
Romans 9–16: 13
1 Corinthians: 219
Colossians and Philemon: 107
1 Timothy: 48
Hebrews: 167
1 Peter: 25
9:6–7
Matthew 8–15: 350, 384
Luke 1–5: 221
Romans 1–8: 171
Galatians: 210
Ephesians: 10
Revelation 1–11: 123
9:6–8
Matthew 8–15: 159
Luke 1–5: 134
9:6–11
Galatians: 101
9:6–13, 14–29
Romans 9–16: 7
9:7
Luke 1–5: 109, 196
2 Corinthians: 16
9:8
1 Corinthians: 219
Hebrews: 167
9:9
Luke 1–5: 174
Titus: 45
1 Peter: 279
9:11
James: 176
1 Peter: 279
9:11–13
Romans 1–8: 486
Galatians: 28
1 Peter: 19, 32
9:13
Luke 11–17: 283
Romans 9–16: 27
9:13–16
Romans 9–16: 30
1 Peter: 124
9:13–22
Colossians and Philemon: 154–55
9:13, 15
Luke 1–5: 134–35
9:14
Acts 13–28: 23
Romans 1–8: 115, 316
9:14–18
Luke 6–10: 346
9:14–24
Mark 1–8: 97
9:15
Romans 9–16: 2
Titus: 6
9:15–16
1 & 2 Thessalonians: 20
1 Peter: 31, 32
9:16
Philippians: 242
1 & 2 Thessalonians: 255
James: 261
1 Peter: 19, 25–26
9:16, 18
Luke 1–5: 135
John 12–21: 258
9:17
Acts 13–28: 196
2 Timothy: 144
1 Peter: 279
9:18
John 12–21: 53
Acts 13–28: 173
1 & 2 Thessalonians: 255
1 Peter: 31
9:18–19
Matthew 16–23: 393
9:18–21
Philippians: 178
9:19–21
Titus: 6
9:19–24
John 12–21: 259
9:20–21
1 Corinthians: 315
2 Peter–Jude: 26
9:20–23
Matthew 16–23: 393
9:21
1 Corinthians: 463
1 & 2 Thessalonians: 107
2 Timothy: 86
1 Peter: 288
9:22
Romans 1–8: 280
1 & 2 Thessalonians: 66, 163
1 Timothy: 256
1 Peter: 128
2 Peter–Jude: 71
9:22–23
Romans 1–8: 120
Philippians: 78
1 & 2 Thessalonians: 107
1 Timothy: 69
9:23
Mark 1–8: 122
John 1–11: 450
John 12–21: 156
Romans 1–8: 280
1 & 2 Thessalonians: 52
1 Peter: 45, 133
9:24
1 & 2 Thessalonians: 255, 256
9:25–26
Matthew 16–23: 299, 309
1 Peter: 53
9:25–27
John 12–21: 25
9:26
2 Corinthians: 253
Revelation 1–11: 51, 217
9:27
Matthew 16–23: 402
Luke 1–5: 70, 154
Romans 9–16: 6
Revelation 1–11: 291
9:28
Titus: 45
9:29
Romans 9–16: 25
James: 3
1 Peter: 26
9:30
Acts 13–28: 336
9:30–32
Mark 9–16: 79
Romans 9–16: 3
Galatians: 134
9:30–33
1 & 2 Thessalonians: 56
9:31–32
Luke 1–5: 328
Romans 9–16: 60, 66, 68

9:32
Luke 11–17: 245
Luke 18–24: 128
9:32–33
Luke 1–5: 183
Romans 9–16: 66, 95
9:33
Mark 1–8: 434
Acts 1–12: 148, 303
Acts 13–28: 119
1 Peter: 53, 120
9:33b
Mark 9–16: 171
9–11
Matthew 1–7: 257, 272
Romans 9–16: 1, 7
1 Peter: 129
10
Romans 9–16: 57
10:1
Matthew 1–7: 113
Luke 18–24: 2
John 12–21: 25
Acts 13–28: 17, 117, 149, 259, 264, 369
Romans 9–16: 111, 128
1 Corinthians: 212
2 Corinthians: 195
Galatians: 182
Philippians: 21, 39, 42
1 & 2 Thessalonians: 64, 188, 255, 293, 294
1 Timothy: 60, 68
2 Timothy: 6
Hebrews: 40
10:1–3
Luke 6–10: 355
2 Corinthians: 211
Revelation 1–11: 132
10:1–4
Romans 1–8: 271
Romans 9–16: 3
10:2
Matthew 16–23: 278
Mark 1–8: 339
Luke 6–10: 42
Luke 11–17: 346
Luke 18–24: 16
Acts 13–28: 265
Romans 9–16: 102, 267
2 Peter–Jude: 24
1–3 John: 226
Revelation 1–11: 137
10:2–3
Luke 1–5: 21
Luke 6–10: 129
Galatians: 95
1 & 2 Thessalonians: 62
Hebrews: 300
10:2–4
Galatians: 77
2 Peter–Jude: 48
10:3
Matthew 1–7: 279, 452
Mark 9–16: 135
Luke 18–24: 38
Romans 9–16: 66, 95, 102
2 Corinthians: 99
Titus: 66
1 Peter: 48, 177
10:4
Matthew 1–7: 273
Matthew 16–23: 67
Romans 9–16: 102
Colossians and Philemon: 117
10:6
Revelation 1–11: 145
10:8
1 & 2 Thessalonians: 22
10:8–10
Acts 13–28: 268
10:9
Matthew 8–15: 92
Mark 1–8: 49, 188
Mark 9–16: 355, 383, 405
Luke 1–5: 160, 315, 322, 328
Luke 6–10: 119
Luke 11–17: 120, 173
Luke 18–24: 373, 430
John 12–21: 87, 258, 343, 372–73, 383
Romans 9–16: 83
1 Corinthians: 398
2 Corinthians: 89, 133, 147, 207, 217
Ephesians: 38
Philippians: 146, 147
Colossians and Philemon: 109
1 Timothy: 7, 265
James: 171, 290
10:9–10
Matthew 8–15: 227
Matthew 16–23: 195
Matthew 24–28: 326
Mark 1–8: 107, 422
Luke 6–10: 238
Luke 11–17: 175
Luke 18–24: 74, 415
John 1–11: 22
John 12–21: 255
Acts 1–12: 74, 270
Acts 13–28: 109
Romans 1–8: 25, 486
1 Corinthians: 287
2 Corinthians: 216
Philippians: 24
1 & 2 Thessalonians: 287
James: 140, 203, 204
1 Peter: 37, 218
1–3 John: 41
Revelation 12–22: 49
10:9–10, 17
2 Timothy: 152
10:9–11
Acts 13–28: 336
10:9–13
Mark 9–16: 242
10:10
Matthew 8–15: 320
Acts 1–12: 71
1 & 2 Thessalonians: 57
Revelation 1–11: 54
10:10–11
Ephesians: 33
10:11
Acts 1–12: 303
Acts 13–28: 196
10:11–13
1 Peter: 53
10:11, 13
Titus: 111
10:12
Acts 13–28: 199
Ephesians: 130
Philippians: 147
James: 109
10:12–13
Romans 9–16: 323
Ephesians: 78
2 Timothy: 94
2 Peter–Jude: 20
10:12–15
Acts 1–12: 255
10:13
Luke 18–24: 447
John 12–21: 186, 281
Acts 13–28: 269
Romans 9–16: 295
1 Corinthians: 287
Ephesians: 198
Philippians: 147
James: 290
10:13–14
Revelation 1–11: 291
10:13–15
Mark 1–8: 81, 287
Acts 13–28: 151
2 Corinthians: 134, 207
2 Timothy: 173
10:13–17
Mark 1–8: 218
Luke 1–5: 297
Revelation 1–11: 90
10:14
Luke 1–5: 162
Acts 13–28: 15
Romans 1–8: 487
2 Corinthians: 82, 91
Ephesians: 93
Philippians: 216
Colossians and Philemon: 23–24
1 & 2 Thessalonians: 22
2 Timothy: 62
James: 63
2 Peter–Jude: 24
10:14–15
Luke 6–10: 103
Acts 1–12: 27, 50
2 Corinthians: 71
10:14–17
John 12–21: 186
1 Peter: 37, 51
2 Peter–Jude: 29
10:14–18
Acts 13–28: 3
10:14, 17
2 Timothy: 138

10:15
Galatians: 182
Ephesians: 354
10:16
Matthew 1–7: 13
Ephesians: 93
10:17
Matthew 16–23: 24
Luke 11–17: 122
John 12–21: 288, 386
Acts 1–12: 51, 258, 276
Romans 1–8: 206
Romans 9–16: 385
2 Corinthians: 82, 133
Ephesians: 371
Philippians: 216, 287
1 & 2 Thessalonians: 57, 204
Titus: 5
Hebrews: 298
James: 63
1 Peter: 92
2 Peter–Jude: 24
Revelation 12–22: 304
10:18
Colossians and Philemon: 21
10:19–20
Romans 9–16: 109
10:19–21
Acts 13–28: 156
10:20
1 Peter: 18, 32, 53
10:21
Luke 11–17: 241
Romans 9–16: 95, 96, 99
11
Luke 18–24: 192, 446
Romans 9–16: 96
11:1
Luke 1–5: 245
Acts 13–28: 20, 23
Romans 1–8: 171, 316
11:1–2
Mark 9–16: 139
Luke 1–5: 111
Acts 13–28: 375
Galatians: 75
Revelation 1–11: 31
11:1–2a
Luke 18–24: 126
11:1–5
Revelation 1–11: 113
11:1–10
Romans 9–16: 127
11:1–24
1 Timothy: 216
11:1–32
Luke 1–5: 211
Luke 18–24: 282
11:2
Matthew 16–23: 299
Acts 1–12: 120, 123
Acts 13–28: 196
Revelation 1–11: 293
11:2, 5, 24
Matthew 8–15: 16
11:3
Luke 6–10: 99
11:3–4
Romans 9–16: 23
11:4–5
Colossians and Philemon: 155
Revelation 1–11: 291, 293, 300, 305
11:5
Luke 1–5: 154
2 Corinthians: 110
Hebrews: 102
1 Peter: 124
11:6
Mark 1–8: 133
Luke 1–5: 328, 342
Acts 13–28: 34, 64
11:7
Romans 9–16: 37
1 & 2 Thessalonians: 287
11:7–10
Acts 1–12: 220
11:8
Luke 1–5: 272
1 & 2 Thessalonians: 284
11:11
Matthew 16–23: 309
Luke 1–5: 111
Acts 13–28: 23
Romans 1–8: 316
11:11–12
Matthew 16–23: 404
1 Corinthians: 382–83
1 Peter: 282
11:11–12, 25
Romans 9–16: 323
11:11–15
John 12–21: 30
11:11–24
Romans 9–16: 131
11:11, 12
Romans 9–16: 4
11:13
Luke 18–24: 446
Acts 1–12: 34, 273
Acts 13–28: 36, 216, 246
Romans 1–8: 26
Romans 9–16: 57, 108
Galatians: 21
Ephesians: xii, 88
1 Timothy: 125
2 Timothy: 213
Revelation 1–11: 31
11:14
1 Corinthians: 212
11:17
Matthew 24–28: 244
Luke 1–5: 111
Acts 13–28: 375
Romans 9–16: 128
1 Peter: 140
11:17–24
Hebrews: 214
11:19–22
Acts 13–28: 375
11:20
1 Peter: 140
11:20–21
Romans 9–16: 127
11:20–24
Acts 13–28: 156
11:22
Philippians: 163
11:23
Matthew 16–23: 404
Luke 1–5: 111
Acts 13–28: 375
11:24
Romans 9–16: 127
1 Peter: 129
11:24–25
Romans 9–16: 330
11:25
Matthew 8–15: 290
Mark 1–8: 310
Luke 1–5: 111
John 12–21: 162
Romans 9–16: 5, 94, 128
1 Corinthians: 191, 282
2 Corinthians: 25, 109
Ephesians: xi
Philippians: 58, 111
1 & 2 Thessalonians: 278
Revelation 1–11: 286
11:25–26
Matthew 16–23: 404
Matthew 24–28: 55, 81
Luke 1–5: 119
Luke 11–17: 248, 250
Romans 9–16: 46
1 Corinthians: 383
11:25–27
Luke 1–5: 107
Luke 11–17: 415
Luke 18–24: 194
1 & 2 Thessalonians: 265
Titus: 6
Revelation 1–11: 223
Revelation 12–22: 12, 79, 212
11:25–29
Romans 1–8: 171
1 Peter: 282
Revelation 12–22: 27
11:26
Matthew 16–23: 402
Matthew 24–28: 75, 116
Mark 9–16: 140
Luke 1–5: 110, 111, 120
Luke 6–10: 147
Luke 11–17: 155
Luke 18–24: 126
John 12–21: 57
Acts 1–12: 118, 121, 205
Acts 13–28: 375
Romans 9–16: 3, 94, 102
Hebrews: 166, 214
1 Peter: 129
Revelation 1–11: 123, 148, 150, 209, 215, 293, 300, 305

Revelation 12–22: 4, 12, 34, 239
11:26–27
Matthew 1–7: 45
Matthew 8–15: 343
Luke 1–5: 135
1 & 2 Thessalonians: 66
1 Peter: 132
Revelation 12–22: 70
11:26–29
Revelation 1–11: 194
11:26a
Luke 1–5: 135
11:28
Mark 1–8: 310
2 Peter–Jude: 10
11:29
Matthew 24–28: 118
Luke 1–5: 111, 135
Romans 1–8: 20, 499
Romans 9–16: 6, 141
1 Corinthians: 290
Ephesians: 119
1 & 2 Thessalonians: 255, 256
Hebrews: 214
2 Peter–Jude: 29
Revelation 12–22: 99
11:30
James: 261
11:30–32
1 Peter: 31
11:31
Hebrews: 166
11:32
Ephesians: 58
James: 261
11:33
Luke 18–24: 290
Ephesians: 95
Philippians: 135, 284
1 & 2 Thessalonians: 184
James: 36, 109, 167
11:33–34
1 Corinthians: 363
11:33–36
Mark 1–8: 421
Luke 11–17: 398
Romans 9–16: 7, 140, 382
2 Corinthians: 158
Philippians: 167, 312
1 Timothy: 70
11:33, 36
Romans 9–16: 148
11:36
Matthew 16–23: 26
Acts 13–28: 139
Romans 1–8: 238
Romans 9–16: 328
2 Corinthians: 44
Ephesians: 58
Philippians: 139, 150
1 & 2 Thessalonians: 42
1 Timothy: 154
Hebrews: 11
1 Peter: 245
12
Ephesians: 136
12:1
Matthew 8–15: 132
Mark 9–16: 49
Romans 1–8: 326, 338, 348, 349
Romans 9–16: 258
1 Corinthians: 157, 424
2 Corinthians: 20, 175, 178, 186
Ephesians: 116, 241
Philippians: 75, 105, 192, 222, 307
1 & 2 Thessalonians: 205
2 Timothy: 189
Hebrews: 335, 401
James: 261
1 Peter: 115, 137
Revelation 1–11: 232
12:1–2
Matthew 1–7: 386
Romans 1–8: 419
2 Corinthians: 173, 257, 284
Galatians: 64, 189
1 & 2 Thessalonians: 107, 204
1 Timothy: 279–80
Titus: 71, 100
James: 237
1 Peter: 22, 112, 115, 128, 275
1–3 John: 114
Revelation 12–22: 79
12:1–3
1 Peter: 22, 127, 275
12:1, 2
Romans 9–16: 154
12:1, 3
Romans 9–16: 162
12:1, 3–21
Romans 9–16: 206
12:2
Matthew 1–7: 426
Luke 1–5: 296
John 12–21: 263
Acts 1–12: 83
Romans 9–16: 188
2 Corinthians: 116, 244, 481
Ephesians: 348, 350
Philippians: 49, 51, 131, 198, 243, 289
Colossians and Philemon: 126, 129, 137, 150
1 & 2 Thessalonians: 199, 208
Titus: 141
Hebrews: 328
James: 53, 195, 200
1 Peter: 65, 137, 201
1–3 John: 72
Revelation 1–11: 82
Revelation 12–22: 181
12:1–13:10
2 Peter–Jude: 51
12:2–13:10
Romans 9–16: 258
12:3
Luke 6–10: 31
Luke 11–17: 375
Romans 9–16: 189, 330
1 Corinthians: 292
2 Corinthians: 344
Ephesians: 135
Philippians: 31, 107
1 & 2 Thessalonians: 195
2 Timothy: 19
Titus: 74
1 Peter: 243, 278
2 Peter–Jude: 20
12:3–6
2 Timothy: 87
12:3–8
Hebrews: 156
1–3 John: 149
12:4–5
Philippians: 90
12:4–8
1 Timothy: 179
12:4–13
1 & 2 Thessalonians: 166, 193
12:5
1 Corinthians: 32, 150, 310
Ephesians: 137
Philippians: 100
1 & 2 Thessalonians: 59, 166, 224
Titus: 165
1 Peter: 187
1–3 John: 29
12:6
Romans 9–16: 328, 331
1 Corinthians: 290, 303
1 & 2 Thessalonians: 196, 320
12:6–8
Acts 13–28: 44
1 Corinthians: 291, 298
Ephesians: 135, 136
1 Timothy: 125
12:6–8, 11
2 Timothy: 16
12:7
Acts 13–28: 43
1 Corinthians: 324
2 Timothy: 210
Titus: 44
12:8
Matthew 1–7: 414
Acts 13–28: 43
2 Corinthians: 484
Ephesians: 147
1 Peter: 193
12:9
Matthew 1–7: 331
Romans 9–16: 376
2 Corinthians: 183, 229
Philippians: 50
1 & 2 Thessalonians: 199
1–3 John: 36
Revelation 1–11: 104
12:9–10
1–3 John: 164

12:9–10, 15–16
Romans 9–16: 371
12:9–21
Romans 9–16: 182
1 & 2 Thessalonians: 97, 203
12:10
Matthew 1–7: 150
John 12–21: 286
Acts 1–12: 84
Philippians: 108
1 & 2 Thessalonians: 90, 117
1 Timothy: 188
Hebrews: 424
1 Peter: 93, 278
1–3 John: 131
12:10–13
Romans 9–16: 298
1–3 John: 136
12:10ff.
Acts 13–28: 206
12:11
John 12–21: 4
Ephesians: 328
Philippians: 199
12:12
Luke 11–17: 2, 30
Acts 1–12: 85, 259
Ephesians: 103, 379
Philippians: 11, 38, 69
1 & 2 Thessalonians: 187, 298
1 Peter: 42
12:13
Luke 6–10: 365
Acts 13–28: 95, 360
Philippians: 22, 108
1 Timothy: 107
Titus: 40
Revelation 1–11: 320
12:14
Luke 11–17: 196
Acts 13–28: 273
Colossians and Philemon: 219
1 & 2 Thessalonians: 90
Revelation 12–22: 184
12:14, 20
Romans 9–16: 247
1–3 John: 134
12:15
1 Corinthians: 183
Philippians: 115
1 & 2 Thessalonians: 117,
126, 184
12:16
Mark 9–16: 100
Acts 1–12: 84
2 Corinthians: 262–63
Philippians: 90, 100
1 Peter: 187, 278
12:17
1 Corinthians: 338
2 Corinthians: 307
Revelation 12–22: 184
12:17, 19
Matthew 1–7: 332
12:17–19
1 Peter: 158
12:17–21
Ephesians: 185
12:18
Matthew 1–7: 216
1 Corinthians: 168
1 & 2 Thessalonians: 90, 174
2 Timothy: 94
Titus: 39, 143
Hebrews: 405
12:19
Matthew 8–15: 115
Luke 6–10: 104
Luke 11–17: 46, 382
Luke 18–24: 8
1 Corinthians: 21
2 Corinthians: 52, 257, 476
Colossians and Philemon: 219
1 & 2 Thessalonians: 111,
163, 180
2 Timothy: 211
1 Peter: 189
Revelation 1–11: 189
Revelation 12–22: 126, 143
12:19–20
Revelation 1–11: 189
12:19–21
Revelation 12–22: 184
12:20
1 & 2 Thessalonians: 90
12:20–21
1 & 2 Thessalonians: 181
12:21
Matthew 1–7: 332
Philippians: 291
2 Timothy: 93
12–16
1 Corinthians: 385
13:1
Matthew 16–23: 322
Luke 1–5: 259
1 Corinthians: 479, 481
2 Corinthians: 283
Philippians: 113
Hebrews: 444
James: 204
1 Peter: 177
Revelation 1–11: 310
13:1–2
Matthew 16–23: 90
13:1–4
Luke 11–17: 32
Luke 18–24: 135–36
Romans 9–16: 373
1 & 2 Thessalonians: 277
1 Peter: 146
13:1–5
Acts 13–28: 320
1 Timothy: 64
James: 98
13:1–7
Matthew 16–23: 34
Acts 1–12: 15, 138
Acts 13–28: 304
2 Corinthians: 439
Philippians: 39, 204
Titus: 99, 142
Revelation 12–22: 229
13:1, 8
Romans 9–16: 330
13:1ff.
Revelation 1–11: 71
13:2–4
1 Peter: 255
13:3
1 Peter: 150
13:3–4
Acts 1–12: 183
1 Peter: 148
13:4
Matthew 1–7: 331
Matthew 24–28: 190
Mark 9–16: 314
Luke 18–24: 316
Romans 9–16: 201, 360
1 Timothy: 124
1 Peter: 150
13:5
Matthew 16–23: 90
Romans 1–8: 141
1 Peter: 177
13:5–7
Matthew 16–23: 90, 322
13:6
Romans 9–16: 332
1 Corinthians: 455
13:6–7
Matthew 16–23: 385
Luke 11–17: 333
2 Corinthians: 283
13:7
Luke 1–5: 220
Luke 18–24: 71
1 Peter: 153
13:8
Matthew 1–7: 446
Acts 1–12: 84
Romans 9–16: 184
1 Corinthians: 213
2 Corinthians: 273
1 & 2 Thessalonians: 90
James: 223
13:8–9
1 Corinthians: 330
13:8–10
Matthew 16–23: 342
Luke 1–5: 220
John 12–21: 157
Galatians: 148
Ephesians: 77, 109, 194
Philippians: 44
1 & 2 Thessalonians: 81, 90
James: 111–12
1–3 John: 63, 67
13:9
Matthew 1–7: 338
James: 249
13:10
1 Corinthians: 213
Colossians and Philemon:
157, 220
1 & 2 Thessalonians: 162

13:11
Mark 1–8: 78
1 Corinthians: 41
Ephesians: 362, 366
Philippians: 163
1 & 2 Thessalonians: 132, 162
Titus: 120
James: 76
1 Peter: 37, 172
2 Peter–Jude: 51
13:11–13
Mark 9–16: 263, 303
13:11–14
Matthew 24–28: 81–82
Luke 11–17: 159
Luke 18–24: 257
Romans 9–16: 257
Colossians and Philemon: 186
13:12
Mark 1–8: 213
Luke 1–5: 122
2 Corinthians: 249
Ephesians: 62, 206
1 & 2 Thessalonians: 73, 132, 161
James: 256
1–3 John: 25
Revelation 1–11: 24
13:12–14
Luke 18–24: 197
Acts 1–12: 23
1 & 2 Thessalonians: 159
Revelation 12–22: 226
13:12, 14
Ephesians: 354
13:13
Luke 1–5: 37
Luke 18–24: 256
Philippians: 64
1 & 2 Thessalonians: 105, 113, 257
1 Peter: 228
1–3 John: 28
13:13–14
Galatians: 154
13:14
Matthew 16–23: 48
Mark 9–16: 47
Luke 18–24: 383
Romans 1–8: 428
Galatians: 147, 156
Colossians and Philemon: 160
1 & 2 Thessalonians: 107
1 Peter: 137, 200
1–3 John: 37
Revelation 12–22: 150
14
Hebrews: 403
14:1
Luke 11–17: 378
2 Corinthians: 392
Philippians: 180
14:1–2
James: 276
14:1–3
Acts 1–12: 296
Galatians: 149
14:1–10
Acts 13–28: 64
14:1–12
Romans 9–16: 274
1 Timothy: 154
14:1–15:3
Revelation 1–11: 61
14:1–15:6
Acts 13–28: 157
14:1–15:7
1 Corinthians: 320
Philippians: 102
14:1–15:13
1 & 2 Thessalonians: 178
14:1, 3
Romans 9–16: 318
14:1ff.
Acts 13–28: 250
14:3
Matthew 16–23: 115
14:4
Matthew 1–7: 433
Philippians: 87
14:5
Acts 13–28: 202
Colossians and Philemon: 119
14:5–6
Matthew 1–7: 257
Matthew 8–15: 287
Mark 1–8: 141
2 Corinthians: 281
14:6
Revelation 12–22: 194
14:7–8
2 Corinthians: 175
Ephesians: 243
Philippians: 193
14:7–9
Acts 13–28: 73
Philippians: 76
14:8
Matthew 16–23: 242, 282
Acts 1–12: 189
2 Corinthians: 193
1 & 2 Thessalonians: 134
2 Timothy: 19
14:9
Romans 9–16: 74
Ephesians: 38
Philippians: 141, 147
James: 140
Revelation 12–22: 238
14:10
1 Corinthians: 79
2 Corinthians: 177
1 & 2 Thessalonians: 74, 144
2 Timothy: 28
James: 257
Revelation 1–11: 30
14:10–12
1 Corinthians: 78
14:11
Philippians: 146, 147
James: 269
14:11–13
Mark 1–8: 295
14:12
Matthew 16–23: 52, 57
Romans 1–8: 128
James: 151
2 Peter–Jude: 113
14:12–13
Hebrews: 401
14:13
Matthew 1–7: 432
Mark 9–16: 45
Philippians: 51
1 & 2 Thessalonians: 110
14:13–23
1 Timothy: 225
14:14–16
Hebrews: 401
14:15
Romans 9–16: 299
2 Corinthians: 191
Galatians: 149
Ephesians: 242
14:16
2 Corinthians: 307
14:17
Matthew 1–7: 56, 426
Matthew 8–15: 189, 387
Luke 1–5: 123
Luke 6–10: 96
Luke 11–17: 26, 147, 293, 404
Acts 1–12: 16, 259
Acts 13–28: 173, 372
Galatians: 166
Ephesians: 80
Philippians: 10, 18, 216, 221
Colossians and Philemon: 41, 118
1 & 2 Thessalonians: 24, 52, 184, 185, 208, 313
2 Timothy: 200
Hebrews: 438
1 Peter: 40, 193
1–3 John: 19
Revelation 12–22: 229
14:17–18
Matthew 16–23: 34
Titus: 100
14:18
2 Corinthians: 173, 350
Philippians: 199
14:19
Acts 1–12: 84
Romans 9–16: 309
1 Corinthians: 385
2 Corinthians: 479, 485
Ephesians: 243
Philippians: 115
1 & 2 Thessalonians: 174
14:20–21
Ephesians: 242–43
14:20–23
Matthew 16–23: 108
Romans 9–16: 10
14:21
Romans 9–16: 248

Philippians: 115
Titus: 37
14:22–23
John 12–21: 129
14:23
1 Corinthians: 195
Ephesians: 244
14–15
Acts 13–28: 253
15:1
2 Corinthians: 392
Galatians: 178
Philippians: 115
15:1–3
Mark 9–16: 45
Philippians: 120
15:2–3
1 Corinthians: 385
15:3
Romans 1–8: 34
Galatians: 147
15:4
Matthew 1–7: 162
Romans 1–8: 267
Ephesians: 370
1 & 2 Thessalonians: 89, 108, 166, 198
1 Timothy: 186
1 Peter: 192
15:4–6
2 Corinthians: 485
15:4–7
1 & 2 Thessalonians: 203
15:5
Acts 1–12: 84
Romans 9–16: 198, 312
Philippians: 107
15:5–6
John 12–21: 291
15:5–7
Matthew 1–7: 176
1 Corinthians: 30
Philippians: 100, 120
1 & 2 Thessalonians: 83, 86
James: 103
15:6
Matthew 1–7: 82
Mark 1–8: 36
Mark 9–16: 196
Luke 11–17: 10, 17
Acts 13–28: 129
2 Corinthians: 18, 393
Ephesians: 41
Philippians: 314
1 Peter: 31
15:7
Acts 1–12: 84
Romans 9–16: 275
15:8
Philippians: 218
2 Peter–Jude: 10
15:8–9
Luke 18–24: 446
15:8–12
1 Peter: 53
15:9
2 Corinthians: 20
Philippians: 283
James: 261
15:9–12
Luke 1–5: 44
1 Peter: 140
15:12
Luke 1–5: 50, 98
15:13
Luke 11–17: 13
Acts 1–12: 259
2 Corinthians: 27, 107, 279
Philippians: 216, 284
Colossians and Philemon: 33
1 & 2 Thessalonians: 83, 86, 90, 184, 314
1–3 John: 108
15:14
Acts 1–12: 84
Romans 1–8: 38
Philippians: 45
Colossians and Philemon: 79
1 & 2 Thessalonians: 168, 170, 258
15:14–21
Romans 9–16: 355
15:15
1 Timothy: 159
2 Peter–Jude: 49
15:15–16
2 Corinthians: 125
Colossians and Philemon: 72
1 Peter: 116
15:16
Mark 1–8: 47
Luke 1–5: 335
Acts 1–12: 273
Romans 1–8: 3
Romans 9–16: 127, 234, 340, 349, 364
Philippians: 204
1 & 2 Thessalonians: 35, 104, 193, 202, 287
2 Timothy: 189
1 Peter: 21
15:17
1 Corinthians: 209
2 Corinthians: 32, 240
Philippians: 222
15:17–18
Acts 1–12: 282
2 Corinthians: 349
15:17–19
2 Corinthians: 416
15:18
Luke 1–5: 166
John 12–21: 151
Acts 13–28: 248, 249
1 Corinthians: 79
2 Corinthians: 85
1 & 2 Thessalonians: 244
1 Peter: 90
1–3 John: 182
15:19
Luke 6–10: 19, 45
Acts 13–28: 15
Romans 1–8: 427
2 Corinthians: 229
Philippians: 105
Hebrews: 50
15:20
Acts 13–28: 79, 181, 246
2 Corinthians: 172
1 & 2 Thessalonians: 119
15:20–21
1 & 2 Thessalonians: 294
1 Peter: 53
15:22
Romans 1–8: 38
15:22–23
Acts 13–28: 79
15:22–24
Acts 13–28: 181
15:23
Acts 13–28: 285, 359
15:24
Acts 13–28: 79, 368
1 Corinthians: 461
2 Corinthians: 480
Philippians: 5, 6, 57
Titus: 2
15:25
Acts 1–12: 183
15:25–27
Acts 13–28: 181
2 Corinthians: 275
15:25–28
Acts 13–28: 199, 306
15:26
Acts 1–12: 179
1 Corinthians: 450, 451
Philippians: 22
James: 108
15:26–27
2 Corinthians: 480
15:26–28
Colossians and Philemon: 32
15:27
1 Corinthians: 451
Galatians: 43
15:28
Acts 13–28: 79
1 Corinthians: 461
2 Corinthians: 45
Philippians: 5
1 Timothy: xi
15:28–29
Hebrews: 454
15:30
2 Corinthians: 27
Ephesians: 189
Philippians: 74
1 & 2 Thessalonians: 211
15:30–31
1 & 2 Thessalonians: 295
Hebrews: 449
15:30–32
1 & 2 Thessalonians: 293
15:31
Acts 13–28: 45, 217
1 & 2 Thessalonians: 213

15:32
1 & 2 Thessalonians: 82, 213
James: 237
15:33
Matthew 1–7: 209, 213
Romans 9–16: 377
2 Corinthians: 44, 485
Philippians: 292
1 & 2 Thessalonians: 204, 313
16
Acts 1–12: 280
2 Corinthians: 480
1 Timothy: 2
16:1
Acts 13–28: 92
2 Corinthians: 18, 80
1 Timothy: 130
1 Peter: 140
16:1–2
1 Corinthians: 260
Philippians: 206
16:1–15
1 & 2 Thessalonians: 69
1 Peter: 5
16:2
1 Timothy: 208
16:3
Acts 13–28: 147
2 Corinthians: 4, 196, 307
Philippians: 203
1 & 2 Thessalonians: 308
2 Timothy: 214
1–3 John: 246
16:3–4
Acts 13–28: 147
16:3–5
Acts 13–28: 160
16:3ff.
Acts 13–28: 92
16:5
Matthew 1–7: 116
Acts 13–28: 203
Romans 1–8: 45
16:6
2 Corinthians: 388
16:7
Acts 13–28: 293
1 Corinthians: 323
2 Corinthians: 196, 409
1 & 2 Thessalonians: 42, 224, 308
1 Timothy: 4
16:8–15
Philippians: 317
16:9
2 Corinthians: 307
Philippians: 203
1 & 2 Thessalonians: 224
16:10
1 & 2 Thessalonians: 224
16:11
Acts 13–28: 293
16:11–13
2 Corinthians: 45
Philippians: 311
16:13
Mark 1–8: 4
Luke 18–24: 368, 369
1 Corinthians: 163
16:16
Luke 18–24: 210
John 12–21: 168
Acts 1–12: 84
2 Corinthians: 234
1 & 2 Thessalonians: 214
Revelation 1–11: 72
16:17
Matthew 1–7: 125
Luke 11–17: 110
1 Corinthians: 27, 96
Ephesians: 173
Hebrews: 436
16:17–18
Matthew 1–7: 432, 461
Matthew 8–15: 151
Acts 1–12: 145
2 Corinthians: 336
Ephesians: 158
Titus: 57, 164
2 Peter–Jude: 204
1–3 John: 153
16:18
Philippians: 199
1 & 2 Thessalonians: 41, 270
16:19
Romans 1–8: 25
Romans 9–16: 244
Philippians: 182
1 & 2 Thessalonians: 199, 244
1 Peter: 90
16:20
Mark 1–8: 183
Luke 1–5: 288
Luke 11–17: 119
2 Corinthians: 70–71, 485
Ephesians: 338
Philippians: 292
Colossians and Philemon: 60
1 & 2 Thessalonians: 88, 204, 216, 313
1 Peter: 284
1–3 John: 66
Revelation 1–11: 21, 32, 168
Revelation 12–22: 15, 211
16:21
Acts 13–28: 4, 293
2 Corinthians: 307, 487
Philippians: 196, 203
1 Timothy: 6, 9
16:22
1 & 2 Thessalonians: 318
1 Peter: 8
Revelation 1–11: 6
16:23
Acts 13–28: 149, 182, 198
1 Corinthians: 32, 179
2 Timothy: 214
16:24
Philippians: 318
16:25
Matthew 1–7: 124
1 Corinthians: 298
2 Corinthians: 109
1 & 2 Thessalonians: 233, 278
1 Timothy: 128
Revelation 1–11: 3
16:25–26
Matthew 24–28: 7
Romans 1–8: 24, 403
1 & 2 Thessalonians: 197
1–3 John: 183
Revelation 1–11: 286
16:25–27
Philippians: 312
1 & 2 Thessalonians: 289
2 Peter–Jude: 63
16:26
Matthew 16–23: 50
Luke 1–5: 71, 166
Acts 1–12: 297
Romans 9–16: 127, 312
1 & 2 Thessalonians: 244
1 Peter: 90
Revelation 1–11: 54
16:27
2 Corinthians: 44, 158
Philippians: 150, 313
1 Peter: 245
Revelation 1–11: 133

1 Corinthians
1:1
Acts 13–28: 47, 153, 200
Romans 1–8: 486
2 Corinthians: 5, 17, 410
Galatians: 28
1:1–2
2 Timothy: 95
1:2
Matthew 8–15: 145
Romans 1–8: 312
Philippians: 15, 310
1 & 2 Thessalonians: 59, 104, 202, 203, 224, 256, 287
1 Timothy: 74, 117
Hebrews: 156
1–3 John: 29
1:3
2 Corinthians: 487
Philippians: 16, 314
1 & 2 Thessalonians: 14, 87, 204, 216, 224
1 Peter: 25
2 Peter–Jude: 24
Revelation 1–11: 24
1:4
Luke 1–5: 47
Luke 11–17: 154
Philippians: 19
Colossians and Philemon: 37
1 & 2 Thessalonians: 320
2 Timothy: 6
Revelation 12–22: 194
1:4–5
2 Corinthians: 294
Philippians: 308

1:4–7
2 Corinthians: 285
Galatians: x
1 & 2 Thessalonians: 86
1:4–8
Revelation 1–11: 30
1:5
Colossians and Philemon: 28
1–3 John: 59
1:5–7
2 Corinthians: 95
1:6–8
Romans 1–8: 460
1:7
Matthew 24–28: 59, 82
Mark 9–16: 252
Luke 11–17: 154
Luke 18–24: 191, 252, 253
2 Corinthians: 394
Philippians: 261
1 & 2 Thessalonians: 73, 116, 185
James: 256
1 Peter: 63
Revelation 1–11: 15, 16
Revelation 12–22: 211, 291, 302
1:7–8
1 & 2 Thessalonians: 73
1 Peter: 46
1:7–9
1 Peter: 18–19
2 Peter–Jude: 210
Revelation 12–22: 99
1:8
Luke 18–24: 216
2 Corinthians: 37
Philippians: 28
1 & 2 Thessalonians: 144
1:9
Luke 1–5: 174
Acts 13–28: 297
Romans 9–16: 27
Philippians: 16, 22
1 & 2 Thessalonians: 20, 256, 287, 296
Titus: 30
1 Peter: 124
2 Peter–Jude: 29
1–3 John: 19, 37, 39
1:10
Romans 9–16: 306
2 Corinthians: 483, 484
Ephesians: 148, 152, 156
Philippians: 90, 100, 271
Colossians and Philemon: 88
1 & 2 Thessalonians: 168
James: 185
1:10–11
Philippians: 110
1:10–13
2 Corinthians: 269
Titus: 166
1:11
2 Corinthians: 4
Philippians: 64
1:11–12
2 Corinthians: 95
Titus: 168
1:11–17
Philippians: 65
1:12
Luke 6–10: 25
Acts 13–28: 163
2 Corinthians: 53, 173, 230, 339
Philippians: 64
1 Peter: 4–5
2 Peter–Jude: 2, 4, 18
1:12–13
Philippians: 110
1:13–17
Romans 1–8: 320
Ephesians: 130
Colossians and Philemon: 108
1:14
Acts 13–28: 149, 186, 198
Romans 9–16: 379
1:14–16
Acts 1–12: 74
1:16
1 & 2 Thessalonians: 293
1:17
Acts 1–12: 74
Acts 13–28: 15
2 Corinthians: 74, 194, 198
Ephesians: 1
Philippians: 126
1 & 2 Thessalonians: 294
1:17–18
Philippians: 257
1:17–25
Acts 1–12: 49
2 Corinthians: 358–59
1:18
Matthew 16–23: 41
Mark 1–8: 432
Mark 9–16: 12, 162
Luke 6–10: 24, 167, 206, 277
Luke 11–17: 395
Luke 18–24: 56, 377
Acts 13–28: 339
Romans 1–8: 52, 89
2 Corinthians: 86, 126, 131, 206, 212, 229
James: 225, 290
Revelation 12–22: 298
1:18–21
Colossians and Philemon: 102
1:18–25
1 & 2 Thessalonians: 58
1:18–31
Mark 1–8: 421
1:18–2:5
Luke 6–10: 344
1:19
James: 234
1:20
Luke 11–17: 349
Romans 1–8: 89
2 Corinthians: 132, 141
James: 173
1:20–21
2 Corinthians: 34
1:20–29
Luke 6–10: 13–14
1:20–31
Mark 1–8: 295
1:20, 25
Titus: 147
1:21
John 12–21: 119
Colossians and Philemon: 23
1 & 2 Thessalonians: 108
Titus: 13
James: 290
1:21a
1–3 John: 227
1:21–23
Acts 13–28: 15
1:22
Mark 1–8: 107
Luke 1–5: 291, 325
1:22–23
Romans 9–16: 51
Colossians and Philemon: 7
1:23
Matthew 1–7: 169
Matthew 8–15: 412
Matthew 16–23: 36, 41
Mark 1–8: 278
Mark 9–16: 2, 34, 266, 368
Luke 6–10: 277
Luke 18–24: 56, 128, 262, 382
Acts 1–12: 252
Acts 13–28: 120
2 Corinthians: 89, 130, 198, 212
Galatians: 198
Philippians: 135, 257
1 Timothy: 139
Hebrews: 235
1:23–25
Romans 1–8: 52
1:23–24
Romans 9–16: 385
1:23–25
2 Corinthians: 126
Titus: 5
1:23–2:1
2 Corinthians: 42
1:24
Luke 1–5: 44
1 & 2 Thessalonians: 256, 287
James: 167, 177
1:25
Romans 1–8: 89
1:26
Matthew 1–7: 146
Mark 1–8: 285
Luke 1–5: 155
Luke 6–10: 240
Luke 18–24: 210
Romans 1–8: 220
2 Corinthians: 86, 274
Ephesians: 119
1 & 2 Thessalonians: 222, 256, 287

1 Timothy: 93
James: 100
2 Peter–Jude: 29
Revelation 1–11: 38, 122
1:26–27
Matthew 8–15: 272
Matthew 16–23: 113
1:26–28
Matthew 8–15: 83
Matthew 16–23: 199
1 & 2 Thessalonians: 48
1 Peter: 158
1:26–29
Matthew 1–7: 118
Matthew 8–15: 432
Luke 1–5: 205, 271
2 Corinthians: 141
Ephesians: 94
Philippians: 131
James: 108
1 Peter: 108–9
1:26–31
Mark 1–8: 112, 166, 172
Luke 1–5: 329
1:27
2 Corinthians: 405
1 Peter: 17
1:27–29
Romans 1–8: 220
Romans 9–16: 334
1:28–29
Matthew 16–23: 114
1 Peter: 278
1:29
Luke 6–10: 345
1 Peter: 19
1:30
Matthew 1–7: 281
Luke 1–5: 25
John 12–21: 117
Acts 13–28: 26
Romans 1–8: 256
Romans 9–16: 257, 328
2 Corinthians: 44–45, 196, 205, 248
Ephesians: 2, 218
Philippians: 288, 311
Colossians and Philemon: 42
1 & 2 Thessalonians: 104, 163, 308
2 Timothy: 90
Titus: 115
James: 140, 167, 177
1 Peter: 129
1–3 John: 28
Revelation 12–22: 203
1:31
Mark 1–8: 16
Luke 6–10: 345
Acts 13–28: 273
Romans 9–16: 333
2 Corinthians: 32, 141, 187, 240, 349
Philippians: 222
1 Peter: 19
1–3
Ephesians: 347
2:1
Matthew 1–7: 226, 326
2:1–2
Romans 1–8: 53
2 Corinthians: 127
Galatians: 29
Titus: 6, 130
2:1–4
Acts 13–28: 94, 148
2:1–5
John 12–21: 183
Acts 1–12: 50
2 Corinthians: 343, 358–59
1 & 2 Thessalonians: 98, 204, 293
2 Timothy: 173
1 Peter: 57
2:1–16
1 & 2 Thessalonians: 293
2:2
Matthew 24–28: 128, 338
John 12–21: 182
Romans 1–8: 89
2 Corinthians: 89, 130, 133, 198
Galatians: 205
Philippians: 200, 257
1 & 2 Thessalonians: 194
1 Timothy: 139
Hebrews: 246
1 Peter: 166
1–3 John: 18
2:2–5
Matthew 1–7: 226
2:3
Acts 13–28: 146
2 Corinthians: 133, 269, 405, 455, 476
Philippians: 160
Titus: 147
2:4
2 Corinthians: 86, 130, 198
Galatians: 69
Ephesians: 113
Titus: 13
2:4–5
Matthew 16–23: 15
Luke 6–10: 24
2 Corinthians: 82
2:5
2 Corinthians: 229, 343
2 Peter–Jude: 20
2:5–8
2 Corinthians: 5, 34
2:6
Matthew 1–7: 350
2 Corinthians: 132
2:6–7, 12, 16
Ephesians: 25
2:6–16
2 Corinthians: 359–60
2:7
Acts 1–12: 141
2 Corinthians: 109, 132
Revelation 1–11: 286
2:8
Mark 9–16: 3
Luke 1–5: 71, 152
Luke 6–10: 280
Luke 11–17: 234
Luke 18–24: 339, 384
John 1–11: 14, 450, 486
John 12–21: 176, 324
Acts 1–12: 111
2 Corinthians: 132
2:9
Luke 11–17: 276
Luke 18–24: 83
Romans 1–8: 20, 482
2 Corinthians: 157
1 & 2 Thessalonians: 17
2 Peter–Jude: 25
2:9–10
Matthew 8–15: 270
Matthew 16–23: 16
John 12–21: 206
Hebrews: 294
James: 66
2:9–12
Ephesians: 43
2:9–16
Matthew 8–15: 354
1 Timothy: 242
2:10
Romans 9–16: 135
Ephesians: 189
1 & 2 Thessalonians: 118, 194
1–3 John: 127
2:10–12
Colossians and Philemon: 29
2:10–14
Mark 1–8: 222, 417
2:10–16
John 12–21: 208
1 Peter: 21
2:11
Romans 1–8: 467
Ephesians: 44, 189
1 & 2 Thessalonians: 206
2:12
Matthew 16–23: 16
Romans 1–8: 225
1 & 2 Thessalonians: 172
James: 66, 92, 194
2:12–13
Luke 1–5: 15
John 12–21: 201
1 & 2 Thessalonians: 108, 166, 193
Titus: 114
2:12–16
Luke 6–10: 198
1–3 John: 159
2:13
John 12–21: 120
2 Corinthians: 25, 229, 414
2 Timothy: 146
2 Peter–Jude: 9
2:14
Matthew 8–15: 244, 386

Matthew 16–23: 2
Luke 6–10: 102, 190, 345, 347
Luke 11–17: 403
John 12–21: 41
Acts 1–12: 252, 267
Acts 13–28: 168
Romans 1–8: 183, 417, 495
Romans 9–16: 135, 140
2 Corinthians: 131, 212, 225
Ephesians: ix, 9, 215
Philippians: 286
Colossians and Philemon: 90, 131
1 & 2 Thessalonians: 22, 96, 282
1 Timothy: 21, 243
Titus: 114
Hebrews: 130
James: 60, 173
1 Peter: 31, 275
1–3 John: 154, 159
Revelation 1–11: 19

2:14–15
1 Peter: 92

2:14–16
Romans 1–8: 433
2 Timothy: 154
1–3 John: 54

2:15
James: 66

2:16
Luke 6–10: 159
Romans 9–16: 187
2 Corinthians: 82, 123
Ephesians: 174
Philippians: 46, 48, 107, 243, 249, 254
1 Timothy: 243
Titus: 114
1 Peter: 275
1–3 John: 57, 127, 219

3:1
Luke 11–17: 280
Romans 1–8: 380, 382, 423
2 Corinthians: 45, 95, 482
Ephesians: 158, 249
Philippians: 311

3:1, 3
Ephesians: 67

3:1–3
John 12–21: 146–47
Ephesians: 249
Philippians: 15, 111
James: 185
1–3 John: 71

3:1–9
Luke 6–10: 301

3:3
Luke 6–10: 301
Romans 9–16: 267
2 Corinthians: 268
Philippians: 64

3:3–4
2 Corinthians: 269

3:4
2 Corinthians: 53, 173, 230
1–3 John: 74

3:4, 6
Acts 13–28: 163

3:4–6
Philippians: 110

3:5
Matthew 16–23: 241
Acts 13–28: 210
Romans 1–8: 5
2 Corinthians: 473
Ephesians: 93

3:5–7
Matthew 8–15: 131
Acts 13–28: 248

3:5–9
Luke 1–5: 14

3:6
Acts 1–12: 188
Romans 9–16: 337
2 Corinthians: 348, 408
Titus: 71

3:6–7
Mark 1–8: 218
Luke 6–10: 346
Acts 13–28: 94
2 Corinthians: 222
1 & 2 Thessalonians: 89

3:6–8
2 Peter–Jude: 26

3:8
Matthew 24–28: 101
Romans 1–8: 128
Philippians: 187
Revelation 1–11: 319

3:9
2 Corinthians: 221
Philippians: 203
1 & 2 Thessalonians: 165
1 Peter: 106

3:9–15
1 Peter: 271
Revelation 12–22: 299

3:10
2 Corinthians: 348, 408

3:10–11
Ephesians: 82

3:10–15
Luke 11–17: 156
Luke 18–24: 192
2 Corinthians: 37
Philippians: 28
1 Peter: 45–46, 68–69

3:11
Matthew 16–23: 29
Luke 1–5: 183, 336
John 12–21: 103
Philippians: 78

3:11–14
1 & 2 Thessalonians: 92, 144
1 Peter: 37

3:11–15
Luke 18–24: 82
Romans 1–8: 128
2 Corinthians: 178
1 & 2 Thessalonians: 130

3:12
2 Corinthians: 265
Philippians: 261
2 Timothy: 195
Hebrews: 451

3:12–14
Revelation 12–22: 104

3:12–15
Romans 1–8: 448
Galatians: 182
Ephesians: 250, 353
Philippians: 248
1 & 2 Thessalonians: 74, 111
2 Timothy: 169
Hebrews: 141
James: 42
Revelation 1–11: 30
Revelation 12–22: 203, 251, 268

3:12, 14
Titus: 10

3:13
Matthew 16–23: 57
2 Corinthians: 277
Philippians: 52, 199
1 & 2 Thessalonians: 169
2 Timothy: 28

3:13–14
Philippians: 187
2 Timothy: 48

3:13–15
Matthew 16–23: 214
Romans 9–16: 284
2 Timothy: 200
James: 151, 257

3:15
Matthew 24–28: 108
2 Corinthians: 265

3:16
Ephesians: 106
Philippians: 170, 243
1 & 2 Thessalonians: 14, 193
2 Timothy: 31
1–3 John: 29, 112
Revelation 1–11: 54

3:16–17
Matthew 8–15: 456
John 1–11: 17
Romans 1–8: 29
2 Corinthians: 253
Ephesians: 129
1 & 2 Thessalonians: 166

3:17
2 Corinthians: 340
1 & 2 Thessalonians: 108

3:18
2 Corinthians: 132

3:19
2 Corinthians: 34
Ephesians: 158

3:21–22
Romans 1–8: 473
2 Corinthians: 232

3:21–23
Matthew 1–7: 174
Romans 1–8: 255

Philippians: 82
2 Peter–Jude: 25
3:22
Luke 6–10: 25
2 Corinthians: 294
Philippians: 64
1 Peter: 4
2 Peter–Jude: 2, 18
3:22–23
Ephesians: 31
3:23
John 12–21: 268
4:1
Matthew 16–23: 241
Acts 1–12: 273
Romans 1–8: 5
2 Corinthians: 173, 189, 194, 359
Ephesians: 89
1 & 2 Thessalonians: 170
1 Timothy: 292
Titus: 35
Revelation 1–11: 286
4:1–2
Galatians: 169
Philippians: 191
Colossians and Philemon: 72
1 & 2 Thessalonians: 44
1 Timothy: 28, 158
4:1–3
2 Corinthians: 125
4:1–5
Romans 1–8: 33
Romans 9–16: 285
2 Corinthians: 189
1 & 2 Thessalonians: 38, 40, 144
1 Timothy: 262, 274
1 Peter: 264–65, 277
4:2
Matthew 8–15: 186, 269
Matthew 16–23: 282
Acts 13–28: 225
1 Timothy: 175
Titus: 35
Hebrews: 80
1 Peter: 244
4:2–5
2 Corinthians: 31
1 Peter: 202
4:2, 17
Titus: 30
4:3
2 Corinthians: 173–74
4:3–4
Matthew 1–7: 433
Romans 1–8: 116
2 Corinthians: 54, 129, 346, 476
4:3–5
Romans 9–16: 280
2 Corinthians: 173, 350
1 Peter: 69, 271
4:4
Acts 13–28: 280
2 Corinthians: 35, 174
Philippians: 172
2 Timothy: 199
Titus: 115
James: 91
4:4–5
Matthew 1–7: 284
2 Corinthians: 40, 79–80
2 Timothy: 169
4:5
Matthew 1–7: 486
Matthew 8–15: 220
Matthew 16–23: 241
Mark 1–8: 356
Luke 11–17: 87, 117
Romans 1–8: 116
Romans 9–16: 260
2 Corinthians: 37, 196
Philippians: 53, 187
1 & 2 Thessalonians: 92
1 Timothy: 267
James: 257
2 Peter–Jude: 132
Revelation 1–11: 30
Revelation 12–22: 268, 291
4:6–7
Romans 9–16: 158
4:7
2 Peter–Jude: 28
4:8
Luke 1–5: 333
Ephesians: 95
4:8–13
Matthew 16–23: 241
1 & 2 Thessalonians: 293
4:9
Matthew 1–7: 225
Acts 1–12: 60
1 Peter: 58
4:9–11
Matthew 8–15: 210
4:9–13
Luke 6–10: 46
Acts 1–12: 273
2 Corinthians: 477
Philippians: 200
4:10
Matthew 1–7: 225
2 Corinthians: 188
4:10–11
Hebrews: 442
4:11
2 Corinthians: 142, 228, 390
4:12
Luke 11–17: 196
Acts 13–28: 281, 282
2 Corinthians: 228, 388, 390
Colossians and Philemon: 156
1 & 2 Thessalonians: 181, 306
Revelation 1–11: 190
4:12–13
Matthew 8–15: 202
4:13
James: 39
4:14
Matthew 1–7: 81
2 Corinthians: 162, 484
1 & 2 Thessalonians: 170, 177
1 Timothy: 159
2 Timothy: 159
4:14–15
2 Corinthians: 94, 237, 445
4:15
Matthew 16–23: 148
Acts 13–28: 81
2 Corinthians: 40, 224, 347–48, 408
1 & 2 Thessalonians: 44
1 Timothy: 2
4:15–16
2 Corinthians: 79
4:15, 21
Galatians: 96
4:16
Luke 6–10: 19
Acts 13–28: 208
2 Corinthians: 413, 484
Philippians: 191, 250, 291
1 Timothy: 91, 172
4:16–17
Philippians: 197
4:16, 17
2 Timothy: 127, 205
4:17
Luke 6–10: 55
Acts 13–28: 83
2 Corinthians: 18
Philippians: 195, 196
1 & 2 Thessalonians: 13, 77, 223
1 Timothy: 2, 6
4:18–21
James: 73
4:19
Matthew 1–7: 326
James: 237
1–3 John: 257
Revelation 1–11: 21
4:20
Luke 11–17: 405
Romans 1–8: 53
2 Corinthians: 86
Ephesians: 113
1 & 2 Thessalonians: 22
4:21
Matthew 16–23: 154
2 Corinthians: 46, 341, 455, 476
5
Luke 11–17: 45
2 Corinthians: 445, 447
5:1
Galatians: 161
1 & 2 Thessalonians: 104
1 Peter: 140
5:1–2
Matthew 16–23: 134
2 Corinthians: 95, 444
Philippians: 259
1 Timothy: 54
Titus: 133
5:1–5
Ephesians: 200

James: 221
1 Peter: 283
Revelation 1–11: 94
5:1–7
Acts 1–12: 161
1 & 2 Thessalonians: 166
5:1–8
2 Corinthians: 65
1 & 2 Thessalonians: 168
5:1–13
Luke 11–17: 379
1 & 2 Thessalonians: 103
1 Timothy: 170
5:2
1 & 2 Thessalonians: 310
5:3
1 & 2 Thessalonians: 206
5:3–5
2 Corinthians: 444, 477
1 Timothy: 54
5:4–5
2 Corinthians: 56
1 Timothy: 47
5:5
Mark 9–16: 277
2 Corinthians: 51, 237
Galatians: 176
Philippians: 29
1 & 2 Thessalonians: 144, 206, 310
Revelation 1–11: 41
5:5–23
2 Peter–Jude: 51
5:6
Matthew 8–15: 373
Matthew 16–23: 127
2 Corinthians: 187
1 Peter: 280
5:6–7
2 Corinthians: 444
1 Timothy: 184
Revelation 1–11: 90
5:6–7, 11, 13
Galatians: 176
5:6–8
1 & 2 Thessalonians: 208
5:7
Matthew 24–28: 131, 145
Mark 9–16: 289
Luke 18–24: 91, 273
John 12–21: 14
Acts 1–12: 39
Colossians and Philemon: 119
5:7–8
Romans 9–16: 272
1 Peter: 72
5:7–8a
Matthew 8–15: 374
5:9
2 Corinthians: 4, 245, 300
5:9–10
Luke 6–10: 103
Acts 1–12: 275
Galatians: 176
1 Timothy: 184
5:9–11
Matthew 8–15: 151
Ephesians: 211
1 & 2 Thessalonians: 108
5:9–13
Matthew 16–23: 135
2 Corinthians: 444
2 Timothy: 89
5:10
John 12–21: 281
5:10–11
Matthew 1–7: 464
5:11
Matthew 1–7: 432
Acts 13–28: 282
2 Corinthians: 56, 309
Ephesians: 232
1 & 2 Thessalonians: 105
1 Timothy: 184
5:12
2 Corinthians: 174
5:13
Matthew 1–7: 331
1 Timothy: 184
6:1
Matthew 16–23: 153
6:1–2
Revelation 1–11: 320
6:1–3
Matthew 16–23: 134
6:1–4
1 Peter: 126
6:1–5
2 Corinthians: 174
6:1–8
Matthew 1–7: 334
2 Corinthians: 65, 95
6:2
Matthew 1–7: 433
Luke 18–24: 43
Revelation 12–22: 219, 237
6:2–3
2 Timothy: 64
Revelation 1–11: 149
6:3
Hebrews: 53
1 Peter: 221
Revelation 1–11: 141
6:4
2 Corinthians: 174
6:5
2 Corinthians: 174, 388
6:6–8
1 & 2 Thessalonians: 181
6:7
Colossians and Philemon: 156
6:9
Matthew 1–7: 174, 302
6:9–10
Matthew 1–7: 475
Matthew 16–23: 310
Ephesians: 203, 232
Colossians and Philemon: 39
1 & 2 Thessalonians: 105
1 Peter: 228
Revelation 12–22: 272
6:9–11
Mark 1–8: 122
Luke 6–10: 170
Romans 1–8: 107, 312
Titus: 146
6:9–11a
1 Peter: 228
6:10
Matthew 1–7: 464
Acts 13–28: 282
2 Corinthians: 309
6:11
Matthew 16–23: 310
Luke 1–5: 25
Acts 13–28: 108
Romans 1–8: 101, 312
2 Corinthians: 89
1 & 2 Thessalonians: 104, 163, 166, 193, 202, 287
1 Peter: 21, 129
1–3 John: 28, 37
Revelation 12–22: 309
6:11–13
Romans 9–16: 143
6:12
Romans 9–16: 289
Ephesians: 241
6:12–20
2 Corinthians: 95
6:13
Matthew 1–7: 300
Romans 1–8: 103
Philippians: 258
Colossians and Philemon: 123
1 & 2 Thessalonians: 102, 104, 107, 205
Revelation 12–22: 77
6:13–20
Ephesians: 200
6:14
Luke 18–24: 411
Acts 1–12: 64
2 Corinthians: 147
1 & 2 Thessalonians: 128, 133
2 Peter–Jude: 26
6:15
Matthew 16–23: 103
Romans 1–8: 320
Romans 9–16: 96
2 Corinthians: 247
1 & 2 Thessalonians: 107, 205
6:15–18
1 & 2 Thessalonians: 105
6:15–20
Acts 13–28: 71
Philippians: 87
1 & 2 Thessalonians: 105, 109
Revelation 1–11: 101
6:15, 19
Matthew 1–7: 301
6:16
2 Corinthians: 95
Philippians: 77
6:16–17
Galatians: 174

6:17
Matthew 16–23: 31
Matthew 24–28: 124
Mark 9–16: 39, 43
Luke 6–10: 303
Romans 1–8: 255, 320
Galatians: 99
Ephesians: viii, 10, 30, 66, 75, 301
Philippians: 24, 90, 101
Colossians and Philemon: 131
1 & 2 Thessalonians: 225
1–3 John: 19, 37
6:17–18
John 12–21: 128
Colossians and Philemon: 158
6:18
Matthew 1–7: 301
Romans 9–16: 187
2 Corinthians: 247
1 & 2 Thessalonians: 104, 109, 199
1 Timothy: 261
Hebrews: 431
Revelation 12–22: 77
6:18–19
Ephesians: 248
Titus: 29
6:19
Mark 1–8: 26
Acts 13–28: 67, 164
Romans 9–16: 144
2 Corinthians: 253, 489
Ephesians: 34, 44, 106
Philippians: 75, 101, 105, 124, 245
1 & 2 Thessalonians: 108, 193
Revelation 1–11: 54
6:19–20
Matthew 8–15: 133
Mark 1–8: 242
Acts 1–12: 18, 169
Romans 1–8: 380
2 Corinthians: 161, 168
Ephesians: 83
1 & 2 Thessalonians: 113, 205
2 Timothy: 83, 91
1–3 John: 169
6:20
Matthew 16–23: 242, 245
Mark 1–8: 242
Acts 13–28: 129
Romans 9–16: 283
1 Timothy: 218
Titus: 3, 35
1 Peter: 51, 130
Revelation 1–11: 172
Revelation 12–22: 79
7
2 Corinthians: 65
Hebrews: 137
7:1
2 Corinthians: 4
1 & 2 Thessalonians: 142
7:1–5
2 Corinthians: 95
7:1–7
1 Timothy: 152
7:2
Hebrews: 430
7:3–4
Ephesians: 278
7:3–5
1 Peter: 181, 283
7:3, 5
Matthew 1–7: 301
7:4
Matthew 16–23: 166
7:4–5
Ephesians: 293
7:5
Luke 11–17: 47
1 & 2 Thessalonians: 81, 187
1 Timothy: 40
7:5–16
2 Corinthians: 5
7:7
Matthew 16–23: 175
2 Corinthians: 5
7:8
1 Timothy: 105
7:8–9
Matthew 16–23: 175
Hebrews: 430
7:8–9, 17
Titus: 78
7:9
Mark 9–16: 60
7:10
Matthew 16–23: 167
7:10–15
Romans 1–8: 360
7:12
2 Corinthians: 5
7:12–13
Matthew 1–7: 318
2 Corinthians: 245
7:13
1 Peter: 177
7:14
Matthew 1–7: 242
Matthew 8–15: 372
Luke 11–17: 212
Acts 13–28: 351
1 & 2 Thessalonians: 202
1 Timothy: 48
7:14–15
Matthew 8–15: 231
7:15
Matthew 1–7: 215, 318
Mark 9–16: 60
Luke 11–17: 352
Ephesians: 80, 302
1 Timothy: 105, 212
Titus: 28
7:17
1 & 2 Thessalonians: 256, 257
1–3 John: 36
7:18
1 & 2 Thessalonians: 256
7:20
1 & 2 Thessalonians: 256
7:20–21
1 Peter: 158
7:20–22
Colossians and Philemon: 223
7:20–24
1 Timothy: 85
7:21
1 & 2 Thessalonians: 256
7:21–22
1 Timothy: 235
7:22
Luke 1–5: 80
2 Corinthians: 45
Philippians: 13, 311
1 & 2 Thessalonians: 256
2 Peter–Jude: 18
7:23
Matthew 8–15: 133
Luke 1–5: 96
1 Peter: 130
Revelation 1–11: 172
Revelation 12–22: 79
7:24
1 & 2 Thessalonians: 256
1 Peter: 158
7:25
1 & 2 Thessalonians: 142
1 Timothy: 28
7:25–35
1 Timothy: 152
7:25–40
1 Timothy: 89
7:26
2 Corinthians: 227
7:27
Acts 13–28: 217
7:28
James: 16
7:28–38
1 Timothy: 152
7:29
Ephesians: 223
7:29–31
1 Timothy: 274
7:31
2 Corinthians: 157
Philippians: 131
1 Timothy: 235
7:32–34
Matthew 16–23: 175
7:33–34
Colossians and Philemon: 170
7:34
Acts 13–28: 239
1 & 2 Thessalonians: 206
7:39
Acts 13–28: 217
Romans 1–8: 360
1 Timothy: 105, 207, 212
Titus: 27
1 Peter: 177
8
2 Corinthians: 245
8:1
John 12–21: 60
Romans 9–16: 59

2 Corinthians: 65
1 & 2 Thessalonians: 142
8:1–13
Acts 13–28: 71
2 Corinthians: 95–96
1 & 2 Thessalonians: 178
8:3
Romans 1–8: 384, 482
Philippians: 80
1 & 2 Thessalonians: 17
1 Peter: 123
Revelation 1–11: 54
8:4
2 Corinthians: 246, 488
1 Timothy: 71, 275
8:4–6
Acts 13–28: 183
Ephesians: 131
8:4–7
Romans 9–16: 292
8:4, 6
1 Timothy: 33
8:4, 7–9, 11
Ephesians: 242
8:5–6
Romans 1–8: 227
8:6
2 Corinthians: 199
Ephesians: 96
Philippians: 147
1 Timothy: 71, 275
8:7
Matthew 8–15: 456
Acts 13–28: 280
Romans 1–8: 141
1 & 2 Thessalonians: 179
8:7–13
2 Corinthians: 32
1 Peter: 204
8:8
1 & 2 Thessalonians: 95
Hebrews: 437
8:8–12
Romans 9–16: 293
8:9
Romans 9–16: 291
8:9–12
Romans 9–16: 282
8:9–13
1 & 2 Thessalonians: 179
8:9, 11
Titus: 37
8:10
Acts 13–28: 280
2 Corinthians: 245
8:11–12
James: 276
8:12
Acts 1–12: 153
Acts 13–28: 280
Romans 1–8: 141
8:12–13
Romans 9–16: 299
1 Timothy: 225
8:13
Mark 9–16: 44
Romans 9–16: 282
8–10
Acts 13–28: 250
9
Matthew 8–15: 431
9:1
Acts 1–12: 267, 274
Acts 13–28: 47, 267, 335
2 Corinthians: 409, 412
Ephesians: 2
2 Peter–Jude: 19
9:1–2
2 Corinthians: 338
9:1–14
1 Timothy: 218
9:1–15
1 & 2 Thessalonians: 169
1 Timothy: 261
9:1–16
1 Timothy: 111
9:1, 4–6, 12
Matthew 1–7: 328
9:2
2 Corinthians: 230
Philippians: 269
9:3
2 Corinthians: 187, 267
9:3–14
1 & 2 Thessalonians: 306
9:3–15
2 Corinthians: 306
9:3ff.
Acts 13–28: 230
9:4–14
James: 244
9:5
Mark 1–8: 72
Luke 1–5: 292
Luke 6–10: 25
Titus: 27, 32
1 Peter: 4, 5
2 Peter–Jude: 2, 4, 18
9:5–6, 12
Romans 9–16: 298
9:5–14
Mark 1–8: 290
9:6
Acts 13–28: 82
9:6–14
2 Corinthians: 274
9:6–18
Matthew 1–7: 146
9:6ff.
Acts 13–28: 149
9:7–11
1 & 2 Thessalonians: 48, 293
9:9
Matthew 16–23: 336
1 & 2 Thessalonians: 172
1 Timothy: 220
9:11, 14
Titus: 39
9:12
Philippians: 300
Colossians and Philemon: 13
9:14
Matthew 8–15: 194
Philippians: 300
1 & 2 Thessalonians: 172
9:15
Philippians: 300
9:16
Matthew 8–15: 186
Acts 1–12: 138, 275
Acts 13–28: 15, 118, 216
Romans 1–8: 6, 34
Romans 9–16: 333
2 Corinthians: 85, 146, 187, 194, 227, 349
Philippians: 58
Colossians and Philemon: 70, 184
1 & 2 Thessalonians: 89
2 Timothy: 25, 129, 166
James: 148
1–3 John: 18
9:16–17
Acts 1–12: 181
Romans 1–8: 46
Ephesians: 89
Colossians and Philemon: 72–73
1 Timothy: 42, 167
Titus: 14
9:16–18
Ephesians: 94
1 & 2 Thessalonians: 41
9:17
2 Corinthians: 173, 189
9:18
Acts 13–28: 230
9:19
Romans 9–16: 297
1 Timothy: 230
9:19–21
2 Corinthians: 245
9:19–22
Matthew 8–15: 201
Acts 1–12: 286
Acts 13–28: 84
Romans 9–16: 308
Titus: 32
9:19–23
Acts 13–28: 215, 253
1 & 2 Thessalonians: 178
Hebrews: 40
9:20–22
Galatians: 115
9:21
Matthew 1–7: 273
Acts 13–28: 65
9:22
Matthew 1–7: 113
Acts 1–12: 257
2 Corinthians: 307, 392
9:23
Romans 9–16: 289, 350
Philippians: 58
9:24
Luke 11–17: 315
Ephesians: 363

Philippians: 242, 245, 248
Hebrews: 372
9:24–25
Mark 1–8: 216
Hebrews: 373
1 Peter: 271
9:24–27
Romans 9–16: 289
2 Corinthians: 184
Galatians: 157
Philippians: 161, 191
1 & 2 Thessalonians: 98, 204
1 Timothy: 164, 263
2 Timothy: 47, 91
9:25
Matthew 1–7: 455
Galatians: 170
Ephesians: 350
Philippians: 242, 269
1 & 2 Thessalonians: 73, 92
2 Timothy: 192, 200
Titus: 92
Revelation 1–11: 149
Revelation 12–22: 113
9:25–27
Luke 11–17: 142
Romans 9–16: 180
2 Timothy: 184
9:26
Romans 9–16: 191
Ephesians: 363
Philippians: 241, 242
Hebrews: 371
9:26–27
Acts 1–12: 181
1 Timothy: 167
2 Timothy: 19, 195
Titus: 92
Hebrews: 374
9:27
Matthew 1–7: 305
Matthew 16–23: 111
Mark 9–16: 108
Luke 18–24: 6
Romans 1–8: 338, 380
Romans 9–16: 143
2 Corinthians: 175, 226
Ephesians: 94, 182, 344
Philippians: 87, 114, 191
1 & 2 Thessalonians: 107, 205
1 Timothy: 105
2 Timothy: 121
Titus: 29
1 Peter: 139
10:1
2 Corinthians: 25
Philippians: 58
1 & 2 Thessalonians: 125
Hebrews: 378
10:1–4
Titus: 109
10:1–5
2 Corinthians: 463
10:1–11
Romans 1–8: 123
10:2
Romans 1–8: 320
10:3–4
Hebrews: 378
10:5
Titus: 110
10:6, 11
Romans 9–16: 312
10:7
2 Corinthians: 247
10:8
Matthew 1–7: 317
Matthew 16–23: 171
1 & 2 Thessalonians: 111
10:9–10
Philippians: 178
10:10
Philippians: 180
10:11
Philippians: 179
1 & 2 Thessalonians: 132
10:12
Matthew 1–7: 85
Matthew 24–28: 216
Luke 18–24: 322
Romans 9–16: 116, 276
2 Corinthians: 37, 174
Ephesians: 342, 377
Revelation 1–11: 104
10:13
Matthew 1–7: 98, 99, 206, 396
Matthew 24–28: 213
Luke 1–5: 174
Luke 18–24: 315
Acts 13–28: 297
Romans 1–8: 336, 511
2 Corinthians: 21, 404
Ephesians: 342
Philippians: 283
1 & 2 Thessalonians: 91, 187, 208, 296, 316
2 Timothy: 57, 102
Titus: 30
Hebrews: 114, 392
James: 26, 46, 49
2 Peter–Jude: 27
Revelation 12–22: 96
10:14
Romans 9–16: 187
2 Corinthians: 247, 257
1 & 2 Thessalonians: 199
1 Timothy: 261
Revelation 12–22: 181
10:14–33
Acts 13–28: 71
10:16
Matthew 24–28: 152
Mark 9–16: 290
Luke 18–24: 281
Colossians and Philemon: 63
Revelation 1–11: 44
10:16–17
Acts 1–12: 84
Philippians: 89
Titus: 166
10:16, 20–21
Ephesians: 233
10:16, 21–22
Galatians: 174
10:17
1 Peter: 187
10:18
Philippians: 192
10:20
Luke 1–5: 259
Romans 1–8: 92
1 Timothy: 146
Revelation 12–22: 46, 273
10:20–21
Luke 1–5: 280, 283
2 Corinthians: 247, 467
Titus: 63
10:21
Matthew 24–28: 152
Romans 1–8: 380
1 & 2 Thessalonians: 105
1–3 John: 210
Revelation 1–11: 101
10:23
Romans 9–16: 289
10:23–32
Romans 9–16: 297
2 Corinthians: 95–96
10:23–33
2 Corinthians: 245
1 & 2 Thessalonians: 178
10:24–29
2 Corinthians: 32
1 Peter: 204
10:25
Romans 1–8: 141
10:26
2 Corinthians: 289
Revelation 1–11: 282
10:27–28
2 Corinthians: 246
10:27–29
Ephesians: 243
10:29
Romans 1–8: 141
10:31
Matthew 1–7: 415
Matthew 24–28: 332
Luke 11–17: 72
John 12–21: 268, 290
Acts 13–28: 210
Romans 1–8: 83, 130, 212
Romans 9–16: 124, 350
2 Corinthians: 28, 186, 250, 317
Galatians: 7
Ephesians: 16, 327
Philippians: 54
Colossians and Philemon: 160, 214
1 & 2 Thessalonians: 41, 248, 260, 302
1 Timothy: 154, 235
2 Timothy: 166
10:31–33
Ephesians: 243

Titus: 32
10:32
Philippians: 51, 52
10:32–33
2 Corinthians: 307
1 & 2 Thessalonians: 110
10:33–11:1
Philippians: 121
11:1
Luke 6–10: 19
Acts 13–28: 208, 246
2 Corinthians: 79, 138, 158, 194, 346, 413
Philippians: 191, 197, 250, 253, 291
1 & 2 Thessalonians: 24, 53, 305
1 Timothy: 91, 166, 172
Titus: 93
Revelation 12–22: 78
11:1–16
2 Corinthians: 96
11:2
2 Corinthians: 442
Philippians: 186
1 & 2 Thessalonians: 288
11:3
Acts 1–12: 182
Ephesians: 278
Colossians and Philemon: 167
1 & 2 Thessalonians: 43, 125
1 Timothy: 86
Hebrews: 430
1 Peter: 178
11:3–10
1–3 John: 252
11:5
Ephesians: 284
1 Timothy: 74, 85
11:7
Colossians and Philemon: 45
11:8
Acts 1–12: 182
11:8–9
1 & 2 Thessalonians: 43
1 Timothy: 88
1 Peter: 178
11:9
Acts 1–12: 182
11:10
2 Corinthians: 43
Ephesians: 97
11:12
2 Corinthians: 199
11:17–22
1 & 2 Thessalonians: 168
11:17–34
2 Corinthians: 65, 96
11:18–19
2 Corinthians: 269
11:19
Matthew 1–7: 472
11:20–21
Ephesians: 234
11:20–22
Matthew 16–23: 116
Acts 13–28: 203
Hebrews: 386
11:21
Luke 18–24: 256
11:22
Matthew 16–23: 153
11:23
Philippians: 292
11:23–25
2 Corinthians: 412
11:23–26
Luke 18–24: 284
1 Peter: 248
11:23–28
1 & 2 Thessalonians: 97
11:24
1 Timothy: 221
11:24–25
2 Corinthians: 96
11:24–29
Acts 1–12: 84
11:25
Matthew 24–28: 154
Luke 1–5: 117
2 Corinthians: 88
Revelation 1–11: 140
11:26
Luke 18–24: 281
John 12–21: 38
1–3 John: 192
11:27–30
Matthew 1–7: 92
Ephesians: 231
11:28
Matthew 1–7: 475
Romans 9–16: 272
2 Corinthians: 461
Philippians: 198, 212
11:28–29
Romans 1–8: 380
11:28–30
Revelation 1–11: 46, 125
11:29–30
Luke 11–17: 142
Romans 1–8: 477
11:30
Matthew 1–7: 126, 395
Matthew 16–23: 125, 147
Luke 6–10: 236
John 1–11: 456
Acts 1–12: 160, 226
Romans 1–8: 193, 380
Galatians: 174, 188
Ephesians: 315
Philippians: 79
1 & 2 Thessalonians: 124, 125
Hebrews: 386, 395
James: 54
1–3 John: 205
Revelation 1–11: 102
11:30–32
Acts 1–12: 153
11:31
Acts 13–28: 282
2 Corinthians: 461
11:32
2 Corinthians: 443
Galatians: 208
1 Timothy: 55
Hebrews: 386
James: 271
1 Peter: 256
12–14
2 Corinthians: 96
12:1
Romans 1–8: 44
Philippians: 58
1 & 2 Thessalonians: 125, 142
12:1–31
Ephesians: 137
1 Timothy: 179
12:1, 4, 8–11
Romans 9–16: 168
12:2
1 Peter: 140
12:3
Matthew 24–28: 281
Mark 1–8: 186
Luke 1–5: 159
Luke 11–17: 58, 122
John 12–21: 179, 289, 389
Acts 1–12: 273
Acts 13–28: 36
Romans 9–16: 74
2 Corinthians: 65, 96, 133
Galatians: 78
Ephesians: 38
Philippians: 147, 148
1 & 2 Thessalonians: 195
1–3 John: 169
12:4–6
1 Peter: 243
12:4–7
Ephesians: 136
12:4–10
Ephesians: 135
1 & 2 Thessalonians: 193
12:4–11
Luke 18–24: 455
John 12–21: 381
1 & 2 Thessalonians: 166
Hebrews: 434
1 Peter: 242–43, 264
12:4–13
Colossians and Philemon: 51
12:5
1 Timothy: 125
12:6
2 Corinthians: 221–22
1 & 2 Thessalonians: 58
12:6, 13
1–3 John: 37
12:7
Acts 13–28: 43
2 Corinthians: 229
1 & 2 Thessalonians: 177
1 Peter: 243–44
12:7, 11
Romans 9–16: 162
12:7, 11, 13
Titus: 155

12:8–10
Ephesians: 136
12:9–11
Hebrews: 156
12:10
Acts 13–28: 43, 239
2 Corinthians: 86
Ephesians: 141
1 & 2 Thessalonians: 197, 199
12:10, 28–29
Matthew 1–7: 127
12:11
John 12–21: 113
2 Corinthians: 221–22, 229
Ephesians: 137, 189
2 Timothy: 15
Hebrews: 49
1 Peter: 243
12:11–12, 19
Romans 9–16: 160
12:12
1 Timothy: 183
Titus: 166
1 Peter: 187
12:12–13
Romans 9–16: 306
Ephesians: 66, 92
12:12–14
Philippians: 101
12:12–27
Mark 9–16: 290
12:12–31
Ephesians: 281
12:13
Matthew 1–7: 71
Mark 1–8: 26
Luke 1–5: 180
John 12–21: 30, 289
Acts 1–12: 18, 39, 41, 169, 245, 273, 304
Acts 13–28: 67, 164
Romans 1–8: 401, 487
2 Corinthians: 45, 116, 489
Galatians: 174
Ephesians: 247, 248
Philippians: 88, 105
Colossians and Philemon: 109, 152
1 & 2 Thessalonians: 118, 166
2 Peter–Jude: 27
12:13, 20
Ephesians: 128
12:14–27
2 Timothy: 204
12:14ff.
Acts 13–28: 43
12:15–16
Romans 9–16: 160
12:15–25
1 Peter: 244
12:15–27
Colossians and Philemon: 51
12:17–18
2 Timothy: 87
12:18
Hebrews: 49
12:19–13:10
2 Corinthians: 442
12:20–21
2 Corinthians: 442
12:20–27
Philippians: 316
12:21
Romans 9–16: 160
12:26
Acts 13–28: 181
Romans 9–16: 197
2 Corinthians: 392
Philippians: 195
1 & 2 Thessalonians: 117
12:26–27
1–3 John: 18
12:27
Matthew 16–23: 103
Romans 1–8: 401
12:28
Acts 1–12: 26
Acts 13–28: 3, 4
2 Corinthians: 410, 473
Ephesians: 140, 143
1 & 2 Thessalonians: 166, 193
Titus: 44
Hebrews: 49
James: 146
2 Peter–Jude: 10
1–3 John: 103
12:29
1 Timothy: 108
12:29–30
Romans 9–16: 160
12:31
Romans 9–16: 158
12:31–13:13
1–3 John: 62
13
Matthew 1–7: 345
Mark 9–16: 44
Romans 9–16: 253
Ephesians: 281
13:1
Ephesians: 40
13:1–2
2 Corinthians: 442
13:1–3
Matthew 8–15: 151
Philippians: 24, 41, 66
Colossians and Philemon: 87
1 & 2 Thessalonians: 96
13:1–4
1 Peter: 193
13:2
Revelation 1–11: 99
13:3
Romans 1–8: 99
Romans 9–16: 140
13:4
Acts 13–28: 201
1 & 2 Thessalonians: 90
13:4–5
1 & 2 Thessalonians: 180
13:4–7
Matthew 1–7: 442
2 Corinthians: 58
Philippians: 20
1 & 2 Thessalonians: 181
Titus: 75
1–3 John: 181
13:4–8
Romans 9–16: 249
2 Corinthians: 235
Philippians: 24
13:5
2 Corinthians: 238, 239
Philippians: 306
13:5–6
Ephesians: 212
13:6
Luke 6–10: 339
Romans 1–8: 63
Romans 9–16: 185, 248, 251, 371
2 Corinthians: 477
Ephesians: 335
Philippians: 195
Titus: 19
2 Peter–Jude: 13
13:7
Acts 13–28: 201
2 Corinthians: 236, 240
Philippians: 41
13:8
Acts 1–12: 43
Acts 13–28: 201
1 Peter: 193
13:9
Romans 9–16: 171
13:11
Galatians: 104
Ephesians: 315
13:12
Matthew 1–7: 16
Mark 1–8: 406
Mark 9–16: 193
Luke 6–10: 89
2 Corinthians: 113
Ephesians: 112
Philippians: 80, 163, 244, 263
1 Timothy: 278
1–3 John: 118
Revelation 1–11: 105
Revelation 12–22: 261
13:13
Romans 9–16: 184
Galatians: 165
Philippians: 24, 41, 66, 263
Colossians and Philemon: 19
1 & 2 Thessalonians: 15, 88, 90, 117, 161
2 Timothy: 130
1 Peter: 62
1–3 John: 103, 141
Revelation 1–11: 99
14:1
Romans 9–16: 247
14:1–3
1 & 2 Thessalonians: 197
14:3
Acts 13–28: 240

Romans 9–16: 170
14:5
Romans 9–16: 171
14:6
1 & 2 Thessalonians: 197, 233
14:12
1 & 2 Thessalonians: 95, 166
14:12–13
1 & 2 Thessalonians: 177
14:12–17
1 & 2 Thessalonians: 189
14:13–15
1 & 2 Thessalonians: 186
14:15
Romans 9–16: 193
Ephesians: 381
1 & 2 Thessalonians: 194
1 Peter: 274
14:16
Matthew 8–15: 104
14:18
Matthew 1–7: 226
2 Corinthians: 79
14:20
Matthew 1–7: 350
Ephesians: 158
Colossians and Philemon: 29
14:21–22
Matthew 8–15: 353
Acts 1–12: 42, 43
14:22
Hebrews: 50
14:23–26
1 & 2 Thessalonians: 197
14:24
John 12–21: 197
Revelation 1–11: 139
14:24–25
Acts 1–12: 86
Romans 9–16: 170
14:25
Matthew 8–15: 76
Mark 1–8: 256
2 Corinthians: 345
14:26
James: 147, 276
14:26–33
2 Corinthians: 96
1 Peter: 264
14:29
Acts 13–28: 237
1 Peter: 264
14:32
Acts 1–12: 316
1 Peter: 177, 264
14:33
Matthew 1–7: 213
Acts 1–12: 176
Ephesians: 80
Philippians: 310
1 & 2 Thessalonians: 174, 204, 313
James: 176
Revelation 1–11: 320
14:33, 40
Matthew 8–15: 432
14:34
Acts 1–12: 182
1 Timothy: 85, 86
1 Peter: 177, 178
14:34–35
2 Corinthians: 96
Colossians and Philemon: 167
1 Timothy: 74
14:34–36
Acts 13–28: 240
14:37
John 12–21: 201
Ephesians: 141
2 Peter–Jude: 9
14:37–40
1 & 2 Thessalonians: 197
14:40
Ephesians: 262
1 & 2 Thessalonians: 166
15
2 Corinthians: 96, 166
Hebrews: 140
15:1
2 Corinthians: 47, 408
Philippians: 292
1 & 2 Thessalonians: 58
15:1–2
James: 28
15:1–4
Mark 1–8: 131, 267
Acts 1–12: 74
Colossians and Philemon: 12
1 & 2 Thessalonians: 21
1–3 John: 108
15:1–5
Hebrews: 264
15:1–8
Romans 1–8: 240–41
15:1–11
John 1–11: 475
15:2
Philippians: 186
15:3
Matthew 24–28: 270
Mark 1–8: 110
Mark 9–16: 396
Luke 1–5: 328
John 12–21: 37
Acts 13–28: 336
2 Corinthians: 412
Philippians: 292
1 Peter: 206
15:3–4
Matthew 16–23: 223
Mark 1–8: 380
Mark 9–16: 383, 386
Luke 11–17: 371
Acts 13–28: 108, 121, 196
Philippians: 86
1 & 2 Thessalonians: 58
2 Peter–Jude: 29
15:3–4, 17, 19
2 Timothy: 56
15:3–7
Acts 1–12: 110
15:3–8
Mark 9–16: 402
Luke 18–24: 431, 443
15:4
Matthew 24–28: 305
15:4–8
Luke 18–24: 195
15:5
Mark 9–16: 340
Luke 6–10: 25
Luke 18–24: 434
1 Peter: 4
2 Peter–Jude: 18
15:5–8
Acts 1–12: 14, 303
Galatians: 2
15:6
Matthew 24–28: 312
Mark 1–8: 192, 253, 264
Luke 1–5: 13
Luke 18–24: 432
John 1–11: 456
Acts 13–28: 24
1 & 2 Thessalonians: 125
15:7
Mark 1–8: 179, 277
Acts 1–12: 29
Galatians: 31
James: 11
15:7–10
2 Corinthians: 17
15:8
Matthew 8–15: 400
Acts 1–12: 267
Acts 13–28: 24, 267, 335
2 Corinthians: 412
Ephesians: 2
15:8–9
2 Timothy: 39
15:8–10
Matthew 1–7: 118
15:9
Luke 6–10: 21, 46
John 1–11: 53
Acts 1–12: 232
Acts 13–28: 210
Romans 1–8: 379
2 Corinthians: 71–72, 138, 345, 386, 408
Galatians: 40
Philippians: 113, 232, 240, 316
1 Timothy: 33
15:9–10
Romans 9–16: 331
1 Timothy: 27
15:10
Luke 6–10: 32, 45
Acts 13–28: 249
Romans 1–8: 380
2 Corinthians: 34, 74, 79, 85, 345, 349, 388
Galatians: 14
Ephesians: 10, 93
Philippians: 153, 168, 222, 245, 315

Colossians and Philemon: 82
1 & 2 Thessalonians: 39, 169, 204, 216, 289
15:12
Luke 11–17: 152
Luke 18–24: 245
1 Timothy: 152
15:12–19
Acts 1–12: 303
15:12–20
Mark 9–16: 12
15:13
Luke 18–24: 245
15:13–14
Matthew 24–28: 305
15:13–15, 17
2 Timothy: 81
15:13–17
Luke 18–24: 437
15:14
Luke 18–24: 245, 430
John 1–11: 88
15:14–17
Romans 9–16: 75
Galatians: 6
15:14–19
Mark 9–16: 393
15:14, 16–19
John 12–21: 373
15:15
Luke 18–24: 245
2 Corinthians: 147
15:16–17
2 Peter–Jude: 26
15:16–19
Luke 18–24: 430
15:16–23
Acts 1–12: 64
15:16–26
Acts 1–12: 65
15:17
Matthew 24–28: 305
Luke 18–24: 245, 406
Acts 1–12: 303
1 Peter: 34, 48
15:17, 19
Matthew 8–15: 164
Luke 1–5: 54
15:18
Luke 18–24: 245
John 1–11: 456
1 & 2 Thessalonians: 125
15:19
Luke 18–24: 245
Ephesians: 364, 367
1 Peter: 34
Revelation 1–11: 32
15:20
Matthew 1–7: 258
Matthew 24–28: 276
Luke 18–24: 391
John 1–11: 456
Acts 1–12: 40, 226
Philippians: 79
1 & 2 Thessalonians: 125
1–3 John: 194
15:20–22
Matthew 24–28: 304
John 1–11: 475
15:20–23
Luke 11–17: 152
Luke 18–24: 407
15:20–28
Mark 1–8: 382
1 Peter: 34
15:21–22
John 12–21: 361
2 Corinthians: 192
1 Timothy: 89
15:21–23
2 Peter–Jude: 30
15:22
Luke 1–5: 58
Romans 1–8: 294, 297, 302, 401
1 & 2 Thessalonians: 224–25
Hebrews: 55
1–3 John: 197
15:22–23
Philippians: 262
15:22, 51–53
Matthew 24–28: 276
15:23
1 & 2 Thessalonians: 74, 128
James: 253
Revelation 12–22: 238, 302
15:23–25
James: 196
15:24
John 1–11: 16
Acts 1–12: 16
2 Corinthians: 488
Philippians: 141
15:24–25
Matthew 24–28: 119
Hebrews: 36
15:24–27
Philippians: 263
15:24–28
Luke 1–5: 50
John 12–21: 248
2 Peter–Jude: 128
Revelation 1–11: 311
Revelation 12–22: 270–71
15:25
Luke 18–24: 154
15:26
Luke 18–24: 391
1 Peter: 225
Revelation 12–22: 261
15:27
Luke 18–24: 112
1 Peter: 177–78
15:27–28
Philippians: 146–47
15:28
Matthew 24–28: 339
Romans 9–16: 304
Titus: 12
Hebrews: 36
Revelation 12–22: 265
15:31
Luke 6–10: 274–75
Romans 9–16: 146
2 Corinthians: 32, 144, 145, 240, 388
Colossians and Philemon: 136
2 Timothy: 15
1 Peter: 225
15:32
Matthew 1–7: 426
Luke 6–10: 351
2 Corinthians: 390
Galatians: 207
Ephesians: 367
Philippians: 2
15:33
Luke 11–17: 116
2 Corinthians: 237
Ephesians: 209
2 Timothy: 31, 89
15:34
Romans 9–16: 259
1 & 2 Thessalonians: 108
Titus: 74
15:35
Acts 13–28: 23
2 Corinthians: 164
15:35–38
Luke 11–17: 208
15:35–41
Romans 1–8: 463
15:35–44
Luke 18–24: 436
Revelation 12–22: 272
15:35–49
2 Corinthians: 161
Philippians: 262
15:35–50
Luke 18–24: 147
15:35–53
Mark 9–16: 190–91
15:36
Luke 11–17: 100
15:36–38
2 Corinthians: 164
15:36–49
2 Corinthians: 164
15:39–42
2 Corinthians: 164
15:39–44
Matthew 16–23: 333
15:42
Matthew 8–15: 222
2 Corinthians: 162
15:42–43
1 Peter: 226
15:42–44
Romans 1–8: 419, 464
2 Corinthians: 154
15:42–49
1 & 2 Thessalonians: 288
15:42b–44
2 Corinthians: 164
15:43
1 & 2 Thessalonians: 52

15:44
1 Peter: 226
15:45
Philippians: 130
15:45–49
2 Corinthians: 164–65
15:47
Luke 1–5: 229
2 Peter–Jude: 30
15:47–49
1 Peter: 34
15:48–49
Matthew 16–23: 333
15:49
Matthew 1–7: 139
Matthew 16–23: 24
Romans 1–8: 445, 492
2 Corinthians: 117, 154, 168
Philippians: 28, 263
Colossians and Philemon: 150–51
15:49–53
1–3 John: 116
15:50–52
1–3 John: 110
15:50–54
1 & 2 Thessalonians: 207
15:50–57
2 Peter–Jude: 52
15:51
Acts 1–12: 226
Romans 9–16: 387
2 Corinthians: 109, 162
Philippians: 79
1 & 2 Thessalonians: 125, 131
Revelation 1–11: 286
15:51–52
Luke 11–17: 410
Luke 18–24: 247
2 Corinthians: 166
Ephesians: xi
1 & 2 Thessalonians: 132, 135
1 Timothy: 128
Revelation 1–11: 230
Revelation 12–22: 213
15:51–53
Matthew 24–28: 60
2 Corinthians: 117
Philippians: 240
Titus: 120
1 Peter: 235
15:51–54
Romans 1–8: 457
2 Timothy: 201
1–3 John: 113
Revelation 1–11: 124
Revelation 12–22: 15
15:51–55
Revelation 12–22: 262
15:51–57
Luke 18–24: 192
1 Peter: 42
15:51–58
1 & 2 Thessalonians: 124
Revelation 1–11: 24
15:52
1 & 2 Thessalonians: 134, 135
Revelation 1–11: 20, 239, 308
15:52–53
Romans 1–8: 393
Philippians: 28
15:52–54
1 & 2 Thessalonians: 203
15:53
Romans 1–8: 131, 337
15:53–54
Romans 1–8: 280
2 Corinthians: 162
Revelation 12–22: 304
15:53–55
2 Timothy: 191
15:54
John 1–11: 475
2 Corinthians: 58, 165
Hebrews: 343
Revelation 12–22: 269
15:54–55
2 Timothy: 24
1 Peter: 225
15:54–57
Matthew 16–23: 33
1 Peter: 34, 226
1–3 John: 109–10, 175
15:55
John 1–11: 474
2 Corinthians: 170
Hebrews: 67, 70
Revelation 12–22: 104
15:55–57
Mark 1–8: 238
John 12–21: 362
Romans 1–8: 409
15:56
2 Corinthians: 101
Galatians: 158
15:56–57
Romans 1–8: 393
Ephesians: 337
15:57
Luke 1–5: 285
Romans 1–8: 306, 346
Philippians: 147
1–3 John: 174
Revelation 12–22: 68, 194
15:58
Luke 18–24: 10
Romans 9–16: 192
2 Corinthians: 388
Galatians: 190
Philippians: 80, 82, 168, 267
1 & 2 Thessalonians: 95, 288
2 Timothy: 49
16:1
Romans 9–16: 346
1 & 2 Thessalonians: 142
Revelation 1–11: 320
16:1–2
Acts 1–12: 88
16:1–3
1 & 2 Thessalonians: 213
16:1–4
Acts 1–12: 179
Acts 13–28: 181, 198, 306
2 Corinthians: 275, 300
16:1–9
Colossians and Philemon: 192
16:2
Matthew 1–7: 358
Matthew 8–15: 287
Mark 1–8: 141
Luke 18–24: 409
Romans 9–16: 233
2 Corinthians: 280, 285, 300–301
1 & 2 Thessalonians: 177
1–3 John: 245
16:2–3
James: 244
16:3
2 Corinthians: 80
16:5–6
2 Corinthians: 42
16:5–8
Acts 13–28: 198
16:6–7
2 Corinthians: 42
16:6, 11
Romans 9–16: 344
16:7
James: 237
16:8
2 Corinthians: 4, 8
Revelation 1–11: 58
16:8–9
Acts 13–28: 182
2 Corinthians: 67
Ephesians: 332
Colossians and Philemon: 183
Revelation 1–11: 123
16:9
Matthew 8–15: 185
2 Corinthians: 25–26
Ephesians: 347
Philippians: 59
16:10
2 Corinthians: 18
Philippians: 196, 199
1 & 2 Thessalonians: 77, 223
2 Timothy: 194
16:10–11
Matthew 16–23: 117
Romans 9–16: 378
1 & 2 Thessalonians: 166
16:12
1 & 2 Thessalonians: 142
Titus: 168
16:13
2 Corinthians: 477
Philippians: 87, 267, 282
1 & 2 Thessalonians: 49, 82, 288
2 Timothy: 36
1–3 John: 15
16:14
Ephesians: 194
1 & 2 Thessalonians: 90, 117

16:15
John 12–21: 150
Galatians: 164
Colossians and Philemon: 31
1 Timothy: 125
James: 64
Revelation 12–22: 79
16:15–16
1 Peter: 276–77
16:16
Ephesians: 276
1 Peter: 178
16:17
2 Corinthians: 4
16:17–18
Romans 9–16: 354
16:19
Acts 13–28: 147, 160, 203
Romans 9–16: 363
2 Corinthians: 4
Philippians: 7
16:19–21
Romans 9–16: 379
16:20
Romans 9–16: 370
2 Corinthians: 234, 486
1 & 2 Thessalonians: 214
Revelation 1–11: 72
16:21
Philippians: 310
1 & 2 Thessalonians: 318
1 Peter: 8–9
2 Peter–Jude: 13
16:22
Matthew 16–23: 299, 340
Mark 1–8: 124
Luke 11–17: 73, 343
Luke 18–24: 9, 152, 197
John 12–21: 400
Acts 1–12: 268
Romans 1–8: 61, 396
Galatians: 10
1 & 2 Thessalonians: 18, 132
2 Timothy: 202
James: 42, 192
1 Peter: 123
Revelation 1–11: 54
Revelation 12–22: 291
16:23
2 Corinthians: 43, 487
Philippians: 318
1 & 2 Thessalonians: 216, 289
16:24
2 Corinthians: 229
Revelation 1–11: 133

2 Corinthians
1:1
Acts 13–28: 47
1 Corinthians: 1
2 Corinthians: 410
Philippians: 196, 199, 310
1 & 2 Thessalonians: 203
1 Timothy: 6, 117
Revelation 1–11: 320
1:1–11
2 Corinthians: 11–12
1:2
Philippians: 16, 314
1 & 2 Thessalonians: 14, 87, 204, 224
2 Peter–Jude: 24
Revelation 1–11: 24
1:2–3
Philippians: 16
1:3
Matthew 1–7: 82, 161
Matthew 16–23: 68
Mark 1–8: 36
Luke 1–5: 308
Acts 13–28: 146, 285
Romans 9–16: 133
2 Corinthians: 18–20, 68, 263, 393
Ephesians: 41
Philippians: 105, 314
1 & 2 Thessalonians: 138
1 Peter: 30, 32, 133, 286
1:3–4
John 12–21: 212
James: 275
1:3–5
1 & 2 Thessalonians: 83, 86
1:3–6
James: 21
1:3–10
2 Corinthians: 455
1:3–11
1 Peter: 257
1:4
Luke 11–17: 182
2 Corinthians: 17, 260, 473
1:4–5
Acts 13–28: 285
Ephesians: 153
1:4–10
2 Corinthians: 2, 388
1:5
Matthew 16–23: 225
Mark 9–16: 98
Luke 18–24: 53
Romans 1–8: 449
2 Corinthians: 24, 120, 144, 260, 279
Galatians: 211
Philippians: 74
Colossians and Philemon: 76
1:5–7
1 Peter: 3
1:5–11
1 Timothy: 174
1:6
Luke 11–17: 182–83
2 Corinthians: 120, 260, 421
2 Timothy: 132
1:6–7
Romans 1–8: 450
2 Corinthians: 22
1:7
2 Corinthians: 260
1:8
Luke 18–24: 256
Acts 13–28: 105
Romans 1–8: 134
1 Corinthians: 191
2 Corinthians: 260, 392, 483
Philippians: 58
1 & 2 Thessalonians: 125
1:8–9
Luke 11–17: 182
2 Corinthians: 66, 143
1:8–10
Acts 13–28: 338
1 Corinthians: 466
2 Corinthians: 120, 160, 231
1 & 2 Thessalonians: 295
1:8–11
Philippians: 74
1:9
2 Corinthians: 147, 260
1:10
2 Corinthians: 260
1:10b
2 Corinthians: 26
1:11
2 Corinthians: 27–28
Philippians: 21
Colossians and Philemon: 26
1 & 2 Thessalonians: 211, 293
1:12
John 12–21: 129
Acts 13–28: 224
Romans 9–16: 9
2 Corinthians: 69, 79, 174, 326–28
Philippians: 18, 51, 52, 73
1 & 2 Thessalonians: 23, 40
1 Timothy: 45, 128, 151
2 Timothy: 5
Titus: 43
James: 54
1 Peter: 204
1–3 John: 142
1:12–13
2 Corinthians: 2, 184
1:12–14
2 Corinthians: 29–38, 40
1:13
2 Corinthians: 69, 235
1:14
2 Corinthians: 187
Philippians: 28
1 & 2 Thessalonians: 73
1:15–16
1 Corinthians: 461
2 Corinthians: 41
1:15–2:4
2 Corinthians: 39–40
1:17
1 Corinthians: 462
2 Corinthians: 7
1:17–18
2 Corinthians: 42
1:18
Luke 1–5: 174
Acts 13–28: 297

Titus: 30
1:19
Luke 1–5: 195
Acts 13–28: 72
1 & 2 Thessalonians: 223
1 Timothy: 139
1 Peter: 289
1:19–20
2 Corinthians: 43
1:20
Luke 1–5: 28, 79, 87, 174
John 1–11: 422
John 12–21: 347
Ephesians: 30
Philippians: 283
Colossians and Philemon: 130
Hebrews: 10
1–3 John: 219
Revelation 1–11: 133
Revelation 12–22: 215
1:21
Philippians: 311
1–3 John: 29
1:21–22
Romans 1–8: 460, 461
2 Corinthians: 45
1–3 John: 102
1:22
Romans 1–8: 490
Philippians: 105
1 & 2 Thessalonians: 112, 193
Hebrews: 168
Revelation 1–11: 217
1:23
Romans 9–16: 9
2 Corinthians: 444
James: 267
1:23–2:1
2 Corinthians: 46
1:23–2:4
2 Corinthians: 341
1:24
Romans 1–8: 476
Philippians: 282
1 & 2 Thessalonians: 89
1–7
2 Corinthians: 270
1–9
2 Corinthians: 6–7, 338, 353
2:1
2 Corinthians: 5, 53, 66, 187, 221, 230, 261, 268, 342, 433, 438, 444, 479
2:1–2
1 Peter: 148
2:1–4
2 Corinthians: 7, 353, 354
2:1–11
1 & 2 Thessalonians: 72
2:2–3
2 Corinthians: 47
2:3
Romans 9–16: 197
2:3–4
2 Corinthians: 66, 300, 322, 337, 341, 433
2:4
Luke 18–24: 234
Acts 13–28: 212
2 Corinthians: 5, 6, 7, 46, 47, 48, 59, 120, 221, 235–36, 262, 264, 455
Philippians: 21, 191, 257
1 & 2 Thessalonians: 69
1 Timothy: 174
2:4–9
2 Corinthians: 7
2:5
2 Corinthians: 53, 61
2:5–8
Matthew 16–23: 136
2 Corinthians: 47, 261
2:5–11
1 Corinthians: 127
2 Corinthians: 7, 8, 49
2:6
Mark 9–16: 65
Luke 18–24: 26
2 Corinthians: 7, 56, 268
2:6–7
2 Corinthians: 267
2:6–8
2 Corinthians: 61
2:7
1 Corinthians: 133
2 Corinthians: 57
Galatians: 179
2:7–8
Matthew 1–7: 159–60
2:8
2 Corinthians: 58
Ephesians: 118
2:8–11
1 & 2 Thessalonians: 168
2:9
2 Corinthians: 47, 59, 277
2:9–11
2 Corinthians: 61
2:10
2 Corinthians: 47, 60, 261
2:10–11
Colossians and Philemon: 208
2:11
Luke 18–24: 294
2 Corinthians: 61, 482
Ephesians: 185, 333, 338
1 & 2 Thessalonians: 81, 166
1 Timothy: 39
Revelation 12–22: 14, 16, 235
2:12
1 Corinthians: 465
2 Corinthians: 262
Colossians and Philemon: 183
Revelation 1–11: 123
2:12–13
Acts 13–28: 198
2 Corinthians: 66, 398
1 & 2 Thessalonians: 77, 82
2:12–17
2 Corinthians: 63
2:13
Luke 11–17: 285
2 Corinthians: 120, 262
2:14
Luke 1–5: 285
2 Corinthians: 143
1 Timothy: 74
1 Peter: 206, 221
Revelation 12–22: 194
2:14–16
Matthew 1–7: 237
Matthew 8–15: 99
2:14–17
2 Corinthians: 68, 221
2:14–7:4
2 Corinthians: 262
2:15
Luke 11–17: 395
James: 290
2:15–16
Matthew 1–7: 242
Matthew 16–23: 393
Acts 1–12: 174
2 Corinthians: 220
Revelation 12–22: 298
2:16
Luke 11–17: 171, 384
Acts 13–28: 173
2 Corinthians: 78
1 & 2 Thessalonians: 32
2:17
Matthew 1–7: 467
Matthew 16–23: 393
Luke 11–17: 254
1 Corinthians: 99
2 Corinthians: 2, 7, 36, 60, 87, 127, 184, 269, 301, 327, 452
Philippians: 51
1 & 2 Thessalonians: 36, 294
1 Timothy: 14, 289
2 Timothy: 146, 159
1–3 John: 248
Revelation 12–22: 310
2:18
2 Corinthians: 484
2:28
2 Corinthians: 484
3
Matthew 1–7: 34
3:1
2 Corinthians: 79, 187, 324, 337, 387, 484
3:1–2
2 Corinthians: 452
3:1–3
1 & 2 Thessalonians: 38
3:1–6
2 Corinthians: 77
3:2
Acts 13–28: 193
2 Corinthians: 236, 408, 437
Colossians and Philemon: 84
3:2–3
2 Corinthians: 81, 341–42
3:3
2 Corinthians: 84
Titus: 89

Revelation 1–11: 51, 217, 315
3:4
2 Corinthians: 84
3:5
Acts 13–28: 210
1 Corinthians: 106
2 Corinthians: 1–2, 74, 184, 345, 392, 403
Ephesians: 123
Philippians: 168
1 & 2 Thessalonians: 89
1 Timothy: 251
Hebrews: 142, 451
3:5–6
2 Corinthians: 78, 420
1 & 2 Thessalonians: 170
3:6
Luke 11–17: 123
2 Corinthians: 98, 113
1 Timothy: 158
3:6–11
2 Corinthians: 93
3:6–18
2 Corinthians: 2, 8, 96–97, 107, 125
3:6ff.
Acts 13–28: 202
3:7
2 Corinthians: 98, 103
Hebrews: 412
3:7–8
1–3 John: 23
3:7–11
Acts 1–12: 196
3:8–9
2 Corinthians: 100
3:9
2 Corinthians: 98, 238–39
3:10–11
2 Corinthians: 103
3:12
2 Corinthians: 107
3:12–18
2 Corinthians: 105
3:13
1 Corinthians: 258
3:14
Matthew 16–23: 252
Philippians: 286
3:14–15
1 & 2 Thessalonians: 81
3:14–16
John 12–21: 50
Galatians: 24
3:15
2 Corinthians: 132
3:15–18
Mark 1–8: 402, 417
3:16
Acts 1–12: 114, 282
Acts 13–28: 337
1 & 2 Thessalonians: 27
James: 289
3:16–18
2 Corinthians: 152
3:17
1 Corinthians: 189
2 Corinthians: 113
Galatians: 39
3:18
Matthew 1–7: 139, 150
John 12–21: 209
Acts 1–12: 274
Acts 13–28: 80
Romans 1–8: 280, 443, 491
Romans 9–16: 150, 178, 268
1 Corinthians: 54, 101
2 Corinthians: 1, 120, 140
Galatians: 120
Ephesians: 157, 197, 253
Philippians: 181, 244, 254
Colossians and Philemon: 45, 65
1 & 2 Thessalonians: 24, 98, 195, 203, 287
2 Timothy: 162
Titus: 155
Hebrews: 379
James: 98
1 Peter: 18–19, 130
2 Peter–Jude: 25
1–3 John: 28, 76, 158, 170
Revelation 1–11: 52
3:18–4:6
2 Corinthians: 119, 152
4
Matthew 1–7: 81, 86, 102, 244
4:1
Luke 6–10: 314
2 Corinthians: 125, 140
4:1–2
1 Corinthians: 99
4:1–2, 8–10, 14
Galatians: 191
4:1–6
1 & 2 Thessalonians: 38
4:1–15
1 & 2 Thessalonians: 293
4:2
1 Corinthians: 55
2 Corinthians: 2, 7, 36, 184, 235–37, 269, 327, 452–53, 477
1 & 2 Thessalonians: 270, 319
1 Timothy: 14
2 Timothy: 159
2 Peter–Jude: 13
Revelation 12–22: 80
4:3–4
Matthew 1–7: 103
Mark 1–8: 58, 281
Luke 1–5: 325
Acts 1–12: 111, 252
2 Corinthians: 129
1 & 2 Thessalonians: 22, 282
1 Timothy: 39
2 Timothy: 183
1 Peter: 282
4:3–6
Luke 6–10: 280
4:4
Matthew 8–15: 169, 357, 386
Matthew 16–23: 2, 252
Matthew 24–28: 322
Mark 1–8: 36, 43, 201, 249
Luke 1–5: 255, 259, 272, 280, 296, 342
Luke 6–10: 224, 340
Luke 11–17: 47, 89, 109, 346
Luke 18–24: 195
John 1–11: 23, 32, 450
John 12–21: 42, 52, 196, 315
Acts 13–28: 168, 291, 335, 336
Romans 1–8: 108, 495
Romans 9–16: 150
2 Corinthians: 225, 408, 482
Ephesians: 169, 206, 339
Philippians: 286, 288
Colossians and Philemon: 57
1 & 2 Thessalonians: 71, 80, 166, 282
Hebrews: 15
James: 98
1 Peter: 275
1–3 John: 123, 153, 175, 214
Revelation 1–11: 32, 86, 139, 162, 244, 255, 310
Revelation 12–22: 15, 16, 54, 86, 212, 233, 236
4:4–6
Philippians: 127
1–3 John: 23–24
4:4–7
2 Corinthians: 227
4:5
Mark 9–16: 129
Romans 1–8: 34
2 Corinthians: 1–2, 133, 184, 453
Philippians: 200
1 & 2 Thessalonians: 41
1 Timothy: 139
2 Timothy: 174, 184
4:5–6
Romans 9–16: 385
4:5–7
Mark 1–8: 217
4:5, 11
Romans 9–16: 350
4:6
Matthew 16–23: 74
Luke 1–5: 272
Luke 11–17: 88
Acts 1–12: 267
1 Corinthians: 18, 52
2 Corinthians: 112, 116, 120, 132, 134, 138, 142
Philippians: 235
Hebrews: 16
James: 98
1 Peter: 92
1–3 John: 102
Revelation 1–11: 48
4:6–7
John 12–21: 268

2 Corinthians: 227
4:7
Luke 6–10: 21, 24
2 Corinthians: 1, 85, 139, 152, 201, 328, 400, 408, 455
Ephesians: 47
1 & 2 Thessalonians: 107
2 Timothy: 86, 87
1 Peter: 277
4:7–11
2 Corinthians: 21–22
4:7–12
2 Corinthians: 2, 160, 388, 392
1 & 2 Thessalonians: 82, 295
4:7–15
2 Corinthians: 137–48, 358
4:7–18
1 Peter: 257, 278
4:8
2 Corinthians: 68, 142, 144
James: 16
4:8–9
2 Corinthians: 142–43, 150, 158
Ephesians: 9
Colossians and Philemon: 74, 86
4:8–9, 17–18
John 12–21: 128
4:8–10
2 Corinthians: 94
Philippians: 200, 260
4:8–11
Romans 1–8: 447
1 Corinthians: 466
2 Corinthians: 85, 227
4:8–12
Acts 1–12: 230
2 Corinthians: 24–25, 121, 175, 260
1 & 2 Thessalonians: 293
James: 19
1 Peter: 225
4:8–12, 16
Ephesians: 106
4:8–15
Ephesians: 88
4:9
1 Corinthians: 371
2 Corinthians: 142, 144
4:10
2 Corinthians: 144–45, 205
Philippians: 75
Colossians and Philemon: 133
4:10–11
2 Corinthians: 144–45, 150
4:10–12
2 Corinthians: 231
4:11
2 Corinthians: 145, 152
4:12
2 Corinthians: 145, 318
4:13
Acts 13–28: 214
2 Corinthians: 85, 146, 235
1 Timothy: 137
4:14
Matthew 24–28: 305
Luke 18–24: 408
1 Corinthians: 409
2 Corinthians: 147
1 & 2 Thessalonians: 128
James: 19
4:15
Matthew 8–15: 481
Matthew 24–28: 332
Mark 1–8: 218
John 1–11: 480
Romans 1–8: 27, 447, 473
1 Corinthians: 91
2 Corinthians: 147–48, 318
Ephesians: 267
Philippians: 23
1 & 2 Thessalonians: 189
1 Timothy: 62
1–3 John: 73, 248
Revelation 12–22: 194
4:16
Romans 1–8: 390
2 Corinthians: 152–54, 328
Ephesians: 105
Philippians: 242
Colossians and Philemon: 150
1 & 2 Thessalonians: 296
4:16–17
Acts 13–28: 105
Romans 1–8: 448, 474
2 Corinthians: 121
4:16–18
2 Corinthians: 149, 160, 161, 227
James: 19
1 Peter: 198, 232, 251
4:17
Matthew 16–23: 237
Luke 6–10: 275
John 12–21: 194, 212
Romans 1–8: 131, 281, 448, 500, 514
2 Corinthians: 154–56, 161, 396
Philippians: 194, 283, 302
Colossians and Philemon: 75
1 & 2 Thessalonians: 52, 247
1 Timothy: 53, 277
Hebrews: 355
James: 254
1 Peter: 42
Revelation 1–11: 158
Revelation 12–22: 261
4:17–18
Luke 11–17: 182
2 Corinthians: 15, 160–61
Ephesians: 367
1–3 John: 176
4:18
Luke 1–5: 64
2 Corinthians: 157
5
Hebrews: 400
5:1
John 12–21: 178
2 Corinthians: 161, 175, 217, 328, 392
Philippians: 79
1 Peter: 35, 225
2 Peter–Jude: 27
5:1–2
2 Peter–Jude: 52
5:1–5
1 Corinthians: 416
2 Corinthians: 169
5:1–8
2 Corinthians: 159–70, 174
5:1–11
2 Corinthians: 2
5:2
Revelation 12–22: 272
5:2–4
2 Corinthians: 165
5:2–8
1 & 2 Thessalonians: 19
5:2, 8
Matthew 1–7: 160
5:4
Luke 18–24: 256
Romans 1–8: 459
5:4–5
Titus: 9
5:5
Acts 1–12: 40
2 Corinthians: 167–69
Ephesians: 247
1 & 2 Thessalonians: 113
Hebrews: 168
5:6
2 Corinthians: 160, 170, 175
Philippians: 262
5:6–7
Luke 6–10: 288
5:6–8
2 Corinthians: 169, 174
5:7
Mark 9–16: 22
Luke 1–5: 64
2 Corinthians: 170
Philippians: 80
1 & 2 Thessalonians: 52, 89, 257
Hebrews: 310, 313
1–3 John: 246
5:8
Matthew 24–28: 60
Mark 1–8: 264
Luke 6–10: 236
Acts 1–12: 225
Romans 1–8: 47, 516
1 Corinthians: 417
2 Corinthians: 160, 175
Philippians: 79, 262, 277
1 & 2 Thessalonians: 125
1 Timothy: 272
2 Timothy: 213
Revelation 1–11: 52
Revelation 12–22: 262

5:9
Mark 1–8: 427
Mark 9–16: 108
Luke 11–17: 77
John 12–21: 268
Romans 1–8: 419
1 Corinthians: 78
2 Corinthians: 73, 174
Galatians: 22
Philippians: 80
1 & 2 Thessalonians: 119
2 Timothy: 28, 45
Titus: 100
5:9–10
Luke 18–24: 82
2 Corinthians: 2, 171–79, 184
1 & 2 Thessalonians: 144
1 Peter: 69, 238
2 Peter–Jude: 132
Revelation 12–22: 299
5:9–11
1 Timothy: 166
1 Peter: 271
5:10
Matthew 1–7: 478
Matthew 16–23: 57
John 12–21: 102
Acts 1–12: 23
Romans 1–8: 128
Romans 9–16: 141, 260, 290
1 Corinthians: 83, 321
2 Corinthians: 37, 175–79
Galatians: 182
Philippians: 28, 52, 142, 187
1 & 2 Thessalonians: 74, 91, 111, 130
1 Timothy: 166
2 Timothy: 28, 169, 200
James: 176, 257
1 Peter: 37, 237
Revelation 1–11: 30
Revelation 12–22: 251
5:11
Matthew 8–15: 56, 70, 115, 400
Matthew 16–23: 57
Luke 1–5: 325
Romans 1–8: 71, 141
Philippians: 160
1 Timothy: 166, 274
5:11–17
2 Corinthians: 181–96
5:12
2 Corinthians: 79, 186–88
5:12–13
2 Corinthians: 7
5:13
Mark 1–8: 266
2 Corinthians: 188–89, 216
5:13–14
Philippians: 104
5:14
Luke 11–17: 171
John 12–21: 400
Romans 1–8: 483
Romans 9–16: 295, 333
1 Corinthians: 78, 479
2 Corinthians: 189–92
Ephesians: 198
1 & 2 Thessalonians: 18
Revelation 1–11: 54
5:14–15
1–3 John: 18
5:14–17
2 Corinthians: 199
5:14–21
2 Corinthians: 2
5:15
1 Corinthians: 78
2 Corinthians: 193–94
Galatians: 210
Ephesians: 174
Titus: 3
1 Peter: 206
5:16
Luke 11–17: 246
James: 4
5:16–17
2 Corinthians: 194–96
5:17
Matthew 1–7: 206
Mark 1–8: 116, 206, 348, 396
Mark 9–16: 331, 332
Luke 1–5: 119, 218, 331
Luke 6–10: 167
Luke 11–17: 77
Luke 18–24: 301
Acts 1–12: 243
Romans 1–8: 306, 319, 322, 461
Romans 9–16: 79
1 Corinthians: 68, 141, 143
2 Corinthians: 45, 126, 134, 153, 216, 243, 471
Galatians: 209
Ephesians: 164, 182, 202
Philippians: 64, 86, 242, 262, 311
Colossians and Philemon: 40, 106, 108, 131, 137, 148, 214
1 & 2 Thessalonians: 15, 23, 59, 158, 193, 203, 225, 287, 308
1 Timothy: 105
Titus: 5, 114, 154
Hebrews: 230, 328
James: 61, 122
1 Peter: 21, 32, 89, 92, 106, 129, 171
2 Peter–Jude: 31
1–3 John: 29, 37, 66, 122, 140
Revelation 1–11: 54, 103
Revelation 12–22: 100
5:17–18
Colossians and Philemon: 61
5:17–20
Acts 13–28: 332
5:17–21
Colossians and Philemon: 66–67
5:18
Matthew 1–7: 215
Romans 1–8: 215
2 Corinthians: 199
Philippians: 200
Colossians and Philemon: 72
James: 289
5:18–19
Mark 1–8: 102
Luke 1–5: 161
1 Peter: 206
1–3 John: 37, 46
5:18–19, 21
2 Peter–Jude: 23
5:18–20
Luke 11–17: 71, 173, 178
2 Corinthians: 197–208
Ephesians: 18
Colossians and Philemon: 56
1 & 2 Thessalonians: 294
Titus: 113
2 Peter–Jude: 134
5:18–21
Mark 1–8: 210
Revelation 1–11: 232
5:19
Matthew 24–28: 332
Luke 6–10: 159
Acts 1–12: 302
Romans 1–8: 305
1 Corinthians: 347
2 Corinthians: 201–6, 216, 221
5:19–20
Matthew 1–7: 215
Luke 1–5: 40
Acts 13–28: 15
1 Timothy: 142
5:20
Matthew 8–15: 196
Luke 11–17: 90, 329
1 Corinthians: 4
2 Corinthians: 201, 206–8, 220–21, 284
Philippians: 124, 200
1 & 2 Thessalonians: 97
1 Timothy: 68
5:20–21
Mark 1–8: 97, 422
5:21
Matthew 1–7: 78, 206
Matthew 16–23: 312
Matthew 24–28: 270
Mark 1–8: 32, 110, 122, 348, 393
Mark 9–16: 300, 371
Luke 1–5: 58, 154, 167, 168, 197, 237
Luke 6–10: 264, 354
Luke 11–17: 30, 40
Luke 18–24: 267, 283, 298, 305, 307, 390, 431
John 1–11: 25
John 12–21: 158, 230, 240, 312

Romans 1–8: 200, 256, 328, 361, 408, 505
Romans 9–16: 67
1 Corinthians: 53
2 Corinthians: 2, 102, 103, 176, 190, 191, 198, 205, 248, 478
Galatians: 205
Ephesians: 199, 352
Philippians: 123, 128, 238, 243, 244, 253, 311
Colossians and Philemon: 65
1 & 2 Thessalonians: 127, 164, 203, 247, 257
1 Timothy: 140
2 Timothy: 14
Hebrews: 67, 242
James: 63, 140
1 Peter: 78, 88, 166, 168, 170, 206, 207, 224
2 Peter–Jude: 22–23
1–3 John: 35, 59, 171, 192
Revelation 12–22: 154, 203, 253

6:1–2
Acts 13–28: 373

6:1–10
2 Corinthians: 219
Philippians: 69

6:2
Matthew 8–15: 314
Matthew 24–28: 96
Mark 1–8: 122
Luke 1–5: 315
Luke 11–17: 90, 165, 191
Luke 18–24: 118, 239
John 12–21: 80
Acts 1–12: 173, 301
Acts 13–28: 32, 310
Hebrews: 88, 103, 158
1 Peter: 57

6:3
2 Corinthians: 237
2 Timothy: 21

6:3–4
2 Corinthians: 2, 184

6:3–7
2 Corinthians: 225
Ephesians: 113

6:3–10
2 Corinthians: 33
1 & 2 Thessalonians: 293
1–3 John: 71

6:4
2 Corinthians: 421
1 Timothy: 158
2 Timothy: 130

6:4–5
2 Corinthians: 95, 142

6:4–6
Romans 9–16: 184

6:4–7
1 Corinthians: 97
2 Corinthians: 227
2 Timothy: 21

6:4–10
1 Corinthians: 191
2 Corinthians: 2, 121, 261, 358, 388, 392, 455
Ephesians: 364
Philippians: 260
1 & 2 Thessalonians: 180, 185, 293
1 Timothy: 174

6:4–11
1 Peter: 257

6:5
2 Corinthians: 226
Revelation 12–22: 123

6:6
1 Corinthians: 338
Galatians: 168
2 Timothy: 8

6:6–7
Romans 9–16: 248
2 Corinthians: 453

6:7
Luke 18–24: 418
2 Corinthians: 267, 269, 285, 327, 477
James: 62

6:8
2 Corinthians: 184, 226

6:8–10
1 Corinthians: 97

6:9
2 Corinthians: 160, 175

6:10
2 Corinthians: 226, 292
Ephesians: 9
Philippians: 11, 69
1 & 2 Thessalonians: 184
James: 109

6:11
2 Corinthians: 2, 184, 235–37, 239
Colossians and Philemon: 84

6:11–13
2 Corinthians: 81, 94, 233
Ephesians: 45
1 Timothy: 264

6:12
Luke 1–5: 120
2 Corinthians: 236
Philippians: 32

6:13
2 Corinthians: 236–37

6:14
Luke 1–5: 122
Luke 11–17: 73
John 1–11: 23
Acts 13–28: 336
1 Corinthians: 123, 164, 180
2 Corinthians: 257
Titus: 32
Hebrews: 328

6:14–15
Acts 1–12: 81
Hebrews: 441
1–3 John: 134, 231

6:14–16
Hebrews: 311

6:14–17
1 Corinthians: 278
James: 194
Revelation 1–11: 88
Revelation 12–22: 181

6:14–18
Mark 1–8: 134
Titus: 63, 162
James: 184

6:14–7:1
2 Corinthians: 2, 235, 237, 243

6:15
1 & 2 Thessalonians: 158
Revelation 1–11: 310

6:15–16
Luke 1–5: 284–85

6:16
John 1–11: 17
Acts 13–28: 164
1 Corinthians: 152
2 Corinthians: 250, 251, 253
Philippians: 170
1 & 2 Thessalonians: 108, 206
Revelation 1–11: 51, 217
Revelation 12–22: 266

6:16–18
2 Corinthians: 257

6:17
Matthew 16–23: 84
Acts 13–28: 158
2 Corinthians: 255, 257
Ephesians: 240
1 & 2 Thessalonians: 104

6:17–18
Romans 1–8: 436

6:18
Revelation 12–22: 272

7
Matthew 1–7: 206
2 Corinthians: 68

7:1
Matthew 8–15: 56
Mark 9–16: 47
Romans 1–8: 340
Romans 9–16: 182, 272
2 Corinthians: 1, 186, 235, 257–58, 443, 482
Ephesians: 240, 363
Philippians: 77, 153, 160, 161, 245
1 & 2 Thessalonians: 96, 107, 206
1 Timothy: 165, 223
1 Peter: 22, 139
2 Peter–Jude: 30
1–3 John: 36, 72, 106
Revelation 1–11: 54
Revelation 12–22: 101

7:1, 11
Luke 1–5: 325

7:2
2 Corinthians: 2, 35, 184, 238, 327, 342

7:2–3
1–3 John: 258
7:2–4
2 Corinthians: 233–41, 259
7:3
Acts 13–28: 193
2 Corinthians: 81, 221, 236, 341
Philippians: 31
7:4
Acts 13–28: 285
2 Corinthians: 32, 484
Philippians: 194
Hebrews: 368
7:5
2 Corinthians: 95, 392
1 Peter: 257
7:5–6
Acts 13–28: 194, 198
2 Corinthians: 121, 231
7:5–7
2 Corinthians: 68
Galatians: 180
7:5–9
Philippians: 196
7:5–16
2 Corinthians: 259–60
7:6
John 12–21: 212
Acts 13–28: 146, 285
1 Corinthians: 483
2 Corinthians: 21, 23, 437, 455
1 & 2 Thessalonians: 82
7:6–7, 23
Titus: 15
7:6–11
2 Corinthians: 433
7:6–16
2 Corinthians: 48
7:6ff.
2 Corinthians: 46
7:7
Romans 9–16: 267
2 Corinthians: 263
7:8
2 Corinthians: 7, 47
7:8–10
2 Corinthians: 236, 264, 341
7:9
Romans 1–8: 224
2 Timothy: 101
7:9–10
Acts 1–12: 116, 247
7:9–11
Luke 1–5: 208
Luke 11–17: 313
2 Corinthians: 432
James: 212
1–3 John: 40
7:10
Matthew 1–7: 53
Matthew 16–23: 311
Matthew 24–28: 283
Mark 1–8: 21, 308
Luke 18–24: 40
John 12–21: 129
2 Corinthians: 48, 58
Philippians: 223
James: 212
1–3 John: 36
Revelation 1–11: 139
7:10–11
Matthew 1–7: 66, 157
Matthew 8–15: 56
7:11
2 Corinthians: 266
1 Timothy: 225
7:11–12
2 Corinthians: 286
7:12
2 Corinthians: 7, 47, 60, 268
7:12–15
2 Corinthians: 60
7:13
Romans 9–16: 355
1 Corinthians: 483
2 Corinthians: 241, 268
Philippians: 105
7:13–16
1 & 2 Thessalonians: 166
7:14
2 Corinthians: 32, 240, 477
1 & 2 Thessalonians: 319
2 Peter–Jude: 13
7:14–15
2 Corinthians: 269
7:15
Luke 1–5: 120
1 Corinthians: 56
2 Corinthians: 304
Philippians: 32, 105, 160
7:15–16
2 Corinthians: 276
7:16
2 Corinthians: 270, 434
8
2 Corinthians: 2, 274, 276, 288, 300, 314, 320, 427, 479–80
8:1
2 Corinthians: 276, 483
Philippians: 78
1 & 2 Thessalonians: 320
1 Peter: 182
8:1–2
Matthew 1–7: 359
Philippians: 297, 306
1 & 2 Thessalonians: 48
James: 102
8:1–3
Philippians: 308
8:1–4
1 Timothy: 283
8:1–5
Acts 1–12: 149
Philippians: 2, 20
1 & 2 Thessalonians: 26, 116, 172
1–3 John: 136
8:1–7
1–3 John: 107
8:1–8
2 Corinthians: 271, 288
8:1–9
2 Corinthians: 314
8:1ff.
Acts 13–28: 306
8:2
1 Corinthians: 452
2 Corinthians: 279, 312, 484
James: 244
8:2–4
Romans 9–16: 346
8:2–5
Romans 9–16: 176
8:3
2 Corinthians: 299, 301, 314
8:3–4
Acts 1–12: 183
1 & 2 Thessalonians: 48
8:4
1 Corinthians: 237, 451, 480
2 Corinthians: 283
Philippians: 22
Revelation 1–11: 320
8:5
Acts 13–28: 5
Romans 9–16: 140, 355
1 Corinthians: 452
8:6
2 Corinthians: 7, 276, 428
8:6–7
1 Timothy: 218
8:7
1 Corinthians: 191
2 Corinthians: 285
1 & 2 Thessalonians: 95, 96, 117, 177, 228
Revelation 1–11: 99
8:7–9
Philippians: 121
8:8
Luke 11–17: 334
1 Corinthians: 330
2 Corinthians: 286, 289
8:9
Luke 18–24: 455
Romans 1–8: 20, 445
2 Corinthians: 2, 232, 279, 283, 287
Ephesians: 135
Philippians: 128
1 Peter: 45
2 Peter–Jude: 30
8:10
2 Corinthians: 281, 299
8:10–9:5
2 Corinthians: 297, 298, 314
8:12
2 Corinthians: 280
Philippians: 298
8:13–14
Acts 1–12: 88
8:13–15
2 Corinthians: 302
8:14–15
Acts 1–12: 89

8:16
2 Corinthians: 428
8:16–19
Acts 13–28: 201
8:16–24
2 Corinthians: 7
8:17
2 Corinthians: 281
Ephesians: 148
8:18
2 Corinthians: 428
8:18–19
2 Corinthians: 428
8:18–23
2 Corinthians: 304–7
8:19
Acts 13–28: 47
8:20
Acts 13–28: 234, 247
2 Corinthians: 299, 318
8:20–21
2 Corinthians: 2, 184
8:21
1 & 2 Thessalonians: 181
8:22
2 Corinthians: 428
Philippians: 199
8:23
Acts 13–28: 47
Romans 1–8: 22
1 Corinthians: 323
2 Corinthians: 409, 428
Ephesians: 141
Philippians: 204
1 & 2 Thessalonians: 260
1 Timothy: 4
8:23–24
Romans 9–16: 361
8:24
2 Corinthians: 32, 240, 307
8–9
Mark 9–16: 86
Acts 1–12: 179
Acts 13–28: 181, 198
1 & 2 Thessalonians: 213
2 Corinthians: 288, 300, 320, 427
9
2 Corinthians: 2, 480
9:1
1 Timothy: 218
9:1–4
2 Corinthians: 308–9
9:2
2 Corinthians: 281, 285
1 & 2 Thessalonians: 172
9:5
Acts 13–28: 234
2 Corinthians: 309–10
9:6
Matthew 1–7: 358, 413
Matthew 8–15: 483
Mark 1–8: 216
Romans 9–16: 176
1 Corinthians: 204, 455
2 Corinthians: 273
Philippians: 307, 308
1 & 2 Thessalonians: 74
9:6–7
1 Timothy: 249
James: 244
9:6–12
1 & 2 Thessalonians: 177, 203
9:6–14
2 Corinthians: 274
9:6–15
2 Corinthians: 311–20
9:7
Matthew 1–7: 359
Luke 11–17: 333
Acts 1–12: 152
Romans 9–16: 233, 347
1 Corinthians: 455
2 Corinthians: 227, 278, 283, 314
9:8
Romans 1–8: 509
Romans 9–16: 384
1 Corinthians: 455
2 Corinthians: 279, 315, 403
Ephesians: 62
Philippians: 45
1 & 2 Thessalonians: 89, 195, 216
1 Timothy: 28, 31, 251
1 Peter: 182, 197
2 Peter–Jude: 24–25
Revelation 1–11: 157
9:10
Matthew 16–23: 13
Philippians: 54
2 Timothy: 200
Titus: 71
Hebrews: 451
James: 181
9:10–11
Matthew 1–7: 389
9:11
Matthew 1–7: 414
1 & 2 Thessalonians: 189
9:12
2 Corinthians: 299
Philippians: 192
9:12–13
1 Timothy: 218
9:12–14
Romans 9–16: 348
9:12, 15
Ephesians: 267
9:13
1 Corinthians: 451
Philippians: 22
1 Peter: 90
9:14
2 Corinthians: 319, 403
9:15
2 Corinthians: 319
Colossians and Philemon: 37
Hebrews: 143
Revelation 12–22: 194
9:23–25
2 Corinthians: 150
9:30
2 Corinthians: 389
10
2 Corinthians: 409
10:1
Matthew 1–7: 170
Acts 13–28: 246
1 Corinthians: 115, 344
2 Corinthians: 189, 323–25, 381, 446, 453
Galatians: 114
1 & 2 Thessalonians: 297
2 Timothy: 98
Titus: 144
2 Peter–Jude: 49
10:1a
1 Peter: 202
10:1–5
1 & 2 Thessalonians: 98
10:1–6
2 Corinthians: 321
10:2
2 Corinthians: 7, 326–27
Philippians: 77
10:3
Philippians: 77
10:3–4
Romans 1–8: 391
2 Timothy: 43
10:3–5
Luke 1–5: 281
Acts 13–28: 168
2 Corinthians: 229–30, 327–31, 356
Ephesians: 345, 368
Titus: 138
1 Peter: 148, 281, 286
2 Peter–Jude: 57
1–3 John: 75
Revelation 12–22: 22
10:4
Matthew 24–28: 189
Luke 18–24: 448
Romans 1–8: 428
Romans 9–16: 214
Galatians: 139
Philippians: 25
1 Timothy: 64
10:4–5
1 Timothy: 40
Titus: 55
Revelation 1–11: 273
10:5
2 Corinthians: 337, 381
Ephesians: 354
1 Peter: 275
10:5b
1 Peter: 22
10:6
2 Corinthians: 331
10:7
2 Corinthians: 2, 184, 338
10:7–18
1 & 2 Thessalonians: 293
10:8
2 Corinthians: 430, 452, 479

Philippians: 75
1 & 2 Thessalonians: 167
10:8–9
2 Corinthians: 127
10:10
Matthew 16–23: 116
Acts 13–28: 330
2 Corinthians: 138, 358, 399, 455
Philippians: 65
1 Timothy: 3
10:10–11
2 Corinthians: 36
10:10–12
Acts 13–28: 209
10:11
1 & 2 Thessalonians: 297
10:12
Luke 6–10: 301
2 Corinthians: 79, 133, 140, 353, 358
Ephesians: 123
10:12–17
1 & 2 Thessalonians: 293
10:12–18
2 Corinthians: 186
10:12–11:21
2 Corinthians: 384
10:13
2 Corinthians: 353
10:13–16
Romans 9–16: 334
10:13–11:21
2 Corinthians: 394
10:14
2 Corinthians: 337, 408
1 & 2 Thessalonians: 167
10:17
Acts 13–28: 249
Romans 9–16: 333
2 Corinthians: 32, 187, 240, 353
Philippians: 222
1 & 2 Thessalonians: 184
10:17–18
Romans 9–16: 335
10:18
2 Corinthians: 79, 140, 187, 353
1 & 2 Thessalonians: 228
10–12
1 Timothy: 125
10–13
2 Corinthians: 6–7, 263, 270, 321–22, 338, 353, 398
11:1
2 Corinthians: 1, 188, 342, 379, 386, 408
11:1–4
2 Peter–Jude: 194
1–3 John: 234
11:1–6
2 Corinthians: 351
11:1ff.
Acts 13–28: 209
11:2
Matthew 8–15: 457
Luke 1–5: 56
Luke 11–17: 154
Acts 1–12: 155
Acts 13–28: 225
Romans 1–8: 361
Romans 9–16: 148
1 Corinthians: 22, 325
2 Corinthians: 266, 442
Philippians: 182
Colossians and Philemon: 65
1 & 2 Thessalonians: 206
Revelation 1–11: 30, 45, 95
Revelation 12–22: 4, 6, 80, 201
11:2–4
2 Corinthians: 1
11:2–15
2 Corinthians: 379
11:3
Luke 1–5: 217
John 12–21: 228
2 Corinthians: 117, 122, 127, 237, 337, 408
1 & 2 Thessalonians: 71, 81, 266
Revelation 12–22: 6, 14, 235
11:3–4
1 Corinthians: 286
2 Corinthians: 348
Galatians: 11
Ephesians: 158
James: 173
11:4
John 12–21: 372
Acts 13–28: 226
2 Corinthians: 337, 355, 357, 358, 380
Philippians: 64
11:5
Acts 1–12: 274
Acts 13–28: 210, 246
2 Corinthians: 141, 230, 337, 408
Galatians: 40
11:5–6
2 Corinthians: 2, 184, 357
11:6
2 Corinthians: 228, 337, 358
Philippians: 65
11:7
Mark 1–8: 47
Luke 1–5: 335
Acts 13–28: 230
2 Corinthians: 338
1 & 2 Thessalonians: 35
11:7–8
2 Corinthians: 338
11:7–9
2 Corinthians: 306, 364, 425
11:7–11
2 Corinthians: 364
11:7–15
2 Corinthians: 2, 361
11:7–18
2 Corinthians: 338
11:8
Philippians: 306
11:8–9
Acts 13–28: 230
1 Corinthians: 208
1 & 2 Thessalonians: 306
11:9
Acts 13–28: 148
2 Corinthians: 35, 276, 390
Philippians: 199
1 & 2 Thessalonians: 77, 293
1 Timothy: 112
11:10
2 Corinthians: 32, 240, 367–68, 477
Ephesians: 175
1 & 2 Thessalonians: 319
2 Peter–Jude: 50
11:11
2 Corinthians: 7, 229, 235, 368
1 Timothy: 174
11:12–15
2 Corinthians: 358, 369
11:13
Matthew 1–7: 461
Luke 11–17: 115
Luke 18–24: 162
Acts 1–12: 94
1 Corinthians: 323
2 Corinthians: 32, 380, 408
Philippians: 64
1 Timothy: 14
11:13–14
Acts 13–28: 97
Hebrews: 436
11:13–15
Matthew 1–7: 465
Luke 1–5: 280
Acts 1–12: 97
Romans 9–16: 376
2 Corinthians: 339, 356, 370
Galatians: 204
Philippians: 255
1 Timothy: 238
James: 173
Revelation 1–11: 60
11:13, 14–15
Galatians: 10
11:13,22
Romans 9–16: 98
11:14
Matthew 8–15: 308
Matthew 24–28: 27
Mark 1–8: 62, 76, 164, 202
Mark 9–16: 15
Romans 1–8: 155
2 Corinthians: 482
Ephesians: 339
1 & 2 Thessalonians: 71, 276
1 Timothy: 14, 146
1 Peter: 281
2 Peter–Jude: 67, 170
Revelation 12–22: 14, 54, 235

11:14–15
Luke 1–5: 284
Luke 11–17: 64
1 & 2 Thessalonians: 270
1 Timothy: 40
James: 7
1–3 John: 155
Revelation 12–22: 156
11:15
Luke 18–24: 132
1 Timothy: 14
Revelation 12–22: 54
11:16
2 Corinthians: 408
11:16–17
2 Corinthians: 1, 188, 379
11:16–21
2 Corinthians: 375
11:16–12:1
Philippians: 228
11:17
2 Corinthians: 240, 379, 384, 408
11:17–18
2 Timothy: 26
11:17–20
2 Corinthians: 391
11:18
2 Corinthians: 379
Philippians: 222, 223
11:18–21
2 Corinthians: 380
11:19–21
2 Corinthians: 380, 425
11:20
2 Corinthians: 361
11:20–21
2 Corinthians: 454
11:21
2 Corinthians: 1, 382, 384, 408
James: 276
11:21–33
2 Corinthians: 358
11:22
2 Corinthians: 337, 380, 382, 384
11:22–23
2 Corinthians: 327
11:22–27
John 12–21: 192–93
2 Corinthians: 398
11:22–33
2 Corinthians: 346
1 & 2 Thessalonians: 293, 295
1–3 John: 226, 241
11:22–12:4
2 Corinthians: 383–84
11:22ff.
2 Corinthians: 409
Acts 13–28: 246
11:23
Acts 13–28: 257
Romans 9–16: 365
2 Corinthians: 25, 160, 228, 384, 388
Revelation 12–22: 123
11:23–25
Acts 1–12: 188
Romans 9–16: 353
2 Corinthians: 25
11:23–27
Matthew 1–7: 226
Acts 1–12: 145
Romans 1–8: 512
Romans 9–16: 337, 348
2 Corinthians: 142, 231, 261, 386
2 Timothy: 26, 131, 185, 189
1–3 John: 176
11:23–28
Acts 13–28: 193
1 Corinthians: 111
2 Corinthians: 121
Colossians and Philemon: 81–82, 84
1 & 2 Thessalonians: 82
11:23–29
Acts 1–12: 273
2 Corinthians: 95
Philippians: 260
1 Timothy: 174
11:23–30
Colossians and Philemon: 221
Philippians: 2
11:23–33
2 Corinthians: 2, 455
Philippians: 71, 302
1 Peter: 257
11:23–12:12
1 Corinthians: 405
11:23ff.
Acts 1–12: 230
11:24
Matthew 8–15: 204
Luke 6–10: 105
Luke 18–24: 208, 209
Acts 13–28: 212
2 Corinthians: 153, 388
1 & 2 Thessalonians: 61
11:24–25
Matthew 16–23: 391
Acts 13–28: 39
11:24–28
1 & 2 Thessalonians: 12
11:25
Luke 18–24: 209
Acts 13–28: 53, 104, 348, 359
11:26
Matthew 1–7: 461
Acts 13–28: 10, 17, 200, 212
2 Corinthians: 459
1–3 John: 2, 231
11:27
2 Corinthians: 228
Philippians: 114
11:28
Acts 13–28: 239, 246
2 Corinthians: 142, 355
Philippians: 80, 198, 296, 303
1 & 2 Thessalonians: 80
2 Timothy: 185
11:28–29
Acts 1–12: 145
2 Corinthians: 65, 391, 398
1 & 2 Thessalonians: 70, 77
11:29
Mark 9–16: 44
2 Corinthians: 1, 434
Philippians: 21
James: 276
11:30
2 Corinthians: 1, 2, 184, 187, 345–46
Ephesians: 94
11:30–33
2 Corinthians: 392
11:31
Romans 9–16: 9
2 Corinthians: 18, 428
Philippians: 314
James: 267
1 Peter: 31
11:32
Acts 1–12: 277
Galatians: 30
11:32–33
Luke 11–17: 196
1 & 2 Thessalonians: 82
1 Timothy: 3
12
Acts 13–28: 53
2 Corinthians: 2
Revelation 1–11: 144
12:1
1 & 2 Thessalonians: 233
2 Peter–Jude: 62
12:1–4
2 Corinthians: 394
12:1–7
Acts 13–28: 335
12:1–10
1 Timothy: 51
12:1ff.
Revelation 1–11: 41
12:2
Luke 18–24: 388
Acts 13–28: 53, 246
2 Corinthians: 393
1 & 2 Thessalonians: 135
Revelation 1–11: 145
Revelation 12–22: 262
12:2–4
Acts 1–12: 222
Romans 1–8: 446
2 Corinthians: 399
Hebrews: 109
Revelation 12–22: 278
12:2, 4
Matthew 1–7: 226
Titus: 2
12:3–9
Romans 1–8: 467
12:4
1 Corinthians: 475
1 & 2 Thessalonians: 126, 135
Revelation 1–11: 65, 144, 283

12:4, 7
2 Timothy: 28
12:5
2 Corinthians: 1, 133, 346
12:5–6
2 Corinthians: 399
12:5–10
2 Corinthians: 2, 397
12:5, 9
Romans 9–16: 333
12:6
2 Corinthians: 188, 408
1 & 2 Thessalonians: 319
12:6–7
Romans 1–8: 478
12:7
Luke 18–24: 294
Romans 9–16: 143
1 Corinthians: 475
2 Corinthians: 394, 399–401
Galatians: 194
Ephesians: 336, 347
Philippians: 254
1 & 2 Thessalonians: 233
1 Timothy: 36
Hebrews: 387
James: 18, 22
1 Peter: 280
Revelation 1–11: 255
Revelation 12–22: 235
12:7–8
Matthew 1–7: 369
James: 22
12:7–9
Matthew 8–15: 15
Luke 6–10: 193
1 & 2 Thessalonians: 71
12:7–9, 9–10
2 Timothy: 22
12:7–10
Acts 1–12: 273
2 Corinthians: 121–22, 392, 423, 437, 455
Ephesians: 94
Philippians: 303
1 & 2 Thessalonians: 32, 293
1 Timothy: 174
James: 259
1 Peter: 42, 200, 257, 278, 283
12:8
Mark 9–16: 304
2 Corinthians: 401
1 & 2 Thessalonians: 227
12:8–9
Hebrews: 387
12:9
Matthew 8–15: 130
Luke 6–10: 24
Romans 1–8: 475, 515
1 Corinthians: 475
2 Corinthians: 1, 124, 133, 141
Galatians: 69
Ephesians: 43, 265, 362
Philippians: 14, 245
1 & 2 Thessalonians: 195, 320
1 Timothy: 28
2 Peter–Jude: 24
12:9–10
Acts 13–28: 50, 73, 106
Romans 1–8: 478
2 Corinthians: 120, 187, 456, 477
Ephesians: 342
Philippians: 58, 253
1 & 2 Thessalonians: 35, 317
1 Peter: 254
Revelation 1–11: 77, 78
12:10
Matthew 16–23: 230
Luke 11–17: 46
Acts 1–12: 222
Romans 9–16: 350
2 Corinthians: 1, 53, 74, 86, 141, 154, 261, 399, 406
Philippians: 205, 239, 296
1 & 2 Thessalonians: 247
2 Timothy: 54, 59, 132
Hebrews: 387
James: 20, 276
Revelation 1–11: 122
12:11
Acts 1–12: 34, 274
2 Corinthians: 1, 187, 358, 379, 410
12:11–12
Mark 1–8: 58, 169
2 Corinthians: 2, 184, 407–17
12:12
Matthew 8–15: 134, 190
Mark 1–8: 76–77, 286, 288
Luke 1–5: 295
Luke 6–10: 19, 243
Acts 1–12: 87, 96, 98, 164
Acts 13–28: 43, 68, 97, 171, 174, 246
Romans 9–16: 168, 336
1 Corinthians: 4, 302, 323, 360, 383
2 Corinthians: 340, 358, 409, 454, 476
Ephesians: 1, 141
1 Timothy: 4
Hebrews: 50
12:12–18
2 Corinthians: 345
12:12–19
2 Corinthians: 419–30
12:13
Acts 13–28: 230
2 Corinthians: 454
12:14
Matthew 1–7: 410
2 Corinthians: 5, 94, 320, 322, 474, 479
12:14–15
1 Corinthians: 115
2 Corinthians: 7, 236
12:14–18
2 Corinthians: 306
12:15
Romans 1–8: 42
2 Corinthians: 66, 94, 221, 229, 235, 342
Colossians and Philemon: 84
1 & 2 Thessalonians: 77
1 Timothy: 174, 264
Hebrews: 445
1 Peter: 269
12:15–16
1 Timothy: 112
12:16
Ephesians: 158
12:17–18
2 Corinthians: 238
12:18
2 Corinthians: 7
Philippians: 90
12:18–13:3
2 Corinthians: 236
12:19
1 Corinthians: 245
2 Corinthians: 60, 235, 256, 307, 340, 353
12:19–21
1 & 2 Thessalonians: 82
12:19–13:3
2 Corinthians: 48
12:19–13:10
2 Corinthians: 442
12:20
1 Corinthians: 108
2 Corinthians: 186, 433–37, 445, 476
Philippians: 64, 68, 100
James: 185, 218, 221
12:20–21
2 Corinthians: 431–38, 442, 474, 478, 482
12:20–13:2
1 & 2 Thessalonians: 176
12:20–13:10
2 Corinthians: 459
12:20–13:14
2 Corinthians: 2
12:21
Romans 1–8: 102
1 Corinthians: 124
2 Corinthians: 337, 444, 467
Philippians: 100
1 & 2 Thessalonians: 104
13:1
Luke 1–5: 165
Luke 6–10: 282
2 Corinthians: 5, 322, 479
Revelation 1–11: 298
13:1–2
2 Corinthians: 320, 439, 442, 474, 478, 482
1–3 John: 257
13:1–3
2 Corinthians: 324
13:2
2 Corinthians: 46, 455, 476
1 & 2 Thessalonians: 297

13:2–3
2 Corinthians: 343–44
13:3
2 Peter–Jude: 9
13:3–4
2 Corinthians: 449–57, 474, 478, 482
James: 276
13:4
2 Corinthians: 392, 477
1 & 2 Thessalonians: 28
2 Peter–Jude: 26
Revelation 12–22: 238
13:5
Matthew 1–7: 475
Matthew 24–28: 90
John 12–21: 82, 117, 383
Romans 1–8: 420
2 Corinthians: 224, 236
Ephesians: 106
Philippians: 32, 198, 212
2 Timothy: 121
Hebrews: 83, 145, 273
James: 8, 123, 142
1–3 John: 15, 54, 141
13:5–6
2 Corinthians: 2, 184, 459–71, 474, 478, 482
13:6
2 Corinthians: 454
13:7
Luke 18–24: 3
1 & 2 Thessalonians: 253, 293
13:7, 9
John 12–21: 235
13:7–10
2 Corinthians: 473–80
13:8
2 Corinthians: 37, 235
1 & 2 Thessalonians: 319
2 Peter–Jude: 13
13:9
2 Corinthians: 7, 482
Philippians: 250
1 & 2 Thessalonians: 253, 293
James: 276
13:10
2 Corinthians: 46, 430, 432, 452, 479
1 & 2 Thessalonians: 297
Titus: 62
13:11
Matthew 1–7: 209
Romans 9–16: 298
2 Corinthians: 482
Ephesians: 152
Philippians: 1, 100, 107, 248, 292
Colossians and Philemon: 88
1 & 2 Thessalonians: 174, 204, 313
Titus: 166
1 Peter: 193
13:11–14
2 Corinthians: 481
13:12
John 12–21: 168
Romans 9–16: 370
2 Corinthians: 234
1 & 2 Thessalonians: 214
Revelation 1–11: 72
13:12–13
2 Corinthians: 486
13:14
2 Corinthians: 487
Philippians: 23, 105, 318
1–3 John: 19
Revelation 1–11: 24
13:15
John 1–11: 98

Galatians
1:1
Matthew 24–28: 310
Mark 9–16: 379, 401
Acts 1–12: 272, 274, 295
Acts 13–28: 47
Romans 1–8: 7
1 Corinthians: 323
2 Corinthians: 17, 147, 411, 488
Ephesians: 141
Philippians: 16, 204
1 & 2 Thessalonians: 98
1:3
Matthew 16–23: 68
Philippians: 16, 314
1 & 2 Thessalonians: 14, 87, 216
1 Peter: 25
2 Peter–Jude: 24
Revelation 1–11: 24
1:3–4
Luke 11–17: 231
2 Corinthians: 487
1 & 2 Thessalonians: 224
1 Peter: 88
1:4
Mark 1–8: 110
Acts 13–28: 336
Romans 1–8: 505
1 Corinthians: 79
2 Corinthians: 132
Colossians and Philemon: 125
1 & 2 Thessalonians: 164
2 Timothy: 14
Titus: 121
Hebrews: 328
1 Peter: 64, 191, 206
1–3 John: 230
1:5
2 Corinthians: 44, 158
Philippians: 312
1:6
Matthew 1–7: 163
Acts 13–28: 226
Romans 1–8: 499
1 Corinthians: 3
2 Corinthians: 360
Philippians: 64, 86
1 & 2 Thessalonians: 256, 287, 320
1 Peter: 162
1:6–7
Acts 1–12: 145
Romans 1–8: 50
Ephesians: 158
2 Timothy: 31
1:6, 8
Romans 9–16: 373
1:6–9
Matthew 8–15: 432
Mark 1–8: 110–11, 134, 287
Acts 13–28: 209
2 Corinthians: 336, 445
Philippians: 218
1 & 2 Thessalonians: 40, 168
1–3 John: 15, 233
1:7
Acts 13–28: 72
Philippians: 91
Colossians and Philemon: 15
2 Timothy: 184
1–3 John: 159
1:7–9
John 1–11: 19
1:8
Matthew 1–7: 432
Matthew 8–15: 151
Matthew 16–23: 354
Romans 1–8: 516
Romans 9–16: 275
Ephesians: 70, 130
Colossians and Philemon: 66, 91
Titus: 57
Hebrews: 23, 436
1:8–9
Matthew 16–23: 361
Luke 1–5: 54
Luke 6–10: 112
John 12–21: 185
Acts 13–28: 291
1 Timothy: 17
1:8–10
1 Timothy: 266
1:8, 10
Romans 9–16: 354
1:9
Mark 1–8: 124
Philippians: 292
1:10
Acts 13–28: 210, 214
Romans 1–8: 7
Romans 9–16: 308
2 Corinthians: 73, 134, 185, 307
1 & 2 Thessalonians: 40
1 Timothy: 230
2 Timothy: 45, 75, 170
Revelation 12–22: 200, 293
1:10–11
2 Timothy: 184
1:11
1 Corinthians: 117

1:11–12
Acts 13–28: 335
Romans 9–16: 384
2 Corinthians: 80, 395, 400, 412
1 & 2 Thessalonians: 58
1 Timothy: 4
1:11–12, 15–16
2 Timothy: 146
1:11–2:10
1 Corinthians: 3
1:12
Philippians: 292
1 & 2 Thessalonians: 233
Revelation 1–11: 3, 16
1:13
Acts 1–12: 231, 232
Acts 13–28: 265
2 Corinthians: 329, 386
Philippians: 232
1:13–14
Mark 9–16: 79
John 12–21: 167
Acts 13–28: 158, 333, 334
Romans 1–8: 369
2 Corinthians: 385
1:14
Luke 1–5: 218
Luke 6–10: 298
Luke 11–17: 83, 346
Luke 18–24: 15
John 1–11: 103
Acts 1–12: 201, 230
Acts 13–28: 246, 266, 279
1 Corinthians: 163, 252
2 Corinthians: 103, 157, 230, 329
Philippians: 217, 227
Colossians and Philemon: 70
1 Timothy: 3
Titus: 126
1:15
Matthew 16–23: 358
John 12–21: 162
Romans 1–8: 8
1 Corinthians: 209
2 Corinthians: 410
1 & 2 Thessalonians: 256, 320
1:15–16
Luke 1–5: 35, 38
Philippians: 67
1 & 2 Thessalonians: 98
Titus: 13
1:15–17
Acts 1–12: 274
1 Corinthians: 323
Ephesians: 141
1 Peter: 112
1:15–18
Acts 13–28: 15
1:16
Romans 1–8: 26
1:17
Luke 18–24: 349
Acts 1–12: 45
Romans 1–8: 26
2 Timothy: 131
1:17–18
Matthew 1–7: 88
John 1–11: 439
Acts 1–12: 276
Acts 13–28: 269
2 Corinthians: 393
James: 150
1:18
Acts 1–12: 278
1 Peter: 4
2 Peter–Jude: 2, 18
1:19
Mark 1–8: 179
2 Corinthians: 410
Philippians: 204
1 Timothy: 4
James: 10
1:20
2 Corinthians: 43
1:21
Acts 1–12: 278
2 Corinthians: 395
1:22
2 Corinthians: 230
1 & 2 Thessalonians: 59
1:22–24
Acts 13–28: 239
1:23
1 Peter: 2, 285
1–3 John: 179
1:24
Philippians: 75
2:1
Acts 13–28: 63
2:1–2
1 & 2 Thessalonians: 81
2:2
Philippians: 242
2:3
Acts 13–28: 63, 85
Titus: 161
2:4
2 Corinthians: 390, 459
1–3 John: 2, 231
2:6
Romans 1–8: 136
Philippians: 315
2:7
Acts 1–12: 187
Philippians: 218
1 Timothy: 22
1 Peter: 15
2:7–9
Philippians: 218
2:9
Mark 1–8: 170
Luke 6–10: 25
John 1–11: 7, 8
Acts 13–28: 248
James: 3
1 Peter: 4, 182
2 Peter–Jude: 2, 18
1–3 John: 18
2:9–10
Acts 13–28: 234
Romans 9–16: 346
2:9–12
James: 11
2:10
Acts 13–28: 199
2 Corinthians: 305
1 & 2 Thessalonians: 308
James: 102, 108, 244, 246
2:11
Matthew 1–7: 331
Matthew 16–23: 128
Ephesians: 70
Philippians: 271
1 Peter: 4, 15
2 Peter–Jude: 2, 18
2:11–12
Matthew 8–15: 463
2:11–13
2 Corinthians: 183
2:11–14
Matthew 24–28: 164
Acts 1–12: 161, 312
2 Corinthians: 445–46, 477
1 Timothy: 187
2:11–21
Acts 13–28: 213
1 Peter: 5
2 Peter–Jude: 4
2:11, 12
Titus: 59
2:11ff.
Acts 13–28: 63
Romans 9–16: 364
2:12
Matthew 8–15: 460
Acts 1–12: 299
2:12–13
Matthew 8–15: 188
2:14
1 Corinthians: 319
1 Peter: 4
2 Peter–Jude: 2, 18
2:15
1 Timothy: 33
2:16
Matthew 1–7: 280
Mark 9–16: 78
Luke 1–5: 63, 114, 319
Luke 6–10: 176, 288
Luke 11–17: 104, 347
John 12–21: 118
Acts 1–12: 74
Acts 13–28: 26, 64, 108, 336
Romans 1–8: 202, 207
2 Corinthians: 89, 192, 207, 217
Philippians: 213, 237
1 & 2 Thessalonians: 163, 258
1 Timothy: 21
James: 137
1–3 John: 36, 159
2:16–21
John 1–11: 346
Philippians: 78, 218
2:17
Romans 9–16: 96

2:18
Mark 1–8: 387
2:19–20
Romans 1–8: 361
2 Corinthians: 193
2:20
Matthew 1–7: 150
Matthew 24–28: 124
Mark 1–8: 427
Mark 9–16: 22
Luke 1–5: 63, 195, 287
Luke 6–10: 268
Luke 11–17: 120, 222
John 12–21: 117, 252
Acts 1–12: 16
Romans 1–8: 99, 132, 313, 323, 386, 402
1 Corinthians: 311
2 Corinthians: 45, 145, 190, 466
Ephesians: 76, 92, 160, 164, 174, 178, 301
Philippians: 15, 27, 77, 154, 170, 237, 242, 311
Colossians and Philemon: 31, 38, 82, 127, 133
1 & 2 Thessalonians: 14, 89, 97, 204, 224, 293
Titus: 115, 122, 152
Hebrews: 58, 381
1 Peter: 106
2 Peter–Jude: 24, 30–31
1–3 John: 131
2:20–21
Hebrews: 376
2:21
Romans 1–8: 208
2 Corinthians: 84
3
Acts 1–12: 204
3:1
Mark 9–16: 8
Acts 13–28: 209
Ephesians: 158
Philippians: 257
1 & 2 Thessalonians: 82
3:1, 3
Colossians and Philemon: 186
Hebrews: 189
3:1–3
Hebrews: 376
1–3 John: 234
3:1–5
1 Corinthians: 3
3:1–7
2 Corinthians: 96
3:1–9
1 & 2 Thessalonians: 168
3:1, 3
Ephesians: 220
3:2–3
Matthew 16–23: 14
Acts 13–28: 68
3:2–14
Philippians: 218
3:3
Matthew 8–15: 71, 291
Romans 1–8: 277
Ephesians: 153
Philippians: 26, 77, 168, 171
1 & 2 Thessalonians: 191, 195, 260
3:6
Luke 1–5: 21
2 Corinthians: 58
James: 34
3:6–7
Luke 1–5: 105, 110
Romans 1–8: 235
Romans 9–16: 24
3:6–9
Luke 18–24: 74–75
Acts 1–12: 70
Romans 9–16: 115
James: 137
3:6–14
John 1–11: 346
3:7
Luke 6–10: 14
2 Corinthians: 97
Hebrews: 161, 327
James: 34, 136, 140
Revelation 12–22: 34
3:7–8
Hebrews: 214
3:7–9, 26–29
Matthew 8–15: 15
3:7, 29
Luke 1–5: 221
3:8
Acts 13–28: 196
Romans 1–8: 254
2 Corinthians: 192
Ephesians: 91, 142
1 & 2 Thessalonians: 258
2 Timothy: 144
1 Peter: 140
3:8–11
2 Peter–Jude: 23
3:9
Luke 1–5: 109, 110
Romans 1–8: 235
1 Timothy: 275
James: 34
3:10
Mark 1–8: 16
Acts 13–28: 26
Romans 1–8: 256, 367, 396, 405
Romans 9–16: 69
2 Corinthians: 90, 99, 104, 215
Colossians and Philemon: 112
Hebrews: 413
2 Peter–Jude: 101
Revelation 12–22: 253
3:10–11
Romans 1–8: 203
3:10–13
Luke 18–24: 298, 382
2 Corinthians: 83–84
Philippians: 237
James: 114
3:11
Luke 1–5: 114, 176, 319
Acts 13–28: 26, 336
Romans 1–8: 367
Romans 9–16: 69
2 Corinthians: 192, 207
Ephesians: 358
1 Timothy: 21
James: 137
3:11–14
1 & 2 Thessalonians: 258
3:11, 24
Luke 1–5: 319
3:13
Matthew 16–23: 245
Matthew 24–28: 267, 270
Luke 1–5: 154
Luke 11–17: 171
Luke 18–24: 390
Acts 13–28: 26
Romans 1–8: 363
1 Corinthians: 446
2 Corinthians: 176, 190, 215–16
Philippians: 135
1 & 2 Thessalonians: 164, 302
1 Peter: 170, 224
1–3 John: 28, 100, 136, 175
Revelation 1–11: 172
Revelation 12–22: 253
3:13–14
Romans 9–16: 116
3:14
Acts 13–28: 67
2 Peter–Jude: 20
3:15
Romans 1–8: 180
2 Corinthians: 58
3:16
Luke 1–5: 174, 249
Luke 18–24: 442
Acts 1–12: 58
Acts 13–28: 22
Romans 1–8: 255
3:17–18
Acts 13–28: 333
3:19
Acts 1–12: 212
Romans 1–8: 257
2 Corinthians: 97, 99, 461
1 & 2 Thessalonians: 234
Hebrews: 25, 212, 415
Revelation 1–11: 21
Revelation 12–22: 84, 296
3:19–22
Romans 1–8: 375
3:20
2 Corinthians: 97
3:21
Acts 13–28: 23
Romans 1–8: 371, 405
2 Corinthians: 101
3:22
Matthew 1–7: 275

Luke 1–5: 58
Luke 6–10: 354
Acts 1–12: 303
Acts 13–28: 196
1 Timothy: 84
2 Timothy: 144
3:22–25
Philippians: 218
3:22–26
Revelation 12–22: 49
3:22a
1–3 John: 45
3:23–24
Hebrews: 133
3:24
Matthew 1–7: 259, 273
Matthew 8–15: 290
Matthew 16–23: 67, 192
Mark 9–16: 79, 202
Luke 1–5: 115, 334
Luke 6–10: 356
Luke 11–17: 175
Acts 13–28: 108, 336
Romans 1–8: 139, 229, 256, 257
2 Corinthians: 90, 99, 101, 106, 192, 207, 217
1 & 2 Thessalonians: 258
1 Timothy: 21, 84
2 Timothy: 141
James: 137
3:26
John 12–21: 379
1 Corinthians: 417
2 Corinthians: 196
Ephesians: 194
Philippians: 181
1 Timothy: 84
3:26–27
Matthew 1–7: 273
1 Corinthians: 312
3:26–28
Romans 9–16: 306
Ephesians: 68
3:27
Luke 18–24: 383
Acts 1–12: 41
Romans 1–8: 320
Romans 9–16: 257
1 Corinthians: 220
1 Timothy: 84
3:28
Matthew 8–15: 84, 151
Luke 1–5: 181
Luke 11–17: 224, 244
Luke 18–24: 210
John 1–11: 484
John 12–21: 168, 285
Acts 1–12: 38, 245, 290
Acts 13–28: 199
Romans 1–8: 416
Romans 9–16: 366
1 Corinthians: 253, 260, 382
2 Corinthians: 196
Ephesians: 278, 280
Philippians: 90
Colossians and Philemon: 87, 153, 168, 194, 213
1 & 2 Thessalonians: 59, 166
1 Timothy: 74, 84, 85, 233
Titus: 100
James: 99
1 Peter: 187
2 Peter–Jude: 20
Revelation 1–11: 38
3:28–29
John 1–11: 35
Romans 9–16: 82
3:29
Luke 18–24: 74–75
Romans 1–8: 255, 444
Romans 9–16: 25
1 Corinthians: 219, 417
2 Corinthians: 71, 97
Ephesians: 92
1 & 2 Thessalonians: 74
Hebrews: 214, 327
4:3
Luke 1–5: 96
Colossians and Philemon: 102
James: 92
4:4
Matthew 1–7: 17, 104
Luke 1–5: 158, 167, 174
Acts 13–28: 333
2 Corinthians: 292
Philippians: 130
1 & 2 Thessalonians: 278
1 Timothy: 140
1 Peter: 279
1–3 John: 16
4:4–5
Luke 18–24: 91
John 12–21: 88, 229
Romans 9–16: 25
2 Corinthians: 214
1 & 2 Thessalonians: 302
1 Timothy: 73
Hebrews: 64
1 Peter: 82
1–3 John: 166
4:5
Matthew 16–23: 68
Romans 9–16: 314
Philippians: 124, 181, 314
Revelation 12–22: 272
4:6
Mark 9–16: 301
Luke 1–5: 239
John 12–21: 225, 227
Acts 13–28: 67
Romans 1–8: 225
2 Corinthians: 489
Philippians: 314
1 & 2 Thessalonians: 194
1 Peter: 22, 31
Revelation 1–11: 54
4:6–7
Luke 1–5: 157
Ephesians: 80
4:7
1 Corinthians: 417
Revelation 1–11: 54
4:8
Ephesians: 74
1 & 2 Thessalonians: 108, 242
1 Peter: 48
4:9
Luke 11–17: 361
John 12–21: 217
Romans 1–8: 384
Philippians: 247
Hebrews: 189, 377
4:9–10
Matthew 8–15: 287
Mark 1–8: 141
Romans 9–16: 282
4:10–11
Acts 13–28: 202
2 Corinthians: 281
Colossians and Philemon: 119
4:11
1 & 2 Thessalonians: 81
4:12
1 Corinthians: 117
Ephesians: 118
4:13
Acts 13–28: 16
4:13–15
Luke 1–5: 295
2 Corinthians: 138
4:14
Matthew 16–23: 117, 372
Luke 6–10: 17
4:14–15
1 & 2 Thessalonians: 173
4:16
Ephesians: 159
1 & 2 Thessalonians: 215
James: 73
4:16–20
1 & 2 Thessalonians: 69
4:19
Romans 9–16: 268
2 Corinthians: 116, 124, 237, 391, 474, 478
Ephesians: 119
Philippians: 28, 40, 248, 253
1 & 2 Thessalonians: 44, 79, 195
2 Timothy: 32
Hebrews: 406
James: 32
1–3 John: 111
4:20
Luke 18–24: 234
4:21–23
Romans 1–8: 262
4:22–31
Luke 11–17: 12
4:25–26
Hebrews: 414
4:26
Revelation 1–11: 4
4:28
Luke 1–5: 109
John 12–21: 156
Romans 1–8: 262

4:29
Matthew 1–7: 220
4:30
Acts 13–28: 196
4:31
Hebrews: 414
5:1
Matthew 16–23: 361
Romans 9–16: 67
1 Corinthians: 145, 189, 247
2 Corinthians: 47, 94, 382
Galatians: x
Philippians: 87, 267, 282
Colossians and Philemon: 99, 117
1 & 2 Thessalonians: 82, 178
Hebrews: 401
1 Peter: 91
5:1–2
Romans 1–8: 202
5:1–4
Romans 1–8: 249
Philippians: 218
5:1–6
2 Peter–Jude: 51
5:2–6
Acts 13–28: 63
Romans 1–8: 504
5:3
Romans 1–8: 160
James: 114
5:4
Mark 1–8: 133
Luke 1–5: 114, 319, 342
Acts 13–28: 34
Philippians: 237
5:5
2 Corinthians: 107
Philippians: 261
2 Timothy: 200
1 Peter: 34, 286
1–3 John: 108
5:6
Romans 1–8: 202, 249
1 & 2 Thessalonians: 18, 81, 228
Hebrews: 189
James: 130
Revelation 1–11: 99
5:7
Philippians: 242
Hebrews: 372
5:8
1 & 2 Thessalonians: 256
5:8–9
1 & 2 Thessalonians: 208
5:9
1–3 John: 99
5:10
Acts 13–28: 72
5:11
Mark 9–16: 2
John 12–21: 185
Acts 13–28: 251
5:11–14
Philippians: 218
5:12
Acts 13–28: 209
Romans 1–8: 249
Philippians: 219
5:13
John 12–21: 60
Acts 1–12: 84
Romans 9–16: 248
1 Corinthians: 145, 146
Philippians: 90, 168, 199
Colossians and Philemon: 19
1 & 2 Thessalonians: 117
1 Timothy: 230
1 Peter: 137, 152
1–3 John: 181
5:13–14
1 & 2 Thessalonians: 90
5:13–15
Luke 11–17: 377
Romans 9–16: 276
5:14
Matthew 1–7: 338
Luke 1–5: 220
Galatians: 137
5:15
Philippians: 90
James: 222
5:16
Matthew 1–7: 207
Matthew 16–23: 176
Matthew 24–28: 179
Acts 1–12: 42
Romans 1–8: 387
Romans 9–16: 269
1 Corinthians: 328
2 Corinthians: 229
Ephesians: 105
Philippians: 90
1 & 2 Thessalonians: 52, 108, 112, 195, 257
Titus: 117
Hebrews: 310
1 Peter: 91
5:16–17
Matthew 16–23: 157
Romans 1–8: 433
1 Corinthians: 72
Ephesians: 253
1 Peter: 137
5:16–25
1 & 2 Thessalonians: 287
5:16–26
1 & 2 Thessalonians: 97
5:16, 25
1–3 John: 36
5:16–6:10
1 & 2 Thessalonians: 203
5:17
Matthew 1–7: 273
Romans 1–8: 387, 418, 428
James: 158
1 Peter: 227
1–3 John: 36, 37
5:17–21
1 Peter: 138
5:18
Matthew 1–7: 273
5:19
1 & 2 Thessalonians: 104
5:19–20
Philippians: 111
5:19–21
1 Corinthians: 236
2 Corinthians: 481
Ephesians: 253
Philippians: 64
Colossians and Philemon: 39
1 & 2 Thessalonians: 105, 108
Titus: 146, 164
1–3 John: 88, 123
Revelation 12–22: 272
5:19–21, 24
Titus: 116–17
5:19–23
Romans 1–8: 102
1 Corinthians: 381
Ephesians: 232
5:19–25
1 Peter: 275
5:20
Philippians: 110
Revelation 12–22: 191, 309
5:21
Luke 11–17: 405
Luke 18–24: 256
Romans 9–16: 266
5:21–22
1 Timothy: 85
5:22
Matthew 1–7: 214, 447
Luke 1–5: 93, 123
Luke 11–17: 293
John 12–21: 217
Acts 1–12: 259
Acts 13–28: 106
Romans 1–8: 119, 284, 483
Romans 9–16: 184, 249, 298
1 Corinthians: 328
2 Corinthians: 57, 229, 483
Ephesians: 209
Philippians: 32, 36, 42, 56, 216, 222
1 & 2 Thessalonians: 17, 25, 81, 90, 117, 180, 184, 229, 258, 313, 315
2 Timothy: 93, 94, 130
1 Peter: 40, 47
2 Peter–Jude: 30
1–3 John: 230
Revelation 1–11: 25
5:22–23
Matthew 1–7: 469
Matthew 16–23: 312
Mark 1–8: 206
John 12–21: 149
Romans 1–8: 45, 362, 410, 438
Romans 9–16: 327
1 Corinthians: 54, 475
2 Corinthians: 158

Ephesians: 80, 108, 218, 247, 254
Philippians: 10, 41, 53, 75, 78, 105, 187
Colossians and Philemon: 32, 208
1 Timothy: 19
Titus: 118
Hebrews: 312
James: 179, 180
1 Peter: 253
1–3 John: 54, 66, 106, 130
5:22–25
1 Peter: 91
5:22, 25
2 Timothy: 19
5:23
Ephesians: 124
Titus: 92, 145
James: 169
2 Peter–Jude: 49
5:24
Romans 1–8: 325
1 & 2 Thessalonians: 109
1–3 John: 122
5:24–25
Romans 1–8: 428
Ephesians: 254
5:25
Acts 1–12: 18
Romans 1–8: 412
1 Corinthians: 328
Philippians: 156
1 & 2 Thessalonians: 52, 196, 257
5:26
Philippians: 100
6:1
Matthew 1–7: 437
Matthew 16–23: 132
Luke 11–17: 379
Romans 9–16: 276
1 Corinthians: 354
2 Corinthians: 57, 437, 447, 478
Ephesians: 126
Philippians: 270
Colossians and Philemon: 156
1 & 2 Thessalonians: 310
1 Timothy: 188
2 Timothy: 161
Titus: 144
James: 277
2 Peter–Jude: 49
6:1–2
Matthew 16–23: 117
1 Corinthians: 127
1 & 2 Thessalonians: 179
1 Timothy: 186, 224
6:2
1 Corinthians: 229
Philippians: 115
1 & 2 Thessalonians: 97, 117
Titus: 75
Hebrews: 428
6:2–3
Philippians: 100
6:3
Acts 1–12: 241
Romans 9–16: 158
Philippians: 112
6:3–5
Luke 18–24: 82
6:4
2 Corinthians: 187
Philippians: 198
James: 8
6:5
1 & 2 Thessalonians: 120
6:6
Luke 6–10: 184
1 & 2 Thessalonians: 293, 306
1 Timothy: 218
James: 244
1–3 John: 18
6:6–10
1 & 2 Thessalonians: 97
6:7
Mark 1–8: 216
Romans 1–8: 136, 400
1 & 2 Thessalonians: 74
1–3 John: 58
6:7–8
Revelation 12–22: 122
6:7–9
Romans 1–8: 128
6:7–10
Hebrews: 401
6:8
Romans 1–8: 136
Romans 9–16: 141
1 & 2 Thessalonians: 195, 245
6:9
Romans 9–16: 191
Ephesians: 361, 367
1 & 2 Thessalonians: 74, 298, 309
James: 255
Revelation 1–11: 60
6:10
Matthew 1–7: 444, 446
John 12–21: 91
Romans 9–16: 190, 193, 208, 248
1 Corinthians: 451
2 Corinthians: 229
Ephesians: 222
Philippians: 24
1 & 2 Thessalonians: 17, 90, 181
1 Timothy: 135, 184, 200, 234
Titus: 40, 143
Hebrews: 426
1–3 John: 148
6:11
Romans 9–16: 379
2 Corinthians: 400
Philippians: 310
1 & 2 Thessalonians: 269, 318
2 Peter–Jude: 13
6:12
Matthew 16–23: 363
Luke 11–17: 348
Luke 18–24: 19
Romans 1–8: 249
2 Corinthians: 188, 195
Galatians: 22
Titus: 161
6:12–13
Philippians: 228
Titus: 163
6:13
Philippians: 222
6:14
Mark 9–16: 266, 267
John 12–21: 134, 256, 263
Romans 9–16: 334
1 Corinthians: 54
2 Corinthians: 193–194, 196, 345, 349
Philippians: 222, 257
Colossians and Philemon: 113, 130
1 & 2 Thessalonians: 294
1 Timothy: 36, 139
James: 194, 200
1 Peter: 82
1–3 John: 84
6:15
Romans 1–8: 322
2 Corinthians: 196
1 & 2 Thessalonians: 23, 158, 287
6:16
Luke 1–5: 126
Luke 18–24: 75
1 & 2 Thessalonians: 316
6:17
Matthew 8–15: 206
Matthew 24–28: 24
John 12–21: 173
Acts 1–12: 174
Acts 13–28: 53, 246, 291
Romans 1–8: 479
Romans 9–16: 350
2 Corinthians: 25, 144, 153, 387, 389
Philippians: 94
Colossians and Philemon: 76
1 Timothy: 28
2 Timothy: 20
Hebrews: 354
Revelation 12–22: 63
6:18
2 Corinthians: 487
Philippians: 318
1 & 2 Thessalonians: 206, 216

Ephesians
1:1
Acts 13–28: 47
2 Corinthians: 17, 196, 410
Philippians: 15, 204, 310
1 & 2 Thessalonians: 59, 203
1:1–2
Philippians: 16

1:1–3
1 & 2 Thessalonians: 225
1:1–5
1 Peter: 13
1:2
2 Corinthians: 487
Philippians: 16, 314
1 & 2 Thessalonians: 14, 87, 224
2 Peter–Jude: 24
Revelation 1–11: 24
1:3
Matthew 1–7: 206, 446
Matthew 16–23: 68, 215
Mark 1–8: 36
Luke 18–24: 452
Romans 1–8: 20, 336, 399, 506
Romans 9–16: 139, 141, 315
2 Corinthians: 18, 294, 393
Philippians: 173, 308, 314
1 & 2 Thessalonians: 25, 287
1 Timothy: 22
Hebrews: 75, 423
James: 109
1 Peter: 30, 104
1–3 John: 230
Revelation 1–11: 91
1:3–4
1 & 2 Thessalonians: 185
1 Timothy: 68
Hebrews: 167
1–3 John: 124
1:3–5
Matthew 16–23: 22
Romans 1–8: 437
Philippians: 124
1:3–5, 7–8
Galatians: 109
1:3–7
Acts 1–12: 252
James: 215
1–3 John: 228
1:3–8
Mark 1–8: 212
Galatians: 207
2 Peter–Jude: 25
1:3–14
1 Peter: 26, 104
1:3, 17
Matthew 1–7: 82
1:3, 18
Galatians: 189
1:4
Matthew 8–15: 175
Mark 9–16: 375
Luke 1–5: 36
Luke 18–24: 8, 384
Acts 1–12: 293
Acts 13–28: 38, 268
Romans 1–8: 335, 411, 465
Romans 9–16: 99, 368
2 Corinthians: 203
Philippians: 27, 182, 273
Colossians and Philemon: 51, 65, 153, 155
1 & 2 Thessalonians: 163, 278, 286
2 Timothy: 24, 82
Titus: 9, 111
Hebrews: 286
James: 256
1 Peter: 22
Revelation 1–11: 54
Revelation 12–22: 50, 80, 171
1:4–5
Matthew 16–23: 37
John 12–21: 246
Romans 1–8: 497
Colossians and Philemon: 154
1 & 2 Thessalonians: 286
2 Timothy: 61
Titus: 6, 11
Hebrews: 392
James: 61, 202, 206
1 Peter: 17
1:4–6
1 & 2 Thessalonians: 20
1:4, 6
John 12–21: 172
1:4, 11
1–3 John: 28
1:5
Matthew 16–23: 68
John 12–21: 257
Acts 1–12: 141
Romans 1–8: 436
Romans 9–16: 314
Philippians: 124, 314
Colossians and Philemon: 56
Revelation 1–11: 54
Revelation 12–22: 272
1:5–6
John 1–11: 451
Romans 9–16: 322
Galatians: 28
1:5–6, 12
Matthew 24–28: 330
1:5–11
1 Peter: 82
1:6
Matthew 16–23: 26
Mark 1–8: 37
Luke 1–5: 88
John 12–21: 135
Acts 1–12: 104
Romans 1–8: 28, 499
2 Corinthians: 257
Philippians: 315
1:6–7
Matthew 8–15: 297
1:7
Matthew 1–7: 206
Matthew 8–15: 304
Matthew 16–23: 246
Mark 1–8: 103, 110
Luke 1–5: 46, 88, 272, 321
Luke 11–17: 40
John 1–11: 14
John 12–21: 42, 379
Acts 1–12: 75, 117, 303
Acts 13–28: 67
Romans 9–16: 283
2 Corinthians: 31, 52, 176, 190, 210, 279
Philippians: 243
Colossians and Philemon: 42, 56, 111
1 & 2 Thessalonians: 216, 320
Hebrews: 416
James: 290
1 Peter: 26, 32, 48, 191, 220
2 Peter–Jude: 30
1–3 John: 37, 73, 219
Revelation 1–11: 54, 232
Revelation 12–22: 308
1:7–8
Matthew 1–7: 446
Mark 1–8: 97
1 Corinthians: 447
2 Corinthians: 279
1:7–9
Romans 1–8: 497–98
1:8–9
1 Corinthians: 60
1:9
John 12–21: 162
Romans 9–16: 387
Philippians: 173
1 Timothy: 128
1:10
Mark 1–8: 48
Revelation 1–11: 286
Revelation 12–22: 228
1:11
Matthew 24–28: 288
Luke 6–10: 78
Luke 11–17: 10, 27
John 1–11: 471
John 12–21: 257
Acts 1–12: 141
Acts 13–28: 336
Romans 1–8: 399, 445, 486
2 Corinthians: 232
Philippians: 298
1 & 2 Thessalonians: 18, 20
1 Peter: 17, 35, 37
1:11–14
Matthew 16–23: 113
Philippians: 54
1:12
John 1–11: 451
1:13
Luke 1–5: 336
Acts 1–12: 304
Acts 13–28: 164
Romans 1–8: 461, 490
2 Corinthians: 206
Galatians: 101
1 & 2 Thessalonians: 51
2 Timothy: 76
James: 62
2 Peter–Jude: 20, 30
1–3 John: 54
Revelation 1–11: 217
Revelation 12–22: 86
1:13–14
John 12–21: 178, 278, 289

Acts 1–12: 40
Romans 1–8: 280
Galatians: 66, 110
Philippians: 105
Colossians and Philemon: 39
1 & 2 Thessalonians: 112, 118, 193, 195
Titus: 9, 155
James: 28
1 Peter: 41
1–3 John: 108, 149

1:14
John 1–11: 451
Acts 1–12: 304
Acts 13–28: 336
Romans 1–8: 399
1 Corinthians: 54
2 Corinthians: 168
1 Timothy: 135
Hebrews: 168
1 Peter: 37, 130
1–3 John: 202
Revelation 1–11: 163

1:15
Romans 9–16: 371
Philippians: 41
1 & 2 Thessalonians: 90, 228
1 Timothy: 32
Revelation 1–11: 61, 99, 320

1:15–16
Acts 13–28: 229

1:15–17
1 & 2 Thessalonians: 253

1:15–19
1 & 2 Thessalonians: 188

1:15–21
1 & 2 Thessalonians: 83

1:15–23
1 & 2 Thessalonians: 86

1:16
John 12–21: 272
Acts 1–12: 180
Romans 1–8: 35
1 & 2 Thessalonians: 293

1:16–18
Philippians: 37

1:17
John 1–11: 450
Romans 1–8: 475
Romans 9–16: 315
1 Corinthians: 18, 53
2 Corinthians: 18, 393
Philippians: 235
Colossians and Philemon: 28
James: 181
1 Peter: 30
2 Peter–Jude: 24
Revelation 1–11: 3

1:17–18
Romans 9–16: 60
James: 36
2 Peter–Jude: 30

1:17–19
Romans 1–8: 432

1:18
Mark 1–8: 356, 396
John 1–11: 451
John 12–21: 110
Acts 13–28: 336
2 Corinthians: 107–8, 279
Colossians and Philemon: 40
1 & 2 Thessalonians: 172, 256, 293
1 Peter: 35, 37

1:18–19
Matthew 1–7: 425
Acts 1–12: 11
2 Corinthians: 475
1 & 2 Thessalonians: 79

1:18–20
Romans 1–8: 272
2 Corinthians: 74
2 Timothy: 18

1:18–23
Mark 1–8: 53

1:19
2 Corinthians: 34, 222
1 & 2 Thessalonians: 282
2 Peter–Jude: 26

1:19–21
1 Peter: 220

1:19–23
1 & 2 Thessalonians: 28

1:20
Matthew 24–28: 305
Luke 18–24: 408, 411, 453
John 12–21: 213
Acts 1–12: 222
Philippians: 140
1 & 2 Thessalonians: 234
Hebrews: 55
Revelation 12–22: 214

1:20–21
Mark 1–8: 175
Luke 11–17: 401
1 Corinthians: 287

1:20–22
John 1–11: 16
John 12–21: 252
Hebrews: 35
Revelation 1–11: 170

1:20–23
1 Corinthians: 138

1:21
Mark 1–8: 53, 242, 250
Luke 1–5: 49
Luke 18–24: 453
John 1–11: 16
2 Corinthians: 132
Colossians and Philemon: 50
Hebrews: 65

1:21–22
Mark 9–16: 152
Philippians: 141
Colossians and Philemon: 60

1:21–23
1 & 2 Thessalonians: 108

1:22
Luke 1–5: 229
Luke 18–24: 112
John 12–21: 383
1 Peter: 178

1:22–23
John 12–21: 142
1 Corinthians: 150, 253
1 & 2 Thessalonians: 166

1:23
1 Corinthians: 310
Philippians: 308

2:1
Matthew 8–15: 318
Luke 1–5: 179, 208
Luke 6–10: 299, 347
Luke 11–17: 37, 38, 83, 105, 144, 346
John 1–11: 22
John 12–21: 315
Acts 1–12: 252, 267
Acts 13–28: 90, 94
Romans 1–8: 417
2 Corinthians: 131, 132, 192
Colossians and Philemon: 109
1 & 2 Thessalonians: 22, 193
1 Timothy: 201
1 Peter: 19, 275
2 Peter–Jude: 29
Revelation 1–11: 111
Revelation 12–22: 105, 253

2:1–2
Mark 1–8: 201
Luke 1–5: 271, 280
Acts 13–28: 168
Romans 1–8: 295
Romans 9–16: 219
Revelation 1–11: 112

2:1–3
Mark 1–8: 120, 207, 357
Mark 9–16: 74
Luke 1–5: 325
Luke 6–10: 270
Luke 11–17: 301
John 1–11: 32
John 12–21: 171, 298
Romans 1–8: 62
Galatians: 208
Colossians and Philemon: 38
1 & 2 Thessalonians: 157
1 Timothy: 243
Titus: 114
James: 52, 58, 205
1 Peter: 31, 50, 138–39, 227
2 Peter–Jude: 102

2:1–4
Mark 1–8: 53, 183, 218
Acts 1–12: 293

2:1, 5
1–3 John: 169

2:1–5
Colossians and Philemon: 142
1 Peter: 18, 21
1–3 John: 28

2:1–6
1–3 John: 128

2:1–7
1 Peter: 173

2:1–10
Mark 1–8: 238
1 Peter: 92

2:2
Matthew 1–7: 86, 455
Matthew 16–23: 76
Luke 1–5: 196, 255
Luke 6–10: 291
John 12–21: 56, 281
Acts 13–28: 45
Romans 1–8: 340, 396
Romans 9–16: 133
1 Corinthians: 21
2 Corinthians: 132, 250, 481
Galatians: 210
Colossians and Philemon: 57
1 & 2 Thessalonians: 157
1 Timothy: 47
Titus: 68
1 Peter: 281
1–3 John: 57, 86, 209
Revelation 1–11: 206, 264, 310
Revelation 12–22: 14, 16, 18, 40, 233, 236
2:2–3
Matthew 8–15: 52, 377
2 Corinthians: 132
2:3
Matthew 16–23: 192
Romans 1–8: 66, 74, 102, 286, 396, 397, 485, 495
Galatians: 97, 155
Philippians: 85
Titus: 146
Hebrews: 311
2 Peter–Jude: 31
2:4
Luke 1–5: 121
John 12–21: 346
2 Corinthians: 20
James: 261
1 Peter: 193
1–3 John: 23, 36
2:4–5
Matthew 1–7: 191
Mark 1–8: 206, 207, 358
Romans 1–8: 28
2 Corinthians: 212
1 & 2 Thessalonians: 22, 195
James: 60
1 Peter: 31
2:4–6
Philippians: 15
Titus: 114, 152
Hebrews: 229
2:4–7
Mark 1–8: 210
John 12–21: 298
1 Corinthians: 15, 329
Titus: 151
2 Peter–Jude: 25
1–3 John: 167
2:4–8
Philippians: 27, 95
2:4–10
Acts 1–12: 267
2:5
Luke 6–10: 347
2 Corinthians: 131
Philippians: 318
1 & 2 Thessalonians: 193, 216, 320
Titus: 153
James: 290
1 Peter: 220
2 Peter–Jude: 29
1–3 John: 19
2:5–6
James: 62
2:6
Philippians: 260
Colossians and Philemon: 126
1 & 2 Thessalonians: 158
Hebrews: 75
James: 215
2:6–7
John 12–21: 253
Romans 9–16: 40–41
1–3 John: 197
2:6–8
Luke 1–5: 183
2:7
Matthew 8–15: 91
Luke 1–5: 88
2 Corinthians: 279, 294
2 Timothy: 102
1 Peter: 182
2:7–9
Philippians: 78
2:7–10
Mark 1–8: 212
2:8
Matthew 16–23: 252
Matthew 24–28: 344
Mark 9–16: 117
Luke 1–5: 47
Luke 11–17: 284
John 1–11: 22
John 12–21: 105, 258
Acts 13–28: 163
Romans 1–8: 55
1 Corinthians: 425
Philippians: 23, 24, 148, 318
1 & 2 Thessalonians: 287, 320
1 Timothy: 31
2 Timothy: 38, 61
Titus: 5
Hebrews: 143, 262, 289
James: 61, 137, 290
1 Peter: 21, 37, 45, 89, 90
1–3 John: 169
2:8–9
Mark 1–8: 210, 359, 429
Mark 9–16: 22
Luke 1–5: 179, 328
Luke 11–17: 172
Luke 18–24: 42, 216
John 1–11: 35
John 12–21: 356
Acts 1–12: 70, 252
Acts 13–28: 67, 75, 108, 336
Romans 1–8: 20, 129, 203, 221, 352, 495
1 Corinthians: 146
2 Corinthians: 467
Galatians: 72
Philippians: 26, 151, 155, 172, 217, 222, 237
Colossians and Philemon: 15, 16, 23
1 & 2 Thessalonians: 15, 208, 287
1 Timothy: 27
Titus: 153
James: 122, 290
1 Peter: 17, 19, 26, 220
2 Peter–Jude: 20–21
Revelation 1–11: 103
Revelation 12–22: 49, 100
2:8–10
Romans 1–8: 22, 260
1 Corinthians: 52
Galatians: 13
Philippians: 164
1 & 2 Thessalonians: 16, 112
Titus: 118
James: 9, 125
1 Peter: 89
2:9
Luke 1–5: 161
John 12–21: 287
2:10
Matthew 1–7: 139, 360, 469
Matthew 8–15: 277, 320, 362
Matthew 16–23: 359
Matthew 24–28: 123
Mark 1–8: 206
Luke 1–5: 219
Luke 6–10: 167
John 12–21: 150
Acts 1–12: 283
Romans 1–8: 24, 55, 129, 226, 343, 361, 423
Romans 9–16: 183, 299, 327
1 Corinthians: 14, 54, 82, 143
2 Corinthians: 193, 248, 277
Galatians: 15, 29, 97, 137
Philippians: 54, 78, 172, 218
1 & 2 Thessalonians: 52, 59, 97, 208, 225, 257, 259
1 Timothy: 8
2 Timothy: 48, 163
Titus: 94, 123
Hebrews: 318
James: 116, 121, 137, 139
1 Peter: 17
2 Peter–Jude: 29, 78
1–3 John: 29, 36
Revelation 1–11: 103
2:11
Philippians: 218
2:11–12
Romans 9–16: 116–17
Colossians and Philemon: 110
2:11–13
Acts 1–12: 75
Romans 9–16: 82
2:11–17
Acts 13–28: 234

2:11–18
1 Corinthians: 451
2 Peter–Jude: 22
2:11–22
Acts 1–12: 291
1–3 John: 50
2:12
Luke 1–5: 142
Luke 11–17: 144
John 12–21: 20
Romans 1–8: 77
Romans 9–16: 313
Colossians and Philemon: 38
1 & 2 Thessalonians: 126, 242
1 Peter: 33
2:12–13
Colossians and Philemon: 60
2:13
John 12–21: 134
Galatians: 206
Hebrews: 416
Revelation 1–11: 232
Revelation 12–22: 308
2:13–14
Matthew 1–7: 213
Romans 9–16: 347
Philippians: 90
2:13–16
2 Corinthians: 200–201
Colossians and Philemon: 151–53
1 Peter: 206
2:14
Luke 1–5: 181
Luke 6–10: 176
Acts 1–12: 291
Romans 1–8: 275
Romans 9–16: 346, 356
2 Corinthians: 275
1 & 2 Thessalonians: 204, 313
2:14–15
Matthew 1–7: 272
1 & 2 Thessalonians: 204
2 Peter–Jude: 24
2:14–16
Revelation 1–11: 296
2:14–18
John 12–21: 380
2:15–16
Matthew 8–15: 356
2:16
Luke 1–5: 161
Acts 1–12: 84
1 Corinthians: 310
Philippians: 257
2:17
Luke 11–17: 169
2:18
Romans 1–8: 276
2 Corinthians: 97, 229
Philippians: 88
1 & 2 Thessalonians: 293
1 Peter: 31
1–3 John: 163
2:18–20
2 Corinthians: 210
2:18–22
Philippians: 90
2:19
Matthew 1–7: 444
Matthew 16–23: 84
Romans 9–16: 360
2 Corinthians: 87, 210, 439
1 Timothy: 135, 184
Hebrews: 80
Revelation 1–11: 320
2:19–20
Matthew 16–23: 297
2:19–22
Acts 1–12: 135
1 Peter: 106, 120
2:20
Matthew 8–15: 134
Matthew 16–23: 28, 29
Mark 1–8: 167, 168, 172
Luke 6–10: 18, 46, 241
Luke 11–17: 383
Luke 18–24: 126
John 12–21: 284
Acts 1–12: 97, 316
Acts 13–28: 3, 63, 240
Romans 1–8: 7
1 Corinthians: 2, 322, 324, 390, 403
2 Corinthians: 348, 412
1 Timothy: 4
2 Peter–Jude: 10
Revelation 12–22: 189, 281
2:20–21
1 & 2 Thessalonians: 108
2:20–22
1 Timothy: 183
2:21
John 1–11: 17
1–3 John: 186
2:22
1 Corinthians: 283
2 Corinthians: 253
Hebrews: 82
3:1
Acts 13–28: 293
Romans 9–16: 82
2 Timothy: 20
3:1–8
1 & 2 Thessalonians: 89
3:1–11
Luke 18–24: 126
3:2
2 Corinthians: 173, 189
1 Peter: 182
3:3
1 Corinthians: 298
1 & 2 Thessalonians: 233
Revelation 1–11: 3
3:3–4
2 Corinthians: 109, 412
3:3–5
Romans 9–16: 387
3:3–6
1 Timothy: 128
3:3–10
Acts 1–12: 38
3:4
Romans 1–8: 4
2 Corinthians: 359–60
Revelation 1–11: 286
3:4–6
Romans 9–16: 20, 82, 347
1 Timothy: 128
3:4–7
1 Peter: 53
3:5
Matthew 8–15: 134
Luke 6–10: 18, 19
Acts 13–28: 3
1 Corinthians: 322
2 Corinthians: 412
Galatians: 4
3:5–6
Matthew 8–15: 351
3:6
John 12–21: 21
Romans 9–16: 387
1 Corinthians: 417
2 Corinthians: 71
3:6–7
Philippians: 67
3:7
2 Corinthians: 74, 78, 85–86, 222
Philippians: 168
1 & 2 Thessalonians: 282, 317
1 Timothy: 125
1 Peter: 182
2 Peter–Jude: 26
3:7–8
1 Corinthians: 80
2 Corinthians: 72, 125
3:8
Matthew 1–7: 113
Luke 6–10: 45
John 1–11: 53
Acts 13–28: 15, 210, 248
Romans 1–8: 379
Romans 9–16: 98, 108
1 Corinthians: 14, 106
2 Corinthians: 198, 232, 279, 345
Philippians: 113, 240
1 & 2 Thessalonians: 39
1 Timothy: 27, 33
3:8–10
Revelation 1–11: 228
3:8–11
Romans 9–16: 389
3:9
John 1–11: 20
Acts 13–28: 137
Romans 9–16: 386
1 Corinthians: 372
2 Corinthians: 109
Revelation 1–11: 286
3:9–10
1 Corinthians: 259
3:10
John 1–11: 16
Romans 1–8: 298
1 Corinthians: 15

James: 167
1 Peter: 58
3:11
1 Timothy: 69
2 Timothy: 24
1 Peter: 279
3:12
John 12–21: 239
Romans 1–8: 276
1 Corinthians: 56
1 & 2 Thessalonians: 89
1–3 John: 203
3:13
Philippians: 194
3:14
1 & 2 Thessalonians: 293
3:14–16
Philippians: 304
3:14–19
Romans 1–8: 39, 284
Philippians: 38
James: 255
3:14–21
1 & 2 Thessalonians: 83, 86, 188, 253
2 Timothy: 20
3:15
1 Timothy: 184
3:16
John 12–21: 113
Acts 1–12: 19
Romans 1–8: 390, 427
2 Corinthians: 117, 153, 279
Galatians: 152
Philippians: 242
Colossians and Philemon: 33, 86
1 & 2 Thessalonians: 195, 259, 296
3:16–17
Colossians and Philemon: 31
3:16–19
Matthew 1–7: 489
Romans 1–8: 422, 433
Romans 9–16: 384
1 & 2 Thessalonians: 318
2 Timothy: 23
James: 167
1–3 John: 203, 230
3:16–20
Colossians and Philemon: 87
3:17
Matthew 8–15: 337
2 Corinthians: 145, 465
Philippians: 124
1 & 2 Thessalonians: 97
1 Timothy: 32
Hebrews: 392
Revelation 1–11: 99
3:17–19
Romans 9–16: 249
2 Corinthians: 153–54
Hebrews: 184
1 Peter: 288
2 Peter–Jude: 25
Revelation 1–11: 61
3:18
2 Corinthians: 117
3:19
John 12–21: 63
1 Corinthians: 314
2 Corinthians: 190
1 & 2 Thessalonians: 194
2 Timothy: 19
Hebrews: 397
3:20
Matthew 1–7: 231
Mark 1–8: 219
Luke 11–17: 58
John 12–21: 178
Acts 1–12: 19, 285
Acts 13–28: 49
2 Corinthians: 74
Galatians: 69
Philippians: 75, 304
1 & 2 Thessalonians: 204, 293
2 Timothy: 18
Titus: 155
Hebrews: 333
1 Peter: 245
2 Peter–Jude: 26
Revelation 1–11: 157
3:20–21
Acts 1–12: 282
Romans 1–8: 238
Romans 9–16: 322, 382
Philippians: 54, 168, 312
1 & 2 Thessalonians: 41
3:21
Matthew 16–23: 26
Matthew 24–28: 331
Romans 9–16: 126
1 Corinthians: 15
2 Corinthians: 44, 158
1 & 2 Thessalonians: 166
Revelation 1–11: 48
4:1
Luke 18–24: 68
Romans 1–8: 22, 422, 428
Philippians: 85, 161
Colossians and Philemon: 30
1 & 2 Thessalonians: 52, 112, 158, 159, 256, 257, 287
Titus: 71
1–3 John: 28, 36
4:1–2
Matthew 1–7: 171
Matthew 16–23: 231
Mark 9–16: 33, 101
1 & 2 Thessalonians: 97
1 Peter: 277
4:1–3
John 12–21: 293
Acts 1–12: 191
1–3 John: 18
4:1–6
Philippians: 100
4:1–6:18
1 & 2 Thessalonians: 203
4:2
Acts 1–12: 84
Romans 9–16: 248
1 Corinthians: 338
2 Corinthians: 228
Galatians: 168, 169
Philippians: 112
Colossians and Philemon: 156
1 & 2 Thessalonians: 90, 180, 257
4:2–6
Romans 9–16: 306
4:3
John 12–21: 278
Romans 9–16: 273, 298
1 Corinthians: 30
2 Corinthians: 186, 269, 485
Galatians: 52
Philippians: 102, 105, 270
Colossians and Philemon: 88
1 & 2 Thessalonians: 174, 257
2 Timothy: 197
Hebrews: 423
4:3–6
Philippians: 88
4:3–7
Galatians: 100
4:4
Luke 18–24: 68
1 Corinthians: 310
2 Corinthians: 108
1 & 2 Thessalonians: 256, 287
1 Peter: 33
4:4–5
Acts 13–28: 166
4:4–6
Matthew 24–28: 344
Acts 1–12: 41
1 Corinthians: 32, 312
Titus: 165
1–3 John: 15
4:5
Acts 1–12: 75, 84
Romans 1–8: 320
1 Peter: 285
2 Peter–Jude: 22
4:6
1 Peter: 31
4:7
1 & 2 Thessalonians: 320
1 Peter: 117, 182, 243
4:7, 11
Romans 9–16: 168
4:8–9
Hebrews: 227
4:8–10
2 Corinthians: 293
4:10
Luke 1–5: 229
Philippians: 141
4:11
Acts 1–12: 26, 232, 316
Acts 13–28: 3, 4, 239
1 Corinthians: 31, 322, 324
2 Corinthians: 473
Philippians: 15
1 & 2 Thessalonians: 167
2 Timothy: 185
Titus: 21

James: 146
Revelation 12–22: 189
4:11–12
Luke 6–10: 18
John 1–11: 17
Acts 13–28: 3
1 Corinthians: 4, 65, 385
2 Corinthians: 340
1 & 2 Thessalonians: 49, 88, 166, 170
2 Peter–Jude: 10
4:11–13
Matthew 24–28: 330
Luke 18–24: 455
1 Corinthians: 5, 282
2 Corinthians: 431–32
Philippians: 168, 291
Colossians and Philemon: 80
Titus: 8, 165
1–3 John: 70
4:11–14
Philippians: 216, 248
1 Timothy: 108
1 Peter: 285
4:11–15
Luke 6–10: 47
Romans 9–16: 300
1 Timothy: 239
1–3 John: 71
4:11–16
Acts 13–28: 55
2 Corinthians: 483
1 & 2 Thessalonians: 53
Hebrews: 437
2 Peter–Jude: 51
4:12
Matthew 8–15: 214
Acts 1–12: 179
Acts 13–28: 195, 213
1 Corinthians: 245, 294, 310
2 Corinthians: 94, 412
1 Timothy: 125
4:12–13
Acts 13–28: 81
Philippians: 40
4:13
Matthew 1–7: 350
Matthew 8–15: 456
Luke 1–5: 195
John 12–21: 278
Acts 13–28: 195
Romans 1–8: 226
1 Corinthians: 475
2 Corinthians: 124, 186, 485
Colossians and Philemon: 93
1 & 2 Thessalonians: 32, 96
2 Peter–Jude: 24
4:13–14
Colossians and Philemon: 29
4:13–16
1–3 John: 75
4:14
Matthew 8–15: 252
Acts 1–12: 200
Acts 13–28: 195
Romans 9–16: 374
1 Corinthians: 381, 447, 473
2 Corinthians: 127
Galatians: 64
Philippians: 48
1 & 2 Thessalonians: 96, 179, 270
1 Timothy: 159
2 Timothy: 36, 95, 155
Hebrews: 437
James: 38
1 Peter: 274
2 Peter–Jude: 101
1–3 John: 152
4:14–15
1 & 2 Thessalonians: 199
1 Peter: 202
1–3 John: 74
4:14–16
2 Peter–Jude: 136–37
4:15
Matthew 1–7: 217
John 12–21: 286
Romans 1–8: 43
Romans 9–16: 248
1 Corinthians: 118, 192, 253, 332, 475
2 Corinthians: 235
Philippians: 40, 217
2 Timothy: 30
Titus: 52
1 Peter: 201
2 Peter–Jude: 13
1–3 John: 228
Revelation 1–11: 47
Revelation 12–22: 80
4:15–16
1 & 2 Thessalonians: 97, 108, 166
4:16
1 Corinthians: 310
1 & 2 Thessalonians: 90
1 Peter: 121
4:17
Luke 18–24: 75
Romans 1–8: 410
Philippians: 286
1 & 2 Thessalonians: 158
1 Peter: 275
4:17–18
Mark 1–8: 396
1 Corinthians: 283
1 & 2 Thessalonians: 157, 242
4:17–19
Colossians and Philemon: 38
1 Timothy: 243
Titus: 146
James: 52, 58
1 Peter: 31
4:17–24
1 Peter: 173
4:17–32
Acts 1–12: 191
1–3 John: 117
4:18
Matthew 16–23: 2
Luke 1–5: 122
Luke 11–17: 144
Romans 1–8: 183, 295
2 Corinthians: 131, 210
Philippians: 286
Colossians and Philemon: 29, 90
1–3 John: 154, 227
4:18–19
John 12–21: 196
Acts 13–28: 335
4:19
John 12–21: 20
4:20–24
Romans 1–8: 324
1 Peter: 129
4:21
Luke 1–5: 336
2 Corinthians: 129
Philippians: 290
1 & 2 Thessalonians: 283, 319
4:22
Matthew 16–23: 47
Romans 1–8: 306, 324, 391
Romans 9–16: 243, 264
Philippians: 45
Colossians and Philemon: 149, 150
1 & 2 Thessalonians: 23
2 Timothy: 45
2 Peter–Jude: 31
4:22–23
Matthew 16–23: 48
4:22–24
Romans 9–16: 256
James: 74
4:23
Luke 1–5: 296
Galatians: 64
Philippians: 243, 289
1 Peter: 275
4:23–24
Romans 9–16: 265
4:24
Matthew 16–23: 48
Romans 1–8: 322
1 Corinthians: 258
2 Corinthians: 153
1 & 2 Thessalonians: 23
James: 61
1 Peter: 22, 92
2 Peter–Jude: 50
4:25
Acts 1–12: 84
1 & 2 Thessalonians: 181
1 Timothy: 173
James: 221, 264, 271
1 Peter: 192
2 Peter–Jude: 13
Revelation 12–22: 80
4:25–28
1 Peter: 138–39
4:25–5:7
1 & 2 Thessalonians: 136
4:25–5:21
1 & 2 Thessalonians: 97

4:26
Matthew 1–7: 294
1 Timothy: 173
4:26–27
Colossians and Philemon: 208
4:27
Luke 11–17: 119
2 Corinthians: 61, 482
1–3 John: 175
Revelation 1–11: 59
Revelation 12–22: 16, 235
4:28
Romans 9–16: 175
2 Corinthians: 273
1 & 2 Thessalonians: 120
4:29
1 Corinthians: 246
Colossians and Philemon: 187
1 Timothy: 173
Titus: 95
James: 221, 265
4:30
John 12–21: 113
Acts 1–12: 19, 304
Romans 1–8: 284, 380, 490
Romans 9–16: 263, 293
1 Corinthians: 124
2 Corinthians: 229
Galatians: 118, 174
Philippians: 105
1 & 2 Thessalonians: 193, 194
James: 28
1 Peter: 22
2 Peter–Jude: 210
Revelation 1–11: 217
4:31
Colossians and Philemon: 143–44
1 Timothy: 173
James: 218
4:32
Matthew 1–7: 394
Matthew 16–23: 127, 143, 146, 153, 154
Mark 1–8: 103
Mark 9–16: 149
Luke 1–5: 321
Luke 6–10: 175
Luke 11–17: 381
Acts 1–12: 75, 84, 117
Romans 9–16: 248
2 Corinthians: 52, 57, 176
Philippians: 90
Colossians and Philemon: 111, 157, 201, 204, 208
Titus: 87
2 Peter–Jude: 49
1–3 John: 168
4:32–5:2
Romans 9–16: 319
5:1
Luke 6–10: 108
Luke 11–17: 380
Philippians: 43, 181
1–3 John: 70, 244
Revelation 1–11: 54
5:1–2
Matthew 1–7: 445
Romans 9–16: 249
2 Corinthians: 58
Philippians: 43, 128
1 Peter: 116
1–3 John: 168
5:1–3
1 & 2 Thessalonians: 117
5:2
Luke 1–5: 154
Romans 1–8: 99
2 Corinthians: 191
Galatians: 165
1 & 2 Thessalonians: 90, 117, 164, 257
2 Timothy: 130
Titus: 122
Hebrews: 311, 313, 450
1 Peter: 170
1–3 John: 66, 131, 220
5:3
Romans 1–8: 102
1 Corinthians: 124
1 & 2 Thessalonians: 104, 257
Titus: 70
Hebrews: 431
5:3–4
1 & 2 Thessalonians: 189
5:3–5
Colossians and Philemon: 140
1 & 2 Thessalonians: 108
5:4
Colossians and Philemon: 144
James: 265
5:5
Luke 11–17: 133
1 Corinthians: 236
2 Corinthians: 309
Colossians and Philemon: 39
5:5–6
Matthew 1–7: 476
1 & 2 Thessalonians: 105
5:5–11
2 Corinthians: 254
5:6
Matthew 1–7: 463
Luke 1–5: 215
Acts 13–28: 45
Romans 1–8: 61, 72, 274
Romans 9–16: 133
Colossians and Philemon: 61
1 & 2 Thessalonians: 163
Titus: 68
Hebrews: 431
1–3 John: 171
5:7–9
1 & 2 Thessalonians: 104
1–3 John: 124
5:8
Matthew 1–7: 240
Luke 1–5: 272
Luke 11–17: 91, 337
John 1–11: 23
John 12–21: 51
Romans 9–16: 265
2 Corinthians: 45, 249
Philippians: 185, 311
1 & 2 Thessalonians: 52, 155, 157, 158
Hebrews: 313
1 Peter: 21, 31
2 Peter–Jude: 78
1–3 John: 36
Revelation 1–11: 54
5:8–9
Acts 13–28: 336
1 & 2 Thessalonians: 257
1–3 John: 25
5:8–10
Philippians: 49
1 & 2 Thessalonians: 195
5:8, 11
Luke 1–5: 122
5:8–11
1 Peter: 138–39
5:8–14
Colossians and Philemon: 39
5:9
Philippians: 45, 54
1 & 2 Thessalonians: 184, 258
2 Timothy: 201
2 Peter–Jude: 13
5:10
2 Corinthians: 73, 173
1 & 2 Thessalonians: 199
Titus: 100
5:11
John 12–21: 172
1 Corinthians: 124
2 Corinthians: 249
1 & 2 Thessalonians: 159
2 Timothy: 178
5:11–12
Galatians: 175
5:13
Luke 11–17: 87
5:14
Acts 13–28: 336
Romans 9–16: 259
5:14–17
1–3 John: 203
5:15
Philippians: 158
1 & 2 Thessalonians: 257
Hebrews: 313
James: 181
5:15–16
Romans 9–16: 190
2 Timothy: 176, 196
5:15–17
1 Peter: 275
5:15–21
1 Peter: 91, 173
1–3 John: 170
5:16
Acts 13–28: 54, 239
1 Corinthians: 464
5:17
Luke 11–17: 100
Romans 9–16: 355
1 & 2 Thessalonians: 195

5:17–18
Colossians and Philemon: 29
1 & 2 Thessalonians: 108
James: 235
5:18
Matthew 16–23: 162
Mark 1–8: 212
Luke 1–5: 37, 254
Luke 18–24: 256
John 12–21: 127
Acts 1–12: 18, 19, 41, 133, 189, 221
Romans 1–8: 428
Romans 9–16: 150
1 Corinthians: 280
Galatians: 152, 154, 189
Philippians: 105
1 & 2 Thessalonians: 118, 196
Titus: 155
5:18–19
Acts 13–28: 106
5:18–20
1 & 2 Thessalonians: 190
5:19
Luke 1–5: 93
James: 276
Revelation 1–11: 171
5:19–33
Acts 1–12: 42
5:20
Philippians: 24
Colossians and Philemon: 36
1 & 2 Thessalonians: 189
Hebrews: 210
Revelation 12–22: 194
5:21
Matthew 8–15: 56
Luke 1–5: 325
Acts 1–12: 84
1 Corinthians: 481
1 Timothy: 223
James: 223
1 Peter: 178
5:21–24
James: 204
5:21–6:2
1 Peter: 149
5:22
1 Corinthians: 481
1 & 2 Thessalonians: 43
1 Timothy: 231
Titus: 86
5:22–23
Matthew 1–7: 314
Mark 1–8: 212
1 Corinthians: 156
5:22–24
Titus: 87
5:22–25
Matthew 16–23: 162
5:22–25, 28, 33
1 Corinthians: 182
5:22–28
Colossians and Philemon: 169
5:22–30
Revelation 1–11: 30
5:22–33
1 Corinthians: 254
5:22–6:4
1 & 2 Thessalonians: 97
5:23
John 12–21: 383
1 & 2 Thessalonians: 108
Hebrews: 430
Revelation 1–11: 47
5:23–32
1 Corinthians: 156
5:24
1 Peter: 178
5:24–27
Romans 1–8: 361
5:25
Luke 11–17: 283
Romans 1–8: 99
2 Corinthians: 190, 203
Philippians: 43
Colossians and Philemon: 84, 168–69
1 & 2 Thessalonians: 90
1 Peter: 193
5:25–26
2 Timothy: 152
Titus: 122
James: 63
5:25–27
Matthew 16–23: 31
Acts 13–28: 225
Romans 9–16: 148
1 & 2 Thessalonians: 165, 206
1–3 John: 124
Revelation 1–11: 45, 95
Revelation 12–22: 201
5:25, 28
Titus: 83
5:25–28
1 Peter: 181
5:26
John 12–21: 67
2 Corinthians: 257
1 & 2 Thessalonians: 89, 202
Titus: 154
Hebrews: 263
1–3 John: 19
5:26–27
Mark 1–8: 358
1 Corinthians: 22
1 & 2 Thessalonians: 104, 203, 207
1–3 John: 28
5:27
Matthew 8–15: 457
Acts 1–12: 155
Romans 9–16: 265
2 Corinthians: 147, 442
Philippians: 182
1 & 2 Thessalonians: 112
1 Peter: 17
Revelation 12–22: 80, 304
5:28
1 & 2 Thessalonians: 90
5:28–33
Mark 9–16: 61
5:29
Matthew 16–23: 341
James: 112
5:30–32
1–3 John: 19
5:32
Mark 1–8: 130
Romans 9–16: 387
2 Corinthians: 109
Revelation 1–11: 286
5:33
1 & 2 Thessalonians: 90
6:1
Colossians and Philemon: 170
Titus: 99
6:1–3
1 Corinthians: 481
6:2
Titus: 73, 76
6:4
Matthew 16–23: 106, 178, 182
Mark 9–16: 45
Luke 18–24: 23
1 Corinthians: 114
Colossians and Philemon: 171, 173
1 & 2 Thessalonians: 50
2 Timothy: 154, 161
6:5
1 Corinthians: 56
2 Corinthians: 269, 279
1 Timothy: 234, 235
Hebrews: 262
6:5–6
Romans 9–16: 355
Titus: 98
1 Peter: 149
6:5–7
Acts 13–28: 210
1 & 2 Thessalonians: 120, 303
6:5–8
1 Corinthians: 173
1 Timothy: 234
6:5–9
Colossians and Philemon: 174
James: 95
1 Peter: 160
6:5, 9
Galatians: 100
6:6
Luke 1–5: 80
Luke 6–10: 41
Romans 1–8: 34
1 & 2 Thessalonians: 213
1 Timothy: 235
James: 230, 237
1 Peter: 201
2 Peter–Jude: 18
6:8
1 & 2 Thessalonians: 74
6:9
Acts 1–12: 300
Romans 1–8: 136
Philippians: 315
Colossians and Philemon: 206
James: 97

Revelation 12–22: 251
6:10
Acts 13–28: 49, 118
1 Corinthians: 475
2 Corinthians: 477
Philippians: 311
1 & 2 Thessalonians: 35
2 Timothy: 36, 38
Hebrews: 24
6:10–13
1 & 2 Thessalonians: 317
6:10–17
John 12–21: 272
Acts 13–28: 172
Galatians: 186
James: 205
1 Peter: 202
2 Peter–Jude: 194
6:10–18
Acts 1–12: 234
1 & 2 Thessalonians: 97
6:10ff.
Acts 13–28: 55, 97
6:11
Luke 11–17: 119
John 12–21: 171
Acts 1–12: 85
2 Corinthians: 482
Philippians: 87, 267, 268, 282
1 & 2 Thessalonians: 71, 288
1 Timothy: 120
Hebrews: 371
Revelation 12–22: 14, 235
6:11–12
1 & 2 Thessalonians: 161
1 Peter: 281
6:11–17
Romans 9–16: 265
6:11, 13
Galatians: 173
6:12
Matthew 8–15: 202
Luke 1–5: 122
John 1–11: 23
Acts 1–12: 153
Acts 13–28: 9
Romans 1–8: 516
1 Corinthians: 240, 282
2 Corinthians: 230, 249
Philippians: 87, 241
Colossians and Philemon: 113
1 & 2 Thessalonians: 157
1 Timothy: 39, 149
2 Timothy: 193, 210
Hebrews: 24, 52
1–3 John: 86
Revelation 1–11: 238, 263, 270
Revelation 12–22: 8, 16
6:12–17
Mark 9–16: 332
6:13
Philippians: 87, 267, 268, 282
1 & 2 Thessalonians: 288
6:13–17
1 & 2 Thessalonians: 161
6:13–18
1 Timothy: 40
6:14
Romans 9–16: 298
Philippians: 267, 268, 282
1 & 2 Thessalonians: 288
2 Peter–Jude: 50
1–3 John: 101
6:14–17
2 Timothy: 157
6:15
Matthew 1–7: 215
John 12–21: 124
Romans 1–8: 275
Revelation 12–22: 86
6:16
Matthew 8–15: 44
1 & 2 Thessalonians: 91, 296
Hebrews: 347, 374
James: 235
6:17
Luke 6–10: 366
Luke 18–24: 418
Acts 13–28: 172
Romans 1–8: 270
2 Corinthians: 330
1 & 2 Thessalonians: 198
2 Timothy: 59
1–3 John: 75, 108, 149, 155, 156
Revelation 1–11: 83
Revelation 12–22: 22
6:18
Matthew 1–7: 207, 373
Luke 11–17: 2, 31
Luke 18–24: 7
John 12–21: 178
Romans 1–8: 38
1 Corinthians: 473
2 Corinthians: 229
Philippians: 39
Colossians and Philemon: 26–27, 179
1 & 2 Thessalonians: 186, 207, 298
1 Timothy: 201
Hebrews: 156
1–3 John: 149
Revelation 1–11: 320
6:18–19
Romans 9–16: 352
2 Corinthians: 27
Philippians: 74
1 & 2 Thessalonians: 187
6:18–20
John 12–21: 180, 272
Colossians and Philemon: 4
1 & 2 Thessalonians: 211
6:19
Acts 13–28: 172
Romans 9–16: 387
1 Corinthians: 17, 56, 80
2 Corinthians: 109, 189
Philippians: 78
1 & 2 Thessalonians: 214, 294
1 Timothy: 128
Titus: 95
Hebrews: 448
6:19–20
Acts 13–28: 46
1 & 2 Thessalonians: 293
6:20
John 12–21: 78
Acts 13–28: 247, 257, 332, 370
1 Corinthians: 4
2 Corinthians: 206
Philippians: 60
6:21
Philippians: 58, 78, 315
1 Timothy: 125
Titus: 30, 167
6:21–24
1 & 2 Thessalonians: 69
6:23
2 Corinthians: 488
1 & 2 Thessalonians: 228, 313
2 Peter–Jude: 20
Revelation 1–11: 61
6:23–24
2 Corinthians: 487
6:24
Matthew 16–23: 340
Romans 1–8: 482
Philippians: 318
1 & 2 Thessalonians: 18
Revelation 1–11: 54
Revelation 12–22: 101

Philippians
1:1
John 12–21: 4
Romans 9–16: 191, 360
2 Corinthians: 134, 196, 473
Philippians: 4, 13, 196, 199, 255, 272, 315
1 & 2 Thessalonians: 13, 59, 78, 167, 225
1 Timothy: xii, 6, 93, 125
Hebrews: 371
James: 12, 89
1 Peter: 263
2 Peter–Jude: 18
1–3 John: 29
Revelation 12–22: 200, 293
1:1–2
Philippians: 139
1:2
2 Corinthians: 487, 488
Philippians: 16, 314, 318
1 & 2 Thessalonians: 14, 87, 224
1 Peter: 25
Revelation 1–11: 24
1:3
Romans 1–8: 35
1:3–4
Acts 1–12: 180
Philippians: 193
2 Timothy: 6
Hebrews: 447

1:3–5
Philippians: 18
Colossians and Philemon: 12
1 & 2 Thessalonians: 188
1:3–6
Ephesians: 266
1:3–7
Acts 13–28: 193
1:3–8
1 & 2 Thessalonians: 69
1:3–9
Philippians: 268
1:3–11
1 & 2 Thessalonians: 83
1:4
Acts 13–28: 229
Ephesians: 103
Philippians: 1, 179, 215, 269
1 & 2 Thessalonians: 253, 293
1:5
Philippians: 89
1:6
Matthew 8–15: 276
Matthew 24–28: 28
Romans 1–8: 226, 277, 306, 318, 335, 443, 465
Romans 9–16: 280
1 Corinthians: 10, 70
2 Corinthians: 21, 34, 168, 240, 257
Galatians: 207
Ephesians: 32, 63, 365
Philippians: 164, 168, 187, 188, 283
1 & 2 Thessalonians: 20, 144, 208, 287, 316
2 Timothy: 83
Hebrews: 18, 146
1 Peter: 22, 36
2 Peter–Jude: 28, 210
1–3 John: 19, 99, 144
Revelation 1–11: 30
Revelation 12–22: 73, 99
1:6–7
Galatians: 141
1:7
Acts 1–12: 200
2 Corinthians: 236
Philippians: 58, 66
Colossians and Philemon: 84
1:7–8
1 & 2 Thessalonians: 69
1:8
Luke 1–5: 120
2 Corinthians: 43, 342
Philippians: 105, 157
1:8–11
1 & 2 Thessalonians: 86
1:9
Romans 1–8: 483
Romans 9–16: 247
1 Corinthians: 330, 333
Philippians: 306
Colossians and Philemon: 28, 33
1 & 2 Thessalonians: 90, 95, 117, 293
James: 36
1 Peter: 90, 93
2 Peter–Jude: 24
1–3 John: 148
1:9–10
Matthew 1–7: 183
Acts 1–12: 12
2 Corinthians: 475
Ephesians: 103
1 Peter: 275
1:9–11
Romans 1–8: 39
Ephesians: 350
1 & 2 Thessalonians: 253
1:10
1 Corinthians: 249
2 Corinthians: 37
Philippians: 28, 187, 188
1 & 2 Thessalonians: 144
Revelation 1–11: 30
1:10–11
2 Corinthians: 476
1:11
Matthew 1–7: 469
Matthew 8–15: 361
Matthew 16–23: 299
Mark 1–8: 206, 212
Luke 6–10: 201
John 1–11: 451
Romans 1–8: 362
Romans 9–16: 298
2 Corinthians: 205
Philippians: 78
1 & 2 Thessalonians: 248
James: 181
1:12
Luke 18–24: 398
Acts 13–28: 104
Philippians: 81, 180
1 & 2 Thessalonians: 125, 184
1:12–13
Acts 13–28: 257
Philippians: 193, 269
1:12–14
Mark 9–16: 144
Ephesians: 88, 384
Philippians: 5
2 Timothy: 21
1:12–14, 18
Romans 9–16: 349
1:12–18
1 Corinthians: 91
Philippians: 7
1:12–21
Philippians: 21
1:12–26
Philippians: 4
1:13
Matthew 1–7: 37
Acts 13–28: 369, 375
Philippians: 5, 6, 317
1:13–14
Philippians: 5, 14, 57, 188
1:14
Philippians: 58, 180, 193
James: 23
1:14–17
Philippians: 6, 7, 197
1:14–18
Colossians and Philemon: 4
1:15
Philippians: 62, 198
1:15–16
Philippians: 198
1:15–17
1 Corinthians: 341
Philippians: 18, 68, 196
1:15–18
Mark 9–16: 40
Luke 6–10: 305
1 Corinthians: 468
Philippians: 78
1 & 2 Thessalonians: 294
1:15, 17–18
Galatians: 119
1:16
Acts 1–12: 200
Colossians and Philemon: 12
1 Timothy: 137
1:17
Luke 1–5: 232
Philippians: 58, 62, 110, 198, 269
James: 23
1:17–18
Philippians: 193
2 Timothy: 129
1:18
Philippians: 1, 18, 179, 198, 215, 275
Colossians and Philemon: 74
1 & 2 Thessalonians: 185
1 Timothy: 139
1:18–21
1 & 2 Thessalonians: 185
1:19
Luke 1–5: 239
Luke 18–24: 3
John 12–21: 215
Romans 1–8: 466
2 Corinthians: 27, 204
Ephesians: 8
Philippians: 6
Colossians and Philemon: 26
1 & 2 Thessalonians: 211, 293
1 Timothy: 168
1:19–20
Acts 13–28: 46
James: 23
1:19–30
1 & 2 Thessalonians: 295
1:19, 25–26
1 Timothy: xi
1:20
Mark 1–8: 433
Luke 1–5: 79
Romans 1–8: 225
2 Corinthians: 128
1 & 2 Thessalonians: 133

1:20–21
Philippians: 6, 188, 193
1:20–23
Colossians and Philemon: 4
1:21
Matthew 1–7: 150
Matthew 24–28: 338
Acts 13–28: 332
Romans 1–8: 47
Romans 9–16: 146
1 Corinthians: 92, 311
2 Corinthians: 143, 160, 194
Ephesians: 30, 160
Philippians: 262, 276, 311
Colossians and Philemon: 133
1 Timothy: 271
2 Timothy: 26, 58, 213
Hebrews: 70, 343
1 Peter: 34
Revelation 12–22: 23, 261, 307
1:21–23
Acts 13–28: 73
1:21–24
Romans 1–8: 480
1–3 John: 79
1:21–26
Philippians: 59
1:21, 23
Titus: 119
1:22–24
Philippians: 81
1:23
Mark 1–8: 264
Luke 11–17: 172
Acts 1–12: 225
2 Corinthians: 158, 160–62
Galatians: 154
Philippians: 6, 260, 262, 277
1 & 2 Thessalonians: 109, 125
1 Timothy: 271
Revelation 1–11: 52
Revelation 12–22: 23, 261, 267
1:23–24
1 Corinthians: 20, 92, 446
James: 18
1:24
2 Corinthians: 175
1:24–25
Philippians: 192
1:24–26
Philippians: 6
1:25
Acts 1–12: 259
Philippians: 1, 7, 19, 179, 215
Colossians and Philemon: 4
1 Peter: 40
1:25–26
Philippians: 84, 86
1:25–30
Philippians: 192
1:26
2 Corinthians: 187
1:27
John 12–21: 286
Romans 9–16: 182, 306
1 Corinthians: 28, 473
2 Corinthians: 47, 484
Ephesians: 116
Philippians: 18, 103, 104, 108, 159, 267, 270, 282
Colossians and Philemon: 12, 30, 88
1 & 2 Thessalonians: 82, 158, 257
James: 185
1:27–28
Philippians: 216–17
1 Peter: 187
1:27–30
Philippians: 2
1:28
Matthew 1–7: 221
Philippians: 193, 256
1:28–30
Philippians: 266
1:29
Acts 1–12: 267
2 Corinthians: 278
Ephesians: 61
Philippians: 26, 180, 193
Colossians and Philemon: 75
James: 61
1 Peter: 3, 16, 45, 206
2 Peter–Jude: 20, 21
1:29–30
Matthew 1–7: 221
1 & 2 Thessalonians: 178
1:30
Philippians: 193
2:1
Luke 1–5: 120
1 Corinthians: 237
Philippians: 32
1–3 John: 19
2:1–2
Acts 1–12: 89, 146
Romans 9–16: 250
Ephesians: 116
Philippians: 18, 89
2:1–4
Philippians: 3
1 & 2 Thessalonians: 203
James: 178, 185
2:1–5
1 Peter: 187
2:1–8
Philippians: 43–44, 81, 157
2:2
Romans 9–16: 306
1 Corinthians: 30, 330
2 Corinthians: 269
Ephesians: 39
Philippians: 1, 31, 215, 266, 269, 270, 315
Colossians and Philemon: 227
1 & 2 Thessalonians: 90
2:2–4
Philippians: 18, 90, 206
Titus: 83
2:2–5
Romans 9–16: 310
2:2–8
Matthew 16–23: 115
Colossians and Philemon: 88–89
2:3
Matthew 1–7: 150
Mark 9–16: 101
Acts 1–12: 84, 147
Romans 9–16: 189
1 Corinthians: 30
Philippians: 108
1 Timothy: 281
James: 104
1 Peter: 188–89
2:3–4
Luke 6–10: 300
John 12–21: 60
Romans 9–16: 252, 308
1 Corinthians: 246
2 Corinthians: 280
Philippians: 80, 306
1 & 2 Thessalonians: 97
Hebrews: 424
James: 112
1–3 John: 171
2:3–4, 5–8
2 Timothy: 111
2:3–11
1 Peter: 278
2:4
1 Corinthians: 193, 345
2 Corinthians: 238
Ephesians: 276
Philippians: 22
2:4–8
Romans 1–8: 14
2:4–11
Ephesians: 139
2:5
Romans 1–8: 416
Romans 9–16: 311
1 Corinthians: 10
Ephesians: 108
Philippians: 31, 90, 107, 138, 306
2:5–7
Luke 18–24: 244
Galatians: 147
1 Peter: 277
2:5, 8
Ephesians: 174
2:5–8
Mark 9–16: 34, 103, 109
Luke 6–10: 15
John 12–21: 136, 255
Romans 1–8: 16
Ephesians: 277
Philippians: 80
1 Peter: 189
2:5–9
1–3 John: 230
2:5–11
Matthew 16–23: 350
Mark 1–8: 192

Romans 1–8: 214
1 Peter: 200
Revelation 1–11: 18
2:5, 7–8
Titus: 63
2:5, 12–13
Romans 9–16: 182
2:6
Matthew 24–28: 72, 271
Mark 9–16: 210
John 1–11: 7, 14
John 12–21: 262
2 Corinthians: 19
Colossians and Philemon: 45
James: 98
2 Peter–Jude: 26
1–3 John: 16
2:6–7
Mark 1–8: 35, 79
Luke 1–5: 150, 239, 249
2 Corinthians: 19, 292
Galatians: 108
1 Timothy: 140
2:6–8
Matthew 8–15: 295
Mark 1–8: 418
Luke 6–10: 300
Romans 9–16: 249, 310
1 Corinthians: 106, 342
Ephesians: 108, 296
Hebrews: 29
1–3 John: 65
Revelation 12–22: 108
2:6–9
Matthew 16–23: 244
2:6–11
2 Corinthians: 292–93
2:7
Matthew 8–15: 411
Matthew 16–23: 88, 151
Luke 1–5: 152, 160, 197, 239, 320
John 1–11: 41
John 12–21: 56
1 Corinthians: 238
2 Corinthians: 279, 455
Galatians: 108
1 Timothy: 230
1 Peter: 166
2 Peter–Jude: 30
Revelation 1–11: 17
2:7–8
Matthew 24–28: 250
Luke 18–24: 454
John 1–11: 17
John 12–21: 248
Acts 1–12: 211
1 Corinthians: 249
2 Corinthians: 213
Ephesians: 120, 268
1 Timothy: 140
1–3 John: 16
Revelation 12–22: 112
2:7–9
Galatians: 169
2:8
Matthew 16–23: 99
Mark 1–8: 45
Mark 9–16: 359, 369
Luke 1–5: 197
Luke 6–10: 282
John 12–21: 67
Romans 1–8: 307
2 Corinthians: 133, 212, 241
2:8–9
Romans 1–8: 508
2 Corinthians: 155
2:8–11
Matthew 24–28: 275
Mark 1–8: 421
Colossians and Philemon: 52
1 Timothy: 142
Revelation 12–22: 217
2:8b–11
Mark 9–16: 281
2:9
Mark 9–16: 122
Luke 18–24: 453
John 12–21: 197
Acts 1–12: 60
2 Corinthians: 289
Hebrews: 279
2:9–10
Mark 1–8: 45
Romans 1–8: 493
Revelation 1–11: 228
2:9–11
Matthew 1–7: 82
Matthew 8–15: 445
Matthew 24–28: 232, 339
Mark 1–8: 36
Mark 9–16: 109
Luke 1–5: 229
Luke 6–10: 310
Luke 18–24: 112
John 1–11: 16, 381
John 12–21: 255
Acts 1–12: 67, 107
Romans 9–16: 74, 322
1 Corinthians: 287
2 Corinthians: 290
Ephesians: 41
Hebrews: 239
1 Peter: 58, 83, 219–20
2 Peter–Jude: 213
1–3 John: 147
Revelation 1–11: 25
2:10
Matthew 8–15: 42
Luke 18–24: 157, 355
John 1–11: 15
Acts 1–12: 104
1 Corinthians: 20
Philippians: 252
Colossians and Philemon: 50, 60
Hebrews: 36, 65, 255
2:10–11
Matthew 16–23: 262
Matthew 24–28: 313
Mark 1–8: 56
Mark 9–16: 404
Luke 11–17: 21
Luke 18–24: 415
John 12–21: 353
Romans 1–8: 27
Romans 9–16: 285, 315
1 Corinthians: 253
2 Corinthians: 133
Ephesians: 26
Revelation 1–11: 32
Revelation 12–22: 131
2:11
Matthew 1–7: 58
Mark 1–8: 332
Romans 9–16: 284
Philippians: 139
1 Timothy: 265
Hebrews: 20
1 Peter: 128
2:12
Matthew 8–15: 56
Luke 1–5: 325
John 12–21: 266
Romans 9–16: 244
1 Corinthians: 56, 314
2 Corinthians: 269
Galatians: 157
Colossians and Philemon: 128
1 & 2 Thessalonians: 297
2 Timothy: 48
1–3 John: 70
Revelation 1–11: 54
2:12–13
Romans 1–8: 129, 335, 338, 466
2 Corinthians: 34, 257
Ephesians: 62, 364
1 & 2 Thessalonians: 104, 204
Hebrews: 451
James: 255
1 Peter: 22, 100, 129
1–3 John: 28, 103, 144
Revelation 12–22: 203
2:12–16
Philippians: 18
2:13
Matthew 24–28: 291
John 12–21: 266
Romans 9–16: 343
2 Corinthians: 74, 222
Ephesians: 15, 47
Philippians: 26, 78, 298
1 & 2 Thessalonians: 16, 58, 96, 190, 204
1 Peter: 279
2:14
Philippians: 3, 266, 271
2:14–15
Philippians: 18
1 & 2 Thessalonians: 203
2:14–16
2 Timothy: 201
James: 257
1 Peter: 160
2:15
Matthew 1–7: 245

Matthew 8–15: 379
Matthew 16–23: 84
John 12–21: 172
Romans 9–16: 298
1 Corinthians: 131
2 Corinthians: 182, 228
Galatians: 99
Philippians: 85, 310
Colossians and Philemon: 165
1 Timothy: 119
Titus: 90, 106
Hebrews: 373
2 Peter–Jude: 78, 134
1–3 John: 2, 116
Revelation 1–11: 43, 54
2:15–16
Philippians: 84
1 & 2 Thessalonians: 81, 121
2:16
Acts 1–12: 166
2 Corinthians: 37, 187, 206
Philippians: 28, 191
1 & 2 Thessalonians: 73, 144
Hebrews: 372
2:17
Acts 13–28: 73, 104, 194
Romans 9–16: 146, 332
2 Corinthians: 145
Philippians: 1, 269
Colossians and Philemon: 4, 74
1 Timothy: 174
2 Timothy: 21, 26, 189
Titus: 3
Hebrews: 380
James: 23
2:17–18
Philippians: 215
1 & 2 Thessalonians: 184
Hebrews: 447
1–3 John: 37
2:18
Philippians: 1, 179
Hebrews: 448
2:19
Acts 13–28: 83
Philippians: 196, 315
1 Timothy: 6
James: 237
Revelation 1–11: 21
2:19–20
2 Timothy: 205
2:19–22
1 Timothy: 2
2:19–24
2 Corinthians: 18
1 & 2 Thessalonians: 77, 223
2:19–30
Philippians: 268
2:20–21
Philippians: 7
2:21
Romans 1–8: 185
Romans 9–16: 309
2 Timothy: 193
2:22
Romans 9–16: 378
1 & 2 Thessalonians: 13
2:23
Philippians: 196
Colossians and Philemon: 4
2:24
Philippians: 5, 6, 7, 192, 196
Colossians and Philemon: 4
1 Timothy: xi
James: 237
Revelation 1–11: 21
2:25
Acts 13–28: 47
Romans 1–8: 22
1 Corinthians: 323, 324, 448, 468
2 Corinthians: 276, 307, 410
Philippians: 202, 315
1 & 2 Thessalonians: 42
1 Timothy: 4
2:25–27
Luke 1–5: 295
2:25–30
Philippians: 4, 192, 197
1 Timothy: 175
1–3 John: 135, 246
2:25ff.
1 Timothy: 264
2:26–27
James: 276
2:27
1 Corinthians: 301
2:28
Philippians: 1
2:28–29
Philippians: 215
2:29
1 Corinthians: 484
Philippians: 1
2:29–30
Matthew 16–23: 372
2:30
Romans 1–8: 48
1 Corinthians: 324, 448
Ephesians: 285
3:1
Ephesians: 230
Philippians: 1, 273
1 & 2 Thessalonians: 293
2 Peter–Jude: 49
Revelation 12–22: 76
3:2
Luke 6–10: 112
Luke 11–17: 254
Acts 13–28: 209
Romans 1–8: 161
Galatians: 47
Philippians: 2, 4, 64, 81, 83, 227, 257
Colossians and Philemon: 99
1–3 John: 153
Revelation 12–22: 308
3:2–3
Romans 1–8: 249
3:2–12
Luke 11–17: 346
3:3
Matthew 1–7: 174
Matthew 16–23: 48
Mark 1–8: 348
Luke 1–5: 164
Romans 1–8: 37, 369
Romans 9–16: 138
2 Corinthians: 229
Galatians: 48, 205
Philippians: 313
Colossians and Philemon: 108
1 & 2 Thessalonians: 184
2 Timothy: 5
James: 207
1–3 John: 106
3:3–11
1–3 John: 91–92
3:4–6
Matthew 1–7: 281
Mark 1–8: 350
Luke 18–24: 15, 38, 75
Romans 1–8: 202, 358, 367
Romans 9–16: 98
2 Corinthians: 122, 126, 329, 385
Philippians: 82
3:4–7
Romans 1–8: 33
Philippians: 180
3:4–7, 8
2 Timothy: 193
3:4–8
Mark 9–16: 79
Luke 1–5: 218
Galatians: 24
2 Timothy: 5
3:4–9
Mark 1–8: 112, 359
Acts 1–12: 264
Titus: 156
3:4–10
Galatians: 206
3:4–11
Mark 1–8: 347–48
Luke 1–5: 319
Acts 1–12: 269
Philippians: 12
3:4–12
2 Corinthians: 112
3:5
Matthew 8–15: 188
Luke 1–5: 245
Acts 13–28: 20, 246, 333
Romans 1–8: 248
Romans 9–16: 8
2 Corinthians: 385
Galatians: 133
1 Timothy: 3
3:5–6
Luke 6–10: 270
Luke 11–17: 367
Acts 1–12: 230
Acts 13–28: 158, 246, 265
Romans 1–8: 369

Romans 9–16: 59, 66, 235
2 Corinthians: 103
Galatians: xii, 26, 95
Colossians and Philemon: 70
3:5–7
Matthew 8–15: 391
3:5–9
Galatians: 48
3:6
Mark 1–8: 150
John 12–21: 192
Acts 13–28: 223, 279
Romans 1–8: 369, 372, 385
2 Corinthians: 329, 386
Philippians: 181
3:7
Matthew 8–15: 62
2 Corinthians: 103
Philippians: 259
3:7–8
Matthew 1–7: 226
Mark 1–8: 117
Luke 6–10: 181, 271
Luke 18–24: 15
Romans 1–8: 256, 373
2 Corinthians: 122
Philippians: 207, 218
James: 23
3:7–9
Matthew 1–7: 281
Acts 13–28: 158
Romans 1–8: 367
Philippians: 82, 96
1 Timothy: 31
1 Peter: 35
3:7–10
1 & 2 Thessalonians: 96
3:7–11
2 Peter–Jude: 26
3:7–14
1 & 2 Thessalonians: 293, 295
1 Peter: 101
3:7–16
1 & 2 Thessalonians: 208
1–3 John: 25
3:8
Matthew 1–7: 147
Mark 1–8: 430
Luke 6–10: 201, 273
Luke 11–17: 265, 347
Luke 18–24: 39
Acts 1–12: 314
Acts 13–28: 223, 293
Romans 1–8: 351, 420
Romans 9–16: 333, 350
1 Corinthians: 363
2 Corinthians: 44, 103, 227
Philippians: 113, 194, 259
3:8–9
John 1–11: 104
John 12–21: 67
Romans 1–8: 57
Romans 9–16: 66, 72
Philippians: 222
2 Peter–Jude: 22–23
1–3 John: 39
Revelation 12–22: 203
3:8–10
1 Peter: 3
3:8–10, 12
Ephesians: 157
3:8–11
Mark 1–8: 150
3:8–14
Philippians: 163
3:8, 10–11
Titus: 10
3:9
Luke 1–5: 198, 206, 237
Luke 11–17: 370
John 12–21: 132, 198
Acts 1–12: 74
Acts 13–28: 26, 336
Romans 1–8: 203
1 Corinthians: 53
2 Corinthians: 103, 205, 207, 216, 248
Ephesians: 2, 352
Philippians: 13
1 & 2 Thessalonians: 258
Titus: 5
1 Peter: 111
1–3 John: 122
Revelation 12–22: 253
3:9–10
Matthew 1–7: 181
Galatians: 154
3:9–11
Romans 9–16: 289
3:10
Matthew 8–15: 206, 217
Matthew 16–23: 225, 238
Matthew 24–28: 305, 338
Mark 9–16: 402
Luke 1–5: 164
Luke 11–17: 50
Acts 13–28: 73, 291
Romans 1–8: 448, 479
1 Corinthians: 237
2 Corinthians: 25, 144
Ephesians: 153
Philippians: 180
Colossians and Philemon: 75
1 & 2 Thessalonians: 194
1 Timothy: 28
2 Timothy: 21
Hebrews: 76, 368
James: 22, 206
2 Peter–Jude: 24, 25
3:10–14
Romans 1–8: 131
3:11–14
Romans 9–16: 290
Titus: 115
1 Peter: 287
3:12
Matthew 16–23: 341
Romans 1–8: 486
1 Corinthians: 109, 363
Philippians: 40, 107
Colossians and Philemon: 80
1 & 2 Thessalonians: 287
Hebrews: 76
3:12–13
Philippians: 82
3:12–14
Matthew 8–15: 145
Romans 1–8: 388, 423
1 Corinthians: 394
2 Corinthians: 124, 345
Ephesians: 352
Philippians: 157, 172
1 & 2 Thessalonians: 94, 98
1 Timothy: 181
3:12–16
Philippians: 162
1 & 2 Thessalonians: 94
3:12–21
Philippians: 242
3:12, 14
Titus: 10
3:13
Philippians: 253
1 & 2 Thessalonians: 207
3:13–14
Romans 9–16: 268
1 Corinthians: 78
Hebrews: 380
1–3 John: 70
3:13b–14
1–3 John: 92, 118
3:14
Matthew 16–23: 341
Romans 1–8: 448, 486
2 Corinthians: 116, 194
Ephesians: 119, 120
Philippians: 107
1 & 2 Thessalonians: 206
2 Timothy: 46, 199
Hebrews: 75
1 Peter: 200
1–3 John: 72
3:15
Philippians: 31, 107
James: 32
3:15–17
1 Corinthians: 27
1 & 2 Thessalonians: 203
3:16–21
James: 254
3:17
Acts 13–28: 208
2 Corinthians: 473
Philippians: 250, 291
1 Timothy: 103, 172
Titus: 25, 93
3:17–18
Philippians: 81, 83
3:17–19
Philippians: 21
3:17–21
Matthew 16–23: 84
3:18
Mark 9–16: 216
Acts 13–28: 212
1 & 2 Thessalonians: 184
3:18–19
Luke 11–17: 254

Luke 18–24: 162
Romans 9–16: 375
1 Corinthians: 236
2 Corinthians: 336
Galatians: 198
Philippians: 2, 4, 157, 266
2 Timothy: 75
James: 197
3:19
Mark 1–8: 432
Romans 1–8: 416
Galatians: 185
Philippians: 31, 107
3:20
Matthew 24–28: 82
Mark 1–8: 198, 210
Luke 1–5: 153
Luke 11–17: 337
Luke 18–24: 191
John 12–21: 281, 296, 297
Romans 1–8: 131, 446
1 Corinthians: 20
2 Corinthians: 206, 439
Galatians: 126
Ephesians: 9, 60, 81
Philippians: 85, 180
Colossians and Philemon: 20, 126
1 & 2 Thessalonians: 73, 185
1 Timothy: 265
2 Timothy: 202
Titus: 141
Hebrews: 75, 229, 311
1 Peter: 15–16, 137
2 Peter–Jude: 111, 128
1–3 John: 175
Revelation 12–22: 207, 211, 243, 255, 260, 291
3:20–21
Mark 9–16: 9
Luke 6–10: 283
Luke 18–24: 436
John 12–21: 249, 253, 300
Romans 1–8: 280, 337, 457, 463
Romans 9–16: 144
1 Corinthians: 150
2 Corinthians: 107, 157, 165
Galatians: 208
Philippians: 244, 276
1 & 2 Thessalonians: 52, 91, 92, 135, 203
Titus: 120
James: 256
1 Peter: 287
2 Peter–Jude: 31
1–3 John: 106, 197
Revelation 1–11: 30
3:21
Mark 9–16: 192
Luke 18–24: 147
John 1–11: 14
Romans 1–8: 131, 464, 491
1 Corinthians: 440
2 Corinthians: 117, 124, 161
Philippians: 245
1 & 2 Thessalonians: 135, 162, 163, 248, 282, 288
1 Peter: 178
Revelation 12–22: 261, 272
4:1
Philippians: 1, 19, 87, 157, 179, 188, 193, 215
1 & 2 Thessalonians: 69, 73, 82, 288
Hebrews: 380
4:1–3
1 Timothy: 189
4:2
Romans 9–16: 364
Philippians: 18, 21, 31, 89, 100, 157
4:2–3
Acts 13–28: 92
Philippians: 3, 81, 203, 266
Titus: 76
4:3
Luke 6–10: 327
John 12–21: 249, 263
Acts 13–28: 39
Romans 9–16: 235
Philippians: 89, 260
1–3 John: 185
Revelation 12–22: 50, 169, 255, 260
4:3–4
Philippians: 21
4:4
Luke 11–17: 293
Acts 13–28: 105
2 Corinthians: 231, 484
Galatians: 166
Ephesians: 230
Philippians: 1, 56, 179, 215, 216
1 & 2 Thessalonians: 25, 184
James: 23
1 Peter: 40
1–3 John: 19
Revelation 12–22: 76
4:4–7
Matthew 8–15: 242
4:4–9
1 & 2 Thessalonians: 203
4:5
1 & 2 Thessalonians: 73
4:5–7
Acts 13–28: 290
4:6
Matthew 1–7: 426
Matthew 8–15: 208
Luke 11–17: 12
Ephesians: 269, 379
Philippians: 18, 33, 34, 81, 198, 266
Colossians and Philemon: 35
1 & 2 Thessalonians: 97, 187, 194, 293
James: 261, 276
1 Peter: 194
4:6–7
Mark 1–8: 235
John 12–21: 127
Galatians: 167
1 & 2 Thessalonians: 187, 190
4:7
Matthew 1–7: 138, 215
Luke 1–5: 123
John 12–21: 124
Romans 1–8: 484
Romans 9–16: 324, 356
1 Corinthians: 7
Ephesians: 3, 43
Philippians: 18, 113, 221
Colossians and Philemon: 158
1 & 2 Thessalonians: 14, 316
2 Peter–Jude: 24
1–3 John: 144
4:7, 12, 19
Romans 9–16: 349
4:8
Matthew 16–23: 13
Romans 1–8: 333
Romans 9–16: 187, 377
1 Corinthians: 164
2 Corinthians: 266
Ephesians: 188, 262
Philippians: 20, 47, 81, 107
Colossians and Philemon: 129, 139, 145
1 & 2 Thessalonians: 181, 199
1 Timothy: 106, 163, 225
2 Timothy: 97
Titus: 41
James: 53
1–3 John: 117
4:9
Matthew 1–7: 209
Acts 13–28: 208
2 Corinthians: 485
Galatians: 167
Ephesians: 173
Philippians: 49, 157
Colossians and Philemon: 82
1 & 2 Thessalonians: 204, 313
1 Timothy: 91, 115, 172
4:10
Luke 6–10: 339
Philippians: 1, 31, 193, 215, 216, 269
4:10–13
Philippians: 56
4:10–19
Acts 13–28: 230
Philippians: 4, 192
1 Peter: 116
4:10–20
1 Corinthians: 244
4:11
Matthew 24–28: 62
Acts 13–28: 54, 129
1 Corinthians: 225, 461
Philippians: 18, 276
Colossians and Philemon: 140
1 Timothy: 250
4:11–12
Matthew 1–7: 419
Luke 6–10: 245

John 12–21: 122
Philippians: 34, 180
1 & 2 Thessalonians: 252
James: 22
4:11–13
Matthew 8–15: 194
Mark 1–8: 292
Philippians: 3, 306
1 Timothy: 251
4:12
Romans 1–8: 446
2 Corinthians: 228
1 & 2 Thessalonians: 172
4:12–14
Ephesians: 183
4:13
Matthew 1–7: 174
1 Corinthians: 476
2 Corinthians: 154
Ephesians: 8, 43, 337
1 & 2 Thessalonians: 185, 318
1 Timothy: 28
2 Timothy: 22
Hebrews: 333
1 Peter: 245
Revelation 1–11: 44
4:14–16
Philippians: 18
Hebrews: 428
4:15
Acts 13–28: 148
2 Corinthians: 276
Philippians: 4, 199, 266, 268
1 & 2 Thessalonians: 77
4:15–16
Philippians: 20, 22, 162, 296
4:15–18
Matthew 1–7: 359
2 Corinthians: 280
4:16
Luke 11–17: 333
2 Corinthians: 231, 273
1 & 2 Thessalonians: 5, 24, 48, 306
4:16–17
Romans 1–8: 45
4:17
Matthew 1–7: 358
John 12–21: 149
4:18
2 Corinthians: 173, 276
Philippians: 5, 192, 202, 297, 306, 315
1 Timothy: 218
Titus: 100
4:19
Matthew 1–7: 420
Matthew 8–15: 276
Luke 1–5: 257
Luke 6–10: 245
Luke 11–17: 14, 140, 144
Luke 18–24: 257
John 12–21: 108
Romans 1–8: 475
1 Corinthians: 204
2 Corinthians: 279, 280
Ephesians: 301, 359
Philippians: 75, 275
1 & 2 Thessalonians: 185, 195, 252
1 Timothy: 251
Hebrews: 354
James: 38, 41
1 Peter: 128
2 Peter–Jude: 25
1–3 John: 107, 184
4:20
2 Corinthians: 44, 158
1 & 2 Thessalonians: 224
1 Peter: 31
4:21
John 12–21: 117
2 Corinthians: 196
1 & 2 Thessalonians: 59
4:21–22
Revelation 1–11: 320
4:22
Acts 13–28: 104, 369, 375
Romans 1–8: 45
Romans 9–16: 366, 367
Philippians: 5, 57, 61
4:23
2 Corinthians: 487

Colossians

1:1
Acts 13–28: 47
2 Corinthians: 17, 410
Philippians: 196
Colossians and Philemon: 70
1 & 2 Thessalonians: 13
1 Timothy: 6
1:1–2
Colossians and Philemon: 13
1:1–8
Colossians and Philemon: 11, 13
1:2
2 Corinthians: 45, 196, 487
Philippians: 15, 310, 311, 314
1 & 2 Thessalonians: 59, 224, 225
Revelation 1–11: 24, 320
1:2–3
Philippians: 16
1:3
Matthew 16–23: 68
Romans 1–8: 35
Philippians: 16, 19, 39
1 & 2 Thessalonians: 87, 253, 293
2 Timothy: 6
1:3–4
Colossians and Philemon: 15
1:3–6
Mark 1–8: 213
Romans 9–16: 327
1:3, 9
Ephesians: 103
1:3–12
1 & 2 Thessalonians: 69
1:4
Romans 9–16: 371
Philippians: 41
1 Timothy: 32
Revelation 1–11: 99, 320
1:4–5
1 & 2 Thessalonians: 15
1:4, 13
Luke 1–5: 284
1:5
Luke 11–17: 13
John 1–11: 43
2 Corinthians: 108, 206, 229, 285, 465, 477
Colossians and Philemon: 12, 19
1 & 2 Thessalonians: 73, 283, 319
2 Timothy: 76
Hebrews: 168
James: 62
1–3 John: 108
1:5–6
Romans 9–16: 88
Philippians: 53, 78
1:5b–6
2 Peter–Jude: 50
1:5–7
Colossians and Philemon: 6
1:6
Matthew 8–15: 361
Mark 1–8: 206
Colossians and Philemon: 21–22
1 & 2 Thessalonians: 59
1:6–7
Revelation 1–11: 134
1:7
Acts 13–28: 210
1 Corinthians: 99
2 Corinthians: 473
Philippians: 202
1 Timothy: 125
Revelation 12–22: 200, 293
1:7–8
Colossians and Philemon: 23
1:8
Galatians: 165
2 Timothy: 18
1:9
Acts 1–12: 180
Romans 1–8: 433, 475
1 Corinthians: 191
Ephesians: 219
Colossians and Philemon: 27
1 & 2 Thessalonians: 186, 293
James: 237
1 Peter: 274
1:9–10
1 Corinthians: 18
1 & 2 Thessalonians: 96
James: 36
2 Peter–Jude: 24
1–3 John: 84
1:9–11
Acts 1–12: 12

Romans 1–8: 39
2 Corinthians: 475
Ephesians: 103
Colossians and Philemon: 25, 26
1 & 2 Thessalonians: 253
1:9–12
1 & 2 Thessalonians: 83, 86, 188
1:10
Matthew 1–7: 469
Matthew 16–23: 299
Mark 1–8: 212
Acts 1–12: 283
1 Corinthians: 82
2 Corinthians: 73, 173, 174
Galatians: 164, 171
Ephesians: 210
Philippians: 38, 85, 218
Colossians and Philemon: 30–32
1 & 2 Thessalonians: 52, 97, 158, 257
James: 237
1–3 John: 28, 36, 111, 220
1:10–11
1 Corinthians: 476
2 Timothy: 22
1:11
2 Corinthians: 227
Colossians and Philemon: 33–34
1 & 2 Thessalonians: 257
1:11–13
Ephesians: 342
1:12
Acts 13–28: 336
Romans 1–8: 400, 443
1 Corinthians: 18
2 Corinthians: 212, 232, 249
Colossians and Philemon: 34, 37
1 & 2 Thessalonians: 74, 164, 257
1 Peter: 35, 37
1–3 John: 37
Revelation 1–11: 320
1:12–13
Acts 13–28: 336
2 Corinthians: 134
Philippians: 85
1:12–14
2 Corinthians: 249
Colossians and Philemon: 35, 37, 39
1–3 John: 29
1:12–16
Ephesians: 259
1:13
Matthew 1–7: 240
Matthew 8–15: 310
Matthew 16–23: 96
Mark 1–8: 48, 58, 118, 210
Mark 9–16: 66
Luke 1–5: 50, 122, 272, 281, 285, 288
Luke 6–10: 218
Luke 11–17: 22, 281
Luke 18–24: 124, 270
John 12–21: 55, 128, 189, 262
Acts 1–12: 15, 16
Romans 1–8: 55
2 Corinthians: 71, 212, 244, 249, 257
Ephesians: 207, 208, 341
Philippians: 85
Colossians and Philemon: 40
1 & 2 Thessalonians: 52, 155, 157
Titus: 153
1–3 John: 66, 83, 94
Revelation 1–11: 26, 47, 125, 266
Revelation 12–22: 89, 180, 229, 236, 243
1:13–14
Matthew 1–7: 125
Mark 1–8: 183, 198, 238
Luke 11–17: 67
Romans 1–8: 215
Colossians and Philemon: 40
1:13–16
Luke 1–5: 296
1:14
Luke 1–5: 272, 321
Luke 11–17: 37
Acts 1–12: 75, 117, 303
Acts 13–28: 336
Romans 9–16: 283
2 Corinthians: 31, 52
1 Peter: 191
1–3 John: 37, 84
1:15
John 12–21: 55, 105
2 Corinthians: 19, 113
Philippians: 123
Colossians and Philemon: 44
1 Timothy: 140
Hebrews: 16, 30
Revelation 12–22: 267
1:15–17
Revelation 1–11: 134
1:15–19
Matthew 1–7: 81
Colossians and Philemon: 43, 44
1:15, 18
Luke 1–5: 196
1:16
Matthew 16–23: 26
Mark 1–8: 57, 226, 232, 330
Luke 1–5: 196, 304
Luke 11–17: 24
Luke 18–24: 58, 81, 355
John 1–11: 16, 17, 20
Acts 13–28: 137
Romans 1–8: 212
2 Corinthians: 290
Ephesians: 96
Colossians and Philemon: 9
Hebrews: 11
2 Peter–Jude: 26
Revelation 1–11: 158, 228, 238
1:16–17
Luke 1–5: 57
Colossians and Philemon: 47–50
Hebrews: 23
1:17
John 1–11: 14
John 12–21: 202
1:18
Luke 1–5: 196
Luke 18–24: 455
John 1–11: 15
John 12–21: 116, 289
Acts 1–12: 104
Romans 1–8: 493
1 Corinthians: 253, 310
Colossians and Philemon: 2, 9, 51–52
1 & 2 Thessalonians: 108
2 Timothy: 57
Hebrews: 30
1–3 John: 256
Revelation 1–11: 47
1:19
2 Corinthians: 44, 133
Philippians: 308
Colossians and Philemon: 52, 56, 103
1:19–20
Matthew 1–7: 213
Ephesians: 79
1:19–22
Romans 1–8: 274
1:20
Luke 18–24: 260
John 12–21: 124
Acts 1–12: 84, 302
Philippians: 257
Colossians and Philemon: 9, 56
1 & 2 Thessalonians: 204, 314
Hebrews: 416, 451
2 Peter–Jude: 24
1–3 John: 219
Revelation 1–11: 232
Revelation 12–22: 308
1:20–21
Colossians and Philemon: 56
1:20, 22
John 12–21: 133
1:20–22
Luke 1–5: 161
2 Corinthians: 200
1 Peter: 130, 206
1–3 John: 37, 46
1:20–23
Colossians and Philemon: 55, 56, 75
1:21
John 12–21: 196
Romans 1–8: 495
2 Corinthians: 210
Philippians: 85, 286
1 & 2 Thessalonians: 209

Titus: 146
James: 197, 225
1 Peter: 275
1:21–22
Romans 1–8: 345
Ephesians: 355
1:21–23
Acts 13–28: 33, 55
1 & 2 Thessalonians: 20, 166, 203, 207
2 Timothy: 64
1 Peter: 36
1–3 John: 99, 111, 149
Revelation 1–11: 79
Revelation 12–22: 101, 238
1:22
2 Corinthians: 201
Philippians: 130, 182
Colossians and Philemon: 2, 7, 62, 64
Revelation 1–11: 45
Revelation 12–22: 80
1:22–23
Romans 9–16: 117, 312
Philippians: 163
Revelation 1–11: 126
1:23
Luke 6–10: 192
Acts 1–12: 272
Romans 9–16: 275
2 Corinthians: 78, 108, 125
Colossians and Philemon: 6, 65, 70
1 & 2 Thessalonians: 89, 298
1 Timothy: 32, 181
1–3 John: 15, 60
1:23–25
1 Timothy: 28
1:24
Matthew 8–15: 206
John 12–21: 173
Acts 1–12: 174
Acts 13–28: 194
Romans 1–8: 48
2 Corinthians: 25, 144, 146
Galatians: 211
Ephesians: 88
Philippians: 94, 194
Colossians and Philemon: 73–74
1 & 2 Thessalonians: 108, 166, 184
1 Timothy: 174
2 Timothy: 26
1:24–25, 29
Romans 9–16: 341
1:24–29
Colossians and Philemon: 69
1 & 2 Thessalonians: 293, 295
1:25
Acts 1–12: 272
Acts 13–28: 15
Romans 9–16: 336
1 Corinthians: 98, 209
2 Corinthians: 78, 125, 173, 189
Colossians and Philemon: 70, 76
Titus: 14, 49
1:25–26
Romans 9–16: 386
Ephesians: 88
1:25–27
2 Timothy: 147
1:25–29
2 Timothy: 173, 186
1:26
Romans 1–8: 4
1 Corinthians: 298
2 Corinthians: 132
1 Timothy: 128
1:26–27
2 Corinthians: 109
Colossians and Philemon: 78
1 Timothy: 128
Revelation 1–11: 286
1:27
Luke 11–17: 13
John 12–21: 117
Romans 9–16: 387
2 Corinthians: 108, 145, 279, 360, 466
Ephesians: 92, 106
Philippians: 170, 283
1 & 2 Thessalonians: 18, 73
1 Timothy: 5
1 Peter: 33
2 Peter–Jude: 30
1:27–28
1 Timothy: 264
1–3 John: 29
1:28
Acts 13–28: 15, 81, 198, 228
Romans 9–16: 151
2 Corinthians: 45, 196
Ephesians: 117, 154
Philippians: 49, 248, 311
Colossians and Philemon: 7, 79–80
1 & 2 Thessalonians: 59, 168, 169, 170, 177
1 Timothy: 159
1:28–29
Romans 1–8: 42
Romans 9–16: 334
1 Corinthians: 464
2 Corinthians: 478
Ephesians: 158
Philippians: 154
1 & 2 Thessalonians: 204
1 Timothy: 100, 166, 169
1:29
Luke 11–17: 219, 384
Acts 1–12: 16
Romans 9–16: 191
1 Corinthians: 80
2 Corinthians: 34, 74, 222
Ephesians: 93, 364
Philippians: 164, 168, 245
Colossians and Philemon: 81
1 & 2 Thessalonians: 282, 289, 317, 320
2 Timothy: 192, 202
1–3 John: 113
Revelation 12–22: 203
2:1
Colossians and Philemon: 6
1 & 2 Thessalonians: 125
Revelation 1–11: 134
2:1–4
Romans 9–16: 351
2:1–7
Colossians and Philemon: 83
2:2
John 12–21: 162
Romans 9–16: 387
1 Corinthians: 298
2 Corinthians: 279, 360
Ephesians: 92, 95
Colossians and Philemon: 84, 87
1 & 2 Thessalonians: 90, 96
2 Peter–Jude: 24
Revelation 1–11: 286
2:2–3
Romans 9–16: 327
1 Corinthians: 363
2 Corinthians: 109
Ephesians: xi
2:2–5
Colossians and Philemon: 89
2:3
2 Corinthians: 140
Galatians: 96
Ephesians: 95, 218
Philippians: 254, 308
Colossians and Philemon: 7, 9, 28, 44
James: 167, 177
2:3, 10
Romans 9–16: 139
2:4–5, 16–19
1–3 John: 101
2:5
Philippians: 267
1 & 2 Thessalonians: 206
2:6
Galatians: 120, 189
Colossians and Philemon: 6
1 & 2 Thessalonians: 52
2:6–7
Romans 9–16: 256
Galatians: 171
Colossians and Philemon: 2, 92–93
1 & 2 Thessalonians: 190
Hebrews: 313
2:7
Romans 9–16: 268
Ephesians: 269
1 & 2 Thessalonians: 97, 189
1–3 John: 72
2:8
Matthew 1–7: 463
Matthew 16–23: 14
Romans 1–8: 86
1 Corinthians: 36, 252
Galatians: 105, 196

Colossians and Philemon: 98–103
1 & 2 Thessalonians: 288
1 Timothy: 159
Hebrews: 293
James: 92
1 Peter: 137
2 Peter–Jude: 79
1–3 John: 103
2:8–10
Colossians and Philemon: 95
2 Peter–Jude: 25–26
2:9
Matthew 1–7: 81
Mark 1–8: 224
Luke 1–5: 49, 229, 240, 249
Luke 11–17: 393
Luke 18–24: 155
John 1–11: 7, 14
2 Corinthians: 19, 109, 123, 140
Galatians: 60
Philippians: 308
Colossians and Philemon: 2, 7, 9, 44, 52, 56, 103–4
Hebrews: 16
2 Peter–Jude: 23, 26
1–3 John: 16, 100
2:9–14
1 & 2 Thessalonians: 185
2:10
John 1–11: 16
1 Corinthians: 16, 19
Ephesians: 95, 377
Colossians and Philemon: 2, 7, 9, 52, 103, 106, 124
Hebrews: 68, 254
2:11
Romans 1–8: 329
2 Corinthians: 163
Colossians and Philemon: 8
2:11–12
Colossians and Philemon: 106–9
2:11–14
Romans 1–8: 210
1–3 John: 143
2:11–15
Colossians and Philemon: 105–13
2:12
Matthew 1–7: 79
Matthew 24–28: 305
2 Corinthians: 147
1 & 2 Thessalonians: 282
1 Timothy: 272
2 Peter–Jude: 26
2:12–14
1 Peter: 172
2:13
Luke 6–10: 175
Acts 1–12: 75, 267
1 Corinthians: 79
2 Corinthians: 52, 205
Ephesians: 195
Colossians and Philemon: 5
1 Peter: 18, 21, 50
2 Peter–Jude: 29
1–3 John: 127
Revelation 1–11: 111
2:13–14
Mark 1–8: 97
Luke 1–5: 321, 334
Luke 11–17: 40
Acts 13–28: 26
Romans 9–16: 67
2 Corinthians: 31
Colossians and Philemon: 9, 109
1 Peter: 48, 191
Revelation 1–11: 167
2:14
Mark 1–8: 32
Mark 9–16: 375
Luke 1–5: 272
John 12–21: 87, 240
Acts 1–12: 117
Philippians: 257
2:14–15
Philippians: 146, 238
Hebrews: 255
2:15
John 1–11: 16, 24
John 12–21: 18, 198, 231
Acts 13–28: 169
Romans 1–8: 516
2 Corinthians: 71, 293
Ephesians: 139, 341
Colossians and Philemon: 59–60, 112
1 & 2 Thessalonians: 88
1 Timothy: 141
1 Peter: 216
Revelation 1–11: 167, 168
Revelation 12–22: 8, 10
2:16
Matthew 8–15: 287
Mark 1–8: 141
Romans 1–8: 202
2 Corinthians: 281
Hebrews: 438
Revelation 12–22: 5
2:16, 17
Romans 9–16: 281
Colossians and Philemon: 8
2:16–17
Matthew 1–7: 257
Matthew 16–23: 23
Mark 9–16: 378
Luke 18–24: 409
Acts 1–12: 296
Acts 13–28: 64, 202
Colossians and Philemon: 44, 116
1 Timothy: 154
Hebrews: 101
2:16–17, 20–23
Galatians: 111
2:16–23
Colossians and Philemon: 115
1 & 2 Thessalonians: 179, 208
1 Timothy: 153
2:17
2 Corinthians: 89
Philippians: 259
Colossians and Philemon: 9
Hebrews: 129, 247
2:18
1 Corinthians: 86, 183, 235
Colossians and Philemon: 7, 44
1 & 2 Thessalonians: 110
1 Timothy: 241
Hebrews: 25, 415
Revelation 12–22: 207, 296
2:18–19
Colossians and Philemon: 119
2:19
Ephesians: 160, 161
2:20–22
Galatians: 209
Colossians and Philemon: 8
2:20–23
Colossians and Philemon: 122
1 Timothy: xi
2 Peter–Jude: 79
1–3 John: 101, 159
2:23
1 Corinthians: 183
Colossians and Philemon: 8
1 & 2 Thessalonians: 205
James: 211
3:1
Luke 1–5: 236
Luke 18–24: 307, 339, 453
John 12–21: 273
Acts 1–12: 67, 222
Colossians and Philemon: 126–30
1 & 2 Thessalonians: 234
Revelation 1–11: 145
Revelation 12–22: 214
3:1–2
Matthew 1–7: 144
Luke 11–17: 144
Philippians: 302
James: 145
Revelation 12–22: 260
3:1, 3, 9, 10
Ephesians: 176
3:1–3
Romans 1–8: 424
Galatians: 209
3:1–4
Colossians and Philemon: 125
2 Peter–Jude: 138
3:1–10
1 Peter: 66–67
3:1–17
Ephesians: 191
3:1–4:6
1 & 2 Thessalonians: 203
3:2
Romans 1–8: 416
Romans 9–16: 151
1 Corinthians: 182
2 Corinthians: 157
Ephesians: 354, 380

Philippians: 107, 289
Colossians and Philemon: 6, 128–29
1 Timothy: 265
Hebrews: 331, 435
James: 53, 195
1 Peter: 41
3:2–3
Philippians: 161
3:3
Romans 1–8: 319
1 Corinthians: 10
2 Corinthians: 193
Colossians and Philemon: 2, 130
1 & 2 Thessalonians: 14, 104, 158, 225
2 Peter–Jude: 31
1–3 John: 19
3:3–4
1 Peter: 106
3:4
Matthew 24–28: 55, 115
Luke 18–24: 191
Romans 1–8: 131, 454
2 Corinthians: 194
Philippians: 28
Colossians and Philemon: 3, 132
1 & 2 Thessalonians: 52, 92
1 Timothy: 273
2 Timothy: 3
1 Peter: 200, 235
1–3 John: 117
Revelation 1–11: 30
Revelation 12–22: 211
3:5
Matthew 16–23: 48
Mark 1–8: 426
Mark 9–16: 46
1 Corinthians: 10
2 Corinthians: 309
Galatians: 156
Ephesians: 116, 172
Colossians and Philemon: 138
1 & 2 Thessalonians: 104, 105, 109, 199, 205
Hebrews: 254
James: 145
1–3 John: 36
3:5–6
Romans 1–8: 62
3:5–7
1 & 2 Thessalonians: 108
3:5–9
Colossians and Philemon: 135
3:5–10
Romans 1–8: 425
1 & 2 Thessalonians: 109
3:5–10, 12–14
Romans 9–16: 266
3:5–17
1 & 2 Thessalonians: 208
3:6
Luke 1–5: 215
Romans 9–16: 202
Colossians and Philemon: 141
1 & 2 Thessalonians: 163
Revelation 12–22: 137
3:7
Colossians and Philemon: 142
3:7–8
Hebrews: 254
3:8
Matthew 8–15: 321
Ephesians: 187, 201
1 Timothy: 55
James: 145, 218
3:8–9
Acts 1–12: 190
Romans 9–16: 264
Colossians and Philemon: 143
3:8–10
James: 74
1 Peter: 89
3:8–17
1 Peter: 173
3:9
Acts 1–12: 84
Philippians: 45
James: 264
1 Peter: 192
2 Peter–Jude: 13
3:9–10
Matthew 1–7: 206
Acts 1–12: 191
Romans 1–8: 325
Romans 9–16: 256
1 Corinthians: 10
Colossians and Philemon: 148
Titus: 115
3:9–14
Ephesians: 352
3:9–17
Colossians and Philemon: 147
3:9–20
1 & 2 Thessalonians: 287
3:10
Matthew 16–23: 24
Romans 1–8: 333
2 Corinthians: 116, 153
Galatians: 64
Colossians and Philemon: 28, 45, 65, 150
1 & 2 Thessalonians: 96
1 Peter: 92
2 Peter–Jude: 24
3:10, 16
Romans 9–16: 151
3:11
Mark 9–16: 140
John 12–21: 168
Acts 13–28: 199
2 Corinthians: 194, 466
Ephesians: 66
Philippians: 218
Colossians and Philemon: 8, 151
Revelation 1–11: 38, 296
3:11–14
Romans 9–16: 306
3:12
Matthew 1–7: 171
Matthew 16–23: 231
Mark 9–16: 33, 101
Luke 1–5: 120
Acts 13–28: 38, 268
Romans 9–16: 198
2 Corinthians: 257
Galatians: 168, 169
Ephesians: 124, 178
Philippians: 32, 105
1 & 2 Thessalonians: 20, 97, 287
Titus: 145
1 Peter: 17
Revelation 1–11: 54
3:12–13
Colossians and Philemon: 88, 153
1 & 2 Thessalonians: 180, 287
1 Peter: 27
3:12–14
Acts 1–12: 191
Romans 9–16: 247
1–3 John: 165
3:12–15
Philippians: 100
3:12–16
Philippians: 109
3:12–17
Romans 9–16: 329
Philippians: 162
3:12–4:6
1 & 2 Thessalonians: 97
3:13
Matthew 16–23: 143
Luke 1–5: 321
Acts 1–12: 84
2 Corinthians: 57
Colossians and Philemon: 201
3:14
John 12–21: 292
Romans 9–16: 250, 273
1 Corinthians: 330
2 Corinthians: 186
Ephesians: 128
Philippians: 41, 270
Colossians and Philemon: 88, 157–58
1 & 2 Thessalonians: 90, 117
3:15
Matthew 1–7: 215
John 12–21: 128
Colossians and Philemon: 158
1 & 2 Thessalonians: 174, 256
3:15–17
1 & 2 Thessalonians: 190
James: 145
3:16
Matthew 1–7: 265
Matthew 8–15: 217
Luke 1–5: 93
John 12–21: 148
Acts 1–12: 19, 84, 133
Romans 1–8: 433, 475
1 Corinthians: 328

2 Corinthians: viii
Galatians: 154
Ephesians: 95, 219
Philippians: 249, 291
Colossians and Philemon: vi, 79, 139, 145, 159
1 & 2 Thessalonians: 89, 108, 166, 168, 170, 185, 194, 259
1 Timothy: 240
2 Timothy: 157
1 Peter: vii, 290
2 Peter–Jude: vii
1–3 John: 76
3:16–25
Acts 1–12: 41
Ephesians: 252
3:16ff.
1 Timothy: 138
3:17
Acts 1–12: 104
Philippians: 24
Colossians and Philemon: 36, 160
1 & 2 Thessalonians: 96, 189
Hebrews: 210
1–3 John: 248
3:18
Ephesians: 282
Colossians and Philemon: 166
1 & 2 Thessalonians: 43
3:18–19
1 Corinthians: 182
3:18–21
1 & 2 Thessalonians: 97
3:18–4:1
Colossians and Philemon: 163, 164
3:19
Colossians and Philemon: 168
1 & 2 Thessalonians: 90
3:20
2 Corinthians: 173
Ephesians: 312
Colossians and Philemon: 170
Titus: 99
3:21
Luke 18–24: 23
Colossians and Philemon: 171
1 & 2 Thessalonians: 50
3:22
2 Corinthians: 279
1 Timothy: 234, 235
3:22–24
1 & 2 Thessalonians: 120
3:22–25
Colossians and Philemon: 174
1 Timothy: 234
3:23
1 Corinthians: 173
Ephesians: 328
1 Timothy: 235
3:23–24
Acts 13–28: 5
3:24
Acts 13–28: 210, 336
Romans 1–8: 444
2 Corinthians: 349
Philippians: 199
Titus: 98
1 Peter: 35
Revelation 1–11: 319
3:24–25
Matthew 16–23: 208
1 & 2 Thessalonians: 74
1 Timothy: 235
3:25
Romans 1–8: 136
James: 95, 97
1–3 John: 39
Revelation 12–22: 251
4:1
Colossians and Philemon: 175
James: 95
4:2
Luke 11–17: 2
Acts 1–12: 85
Ephesians: 103, 379, 381
Philippians: 283
Colossians and Philemon: 27, 35, 179
1 & 2 Thessalonians: 187, 190, 194
James: 276
4:2–3
John 12–21: 272
Romans 9–16: 352
Revelation 1–11: 123
4:2–4
Colossians and Philemon: 4
1 & 2 Thessalonians: 211, 214, 294
4:2–6
Colossians and Philemon: 177
4:3
Romans 9–16: 387
1 Corinthians: 298, 465
2 Corinthians: 27, 67, 109, 189, 360
Ephesians: 92
Philippians: 58
1 & 2 Thessalonians: 293
1 Timothy: 128
4:3–4
Colossians and Philemon: 183
4:5
Matthew 8–15: 201
1 Corinthians: 197
Colossians and Philemon: 185
1 Timothy: 119
4:6
Ephesians: 189
Colossians and Philemon: 187
1 & 2 Thessalonians: 172
James: 221
1 Peter: 202
2 Peter–Jude: 134
4:7
Acts 13–28: 210
1 Corinthians: 99
2 Corinthians: 45
Philippians: 58, 311, 315
2 Timothy: 210
Titus: 167
Revelation 12–22: 200
4:7–8
Colossians and Philemon: 192
4:7–9
Ephesians: 385
4:7–18
Colossians and Philemon: 189
4:9
Philippians: 316
Colossians and Philemon: 193, 203
4:10
Mark 1–8: 1
Luke 6–10: 202
Acts 1–12: 150, 328
Acts 13–28: 7, 82, 346
Philippians: 198, 316
Colossians and Philemon: 194–95
2 Timothy: 209, 210
4:10–11
Mark 1–8: 2
Acts 13–28: 187
4:10–12
Acts 13–28: 376
4:10–14
Luke 1–5: 2
4:10, 11
Luke 1–5: 11
4:11
Luke 11–17: 405
2 Corinthians: 307
Philippians: 203, 218
Colossians and Philemon: 194, 195, 197
4:12
John 12–21: 272
Romans 9–16: 352
2 Corinthians: 478
Ephesians: 154
Philippians: 202, 248
Colossians and Philemon: 6
1 & 2 Thessalonians: 44
1 Timothy: 264
2 Timothy: 193
James: 12, 237
2 Peter–Jude: 18
4:12–13
Acts 13–28: 55
Ephesians: 153
Colossians and Philemon: 196
4:12–14
2 Timothy: 206
1–3 John: 80
4:12–17
Luke 1–5: 11
4:13
1 & 2 Thessalonians: 70
4:14
Luke 1–5: 1, 4, 10, 11, 12
Luke 11–17: 61
Luke 18–24: 306
Acts 13–28: 204, 376
Romans 9–16: 378

Philippians: 7, 198
Colossians and Philemon: 4, 197–98, 230
2 Timothy: 208
4:15
Acts 13–28: 203
4:15–16
Colossians and Philemon: 84
4:15–18
Colossians and Philemon: 198
4:16
1 Timothy: 176
2 Peter–Jude: 9
Revelation 1–11: 134
4:17
1 Corinthians: 480
Revelation 1–11: 134
4:18
Philippians: 58, 310, 318
1 & 2 Thessalonians: 318
Hebrews: 428
1 Peter: 8–9

1 Thessalonians
1:1
Acts 13–28: 72
2 Corinthians: 487
Philippians: 16, 196
1 & 2 Thessalonians: 7, 59, 87, 222
1 Timothy: 6
1 Peter: 289
Revelation 1–11: 24
1:1–10
Acts 1–12: 81
1 & 2 Thessalonians: 34
1:2
Philippians: 19, 38
1 & 2 Thessalonians: 1, 57, 76, 212, 253, 293
1:2–3
Acts 13–28: 229
1 & 2 Thessalonians: 76, 176
2 Timothy: 6
1:2–4
1 & 2 Thessalonians: 70, 94
1:2–5
1 & 2 Thessalonians: 1
1:2–7
Ephesians: 152
1:2–10
Romans 9–16: 327
1 & 2 Thessalonians: 7
1 Peter: 22–23, 173
1:3
John 12–21: 223
1 Corinthians: 479
2 Corinthians: 227
Philippians: 16, 41
Colossians and Philemon: 19
1 & 2 Thessalonians: 73, 76, 87, 88, 161, 224, 227, 258, 259, 297
1 Timothy: 32
1 Peter: 63
Revelation 1–11: 99
1:3–4
Romans 1–8: 465
1 & 2 Thessalonians: 116
Hebrews: 154
1:3–10
1 & 2 Thessalonians: 103
1:4
Luke 1–5: 36
2 Corinthians: 257
Colossians and Philemon: 153
1 & 2 Thessalonians: 52
1 Peter: 17
Revelation 1–11: 54
1:4–5
2 Peter–Jude: 29
1:4–6
1 Peter: 21
1:5
Matthew 16–23: 15
Acts 13–28: 123
Romans 9–16: 175
2 Corinthians: 82, 86, 158
Ephesians: 47
Colossians and Philemon: 13
1 & 2 Thessalonians: 76
1:5–6
1 Corinthians: 482
1 & 2 Thessalonians: 97
1 Timothy: 172
1:5–7
Philippians: 121
1:5–9
1 & 2 Thessalonians: 295
1:6
Luke 6–10: 19
Acts 1–12: 259
Acts 13–28: 208
Romans 9–16: 298
2 Corinthians: 194, 277, 278
Philippians: 11, 221, 250, 291
Colossians and Philemon: 22
1 & 2 Thessalonians: 20, 60, 305
1 Timothy: 115
1 Peter: 40
1:6–8
1 & 2 Thessalonians: 297
1:7
1 & 2 Thessalonians: 94
1:7–8
1 & 2 Thessalonians: 116
1:7–9
1 & 2 Thessalonians: 168
1:8
Luke 6–10: 199
Acts 13–28: 123
1 Corinthians: 479
Colossians and Philemon: 21–22
1 & 2 Thessalonians: 118, 228
1 Timothy: 74, 240
Hebrews: 126
1:8–10
1 & 2 Thessalonians: 2
1:9
Matthew 8–15: 471
Matthew 16–23: 98
Mark 1–8: 21, 426
Luke 1–5: 208
Acts 1–12: 73, 114, 282, 313
Acts 13–28: 177, 184, 217, 337
Romans 1–8: 120
2 Corinthians: 244, 253
Ephesians: 176
Colossians and Philemon: 16
1 & 2 Thessalonians: 5, 20, 34, 76, 90, 319
1 Timothy: 9
James: 126, 290
1 Peter: 24, 229
Revelation 1–11: 51, 139
1:9–10
Luke 11–17: 188
1 & 2 Thessalonians: 124, 176
James: 254, 256
Revelation 12–22: 291
1:9b–10a
1 Peter: 63
1:10
Matthew 1–7: 381, 486
Matthew 24–28: 55
Luke 11–17: 178, 408, 411
Luke 18–24: 8, 9, 197, 241, 253, 259
Romans 1–8: 65, 215, 286
Philippians: 261
Colossians and Philemon: 61, 142
1 & 2 Thessalonians: 1, 73, 74, 132, 133, 141, 163, 231, 268, 274
1 Peter: 48, 171, 206
1–3 John: 91
Revelation 1–11: 214
Revelation 12–22: 122, 154, 238, 309
2:1
Acts 13–28: 209
1 & 2 Thessalonians: 51, 142, 305
2:1–2
1 & 2 Thessalonians: 7, 90
2:1–6
1 & 2 Thessalonians: 13
2:1–12
1 & 2 Thessalonians: 7
2:2
Mark 1–8: 47
Luke 18–24: 209
Acts 13–28: 46, 104
2 Corinthians: 389
Philippians: 59
1 & 2 Thessalonians: 21, 51, 57, 78, 305
1 Peter: 3
2:2–4
1 & 2 Thessalonians: 76
2:2, 8, 9
Luke 1–5: 335
2:3
Matthew 8–15: 202

2 Timothy: 73
2:3–4
1 Timothy: 292
2:3–5
1 & 2 Thessalonians: 305
2 Timothy: 184
2:4
Acts 13–28: 210, 248
1 Corinthians: 269
2 Corinthians: 73, 241, 307, 344
Philippians: 199
2 Timothy: 45, 75
2:5
Acts 13–28: 209
2 Corinthians: 43
Ephesians: 172
1 & 2 Thessalonians: 51
1 Timothy: 111, 112
2:5–7
1 & 2 Thessalonians: 76
2:5–8
Mark 1–8: 289
2:6
Matthew 16–23: 240
1 Corinthians: 323
1 & 2 Thessalonians: 305
2:6–7
Galatians: 168
2:7
2 Corinthians: 391
1 & 2 Thessalonians: 305
2 Timothy: 99
2 Peter–Jude: 49
2:7–8
Acts 13–28: 193
Galatians: 120
1 & 2 Thessalonians: 1, 97
Titus: 25
2:7–9
Matthew 16–23: 362
Romans 1–8: 42
2:7–11
1 & 2 Thessalonians: 24
2:7–12
2 Corinthians: 474
Ephesians: 160
1 & 2 Thessalonians: 82
1 Timothy: 175
2:8
Romans 9–16: 175
1 & 2 Thessalonians: 5, 57, 76, 78, 305
2:8–9
Mark 1–8: 47
1 & 2 Thessalonians: 35
1 Peter: 268
2:9
Acts 13–28: 228, 230
1 Corinthians: 208
2 Corinthians: 228, 231, 390
Philippians: 300, 306
1 & 2 Thessalonians: 5, 21, 24, 51, 57, 78, 168, 305, 306
1 Timothy: 201, 261
2:9–11
1 & 2 Thessalonians: 76
2:10
1 & 2 Thessalonians: 305
1 Timothy: 124
Titus: 42
2:10–11
Acts 13–28: 209
2:10–12
Matthew 1–7: 271
1 Corinthians: 115
1 & 2 Thessalonians: 90
1 Peter: 70
2:11
Acts 13–28: 55
Ephesians: 148
1–3 John: 247
2:11–12
1 & 2 Thessalonians: 1, 5
2 Timothy: 178
2:12
Luke 18–24: 9–10
Philippians: 85
Colossians and Philemon: 30, 41
1 & 2 Thessalonians: 112, 158, 229, 256, 257
Revelation 12–22: 243
2:13
Mark 1–8: 205
Luke 6–10: 364
Acts 13–28: 229
Romans 1–8: 486
Romans 9–16: 334
2 Corinthians: 82
Philippians: 19, 292
1 & 2 Thessalonians: 12, 70, 76, 98, 116, 293
2 Timothy: 147, 152
Hebrews: 100
James: 63, 75
1 Peter: 23
2 Peter–Jude: 9, 50, 136, 196
1–3 John: 123
2:13–14
1 & 2 Thessalonians: 2, 94
1 Peter: 173
2:13–16
1 & 2 Thessalonians: 7
2:14
1 Corinthians: 450
1 & 2 Thessalonians: 14, 97
1 Peter: 3
2:14–15
2 Corinthians: 277
1 & 2 Thessalonians: 25
2:14–16
Matthew 16–23: 378
Luke 1–5: 50
Acts 13–28: 125
1 & 2 Thessalonians: 2, 136, 222
1 Peter: 140
1–3 John: 84
2:15
Luke 18–24: 338
2:16
1 & 2 Thessalonians: 141
2 Peter–Jude: 89
2:17
Acts 13–28: 80
1 & 2 Thessalonians: 28, 109, 142
2:17–18
Acts 13–28: 124
Romans 9–16: 345
1 & 2 Thessalonians: 6
1 Timothy: 36
2:17–20
1 & 2 Thessalonians: 1, 76
2:18
Luke 18–24: 294
2 Corinthians: 408, 482
Ephesians: 332, 336, 338, 347
Philippians: 59
1 & 2 Thessalonians: 7, 166, 217, 295
1 Peter: 280
Revelation 1–11: 255
Revelation 12–22: 235
2:19
Mark 1–8: 218
Galatians: 191
Philippians: 188, 269
1 & 2 Thessalonians: 1, 28, 124, 268
Hebrews: 380
James: 253
Revelation 12–22: 113, 302
2:19–20
1 Corinthians: 85
2 Corinthians: 37
Philippians: 269
1 & 2 Thessalonians: 2, 176
Hebrews: 447
2:20
1 & 2 Thessalonians: 76
3:1–2
1 & 2 Thessalonians: 6, 7
3:1–3
1 & 2 Thessalonians: 68
3:1–6
Acts 13–28: 148
3:1–12
1 & 2 Thessalonians: 1
3:2
Acts 13–28: 83
Romans 9–16: 378
2 Corinthians: 18
1 & 2 Thessalonians: 141, 155, 223, 225
1 Timothy: 6
3:2–4
1 & 2 Thessalonians: 178
2 Timothy: 132
3:3
Romans 1–8: 282
1 & 2 Thessalonians: 305
1 Peter: 42
3:3–4
Matthew 1–7: 221
1 & 2 Thessalonians: 124

3:3–5
1 & 2 Thessalonians: 228
3:4
1 & 2 Thessalonians: 25
3:5
Luke 1–5: 255
2 Corinthians: 482
1 & 2 Thessalonians: 6, 56, 68, 76, 77, 166
James: 26
Revelation 1–11: 310
3:6
1 & 2 Thessalonians: 8, 13, 56, 141, 155, 225
1 Timothy: 32, 263
Revelation 1–11: 99
3:6–7
1 & 2 Thessalonians: 70
3:6–9
1 & 2 Thessalonians: 7
3:6–10
1 & 2 Thessalonians: 5
3:7
Acts 13–28: 146
2 Corinthians: 227
1 & 2 Thessalonians: 76
3:8
1 & 2 Thessalonians: 176, 288
3:9
1 & 2 Thessalonians: 2, 185
Hebrews: 447
3:9–10
1 & 2 Thessalonians: 176
3:9–13
1 & 2 Thessalonians: 70, 293
3:10
1 Corinthians: 464
2 Corinthians: 390, 475, 483
1 & 2 Thessalonians: 71, 95, 118, 187, 225, 253, 305
1 Timothy: 201
James: 26
3:10–13
1 & 2 Thessalonians: 70
3:11
1 & 2 Thessalonians: 224, 297
3:11–13
1 & 2 Thessalonians: 1, 202, 203, 253, 289
3:12
John 12–21: 91
Romans 9–16: 184
1 Corinthians: 330
Philippians: 45
1 & 2 Thessalonians: 47, 95, 96, 176, 227
1 Peter: 93
3:12–13
1 & 2 Thessalonians: 297
James: 255
3:13
Matthew 16–23: 69
Philippians: 181
1 & 2 Thessalonians: 28, 74, 78, 104, 108, 124, 132, 224, 268
James: 253
2 Peter–Jude: 64, 117, 212
Revelation 1–11: 320
Revelation 12–22: 302
4:1
Romans 1–8: 419
2 Corinthians: 73, 174, 484
Ephesians: 116, 148
Philippians: 85
1 & 2 Thessalonians: 78, 118, 142, 158, 164, 166, 176, 257, 293, 297
1–3 John: 37
4:1–2
Philippians: 292
1 & 2 Thessalonians: 103
4:1–8
1 & 2 Thessalonians: 7, 204
4:1–12
1 & 2 Thessalonians: 1
4:3
Ephesians: 226
Colossians and Philemon: 29, 138
1 & 2 Thessalonians: 210
Hebrews: 254
1 Peter: 129
Revelation 12–22: 77
4:3–4
1 & 2 Thessalonians: 202, 287
4:3–5
1 Corinthians: 149
James: 187
4:3–8
1 & 2 Thessalonians: 117, 136
James: 235
4:3–12
1 & 2 Thessalonians: 203
4:3, 7
2 Timothy: 91
4:5
Romans 1–8: 102
Ephesians: 165
Colossians and Philemon: 139
1 & 2 Thessalonians: 242
James: 52
1 Peter: 140
4:6
Matthew 16–23: 117
Luke 11–17: 377
2 Corinthians: 473
1 & 2 Thessalonians: 141, 180
4:7
Colossians and Philemon: 139
1 & 2 Thessalonians: 202, 256
Titus: 8
4:9
Acts 1–12: 84
Romans 9–16: 188, 249, 371
1 Corinthians: 330
Philippians: 32
1 & 2 Thessalonians: 17, 90, 142, 228
1 Timothy: 202
1 Peter: 93
1–3 John: 130
4:9–10
Philippians: 41, 42, 101
1 & 2 Thessalonians: 2, 124, 227
Hebrews: 423
4:9–12
1 & 2 Thessalonians: 7
4:10
1 & 2 Thessalonians: 78, 95, 176
4:10–12
Ephesians: 327
4:11
Matthew 8–15: 186
2 Corinthians: 172
1 & 2 Thessalonians: 307
1 Timothy: 66
1 Peter: 255
4:11–12
Romans 9–16: 214
1 & 2 Thessalonians: 204, 218, 303, 304, 305, 308
4:13
Romans 1–8: 44
1 Corinthians: 191, 282
2 Corinthians: 25, 170
Ephesians: 74
Philippians: 58, 206
1 & 2 Thessalonians: 142
4:13–14
1 Corinthians: 427
4:13–15
Mark 1–8: 264
John 1–11: 456
Philippians: 79
1 & 2 Thessalonians: 164
4:13–17
Matthew 24–28: 67
Titus: 119
2 Peter–Jude: 185
Revelation 1–11: 124
Revelation 12–22: 266
4:13–18
Luke 18–24: 10
1 Corinthians: 279, 416
1 & 2 Thessalonians: 91, 142, 155, 265, 268
1 Timothy: 273
2 Timothy: 169
James: 256
1 Peter: 231
2 Peter–Jude: 112
Revelation 1–11: 201
Revelation 12–22: 15, 213, 250, 262
4:13–5:11
1 & 2 Thessalonians: 1, 7, 116, 215, 218, 268
James: 174
4:14
Acts 1–12: 226
4:14–15
Luke 6–10: 236
4:14–17
Luke 11–17: 410

4:15
Luke 11–17: 157
1 & 2 Thessalonians: 8, 58, 74, 268
James: 253
Revelation 12–22: 291, 302
4:15–17
2 Corinthians: 162
Philippians: 262
1 & 2 Thessalonians: 28
1 Peter: 236
2 Peter–Jude: 135
4:15–18
Luke 18–24: 228
Revelation 1–11: 24
4:16
Matthew 24–28: 275
1 Corinthians: 409, 418
2 Corinthians: 166
Philippians: 260
1 & 2 Thessalonians: 155
Revelation 1–11: 145, 238, 239, 308
Revelation 12–22: 17, 213
4:16–17
Luke 11–17: 151
Luke 18–24: 191
1 Corinthians: 444
2 Timothy: 201
Revelation 12–22: 17, 211, 212, 262
4:16–18
James: 256
4:17
Matthew 24–28: 15
Mark 9–16: 242
Luke 11–17: 156
Luke 18–24: 231, 248
1 Corinthians: 443
2 Corinthians: 395
Philippians: 259, 263
1 & 2 Thessalonians: 8, 164
Hebrews: 315
2 Peter–Jude: 112
Revelation 1–11: 32
Revelation 12–22: 304
4:18
Matthew 1–7: 162
Luke 18–24: 253
Acts 1–12: 84
1 & 2 Thessalonians: 155, 164, 204
Revelation 1–11: 32
5:1
1 & 2 Thessalonians: 117
5:1–2
1 & 2 Thessalonians: 131
5:1–3
Matthew 24–28: 15
Mark 9–16: 234
1 & 2 Thessalonians: 124
5:1–4
Revelation 1–11: 201
5:1–8
Romans 9–16: 263
5:1–11
Luke 18–24: 10
1 & 2 Thessalonians: 265
2 Peter–Jude: 135
5:2
Matthew 1–7: 478
Matthew 24–28: 77
Acts 1–12: 20, 40, 54
1 & 2 Thessalonians: 155, 218, 305
2 Peter–Jude: 5
1–3 John: 201
Revelation 1–11: 41, 114, 200, 201
Revelation 12–22: 149
5:2–3
Philippians: 187
5:2–4
Luke 11–17: 161
2 Corinthians: 37
Philippians: 28
5:2–5
1 & 2 Thessalonians: 268
5:3
Mark 9–16: 230
Luke 1–5: 160
John 12–21: 126
1 & 2 Thessalonians: 156, 315
1 Timothy: 256
Revelation 1–11: 179, 209, 212
5:4
1 & 2 Thessalonians: 274
2 Peter–Jude: 31
Revelation 1–11: 114
5:4–5
John 1–11: 411
5:4–8
Revelation 1–11: 201
5:5
Mark 1–8: 213, 396
Acts 13–28: 336
2 Corinthians: 249
Philippians: 185
5:5–6
1–3 John: 25
5:6
1 & 2 Thessalonians: 204
2 Peter–Jude: 51
5:6–8
Ephesians: 232
5:7
John 1–11: 82
5:8
Romans 1–8: 465
2 Corinthians: 108
Ephesians: 366
Colossians and Philemon: 19
1 & 2 Thessalonians: 15, 28, 88, 204
1 Timothy: 32, 263
1 Peter: 202
Revelation 1–11: 99
Revelation 12–22: 22
5:8–9
Romans 9–16: 266
5:8–11
Ephesians: 367
5:9
Romans 9–16: 37
Colossians and Philemon: 61, 142
1 & 2 Thessalonians: 29, 141, 288
1 Peter: 191
Revelation 1–11: 214
Revelation 12–22: 122, 238, 256
5:9–10
2 Corinthians: 191
2 Peter–Jude: 31
5:10
John 1–11: 456
Acts 1–12: 226
1 Corinthians: 472
Ephesians: 174
Philippians: 79
Hebrews: 381
5:11
Acts 1–12: 84
1 Corinthians: 385
1 & 2 Thessalonians: 2, 97, 155, 204
2 Peter–Jude: 200
5:11–27
James: 264
5:12
Acts 13–28: 55
1 Corinthians: 107
2 Corinthians: 388
Ephesians: 147
Philippians: 188
1 & 2 Thessalonians: 2, 7
1 Timothy: 100, 219
Hebrews: 447
5:12–13
Matthew 16–23: 367, 372
Acts 13–28: 224
1 Corinthians: 28, 74, 90, 485
2 Corinthians: 285
Philippians: 106
1 & 2 Thessalonians: 118, 177
1 Timothy: 93, 131, 217
Hebrews: 445
James: 97
1 Peter: 277
5:12–22
1 & 2 Thessalonians: 7, 204
5:13
Acts 1–12: 84
Ephesians: 285
1 & 2 Thessalonians: 2
5:14
Romans 9–16: 276
1 Corinthians: 321
2 Corinthians: 260, 392
Galatians: 178
Ephesians: 127
Philippians: 270
1 & 2 Thessalonians: 97, 168, 170, 304, 307
2 Timothy: 178

James: 253, 277
5:14–15
1 & 2 Thessalonians: 2, 118
5:15
Romans 9–16: 201
Ephesians: 209
Hebrews: 426
Revelation 12–22: 184
5:16
Luke 6–10: 339
Acts 13–28: 105
2 Corinthians: 231, 484
Philippians: 1, 216
1 Peter: 51
1–3 John: 19
Revelation 12–22: 76
5:16–18
Philippians: 24
5:16–22
1 & 2 Thessalonians: 2
5:17
Matthew 1–7: 373
Mark 9–16: 149
Luke 11–17: 2
Luke 18–24: 7
Romans 1–8: 38
Romans 9–16: 193
Ephesians: 379
Philippians: 39
Colossians and Philemon: 27
1 & 2 Thessalonians: 97, 194
1 Timothy: 201
2 Timothy: 6
5:18
Luke 1–5: 79
Acts 13–28: 105
Ephesians: 226, 267
Philippians: 34
Colossians and Philemon: 29, 37
Hebrews: 443
Revelation 12–22: 194
5:19
2 Corinthians: 229
Ephesians: 189, 248
Philippians: 105
2 Timothy: 15
5:19–22
1 Peter: 202
5:20
Acts 13–28: 3
1 Corinthians: 304
5:20–22
2 Peter–Jude: 68, 194
5:21
Philippians: 49, 186, 199
1 Timothy: 17
5:21–22
Romans 9–16: 187
Philippians: 46
2 Timothy: 69, 95
1–3 John: 154
5:22
Matthew 1–7: 331
Titus: 94
5:23
Luke 18–24: 10
Romans 9–16: 144
1 Corinthians: 22
2 Corinthians: 485
Philippians: 292
1 & 2 Thessalonians: 1, 28, 74, 87, 89, 91, 132, 253, 268, 287, 293, 313
James: 253
Revelation 12–22: 100, 302
5:23–24
Luke 18–24: 216
Romans 1–8: 282
1 & 2 Thessalonians: 70
1 Peter: 22
2 Peter–Jude: 210
1–3 John: 208
5:24
Luke 1–5: 174
Romans 1–8: 461
Romans 9–16: 132
Galatians: 169
1 & 2 Thessalonians: 52, 256, 296
Hebrews: 267
2 Peter–Jude: 206
Revelation 12–22: 100
5:25
2 Corinthians: 27
Philippians: 74
1 & 2 Thessalonians: 293
5:25–28
1 & 2 Thessalonians: 2
5:26
Romans 9–16: 370
2 Corinthians: 234, 486
1 & 2 Thessalonians: 118
Revelation 1–11: 72
5:27
1 & 2 Thessalonians: 97
1 Timothy: 176
5:28
2 Corinthians: 487
Philippians: 318
1 & 2 Thessalonians: 293

2 Thessalonians
1:1
Acts 13–28: 72
Philippians: 196, 314
1 & 2 Thessalonians: 14, 218
1 Timothy: 6
1 Peter: 289
1:1–2
1 & 2 Thessalonians: 87
1:2
2 Corinthians: 487
Philippians: 16
1 Peter: 25
Revelation 1–11: 24
1:3
Philippians: 41, 101, 108
Colossians and Philemon: 33, 37
1 & 2 Thessalonians: 70, 89, 90
1 Timothy: 32
1 Peter: 93
Revelation 1–11: 99
Revelation 12–22: 194
1:3–4
1 & 2 Thessalonians: 1, 2, 116, 217, 297
James: 27
1:3–5
1 & 2 Thessalonians: 69
1:3–10
2 Peter–Jude: 93, 135
1:4
Romans 1–8: 134
2 Corinthians: 150, 278
Colossians and Philemon: 156
1 & 2 Thessalonians: 19, 25, 136
James: 252
1:4–5
Philippians: 93
1:4–6
1 Peter: 43
1:4–8
Philippians: 94
1:5
Colossians and Philemon: 41
James: 271
1 Peter: 3, 46
1:5–7
Matthew 1–7: 229
1:5–8
Romans 9–16: 262
1:5–9
1 & 2 Thessalonians: 141
1 Peter: 258
1:5–10
Luke 18–24: 10
1 & 2 Thessalonians: 312
1:5–2:12
Revelation 1–11: 286
1:6–7
1 Corinthians: 21
1:6–8
Philippians: 93
2 Peter–Jude: 185
Revelation 12–22: 198, 207
1:6–9
Mark 1–8: 293
Luke 11–17: 275
1 Peter: 123, 230
Revelation 1–11: 189
Revelation 12–22: 108, 211, 219
1:6–10
1 & 2 Thessalonians: 311
1–3 John: 91
1:7
Mark 9–16: 255
Luke 1–5: 223
1 & 2 Thessalonians: 268
2 Peter–Jude: 64
Revelation 1–11: 3, 16

Revelation 12–22: 84, 115, 171
1:7–8
Matthew 24–28: 114
Luke 18–24: 231
Romans 1–8: 62, 126
Romans 9–16: 85
James: 247
2 Peter–Jude: 117
Revelation 1–11: 215, 279
1:7–9
Luke 11–17: 411
Romans 1–8: 398
1 Corinthians: 21
Colossians and Philemon: 15
Hebrews: 277
1 Peter: 84
Revelation 1–11: 213
Revelation 12–22: 124, 137, 215
1:7–10
Mark 1–8: 433
Mark 9–16: 257
Acts 1–12: 303
1 & 2 Thessalonians: 1
2 Peter–Jude: 189
Revelation 12–22: 176
1:8
Luke 1–5: 166
Acts 13–28: 45
Romans 1–8: 55
Philippians: 158
1 & 2 Thessalonians: 108, 284
Hebrews: 125
2 Peter–Jude: 89
1:8–9
Matthew 8–15: 379
2 Corinthians: 203
Galatians: 204
Philippians: 145
James: 287, 288
Revelation 12–22: 50
1:8–10
Matthew 16–23: 58
1:9
Matthew 8–15: 52
Luke 1–5: 216
Luke 11–17: 366
Luke 18–24: 10
John 12–21: 198
Acts 1–12: 124
Romans 1–8: 131
1 Corinthians: 417
2 Corinthians: 192, 202, 210
Philippians: 258
1 & 2 Thessalonians: 150, 163
2 Timothy: 72
James: 225, 245
1–3 John: 167
Revelation 12–22: 92, 243, 253, 273
1:9–10
Mark 9–16: 242
1:10
Matthew 16–23: 69
2 Corinthians: 37
Philippians: 28, 145
1 & 2 Thessalonians: 288
1 Peter: 235
Revelation 1–11: 320
1:11
Acts 13–28: 229
Galatians: 168
Ephesians: 209
Philippians: 173
1 & 2 Thessalonians: 18, 293
1:11–12
Romans 1–8: 38
Ephesians: 15
Philippians: 39
1 & 2 Thessalonians: 1, 70, 83, 86, 216, 312
1 Peter: 52
1:12
Acts 1–12: 104
1 & 2 Thessalonians: 288
1:17
1 Peter: 230
2:1
1 & 2 Thessalonians: 74, 126, 274
James: 253
Revelation 1–11: 125
Revelation 12–22: 302
2:1–2
1 & 2 Thessalonians: 124, 142, 311
2:1–3
1 & 2 Thessalonians: 155
2:1–4
2 Peter–Jude: 198
2:1–5
James: 174
2 Peter–Jude: 112
2:1–8
Philippians: 187
2:1–12
1 & 2 Thessalonians: 1, 116
1–3 John: 98
2:1–15
1 & 2 Thessalonians: 312
2:1ff.
1 & 2 Thessalonians: 161
2:2
Acts 1–12: 54
Galatians: 195
1 & 2 Thessalonians: 116, 124, 144, 318
1 Timothy: xiv
1 Peter: 9
2 Peter–Jude: 5, 13
Revelation 1–11: 41, 200
2:2–3
1 & 2 Thessalonians: 311
2:2–5, 9
2 Timothy: 123
2:3
Matthew 24–28: 18
Luke 1–5: 195
Luke 11–17: 21
1 & 2 Thessalonians: 146, 218
1 Timothy: 256
Hebrews: 271
2 Peter–Jude: 71
Revelation 12–22: 45, 169
2:3–4
Matthew 24–28: 37
Mark 9–16: 232
Luke 18–24: 242
Romans 1–8: 92
2 Corinthians: 345
1 & 2 Thessalonians: 145
Revelation 1–11: 192, 304
Revelation 12–22: 28, 32, 49, 58
2:3–4, 8–9
1–3 John: 158
2:3–9
Romans 1–8: 98
2:3–10
Revelation 12–22: 39
2:3–12
1 & 2 Thessalonians: 311
1 Timothy: 148
2 Peter–Jude: 198
2:4
Luke 18–24: 225
Acts 1–12: 60
1 & 2 Thessalonians: 146
Revelation 1–11: 294, 295
Revelation 12–22: 37, 41, 43, 46, 47, 61, 168
2:5
Luke 18–24: 9
1 & 2 Thessalonians: 141, 155, 218
2 Peter–Jude: 49
Revelation 12–22: 37
2:5–17
2 Peter–Jude: 158
2:6–7
Matthew 24–28: 74
Luke 11–17: 416
Revelation 1–11: 192
Revelation 12–22: 77
2:6–8
Revelation 1–11: 204
2:6–12
James: 174
2:7
Luke 18–24: 220
2 Corinthians: 109
Ephesians: xi
1 Timothy: 128
Revelation 1–11: 222, 286, 320
Revelation 12–22: 44
2:7–8
Matthew 16–23: 6
Romans 9–16: 386
2:8
2 Timothy: 170
James: 253
Revelation 1–11: 48, 297
Revelation 12–22: 219
2:8–9
1 & 2 Thessalonians: 74

2:8–10
Matthew 1–7: 480
2:8–12
Revelation 12–22: 46
2:9
Matthew 8–15: 44
Matthew 24–28: 46
Luke 6–10: 75
Acts 1–12: 96
1 & 2 Thessalonians: 71
1 Peter: 285
1–3 John: 153
Revelation 1–11: 193
Revelation 12–22: 45, 46, 61
2:9–10
Matthew 24–28: 37
Galatians: 10
Revelation 12–22: 60, 147, 169
2:9–11
2 Corinthians: 131
Revelation 1–11: 179
Revelation 12–22: 80
2:10
Luke 1–5: 336
John 1–11: 43
Romans 9–16: 54, 79
2 Corinthians: 128
1–3 John: 159
Revelation 12–22: 46, 49, 61
2:10–12
Matthew 1–7: 472
Romans 9–16: 85
1 & 2 Thessalonians: 150
Revelation 1–11: 230
2:10, 12–13
1–3 John: 144
2:11–12
Revelation 1–11: 208, 213
Revelation 12–22: 61
2:12
Matthew 1–7: 159
John 1–11: 43
Revelation 12–22: 49
2:13
Luke 1–5: 336
John 1–11: 35, 43
Acts 1–12: 252
Acts 13–28: 38, 268
Romans 9–16: 54
2 Corinthians: 89, 257
Ephesians: 12
Colossians and Philemon: 23, 153, 155
1 & 2 Thessalonians: 2, 20, 104, 193, 278
1 Timothy: 5
2 Timothy: 82, 90
Titus: 6
Hebrews: 100
1 Peter: 17, 21–22, 124
1–3 John: 28
Revelation 1–11: 54
Revelation 12–22: 50, 194
2:13–14
Romans 1–8: 498
Galatians: 140
1 & 2 Thessalonians: 1, 69, 225
1 Peter: 51
2:13–15
1 & 2 Thessalonians: 82, 203
2:13–16
1 & 2 Thessalonians: 70
2:14
Matthew 16–23: 241
Romans 1–8: 131, 500
Philippians: 246
1 & 2 Thessalonians: 21, 52
1–3 John: 28
2:15
1 Corinthians: 252, 474
Philippians: 87, 267, 282
1–3 John: 234
2:16
Matthew 1–7: 162
Acts 13–28: 75
2 Corinthians: 23, 263
Philippians: 106, 314
1 & 2 Thessalonians: 224
1–3 John: 107
2:16–17
Romans 1–8: 511
2 Corinthians: 20
1 & 2 Thessalonians: 1, 79, 293, 312
James: 255
1–3 John: 107
3:1
Romans 9–16: 352
1 Corinthians: 244
2 Corinthians: 27, 189
Philippians: 74
1 & 2 Thessalonians: 186, 187, 214
1 Timothy: 240
3:1–2
1 & 2 Thessalonians: 2, 213, 312
3:2
Titus: 111
3:3
Luke 1–5: 174
Acts 13–28: 297
1 & 2 Thessalonians: 79
Titus: 30
James: 235
Revelation 12–22: 100
3:3–4
1 & 2 Thessalonians: 312
3:4
1 & 2 Thessalonians: 166
3:4, 6, 10, 12
Matthew 8–15: 186
3:5
1 Corinthians: 351
Ephesians: 109
Philippians: 31
1 & 2 Thessalonians: 1, 87, 193
James: 27
1 Peter: 47
Revelation 1–11: 122
3:6
Matthew 16–23: 135
1 Corinthians: 350
2 Corinthians: 56–57, 444
Galatians: 176
Colossians and Philemon: 101
1 & 2 Thessalonians: 2, 97, 257, 288
1 Timothy: 54, 188
3:6–7
1 & 2 Thessalonians: 169, 177
3:6–12
1 & 2 Thessalonians: 28
3:6–13
1 & 2 Thessalonians: 2
3:6, 14
Matthew 8–15: 151
3:6–15
1 Corinthians: 130
1 & 2 Thessalonians: 311
3:7
2 Corinthians: 473
Philippians: 250
1 & 2 Thessalonians: 172, 203
3:7–8
1 & 2 Thessalonians: 23
3:7–9
1 & 2 Thessalonians: 48, 293
1 Timothy: 172
3:8
Acts 13–28: 228, 230
1 Corinthians: 204, 208
2 Corinthians: 228, 390
Philippians: 300, 306
1 & 2 Thessalonians: 5, 24
1 Timothy: 201
3:8, 9
Titus: 93
3:9
2 Corinthians: 473
1 Timothy: 103
3:10
Matthew 1–7: 359, 410
Luke 6–10: 106
Luke 11–17: 332
2 Corinthians: 273, 446
Galatians: 43
1 & 2 Thessalonians: 116, 120, 303, 304, 305
2 Timothy: 111
3:10–11
Ephesians: 186
3:10–12
Luke 11–17: 36
Revelation 12–22: 292, 299
3:10–13
Matthew 24–28: 97
3:11
1 Corinthians: 464
1 & 2 Thessalonians: 177, 257
3:11–12
1 & 2 Thessalonians: 120
1 Timothy: 66
1 Peter: 255

3:12
2 Corinthians: 484
1 & 2 Thessalonians: 95, 97, 119
3:13
1 & 2 Thessalonians: 203
3:14
1 & 2 Thessalonians: 215
1 Timothy: 54
2 Timothy: 90
3:14–15
1 Corinthians: 127
2 Corinthians: 56–57, 444
Colossians and Philemon: 79
1 & 2 Thessalonians: 2
1 Timothy: 170, 188
Titus: 165
3:15
Matthew 16–23: 136
Galatians: 179
1 & 2 Thessalonians: 170, 304
3:16
Matthew 1–7: 213
John 12–21: 125
1 & 2 Thessalonians: 1, 70, 87, 204, 293
1 Peter: 124
2 Peter–Jude: 24
3:17
Philippians: 310
1 & 2 Thessalonians: 218, 269
1 Timothy: xiv
1 Peter: 8, 9
2 Peter–Jude: 13
3:18
2 Corinthians: 487
Philippians: 318
1 & 2 Thessalonians: 1, 293

1 Timothy
1:1
Luke 1–5: 153
John 12–21: 231
Acts 13–28: 47
Romans 1–8: 279
Romans 9–16: 313
1 Corinthians: 2
2 Corinthians: 17, 27, 199, 410
1 Timothy: x, 69, 139
2 Timothy: 23
Titus: 14
Hebrews: 168
1 Peter: 62
1:1–2
Philippians: 16
1:2
Matthew 1–7: 191
Acts 13–28: 83
1 Corinthians: 2
2 Corinthians: 237
Philippians: 13, 190, 195, 196
1 & 2 Thessalonians: 13, 78, 87
1 Timothy: 15
1–3 John: 80
1:3
Matthew 8–15: 186
1 Corinthians: 80
2 Corinthians: 18
1 & 2 Thessalonians: 13, 77, 223
1 Timothy: xiv, 7, 9, 10, 54, 92, 170
Revelation 1–11: 56
1:3–4
Philippians: 196
1 Timothy: 238
1:3–4, 6–7
Titus: 54
1:3–4, 18–19
2 Timothy: 69
1:3–6
2 Timothy: 95
Titus: 162
1:3–7
Luke 6–10: 55
Acts 13–28: 226
1 & 2 Thessalonians: 70
1 Timothy: 146, 260, 289
James: 148
1:3–11
1 Timothy: 154
1:4
Philippians: 256
1 & 2 Thessalonians: 89
Titus: 63
1:4–5
1 Timothy: 36
1:4–7
1 Timothy: 36
1:5
Acts 13–28: 280
Romans 9–16: 327
2 Corinthians: 32
Philippians: 73
1 Timothy: 45, 151, 165
2 Timothy: 5, 8
Hebrews: 168
1 Peter: 47, 203
1–3 John: 144
1:5–6
1 Timothy: 184
2 Peter–Jude: 105
1:6
1 Timothy: 7, 10, 45, 92, 147
1:6–7
1 Timothy: 9, 54, 238
1:7
1 Timothy: xi, 10, 16, 55
2 Timothy: 112
1:7–11
1 Timothy: 60, 92
1:8
Romans 1–8: 358
1 & 2 Thessalonians: 199
1:8–10
1 Timothy: 26
1:9
Matthew 8–15: 52
Luke 11–17: 21
James: 209, 286
1:9–10
Luke 1–5: 334
2 Timothy: 181
1:10
1 Timothy: 240
Titus: 71
1:11
Matthew 1–7: 142
Luke 1–5: 328
Luke 11–17: 301
Luke 18–24: 440
2 Corinthians: 393
Philippians: 91
1 Timothy: 6, 26, 43
Revelation 12–22: 86
1:11–12
1 & 2 Thessalonians: 39
1:12
Romans 1–8: 379
1 Corinthians: 476
2 Corinthians: 78, 125, 349, 411
Philippians: 275, 303
Colossians and Philemon: 72
1 & 2 Thessalonians: 317
Revelation 12–22: 194
1:12–13
Mark 9–16: 371
John 12–21: 192
Romans 1–8: 312
Romans 9–16: 57
1 Corinthians: 61
2 Corinthians: 139
Ephesians: 89
Colossians and Philemon: 37, 70
1:12–14
Romans 9–16: 133, 158
1 & 2 Thessalonians: 320
1:12–15
Mark 9–16: 358, 381
1 Timothy: 262
1–3 John: 30
1:12–16
Luke 11–17: 265
John 1–11: 53
Romans 9–16: 158, 333
2 Corinthians: 70, 72, 222–23
2 Peter–Jude: 26
1–3 John: 38
1:12–17
Acts 13–28: 246
1 Corinthians: 405
1 & 2 Thessalonians: 293
1 Peter: 134, 269
1:13
Matthew 8–15: 52
Luke 1–5: 121
Luke 6–10: 313
John 12–21: 167
Acts 1–12: 232
2 Corinthians: 125
Galatians: xii
Philippians: 232
Titus: 146
1 Peter: 31, 48

1:13–14
Matthew 8–15: 311
Mark 1–8: 183
1:13–15
Acts 1–12: 226
1:13–17
Acts 1–12: 269
1:13, 15
Ephesians: 2
1 Timothy: xiv
1:14
Matthew 1–7: 151
Luke 1–5: 334
John 1–11: 353
2 Corinthians: 404
1 Timothy: 27, 263
Revelation 1–11: 99
1:14–17
1 Timothy: 6
1:15
Matthew 1–7: 147, 164
Matthew 8–15: 59, 267
Mark 1–8: 70, 422
Mark 9–16: 371
Luke 1–5: 48, 334
Luke 6–10: 11, 21, 107, 271
Luke 18–24: 20, 68, 75
John 12–21: 229
Acts 13–28: 211
Romans 1–8: 5, 207, 379
Romans 9–16: 267, 320
1 Corinthians: 14
2 Corinthians: 141, 345
Galatians: 40
Ephesians: 95, 124
Philippians: 113, 191, 243, 254
1 Timothy: 92
Titus: 30, 153
James: 209, 286, 287, 290
1–3 John: 30, 39
1:15–16
Romans 1–8: 129
2 Corinthians: 196
Galatians: 167
Philippians: 218, 316
1:16
Matthew 1–7: 397
Luke 6–10: 32
Luke 18–24: 9
John 12–21: 48
Philippians: 147
Colossians and Philemon: 156
1 & 2 Thessalonians: 180, 245, 287
Titus: 118
1:17
Acts 1–12: 15
2 Corinthians: 44, 158, 223
Ephesians: 312
Philippians: 312, 313
1 Timothy: 140, 269
1 Peter: 245
1–3 John: 168
Revelation 1–11: 158
Revelation 12–22: 267
1:18
1 Corinthians: 215
Philippians: 195
1 & 2 Thessalonians: 78, 199, 223
1 Timothy: 10, 180, 270
2 Timothy: 16
1:18–19
1 Timothy: 110, 266, 289
1:18–20
2 Corinthians: 447
1 Timothy: 135, 146, 260
1 Peter: 283
1:19
Acts 13–28: 280
2 Corinthians: 30, 31, 32
Philippians: 186
1 Timothy: 8, 147, 151, 184
1 Peter: 203
2 Peter–Jude: 1
1:19–20
1 Timothy: 36
James: 148
1:19, 20
Titus: 161
1:20
Matthew 16–23: 135
Luke 6–10: 80
Acts 1–12: 161
Acts 13–28: 188, 226
1 Corinthians: 126
2 Corinthians: 51, 444, 446, 477
Galatians: 10
Philippians: 256
1 & 2 Thessalonians: 310
1 Timothy: 10, 15, 54, 92, 238
2 Timothy: 88, 211
Revelation 1–11: 95
1–6
2 Peter–Jude: 11
2:1
Luke 11–17: 24
Colossians and Philemon: 26, 35
1 & 2 Thessalonians: 90, 181
2:1–2
Mark 9–16: 181
Romans 9–16: 213
Philippians: 39
2:1–3
Matthew 16–23: 322
1 Peter: 255
2:1–4
1 & 2 Thessalonians: 90, 188
Titus: 143
2:1–8
1 Timothy: 78
2:1–15
1 Timothy: 91
2:2
Luke 1–5: 75
1 & 2 Thessalonians: 119
1 Timothy: 164
2:2–6, 15, 21, 24
Titus: 23
2:3
Luke 1–5: 35, 153
2 Corinthians: 199
1 & 2 Thessalonians: 199
1 Timothy: 6
2 Timothy: 23
Revelation 1–11: 222
2:3–4
Matthew 8–15: 340
Luke 1–5: 168
Romans 1–8: 499
Romans 9–16: 58
Ephesians: 226
1 & 2 Thessalonians: 295
Titus: 7
2:3–6
Romans 1–8: 228
Romans 9–16: 295
2 Timothy: 23
2:4
Matthew 16–23: 246
Matthew 24–28: 332
Luke 1–5: 336
John 1–11: 43, 353
John 12–21: 119
Acts 1–12: 303
2 Corinthians: 73
Colossians and Philemon: 29
2 Timothy: 120
Titus: 110, 111, 151, 153
James: 235, 290
1 Peter: 50–51
2 Peter–Jude: 24
Revelation 1–11: 222
2:4, 6
Ephesians: 198
2:5
Matthew 1–7: 453
Mark 1–8: 103, 124
Luke 1–5: 47, 159, 322, 336
Luke 6–10: 61
Luke 11–17: 400
John 12–21: 184
Romans 1–8: 35
Romans 9–16: 331
2 Corinthians: 97, 200
Colossians and Philemon: 120
1 & 2 Thessalonians: 254
1 Timothy: xii, 33
1–3 John: 225, 236
2:5–6
Luke 1–5: 120, 183
2 Corinthians: 191
1 Timothy: 139
Titus: 112
Hebrews: 217
1 Peter: 26, 170, 206
1–3 John: 177
2:5–7
Colossians and Philemon: 72
2:6
Matthew 16–23: 245
Romans 1–8: 209
2 Corinthians: 202, 204
1 Timothy: xii, 168
1 Peter: 130, 279

1–3 John: 37
2:7
Acts 1–12: 272
Acts 13–28: 15, 47, 216, 246
2 Corinthians: 78, 125, 410, 413
1 & 2 Thessalonians: 44, 319
2 Timothy: 171
2 Peter–Jude: 13
1–3 John: 159
Revelation 1–11: 31, 291
2:8
Matthew 1–7: 373
Romans 9–16: 193
Ephesians: 379
Philippians: 180
1 & 2 Thessalonians: 97, 187, 293
1 Timothy: 165, 184
James: 38, 208
2:9
Matthew 8–15: 383
1 Timothy: 130
2 Timothy: 25
James: 244
2:9–10
Titus: 85
1 Peter: 180
2:9–11
Titus: 77
2:9–15
1 Timothy: 116, 184
2:10
1 Timothy: 45
2:11–12
Acts 1–12: 182
Acts 13–28: 240
1 Corinthians: 392
Ephesians: 276
1 & 2 Thessalonians: 119
2:11–13
1 Timothy: 212
2:11–14
1 Peter: 178
2:11–15
Colossians and Philemon: 167
1 Timothy: 95
2:12
1 Corinthians: 256
1 Timothy: 92
Titus: 78
Revelation 1–11: 100
2:12–14
1 & 2 Thessalonians: 43
2:13–14
1 Corinthians: 392
2:13–15
Ephesians: 276
2:14
Mark 1–8: 270
Romans 1–8: 296
2:14, 15
Luke 1–5: 169
2:15
Romans 9–16: 247
1 Corinthians: 261
Ephesians: 311
1 Timothy: 208, 213
Titus: 77, 78, 85
Revelation 1–11: 99
3:1
Matthew 8–15: 185
Matthew 16–23: 240
Romans 9–16: 162
2 Corinthians: 172, 473
Ephesians: 144, 147
1 Timothy: 32, 43, 158, 217, 219
James: 148
1 Peter: 267
3:1–2
1 & 2 Thessalonians: 167
3:1–7
Philippians: 15
1 & 2 Thessalonians: 167, 173, 292
Titus: 21
1 Peter: 174, 284
Revelation 1–11: 48
3:1–10, 12–13
Romans 9–16: 360
3:1–12
Matthew 8–15: 130
3:1–13
Acts 13–28: 3, 220
Galatians: 179
1 & 2 Thessalonians: 49
1 Timothy: 184
Hebrews: 180
3:1ff.
Acts 13–28: 3
1 Corinthians: 29
1 & 2 Thessalonians: 44
3:2
Acts 13–28: 84, 220, 240, 360
Romans 9–16: 173
2 Corinthians: 182, 184, 228, 473
Ephesians: 144, 240
Philippians: 15, 16, 88
Colossians and Philemon: 79
1 & 2 Thessalonians: 168
1 Timothy: 10, 16, 87, 124, 129, 130, 165, 175, 176, 202, 207, 208, 289
2 Timothy: 19, 99
Titus: 23, 34, 40, 41, 44
Hebrews: 426
James: 89
3:2–3
2 Timothy: 88, 98
3:2–7
Luke 6–10: 23–24
Ephesians: 148
Philippians: 88
1 & 2 Thessalonians: 170
1 Timothy: 222, 226
3:2ff.
1 Timothy: 218
3:3
Matthew 8–15: 193
Acts 13–28: 230
2 Corinthians: 382
Ephesians: 237
1 Timothy: 186, 245
Titus: 36, 37
Hebrews: 434
3:3–7
Ephesians: 94
3:4
1 Timothy: 66
3:4–5
Acts 13–28: 224
1 Corinthians: 117
1 & 2 Thessalonians: 170
1 Timothy: 135, 198
Titus: 30
3:4, 5, 12
Romans 9–16: 176
Ephesians: 147
3:5
Ephesians: 147
1 Timothy: 219
Titus: 35
3:6
Matthew 16–23: 230
1 Timothy: 9, 241
2 Timothy: 116
James: 149
1–3 John: 252
3:6–7
1 & 2 Thessalonians: 72
3:7
Ephesians: 339
1 & 2 Thessalonians: 71
1 Timothy: 40
2 Timothy: 102
1 Peter: 151
3:8
Philippians: 290
1 Timothy: 74, 78, 130
3:8–10
Philippians: 88
3:8–13
Philippians: 16
1 Timothy: 125
3:9
Acts 13–28: 280
Romans 9–16: 387
2 Corinthians: 31–32, 109
Philippians: 73, 186
1 Timothy: 45
2 Timothy: 5
1 Peter: 203
3:10
Acts 13–28: 84
Philippians: 88, 199
1 Timothy: 10, 165, 208, 225
Titus: 22
3:10, 13
Romans 9–16: 360
3:11
Philippians: 290
1 Timothy: 74, 78
Revelation 12–22: 235
3:12
Philippians: 88, 245
1 & 2 Thessalonians: 170

1 Timothy: 116, 135, 198, 207
3:14
1 Timothy: 175
Revelation 1–11: 21
3:14–15
1 & 2 Thessalonians: 166
3:15
Matthew 16–23: 402
Luke 1–5: 336
Acts 13–28: 229, 240
2 Corinthians: 253, 485
1 & 2 Thessalonians: 32, 165, 172, 206, 319
1 Timothy: x, 82, 287
2 Timothy: 81
Titus: 35
Hebrews: 83
1 Peter: 107
2 Peter–Jude: 13
1–3 John: 28, 214, 238
Revelation 1–11: 51, 217
3:16
John 1–11: 40
John 12–21: 162
Romans 9–16: 386
Ephesians: 18
Philippians: 140
Colossians and Philemon: 90–91
1 Timothy: 5, 7, 66, 128, 276
2 Timothy: 63
Hebrews: 33
James: 138
1–3 John: 16
Revelation 1–11: 286
4:1
Matthew 16–23: 7, 354
Mark 1–8: 62
Luke 1–5: 56, 280, 283
Luke 6–10: 113
Luke 11–17: 47
Luke 18–24: 431
John 12–21: 373
Acts 1–12: 94
2 Corinthians: 251, 336, 357
Ephesians: 198, 339, 349
Philippians: 217, 220
Colossians and Philemon: 91
1 & 2 Thessalonians: 80, 272
1 Timothy: 16, 40, 243
2 Timothy: 36, 73, 188
Titus: 163
James: 174
Revelation 1–11: 273
Revelation 12–22: 20, 54, 156
4:1–2
Matthew 1–7: 352, 461, 466
1 Corinthians: 55
Galatians: 10, 34, 139, 204
2 Timothy: 5
Titus: 57
Hebrews: 272
1 Peter: 281
2 Peter–Jude: 108
4:1–3
Mark 1–8: 242
Luke 1–5: 283
Luke 18–24: 162
Romans 9–16: 277
1 Timothy: 7–8, 36, 92
James: 211
1 Peter: 237
1–3 John: 98, 232
4:1–5
Matthew 8–15: 460
Acts 1–12: 296
1 Timothy: xi, 158, 159, 184, 238, 260
Hebrews: 437
4:1–6
1 & 2 Thessalonians: 199
4:1–7
1 Timothy: 40, 290
4:1–15
Acts 13–28: 222
4:1, 3–5
Matthew 1–7: 389
4:1, 6
1–3 John: 15
4:2
Matthew 16–23: 360
Luke 11–17: 112
Acts 13–28: 280
Romans 1–8: 141
Romans 9–16: 9, 293
2 Corinthians: 30, 183
Ephesians: 170, 244
Hebrews: 88
1–3 John: 142
4:3
Matthew 16–23: 361
1 Corinthians: 183
1 & 2 Thessalonians: 157
1 Timothy: 17, 116
Hebrews: 430
1–3 John: 14
4:3–4
Revelation 12–22: 194
4:3–5
Mark 1–8: 320
Romans 9–16: 292
4:4
1 Corinthians: 195
Ephesians: 209
1 & 2 Thessalonians: 199
2 Timothy: 193
4:4–5
1 Corinthians: 247
2 Timothy: 161
Titus: 67
4:5
Romans 1–8: 475
1 & 2 Thessalonians: 202
1 Timothy: 62
4:6
Acts 1–12: 12, 83
Romans 9–16: 330
2 Corinthians: 129, 473
1 & 2 Thessalonians: 170
1 Timothy: 8, 10, 45, 103, 108, 125, 179, 239, 266
2 Timothy: 162
Titus: 46
Hebrews: 437
4:6–7, 13
Galatians: 17
4:6–11
1 & 2 Thessalonians: 292
4:6–16
1 Timothy: 226
James: 150
4:6, 11–16
Titus: 47
4:6, 11, 13
Ephesians: 154
4:7
1 Timothy: 10, 16, 66, 92, 109, 110, 210
Titus: 63, 164
4:7–8
Luke 11–17: 142
1 Timothy: 45
4:8
Luke 11–17: 71
Romans 9–16: 179
1 Timothy: 66
2 Peter–Jude: 30
4:9
1 Timothy: 32, 92
4:10
Luke 1–5: 153, 154, 168
Luke 11–17: 219
Romans 9–16: 295
2 Corinthians: 192, 199, 203, 253
1 & 2 Thessalonians: 169
1 Timothy: 6, 7, 69, 72
2 Timothy: 23, 193
Titus: 109, 145
Revelation 1–11: 51, 217, 222
4:11
Acts 1–12: 12, 83
1 & 2 Thessalonians: 297
1 Timothy: 10, 108, 110, 179, 235
4:11–12
Matthew 1–7: 271
4:11–15
Acts 1–12: 181
4:12
Matthew 16–23: 107
Acts 13–28: 208
1 Corinthians: 197
2 Corinthians: 473
Philippians: 201, 250, 255
1 & 2 Thessalonians: 32, 223
1 Timothy: 9, 15, 109, 115, 270
2 Timothy: 93, 171
Titus: 23, 32, 94
1–3 John: 80
4:12–16
1 & 2 Thessalonians: 203
4:13
Acts 1–12: 83
Acts 13–28: 196
1 Corinthians: 55
1 & 2 Thessalonians: 199, 215

1 Timothy: 10, 45, 108, 110, 179, 290
Revelation 1–11: 23
4:14
Matthew 8–15: 185
Matthew 16–23: 358
Acts 1–12: 184
Acts 13–28: 84
1 Corinthians: 303
Ephesians: 148
Philippians: 201
1 & 2 Thessalonians: 193
1 Timothy: 43, 98, 100, 109, 224, 265, 270
2 Timothy: 16, 38
Hebrews: 140
1 Peter: 243
4:14–16
1 Timothy: 260
4:16
Luke 18–24: 126
Acts 1–12: 12, 83
Acts 13–28: 222
Romans 9–16: 173
Philippians: 164
1 & 2 Thessalonians: 170
1 Timothy: 45, 108, 179, 239, 262, 266, 290
5:1
Titus: 73
5:1ff.
Acts 1–12: 284
5:2
Ephesians: 145
Titus: 76
5:3
1 Timothy: 218, 231
James: 90
5:3–10
Titus: 76
5:3–16
1 & 2 Thessalonians: 97
5:3ff.
Acts 1–12: 178
5:4
Ephesians: 286
1 & 2 Thessalonians: 308
5:6
Ephesians: 53
1 Timothy: 78
James: 247
Revelation 1–11: 111
Revelation 12–22: 105, 185
5:6–7
1 Timothy: 184
5:7
2 Corinthians: 182, 228
1 Timothy: 170
5:8
Matthew 1–7: 410
1 Corinthians: 184
2 Corinthians: 273
Ephesians: 186, 286
1 & 2 Thessalonians: 307
1 Timothy: 198, 283
James: 244
1–3 John: 172
5:9
1 Timothy: 105
Titus: 76
5:9–10
Acts 13–28: 95–96
1 Corinthians: 486
Ephesians: 286
5:10
Matthew 24–28: 284
John 12–21: 69
Acts 13–28: 95
Hebrews: 426
Revelation 1–11: 320
5:11–12
1 Timothy: 10
5:11–12, 13
Ephesians: 286
5:11–13
1 Timothy: 184
5:11–14
1 & 2 Thessalonians: 309
5:11–15
1 Timothy: 78
5:13
1 & 2 Thessalonians: 177, 308
5:14
Acts 13–28: 282
Romans 1–8: 360
Ephesians: 285
1 Timothy: 105
Titus: 27
1–3 John: 216
5:14–15
Ephesians: 286
Titus: 88
5:15
1 Timothy: 9
2 Timothy: 183
Revelation 1–11: 310
Revelation 12–22: 235
5:16
Ephesians: 286
5:17
Matthew 16–23: 372
John 1–11: 17
Acts 13–28: 16, 55, 220, 225, 248
Romans 1–8: 6
Romans 9–16: 176
1 Corinthians: 107, 203, 485
2 Corinthians: 274, 388
Ephesians: 143, 148, 149
1 & 2 Thessalonians: 167, 170, 172, 177, 306
1 Timothy: 9, 16, 87, 98, 108, 116, 161, 178, 186, 197, 283, 290
2 Timothy: 42, 75
Titus: 39, 44, 47
James: 98
1 Peter: 276
5:17–18
Matthew 8–15: 194
1 & 2 Thessalonians: 48, 293
1 Peter: 269
5:17–20
1–3 John: 248
5:17–22
1 & 2 Thessalonians: 166
5:17–25
Ephesians: 97
5:18
Acts 13–28: 196
1 & 2 Thessalonians: 172
2 Timothy: 146
5:19
Luke 1–5: 165
Luke 6–10: 282
Acts 13–28: 251
2 Corinthians: 447
1 & 2 Thessalonians: 167
1 Timothy: 186
Revelation 1–11: 298
5:19–20
Matthew 16–23: 133
Acts 1–12: 155
Galatians: 176
1 Timothy: 9, 36
Titus: 42
Hebrews: 447
1–3 John: 257
5:19–21
1 Corinthians: 100
James: 96
5:19–22
1 Timothy: 16, 184
5:20
Matthew 1–7: 331
Matthew 8–15: 56
Luke 6–10: 109
Acts 1–12: 161
Acts 13–28: 220, 225
1 Corinthians: 96
Galatians: 53, 54
1 Timothy: 92
2 Timothy: 32, 178
5:20–24
1 Timothy: 92
5:21
Romans 9–16: 199
Ephesians: 12, 97
1 Timothy: 42
2 Timothy: 71, 168
5:22
Acts 1–12: 184
2 Corinthians: 266
Philippians: 290
1 Timothy: 100
2 Timothy: 197
James: 72
5:23
Matthew 1–7: 129
Luke 1–5: 295
Acts 1–12: 97
1 Corinthians: 301
2 Corinthians: 417
Ephesians: 234, 241
Philippians: 38
1 Timothy: 111
Titus: 37, 38
Hebrews: 77

1–3 John: 245
5:24
James: 271
1 Peter: 229
5:24–25
Luke 11–17: 117
6:1
Colossians and Philemon: 174
1 & 2 Thessalonians: 310
1 Timothy: 218
Titus: 98
6:1–2
Ephesians: 325
1 & 2 Thessalonians: 120
Titus: 100
1 Peter: 159
6:2
Philippians: 199
1 Timothy: 10, 179
Titus: 47
Hebrews: 400
6:2–3
Acts 1–12: 12
6:2b–5
1 Timothy: 290
6:3
1 Timothy: 66, 164
Titus: 71
2 Peter–Jude: 78
6:3–4
Luke 11–17: 375
1 & 2 Thessalonians: 37
2 Timothy: 116
Titus: 8
6:3–5
1 Timothy: 92, 154, 184, 250
2 Timothy: 96, 181
Titus: 162
James: 149
2 Peter–Jude: 105
6:3–5a
1–3 John: 101
6:3–10
1 Timothy: 260
6:4
Matthew 16–23: 230
Luke 11–17: 254
Philippians: 64, 68
1 Timothy: 9, 10, 17, 19
6:4–6
Titus: 61
6:5
Mark 1–8: 291
Luke 1–5: 337
John 1–11: 353
Acts 13–28: 53
2 Corinthians: 132
Philippians: 286
1 Timothy: 66, 280
2 Timothy: 111
Titus: 39
2 Peter–Jude: 78
1–3 John: 214
6:5–6
1 Timothy: 164
6:6
Matthew 8–15: 194
Philippians: 296
1 & 2 Thessalonians: 97
1 Timothy: 45, 66
2 Timothy: 112
6:6–8
Matthew 1–7: 409
Hebrews: 434
6:6–10
Mark 1–8: 291
1 Timothy: 111
6:6–11
Titus: 39
1 Peter: 268
6:6–17
Matthew 1–7: 146
6:7
John 1–11: 460
James: 92
6:8
Luke 11–17: 140
Philippians: 296, 300
1 & 2 Thessalonians: 97
6:8, 9–10
2 Timothy: 111
6:9
Luke 6–10: 194
Acts 13–28: 103
Galatians: 63
Ephesians: 220
Colossians and Philemon: 185
1 & 2 Thessalonians: 150, 245
Titus: 117
1 Peter: 229
6:9–10
1 & 2 Thessalonians: 170
1 Timothy: 9, 280
6:9–11
2 Peter–Jude: 78
6:10
Matthew 8–15: 182, 360
Mark 1–8: 204
Luke 11–17: 129, 333
Acts 13–28: 103
2 Corinthians: 272
Colossians and Philemon: 122
1 & 2 Thessalonians: 199
1 Timothy: 11, 45, 95
Hebrews: 433
James: 240
6:10–11
Romans 9–16: 187
Hebrews: 354
6:10, 21
1–3 John: 15
6:11
Ephesians: 210
1 & 2 Thessalonians: 199
1 Timothy: 7, 66, 109, 164, 165
2 Timothy: 92
2 Peter–Jude: 49
1–3 John: 72
Revelation 1–11: 99
Revelation 12–22: 181
6:11–12
Matthew 1–7: 271
Philippians: 162
1 Timothy: 260
6:11–14
1 & 2 Thessalonians: 203
6:12
Matthew 1–7: 455
Luke 11–17: 219
1 Corinthians: 473
2 Corinthians: 481
Philippians: 242, 245
1 & 2 Thessalonians: 78, 245, 256
1 Timothy: 7, 270
James: 42
1–3 John: 112, 117
6:12–13
1 & 2 Thessalonians: 199
6:12–14
1 Timothy: 290
6:13
Matthew 8–15: 186
John 12–21: 331
2 Timothy: 71
6:13–14
1 Timothy: 42
6:14
2 Timothy: 170
Titus: 26, 119
1–3 John: 113, 220
6:14–16
1–3 John: 23
6:15
Matthew 1–7: 142
Luke 11–17: 398
Acts 1–12: 15
Romans 9–16: 284
1 & 2 Thessalonians: 254
1 Timothy: 22
Revelation 12–22: 171, 221
6:15–16
1 Timothy: 139
Revelation 1–11: 158
6:16
2 Corinthians: 158
Ephesians: 47
Colossians and Philemon: 39
1 Timothy: 140
Revelation 1–11: 281
Revelation 12–22: 267, 279, 288
6:17
Matthew 1–7: 410
Matthew 8–15: 186
Matthew 16–23: 200
Mark 1–8: 204
Luke 11–17: 128, 129, 333
Acts 13–28: 139
2 Corinthians: 272, 279
Ephesians: 95
1 Timothy: 170, 249
Hebrews: 432
James: 101, 240, 244
6:17–18
Romans 9–16: 193

Titus: 47
6:17–19
Philippians: 307
1 Timothy: 291
James: 250
1–3 John: 135
6:18
Philippians: 22
Hebrews: 318
1–3 John: 18
6:18–19
2 Timothy: 198
Revelation 1–11: 138
6:19
1 & 2 Thessalonians: 199
6:20
Matthew 8–15: 462
John 1–11: 353
Philippians: 91, 92, 292
1 & 2 Thessalonians: 37, 289
1 Timothy: 10, 43, 45, 110, 162, 266
2 Timothy: 31, 78, 172, 197
Titus: 55
1–3 John: 234
Revelation 1–11: 114
Revelation 12–22: 294
6:20–21
Acts 1–12: 12
1 & 2 Thessalonians: 199
1 Timothy: 8, 154
2 Timothy: 96
6:21
Philippians: 318
1 Timothy: 45

2 Timothy
1:1
Acts 13–28: 47
1 Corinthians: 2
2 Corinthians: 17
1 Timothy: x
1–3 John: 165
1:2
Matthew 1–7: 191
Acts 13–28: 83
2 Corinthians: 237
Philippians: 16, 195, 196
1 & 2 Thessalonians: 13, 78, 87, 223
1 Timothy: 11
Titus: 14
1–3 John: 219
1:3
John 12–21: 235
Acts 13–28: 229, 280
Romans 1–8: 37
2 Corinthians: 31–32, 40, 185, 390, 475
Ephesians: 379, 381
Philippians: 18, 19, 38, 39, 52, 73
1 & 2 Thessalonians: 253, 293
1 Timothy: 151
1 Peter: 203
1:3–4
Matthew 1–7: 156
1:3–5
1 & 2 Thessalonians: 69
1:3–8
1 Timothy: 178
1:4
1 & 2 Thessalonians: 185
1:5
Luke 11–17: 371
Luke 18–24: 31
Acts 13–28: 48, 54, 83
2 Corinthians: 17
Philippians: 195, 197
1 & 2 Thessalonians: 223
1 Timothy: 7, 18
1:6
Luke 6–10: 55
Acts 1–12: 184
Acts 13–28: 84
Romans 9–16: 178
1 & 2 Thessalonians: 193, 194
1 Timothy: 109, 224, 265, 270
1 Peter: 243
1:6–7
Romans 1–8: 9
1 & 2 Thessalonians: 78
1:6–8
Ephesians: 337
1 Timothy: 162
1:6–8, 13–14
1–3 John: 80
1:6–10
1 & 2 Thessalonians: 203
1:6–2:12
Hebrews: 454
1:7
Acts 13–28: 116
Romans 1–8: 435
1 Timothy: 15, 270
1 Peter: 275
1:7, 8
Matthew 24–28: 157
1:8
Matthew 8–15: 228
Luke 18–24: 209
Acts 13–28: 293
1 Corinthians: 15
2 Corinthians: 228
Philippians: 245
Colossians and Philemon: 12
1 Timothy: 270
James: 252
1 Peter: 3
1:8–9
Luke 1–5: 168
Colossians and Philemon: 155
Titus: 6
1:8–12
1 & 2 Thessalonians: 294
1:9
Mark 1–8: 110
Luke 1–5: 46, 88, 328
Luke 18–24: 68
John 1–11: 34, 42
John 12–21: 258
Acts 1–12: 62
Romans 1–8: 203, 486, 498
Romans 9–16: 101
Ephesians: 12, 120
Philippians: 273, 318
Colossians and Philemon: 153
1 & 2 Thessalonians: 20, 163, 256, 278, 287, 320
1 Timothy: 265
Titus: 11, 155
1 Peter: 18, 32, 50–51, 121, 162, 182
2 Peter–Jude: 29
Revelation 1–11: 103
Revelation 12–22: 50
1:9–10
Titus: 107
1:10
Mark 1–8: 253
Mark 9–16: 379
Luke 1–5: 153
Luke 18–24: 68, 391
John 12–21: 361
Romans 1–8: 304
1 Timothy: 69
Titus: 119
1 Peter: 225
Revelation 1–11: 222
1:11
Acts 1–12: 272
Acts 13–28: 15, 47
Romans 9–16: 173
1 Corinthians: 31
2 Corinthians: 78, 125, 410, 413
Colossians and Philemon: 72
Titus: 47
Revelation 1–11: 291
1:12
Matthew 24–28: 157
Romans 1–8: 277, 515
Romans 9–16: 384
1 Corinthians: 20
1 & 2 Thessalonians: 172
James: 28
1 Peter: 3
Revelation 1–11: 30, 157
1:12–15
1 Timothy: 178
1:13
Romans 1–8: 348
Philippians: 186, 198
1 Timothy: 162, 240, 263
Titus: 71
Revelation 1–11: 99
1:13–14
Luke 18–24: 126
Acts 1–12: 12
1 & 2 Thessalonians: 37
1 Timothy: 239, 266, 270, 289, 290
Titus: 47
1–3 John: 234
Revelation 12–22: 294
1:14
Philippians: 91, 92, 124, 243

1 & 2 Thessalonians: 14, 112, 118, 289, 302
1 Timothy: 43, 162, 266
Titus: 46
1–3 John: 29, 181
Revelation 1–11: 54
1:15
Acts 13–28: 226
2 Corinthians: 151
Philippians: 198
1 & 2 Thessalonians: 82
1:15–16
Luke 11–17: 196
1:16
Acts 13–28: 370
1 Corinthians: 480
2 Corinthians: 228
1 Timothy: 135
Revelation 1–11: 56
1:16–17
Philippians: 202
1:16–18
Romans 9–16: 194
1:18
1 Corinthians: 480
Revelation 1–11: 30, 56
2:1
Acts 13–28: 118
1 Corinthians: 475
2 Corinthians: 150, 237, 477
Galatians: 14
Ephesians: 337
1 & 2 Thessalonians: 13, 78
1 Timothy: 165, 179
2:1–2
1 Timothy: 162
2:1–10
1 Peter: 128
2:2
Matthew 8–15: 132
Acts 1–12: 12, 83, 280
Acts 13–28: 122
Romans 9–16: 173
1 Corinthians: 80
Philippians: 292
Colossians and Philemon: 80
1 & 2 Thessalonians: 44, 49
1 Timothy: 1, 43, 239, 290
1 Peter: 240
Revelation 1–11: 291
2:2–6
1 & 2 Thessalonians: 44
2:3
Acts 13–28: 55
Ephesians: 363
Philippians: 25, 203
1 Timothy: 39, 45, 264
Hebrews: 371
1 Peter: 3
2:3–4
2 Corinthians: 322–23
Galatians: 156
Hebrews: 331
2:3–5
1 Timothy: 165
1 Peter: 65
2:3–6
1 Timothy: 179
Hebrews: 77
2:4
Ephesians: 349
1 Timothy: 42
Hebrews: 441
James: 202
2:5
Philippians: 91
2:6
John 12–21: 145
2:8
Matthew 8–15: 90
Matthew 16–23: 350
Hebrews: 71, 77
2 Peter–Jude: 48
Revelation 12–22: 307
2:8–10
Ephesians: 48
Philippians: 59
2:8–14
Romans 9–16: 330
2:9
Luke 1–5: 227
2 Corinthians: 228
1 Timothy: 154
James: 275
2:9–10
1 Peter: 3
2:10
John 12–21: 29
Acts 1–12: 252
Acts 13–28: 38, 268
Romans 1–8: 500
Romans 9–16: 58
2 Corinthians: 158
Ephesians: 12
Colossians and Philemon: 76, 84
1 & 2 Thessalonians: 20, 59, 162, 287
Titus: 5
1–3 John: 28, 106
Revelation 1–11: 54
2:11
1 Timothy: 32, 92
Titus: 30
2:11–12
Matthew 16–23: 234
Matthew 24–28: 26
2:12
Luke 11–17: 163
Luke 18–24: 83
1 & 2 Thessalonians: 73
1–3 John: 185
Revelation 1–11: 141, 149, 172
Revelation 12–22: 237, 288
2:12–13
Hebrews: 273
2:13
Matthew 8–15: 247
Romans 1–8: 272
2:14
1 Timothy: 17
2:14–18
1 Timothy: 154
2 Peter–Jude: 79, 105
2:14, 16
Titus: 60
2:15
Matthew 1–7: 265
Luke 18–24: 418
John 1–11: 353
John 12–21: 200
Acts 13–28: 5, 122, 215
Romans 1–8: 9, 37
1 Corinthians: 17, 65, 99, 101, 460
2 Corinthians: vii, 229, 285, 396, 453, 477
Ephesians: 128, 370
Philippians: 255
Colossians and Philemon: vi
1 & 2 Thessalonians: 37, 194, 195, 319
1 Timothy: 17, 23, 108, 109, 137, 161, 293
James: 62, 69, 71, 150
1 Peter: vii, 274
2 Peter–Jude: vii
1–3 John: 153
Revelation 12–22: 80
2:15–16
1 Timothy: 290
2:15–17
Galatians: 17
Titus: 162
2:15–18
1 Timothy: 266
2:15–23
1 Timothy: 162
2:16
Romans 1–8: 9
1 Timothy: 17, 110, 163, 292
2:16–17
2 Corinthians: 254
2:16–18
Luke 18–24: 162
2 Peter–Jude: 1
2:17
Acts 13–28: 226
1 Timothy: 17, 292
2:17–18
1 Timothy: 151
1–3 John: 152
2:18
Luke 1–5: 337
Luke 11–17: 152
Luke 18–24: 245
1 Timothy: xi, 17, 55, 244
2:19
Acts 1–12: 104
Romans 1–8: 20, 497
2 Corinthians: 469
Philippians: 29
Colossians and Philemon: 132
1 & 2 Thessalonians: 208
1 Timothy: 69
Titus: 27
James: 125

Revelation 1–11: 30, 260
2:19–21
Acts 1–12: 160
2:19a
2 Peter–Jude: 57
2:20
2 Corinthians: 140
2:20–21
Acts 1–12: 253
Acts 13–28: 222
1 Corinthians: 83
2:20–22
Romans 9–16: 155
2:21
Acts 1–12: 140
Romans 1–8: 380
Galatians: 174
Philippians: 218
1 & 2 Thessalonians: 104, 107, 202
1 Timothy: 231
Titus: 27
1 Peter: 129
2:21–22
1 Corinthians: 221
Philippians: 201
1 Timothy: 165
2:22
Matthew 1–7: 304
Mark 1–8: 359
John 12–21: 127
Romans 1–8: 9, 37
Romans 9–16: 187
2 Corinthians: 247
1 & 2 Thessalonians: 109, 199
1 Timothy: 175, 179, 261, 262, 270
Titus: 92, 117
1 Peter: 193, 227
1–3 John: 123
Revelation 1–11: 99
Revelation 12–22: 77, 182
2:23
Romans 9–16: 372
2 Corinthians: 262
1 Timothy: 17, 162
Titus: 162, 164
2:23–26
1 Timothy: 154
2:24
Galatians: 168
1 & 2 Thessalonians: 180, 181
1 Timothy: 108, 230
Titus: 36, 44
Revelation 12–22: 200
2:24–25
1 Corinthians: 17
1 Timothy: 109, 111, 179, 186
Titus: 39, 62
James: 179
2:24–26
Matthew 16–23: 203
John 12–21: 180
2 Corinthians: 131
1 & 2 Thessalonians: 171
1 Timothy: 66, 270
1 Peter: 202
Revelation 1–11: 90
2:25
Matthew 1–7: 109, 196
Matthew 16–23: 96
Mark 1–8: 21, 207, 429
Luke 1–5: 208, 218
Luke 18–24: 444
Acts 1–12: 301
2 Corinthians: 266
Philippians: 223
Colossians and Philemon: 16
1 & 2 Thessalonians: 287
1 Timothy: 70
Titus: 7, 144, 165
2 Peter–Jude: 24, 49
1–3 John: 36
Revelation 1–11: 139
2:25–26
Matthew 1–7: 67
Luke 6–10: 272
1 & 2 Thessalonians: 208
1 Peter: 50, 131
2:26
Luke 11–17: 74
2 Corinthians: 132
Revelation 12–22: 236
3:1–5
Matthew 24–28: 28
Galatians: 201
1 & 2 Thessalonians: 272
1 Peter: 237
3:1–5, 13
Ephesians: 292
3:1–6
2 Peter–Jude: 105
3:1–7
1 & 2 Thessalonians: 108
3:1–9
Acts 13–28: 226
1–3 John: 15
3:2
Luke 6–10: 266
Luke 11–17: 345
2 Corinthians: 257
Colossians and Philemon: 36, 170
James: 199
3:2–4
James: 187
3:2–5
Revelation 12–22: 272
3:3
Revelation 12–22: 235
3:3–4
1 & 2 Thessalonians: 209
3:4
Matthew 1–7: 208
3:4–5
Titus: 107
3:5
Matthew 1–7: 474
Luke 1–5: 214
Luke 11–17: 95
Romans 1–8: 155
Philippians: 212, 215, 220
1 Timothy: 66
Titus: 67, 160
Revelation 1–11: 132, 137
3:6
Mark 1–8: 291
1 Corinthians: 283
Colossians and Philemon: 99
1 Timothy: 78, 213
Titus: 60
James: 71
3:7
Matthew 1–7: 484
Luke 1–5: 337
John 1–11: 353
Romans 9–16: 54, 383
Ephesians: 168, 216
1 Timothy: 70, 244
Titus: 7
2 Peter–Jude: 24
1–3 John: 165
3:7–8
Romans 9–16: 375
Galatians: 139
3:8
Luke 1–5: 337
Acts 1–12: 94
2 Corinthians: 132
Philippians: 286
1 Timothy: 244
Titus: 68
James: 67
1–3 John: 15
Revelation 12–22: 57
3:8–9
Revelation 12–22: 60
3:10
Philippians: 292
Revelation 1–11: 99
3:11
Acts 13–28: 39, 338
1 & 2 Thessalonians: 82, 293
1 Peter: 3, 16
3:12
Matthew 1–7: 220
Matthew 8–15: 23, 201, 359
Matthew 16–23: 46
Mark 1–8: 203, 428
Mark 9–16: 8
Luke 11–17: 222
Luke 18–24: 297
John 12–21: 193
Acts 1–12: 128, 165
Acts 13–28: 55, 211
Romans 1–8: 281, 447, 512
2 Corinthians: 23–24, 120, 149, 387
Philippians: 95, 193, 252, 265
Colossians and Philemon: 75
1 & 2 Thessalonians: 79, 97, 124, 178, 213, 248, 298
1 Timothy: 67, 164, 265
Hebrews: 442
James: 16, 252
1 Peter: 162, 166, 249
1–3 John: 134
Revelation 1–11: 68

3:12–14
Hebrews: 454
3:13
Matthew 1–7: 237, 465
Matthew 24–28: 74
Mark 9–16: 231
Romans 1–8: 82
Romans 9–16: 262
2 Corinthians: 336
Galatians: 185
Ephesians: 172
1 & 2 Thessalonians: 270, 272, 278
1 Timothy: xiv
Titus: 55, 148
James: 174
1–3 John: 227
Revelation 1–11: 273
Revelation 12–22: 215
3:13–17
1 Timothy: 154, 291
3:14
Philippians: 201
3:14–15
1 Timothy: 260
3:15
Matthew 16–23: 182
John 12–21: 120
Acts 13–28: 108
Romans 1–8: 170
Ephesians: 217, 218
Philippians: 197
1 & 2 Thessalonians: 108, 287
1 Timothy: 6, 162
3:15–17
Romans 9–16: 312
1 & 2 Thessalonians: 89, 198
1 Timothy: xii
Titus: 46
1 Peter: 240
2 Peter–Jude: 24
3:16
Mark 9–16: 396
Luke 1–5: 15
John 12–21: 207
Acts 1–12: 207
Acts 13–28: 214
Romans 9–16: 328
1 Corinthians: 63, 98, 245
2 Corinthians: 384, 394
Galatians: 4
Ephesians: 213, 369, 370
1 & 2 Thessalonians: 194, 254
Titus: 47
Hebrews: 5
1 Peter: 55, 192
2 Peter–Jude: 61
Revelation 1–11: 15
3:16–4:4
1 & 2 Thessalonians: 168
1 Timothy: 162
3:16–17
Mark 1–8: 288, 406
Luke 18–24: 200
Acts 1–12: 12
Acts 13–28: 196, 229
Romans 9–16: 135
1 Corinthians: 115, 386, 475
2 Corinthians: 90–91, 417, 420
Ephesians: 117, 153, 369
Colossians and Philemon: 29, 80, 150
1 & 2 Thessalonians: 58, 97, 166, 198, 208, 305
1 Timothy: 162, 260
James: 68
2 Peter–Jude: 31, 96
1–3 John: 103, 160
Revelation 1–11: 52
3:16–4:5
1 & 2 Thessalonians: 292
3:17
John 12–21: 208
Acts 13–28: 214
Ephesians: 62
Philippians: 218
Titus: 23, 40, 48
4:1
Mark 1–8: 225
Mark 9–16: 354
Luke 18–24: 342
John 1–11: 14
Acts 1–12: 15, 53
Romans 1–8: 126
Philippians: 142
1 & 2 Thessalonians: 91, 234
Titus: 119
James: 257
1 Peter: 37, 235
2 Peter–Jude: 117
Revelation 1–11: 195
Revelation 12–22: 108, 120, 215, 249
4:1–2
Mark 1–8: 287
Acts 1–12: 83
2 Corinthians: 61
1 Timothy: 42
Hebrews: 400
4:1–2, 3
1 Corinthians: 55
4:1–4
Acts 1–12: 12
Acts 13–28: 198
1 Timothy: 154
4:1–5
1 & 2 Thessalonians: 199
1 Timothy: 160
4:1–7
1 Timothy: 291
4:2
John 12–21: 402
Acts 13–28: 16, 214
Romans 9–16: 172, 174
2 Corinthians: 189, 228, 484
Galatians: 168
Ephesians: 148, 154, 372
Philippians: 201
1 & 2 Thessalonians: 32, 78, 95, 141, 168, 180, 197
1 Timothy: 45, 179, 180, 185, 266, 293
Titus: 13, 48, 49, 62, 127
4:2–4
Titus: 70
4:3
Matthew 16–23: 239
Luke 1–5: 232
Romans 1–8: 348
Titus: 71, 128, 131
Hebrews: 275, 453
4:3–4
2 Corinthians: 128
Titus: 58, 164
1 Peter: 237, 265
2 Peter–Jude: 105
4:3–5
1 Corinthians: 473
4:4
Luke 1–5: 337
John 1–11: 353
1 Timothy: 163
1–3 John: 214
4:5
Acts 1–12: 232
Acts 13–28: 5, 239
2 Corinthians: 150
Ephesians: 142
Philippians: 201
1 & 2 Thessalonians: 78, 97, 168
1 Timothy: 42, 99, 125, 179
James: 275
2 Peter–Jude: 134
4:6
2 Corinthians: 26
Philippians: 79, 192
1 Timothy: xi
1 Peter: 225
4:6–7
Matthew 8–15: 227
Philippians: 76
1 & 2 Thessalonians: 133
4:6–8
Matthew 24–28: 103
John 12–21: 297
2 Corinthians: 147, 169
Philippians: 59
1–3 John: 79
4:7
Acts 13–28: 218
Romans 9–16: 337
2 Corinthians: 65, 229, 323
Ephesians: 223, 361
Philippians: 91, 241, 242, 245
Colossians and Philemon: 77
1 & 2 Thessalonians: 199, 204
1 Timothy: ix, 110, 264, 291
Titus: 72
1–3 John: 15, 207
4:7–8
Romans 9–16: 260–61
1 Corinthians: 85
2 Corinthians: 26, 151–52, 174, 229
Galatians: 191
Philippians: 249

James: 257
Revelation 12–22: 68, 104
4:8
Matthew 16–23: 214, 340
Matthew 24–28: 59, 103
Mark 1–8: 216
Mark 9–16: 354
Luke 11–17: 155, 408
Luke 18–24: 7, 241, 342
John 1–11: 14
Acts 1–12: 104, 303
Romans 1–8: 485, 493
Romans 9–16: 192
1 Corinthians: 215
Colossians and Philemon: 20
1 & 2 Thessalonians: 18, 28, 73, 92
1 Timothy: 273
Titus: 119
Hebrews: 381
James: 42, 254
1 Peter: 37, 45
2 Peter–Jude: 117
Revelation 1–11: 30, 32, 35, 126, 149, 319
Revelation 12–22: 113, 207, 211, 304, 312
4:9
Revelation 1–11: 21
4:9–10
Colossians and Philemon: 198
4:9–12
1 Corinthians: 483
4:10
John 12–21: 85
Acts 13–28: 194
Romans 9–16: 186, 364
Philippians: 198
Colossians and Philemon: 230
1 & 2 Thessalonians: 4
1 Timothy: 146, 257
Titus: 167
Hebrews: 275
James: 194
4:11
Mark 1–8: 2
Luke 1–5: 1, 10
Acts 1–12: 4
Acts 13–28: 82
Romans 9–16: 378
1 Corinthians: 468
Colossians and Philemon: 195, 230
1 Peter: 290
1–3 John: 246
4:12
Ephesians: 385
Colossians and Philemon: 193
Titus: 167
Revelation 1–11: 56
4:13
2 Corinthians: 390
4:14
Acts 13–28: 188
1 & 2 Thessalonians: 238
Revelation 1–11: 103
4:14–15
James: 67
4:16
2 Corinthians: 151, 267
Philippians: 198
1 Timothy: 28
1 Peter: 201
4:16–17
Mark 9–16: 235
Luke 18–24: 209
Acts 1–12: 273
4:16–18
Acts 13–28: 150
2 Corinthians: 26–27
1 & 2 Thessalonians: 296
4:17
Mark 9–16: 236
2 Corinthians: 154, 231
Ephesians: 105
Philippians: 303
1 & 2 Thessalonians: 318
1 Timothy: 28
Titus: 13
4:17–18
Acts 13–28: 338
4:18
Matthew 1–7: 331
Mark 1–8: 236
Mark 9–16: 238, 250
2 Corinthians: 44, 158
Philippians: 312
1 & 2 Thessalonians: 73, 317
1 Timothy: 89
James: 28
1 Peter: 22, 37
1–3 John: 208
4:19
Acts 13–28: 147
Romans 9–16: 363
2 Corinthians: 4
4:20
Matthew 1–7: 129
Luke 1–5: 295
Luke 6–10: 243
Acts 1–12: 97
Acts 13–28: 182
Romans 9–16: 379
1 Corinthians: 301
2 Corinthians: 417
Philippians: 205
4:22
Philippians: 318
1 & 2 Thessalonians: 206

Titus
1:1
Acts 1–12: 252
Acts 13–28: 38, 47, 151, 210, 268
Romans 9–16: 127, 191
2 Corinthians: 134
Philippians: 13
1 & 2 Thessalonians: 287
1 Timothy: x, 66, 70
Hebrews: 371
1 Peter: 17
2 Peter–Jude: 18, 24
Revelation 1–11: 54
Revelation 12–22: 200
1:1–2
1 & 2 Thessalonians: 47
1 Peter: 13, 17
1:1–3
1 & 2 Thessalonians: 294
1:2
Matthew 16–23: 381
Mark 9–16: 375
Luke 1–5: 28
Luke 11–17: 154
Luke 18–24: 189
John 12–21: 222, 246
Romans 9–16: 92
Ephesians: 28
Colossians and Philemon: 145
1 & 2 Thessalonians: 73, 245, 316, 319
1 Timothy: 173
Hebrews: 163, 287
1 Peter: 286
2 Peter–Jude: 31, 82
1–3 John: 30
Revelation 12–22: 211, 215
1:3
Matthew 1–7: 124–25
Luke 1–5: 153, 168
2 Corinthians: 199
1 & 2 Thessalonians: 39
1 Timothy: 69
2 Timothy: 23
1 Peter: 279
Revelation 1–11: 222
1:4
Matthew 1–7: 191
Luke 1–5: 153
John 12–21: 125
1 Corinthians: 117
2 Corinthians: 199, 237, 262
Philippians: 16
1 & 2 Thessalonians: 69, 87
1 Timothy: 2, 69
2 Timothy: 23
1 Peter: 25
1–3 John: 18
1:4–5
Galatians: 35
1:4ff.
1 & 2 Thessalonians: 44
1:5
John 1–11: 17
Acts 13–28: 220, 248
Romans 9–16: 360
Philippians: 15
1 & 2 Thessalonians: 167
1 Timothy: 224
2 Timothy: 207
Hebrews: 445
1 Peter: 263, 264
1:5, 7
1 Timothy: xii
1:5–7
Hebrews: 434

1:5–9
Acts 13–28: 3, 220
Galatians: 179
Philippians: 88
1 & 2 Thessalonians: 167, 173, 292
1 Timothy: 98
2 Timothy: 88
Hebrews: 180
1 Peter: 174
Revelation 1–11: 48
1:5ff.
1 Corinthians: 29
1:6
Acts 13–28: 220
Philippians: 88
1 Timothy: 103, 116, 117
1 Peter: 151
1:6–7
2 Corinthians: 182, 184, 228
1:6–9
Luke 6–10: 53
Philippians: 15
1:7
Acts 13–28: 230
1 Corinthians: 98
2 Corinthians: 173, 382, 473
Ephesians: 237
Philippians: 15
Colossians and Philemon: 73
1 & 2 Thessalonians: 167
James: 89
1 Peter: 244, 263, 269
2 Peter–Jude: 78
1:7–9
Ephesians: 148
1 & 2 Thessalonians: 170
2 Timothy: 98
1:7–11
1–3 John: 156
1:8
Acts 13–28: 95, 360
Romans 9–16: 194
2 Timothy: 19
Hebrews: 426
1 Peter: 197
1:9
Acts 1–12: 200
Acts 13–28: 240
Romans 1–8: 348
Romans 9–16: 173
2 Corinthians: 484
Ephesians: 148
Philippians: 16
1 & 2 Thessalonians: 168, 170, 179, 199
1 Timothy: 176, 240
2 Peter–Jude: 97
1–3 John: 22, 236
1:9b
2 Peter–Jude: 71
Revelation 1–11: 139
1:9–16
Luke 6–10: 55
1 Timothy: 154
1:10
Acts 1–12: 94
Philippians: 218
1 Timothy: xiv
1:10–11
Acts 1–12: 200
Galatians: 15
1 Timothy: 40
1:10–11, 13
2 Timothy: 178
1:10–11, 13–14
Matthew 8–15: 464
1:10, 14
1 Timothy: xi
1:11
Matthew 1–7: 144
Matthew 8–15: 321
Acts 13–28: 230
1 Timothy: 15, 135
2 Timothy: 112
1:11, 13
Matthew 1–7: 196
1:13
Acts 1–12: 161
2 Corinthians: 479
1 Timothy: 185
1–3 John: 15, 245
1:14
Mark 9–16: 92
Luke 1–5: 337
2 Timothy: 148
1:14–15
Colossians and Philemon: 117
1:15
Acts 13–28: 280
Romans 1–8: 340
Romans 9–16: 9, 292
2 Corinthians: 30, 427
Ephesians: 170
Philippians: 286
1 & 2 Thessalonians: 209
1 Timothy: 18
Hebrews: 449
1 Peter: 31
1:15–16
Matthew 1–7: 483
1:16
Mark 1–8: 216
Luke 1–5: 214
Romans 1–8: 186, 449
2 Corinthians: 468
Philippians: 212
1 & 2 Thessalonians: 242
2 Timothy: 66, 118
James: 125
1 Peter: 66
1–3 John: 56
2:1
Acts 13–28: 15
Romans 1–8: 348
1 Timothy: 108, 240
2:1–8
1 & 2 Thessalonians: 97
2:1–10
2 Corinthians: 226
1 & 2 Thessalonians: 166
2:2
Philippians: 290
1 Peter: 280
Revelation 1–11: 99
2:2–8
Acts 13–28: 320
2:3
Matthew 1–7: 326
1 Corinthians: 212
1 Timothy: 130
1–3 John: 258
Revelation 12–22: 235
2:3–4
1 Timothy: 87
2:3–5
Acts 1–12: 181
Ephesians: 285
1 & 2 Thessalonians: 309
1 Timothy: 206, 208
1 Peter: 178
2:4
Luke 11–17: 283
2:5
Acts 1–12: 21
2 Corinthians: 266
Ephesians: 285
Colossians and Philemon: 167–68
1 Timothy: 154
2 Peter–Jude: 78
2:6
1 Timothy: 130
2:7
Acts 1–12: 12
2 Corinthians: 473
1 & 2 Thessalonians: 259
1 Timothy: 66, 115
James: 125
1 Peter: 197
2 Peter–Jude: 78
2:7–8
Galatians: 192
Hebrews: 420
2:7, 14
Ephesians: 209
2:8
Luke 11–17: 196
Acts 1–12: 12, 21
2:9
James: 204
1 Peter: 159, 178
2 Peter–Jude: 72
2:9–10
Ephesians: 326
1 Timothy: 232
2:10
Luke 1–5: 153, 168
Acts 1–12: 12, 21
Romans 9–16: 202
2 Corinthians: 199
Ephesians: 353
Philippians: 85, 243
1 & 2 Thessalonians: 229
1 Timothy: 69, 137
2 Timothy: 23
Revelation 1–11: 222

2:10–14
Philippians: 183
2:11
John 1–11: 42
1 & 2 Thessalonians: 320
1 Timothy: 27, 63
1 Peter: 220
1–3 John: 166
2:11–12
Romans 1–8: 411
Ephesians: 202
Colossians and Philemon: 23
1 & 2 Thessalonians: 159, 208
James: 9, 230
1–3 John: 176
Revelation 1–11: 54
2:11–13
Romans 9–16: 260
1 & 2 Thessalonians: 18, 28
2 Timothy: 101, 170
James: 254
2:11–14
Mark 1–8: 433
Mark 9–16: 250
1 Corinthians: 129
1 Timothy: 232
2 Timothy: 23
1 Peter: 64
2 Peter–Jude: 110
2:12
Mark 9–16: 46
2 Corinthians: 132
James: 194
1 Peter: 65
1–3 John: 123
Revelation 1–11: 82
2:12–13
Matthew 24–28: 59
2:13
Mark 1–8: 224
Mark 9–16: 98, 242
Luke 1–5: 153
Luke 11–17: 155, 408, 411, 420
Luke 18–24: 8, 155, 196, 241
John 1–11: 7, 14
Acts 13–28: 333
1 Corinthians: 444
2 Corinthians: 19, 199, 249, 488
1 & 2 Thessalonians: 73, 90, 132, 138, 254, 289
1 Timothy: xii, 69
2 Timothy: 23
Hebrews: 33
James: 256
1 Peter: 33, 235, 286
2 Peter–Jude: 23
1–3 John: 23, 100, 170
Revelation 1–11: 32, 222
Revelation 12–22: 212, 292
2:13–14
1 Peter: 130, 226
2:14
Matthew 16–23: 246
Mark 9–16: 270
Luke 1–5: 83, 96
John 12–21: 67, 134
Romans 1–8: 215, 347
1 Corinthians: 14
2 Corinthians: 52, 191, 193, 241, 248
Ephesians: 20, 62
Philippians: 218
1 & 2 Thessalonians: 210, 259
1 Timothy: 135
James: 9
1 Peter: 89, 111, 152, 197
2 Peter–Jude: 78
2:15
Matthew 16–23: 117
Mark 9–16: 159
Acts 13–28: 15
2 Corinthians: 484
Galatians: 175
1 & 2 Thessalonians: 95, 170
1 Timothy: 185
Hebrews: 445
3:1
Matthew 16–23: 34
John 1–11: 16
Romans 9–16: 330
Ephesians: 354
1 & 2 Thessalonians: 259
1 Peter: 178
3:1–2
Romans 9–16: 208, 214
3:1–3
James: 185
1 Peter: 151
3:1–5
1 Peter: 255
3:1–7
Acts 13–28: 304
3:1–8
1 & 2 Thessalonians: 203
3:2
1 & 2 Thessalonians: 90, 181
3:2–7
Matthew 16–23: 153
3:3
Acts 13–28: 45
Romans 1–8: 82
1 Corinthians: 283
Galatians: 63
Philippians: 64, 199
1 & 2 Thessalonians: 109
James: 285
1 Peter: 76
3:3–5
Acts 1–12: 267
3:3–7
Romans 9–16: 267
3:4
Luke 1–5: 153
John 12–21: 63
2 Corinthians: 199
1 Timothy: 69
2 Timothy: 23
1–3 John: 23
Revelation 1–11: 222
3:4–5
Luke 1–5: 168
Romans 1–8: 321
3:4–6
1 Corinthians: 339
Philippians: 27
3:4–7
Mark 1–8: 354, 382
John 12–21: 148
Colossians and Philemon: 111
2 Timothy: 23
3:5
Matthew 1–7: 112, 191
Matthew 8–15: 91
Mark 1–8: 218
Mark 9–16: 117, 149
Luke 1–5: 40, 121
Luke 6–10: 117
John 12–21: 84, 269
Acts 1–12: 273
Romans 1–8: 203
2 Corinthians: 89, 131, 257
Ephesians: 178
1 & 2 Thessalonians: 193, 279, 287, 302
1 Timothy: 18
Hebrews: 140, 263
James: 63, 290
1 Peter: 21, 31, 33, 87, 111, 133, 171
2 Peter–Jude: 26, 29
1–3 John: 19, 73, 125, 133, 149, 166
Revelation 1–11: 103, 231
Revelation 12–22: 305, 308
3:5–6
Acts 1–12: 18, 53
Romans 1–8: 404
3:5–7
Mark 1–8: 26, 109, 359, 429
1 Timothy: xii
3:6
Luke 1–5: 153
2 Corinthians: 199
1 Timothy: 69
2 Timothy: 23
Revelation 1–11: 222
3:7
Mark 1–8: 210
Luke 1–5: 46
John 1–11: 42
John 12–21: 110
Acts 13–28: 108
Romans 1–8: 445
2 Corinthians: 71
Galatians: 101
1 & 2 Thessalonians: 73, 216, 245, 320
James: 137
1 Peter: 52, 220
2 Peter–Jude: 24, 27
3:8
Romans 9–16: 217
1 Corinthians: 14
Galatians: 192
Ephesians: 363

Philippians: 158
1 & 2 Thessalonians: 97, 181, 199, 259
1 Timothy: 32, 92
1 Peter: 140
3:9
Romans 9–16: 372
2 Corinthians: 262
Philippians: 64, 256
1 Timothy: xi
2 Timothy: 78
2 Peter–Jude: 105
3:9–11
1 Timothy: 154
3:9, 10–11
2 Timothy: 98
3:10
2 Corinthians: 447
1 Timothy: 162–63
James: 221
3:10–11
Matthew 1–7: 439
Luke 11–17: 379
1 Corinthians: 269
2 Corinthians: 444
Galatians: 175
Revelation 1–11: 87
3:12
Colossians and Philemon: 192
2 Timothy: 208
3:13
Romans 9–16: 344
1–3 John: 248
3:14
1 & 2 Thessalonians: 97, 259
3:15
Philippians: 318
Hebrews: 455
1–3 John: 15

Philemon
1
Acts 13–28: 293
2 Corinthians: 307
1 & 2 Thessalonians: 13
1 Timothy: 6
1–2
1 Corinthians: 173
1–3
Colossians and Philemon: 209
1–7
Colossians and Philemon: 207
1 & 2 Thessalonians: 69
2
Acts 13–28: 203
1–3 John: 243
Revelation 1–11: 134
3
2 Corinthians: 487
Philippians: 16, 314
1 & 2 Thessalonians: 87, 224
Revelation 1–11: 24
4
Acts 13–28: 229
Romans 1–8: 35
2 Corinthians: 475
Philippians: 19, 38
1 & 2 Thessalonians: 253, 293
2 Timothy: 6
4–5
Colossians and Philemon: 211–13
4–6
1 & 2 Thessalonians: 86
4–7
1 & 2 Thessalonians: 83
5
1 Timothy: 32
Revelation 1–11: 320
6
Philippians: 38
Colossians and Philemon: 213–14
1 & 2 Thessalonians: 253, 293
1–3 John: 18
7
Philippians: 32
Colossians and Philemon: 215
1 & 2 Thessalonians: 185
Revelation 1–11: 320
7, 12, 20
Luke 1–5: 120
Ephesians: 45
8
Ephesians: 282
8–9
Romans 9–16: 140
Titus: 126
8–18
Colossians and Philemon: 217
9
Acts 13–28: 293
1 Corinthians: 25
Philippians: 58
1 Timothy: 173
Titus: 73
10
1 Corinthians: 117, 173
2 Corinthians: 237
Philippians: 316
10–11
Philippians: 272
10–13
1 Corinthians: 468
10–14
Colossians and Philemon: 221
12
Philippians: 32
12–16
1 Peter: 159
13
Philippians: 58
14
2 Corinthians: 227
15–16
Luke 18–24: 398
Colossians and Philemon: 223
16
1 Corinthians: 173
Colossians and Philemon: 153
17
Romans 9–16: 318
17–18
Colossians and Philemon: 175, 223
18–19
Hebrews: 197
19
Colossians and Philemon: 199, 226–27
1 & 2 Thessalonians: 318
19–25
Colossians and Philemon: 225–35
20
Philippians: 32
Colossians and Philemon: 227–28
21
Colossians and Philemon: 228
22
2 Corinthians: 27
Philippians: 5
Colossians and Philemon: 4, 26, 228–29
1 & 2 Thessalonians: 211, 293
1 Timothy: xi
23
Acts 13–28: 293
23–24
Colossians and Philemon: 195, 197, 229–31
24
Mark 1–8: 2
Luke 1–5: 1, 4, 10, 13
Acts 13–28: 82, 376
Romans 9–16: 378
2 Corinthians: 307
Philippians: 198, 203, 316
2 Timothy: 206, 208, 210
1–3 John: 260
25
Philippians: 318
Colossians and Philemon: 231–35

Hebrews
1:1
John 12–21: 200
1 Peter: 51
2 Peter–Jude: 10, 114
1:1–2
Luke 1–5: 159
John 1–11: 17, 39
John 12–21: 181
Romans 1–8: 13
2 Corinthians: 18
2 Timothy: 107, 146
James: 245
1 Peter: 56
1–3 John: 96, 224
Revelation 1–11: 47
1:1–3
Luke 6–10: 280
2 Corinthians: 122, 123
Philippians: 16
1–3 John: 16

1:1–8
Matthew 1–7: 81
1:1–3:6
Galatians: 48
1:2
Mark 1–8: 330
Luke 1–5: 304
Luke 6–10: 255
Luke 11–17: 154
Luke 18–24: 81, 124
John 1–11: 16, 17, 20
Acts 1–12: 53
Romans 1–8: 445
2 Corinthians: 290, 461
Galatians: 68
Colossians and Philemon: 46, 47
1 Timothy: 148
Revelation 1–11: 134
1:2–3
Matthew 1–7: 388
Romans 1–8: 491
Philippians: 123, 139
1:3
Matthew 8–15: 31
Matthew 24–28: 51, 331
Mark 1–8: 36, 260, 378, 389
Mark 9–16: 122, 212, 415
Luke 1–5: 49, 91, 175, 236
Luke 11–17: 400
Luke 18–24: 158, 453
John 1–11: 14, 32
John 12–21: 55, 105, 136, 202, 213, 262
Acts 1–12: 222
2 Corinthians: 19, 113, 132, 290, 461
Galatians: 108
Colossians and Philemon: 45, 50
1 & 2 Thessalonians: 133, 233, 302
1 Timothy: 140, 142, 271
2 Peter–Jude: 26, 29
Revelation 1–11: 33, 146
Revelation 12–22: 11, 50, 214, 218
1:3–6
1 Peter: 219
1:4
Philippians: 143
1:4–7
2 Corinthians: 461
1:4–2:18
Luke 18–24: 306
1 Corinthians: 259
1:5
Luke 1–5: 175
Romans 1–8: 16
Galatians: 108
1:5, 8
1–3 John: 157
1:6
Mark 9–16: 129
Luke 1–5: 196
Luke 18–24: 157
John 1–11: 15
Ephesians: 96
Philippians: 139, 145
1 Peter: 58
1:7
Philippians: 204
1:7–8
Colossians and Philemon: 50
1:7, 14
Romans 9–16: 234, 332
1:8
Luke 18–24: 155
John 1–11: 14
2 Corinthians: 19, 461
Philippians: 139
2 Peter–Jude: 23
1–3 John: 23
1:9
Mark 1–8: 416
Romans 1–8: 60
Romans 9–16: 187
2 Corinthians: 45
1 Peter: 206
1–3 John: 102
1:10–12
Revelation 12–22: 249
1:13
2 Corinthians: 461
Philippians: 139
James: 196
Revelation 12–22: 214
1:14
Matthew 16–23: 118
Mark 9–16: 402
John 12–21: 156
Acts 1–12: 324
Romans 1–8: 443, 475
Ephesians: 97
Philippians: 168
1 Peter: 37, 57
Revelation 1–11: 149
Revelation 12–22: 84, 123, 207, 280, 296
1:24
1 Corinthians: 5
1:26
1 Corinthians: 5
2:1–3
Acts 13–28: 27
2 Corinthians: 461
2:2
Acts 1–12: 212
Romans 1–8: 358
1 & 2 Thessalonians: 234
Revelation 1–11: 21
Revelation 12–22: 84, 296
2:2–3
Romans 1–8: 117
2 Corinthians: 461
2:2–4
Luke 11–17: 123
2:3
1 & 2 Thessalonians: 151
1–3 John: 198
Revelation 1–11: 185
2:3–4
Matthew 1–7: 126
Matthew 8–15: 135, 314
Mark 1–8: 77, 169, 185, 288
Mark 9–16: 415
Luke 6–10: 19, 243
Acts 1–12: 43, 87, 96
Acts 13–28: 44, 68, 171, 174
Romans 9–16: 168
1 Corinthians: 302, 360
2 Corinthians: 415, 417
1 Timothy: 4
James: 287
2:4
Acts 1–12: 86
2:5
1 Peter: 178
2:6
James: 89
2:7
2 Corinthians: 292
2:8
Luke 18–24: 81
1 Corinthians: 253
1 Peter: 178
2:9
Matthew 24–28: 171
John 12–21: 39, 140
2 Corinthians: 191, 292
Ephesians: 312
Philippians: 141
Titus: 112
1 Peter: 206, 220
2:9–10
Mark 9–16: 369
2:9–11
Romans 1–8: 492
2:10
Matthew 8–15: 182
Matthew 16–23: 225
Luke 18–24: 53
John 1–11: 422
John 12–21: 44
Acts 1–12: 110, 169
Acts 13–28: 101
Romans 1–8: 450
1 & 2 Thessalonians: 44
1 Peter: 2
2:10–11
2 Timothy: 14
2:11
Matthew 16–23: 31
Matthew 24–28: 124
John 12–21: 379
Romans 1–8: 329
1 Corinthians: 5
Ephesians: 82
1 & 2 Thessalonians: 104, 166, 202
1 Timothy: 140
1 Peter: 129
2:12
Luke 11–17: 404
Ephesians: 259
2:14
Matthew 16–23: 33

Mark 9–16: 133, 379
Luke 6–10: 217
Luke 11–17: 67, 172
Luke 18–24: 391
John 1–11: 24, 41
John 12–21: 42, 82, 139, 198, 240, 250, 356
Acts 1–12: 65
Acts 13–28: 169
Romans 1–8: 215, 295, 336
1 Corinthians: 420, 443
2 Corinthians: 71, 140
Ephesians: 337, 338
Philippians: 130
Colossians and Philemon: 112
1 Timothy: 140
2 Timothy: 24
1–3 John: 16, 158
Revelation 1–11: 69, 168, 261
Revelation 12–22: 10, 15, 269
2:14–15
Mark 1–8: 58, 183, 238
Mark 9–16: 163
Luke 1–5: 96, 271, 281
John 12–21: 36
Romans 1–8: 434
1 Corinthians: 446
2 Corinthians: 113
James: 205
1–3 John: 207
Revelation 1–11: 32, 52, 167
2:14–18
Mark 1–8: 97
2:14, 18
2 Timothy: 57
2:15
Mark 1–8: 252
Mark 9–16: 163
John 12–21: 361
Romans 1–8: 295
2:16
Mark 1–8: 58
1 Timothy: 72
2:17
Matthew 8–15: 91
Mark 9–16: 210
Luke 6–10: 308
Luke 18–24: 20, 155, 455
Romans 9–16: 331
1 Corinthians: 238, 353
2 Corinthians: 201
Philippians: 131, 239
Titus: 30
James: 261
1 Peter: 126, 170, 206
2 Peter–Jude: 30
1–3 John: 37, 39, 46, 157, 167
2:17–18
Luke 18–24: 301
1 & 2 Thessalonians: 298
Revelation 1–11: 44, 69, 96
2:18
Matthew 1–7: 99
Mark 1–8: 421
1 Corinthians: 229
Philippians: 130, 142
James: 20
1 Peter: 2
Revelation 1–11: 45, 157
3:1
Luke 1–5: 159
Luke 18–24: 68
Romans 1–8: 22
Romans 9–16: 331
1 Corinthians: 323
2 Corinthians: 248, 409
Ephesians: 120, 141
Philippians: 204
1 & 2 Thessalonians: 256
2 Timothy: 2
Revelation 1–11: 44
3:1–2
Romans 9–16: 311
1 Peter: 126
3:2
Titus: 30
3:4
Acts 13–28: 133
3:6
Luke 18–24: 259
Acts 13–28: 55
Romans 1–8: 281
2 Corinthians: 187
Ephesians: 82
Philippians: 282
1 & 2 Thessalonians: 20, 73, 165, 166, 298
1 Timothy: 135
1 Peter: 36, 107
2 Peter–Jude: 27–28
3:6–4:2
2 Corinthians: 462
3:7
Luke 18–24: 158
Acts 1–12: 173
3:7–8
Acts 13–28: 32, 311
Revelation 1–11: 251
Revelation 12–22: 303
3:7–11
Acts 13–28: 19
3:7–12
Acts 1–12: 220
Acts 13–28: 373
3:7–13
Luke 18–24: 118, 239
3:7–15
James: 287
3:7ff.
Acts 13–28: 301
3:8
Acts 1–12: 124
Acts 13–28: 173
Romans 1–8: 120
2 Corinthians: 110
3:10
James: 285
3:11–12
Matthew 8–15: 276
3:12
Matthew 1–7: 208
Matthew 8–15: 276
Matthew 24–28: 26
John 1–11: 228
1 Timothy: 148
Revelation 1–11: 51, 217
3:12–13
2 Corinthians: 463
3:12–14
Romans 9–16: 117, 312
3:13
Acts 1–12: 84
Acts 13–28: 173
1 Peter: 236, 280
3:14
Luke 6–10: 192
Acts 13–28: 34
Romans 1–8: 281, 514
2 Corinthians: 248
Philippians: 164, 282
1 & 2 Thessalonians: 20, 298
1 Timothy: 11, 181
James: 29
1 Peter: 36
Revelation 12–22: 101, 238
3:15
Mark 1–8: 359
Acts 13–28: 173
Romans 1–8: 120
2 Corinthians: 110, 463
Revelation 12–22: 133, 298
3:16–19
1 Peter: 125
3:17–18
Acts 13–28: 19
4:1
2 Corinthians: 463
James: 9, 287
4:1–10
1 Peter: 41, 217
4:1–11
Matthew 1–7: 256
Colossians and Philemon: 119
4:2
2 Corinthians: 463
Philippians: 214
4:3
Matthew 16–23: 23
Acts 1–12: 124
James: 92
4:6–7
James: 287
4:7
Acts 1–12: 173
Acts 13–28: 173
Romans 1–8: 120
2 Corinthians: 110
Revelation 1–11: 272
Revelation 12–22: 133, 154, 298
4:9
Mark 1–8: 158
Romans 9–16: 282
1 & 2 Thessalonians: 52
4:9–10
Matthew 16–23: 23
2 Peter–Jude: 52

4:9–11
John 12–21: 212
1 & 2 Thessalonians: 246
4:11
Romans 9–16: 117, 312
2 Corinthians: 463
Philippians: 158
4:12
Matthew 1–7: 262
Acts 1–12: 72, 170, 212
1 Corinthians: 384
2 Corinthians: 129
Ephesians: 370
Philippians: 50
1 & 2 Thessalonians: 166
2 Timothy: 59
James: 75
1 Peter: 192
1–3 John: 155
Revelation 1–11: 83
4:12–13
2 Corinthians: 101
Ephesians: 213, 371
2 Timothy: 158
Revelation 1–11: 48
4:13
Matthew 1–7: 360
Matthew 8–15: 440
Mark 1–8: 329
Luke 1–5: 304
Romans 1–8: 116
2 Corinthians: 176
Revelation 1–11: 46
Revelation 12–22: 217
4:14
Luke 1–5: 195
Ephesians: 140
Philippians: 140, 141
Revelation 1–11: 44
4:14–15
1–3 John: 46
4:14–16
John 12–21: 226
4:14–5:10
1–3 John: 100
4:15
Matthew 1–7: 77, 99
Matthew 8–15: 18, 298
Matthew 16–23: 349
Matthew 24–28: 169, 313
Mark 1–8: 31, 45, 77, 178, 421
Luke 1–5: 167, 190, 197, 249, 253
Luke 6–10: 137, 148
Luke 18–24: 431
John 12–21: 385
Romans 1–8: 14, 200, 407, 480
1 Corinthians: 229
2 Corinthians: 293
Philippians: 130, 142, 239, 268
1 Timothy: 140
James: 20
1 Peter: 88, 168, 206
2 Peter–Jude: 30
1–3 John: 16, 30, 125, 193
Revelation 1–11: 45, 69
4:15–16
Ephesians: 98
1 & 2 Thessalonians: 19, 298
4:16
Matthew 24–28: 273
Mark 9–16: 379
Luke 1–5: 88
Romans 1–8: 35, 276, 426
2 Corinthians: 404
Galatians: 98
Ephesians: 80
1 & 2 Thessalonians: 97
2 Timothy: 57
James: 41, 207
1 Peter: 104, 182, 207
2 Peter–Jude: 24
1–3 John: 203
5:1
Philippians: 192
5:1–3
1 & 2 Thessalonians: 180
5:1–6
Philippians: 141
5:3
Romans 9–16: 307
5:4
1 & 2 Thessalonians: 170
5:4–5
1 Peter: 126
5:5
1–3 John: 167
5:5–6
Luke 1–5: 175
5:6
1 Peter: 125–26
5:7
Matthew 24–28: 172
Mark 9–16: 301
Luke 6–10: 338
Luke 18–24: 300, 303
John 12–21: 38
Philippians: 21
5:7–9
Philippians: 133
5:8
Luke 1–5: 190
Philippians: 127
2 Timothy: 56
1 Peter: 2
5:9
Matthew 1–7: 478
Matthew 24–28: 346
Luke 1–5: 79, 166
John 12–21: 159, 266
Acts 1–12: 169
Romans 9–16: 85
2 Corinthians: 330
1 & 2 Thessalonians: 244, 316
1 Timothy: 140
1–3 John: 30, 183
Revelation 1–11: 54
Revelation 12–22: 50
5:10
Matthew 16–23: 38
5:11–6:8
1 Timothy: 148
5:12
Acts 1–12: 12
Romans 1–8: 168
5:12–13
1–3 John: 74
5:12–14
1 Peter: 275
2 Peter–Jude: 197
5:12–6:9
James: 287
5:13
1 Corinthians: 71
5:14
Matthew 1–7: 432, 468
1 & 2 Thessalonians: 199
6:1
1 Corinthians: 60
2 Corinthians: 464
2 Timothy: 36
6:2
Luke 1–5: 209
1 & 2 Thessalonians: 163, 245
1 Timothy: 224
6:3
James: 237
6:4–6
Matthew 1–7: 123
Matthew 8–15: 314
Matthew 24–28: 262
Mark 1–8: 185
Luke 11–17: 62, 123
Luke 18–24: 367
John 12–21: 175
Romans 1–8: 138
Romans 9–16: 73
Galatians: 135
Philippians: 214
1 Timothy: 30, 244
2 Timothy: 66, 80
James: 132
2 Peter–Jude: 106–7
Revelation 12–22: 101
6:4–8
Luke 11–17: 164
2 Peter–Jude: 166
6:4–9
2 Corinthians: 463
6:5
Matthew 16–23: 59
1 Corinthians: 360
2 Corinthians: 132
6:5–6
Matthew 8–15: 196
6:6
Luke 1–5: 195
John 12–21: 343
Romans 1–8: 217
1 Corinthians: 360
1 Timothy: 244
6:9
1 Timothy: 150

6:9–12
1 Peter: 41
6:10
Romans 9–16: 247
1 Corinthians: 481
1 & 2 Thessalonians: 117
Revelation 1–11: 99, 113, 320
Revelation 12–22: 104
6:10–11
1 & 2 Thessalonians: 20, 298
6:10–12
Romans 9–16: 190
6:11
1 & 2 Thessalonians: 73, 90
6:12
Romans 1–8: 446
Colossians and Philemon: 39
1 & 2 Thessalonians: 96
1 Peter: 280
2 Peter–Jude: 51
6:13
Luke 1–5: 134
Revelation 1–11: 279, 284
6:13–14
Matthew 1–7: 321
6:13–17
Matthew 1–7: 324
James: 269
6:13–20
Romans 9–16: 93
6:15
Ephesians: 126
1 & 2 Thessalonians: 96
6:16
Matthew 1–7: 321
Titus: 101
6:16–17
Luke 1–5: 134
6:17–18
Romans 1–8: 506
6:17–19
Romans 1–8: 460, 465
2 Corinthians: 108
6:18
Matthew 16–23: 381
John 12–21: 222, 246
1 & 2 Thessalonians: 319
1 Timothy: 173
Titus: 11
Revelation 12–22: 211
6:18–19
Colossians and Philemon: 19
6:18–20
1 & 2 Thessalonians: 19
6:19
Romans 1–8: 518
Ephesians: 366
1 & 2 Thessalonians: 206, 298
1 Peter: 33, 41
1–3 John: 106, 170
6:20
Acts 13–28: 22
Philippians: 141
1 Peter: 41, 125–26
6–12
2 Corinthians: 462
7:1
Mark 1–8: 244
7:3
Luke 1–5: 195
7:7
Titus: 101
7:7–10
Romans 1–8: 294
7:8–9
Matthew 16–23: 384
7:11
2 Corinthians: 106
1 Peter: 126
7:14
Luke 1–5: 170
1 Peter: 126
Revelation 1–11: 166
7:14–17
1 Peter: 125
7:16
1 Peter: 126
Revelation 1–11: 51, 69
7:18–19,22
Galatians: 65
7:19
2 Corinthians: 106, 108
7:21
Philippians: 141
7:22
Luke 1–5: 114
7:24–25
Romans 1–8: 402
7:25
Luke 1–5: 159
Luke 18–24: 295, 455
John 12–21: 242, 270, 273, 310
Romans 1–8: 274, 279, 467, 472, 509
Romans 9–16: 280
2 Corinthians: 52, 89, 107
Colossians and Philemon: 131
1 & 2 Thessalonians: 19, 163, 234
1 Timothy: 62
2 Timothy: 58
James: 28, 225
1 Peter: 25, 104, 220
Revelation 1–11: 45, 51, 157
Revelation 12–22: 100
7:25–26
Romans 1–8: 468
Philippians: 141
7:25–28
1–3 John: 46
7:26
Matthew 8–15: 202, 456
Mark 9–16: 212
Luke 1–5: 58, 71, 253
Luke 18–24: 157
John 12–21: 254, 291
Acts 1–12: 107
2 Corinthians: 478
Philippians: 253
1 Timothy: 140
Titus: 42
James: 48
1 Peter: 166, 168, 206
2 Peter–Jude: 30
1–3 John: 48
7:26–27
Romans 1–8: 328
1 Peter: 88
7:26–28
1 Peter: 200
7:27
Matthew 16–23: 37, 247
Mark 9–16: 317
Luke 18–24: 91
John 12–21: 43
2 Corinthians: 97
2 Timothy: 139
1 Peter: 126, 206, 225
7:28
1 Peter: 109
8
Acts 13–28: 202
8:1
Luke 1–5: 236
Acts 1–12: 222
1 & 2 Thessalonians: 233
Revelation 12–22: 214
8:1–2
1 Peter: 126
8:1–2, 6
Romans 9–16: 332
8:1–6
Philippians: 141
8:2
Romans 9–16: 234
Philippians: 204
1 Peter: 217
Revelation 12–22: 132
8:5
Matthew 8–15: 459
1 Peter: 217
Revelation 1–11: 232
Revelation 12–22: 132
8:6
Luke 1–5: 114, 117
2 Corinthians: 97, 200
1 Timothy: 71
1 Peter: 126
8:6–13
2 Corinthians: 88
8:7
Philippians: 181
8:7–13
Luke 1–5: 114
8:8
2 Corinthians: 97
8:8–12
2 Corinthians: 97
8:8–13
2 Corinthians: 89
8:9
2 Corinthians: 98
Philippians: 164
8:10
Romans 1–8: 403
2 Corinthians: 98
1–3 John: 122

8:11
2 Corinthians: 98
8:12
Acts 13–28: 336
Romans 1–8: 275
2 Corinthians: 248
Colossians and Philemon: 111
8:13
Acts 13–28: 64
2 Corinthians: 104, 106
1 Peter: 114
9:1
John 12–21: 191
1 & 2 Thessalonians: 62
9:1–5
Luke 1–5: 26
9:1–10
1 Peter: 108
9:1–18
1 Peter: 80
9:3
Mark 9–16: 378
9:3–7
Revelation 1–11: 321
9:4
Revelation 1–11: 321
9:6
Romans 9–16: 148
1 & 2 Thessalonians: 62
9:7
Revelation 1–11: 321
9:9
Mark 9–16: 93
2 Corinthians: 106
9:9–11
Mark 1–8: 353
9:11
2 Corinthians: 163
Galatians: 182
9:11–12
Matthew 1–7: 258
Romans 9–16: 145
2 Timothy: 139
Revelation 1–11: 45
9:11–14
Mark 9–16: 379
Luke 18–24: 390
1 Peter: 207
9:11–15
2 Corinthians: 88
1 Peter: 25, 41, 114
1–3 John: 35
9:12
Luke 1–5: 47
Luke 11–17: 172
Luke 18–24: 455
John 1–11: 14
John 12–21: 356
Romans 1–8: 328
2 Corinthians: 97, 104, 107
1 & 2 Thessalonians: 244
1 Peter: 80, 206, 225
1–3 John: 28, 37, 208
Revelation 12–22: 308
9:12–14
Revelation 1–11: 232
9:13
1 & 2 Thessalonians: 202
9:13–14
Mark 1–8: 353
1–3 John: 39
9:14
Matthew 1–7: 206
Mark 1–8: 35, 183
Luke 1–5: 239
John 12–21: 4, 134
Acts 13–28: 280
2 Corinthians: 31, 190
1 & 2 Thessalonians: 244
1 Timothy: 141
Titus: 123
1–3 John: 143
Revelation 1–11: 51, 217
Revelation 12–22: 308
9:14–15
2 Corinthians: 98, 106
9:15
Luke 1–5: 117
John 1–11: 17
Acts 13–28: 336
Romans 1–8: 445
2 Corinthians: 104, 200
Colossians and Philemon: 39
1 & 2 Thessalonians: 256
1 Timothy: 71
1 Peter: 35, 37
9:16–20
Mark 9–16: 291
9:18–20
Luke 18–24: 284
9:19–20
1 Peter: 23
9:21
Romans 9–16: 332
9:22
Matthew 16–23: 37
Matthew 24–28: 152
Luke 1–5: 272
Luke 11–17: 370
Colossians and Philemon: 63
1 Peter: 80
9:22–23
1 Peter: 89
9:23–24
Revelation 12–22: 48
9:23–28
1–3 John: 47
9:24
Philippians: 141
1 & 2 Thessalonians: 234
2 Timothy: 71
1 Peter: 207, 220
Revelation 12–22: 262
9:24–28
1 Peter: 206
9:25
1 Peter: 108
9:25–26
1 Peter: 126
9:26
Luke 18–24: 185
John 12–21: 335
Acts 1–12: 53
2 Corinthians: 201
1 Timothy: 148
James: 92, 245
1–3 John: 124
Revelation 12–22: 50
9:26–28
1 Peter: 237
9:27
Mark 9–16: 330
Luke 11–17: 178, 188
John 1–11: 92
John 12–21: 361
Romans 1–8: 146
1 Corinthians: 425
James: 237, 271
Revelation 1–11: 230, 301
9:28
Luke 1–5: 154
Luke 18–24: 191, 195, 197
Acts 13–28: 336
Romans 1–8: 328, 408
1 Corinthians: 20, 239, 272
Philippians: 142, 261
1 Peter: 37, 207
1–3 John: 110
Revelation 12–22: 211
10
Luke 11–17: 123
10:1
Matthew 8–15: 459
2 Corinthians: 106
10:1–2
Luke 18–24: 50, 263, 424–25
10:1–3
Mark 9–16: 93
10:1–4
Luke 11–17: 370
10:1–10
1 Peter: 77–78
10:1–18
2 Corinthians: 281
1 Peter: 114
10:4
Matthew 1–7: 80
Matthew 24–28: 141
Mark 1–8: 37
Mark 9–16: 284
Luke 18–24: 279
Acts 1–12: 117
2 Corinthians: 97–98, 107, 190, 213
Revelation 1–11: 231, 294
10:5
2 Corinthians: 212
10:7
Mark 1–8: 16
2 Corinthians: 212
Philippians: 133
10:9–10
1 Peter: 88
10:10
Matthew 1–7: 402
John 12–21: 134
Romans 1–8: 210, 328
1 Corinthians: 6

2 Corinthians: 190
Philippians: 311
1 & 2 Thessalonians: 104, 202, 203
1 Peter: 206, 225
1–3 John: 37
10:10–12
Mark 9–16: 93
Luke 1–5: 175
10:10–18
Luke 11–17: 40
10:11
Romans 9–16: 332
10:11–12
Acts 1–12: 222
Romans 1–8: 509
10:11–14
1 Peter: 126
10:12
Matthew 24–28: 141
Acts 1–12: 67, 222
Acts 13–28: 336
2 Corinthians: 96–97, 176, 190, 201
Philippians: 141
1 & 2 Thessalonians: 233
1 Peter: 126, 225
Revelation 1–11: 146
Revelation 12–22: 214
10:12–18
1 Peter: 25
10:13
James: 196
10:14
John 12–21: 240
Romans 1–8: 210, 399
1 Corinthians: 60, 314
2 Corinthians: 106, 190, 210
Philippians: 249
1 & 2 Thessalonians: 104, 202, 203
1 Peter: 225
10:14–15
1 & 2 Thessalonians: 193
10:16
1 Peter: 275
10:17
2 Corinthians: 248
10:17–18
1–3 John: 33
10:18
Luke 1–5: 272
10:19
1 & 2 Thessalonians: 293
1–3 John: 37, 145
Revelation 1–11: 232
Revelation 12–22: 308
10:19–20
Acts 1–12: 266
1–3 John: 194
10:19–22
Matthew 1–7: 257
John 12–21: 226
Romans 1–8: 277
1 Peter: 207
10:20
Romans 1–8: 186
10:21
Titus: 121
10:22
Mark 1–8: 353
Luke 1–5: 77
Acts 13–28: 280
2 Corinthians: 31
Philippians: 31
1 & 2 Thessalonians: 97
James: 207
1 Peter: 104, 112
10:23
Luke 1–5: 28, 87, 174
Romans 1–8: 272
Romans 9–16: 92, 130
1 & 2 Thessalonians: 296
2 Timothy: 66
10:24
Matthew 16–23: 108
Mark 9–16: 45
Romans 1–8: 476
1 Corinthians: 330
1 & 2 Thessalonians: 97, 117
1–3 John: 164
10:24–25
Matthew 1–7: 257
Matthew 24–28: 82
Luke 1–5: 74
Luke 11–17: 377
Acts 1–12: 84
Romans 9–16: 159, 174, 250, 260, 268
1 & 2 Thessalonians: 166
1 Peter: 236
10:25
Luke 11–17: 157
1 & 2 Thessalonians: 82
James: 256
1–3 John: 18, 106
Revelation 1–11: 24
10:25–31
1 & 2 Thessalonians: 272
2 Peter–Jude: 76
1–3 John: 98
10:26
Luke 11–17: 124
John 1–11: 228
John 12–21: 152
Revelation 12–22: 143
10:26–27
Matthew 8–15: 264
Luke 18–24: 158
John 12–21: 51, 382
Acts 13–28: 311
Romans 1–8: 72, 170
1 & 2 Thessalonians: 163
1 Timothy: 30
Revelation 1–11: 209, 242
Revelation 12–22: 109
10:26–27, 29
Matthew 24–28: 149
10:26–29
Romans 1–8: 114
James: 287
2 Peter–Jude: 106
10:26–31
Luke 11–17: 84, 165, 168, 269
Romans 1–8: 138
2 Corinthians: 464
1 & 2 Thessalonians: 244
1 Timothy: 148, 245
2 Peter–Jude: 107, 187
Revelation 12–22: 137, 257
10:27
Luke 1–5: 223
Luke 11–17: 124, 170
Romans 1–8: 396
1 & 2 Thessalonians: 235
James: 271
Revelation 12–22: 124, 143, 256
10:28
Luke 1–5: 165
Luke 6–10: 284
Luke 11–17: 124
Luke 18–24: 330
2 Corinthians: 447
Revelation 1–11: 298
10:28–29
Matthew 8–15: 398
10:28–30
1 & 2 Thessalonians: 65
10:28–31
2 Corinthians: 111
Revelation 1–11: 268
10:29
Matthew 8–15: 100
Luke 1–5: 195
Luke 6–10: 333
Luke 11–17: 124
Romans 1–8: 273
Galatians: 210
Ephesians: 189
1 & 2 Thessalonians: 202
2 Timothy: 80
Revelation 1–11: 25
Revelation 12–22: 101, 254
10:29–30
Revelation 1–11: 115
10:29–31
Mark 1–8: 434
Luke 11–17: 109
1 Peter: 168
10:30
Romans 9–16: 202
1 & 2 Thessalonians: 172, 180, 236
1 Peter: 189
Revelation 12–22: 143
10:30–31
Luke 11–17: 124
Revelation 1–11: 202
10:31
Romans 1–8: 126
James: 196
Revelation 1–11: 51, 185, 209, 217
Revelation 12–22: 85, 118, 120, 132

10:32–36
1 Peter: 42
10:34
Matthew 1–7: 171
10:34–36
1 Peter: 16
10:35–37
Romans 9–16: 262
10:35–39
Matthew 1–7: 123
10:35, 36
2 Timothy: 130
10:36
1 & 2 Thessalonians: 96
1 Peter: 201
10:38
1 Corinthians: 400
Ephesians: 358
10:38–39
Acts 13–28: 34
2 Corinthians: 465
Philippians: 164
10:39
John 1–11: 228
Acts 1–12: 238
1 & 2 Thessalonians: 206
1 Timothy: 150, 256
Revelation 12–22: 273
11
Romans 1–8: 204, 228
2 Corinthians: 115, 227
James: 259
Revelation 12–22: 81
11:1
Mark 1–8: 370
Luke 1–5: 64
Romans 1–8: 265
2 Corinthians: 170
Colossians and Philemon: 15
1 Peter: 47
11:1, 6
1–3 John: 30
11:1–39
James: 9
11:2
2 Corinthians: 106
11:3
Romans 1–8: 258
2 Corinthians: 279
11:4
Matthew 16–23: 74
Romans 9–16: 23, 145
Philippians: 155
2 Peter–Jude: 177
1–3 John: 132
11:4–5
Matthew 1–7: 280
11:4–38
2 Corinthians: 106
11:4–39
Romans 9–16: 50
Titus: 106
11:4–40
Romans 1–8: 57
11:4, 7, 23–29, 39
Galatians: 72
11:5
Matthew 16–23: 74
Luke 1–5: 35
Philippians: 36, 155
11:6
Matthew 1–7: 378
Mark 1–8: 370
Acts 13–28: 132
2 Corinthians: 424
Ephesians: 358
1 & 2 Thessalonians: 89
2 Timothy: 199
Titus: 103
James: 38
11:7
Matthew 16–23: 74
Romans 1–8: 264
Philippians: 155
1 Timothy: 168
11:8
James: 140
11:8–10
Matthew 16–23: 74
Romans 1–8: 235, 256
Philippians: 156
Revelation 12–22: 277
11:8–10, 17–19
Galatians: 75
11:9
Luke 1–5: 174
11:10
2 Corinthians: 170
James: 253
1 Peter: 16
Revelation 12–22: 264, 265, 278
11:10–11
2 Peter–Jude: 128
11:11
Romans 1–8: 265
Galatians: 124
11:11–12
Romans 1–8: 258
11:11, 20
Galatians: 129
11:12
Revelation 12–22: 241
11:13
Luke 6–10: 348
Acts 1–12: 209
2 Corinthians: 162, 170
Colossians and Philemon: 126
James: 140
1 Peter: 15, 56
1–3 John: 176, 209
Revelation 12–22: 260
11:13–16
Matthew 16–23: 334
1 & 2 Thessalonians: 185
1 Peter: 15–16, 41, 137, 225
Revelation 12–22: 261
11:16
Matthew 16–23: 31
Mark 1–8: 434
Luke 6–10: 277
1 & 2 Thessalonians: 52
1 Timothy: 95
1–3 John: 116
Revelation 12–22: 260
11:16, 35–38
2 Timothy: 13
11:17
Luke 1–5: 196
James: 34, 140
11:17–18
Romans 9–16: 33
11:17–19
Matthew 24–28: 161
Romans 1–8: 237, 255, 264
2 Corinthians: 16
1 Timothy: 272
James: 34
11:19
Matthew 16–23: 222
Matthew 24–28: 304
Luke 1–5: 109
Romans 9–16: 146
1 Timothy: 266
James: 34, 138
11:20–21
Romans 9–16: 33
11:23
Ephesians: 316
11:23–38
Philippians: 156
11:24–26
2 Corinthians: 107
James: 18
11:24–27
Colossians and Philemon: 20
11:25
Luke 11–17: 310
John 12–21: 156
1 & 2 Thessalonians: 185
Revelation 1–11: 266
11:25–27
Ephesians: 126
11:26
Matthew 1–7: 221
2 Corinthians: 279, 349
1 Peter: 251
11:27
Romans 1–8: 134
Ephesians: 381
11:29
2 Corinthians: 58
11:31
Luke 6–10: 14
James: 140
11:32–37
1 & 2 Thessalonians: 62
11:33–34
1 Corinthians: 428
James: 20
11:34
James: 184
11:35
1 Corinthians: 428
Revelation 12–22: 238
11:35–38
2 Timothy: 53
1 Peter: 225

11:36–38
Matthew 1–7: 232
Romans 1–8: 512
11:36–39
Matthew 8–15: 171
11:36–40
1–3 John: 134
11:37
Mark 9–16: 168
Luke 18–24: 124
1 & 2 Thessalonians: 64
11:37–38
Mark 1–8: 298
11:37–39
James: 27
11:38
John 1–11: 472
1 Corinthians: 428
James: 285
11:39
Matthew 16–23: 74
2 Corinthians: 106
Galatians: 107
Philippians: 156
11:39–40
Luke 6–10: 158
2 Corinthians: 106
1 Peter: 52, 56
11:40
Matthew 8–15: 146
2 Corinthians: 122
12:1
Matthew 1–7: 99
Romans 9–16: 264
1 Corinthians: 197
2 Corinthians: 106
Ephesians: 349, 363
1 & 2 Thessalonians: 136
2 Timothy: 195
James: 27, 74, 259
1 Peter: 65
1–3 John: 36, 190
Revelation 1–11: 172
12:1–2
Matthew 16–23: 74
1 & 2 Thessalonians: 98
12:1–3
Galatians: 190
Philippians: 162
12:2
Matthew 1–7: 99, 232
Matthew 16–23: 151
Matthew 24–28: 105, 179
Mark 9–16: 305
Luke 1–5: 236
Luke 6–10: 277
Luke 11–17: 146, 172, 292
John 1–11: 422
John 12–21: 140, 280
Acts 1–12: 66, 67, 110, 169, 222
Romans 1–8: 256, 445
1 Corinthians: 429
2 Corinthians: 120, 123, 135
Galatians: 166
Philippians: 138, 188, 191, 268
1 & 2 Thessalonians: 234
2 Timothy: 56, 195
James: 20
Revelation 1–11: 146
Revelation 12–22: 214
12:2–3
Philippians: 140
Colossians and Philemon: 73
1 & 2 Thessalonians: 207, 298
1 Peter: 279
12:2–4
James: 22
Revelation 1–11: 122
12:3
John 12–21: 173, 346
Philippians: 268
Titus: 101
James: 278
12:3–4
Luke 18–24: 306
1 Corinthians: 230
1 Peter: 167
Revelation 1–11: 69
12:3–13
2 Corinthians: 98
12:4
1 Peter: 80–81, 206
12:5
2 Peter–Jude: 48
12:5–6
Acts 1–12: 161
2 Corinthians: 443
Galatians: 175
Colossians and Philemon: 142
12:5–7, 11
Romans 9–16: 181
12:5–9
Revelation 12–22: 272
12:5–10
Revelation 1–11: 46
12:5–11
Matthew 16–23: 129
Romans 1–8: 193
2 Corinthians: 16, 24, 98
Ephesians: 319
1 Timothy: 55
2 Timothy: 159
1 Peter: 69, 162, 200, 250
12:5–12
1 Peter: 42
12:5–13
Matthew 1–7: 395
12:5, 7, 11
2 Timothy: 161
12:5ff.
Revelation 1–11: 46
12:6
Matthew 16–23: 146, 155, 272
Romans 1–8: 400
Romans 9–16: 141
1 Corinthians: 125, 471
2 Corinthians: 236, 255
Ephesians: 318
2 Timothy: 32
12:6–7
James: 271
12:6–8
Romans 1–8: 479
12:7
Romans 1–8: 380
12:7–8
1 & 2 Thessalonians: 229
1 Peter: 257
12:7–11
Matthew 16–23: 125
12:9
1 Peter: 31, 178
12:10
Romans 1–8: 481
2 Corinthians: 34, 443
Philippians: 161
1 & 2 Thessalonians: 229
1–3 John: 19
12:11
John 12–21: 127, 149
Galatians: 175
Colossians and Philemon: 32
2 Timothy: 161
James: 22
1 Peter: 200
12:12–13
Galatians: 179
James: 279
12:12–15
1 & 2 Thessalonians: 203
12:14
Matthew 1–7: 211
Matthew 16–23: 312
Romans 1–8: 26, 411
1 & 2 Thessalonians: 174, 210
James: 29, 58, 121, 177
1 Peter: 22
Revelation 1–11: 54
12:15
Matthew 1–7: 294, 397
2 Corinthians: 50
Ephesians: 190
2 Timothy: 89
James: 9
12:16
James: 33
12:16–17
Romans 9–16: 33
12:18, 22
Galatians: 126
12:22
Revelation 1–11: 217, 228, 315
12:22–23
Matthew 16–23: 84
Revelation 12–22: 265
12:22–24
1–3 John: 18
Revelation 12–22: 71, 264, 277
12:23
Matthew 16–23: 32
Luke 1–5: 176
2 Corinthians: 106, 166
Galatians: 127

Philippians: 145, 260, 262
1 Timothy: 183
2 Timothy: 57
1 Peter: 231
1–3 John: 43
Revelation 1–11: 226
Revelation 12–22: 255, 260, 272
12:24
Luke 1–5: 117
John 1–11: 17
Romans 9–16: 68
2 Corinthians: 200
1 Timothy: 71
1 Peter: 23, 207
12:25
John 12–21: 56
Romans 1–8: 72
12:25–29
Romans 1–8: 117
12:26–27
Matthew 24–28: 275
Revelation 12–22: 152, 249
12:26–28
1 Peter: 236
12:28
Colossians and Philemon: 41
1 Timothy: 223, 262
12:28–29
Revelation 1–11: 50
12:29
1 & 2 Thessalonians: 235
1 Timothy: 278
Revelation 1–11: 148
Revelation 12–22: 124
13
1 Corinthians: 90
1 Peter: 115–16
13:1
Luke 6–10: 102
1 & 2 Thessalonians: 117
1 Timothy: 188
13:1–3
1 & 2 Thessalonians: 97
13:1–4
1 Peter: 276
13:1–9
1 & 2 Thessalonians: 203
13:2
John 12–21: 91
Acts 1–12: 298
Acts 13–28: 95, 360
Romans 9–16: 194
1 Timothy: 107
Titus: 40
James: 113
1 Peter: 213
1–3 John: 243
13:3
1 Peter: 286
13:4
Matthew 1–7: 302
Romans 9–16: 267
1 Corinthians: 183
1 & 2 Thessalonians: 97, 104, 111
Revelation 12–22: 77
13:5
Matthew 8–15: 441
John 12–21: 99
Acts 13–28: 230
2 Corinthians: 21, 120, 241
Philippians: 170, 296
1 & 2 Thessalonians: 97
Revelation 1–11: 44
13:5–6
Mark 1–8: 233, 291, 392
John 12–21: 116
13:6
Mark 1–8: 331
Acts 13–28: 290
Romans 1–8: 518
1 Timothy: 278
13:7
Luke 6–10: 24
John 12–21: 105
Acts 13–28: 208
1 Corinthians: 91, 482
Ephesians: 147
Philippians: 250
1 & 2 Thessalonians: 167, 174, 177, 292
1 Timothy: 103, 115, 172, 217
Titus: 26, 94
1 Peter: 276
1–3 John: 260
13:8
Matthew 24–28: 232
John 1–11: 14, 39
Galatians: 169
1 & 2 Thessalonians: 161
James: 55
13:8–9
1–3 John: 15
13:9
1 & 2 Thessalonians: 320
1 Timothy: 155
13:10
Revelation 1–11: 232
13:11–12
Colossians and Philemon: 62
1 Peter: 207
13:12
Matthew 24–28: 253
2 Corinthians: 190
1 & 2 Thessalonians: 104, 202
1 Peter: 2, 130, 206
Revelation 1–11: 232
Revelation 12–22: 308
13:14
Colossians and Philemon: 126
1 Peter: 15, 137
Revelation 12–22: 264, 277
13:15
Luke 1–5: 76, 164
John 12–21: 149
Romans 1–8: 45, 362
Romans 9–16: 138
Galatians: 164
Ephesians: 269
Philippians: 192
Colossians and Philemon: 31–32, 36, 93
1 & 2 Thessalonians: 189
Revelation 12–22: 194
13:15–16
Acts 13–28: 5
Romans 9–16: 138
Philippians: 308
13:16
2 Corinthians: 280
Philippians: 22, 221
1 & 2 Thessalonians: 308
13:17
Matthew 16–23: 372
Mark 1–8: 295
Acts 13–28: 55, 224, 225
Romans 1–8: 457
1 Corinthians: 29, 30, 91, 485
2 Corinthians: 77, 269, 270, 285, 473
Ephesians: 149, 226, 276
Philippians: 106, 188
Colossians and Philemon: 229
1 & 2 Thessalonians: 32, 40, 166, 167, 171, 174, 177, 292
1 Timothy: 42, 93, 97, 217, 219, 233
Titus: 34, 49
James: 72, 148, 151
1 Peter: 268, 277
1–3 John: 36, 247
13:18
John 12–21: 129
Acts 13–28: 280
2 Corinthians: 31
Colossians and Philemon: 26
1 & 2 Thessalonians: 214
13:19
Revelation 1–11: 21
13:20
Matthew 16–23: 120
Luke 1–5: 117, 155
Luke 11–17: 296
Acts 13–28: 224
Romans 9–16: 68
2 Corinthians: 485
Ephesians: 80
1 & 2 Thessalonians: 108, 204, 244, 313
Titus: 11, 24, 121
Revelation 1–11: 233
13:20–21
Romans 9–16: 174, 382
2 Corinthians: 222
Ephesians: 144, 152
Philippians: 172
1 & 2 Thessalonians: 85, 317
James: 237
13:21
1 & 2 Thessalonians: 97
13:23
Philippians: 196, 200
1 & 2 Thessalonians: 13
2 Timothy: 185, 205
Revelation 1–11: 21

13:24
2 Corinthians: 473
Philippians: 310
1 & 2 Thessalonians: 167

James
1:1
Acts 13–28: 72, 333
Philippians: 13, 16
1 & 2 Thessalonians: 87
1 Timothy: 230
James: 3, 123, 136, 274
1 Peter: 15
2 Peter–Jude: 18
Revelation 1–11: 220
Revelation 12–22: 200, 293
1:1–3
1 Peter: 16
1:2
2 Corinthians: 149
Philippians: 11, 216
1 & 2 Thessalonians: 184
James: 13, 285
1 Peter: 43, 252
Revelation 12–22: 76
1:2–3
Matthew 1–7: 395
Mark 1–8: 235
Romans 1–8: 477
1 Corinthians: 228
Philippians: 180
1 & 2 Thessalonians: 89, 189, 194
1:2–4
Matthew 1–7: 87
Matthew 16–23: 42
Mark 9–16: 238
Luke 6–10: 193
Luke 11–17: 46, 182, 383
Acts 13–28: 55
Romans 1–8: 265
2 Corinthians: 17, 52, 406
Ephesians: 88, 153
Philippians: 56, 97, 194, 250
1 & 2 Thessalonians: 79, 185, 227, 247
1 Timothy: 264
1 Peter: 43, 161, 279
Revelation 1–11: 68
1:2–12
1 Timothy: 67
James: 65
1:2–27
1 & 2 Thessalonians: 203
1:2ff.
James: 4, 274
1:3
2 Corinthians: 227
Ephesians: 269
James: 124
1:3–4
James: 253
1:3–12
1 Peter: 250
1:4
1 Peter: 279
1:5
Matthew 1–7: 414, 443
1 Corinthians: 298
Ephesians: 219
Colossians and Philemon: 186
1 & 2 Thessalonians: 187, 195
2 Peter–Jude: 30
1:5–6
James: 190
1:5–8
2 Corinthians: 183
1:6
Matthew 8–15: 239
Mark 1–8: 233
1 & 2 Thessalonians: 97
James: 255
1 Peter: 62
2 Peter–Jude: 101
1:6–8
Mark 9–16: 145
Luke 11–17: 143
1:7–8
Matthew 1–7: 444
James: 255
1:8
Matthew 8–15: 252
Luke 6–10: 26
Philippians: 198, 247, 267
1 Timothy: 180
James: 158, 176, 210
1:10
John 12–21: 360
1:10–11
1 Peter: 92
1:12
Matthew 8–15: 444
Matthew 16–23: 214
John 12–21: 400
Romans 1–8: 282, 482, 493
1 Corinthians: 85
1 & 2 Thessalonians: 18, 73, 91, 92, 194
2 Timothy: 47, 200
James: 124
1 Peter: 279
1–3 John: 171
Revelation 1–11: 78, 126, 149, 319
Revelation 12–22: 95, 113
1:12–18
1 & 2 Thessalonians: 81
1:13
Matthew 1–7: 395
Matthew 16–23: 108
Mark 1–8: 247
Luke 1–5: 253
Luke 11–17: 46
Romans 9–16: 39
2 Corinthians: 215
1 Timothy: 70, 119
James: 25
1:13–14, 14–15
1 Corinthians: 228
1:13–15
Matthew 1–7: 88
1 Peter: 139
1:13–16
1 Peter: 285
1–3 John: 86
1:13–18
James: 65
1:14
Romans 1–8: 101
1:14–15
Luke 11–17: 48
Romans 9–16: 269
2 Corinthians: 38
James: 144
1 Peter: 74
1–3 John: 121
1:14, 21
Galatians: 174
1:15
Matthew 8–15: 181
Mark 1–8: 350
Colossians and Philemon: 139
James: 288
1:16
James: 3, 24, 285
1:17
Matthew 1–7: 388
Matthew 8–15: 482
Acts 13–28: 140
2 Corinthians: 199
Ephesians: 268, 359
Philippians: 172
1 & 2 Thessalonians: 245
Hebrews: 34, 163
James: 190
1 Peter: 52, 120
1–3 John: 219
1:17–18
James: 137
1:18
Luke 18–24: 418
John 1–11: 43, 102
Acts 1–12: 267
1 Corinthians: 117
2 Corinthians: 229, 285, 477
Philippians: 27
1 & 2 Thessalonians: 58, 319
2 Timothy: 76
Titus: 154
James: 172, 286
1 Peter: 33, 50, 92, 171
2 Peter–Jude: 31
1:19
1 & 2 Thessalonians: 172
James: 3, 24, 144, 150, 285
1:19–20
Colossians and Philemon: 143
1:19–27
James: 65
1:20
Titus: 36
1:21
Matthew 1–7: 175, 265
Romans 9–16: 264
2 Corinthians: 257
Galatians: 169
Ephesians: 126
Hebrews: 396

James: 3, 103, 124, 169, 290
1:21–22
1 & 2 Thessalonians: 89
1:21–23
1 Peter: 24
1:21–25
1 & 2 Thessalonians: 194
1:22
Matthew 1–7: 487
Luke 6–10: 119, 203, 364
Luke 11–17: 77
John 1–11: 357
Acts 13–28: 122
Romans 1–8: 223
2 Corinthians: 318, 471
Galatians: 186
James: 122, 284
1–3 John: 67, 147, 220
1:22–23
Romans 1–8: 138
James: 124
1–3 John: 247
1:22–24
Matthew 1–7: 483
1:22–25
Philippians: 164
1 & 2 Thessalonians: 195
1 Peter: 90
2 Peter–Jude: 76
1–3 John: 28–29, 91
1:23–24
Matthew 1–7: 436
Romans 1–8: 139
1:25
Luke 1–5: 62
Acts 13–28: 358
1 Corinthians: 71
1 & 2 Thessalonians: 89
1 Timothy: 275
2 Peter–Jude: 48
1:26
Matthew 8–15: 319
James: 72, 144, 147, 264
1 Peter: 167
1:27
Matthew 1–7: 241
Matthew 8–15: 456
Philippians: 25, 51
1 & 2 Thessalonians: 97, 117, 119
1 Timothy: 267
Hebrews: 444
James: 3, 124, 183, 200
1 Peter: 31, 137, 280
1–3 John: 137, 209
Revelation 1–11: 82
Revelation 12–22: 181
2
James: 2
2:1
Matthew 16–23: 115
Mark 9–16: 3
James: 24, 285
2:1–4
1 Timothy: 281
2:1–4, 8–9
Romans 9–16: 321
2:1–4, 9
Romans 9–16: 199
Galatians: 100
2:1–9
Romans 9–16: 366
James: 124, 180
2:1–10
1 Timothy: 248–49
2:2
Romans 9–16: 199
James: 3
2:2–8
Matthew 16–23: 116
2:4
James: 255
2:5
Matthew 1–7: 97
Luke 1–5: 271
2 Corinthians: 71, 471
James: 3, 24, 285
1 Peter: 17, 108–9
1–3 John: 217
2:6
Acts 13–28: 103
James: 252
Revelation 12–22: 191
2:6–7
James: 4
2:7
1 & 2 Thessalonians: 256
1 Timothy: 55
2:8
Matthew 1–7: 338
Luke 1–5: 220
Romans 9–16: 253
2 Corinthians: 58
Ephesians: 77
James: 223
2:9
James: 98
2:10
Matthew 1–7: 271
Matthew 16–23: 191
Luke 1–5: 271
Luke 18–24: 12, 38
Romans 1–8: 229, 367, 406
Romans 9–16: 69
2 Corinthians: 90, 104
Galatians: 78
Hebrews: 47
1–3 John: 44, 45
Revelation 12–22: 253
2:10–11
1–3 John: 39
2:10–13
Matthew 1–7: 194
2:11
James: 249
2:12
James: 3, 144, 265
2:13
Matthew 1–7: 194, 197, 398
Matthew 16–23: 155
Mark 1–8: 121
Luke 1–5: 333
Luke 6–10: 308
Luke 11–17: 45
2 Corinthians: 51
Colossians and Philemon: 202
James: 271
2:14
Acts 1–12: 243
Galatians: 67
Hebrews: 302
James: 24, 285, 290
2:14–17
Acts 13–28: 109
2:14–20
Romans 1–8: 132
James: 179
2:14–26
Matthew 16–23: 52
Luke 11–17: 287
John 1–11: 98
John 12–21: 23, 160
Acts 1–12: 70, 297
Romans 1–8: 24
Galatians: 15
Philippians: 32, 213, 258
Colossians and Philemon: 16
1 & 2 Thessalonians: 259
1 Peter: 90
1–3 John: 178, 247
2:14ff.
Revelation 1–11: 136
2:15
James: 124
2:15–16
Matthew 16–23: 116
Luke 18–24: 74
Acts 1–12: 148
Acts 13–28: 181, 199
2 Corinthians: 294
Galatians: 43
1 & 2 Thessalonians: 119, 308
2:15–17
Matthew 24–28: 123
1 & 2 Thessalonians: 97
2:16
Matthew 16–23: 341
2:17
Matthew 1–7: 65, 479
Matthew 16–23: 57
Romans 1–8: 24, 205
Philippians: 153, 155
Hebrews: 302
James: 169
1 Peter: 36
1–3 John: 140
Revelation 1–11: 103
2:17–18
Acts 1–12: 243
2:17–20
James: 195
2:17, 26
1–3 John: 58
2:18
Acts 13–28: 337
Hebrews: 154
Revelation 1–11: 103

2:18–22
1 & 2 Thessalonians: 16
2:18–26
1–3 John: 136
2:19
Matthew 1–7: 454, 479
Matthew 8–15: 43, 227
Matthew 16–23: 339–40
Mark 1–8: 58, 64, 164, 216, 243
Luke 1–5: 280
John 1–11: 23
Acts 1–12: 243
Acts 13–28: 171
Romans 1–8: 482
Romans 9–16: 73
1 Corinthians: 400
2 Corinthians: 467
Ephesians: 131
Philippians: 48, 214
1 Timothy: 128
Revelation 1–11: 208
2:19–22
Hebrews: 302
2:20
Matthew 1–7: 139
Romans 1–8: 24
2:20–26
1 Peter: 36
2:21
Acts 1–12: 70
James: 3, 123
2:23
Mark 1–8: 36
Luke 11–17: 40, 363
John 12–21: 124, 161
Hebrews: 161
James: 197
Revelation 12–22: 68
2:25
James: 3
Revelation 1–11: 47
2:26
Luke 1–5: 166
Romans 1–8: 132
1 Corinthians: 448
1 & 2 Thessalonians: 16
Hebrews: 154, 317
James: 116
1–3 John: 113
Revelation 1–11: 103
3:1
Matthew 1–7: 270, 434
Mark 1–8: 287
Acts 13–28: 4, 220, 221
Romans 1–8: 114, 156
1 Corinthians: 210
2 Corinthians: 77
Ephesians: 240
1 & 2 Thessalonians: 32, 40
1 Timothy: 19, 42, 97, 222
Titus: 49
Hebrews: 448
James: 24, 71, 72, 285
2 Peter–Jude: 167
Revelation 1–11: 102
3:1–2
2 Timothy: 168
3:1–12
1 & 2 Thessalonians: 180
3:2
Matthew 8–15: 318
Galatians: 173
Colossians and Philemon: 187
James: 32, 271
3:2–3
1 & 2 Thessalonians: 205
3:2–11
James: 265
3:2–12
Mark 1–8: 352
Colossians and Philemon: 178
James: 124
1 Peter: 167
3:5–6
Titus: 54
James: 144
3:6
1 & 2 Thessalonians: 205
3:6–8
Ephesians: 187
3:8
James: 144, 176
3:8–12
James: 255
3:9b
1 Peter: 152
3:10
Colossians and Philemon: 144
James: 24, 285
3:11
Matthew 8–15: 319
James: 82
3:11–12
James: 195
3:12
James: 24, 285
3:13
1 Corinthians: 298
1 Timothy: 174
2 Peter–Jude: 49
3:13–16
Mark 1–8: 242
Luke 1–5: 283
Luke 6–10: 220
3:13–18
1 & 2 Thessalonians: 203
Hebrews: 405
3:14
James: 72, 189, 286
3:14–16
1 Corinthians: 341
3:14, 16
Romans 9–16: 267
3:15
Luke 1–5: 280
Luke 11–17: 47
John 1–11: 353
1 Corinthians: 42
1 Timothy: 242
3:16
Philippians: 111
1 & 2 Thessalonians: 199
James: 103, 189
3:16–18
Matthew 1–7: 212
3:17
Matthew 1–7: 211
Luke 11–17: 163
1 Corinthians: 42, 298
2 Corinthians: 183, 266
Colossians and Philemon: 32
1 & 2 Thessalonians: 181
1 Timothy: 225
2 Timothy: 8
James: 35
1 Peter: 193
2 Peter–Jude: 30
3:17–18
James: 184
3:18
Philippians: 53
1 & 2 Thessalonians: 174
4:1
2 Corinthians: 262
Ephesians: 276
4:1–2
Matthew 1–7: 328
1 Corinthians: 24
Colossians and Philemon: 164
1 Timothy: 256
James: 72
4:1–3
Ephesians: 76
4:1–12
James: 230
4:2
Mark 9–16: 30, 146
Colossians and Philemon: 139
James: 249
4:3
Matthew 1–7: 444
Matthew 16–23: 281
Mark 9–16: 144
John 12–21: 150
1 & 2 Thessalonians: 252, 258
James: 280
1–3 John: 204
4:4
Matthew 1–7: 204
Matthew 16–23: 84
John 1–11: 347
John 12–21: 54, 180
2 Corinthians: 244, 471, 481
Ephesians: 173
Philippians: 259, 266
2 Timothy: 79
Hebrews: 329
James: 3, 39, 205, 242, 256
1 Peter: 280
1–3 John: 81, 209
Revelation 1–11: 82, 89
Revelation 12–22: 181, 260
4:6
Matthew 16–23: 231
Mark 9–16: 32, 101
Luke 1–5: 47, 79, 80, 88, 277, 334

Luke 11–17: 299, 376
Luke 18–24: 22
Acts 1–12: 241
Acts 13–28: 49
Ephesians: 122
1 & 2 Thessalonians: 97
2 Timothy: 113
James: 72, 124, 203, 230
1 Peter: 182, 278
Revelation 12–22: 185
4:6–10
Matthew 16–23: 100
Acts 1–12: 242
4:7
Matthew 1–7: 98, 331, 396
Matthew 24–28: 179
Luke 1–5: 261
2 Corinthians: 482
Ephesians: 338, 344
Philippians: 154
1 & 2 Thessalonians: 72
1 Peter: 178, 285
1–3 John: 84, 90, 175
Revelation 12–22: 16, 235
4:7–10
Luke 11–17: 264–65
Galatians: 93
James: 284
4:8
Mark 9–16: 47
2 Corinthians: 183
2 Timothy: 77
James: 38, 256, 286
4:8–10
Matthew 1–7: 158
Matthew 16–23: 131
2 Corinthians: 208
4:9
James: 242
4:10
Matthew 1–7: 149, 151
Luke 6–10: 64, 304
Luke 11–17: 386
Acts 13–28: 49
Philippians: 138
1 Timothy: 131
James: 124
1 Peter: 277
4:10a
1 Peter: 278
4:11
James: 24, 72, 124, 144, 265, 285
4:11–12
Matthew 1–7: 433
Galatians: 178
James: 231
4:12
James: 290
4:13
Hebrews: 142
James: 242
4:13–14
Ephesians: 224
4:13–15
1 & 2 Thessalonians: 213
4:13–16
Luke 11–17: 134
4:13–17
2 Peter–Jude: 51
4:14
Matthew 1–7: 163, 231
Luke 11–17: 153
John 12–21: 360
1 Corinthians: 182
2 Corinthians: 155
1 Timothy: 273
1 Peter: 93
1–3 John: 200
4:14–15
Matthew 1–7: 92
4:14–26
2 Corinthians: 318
4:15
1 Corinthians: 462
1 & 2 Thessalonians: 195
4:16
2 Corinthians: 32, 240
Philippians: 187
James: 103
4:17
Philippians: 155
1–3 John: 39
5:1
James: 211, 231
5:1–3
Hebrews: 352
5:1–5
1 Timothy: 257
Revelation 12–22: 180
5:1–6
James: 4, 252
5:2
2 Corinthians: 279
5:3
1 Peter: 44
5:4
Luke 11–17: 333
1 Timothy: 221
5:4–6
Revelation 12–22: 191
5:5
1 Timothy: 201
5:5–6
Hebrews: 352
5:7
James: 24, 285
Revelation 12–22: 292
5:7–8
Luke 11–17: 413
Luke 18–24: 191
Romans 9–16: 260, 312
1 & 2 Thessalonians: 74, 116
Hebrews: 330
Revelation 12–22: 211
5:7–8, 10
Luke 1–5: 259
5:7–9
Revelation 1–11: 24
5:7–11
James: 264
5:8
Matthew 24–28: 82
Romans 9–16: 263
Philippians: 276
Hebrews: 241
James: 124
Revelation 1–11: 30
Revelation 12–22: 302
5:9
Philippians: 176, 178
James: 24, 72, 285
Revelation 12–22: 292
5:10
Luke 18–24: 338
Ephesians: 126
1 Timothy: 115
James: 24, 285
1 Peter: 51
5:11
Luke 1–5: 120
Luke 11–17: 236
Romans 9–16: 198, 313
1 & 2 Thessalonians: 185
James: 3
1 Peter: 43, 161, 286
5:12
Matthew 1–7: 326
James: 3, 24, 144, 285
5:13
1 & 2 Thessalonians: 184
5:13–14
1 & 2 Thessalonians: 186
5:14
Acts 13–28: 248
Ephesians: 148
Philippians: 15
1 & 2 Thessalonians: 167, 179
1 Timothy: 98
5:14–16
Luke 1–5: 295
Philippians: 34
5:15
Hebrews: 137
James: 290
5:16
Matthew 1–7: 372, 384
Matthew 16–23: 81
Luke 11–17: 30
John 12–21: 163
Acts 1–12: 323
Romans 9–16: 352
1 Corinthians: 229
2 Corinthians: 27
Galatians: 180
Philippians: 21, 73, 303
Colossians and Philemon: 229
1 & 2 Thessalonians: 166, 186, 255
2 Timothy: 6
1 Peter: 117
Revelation 1–11: 241
5:17
Matthew 8–15: 130
Luke 1–5: 275
Luke 6–10: 24, 173
Revelation 1–11: 300, 302

5:17–18
John 12–21: 234
James: 3
5:19
James: 24, 172
5:19–20
Matthew 16–23: 132
Luke 1–5: 39
James: 3, 202
5:20
1 & 2 Thessalonians: 27
Titus: 106

1 Peter
1:1
Acts 1–12: 252
Acts 13–28: 38
Romans 9–16: 212
1 Corinthians: 323
2 Corinthians: 162
Ephesians: 141, 147
1 & 2 Thessalonians: 287
James: 13
1 Peter: 9, 13, 262
2 Peter–Jude: 4, 14, 20, 128
1:1a
1 Peter: 14–16
1:1b
1 Peter: 16
1:1–2
Luke 1–5: 166
John 12–21: 118
Acts 13–28: 268
Romans 1–8: 496
Romans 9–16: 100
1 & 2 Thessalonians: 23, 287
Titus: 7
1 Peter: 13–27
Revelation 1–11: 54
1:1–12
1 Peter: 61
1:2
Matthew 16–23: 50
Mark 9–16: 291
Luke 1–5: 37
Luke 6–10: 119
John 12–21: 114
Romans 1–8: 347
Romans 9–16: 244
Philippians: 158
1 & 2 Thessalonians: 104, 193, 287
1 Peter: 19, 42, 80, 89
2 Peter–Jude: 11
1–3 John: 149
Revelation 1–11: 54, 232
Revelation 12–22: 308
1:2a
1 Peter: 19
1:2b
1 Peter: 21
1:2c
1 Peter: 22
1:2d
1 Peter: 23
1:2e
1 Peter: 25
1:2–3
Philippians: 27
1:3
Matthew 1–7: 82
Matthew 16–23: 68
Matthew 24–28: 310
Mark 1–8: 37
Mark 9–16: 396
Luke 1–5: 96, 121
Luke 18–24: 407, 408
Romans 9–16: 133, 315
2 Corinthians: 18, 20, 108, 243, 393
Ephesians: 41, 105
Philippians: 16, 314
1 & 2 Thessalonians: 87
James: 261
1 Peter: 31, 42, 48, 62, 201, 286
2 Peter–Jude: 11, 12
1–3 John: 108, 219
1:3a
1 Peter: 30
1:3b
1 Peter: 31
1:3c
1 Peter: 32
1:3–4
Matthew 24–28: 305
Romans 9–16: 75
1 Corinthians: 437
Ephesians: 30, 34
1 & 2 Thessalonians: 52
Titus: 156
1 Peter: 288
1:3–5
Matthew 24–28: 122
Romans 1–8: 460
2 Corinthians: 155
Ephesians: 366
Philippians: 29
1 Peter: 29, 41, 62, 266
2 Peter–Jude: 207, 211
1–3 John: 118
Revelation 12–22: 100
1:3–6
Romans 1–8: 448
Philippians: 11
James: 40
1:3–7
1 & 2 Thessalonians: 18
1:3–9
Luke 18–24: 296
1:4
Matthew 8–15: 385
Mark 1–8: 117
Luke 1–5: 331
Luke 6–10: 186
Acts 13–28: 336
Romans 1–8: 446
1 Corinthians: 215
2 Corinthians: 45, 232, 294, 465
Ephesians: viii, 60
Philippians: 243, 244, 260
Colossians and Philemon: 19, 39, 131
1 & 2 Thessalonians: 74, 92
Hebrews: 368
1–3 John: 234
Revelation 1–11: 125
Revelation 12–22: 243, 260, 272
1:4a
1 Peter: 34
1:4b–5
1 Peter: 36
1:4–5
Romans 1–8: 20
Hebrews: 146
1 Peter: 271
1:5
Luke 18–24: 260
John 12–21: 277
Romans 9–16: 280
Philippians: 164, 283
2 Timothy: 22, 29
James: 28
1 Peter: 279
2 Peter–Jude: 11
Revelation 12–22: 74, 101
1:5–7
Luke 11–17: 124
1:6
Luke 6–10: 98
1 & 2 Thessalonians: 184, 287
1 Peter: 42, 187, 286
1:6–7
Matthew 8–15: 444
Luke 11–17: 181
Luke 18–24: 328
2 Corinthians: 13, 155
1 & 2 Thessalonians: 185, 226
James: 42, 254
1 Peter: 167, 198, 248–50
1:6–8
Philippians: 97
1:6–9
1 & 2 Thessalonians: 189
1 Peter: 39, 223
1:6a
1 Peter: 41
1:6b–7a
1 Peter: 42
1:6, 8
Luke 1–5: 79
1:7
Luke 11–17: 155
Romans 1–8: 477
2 Corinthians: 277, 394
Philippians: 199
1 Peter: 63
2 Peter–Jude: 59
Revelation 1–11: 3, 15, 16, 138
1:7b
1 Peter: 44
1:8
Mark 9–16: 22
Luke 1–5: 63, 158

Luke 18–24: 36
John 12–21: 151
Acts 1–12: 16, 259
1 Corinthians: 365
2 Corinthians: 484
Galatians: 166
Philippians: 11
1 & 2 Thessalonians: 81, 184, 233, 287
James: 42
1 Peter: 41, 46, 88, 123, 189
Revelation 1–11: 54
1:8–9
1 & 2 Thessalonians: 185
1:9
1 & 2 Thessalonians: 287
1 Peter: 48, 89
1:10
Hebrews: 248
1:10–11
Matthew 1–7: x
Matthew 8–15: 242
Matthew 16–23: 223
Luke 11–17: 409
Romans 9–16: 387
Hebrews: 10, 369
1:10–11a
1 Peter: 51
1:10–12
Matthew 8–15: 354
Luke 6–10: 348
Romans 1–8: 13
2 Corinthians: 107, 109
2 Timothy: 149
Hebrews: 4, 192
1 Peter: 49
2 Peter–Jude: 11
1:11
Matthew 16–23: 225
Luke 1–5: 239
Luke 18–24: 52, 53
John 12–21: 116
Philippians: 138
Hebrews: 31
1 Peter: 2, 266
1:11–12
Acts 13–28: 333
1:11b–12a
1 Peter: 55
1:12
Matthew 24–28: 332
Romans 1–8: 298
Ephesians: 97
Hebrews: 31
1 Peter: 221, 271
1–3 John: 195
Revelation 1–11: 228
1:12b
1 Peter: 56
1:12c
1 Peter: 57
1:13
Luke 11–17: 158
Romans 1–8: 465
2 Corinthians: 108, 394
Ephesians: 349
Philippians: 289
1 & 2 Thessalonians: 73, 160
1 Peter: 46, 62, 266, 271, 280, 286
2 Peter–Jude: 59
Revelation 1–11: 30
Revelation 12–22: 211
1:13–16
1–3 John: 114
1:13–17
1 Peter: 61
1:13–19
1 & 2 Thessalonians: 92
1:13–21
1 Peter: 102
1:14
Acts 13–28: 337
Philippians: 131
2 Peter–Jude: 102
1:14–16
Matthew 1–7: 206
2 Corinthians: 255
Ephesians: 194
Philippians: 213
1 & 2 Thessalonians: 203, 287
James: 195
1 Peter: 65
1:15
Romans 1–8: 411
Philippians: 311
1 & 2 Thessalonians: 256
1 Timothy: 174
2 Timothy: 83
1 Peter: 131
1–3 John: 70
Revelation 1–11: 119
1:15–16
Acts 13–28: 310
Romans 1–8: 333
2 Corinthians: 443
Revelation 1–11: 45, 54
Revelation 12–22: 80, 253
1:16
Matthew 1–7: 378
Matthew 16–23: 123, 131
Mark 1–8: 16
Luke 18–24: 12
Romans 9–16: 63
2 Corinthians: 257
Titus: 71, 90
Hebrews: 254, 396
James: 48
Revelation 1–11: 155
1:16–17
James: 96
1:17
Romans 1–8: 47, 136
2 Corinthians: 162
Ephesians: 223
James: 97
1 Peter: 68
1–3 John: 45
Revelation 1–11: 54
Revelation 12–22: 251
1:17–19
James: 91
1:18–19
Matthew 16–23: 242, 246
Mark 1–8: 37
Luke 1–5: 96, 198
John 12–21: 66
Acts 13–28: 225
Romans 1–8: 209
1 Corinthians: 54, 152, 253
2 Corinthians: 190, 440
Ephesians: 21
Colossians and Philemon: 62
Titus: 3, 121
Hebrews: 19
1 Peter: 130
1–3 John: 35
Revelation 1–11: 172
Revelation 12–22: 22, 50, 79, 308
1:18–20
1–3 John: 46
1:18–21
Romans 1–8: 280
1 Peter: 71
1:18a
1 Peter: 76
1:18b
1 Peter: 73
1:19
Matthew 1–7: 81
Matthew 24–28: 153
Mark 9–16: 292, 294
Luke 1–5: 58
1 Corinthians: 175
2 Corinthians: 214
Galatians: 78
Ephesians: 14
Philippians: 182
1 Peter: 76, 81, 88, 166, 266
Revelation 1–11: 168, 232
1:19–20
Matthew 24–28: 131
Luke 18–24: 267
Hebrews: 235
1:20
Mark 9–16: 344
John 12–21: 34
Acts 1–12: 53
Romans 1–8: 496
Ephesians: 14
1 Timothy: 8, 148
James: 245
1 Peter: 20
Revelation 12–22: 50
1:20a
1 Peter: 82
1:20b
1 Peter: 83
1:21
John 12–21: 232
2 Corinthians: 108, 147
1 Peter: 62
1:21a
1 Peter: 82
1:21b
1 Peter: 83

1:22
Matthew 16–23: 312
Mark 1–8: 359
Luke 6–10: 35
John 12–21: 93
Acts 1–12: 84
Romans 9–16: 184, 247, 250
Ephesians: 108
Philippians: 45
1 & 2 Thessalonians: 17, 90, 117, 119, 244
2 Timothy: 8, 18
1–3 John: 183, 217, 245
1:22a
1 Peter: 88
1:22b
1 Peter: 90
1:22c
1 Peter: 90
1:22–23
John 12–21: 94
Romans 1–8: 347
Hebrews: 423
1:22–25
1 & 2 Thessalonians: 22
1 Peter: 87–93, 102
1:23
Luke 6–10: 190
Luke 11–17: 123, 368
Luke 18–24: 250
Romans 1–8: 52, 487
2 Corinthians: 243
Philippians: 181, 187
1 & 2 Thessalonians: 58
Titus: 12, 154
James: 62, 76
2 Peter–Jude: 11, 31
1–3 John: 142, 206
1:23–25
2 Corinthians: 82–83
1 & 2 Thessalonians: 22, 209
2 Timothy: 141, 162
James: 63, 68
1 Peter: 32, 91
2 Peter–Jude: 49
1–3 John: 127, 158
1:24
1 Corinthians: 182
James: 40, 233
1:24–25
John 12–21: 360
1:25
1 & 2 Thessalonians: 294
1–3 John: 160
2:1
Luke 11–17: 114
Romans 9–16: 264
2 Corinthians: 183
Philippians: 64
James: 180, 218, 221
1 Peter: 168
1–3 John: 258
2:1a
1 Peter: 96
2:1b
1 Peter: 97
2:1–2
Acts 13–28: 122
1 Corinthians: 71
Philippians: 243
1 Timothy: 83
2 Timothy: 160
James: 74
2:1–3
Titus: 8
1 Peter: 95
2 Peter–Jude: 101
2:2
Luke 6–10: 366
John 12–21: 284
Acts 1–12: 83
Acts 13–28: 229
1 Corinthians: 475
2 Corinthians: 129
Ephesians: 156, 370
Philippians: 250
Colossians and Philemon: 22, 32, 150
1 & 2 Thessalonians: 58, 108, 166, 194, 198
1 Timothy: 162, 240
Titus: 46
Hebrews: 372
1–3 John: 72
2:2a
1 Peter: 98
2:2b
1 Peter: 100
2:2–3
1 Corinthians: 339
2:3
1 Peter: 101
2:4
Luke 6–10: 125
Acts 1–12: 135
1 Peter: 104
2:4–5
Hebrews: 80
1 Peter: 103, 120
2:4, 6
1–3 John: 216
2:5
Matthew 16–23: 29
Luke 1–5: 74
Romans 1–8: 29
Romans 9–16: 142
1 Corinthians: 452
2 Corinthians: 284
Ephesians: 83
Philippians: 124, 192, 308
1 & 2 Thessalonians: 206
1 Timothy: 183
Hebrews: 110, 372
Revelation 1–11: 172
2:5a
1 Peter: 106
2:5b
1 Peter: 107
2:5c
1 Peter: 113
2:5–7
1 & 2 Thessalonians: 165
2:5–8
Luke 6–10: 120
2:5, 9
Romans 9–16: 138, 331–32
Ephesians: 146
Titus: 139
2:6
Ephesians: 12
1 Peter: 20, 51, 120
2:6–7
2 Peter–Jude: 62
2:6–8
Matthew 16–23: 297
Luke 18–24: 128
Acts 1–12: 135
Acts 13–28: 120
1 Corinthians: 82
2 Corinthians: 73, 178
2:6–9b
1 Peter: 119
2:7
Matthew 16–23: 340
Romans 1–8: 223
2:7–8
Luke 1–5: 183
1 Peter: 122
2:7, 9
Ephesians: 83
2:8
Luke 1–5: 40
Acts 1–12: 148
1 Peter: 105
Revelation 12–22: 50
2:9
Matthew 1–7: 102, 116, 237
Matthew 16–23: 89, 299
Mark 1–8: 215
Luke 1–5: 31
Luke 11–17: 91
Luke 18–24: 68, 75
Acts 1–12: 16
Acts 13–28: 336
Romans 1–8: 29, 55, 337
Romans 9–16: 209
2 Corinthians: 249
Galatians: 29
Ephesians: 208, 240
Philippians: 124
1 & 2 Thessalonians: 155, 256
1 Timothy: 135, 183, 216
Titus: 7, 90, 122, 141
Hebrews: 110
1 Peter: 16, 318, 108, 176, 207, 287
2 Peter–Jude: 11
1–3 John: 24
Revelation 1–11: 139, 172
Revelation 12–22: 239
2:9a
1 Peter: 123
2:9b
1 Peter: 125
2:9c
1 Peter: 127
2:9c–10
1 Peter: 127

2:9d
1 Peter: 130
2:9e
1 Peter: 133
2:9f
1 Peter: 131
2:9–10
Matthew 1–7: 257
1 Peter: 21, 26, 127
Revelation 1–11: 26
2:9–12
2 Corinthians: 443
2:10
Matthew 16–23: 89
Luke 1–5: 121
Romans 9–16: 46
James: 261
1 Peter: 31, 132
2:11
John 12–21: 296
Romans 1–8: 337, 425
Romans 9–16: 211
2 Corinthians: 162, 206, 247
Ephesians: 354
Colossians and Philemon: 126
1 & 2 Thessalonians: 113, 206
Titus: 96, 117, 122
1 Peter: 137, 187
Revelation 1–11: 89
Revelation 12–22: 261
2:11–12
Matthew 16–23: 89
Titus: 32
1 Peter: 135, 248
2 Peter–Jude: 11
2:11–19
1 Corinthians: 249
2:12
Luke 6–10: 34
Acts 13–28: 320
Colossians and Philemon: 165
1 & 2 Thessalonians: 121
1 Timothy: 119, 174
Titus: 123
James: 221, 222
1 Peter: 10, 40, 139, 279
2:12–15
1 Peter: 176
2:12–15, 17
Titus: 141
2:13
Matthew 16–23: 34
1 Corinthians: 481
Philippians: 113
2:13a
1 Peter: 145
2:13b
1 Peter: 147
2:13c–14
1 Peter: 148
2:13–14
Matthew 1–7: 331
Matthew 16–23: 90
2:13–15
Matthew 16–23: 322
Mark 9–16: 181
Romans 9–16: 227
Ephesians: 226, 276
James: 235
2:13–15, 17
Matthew 8–15: 141
2:13–17
Acts 1–12: 138
Acts 13–28: 304
Romans 9–16: 212
Philippians: 39
1 Peter: 143, 175, 187
2:13–18
Luke 6–10: 34
2:13–20
1 Peter: 276
2:13–23
1 Timothy: 66
2:15
Luke 11–17: 100
Acts 13–28: 320
Galatians: 191
Titus: 56
Hebrews: 420
1 Peter: 150
2:15–16
Revelation 1–11: 88
2:16
Matthew 16–23: 115
Acts 13–28: 71
Romans 9–16: 288
1 Corinthians: 189
Galatians: 39, 146
1 Timothy: 230
1 Peter: 151
2:17
Luke 1–5: 157
Luke 6–10: 35
Luke 18–24: 136
2 Corinthians: 439
Ephesians: 312
1 & 2 Thessalonians: 90, 119
1 Timothy: 64, 188, 223
Hebrews: 98
James: 98
1 Peter: 152
1–3 John: 165
Revelation 12–22: 87
2:18
James: 204
1 Peter: 158
2:18–19
Matthew 16–23: 91
Titus: 99
2:18–20
Ephesians: 325
1 Timothy: 232
2:18–21
1 Peter: 40
2:18–21a
1 Peter: 155
2:18–24
Acts 1–12: 132
2:18–25
1 Peter: 176
2:19–20
1 Peter: 248
2:19–21a
1 Peter: 160
2:19–23
2 Corinthians: 52–53, 324
1 & 2 Thessalonians: 181
1 Peter: 223
1–3 John: 136
2:20
Acts 1–12: 165
2 Corinthians: 156
Ephesians: 226
James: 22–23
1 Peter: 200
2:20–21
2 Timothy: 59
1 Peter: 187
2:20–21a
1 Peter: 166
2:20–22
2 Timothy: 55–56
2:20–23
Matthew 1–7: 333
2:21
Luke 18–24: 68
Acts 1–12: 128
Acts 13–28: 73, 211
1 & 2 Thessalonians: 256
Hebrews: 66
1 Peter: 2, 131
2:21–22
1 Timothy: 141
2:21–23
Matthew 1–7: 171
Matthew 16–23: 91
Luke 6–10: 34
Romans 9–16: 196
1 Timothy: 266
2 Timothy: 99
James: 152
1 Peter: 189
2 Peter–Jude: 30
2:21b–23
1 Peter: 166
2:21–24
1 Peter: 266
2:21–25
Mark 1–8: 192
2:21b–25
1 Peter: 165
2:22
Luke 1–5: 167, 253
Luke 18–24: 298, 431
John 12–21: 254, 324, 374
2 Corinthians: 478
Philippians: 253
1 Peter: 206
Revelation 12–22: 80
2:22–23
Luke 11–17: 46, 383
2:23
Matthew 8–15: 149, 202
Matthew 24–28: 210
Luke 18–24: 8, 384
John 1–11: 346
John 12–21: 125
Acts 13–28: 273, 281, 282

Romans 1–8: 100
Ephesians: 125
James: 250, 252
1 Peter: 2, 190, 280
Revelation 12–22: 51
2:23–24
Mark 9–16: 330
2:24
Matthew 1–7: 273
Matthew 8–15: 19
Matthew 16–23: 42
Matthew 24–28: 270
Mark 1–8: 110
Mark 9–16: 109, 376
Luke 1–5: 150, 154, 175, 328
Luke 11–17: 40
Luke 18–24: 283, 390, 406
John 12–21: 66
Acts 13–28: 336
Romans 1–8: 200
1 Corinthians: 41, 79
2 Corinthians: 52, 176, 191, 193
Galatians: 6, 78, 205
Philippians: 135, 142, 238, 253, 257
1 & 2 Thessalonians: 127, 164, 247
2 Timothy: 201
James: 280
1 Peter: 88, 169, 173, 224
2 Peter–Jude: 22–23
Revelation 1–11: 54
Revelation 12–22: 154, 253, 269
2:24–25
Luke 11–17: 298
2:25
Luke 1–5: 155
Luke 11–17: 296
Acts 1–12: 114
Acts 13–28: 224, 337
Ephesians: 144
1 & 2 Thessalonians: 108
Titus: 24, 34
James: 286, 289
1 Peter: 173, 270
Revelation 1–11: 233
3:1
Hebrews: 430
1 Peter: 6, 10, 276
3:1–2
Matthew 16–23: 91
Ephesians: 282
Titus: 88
Hebrews: 404
1 Peter: 177
3:1–6
1 Peter: 176
3:1–7
1 Peter: 175, 176, 187, 276
3:1–12
1 & 2 Thessalonians: 203
3:2
Matthew 8–15: 56
2 Corinthians: 266
3:3
James: 244
Revelation 12–22: 265
3:3–4
Ephesians: 283
1 & 2 Thessalonians: 208
1 Timothy: 79
3:3–6
Titus: 85
1 Peter: 179
3:4
Ephesians: 126, 283
1 Timothy: 66
3:5–6
Ephesians: 284
3:6
Luke 1–5: 159
Colossians and Philemon: 168
Hebrews: 430
3:7
1 Corinthians: 253
Ephesians: 282, 291, 304
Colossians and Philemon: 169
1 Timothy: 85, 154
2 Timothy: 119
Hebrews: 430
1 Peter: 181, 276
1–3 John: 204
3:7a
1 Peter: 181
3:7b
1 Peter: 182
3:7c
1 Peter: 182
3:8
Mark 9–16: 101
Romans 9–16: 306
Philippians: 271
3:8b
1 Peter: 187
3:8–9
Matthew 8–15: 112
Romans 9–16: 201
1 Peter: 176, 248
3:8–12
1 & 2 Thessalonians: 181
1 Peter: 185
3:8–22
1 Peter: 223
3:9
Luke 6–10: 104
Acts 13–28: 282
1 & 2 Thessalonians: 256
1 Peter: 40, 131, 189
Revelation 12–22: 184
3:10
Acts 1–12: 156
3:10–11
1 & 2 Thessalonians: 174
1 Peter: 191
3:12
Romans 1–8: 380
Philippians: 21
1 Peter: 193
3:13
1 Peter: 196
3:13–15
Acts 1–12: 139
3:13–17
1 Peter: 10, 195, 206
3:13–18
Matthew 1–7: 227
3:14
1 Peter: 167, 197, 216, 248
Revelation 12–22: 95
3:14–15
Luke 6–10: 36
1 Peter: 40, 187
3:15
Matthew 1–7: 176, 378
Luke 1–5: 31
Luke 11–17: 16
Acts 1–12: 21, 200, 257
Acts 13–28: 120
1 Corinthians: 17
Ephesians: 126
Philippians: 287
Colossians and Philemon: 12, 156, 187
1 & 2 Thessalonians: 202
1 Timothy: 137
2 Timothy: 97, 176
Titus: 144
2 Peter–Jude: 12
3:15a
1 Peter: 200
3:15b
1 Peter: 201
3:16
Acts 13–28: 280
2 Corinthians: 31
1 Timothy: 174
James: 221, 222
1 Peter: 202
Revelation 12–22: 51
3:16–17
2 Timothy: 62
3:17
Acts 1–12: 165
Acts 13–28: 73
Romans 9–16: 213
James: 235
1 Peter: 40, 167, 187, 197, 216, 248
3:18
Matthew 24–28: 267, 270
Mark 1–8: 32, 422
Luke 1–5: 154, 197, 328
Luke 18–24: 267
John 12–21: 37, 66, 158, 365
Acts 13–28: 336
Romans 1–8: 328
2 Corinthians: 191
1 & 2 Thessalonians: 164
1 Peter: 80, 170, 224, 266
Revelation 1–11: 51, 69
3:18a
1 Peter: 206
3:18–19
2 Corinthians: 293
Ephesians: 139

3:18b–20a
1 Peter: 208
3:18–20
Luke 1–5: 286
Philippians: 238
1 Timothy: 141
1 Peter: 211, 231
2 Peter–Jude: 86
Revelation 1–11: 258
Revelation 12–22: 10
3:18–22
Acts 13–28: 169
1 Peter: 205
3:19
Philippians: 146
Revelation 1–11: 167
3:19–20
Hebrews: 322
1 Peter: 281
Revelation 12–22: 234
3:20
Luke 18–24: 9
John 12–21: 47
Galatians: 167
3:20b–21
1 Peter: 216
3:21
Acts 13–28: 280
Romans 1–8: 321
2 Peter–Jude: 11
3:22
Luke 1–5: 229
Luke 18–24: 112, 453
John 12–21: 140, 213
Acts 1–12: 67
Ephesians: 139, 341
Philippians: 140, 141
Colossians and Philemon: 50
1 & 2 Thessalonians: 234
Hebrews: 20
1 Peter: 216, 219
Revelation 1–11: 168
Revelation 12–22: 214, 262
4:1
1 Peter: 2, 40, 187, 224, 248, 250, 266
4:1–2
Romans 1–8: 327
Ephesians: 227
Philippians: 77
4:1–4
1 & 2 Thessalonians: 108
4:1–6
1 Peter: 223
4:2
James: 230
1 Peter: 226
4:2–3
James: 195
4:2–5
2 Peter–Jude: 12
4:3
Luke 18–24: 256
Romans 9–16: 266
Ephesians: 232
1 & 2 Thessalonians: 105, 109
4:3–4
Luke 6–10: 170
Luke 18–24: 211
Ephesians: 166
1–3 John: 116
4:3–5
1 Peter: 228
4:5
James: 257
4:6
1 Peter: 231
4:7
Matthew 24–28: 82
John 12–21: 93, 233
Romans 1–8: 426
Romans 9–16: 263
Ephesians: 381
Philippians: 38
Hebrews: 241
James: 245, 254, 256
1 Peter: 271, 280
2 Peter–Jude: 12
Revelation 1–11: 24
Revelation 12–22: 65
4:7a
1 Peter: 234
1–3 John: 90
4:7b
1 Peter: 240
4:7–8
Romans 9–16: 250, 260
4:7–11
1 Peter: 233
4:7b–11a
1 Peter: 239
4:8
Matthew 8–15: 141
Matthew 16–23: 156
Luke 6–10: 35
Luke 11–17: 380
Acts 1–12: 323
Romans 9–16: 184, 248
1 Corinthians: 330, 353, 358, 476
2 Corinthians: 239
Ephesians: 127, 195
1 & 2 Thessalonians: 90, 119, 173
1 Peter: 90–91
4:8–9
1 Peter: 241
4:9
Acts 1–12: 89
Acts 13–28: 95, 360
Romans 9–16: 194
Philippians: 176
1 Timothy: 107
Titus: 40
1–3 John: 218, 258
4:9–10
Acts 1–12: 84
Philippians: 178
4:10
Acts 13–28: 44
1 Corinthians: 98, 290, 292
Ephesians: 89, 136, 137
Colossians and Philemon: 73
1 & 2 Thessalonians: 320
Titus: 35
1 Peter: 43
4:10–11
Romans 9–16: 162
1 Timothy: 179
2 Timothy: 15
Hebrews: 156
4:10–11a
1 Peter: 242
4:11
Acts 1–12: 282
Acts 13–28: 49
Romans 9–16: 170
1 Corinthians: 291
2 Corinthians: 44
1 Timothy: 278
1 Peter: 288
4:11b
1 Peter: 245
4:11–12
2 Peter–Jude: 9
4:12
1 Peter: 40, 187, 248
4:12–13
John 12–21: 193
James: 252
4:12–14
Matthew 16–23: 49
Luke 11–17: 124
4:12–14, 16, 19
Matthew 1–7: 228
4:12–16
2 Corinthians: 24
Philippians: 95
1 Peter: 198
4:12–19
1 Peter: 167, 247, 263
4:13
Matthew 16–23: 225
Mark 9–16: 8
Acts 1–12: 174
Romans 9–16: 193
2 Corinthians: 156, 394, 484
Philippians: 11, 97, 194
1 & 2 Thessalonians: 184, 185, 298
Hebrews: 368
1 Peter: 16, 42, 46, 63, 266, 271
2 Peter–Jude: 12, 59
1–3 John: 18
Revelation 12–22: 76
4:13–14
1 Peter: 251
4:13–14, 16, 19
Matthew 8–15: 141
4:14
Matthew 8–15: 206
Luke 11–17: 74
John 1–11: 450
John 12–21: 174
Acts 1–12: 165, 221
Colossians and Philemon: 75
1 & 2 Thessalonians: 51

Hebrews: 354
1 Peter: 40
Revelation 12–22: 51, 95
4:14–15, 19
2 Timothy: 21
4:14–16
1 Corinthians: 244
2 Corinthians: 156
4:14–19
1 Peter: 223
4:15
Matthew 1–7: 437
Romans 1–8: 327
4:15–16
Romans 9–16: 213
4:15–18
1 Peter: 254
4:15–19
1 Peter: 200
4:16
Matthew 1–7: 150
Mark 1–8: 433
Luke 6–10: 274, 277
Acts 1–12: 315
Romans 9–16: 256
2 Timothy: 27
1 Peter: 16, 40
4:17
Matthew 16–23: 270
Mark 1–8: 47
Luke 1–5: 335
John 12–21: 111, 159
Acts 1–12: 156
Acts 13–28: 45
Galatians: 176
Colossians and Philemon: 15
1 & 2 Thessalonians: 35
1 Timothy: 135
1 Peter: 69
Revelation 1–11: 46, 97, 103
Revelation 12–22: 50
4:18
James: 286
4:19
Mark 9–16: 144
Luke 1–5: 174
Romans 1–8: 282
Colossians and Philemon: 29
1 & 2 Thessalonians: 178, 227, 296
1 Timothy: 271
1 Peter: 16, 40, 187, 258, 280
Revelation 12–22: 51
5:1
Matthew 16–23: 30
Acts 13–28: 248
2 Corinthians: 484
1 & 2 Thessalonians: 167
1 Peter: 2, 7, 270
5:1–2
Ephesians: 143, 147
Philippians: 15
1 & 2 Thessalonians: 32
1 Timothy: 98
1–3 John: 249
5:1–2a
1 Peter: 263
5:1–3
John 1–11: 17
John 12–21: 403
Acts 13–28: 55
Ephesians: 148
1 Timothy: 93
Titus: 26
5:1–4
1 & 2 Thessalonians: 44, 49, 170, 213, 292
1 Peter: 261, 276
2 Peter–Jude: 111
5:1–5
1 & 2 Thessalonians: 166
5:1, 5
1–3 John: 216
5:2
Matthew 1–7: 33, 466
Matthew 8–15: 193
Luke 18–24: 170
John 12–21: 402
Acts 13–28: 224, 225
1 Corinthians: 208
2 Corinthians: 473
Ephesians: 148
1 Timothy: 111, 219
Titus: 34, 40, 61
1 Peter: 7, 174
2 Peter–Jude: 96, 177
5:2b
1 Peter: 266
5:2c–3
1 Peter: 267
5:2–3
Matthew 16–23: 369
1 & 2 Thessalonians: 170
1 Timothy: 183
Hebrews: 445
2 Peter–Jude: 50
5:2–4
Acts 13–28: 224
5:3
Matthew 16–23: 30, 239
Luke 6–10: 35
Acts 13–28: 197, 208, 224
2 Corinthians: 473
Ephesians: 152
Philippians: 250, 291
1 Timothy: 103, 115
1 Peter: 264
1–3 John: 257
5:3–4
Romans 1–8: 44
5:4
Matthew 16–23: 214
Mark 1–8: 117, 295
Luke 1–5: 155
Acts 13–28: 224
Romans 1–8: 493
1 Corinthians: 85
Philippians: 28
1 & 2 Thessalonians: 73, 92, 108
2 Timothy: 47, 200
Titus: 24
Hebrews: 445
James: 42
1 Peter: 35, 46, 174, 270
2 Peter–Jude: 59, 96, 111
Revelation 1–11: 126, 149, 233, 319
Revelation 12–22: 113, 211
5:4, 7
Matthew 8–15: 295
5:5
Matthew 1–7: 149
Matthew 8–15: 141
Matthew 16–23: 231
Mark 9–16: 33, 101
Luke 1–5: 79
John 12–21: 61
Acts 1–12: 84
Acts 13–28: 248
Romans 1–8: 44
Romans 9–16: 158
1 Corinthians: 481
2 Corinthians: 285
Ephesians: 145
Philippians: 138
1 & 2 Thessalonians: 167
2 Timothy: 113
Titus: 92
Hebrews: 425
James: 199
5:5a
1 Peter: 276
5:5b–6
1 Peter: 277
5:5–6
Matthew 16–23: 369
Luke 6–10: 35
Acts 13–28: 49
Philippians: 113
5:5–8
Mark 9–16: 332, 340–41
5:5–14
1 Peter: 273
5:6
Matthew 16–23: 361
Luke 6–10: 300, 304
Luke 11–17: 264
1 Corinthians: 112
Philippians: 138
1 Timothy: 131
5:6–10
1 Peter: 223
5:7
Matthew 16–23: 121
Mark 1–8: 233
Luke 6–10: 212
Luke 11–17: 34, 140
Acts 1–12: 323
Acts 13–28: 297
Galatians: 180
Philippians: 283
1 & 2 Thessalonians: 194
James: 261, 275
1 Peter: 279
2 Peter–Jude: 25

5:8
Matthew 24–28: 176
Mark 9–16: 303
Luke 1–5: 50, 255
2 Corinthians: 58
Ephesians: 336
Philippians: 32, 266
1 & 2 Thessalonians: 72, 81, 160
1 Timothy: 39
2 Timothy: 213
2 Peter–Jude: 69
1–3 John: 133
Revelation 1–11: 255, 310
Revelation 12–22: 14, 16, 19, 21
5:8a
1 Peter: 280
5:8b
1 Peter: 280
5:8–9
Acts 1–12: 153
1 Corinthians: 472
Ephesians: 344, 363
1 & 2 Thessalonians: 91
1–3 John: 84
5:8–10
Luke 6–10: 35–36
5:9
Romans 1–8: 449
Philippians: 282
1 & 2 Thessalonians: 72
1 Peter: 167, 285
5:10
Matthew 8–15: 359
Matthew 16–23: 234
Luke 1–5: 88
Luke 11–17: 4
Acts 13–28: 55, 73, 105
Romans 1–8: 447, 478
2 Corinthians: 152, 257
Ephesians: 153
Philippians: 97, 250, 283
1 & 2 Thessalonians: 52, 79, 162, 178, 185, 227, 229, 247, 256
James: 33, 255
1 Peter: 40, 43, 131, 187, 286
2 Peter–Jude: 27, 211
Revelation 1–11: 68
5:11
2 Corinthians: 44
1 Timothy: 278
1 Peter: 288
5:12
Acts 13–28: 72
2 Corinthians: 484
Philippians: 267, 282
1 & 2 Thessalonians: 13, 223
1 Peter: 8, 9, 10, 288
2 Peter–Jude: 11
5:13
Mark 1–8: 2
Acts 13–28: 82
2 Timothy: 210
1 Peter: 10
5:13–14
1 Peter: 289
1–3 John: 238
5:14
Luke 6–10: 342
Luke 18–24: 210
Romans 9–16: 370
2 Corinthians: 234, 487
1 & 2 Thessalonians: 59, 214
1–3 John: 210

2 Peter
1:1
Matthew 16–23: 30
Luke 6–10: 27
Luke 18–24: 155, 328
John 1–11: 7, 14
John 12–21: 4
Romans 1–8: 240
1 Corinthians: 7
2 Corinthians: 205, 249, 488
Ephesians: 61
Philippians: 13
1 & 2 Thessalonians: 87, 254
1 Timothy: 230
James: 12
2 Peter–Jude: 4, 5, 10, 14, 18
Revelation 1–11: 222
Revelation 12–22: 200, 293
1:1–2
Philippians: 16
1:1–4
2 Peter–Jude: 17, 48
1:2
2 Peter–Jude: 23–25
1:2–3
Mark 1–8: 406
1:2–8
1 Peter: 290
1:2–9
1 & 2 Thessalonians: 96
1:2, 11
Luke 1–5: 153
1:3
Matthew 1–7: 206
Matthew 16–23: 34
Luke 18–24: 68
John 1–11: 35
John 12–21: 209
Acts 13–28: 196
Romans 9–16: 139
1 Corinthians: 16, 204, 364
Ephesians: 8, 41, 95, 377
Philippians: 249, 308
Colossians and Philemon: 122, 128
1 & 2 Thessalonians: 185, 256
1 Timothy: 164
Titus: 8
Hebrews: 423
1 Peter: 162
2 Peter–Jude: 5, 30, 48
1:3a
2 Peter–Jude: 26–27
1:3b
2 Peter–Jude: 27–28
1:3c
2 Peter–Jude: 28–31
1:3–4
Romans 1–8: 462
1 Corinthians: 6, 313
Ephesians: 30
Philippians: 153
Colossians and Philemon: 104
Hebrews: 254
2 Peter–Jude: 25–31
1:3–4, 5–6
Galatians: 157
1:3, 5–8, 10
Ephesians: 363
1:3–8
2 Corinthians: 257
1:3–11
Matthew 1–7: 475
James: 130
1:4
Matthew 1–7: 142, 281
Luke 11–17: 12
John 1–11: 18–19
1 Corinthians: 68, 141
2 Corinthians: 107, 294
Galatians: 60, 208
Ephesians: 178
Colossians and Philemon: 131
1 & 2 Thessalonians: 203, 224, 225
Hebrews: 69, 311
James: 62
2 Peter–Jude: 30–31
1:4–9
1 Peter: 89
1:5
1 Peter: 275
1:5a
2 Peter–Jude: 39–40
1:5b–7
2 Peter–Jude: 40–42
1:5–6
Galatians: 170
2 Peter–Jude: 24
1:5–7
Philippians: 40
2 Peter–Jude: 11–12
1:5–8
Matthew 1–7: 469
Colossians and Philemon: 32, 90
1:5–10
2 Corinthians: 178–79
Philippians: 153
1 & 2 Thessalonians: 159
1:5–11
Luke 18–24: 82
Ephesians: 210
1 & 2 Thessalonians: 203, 204
2 Peter–Jude: 33–46, 48
1:6–7
2 Peter–Jude: 5
1:7
Luke 6–10: 35
1 & 2 Thessalonians: 117, 119
1 Peter: 93

2 Peter–Jude: 11
1:8
Galatians: 170
2 Peter–Jude: 12, 24
Revelation 1–11: 99
1:8–9
2 Peter–Jude: 42–44
1:8–10
1–3 John: 149
1:9
1 & 2 Thessalonians: 160
2 Peter–Jude: 48–49
1:9–10
Matthew 1–7: 246
1:10
Galatians: 174
Colossians and Philemon: 90
1 & 2 Thessalonians: 29, 256
James: 80
2 Peter–Jude: 11, 29
1–3 John: 52
1:10–11
1 Peter: 200
2 Peter–Jude: 44–45
1–3 John: 19
1:11
Matthew 1–7: 56
Acts 1–12: 15
1 & 2 Thessalonians: 245
2 Peter–Jude: 12, 23
1:12
Romans 9–16: 331
1 & 2 Thessalonians: 157
2 Peter–Jude: 163
1:12a
2 Peter–Jude: 48–49
1:12b
2 Peter–Jude: 49–50
1:12–13, 15
Ephesians: 155
1:12–15
Luke 6–10: 33
1 & 2 Thessalonians: 271
2 Timothy: 71
2 Peter–Jude: 47–54
1:12, 19
1–3 John: 14
1:13
2 Peter–Jude: 50–51
1:13–14
2 Corinthians: 162
1:14
Matthew 16–23: 232
2 Timothy: 190
2 Peter–Jude: 1, 5, 10–12, 14
Revelation 1–11: 21
1:14–15
2 Peter–Jude: 51–53
1:15
2 Peter–Jude: 1
1:16
Acts 1–12: 21
James: 253
2 Peter–Jude: 12, 14, 26
1:16–18
Matthew 8–15: 242
Matthew 16–23: 70
Matthew 24–28: 57
Mark 9–16: 4
John 1–11: 452
John 12–21: 181
Philippians: 127
1 Peter: 7, 245
2 Peter–Jude: 4, 29, 57–61
1:16–21
2 Peter–Jude: 55–66
1–3 John: 18
1:17
Matthew 16–23: 63
Luke 6–10: 262
Luke 18–24: 124
John 1–11: 450
Ephesians: 312
2 Peter–Jude: 8
1:17–18
2 Corinthians: 113
1:19
Luke 1–5: 122
Acts 13–28: 3
2 Corinthians: 123, 413
1 & 2 Thessalonians: 97, 108
1 Peter: 56, 131
2 Peter–Jude: 62
1–3 John: 24, 160, 210
Revelation 1–11: 105
Revelation 12–22: 307
1:19–21
1 Peter: 106
2 Peter–Jude: 11, 61–66
1:20–21
Luke 1–5: 15
Luke 11–17: 154
Romans 9–16: 312
Ephesians: 91, 369
1 & 2 Thessalonians: 98, 194, 197
2 Timothy: 144
1 Peter: 289
1–3 John: 15
1:20–2:3
Romans 9–16: 375
1:21
Mark 1–8: 6
Luke 1–5: 70
Luke 11–17: 122
Acts 1–12: 31, 121
Acts 13–28: 374
1 Corinthians: 303
2 Corinthians: 114
Ephesians: 250
1 & 2 Thessalonians: 254
1 Timothy: 260
Hebrews: 5, 87
1 Peter: 55
1–3 John: 107
1:23
John 1–11: 35
1 Peter: 289
2
1 Timothy: 45
2 Peter–Jude: 50
2:1
Matthew 1–7: 461
Matthew 16–23: 354
Acts 1–12: 140
Acts 13–28: 62
Romans 9–16: 295
1 Corinthians: 473, 474
2 Corinthians: 336
Galatians: 139
1 & 2 Thessalonians: 136
1 Timothy: 14, 231, 244
2 Timothy: 65, 74
2 Peter–Jude: 6, 7, 12, 14
1–3 John: 155
Revelation 12–22: 56
2:1a
2 Peter–Jude: 69
2:1b
2 Peter–Jude: 71
2:1c
2 Peter–Jude: 72
2:1–2
Galatians: 11
1 Timothy: 293
2 Timothy: 69, 106
1–3 John: 27
2:1–3
Matthew 1–7: 438
Matthew 16–23: 7, 360
1 Timothy: 40, 111
Titus: 57
James: 149
2 Peter–Jude: 8
2:1–3a
2 Peter–Jude: 67
2:1–9
1–3 John: 100
2:1–21
Acts 1–12: 95
1–3 John: 232
2:1–22
Luke 18–24: 162
1 Peter: 281
2:2
Matthew 1–7: 472
Acts 1–12: 266
2 Timothy: 78
Titus: 164
2 Peter–Jude: 8
2:2a
2 Peter–Jude: 76
2:2b
2 Peter–Jude: 76
2:2c
2 Peter–Jude: 77
2:2, 3, 9
Galatians: 141
2:2–3
1 & 2 Thessalonians: 38
2:3
Matthew 1–7: 466
Matthew 8–15: 193
Matthew 16–23: 362
Luke 11–17: 345
Acts 13–28: 230
Ephesians: 172

2 Timothy: 112
2 Peter–Jude: 14
2:3a
2 Peter–Jude: 78
2:3b
2 Peter–Jude: 83
2:3b–10a
2 Peter–Jude: 81, 162
2:3–6
2 Peter–Jude: 160
2:3–10
2 Peter–Jude: 162
2:3, 9, 12, 17
Matthew 1–7: 467
2:3, 14
Galatians: 11
2:4
Matthew 24–28: 269
Mark 1–8: 244
Mark 9–16: 376
Luke 6–10: 222
Romans 1–8: 99
1 Corinthians: 138
1 & 2 Thessalonians: 157, 245
James: 271
2 Peter–Jude: 84, 165
Revelation 1–11: 257, 268
2:4–5
Luke 1–5: 280
2:4–6
1 Peter: 215
2:4–8
2 Peter–Jude: 84
2:4–9
Matthew 24–28: 76
1 Timothy: 244
2:5
Matthew 24–28: 74
Luke 18–24: 254
Romans 1–8: 119, 264
2 Timothy: 172
Hebrews: 322
1 Peter: 216
2 Peter–Jude: 87
2:6
2 Timothy: 74
2:6–8
2 Peter–Jude: 88
2:7
2 Peter–Jude: 11, 77
2:7–8
Luke 11–17: 417
2:8
1 & 2 Thessalonians: 206
2:9
Matthew 24–28: 176, 213
Luke 18–24: 249
John 12–21: 156
2 Corinthians: 27
1 & 2 Thessalonians: 163
2 Timothy: 102
James: 25, 174, 271
Revelation 12–22: 109, 176
2:9–10a
2 Peter–Jude: 91
2:9–10, 12, 14, 17–18
Titus: 36
2:10
Acts 13–28: 226
Romans 1–8: 416
2 Peter–Jude: 12, 14, 77
Revelation 1–11: 54
2:10, 12–14, 17–19
Matthew 16–23: 360
2:10–12
Ephesians: 171
2:10b–13a
2 Peter–Jude: 97
2:10–14
James: 187
2:10–19
James: 175
2:10–22
1 Timothy: 241
2 Peter–Jude: 12
2:10b–22
2 Peter–Jude: 95–96
2:11
Matthew 8–15: 44
Mark 1–8: 247
James: 271
2:12
Matthew 1–7: 438, 464
Acts 13–28: 226
Romans 9–16: 37
2 Peter–Jude: 11
2:12–13, 17
Revelation 12–22: 56
2:12–14
1 & 2 Thessalonians: 108
2:12–15
1 & 2 Thessalonians: 38
2:12–15, 17–18
Galatians: 12
2:13
Acts 13–28: 226
1 Corinthians: 267
2:13b–14
2 Peter–Jude: 100
2:13–14
2 Peter–Jude: 77
2:14
Matthew 1–7: 466
Acts 13–28: 226
2 Corinthians: 309
Galatians: 11
Philippians: 267
1 Timothy: 111
James: 49
1 Peter: 229
2 Peter–Jude: 14
2:15
Matthew 16–23: 8
Romans 1–8: 186
1 Timothy: 245
James: 285
Revelation 12–22: 56
2:15–16
Luke 18–24: 396
2 Peter–Jude: 102
Revelation 12–22: 56
2:15–18
1 & 2 Thessalonians: 38
2:17
Acts 13–28: 226
2 Corinthians: 249
1 & 2 Thessalonians: 157, 245
Revelation 12–22: 256
2:17–19
2 Peter–Jude: 103
2:17–21
James: 187
2:18
Matthew 8–15: 321
2 Corinthians: 345
1 Timothy: 241
Titus: 60
James: 49
2 Peter–Jude: 14
2:18–19
Matthew 1–7: 469
Romans 1–8: 344
2 Peter–Jude: 77
2:18–21
Galatians: 147
2:19
Matthew 1–7: 466
Acts 13–28: 226, 320
Titus: 94
2 Peter–Jude: 161
1–3 John: 83
2:20
Luke 1–5: 153
2 Timothy: 44
James: 132, 175
2 Peter–Jude: 12, 23–24
2:20–21
John 12–21: 153
2 Timothy: 14
Hebrews: 143
2:20–22
Matthew 1–7: 469
Matthew 8–15: 338
1 & 2 Thessalonians: 272
2 Peter–Jude: 106
2:21
Romans 1–8: 186
Romans 9–16: 375
James: 197
2:22
Matthew 1–7: 179
Acts 13–28: 226
2 Peter–Jude: 77
3:1
Romans 9–16: 331
Colossians and Philemon: 99
2 Peter–Jude: 4, 14, 48
3:1–2
2 Peter–Jude: 115
3:1–10
2 Peter–Jude: 109–10, 138
3:2
Mark 9–16: 170
1 Peter: 7, 289
2 Peter–Jude: 5, 10, 23
Revelation 12–22: 293

3:3
2 Corinthians: 336
1 Timothy: 148
2 Peter–Jude: 8
3:3a
2 Peter–Jude: 111
3:3b
2 Peter–Jude: 113
3:3–4
Matthew 16–23: 7
Matthew 24–28: 81, 97
Luke 11–17: 409
Luke 18–24: 186
1 & 2 Thessalonians: 272
James: 255
2 Peter–Jude: 111
Revelation 1–11: 28, 277
3:3–7
Romans 9–16: 262
3:3–10
1 & 2 Thessalonians: 253
3:4
Matthew 8–15: 245
Mark 1–8: 264
Luke 6–10: 281
Luke 18–24: 255
John 1–11: 456
Romans 9–16: 258
Galatians: 167
1 & 2 Thessalonians: 74, 125
Hebrews: 36
James: 253
2 Peter–Jude: 5, 7, 10, 12, 14, 113
Revelation 1–11: 24, 202
Revelation 12–22: 312
3:5–6
Matthew 24–28: 81
2 Peter–Jude: 10
3:5–7
Matthew 24–28: 97
2 Peter–Jude: 14, 117–18
3:5–9
2 Peter–Jude: 115
3:7
Matthew 1–7: 262
Luke 11–17: 250
Luke 18–24: 250
Romans 1–8: 126
1 & 2 Thessalonians: 163, 235
James: 271
Revelation 12–22: 109, 124
3:7–12
Luke 1–5: 91
3:7, 10
Matthew 1–7: 238
3:8
Luke 18–24: 7
2 Peter–Jude: 10, 115, 121
Revelation 1–11: 20
Revelation 12–22: 203
3:8–9
Matthew 24–28: 81
Romans 9–16: 262
3:9
Matthew 1–7: 383, 454, 458, 489
Matthew 8–15: 115, 196, 340, 396
Matthew 16–23: 96, 193, 216, 246, 313, 375, 392
Matthew 24–28: 111, 332
Luke 1–5: 214
Luke 11–17: 183, 186
Luke 18–24: 9, 192, 193
John 12–21: 258
Acts 1–12: 303
Romans 1–8: 26, 81, 101, 119, 127, 185, 218, 241, 487, 499
Romans 9–16: 42, 58, 79, 130
1 Corinthians: 338
2 Corinthians: 73
Galatians: 167, 210
Philippians: 166, 223
Colossians and Philemon: 29
1 Timothy: 69
2 Timothy: 61
Titus: 103, 110, 111, 151
Hebrews: 86, 257, 280, 320, 404
James: 202, 235
2 Peter–Jude: 121
1–3 John: 166
Revelation 1–11: 54, 139, 190
Revelation 12–22: 124, 133, 226
3:10
Matthew 1–7: 478
Matthew 24–28: 77
Luke 6–10: 228
Luke 11–17: 156, 161
Luke 18–24: 253
Romans 1–8: 456
2 Corinthians: 37
Philippians: 28
Colossians and Philemon: 50
1 & 2 Thessalonians: 143, 144, 235
Hebrews: 35, 324, 418
James: 64
1 Peter: 238
2 Peter–Jude: 123
Revelation 1–11: 41, 114, 200, 201, 206, 244
Revelation 12–22: 149
3:10–11
Philippians: 183
3:10–12
Mark 1–8: 431
1 Corinthians: 473
Revelation 1–11: 10
3:10–13
Mark 9–16: 260
Luke 18–24: 250
Acts 13–28: 114
James: 64
1 Peter: 217
Revelation 12–22: 249
3:11
Matthew 1–7: 427
Luke 11–17: 420
Luke 18–24: 10
Philippians: 85
1 & 2 Thessalonians: 253, 270
1 Timothy: 164
2 Peter–Jude: 5, 11
1–3 John: 114
Revelation 1–11: 54, 321
Revelation 12–22: 65, 226
3:11–12
Revelation 12–22: 295
3:11–13
Romans 9–16: 266
3:11–18
Luke 18–24: 228
2 Peter–Jude: 127
3:12
Luke 11–17: 26, 399
1 & 2 Thessalonians: 74, 144
Hebrews: 418
3:12–13
2 Peter–Jude: 129–31
Revelation 1–11: 320
3:13
Romans 1–8: 455, 457
Colossians and Philemon: 58
2 Timothy: 200
1 Peter: 33
2 Peter–Jude: 30
Revelation 12–22: 249
3:13–14
1 & 2 Thessalonians: 116
3:14
Matthew 8–15: 130, 457
Luke 11–17: 161
Luke 18–24: 197
Romans 9–16: 265
1 Corinthians: 449
Philippians: 85, 183
1 & 2 Thessalonians: 160, 253, 270
James: 254
Revelation 1–11: 11, 21, 201
Revelation 12–22: 261, 295
3:14a
2 Peter–Jude: 132
3:14b
2 Peter–Jude: 132–33
3:14–15
Mark 9–16: 264
3:14–18
Acts 1–12: 23
3:15
Matthew 16–23: 128
Luke 18–24: 9
1 Corinthians: 298
Colossians and Philemon: 156
2 Peter–Jude: 12
1–3 John: 244
3:15a
2 Peter–Jude: 133–34
3:15b–17
2 Peter–Jude: 134–36

3:15–16
Luke 11–17: 109
John 12–21: 201
Galatians: 32, 41
Colossians and Philemon: 14
1 Timothy: 220
2 Timothy: 74
2 Peter–Jude: 5, 9, 12, 14, 50
Revelation 1–11: 114
3:16
Romans 9–16: 41, 312
Philippians: 92
2 Timothy: 147
Titus: 60
1 Peter: 6
2 Peter–Jude: 9, 12
3:16–17
Philippians: 267
3:17–18
Matthew 24–28: 219
Luke 18–24: 328
3:18
Matthew 1–7: 181
Matthew 8–15: 143
Matthew 16–23: 232
Luke 1–5: 153
Luke 6–10: 36
Acts 13–28: 229
1 Corinthians: 245, 475
2 Corinthians: 44
Ephesians: 117, 218
Philippians: 49, 243, 253
Colossians and Philemon: 32, 93
1 & 2 Thessalonians: 216, 320
Titus: 8
2 Peter–Jude: 12, 24, 25
1–3 John: 77, 246
3:18a
2 Peter–Jude: 136–37
1–3 John: 70
3:18b
2 Peter–Jude: 137–38

1 John
1:1
Matthew 8–15: 242
John 1–11: 23
Acts 1–12: 138
Colossians and Philemon: 48
2 Peter–Jude: 19
1–3 John: 8
Revelation 12–22: 218
1:1a
1–3 John: 14
1:1b–2a
1–3 John: 16
1:1–2
Acts 1–12: 21
Philippians: 186
2 Peter–Jude: 30
1:1–3
Luke 1–5: 14
John 1–11: 38
John 12–21: 394
Ephesians: 91
1–3 John: 157, 169
1:1–4
Acts 1–12: 166
1–3 John: 4, 13, 188
1:2
John 1–11: 17
1 & 2 Thessalonians: 245
Revelation 1–11: 22
1:2b–3a
1–3 John: 17
1:2–3
Matthew 1–7: 444
1:3
Matthew 16–23: 68
John 12–21: 179
Acts 1–12: 84, 138
Romans 1–8: 320
Ephesians: 380
Philippians: 16
1 & 2 Thessalonians: 82, 87
Revelation 12–22: 266
1:3b
1–3 John: 18
1:4
Matthew 8–15: 387
Galatians: 166
Ephesians: 230, 353, 365
Philippians: 10, 56, 188
1–3 John: 19, 237
1:5
Matthew 24–28: 108
Luke 1–5: 122
Luke 11–17: 88
Romans 9–16: 265
2 Corinthians: 249
Hebrews: 34
James: 55
1–3 John: 22, 131
1:5–6, 8, 10
1–3 John: 21
1:5–7
Matthew 1–7: 244
Luke 11–17: 91
John 12–21: 51
Ephesians: 206
1:5–9
1 & 2 Thessalonians: 203
1:6
Romans 1–8: 345
Colossians and Philemon: 61
1–3 John: 4, 28
1:6–7
Luke 1–5: 20
Romans 9–16: 85
Hebrews: 312
1:6–10
James: 9
1:6, 8, 10
1–3 John: 25
1:7
Matthew 24–28: 212
Acts 13–28: 336
Romans 1–8: 410
Romans 9–16: 306
1 Corinthians: 445
2 Corinthians: 31, 190, 249
Colossians and Philemon: 39
1 & 2 Thessalonians: 157
Hebrews: 19
1 Peter: 25, 26, 62, 206
1–3 John: 36
Revelation 1–11: 54, 232
Revelation 12–22: 308
1:7–9
Philippians: 243
1:7–10
2 Corinthians: 468
1:8
Romans 1–8: 400
Galatians: 186
Ephesians: 362
1 & 2 Thessalonians: 286
Hebrews: 250
James: 151
1–3 John: 8, 10, 29
1:8–9
Matthew 1–7: 160, 393, 475
Romans 1–8: 224
Ephesians: 123
Philippians: 160
Titus: 42
1:8–10
Matthew 1–7: 454
Romans 1–8: 383, 426
Romans 9–16: 85
1 Peter: 22
Revelation 12–22: 80
1:8, 10
Galatians: 173
1:9
Matthew 1–7: 160, 393, 479
Matthew 8–15: 304, 312, 360
Matthew 16–23: 58
Matthew 24–28: 163, 212
Mark 1–8: 103
Luke 1–5: 174, 321
Luke 11–17: 39
John 1–11: 417
John 12–21: 129
Acts 1–12: 75
Romans 1–8: 376, 386, 399, 509
1 Corinthians: 274
2 Corinthians: 31, 438
Galatians: 65, 188
Ephesians: 23, 300, 303, 346
Philippians: 35
Colossians and Philemon: 202
1 & 2 Thessalonians: 97, 166, 188, 247, 296
2 Timothy: 38, 102, 160
Titus: 19, 41
James: 152, 208, 279
1 Peter: 37, 62
1–3 John: 37
Revelation 1–11: 54
1:10
Romans 1–8: 386
Galatians: 186
1 & 2 Thessalonians: 286
Hebrews: 250
James: 32, 151

1–3 John: 30
2:1
Matthew 1–7: 444
Luke 1–5: 236
John 1–11: 422
Romans 1–8: 509
Romans 9–16: 174
1 Corinthians: 25
1 & 2 Thessalonians: 234
1 Timothy: 140
Titus: 25
James: 28
2 Peter–Jude: 175
1–3 John: 163
Revelation 12–22: 19
2:1a
1–3 John: 33, 41
2:1b–2
1–3 John: 43
2:1–2
Luke 1–5: 154
John 12–21: 147
Acts 13–28: 336
Romans 1–8: 399
Romans 9–16: 295
2 Corinthians: 176
1 Peter: 226
2:1, 12, 28
1–3 John: 7
2:2
Matthew 16–23: 246
Mark 1–8: 110
Luke 1–5: 10
John 1–11: 160
John 12–21: 39
1 Corinthians: 353
2 Corinthians: 133, 191–92, 201–2
Colossians and Philemon: 60
1 & 2 Thessalonians: 164
1 Timothy: 142
Titus: 111
Hebrews: 223
1 Peter: 52, 206
1–3 John: 46
2:3
2 Corinthians: 466
Ephesians: 364
1 & 2 Thessalonians: 194
James: 9, 83
1–3 John: 55
2:3–4
Acts 1–12: 297
James: 81
Revelation 12–22: 34, 294
2:3–5
Matthew 16–23: 340
John 12–21: 86
Romans 1–8: 226
2 Corinthians: 470
Colossians and Philemon: 33
1 & 2 Thessalonians: 98
1 Peter: 23
2:3–6
Matthew 1–7: 483
Mark 1–8: 429
John 12–21: 84
1 Peter: 90
2 Peter–Jude: 76
1–3 John: 51
2:4
Mark 1–8: 187
Romans 1–8: 345
Ephesians: 173, 181
James: 9, 83
1–3 John: 8
2:4–5
Titus: 19
1–3 John: 58
2:4–6
Matthew 1–7: 454
John 1–11: 357
2:4–11
James: 130–31
2:5
Matthew 16–23: 340
1 & 2 Thessalonians: 81, 193
1 Peter: 88
2 Peter–Jude: 201
1–3 John: 4, 36, 164
2:5–6
James: 9, 43
2:6
Matthew 1–7: 394
Matthew 8–15: 217
Matthew 16–23: 50, 244
John 12–21: 29, 404
Romans 9–16: 307
1 Corinthians: 197
2 Corinthians: 123
Ephesians: 121, 123, 157
Philippians: 119, 157, 190, 253
Colossians and Philemon: 92
1 & 2 Thessalonians: 26, 52, 195, 210, 257
2 Timothy: 55
Titus: 10
Hebrews: 313, 405
1–3 John: 59
Revelation 1–11: 54
Revelation 12–22: 78
2:7
1–3 John: 63
2:7–11
1–3 John: 61
2:8
John 1–11: 23
1–3 John: 64, 230
2:8–9
2 Corinthians: 249
2:8–10
Acts 13–28: 336
2:9
Mark 1–8: 396
1 & 2 Thessalonians: 17
Hebrews: 157
James: 9
1 Peter: 88
1–3 John: 9
2:9–10
Romans 1–8: 225
1 & 2 Thessalonians: 118
James: 221
2:9–11
Matthew 1–7: 444, 454
2 Corinthians: 471
Colossians and Philemon: 18
1 Timothy: 188
1–3 John: 67, 229
2:10
Romans 9–16: 247
2 Corinthians: 318
1 & 2 Thessalonians: 17, 81, 228
2:10–11
James: 90
1 Peter: 90
1–3 John: 180
2:11
John 12–21: 51
1 & 2 Thessalonians: 17
1 Peter: 88
1–3 John: 4
Revelation 1–11: 139
2:12
Matthew 8–15: 304
Luke 1–5: 321
Acts 1–12: 75
Acts 13–28: 336
1 Corinthians: 79, 445
Ephesians: 23, 195
Philippians: 35
Colossians and Philemon: 111
1–3 John: 16, 72
2:12–13
1 Peter: 284
2:12–14
Luke 1–5: 164
1 & 2 Thessalonians: 96
1–3 John: 69
2:12, 28
1–3 John: 42
2:13
Matthew 1–7: 444
Luke 1–5: 285
Luke 11–17: 50
Acts 13–28: 129
Ephesians: 364
1 Peter: 31
2 Peter–Jude: 101
2:13a, 14a
1–3 John: 75
2:13b, 14b
1–3 John: 75
2:13c
1–3 John: 74
2:13–14
Romans 9–16: 277
1 & 2 Thessalonians: 296
James: 235
2:14
Acts 13–28: 55
1 Timothy: 159, 239, 293
2 Timothy: 27
1 Peter: 202
2:15
Matthew 1–7: 236

Matthew 16–23: 84, 340
Luke 11–17: 22
John 12–21: 163, 281
Romans 1–8: 382, 484
1 Corinthians: ix, 182
Ephesians: 173
Philippians: 51, 259, 266
2 Timothy: 206
Hebrews: 329, 350
James: 9
1–3 John: 73
Revelation 12–22: 181
2:15a
1–3 John: 82
2:15b
1–3 John: 84
2:15b–17
1–3 John: 83
2:15–16
Matthew 8–15: 219, 360
Mark 9–16: 83
2 Corinthians: 244, 471, 481
Ephesians: 348
Philippians: 25, 59
1 & 2 Thessalonians: 109
2 Timothy: 79
James: 92, 189
1 Peter: 280
2:15, 17
Matthew 1–7: 144
2:15–17
Matthew 1–7: 179
Mark 9–16: 264
Luke 6–10: 194, 321
Luke 11–17: 418
John 12–21: 42, 155, 296
Ephesians: 167
Hebrews: 442
James: 193, 242
1 Peter: 35, 137, 139, 227
2 Peter–Jude: 128
1–3 John: 79
Revelation 1–11: 82
Revelation 12–22: 260
2:16
Matthew 1–7: 98
Matthew 16–23: 231
Luke 6–10: 276
John 1–11: 21
1 Corinthians: 472
Colossians and Philemon: 108
James: 213
2 Peter–Jude: 31
1–3 John: 85
Revelation 12–22: 182
2:16–17
Mark 1–8: 198
2:17
Mark 1–8: 431
1 Corinthians: 182
2 Corinthians: 157
Hebrews: 350
James: 230
1–3 John: 90
2:18
Matthew 16–23: 354
Matthew 24–28: 82
Luke 6–10: 48
Luke 18–24: 162, 185
Acts 1–12: 53
2 Corinthians: 336
1 & 2 Thessalonians: 264, 265, 278
1 Timothy: 14, 148
2 Timothy: 107
Hebrews: 241
James: 245, 256
1–3 John: 27, 233
Revelation 1–11: 24
Revelation 12–22: 36, 37
2:18–19
2 Timothy: 106
2:18–19, 22–23, 26
1–3 John: 95
2:18–27
1–3 John: 93–94
2:19
Matthew 24–28: 25
Mark 1–8: 203
Mark 9–16: 238
Luke 6–10: 193
Luke 11–17: 287
Luke 18–24: 217
John 12–21: 23
Acts 1–12: 80, 297
Acts 13–28: 33
Romans 1–8: 278, 281, 513, 515
Romans 9–16: 117
Colossians and Philemon: 66
1 Timothy: 9, 148
Hebrews: 83, 94, 270, 407
James: 28–29, 287
1–3 John: 205, 211
Revelation 1–11: 79, 126, 192
Revelation 12–22: 23, 102
2:19, 22–23, 26
1–3 John: 98–99
2:20
Matthew 16–23: 15
Luke 6–10: 158
Luke 11–17: 124
2 Corinthians: 45
Ephesians: 158
Philippians: 311
1 & 2 Thessalonians: 172
2:20–21
John 12–21: 190
Ephesians: 218
2:20–21, 24–25, 27
1–3 John: 101
2:20–21, 27
1–3 John: 102, 219
2:20, 24, 27
2 Timothy: 154
2:20, 27
Matthew 8–15: 354
John 12–21: 208, 218
2:21
1 & 2 Thessalonians: 157
1–3 John: 4, 14
2:22
Matthew 16–23: 354
Galatians: 15
1 & 2 Thessalonians: 264, 276
James: 286
Revelation 12–22: 36
2:22–23
Luke 18–24: 152
John 12–21: 228
2 Timothy: 65
2:22–24
John 1–11: 38
2:23
Luke 11–17: 122
John 1–11: 43
1–3 John: 158
2:23–25
1–3 John: 112
2:24
Acts 1–12: 314
James: 67
2:24–25
1–3 John: 103
2:25
1 & 2 Thessalonians: 245
2 Peter–Jude: 27, 31
Revelation 12–22: 99
2:26
1 & 2 Thessalonians: 270
2:26–27
Ephesians: 43
2:27
Matthew 16–23: 15
Mark 1–8: 222
Luke 6–10: 158
Luke 11–17:124
Acts 1–12: 304, 314
Romans 9–16: 139
1 Corinthians: 64
2 Corinthians: 45
Ephesians: 218
1 & 2 Thessalonians: 113, 118, 166, 193, 194
2 Peter–Jude: 50
2:28
Luke 11–17: 420
Luke 18–24: 197, 257
Acts 1–12: 23
Galatians: 174
1 & 2 Thessalonians: 74
James: 253
Revelation 12–22: 150, 292
2:28–3:3
1–3 John: 105
2:29
Matthew 1–7: 357
Mark 1–8: 359
John 1–11: 102
2 Corinthians: 469
Ephesians: 210
Titus: 154
James: 9
3:1
Matthew 1–7: 444
Matthew 8–15: 152
Romans 1–8: 28, 454

1 & 2 Thessalonians: 195
1 Peter: 31, 193
1–3 John: 114
Revelation 12–22: 272
3:1–2
Colossians and Philemon: 19
1 & 2 Thessalonians: 288
1 Peter: 237
1–3 John: 4
3:1–3
Luke 11–17: 409
Luke 18–24: 10
James: 40
3:2
Matthew 1–7: 201
Matthew 8–15: 217
Matthew 16–23: 216
Matthew 24–28: 60
Mark 9–16: 252, 396
Luke 1–5: 196
Luke 6–10: 115
Luke 18–24: 406, 436
Romans 1–8: 441, 445, 456, 464, 491
Romans 9–16: 268
1 Corinthians: 440
2 Corinthians: 107, 116, 165, 167, 257, 294
Ephesians: 29, 130, 194, 365
Philippians: 28, 80, 124, 163, 244, 248, 262, 263
Colossians and Philemon: I51, 80, 131, 133, 151
1 & 2 Thessalonians: 90, 134, 172, 248
1 Timothy: 274
2 Timothy: 201
Titus: 119
Hebrews: 140, 416
James: 98
1 Peter: 23, 45, 85
1–3 John: 116
Revelation 1–11: 30, 54, 127
Revelation 12–22: 204, 211, 261, 267, 272, 292
3:2–3
Matthew 8–15: 247
Luke 18–24: 257
Acts 13–28: 308
Romans 9–16: 268
1 & 2 Thessalonians: 162, 203, 270
1 Timothy: 5
Titus: 10
James: 178
1 Peter: 238, 287
2 Peter–Jude: 31, 113
Revelation 12–22: 212
3:3
Romans 1–8: 446
2 Corinthians: 128, 266
Philippians: 290
1 & 2 Thessalonians: 91
James: 178, 254
1 Peter: 66
2 Peter–Jude: 30, 110
1–3 John: 117
Revelation 12–22: 261
3:3–10
1–3 John: 8
3:4
Matthew 8–15: 52
Luke 11–17: 38
Romans 9–16: 242
1 & 2 Thessalonians: 272, 278
1 Peter: 227
1–3 John: 98, 122
3:4, 9
1–3 John: 28
3:4–10
Matthew 1–7: 454
Mark 1–8: 429
Galatians: 163
1 & 2 Thessalonians: 287
1–3 John: 119
3:5
Luke 1–5: 58, 167, 253
Luke 18–24: 68
Acts 13–28: 336
2 Corinthians: 133, 214, 478
Philippians: 253
1 Peter: 26, 168
1–3 John: 4
3:5–7
2 Corinthians: 469
3:5–8
1–3 John: 124
3:6
John 12–21: 159
James: 9, 208
3:6–10
Matthew 1–7: 476
1 Peter: 23
3:7
Matthew 1–7: 65
1 & 2 Thessalonians: 270
1–3 John: 42
3:7–9
1 Peter: 90
3:7–10
Titus: 116
James: 121
3:7, 18
1–3 John: 7
3:8
Matthew 8–15: 40
Mark 1–8: 43, 59, 64, 238
Mark 9–16: 66
Luke 1–5: 252, 286
Luke 6–10: 217
Luke 11–17: 67
Luke 18–24: 270
John 1–11: 24
John 12–21: 139
Acts 1–12: 302
Acts 13–28: 169
Romans 1–8: 292, 396
2 Corinthians: 71
1 & 2 Thessalonians: 88
James: 205
1–3 John: 4
Revelation 1–11: 32, 168
Revelation 12–22: 10
3:8–9
James: 287
3:9
John 1–11: 102
Romans 1–8: 317, 345
Philippians: 213
Titus: 154
Hebrews: 274
James: 9
3:9–10
Romans 1–8: 278, 345
Ephesians: 202
1 & 2 Thessalonians: 109
3:10
Matthew 1–7: 444
Matthew 8–15: 377
Luke 11–17: 12, 120
John 12–21: 157
2 Corinthians: 250, 469
Colossians and Philemon: 18
1 & 2 Thessalonians: 17
James: 67, 80, 146
1 Peter: 88
1–3 John: 9, 180
3:10–11
1 Corinthians: 139
James: 90
1 Peter: 90
3:10–12
Matthew 1–7: 444
3:10, 17–19
Romans 9–16: 189
3:11
Philippians: 45
1 & 2 Thessalonians: 90
3:11–15
1 Timothy: 188
3:11–18
1–3 John: 129
3:12
John 12–21: 171
1 & 2 Thessalonians: 296
Hebrews: 301
James: 235
1–3 John: 10
Revelation 12–22: 8
3:12, 14
1–3 John: 132
3:13
John 12–21: 42
2 Corinthians: 481
1 Peter: 162, 249
3:13, 15
1–3 John: 133
3:14
John 12–21: 91
Acts 1–12: 274
Romans 1–8: 225, 484
Romans 9–16: 184
2 Corinthians: 210, 466, 471
Galatians: 165
Ephesians: 39
Philippians: 42, 108
1 & 2 Thessalonians: 17, 81, 118

1 Timothy: 32
Titus: 75
Hebrews: 424
James: 9, 90
1 Peter: 91
1–3 John: 4, 180
Revelation 1–11: 111
3:14–15
John 12–21: 157
Colossians and Philemon: 18
1–3 John: 9
3:14–17
1 Peter: 90
3:14–20
Mark 1–8: 170
3:15
Matthew 1–7: 293
Luke 11–17: 43
2 Corinthians: 51
1 & 2 Thessalonians: 245
3:16
Mark 1–8: 393
John 12–21: 86
Romans 9–16: 249, 307
Philippians: 108
Hebrews: 425
James: 90
1 Peter: 193
1–3 John: 4
3:16–17
Matthew 1–7: 454
1 & 2 Thessalonians: 90
3:16–18
Acts 1–12: 89
Acts 13–28: 199
Romans 9–16: 307
Ephesians: 40
Colossians and Philemon: 89
James: 179, 244
1–3 John: 135
3:16–19
James: 95
3:16, 17
Galatians: 165
3:17
Matthew 1–7: 143
Matthew 16–23: 340
Luke 1–5: 120
Luke 11–17: 130, 333
Luke 18–24: 74
Acts 1–12: 148
Acts 13–28: 199
1 Corinthians: 457
2 Corinthians: 272, 294
Galatians: 42
Ephesians: 45
Philippians: 32, 108
1 & 2 Thessalonians: 118, 308
Hebrews: 425
James: 127
1–3 John: 103, 180
3:17–18
Matthew 16–23: 116
Matthew 24–28: 123
2 Corinthians: 318
1 & 2 Thessalonians: 119
3:18
Acts 13–28: 193
Romans 9–16: 184
Ephesians: 40
Philippians: 108
1 & 2 Thessalonians: 117
Hebrews: 444
3:18–19
Hebrews: 425
3:18–20
Romans 1–8: 439
3:19
Ephesians: 365
1–3 John: 4
3:19–20
1–3 John: 141
3:19–24
1–3 John: 139
3:22
Matthew 1–7: 444
3:22b
1–3 John: 146
3:22–24
Revelation 12–22: 34
3:23
John 1–11: 34
Romans 9–16: 247
1 & 2 Thessalonians: 90
1 Peter: 93, 153
1–3 John: 180
3:24
John 1–11: 357
John 12–21: 112
2 Corinthians: 470
Philippians: 46
1 & 2 Thessalonians: 112, 166
James: 9
1 Peter: 90
1–3 John: 169
Revelation 1–11: 54
4:1
Matthew 1–7: 461
Acts 1–12: 95
1 Corinthians: 304, 381, 390
2 Corinthians: 336, 357
Philippians: 199
1 & 2 Thessalonians: 199
1 Timothy: 14
Revelation 12–22: 56
4:1b
1–3 John: 154
4:1–2
Philippians: 49
1–3 John: 188
4:1–3
John 1–11: 38, 40
Philippians: 256
1 & 2 Thessalonians: 136, 268
2 Peter–Jude: 68
1–3 John: 27, 232
4:1, 5
2 Timothy: 79
4:1–6
Luke 6–10: 49
John 1–11: 429
1 Timothy: 148
1–3 John: 151
4:2
Luke 1–5: 54
Romans 1–8: 362
1–3 John: 4, 8
4:2–3
Luke 11–17: 122
Romans 1–8: 15
1–3 John: 157
4:2–6
1–3 John: 156
4:3
John 12–21: 228
1 & 2 Thessalonians: 264, 276, 278
James: 286
Revelation 12–22: 36
4:3a
1–3 John: 94
4:4
Luke 1–5: 285
Luke 6–10: 342
Luke 11–17: 118–19
John 12–21: 198, 232
Romans 1–8: 408
Ephesians: 343
Colossians and Philemon: 40
1 & 2 Thessalonians: 88
1–3 John: 7, 42
Revelation 12–22: 15, 22, 100
4:4–5
1–3 John: 158
4:4–6
1 Peter: 284
4:5
1–3 John: 4
4:6
2 Corinthians: 357
1 & 2 Thessalonians: 319
1–3 John: 14
4:7
Romans 1–8: 485
Romans 9–16: 247
1 Corinthians: 476
Galatians: 165
Philippians: 40
1 & 2 Thessalonians: 90
Titus: 154
James: 9, 112
1 Peter: 91, 93, 153
4:7–8
Matthew 16–23: 342
John 12–21: 157
Romans 1–8: 225, 484
Philippians: 24, 41, 42
1 & 2 Thessalonians: 118
1 Timothy: 18
James: 112, 179
1 Peter: 90
1–3 John: 165, 180
4:7–10
Matthew 1–7: 345
Romans 1–8: 283
4:7–12
James: 91

4:7–21
1 Timothy: 264
1–3 John: 161–62
4:7, 8
2 Timothy: 202
Titus: 75
4:7, 8, 16
2 Timothy: 130
4:8
Matthew 8–15: 108
1 Corinthians: 367
Philippians: 40
1 & 2 Thessalonians: 242
Hebrews: 157
James: 42
1–3 John: 9, 39
4:8, 16
Matthew 8–15: 152
2 Timothy: 94
4:9
Luke 1–5: 196
1–3 John: 4, 207
4:9–10
John 12–21: 227
Romans 1–8: 511
1 Peter: 191
1–3 John: 115, 188
4:9–11
1–3 John: 167
4:9–12, 19
Ephesians: 108
4:10
Matthew 24–28: 270
Luke 1–5: 168
John 12–21: 39
Acts 13–28: 336
Romans 1–8: 485
1 Corinthians: 13
2 Corinthians: 192, 201, 213
Galatians: 205
Philippians: 41
1 & 2 Thessalonians: 203
Hebrews: 65
James: 61
1 Peter: 18–19, 130, 206
1–3 John: 124
4:10–12
James: 95
4:11
Romans 9–16: 307
1 Corinthians: 381
1 & 2 Thessalonians: 90
James: 9, 112, 179
4:11–12
Matthew 1–7: 345
4:11, 21
Matthew 8–15: 153
4:12
1 & 2 Thessalonians: 118
1 Peter: 88
1–3 John: 180
Revelation 12–22: 267, 288
4:12–13
Matthew 16–23: 340
4:12–16
1–3 John: 168
4:13
John 12–21: 116
Galatians: 66
1 & 2 Thessalonians: 112, 166, 193
1–3 John: 219
4:14
Matthew 1–7: 444
Luke 1–5: 153, 154, 157, 168, 266
John 1–11: 160
Romans 9–16: 295
2 Corinthians: 202, 213
1 Timothy: 72, 142
Titus: 14
1 Peter: 31
Revelation 1–11: 22
4:14–15
Matthew 16–23: 22
4:15
Matthew 8–15: 227
Luke 1–5: 195
4:16
Matthew 1–7: 348
Matthew 8–15: 443
Romans 9–16: 184, 249
1 Corinthians: 327, 359
2 Corinthians: 314
Philippians: 40, 41
James: 42, 43
1 Peter: 90
1–3 John: 36
4:16–21
Matthew 16–23: 340
4:16, 18, 19
Titus: 75
4:17
Romans 1–8: 511
James: 271
4:17–21
1–3 John: 170
4:18
Romans 1–8: 435
2 Timothy: 18
1 Peter: 181
4:19
Matthew 1–7: 448
Luke 18–24: 75
Romans 1–8: 510
Romans 9–16: 250
1 Corinthians: 192, 476, 479
Philippians: 41
1 & 2 Thessalonians: 195
2 Timothy: 102
James: 61
1 Peter: 47, 88
4:20
Matthew 1–7: 65, 348, 444
Matthew 8–15: 443
John 12–21: 157
Romans 9–16: 188
Philippians: 42
Colossians and Philemon: 18
1 & 2 Thessalonians: 17, 81
Hebrews: 443
James: 221
1 Peter: 88, 90
4:20–21
Romans 1–8: 484
2 Corinthians: 286, 318
Galatians: 192
Ephesians: 109
1 & 2 Thessalonians: 118
James: 96
1–3 John: 9, 180
4:21
Romans 9–16: 247
Colossians and Philemon: 84
1 Peter: 93, 153
5:1
Matthew 16–23: 340
John 1–11: 22, 28, 38
John 12–21: 157
Romans 9–16: 188
1 Corinthians: 192
Ephesians: 40
1 & 2 Thessalonians: 118, 287
Titus: 154
Hebrews: 157
1 Peter: 88, 123, 153
1–3 John: 4
Revelation 1–11: 54
5:1–2
Romans 1–8: 484
1 Peter: 91
5:1–3
1 & 2 Thessalonians: 81
James: 43
5:1–5
2 Peter–Jude: 76
1–3 John: 173
5:2
Matthew 1–7: 444
2 Corinthians: 471
5:2–3
John 12–21: 112, 210
1 Corinthians: 142
2 Corinthians: 470
James: 9
1 Peter: 23
1–3 John: 181
Revelation 12–22: 34, 294
5:3
Matthew 8–15: 277
Luke 1–5: 273
John 1–11: 357
John 12–21: 400
Titus: 19, 75
James: 42
1–3 John: 231
Revelation 12–22: 103
5:4
2 Corinthians: 481
Ephesians: 359
1 Peter: 32, 36, 137
Revelation 12–22: 50
5:4–5
Romans 1–8: 225
Galatians: 208
Philippians: 143
Colossians and Philemon: 125
1 & 2 Thessalonians: 19

James: 200
2 Peter–Jude: 106
Revelation 1–11: 65, 90
Revelation 12–22: 68, 101, 272
5:5
1–3 John: 4
Revelation 1–11: 105, 126, 141, 167
5:5, 10, 12, 13, 20
Luke 1–5: 195
5:6
John 1–11: 358
1 & 2 Thessalonians: 319
2 Peter–Jude: 13
1–3 John: 218
5:6–8
Luke 1–5: 235
5:6–9
1–3 John: 191
5:6–12
1–3 John: 187
5:8
Matthew 8–15: 152
5:9b–11
Luke 1–5: 235
5:10
Luke 1–5: 229
Romans 1–8: 265
Ephesians: 346, 359
Hebrews: 309
5:10–11
1–3 John: 30
5:10–12
Luke 18–24: 152
John 1–11: 38
5:10, 12
1–3 John: 197
5:11
Matthew 16–23: 188
Acts 1–12: 110
1 Corinthians: 15
1 & 2 Thessalonians: 245
2 Peter–Jude: 31
1–3 John: 4, 197
5:11–12
Luke 1–5: 183
5:11–13
John 1–11: 22
1 Peter: 36
2 Peter–Jude: 24
5:12
1 Corinthians: 311
1–3 John: 17
5:13
John 1–11: 34
John 12–21: 253
2 Corinthians: 207, 466
Ephesians: 365
1 & 2 Thessalonians: 245
2 Peter–Jude: 27
1–3 John: 4, 9, 94, 202
5:13–14
1 Peter: 40
5:13–15
John 1–11: 15
5:13–21
1–3 John: 199
5:14
Matthew 1–7: 444
Matthew 16–23: 281
1 & 2 Thessalonians: 87
5:14–15
Luke 18–24: 304
1 & 2 Thessalonians: 178, 187, 195, 258
1 Peter: 194
2 Peter–Jude: 201
1–3 John: 106
5:16
Matthew 1–7: 92
Acts 1–12: 153
Romans 1–8: 380
Hebrews: 395
James: 54
Revelation 1–11: 102
5:18
1–3 John: 8, 206
5:18–19
1 & 2 Thessalonians: 296
James: 235
5:19
Matthew 8–15: 377
Mark 1–8: 58
Luke 1–5: 280
Luke 18–24: 195
John 12–21: 198
Acts 13–28: 168
Romans 1–8: 181
Romans 9–16: 150, 219
1 Corinthians: 92
2 Corinthians: 132
Galatians: 207
Ephesians: 339
1 Timothy: 47
2 Timothy: 79
Hebrews: 56, 160
James: 205
1 Peter: 35
1–3 John: 209, 214
Revelation 1–11: 125
Revelation 12–22: 212
5:20
Matthew 16–23: 188
Luke 1–5: 58
Luke 6–10: 350
Luke 18–24: 36
John 1–11: 14, 38
John 12–21: 144, 251
Acts 1–12: 110, 167
Romans 1–8: 131
1 Corinthians: 364
2 Corinthians: 19
Ephesians: 175
Philippians: 235
1 & 2 Thessalonians: 97, 185, 245, 319
Hebrews: 34
1 Peter: 208
2 Peter–Jude: 26, 30, 201
1–3 John: 4, 23, 29
5:20–21
1–3 John: 209
5:21
1 Corinthians: 223
1–3 John: 7, 10, 42

2 John
1
1 & 2 Thessalonians: 157, 167
1 Peter: 264
1–3 John: 14
Revelation 1–11: 56
1–4
1–3 John: 213
2
2 Peter–Jude: 24, 50
1–3 John: 218
3
Matthew 1–7: 82
Matthew 16–23: 68
Mark 1–8: 37
John 1–11: 38
Romans 9–16: 315
Philippians: 16
1 & 2 Thessalonians: 87
1 Peter: 30
1–3 John: 233
4
1 & 2 Thessalonians: 318
1–3 John: 220
5
Luke 6–10: 51
1 & 2 Thessalonians: 90
5–6
1–3 John: 229
5–13
1–3 John: 223
6
Mark 1–8: 170
1 Corinthians: 351
Hebrews: 312
1–3 John: 64
Revelation 1–11: 62
7
Matthew 1–7: 461
Mark 9–16: 216
Luke 1–5: 54
Luke 11–17: 254
John 1–11: 38
John 12–21: 228
1 Corinthians: 410
2 Corinthians: 336
Philippians: 256
1 & 2 Thessalonians: 264, 270, 276
1 Timothy: 14
Revelation 1–11: 60
Revelation 12–22: 36
7–8
1 Corinthians: 351
1–3 John: 231
7–11
John 12–21: 286
1 Timothy: 149–50
2 Peter–Jude: 68

7, 10–11
Galatians: 17
8
Matthew 1–7: 271
Luke 18–24: 255
2 Corinthians: 156, 265
Galatians: 190
Ephesians: 344
Philippians: 261
1 & 2 Thessalonians: 111
James: 258
1 Peter: 46, 251
2 Peter–Jude: 136
Revelation 1–11: 126, 319
Revelation 12–22: 299
9
Luke 6–10: 335
Luke 11–17: 122
John 1–11: 38, 43, 357
1–3 John: 233
9–10
1 Corinthians: 488
9–11
John 12–21: 228
Philippians: 217
2 Peter–Jude: 100
1–3 John: 235
10
Luke 6–10: 109
John 1–11: 19
1 Corinthians: 351
Revelation 1–11: 60
10–11
Matthew 1–7: 432
Matthew 8–15: 196
1 Corinthians: 240
1–3 John: 74
11
John 1–11: 19
1 Corinthians: 488
12
Luke 11–17: 293
2 Corinthians: 57
Philippians: 188
1 & 2 Thessalonians: 71, 185
12–13
1–3 John: 237

3 John
1
Acts 13–28: 186
1 & 2 Thessalonians: 167
1 Peter: 264
Revelation 1–11: 56
1–2
Luke 18–24: 3
1–8
1–3 John: 241
2
Luke 11–17: 2
1–3 John: 245
3–4
1 & 2 Thessalonians: 257
1–3 John: 22
4
1 Corinthians: 114
Philippians: 188
1 & 2 Thessalonians: 318
Hebrews: 313, 445
5–8
Romans 9–16: 194
6
Romans 9–16: 344
1 Peter: 188
6b–8
1–3 John: 247
7
Acts 13–28: 73
Hebrews: 155
1 Peter: 140
8
1 Corinthians: 484
Philippians: 203
9
Matthew 16–23: 236
Luke 6–10: 43
Romans 1–8: 32
Romans 9–16: 159, 361
1 Corinthians: 484
1 Timothy: 20
2 Peter–Jude: 140
1–3 John: 256
9–10
Matthew 16–23: 136
Philippians: 271
1 & 2 Thessalonians: 171
1 Peter: 269
2 Peter–Jude: 103
9–11
2 Peter–Jude: 68
9–14
1–3 John: 251
10
1 Corinthians: 484
1–3 John: 257
11
1 Corinthians: 484
1 & 2 Thessalonians: 157
James: 67
1 Peter: 197
11–15
1–3 John: 259
12
Acts 13–28: 183
1 Corinthians: 484
1 & 2 Thessalonians: 172
13
Revelation 1–11: 293
14
Acts 13–28: 346

Jude
1
2 Corinthians: 488
Philippians: 13, 16
1 & 2 Thessalonians: 87, 89, 256
1 Timothy: 230
2 Timothy: 197
James: 12, 28
1 Peter: 131
2 Peter–Jude: 18, 27, 141
Revelation 12–22: 200, 293
1a
2 Peter–Jude: 149
1b
2 Peter–Jude: 150
1b–2
2 Peter–Jude: 150
1c
2 Peter–Jude: 151
1d
2 Peter–Jude: 153
1–3
2 Peter–Jude: 147
1–19
Luke 18–24: 162
1–25
2 Peter–Jude: 1, 8, 139
2
2 Peter–Jude: 154
3
Matthew 1–7: 265
Luke 1–5: 82
Acts 13–28: 196, 310
Romans 1–8: 24
Romans 9–16: 171
1 Corinthians: 299, 304, 473
2 Corinthians: 412, 417, 484
Ephesians: 130
Philippians: 91
1 & 2 Thessalonians: 78, 197, 289
1 Timothy: 147, 257, 265, 289, 293
2 Timothy: 153
James: 286
1 Peter: 113
2 Peter–Jude: 20, 49, 144, 155, 170
1–3 John: 18, 131, 160, 217
Revelation 1–11: 320
3–4
Acts 13–28: 227
2 Timothy: 106, 126
Hebrews: 302
3–16
1 Peter: 281
3, 4, 20
1–3 John: 15
4
Matthew 1–7: 463, 465
Luke 11–17: 254
Acts 1–12: 140
Romans 1–8: 174, 175, 315
2 Corinthians: 436
Galatians: 16, 147
Ephesians: 367
Philippians: 92, 212, 258
1 Timothy: 231, 241, 245
2 Timothy: 119
2 Peter–Jude: 8, 71, 72, 77, 144–46, 170
1–3 John: 27, 95
4a
2 Peter–Jude: 158
4b
2 Peter–Jude: 160

4c
2 Peter–Jude: 160, 161
4–7
2 Peter–Jude: 157
4–16
Acts 1–12: 94–95
4–19
1–3 John: 153
5
John 1–11: 399
Hebrews: 47, 94
2 Peter–Jude: 49
5–7
2 Peter–Jude: 146, 162
6
Matthew 24–28: 269
Mark 1–8: 244
Luke 1–5: 280, 286
Luke 6–10: 217
Romans 1–8: 126, 516
Romans 9–16: 261
1 Corinthians: 138
1 & 2 Thessalonians: 88, 157
1 Timothy: 38
James: 271
1 Peter: 220
2 Peter–Jude: 86, 164
Revelation 1–11: 258, 268
Revelation 12–22: 234, 235
6–7
Luke 1–5: 219
1 Peter: 211
2 Peter–Jude: 86, 145
Revelation 1–11: 258
7
Luke 1–5: 223
Luke 11–17: 366
1 & 2 Thessalonians: 245
2 Peter–Jude: 77, 165
Revelation 1–11: 258
Revelation 12–22: 256
8
Matthew 16–23: 354, 360
James: 149
2 Peter–Jude: 72, 145
8b
2 Peter–Jude: 172
8c
2 Peter–Jude: 173
8d–10
2 Peter–Jude: 173
8–9
2 Peter–Jude: 99
8–10
2 Peter–Jude: 171
8–13
2 Peter–Jude: 169
8–16
2 Peter–Jude: 146
9
Luke 1–5: 29
Luke 6–10: 283
Acts 13–28: 171
Ephesians: 332, 339
1 & 2 Thessalonians: 134, 278
1 Timothy: 39
1 Peter: 57
Revelation 1–11: 238, 301
Revelation 12–22: 17, 234
9–10
2 Peter–Jude: 145
10
Matthew 16–23: 360
James: 149
10–11
Revelation 1–11: 88
10–13
Acts 13–28: 227
11
2 Corinthians: 313
1 & 2 Thessalonians: 38
Titus: 101
Hebrews: 300
2 Peter–Jude: 78, 102, 145–46
1–3 John: 248
Revelation 1–11: 251
Revelation 12–22: 56
11a
2 Peter–Jude: 176
11b
2 Peter–Jude: 177
11c
2 Peter–Jude: 178
12
1 Corinthians: 267
2 Peter–Jude: 104, 146
12a
2 Peter–Jude: 179
12b
2 Peter–Jude: 104, 180
12c
2 Peter–Jude: 181
12–13
Matthew 16–23: 360
Romans 9–16: 375
2 Timothy: 76
2 Peter–Jude: 179
12–15
1–3 John: 91
13
Matthew 16–23: 332
1 & 2 Thessalonians: 157, 245
Hebrews: 48
2 Peter–Jude: 104
Revelation 12–22: 256
13a
2 Peter–Jude: 181
13b
2 Peter–Jude: 181
14
Matthew 8–15: 146
Matthew 16–23: 69
2 Peter–Jude: 85
Revelation 1–11: 228
Revelation 12–22: 302
14a
2 Peter–Jude: 187
14b–16
2 Peter–Jude: 188
14–15
Matthew 1–7: 47
Matthew 24–28: 113
Luke 11–17: 420
Luke 18–24: 237
Romans 1–8: 66
Hebrews: 313
2 Peter–Jude: 87–88
1–3 John: 252
14–16
2 Peter–Jude: 183
15
1 Timothy: 245
James: 271
1 Peter: 227
2 Peter–Jude: 144
Revelation 1–11: 139
16
Acts 13–28: 227
2 Corinthians: 345
Philippians: 178
1 Timothy: 111, 241
James: 149
1 Peter: 73
2 Peter–Jude: 78, 146
16–18
James: 187
17
2 Peter–Jude: 48, 142, 143
17–18
1 & 2 Thessalonians: 272
2 Timothy: 147
17–19
1 & 2 Thessalonians: 108
2 Peter–Jude: 197
17–23
2 Peter–Jude: 146, 193
18
Galatians: 185
1 Timothy: 148
James: 245
1 Peter: 73, 229
2 Peter–Jude: 144, 146
18–19
2 Peter–Jude: 112
19
Matthew 16–23: 363
John 1–11: 347
Acts 1–12: 304
Acts 13–28: 164
1 Timothy: 149
James: 173
2 Peter–Jude: 145
20
Romans 9–16: 193
1 Corinthians: 304
1 & 2 Thessalonians: 89, 197
20–21
2 Timothy: 38
2 Peter–Jude: 200
1–3 John: 112
20–21, 23
Romans 9–16: 186
21
Luke 6–10: 310, 352
Ephesians: 197
1 & 2 Thessalonians: 245
Revelation 1–11: 125

21–23
Matthew 1–7: 196, 464
22
2 Peter–Jude: 202
22–23
2 Peter–Jude: 201
23
Matthew 8–15: 462
Matthew 16–23: 14, 381
2 Corinthians: 255, 330
1 Timothy: 150
2 Timothy: 79
James: 156
Revelation 1–11: 113, 141, 274
Revelation 12–22: 89
23a
2 Peter–Jude: 202
23b
2 Peter–Jude: 203
24
Luke 6–10: 338
Acts 1–12: 259
Romans 1–8: 277
Romans 9–16: 280, 385
2 Corinthians: 147, 316
Ephesians: 338
Philippians: 29, 182, 267
Colossians and Philemon: 65
1 & 2 Thessalonians: 73, 91, 185, 296, 317
Hebrews: 201
James: 28
1 Peter: 36, 40, 47
Revelation 12–22: 74, 80, 100
24a
2 Peter–Jude: 207
24–25
Luke 18–24: 260, 295
Galatians: 79
Philippians: 11, 188, 313
1 & 2 Thessalonians: 85, 208
1 Timothy: 150, 278
Hebrews: 18
1 Peter: 19, 259
2 Peter–Jude: 27, 146, 205
1–3 John: 207
Revelation 1–11: 157
24b–25
2 Peter–Jude: 211
25
Luke 1–5: 153, 168
2 Corinthians: 44, 199
Philippians: 141, 313
1 Timothy: 69
1 Peter: 245, 288
2 Peter–Jude: 137

Revelation
1:1
Luke 1–5: 80
Luke 6–10: 84
John 12–21: 4, 201
Romans 1–8: 453
1 Timothy: 230
James: 12
Revelation 1–11: 2, 3, 4
Revelation 12–22: 200, 293, 302, 307
1:1–2
2 Timothy: 147
1:1–2, 9
Luke 1–5: 234
1:1–3
Luke 18–24: 183
Revelation 12–22: 290
1:2
Titus: 45
Revelation 1–11: 1, 194
Revelation 12–22: 238
1:2, 9
Titus: 95
1:3
Luke 18–24: 200
Romans 9–16: 259
1 & 2 Thessalonians: 197
1 Peter: 236
Revelation 1–11: 1, 9, 21
Revelation 12–22: 95, 149, 204, 238, 294, 297, 308, 309
1:4
1 Peter: 25, 290
1–3 John: 219
Revelation 1–11: 3, 4, 108, 151, 315
Revelation 12–22: 142, 248
1:5
Luke 1–5: 48, 83, 196, 321, 328
John 12–21: 134
Acts 13–28: 336
2 Corinthians: 31, 133, 190
Colossians and Philemon: 46
1 Timothy: 272
1 Peter: 111, 206
1–3 John: 37, 244
Revelation 1–11: 2, 3, 7, 17, 51, 52, 54, 87, 232, 240, 279
Revelation 12–22: 308
1:5–6
Mark 1–8: 335
Ephesians: 240
2 Peter–Jude: 138
1:6
Luke 18–24: 83
Romans 9–16: 332
2 Corinthians: 44
Ephesians: 146
Philippians: 124, 314
1 Peter: 31
Revelation 1–11: 172
Revelation 12–22: 238
1:6–7
Revelation 1–11: 173
1:7
Matthew 24–28: 55
Mark 9–16: 255
Luke 11–17: 404, 414
Luke 18–24: 220, 229, 231
Acts 1–12: 23
2 Corinthians: 210
1 & 2 Thessalonians: 231
James: 154
2 Peter–Jude: 63, 117
Revelation 1–11: 7, 278, 280
Revelation 12–22: 112, 211
1:8
Mark 9–16: 211
John 1–11: 14
2 Peter–Jude: 213
Revelation 1–11: 2, 3, 17, 24, 315
Revelation 12–22: 130, 142, 200, 271, 306
1:9
Matthew 16–23: 238
John 12–21: 182
1–3 John: 135
Revelation 1–11: 3, 4, 22, 194, 288
Revelation 12–22: 238, 278, 296
1:10
Matthew 1–7: 257
Matthew 16–23: 348
Mark 9–16: 398
Luke 1–5: 180
Luke 18–24: 409
1 Corinthians: 453
Revelation 1–11: 145, 146
Revelation 12–22: 162
1:10–11
2 Timothy: 147
Revelation 1–11: 283
1:11
1 Peter: 16
Revelation 1–11: 24
Revelation 12–22: 103, 297, 307
1:12–13
Revelation 1–11: 151
1:12–16
2 Corinthians: 442
1:12–17
Revelation 1–11: 83
1:12–18
1 Peter: 200
1:12–20
Revelation 1–11: 68
1:13
Revelation 1–11: 96, 240, 279
Revelation 12–22: 113
1:13–16
Matthew 16–23: 64
Luke 1–5: 156
1:13–20
John 12–21: 255
1:14
Revelation 1–11: 3
1:14–15
Revelation 1–11: 55
1:15
Acts 1–12: 40
Revelation 12–22: 75, 200
1:16
Matthew 1–7: 29

Ephesians: 360
1 & 2 Thessalonians: 281
Revelation 1–11: 55, 82, 281
Revelation 12–22: 219
1:17
Mark 1–8: 235, 335
Luke 1–5: 157, 287, 308
Luke 6–10: 213, 286
John 1–11: 14, 422
Revelation 1–11: 2, 3, 17, 240, 279, 287, 292
Revelation 12–22: 306
1:17–18
Matthew 24–28: 305
1 Corinthians: 410
Revelation 1–11: 3
1:18
Matthew 8–15: 86
Mark 1–8: 253
Mark 9–16: 153
Luke 11–17: 364
John 1–11: 475
John 12–21: 36
James: 154, 237
Revelation 1–11: 2, 3, 17, 55, 68, 119, 184, 240, 258, 279, 285
Revelation 12–22: 238, 242
1:19
Luke 1–5: 309
Revelation 1–11: 4, 23, 42, 283, 288
Revelation 12–22: 103, 270
1:20
Romans 9–16: 387
Revelation 1–11: 56, 64, 109
2:1
Revelation 1–11: 2, 17, 42, 47, 283
Revelation 12–22: 103
2:1–7
1 & 2 Thessalonians: 70
2:2
Acts 13–28: 226
2 Corinthians: 408, 453
Philippians: 49
1 & 2 Thessalonians: 172
2 Peter–Jude: 194
2:2–3
Revelation 1–11: 64
2:2–4
Ephesians: 40
2:3
Ephesians: 361
2:4
Matthew 16–23: 47
John 12–21: 147
1 Corinthians: 329
Philippians: 48, 198
1 & 2 Thessalonians: 195
2:4–5
Philippians: 35
Revelation 1–11: 47, 63, 64
2:5
Luke 18–24: 191
2 Corinthians: 438, 486
Ephesians: 333, 334
Revelation 1–11: 64, 125
Revelation 12–22: 291
2:6
Acts 1–12: 184
Revelation 1–11: 8, 64
2:7
Luke 18–24: 123, 388
John 12–21: 201, 231
2 Corinthians: 395
Philippians: 164
1 & 2 Thessalonians: 126, 215
1 Timothy: 137
1–3 John: 184
Revelation 1–11: 64, 141
Revelation 12–22: 51, 101, 287, 308
2:7, 11, 17, 29
2 Timothy: 147
2:8
Revelation 1–11: 42, 50, 55, 283
Revelation 12–22: 103, 238
2:8–10
1 Timothy: 53
2:9
Ephesians: 333
1 & 2 Thessalonians: 71
Revelation 1–11: 59, 95, 123
2:9–10
1 & 2 Thessalonians: 72
2:10
Matthew 16–23: 214
Romans 1–8: 493
Galatians: 169
1 & 2 Thessalonians: 73
2 Timothy: 47
James: 42
1 Peter: 198, 251
2 Peter–Jude: 28
1–3 John: 170
Revelation 1–11: 8, 141, 149, 319
Revelation 12–22: 113
2:10–11
Matthew 24–28: 29
2:10b–11
2 Peter–Jude: 31
2:11
Luke 18–24: 123
Philippians: 164
1 Timothy: 137
Revelation 1–11: 64, 141
Revelation 12–22: 51, 101
2:12
Revelation 1–11: 2, 17, 42, 48, 55, 283
Revelation 12–22: 103
2:12–15
Revelation 1–11: 61
2:13
Matthew 1–7: 5
Matthew 8–15: 227
Luke 1–5: 226
Luke 18–24: 212
John 12–21: 169, 182
Ephesians: 334
1 & 2 Thessalonians: 71, 72
Revelation 1–11: 8, 39, 59, 85, 95
Revelation 12–22: 44, 103
2:14
Matthew 1–7: 317
Matthew 16–23: 106
Ephesians: 334
2 Peter–Jude: 178
Revelation 1–11: 47, 61
Revelation 12–22: 56
2:14–15
2 Peter–Jude: 140
Revelation 1–11: 61
2:14–16
Acts 1–12: 82
2:15
Acts 1–12: 184
Revelation 1–11: 8
2:15–16
Romans 9–16: 117
2:16
Acts 1–12: 322
2 Corinthians: 438, 456, 486
1 & 2 Thessalonians: 281
Revelation 1–11: 20, 30, 48, 125, 306
Revelation 12–22: 216, 291
2:17
Luke 18–24: 123
Romans 1–8: 322
Philippians: 143, 164
1 & 2 Thessalonians: 215
1 Timothy: 137
1–3 John: 184
Revelation 1–11: 64, 141
Revelation 12–22: 51, 101
2:18
Luke 1–5: 194
Revelation 1–11: 2, 17, 42, 46, 55, 109, 240, 279, 283
Revelation 12–22: 103
2:18–24
1 Peter: 283
2:18–29
Acts 13–28: 92
2:19
Revelation 1–11: 59
2:19–20
Ephesians: 335
2:19–23
1 Corinthians: 124
2:20
Matthew 16–23: 106
Mark 1–8: 288
Luke 6–10: 244
1 & 2 Thessalonians: 38
Revelation 1–11: 47
Revelation 12–22: 4, 200, 293
2:20–23
Luke 6–10: 112
Revelation 12–22: 309
2:20–24
2 Peter–Jude: 140

2:21
1 & 2 Thessalonians: 104
2:21–22
2 Corinthians: 438
2:22–23
Ephesians: 335
2:23
Matthew 16–23: 57
Luke 6–10: 201
Colossians and Philemon: 85
Revelation 1–11: 3
2:24
1 & 2 Thessalonians: 71, 72
Revelation 1–11: 95
Revelation 12–22: 309
2:24–25
Ephesians: 335
2:25
Ephesians: 338
Revelation 1–11: 99
2:26
Matthew 16–23: 204
Mark 9–16: 160
Philippians: 164
Revelation 1–11: 64, 141
Revelation 12–22: 237
2:26–27
1 Corinthians: 138
Revelation 1–11: 141, 149
Revelation 12–22: 11, 220
2:26–28
1–3 John: 184
Revelation 12–22: 101
2:27
Matthew 1–7: 33, 381
Revelation 1–11: 233
Revelation 12–22: 11, 198, 236, 240
2:28
Revelation 1–11: 141
Revelation 12–22: 307
2:29
Luke 18–24: 123
1 & 2 Thessalonians: 215
1 Timothy: 137
Revelation 1–11: 64
Revelation 12–22: 51
2–3
1 Corinthians: 82
2 Corinthians: 353, 438
3:1
2 Corinthians: 471
Ephesians: 335
Philippians: 215
Revelation 1–11: 2, 17, 42, 47, 55, 59, 283
Revelation 12–22: 103
3:1–3
1 Corinthians: 227, 472
Revelation 1–11: 47
3:1–6
1 & 2 Thessalonians: 225
3:3
Matthew 24–28: 77
Luke 11–17: 160
2 Corinthians: 438
Revelation 1–11: 125
Revelation 12–22: 149, 291
3:4
Matthew 8–15: 456
Hebrews: 311
3:4–5
Ephesians: 336
Revelation 1–11: 139
3:5
Acts 13–28: 39
Philippians: 164, 273
1 Peter: 18, 279
2 Peter–Jude: 185
1–3 John: 185
Revelation 1–11: 64, 141, 149, 196
Revelation 12–22: 49, 50, 101, 169, 255, 260, 286
3:6
Mark 1–8: 355
Luke 18–24: 123
1 & 2 Thessalonians: 215
1 Timothy: 137
Revelation 1–11: 64
Revelation 12–22: 51
3:6, 13, 22
2 Timothy: 147
3:7
John 12–21: 144
1 Corinthians: 465
2 Corinthians: 188
Philippians: 311
Colossians and Philemon: 183
1 & 2 Thessalonians: 319
1–3 John: 48
Revelation 1–11: 2, 17, 42, 196, 240, 279, 283
Revelation 12–22: 103
3:8
Ephesians: 337
1 & 2 Thessalonians: 172
Revelation 1–11: 59
3:9
Ephesians: 333
1 & 2 Thessalonians: 71, 72
Revelation 12–22: 309
3:10
Matthew 24–28: 55, 66
Mark 9–16: 243
Luke 18–24: 192, 228, 249, 259
John 12–21: 101
1 Corinthians: 279
1 & 2 Thessalonians: 135, 137, 268, 271
2 Peter–Jude: 185
Revelation 1–11: 2, 30, 125, 145, 176, 196, 209, 296
Revelation 12–22: 49, 51, 61, 86, 154, 162, 169
3:11
Luke 11–17: 410
Luke 18–24: 191
1 & 2 Thessalonians: 73
Revelation 1–11: 20, 30, 306
Revelation 12–22: 211, 291
3:12
Philippians: 143, 164
Revelation 1–11: 64, 141, 261
Revelation 12–22: 101, 264, 288
3:13
Mark 1–8: 355
Luke 18–24: 123
1 & 2 Thessalonians: 215
1 Timothy: 137
Revelation 1–11: 64
Revelation 12–22: 51
3:14
Luke 11–17: 17
John 1–11: 422
1 & 2 Thessalonians: 319
1 Timothy: 272
Revelation 1–11: 2, 17, 25, 42, 87, 240, 279, 283
Revelation 12–22: 103, 215, 270, 292
3:14–22
1 & 2 Thessalonians: 225, 272
3:15
Revelation 1–11: 47, 59
3:15–16
John 1–11: 479
Ephesians: 336
3:16
Matthew 8–15: 151
Romans 9–16: 117
2 Corinthians: 486
Ephesians: 336
Philippians: 212
James: 38
3:16–17
1 & 2 Thessalonians: 195
3:17
Matthew 1–7: 148, 208
Matthew 16–23: 199
Luke 1–5: 271
John 1–11: 410
1 Corinthians: 109
Ephesians: 95, 336
James: 211
Revelation 1–11: 9, 47, 76
3:18
Mark 1–8: 243
Revelation 1–11: 149
3:19
2 Corinthians: 438
James: 192
1 Peter: 250
Revelation 1–11: 3, 47
3:21
Matthew 16–23: 204
Matthew 24–28: 79
Romans 1–8: 445
1 Corinthians: 138
Philippians: 164
1 & 2 Thessalonians: 235
2 Timothy: 171
Hebrews: 55, 207
1 Peter: 125, 221
Revelation 1–11: 64, 149

Revelation 12–22: 44, 101, 237, 248, 285, 288
3:22
Mark 1–8: 355
Luke 18–24: 123
1 & 2 Thessalonians: 215
1 Timothy: 137
Revelation 1–11: 64
Revelation 12–22: 51
4:1
Matthew 1–7: 79
Ephesians: 258
Revelation 1–11: 168, 215, 225, 278, 287, 292, 305
Revelation 12–22: 71, 74, 112, 132, 178, 196, 214, 262
4:1–3
Revelation 1–11: 232
4:1–6
Revelation 1–11: 228
4:1ff.
Acts 1–12: 222
4:2
Luke 1–5: 180
Revelation 1–11: 194, 226
Revelation 12–22: 162
4:2–3
Revelation 1–11: 183, 208
4:2–6
Revelation 12–22: 247
4:2–11
Revelation 12–22: 287
4:3
Revelation 1–11: 280
4:4
Revelation 1–11: 139
4:5
Revelation 1–11: 162, 168, 237, 241, 321
4:6
Revelation 1–11: 182
Revelation 12–22: 124, 132
4:6–8
Revelation 1–11: 178
4:6–11
Matthew 16–23: 27
4:8
Philippians: 311
1–3 John: 25, 39
Revelation 1–11: 24, 35, 118, 237, 315
Revelation 12–22: 65, 130, 142, 200
4:8–9
Revelation 12–22: 132
4:8–10
1 Peter: 52
4:8–11
Luke 11–17: 300
Ephesians: 96
Philippians: 145
Revelation 12–22: 21, 196, 200, 248, 296
4:9
Revelation 1–11: 305
Revelation 12–22: 247
4:9–10
Revelation 1–11: 217, 285
Revelation 12–22: 242, 248
4:9–11
Colossians and Philemon: 21
4:9, 11
Ephesians: 312
4:10
Matthew 8–15: 9, 76
Mark 1–8: 256
2 Timothy: 47
Revelation 1–11: 1, 170, 208, 228
Revelation 12–22: 268, 286
4:10–11
Matthew 1–7: 360
Matthew 24–28: 330
Romans 1–8: 493
Romans 9–16: 136
Hebrews: 381
1 Peter: 288
4:11
Luke 1–5: 91
John 1–11: 20
Acts 13–28: 137
Romans 1–8: 83
1 Corinthians: 20
Philippians: 283
Revelation 1–11: 1, 177, 228, 237, 285
Revelation 12–22: 89, 194
4–5
Revelation 12–22: 123
4–19
1 & 2 Thessalonians: 280
5
Acts 13–28: 114
5:1
Hebrews: 11, 32
Revelation 1–11: 176, 228, 232, 236, 281
5:1–7
Philippians: 139
Colossians and Philemon: 46
Revelation 1–11: 176
Revelation 12–22: 215, 247
5:1–14
Revelation 12–22: 195
5:2
Hebrews: 12, 32
Revelation 1–11: 42, 237, 279
Revelation 12–22: 190, 266
5:3
Hebrews: 12
5:4–5
Hebrews: 12
Revelation 1–11: 191, 287, 292
5:5
Matthew 8–15: 90
Luke 1–5: 42
Luke 18–24: 442
John 1–11: 422
Acts 1–12: 104
Hebrews: 27, 32
Revelation 1–11: 2, 17, 119, 209, 240, 279
Revelation 12–22: 11
5:5–7
Revelation 1–11: 237
5:6
Matthew 16–23: 223
Acts 1–12: 104
Hebrews: 12, 172
Revelation 1–11: 2, 17, 25, 228, 233, 240, 267
Revelation 12–22: 45, 71, 132
5:6–7
Revelation 12–22: 248
5:6–8
Revelation 1–11: 209
5:7
Luke 18–24: 220
Revelation 1–11: 177, 237, 267
5:7–12
1 Peter: 58
5:8
Hebrews: 172
Revelation 1–11: 158, 194, 228, 240, 241, 314, 320
Revelation 12–22: 71, 116, 125, 132
5:8–9
Romans 9–16: 84, 382
Ephesians: 257
5:8–9, 11–12
Romans 9–16: 382
5:8–10
Ephesians: 21
Revelation 1–11: 150, 227, 228
5:8–12
Revelation 12–22: 200
5:8–14
Matthew 16–23: 263
Luke 18–24: 196
Ephesians: 96
Philippians: 145
1 Peter: 224
Revelation 12–22: 129, 296
5:9
Matthew 16–23: 246
Mark 9–16: 270
Luke 1–5: 82, 94
1 Corinthians: 253
Philippians: 313
1 Timothy: 135
1 Peter: 17, 51, 129–30, 171, 206
1–3 John: 37, 49
Revelation 1–11: 225, 232, 288, 295, 304
Revelation 12–22: 79, 86, 161, 308
5:9–10
Matthew 24–28: 275
Hebrews: 59
Revelation 1–11: 177, 237
Revelation 12–22: 21, 75
5:9–13
2 Peter–Jude: 60–61

5:9–14
Matthew 16–23: 27
Romans 9–16: 41
Revelation 12–22: 195, 196
5:10
Philippians: 124
1 Timothy: 183
2 Timothy: 171
1 Peter: 125, 279
2 Peter–Jude: 110
Revelation 1–11: 141, 149
Revelation 12–22: 238
5:11
Matthew 16–23: 148
Luke 1–5: 160
1 Corinthians: 378
Hebrews: 23, 415
1 Peter: 220
Revelation 1–11: 227, 228, 270
Revelation 12–22: 8, 85, 132
5:11–12
Luke 1–5: 160
Philippians: 141
Hebrews: 32
1 Peter: 58
Revelation 1–11: 237
5:11–14
Luke 1–5: 162
Revelation 12–22: 21
5:12
Matthew 16–23: 223
Matthew 24–28: 131
Luke 18–24: 267
1 Corinthians: 20
Revelation 1–11: 42, 195, 227, 228
Revelation 12–22: 75
5:12–13
Ephesians: 312
Revelation 12–22: 71
5:13
Ephesians: 7
Revelation 1–11: 3, 232, 237
Revelation 12–22: 75, 247, 248
5:13–14
Hebrews: 32
5:13ff.
Revelation 1–11: 227, 229
5:14
Revelation 1–11: 158, 228, 314
Revelation 12–22: 132, 200, 268
6
Luke 18–24: 220
Hebrews: 440
6:1
Matthew 24–28: 20
Luke 18–24: 196
Revelation 1–11: 2, 17, 154, 237, 238, 240, 267, 279
Revelation 12–22: 132, 200, 233, 247, 262
6:1ff.
Revelation 1–11: 164
6:1–8:5
2 Peter–Jude: 185
6:2
1 & 2 Thessalonians: 73, 146
Revelation 1–11: 241
Revelation 12–22: 71, 112, 132, 233, 262
6:3
Revelation 1–11: 237, 238
6:3–4
Luke 18–24: 202
1 & 2 Thessalonians: 147
6:3–8
Revelation 1–11: 214
6:4
Matthew 24–28: 21
Revelation 1–11: 178, 241
Revelation 12–22: 47
6:5
Revelation 1–11: 237
Revelation 12–22: 71, 112, 132, 233, 262
6:5–6
Mark 9–16: 233
Luke 18–24: 206
1 & 2 Thessalonians: 147
Revelation 12–22: 63
6:5–7
Revelation 1–11: 238
6:6
Revelation 1–11: 154
Revelation 12–22: 132
6:7
Revelation 1–11: 237
6:7–8
1 & 2 Thessalonians: 147
1 Peter: 133
6:8
Matthew 24–28: 21
Acts 1–12: 54
Revelation 1–11: 241, 270
Revelation 12–22: 47, 71, 112, 132, 233, 262
6:9
Revelation 1–11: 181, 226, 240
Revelation 12–22: 237, 238
6:9–10
Matthew 16–23: 56
Matthew 24–28: 42
Luke 18–24: 7
1 Corinthians: 21
Hebrews: 303
Revelation 1–11: 171, 237
Revelation 12–22: 125, 182, 190, 212
6:9–11
Matthew 24–28: 24
Mark 9–16: 235, 236, 245
Acts 1–12: 225
Philippians: 79
1 & 2 Thessalonians: 126, 148
James: 255
1 Peter: 283
Revelation 1–11: 124, 125, 214, 226, 231, 241, 267, 286
Revelation 12–22: 29, 48, 62, 70, 73, 81, 115, 124, 143, 146, 211
6:10
Matthew 8–15: 245
Luke 18–24: 8
Acts 1–12: 140
Philippians: 311
1 & 2 Thessalonians: 238, 319
2 Peter–Jude: 72
Revelation 1–11: 1, 2, 17, 42, 119, 124, 227, 241, 251, 256, 277, 285, 304
Revelation 12–22: 49, 61, 86, 162, 169, 192, 198
6:11
Matthew 24–28: 42
2 Corinthians: 269
Revelation 1–11: 113, 139, 197, 241
6:12
Matthew 24–28: 308
Revelation 1–11: 237, 242
Revelation 12–22: 34, 233, 262
6:12–13
1 & 2 Thessalonians: 146
6:12–14
Matthew 24–28: 22, 45
Mark 9–16: 233
Luke 18–24: 204, 207
Hebrews: 417
Revelation 1–11: 214
Revelation 12–22: 85, 153
6:12–17
Luke 18–24: 234
1 & 2 Thessalonians: 150
Revelation 12–22: 69
6:13
Revelation 1–11: 256
6:13–14
Matthew 24–28: 274
6:14
Hebrews: 35
Revelation 1–11: 163
6:15
John 1–11: 472
6:15–16
Matthew 24–28: 48
6:15–17
Luke 1–5: 308
Luke 18–24: 204–5, 235
2 Corinthians: 468
Revelation 1–11: 124, 242, 245, 251, 315, 316
Revelation 12–22: 87, 138
6:16
1 Peter: 194
Revelation 1–11: 240, 279
Revelation 12–22: 247, 248
6:16–17
Luke 1–5: 215
Luke 18–24: 372

2 Peter–Jude: 184
Revelation 1–11: 50, 156, 236
Revelation 12–22: 69, 87, 133
6:17
1 & 2 Thessalonians: 144, 163
2 Peter–Jude: 89
Revelation 1–11: 200, 202, 212, 231
Revelation 12–22: 96, 123, 195
6–16
Mark 9–16: 243
6–18
Luke 18–24: 247
6–19
Luke 11–17: 151, 156
Luke 18–24: 223
6–20
2 Peter–Jude: 184
7:1
Revelation 1–11: 225, 278
Revelation 12–22: 142, 241
7:1–8
Matthew 24–28: 75
Luke 6–10: 243
Romans 9–16: 102, 128
Revelation 1–11: 193, 223, 225, 272
Revelation 12–22: 96
7:1–10
Revelation 1–11: 292
7:1–17
Revelation 12–22: 149
7:2
Revelation 1–11: 42, 51, 240, 241, 282, 315
Revelation 12–22: 47, 221, 233, 247, 262, 266
7:2–3
Revelation 1–11: 237
Revelation 12–22: 63
7:2–8
Luke 18–24: 127, 236
Revelation 12–22: 34, 122
7:3
Revelation 1–11: 225
Revelation 12–22: 72, 200, 293
7:3–4
Revelation 1–11: 260
Revelation 12–22: 69, 71, 77
7:3–8
Matthew 24–28: 67
7:3ff.
Revelation 1–11: 148
7:4
Matthew 24–28: 50
Revelation 12–22: 27
7:4–8
Mark 9–16: 257
Luke 1–5: 107
Hebrews: 213
Revelation 12–22: 72
7:4, 9
Matthew 8–15: 350
Romans 9–16: 5, 111
7:4–10
1 & 2 Thessalonians: 265
7:5–8
James: 13
7:9
Matthew 16–23: 260
Mark 9–16: 258
Luke 18–24: 238
Romans 9–16: 128
1 & 2 Thessalonians: 148
1 Peter: 17, 52
Revelation 1–11: 113, 139, 144, 172, 193, 196, 209, 215, 270, 278, 288, 295, 304
Revelation 12–22: 70, 71, 81, 86, 96, 104, 112, 122, 132, 143, 161, 178, 180, 196, 219
7:9–10
Matthew 24–28: 24
Mark 9–16: 236
Luke 18–24: 221
Philippians: 313
Colossians and Philemon: 21
Revelation 1–11: 2, 17
Revelation 12–22: 71, 75
7:9–12
Ephesians: 96
Revelation 12–22: 21, 296
7:9–13
Revelation 1–11: 237
7:9–14
Matthew 24–28: 75
Revelation 1–11: 125, 194
Revelation 12–22: 34
7:9–15
1 Timothy: 52
7:9–17
Revelation 1–11: 214
Revelation 12–22: 48, 73, 122, 124, 237, 239
7:9, 10, 14
Revelation 1–11: 34, 124
7:10
Revelation 1–11: 42, 232
Revelation 12–22: 247, 248
7:10–12
Ephesians: 60
Revelation 12–22: 196
7:11
Colossians and Philemon: 36
Revelation 1–11: 158, 314
Revelation 12–22: 132, 200, 268
7:11–12
Luke 1–5: 160
1 Peter: 58
7:11–14
Revelation 1–11: 150
7:12
2 Corinthians: 44
James: 167
Revelation 1–11: 1
Revelation 12–22: 200
7:13
Revelation 1–11: 113
7:13–14
Revelation 1–11: 139, 287, 292
Revelation 12–22: 70, 96
7:14
Matthew 24–28: 24
Luke 18–24: 220, 230, 242
1 & 2 Thessalonians: 279
1–3 John: 185
Revelation 1–11: 2, 113, 176, 191, 196, 255, 266, 292
Revelation 12–22: 22, 71, 104, 143, 308
7:14–17
Matthew 24–28: 29
Mark 9–16: 239
7:15
Philippians: 263
Revelation 1–11: 146
Revelation 12–22: 247, 268, 284, 288
7:15–17
Philippians: 79
7:16–17
1 & 2 Thessalonians: 52
7:17
Matthew 1–7: 33
John 1–11: 423
John 12–21: 96
Revelation 1–11: 165, 240, 277, 279
Revelation 12–22: 71, 269, 271
8:1
Revelation 1–11: 2, 17, 240, 244, 279
8:1–6
Romans 1–8: 194
8:2
1 Peter: 220
Revelation 12–22: 233, 247, 262
8:2–5
Revelation 1–11: 310
8:2–6
Revelation 12–22: 123
8:2ff.
Revelation 1–11: 215
8:3
Revelation 1–11: 267
8:3–4
1 Peter: 117
Revelation 1–11: 171, 194, 320
8:3–5
Revelation 1–11: 285
Revelation 12–22: 116
8:4
Revelation 1–11: 258
8:4–5
Revelation 1–11: 268
8:5
Matthew 24–28: 308
Acts 1–12: 55

Revelation 1–11: 151, 245, 282, 283, 321
Revelation 12–22: 34, 151
8:5ff.
Revelation 1–11: 217
8:6–11:19
2 Peter–Jude: 185
8:6–11
Luke 18–24: 207
8:6–12
Revelation 1–11: 239
8:6ff.
Revelation 1–11: 239
Revelation 12–22: 84
8:7
Acts 1–12: 55
Revelation 1–11: 183, 239, 260
Revelation 12–22: 153
8:7–8
Acts 1–12: 54
8:7–9
1 Peter: 133
8:7–11
2 Peter–Jude: 130
8:7–12
Matthew 24–28: 22
Revelation 1–11: 255, 270
Revelation 12–22: 138
8:8
Luke 18–24: 207
Acts 1–12: 55
Revelation 1–11: 239, 256
8:10
Luke 18–24: 207
Acts 1–12: 55
Revelation 1–11: 239
8:10–11
Revelation 1–11: 302
Revelation 12–22: 142
8:11
Mark 9–16: 233
8:12
Matthew 24–28: 45
Luke 18–24: 207
1 & 2 Thessalonians: 146
Revelation 1–11: 206
8:13
Revelation 1–11: 42, 124, 196, 239, 255, 256, 264, 270, 304, 308
Revelation 12–22: 49, 61, 85, 86, 162, 169, 221, 233, 262
8–11
Revelation 12–22: 138
9:1
Mark 1–8: 57
Revelation 1–11: 119, 241, 270
Revelation 12–22: 8, 233, 234, 235, 262
9:1–2
Luke 18–24: 220
1 Peter: 210
Revelation 1–11: 303
9:1–3
Revelation 12–22: 8, 20
9:1–5
Matthew 24–28: 74
9:1–6
Mark 9–16: 243
Revelation 1–11: 239
9:1–10
Revelation 12–22: 210
9:1–11
Luke 6–10: 222
Luke 11–17: 416
Romans 1–8: 98
Revelation 1–11: 239
Revelation 12–22: 2, 41, 69, 77, 179
9:1–12
Mark 1–8: 244
Revelation 1–11: 266
Revelation 12–22: 235
9:1–19
1 & 2 Thessalonians: 278
Revelation 1–11: 311
9:1–21
Revelation 1–11: 251
9:1ff.
Revelation 1–11: 215
9:2
Revelation 12–22: 145, 234
9:2–3
Acts 1–12: 55
9:2–11
1 Timothy: 150
9:3
Revelation 1–11: 168, 241
9:3ff.
1 Timothy: 38
9:4
2 Timothy: 82
Revelation 1–11: 183, 218
Revelation 12–22: 71
9:5
Revelation 1–11: 241, 272
Revelation 12–22: 47, 185
9:5–6
Matthew 24–28: 22
Revelation 1–11: 270
9:6
Luke 18–24: 235
9:10
Revelation 1–11: 236
9:11
Matthew 1–7: 86
Hebrews: 48
1 Peter: 210
Revelation 12–22: 168, 234
9:12
Revelation 1–11: 306, 308
9:13–15
Revelation 1–11: 239
9:13–16
Revelation 12–22: 20, 179
9:13–19
Revelation 1–11: 239
9:14
Revelation 12–22: 146
9:14–16
Matthew 24–28: 20
9:14–19
Revelation 12–22: 69, 77
9:14–20
Revelation 12–22: 210
9:15
Acts 1–12: 54
Revelation 1–11: 249
Revelation 12–22: 138
9:16
Revelation 12–22: 8
9:17
Revelation 12–22: 225
9:17–18
Acts 1–12: 55
Revelation 1–11: 258
9:18
Revelation 12–22: 138
9:18–20
Revelation 12–22: 123
9:20
Luke 1–5: 259, 280
1 Corinthians: 236
2 Corinthians: 251
Revelation 1–11: 124
9:20–21
Matthew 8–15: 41
Luke 11–17: 418
2 Corinthians: 433, 468
Revelation 1–11: 2, 229, 242, 251, 256, 260, 261, 266
Revelation 12–22: 86, 87, 144, 177, 196, 210, 216, 241
9:21
Matthew 24–28: 24, 27, 74
1 & 2 Thessalonians: 104
Revelation 1–11: 34, 193, 207
Revelation 12–22: 138, 191, 309
10
Revelation 1–11: 256
10:1
Revelation 1–11: 164
Revelation 12–22: 190, 233, 247, 262
10:1–3
Revelation 12–22: 221
10:1–11:14
Revelation 1–11: 309
Revelation 12–22: 149
10:3
Revelation 1–11: 4, 42
10:4
Ephesians: 258
Revelation 1–11: 42
Revelation 12–22: 74, 103
10:5–6
James: 267
10:6
Acts 13–28: 137
Revelation 1–11: 157, 158, 217
Revelation 12–22: 242

10:7
Romans 9–16: 387
Ephesians: xi
Revelation 1–11: 236, 307
Revelation 12–22: 86, 151
10:8
Revelation 1–11: 281
Revelation 12–22: 74, 103
10:8–10
1 & 2 Thessalonians: 55
Revelation 1–11: 190, 292
10:9–10
Luke 18–24: 221
1 & 2 Thessalonians: 235
2 Peter–Jude: 130
Revelation 1–11: 20
10:10
Matthew 1–7: 342
Matthew 16–23: 57
2 Timothy: 26
10:11
Revelation 1–11: 293, 304
Revelation 12–22: 297
11
Matthew 1–7: 53
Luke 1–5: 39
11:1
Revelation 1–11: 241
Revelation 12–22: 268, 281
11:1–4
Romans 9–16: 119
11:1–13
Mark 9–16: 236
11:1–14
Revelation 1–11: 272
11:1–19
Mark 1–8: 24
11:2
Matthew 24–28: 44
Mark 9–16: 245, 249
Luke 18–24: 228
1 & 2 Thessalonians: 266
Revelation 1–11: 176, 241
Revelation 12–22: 32, 117, 264
11:2–3
Matthew 24–28: 70, 114
1 & 2 Thessalonians: 142
Revelation 1–11: 230, 231
Revelation 12–22: 12
11:2–6
1 & 2 Thessalonians: 148
11:3
Matthew 24–28: 23
Luke 18–24: 236
1 Corinthians: 364
1 & 2 Thessalonians: 145, 266
Revelation 12–22: 32
11:3–12
Mark 9–16: 19
Luke 6–10: 156
11:3–13
Romans 9–16: 128
Revelation 1–11: 320
Revelation 12–22: 96, 122
11:3–14
Revelation 12–22: 27
11:3ff.
Revelation 1–11: 193
11:4
Matthew 24–28: 23
Romans 9–16: 119
11:5
Acts 13–28: 150
Revelation 12–22: 60
11:5–6
Revelation 12–22: 60
11:6
Revelation 1–11: 250, 271, 301
Revelation 12–22: 123, 142
11:7
Matthew 24–28: 18, 23
1 & 2 Thessalonians: 146, 264
Hebrews: 48
James: 184
1 Peter: 210
Revelation 1–11: 257
Revelation 12–22: 40, 41, 48, 143, 168, 192, 224, 234
11:8
Matthew 16–23: 38, 400
Romans 9–16: 122
Revelation 12–22: 152
11:9
Revelation 1–11: 172
Revelation 12–22: 86, 161
11:10
Revelation 1–11: 124, 196, 251, 256, 261
Revelation 12–22: 49, 61, 86, 162, 169
11:11
Revelation 12–22: 60
11:11–13
Matthew 24–28: 23
11:12
Revelation 1–11: 42, 227, 283
Revelation 12–22: 74, 103
11:13
Mark 9–16: 233
Luke 18–24: 205
Revelation 1–11: 296
Revelation 12–22: 12, 34, 144, 145, 152
11:13–19
Matthew 24–28: 308
11:14
Revelation 1–11: 20, 308
Revelation 12–22: 123
11:15
Matthew 8–15: 370
Luke 1–5: 49, 249
Luke 6–10: 205, 262, 324
Luke 11–17: 22
Luke 18–24: 196, 307
John 12–21: 330
Acts 1–12: 15
Romans 9–16: 122, 263
1 Corinthians: 421
Philippians: 139, 141
Hebrews: 12
Revelation 1–11: 42, 176, 227, 239, 277, 286
Revelation 12–22: 3, 7, 11, 21, 34, 51, 70, 85, 122, 217, 242
11:15–17
Revelation 1–11: 236
Revelation 12–22: 15
11:15–18
Revelation 1–11: 150
Revelation 12–22: 21, 196
11:15–19
Revelation 1–11: 215
11:15ff.
Revelation 1–11: 251
Revelation 12–22: 84
11:16
Revelation 1–11: 158, 228
Revelation 12–22: 268
11:17
2 Corinthians: 315
Revelation 1–11: 35
Revelation 12–22: 130, 142, 200
11:18
1 Corinthians: 75
Revelation 1–11: 30, 308
Revelation 12–22: 87, 123, 143, 200, 223, 293
11:19
Matthew 1–7: 79
Revelation 1–11: 146, 151, 232, 242, 282, 283
Revelation 12–22: 4, 34, 132, 151, 284
12
1 Peter: 281
12:1
Revelation 12–22: 29, 123
12:1–6
Revelation 1–11: 254
12:2
Revelation 1–11: 261
Revelation 12–22: 29
12:3
Revelation 1–11: 303, 310
Revelation 12–22: 3, 19, 42, 123, 217, 235
12:3–4
Luke 1–5: 280
Acts 13–28: 291
1 Timothy: 38
1 Peter: 209, 281
Revelation 1–11: 162, 172
Revelation 12–22: 3
12:3–17
Luke 1–5: 255
12:4
Luke 1–5: 255
Acts 1–12: 319
1 Timothy: 38
Hebrews: 23
1 Peter: 281
2 Peter–Jude: 165
Revelation 1–11: 256, 270

Revelation 12–22: 19, 20, 179, 235
12:5
Matthew 1–7: 33
Luke 1–5: 50
Luke 18–24: 238
Philippians: 263
1 & 2 Thessalonians: 246
1 Timothy: 38
Revelation 1–11: 105, 233, 312
Revelation 12–22: 4, 29, 198, 219, 236, 240
12:5–9
Matthew 24–28: 42
12:6
Matthew 24–28: 70
1 & 2 Thessalonians: 281
1 Peter: 282
Revelation 1–11: 176, 230, 296, 299
Revelation 12–22: 22, 23, 29, 32, 239
12:6–7
Revelation 12–22: 62
12:7
Luke 1–5: 29
1 Timothy: 39
Revelation 1–11: 310
Revelation 12–22: 8, 85, 234, 235
12:7–9
Luke 1–5: 280
John 12–21: 198
Acts 13–28: 291
Romans 1–8: 298
Ephesians: 338
Revelation 1–11: 257
Revelation 12–22: 8, 29, 85
12:7–12
Mark 1–8: 240
12:9
Matthew 1–7: 86
Luke 1–5: 217, 255
Luke 6–10: 49, 340
2 Corinthians: 356
Galatians: 10, 186
Philippians: 52
1 & 2 Thessalonians: 266, 276, 282
1 Timothy: 118
Titus: 148
1 Peter: 282
2 Peter–Jude: 165
Revelation 1–11: 86, 168, 303, 310
Revelation 12–22: 3, 6, 8, 40, 41, 69, 77, 151, 179, 210, 215, 235, 240
12:10
Luke 1–5: 255
Acts 1–12: 15
Romans 1–8: 506
2 Corinthians: 482
Colossians and Philemon: 65
1 & 2 Thessalonians: 88
1 Timothy: 37
James: 220
1–3 John: 43
Revelation 1–11: 42, 77, 227, 254, 257, 310
Revelation 12–22: 8, 11, 14, 16, 19, 74, 103
12:11
John 12–21: 134
Ephesians: 370
1–3 John: 175
Revelation 1–11: 2, 17, 232
Revelation 12–22: 124, 237
12:12
John 1–11: 41
1 Peter: 210
Revelation 1–11: 257
Revelation 12–22: 3, 5, 18, 29, 40, 170
12:13
Revelation 12–22: 235
12:13–17
Luke 1–5: 107
Revelation 1–11: 254
Revelation 12–22: 12, 22, 239
12:14
Matthew 24–28: 42, 44, 70, 114
1 & 2 Thessalonians: 266
Revelation 1–11: 296
Revelation 12–22: 3, 12, 23, 62
12:14–15
Revelation 1–11: 86
12:14–16
Revelation 12–22: 12
12:16
Revelation 12–22: 235
12:16–17
Revelation 1–11: 215
12:17
1 Timothy: 39
1 Peter: 282
Revelation 1–11: 22, 194, 219, 303
Revelation 12–22: 4, 96, 124, 235, 238
13
Matthew 16–23: 7
13:1
Matthew 24–28: 36
1 & 2 Thessalonians: 264
Revelation 12–22: 7, 58, 144, 163, 166, 217, 233, 235, 247, 262
13:1–4
Revelation 1–11: 311
13:1–8
Revelation 1–11: 303
Revelation 12–22: 41, 224
13:1–10
Matthew 24–28: 18
Revelation 12–22: 58
13:1–17
1 & 2 Thessalonians: 274
13:1, 6–7
Matthew 8–15: 207
13:1ff.
Revelation 1–11: 262
13:2
1 & 2 Thessalonians: 266, 273
Revelation 12–22: 58, 59, 235
13:2–8
1 & 2 Thessalonians: 146
13:3
1 & 2 Thessalonians: 282
Revelation 12–22: 60, 61–62, 123
13:3–4
Revelation 1–11: 193
Revelation 12–22: 169
13:4
1 & 2 Thessalonians: 282
Revelation 12–22: 89, 125, 163, 167, 189, 235
13:4–7
Revelation 12–22: 29
13:4–8
Revelation 1–11: 272
13:4–10
Revelation 12–22: 15
13:5
Matthew 24–28: 36, 44, 70, 114
1 & 2 Thessalonians: 142, 266, 281
Revelation 1–11: 176, 193, 230, 241, 296
Revelation 12–22: 12, 23, 32, 59, 170
13:5–6
Matthew 8–15: 311
2 Corinthians: 345
Revelation 12–22: 144
13:5–8
1 & 2 Thessalonians: 274
13:6
John 1–11: 41
Revelation 1–11: 233
13:7
Matthew 24–28: 24, 42
Revelation 1–11: 172, 193, 241, 303
Revelation 12–22: 86, 125, 161, 192
13:7–8
Matthew 24–28: 36
Mark 9–16: 245
13:7–10
Revelation 1–11: 214
13:8
Matthew 24–28: 267
Luke 1–5: 36
Luke 6–10: 327
Luke 18–24: 366
John 12–21: 34, 247, 263, 287
Acts 1–12: 62
Acts 13–28: 38, 39
2 Corinthians: 203
Ephesians: 14
Philippians: 260, 273

Colossians and Philemon: 154
1 & 2 Thessalonians: 20, 278, 287
Hebrews: 235, 410
1 Peter: 18, 51, 121
1–3 John: 35, 208
Revelation 1–11: 2, 17, 115, 124, 196, 251, 256, 304
Revelation 12–22: 61, 71, 86, 140, 162, 167, 169, 255, 260, 286, 308
13:11
Revelation 12–22: 233, 247, 262
13:11–14
Revelation 12–22: 163
13:11–15
Matthew 24–28: 37
13:11–17
Revelation 12–22: 224
13:12
1 & 2 Thessalonians: 282
Revelation 1–11: 124, 196, 251, 256, 304
Revelation 12–22: 45, 46, 49, 61, 86, 123, 140, 162, 167, 169
13:12–15
1 & 2 Thessalonians: 282
Revelation 12–22: 46
13:13
1 & 2 Thessalonians: 150
Revelation 12–22: 3, 147
13:14
1 & 2 Thessalonians: 282
1 Timothy: 150
Revelation 1–11: 124, 241, 251, 256, 304
Revelation 12–22: 3, 20, 45, 46, 49, 59, 86, 147, 162, 168, 169, 238
13:14–15
Luke 18–24: 242
13:14–17
Revelation 12–22: 125
13:15
Mark 9–16: 245
Luke 18–24: 225
Revelation 1–11: 241, 295
Revelation 12–22: 103, 192, 211
13:15–16
1 & 2 Thessalonians: 274
Revelation 12–22: 180
13:16
Revelation 1–11: 320
Revelation 12–22: 223
13:16–17
Revelation 1–11: 218
Revelation 12–22: 72, 140, 238
13:17
Revelation 12–22: 32, 180, 211
14:1
Revelation 1–11: 2, 17, 218, 260, 312
Revelation 12–22: 112, 132, 233, 247, 262
14:1–3
Ephesians: 96
Revelation 1–11: 150
14:1–5
Romans 9–16: 102, 128
1 & 2 Thessalonians: 265
Revelation 1–11: 193, 218, 219
Revelation 12–22: 34, 96, 122, 124
14:2
Revelation 1–11: 42, 47, 170, 283
Revelation 12–22: 103, 125, 200
14:3
Ephesians: 257
Revelation 1–11: 171, 228
Revelation 12–22: 132
14:4
Matthew 8–15: 456
James: 64
Revelation 1–11: 124, 219
14:6
Matthew 24–28: 54
Mark 9–16: 243
Luke 18–24: 447
Acts 1–12: 294
Romans 9–16: 128
1 & 2 Thessalonians: 148, 244
Revelation 1–11: 124, 172, 256, 292, 304
Revelation 12–22: 161, 162, 169, 221, 233, 247, 262
14:6–7
Matthew 24–28: 29, 67
Romans 9–16: 122
Revelation 1–11: 193, 272
Revelation 12–22: 122, 195
14:7
Hebrews: 98
Revelation 1–11: 227, 305
Revelation 12–22: 140
14:8
1 Peter: 289
Revelation 12–22: 123, 157, 177, 178, 179, 184, 198
14:9
1 & 2 Thessalonians: 264
Revelation 12–22: 41, 58, 125, 163, 266
14:9–10
James: 245
14:9–11
Romans 1–8: 72, 131
2 Corinthians: 192, 202, 210
1 & 2 Thessalonians: 163
Revelation 1–11: 218
Revelation 12–22: 59, 65, 140, 238
14:10
Luke 11–17: 365
Philippians: 310
Revelation 1–11: 271
Revelation 12–22: 87, 90, 123, 184, 225, 256
14:10–11
Mark 1–8: 433
Luke 1–5: 216, 223
1 Peter: 256
Revelation 1–11: 261
Revelation 12–22: 199, 225, 242
14:11
Mark 1–8: 244
Luke 11–17: 366
1 & 2 Thessalonians: 245
James: 245
Revelation 1–11: 158, 258
Revelation 12–22: 41, 58, 104, 125, 185, 224
14:12
1 & 2 Thessalonians: 19
Revelation 1–11: 122
Revelation 12–22: 34, 294
14:12–13
Revelation 1–11: 214
Revelation 12–22: 124
14:13
Hebrews: 104
1 Peter: 42, 199
Revelation 1–11: 22, 42, 283
Revelation 12–22: 74, 149, 204, 238, 286, 294, 308
14:14
Matthew 8–15: 377
Acts 1–12: 23
Revelation 12–22: 71, 132, 233, 247, 262
14:14–15
Luke 6–10: 327
14:14–16
Matthew 16–23: 68
Revelation 1–11: 280
Revelation 12–22: 123
14:14–19
1 Peter: 133
14:14–20
Matthew 8–15: 115
1 & 2 Thessalonians: 180
Revelation 12–22: 211
14:15
Revelation 1–11: 42, 146, 232
Revelation 12–22: 221, 266, 284
14:15–16
Matthew 24–28: 80
14:15ff.
Revelation 1–11: 215
14:17
Revelation 1–11: 146, 232
Revelation 12–22: 284
14:17–20
Revelation 12–22: 123
14:18
Revelation 1–11: 42, 215
Revelation 12–22: 266
14:18–20
Romans 1–8: 134

Revelation 12–22: 220
14:19
Revelation 12–22: 87
14:20
Matthew 24–28: 53
Luke 18–24: 203
Acts 1–12: 54
Revelation 12–22: 150, 222
15:1
Matthew 16–23: 5
Revelation 1–11: 154, 271, 308
Revelation 12–22: 3, 87, 137, 138, 139, 151, 182, 233, 247, 262, 278
15:1–4
Ephesians: 265
15:1ff.
Revelation 1–11: 215
15:2
Revelation 1–11: 170
Revelation 12–22: 41, 58
15:2–4
Revelation 1–11: 311–12
Revelation 12–22: 50, 296
15:2, 4
Titus: 42
15:3
Titus: 3
Revelation 1–11: 2, 17, 35, 119, 315
Revelation 12–22: 143, 200, 293
15:3–4
Romans 9–16: 42
Revelation 12–22: 21, 76, 142, 196
15:4
Philippians: 311
1–3 John: 25, 45
15:5
Revelation 1–11: 144, 215, 225, 233, 278
Revelation 12–22: 71, 178, 196
15:5–8
Revelation 1–11: 232
Revelation 12–22: 284
15:5–16: 21
2 Peter–Jude: 185
15:6
Revelation 1–11: 271
Revelation 12–22: 182
15:6–7
Matthew 24–28: 75
15:6–8
Revelation 1–11: 146
Revelation 12–22: 139
15:7
Revelation 1–11: 154, 157, 217, 285
Revelation 12–22: 87, 242
15:8
Revelation 1–11: 258, 271
Revelation 12–22: 138, 182
16:1
Luke 18–24: 220
Revelation 1–11: 42, 227, 232, 236, 308
Revelation 12–22: 87, 284
16:1–21
Acts 1–12: 121
1 Peter: 133
Revelation 1–11: 277, 308
Revelation 12–22: 111, 132, 161
16:1ff.
Revelation 1–11: 215
Revelation 12–22: 84, 85
16:2
Luke 11–17: 361
Revelation 1–11: 218
Revelation 12–22: 41, 58, 59, 114, 144, 238
16:2–4
Revelation 1–11: 238
16:2–21
Revelation 1–11: 239
16:3
Acts 1–12: 54
Revelation 12–22: 114
16:4
Revelation 12–22: 114
16:5
Philippians: 311
Titus: 42
Revelation 1–11: 215, 315
16:5–6
Revelation 12–22: 196, 198
16:6
Revelation 12–22: 192
16:7
Revelation 1–11: 35, 119, 315
Revelation 12–22: 87, 130, 197, 200
16:8
Revelation 1–11: 238, 241
Revelation 12–22: 114
16:8–9
Revelation 1–11: 250
16:8–11
Luke 18–24: 235
Acts 1–12: 220
16:9
Romans 9–16: 122
1 & 2 Thessalonians: 209
Revelation 1–11: 2, 192, 230, 233, 242, 251, 256, 261, 266, 271, 272, 305, 316
Revelation 12–22: 48, 61, 86, 177, 182, 196, 210, 216, 241
16:10
Matthew 24–28: 22, 45, 46
Revelation 1–11: 238
Revelation 12–22: 41, 114, 163, 178, 221
16:11
2 Corinthians: 433
Revelation 1–11: 2, 124, 192, 207, 242, 251, 256, 261, 266, 272, 316
Revelation 12–22: 61, 86, 144, 177, 196, 210, 216, 241
16:12
Revelation 1–11: 238, 271
Revelation 12–22: 114
16:12–14
Luke 18–24: 203
1 Peter: 209
16:12–16
Revelation 1–11: 269
16:13
1–3 John: 96
Revelation 1–11: 168
Revelation 12–22: 56, 233, 235, 262
16:13–14
Matthew 24–28: 21
Revelation 12–22: 147, 171, 179
16:14
Luke 1–5: 280
1 & 2 Thessalonians: 71, 144
1 Timothy: 150
James: 184
Revelation 1–11: 35, 312, 315, 316
Revelation 12–22: 3, 20, 130, 200
16:14–16
Revelation 1–11: 176
16:15
Matthew 24–28: 77
Mark 9–16: 262
Acts 1–12: 23
1 & 2 Thessalonians: 143
1 Peter: 235
2 Peter–Jude: 117
Revelation 1–11: 22, 114, 278, 309
Revelation 12–22: 95, 204, 238, 291, 294, 308
16:16
Matthew 24–28: 21
Luke 18–24: 203
Revelation 1–11: 316
Revelation 12–22: 171
16:17
Revelation 1–11: 42, 146, 232, 238
Revelation 12–22: 157, 284
16:17–18
Revelation 1–11: 321
16:17–19
Revelation 12–22: 90, 179
16:17–21
Matthew 24–28: 23
Acts 1–12: 220
2 Peter–Jude: 130
16:18
Revelation 1–11: 151, 242, 282, 283
Revelation 12–22: 34, 114

16:18–20
Luke 18–24: 205
16:19
Matthew 16–23: 390
1 Peter: 289
Revelation 1–11: 308
Revelation 12–22: 87, 123, 157, 182, 184
16:20
Revelation 1–11: 207
Revelation 12–22: 242
16:21
Revelation 1–11: 192, 250, 271
Revelation 12–22: 241
17
Ephesians: xi
1 & 2 Thessalonians: 276
1 Peter: 10
17:1
1 Corinthians: 279
Revelation 12–22: 87, 178, 187, 198, 204, 278, 307
17:1–5
Revelation 12–22: 90
17:1–7
Revelation 12–22: 4
17:1–9
Revelation 12–22: 58
17:2
John 1–11: 82
Revelation 1–11: 124, 196, 251, 256, 304
Revelation 12–22: 49, 61, 86, 179, 184, 198
17:3
Luke 1–5: 180
Revelation 12–22: 233, 247, 262
17:4
Revelation 12–22: 184
17:4–5
Matthew 24–28: 34
17:5
Matthew 1–7: 5
1 Corinthians: 279
1 Peter: 289
17:5–6
Matthew 8–15: 205
17:5, 7
Romans 9–16: 387
17:6
Matthew 24–28: 24, 42
John 12–21: 182
Revelation 1–11: 192, 214
Revelation 12–22: 48, 143, 192
17:7
Revelation 12–22: 307
17:8
John 12–21: 247
Acts 13–28: 39
2 Corinthians: 203
Colossians and Philemon: 154
1 & 2 Thessalonians: 20, 278, 282, 287
1 Timothy: 256
1 Peter: 18, 121, 210
Revelation 1–11: 115, 124, 196, 251, 256, 257, 304, 315
Revelation 12–22: 41, 45, 49, 50, 60, 61, 86, 162, 234, 255, 260
17:9–10
Revelation 12–22: 7
17:9–14
Acts 1–12: 140
17:11
1 & 2 Thessalonians: 280, 282
Revelation 12–22: 45
17:12
Revelation 12–22: 7, 187
17:12–14
Revelation 12–22: 147, 152, 224
17:12–18
Revelation 1–11: 308
17:13
1 Corinthians: 279
1 & 2 Thessalonians: 274
17:14
Mark 9–16: 129
Luke 1–5: 159
Luke 18–24: 307
John 1–11: 14
Acts 1–12: 15, 104
1 Corinthians: 20, 41
1 & 2 Thessalonians: 254
1 Timothy: 276
1–3 John: 216
Revelation 1–11: 2, 17, 124
Revelation 12–22: 71, 149, 218, 221
17:15
Revelation 12–22: 41, 187, 204
17:15–16
Revelation 12–22: 198
17:15–17
Revelation 12–22: 58
17:16
Romans 9–16: 117
Revelation 12–22: 187, 199
17:18
Revelation 1–11: 312
17–18
Matthew 16–23: 7
18
Ephesians: 322
1 Peter: 10
18:1
Revelation 1–11: 144, 215, 225, 278, 281
Revelation 12–22: 196
18:1–2
Revelation 12–22: 221
18:1–24
1 Peter: 133
18:1ff.
Revelation 1–11: 215
18:2
Luke 1–5: 280
1 Timothy: 150
1 Peter: 289
18:3
Revelation 12–22: 198
18:4
2 Corinthians: 254
Revelation 1–11: 271, 283
Revelation 12–22: 74, 103
18:5
Revelation 12–22: 165
18:7
Colossians and Philemon: 85
Revelation 1–11: 261
18:8
Revelation 1–11: 271
Revelation 12–22: 199
18:8–10
2 Peter–Jude: 130
18:8–23
Luke 18–24: 235–36
18:9
Acts 1–12: 55
Revelation 1–11: 259
Revelation 12–22: 198, 199
18:9–10
Revelation 12–22: 182
18:9–11
Revelation 12–22: 195
18:9–19
Revelation 12–22: 221
18:10
1 Peter: 289
Revelation 1–11: 251, 261
Revelation 12–22: 87, 167, 185
18:11, 15
Matthew 1–7: 158
18:12
Revelation 12–22: 203
18:15
Revelation 1–11: 261
Revelation 12–22: 185
18:15–19
Revelation 12–22: 195
18:16
Revelation 1–11: 251
Revelation 12–22: 203
18:17
2 Corinthians: 279
18:18
Acts 1–12: 55
Revelation 1–11: 259
Revelation 12–22: 167, 199
18:19
Revelation 1–11: 251
18:20
Revelation 12–22: 87, 198
18:21
1 Peter: 289
Revelation 1–11: 164, 279
Revelation 12–22: 167
18:21–23
Luke 18–24: 252

18:22
Ephesians: 260
18:23
1 Timothy: 150
Revelation 12–22: 20, 215
18:23–24
Matthew 8–15: 41
18:24
Revelation 12–22: 198
18–22
2 Peter–Jude: 204
19
Luke 18–24: 94
19:1
Revelation 1–11: 42, 144, 215, 225, 227, 278
Revelation 12–22: 74, 178
19:1–2
Romans 9–16: 383
Revelation 12–22: 143, 192
19:1–4
Revelation 1–11: 150
19:1–6
Mark 1–8: 382
Revelation 12–22: 296
19:1–8
Ephesians: 96
Revelation 12–22: 21
19:2
Luke 18–24: 8
Revelation 1–11: 119, 320
Revelation 12–22: 87, 293
19:3
Revelation 1–11: 259
19:3–4
Revelation 12–22: 196
19:4
Revelation 1–11: 158, 228, 314
Revelation 12–22: 132, 247, 248, 268
19:5
2 Peter–Jude: 150
Revelation 1–11: 320
Revelation 12–22: 103, 293
19:6
Revelation 1–11: 35, 47, 315
Revelation 12–22: 75, 130, 196
19:6–9
Luke 11–17: 154
1 & 2 Thessalonians: 74
2 Peter–Jude: 26
19:7
Mark 1–8: 130
Luke 1–5: 340
Luke 11–17: 156
Luke 18–24: 193
John 12–21: 102, 116, 142, 299
Romans 9–16: 122
1 Peter: 41
Revelation 1–11: 2, 17, 305
Revelation 12–22: 210, 278
19:7–8
Luke 18–24: 237
1 & 2 Thessalonians: 203, 206
Revelation 12–22: 4, 218
19:7–9
Revelation 1–11: 30, 115
Revelation 12–22: 6, 251, 265
19:7–10
Revelation 12–22: 211
19:8
Matthew 24–28: 55
Luke 18–24: 192
2 Timothy: 200
Revelation 1–11: 113, 139, 149, 226, 241
19:8, 14
John 12–21: 102
19:9
Matthew 24–28: 55
Mark 1–8: 392
Luke 11–17: 269
Ephesians: 129
Revelation 1–11: 22, 42, 140
Revelation 12–22: 95, 103, 149, 238, 294, 308
19:10
Matthew 8–15: 9
Luke 1–5: 10, 27, 174, 233
Acts 13–28: 3, 21
Romans 9–16: 171
1 Corinthians: 235, 304
Colossians and Philemon: 121
1 & 2 Thessalonians: 197
Hebrews: 415
1 Peter: 55
2 Peter–Jude: 62
Revelation 1–11: 22, 170, 194, 230
Revelation 12–22: 21, 87, 238, 296
19:10–20:6
Luke 1–5: 39
19:11
Matthew 1–7: 79
Luke 1–5: 238
John 12–21: 17
2 Corinthians: 128, 188, 456
Galatians: 169
1 & 2 Thessalonians: 241, 319
1–3 John: 39
Revelation 1–11: 2, 3, 17, 119, 178, 240, 279
Revelation 12–22: 71, 132, 157, 213, 233, 247, 262, 270, 292
19:11–14
Luke 18–24: 193
19:11–15
Luke 11–17: 209
Luke 18–24: 237
19:11–16
Matthew 24–28: 112
Mark 1–8: 431
Mark 9–16: 5
Colossians and Philemon: 132
Hebrews: 242
2 Peter–Jude: 63–64, 117
Revelation 1–11: 297
19:11–20
Matthew 24–28: 21
19:11–21
Mark 9–16: 257
Luke 1–5: 101
Luke 11–17: 156
Luke 18–24: 80, 82, 196, 247
Acts 1–12: 141
Acts 13–28: 114
1 & 2 Thessalonians: 135, 231, 244, 274, 281
2 Peter–Jude: 185
Revelation 1–11: 308, 311
Revelation 12–22: 2, 11, 15, 40, 111, 117, 149, 195, 196, 233, 242, 247
19:11–20:6
Mark 1–8: 191
19:11–20:7
1 & 2 Thessalonians: 246
19:11ff.
Acts 1–12: 303
1 & 2 Thessalonians: 267
19:12
Revelation 1–11: 46, 97, 178
Revelation 12–22: 113
19:13
Luke 11–17: 18
Acts 1–12: 104
1–3 John: 16
Revelation 1–11: 2, 7, 17, 240, 279
19:14
Matthew 24–28: 56
Luke 11–17: 156, 410
Luke 18–24: 192
1 & 2 Thessalonians: 249
Revelation 1–11: 30, 113, 178, 226
Revelation 12–22: 171
19:15
Matthew 1–7: 33
Matthew 24–28: 250
Luke 1–5: 50
1 Corinthians: 420
Philippians: 263
1 & 2 Thessalonians: 246, 281
Revelation 1–11: 35, 48, 83, 97, 105, 178, 233, 312, 315
Revelation 12–22: 11, 87, 123, 130, 198, 200, 213, 240
19:15–16
Luke 1–5: 175
Hebrews: 37
19:16
Matthew 16–23: 205
Luke 1–5: 159
Luke 18–24: 237
John 12–21: 353
Acts 1–12: 15
Philippians: 143
1 & 2 Thessalonians: 254
1 Timothy: 276
1 Peter: 125
Revelation 1–11: 2, 3, 17, 25, 168, 240, 279

Revelation 12–22: 237
19:17
Revelation 1–11: 42
Revelation 12–22: 85, 115, 233, 262, 266
19:17–18
Revelation 1–11: 124, 215
Revelation 12–22: 241
19:17–21
Mark 9–16: 232
Luke 18–24: 203
1 & 2 Thessalonians: 147
1 Peter: 133
Revelation 1–11: 297
Revelation 12–22: 213
19:18
Revelation 1–11: 320
19:19
Revelation 1–11: 168, 312
Revelation 12–22: 20, 233, 262
19:19–21
Revelation 1–11: 316
19:20
Matthew 8–15: 379
Matthew 24–28: 56, 339
Luke 18–24: 207
1 Corinthians: 21
2 Corinthians: 465
1 & 2 Thessalonians: 264, 280, 281, 282
1 Timothy: 150
Hebrews: 48
James: 245
1 Peter: 215
Revelation 1–11: 218, 271
Revelation 12–22: 3, 56, 58, 59, 65, 92, 125, 169, 170, 189, 233, 238, 242, 255, 256, 303
19:21
Luke 6–10: 255
John 12–21: 309
1 & 2 Thessalonians: 281
Revelation 1–11: 48
20
Luke 18–24: 94
Romans 9–16: 111
20:1
Revelation 1–11: 119, 257
Revelation 12–22: 168, 262, 278
20:1–2
Revelation 12–22: 2
20:1–3
Mark 1–8: 70
Luke 1–5: 50, 286
Luke 18–24: 196
Acts 1–12: 234
Acts 13–28: 169
1 Peter: 284
Revelation 1–11: 264, 277, 311
Revelation 12–22: 15, 21, 29, 41, 115, 212
20:1–6
Mark 1–8: 324
Luke 11–17: 26
John 1–11: 483
1 Peter: 282
2 Peter–Jude: 185
Revelation 1–11: 178
20:1–7
1 Peter: 120–21
20:1–10
Revelation 1–11: 297
Revelation 12–22: 196, 247
20:1ff.
Revelation 1–11: 268
20:2
Mark 1–8: 240
Luke 1–5: 217, 255
Luke 11–17: 155
2 Corinthians: 356
1 Timothy: 150
Revelation 1–11: 86, 310
Revelation 12–22: 6, 19
20:2–3
1 & 2 Thessalonians: 266
20:2, 7–10
Matthew 8–15: 40
20:3
2 Corinthians: 408
1 Timothy: 150
Revelation 1–11: 257
Revelation 12–22: 2, 20, 168
20:3–6
Mark 9–16: 258
20:3, 10
Matthew 8–15: 44
Ephesians: 26
20:4
Matthew 1–7: 230, 380
Matthew 8–15: 189
Matthew 24–28: 117
Mark 9–16: 250
Luke 11–17: 156
1 Corinthians: 418
Ephesians: x
Philippians: 262
Hebrews: 59
1–3 John: 110
Revelation 1–11: 149, 194, 214, 218, 226, 241
Revelation 12–22: 50, 58, 87, 125, 234, 247, 262
20:4–5
Revelation 1–11: 196
20:4–6
Luke 1–5: 211
Luke 11–17: 207
Acts 1–12: 120
Revelation 12–22: 125, 219
20:5
Revelation 12–22: 238
20:6
Mark 9–16: 250
John 12–21: 330
Romans 9–16: 332
1 Corinthians: 416
Philippians: 124
Colossians and Philemon: 38
1 & 2 Thessalonians: 249
2 Peter–Jude: 31
Revelation 1–11: 2, 17, 22, 141, 172
Revelation 12–22: 95, 149, 204, 251, 256, 264, 272, 294, 308
20:7–8
Matthew 8–15: 351
1 Peter: 285
Revelation 12–22: 54
20:7–9
Matthew 24–28: 117
Luke 1–5: 286
1 Corinthians: 420
20:7–10
Mark 1–8: 240, 244
Revelation 12–22: 2, 14, 72, 151, 199
20:7–15
1 Peter: 133
2 Peter–Jude: 184
20:8
1 & 2 Thessalonians: 266
1 Timothy: 150
Revelation 12–22: 20, 41
20:8–9
Revelation 1–11: 316
Revelation 12–22: 250
20:8–10
James: 196
Revelation 1–11: 318
20:9
Revelation 12–22: 241
20:10
Matthew 8–15: 379
Matthew 24–28: 339
Mark 1–8: 65
Luke 1–5: 216, 286
Luke 6–10: 221
Luke 11–17: 118
Luke 18–24: 196, 207
1 Corinthians: 21
2 Corinthians: 408
1 & 2 Thessalonians: 88, 266
1 Timothy: 150
1 Peter: 211, 215
2 Peter–Jude: 86, 158, 166
Revelation 1–11: 182, 257, 258, 261, 263, 271, 311
Revelation 12–22: 15, 20, 21, 56, 65, 92, 169, 170, 185, 212, 225, 256, 269
20:10–15
Mark 1–8: 58
Luke 11–17: 275
Acts 13–28: 169
Romans 1–8: 121
1 Corinthians: 420
Ephesians: 49
Colossians and Philemon: 59
Revelation 12–22: 262
20:11
Mark 9–16: 260
Luke 18–24: 250

Revelation 12–22: 262, 263, 270
20:11–13
1 Peter: 235
20:11–15
Matthew 1–7: 478
Matthew 8–15: 396
Mark 1–8: 434
Luke 6–10: 277, 332
Luke 11–17: 156, 178
John 1–11: 194
Acts 13–28: 307
Romans 1–8: 126
1 Corinthians: 420
2 Corinthians: 177, 192, 202, 203, 210
1 & 2 Thessalonians: 163, 244
1 Timothy: 167
2 Timothy: 169
Hebrews: 141
James: 150, 287, 288
1 Peter: 230
1–3 John: 36, 50
Revelation 1–11: 208, 319
Revelation 12–22: 238, 242
20:12
Acts 13–28: 39
Philippians: 273
Hebrews: 410
1 Peter: 18
2 Peter–Jude: 185
Revelation 1–11: 115
Revelation 12–22: 50, 260
20:12–13
Romans 1–8: 127
Colossians and Philemon: 175
Titus: 98
20:12–15
Romans 1–8: 341
20:12, 15
Matthew 1–7: 486
Matthew 8–15: 321
20:13–14
1 Peter: 211
Revelation 1–11: 184, 257
20:14
Romans 1–8: 397
1 Corinthians: 446
1 Peter: 215
Revelation 1–11: 79
Revelation 12–22: 269
20:14–15
2 Corinthians: 465
Revelation 12–22: 255, 277
20:15
Matthew 1–7: 479
Luke 18–24: 207
John 12–21: 258
Acts 13–28: 39
1 Corinthians: 417
Philippians: 273
James: 245
1 Peter: 18, 209, 215
Revelation 1–11: 115
Revelation 12–22: 50, 169, 224, 256, 260, 308
21
Luke 11–17: 151
1 Corinthians: 92
21:1
Matthew 16–23: 204
Romans 1–8: 455, 456
Colossians and Philemon: 58
James: 64
Revelation 1–11: 152, 206, 320
Revelation 12–22: 124, 233, 247, 249, 251, 284, 286
21:1–2
1 Corinthians: 420
Hebrews: 418
Revelation 12–22: 203, 204
21:1–4
Acts 13–28: 114
Romans 9–16: 304
1 Peter: 146, 172
2 Peter–Jude: 31, 131
21:1–5
Luke 6–10: 228
21:1–27
1 Peter: 38
21:1–22:5
Mark 1–8: 70
Mark 9–16: 258
21:1ff.
Revelation 1–11: 244
Revelation 12–22: 247
21:2
Matthew 16–23: 103, 215
Mark 1–8: 130
1 & 2 Thessalonians: 203, 206
Revelation 1–11: 4
21:2, 9
Luke 1–5: 340
21:3
Romans 1–8: 444
Philippians: 263
Hebrews: 415
Revelation 1–11: 42, 227, 233
Revelation 12–22: 103, 284
21:3–4
Matthew 8–15: 74
John 1–11: 41
2 Corinthians: 170
21:3–4, 7
Galatians: 101
21:3–7
Matthew 16–23: 69
21:4
Matthew 1–7: 161
Mark 9–16: 193
1 Corinthians: 446
1 & 2 Thessalonians: 246
1 Peter: 225
Revelation 1–11: 28, 165, 233, 277
21:4–5
Romans 1–8: 456
21:5
Revelation 1–11: 42
Revelation 12–22: 103, 247, 249, 292
21:6
Revelation 1–11: 2, 17, 233
Revelation 12–22: 305, 306
21:7
Mark 1–8: 434
1 Peter: 46
Revelation 1–11: 319
21:7–8
1–3 John: 135
21:8
Matthew 1–7: 326
Romans 1–8: 295
1 Corinthians: 236, 241, 419
2 Corinthians: 465
Ephesians: 182
1 & 2 Thessalonians: 105, 163
James: 272, 287, 288
2 Peter–Jude: 83
Revelation 1–11: 79, 271
Revelation 12–22: 92, 256, 277, 308, 309
21:9
Matthew 16–23: 103
Ephesians: 304
1 & 2 Thessalonians: 203
Revelation 1–11: 2, 17, 271
Revelation 12–22: 292, 307
21:9–27
John 12–21: 101
21:10
Luke 1–5: 180
Revelation 12–22: 162, 265
21:10–11
Revelation 1–11: 152
21:10–11, 23
Luke 1–5: 157
21:10–14
Revelation 12–22: 206
21:11
2 Peter–Jude: 29
Revelation 1–11: 147
Revelation 12–22: 267
21:12
Acts 13–28: 333
James: 12
Revelation 1–11: 220
21:12–14
Matthew 16–23: 204
Luke 6–10: 19
21:14
Mark 1–8: 172, 285
Luke 6–10: 18, 241
Acts 13–28: 301
2 Corinthians: 414
21:15
Romans 9–16: 119
Revelation 1–11: 293
21:16
John 12–21: 100
Revelation 12–22: 264
21:18
Revelation 1–11: 152
Revelation 12–22: 203
21:21
Matthew 8–15: 383
Revelation 12–22: 203

21:22
Revelation 1–11: 35, 146, 232, 315
Revelation 12–22: 130, 200, 266
21:22–23
2 Corinthians: 170
21:22–26
Revelation 12–22: 288
21:22–27
2 Peter–Jude: 131
21:23
Matthew 1–7: 29
Matthew 24–28: 55
John 1–11: 334
1 Corinthians: 366
2 Peter–Jude: 29
1–3 John: 23
Revelation 12–22: 267
21:23–25
Mark 1–8: 406
21:24–27
2 Peter–Jude: 185
21:27
Matthew 8–15: 456
Matthew 24–28: 34
Luke 18–24: 224
John 12–21: 297
Acts 13–28: 39
2 Corinthians: 203
Philippians: 260, 273
Titus: 7, 68
Hebrews: 415
James: 272
1 Peter: 18, 35–36
2 Peter–Jude: 83
Revelation 1–11: 115
Revelation 12–22: 50, 92, 169, 255, 260, 308
21:33
Luke 1–5: 156
21–22
John 1–11: 194
Galatians: 126
22
Luke 11–17: 151
22:1
Revelation 1–11: 2, 3, 17, 233
Revelation 12–22: 44, 248, 263, 292
22:1–3
1 Peter: 172
22:1–5
Mark 1–8: 49
1 Peter: 38
2 Peter–Jude: 31
22:2
Matthew 8–15: 476
Luke 18–24: 388
2 Corinthians: 395
Revelation 1–11: 65
Revelation 12–22: 308
22:3
Matthew 1–7: 133
Matthew 16–23: 205
Revelation 1–11: 3, 28
Revelation 12–22: 44, 200, 248, 268
22:3–4
2 Corinthians: 170
Philippians: 263
Revelation 12–22: 266
22:3–5
Titus: 120
Revelation 1–11: 232
22:4
Revelation 1–11: 260
22:5
Matthew 24–28: 55
John 1–11: 419
2 Corinthians: 249
1 & 2 Thessalonians: 164
Revelation 12–22: 267
22:6
Revelation 1–11: 21
Revelation 12–22: 200, 270, 309
22:7
Luke 11–17: 154
Luke 18–24: 253
James: 154
2 Peter–Jude: 184
Revelation 1–11: 1, 9, 21, 22, 30, 306
Revelation 12–22: 95, 149, 204, 211, 238, 294
22:7, 12, 20
Romans 9–16: 377
22:8
Revelation 1–11: 3, 4, 22
Revelation 12–22: 207
22:8–9
Luke 1–5: 27
Luke 18–24: 157
John 1–11: 15
Acts 1–12: 298
Revelation 1–11: 230
Revelation 12–22: 21
22:9
1 Corinthians: 223
Colossians and Philemon: 121
Revelation 12–22: 87, 207
22:10
1 & 2 Thessalonians: 197
Revelation 1–11: 9, 283
Revelation 12–22: 294, 307, 309
22:11
Matthew 16–23: 393
Ephesians: 170
22:11b–12a
Romans 9–16: 261
22:12
Matthew 16–23: 57
Mark 1–8: 216
Mark 9–16: 109
Acts 1–12: 23
1 Corinthians: 78, 86, 448
2 Corinthians: 178
1 & 2 Thessalonians: 74, 92
1 Timothy: 267
James: 154, 257
1–3 John: 110, 113, 234
Revelation 1–11: 21, 30, 103, 306, 319
Revelation 12–22: 149, 211
22:13
Luke 18–24: 156
John 1–11: 14, 422
Acts 1–12: 104
Colossians and Philemon: 48–49
Revelation 1–11: 50, 68, 134
Revelation 12–22: 271
22:14
Luke 18–24: 388
2 Corinthians: 395
Revelation 1–11: 22, 65, 231
Revelation 12–22: 95, 149, 204, 238
22:14–15
Romans 1–8: 72
1 Peter: 36, 225
22:15
Matthew 1–7: 291
Luke 11–17: 362
1 Corinthians: 236
Philippians: 217
1 & 2 Thessalonians: 105, 245
James: 272
1 Peter: 35
Revelation 12–22: 92, 272
22:16
Matthew 1–7: 29
Matthew 8–15: 90
Luke 1–5: 50, 122
John 1–11: 422
Acts 1–12: 104
1 Timothy: 38
2 Timothy: 57
Revelation 1–11: 2, 15, 17, 21, 22, 105, 119, 167
22:17
Matthew 8–15: 268
Matthew 24–28: 331
Mark 1–8: 130
Luke 1–5: 340
Luke 11–17: 329
Luke 18–24: 440
Acts 1–12: 303
Romans 1–8: 28
2 Corinthians: 192, 202, 213
1 Timothy: 72
James: 203
Revelation 1–11: 233
Revelation 12–22: 104, 263, 271
22:18
1 Corinthians: 299
2 Corinthians: 417
Revelation 1–11: 271
Revelation 12–22: 294
22:18–19
Luke 11–17: 151
John 12–21: 207
Romans 1–8: 72
1 Corinthians: 361
Ephesians: 369

1 & 2 Thessalonians: 197
1 Timothy: 288–89
2 Timothy: 153
Titus: 51
Hebrews: 7
2 Peter–Jude: 67
1–3 John: 15, 235
Revelation 1–11: 9, 23
22:19
Acts 13–28: 39
2 Corinthians: 395
James: 113
2 Peter–Jude: 63
Revelation 1–11: 65
Revelation 12–22: 294
22:20
Matthew 1–7: 381
Matthew 16–23: 56
Matthew 24–28: 82
Luke 11–17: 26, 408, 413
Luke 18–24: 3, 241, 253
1 & 2 Thessalonians: 116, 231, 255
James: 256
1 Peter: 65, 235
Revelation 1–11: 21, 30, 125, 306
Revelation 12–22: 149, 211

Index of Ancient Texts (includes Apocryphal Works, Pseudepigrapha, and Rabbinic Writings)

Acts of Peter and the Twelve Apostles
2 Peter–Jude: 9

Acts of Philip
Luke 6–10: 59

Against Heresies (Irenaeus)
3.1.1
John 1–11: 3–4, 9
3.3.4
Luke 6–10: 51
John 1–11: 3–4, 8

Agriculture (Varro)
1.17
Luke 6–10: 125

Analects (Confucius)
XV.24
Luke 6–10: 107

Antiquities (Josephus)
18.1.6
Luke 6–10: 70
20.8.6
John 12–21: 12

Apocalypse of Peter
2 Peter–Jude: 7, 9

Apocryphon of John
2 Peter–Jude: 7

Assumption of Moses
10:8–10
Luke 18–24: 182

2 Baruch
29:5
Romans 1–8: 452–53
50:2–51:10
Mark 9–16: 184–85
Luke 18–24: 141–42

Book of Jubilees
23:10
Romans 1–8: 233
15:25ff.
Romans 1–8: 248

1 Clement
2 Peter–Jude: 7–8, 12
9.2
2 Peter–Jude: 8
23.3
2 Peter–Jude: 7
23.5
2 Peter–Jude: 7
35.5
2 Peter–Jude: 8
47.1
2 Peter–Jude: 12

Dialogue of Justin with Trypho, a Jew (Justin Martyr)
Chapter 120
Mark 9–16: 168

Ecclesiastical History (Eusebius)
3.24
John 1–11: 9
5.20
John 1–11: 3–4
6.14
John 1–11: 9
II.9
Luke 6–10: 43
III.1
John 12–21: 404
III.31.3
John 12–21: 318

Ecclesiasticus (The Wisdom of Sirach)
44:19–21
Romans 1–8: 233

Enoch
52:7–9
Luke 18–24: 181
90:28
Luke 18–24: 181
90:29
Luke 18–24: 181

Epistle of Barnabas
5.4
2 Peter–Jude: 7
15.4
2 Peter–Jude: 7

Epistle of Peter to Philip
2 Peter–Jude: 9

Epistle to the Ephesians
12.2
2 Peter–Jude: 12

Epistle to the Philippians
3.1
2 Peter–Jude: 12

4 Esdras
7:28
John 1–11: 303
13:32
John 1–11: 303
13:52
John 1–11: 303

4 Ezra
12:32
Luke 18–24: 180
12:33
Luke 18–24: 180
13:33–35
Luke 18–24: 180

Ethics (Aristotle)
1161b
Luke 6–10: 125

First Apology (Justin Martyr)
61
John 1–11: 4

Gallic Wars (Julius Caesar)
Mark 9–16: 408

Gospel of Peter
2 Peter–Jude: 9

Gospel of Thomas
John 1–11: 4

Gospel of Truth
2 Peter–Jude: 7

Histories (Polybius)
vi.xix–xlii
Luke 6–10: 124

History (Herodotus)
Mark 9–16: 408

History of the Peloponnesian War (Thucydides)
Mark 9–16: 408

Iliad (Homer)
Mark 9–16: 409
Romans 1–8: 200

Institutes (Gaius)
1.52
Luke 6–10: 125

Letter of Peter to James
2 Peter–Jude: 9
John 1–11: 484

1 Maccabees
13:51
John 12–21: 16

2 Maccabees
10:1–8
John 1–11: 439–40
10:7
John 12–21: 16
14:45–46
Luke 18–24: 141

Mishnah Sanhedrin
4.1
Luke 18–24: 333
4.2
Luke 18–24: 333
7.5
Luke 18–24: 333
11.2
Luke 18–24: 333

Nicocles (Isocrates)
3.60
Luke 6–10: 106–7

Nicomachean Ethics (Aristotle)
4:3
Mark 9–16: 32

Odyssey (Homer)
Ephesians: 236

Prayer of Manasseh
Romans 1–8: 233

Preaching of Peter
2 Peter–Jude: 9

Psalms of Solomon
11
Luke 18–24: 181

Shepherd of Hermas
Similitude 8.11.1
2 Peter–Jude: 7

Sibylline Oracles
3:363ff.
Matthew 24–28: 4
3:363–72
Matthew 24–28: 5
Luke 18–24: 180
3:620–33
Romans 1–8: 453
3:690ff.
Matthew 24–28: 6–7
Luke 18–24: 182
3:744–56
Romans 1–8: 453

Talmud
Berakot 5:5
2 Corinthians: 409

Teaching of Peter
2 Peter–Jude: 9

To Autolycus (Theophilus of Antioch)
2.22
John 1–11: 4

Wars of the Jews (Josephus)
2.13.5
John 12–21: 12
2.166

Wisdom of Solomon
9:15
2 Corinthians: 166

Index of Subjects

Aaron
Mark 1–8: 270
Luke 1–5: 24, 30, 74, 170
Luke 6–10: 21, 143
John 1–11: 342, 399
2 Corinthians: 101–2, 454
1 Peter: 72, 108–13
2 Peter & Jude: 163–64
1–3 John: 253
Aaron's sons
1 Peter: 108–13
Abandonment
Mark 9–16: 377
Abba
Mark 9–16: 301
Abbott–Smith, G.
on meaning of *huparchō*
Acts 1–12: 221
Abel
Luke 6–10: 84, 85
Luke 11–17: 108
Luke 18–24: 262, 331
John 1–11: 372
Hebrews: 297–301, 303
2 Peter & Jude: 70, 176–77
1–3 John: 132, 133
sacrifice of
Galatians: 46
Abiding
John 12–21: 114–15, 117, 142, 146–50
Abihu
Luke 1–5: 29–30, 74
1 Peter: 108, 112–13
Abijah
Luke 1–5: 23–24
2 Corinthians: 352
Ability
2 Corinthians: 280
Abimelech (son of Gideon)
1–3 John: 253
Abiram
2 Corinthians: 454
2 Peter & Jude: 178
Abishai
1 Peter: 157
Abner
1 Peter: 157
Abomination
Mark 9–16: 244
Abomination of desolation
Mark 9–16: 244, 248
Luke 18–24: 224–28
Revelation 1–11: 192, 193, 294–95
Revelation 12–22: 12, 28, 32, 58, 61
Abortion
Romans 9–16: 226
Titus: 146
Abraham
Matthew 1–7: 6, 172
Mark 9–16: 102, 184, 209
Luke 1–5: 54, 59, 127, 196, 221–22, 249
Luke 6–10: 20, 60, 99, 142–44, 213
Luke 18–24: 2, 50, 74, 75, 150, 154
John 1–11: 33, 42, 116, 123–25, 137, 148, 152, 184, 194, 206, 216, 346, 359–78
John 12–21: 21–22, 47
2 Corinthians: 15–19, 88, 97, 115, 139, 272, 281–82, 316, 377, 393
Ephesians: 126
1 Peter: 43, 63, 175
2 Peter & Jude: 89–90, 186
1–3 John: 242
call of
Hebrews: 327–28
descendants' salvation and
Luke 11–17: 223, 367
faith of
Acts 1–12: 204
Romans 1–8: 260, 263, 267
Hebrews: 161–62, 326–35
fear and
Hebrews: 356
God's plan for
Hebrews: 163–65
importance of
Hebrews: 326–27
Melchizedek and
Hebrews: 179–80
obedience of
Romans 1–8: 236, 237
James: 33
patience and
Hebrews: 330
in rich man and Lazarus parable
Luke 11–17: 362–65, 368
spiritual descendants of
Romans 9–16: 115
spiritual descent from
Romans 1–8: 255
wealth and
Luke 11–17: 128
Abrahamic Covenant
Mark 9–16: 291
Luke 1–5: 95, 105–11, 119–20, 127–28, 131
Luke 11–17: 236, 248, 415
John 1–11: 123–25
2 Corinthians: 88–91, 97–98
Hebrews: 164, 165, 196, 214, 338
second
Romans 9–16: 131
Absalom
Mark 9–16: 69, 287
Luke 6–10: 74
Luke 18–24: 29
John 1–11: 365–66
John 12–21: 72
1–3 John: 85, 253–54
Absolute authority
Mark 9–16: 152–54
Absolute inability
2 Peter & Jude: 74
Absolute truth. *see* Truth
Absolutes
Matthew 1–7: 250
Abstinence
1 Peter: 137–38

Abundant life
Romans 9–16: 138
Abuse
2 Corinthians: 372–73
Abused children
Romans 1–8: 191
Abused wives
Romans 1–8: 191
Abyss
Luke 1–5: 286
Luke 6–10: 222
1 Peter: 210–11
Revelation 12–22: 234–35
Access to God
1 Peter: 103–17
Accountability
Mark 9–16: 66
Romans 1–8: 137, 158, 293
2 Corinthians: 304–7
Colossians & Philemon: 228–29
age of
Matthew 16–23: 181
Luke 18–24: 27, 28, 30
believers'
Matthew 16–23: 52
human
Matthew 24–28: 79
Accursed children
2 Peter & Jude: 101–2
Accusation
Matthew 1–7: 226–28
Accuser, Satan as
2 Timothy: 115
Achaicus
1–3 John: 246
Achan
Mark 1–8: 270
Luke 11–17: 129, 333
2 Corinthians: 272
1–3 John: 88
Actium (Battle of)
Luke 1–5: 144
Activism, Christian
Romans 9–16: 213
Acts, book of
Luke 18–24: 451
Adam
Mark 1–8: 43–44, 70
Luke 1–5: 42, 246, 249, 253, 255
Luke 6–10: 84, 142
Luke 18–24: 272
John 1–11: 17, 20–21, 76, 110–13, 175, 342, 376
2 Corinthians: 164–65, 210, 356, 451
1 Timothy: 88, 89
1–3 John: 90, 133, 188, 252
Christ and, antithetical analogy of
Romans 1–8: 291
deception by Satan
Romans 1–8: 303
and Eve
Mark 9–16: 55
Luke 18–24: 49–50, 68, 262, 286, 383
John 12–21: 204–5
Romans 1–8: 294
1 Peter: 209–10
2 Peter & Jude: 119, 157–58, 176–77, 183–84
historicity of
Romans 1–8: 294
inexcusability of sin of
Romans 1–8: 296
as representative of human race
Romans 1–8: 293
Admonishments
Colossians & Philemon: 79–80, 159–60
to false teachers
2 Peter & Jude: 1–7, 31, 58, 104–19, 159–78, 189–98
Adonijah
1–3 John: 254
Adoption
1 Peter: 85
divine
Matthew 16–23: 68
Roman
Romans 1–8: 436
Adultery
Matthew 1–7: 299–306, 312
Mark 9–16: 55, 58–60
Luke 11–17: 351–52
Ephesians: 303
2 Peter & Jude: 100–101
of David
Mark 9–16: 58–59
disqualification of pastor by
Titus: 28
and divorce
Matthew 16–23: 166
Mark 9–16: 58–60
and marriage
Matthew 16–23: 166
spiritual
Mark 9–16: 60
James: 191
woman caught in
John 1–11: 325–29
Adversaries
1 Peter: 281
Advocate, Jesus as. *see* Jesus Christ
Aeneas
Luke 1–5: 294
Luke 6–10: 36
Aeschylus
2 Peter & Jude: 39–40
Affection
2 Corinthians: 236, 481–82, 486–87
Christian
1 Corinthians: 487
showing of
Colossians & Philemon: 172
Affliction. *see* Suffering
Africa
Matthew 24–28: 19
Afterlife, pagan views about
Matthew 16–23: 326
Agag
Mark 9–16: 46
Age, loneliness and
Titus: 78
Agnosticism, philosophical
2 Peter & Jude: 56–58

Subjects

Agony
Luke 18–24: 306
Agrippa. *see* Herod Agrippa
Agur
Luke 11–17: 32–33, 129
Ahab
Mark 1–8: 298
Luke 1–5: 231, 275
Luke 6–10: 54, 75
Luke 18–24: 351
John 1–11: 376
2 Corinthians: 252
Ephesians: 35
Ahasuerus
Luke 6–10: 74
Ahaz
Mark 9–16: 48
1 Peter: 199
Ahaziah
Luke 6–10: 54, 74, 313
Ahimelech
Mark 1–8: 144
Luke 6–10: 5, 6
1 Peter: 157
Ahithophel
Mark 9–16: 287
Luke 6–10: 74
John 12–21: 73
Akiba
John 1–11: 214
Alabaster vials
Mark 9–16: 273
Alamo
Luke 6–10: 38
Albright, W. F.
John 12–21: 203
Alcibiades
Luke 6–10: 73
John 12–21: 72
Alcohol, beverage
Ephesians: 229–44
Alcoholics Anonymous
Romans 1–8: 369
Alertness (watchfulness)
Matthew 24–28: 72
Mark 9–16: 261–63
Luke 11–17: 157–65
1 Peter: 280–85
Alexander (false apostle)
2 Corinthians: 477
2 Peter & Jude: 140
Alexander (Simon of Cyrene's son)
Mark 9–16: 363
Luke 18–24: 368
Alexander the Great
Luke 6–10: 259
Luke 18–24: 378
John 1–11: 48
Ephesians: 194
1 & 2 Thessalonians: 3
Alexandria
Luke 18–24: 368
Alexandrian church
1 Peter: 144
Alienation
Colossians & Philemon: 163–64
Aliens and strangers
1 Peter: 15–16, 137
Allah
Luke 18–24: 150
Romans 1–8: 336
Allegory
Matthew 24–28: 86
Galatians: 122
Allen, James
on the phrase "seven mountains"
Revelation 12–22: 169
Alliance of Russia and Arab nations
Matthew 24–28: 35
Almsgiving
Mark 1–8: 128
Mark 9–16: 84
Alpha and Omega
John 1–11: 14
Alphaeus
Mark 1–8: 171
Luke 6–10: 69
Altar call
Luke 11–17: 216
Altars
Luke 1–5: 135
Altruism
2 Timothy: 3
Amasai
2 Corinthians: 114
Amazement
Mark 1–8: 57, 62, 67, 106, 250
Mark 9–16: 24, 182, 348, 401, 418
Luke 6–10: 122–23, 213
Amaziah (king of Judah)
Luke 6–10: 74
2 Corinthians: 352
1 Timothy: 145
Ambition
noble (*see* Noble ambition)
selfish
Matthew 8–15: 124, 150
Matthew 16–23: 95
Romans 1–8: 133
worldly
Matthew 16–23: 236
Ambrose
John 1–11: 323–24
Acts 13–28: 211
1 & 2 Thessalonians: 4
America, illusion of Christian
Titus: 138
American Revolution
Romans 9–16: 206
Amillennialism
Luke 1–5: 50, 126, 127, 131–34
Luke 18–24: 43
Romans 9–16: 114
Hebrews: 98
Revelation 12–22: 229–31
Amon's servants
Luke 6–10: 74
Amos
Mark 9–16: 168
Luke 11–17: 342
Luke 18–24: 4–5, 124
John 1–11: 117

Analogia Scriptura
1 Timothy: 167
Analogy(ies)
Mark 1–8: 182, 194
Luke 6–10: 187
Luke 18–24: 243, 244
Galatians: 122
Ananias
Acts 13–28: 281
2 Corinthians: 272, 339, 387, 410, 442
1 Peter: 253
2 Peter & Jude: 149
1–3 John: 205
Ananias and Sapphira
Luke 6–10: 36, 320
Luke 11–17: 114, 129, 333
1–3 John: 205
Anarthrous construction, Greek
Romans 1–8: 255, 359
Ancestry
Luke 1–5: 45, 158, 244–50
See also Genealogies
Anchor, Robert
2 Peter & Jude: 56
Anchorites (hermits)
Luke 18–24: 70
Ancient Egyptians, death and
Luke 18–24: 140
Ancient Greeks, death and
Luke 18–24: 140
Ancient manuscripts
Mark 9–16: 408–10
Ancient of Days
John 1–11: 183
"And the Glory of the Lord" (*Messiah* chorus)
Luke 6–10: 280
Anderson, Robert
Mark 9–16: 126
John 12–21: 15
Andrew
Mark 9–16: 36, 105
Luke 1–5: 225, 282, 303–4
Luke 6–10: 25, 39, 251
John 1–11: 2–3, 63–71, 163, 464
John 12–21: 25, 26, 188, 274
2 Corinthians: 141
1 Peter: 4
2 Peter & Jude: 2
1–3 John: 5
call of
Mark 1–8: 40, 50, 161
choosing of
Luke 6–10: 16, 17
as missionary
Mark 1–8: 170–71
Luke 6–10: 40, 41, 58
residence/business of
Mark 1–8: 60, 72, 315
significance
Luke 6–10: 18, 47, 55, 282
Androgyny
Titus: 81
Andronicus
2 Corinthians: 409
Angel of the Lord
Revelation 1–11: 240
Angelic majesties
2 Peter & Jude: 97–99, 174
Angels
Matthew 1–7: 18, 98
Mark 9–16: 400, 401
Luke 1–5: 27–30, 56, 156, 160–63
Luke 18–24: 305–6, 410–12
2 Corinthians: 158, 357, 401, 461
Ephesians: 96
1 Peter: 57–59, 77, 127, 212–13, 282
Revelation 1–11: 21, 33, 149, 172, 215, 227–28, 238
apostate
2 Peter & Jude: 164–65
archangels
2 Peter & Jude: 98–99, 145, 169, 173–75
authority over
Colossians & Philemon: 50, 103, 112–13
biblical view of
Hebrews: 22–24
and end–time events
Revelation 12–22: 84
fallen (*See also* Demons)
Matthew 8–15: 42, 44
Mark 1–8: 58, 63, 65, 245, 246
Romans 1–8: 99, 298
2 Peter & Jude: 84–86, 145, 164–67, 169–71
of God
2 Peter & Jude: 85, 98–99, 117, 164, 173–74
guardian
Matthew 16–23: 118
in heaven
Hebrews: 414–15
human response to in Scripture
Acts 1–12: 294
Jewish views of
Hebrews: 24–25
of light
Luke 1–5: 284, 285
man and
Hebrews: 52–55
as mediators of the Old Covenant
Hebrews: 25, 46
ministry of
Hebrews: 37
Revelation 12–22: 296
serve as God's messengers
Revelation 12–22: 84
worship of
1 Corinthians: 235
Colossians & Philemon: 120–21
Anger
Matthew 1–7: 292–94
Mark 1–8: 156, 157
2 Corinthians: 435
Colossians & Philemon: 143–44
holy
Romans 1–8: 63
power of
Matthew 16–23: 152
righteous
Ephesians: 125
Animal sacrifices
Luke 18–24: 50

Ankerberg, John
John 12–21: 204
Anna (prophetess)
Luke 1–5: 111, 184–86
Luke 6–10: 61, 183, 258
1 Timothy: 201
Annas
Mark 9–16: 137, 152, 323, 324, 325
Luke 1–5: 201, 203–4
John 12–21: 315, 316, 320, 321, 324, 325
legal violations of
Luke 18–24: 334, 335
power of
Luke 18–24: 105, 268, 333–34
Annihilation
Matthew 8–15: 222
Annihilationism
Mark 9–16: 187
The Anointed One
Luke 18–24: 180
Anointing
Mark 1–8: 33–36, 295
Mark 9–16: 273, 274
2 Corinthians: 45
Anonymity
Colossians & Philemon: 163–64
Anthony, Saint, asceticism of
Colossians & Philemon: 123
Anthropic Principle
Colossians & Philemon: 48
Anti-Gentile prejudice
Romans 9–16: 109
Anti-intellectualism
1 Peter: 274
Anti-Semitism
Luke 6–10: 126
Luke 11–17: 243–44
Acts 13–28: 103, 104
Romans 1–8: 164
Romans 9–16: 3, 8, 109, 112, 127
Revelation 12–22: 25–27
See also Holocaust
Antichrist(s)
Matthew 24–28: 36
Mark 9–16: 232, 235, 236, 244, 245, 246
Luke 18–24: 187, 203, 225, 227, 228
John 1–11: 427
John 12–21: 12
Romans 1–8: 92
Romans 9–16: 102
Ephesians: 322
1 & 2 Thessalonians: 156–57, 264, 266–67, 272–74
1 Peter: 283
Revelation 1–11: 178, 181, 193, 204, 214, 262, 294, 296, 303
alleged resurrection of
Revelation 12–22: 45–46, 60, 168
character of
Revelation 12–22: 168
characteristics of
1–3 John: 95, 98–101
Christians contrasted with
1–3 John: 104
coming of
2 Timothy: 123
definition of
1–3 John: 94
departing from the faith
1–3 John: 99–100
error and
1–3 John: 22
false teachers as
1–3 John: 95, 158, 188
Father and Son denial by
1–3 John: 100, 179
final
1–3 John: 96–97
introduction of
1–3 John: 95–98
Jerusalem temple and
Luke 18–24: 242
Jesus Christ and
1–3 John: 96, 97, 100
kingdom of
Revelation 12–22: 89–90, 177
persecution of God's people
Revelation 12–22: 48–49
spirit of as false religion
1–3 John: 158
tactics of deception by
1–3 John: 101
worship of
Revelation 12–22: 47, 58, 61, 90, 162, 163, 172
Anticipation, second coming
2 Peter & Jude: 127–46
Antietam, battle of
Acts 13–28: 242
Antinomianism
Matthew 1–7: 267–68
Romans 1–8: 173, 315
Galatians: 16, 145
1–3 John: 34, 38, 39, 54, 121
Antinomy
Ephesians: 11–12, 32
See also Paradox
Antioch
Luke 18–24: 369, 407, 444
1 Peter: 257
Antiochus IV (Epiphanes)
Matthew 24–28: 34, 37
Mark 9–16: 244, 245
Luke 1–5: 107, 318
Luke 11–17: 97
Luke 18–24: 225, 226, 227
John 1–11: 100, 439–40
Antipas (Herod Antipas). *see* Herod Antipas
Antipas (pastor)
Luke 1–5: 226
Luke 18–24: 212
Antisupernaturalism
2 Peter & Jude: 56
Antitype, biblical
Matthew 1–7: 42–43
Antonia (fortress)
Mark 9–16: 310, 346, 360
Antony
Mark 9–16: 114
Luke 1–5: 22, 143, 144
Antony, Mark
Luke 18–24: 78

Anxiety. *see* Worry
"Anxious bench"
Luke 11–17: 216
Aorist tense, Greek
Romans 1–8: 296
Apathy
1 Corinthians: 472
Aphrodite
Mark 1–8: 374
2 Corinthians: 247
Apis (bull–god)
Romans 1–8: 94
Apocalypse
Luke 11–17: 152
Apocalypse of Baruch
Romans 1–8: 452
Apocrypha
Matthew 1–7: 76
Romans 1–8: 90
Apocryphal resurrection beliefs
Mark 9–16: 184–85
Apollos
John 1–11: 42, 127–28
2 Corinthians: 222, 294
Apologetics
Acts 1–12: 200
Apology of Aristides
Acts 1–12: 90–91
Apostasy
Mark 1–8: 185
Luke 1–5: 116, 119, 126, 130
Luke 11–17: 164
Romans 1–8: 120, 138
Romans 9–16: 117
2 Peter & Jude: 147–48, 156, 159–60
causes of
Hebrews: 274–76
characteristics of
Hebrews: 272–73
deterrents to
Hebrews: 280–83
at Ephesus
1 Timothy: 152
error of
1 Timothy: 154
finality of
Hebrews: 147–49
and last times
1 Timothy: 148
nature of
Hebrews: 271–72
profession and
Hebrews: 83, 93–94
purveyors of
1 Timothy: 151
results of
Hebrews: 276–78
Scriptural examples
Hebrews: 270–71
source of
1 Timothy: 149
unbelief and
Hebrews: 92
warning of
1 Timothy: 147, 150
See also Error
Apostates and apostate times
apostate angels
2 Peter & Jude: 164–65
coming judgments on
2 Peter & Jude: 183–91
definition of
1 Timothy: 147
at Ephesus
1 Timothy: 146
illustrations of
2 Peter & Jude: 169–82
in New Testament
1 Timothy: 146
survival strategies for
2 Peter & Jude: 193–204
warnings to
2 Peter & Jude: 157–67
See also Believer(s), false
Apostle(s)
Mark 1–8: 168
Luke 6–10: 17, 144, 251
Luke 11–17: 383–84
Luke 18–24: 126
John 12–21: 78, 274–75
Hebrews: 78–79
2 Peter & Jude: 19–20, 48, 50–53, 68, 146, 198–99, 201
authority of
Ephesians: 1
choosing
Luke 6–10: 15–17, 46
commissioning
Matthew 8–15: 184
Galatians: 7
commitment of
Luke 6–10: 64
definition of
2 Corinthians: 409–10
general meaning of
Romans 1–8: 22
impact of
Matthew 8–15: 127
importance of
Luke 6–10: 18–21
initiation of
Matthew 8–15: 120
ministry of
1 Timothy: 4
pastoral and ministerial functions of (*see* Pastors and ministers)
preaching by
Luke 6–10: 240, 247
qualifications of
Romans 1–8: 7
responsibilities and duties of
2 Corinthians: 413–14
sending
Luke 6–10: 17–18
training of
Luke 6–10: 182, 184, 297
true (definition)
2 Corinthians: 410
the Twelve
Luke 6–10: 47, 162, 241
John 12–21: 3, 20, 65–69, 73–80, 166, 231
2 Corinthians: 17, 358, 385, 387, 407–17

2 Peter & Jude: 2–3, 50–53
uses of term
Galatians: 2
weaknesses of
Luke 6–10: 19–21, 24, 182
See also Apostolic entries; Recognition; Twelve apostles
Apostle of love
John 1–11: 8
Apostleship
Luke 6–10: 241
Paul's
1 Corinthians: 2–4
purpose and responsibilities of
1 Corinthians: 4–5
Apostolic attributes
authenticity
2 Corinthians: 45–46
love (See also Love)
2 Corinthians: 48, 233–41
overview of
2 Corinthians: 40–41
reliability
2 Corinthians: 43–44
sensitivity
2 Corinthians: 46–48
Apostolic authority
Ephesians: 1
delegated
Titus: xii
false spiritual
Matthew 16–23: 357
Paul's
Romans 1–8: 6
Galatians: 2, 20
Apostolic credentials
and experience of supernatural
2 Corinthians: 394–96
Jesus Christ's servants
2 Corinthians: 386–91
overview of
2 Corinthians: 383–86
and submission
2 Corinthians: 392–94
and suffering
2 Corinthians: 386–91
and sympathy
2 Corinthians: 391–92
Apostolic marks
abuse and
2 Corinthians: 372–73
deception and
2 Corinthians: 370–72
of false apostles
2 Corinthians: 369–73
humility
2 Corinthians: 364–67
love (*See also* Love)
2 Corinthians: 233–41, 368–69
overview of
2 Corinthians: 361–64
pride and
2 Corinthians: 369–70
of true apostles
2 Corinthians: 364–73
truth
2 Corinthians: 367–68
Apostolic succession
2 Timothy: 39
Apostolic uniqueness
overview of
2 Corinthians: 407–9
power
2 Corinthians: 414–17
qualifications
2 Corinthians: 409–14
Appalachian snake-handling
Mark 9–16: 412
Appearances, Jesus' postresurrection
1 Corinthians: 439
Appreciation
2 Timothy: 4
Appropriation
1 Peter: 32–34
Aquila
2 Corinthians: 4
Arab nations, alliance with Russia
Matthew 24–28: 35
Arabia
Mark 9–16: 114
Luke 18–24: 70
Arabs
Luke 1–5: 69, 108
animosity towards Jews
Galatians: 125
origin of people
James: 138
Aramaic
Mark 1–8: 378
Luke 6–10: 94, 236
Romans 9–16: 55
Archaeology
John 12–21: 203
Archangel
2 Peter & Jude: 98–99, 145, 169, 173–75
Archelaus. *see* Herod Archelaus
Archer, Gleason L.
John 12–21: 203
on Jacob's purchase of a tomb in Shechem
Acts 1–12: 206
on the pointlessness of a posttribulational Rapture
1 & 2 Thessalonians: 137–38
on Quirinius's census
Acts 1–12: 172–73
on the size of Jacob's family in Egypt
Acts 1–12: 206
on translation of 1 Samuel 13:1–2
Acts 13–28: 20
Archippus
Colossians & Philemon: 199, 211
Aretas IV Philopatris (king of the Nabataeans)
Mark 1–8: 304
Luke 1–5: 230
Luke 18–24: 349
2 Corinthians: 393
Arimathea
Mark 9–16: 389
Aristarchus
Luke 1–5: 11
Colossians & Philemon: 194–95, 230

Aristides
Apology of
Acts 1–12: 90–91
on Christian joy
Colossians & Philemon: 74
Aristion
1–3 John: 5
Aristobulus
Mark 1–8: 304
Aristotle
Matthew 8–15: 12
Mark 9–16: 32, 408
Luke 6–10: 125
Ephesians: 127
1 Peter: 158
Ark of the Covenant
Luke 1–5: 75
Revelation 1–11: 90, 321
Armageddon
Matthew 24–28: 21
Mark 9–16: 232
Luke 11–17: 152–53
Luke 18–24: 202, 203, 228
2 Peter & Jude: 185–86
Revelation 1–11: 176, 308, 316
Revelation 12–22: 117–18, 150, 171
Armed resistance (by the apostles)
Luke 18–24: 316
Armies
Luke 18–24: 223, 227, 228, 237
Arminianism
Mark 9–16: 67, 70
John 1–11: 247
2 Peter & Jude: 35, 75–76
1–3 John: 121, 140, 141, 177–78
Armstrong, Mrs. Herbert
Galatians: 204
Arndt, W. F.
2 Peter & Jude: 215
on Jacob's purchase of a tomb in Shechem
Acts 1–12: 206
Arnold, Benedict
Luke 6–10: 74
John 12–21: 72
2 Corinthians: 351
2 Peter & Jude: 140
Arnot, William
Matthew 8–15: 356, 373
Romans 9–16: 181
Arrogance. *see* Pride
Art
Hebrews: 290
Artaxerxes
Matthew 24–28: 35
Luke 1–5: 146
John 12–21: 14–15
Artemis (Diana)
Mark 1–8: 374
Luke 6–10: 54
Romans 1–8: 94
2 Corinthians: 151
1–3 John: 2, 210, 214
Artemis, cult of
Acts 13–28: 183
Asaph
Mark 9–16: 143
Ascension
Luke 6–10: 310
Ascension of Christ
1 Peter: 236, 267
Asceticism
Matthew 1–7: 301, 305
Ephesians: 42
Colossians & Philemon: 8, 75–76, 122–24, 136–37
See also Self–denial
Asher
Luke 1–5: 185, 245
Asherah
2 Corinthians: 251
Ashes
2 Peter & Jude: 89
Ashtaroth
Mark 1–8: 366
Asia, province of
Luke 18–24: 212
Asia Minor
1–3 John: 1, 10, 80
churches
1 Peter: 15–16, 262
Asimov, Isaac
on second law of thermodynamics
Acts 13–28: 136
Asphyxiation
Mark 9–16: 365, 388
Assurance
2 Peter & Jude: 33–45, 123–25
Arminian position
1–3 John: 140, 141
certainties of
1–3 John: 51–60
confidence and
1–3 John: 145, 170–71, 203
English Puritans and
1–3 John: 54
Holy Spirit's working in
1–3 John: 54, 55, 169, 202
moral tests for
1–3 John: 55–60
no–lordship or Free Grace view
1–3 John: 140, 141
from obeying God's commandments
1–3 John: 55–60, 142
presence of holy affections and
1–3 John: 149
pursuit of needed
1–3 John: 52
Reformed view and
1–3 John: 53, 140
Roman Catholicism and
1–3 John: 52–53
salvation and
1–3 John: 52–60, 140–42
spiritual growth and
1–3 John: 72–77
tranquility in God's presence
1–3 John: 144
See also Salvation, assurance of
Assyria
John 12–21: 47
Assyrian conquest of Israel
Romans 9–16: 45

Astarte
Mark 1–8: 366
Astonishment
Mark 1–8: 380
See also Amazement
Astrology
Romans 1–8: 95
Galatians: 105
Athaliah
Luke 6–10: 74
John 12–21: 73
Athanasius
2 Peter & Jude: 9
on church father Anthony
Colossians & Philemon: 123
Atheism
Mark 1–8: 174
Ephesians: 215
despair of
Colossians & Philemon: 96–97
practical
Titus: 136
sin and
Colossians & Philemon: 140
Athenagoras
2 Peter & Jude: 141
Athenians
1–3 John: 226–27
Athens
Luke 6–10: 54, 73
Luke 18–24: 407
John 12–21: 47, 166
Atomic forces, confining of
Colossians & Philemon: 49–50
Atonement
Luke 18–24: 283, 284
Ephesians: 18
1 Peter: 79–82, 172–73
2 Peter & Jude: 17–18, 73–76
1–3 John: 8
the blood of
Colossians & Philemon: 62–64
Day of (*see* Day of Atonement)
extent of
Colossians & Philemon: 60
Titus: 111
necessity of
Matthew 16–23: 66
substitutionary
Matthew 24–28: 110
Romans 1–8: 118, 209, 274, 291, 399
Galatians: 5, 65, 198
Titus: 155
Atrophy
Mark 1–8: 152
Attitudes
of believers
Romans 1–8: 36, 42
1 Peter: 187–89, 273–90
of Christ
1 Peter: 224–26
of love
1 Peter: 289–90
Audience
Hebrews: x–xv, 41–42, 75, 127
Augustine
John 1–11: 240, 256, 323
Acts 1–12: 263–64
Romans 1–8: ix
Romans 9–16: 159
2 Corinthians: 167, 291
Galatians: 54
2 Timothy: 109
James: 61
2 Peter & Jude: 9
Augustus Caesar (Octavian)
Mark 1–8: 14, 414
Mark 9–16: 387
Luke 1–5: 22, 142–46, 201
Luke 18–24: 78
John 1–11: 26, 48
2 Corinthians: 66
Austria
Luke 11–17: 244
Authenticity
Luke 6–10: 200, 243
faith and
2 Corinthians: 460–71
genuineness and
2 Corinthians: 466–71
overview of
2 Corinthians: 45–46, 459–60
Authority
Luke 6–10: 88, 92, 93, 294–95
Luke 18–24: 111, 112, 115, 116, 342
John 12–21: 106, 120, 250–52, 335, 382
2 Peter & Jude: 19–20, 92–93, 173–75
affirmations of
2 Corinthians: 454–57
anti–
Titus: 131
assaults on
2 Corinthians: 453–54
civil
1 Peter: 143–53
ecclesiastical
Titus: 129
obedience to human
Titus: 140
over Satan and demons
Colossians & Philemon: 50, 103, 112–13
overview of
2 Corinthians: 449–53
submission and
Colossians & Philemon: 166–75
See also specific types, e.g., Spiritual authority
Authority of Jesus
Mark 9–16: 152–54
Luke 18–24: 116, 150
delegated to apostles and believers
Mark 9–16: 159–60
to forgive sins
Mark 1–8: 98
over Satan/demons
Mark 1–8: 41–46, 53, 57–59, 250
over sin
Mark 1–8: 46–49, 53, 105
over sinners
Mark 1–8: 49–54
submitting to
Mark 1–8: 56

Authorship
Hebrews: x, 26
of Jude's writings
2 Peter & Jude: 139–46
of Peter's writings
2 Peter & Jude: 1–15
Autolycus
John 1–11: 4
Autumn trees, fruitless
2 Peter & Jude: 181
"Axis Sally" (Mildred Elizabeth Gillars)
Luke 6–10: 74
John 12–21: 72
Azariah
1–3 John: 254

Baal
Mark 9–16: 68
Luke 1–5: 275
John 1–11: 376
2 Corinthians: 334
Baal–zebub (Beelzebul). *see* Beelzebul
Baalbek
Ephesians: 233
Baasha
Luke 6–10: 74
John 12–21: 73
Babel
1 Corinthians: 279
Babies and infants
Mark 9–16: 63, 65–70
Luke 6–10: 343, 345
Luke 18–24: 23–25, 28–30
abandoned
Titus: 77
baptism
Romans 1–8: 150, 253
sacrifices
Mark 9–16: 48
See also Children
Babylon
Mark 9–16: 244
Luke 1–5: 107
Luke 18–24: 232
1 Peter: 145–46, 289–90
1–3 John: 254
Revelation 12–22: 167, 177, 185
destruction of
Revelation 12–22: 191
final
Revelation 12–22: 89–90, 177
prophecies regarding the destruction of
Revelation 12–22: 167
the source of false religion
Revelation 12–22: 90, 157–60
Babylonian Captivity
Romans 1–8: 90, 157
Romans 9–16: 13, 21, 45, 226
Galatians: 107
2 Peter & Jude: 174–75
Babylonian Talmud
Matthew 24–28: 8
Bacchus (Dionysus)
1–3 John: 2
Bach, Johann Sebastian
Ephesians: 262
Bacterium
Luke 11–17: 389
Bahá'ism
Luke 18–24: 150
Bainton, Roland H.
Luke 1–5: 141
2 Corinthians: 234
2 Timothy: 33
Balaam
Luke 11–17: 129, 333
John 1–11: 293
2 Corinthians: 114, 272
2 Peter & Jude: 95–96, 102–3, 145, 177–78
1–3 John: 248
Balak
2 Peter & Jude: 102–3, 177–78
Balance of salvation
John 1–11: 59–74
Balsam plants
Luke 18–24: 70
Banquets
Luke 6–10: 172
Luke 11–17: 270–75
Baptism
Mark 9–16: 106
Luke 1–5: 205, 209, 210, 222, 228–29, 236–38
Luke 6–10: 152, 156
Luke 11–17: 171
Luke 18–24: 115
John 1–11: 37–58, 121–32
John 12–21: 38
1 Peter: 92, 97–98, 217–18
2 Peter & Jude: 22
of fire
Matthew 1–7: 71–72
for Gentile proselyte
Mark 1–8: 29
of the Holy Spirit
Matthew 1–7: 71
Mark 1–8: 25–26
Acts 1–12: 18, 41–42, 244–45, 304
Acts 13–28: 164
Ephesians: 248
importance of
Matthew 24–28: 343
Acts 1–12: 75
infant
Romans 1–8: 150, 251, 253
of Jesus
Matthew 1–7: 58, 74–78
1–3 John: 192–93, 195
of John
Mark 9–16: 157
of John the Baptist
Mark 1–8: 20, 21, 25, 38, 127
of repentance
Mark 1–8: 20, 21, 30
salvation and
Acts 1–12: 73–75, 305
Acts 13–28: 268–69
Colossians & Philemon: 108–9
Spirit
1 Corinthians: 311–13
water
Romans 1–8: 21, 253, 320

Ephesians: 130
Baptismal regeneration
Romans 1–8: 250
Baptist Confession (1689)
2 Peter & Jude: 38
Bar Cochba. *see* Simon Bar Cochba
Bar Kochba revolt
Luke 1–5: 319
John 1–11: 100
Bar mitzvah
Luke 1–5: 192
Galatians: 104
Barabbas
Mark 9–16: 310, 352, 353
Luke 18–24: 313, 358–59, 372
John 1–11: 310–11
John 12–21: 337, 351
Barak
Luke 1–5: 94
Hebrews: 365
Barclay, William
Matthew 8–15: 240–41, 262
John 1–11: 487
John 12–21: 316
Acts 13–28: 160
Romans 9–16: 369
2 Corinthians: 68–69, 166, 491
Ephesians: 323
1 Timothy: 83, 107, 136, 152, 198
2 Timothy: 39, 113, 127, 170, 190–91
Titus: 132
2 Peter & Jude: 19, 39–40, 101
on the danger of disunity in the church
Philippians: 101
on the difference between schēma and morphē
Philippians: 122–23
on the Egnatian Way
1 & 2 Thessalonians: 3
on greed
Colossians & Philemon: 139
on huperēphanos
James: 199
on the meaning of ataktōs
1 & 2 Thessalonians: 304
on the meaning of huparchō
Philippians: 122
on the pagan view of death
1 & 2 Thessalonians: 126
on "The Gamblers"
Philippians: 207
Barker, H. P.
Ephesians: 372
Barnabas
Mark 1–8: 1
Luke 1–5: 195, 245, 294
Luke 18–24: 192
John 1–11: 302
John 12–21: 20
Acts 1–12: 150–51
2 Corinthians: 44, 120, 149, 274, 409, 416
1 Timothy: 3, 4
1 Peter: 6, 18, 75
2 Peter & Jude: 149
apostleship of
Acts 13–28: 47
background of
Acts 13–28: 4
Barnabas, Letter of
Romans 1–8: 250
Barnes, Albert
Acts 13–28: 52
on Peter's boldness
Acts 1–12: 51–52
on Sadducees' opposition to the apostles
Acts 1–12: 129
on true and false repentance
Acts 1–12: 73
Barnett, Paul
2 Corinthians: 491
Barnhouse, Donald Grey
Matthew 8–15: 290
Acts 1–12: 180
Romans 1–8: xi, 23, 116, 179, 260, 273, 318, 335, 516
on the cup full of abominations
Revelation 12–22: 164
on things out of place in the universe
Revelation 1–11: 170
on the uncreation of the universe
Revelation 12–22: 249
Barrenness
Luke 18–24: 371
spiritual
Matthew 16–23: 278
Barrett, C. K.
2 Corinthians: 81, 491
Barrett, William
on Sartre's atheism
Colossians & Philemon: 97
Barsabbas
2 Corinthians: 411
Barth, Karl
John 1–11: 182
Bartholomew (Nathanael)
Mark 1–8: 15, 161, 169, 171, 315
Luke 1–5: 226, 265, 305
Luke 6–10: 16, 18, 55, 59–61, 251
John 1–11: 6, 28, 70–74, 77, 287, 464
John 12–21: 188, 274
Bartimaeus
Mark 9–16: 115, 116, 117, 119
Luke 18–24: 60, 61, 64, 72
Baruch, Apocalypse of
Romans 1–8: 452
Basil
John 1–11: 240
Basilides
John 1–11: 4
Baskets
Mark 1–8: 389
Bastogne, Belgium
Luke 6–10: 38
Bathsheba
Mark 9–16: 58, 69
Luke 6–10: 21
Luke 18–24: 29
John 12–21: 151
2 Corinthians: 57
1–3 John: 88
Battle(s)
Luke 18–24: 202–3

Battle of Antietam
Acts 13–28: 242
Battle of Armageddon
Matthew 24–28: 21
Mark 9–16: 232
Luke 11–17: 152–53
Luke 18–24: 202, 203, 228
2 Peter & Jude: 185–86
Revelation 1–11: 176, 308, 316
Revelation 12–22: 117–18, 150, 171
Battle of San Jacinto
Luke 6–10: 38
Battle of Thermopylae
Luke 6–10: 37
John 12–21: 72
Baur, F. C.
2 Peter & Jude: 56
Baxter, Richard
John 1–11: 240, 394
John 12–21: 259–60
Romans 1–8: 420
1 Timothy: 61–62, 102–3, 108, 115, 169, 262
Titus: 17–18
on being ruthless with sin
Colossians & Philemon: 136
on believers' communion with God in heaven
Revelation 12–22: 266–67
on ministers' self–examination
Acts 13–28: 223
on the pastor as teacher
1 & 2 Thessalonians: 171
Bazaar of Annas
Mark 9–16: 137, 323
Luke 18–24: 105
Beasley–Murray, G. R.
on the date of Revelation
Revelation 1–11: 9
Beatitudes
Matthew 1–7: 141–45
Luke 6–10: 93
2 Corinthians: 468
Beautiful Gate
Luke 18–24: 104
Beelzebul (Baal–zebub)
Mark 1–8: 181
Luke 11–17: 61–65
John 1–11: 137, 379
Romans 1–8: 95
2 Corinthians: 189
1 Peter: 1
Beersheba
Mark 1–8: 23
Beggars
Mark 9–16: 115, 116
Luke 18–24: 60, 108
Beginning
Mark 1–8: 14
Behavior
deviant sexual
Titus: 137
forced social
Titus: 138
Spirit–controlled
Romans 1–8: 428
Behaviorism
Ephesians: 22
Belgium
Luke 6–10: 37, 38
Belial
2 Corinthians: 249–50
Belief
Mark 1–8: 49
Mark 9–16: 22, 26
John 12–21: 23, 227, 230, 264–65, 287–88
false (*See also* Unbelief)
1 Corinthians: 400
true
Romans 1–8: 237
See also Faith
Beliefs. *see* Doctrine
Believer(s)
Luke 1–5: 180, 284, 285
Luke 11–17: 42, 46, 48, 162–63
Luke 18–24: 82–83, 197, 217, 406
John 12–21: 55–57, 185–86, 299
as "aliens and strangers"
1–3 John: 116, 176, 209
anointing of by Holy Spirit
1–3 John: 102
Antichrist's war with
Mark 9–16: 245
attitudes of
1 Peter: 187–89, 273–90
and authority
Mark 9–16: 159–60
battle with sin and Satan
Romans 1–8: 332
called to divine service
Romans 1–8: 22
certainty of faith of
2 Peter & Jude: 33–46
characteristics of
1–3 John: 101–4
chastening of
James: 54
chosen
1–3 John: 237, 238
and Christ's return
Revelation 1–11: 21
consciences of
1–3 John: 142
desire of Christ's return by
Revelation 12–22: 304
edification of
Titus: 7
election of
Revelation 12–22: 171
eternal security of
Romans 1–8: 146, 270, 304, 442, 472, 489, 498
Philippians: 29, 163–64
Titus: 108, 122
Hebrews: 146–47, 154, 163, 167–69, 266
James: 27ff., 42, 131
Revelation 1–11: 115–16
Revelation 12–22: 73–74, 95–103
and faith
2 Peter & Jude: 20–21
false
Philippians: 21

Revelation 12–22: 101–2
and false teachers
1–3 John: 235–37, 239
future inheritance of
Revelation 12–22: 243
glorification of
Romans 1–8: 279
as God's children
Philippians: 123–24
1–3 John: 114–16, 128
and God's eternal wrath
Revelation 12–22: 238
and God's judgment
Revelation 12–22: 250–51
God's preservation of
1–3 John: 208–9
Revelation 1–11: 113, 213–14, 260–61
God's protection of
Revelation 12–22: 69–70
happiness of
Revelation 12–22: 93–95
hatred of sin
Romans 1–8: 381, 388
holiness of
Revelation 1–11: 45, 113
holy disposition of
Romans 1–8: 326
imperfection of
Romans 1–8: 278
indwelling of Holy Spirit
1–3 John: 29, 36, 112, 148–49, 230
judgment by
Mark 9–16: 405
judgment of
Romans 1–8: 128
James: 151, 257–58
lifestyle of
Romans 1–8: 343
living godly lives in light of Christ's return
Revelation 12–22: 226
love as manifestation in
1–3 John: 66, 130, 165, 166, 170
love as test of
1–3 John: 128, 168–70, 229
love of God's Word
Revelation 12–22: 310
marks of
Matthew 8–15: 70
Matthew 24–28: 26
Romans 1–8: 380
means of grace and
1–3 John: 70
and new birth
1–3 John: 127–28, 136–37, 158, 177
nonconformity to the world
Revelation 12–22: 181
obedience to the Word of
1–3 John: 122–24
as overcomers
1–3 John: 174–77, 179
persecution of
James: 252
reasons of for not loving the world
1–3 John: 83–92
to reign with Christ
Matthew 16–23: 204
Revelation 12–22: 237, 239
resurrection of
James: 196
Revelation 12–22: 238
reward of
Luke 18–24: 85
Ephesians: 353
1–3 John: 234–35
Revelation 1–11: 319
Revelation 12–22: 104–5
riches of
Romans 1–8: 20
righteousness and
1–3 John: 114
sacrificial love of
1–3 John: 135–36, 165, 168
salvation of
Philippians: 23, 26–30
sanctification and purification
1–3 John: 117–18
and the second coming
Mark 9–16: 242
and self–denial
Revelation 12–22: 78
and sexual purity
Revelation 12–22: 77
sin in
Mark 9–16: 42–45
source, substance, and sufficiency of faith
2 Peter & Jude: 17–31
spiritual union with Christ
Philippians: 15, 236–37
suffering of
Mark 9–16: 234–37
superficial
Romans 1–8: 36
testing of the spirits
1–3 John: 154
Trinity abiding in
1–3 John: 163
and truth
1–3 John: 101, 103–4, 160, 220, 246, 247
truthfulness of
Revelation 12–22: 80
uniqueness of
Matthew 16–23: 132
unity of
Philippians: 99–103, 119
unredeemed humanness of
Romans 1–8: 326
and vengeance
Revelation 12–22: 183–84
weakness in
Matthew 16–23: 76
work of Holy Spirit in
Romans 1–8: 415
world's rejection/hatred of
Matthew 16–23: 72
Mark 9–16: 237
worship of
Philippians: 24
See also Christian(s)
Beloved
Mark 1–8: 37
Belshazzar
Romans 1–8: 93

"Beneath the Cross of Jesus"
1 Timothy: 30
Benediction
2 Corinthians: 481–82, 487–89
Benedictus. *see* Zacharias's Song of Salvation (Benedictus)
Benevolence
1 Corinthians: 335
Bengel, Johann
Matthew 8–15: 266
Benjamin
2 Corinthians: 55
Benjamin, Tribe of
Luke 1–5: 245
Beor
John 1–11: 293
2 Peter & Jude: 95
Bereans
Luke 6–10: 49, 144, 147
1–3 John: 160
Berkhof, Hendrikus
on the meaning of history
1 & 2 Thessalonians: 139–40
Berkhof, L.
on meaning of foreknowledge
Acts 1–12: 63
Bernard of Clairvaux
Ephesians: 123
Bernice (consort of Herod Agrippa II)
Acts 13–28: 327
Besetting sins, power of
Titus: 72
Beth Din
John 1–11: 101
Bethany
Mark 9–16: 124, 139, 141, 153, 272
Luke 6–10: 67, 171
Luke 18–24: 92–95, 102, 310
John 12–21: 2, 3, 6, 14, 15, 23
Bethel
Mark 1–8: 23
Bethesda
Luke 1–5: 293
Bethlehem
Matthew 1–7: 25
Luke 1–5: 142, 146–48, 156, 158, 162, 171
Luke 6–10: 60, 144
Luke 11–17: 226
Luke 18–24: 102, 366
Bethphage
Mark 9–16: 124, 125
Luke 18–24: 92, 93
John 12–21: 17
Bethsaida
Mark 1–8: 72, 280, 315, 326, 407, 409
Luke 6–10: 25, 39, 41, 56–57, 251, 252, 334
Luke 18–24: 175
John 12–21: 13, 25–26
Bethsaida, Plain of
Mark 1–8: 326
Betrayal
Mark 9–16: 286, 287, 288, 309
Luke 18–24: 289, 290, 291
John 12–21: 72–73
See also Judas Iscariot
Bettenson, Henry
John 1–11: 38–39
John 12–21: 169
Bezalel
2 Corinthians: 114
The Bible
Luke 1–5: 252
Luke 6–10: 83, 84, 93
Luke 18–24: 418
authority and sufficiency of
Titus: 46
believers' affection for
James: 65
believers' defense of
Revelation 12–22: 294
believers' obedience to
Revelation 12–22: 294
compromising
Titus: 51
discernment mandate
1–3 John: 156
evangelization and
1–3 John: 224
feminine–deity versions
Titus: 81
fulfilled prophecies
John 12–21: 203–4
gender–neutral versions
Titus: 81
historical accuracy
John 12–21: 202–3
as Holy Spirit–inspired
1–3 John: 14
inerrancy of
Romans 9–16: 41
2 Timothy: 72, 142, 151
Titus: 46
James: 85
inspiration of
John 12–21: 120, 200–201, 207
Titus: 46
interpretation of
John 12–21: 224, 225, 229
James: 274
Revelation 12–22: 3
obedience to
James: 77–78
power to deliver from sin
James: 75
prerequisites for effective study of
Acts 13–28: 122
proper interpretation of
James: 274
protecting and guarding
1–3 John: 235
reliability of manuscript
Mark 9–16: 408–10
scientific accuracy of
John 12–21: 201–2
as source of truth
Titus: 46, 49
and testimony of Jesus
John 12–21: 204, 283
translation of
1–3 John: 224

truthfulness of
John 12–21: 209–10
unbelievers' disregard of
James: 67
unity
John 12–21: 201
See also Scripture; Word of God
Biblical Christianity
Romans 1–8: 199
Biblical thinking
Philippians: 285
Big Bang theory
Colossians & Philemon: 49–50
Bigg, Charles
2 Peter & Jude: 9–10, 215
Bigotry, destruction of. *see* Unity
Bigthan (Perisan official)
Luke 6–10: 74
John 12–21: 73
Bios
illustration regarding the tongue
Colossians & Philemon: 178
Birds
Luke 11–17: 140–41, 211, 212
Birth, new. *see* New birth
Birth of Christ
1 Peter: 1–2, 40, 58, 82
Birth pangs metaphor
Mark 9–16: 230, 232, 233, 234, 243
Birthdays
Mark 1–8: 306
Luke 1–5: 140
Births
Luke 1–5: 53–54
Bishops
Ephesians: 143
1 Peter: 263, 267
Bithynian churches
1 Peter: 15–16
Bitterness
Colossians & Philemon: 169, 212
See also Forgiveness
Black darkness
2 Peter & Jude: 104–5, 182
Black Death
Luke 11–17: 244
Luke 18–24: 205
John 1–11: 388
Blackstone, William E.
Matthew 8–15: 278
Blaiklock, E. M.
Luke 1–5: 44
Blake, Morgan
on gossip
James: 155
Blamelessness
2 Peter & Jude: 212–13
Blanchard, John
2 Corinthians: 171
Blasphemy(ies)
Mark 1–8: 104–6, 183–85, 225
Mark 9–16: 156–58, 328, 329, 367, 370
Luke 1–5: 323
Luke 11–17: 62–67, 80, 123–24, 239
John 1–11: 88–89, 375–85, 445–46
1 Peter: 75, 229–30
2 Peter & Jude: 10, 92–93, 112–13, 115
of Christ's accusers
Luke 18–24: 354, 363
Christ's divine authority claim as
Luke 18–24: 116, 150, 324–25, 337
at the crucifixion
Luke 18–24: 380, 385
Blavatsky, Madam Elena Petrovna
Ephesians: 277
Bleeding (hemorrhage)
Mark 1–8: 258
Luke 6–10: 232, 233
Blessed
Luke 6–10: 84–85, 95–99, 102
See also Happiness
Blessed hope
Matthew 24–28: 59
Blessed One
Mark 9–16: 327
Blessedness
2 Peter & Jude: 154
Blessing(s)
Mark 9–16: 64, 66, 71
Luke 1–5: 71, 72, 107
Luke 6–10: 84–85, 95–99, 102
1–3 John: 219
of children
Luke 18–24: 25, 26, 29
at Christ's ascension
Luke 18–24: 452–53
wealth as
Luke 18–24: 41
Blessing and cursing
Luke 11–17: 240, 247
Blessing and mercy, God's
Romans 1–8: 115
Blessing God
1 Peter: 30–31
Blind Bartimaeus
Luke 18–24: 60, 61, 64, 72
Blind man at Bethsaida
Mark 1–8: 406–10
Blindness
Mark 1–8: 376, 396, 397, 401, 407
Mark 9–16: 115, 116
Luke 1–5: 272
Luke 6–10: 114
John 1–11: 387–96, 409–19
spiritual
Matthew 16–23: 2, 3, 252
Matthew 24–28: 73, 77, 184
Mark 1–8: 396, 397, 399, 401, 409, 410
Luke 6–10: 114
Luke 11–17: 81, 89
John 1–11: 409–20
Romans 9–16: 104
1 & 2 Thessalonians: 22, 283
Bliss, Philip P.
Luke 18–24: 75, 307
Ephesians: 24
Blood
Hebrews: 236–38, 416
of Christ (see Jesus Christ, blood of)
and water
Mark 9–16: 388
John 12–21: 364

Blood sacrifice
Luke 18–24: 50
of Christ (See also Jesus Christ, blood of)
1 Peter: 23–25, 76–82
Bloodless offerings
Hebrews: 122
Boanerges
Mark 1–8: 170
Luke 6–10: 42, 313
Boasting
Mark 9–16: 333
fleshly
2 Corinthians: 380–82
foolishness of
2 Corinthians: 379–80
humility and (See also Humility)
2 Corinthians: 375–76
Boats
Luke 6–10: 207
Boaz
Mark 9–16: 189
Luke 1–5: 246
Luke 6–10: 143
Luke 18–24: 145, 262
2 Corinthians: 272
Bock, Darrell L.
Luke 1–5: 1, 144, 145, 203, 240
Luke 11–17: 118, 284
Luke 18–24: 80–81
Bodies, Christians' unredeemed
Romans 9–16: 142
Bodily injury
Luke 18–24: 54–55
Bodily resurrection. *see* Resurrection; second coming
Bodmer papyrus
2 Peter & Jude: 6
Body, temporariness of physical
Ephesians: 28
Body of Christ
Ephesians: xi, 5–16, 151–62
Boettner, Loraine
Luke 11–17: 248
on the postmillennial view of the Millennium
Revelation 12–22: 229
Boice, James Montgomery
John 12–21: 243, 266
Bold speech
2 Corinthians: 108
Boldness
in prayer
Luke 11–17: 53–55, 58
1–3 John: 145–46
spiritual
Romans 1–8: 48
Bonaparte, Napoleon
1–3 John: 94
Bonar, Andrew A.
2 Corinthians: 40
Bonar, Horatius
John 1–11: 313
Romans 1–8: 210, 278
Ephesians: 214
Bond–servants
2 Corinthians: 134
2 Peter & Jude: 18–23, 149–50
Bondage
1 Peter: 73–76, 151–52
Bonds, eternal
2 Peter & Jude: 164
Bondslaves
1 Peter: 151–52
Bonhoeffer, Dietrich
Romans 1–8: 353
Book of Life
1–3 John: 185
Revelation 12–22: 50, 255
Book of the Dead (Egyptian)
Luke 18–24: 140
Booths, Feast of. *see* Feast of Tabernacles (Booths)
Borchert, Gerald L.
John 1–11: 43, 71–72, 142, 176, 223, 238, 330, 440, 475, 487
John 12–21: 239, 319, 348
Borden, William
2 Timothy: 197
Borrowing/lending
Luke 6–10: 106, 108
Romans 9–16: 245, 246
Bottomless pit. *see* Abyss
Bowie, James
Luke 6–10: 38
Bowl judgments
Luke 18–24: 220
Boxer Rebellion
2 Timothy: 10
Boy possessed by demon
Luke 6–10: 290–94
Brainerd, David
Luke 18–24: 427
Romans 1–8: 214
Branches
John 12–21: 145–49, 151–52
Brand, Paul
Matthew 8–15: 83, 110
Romans 9–16: 164
Brats
Luke 6–10: 161, 162, 164–67
Bray, Billy
Romans 1–8: 438
Bread
Mark 9–16: 286, 287, 289, 290
Luke 6–10: 244, 245
Luke 18–24: 282, 283
Bread of Life
Luke 6–10: 256
appropriation of
John 1–11: 255–64
Jesus Christ as
1–3 John: 103–4
responses to
John 1–11: 265–74
as true Bread from Heaven
John 1–11: 239–54
Bread of the Presence
Mark 1–8: 144
Brengle, Samuel Logan
and Salvation Army
1 Timothy: 94, 96
Brevity
2 Peter & Jude: 51–53

Bridges, Charles
1 Timothy: 263
Bright, John
on the kingdom of God
Revelation 12–22: 228–29
British Israelism
Romans 9–16: 112
Brooks, Thomas
Luke 11–17: 8
2 Corinthians: 171
on the importance of example
Philippians: 190
1 & 2 Thessalonians: 305
Brotherhood
Hebrews: 68–69, 75
false
Galatians: 17
Brotherly kindness
2 Peter & Jude: 40–42
Brotherly love
Hebrews: 422–25
Brothers
Luke 6–10: 202, 203
Brown, Colin
2 Corinthians: 409
Brown, Harold O. J.
on Simon Magus
Acts 1–12: 240
Brown, John
Romans 9–16: 134
Galatians: 30, 190
Titus: 112
Brown, Louise
Luke 1–5: 54
Bruce, F. F.
Mark 9–16: 409
John 1–11: 90, 182, 185, 272, 334, 393, 487
John 12–21: 103, 325, 337, 348
Romans 1–8: 112, 308, 371
2 Peter & Jude: 13, 215
on baptism and salvation
Acts 1–12: 74
on correctness of Luke's title for Malta's governor
Acts 13–28: 363
on the dating of Acts
Acts 1–12: 4
on death of the Dean of St. Paul's Cathedral
Acts 1–12: 155
on Domitian's exile of Flavia Domitilla
Revelation 1–11: 41
on evidence for the resurrection
Acts 1–12: 138
on exemption of Roman citizens from flogging
Acts 13–28: 272
on false witnesses
Acts 1–12: 194
on God's call of Abraham
Acts 1–12: 203
on Jacob's purchase of a tomb in Shechem
Acts 1–12: 207
on Jewish population of Damascus
Acts 1–12: 265
on makeup of Jerusalem church
Acts 1–12: 231
on meaning of tassō
Acts 13–28: 39
on Paul's use of Tyrannus's lecture hall
Acts 13–28: 174
on Pharisees becoming Christians
Acts 13–28: 284
on physical appearance of Paul
Acts 13–28: 47
on Samuel
Acts 1–12: 122
on Stoicism and Epicureanism
Acts 13–28: 131
on synagogues in Jerusalem
Acts 1–12: 192
Brutality
Matthew 1–7: 188
Brutus
Luke 1–5: 143
Bubastis, cat–goddess
Romans 1–8: 94
Bubonic plague
Luke 18–24: 205
Buddhism
Matthew 8–15: 111
Luke 1–5: 328
Romans 1–8: 89, 336
Galatians: 111
Bultmann, Rudolf
Luke 1–5: 300
John 1–11: 182
2 Peter & Jude: 56
Bunyan, John
Matthew 8–15: 159, 232, 234, 252, 398
John 1–11: 240
Acts 13–28: 257
Romans 1–8: xi, 372
2 Corinthians: 100–101
Galatians: 93, 157, 211
Ephesians: 160, 219, 262, 376
Philippians: 59–60
1 Timothy: 264
2 Timothy: 60
James: 39, 81
on false believers
Revelation 12–22: 102
Burial
Mark 9–16: 385–94
Luke 18–24: 396, 398
John 12–21: 8, 365–67
Burns, Robert
James: 46
Burroughs, Jeremiah
on Christian contentment
Philippians: 296
on Christ's strengthening of believers
Philippians: 304
Busenitz, Nathan
2 Peter & Jude: 110
Bush, L. Russ
2 Peter & Jude: 56–57

Caesar
Mark 1–8: 15, 187
Mark 9–16: 178, 180, 182, 351, 352
Luke 18–24: 78, 134, 135, 210, 348
John 1–11: 26, 48
John 12–21: 342
2 Corinthians: 151, 283

See also specific Roman emperors by name
Caesar Augustus. *see* Augustus Caesar (Octavian)
Caesarea
Mark 1–8: 414
Luke 6–10: 259
Caesarea Maritima
Mark 9–16: 346
Caesarea Philippi
Luke 6–10: 259
Caesaria
Luke 1–5: 23
Caesarion
Luke 1–5: 144
Caiaphas
Luke 1–5: 201, 203–4
John 1–11: 433, 483–84
Acts 1–12: 202
1–3 John: 50
Annas's influence on
Mark 9–16: 323, 336
authority of
John 12–21: 316
and Christ's trial
Mark 9–16: 326, 328, 329
John 12–21: 315, 324, 325
and guilt for crucifixion
John 12–21: 341
Judas Iscariot and
Luke 18–24: 312
plot to kill Christ
Luke 18–24: 120
political concerns of
Luke 18–24: 268
prophecy of
Mark 9–16: 327
John 12–21: 8, 10, 24
summary of life
John 12–21: 317
temple businesses of
Mark 9–16: 137, 152
Luke 18–24: 105
at trial of Christ
Luke 18–24: 323–25, 336, 337
Cain
Luke 6–10: 84
Luke 11–17: 108
Luke 18–24: 331
John 1–11: 372
Hebrews: 296–97, 299, 300
2 Peter & Jude: 169, 176–77
envy as motivation of
1–3 John: 252
of the evil one
1–3 John: 132
hatred of righteousness by
1–3 John: 133
murder of Abel by
1–3 John: 132, 133
sacrifice of
Galatians: 46
wickedness of
1–3 John: 258
Caleb
John 1–11: 399
2 Peter & Jude: 163–64
Caligula
Matthew 8–15: 383
Luke 1–5: 230, 231
Calling
choosing vs.
2 Peter & Jude: 44, 150–51
to Christian service
Galatians: 29
confidence in
2 Corinthians: 84–86
of divine pastor
Titus: 49
effectual
1 & 2 Thessalonians: 52, 256, 287–88
James: 110
God's
Matthew 8–15: 185
Romans 1–8: 486
1 Corinthians: 209
of Jewish people
Romans 1–8: 148
of Matthew
Mark 1–8: 161
ministry as fulfilled
1 Timothy: 178
of Peter
Mark 1–8: 40, 50, 161
Callousness, spiritual
Matthew 16–23: 153
Calming the storm miracle
Luke 6–10: 209–10, 212, 213
Calvary
Mark 9–16: 267, 374–77, 379, 383, 389
Luke 18–24: 366, 376, 384, 389, 412
2 Peter & Jude: 17–18
sin debt paid on
Romans 1–8: 363
Calvin, John
Matthew 8–15: 235
Mark 9–16: 69–70
Luke 1–5: 25, 177
Luke 11–17: 340
Luke 18–24: 30
John 1–11: 279, 417, 487
John 12–21: 229
Romans 1–8: x, 215, 303, 351
Romans 9–16: 159, 170
1 Timothy: 177
2 Timothy: 109
Titus: 152, 155
Hebrews: 120
1–3 John: 53, 54
on genuine faith
James: 138
Calvinism
Luke 1–5: 125–26
Titus: 110
2 Peter & Jude: 75–76
ultra–
Romans 9–16: 84
Camels
Luke 18–24: 41
Campbell, Donald K.
2 Corinthians: 432
Cana
Luke 1–5: 266

Cana wedding, miracle of
John 1–11: 75–84
Canaanite woman
Mark 9–16: 208
Luke 6–10: 179
John 1–11: 167
daughter of
Mark 1–8: 366–72
Canaanites
Hebrews: 91
Candace (Ethiopian queen)
Mark 9–16: 138
Canons Concerning Justification
2 Corinthians: 466
Capernaum
Mark 9–16: 34, 36
Luke 1–5: 269, 275, 282, 291, 317, 330–31
Luke 6–10: 86, 123, 208, 231
Luke 18–24: 175
John 12–21: 13
as Christ's hometown
Luke 6–10: 250
as Christ's ministry headquarters
Mark 1–8: 99, 116, 176
Christ's teaching in
Mark 1–8: 59, 113, 272–73
fishing operations in
Mark 1–8: 60, 72
and Gennesaret
Mark 1–8: 333–34
humility lesson in
Luke 6–10: 300
judgment of
Mark 1–8: 280
location
Luke 6–10: 25
Matthew's tax collection in
Mark 1–8: 113, 114
Peter and Andrew in
Luke 6–10: 40
punishment for
Luke 6–10: 334
synagogue in
Luke 6–10: 126, 230
Capital cases, rules
Luke 18–24: 331–32
Capital punishment
Mark 9–16: 321, 322
Luke 18–24: 316
Romans 9–16: 222, 226
Cappadocian church
1 Peter: 15–16
Captivity, Babylonian. *see* Babylonian captivity
Caravans
Luke 1–5: 192, 193
Cardiac, Jean Louis
Luke 1–5: 188
Carey, William
Romans 1–8: 44
social reforms of
Colossians & Philemon: 166
Cargo cults
1 & 2 Thessalonians: 251–52
Carmichael, Amy
Matthew 8–15: 62
James: 24
Carnality. *see* The Flesh
Carpenters
Mark 1–8: 276
Carson, D. A.
John 1–11: 2, 7, 82, 105, 128, 146, 174, 190, 260, 322, 338, 403, 475, 485, 487
John 12–21: 7–8, 52, 54, 65, 79, 89–90, 137, 195, 289, 326, 341, 343, 354, 386, 394
2 Corinthians: 373, 393, 467, 491
2 Peter & Jude: 215
on forgery in the early church
1 Timothy: xiv
on pseudonymity
1 Timothy: xiii
Carson, Herbert
on philosophy
Colossians & Philemon: 100–101
Carthage, Council of
2 Peter & Jude: 9
Cassander (founder of Thessalonica)
1 & 2 Thessalonians: 3
Cassius
Luke 1–5: 143
Cassius Dio
Mark 1–8: 308
Casting out demons
Luke 11–17: 61–65
Castration, pagan ritual of
Galatians: 142
Catacombs, Roman
Matthew 8–15: 222
Romans 9–16: 366
2 Timothy: 59
Catechism, Westminster Shorter
Romans 1–8: 83
Romans 9–16: 124
Catharsis
2 Peter & Jude: 44
Catholic Church. *see* Roman Catholicism/Roman Catholic Church
Catholicism
1–3 John: 40, 52–53, 121–22
Roman (*see* Roman Catholicism/Roman Catholic Church)
Cato
Ephesians: 323
Celibacy
1 Corinthians: 155–59
gift of
Matthew 16–23: 175
Celsus
John 1–11: 4
James: 100
Censuses
Luke 1–5: 144–46, 244
Centurion(s)
Mark 9–16: 370, 380–81
Luke 6–10: 123, 124–29, 248
Luke 18–24: 391, 431
Acts 1–12: 293
Centurion's servant
Luke 1–5: 292
Cephas. *see* Peter; Peter, teachings and writings of

Ceremonial defilement
Mark 1–8: 376
Ceremonial law
Hebrews: 188–89
Ceremonial uncleanness
Luke 1–5: 169, 171
Ceremonial washings
Mark 1–8: 341, 342, 345
Ceremonialism
Matthew 8–15: 453
2 Corinthians: 89, 94, 99, 117
See also Tradition
Cerinthianism
1–3 John: 27
Cerinthus
Luke 6–10: 51
John 1–11: 8, 41
1–3 John: 7, 8, 236
Certainties
about person and work of Christ, summarized
1–3 John: 14
of believers' faith
2 Peter & Jude: 33–45
categories of
1–3 John: 14
of Christ
1–3 John: 13–20
Christian
1–3 John: 199–210
of Christian assurance
1–3 John: 51–60
scriptural absolutes, list of
1–3 John: 201
See also Assurance; Salvation
Certificate of divorce
Matthew 1–7: 309–11
Mark 9–16: 57
Chadwick, John
Ephesians: 13
Chaff
Luke 18–24: 295
Chalcedon, Council of
John 1–11: 38
Chaldeans
Romans 1–8: 235
Chalmers, James
Romans 1–8: 73
Chambers, R. W.
on Thomas More's forgiving spirit
Colossians & Philemon: 225–26
Chantry, Walter J.
Romans 1–8: 411
Chapman, John Wilbur
Mark 1–8: 236
Ephesians: 111
Chapman, Robert C.
Romans 9–16: 181
Character
conduct and
James: 82
of God (*see* God, character of)
moral and spiritual
Matthew 1–7: 468–70
Charismatic movement
Luke 18–24: 171
1 & 2 Thessalonians: 192
mysticism of
Colossians & Philemon: 121–22
Charnock, Stephen
Luke 1–5: 76
John 12–21: 46, 49
on the rich young ruler
Philippians: 213–14
on sin as atheism
Colossians & Philemon: 139–40
Charoseth
Matthew 24–28: 141
Chastening
1 Timothy: 55
of believers
1 Corinthians: 275
divine
Matthew 16–23: 155
Chauvinism
Ephesians: 276, 294
male
Matthew 16–23: 161–62
Titus: 79–80
Cheops (Pharaoh)
Luke 18–24: 140
Chesnut, D. Lee
on atomic forces
Colossians & Philemon: 49–50
Chesterton, G. K.
Luke 6–10: 216
Chiasm
Luke 11–17: 324
Chief corner stone
Mark 9–16: 170, 171
Luke 18–24: 127–28
Chief priests
Matthew 1–7: 32
Mark 9–16: 155–56, 186, 270, 271, 311
at Christ's arrest
Luke 18–24: 313
at crucifixion
Luke 18–24: 367
influence of
Luke 18–24: 114
motivations of
Luke 18–24: 268
See also Annas; Caiaphas
Chief seats
Mark 9–16: 219
Chief Shepherd
2 Peter & Jude: 96
Child pornography
Romans 1–8: 103
Child prodigies
Luke 1–5: 188–89
Child sacrifices
Mark 9–16: 48, 68
Childlikeness
necessity for
Matthew 16–23: 114
spiritual
Matthew 16–23: 93–94, 99, 181
Children
Luke 6–10: 161, 164, 167, 302, 303
abused
Romans 1–8: 191

accursed
2 Peter & Jude: 101–2
and blessing
Mark 9–16: 64, 71
blessing from God
Ephesians: 310
blessings bestowed on
Mark 9–16: 64
of God (*see* Children of God)
God's adopted
Matthew 16–23: 68
Jewish blessing of
Matthew 16–23: 179
parents' treatment of
Matthew 16–23: 106
playing
Luke 6–10: 164
principles for
Colossians & Philemon: 170–71
principles for evangelizing
Matthew 16–23: 182
salvation of
Mark 9–16: 64, 67, 69, 70, 71
Luke 18–24: 23–31
spiritual growth of
Ephesians: 315
submission of
Ephesians: 311
teaching of
Matthew 16–23: 182
Ephesians: 308
See also Babies and infants
"Children Learn What They Live" (Dorothy Law Nolte)
Colossians & Philemon: 173
Children of Abraham
Luke 11–17: 223
children of Satan *vs.* (Jesus' teachings of)
John 1–11: 363–74
Children of God
Matthew 1–7: 217–18, 348
1–3 John: 73, 95, 116, 131, 172
believers as
1–3 John: 50, 73, 95
perfect love of God as mark of
1–3 John: 172
as spiritual family
1–3 John: 73
transformation to Christlikeness
1–3 John: 116–17
vulnerabilities of spiritual children
1–3 John: 74
Children of Satan. *see* Satan, children of
Chiliasm
2 Peter & Jude: 10
China
Christianity in
Philippians: 63
Christians in
2 Timothy: 60
earthquakes in
Luke 18–24: 204
plague in
Luke 18–24: 205
China Inland Mission
Romans 1–8: 214
Chinese army
Matthew 24–28: 20
Chinnereth (Chinneroth), Sea of. *see* Sea of Galilee (Sea of Chinnereth)
Chivalry
1 Peter: 182
Choice
Hebrews: 346–47
See also Will, human
Choirmaster concept
2 Peter & Jude: 39–40
Choosing *vs.* calling
2 Peter & Jude: 44–45, 150–51
Chorazin
Mark 1–8: 280
Luke 6–10: 252, 334
Luke 18–24: 175
John 12–21: 13
Chosen
1 Peter: 13–27, 124–25
See also Election by Christ
"Chosen lady"
1–3 John: 215–17
Chosen people
John 1–11: 152–53
Christ. *see* Jesus Christ
Christ, Carol
Titus: 82
Christ–likeness
1–3 John: 118
Christian(s)
activism
Romans 9–16: 213
afflictions of
Romans 1–8: 511
availability of
Matthew 24–28: 335
biblical definition of
Revelation 1–11: 54
commitment of
John 12–21: 398–404
confession of sins by
Romans 1–8: 426
conflicts with sin
Romans 1–8: 400
conflicts with temptation
Romans 1–8: 335
conflicts with the flesh
Romans 1–8: 418
and culture
Luke 6–10: 216
divine discipline of
Romans 1–8: 400
election of (*see* Election)
empowerment of
Matthew 24–28: 346
external marks of
John 12–21: 83–84
false
Romans 1–8: 423
and the flesh
Romans 1–8: 418
"God's chosen ones"
John 12–21: 267
government and
Luke 18–24: 136

identity with Christ
Romans 1–8: 297
inheritance of
John 12–21: 297
longing for heaven
Romans 1–8: 393
love for God by
1 & 2 Thessalonians: 17–18
mutual support
Titus: 168
not to cause others to stumble
1 & 2 Thessalonians: 110
not to retaliate when wronged
1 & 2 Thessalonians: 180, 236
obedience of
Matthew 24–28: 340
1 & 2 Thessalonians: 297
persecution of
Matthew 24–28: 41
Luke 18–24: 208–17
John 12–21: 165–71
1 & 2 Thessalonians: 226–27
perseverance of (*see* Perseverance)
pleasing God
1 & 2 Thessalonians: 97
service of
John 12–21: 4, 68, 69
sham
Matthew 24–28: 25
sin, remnant of
Romans 1–8: 382
and sin
Romans 1–8: 400
in Soviet Union
John 12–21: 295–96
spiritual nature of
Romans 1–8: 323, 334, 344
spiritual responsibility of
Romans 1–8: 412
steps in spiritual growth of
1 & 2 Thessalonians: 96
submission of
Matthew 24–28: 338
suffering of
Romans 1–8: 511
1 & 2 Thessalonians: 247
and temptation
Romans 1–8: 335–36
union with Jesus Christ
1 & 2 Thessalonians: 13–14, 224–25
will of
Romans 1–8: 338
witness of
John 12–21: 181–82, 189, 284
worship of
Matthew 24–28: 336
worthy walk of
1 & 2 Thessalonians: 257
See also Believer(s)
Christian College Coalition (Coalition for Christian Colleges & Universities)
2 Timothy: 110
Christian life
Luke 1–5: 164
Luke 6–10: 268
axioms of
Romans 1–8: 343
characteristics of
Romans 1–8: 343
remaining humanness in
Romans 1–8: 404
See also Discipleship
Christian Science
Luke 18–24: 150
Ephesians: 277
2 Timothy: 153
Christian teachers
Romans 1–8: 114
Christian workers, finances for
1–3 John: 248–49
Christianity
Luke 18–24: 210, 441
apostate
Romans 1–8: 120
biblical
Romans 1–8: 199
Titus: 153
cultural
Titus: 139
democracy and
Romans 9–16: 206
Jewish views of
Romans 9–16: 19
ritualistic
Romans 1–8: 89
as a saving religion
Titus: 153
social
Romans 9–16: 208
Christianity Lite
Luke 11–17: 278–79
Christlikeness
Romans 1–8: 131
Galatians: 154
Colossians & Philemon: 160–61
Christmas
Luke 1–5: 41–42, 140–41
Luke 18–24: 251–52, 449
Christ's return. *see* second coming
Christ's work, adding to
Galatians: 67
The Chronicles of Narnia **(Lewis)**
Mark 1–8: 174
Chrysostom
1 Peter: 117
Chrysostom, John
Matthew 8–15: 252
John 1–11: 240
Romans 1–8: 380
Galatians: 142
Ephesians: 303
1 Timothy: 79, 177
Church, composition of
organization of
Acts 1–12: 176–77
purpose of
Acts 1–12: 159
unity of
Acts 1–12: 38–39, 139–40
Church, the
Mark 1–8: 130

Luke 6–10: 242, 243, 301, 314
apostate
Romans 9–16: 117, 127
authority of
Matthew 16–23: 33
John 12–21: 382, 383
body of Christ
Ephesians: xi, 5–16, 151–62
building the
Ephesians: 151–62
built by Christ
Matthew 16–23: 30
Calvinism and
Luke 1–5: 125–26
and care for the poor
1 & 2 Thessalonians: 307–9
central purpose of
Matthew 24–28: 333
Christ as message of
1 Timothy: 138
Christ's gifts to (*see* Jesus Christ)
Christ's relationship to
Colossians & Philemon: 51–53
composition of
Acts 1–12: 80–82
conduct in
1 Timothy: 134
conflict in
James: 185
confronting sin within
1 Timothy: 186
consumer mindset and
Luke 11–17: 278–79
danger of weak doctrine to
1 Timothy: 159
deception in
1 & 2 Thessalonians: 269–70
decisions
1 Corinthians: 29–30
definition of
1 & 2 Thessalonians: 13
discipline in
1 & 2 Thessalonians: 176, 304
James: 96
Revelation 1–11: 46, 87, 94–95
disharmony in
Romans 9–16: 307
distinguishing mark of
Mark 9–16: 11
diversity within
Romans 9–16: 273
divine characteristics of
Matthew 16–23: 28
division within
Ephesians: 347
and divorce
Mark 9–16: 52
doctrine of
Ephesians: viii
1–3 John: 119–21
early growth of
John 12–21: 166
endurance of
1 Corinthians: 400
evangelism and
Luke 18–24: 258–59, 440
and false religions
1–3 John: 2
as family
1 Timothy: 184
fellowship of
Matthew 16–23: 31
as foundation and pillar of truth
1 Timothy: 136
foundation of
Matthew 16–23: 28
as God's channel for truth
1 Timothy: 216
God's equipping of
1 Corinthians: 322
as God's family
1 Timothy: 135
God's program for
Luke 11–17: 154
growth of
John 12–21: 166
Ephesians: 151
as home for worship in early years
1–3 John: 243–44
identity of
Matthew 16–23: 32
invincibility of
Matthew 16–23: 32
Israel and
Luke 1–5: 110, 132, 135
Luke 18–24: 125
1 Timothy: 216
Titus: 6
legacy and heritage of
1–3 John: 234
loving
Colossians & Philemon: 83
metaphors and analogies of
1 Timothy: 183
mission of
Luke 1–5: 328
as monument to the truth
1–3 John: 214–15, 238
mutual caring in
Mark 9–16: 86
mystery of
Ephesians: viii, 85–98
nature of true
1 Corinthians: 277
as new Israel
Luke 1–5: 110, 132, 135
offices in
Romans 9–16: 164
opposition to
1 & 2 Thessalonians: 166
ordinances
John 12–21: 38, 132
and outsiders
1 Timothy: 66
overview of
John 12–21: 288, 296
Pentecost as birth of
John 12–21: 289
persecution of
Luke 11–17: 195, 197
1 & 2 Thessalonians: 60
Revelation 1–11: 67–68, 71, 72, 86, 123

politicization of
Romans 9–16: 207
and prayer
Mark 9–16: 149
rapture of
Mark 9–16: 257
Luke 18–24: 228
renewal
Ephesians: 117
and replacement theology
Luke 1–5: 135–36
responsibilities of
1 & 2 Thessalonians: 2
Roman persecution of
John 12–21: 167–70
second coming and
Luke 1–5: 137
Luke 11–17: 410, 417
security of
Matthew 16–23: 30
significance of
1 & 2 Thessalonians: 165
Spirit–controlled
1 Corinthians: 306–7
spiritual kingdom and
Luke 11–17: 404
spiritual reality of
Matthew 16–23: 34
standards of belief and behavior
1–3 John: 119–21
supernatural resources of
1 & 2 Thessalonians: 166
supreme purpose of
Galatians: 79
temporary replacement of Israel as God's chosen
Titus: 6
the tribulation and
Luke 18–24: 247–49
unity of
John 12–21: 286, 289–93
1 Corinthians: 25–32
Ephesians: 65–83
Titus: 165
1–3 John: 220–21

The Church Age
Matthew 8–15: 343, 378
Mark 1–8: 220, 221

Church building, earliest known
Acts 13–28: 203

Church discipline
Luke 11–17: 45
Acts 1–12: 160–62
1 Timothy: 47, 55, 170, 184

Church leaders
and believing wife
Titus: 32
commending
Titus: 166
qualifications of
Philippians: 88

Church membership, trust in
Romans 1–8: 170

Churchill, Winston
Acts 13–28: 344–45
1 Peter: 49–50
Revelation 1–11: 1

"The Church's One Foundation"
Acts 1–12: 301–2

Chuza (Herod's steward)
Luke 6–10: 183
John 1–11: 166

Cicero
Mark 1–8: 308
Mark 9–16: 364
Acts 1–12: 313
James: 163
2 Peter & Jude: 41

Circumcision
Mark 1–8: 353
Luke 1–5: 89, 167, 169
Colossians & Philemon: 106–8
Titus: x
physical vs. spiritual
John 1–11: 367–68
significance of
Romans 1–8: 160, 248
Galatians: 72

Circumstances
Ephesians: 88, 262
human
Galatians: 166
transcending
2 Corinthians: 277–78

Citizenship
believers'
Ephesians: 9
earthly
Titus: 141
heavenly
Matthew 16–23: 96
Titus: 156

***The City of God* (Augustine)**
Romans 9–16: 159
2 Timothy: 109

Civil authority, divine standards for
Romans 9–16: 237

Civil courts
Luke 18–24: 4

Civil disobedience
Romans 9–16: 207, 211, 214, 217

Civil responsibility
Romans 9–16: 208

Clarity of New Covenant
2 Corinthians: 108–11

Claudius (Roman emperor)
Romans 1–8: 35
2 Corinthians: 4

Cleansing
of conscience as gift of salvation
1–3 John: 143
and forgiveness
1–3 John: 36–37
Holy Spirit and
Mark 1–8: 359
self–
Matthew 8–15: 336
from sin
Ephesians: 299
1–3 John: 36–37, 144
spiritual
John 12–21: 67

of temple
Luke 11–17: 226
Clement of Alexandria
Mark 1–8: 3
Mark 9–16: 410–11
Luke 1–5: 2, 144–45
John 1–11: 4, 8
2 Corinthians: 5
1 Peter: 6
2 Peter & Jude: 6, 141
1–3 John: 3, 6, 7, 8
on Johannine authorship of Revelation
Revelation 1–11: 4
Clement of Rome
John 12–21: 188
Romans 9–16: 235
2 Peter & Jude: 7–8
1–3 John: 2
on Paul's visit to Spain
1 Timothy: xi
Clements, Roy
2 Corinthians: 130–31
Cleopas
Luke 18–24: 421, 422, 433
Cleopatra
Mark 9–16: 114
Luke 1–5: 143, 144
Luke 18–24: 69
Clingen, Herb and Ruth
1 Peter: 141
Clotfelter, David
2 Peter & Jude: 75–76, 210
Clothing
Matthew 1–7: 423–24
Luke 6–10: 154
Luke 11–17: 142–43
Clouds
Luke 18–24: 231, 237
waterless
2 Peter & Jude: 180
Co-belligerency
Romans 9–16: 207
Coalition for Christian Colleges & Universities (Christian College Coalition)
2 Timothy: 110
Cock crow (watch of the night)
Mark 9–16: 298, 337, 339
Codex Alexandrinus
2 Peter & Jude: 6
Codex Sinaiticus
2 Peter & Jude: 6
Codex Vaticanus
2 Peter & Jude: 6
Cohorts
Matthew 24–28: 183
Mark 9–16: 310, 323, 347
Luke 6–10: 124
Coins
Luke 11–17: 299–300
Cole, Alan
Galatians: 7
Colossae
Colossians & Philemon: 5–6
Colossian church
1 Peter: 66–67, 97–98
Colson, Charles
1 Timothy: 26
Colt
Mark 9–16: 125
Luke 18–24: 93, 94
"Come Thou Long Expected Jesus"
Luke 6–10: 141–42
Comfort
John 12–21: 95–107, 212–14
abundance of
2 Corinthians: 24–25
forgiveness and
2 Corinthians: 58
Jesus Christ as person of
2 Corinthians: 18–20
overview of
2 Corinthians: 11–18
parameters of
2 Corinthians: 24–25
participation in
2 Corinthians: 27–28
perpetuity of
2 Corinthians: 26–27
power of
2 Corinthians: 25–26
promise of
2 Corinthians: 20–22
purpose of
2 Corinthians: 22–24
for sorrow (See also Sorrow)
2 Corinthians: 259–70
times of trouble and
2 Corinthians: 11–28
Comfort, dangers of
Matthew 8–15: 21–24
Comfort, Philip
John 1–11: 322
The Comforter
and comma Johanneum
1–3 John: 195–96
See also Holy Spirit
Coming judgments
2 Peter & Jude: 183–92
See also Judgment
Comma Johanneum
1–3 John: 195–96
Commandments
1 Peter: 238–39
of Christ
2 Peter & Jude: 117
greatest commandment
1–3 John: 166
obedience to
1–3 John: 55–60, 68, 146–47
as precious treasure
1–3 John: 181
Ten (*see* Ten Commandments)
Commendation of church leaders
Titus: 166
Commitment
Mark 1–8: 187, 203
Luke 6–10: 316
Luke 11–17: 288
Acts 1–12: 162–63
2 Corinthians: 300–301
Hebrews: 86, 265

2 Peter & Jude: 203–4
Christian
John 12–21: 398–405
Romans 1–8: 37
godly
Romans 9–16: 154
to God's mastery
Titus: 2
to God's mission
Titus: 4
to God's people
Titus: 14
lack of
Matthew 8–15: 125
marital
Matthew 16–23: 174
pastoral
Titus: 2, 4, 14
selfless
Romans 9–16: 155
spiritual
Matthew 8–15: 22, 194
Matthew 24–28: 87
Galatians: 51
2 Timothy: 11
Common grace
Mark 9–16: 181
Luke 6–10: 108, 251
John 12–21: 267
1–3 John: 115, 166
Revelation 1–11: 222
The common people
Luke 18–24: 382
Communication, effective
2 Timothy: 99
Communion. *see* Lord's Supper
Communism
Luke 18–24: 213
John 12–21: 170, 189
Companionship
1 Corinthians: 482–83
1 Peter: 182–83
Comparative judgment
Luke 6–10: 332–35
Compassion
Matthew 8–15: 431
Mark 9–16: 27, 119
Luke 6–10: 9, 35, 89–90, 136–37, 326–27, 358
2 Corinthians: 323–25, 341–42
Colossians & Philemon: 155
from Christ
1 Peter: 132–34
definition of
Mark 1–8: 316–17, 386
of God
Matthew 8–15: 191
Mark 1–8: 392–93
Luke 11–17: 182
of Jesus
Matthew 8–15: 18, 483
Mark 1–8: 90, 265–68, 288–89, 385–87
Luke 11–17: 260, 388
lack of
Luke 11–17: 113
as mark of salvation
Matthew 24–28: 123
Old Testament descriptions
Luke 11–17: 235–37
Competent pastors and ministers
competence (defined)
2 Corinthians: 327–31
confidence in calling of
2 Corinthians: 84–86
humility of
2 Corinthians: 86–87
New Covenant message of (*See also* New Covenant)
2 Corinthians: 87–91
overview of
2 Corinthians: 77–78
reputation of
2 Corinthians: 79–81
transformation ministries of
2 Corinthians: 81–84
See also Pastors and ministers
Complacency, spiritual
Ephesians: 343
Complaining
Matthew 1–7: 91–92
1 Corinthians: 225
sin of
Philippians: 176–78
Completeness
of Christ (see Jesus Christ)
of Christians (*see* Maturity)
Compromise
Matthew 1–7: 225–26
spiritual
Matthew 24–28: 213
Conceit. *see* Pride
Concern, pastoral
deceit and
2 Corinthians: 427–28
edification and
2 Corinthians: 429–30
faithfulness and
2 Corinthians: 421–24
honesty and
2 Corinthians: 427–28
overview of
2 Corinthians: 419–21
perseverance and
2 Corinthians: 421–22
reverence and
2 Corinthians: 428–29
sacrifice and
2 Corinthians: 424–27
self–centeredness and
2 Corinthians: 424–27
See also Integrity; Obedience
Condemnation
Matthew 1–7: 64–70
2 Peter & Jude: 89–91, 160
of Christ
Luke 18–24: 336–39, 354
of false teachers
Luke 18–24: 166–67
of Israel
Luke 18–24: 97–98

of unbelievers
Romans 9–16: 37
of the unsaved
Matthew 24–28: 125
See also Judgment
Condescension
1 Corinthians: 247
Conduct, Christian
1 Corinthians: 83
Confederacy of ten European nations
Matthew 24–28: 33
Confession
erroneous views of
1–3 John: 37–41
as godly sorrow
1–3 John: 40
as repentance
1–3 John: 38–40
Roman Catholic Church and
1–3 John: 40
salvation and
Matthew 16–23: 149, 193
of sin
Romans 1–8: 219, 268, 426
See also Forgiveness
Confidence
Luke 18–24: 324, 326
2 Corinthians: 84–86, 159–61
1 Peter: 41–48
1–3 John: 145, 170–71, 203–4
See also Overconfidence
Confirmation, Roman Catholic
Romans 1–8: 250
Confrontation
Luke 18–24: 114–15
Confucius
Luke 6–10: 107
Coniah
John 1–11: 138
Conquerers, Christians as
1–3 John: 174–75, 179
Conquering King (Jesus)
Mark 9–16: 230
Conscience
John 12–21: 129
Acts 13–28: 279–80
Romans 1–8: 141, 224, 431
Romans 9–16: 9, 216
1 Corinthians: 196
Galatians: 149
Ephesians: 244, 325, 343, 351
1 Timothy: 18, 45, 151
Hebrews: 249–50, 449
1 Peter: 161, 202–3, 217–18
1–3 John: 141–44
guilty
Matthew 24–28: 185
lies and
1–3 John: 142
obeying
Matthew 16–23: 107
overview of
2 Corinthians: 29–33
of Paul
2 Corinthians: 33–38
pure
1 Peter: 202–3
resisting
Matthew 16–23: 107
See also Soul and conscience
Consecrated bread
Mark 1–8: 144
Consolation/comfort
Luke 1–5: 177–79
Constable, Thomas L.
2 Corinthians: 432
Constance, Council of
Luke 1–5: 227
Constantine
Matthew 8–15: 378
Luke 18–24: 165, 212, 213
John 12–21: 170
granting of religious toleration to Christians
Revelation 1–11: 83
Constantinople
Luke 1–5: 226
Consubstantiation
1 Corinthians: 238
Consultation (of Sanhedrin)
Mark 9–16: 345
Consumer mindset
Luke 11–17: 278–79
Contamination, spiritual
Matthew 16–23: 386
Contentment
Matthew 1–7: 419–21
Matthew 8–15: 194
Mark 1–8: 291–92
Luke 6–10: 245
1 Corinthians: 171, 173–75
Colossians & Philemon: 140–41
Hebrews: 434–35
Continual praise
2 Peter & Jude: 137–38
Contributions, financial
Luke 6–10: 184
Contrition
as mark of true believer
Romans 1–8: 385
repentance and
Matthew 16–23: 149
Conversation
godly
Titus: 95
as reflector of character
Romans 1–8: 187
Conversion
Matthew 1–7: 54
Mark 1–8: 187
Mark 9–16: 370–71, 380–81
Luke 18–24: 58, 69
Romans 1–8: 20
1–3 John: 53, 55
false
Matthew 16–23: 186
genuine
Matthew 16–23: 49, 189
repentance and
Matthew 16–23: 30, 98
Converts, false
Matthew 16–23: 30

Conviction
biblical
2 Timothy: 30, 126
salvation and
Matthew 16–23: 193
of sin
Romans 1–8: 222, 417
spiritual
Matthew 8–15: 251
Cook, W. Robert
John 1–11: 17
Cooperation
Matthew 1–7: 239–40
Copernicus
2 Timothy: 150
Corban
Mark 1–8: 346
Corinth
Luke 6–10: 170
John 12–21: 166
historical information about
2 Corinthians: 1–9
problem church
Titus: x
Corinthian church
1 Peter: 68–69, 78–79, 84, 158–59, 235–36, 283–84
historical information about
2 Corinthians: 1–9
Corn, measuring of
Luke 6–10: 110
Cornelius
John 1–11: 413
John 12–21: 21
2 Peter & Jude: 21–22
1–3 John: 243
Cornerstone
Mark 9–16: 170, 171
Luke 18–24: 127–28
1 Peter: 121–23
Coronation
Mark 1–8: 40, 41
Mark 9–16: 122, 126–27
Luke 18–24: 88–90
of Christ
Matthew 16–23: 259
Correction, resentment of
Matthew 16–23: 117
Corrupt nature
Mark 9–16: 67
Corruption
2 Peter & Jude: 31, 92–93
Cosmological dualism
2 Peter & Jude: 144–45
Council of Carthage
2 Peter & Jude: 9
Council of Chalcedon
John 1–11: 38
Council of Constance
Luke 1–5: 227
Council of Hippo
2 Peter & Jude: 9
Council of Jerusalem. *see* Jerusalem Council
Council of Laodicea
2 Peter & Jude: 9, 141
Council of Trent
Romans 1–8: 250
2 Corinthians: 466
1–3 John: 53
Counseling, Christian
Romans 9–16: 328
Courage
Matthew 8–15: 162
Mark 9–16: 296–97
Luke 6–10: 36
Acts 1–12: 195
2 Corinthians: 326–27
Court of Judgment
John 1–11: 101
Court of the Gentiles
Mark 9–16: 136
Luke 18–24: 104
John 12–21: 25
Court of the Israelites
Luke 18–24: 104
Court of the Priests
Luke 18–24: 105
Court of the Women
Mark 9–16: 222
Luke 18–24: 104, 169
John 1–11: 333
Courtyards
Mark 9–16: 336
Cousins
Luke 6–10: 202
Covell, Margaret "Peggy"
Colossians & Philemon: 233
Covenant(s)
Luke 1–5: 95–101, 103–11
Luke 6–10: 18, 21, 151, 348
John 1–11: 121–24, 130
John 12–21: 25, 381, 382
Hebrews: xvi, 235–36
1 Peter: 24–25, 34–35, 79–80, 108, 111, 114, 126
Abrahamic
2 Corinthians: 89, 97–98
God's new
1–3 John: 56, 125
Mosaic
2 Corinthians: 89, 97–98, 108–10
New (*See also* New Covenant)
2 Corinthians: 87–117
ratified with blood
Matthew 24–28: 152
second Abrahamic
Romans 9–16: 131
Covenant people
Mark 1–8: 22
Covenant theology
Luke 11–17: 247
Romans 1–8: 151, 171
Romans 9–16: 92
Covering
1 Peter: 151–52
Coveting
Mark 1–8: 357
Mark 9–16: 55
Covetousness
2 Timothy: 111
Hebrews: 432

See also Greed
Cowardice
Matthew 24–28: 184
Mark 9–16: 316–17
Cowardliness
Luke 18–24: 313–14
Cowper, William
Romans 1–8: 169
2 Timothy: 62
Craddock, Fred B.
2 Corinthians: 291, 295, 491
Craig, William Lane
Luke 18–24: 403–4
John 1–11: 256
John 12–21: 375
Cranfield, C. E. B.
Mark 9–16: 411
Romans 1–8: 383
Cranmer, Thomas
1 Peter: 3
Creation
Luke 6–10: 206, 255
John 1–11: 17
Hebrews: 14, 56–57, 292
1 Peter: 71, 152
2 Peter & Jude: 118–20
awesomeness of
Romans 1–8: 81
curse of
Colossians & Philemon: 57
evidence in nature
Romans 1–8: 79
ex nihilo
Romans 1–8: 258
glorifying God
Romans 1–8: 298
groaning of
Luke 11–17: 156
magnitude of
Colossians & Philemon: 47–50
purpose of
Romans 9–16: 126
wonder of
Matthew 8–15: 30
Creationism, progressive
Romans 1–8: 88
Creator
1 Peter: 259
Creator, God as
Romans 1–8: 414
Creatures born to be killed concept
2 Peter & Jude: 95–108
Cretan churches, Gentiles in
Titus: 4
Crimes
Luke 18–24: 332, 345
Criminal behavior
Ephesians: 167
Criminals
Mark 9–16: 367, 368
Luke 18–24: 372–73
Crispus
2 Corinthians: 4
Criswell, W. A.
on John's weeping
Revelation 1–11: 165
on the mark of the beast
Revelation 12–22: 63
on the promise of Christ's second coming
Revelation 12–22: 302
on the revelation of Christ's glory
Revelation 1–11: 16
Criticism
Matthew 1–7: 429–39
Colossians & Philemon: 172–73
Crockett, Davy
Luke 6–10: 38
Crosby, Fanny J.
Matthew 8–15: 301
The cross
Mark 1–8: 393, 418–22, 427, 428
Luke 6–10: 238, 268, 270, 274, 275
centrality of
Luke 18–24: 49, 262–63
centrality to Scripture of
Mark 9–16: 266–67
Christ facing
John 12–21: 33–44
effect on Satan
Romans 1–8: 215
glorification of Christ by
John 12–21: 241–43, 255
and Jewish people
Luke 18–24: 377
necessity of
John 12–21: 27–29
Old Testament predictions of
Luke 18–24: 50, 51, 52
purpose of
John 12–21: 39, 87, 131–40
and the resurrection
Mark 9–16: 12, 13
salvation and
John 12–21: 255–56
Satan's opposition to
Matthew 16–23: 41
Simon of Cyrene and
Mark 9–16: 362–63
understanding of
1 Corinthians: 40–41
See also Crucifixion
Cross–bearing
genuine
Matthew 16–23: 237
obedience and
Matthew 16–23: 234
self–giving and
Matthew 16–23: 234
Crowd(s)
astonishment of
Luke 18–24: 147–48
in Capernaum
Mark 1–8: 99, 177
Luke 6–10: 229–31, 290
danger of
Luke 6–10: 203
fickleness of
Mark 1–8: 191
groups in
Luke 6–10: 93–94
at healing of paralytic
Mark 1–8: 113

Jesus' identity and
Luke 6–10: 260, 261
manipulation of
Luke 18–24: 369–70
motivation of
Luke 6–10: 187, 229, 230
at Passover
Luke 18–24: 102
Pilate and
Luke 18–24: 345, 346, 361–63
and populated places
Mark 1–8: 93
scribes and Pharisees in
Mark 1–8: 100
size of
Mark 1–8: 161, 194, 316
Luke 6–10: 86, 87, 118, 290

Crown of glory
1 Peter: 270–71

Crown of life
James: 42

Crown of thorns
Luke 18–24: 376, 379
John 12–21: 338
Crucifixion
Mark 1–8: 130, 427
Luke 6–10: 274, 281
Acts 13–28: 24
2 Corinthians: 12, 140, 145, 198, 455
1 Peter: 30, 80–82, 105–6, 148, 166–74, 210, 224–25, 231, 237, 258–59
Revelation 1–11: 33
cruelty of
Mark 9–16: 97–98
description of
Matthew 24–28: 254
Mark 9–16: 358, 364–65
expression of Christ's love
John 12–21: 353–55
the Father's presence at
Mark 9–16: 375–81
"King of the Jews" inscription
John 12–21: 352–53
location
Luke 18–24: 366
manifestations of Christ's control during
John 12–21: 356–57, 362–65
miraculous events during
1–3 John: 194
Old Testament predictions of
Mark 9–16: 93–94
Luke 18–24: 51, 377
origin of
Matthew 24–28: 254
Galatians: 197
Persians and
Luke 18–24: 377–78
physical aspects of
Luke 18–24: 54–55, 378–79
prophecies fulfilled by
John 12–21: 347–52
Roman use of
Mark 9–16: 347, 364
See also Cross

Cruelty
Mark 9–16: 97–98, 358

Crurifragium
Mark 9–16: 388
Luke 18–24: 399

Crusades
Matthew 8–15: 378
Romans 1–8: 164

Cryonics
John 12–21: 369–70

Cultists. *see* False teachers

Cults
John 1–11: 348
Romans 1–8: 221
Galatians: 119
Ephesians: 277, 285
2 Timothy: 68, 119
confronting
Matthew 16–23: 379

Cultural Christianity
Titus: 139

Cultural morality
Luke 11–17: 69–74

Cultural settings
Luke 11–17: 293

Culturalism, gospel and
Titus: 79

Culver, Robert D.
Romans 9–16: 213, 226, 237

Cumming, Robert DeNoon
on Sarte's existentialism
Colossians & Philemon: 97

The cup
Mark 9–16: 106, 304, 305, 358

Cup of blessing
Luke 18–24: 280, 281, 282

Curiosity
Luke 6–10: 28

Currency exchange
Luke 18–24: 334

Curse, reversal of the
Colossians & Philemon: 57–58

The curse on mankind
Mark 9–16: 56, 57

The cursed
Luke 6–10: 99–100

Cursing and blessing
Luke 11–17: 240, 247

Cursing of the fig tree
Mark 9–16: 132, 134, 139, 141, 142, 258

Custer, George Armstrong
2 Corinthians: 327

Cybele, cult of
Galatians: 142

Cybelene priests
Romans 1–8: 249

Cyberchurches
2 Corinthians: 440

Cynicism
2 Peter & Jude: 111

Cyprian of Carthage
Mark 9–16: 411
1–3 John: 3

Cyrene
Mark 9–16: 363
Luke 18–24: 368, 369

Cyril of Alexandria
John 1–11: 39

Cyril of Jerusalem
2 Peter & Jude: 9, 141
Cyrus
Mark 9–16: 387
Luke 1–5: 146
Luke 6–10: 134–35

Dabney, R. L.
Titus: 110
Dagon
2 Corinthians: 252
Dalmanutha, district of
Mark 1–8: 390
Damascus
Mark 9–16: 114
Luke 6–10: 54
Luke 18–24: 70
John 12–21: 166
Dame Wisdom
Titus: 81
Damnation, predestination and
Romans 1–8: 498–99
Dana, H. E.
John 1–11: 18
on meaning of eis
Acts 1–12: 74–75
Danger
Matthew 1–7: 402
forsaking spiritual
Matthew 16–23: 110
Daniel
Matthew 1–7: 27–28
Mark 9–16: 126
Luke 1–5: 43
Luke 6–10: 144, 260
Luke 11–17: 211–12
Luke 18–24: 2, 91, 224, 225
John 12–21: 14–15, 34, 203, 204
2 Corinthians: 50, 148, 177, 377–78, 442, 479
Ephesians: 266
1 Timothy: 59
1–3 John: 96, 97
Darius (king)
Luke 18–24: 378
2 Timothy: 196
Darkness
Mark 9–16: 254, 376
Luke 11–17: 89, 90, 91
Luke 18–24: 231, 389
John 12–21: 50–51, 55
1–3 John: 24, 28, 29, 62, 64–68
of hell
Mark 1–8: 401
Mark 9–16: 376
light and
John 12–21: 50–51, 55, 88
2 Corinthians: 249
1 Peter: 131
1–3 John: 24, 28, 29, 62, 64–68
pits of
2 Peter & Jude: 84–86
Satan and
Luke 18–24: 389
1–3 John: 62, 132
spiritual
Matthew 24–28: 184
Luke 1–5: 20–21, 122, 272
John 1–11: 23–24
Romans 1–8: 86
1 & 2 Thessalonians: 156–57
walking in
1–3 John: 28–29
Darrow, Karl K.
on atomic forces
Colossians & Philemon: 49–50
Darwin, Charles
2 Peter & Jude: 114
Dathan
2 Corinthians: 454
David (King)
Matthew 1–7: 6, 173, 203–4, 339
Mark 1–8: 144, 145
Luke 1–5: 20, 45, 49, 58, 75, 98, 147, 155, 247, 250
Luke 6–10: 5, 6, 14, 21, 74, 75, 143
Luke 11–17: 35
John 1–11: 48, 60, 92, 118, 123–25, 137–38, 207, 224, 291, 309–10, 365, 423, 424, 430, 450
John 12–21: 72–73, 350, 351
2 Corinthians: 12, 35, 57, 110, 183, 251–52, 256, 280, 352
Galatians: 168
Ephesians: 125, 263
1 Timothy: 18
Hebrews: 366, 386
1 Peter: 74, 156–57, 259–60, 279–80
2 Peter & Jude: 18, 142
1–3 John: 85, 88, 253–54
and Absalom's death
Mark 9–16: 69
adultery of
Mark 9–16: 58–59
betrayal of
Mark 9–16: 286–87
child's death and
Luke 18–24: 29
Christ in line of
Luke 18–24: 151–55
covenant promise to
Luke 18–24: 150
covenants with
2 Corinthians: 88
faith of
Romans 1–8: 242
God's providential protection of
Acts 13–28: 288–90
Jesus as Son of
Mark 9–16: 115–16, 208
prayers of
Luke 18–24: 2, 287
Psalms of
2 Corinthians: 51, 84, 90, 120, 150, 183, 184, 216, 348, 378
Davidic covenant
Luke 1–5: 95, 97–101, 119–20, 128, 131
Luke 18–24: 60
John 1–11: 123–25

Dawkins, Richard
on the directionlessness of evolution
1 & 2 Thessalonians: 140–41
Day of Atonement
Matthew 24–28: 139
Mark 1–8: 128
Mark 9–16: 378
Luke 1–5: 26, 339
Acts 13–28: 348
Romans 1–8: 209, 402
Romans 9–16: 54
Ephesians: 22
1 Timothy: 31
Hebrews: xvi, 109, 223–26, 234, 242, 440
1–3 John: 49
Day of Judgment
Matthew 16–23: 52
2 Peter & Jude: 115, 120
1–3 John: 170
Day of the Lord
Luke 1–5: 216
John 1–11: 29
Acts 1–12: 54–56
Philippians: 28, 183
Revelation 1–11: 199–202, 235, 244, 250
Revelation 12–22: 120–22, 145
Day of God vs.
2 Peter & Jude: 5, 120, 134
description of
1 & 2 Thessalonians: 144–45
precursors to
1 & 2 Thessalonians: 145–46
Day of Pentecost. *See* Pentecost
Day of visitation
1 Peter: 140–41
Days
Luke 11–17: 412, 413, 416
reckoning of
Mark 9–16: 280
Days of vengeance
Luke 18–24: 223
De Young, Donald B.
on the Anthropic Principle of the universe
Colossians & Philemon: 48
Deacon(s)
Mark 9–16: 383
Acts 1–12: 182–83
Ephesians: 240
definition of
1 Timothy: 124
as good managers at home
1 Timothy: 130
and moral purity
1 Timothy: 129
personal character of
1 Timothy: 126
relative to Acts 6
1 Timothy: 125
rewards for service
1 Timothy: 131
spiritual life of
1 Timothy: 128
tested
1 Timothy: 129
Deaconess
Mark 9–16: 383
The dead, raising of
Luke 18–24: 64
Dead Sea
Mark 1–8: 23, 29, 228
Mark 9–16: 49, 114
Luke 1–5: 204
Luke 6–10: 145, 208
Dead Sea Scrolls
John 12–21: 203
2 Corinthians: 250
Deafness
Mark 1–8: 376
Death
Luke 6–10: 135, 137–38, 228, 236–37, 281, 319–20
Luke 11–17: 359–60, 362–66
Luke 18–24: 140
Hebrews: 69–70, 242, 337–38, 342–43
2 Peter & Jude: 114
blood representing Christ's
1–3 John: 193–94
Christ's power over
Mark 1–8: 253, 254, 260, 262–66
John 12–21: 14, 63, 304, 306, 356–57, 362–69
confidence in facing
2 Corinthians: 159–60
deliverance from fear of
Romans 1–8: 434
eternity and
Luke 18–24: 406
fear of
Mark 1–8: 252–53
Romans 1–8: 434
1–3 John: 109
of Jesus (*see* Death of Jesus)
kinds of
Romans 1–8: 295
life after (*See also* Eternal life)
Luke 18–24: 140
origin of
Romans 1–8: 294
pagan view of
1 & 2 Thessalonians: 126
sin and
Mark 1–8: 32, 89, 252, 376
1–3 John: 205–6
sleep and
Mark 1–8: 264–65
1 & 2 Thessalonians: 127
spiritual
Romans 1–8: 417
Ephesians: 52
1–3 John: 133, 207
Revelation 1–11: 111
substitutionary
Mark 9–16: 127
universality of
Romans 1–8: 298
victory over
1–3 John: 175
Death of Jesus
Mark 9–16: 6, 91–98, 109, 162–64, 269
Luke 18–24: 265, 267, 399
John 12–21: 360, 361, 362
Acts 1–12: 62–64

2 Corinthians: 22, 51, 90, 104, 144–47, 160, 189–94, 203–5, 260
1 & 2 Thessalonians: 62, 127, 164
Hebrews: 62–63
believers, meaning for
John 12–21: 131–34
and church's ordinances
John 12–21: 38, 132
God's nature revealed by
John 12–21: 87–88
meaning for believers
John 12–21: 131–35
overview of
John 12–21: 34–38
as plan of God
Luke 18–24: 265, 266
predictions of
Mark 9–16: 91–98, 269
purposes of
John 12–21: 43, 134–40
substitutionary character of
Mark 9–16: 109, 383–84
transfiguration discussion of
Mark 9–16: 6
victory accomplished by
John 12–21: 41–42
See also Cross; Crucifixion
Deathbed testimony
Matthew 16–23: 10, 16
Deborah
Luke 1–5: 94
1 Timothy: 83
Debts
Luke 11–17: 44
Romans 9–16: 245
Decapolis
Mark 1–8: 250, 312, 374, 375
Luke 6–10: 57, 250
John 12–21: 26
Deceit
Matthew 1–7: 319–20
Mark 1–8: 358
2 Corinthians: 427–28
1 Peter: 98, 167–68
Deceitfulness, man's natural
Romans 1–8: 188
Deceivers
2 Peter & Jude: 69
See also Antichrist(s); Error; False teachers
Deception
Matthew 1–7: 325–26, 459–72
2 Corinthians: 370–72
2 Peter & Jude: 100–101
Decision(s)
Hebrews: 345–46
for Christ
Romans 1–8: 497
unity in
1 Corinthians: 29–30
See also Will, human
Decius
Luke 11–17: 197
Luke 18–24: 212
John 12–21: 170
Declaration of Independence
1 Peter: 185–86
Decree
Hebrews: 102–3
divine eternal
Titus: 155
Decretive will of God
Luke 11–17: 28
Dedication
Matthew 8–15: 214
Dedication, Feast of the (Feast of Lights)
Matthew 24–28: 139
John 1–11: 5, 438–41
Deeds, good
Matthew 24–28: 122
Deeds of the flesh. *see* The Flesh
Deeper life
Romans 1–8: 425
Defamation of the lost
Titus: 138
Defection, spiritual
Galatians: 61
Defense (in trial)
Luke 18–24: 333
Deficiency, spiritual
Luke 6–10: 96
Defilement
2 Peter & Jude: 106–8
Defiling flesh
2 Peter & Jude: 172–73
Deity
Luke 6–10: 92, 132, 133, 139
Luke 18–24: 149, 151, 155–57
Deity of Jesus
Matthew 24–28: 232
Mark 1–8: 148, 224, 225
Mark 9–16: 209–12, 217
Luke 6–10: 92, 132, 133, 139
Luke 18–24: 149, 151, 155–57
John 12–21: 104, 143, 239, 267–68
Philippians: 123, 125
Colossians & Philemon: 2, 43–54, 103
Hebrews: 14, 26–28, 30, 33–34, 52
1–3 John: 157–58, 190, 210
Revelation 1–11: 3, 50, 51, 68, 96, 119
affirmation of
Mark 1–8: 148, 224, 225
claims of
Matthew 16–23: 23
John 1–11: 181–92
confirmations of
Matthew 16–23: 63
demon's attestation to
Mark 1–8: 64, 67
disciples' belief in
Mark 1–8: 416
displays of
John 1–11: 85–96
as Lord of the Sabbath
Mark 1–8: 138
Old Testament prophecy and
Mark 1–8: 18, 19
Peter's testimony to
Mark 1–8: 411–13
proofs of
Matthew 8–15: 436–45
reactions to
John 1–11: 299–308

and religious leaders
Mark 1–8: 148
verification of
John 1–11: 285–98
visible displays of
Mark 1–8: 160, 225–26
witnesses to
John 1–11: 203–16
Delilah
Luke 11–17: 129
2 Corinthians: 272
Delitzsch, Franz Julius
Ephesians: 231
Deliverance
1 Peter: 48
divine
Colossians & Philemon: 40
Delivered
Mark 9–16: 34
Demas
John 1–11: 267
John 12–21: 85
Colossians & Philemon: 198, 230
1–3 John: 80–81, 266
Demeter
1–3 John: 259
Demetrius
1–3 John: 245, 256, 259–60
Democracy, Christianity and
Romans 9–16: 206
Demon possession
Mark 1–8: 62, 63, 64, 242
Mark 9–16: 24–28, 153
Luke 1–5: 283–85
Luke 6–10: 165, 166, 183, 217–21, 290–94
Revelation 12–22: 40
effects of
Revelation 1–11: 263
Demonism
Ephesians: 246
Demonization
Matthew 8–15: 41
Demons
Matthew 1–7: 127
Luke 1–5: 252, 280–88, 295–96
Luke 11–17: 61–65, 75, 76
Luke 18–24: 58, 203, 211
John 1–11: 1–2, 23–24, 26–27, 95, 137, 171–72, 182, 379–80, 435
2 Corinthians: 158, 234, 357, 401–2, 464, 467
1 Peter: 209–13, 225–26, 240, 280–84
2 Peter & Jude: 85–86, 98–99, 165
Revelation 1–11: 257–58
Revelation 12–22: 2, 8
activities of
Ephesians: 231, 233, 346, 349, 360, 365
affliction by
Matthew 16–23: 75
authority of believers over
Acts 13–28: 97, 171–72
authority over
Colossians & Philemon: 50, 103, 112–13
believers' power over
Luke 6–10: 341–42
categories of
Ephesians: 341
Christ and
Luke 6–10: 217–19, 340
and Christ's identity
Mark 1–8: 57, 63–64, 243, 244
Christ's power over
Mark 1–8: 58, 59, 164, 182
Luke 6–10: 88–89, 218, 221–23, 225
deliverance from
Ephesians: 342
disciples' authority over
Mark 1–8: 169
Gerasene demoniac
Luke 6–10: 165, 328
and the Holy Spirit
Mark 1–8: 66
influence of
Ephesians: 261
nature and destiny of
Matthew 8–15: 42
power of
Luke 6–10: 218–21
speaking by
Mark 1–8: 75–76
worship of
1 Corinthians: 236
Demosthenes
Ephesians: 273
Denarii
Mark 1–8: 319
Denarius
Mark 9–16: 179–80, 182, 274
Luke 18–24: 135
John 12–21: 7
Denials (of Peter)
John 12–21: 317–19, 321–22
Denominationalism
Romans 1–8: 170
Denunciation
2 Peter & Jude: 97
Departure
2 Peter & Jude: 52–53
Dependence and obedience
Ephesians: 363
See also Obedience
Dependence on God
Matthew 8–15: 193, 270
Dependent living
Mark 1–8: 289–91
Deportation of Jews
Assyrian
Romans 9–16: 21
Babylonian
Romans 9–16: 21
Deportment, outward
1 Peter: 139–41
Depravity
Luke 6–10: 302
Luke 11–17: 56–57
human
1 Corinthians: 24
1–3 John: 29, 85, 128, 227
man-made religion and
Romans 1–8: 89

total
Titus: 114
James: 188
universal to man
Romans 1–8: 88, 180, 182, 294
Depression, spiritual
Matthew 16–23: 63
Derision. *see* Mockers/mockery
DeShazer, Jacob
Colossians & Philemon: 234
Desire
Mark 9–16: 56
Despair
Hebrews: 391
philosophical
Colossians & Philemon: 96–97
Destiny, no human mastery of
Romans 1–8: 344
Destruction
2 Peter & Jude: 83–99
Destructiveness
2 Peter & Jude: 71–72
Determinism
Titus: 31, 111
"Dethrone the King: Dying to Self" (Bill Britton)
Luke 6–10: 273–74
Deuteronomy
Mark 9–16: 320, 321
Deviant sexual behavior
Titus: 137
Devil. *see* Satan
Devotion
2 Corinthians: 174–75, 188–89
1 Peter: 200–201
to God's glory
Romans 1–8: 225
spiritual
Galatians: 60
Devouring
1 Peter: 281–83
Dialetical processes
2 Peter & Jude: 56
Diana (Artemis)
Romans 1–8: 94
1–3 John: 2, 210, 214
Diana, temple of
Ephesians: 165
Diaspora
Luke 6–10: 17
John 1–11: 5
Philippians: 230
Dickason, C. Fred
Luke 1–5: 284
Dickens, Charles
and character Uriah Heep
Colossians & Philemon: 120
Didymus. *see* Thomas (Didymus)
Dies Natalis Solis Invicti
Luke 1–5: 140
Diet of Worms
2 Corinthians: 146–47
Dietary laws
Hebrews: 437–38
Old Testament
Acts 1–12: 295–96
Dignity of believers, divine
Romans 1–8: 5
Diligence
2 Peter & Jude: 39–40, 44–45, 52–53
Dillenberger, John
John 12–21: 226
Dio Chrysostom
Luke 1–5: 12
Diocletian
Luke 11–17: 197
Luke 18–24: 212
John 12–21: 170
Diognetus, Epistle to
Romans 9–16: 240
Dionne sisters
Luke 1–5: 53
Dionysius of Alexandria
John 1–11: 4
1–3 John: 3
Dionysus
Mark 1–8: 374
Diotrephes
Luke 6–10: 43
1 Peter: 269
2 Peter & Jude: 140
character assassination of John
1–3 John: 239, 257–59
personal ambition of
1–3 John: 256–57
refusal of to show hospitality
1–3 John: 239, 258, 259
rejection of the truth
1–3 John: 245, 246
selfishness and spiritual pride of
1–3 John: 256–57
Diprose, Ronald
Luke 1–5: 135–36
Disappointment
1 Peter: 121–22
acceptance of
Titus: 75
Disasters
Luke 11–17: 180, 186
Luke 18–24: 202, 230
Discernment
Mark 1–8: 292–94
Luke 6–10: 109
Philippians: 92, 256
Hebrews: 134, 437
2 Peter & Jude: 40–42, 194–204
Revelation 1–11: 59–60
definition of
1 & 2 Thessalonians: 198–200
gift of
1 Corinthians: 304–5
lack of
Luke 11–17: 113, 174–75
1 & 2 Thessalonians: 192–93
of need for judgment
Luke 11–17: 177–78
spiritual
Matthew 8–15: 169–70
Romans 1–8: 116
Ephesians: 343
Titus: 51

of the time
Luke 11–17: 175–77, 191
Disciples
Mark 1–8: 118, 228
Luke 6–10: 15, 16, 40, 87, 113, 123, 209
Luke 11–17: 207, 279, 280, 285
call of the Twelve
Matthew 1–7: 114–20
categories of
Matthew 8–15: 32
courage of
John 12–21: 231–32
defective
Matthew 24–28: 193
definition of
John 1–11: 357–58
failure to believe
Mark 9–16: 26
faithfulness of
Luke 18–24: 293
faithless
John 1–11: 221–23
fearfulness of
Mark 9–16: 92, 316
frailties of
Matthew 8–15: 122–26
genuine
Mark 1–8: 228
and Jesus' death and resurrection
Mark 9–16: 13–18
Jesus' prayers for
John 12–21: 260–61, 271–84
Jesus' sufferings and
Luke 18–24: 48–56
of John the Baptist
Mark 1–8: 126, 127, 129
learning/truth–seeking by
Mark 1–8: 402, 405
ministry internship of
Mark 1–8: 284, 390, 391, 392
and miracles
Mark 1–8: 388, 389
number of
Mark 1–8: 221, 285
as ordinary men
Mark 1–8: 172, 284–85
pride of the twelve
Matthew 16–23: 232
resurrection appearances to
John 12–21: 380–86
on road to Emmaus
Mark 9–16: 404
safeguarding of
John 12–21: 278, 280, 309–10
special revelation to
Luke 18–24: 126
and stealing Jesus' body
Mark 9–16: 393, 394
and treatment of children
Mark 9–16: 66
true vs. false
John 1–11: 227–38
The Twelve
Mark 1–8: 166–72, 312, 314, 315, 340
Mark 9–16: 92, 277, 284
Luke 18–24: 48, 270, 271, 272, 274
John 1–11: 1–7, 63–74, 221–38, 272–79, 287, 336–37
1 Peter: 4–9, 56–59
See also The Twelve
Discipleship
Matthew 1–7: 113–14, 116, 223–33
Mark 1–8: 425–29
Luke 6–10: 241, 268–77
Luke 18–24: 34, 35, 42
1 Peter: 239, 248–49
change in meaning of
Luke 11–17: 279
commitment needed
Luke 11–17: 282–84
cost of
Matthew 8–15: 22, 230
Matthew 16–23: 46, 49, 51, 56, 194, 205
Luke 11–17: 284–89
Romans 1–8: 353
2 Timothy: 10, 12, 53
divine imperative of
Matthew 16–23: 135
love and
Mark 9–16: 43–45
obedience and
Matthew 16–23: 47
Mark 9–16: 49
paradox of
Matthew 16–23: 51
purity of
Mark 9–16: 46–48
sacrifice and
Mark 9–16: 48–49
salvation and
Luke 11–17: 280–81
true
Matthew 16–23: 46
Discipline
Christian
Romans 1–8: 400
church
Matthew 1–7: 216
1 Corinthians: 119, 122–33
Galatians: 173–82
divine
Romans 1–8: 479
divine authority for
Matthew 16–23: 136–138
God's love and
Matthew 16–23: 147
Hebrews: 392–93
God's participation in
Matthew 16–23: 138
initiation of
Matthew 16–23: 128
inner
1 Peter: 137–39
judgment and
Hebrews: 385
local church and
Matthew 16–23: 134
loving
Matthew 16–23: 129
methods of
2 Corinthians: 446–47

motives for
2 Corinthians: 443–46
ostracism and
Matthew 16–23: 134
overview of
2 Corinthians: 439–42
perils in
Hebrews: 390–91
place of
Matthew 16–23: 133
process of
Matthew 16–23: 133
products of
Hebrews: 395–97
purity and
Matthew 16–23: 131
purpose of
Matthew 16–23: 132
Hebrews: 385–89
recipients of
Matthew 16–23: 126–27
restoration and
Matthew 16–23: 136
self–righteousness and
Matthew 16–23: 136
sonship and
Hebrews: 393–95
spiritual
1 Timothy: 164
zeal and
Matthew 16–23: 131
Discipling
Matthew 16–23: 12
Discontentment, with spiritual gifts
1 Corinthians: 314–16
Discouragement
2 Corinthians: 66–68
Ephesians: 361, 364
Discussing (meaning of)
Mark 9–16: 25
Disease
Mark 1–8: 70, 73, 77, 169
Mark 9–16: 118
Luke 1–5: 292–95, 312
Luke 6–10: 87, 88, 228
See also Healing(s)
Disheartened pastors
2 Corinthians: 63–75
Dishonesty
Matthew 1–7: 325–26
Dishonor
honor vs.
2 Corinthians: 219–32
of Jesus Christ
John 1–11: 378–82
Disloyalty
Luke 18–24: 53
to God
2 Corinthians: 354
to the gospel
2 Corinthians: 357
to Jesus Christ
2 Corinthians: 355–56
loyalty vs.
2 Corinthians: 351–60
to truth
2 Corinthians: 357–60
Dismay
Luke 18–24: 234
Disobedience
Matthew 1–7: 269–71, 477–80
Luke 6–10: 161–62
Luke 11–17: 240–43
1 Corinthians: 221
Ephesians: 207, 212, 249, 272, 281, 292–93, 339, 348
1 Peter: 66–68, 112–13, 178, 212
1–3 John: 71
Disobedient separation
2 Corinthians: 254–55
Dispensationalism
Luke 1–5: 131, 135
Dissension in church
Titus: 57
Dissipation
Luke 18–24: 256
Distress
1 Peter: 43
Distressed
Luke 11–17: 171–72
Diveine attributes
Romans 1–8: 70
Diversity
Mark 1–8: 124
Divided kingdoms
Luke 11–17: 64
Divine authority, Jesus' claim of
Luke 18–24: 116, 150–53, 324–25, 337
Divine compassion
Luke 6–10: 136–37
Divine judgment
Mark 1–8: 198, 199
See also Judgment
Divine justice
2 Peter & Jude: 35, 82
Divine knowledge
Mark 9–16: 296
Divine nature
2 Peter & Jude: 30–31
Divine power
Mark 9–16: 190, 297
Luke 6–10: 137–38
Romans 9–16: 17–18
2 Peter & Jude: 26–28
Divine procurement
2 Peter & Jude: 26, 28–30
Divine promises
2 Peter & Jude: 26, 30–31
Divine providence. *see* God, provision by; Providence
Divine purpose
Luke 6–10: 133–34
Divine resources
Mark 1–8: 391–92
Divine sovereignty
Mark 9–16: 250
Divine standard
Luke 18–24: 12–13
Divine substitution. *see* Atonement
Divine timetable
John 1–11: 275–84

Division
cause of
1 Corinthians: 69–72
cure for
1 Corinthians: 73–74
symptoms of
1 Corinthians: 72–73
Division of Abijah
Luke 1–5: 24
Divorce
Luke 11–17: 351–52
Romans 1–8: 122, 360
1 Corinthians: 165
Ephesians: 272, 302
Titus: 149
Hebrews: 137
adultery and
Matthew 16–23: 166
Mark 9–16: 58–60
certificate of
Matthew 1–7: 309–11
Mark 9–16: 57
by Christians
Matthew 1–7: 307–18
and the church
Mark 9–16: 52
and God's curse on mankind
Mark 9–16: 56–57
God's reasons for hating
Mark 9–16: 55
and intermarriage with pagan women
Mark 9–16: 52–53, 59
Israel's accommodation of
Mark 9–16: 54
Jewish views of
Matthew 16–23: 164
in Judaism
Matthew 1–7: 18
in New Testament times
Titus: 28
Pharisees and
Mark 9–16: 53–54, 57–59
and remarriage
Matthew 16–23: 167, 170, 171
1 Corinthians: 162, 165
scriptural grounds for
Matthew 16–23: 171
Docetists
John 1–11: 40
1–3 John: 8
Doctrine
Matthew 1–7: 431–32, 470
Hebrews: 399–400, 421–22, 435–37
apostles'
1 Timothy: 4
biblical
2 Timothy: 29
Christian
Ephesians: 116, 346–47
and church
1–3 John: 22, 119–20
compromise of
Titus: 20
of demons
1 Timothy: 149
duty and
Titus: 71
false
Matthew 16–23: 14
Galatians: 11, 14, 53, 140
Ephesians: 335, 346, 349
1 Timothy: 7, 45
2 Peter & Jude: 67–68
1–3 John: 2, 152, 160, 234
pastors and
1–3 John: 22
purity of
Titus: 19
saving faith and
1–3 John: 120
on sin
1–3 John: 121–22
sound
1 Timothy: 10
true
Galatians: x
unity in
1 Corinthians: 25–30
Dods, Marcus
John 1–11: 16, 129
Dogmatism
1–3 John: 13, 14
Dogs
Mark 1–8: 369
Luke 6–10: 246, 247
Dome of the Rock (Islamic shrine)
Revelation 1–11: 294
Dominance/dictatorship
Luke 18–24: 292
Dominion over earth, man's
Matthew 8–15: 29, 87
Dominion with Christ
1 Peter: 119–26, 288
Domitian (Emperor)
Luke 11–17: 197
Luke 18–24: 212
John 12–21: 169
2 Peter & Jude: 142
1–3 John: 7
persecution of Christians
Revelation 1–11: 39
Donkey
Luke 18–24: 93, 94
Donkey's colt
Mark 9–16: 125, 126
Donne, John
Romans 1–8: 293, 434
Door and doorkeeper, Jesus as
John 1–11: 421–36
Dorcas
Luke 1–5: 294
Luke 6–10: 36
John 1–11: 388–89
1 Timothy: 196
Double–mindedness
Matthew 1–7: 204
Double predestination
Titus: 111
Doubt
Mark 9–16: 28, 92, 145, 146
Luke 6–10: 144–49, 163, 296

James: 37
believers'
Romans 1–8: 430, 502
in believers
Matthew 16–23: 21, 39
causes of
Matthew 8–15: 238–44
faith and
Romans 1–8: 265
Doubtful things
1 Corinthians: 188–97
Doubting God
Matthew 1–7: 90–92
Ephesians: 359, 364
"Doubting Thomas"
Luke 6–10: 66
See also Thomas
Douglas, J. D.
John 1–11: 128
Dove
Mark 1–8: 34
Doxology
1 Timothy: 274
1 Peter: 29
Dragon. *see* Satan
Drawing near to God
Hebrews: 183–84
Dreaming
2 Peter & Jude: 171–72
Dreyfus, Alfred
Luke 11–17: 244
Dreyfus affair. *see* Anti–Semitism
Drifting
Hebrews: 43–45
Drink the cup
Mark 9–16: 106, 358
Drinking and drunkenness
Ephesians: 229–44
Drinking poison
Mark 9–16: 412, 416
Dropsy (edema)
Luke 11–17: 258
Drugs, mind–altering
Galatians: 161
Drummond, Henry
Matthew 8–15: 132
Romans 9–16: 181
Drunkenness
Luke 1–5: 36, 37
Luke 18–24: 256
Dual days reckoning method
Mark 9–16: 279–80
Dualism
1 Corinthians: 408, 410
cosmological
2 Peter & Jude: 144–45
Greek
Romans 1–8: 386
Romans 9–16: 143
light and darkness
1–3 John: 24, 28, 29, 62, 64–68
love and hatred
1–3 John: 81, 82, 133–35, 137
philosophical
2 Corinthians: 166
Colossians & Philemon: 7, 58, 123
1–3 John: 8, 27
Due process
Luke 18–24: 356
Dullness, spiritual
Hebrews: 130–32
Durant, Will and Ariel
John 12–21: 121
Duty(ies)
Ephesians: 116
description of
1 Peter: 233–34
doctrine and
Titus: 71
incentives for
1 Peter: 234–38
instructions for
1 Peter: 239–44
intentions of
1 Peter: 245–46
mutual love and
1 Peter: 241–42
personal holiness and
1 Peter: 240–41
spiritual service
1 Peter: 242–45
Dwelling places (heavenly)
John 12–21: 100–101
Dwellings, earthly
2 Peter & Jude: 50–51
Dying to sin, teachings on
John 1–11: 341–50

Eadie, John
John 1–11: 197
Ephesians: 177
on the power of God's Word
Philippians: 68
Eareckson Tada, Joni
Ephesians: 266
Earth
destiny of in God's hands
Romans 1–8: 456
restoration of
Matthew 16–23: 204
***Earth in Upheaval* (Velikovsky)**
Luke 18–24: 231
Earthly kingdom
Luke 11–17: 209–12, 411
Earthquakes
Mark 9–16: 233, 248, 249
Luke 18–24: 204–5, 230, 390
Eastern mysticism
Galatians: 11
Eastern religion
Ephesians: 232, 261
Easy–believism
Romans 1–8: 316
Ephesians: 159, 218
Eating and drinking
Mark 1–8: 118–19
See also Food
Eclecticism
Matthew 16–23: 374
Economics
persecution and
Luke 18–24: 211

of temple merchants
Luke 18–24: 268–69
Ecstatic experience
Ephesians: 232, 246
Ecumenical councils
Acts 13–28: 61
Ecumenism
Mark 1–8: 124
Colossians & Philemon: 1
2 Timothy: 104
Eczema
Mark 1–8: 87
Eddy, Mary Baker
Ephesians: 277
Eden
Luke 1–5: 253
Luke 6–10: 84
John 1–11: 342, 376
2 Corinthians: 334
1 Peter: 213–14
2 Peter & Jude: 157–58
1–3 John: 153, 252
Revelation 1–11: 65, 153, 254
Edersheim, Alfred
Matthew 8–15: 60, 480
Mark 9–16: 113
Luke 1–5: 203, 269–70, 314
Luke 18–24: 69, 164, 165
John 12–21: 204
Edgar, Thomas R.
Luke 18–24: 248
on the pointlessness of a posttribulational Rapture
1 & 2 Thessalonians: 128–29
Revelation 12–22: 212–13
Edict of Milan
Luke 18–24: 212–13
Edification
2 Corinthians: 429–30
of believers
Titus: 7
Edom
Romans 9–16: 26
Edomites
Mark 1–8: 190
Luke 1–5: 22
Edwards, Jonathan
Matthew 8–15: 215
Luke 1–5: 135
John 1–11: 240
Romans 1–8: 225, 416
Romans 9–16: 156
2 Corinthians: 398
1 & 2 Thessalonians: 93–94
2 Peter & Jude: 56
1–3 John: 139, 140, 162
social reforms of
Colossians & Philemon: 165
Efficacious calls
2 Peter & Jude: 29
Egalitarianism
Ephesians: 282
Titus: 79
Egerton Papyrus 2
John 1–11: 4, 9
Egnatian Way
1 & 2 Thessalonians: 3, 5, 26
Egypt
Matthew 1–7: 41
Mark 1–8: 86
Luke 1–5: 146, 154, 189
Luke 18–24: 225, 226, 266, 366
Egyptians, death and
Luke 18–24: 140
Ekron
Mark 1–8: 181
Elah
Luke 6–10: 74
Elders
Mark 9–16: 156, 311
Luke 18–24: 114, 268, 313, 330, 332
Acts 13–28: 55, 209, 225, 248
Ephesians: 143
Hebrews: 444–45
1 Peter: 263–66, 276
as overseer, bishop, pastor
Titus: 21, 35
See also Spiritual leaders/leadership
Eldership
categories of
1 Timothy: 219
dealing with accusations against
1 Timothy: 221
as deserving of honor
1 Timothy: 217
and financial support
1 Timothy: 218
instructions for rebuke of
1 Timothy: 222
and laying on of hands
1 Timothy: 224
ordination of
1 Timothy: 224
See also Pastor (overseer, elder)
Eleazar
Luke 11–17: 361
John 1–11: 453
1 Peter: 108
See also Lazarus
The elect
Mark 9–16: 249, 250, 258
John 1–11: 183, 253–54
Titus: 5, 6
2 Peter & Jude: 20–21
gospel not restricted to
1 Timothy: 63, 68
See also Believer(s)
Election, divine
Matthew 16–23: 181
Colossians & Philemon: 153–55
Titus: 110, 112
kinds of
Ephesians: 10
as not arbitrary
Romans 9–16: 60
sovereign
Romans 9–16: 24, 35, 57
Election by Christ
Luke 1–5: 128, 132, 136
John 12–21: 172
1 & 2 Thessalonians: 20

1 Timothy: 68–69
2 Timothy: 61, 82
Hebrews: 103
1 Peter: 13–27, 124
advantages of
1 Peter: 25–27
condition of
1 Peter: 14–16
description of
1 Peter: 13–14, 119–26
effect of
1 Peter: 22–23
elements of
1 Peter: 13–27
nature of
1 Peter: 16–19
of the saved
Matthew 24–28: 45
security of
1 Peter: 23–25
source of
1 Peter: 19–21
sphere of
1 Peter: 21–22
Eli (Jesus' grandfather)
Luke 1–5: 246, 247, 248
John 1–11: 17
Elijah
Mark 1–8: 23, 298, 302, 415
Mark 9–16: 6. 7, 17–19, 377
Luke 1–5: 38–39, 275
Luke 6–10: 21, 144
Luke 11–17: 226
Luke 18–24: 180, 453
John 1–11: 17, 26, 29, 51–53, 83, 86, 132, 154, 189, 209, 376
John 12–21: 204
2 Corinthians: 112–13, 139, 415
Ephesians: 360
Christ and
Luke 6–10: 139, 260
in Christ's transfiguration
Luke 6–10: 283–86
and fire from heaven
Luke 6–10: 54, 313
as forerunner of Christ
Matthew 16–23: 67, 71
and John the Baptist
Matthew 16–23: 71
Luke 6–10: 155
Elimelech
Mark 9–16: 189
Luke 18–24: 145
Eliphaz the Temanite
Luke 18–24: 6
2 Corinthians: 12, 183
1–3 John: 86
Elisha
Mark 1–8: 298, 302
Luke 1–5: 276
Luke 6–10: 133, 139
Luke 11–17: 226
Luke 18–24: 2
John 1–11: 83, 154, 189, 388
2 Corinthians: 415
1–3 John: 242
Elisha–Spring
Mark 9–16: 113
Elizabeth
Mark 1–8: 30
Luke 1–5: 5, 24, 27, 30–31, 37, 58–59, 66–72, 90, 94, 204
Luke 6–10: 144, 183
Luke 18–24: 371
John 1–11: 29, 48
2 Corinthians: 110
1 Peter: 198–99
Elliot, Charlotte
Ephesians: 376
Elliot, Elisabeth
Acts 1–12: 228
Elliot, Jim
Matthew 8–15: 214
Mark 9–16: 87
Luke 11–17: 148, 187
Acts 1–12: 228
on heavenly gain
Colossians & Philemon: 20
Ellul, Jacques
Ephesians: 103
Elwell, Walter A.
Luke 1–5: 55
Elymas
1 Peter: 98
Eminent apostles
2 Corinthians: 408–9
Emmaus
Mark 9–16: 404
Luke 1–5: 43
Luke 6–10: 310
Luke 18–24: 420, 442–43, 453
1–3 John: 243
Emotional encouragement, divine provision of
Romans 1–8: 284
Emotions
Luke 6–10: 136, 157, 327
Ephesians: 45
Colossians & Philemon: 18–19, 88–89, 160, 172
limitations of
Galatians: 64
saving faith and
Romans 1–8: 206
Emperor worship
Romans 1–8: 9
Employers and employees
Ephesians: 321–29
Christian
1 Timothy: 233
non–Christian
1 Timothy: 231
See also Work
Empty tomb
Mark 9–16: 400
Luke 18–24: 403, 404, 408, 410, 412, 414
Emulating Christ
Matthew 8–15: 216
Enablement
Hebrews: 142
Encouragement
2 Corinthians: 68–70
Colossians & Philemon: 85–87

Titus: 9
Hebrews: 374–75, 402
Encumbrances
Hebrews: 375–77
End, means justifying
Romans 9–16: 207
End of all things
1 Peter: 235
End times
Matthew 24–28: 36
chronology of
Matthew 24–28: 50, 70
See also Eschatology; second coming
Endurance
Colossians & Philemon: 34, 66
Hebrews: 373–74
eternal vs. temporal
2 Corinthians: 157–58
as mark of salvation
Matthew 24–28: 28
overview of
2 Corinthians: 149–52
present vs. future
2 Corinthians: 154–56
spiritual vs. physical
2 Corinthians: 152–54
of suffering
Titus: 10
Enemies
Matthew 1–7: 337–50
Mark 9–16: 209
Luke 6–10: 102–4
Engagement
Luke 1–5: 44–45, 148
England
Luke 11–17: 243, 244
Enlightenment
John 1–11: 352
John 12–21: 222
Hebrews: 142–43, 281
Enlightenment philosophies
2 Peter & Jude: 55–57
Enoch
Luke 18–24: 453
Hebrews: 305–6, 310, 311, 313–14
2 Peter & Jude: 85, 143, 159–60, 187–90
1–3 John: 252
Entertainment, religious
Ephesians: 154, 257
Enticements
2 Peter & Jude: 101
Entropy, evolution and
Romans 1–8: 455
Entrusting to God
1 Peter: 168–69, 258–60
Environment
Luke 18–24: 220
Environmentalism
Romans 1–8: 455
Revelation 1–11: 244
Envy
Mark 1–8: 358
1 Corinthians: 314–15
1 Peter: 98
Epaphras
Luke 18–24: 3
Colossians & Philemon: 196–97
Epaphroditus
Luke 1–5: 295
Luke 6–10: 125
2 Corinthians: 410
1–3 John: 135, 246
Ephesian church
1 Timothy: 60, 136
1 Peter: 16–17, 75, 107, 116, 275, 287
and Gnosticism
1 Timothy: 60
John and
1–3 John: 10
and Judaizers
1 Timothy: 60
leadership of
1 Timothy: 92
letter to
1–3 John: 184
sin within
1 Timothy: 184
women's roles in
1 Timothy: 78
and worldliness
1–3 John: 2
See also Ephesus
Ephesians, Paul's letter to
2 Corinthians: 5–8, 17, 87–147, 153–72, 189–235, 340–66, 390–412, 431–42, 466–77, 485
Ephesus
Luke 6–10: 51, 54
Luke 18–24: 211, 212
John 12–21: 168, 169
church in (*see* Ephesian church)
John and Cerinthus in
1–3 John: 236
and John's letters
1–3 John: 6, 7, 212, 240
riot over Paul's teaching in
1–3 John: 210, 259
Ephod
Hebrews: 203
Ephphatha
Mark 1–8: 377–78
Ephraim, village of
John 12–21: 2
Epictetus
Romans 1–8: 54
Epicureans
Acts 13–28: 131
Hebrews: 112–13
Epicurus
Hebrews: 287
"Epiphanes"
Luke 18–24: 225
Epiphanius
2 Peter & Jude: 141
Equality of believers
Galatians: 50
Era of fulfillment
Luke 6–10: 158–59
Erasmus
Romans 9–16: 38
Erastus
2 Corinthians: 480

Erdman, Charles R.
on Christ's dignity
Colossians & Philemon: 98
on the letter to Thyatira
Revelation 1–11: 95
Erickson, Millard J.
John 1–11: 253
Error
as antichrist and deceiver
1–3 John: 22
truth mixed with
1–3 John: 155
Word of God as defense against
1–3 John: 155, 160
See also Apostasy
"Eruvs"
Mark 1–8: 140
Esau
Mark 1–8: 190
Luke 1–5: 69
Luke 6–10: 21
Hebrews: 408
Eschatological extremism
1 Peter: 238
Eschatology
Luke 1–5: 126, 131, 136–37
Luke 18–24: 9–10, 178–83, 200–201
Esdraelon, Plain of
Luke 18–24: 203
***Essay on Man* (Alexander Pope)**
Romans 9–16: 186
Essenes
Matthew 1–7: 134
Matthew 16–23: 328
Mark 9–16: 185–86
Luke 1–5: 166, 318
Luke 6–10: 70
Luke 11–17: 96, 255, 256
Luke 18–24: 102
John 1–11: 325
Colossians & Philemon: 6, 100
1 Timothy: 98, 152
Esther
Mark 9–16: 387
1–3 John: 254
Eternal bonds
2 Peter & Jude: 164
Eternal decree, divine
Titus: 155
Eternal destruction
Mark 9–16: 355
Eternal endurance
temporal endurance vs.
2 Corinthians: 157–58
Eternal fire
2 Peter & Jude: 165–67
Eternal future
Luke 11–17: 337, 338
Eternal individuality
Romans 1–8: 492
Eternal inheritance
appropriation of
1 Peter: 32–34
description of
1 Peter: 29
motives for
1 Peter: 31–32
nature of
1 Peter: 34–35
security of
1 Peter: 36–38
source of
1 Peter: 30–31
Eternal kingdom
Mark 1–8: 48–49
Christ's
Matthew 8–15: 88
Eternal life
Mark 1–8: 382, 431
Mark 9–16: 77, 81, 86
Luke 6–10: 256
Luke 18–24: 34, 36, 42, 73, 146
John 1–11: 114–17, 265–74
John 12–21: 178, 252–54
1 Peter: 231–32
2 Peter & Jude: 201
acquiring
Luke 6–10: 350, 354–59
believing God's testimony and
1–3 John: 197–98
and children of Satan
1–3 John: 135–37
"chosen" as selected for
1–3 John: 216
of Christians
1–3 John: 91, 106, 107, 158, 197
exclusivity of
1–3 John: 197–98
as goal of hope
1–3 John: 107
heaven and
1–3 John: 202
incorruptible seed of
1–3 John: 158
the law and
Luke 6–10: 353–54
motivation for
Luke 6–10: 352–53
nature of
Luke 6–10: 351–52
obedience and living forever in
1–3 John: 91
as present possession
1–3 John: 203
as union with Christ
1–3 John: 197
Eternal punishment
Luke 6–10: 327, 333
Luke 11–17: 124, 125, 223, 255, 366
Luke 18–24: 221
See also Hell
Eternal security
Romans 1–8: 146, 148, 270, 304, 442, 471–88, 489, 498
Philippians: 29, 163–64
2 Timothy: 27, 82
Titus: 108–9, 122–23
Hebrews: 146–47, 154, 163, 167–69, 266
James: 27ff., 42, 131
Revelation 1–11: 115–16
Revelation 12–22: 73–74, 95–103

Eternal state
Romans 1–8: 132
See also Heaven
Ethics
Hebrews: 421
Ethiopian eunuch
Mark 9–16: 138
Ethnology
Romans 1–8: 216
Eucharist. *see* Lord's Supper
Eudoxia
Luke 1–5: 226
Eunuchs, self–made
Galatians: 142
European Common Market
Matthew 24–28: 19
European nations, confederacy of
Matthew 24–28: 33
Eusebius of Caesarea
Matthew 8–15: 142
Mark 1–8: 3
Mark 9–16: 410
John 1–11: 3–4, 9, 40–41, 87–88
John 12–21: 318, 404
Romans 1–8: 90
Titus: 162–63
1 Peter: 6
2 Peter & Jude: 5–6, 13, 52, 141–42
1–3 John: 3, 4, 5, 8
on the martyr Sanctus
Acts 1–12: 315
Euthymius Zigabenus
John 1–11: 323
Eutychus
Luke 1–5: 294
John 1–11: 388–89
Evangelicalism
2 Peter & Jude: 35
Evangelism
Matthew 1–7: 111–20, 486
Mark 1–8: 5, 65, 206, 212, 215, 250
Mark 9–16: 207
Luke 6–10: 186, 195, 199–200, 266, 316, 335
John 12–21: 178–86, 189–90, 284
2 Timothy: 38, 140, 186
Titus: 4
1 Peter: 93, 139–40, 153, 163, 178, 233–37, 242, 249
the ascension and
Luke 18–24: 454
biblical
Matthew 16–23: 189
of children
Luke 18–24: 31
duty of
Titus: 7
effective
Titus: 95
ego–focused
Colossians & Philemon: 185
experience–centered
Colossians & Philemon: 184–85
false motives for
Matthew 16–23: 114
global extent of
Luke 18–24: 445–47
judgment truth and
Luke 18–24: 258–59
love and
Romans 9–16: 12
manipulative
Colossians & Philemon: 185
methods of
Luke 11–17: 216, 224, 278–79, 281–83
Acts 13–28: 78
necessity of
Acts 13–28: 78
1–3 John: 224, 227, 248
opportunities for
Colossians & Philemon: 183–87
Pauline principles of
Acts 13–28: 376
"seeker–friendly" approach
Luke 6–10: 266
strategies of
Titus: 89
in the tribulation
Luke 18–24: 127
See also Gospel
Evangelistic praying
attitude of
1 Timothy: 74
benefits of
1 Timothy: 65
elements of
1 Timothy: 61
importance of
1 Timothy: 58
Jesus' example
1 Timothy: 75
New Testament examples of
1 Timothy: 60
Old Testament examples of
1 Timothy: 58
reasons for
1 Timothy: 67
for rulers
1 Timothy: 63
scope of
1 Timothy: 63
Evangelists
Romans 9–16: 337
characteristics of
Matthew 1–7: 118–19
Evangelizing children
Matthew 16–23: 182
Eve (biblical)
Mark 1–8: 70, 270
Mark 9–16: 55
Luke 1–5: 42, 255
Luke 6–10: 84, 142
Luke 18–24: 49–50, 68, 262, 286, 383
John 1–11: 110, 342, 376
John 12–21: 204–5
2 Corinthians: 334, 356
1 Timothy: 88, 89
1 Peter: 209–10
2 Peter & Jude: 119, 157–58, 176
1–3 John: 90, 133, 188, 252

curse on
Titus: 80
See also Adam
Eve (pagan)
Titus: 81
Evidence
Hebrews: 89, 90, 91
Evil
Mark 1–8: 357, 358
Mark 9–16: 100, 243, 326
Luke 1–5: 184, 255, 256
Luke 6–10: 116, 117
1 Peter: 189–90
problem of
Revelation 1–11: 276ff.
See also Sin
Evil One. *see* Satan
Evil spirits
Mark 1–8: 62, 65
See also Demons
Evildoers
1 Peter: 140
Evolution
Matthew 1–7: 237–38
1 Corinthians: 435
entropy and
Romans 1–8: 455
theistic
Romans 1–8: 88
theory of
Acts 13–28: 51, 135–37
Evolutionism
2 Timothy: 109
Exaltation
Luke 18–24: 21–22
John 12–21: 136–37
1 Peter: 279
Example
Christian
1 Corinthians: 117–18
godly
Matthew 16–23: 183
importance of
2 Timothy: 126
Jesus'
Matthew 1–7: 77–78
sinful
Matthew 16–23: 105, 106
Excellence
2 Peter & Jude: 30
Excellencies of Christ
1 Peter: 133–34
Exclusion, false spiritual
Matthew 16–23: 376
Exclusivism
Luke 1–5: 337–38
Exclusivity
Mark 1–8: 124
Luke 6–10: 304–5
Excommunication
1 Corinthians: 130–32
Excuses
Luke 11–17: 271–72, 274
Execution. *see* Capital punishment
Exegesis
John 1–11: 46
Exhortation
Hebrews: 400–401
1 Peter: 263
Exile, Babylonian. *see* Babylonian Captivity
Existentialism
John 1–11: 182
Ephesians: 42
2 Timothy: 110
2 Peter & Jude: 56
despair of
Colossians & Philemon: 96–97
Exorcism
Mark 1–8: 65, 239
Luke 1–5: 284
Acts 13–28: 171–72
Ephesians: 341
Exorcists, false
Acts 13–28: 175–77
2 Peter & Jude: 98
Expected One
Luke 6–10: 142–46, 152
See also Messiah
Experience, values and limitations
Galatians: 63
Experiences
Luke 6–10: 30
Experientialism
2 Timothy: 104
Titus: 130
Exploitation
2 Peter & Jude: 78–79
Expository preaching
2 Timothy: 174
Titus: 12, 49
External marks, of Christians
John 12–21: 83–84
External religion. *see* False religion
Externalism
Matthew 1–7: 277
1 Timothy: 152
Extortion
Matthew 16–23: 385
Extrabiblical Jewish writings
Matthew 24–28: 3
Extrabiblical regulations/traditions
Mark 1–8: 354, 355
Luke 11–17: 98, 101, 198, 259
See also Tradition
Extreme unction
Titus: 129
Exultation
1 Peter: 252
Eye of a needle
Mark 9–16: 84–85
Luke 18–24: 41
Eyes of the Lord
1 Peter: 193–94
Eyewitness experiences
2 Peter & Jude: 57–61
Eyewitnesses. *see* Witnesses
Ezekiel
Mark 9–16: 168, 184
Luke 6–10: 213
Luke 11–17: 212
Luke 18–24: 124, 161
2 Corinthians: 83, 210, 252, 423

1 Peter: 89
1–3 John: 144
Ezra
Mark 1–8: 61, 342
Mark 9–16: 59–60

Faber, F. W.
Matthew 8–15: 268
Face of Jesus Christ
clarity of
2 Corinthians: 123–24
humility and
2 Corinthians: 133–34
overview of
2 Corinthians: 119–23
privilege and
2 Corinthians: 129–33
purification aspects of
2 Corinthians: 125–28
sovereign aspects of
2 Corinthians: 134–35
strength of
2 Corinthians: 125
transformational aspects of
2 Corinthians: 124
truth–loving aspects of
2 Corinthians: 128–29
Face of the Lord
1 Peter: 194
Factions, factionalism
1 Corinthians: 30–31
Failure, as source of growth for believer
Romans 1–8: 384–85
Fainting
Luke 18–24: 234
Fairbairn, Patrick
1 Timothy: 96
Titus: 66
Faith
Luke 1–5: 63–64, 109, 110
John 12–21: 23, 227, 230, 264–65, 287–88
2 Corinthians: 460–71
1 Peter: 36–37, 42–44, 48, 84, 89–90, 201–2, 250, 255, 285
of Abraham
Acts 1–12: 204
Romans 1–8: 260, 263, 267
Hebrews: 161–62, 326–35
antichrist's departure from
1–3 John: 99–100
of apostles
Luke 6–10: 254, 262
authenticity and
2 Corinthians: 460–71
believers'
2 Peter & Jude: 17–45
in believers' evidence of Holy Spirit
1–3 John: 168–170
as body of doctrine
Ephesians: 156
of centurion
Luke 6–10: 128–29
certainty of believers'
2 Peter & Jude: 33–46
and Christians as overcomers
1–3 John: 179
and Christ's healing miracles
Mark 1–8: 280
Christ's lessons on
Mark 9–16: 23
continuity of
Romans 1–8: 57
counterfeit
James: 7, 7ff.
in daily life
Hebrews: 94, 262, 289
of David
Romans 1–8: 242
defending
2 Timothy: 128
defined
Colossians & Philemon: 15–16
Hebrews: 286–89, 360
divine healings and
Matthew 8–15: 9, 15, 82, 92, 95
Matthew 16–23: 252
Mark 1–8: 280
divine righteousness and
Luke 11–17: 83
divine sustenance of
Romans 1–8: 272
doctrine
1–3 John: 120
doubt and
Romans 1–8: 265
elements of
Luke 6–10: 288–89
emotions and
Romans 1–8: 206
and falling away
Mark 1–8: 203
false
Romans 1–8: 205
false vs. genuine
1 Timothy: 7
fear and
Luke 6–10: 235
forgiveness through
Luke 18–24: 20
foundational
1–3 John: 147
four types of
Hebrews: 362–63
of Gentiles
Matthew 8–15: 12
genuine
Matthew 16–23: 281
Mark 1–8: 103, 228, 327, 367–72
James: 9ff., 43, 69, 77ff., 80ff., 116, 138
genuine vs. false
1 Timothy: 7
genuineness revealed by speech
James: 144
toward God
Hebrews: 139
God's response to
Matthew 16–23: 250–51
good works as evidence of
Romans 1–8: 129
1 Timothy: 8
and gospel
Romans 1–8: 259–60

and grace
  Romans 1–8: 259
healers
  Matthew 16–23: 251
healings and
  Matthew 8–15: 9, 15, 82, 92, 95
  Matthew 16–23: 252
  Mark 1–8: 280
heroes of
  Luke 6–10: 348
Holy Spirit and
  Luke 11–17: 202
human will and
  Romans 1–8: 205
humility and
  Matthew 16–23: 98
imperfect
  Luke 6–10: 292, 293
importance of
  Mark 9–16: 22, 28
  2 Peter & Jude: 20–21
in Jesus Christ
  1–3 John: 147–48
of Job
  James: 24
justification by
  Luke 11–17: 347
  Luke 18–24: 13, 75
  Romans 1–8: x, 132, 215
  Galatians: 55
  Titus: 5
lack of
  Luke 11–17: 143, 384
and love
  Matthew 16–23: 340
  Ephesians: 40
  1–3 John: 148
and meekness
  Matthew 16–23: 97
and miracles
  Mark 1–8: 280
of Moses
  Hebrews: 287, 347
nature of
  Hebrews: 286–89
necessity of
  Hebrews: 99–100, 282–83
new birth and
  1–3 John: 177
non–saving
  Luke 11–17: 287
obedience and
  Mark 1–8: 91
  John 12–21: 111, 159, 263–64
  Acts 1–12: 297
  Romans 1–8: 24, 307, 346
  Colossians & Philemon: 17
object of
  Colossians & Philemon: 17
origin of
  Hebrews: 378
and patience
  Matthew 16–23: 79–81
persevering in
  Romans 1–8: 281
  1–3 John: 111–13, 177–78, 197–98
persistence and
  Matthew 16–23: 97
persistent
  Matthew 8–15: 50–51
  Matthew 16–23: 80, 97
of Peter
  Mark 1–8: 325, 331, 411–13
  Mark 9–16: 2, 146
  Luke 6–10: 132, 248, 262
  Luke 18–24: 295–96
Peter's teachings on
  2 Peter & Jude: 17, 50–51
politicized
  Titus: 138
power and
  Hebrews: 333
power of
  Matthew 16–23: 73
and prayer
  Mark 9–16: 145–46
prayerful
  Matthew 16–23: 81
prayers of
  Luke 6–10: 296
prompted by God
  Matthew 16–23: 203
regeneration as cause of continual
  1–3 John: 177–78
repentance and
  Matthew 16–23: 96
requirements of
  Hebrews: 264–65
reward and
  Hebrews: 309–10
sacrifice and
  Hebrews: 335–36
salvation and
  Mark 1–8: 261
  Luke 6–10: 176
  Luke 18–24: 64
  Acts 13–28: 108
  1–3 John: 120–22, 227
saving (*see* Saving faith)
security in Christ and
  1 Peter: 201–2
serving
  Matthew 24–28: 97
source, substance, and sufficiency of
  2 Peter & Jude: 17–32
and sovereignty of God
  Matthew 16–23: 282
strong
  Matthew 16–23: 79
struggling
  Romans 1–8: 265
subjective and personal
  1–3 John: 179
subversion of
  Matthew 16–23: 379
temporary
  Hebrews: 266–67
  1–3 John: 178
tests of
  Mark 1–8: 91, 233, 331
  Luke 11–17: 124, 181
  2 Corinthians: 10–18

true
Romans 1–8: 257, 482
as trust in God
Mark 9–16: 144
in the truth
1–3 John: 177–78
unity and
John 12–21: 287–88
walking by
Hebrews: 305–6, 313
weak
Matthew 8–15: 125
Matthew 16–23: 79
Word of God and
Luke 11–17: 368
and works
Romans 1–8: 26, 129, 132, 140
Galatians: 45–60
Hebrews: 285–86, 302, 317–18
Faith healers
Matthew 16–23: 251
Mark 1–8: 74, 76, 408–9
Luke 1–5: 292, 294
Faithfulness
Matthew 24–28: 78
2 Corinthians: 146–47, 300–301, 421–24
1 Peter: 62–65, 235, 251, 288–89
2 Peter & Jude: 50–51
blessings of
Acts 13–28: 365–66
cost of
Matthew 16–23: 51
Romans 1–8: 512
God's
1 Corinthians: 22
lapses in
Matthew 8–15: 228
practical
Romans 1–8: 24
Faithlessness
Matthew 24–28: 108
danger of
Matthew 16–23: 77
Falconer, Robert
Ephesians: 196
The Fall
Matthew 1–7: 311–12
Ephesians: 13, 18, 52, 182, 235, 281, 293, 308
Fall away
Mark 1–8: 203
Fall of Adam
John 1–11: 20–21, 76, 110, 175, 342, 388
1 Peter: 82–83, 209–10
Fall of man
Matthew 8–15: 29, 87–88
Acts 13–28: 18, 114, 129, 168
Romans 1–8: 292, 406
Romans 9–16: 37
Hebrews: 164
Revelation 1–11: 273
Revelation 12–22: 2, 156
Fallen angels
Matthew 8–15: 42, 44
Mark 1–8: 58, 63, 65, 245, 246
Romans 1–8: 298
2 Peter & Jude: 84–86, 145, 164–67
See also Demons
Fallen mankind, destructive disposition of
Romans 1–8: 190
False apostles and teachers
2 Corinthians: 32–38, 80–94, 127–29, 244–45, 361–73, 408–9
See also False teachers
False believers
Luke 18–24: 84, 217
False brethren
2 Corinthians: 390
False Christians, marks of
Matthew 24–28: 188
False Christs
Matthew 24–28: 17
False converts
Matthew 16–23: 30
False coronations
Mark 9–16: 122, 129
False disciples
Mark 1–8: 216
John 12–21: 85
False doctrines
John 1–11: 260
1 Peter: 283
2 Peter & Jude: 67–69
1–3 John: 2, 152, 160, 234
Revelation 1–11: 87
False evidence
Mark 9–16: 324
False exorcists
Acts 13–28: 175–77
2 Peter & Jude: 98
False followers
Luke 18–24: 84, 85, 230
False gods
Romans 1–8: 216
James: 47
False humility
Romans 9–16: 160
Colossians & Philemon: 120
False messiahs
Luke 18–24: 187, 230
John 1–11: 137, 214
John 12–21: 11–12
False professors
Hebrews: 260
False prophets
2 Peter & Jude: 6–7
character of
Revelation 12–22: 56
danger of
Revelation 12–22: 56, 59
examples of
Revelation 12–22: 56
False relevancy
Titus: 46
False religion
Matthew 16–23: 201, 284, 307
Mark 1–8: 62, 125, 133, 134, 339
Mark 9–16: 175–76
Luke 6–10: 3, 8, 10, 261
Romans 1–8: 199, 221, 231
Romans 9–16: 104
1 & 2 Thessalonians: 276

Hebrews: 299
2 Peter & Jude: 69–79
futility of
Acts 13–28: 51
God's hatred of
Luke 11–17: 374
hypocrisy and
Luke 11–17: 95–96
man–made regulations and
Luke 11–17: 101
origin of
1 Corinthians: 279
prophetic rebukes of
Luke 11–17: 342–43
spiritual qualities lacking in
Luke 11–17: 103–10, 256
symbolism and
Luke 11–17: 98, 99
Word Faith movement
Luke 11–17: 9–10
False religious security
Romans 1–8: 151
False spiritual authority
Matthew 16–23: 357
False teachers
Matthew 8–15: 113, 193, 196
Mark 1–8: 136, 216, 288, 291
Mark 9–16: 129, 214, 218
Luke 11–17: 95, 96, 109–10, 254–55, 343–44
John 1–11: 293
Acts 1–12: 94–95
Romans 1–8: 155, 186, 344
1 Corinthians: 473
2 Corinthians: 32–38, 80–94, 127–29, 244–45, 361–73, 408–9
Galatians: 10–11, 139–42, 185
Ephesians: 42
Philippians: 217ff., 255–56
1 & 2 Thessalonians: 33, 37–38, 148–49
Titus: 51, 161
James: 148ff.
2 Peter & Jude: 65–79, 103–4
Revelation 1–11: 60, 95, 100, 103, 133, 144
absence of God's love in
1–3 John: 165
admonishments concerning
2 Peter & Jude: 1–7, 31, 58, 104–19, 158–78, 189–98
altering and adding to Scripture
1–3 John: 235–36
as antichrists
1–3 John: 95, 158, 188
attitude of
1 Timothy: 241
believers to avoid and shun
1–3 John: 235–37, 239
cause of
1 Timothy: 243
character of
Titus: 61
characteristics of
Luke 6–10: 113–17, 243–44
Luke 18–24: 164–66
Christian organizations infiltration by
1–3 John: 155
Christ's true nature denied by
1–3 John: 158, 159, 192, 219–20, 233
claim to transcendent anointing
1–3 John: 102
condemnation of
Luke 18–24: 166–67
condition of
1 Timothy: 244
confronting
Matthew 16–23: 373
danger of
Acts 13–28: 62, 209, 226–28, 230, 250
1 Timothy: 14, 17
dealing with
Colossians & Philemon: 98–104, 115–24
deceitfulness of
1 Timothy: 14
1–3 John: 231–32
divine judgments on
2 Peter & Jude: 81–93
"divine truth" pretense of
1–3 John: 58
effects of
1 Timothy: 243
as emissaries of Satan
1–3 John: 232, 236–37
at Ephesus
1 Timothy: 15, 36, 54
exposed by ungodliness
Titus: 8
giving and
Luke 18–24: 167–71
goal of
1 Timothy: 18–19
God's attitude toward
Luke 6–10: 112
hypocrisy of
Luke 18–24: 132–33
John's opposition to
1–3 John: 9, 188
marks of
1 Timothy: 22, 238–41
mentality of
1 Timothy: 242
methods of
Luke 6–10: 48–49, 266
motives of
1 Timothy: 245
Titus: 60–61
opposing
Titus: 55
portraits of
2 Peter & Jude: 67–79
revoking right to preach
Titus: 55
Scripture warnings about
1–3 John: 21–22, 152–53, 231–33
self–righteous
Titus: 67
silencing
Titus: xi, 54
threats to church
1–3 John: 15, 233
warnings against
Luke 18–24: 159–64
See also False apostles and teachers

False teaching
Hebrews: 274–75, 435–37
1–3 John: 160
Revelation 1–11: 87
on God's wrath
Romans 1–8: 72
False testimony, penalty for
Matthew 24–28: 199
False witnesses
Luke 18–24: 324–25, 330, 336, 337, 343–44
Falsehood
Matthew 1–7: 319–20
Family
division
Luke 11–17: 172–74, 283–84
of God
Mark 1–8: 186–88
and God–ordained marriage
Titus: 79
persecution by
Mark 9–16: 237
spiritual
Mark 1–8: 186, 187, 188, 192
stabilizing force of
Matthew 16–23: 160
See also Marriage
Famine
Mark 9–16: 233
Luke 11–17: 310
Luke 18–24: 205–6, 230
Judean
Galatians: 42
spiritual
Matthew 1–7: 179–80
Farnell, F. David
Luke 1–5: 301
Farrar, Frederic
Luke 18–24: 54
on crucifixion
Philippians: 134
Fasting
Matthew 1–7: 88–89, 399–405
Mark 1–8: 44, 127–28
Luke 1–5: 185, 338–41
Luke 18–24: 18, 19
Acts 13–28: 5
Fatalism
2 Timothy: 61
Titus: 31
Father(s)
discipline by
1 Corinthians: 119
God as (*see* God the Father)
of Israel
Luke 1–5: 105
love of
1 Corinthians: 115
spiritual
1 Corinthians: 116–17
teaching by
1 Corinthians: 118
Father of lies
2 Peter & Jude: 139, 157–58
Fatherhood of God
Luke 11–17: 11–14, 56, 57
Fault–finding
2 Peter & Jude: 190–91
Favoritism
Colossians & Philemon: 172
Fear
Mark 9–16: 85, 92, 403, 416–18
Luke 1–5: 27, 157, 308, 309, 324–25
Luke 6–10: 223, 224, 286
2 Corinthians: 434
Hebrews: 98, 356–57
2 Peter & Jude: 203–4
of God's presence
Mark 1–8: 106–7, 234–35, 248
of Herod Antipas
Mark 1–8: 303–5, 309–10
of man
Mark 1–8: 192
Fear of death, deliverance from
Romans 1–8: 434
Fear of God
Mark 1–8: 106–7, 234–35, 248
Luke 11–17: 118–19
Luke 18–24: 386–87
Fear of men before God
Matthew 8–15: 46
Fear of the Lord
Philippians: 160
***Fearfully and Wonderfully Made* (Paul Brand)**
Romans 9–16: 164
Fearing God
Romans 1–8: 192
Feast of Passover. *see* Passover
Feast of Purim
Matthew 24–28: 139
Feast of Tabernacles (Booths)
Matthew 16–23: 66
Matthew 24–28: 139
Mark 9–16: 7, 268
Luke 1–5: 191
Luke 6–10: 285
John 1–11: 5, 278–81, 288, 300–302, 311–12, 334
Revelation 1–11: 226
Feast of the Dedication (Feast of Lights)
Matthew 24–28: 139
John 1–11: 5, 438–41
Feast of Unleavened Bread
Mark 9–16: 268
Luke 18–24: 265, 278
John 1–11: 89–91
Feasts
Mark 9–16: 268, 322
Luke 1–5: 191
2 Peter & Jude: 180
Feeding of the five thousand
Mark 1–8: 390
Luke 6–10: 57, 250–55
location of
Mark 1–8: 318
organization of
Mark 1–8: 319–20
scale of
Mark 1–8: 312–13, 321
Feeding of the four thousand
Mark 1–8: 388–90
Feelings. *see* Emotions

Feinberg, Charles L.
Romans 9–16: 102–3
on Babylonian shrines to Ishtar
Revelation 12–22: 158
Felicitas and Perpetua, martyrdom of
Colossians & Philemon: 153
Felix
John 12–21: 85
2 Corinthians: 31
2 Peter & Jude: 65
Fellow elders
1 Peter: 264, 266
Fellowship
Acts 1–12: 84
Hebrews: 69, 184, 268, 276, 311
1–3 John: 18–19, 99
with Christ
1 Peter: 46–47
examples of
Colossians & Philemon: 189–99, 213
importance of
Colossians & Philemon: 189–99, 229–31
James: 279
overview of
2 Corinthians: 236–37
restoration of
2 Corinthians: 60–61
spiritual
Titus: 165
Feminine–deity versions of Bible
Titus: 81
Feminism
Matthew 16–23: 161
Acts 13–28: 90
1 Corinthians: 256
Ephesians: 273, 283–84, 339
Titus: 79, 84
demanding revenge
Titus: 82
origin of
Titus: 80
radical
Titus: 79, 81, 86
true victims of
Titus: 87
Festival tithe
Romans 9–16: 232
Festus
1 Timothy: xi
Fever
Mark 1–8: 73
Fickleness
about Christ
Matthew 8–15: 101
spiritual
Galatians: 118
Fiery trials
1 Peter: 247–60
Fig tree
Luke 6–10: 61
Luke 11–17: 189–90
John 1–11: 73
cursing of the
Mark 9–16: 132, 134, 139, 141, 142, 258
parable of
Luke 18–24: 243, 247
Fighting God, folly of
Acts 1–12: 319–20
Figurative language
John 12–21: 224, 225, 229
Figures of speech
Hebrews: 371–72
Fillmore, Mrs. Charles
Ephesians: 277
Final tribulation
Mark 9–16: 253
See also Tribulation, the Great
Finney
Galatians: 153
Fire(s)
Luke 18–24: 206–7, 230
2 Peter & Jude: 202–3
eternal
2 Peter & Jude: 165–67
as metaphor
Luke 1–5: 223
First and Last
John 1–11: 14
The first day of the week
Luke 18–24: 409
First resurrection. *see* Believer(s), resurrection of
First Triumvirate
Luke 1–5: 143
First World War
Luke 11–17: 152
Firstborn
Luke 1–5: 168, 170, 196
Hebrews: 30
Fish
Luke 18–24: 436
Fishermen
Mark 1–8: 51, 230
Luke 1–5: 331
Fishers of men
Mark 1–8: 51, 54
Fishing
Luke 1–5: 303–9
disciples return to
John 12–21: 390–93
industry
Mark 1–8: 50, 51, 60, 72
Flagellation. *see* Asceticism
Flat bread
Mark 9–16: 286, 287
See also Bread
Flattery
Mark 9–16: 177, 178
Luke 18–24: 133–34
Romans 1–8: 188
evil of
Matthew 16–23: 318, 320
Flavel, John
1 Timothy: 178, 263
Fleming, Alexander
1 Peter: 49–50
The Flesh
Matthew 24–28: 194
John 1–11: 97–99, 337–39
1 Corinthians: 68–71
Ephesians: 245, 247, 249, 250, 253, 367
James: 49, 50–51
2 Peter & Jude: 172–73

Christian's battle with
Romans 1–8: 418
Christian's victory over
Romans 1–8: 422
denying
Matthew 1–7: 149
self–deceptive
Matthew 16–23: 152
unable to do good
Matthew 16–23: 359
Flesh and blood. *see* Incarnation
Fleshliness
Colossians & Philemon: 108, 127–28, 135–50
Fleshly boasting
2 Corinthians: 380–82
Fleshly methods, disdain of
2 Corinthians: 342–43
Fleshly wisdom
2 Corinthians: 34
Flock of God
1 Peter: 262
The Flood (Great Flood)
Mark 1–8: 270
Luke 18–24: 186, 254
John 12–21: 205
Romans 1–8: 90
2 Peter & Jude: 87–88, 114, 118–20, 160, 162
Revelation 1–11: 27, 190, 203, 272
Revelation 12–22: 120, 158
Flute–players
Mark 1–8: 263, 264
Following
Mark 1–8: 51, 52
Food
diversity/variety of
Luke 11–17: 34
spiritual
Mark 1–8: 321, 322
Foolish boasting
2 Corinthians: 379–80
"Fool's gold" doctrinal
1–3 John: 152, 160
Foot washing
John 12–21: 5, 65–69, 75
1 Peter: 277–79
Foreknowledge
Acts 1–12: 63
Romans 9–16: 99
1 Peter: 19–21, 82–83, 89
Foreordination
Romans 1–8: 495
Forfeiting Christ
Matthew 16–23: 198
Forgeries, pious
2 Peter & Jude: 1, 12–13
Forgiveness
Matthew 1–7: 190–91, 314, 391–95, 397–98
Mark 9–16: 148–149
Luke 1–5: 114, 206–9, 321–24, 322
Luke 6–10: 110, 175, 176
John 12–21: 90–91, 133
Acts 1–12: 75, 117, 303
1 Corinthians: 140
Ephesians: 195
Colossians & Philemon: 42, 201–35, 209
Hebrews: 137, 216, 238–39
2 Peter & Jude: 24, 34
affirmation of
2 Corinthians: 58–59
antinomianism and
1–3 John: 34, 39
apart from works
Luke 11–17: 315–16
by believers
Luke 11–17: 42, 46
Christ and
2 Corinthians: 54
2 Peter & Jude: 24
1–3 John: 34–35
Christ's authority in
Luke 18–24: 112
in Christ's name
Luke 18–24: 444–45
Christ's substitutionary death and
1–3 John: 34–35
cleansing and
1–3 John: 36–37
comfort and
2 Corinthians: 58
completeness of
Colossians & Philemon: 109–12
confession and (*see* Confession)
divinely empowered
Matthew 16–23: 157
extent of
Matthew 16–23: 145–46
through faith
Luke 18–24: 20
fellowship restoration and
2 Corinthians: 60–61
godliness and
Matthew 16–23: 142–43
God's
Matthew 8–15: 304
Mark 1–8: 104
Luke 11–17: 369–70
1 & 2 Thessalonians: 247
humility and
Luke 11–17: 378–83
illustrations of
Colossians & Philemon: 112, 201–2, 232–35
importance of
Luke 11–17: 381–83
judicial
Luke 11–17: 39–40
1–3 John: 35–36
kinds of
Matthew 16–23: 156
lack of
Matthew 16–23: 152
love and (See also Love)
Romans 1–8: 483
2 Corinthians: 58–59, 238–39
of Matthew
Mark 1–8: 116
mercy and
2 Corinthians: 56–57
obedience and
2 Corinthians: 59–60

overview of
2 Corinthians: 49–53
of the paralytic
Mark 1–8: 102–7
of the penitent thief
Luke 18–24: 387
of Peter
Luke 18–24: 327–28
Pharisees and
Luke 11–17: 350
and prayer
Mark 9–16: 148–49
pride and
2 Corinthians: 53–56
principles of
Colossians & Philemon: 218–20
reconciliation and
2 Corinthians: 201–6
relational
Luke 11–17: 41, 42
and repentance
Matthew 24–28: 219
Mark 1–8: 22
Luke 18–24: 444
and restoration of joy
2 Corinthians: 57–58
sanctifying
1–3 John: 35, 36
Satan's schemes vs.
2 Corinthians: 61
of sin
Matthew 8–15: 52
Mark 1–8: 96, 97, 107, 125
Luke 11–17: 39–41, 236
Luke 18–24: 112, 443–44
Acts 13–28: 26, 336
spiritual growth and
1–3 John: 73
spiritual unity and
Matthew 16–23: 143
tests of
1–3 John: 33–36
and trust
Matthew 16–23: 157
and unity
Matthew 16–23: 143
unlimited
Matthew 16–23: 145
Luke 11–17: 43, 44
as unnatural to man
Matthew 16–23: 142
virtue of
Matthew 16–23: 143

Formalism
Galatians: 61
Hebrews: 251

Fornication
Romans 1–8: 108
2 Peter & Jude: 100–101

Fort Antonia
Luke 18–24: 103

Fortitude
1 Peter: 285–86

Fortunatus
1–3 John: 246

Fortune–tellers
Matthew 24–28: 2

Foundations
Luke 6–10: 119–20

Four living creatures, identification of
Revelation 1–11: 153

Foursquare pentecostalism
Ephesians: 277

Fox, John
John 12–21: 189

Foxes
Luke 11–17: 229–30

Frame, John M.
Luke 1–5: 54

France
Luke 11–17: 244

Franklin, Benjamin
Luke 18–24: 140

Free Grace
1–3 John: 140, 141

Free will
2 Peter & Jude: 34–35

Freedom
Christian
Romans 9–16: 288
and free men
1 Peter: 103, 151–52
human
Ephesians: 207
moral
Titus: 136
religious
2 Timothy: 59
sexual
Titus: 81

Freedom of worship
Romans 9–16: 208

French Revolution
Ephesians: 282

Freystein, Johann B.
Ephesians: 375

Friends
Luke 11–17: 53, 54, 56, 183, 310, 363

Friends of Jesus
chosen by Him
John 12–21: 162–63
divine truth and
John 12–21: 160–62
love and
John 12–21: 156–58
obedience and
John 12–21: 158–60

Fromm, Erich
2 Timothy: 109

Fruit
John 12–21: 145, 146, 149–50, 163
godly
Romans 1–8: 45, 362

Fruit–bearing
Mark 1–8: 205–7, 212

"The Fruit of the Spirit"
1–3 John: 54

Fruit of the vine
Luke 18–24: 281–82

Fruitfulness
Luke 6–10: 194–96, 201

2 Corinthians: 145–46
salvation and
Matthew 16–23: 278
spiritual
Matthew 24–28: 108
Colossians & Philemon: 31–32
Fruitless autumn trees metaphor
2 Peter & Jude: 181
Fruitlessness, spiritual
Romans 1–8: 364
Fry, Elizabeth Gurney
prison reforms of
Colossians & Philemon: 165
Fuchida, Mitsuo
conversion of
Colossians & Philemon: 232–35
Fulfilling all righteousness
Mark 1–8: 31–33
Fuller, Francis
on repentance
James: 212
Fulness of time
Mark 1–8: 48
Fulvia
Mark 1–8: 308
Funerals
Mark 1–8: 263–64
ancient Jewish
Matthew 8–15: 84
attending
Luke 6–10: 320
children and
Luke 6–10: 164
Christ and
Luke 6–10: 138, 326
Jewish customs regarding
Luke 6–10: 135, 137, 235–36
Futile life
1 Peter: 75
Future, current fascination with
Revelation 1–11: 13–15
Future Millennium
1 Peter: 120

Gabriel
Luke 1–5: 21–22, 28–29, 35, 39, 43–44, 51, 59, 68, 77
Luke 6–10: 144, 258, 260
John 1–11: 49
2 Peter & Jude: 98
Gadara
Mark 1–8: 241
Luke 6–10: 219, 229
Gaebelein, Frank E.
Luke 1–5: 201
John 1–11: 481
Gaius
Luke 6–10: 125
2 Corinthians: 480
character of
1–3 John: 244, 245
friends of John and
1–3 John: 260
hospitality of
1–3 John: 247–48
John's commendation of
1–3 John: 246–47
John's concern for
1–3 John: 245–46
John's counsel to
1–3 John: 247–49, 259
Galatia
Galatians: xi
Galatian church
1 Peter: 15–16, 91, 170
Galatians, Paul's letter to
2 Corinthians: 17–18, 25, 44–73, 83–116, 124–58, 207–37, 292, 305, 320–60, 372–95, 400–446, 459–89
Galen
Luke 1–5: 12
Galilean ministry
Luke 6–10: 324, 338
Galileans
Luke 6–10: 14, 60, 64, 75, 179, 339
Galilee
Matthew 1–7: 105–8
Mark 9–16: 34, 113, 114, 297, 349, 404
Luke 1–5: 147, 265–68, 282, 302, 320
Luke 6–10: 124, 133, 145, 152, 171, 240
Luke 11–17: 228
Luke 18–24: 71, 271, 451
John 12–21: 6
Christ's return to
Luke 6–10: 339
description of
Luke 6–10: 188, 250
Herod Antipas's rule of
Mark 1–8: 300
Luke 6–10: 247
as Jesus' home
Mark 1–8: 29
Jesus' ministry in
Mark 1–8: 47, 271, 284, 286, 312
Luke 6–10: 2, 40, 171, 179, 240
Jewish disdain for
Mark 1–8: 28
Judean view of
Luke 6–10: 177, 180
Sea of Galilee in
Luke 6–10: 208
the Twelve's ministry in
Luke 6–10: 240
unbelief of
Mark 1–8: 401
Galilee, Sea of. *see* Sea of Galilee (Sea of Chinnereth, Sea of Tiberius)
Galilei, Galileo
Romans 9–16: 88
Gallio (Roman proconsul)
Luke 18–24: 210
2 Corinthians: 3–4
1 & 2 Thessalonians: 8
Gamaliel
John 12–21: 24
Acts 1–12: 172–73, 193
2 Corinthians: 386
Gamow, George
on atomic forces
Colossians & Philemon: 49

Gandhi, Mahatma
Matthew 8–15: 73
2 Timothy: 187
Garden of Eden
Luke 1–5: 253
Luke 6–10: 84
John 1–11: 342, 376
2 Corinthians: 334
1 Peter: 212–14
2 Peter & Jude: 157–58
1–3 John: 153, 252
Revelation 1–11: 65, 153, 254
Garden of Gethsemane. *see* Gethsemane
Garland, David E.
2 Corinthians: 6, 453, 486, 491
Garments
2 Peter & Jude: 203–4
Gaul
Luke 18–24: 212
John 12–21: 170
Gehazi
Luke 1–5: 313–14
Gehenna
Mark 9–16: 47–48
Luke 11–17: 118
1 Peter: 210
Revelation 12–22: 255–56
See also Hell
Geisler, Norman L.
2 Peter & Jude: 56
Gemara
Mark 1–8: 342
Gender–neutral Bibles
Titus: 81
Genealogies
Luke 1–5: 45, 244–50
Jesus'
Matthew 1–7: 2–3, 7–9
Jewish
Matthew 1–7: 2–4
General revelation
Acts 13–28: 360–62
1–3 John: 227, 228
Generation
Mark 9–16: 259
Luke 6–10: 163, 292, 293
The generation (in Olivet Discourse)
Luke 18–24: 244, 245, 246, 247
Generosity
Luke 6–10: 110, 126–27
1 Peter: 116
and giving
2 Corinthians: 279–80, 306–7
of God
Ephesians: 25
as mark of salvation
Matthew 24–28: 125
prosperity and
2 Corinthians: 279–80, 315–17
Gennesaret
Mark 1–8: 333, 334
Luke 1–5: 302
Gennesaret, Lake. *see* Sea of Galilee
Gentile evangelism
Luke 18–24: 445–47
Gentiles
Mark 9–16: 138, 139, 140
Luke 11–17: 223–24
Luke 18–24: 125, 182, 224
John 12–21: 20–22, 24–30
baptism of
Mark 1–8: 29
centurion
Luke 6–10: 124, 126
in Crete churches
Titus: 4
faith of
Matthew 8–15: 12
of Galilee
Mark 1–8: 28
gospel extension to
Mark 1–8: 362–64, 391–92
Jewish disdain for
Romans 9–16: 109
Jewish people and
Luke 1–5: 142, 209, 276–77
Luke 6–10: 129, 147, 242
Jewish people eating with
Mark 1–8: 387–88
Jewish prejudice against
Romans 1–8: 227
Judaism's attitude toward
Luke 6–10: 103
Luke as
Luke 1–5: 1–2, 11, 15–16
Mark's gospel addressing
Luke 1–5: 290
Philip and
Luke 6–10: 57, 58
receptiveness of
Mark 1–8: 392
salvation and
Matthew 8–15: 14
Mark 9–16: 381
Luke 1–5: 134, 180–82
Luke 6–10: 85, 311
Acts 1–12: 310
Gentleness. *see* Meekness
Genuineness
Matthew 8–15: 159
2 Corinthians: 466–71
George III (king of Great Britain)
Luke 11–17: 397
Gerasa
Mark 1–8: 241, 242, 374
Luke 6–10: 208, 219
Gerasene demoniac
Luke 6–10: 165, 170, 328
Gerasenes
Mark 1–8: 227, 241
Gersa. *see* Gerasa
Gerstner, John
Matthew 8–15: 398
Gethsemane
Mark 9–16: 296, 299–301, 305
Luke 6–10: 27, 29, 80, 284, 310
John 12–21: 39, 43, 140, 306
Hebrews: 124
2 Peter & Jude: 3, 51
crowd in
Luke 18–24: 311, 313

disciples' flight from
Luke 18–24: 295
location of
Luke 18–24: 300, 317
prayer in
Mark 9–16: 301–4
temptation in
Mark 9–16: 300–301, 304
Ghost
Mark 1–8: 330
Gibbs, Sir Philip
Ephesians: 66
Gideon
Mark 9–16: 102
Luke 1–5: 64–65
Luke 6–10: 38, 39, 144
John 1–11: 212
Hebrews: 364
Giftedness, divine
2 Timothy: 16
Gifts
2 Peter & Jude: 21, 29
of Christ to church
Ephesians: 133–49
discontentment with
1 Corinthians: 314–16
giving of (See also Giving)
Luke 1–5: 140
grace
Romans 9–16: 131
identifying
Romans 9–16: 162
purpose of
1 Corinthians: 297
spiritual
Acts 13–28: 43–44
Romans 9–16: 154, 162–63
1 Corinthians: 18–19, 314–16
Ephesians: 136
Hebrews: 49–50, 81, 156
1 Peter: 242–45
uniqueness of
Matthew 16–23: 132
use of
Romans 9–16: 162–63
See also Giving
Gilder, George
Titus: 82
Gilgal
1 Peter: 108
Gillars, Mildred Elizabeth ("Axis Sally")
Luke 6–10: 74
John 12–21: 72
Gingrich, F. W.
2 Peter & Jude: 215
Ginott, Haim
on criticism
Colossians & Philemon: 172
Girty, Simon
Luke 6–10: 73–74
John 12–21: 72
Giving
Matthew 1–7: 351–60, 411–13
Mark 9–16: 221–23
Luke 11–17: 100, 333–34
Luke 18–24: 167–71
1 Corinthians: 451–57
2 Corinthians: 280
Hebrews: 179
Christian values and
2 Corinthians: 285–86
circumstances and
2 Corinthians: 277–78
generosity and
2 Corinthians: 279–80, 306–7
grace and
2 Corinthians: 276–77
joy and
2 Corinthians: 278
love and
2 Corinthians: 286
motivation for
2 Corinthians: 276–77
overview of
2 Corinthians: 271–76
poverty and (*See also* Poverty)
2 Corinthians: 278–79
privilege vs. obligation
2 Corinthians: 283–84
proportionality of
2 Corinthians: 280
sacrifice and
2 Corinthians: 280
selfless
Romans 1–8: 42
submission and
2 Corinthians: 285
voluntary
2 Corinthians: 281–83, 299–300
worship and
2 Corinthians: 284
Gleaning
Romans 9–16: 232
Global devastation
Mark 9–16: 254, 255
Glorification
Luke 18–24: 141–42
Ephesians: 365
2 Peter & Jude: 25–26
of believers
John 12–21: 268, 277, 298, 299
Romans 9–16: 260
Titus: 120
in High Priestly prayer
John 12–21: 241–42
of Jesus
John 12–21: 136, 137, 140, 249, 254–55
justification and
Romans 1–8: 442, 443
ultimate
Romans 1–8: 279, 447, 500
Glorified bodies
2 Corinthians: 161–65
Glorifying God
Matthew 1–7: 246–47
Matthew 24–28: 331
Luke 11–17: 15
John 12–21: 248, 249, 250
Romans 1–8: 83
Romans 9–16: 124
2 Corinthians: 317–18

Ephesians: 12, 15, 26, 31, 54, 55, 60, 97, 100, 154, 224, 258–59, 262, 267, 380
Hebrews: 380
Glory
Luke 1–5: 49, 156–57, 160–61
2 Peter & Jude: 29–30
divine
Romans 9–16: 124
intrinsic
Romans 9–16: 124
seeking eternal
Matthew 16–23: 240
Glory of Christ
Mark 9–16: 3, 4, 5, 13
Glory of God
Luke 1–5: 156–57
Luke 11–17: 32
Acts 1–12: 203
Romans 9–16: 124
1 Corinthians: 15, 30
Ephesians: 96
1 Peter: 45–46, 63, 83, 93, 115–16, 128, 141, 245–46, 252–53, 256, 266, 270–71, 287
Revelation 12–22: 172, 267, 279
believers' desire for
Romans 1–8: 130
believers devotion to
Romans 1–8: 130, 225
creation and
Romans 1–8: 298
devotion to
Romans 1–8: 225
elements of
Romans 1–8: 83
incarnation and
Romans 1–8: 84
Moses and
Luke 6–10: 280
as motivation for believers' suffering
Romans 1–8: 447
prayer and
Luke 11–17: 10–11
in salvation
Romans 1–8: 27
salvation and
Romans 1–8: 27
Shekinah (*see* Shekinah glory)
unveiled
Matthew 24–28: 57
Glueck, Sheldon and Eleanor
Ephesians: 316
Gnostic literature, ancient
Titus: 81
Gnostics/Gnosticism
Matthew 1–7: 76
Luke 1–5: 237
John 1–11: 4, 20
1 Corinthians: 285
Colossians & Philemon: 6–7
1 Timothy: xi, 152
Hebrews: 25
2 Peter & Jude: 5, 9–10, 14–15, 31, 143–45, 159–60
Revelation 1–11: 134, 137
arrogance of
1–3 John: 9
"Christ spirit" tenet of
1–3 John: 100
core doctrine of
Titus: 81
denial of Christ's deity and humanity
1–3 John: 15, 192, 233
denial of reality of sin
1–3 John: 27
Greek
Titus: 67, 80
John's opposition to
1–3 John: 7
as philosophical dualism
1–3 John: 8, 27
as philosophy
1–3 John: 8
as secret, transcendent knowledge
1–3 John: 15, 55
God
abandonment of rebellious mankind by
Romans 1–8: 99
absolute sovereignty of
Matthew 24–28: 288
abundance of grace
Romans 1–8: 317
access to
Hebrews: 118, 226–27, 234, 238–40, 247, 260–61, 415
agape love for believers
1–3 John: 115–16
arguments for existence of
Acts 13–28: 132–34
aspects of true grace of
Romans 1–8: 122, 199, 201, 239, 287, 297, 303, 314, 315, 316, 321, 342, 353, 478
attributes of
Luke 11–17: 292
Romans 1–8: 60, 62
Revelation 1–11: 1
authority of
Luke 11–17: 46, 382
believers' love for
1–3 John: 58–59
believers' pursuit of
1 & 2 Thessalonians: 96
blessedness of
1 Timothy: 274
blessings and mercy of
Romans 1–8: 115
and call to ministry
1 Timothy: 270
character of
Hebrews: 360
2 Peter & Jude: 121–23
children of (*see* Children of God)
and Christ's death timetable
Luke 18–24: 264, 266, 269, 275
common grace of
1 Timothy: 168
compassion of
Matthew 8–15: 191
Mark 1–8: 392–93
Mark 9–16: 27
1 Timothy: 29

1–3 John: 166
conditional promises of
Romans 9–16: 120
confirmation of promises
Luke 1–5: 63–72
covenant name of (See also Yahweh)
Matthew 16–23: 137
as Creator
Romans 1–8: 414
Colossians & Philemon: 47–50
James: 54
Revelation 1–11: 285
Revelation 12–22: 88–89
credibility of
Luke 18–24: 221–22
curse on mankind
Mark 9–16: 56–57
decrees of
1 Timothy: 70
decretive will of
Luke 11–17: 28
divine compassion of
Luke 11–17: 236–39
and divorce
Mark 9–16: 55
and election
1 Timothy: 69
eternality of
1 Timothy: 33, 277
Revelation 1–11: 157–58, 285, 315
evidence of
Matthew 16–23: 2
Hebrews: 307–9
exaltation of
Ephesians: 139
existence of
Luke 11–17: 13–14
faithfulness of
Matthew 16–23: 217
Luke 1–5: 174
Romans 1–8: 475
1 & 2 Thessalonians: 296
false concepts of
Romans 1–8: 72, 119
false views of
Matthew 1–7: 433
family of
Mark 1–8: 186–88
as Father and Son (*See also* God the Father)
Mark 1–8: 36, 37
as Father of Israel
Romans 9–16: 13
fatherhood of
Matthew 1–7: 80–82, 375–77, 421–25, 445–46
Luke 11–17: 11–14, 56, 57
fear in presence of
1–3 John: 144
fear of
Luke 11–17: 118–19
Luke 18–24: 386–87
Romans 1–8: 192
Revelation 12–22: 87
fellowship with
Ephesians: 380
folly of fighting
Acts 1–12: 319–20
foreknowledge of
Acts 1–12: 63
Romans 9–16: 99
1 Peter: 19–21, 82–83, 89–90
and forgiveness
Matthew 8–15: 304
Mark 1–8: 104
Luke 11–17: 369–70
fullness of
Ephesians: 99–113
generosity of
Ephesians: 25
glorifying (*see* Glorifying God)
glorifying Himself
Romans 9–16: 124
glory of (*see* Glory of God)
goodness of
James: 54
grace of
Matthew 1–7: 4–9, 191–92
Luke 1–5: 46–47, 55, 88–90
Luke 11–17: 326
Romans 1–8: 122, 199, 201, 239, 287, 297, 303, 314, 315, 316, 317, 321, 342, 353, 478
Galatians: 28
1 Timothy: 168
Titus: 112
1–3 John: 141–45
Revelation 12–22: 100
gratitude to
Matthew 8–15: 46
greatness of grace
Romans 1–8: 303
hidden will of
Luke 11–17: 28
holiness of
Romans 1–8: 173
1 & 2 Thessalonians: 71
1 Timothy: 277
James: 48, 54
Revelation 1–11: 155
immortality of
1 Timothy: 33
immutability of
James: 54
impartiality of
Matthew 1–7: 348
Matthew 16–23: 208
Acts 1–12: 300–301
Romans 9–16: 198
James: 93, 97
impartiality of grace
Romans 1–8: 136, 239
impeccability of
James: 47
importance of knowledge of
Acts 13–28: 129
integrity of
Romans 1–8: 171
Romans 9–16: 100
invincibility of
1 Timothy: 273

and Israel
Luke 11–17: 248–50
joy of
Luke 11–17: 291–301
as Judge
1–3 John: 27, 43–48, 167
Revelation 1–11: 148, 151, 156, 157, 268, 317
Revelation 12–22: 89
judgment of
Matthew 1–7: 72
Matthew 8–15: 114, 377
Matthew 16–23: 34, 57, 391
John 12–21: 42
Romans 1–8: 71, 173
1 & 2 Thessalonians: 240–42
Revelation 12–22: 84, 87, 108–11, 113–14, 120–23, 137, 143, 175–76
justice of
Mark 9–16: 269–70
Acts 13–28: 27
Romans 1–8: 219, 297
Revelation 12–22: 246
kingdom of (*see* Kingdom of God)
knowing
1–3 John: 55–56, 75–77, 165
knowing will of
Colossians & Philemon: 28–30
law of ancient Israel and
Romans 1–8: 357
law of Christian life and
Romans 1–8: 60, 364, 376
leading of
Matthew 1–7: 403–4
and light
Mark 9–16: 3
as Light
1–3 John: 23–25
lordship
Romans 1–8: 78
love for
Mark 9–16: 196, 201, 203, 275
love for Israel
Luke 11–17: 245
love of
Luke 6–10: 45
Romans 1–8: 373
Romans 9–16: 100
Philippians: 166–67
1 & 2 Thessalonians: 20, 287
Hebrews: 392
1–3 John: 244
love of believers and
Romans 1–8: 223
love of sinners
Romans 1–8: 305
majesty of
Matthew 8–15: 37
Revelation 12–22: 175
mankind's conception of
Luke 11–17: 50
man's compromising of revelation
Romans 1–8: 88
man's disposition against
Romans 1–8: 92, 183
man's search for
Mark 9–16: 74–75
men's fear of
Matthew 8–15: 46
mercy of
Matthew 24–28: 114
Mark 1–8: 96–97
Romans 9–16: 141
Philippians: 206
misjudgment of
Matthew 24–28: 106
movement in history
Luke 18–24: 396–98
and mystery of election
1 Timothy: 69
names of
Matthew 1–7: 377–79
Luke 11–17: 16–18
1–3 John: 247, 248
natural revelation of
Romans 1–8: 79, 137
nature of
Romans 1–8: 380
1–3 John: 22–24
New Testament teaching about
Romans 1–8: 61, 70
obedience to
Romans 1–8: 426
of the Old Testament
1 Timothy: 69
Old Testament teaching about
Romans 1–8: 61
omnipotence of
Revelation 1–11: 156, 157, 315
omniscience of (See also Omniscience)
Mark 1–8: 328–29
Romans 1–8: 494
1 & 2 Thessalonians: 40
patience of
Mark 9–16: 158–59
Luke 18–24: 117
Romans 1–8: 101
peace with
Matthew 16–23: 262
Romans 1–8: 418
perfect love of
1–3 John: 81, 164, 167, 171
perfection
Romans 9–16: 63
personhood of
Philippians: 166
plan of
Matthew 1–7: 105, 381–86
Ephesians: 45
power of
Mark 9–16: 190, 297, 328
Luke 1–5: 91–92
Luke 6–10: 206–13
Acts 13–28: 49
Romans 1–8: 53
1 Timothy: 271
1 Peter: 36–37, 259–60
Revelation 12–22: 99–100
preceptive will of
Luke 11–17: 28

preeminence of
Ephesians: 32
promise of
Hebrews: 358
promises of
Luke 11–17: 248–50
Romans 1–8: 171
Romans 9–16: 120
provision by (*See also* Providence)
Matthew 1–7: 387–91
Matthew 8–15: 193
Mark 1–8: 290–91
Luke 1–5: 257, 258
Luke 11–17: 32–36, 140–41, 143–46
1 Timothy: 282
2 Peter & Jude: 27–28
purposes of
Revelation 12–22: 185–86
reasons for giving thanks to
Revelation 12–22: 194–95
reconciliation and will of
2 Corinthians: 199–201
redemptive plan of
Matthew 24–28: 128
redemptive revelation of
Romans 1–8: 237
and regeneration
Mark 1–8: 218
rejection of
Mark 1–8: 199
Romans 1–8: 82, 91, 102
and rejection of the proud
Matthew 16–23: 290
response to faith
Matthew 16–23: 250
revelation of
Romans 1–8: 79, 88, 137
righteousness of
Romans 1–8: 113, 187, 200, 267, 370
1–3 John: 25, 113–14
as sacred
Luke 11–17: 14–18
and salvation (*see* Salvation) satisfaction of
Hebrews: 263
saving purpose of
1 Timothy: 68
1–3 John: 107, 158
as Savior
Luke 11–17: 36–46
Romans 9–16: 134
1 Timothy: 69, 168
self–glorification
Matthew 24–28: 332
self–revelation in Scripture
Ephesians: 194
Shekinah glory (*see* Shekinah glory)
as shelter
Luke 11–17: 46–48
and sinners
1–3 John: 166
sinners condemned by
Romans 1–8: 396
sovereignty of (*see* Sovereignty of God)
spirit of (*see* Holy Spirit)
spiritual fathers' knowledge of
1–3 John: 75–77
sufficiency of grace
Titus: 112
as supreme
Luke 11–17: 27–30
taking grace for granted
Romans 1–8: 122
terror of
Matthew 16–23: 68
testing
Matthew 1–7: 93–95
titles
Luke 18–24: 155–56
Trinity and
1–3 John: 162–65
trust in
Mark 9–16: 22, 144, 145
truth and
Luke 18–24: 188–89
Hebrews: 162
unconditional promises of
Romans 1–8: 171
uniqueness of
1 Timothy: 33, 71
vengeance of
Revelation 1–11: 188–89
Revelation 12–22: 198
and vineyard owner parable
Luke 18–24: 123–25
walking with
Hebrews: 310–13
and widows
1 Timothy: 194, 195
will of
Matthew 1–7: 381–86, 403–4
Luke 1–5: 257, 260–61
Luke 11–17: 27–30
Luke 18–24: 303–5
Acts 13–28: 6
2 Corinthians: 199–201
Galatians: 7, 28
Colossians & Philemon: 28–30
1 Peter: 226–28
will of disposition
Luke 11–17: 28
wisdom/knowledge of
Luke 11–17: 398
witness of (*see* Testimony of God)
Word of (*see* Scripture; Word of God)
and Word of Old Testament
Romans 1–8: 356
worship of (*see* Worship)
wrath of
Mark 9–16: 302, 358
Luke 11–17: 74
Romans 1–8: 61, 62, 64, 65, 66, 72, 76, 100, 201, 373
1 & 2 Thessalonians: 29, 65–66, 163
Hebrews: 278, 418
1 Peter: 73, 77, 171
Revelation 12–22: 91, 238
See also God the Father; Holy Spirit; Jesus Christ
God–Man
John 1–11: 38
God the Father
1 Peter: 258–59

2 Peter & Jude: 17–37, 43–48, 57, 60, 105–10, 118–28, 130–31, 150–61, 175, 184–85, 208–109
affirmation of the Son
John 12–21: 39–41
as benefactor of
2 Corinthians: 211–13
Christian witness from
John 12–21: 181–82
at crucifixion
Mark 9–16: 375–81
disloyalty to
2 Corinthians: 354
as Father of mercies
2 Corinthians: 19–20
giving the kingdom
Luke 11–17: 146–48
glorification of
John 12–21: 248, 249, 250, 268
2 Corinthians: 317–18
as God of all comfort
2 Corinthians: 20
honoring
Luke 11–17: 116–19
Jesus as equal to
John 12–21: 239–40
and Jesus' authority
Mark 9–16: 153, 262
at Jesus' transfiguration
Mark 9–16: 8, 23
obedience required by
John 12–21: 117–19
provision of
Luke 11–17: 143–46
redemptive plan of
Mark 9–16: 267–70, 280, 344
rejection of Jesus by
Mark 9–16: 96
sovereignty of
Luke 11–17: 234

Goddess–worship, pagan
Titus: 82

Goddesses, pagan
Romans 1–8: 94

Godet, Frederic
John 12–21: 238, 242
Romans 9–16: 9

Godlessness, man's natural
Romans 1–8: 192

Godliness
2 Peter & Jude: 27–28, 41–42, 129
forgiveness and
Matthew 16–23: 142
hypocritical
Matthew 8–15: 325

Godly heritage
2 Timothy: 5

Godly living
description of
1 Peter: 135–36
inner discipline of
1 Peter: 137–39
motivation to
Galatians: 160
outward deportment of
1 Peter: 139–41

Godly love
Titus: 165

Godly women, acclamation of
Matthew 24–28: 284

Gods
false
Romans 1–8: 216
James: 47
man–made
Romans 1–8: 216
pagan
Romans 1–8: 216
1 Corinthians: 279–80, 466

God's law. *see* Law of God

God's people, designations of
1–3 John: 173–74

God's Word. *see* Word of God

***Godspell* (musical)**
John 1–11: 182

Golan Heights
Mark 1–8: 229
Luke 6–10: 208

Golden calf
Mark 1–8: 270

Golden Rule
Luke 6–10: 106–7
Romans 9–16: 253

Golgotha
Mark 9–16: 364, 379
John 12–21: 349

Goliath
John 1–11: 224

Gomer
Matthew 1–7: 42, 314
Mark 9–16: 60

Gomorrah. *see* Sodom and Gomorrah

Good and evil, problem of
Romans 9–16: 133

Good deeds, fruit of salvation
Matthew 24–28: 122

Good man
John 1–11: 25

Good news
Mark 1–8: 12, 13, 16, 26, 149
Luke 1–5: 29, 157–64

Good Samaritan
Luke 6–10: 357–58

Good Shepherd
2 Peter & Jude: 51, 96, 208

Good soil
Mark 1–8: 196, 201, 205, 211, 212
Luke 6–10: 189

Good stewards
1 Peter: 244

Good works
Mark 1–8: 110, 111
Mark 9–16: 71, 77, 238
Luke 18–24: 12, 14, 37
divinely provided
Matthew 16–23: 57
as evidence of faith
Romans 1–8: 129
as evidence of salvation
Matthew 16–23: 57, 278, 299, 312
godly
Galatians: 68

and salvation
Titus: 118
Gooding, David
Luke 18–24: 109, 420
Goodness
of God
James: 54
human
Matthew 16–23: 58
Ephesians: 55
man's presumed
Galatians: 205
of Old Covenant
Hebrews: 197
relative human
Romans 1–8: 144, 182–83
Gordon, S. D.
Matthew 8–15: 129
Gordon's Calvary
Luke 18–24: 366, 378
Gospel(s)
Matthew 1–7: 107–8, 125
Mark 1–8: 135–36, 175
Luke 1–5: 328
John 12–21: 20–22, 24–30
Philippians: 209
Colossians & Philemon: 11–24
Hebrews: xiii–xiv, 48–50, 63–64
Revelation 1–11: 26
Revelation 12–22: 86
addition to
Galatians: 57
beginning of proclamation of
1–3 John: 131
biblical
Matthew 16–23: 192
biblical foundation
Luke 18–24: 441–42
comprehensiveness of
1 & 2 Thessalonians: 47
divisiveness of
Acts 13–28: 373
essence of
Mark 9–16: 15, 385–86
Colossians & Philemon: 12–13
exclusivity of
Mark 1–8: 124–25, 193
1–3 John: 197
and faith
Romans 1–8: 259
false
Matthew 8–15: 113
Matthew 16–23: 45, 100, 354
Romans 1–8: 74–75, 353
Gentile understanding of
Mark 1–8: 14
global reach of
Mark 1–8: 362–64
Luke 18–24: 445–47
harmony of
Luke 18–24: 408
law and
Matthew 16–23: 193
meaning of
Mark 1–8: 12–14, 27, 47
offense of
Matthew 8–15: 102
perversion of
Matthew 16–23: 192
preaching of (*See also* Preaching)
Mark 9–16: 230
1–3 John: 224–26
proclamation of
Mark 1–8: 53, 167
1–3 John: 131
prosperity
Mark 9–16: 129
purpose of
Romans 1–8: 411
receptiveness to
Matthew 8–15: 195
rejection of
Matthew 8–15: 195
rejection of disobedience to God
Acts 13–28: 45, 141, 173
repentance and
Luke 18–24: 443–44
resurrection as main event of
Mark 9–16: 396
salvation through
1–3 John: 227
social evils and
Matthew 16–23: 267
supernatural power of
Luke 18–24: 448
true presentation of
Romans 1–8: 74
truth of
Romans 1–8: 398
Colossians & Philemon: 12
two pillars of
Galatians: 60
universality of
Colossians & Philemon: 21
1 Timothy: 60, 63, 72
See also Evangelism
Gospel invitation
Luke 11–17: 275
Gospel proclamation
Mark 1–8: 81, 206, 207, 217, 219, 286–87
Gossip
1 Corinthians: 350
2 Corinthians: 435
Gould, Stephen Jay
on absence of transitional forms
Acts 13–28: 137
Government
Mark 9–16: 180–81
Luke 6–10: 105
Luke 18–24: 135–36
Christian
Matthew 16–23: 83
divine authority of
Matthew 16–23: 90
human
Matthew 1–7: 331
Matthew 16–23: 83
human respect for
Titus: 141–42
limits of
Matthew 16–23: 90

prayer for leaders
Mark 9–16: 181
roles of
1 Peter: 149–50
submission to human
Matthew 16–23: 87
Grace
Mark 1–8: 112, 426
Mark 9–16: 64, 68, 70, 71, 181
Luke 1–5: 46, 47, 55, 88–90, 190
Luke 11–17: 326, 347, 350, 369
John 1–11: 42–43
John 12–21: 267
2 Corinthians: 276–77, 319, 402–5
Colossians & Philemon: 22–23
Hebrews: 238
1 Peter: 25–32, 52, 64–65, 124–25, 182–83, 244–45, 278–89
2 Peter & Jude: 21, 23–24, 161
aspects of
1 Timothy: 27
believers to use means of
1–3 John: 70
as blessing
1–3 John: 219
cheap
Romans 1–8: 353
common
1 Timothy: 168
1–3 John: 115, 166
definition of
1 & 2 Thessalonians: 14, 216
1 Timothy: 27
future benefits of
1 Corinthians: 19–20
of God
Matthew 1–7: 4–8, 191–92
Luke 1–5: 46–47, 55, 88–90
Luke 11–17: 326
Romans 1–8: 122, 199, 201, 239, 287, 297, 303, 314, 315, 316, 317, 321, 342, 353, 478
Galatians: 28
1 Timothy: 168
Titus: 112
1–3 John: 141–45
Revelation 12–22: 100
God's abundant
Romans 1–8: 317
God's sovereign
Galatians: 28
God's true
Romans 1–8: 122, 201, 239, 297, 321, 342, 353
gospel of
Galatians: 13
gratitude for God's
1–3 John: 141–45
greatness of God's
Romans 1–8: 303
growing in
Matthew 16–23: 48
1 Corinthians: 245
and guilt
1 Corinthians: 11
hearing of the gospel and
1–3 John: 227
holiness as product of God's
Romans 1–8: 316
impartiality of God's
Romans 1–8: 239
no–lordship or Free Grace view
1–3 John: 140, 141
past benefits of
1 Corinthians: 11–15
perverted views of God's
Romans 1–8: 314
present benefits of
1 Corinthians: 16–19
reasons for
1 Corinthians: 14–15
salvation and
1–3 John: 227
salvation by God's
Romans 1–8: 199
security in God's
Romans 1–8: 287
source of
1 Timothy: 27
sovereignty and
Romans 9–16: 32
special
1–3 John: 115
spiritual growth and
1–3 John: 70–71
sufficiency of God's
Romans 1–8: 478
Titus: 112
supposed additional works of
Ephesians: 46
taking for granted
Romans 1–8: 122
and works
1 Corinthians: 12–13
works not augmented by God's
Romans 1–8: 315
Grace gifts
Romans 9–16: 131
"Grace Greater Than Our Sin"
James: 290
Graciousness
1 Corinthians: 344
Ephesians: 188
Grafting, plant
Romans 9–16: 114
Grain
Mark 1–8: 141–43
Grain fields
Luke 6–10: 5
Grain offerings
Mark 9–16: 48–49
Grand Council
Luke 18–24: 332
Gratitude
Romans 1–8: 34
2 Corinthians: 189–92
Colossians & Philemon: 35–37, 93, 160
1–3 John: 141–45
to God
Matthew 8–15: 46

Gray, Thomas
Romans 1–8: 290
Great Awakening
John 1–11: 240
1–3 John: 139
Great Britain
Luke 18–24: 89
Great Commission
Matthew 8–15: 186
Matthew 24–28: 11
Mark 1–8: 384
Luke 6–10: 241
Luke 18–24: 440, 450, 451
2 Corinthians: 257–58, 432–33
James: 147
Great joy
2 Peter & Jude: 212–13
Great Sanhedrin
Mark 9–16: 321, 322
Luke 18–24: 330
See also Sanhedrin
Great Tribulation. *see* Tribulation, the Great
Great White Throne Judgment
Luke 6–10: 333
John 1–11: 199
James: 150, 196
2 Peter & Jude: 92–93, 184–86
1–3 John: 50
Revelation 1–11: 319
Revelation 12–22: 245
See also Judgment
Greatness
Mark 9–16: 103, 108, 109
Luke 1–5: 33, 35, 40, 48–49
Luke 6–10: 294, 301–3
human
1 Corinthians: 51
principles of spiritual
Matthew 16–23: 240
of salvation
1 Peter: 49–59
standards of worldly
Matthew 16–23: 235
true
Matthew 1–7: 49–50, 58
Greece
Luke 6–10: 37
Greed (Covetousness)
Matthew 1–7: 408–9
Matthew 16–23: 152
Mark 1–8: 357
Luke 11–17: 131–35, 344–45
Colossians & Philemon: 139–41
2 Timothy: 111
Hebrews: 432–34
See also Materialism
Greek culture
Ephesians: 66
Greek gnostics
Titus: 67
Greek gods, apathy of
Matthew 8–15: 112
Greek language
Luke 6–10: 236
aorist tense
Romans 1–8: 296
future tenses
Romans 1–8: 327
Granville Sharp rule
Romans 1–8: 496
Greek paganism
Mark 1–8: 374
Greek philosophy
Luke 6–10: 106–7
Romans 1–8: 54, 386
Hebrews: 209
Greek virtue
Ephesians: 127
Greeks
Luke 6–10: 41, 57
death and
Luke 18–24: 140
at Passover feast
John 12–21: 24–26
Green, E. M. B. (Michael)
2 Peter & Jude: 62, 113, 215
Greenland, death beliefs in
Luke 18–24: 140
Greetings
Luke 6–10: 329
Gregory of Nazianzus
2 Peter & Jude: 141
Grief
Mark 9–16: 294
Luke 18–24: 299, 300
Hebrews: 446–47
Grieving the Lord
Matthew 16–23: 154
Gross, Martin
Ephesians: 105
Gross immorality
2 Peter & Jude: 165–67
Growth, spiritual
Romans 1–8: 226, 325
1 Corinthians: 72
Philippians: 243, 250
Colossians & Philemon: 32–33
1 Peter: 100–101
assurance regarding
1–3 John: 72–77
forgiveness and
1–3 John: 73
grace and
1–3 John: 70–71
holiness as goal of
1–3 John: 70
misconceptions regarding
1–3 John: 70–72
overview of
1–3 John: 69–70
stages of
1–3 John: 69–77
Grudem, Wayne
Luke 1–5: 253
Grumblers
2 Peter & Jude: 190
Guaranteeing
Hebrews: 197
Guarantees, saints'
2 Peter & Jude: 205–13
Guardians
1 Peter: 173

Guilt
Mark 9–16: 85, 322
Luke 18–24: 333, 337, 347
Galatians: 46, 207
1 Peter: 74, 79, 239
causes of
Romans 1–8: 178
false ideas about causes
Romans 1–8: 178
feelings
Romans 1–8: 178
God–given warning
Romans 1–8: 2
grace and
1 Corinthians: 11
inescapability of
Romans 1–8: 178
as spiritual warning sign
Matthew 24–28: 226
Guilty conscience
Matthew 24–28: 185
Guinness, Os
on philosophical queries
Colossians & Philemon: 96–97
Gundry, Stanley N.
Luke 1–5: 3, 247, 296
John 1–11: 7
John 12–21: 63, 315
2 Peter & Jude: 143
Guthrie, Donald
John 1–11: 487
2 Corinthians: 6, 492
1 Peter: 8–9
2 Peter & Jude: 216
on apostolic authorship of Revelation
Revelation 1–11: 5
on dating of Acts
Acts 1–12: 4
on doctrinal importance of Acts
Acts 1–12: 2
on Greek vocabulary of Pastoral Epistles
1 Timothy: xiii
on Paul's release from his first Roman imprisonment
1 Timothy: xi
on slavery
Colossians & Philemon: 206
Guthrie, Thomas
Matthew 8–15: 385
Ephesians: 123, 368
Guyana
Luke 11–17: 255
Guyon, Madam
Romans 9–16: 180

Habakkuk
2 Corinthians: 14–15
Hades
Luke 6–10: 334
Luke 11–17: 364
John 1–11: 343–44
Hadrian, emperor
Romans 1–8: 164
Hagar
Luke 1–5: 108
Hakeldama (Field of Blood)
Acts 1–12: 33
Halakah
Matthew 8–15: 461
Galatians: 27
Haldane, Robert
Romans 1–8: 55, 190, 193, 392, 403, 408
Romans 9–16: 220, 225
Half–shekel tax
Romans 9–16: 232
"Hall of Shame"
1–3 John: 252–55
The Hallel
Mark 9–16: 286, 292
Luke 18–24: 280, 282
"Hallelujah, What a Savior!"
Luke 18–24: 75, 307
Hallowed
Luke 11–17: 15, 16
Hallucination theory
Luke 18–24: 432
John 12–21: 374–75
Haman
1–3 John: 254
Hamilton, Patrick
John 12–21: 189
Hammurabi
John 1–11: 48
Hand–washing
Mark 1–8: 341, 342, 345
Mark 9–16: 286
Handling snakes
Mark 9–16: 412
Hanna, Mark M.
1 Timothy: 287
on philosophy in Colossians
Colossians & Philemon: 100
Hannah
Luke 1–5: 25, 54, 60, 77, 94, 185
Luke 18–24: 2, 18, 287, 371
Hansen, G. H. A.
Luke 1–5: 313
Hansen's disease. *see* Leprosy
Hanukkah
Matthew 24–28: 139
Happiness
Matthew 1–7: 141–45
1–3 John: 109, 236–37
Hardness of heart
Matthew 16–23: 390
Matthew 24–28: 208
Mark 1–8: 85, 156, 184, 198, 199, 249, 359
John 12–21: 54
Acts 1–12: 220
Hebrews: 88, 92, 93
Hardy, G. B.
Matthew 8–15: 75
Harlot of Babylon
Matthew 24–28: 27
Harlotry, spiritual
John 1–11: 203–16
Revelation 12–22: 165
Harm, spiritual, to others
Matthew 16–23: 121
Harmagedon (Armageddon). *See* Armageddon
Luke 18–24: 203

Harmony
2 Corinthians: 249–50
Harris, Murray J.
2 Corinthians: 414, 492
Harris, R. Laird
Luke 1–5: 55
Harrison, Everett F.
2 Peter & Jude: 216
on meaning of Acts 10:35
Acts 1–12: 301
on Paul's discouragement in Corinth
Acts 13–28: 146
on Paul's friendship with Asiarchs
Acts 13–28: 187
Harrison, R. K.
Matthew 8–15: 6
Harvest
Mark 9–16: 167–68
Luke 6–10: 327, 328
John 1–11: 158–59
spiritual
Mark 1–8: 218
as symbol of judgment
Matthew 24–28: 62
Hasidim
Luke 1–5: 318
Luke 11–17: 97
John 1–11: 100
Hastening
2 Peter & Jude: 129
Hathor (cow–goddess)
Romans 1–8: 94
Hatred
Luke 6–10: 97, 98, 104
1–3 John: 81, 82, 131, 133–35
of Jesus
Luke 18–24: 131
"Have Thine Own Way Lord"
James: 230
Heading, John
John 1–11: 190, 487
Healers, faith
Matthew 16–23: 251
Mark 1–8: 74, 76, 409
Luke 1–5: 292, 294
Healing(s)
Mark 9–16: 111–12, 117–19
Luke 1–5: 291–95, 320–25
Luke 11–17: 258–60, 387–95
Luke 18–24: 63–64
1 Peter: 172–73
of blind Bartimaeus
Luke 18–24: 60, 61, 64, 72
Christ's compassion manifested by
Luke 18–24: 108
demonstrating Christ's power
Luke 6–10: 88
by the disciples
Luke 18–24: 125
divine
Matthew 1–7: 126–30
Colossians & Philemon: 105–6
divine, and faith
Matthew 8–15: 9, 15, 82, 92, 95
Matthew 16–23: 252
features of
Luke 18–24: 62–64
gift of
Acts 1–12: 96–98, 282
of Jairus's daughter
Luke 6–10: 230, 234–35
of the leper
Mark 1–8: 85–86, 86–89, 90–92, 92–93
of man with withered hand
Luke 6–10: 6–10
miracles of (*See also* specific miracles by name)
Mark 1–8: 84, 163, 164
John 1–11: 161–79
need for
Luke 6–10: 253
of paralytic
Mark 1–8: 101–3, 113
Luke 1–5: 320–25
of woman with hemorrhage
Luke 6–10: 232–33
Health
Luke 11–17: 141–42
spiritual
2 Timothy: 108
Health and wealth gospel
Luke 11–17: 8
Romans 1–8: 50
Hearst, William Randolph
Ephesians: 41
Heart
Matthew 1–7: 134–35, 202–7, 279–80, 280–82, 283–87, 360, 401, 404, 481
Mark 1–8: 352, 354, 357, 358, 359
Mark 9–16: 201
Luke 6–10: 186–87, 191, 302
Luke 11–17: 100, 348, 404
biblical meaning of
Colossians & Philemon: 85–86
1 & 2 Thessalonians: 91
hardening of
Matthew 16–23: 390
Matthew 24–28: 208
Mark 1–8: 85, 156, 184, 198, 199, 249, 359
John 12–21: 54
Acts 1–12: 220
Hebrews: 88, 92, 93
See also Righteousness
Heaven
Matthew 1–7: 457
Luke 6–10: 89, 112, 118–19, 237, 334, 342
Luke 11–17: 121, 357–60, 364–65, 367
Luke 18–24: 146, 151
John 1–11: 17–22, 32, 73–74, 239–54, 267, 286, 344, 353
John 12–21: 100–101, 110–11, 296–302
1 Corinthians: 21, 365–66
Hebrews: 414
1 Peter: 36–38, 57, 75, 172–73, 220–21, 267
1–3 John: 90, 201
believers to desire
Revelation 12–22: 262
believers to focus on
Revelation 12–22: 260–61
biblical description of
Revelation 12–22: 262

Christian's longing for
Romans 1–8: 393
equality in
Matthew 16–23: 215
focusing on
Colossians & Philemon: 125–33
personal relationships in
Matthew 16–23: 332
Heavenly mindedness
Hebrews: 331
Heavenly reward
Luke 11–17: 337, 338
Heavenly sanctuary
Hebrews: 208–9, 228–29
Hebraism
Luke 6–10: 163
Hedonism
John 1–11: 366
Ephesians: 56, 348
2 Timothy: 116
Titus: 50, 136, 149
James: 186– 87
1 Peter: 185–94
2 Peter & Jude: 119–20
1–3 John: 55
Heep, Uriah
Colossians & Philemon: 120
Hegel, Georg W. F.
2 Peter & Jude: 56
Heidegger, Martin
2 Peter & Jude: 56
Heine, Heinrich
Romans 1–8: 121
Titus: 88
Heinecken, Christian Friedrich
Luke 1–5: 188
Hell
Matthew 1–7: 69, 457
Luke 1–5: 10, 215–16, 223, 334
Luke 6–10: 81, 276
Luke 18–24: 221, 389, 390
John 1–11: 346–47, 354, 419
John 12–21: 152
Acts 1–12: 221
Romans 9–16: 40
1 Timothy: 167
Hebrews: 48, 108
1 Peter: 88
2 Peter & Jude: 84–86, 183–92
Revelation 12–22: 169, 170, 189, 224, 242
aspects of
Revelation 12–22: 256
as believers' motivation
Luke 11–17: 367
biblical truth about
1–3 John: 201
Christ's enduring of
Mark 9–16: 377
Christ's teaching on
Luke 11–17: 356–57
darkness of
Mark 9–16: 376
degrees of punishment in
Matthew 8–15: 265
Luke 6–10: 333
Luke 11–17: 164–65
Revelation 12–22: 254
demons sentenced to
Luke 6–10: 89, 222
as destiny for unredeemed
1–3 John: 86, 90, 200
destiny of all unbelievers
Romans 1–8: 397
as eternal punishment
1–3 John: 44, 91
eternality of
Philippians: 93–94
Revelation 12–22: 92, 199, 242–43
false prophets and
Luke 6–10: 112, 132
false religion and
1–3 John: 226
fear of God and
Luke 11–17: 118–19
forces of
Luke 6–10: 218, 340
as gehenna
Mark 9–16: 47–48
holiness of God and
1–3 John: 27
horror of
Matthew 8–15: 115, 398
as Lake of Fire
1–3 John: 50
leading sinners toward
Mark 9–16: 44, 218
nature of
Matthew 8–15: 397–98
Luke 6–10: 100, 237
as "outer darkness"
Mark 1–8: 401
reality of
Matthew 8–15: 397
Luke 11–17: 223
Satan to be cast into
1–3 John: 175
torment of
Luke 11–17: 365–66
and unbelief
Mark 1–8: 270
Luke 11–17: 124, 368
and unforgiven sin
Mark 1–8: 96
See also Satan
Hellenistic philosophy
2 Peter & Jude: 11
Hellenists (Greek–speaking Jews)
Acts 1–12: 178
Hellenization
John 1–11: 5, 100, 439
Help, withholding
Matthew 16–23: 116
Helpfulness
Matthew 1–7: 190
Helpless, God's compassion for
Matthew 16–23: 216
Hematridrosis
Luke 18–24: 306, 379
Hemer, Colin J.
on the difficulty of capturing Sardis's acropolis
Revelation 1–11: 110

Hemingway, Ernest
Acts 1–12: 319
Galatians: 184
1 Peter: 186
Hemorrhage
Mark 1–8: 258
Luke 6–10: 232–33
Hendriksen, William
Matthew 8–15: 7
Luke 1–5: 90, 268
John 1–11: 30–31, 158, 487–88
John 12–21: 229, 354
Romans 9–16: 364
Galatians: 17, 35, 64
Ephesians: 31, 264
2 Timothy: 193
on afflictions
1 & 2 Thessalonians: 80
on Christ's coronation
Philippians: 142–43
on God's completion of believers' salvation
Philippians: 29
on koinōnia
Philippians: 23
on the meaning of "sober"
1 & 2 Thessalonians: 160
on Paul's need of prayer
1 & 2 Thessalonians: 212
on progressive salvation
Colossians & Philemon: 150
on the restraining of the Antichrist
1 & 2 Thessalonians: 279
on the Scythians
Colossians & Philemon: 152
on the vocabulary of 1 Thessalonians
1 & 2 Thessalonians: 8
on worshiping angels
Colossians & Philemon: 120
Henley, William Ernest
Luke 11–17: 19
Henry, Matthew
Mark 1–8: 231
Romans 1–8: 343
Heppe, Heinrich
on meaning of repentance
Acts 13–28: 216
Heracleon
John 1–11: 4
Heraclius (Byzantine emperor)
Luke 11–17: 243
Heralds. *see* Messengers/heralds
Heresy(ies)
Galatians: 140
Ephesians: 40, 42, 220, 224, 277
2 Peter & Jude: 1–2, 14–15, 71–72, 114, 144–45
at Ephesus
1 Timothy: 16
kinds of
2 Timothy: 118
Heretics
John 12–21: 188
See also False teachers
Heritage, Jewish trust in
Romans 9–16: 3
Hermeneutics
Hebrews: 128
Hermogenes
2 Corinthians: 151
1–3 John: 80
Heroclitus (emperor)
Romans 1–8: 164
Herod I (the Great)
Matthew 1–7: 24–26, 31–32, 34, 43–46
Mark 1–8: 158, 190, 300, 301
Mark 9–16: 349
Luke 1–5: 22–23, 142, 145, 146, 201–2, 230, 318
Luke 6–10: 70, 247, 259
Luke 11–17: 226
Luke 18–24: 69, 78, 176, 266, 348, 349, 366
John 1–11: 24, 29, 93, 166, 325, 423
Acts 1–12: 320
Acts 13–28: 296, 327
Romans 1–8: 164
1 Peter: 2
Herod II (Herod Philip I)
Mark 1–8: 304
Mark 9–16: 349
Luke 1–5: 22, 202
Luke 6–10: 145
Herod Agrippa I
Mark 1–8: 170, 300
Mark 9–16: 107
Luke 1–5: 22, 225, 231
Luke 6–10: 199
Luke 18–24: 351
John 1–11: 365
John 12–21: 166, 192
Acts 1–12: 320–21
Acts 13–28: 31, 104, 248, 277, 310, 327
2 Corinthians: 177, 326, 433
1 Timothy: xi
1 Peter: 130
1–3 John: 255
Herod Agrippa II
Luke 1–5: 22
Acts 13–28: 327
Herod Antipas (Herod the Tetrarch)
Mark 9–16: 54, 349, 350
Luke 1–5: 22, 34, 201, 202, 204, 228, 230–32, 282, 330
Luke 6–10: 124, 183, 248, 260
Luke 11–17: 227–30, 232
Luke 18–24: 71, 342, 348–52
John 1–11: 132, 166, 220
John 12–21: 169, 182, 324
Acts 13–28: 4, 327
corrupt life of
Mark 1–8: 304
fear of
Mark 1–8: 303–5, 309–10
and Jesus
Mark 1–8: 285, 302, 309–10, 314
on Jesus' identity
Luke 6–10: 259
Jewish people and
Luke 6–10: 157, 250
John the Baptist and
Mark 1–8: 301–10
Luke 6–10: 145, 152, 153, 247

mockery of Jesus by
Mark 9–16: 350
tetrarchy of
Mark 1–8: 60, 300
Herod Archelaus
Matthew 1–7: 46–47
Mark 9–16: 349
Luke 1–5: 22, 202
Luke 6–10: 247
Luke 11–17: 228
Luke 18–24: 70, 78–79, 81
Herod Philip. *see* Herod II (Herod Philip I)
Herodian rulers
Matthew 8–15: 290
Mark 1–8: 157, 158, 165, 271, 306, 403, 404
Mark 9–16: 175–76, 180
Luke 1–5: 22, 23
Luke 6–10: 10
Luke 18–24: 131, 135, 162, 367
Herodias
Mark 1–8: 304, 306, 307, 308
Mark 9–16: 54, 349
Luke 1–5: 230–32
Luke 6–10: 145, 149
Luke 11–17: 228
Luke 18–24: 349, 351
John 1–11: 29
Herodotus
Mark 9–16: 408
Luke 1–5: 11
Romans 1–8: 89
Heroes of faith
Luke 6–10: 348
Hesiod
Matthew 8–15: 26
Hezekiah (king)
Luke 1–5: 65, 185
Luke 18–24: 2
John 1–11: 388, 394–95
2 Corinthians: 13, 251–52, 352
1 & 2 Thessalonians: 255–56
Hidden reefs metaphor
2 Peter & Jude: 179–80
Hidden shame
2 Corinthians: 125–28
Hidden things
Mark 1–8: 214, 221, 222
Hidden will of God
Luke 11–17: 28
Hiebert, D. Edmond
John 1–11: 488
1 Timothy: 119
Titus: 8
2 Peter & Jude: 10, 216
on importance of James
James: 2
on persecution
James: 4–5
on the "we passages" of Acts
Acts 1–12: 2
High priesthood
Matthew 24–28: 132
Mark 9–16: 336
High Priestly prayer (of Jesus)
for all believers
John 12–21: 273–74, 295–302
eternal plan of God and
John 12–21: 245–56
for His disciples
John 12–21: 260–61, 271–84
as Lord's Prayer
John 12–21: 244
setting of
John 12–21: 236–40
significance of
John 12–21: 243–44
substance of
John 12–21: 240–43
summary of
John 12–21: 302
See also Prayer
High priests
Mark 9–16: 186, 321
Luke 1–5: 26, 203
Luke 18–24: 143, 268, 333, 367
See also Annas; Caiaphas
Hillel (rabbi)
Mark 9–16: 54
Luke 6–10: 107
***Hina* clauses, Greek**
Titus: 78
Hinduism
Matthew 8–15: 111, 289
Luke 18–24: 150
Romans 1–8: 89, 95, 246, 336
Titus: 81
Hinnom, Valley of
Mark 9–16: 48
James: 157
Hippo, Council of
2 Peter & Jude: 9
Hiram
2 Corinthians: 114
Hired men
Luke 11–17: 312
Historical events, most significant
Luke 1–5: 103, 104
"Historical Jesus"
Luke 1–5: 300
History
purpose of
Acts 13–28: 18
redemptive
Romans 9–16: 259
various views of
1 & 2 Thessalonians: 139–41
Hitler, Adolf
Luke 6–10: 37
Luke 11–17: 244
1–3 John: 94
Revelation 1–11: 179
Revelation 12–22: 44
Hittites
John 12–21: 202–3
Hoarding
Matthew 1–7: 411
Hobbes, Thomas
2 Peter & Jude: 56

Hodge, Charles
Mark 9–16: 70
Luke 18–24: 30
Romans 1–8: 79, 105, 161, 268, 275, 285, 322, 361, 369
Romans 9–16: 98
2 Corinthians: 290–91
2 Peter & Jude: 56
Hoehner, Harold W.
Mark 9–16: 126
Luke 1–5: 145
John 12–21: 15, 63
Hoekema, Anthony A.
on the amillennial view of the Millennium
Revelation 12–22: 230
on the chronology of Revelation 19 and 20
Revelation 12–22: 234
on the naturalistic view of history
1 & 2 Thessalonians: 140
Holidays
Luke 1–5: 41–42
Holiness
Matthew 1–7: 202–8
Luke 18–24: 13
2 Corinthians: 33–34
Colossians & Philemon: 65, 126–28, 185–86
Hebrews: 67–68, 372, 396–97
1 Peter: 65–68, 102, 240–41
2 Peter & Jude: 34, 103, 110, 133
1–3 John: 25, 70, 113, 114
of believers
Galatians: 174
divine
Romans 1–8: 173
false
Galatians: 175
love and
Matthew 16–23: 129
necessity of
Matthew 16–23: 123, 129
personal
2 Timothy: 82
product of grace in believers
Romans 1–8: 316
See also Sanctification
Holocaust
Luke 1–5: 107
Luke 11–17: 244
John 1–11: 352
Jerusalem
Romans 9–16: 210
Nazi
Romans 1–8: 165
Holy affections
1–3 John: 139–49
Holy hands (related to prayer)
1 Timothy: 75
Holy kiss
Luke 18–24: 210
Holy living
Romans 1–8: 315
sovereign purpose of
Titus: 106
Holy nation
1 Peter: 128–30
Holy of Holies
Mark 9–16: 136, 139, 291, 378
Luke 18–24: 104, 105, 390
Romans 1–8: 209, 276, 402
1 Peter: 108, 235
Holy One
John 1–11: 14
Holy One of God
Mark 1–8: 64
Holy Place
Mark 9–16: 136, 139
Luke 18–24: 104, 105, 344, 390
Holy priesthood
1 Peter: 107–13
Holy Spirit
Matthew 1–7: 51, 71, 80
Luke 6–10: 92, 144, 158, 240, 343, 348
Luke 18–24: 191, 220, 386, 408, 443, 448
John 1–11: 13, 17–19, 64–65, 105–6, 132, 162, 211, 315, 353–54, 358
2 Corinthians: 65, 82
Hebrews: 144, 168, 215–16
1 Peter: 21–22, 41–42, 55–57, 82–83, 143–44, 162, 239–46, 253–56
2 Peter & Jude: 3, 20, 35–36, 61–66, 79, 139, 149, 156
Revelation 1–11: 24, 30, 108, 151, 168, 204
actions of
Luke 11–17: 58
Ananias and Sapphira's lie to
1–3 John: 205
assurance of salvation and
1–3 John: 54, 55, 169, 202
baptism with
Matthew 1–7: 71
Mark 1–8: 25–26
Acts 1–12: 18, 41–42, 244–45, 304
Acts 13–28: 164
Ephesians: 248
believers confirming hope in
1–3 John: 108
believers discerning presence of
1–3 John: 170
in believers' lives
1 & 2 Thessalonians: 193
in believers' sanctification
1 & 2 Thessalonians: 194–96
blasphemy against
Mark 1–8: 183–85
Luke 11–17: 123–24
Caiaphas and
1–3 John: 50
Christ and
Luke 1–5: 57, 229
Christian witness and
John 12–21: 177–86, 189
Christ's anointing by
Mark 1–8: 33–36
Luke 1–5: 238–40
and Christ's baptism
1–3 John: 193, 195
Christ's reliance on
Mark 1–8: 78
Christ's sending of
1–3 John: 65

and Christ's wilderness temptation
Mark 1–8: 42
and comma Johanneum
1–3 John: 195–96
control of
Ephesians: 250, 260
conversion and
1–3 John: 53, 55
convicting/regenerating work of
John 12–21: 196–98
conviction of sin by
Romans 1–8: 417
deity of
John 12–21: 114
Acts 1–12: 154
and demons
Mark 1–8: 66, 242
dependence of Christians on
Romans 1–8: 428
disciples and
Mark 1–8: 168
as divine advocate
Titus: 48
as a dove
Mark 1–8: 34
Jonathan Edwards and
1–3 John: 139
faith in believers' evidence of
1–3 John: 169, 170
filling with
Luke 1–5: 37, 69, 70, 254
Acts 1–12: 41–42
Ephesians: 245–69
final Antichrist and
1–3 John: 98
and fruit of the Spirit
1–3 John: 54
gift of
Luke 11–17: 57
Galatians: 66
as guarantor of security
Romans 1–8: 280
honoring
Luke 11–17: 121–25
illumination by
Romans 1–8: 433
and Incarnation
Romans 1–8: 415
indwelling of
John 12–21: 115, 116, 178
Romans 1–8: 284, 410, 421
Ephesians: 247
2 Timothy: 18, 30
Titus: 114
1–3 John: 29, 36, 112, 148–49, 230
inspiring the words of Scripture
Mark 1–8: 6, 406
John 12–21: 120
1–3 John: 14
knowing through truth and error
1–3 John: 102, 160
new birth and
1–3 John: 66, 127–28
under New Covenant
John 12–21: 381
obedience and
1–3 John: 56
personality of
Acts 1–12: 154
personhood of
John 12–21: 113–14
Romans 1–8: 414
power necessary for spiritual growth
1 & 2 Thessalonians: 108
power of in believers' lives
Acts 1–12: 17
presence of
John 12–21: 112–15
revelation of
John 12–21: 205–10
sanctifying work of
1–3 John: 117
second coming and
Luke 11–17: 410
soul–cleansing of
Mark 1–8: 358–59
"Spirit of truth"
1–3 John: 159–60, 195, 218
testimony of
Luke 11–17: 154
transforming power of
1–3 John: 48, 76, 131, 217–18
and the Trinity
Romans 1–8: 414
1–3 John: 162–65
union of with believers
1–3 John: 19
walking by
Romans 1–8: 412
withdrawal of His restraint
Matthew 24–28: 24
as witness to Jesus
Luke 1–5: 234–35
work of
Acts 1–12: 2
Romans 1–8: 415, 431
Galatians: 67
1–3 John: 54, 122, 127–28, 142
and work of Spirit of Christ
1–3 John: 149
in worship
Luke 1–5: 76
Yahweh and
Romans 1–8: 414
yielding to
Ephesians: 253
Home. *see* Marriage
Homes, godly
2 Timothy: 8
Homosexuality
Matthew 8–15: 102
Romans 1–8: 104, 105, 106, 107
Ephesians: 271, 282, 294, 339
Titus: 81–82, 131, 137, 146
Honesty
2 Corinthians: 235–36, 427–28
Honor
Luke 11–17: 385–86
1 Peter: 44–46, 68–69, 115, 152–53, 201
worldly
Romans 1–8: 131

Honor–based culture
Luke 18–24: 5
Honoring parents
Mark 1–8: 345–46
Hope
Luke 11–17: 13, 155, 182, 371
John 12–21: 212, 230–32
Colossians & Philemon: 19–20, 78
1 Timothy: 5
Hebrews: 157, 266
1 Peter: 33–34, 62–65, 84, 201–3, 231–32, 286–88
abiding
1–3 John: 110–13
benefactor of
2 Corinthians: 211–13
beneficiaries of
2 Corinthians: 216
benefit of
2 Corinthians: 216–17
blessed
Matthew 24–28: 59
description of
1–3 John: 107–10
false or worldly form of
1–3 John: 106
fulfilled by Christlikeness
1–3 John: 116–17
fundamental nature of
1–3 John: 105–6, 110, 118
godly
Romans 1–8: 241
love and
1–3 John: 114–17
New Covenant and
2 Corinthians: 107–8
overview of
2 Corinthians: 27, 209–11
1–3 John: 118
and purity
1–3 John: 117–18
and righteousness
2 Corinthians: 216–17
1–3 John: 113–14
sacrificial substitute and
2 Corinthians: 213–16
as sure and absolutely fixed
1–3 John: 107
Hopelessness
1 Peter: 239
Horace
Luke 1–5: 144
Romans 1–8: 90
Horne, Charles M.
2 Peter & Jude: 28–29
Hosanna
Mark 9–16: 127
Luke 18–24: 96
Hosea
Mark 9–16: 60
Luke 6–10: 144
2 Corinthians: 199, 225, 317, 353
1 Peter: 132
Hosea and Gomer
Matthew 1–7: 42, 314
Mark 9–16: 60
Hoshea
John 12–21: 73
Hospitality
Luke 11–17: 54
1 Corinthians: 485–87
Hebrews: 426–27
"chosen lady" responsible for
1–3 John: 216
as Christian duty
1–3 John: 242, 243
Diotrephes and
1–3 John: 239, 258, 259
false teachers and
1–3 John: 239
as inclusive to all in the truth
1–3 John: 244
as manifestation of love
1–3 John: 246
Hostility to God, man's natural
Matthew 16–23: 46
House
Hebrews: 80–81
House of prayer (temple)
Luke 18–24: 105, 106
Household, believer's
provision required
1 Timothy: 202
Houses, spiritual
1 Peter: 107–13
How, William W.
Romans 9–16: 113
Howard, John
prison reforms of
Colossians & Philemon: 165
Hughes, Philip E.
2 Corinthians: 36, 46, 112–13, 146, 206, 368–69, 382, 457, 492
Huizenga, L. S.
Matthew 8–15: 7
Huldah
Luke 1–5: 185
Hull, Bill
on anti–intellectualism in the church
Philippians: 285–86
Human depravity
1–3 John: 29, 85, 128, 227
Human effort, failure of
Romans 1–8: 262
Human nature
elements of
Mark 9–16: 201
sinfulness of
Romans 1–8: 67
views of
Galatians: 160
Human reason
reliance on
Matthew 16–23: 42
Human religion, works righteousness and
Matthew 16–23: 284
Human responsibility
Mark 9–16: 250
doctrine of
Acts 13–28: 37

Human will
Matthew 1–7: 383–84, 450–52, 474–75, 487–89
Galatians: 153
Ephesians: 11
Christian's
Romans 1–8: 338
and saving faith
Romans 1–8: 205
Human wisdom, inadequacy of
1 & 2 Thessalonians: 58
Humanism
Matthew 16–23: 25
Mark 9–16: 187
Romans 1–8: 89, 102, 105
Galatians: 160
Ephesians: 56, 158, 282, 292, 309, 336, 341
2 Timothy: 109
Titus: 50, 131
Humanistic hedonism
Titus: 50
Humanness, believer's unredeemed
Romans 1–8: 326, 404
Humble people
and forgiveness of others
Luke 11–17: 378–83
recognition of weakness in
Luke 11–17: 383–85
rejection of honor by
Luke 11–17: 385–86
stumbling blocks and
Luke 11–17: 377–78
Hume, David
2 Peter & Jude: 56
denial of miracles
Acts 1–12: 60
philosophical despair
Colossians & Philemon: 96
Humiliation
Mark 1–8: 45, 192
Luke 18–24: 53–54
Jesus'
Matthew 8–15: 22
Humility
Matthew 1–7: 146, 148–51, 436–37
Matthew 8–15: 141, 147, 165, 270, 473
Matthew 24–28: 157
Mark 9–16: 33, 34, 36, 100–103, 106
Luke 1–5: 79, 80, 81
Luke 11–17: 264, 265, 315, 376–86
Luke 18–24: 19, 20, 22
John 12–21: 59–69
Acts 13–28: 49
Romans 1–8: 43, 224, 385
1 Corinthians: 343
2 Corinthians: 86–87, 133–34, 238, 344–50, 364–67, 371–82, 400–401
Galatians: 95, 181
1 Peter: 188–89, 277–79
1–3 John: 65–66, 131, 255
of centurion
Luke 6–10: 126–28
Christ's
1 Corinthians: 106
examples of
Matthew 16–23: 231
faith and
Matthew 16–23: 97
false
Romans 9–16: 160
Colossians & Philemon: 120
God's blessing of
Luke 6–10: 299–300
God's demand for
Luke 6–10: 63, 65, 301
greatness and
Luke 6–10: 304
lack of
Matthew 16–23: 365–66
Moses'
1 Corinthians: 107–8
necessity of
Matthew 16–23: 48
Paul's
1 Corinthians: 109–12
Peter and
Luke 6–10: 34–35
spiritual
Matthew 16–23: 95
supremacy of
Matthew 16–23: 98
true
Colossians & Philemon: 88–89, 156
Humor, worldly
Matthew 1–7: 159
Hus, John
2 Timothy: 13
Husbands
Ephesians: 291–305
principles for
Colossians & Philemon: 168–70
responsibilities of
1 Peter: 181–83
unsaved spouses
1 Peter: 175–83
See also Marriage
Huss, Jan (John)
Luke 1–5: 226–27
Luke 18–24: 214
John 12–21: 189
Huxley, Julian
Romans 9–16: 181
Hymenaeus
Luke 18–24: 162, 245
2 Corinthians: 477
2 Peter & Jude: 140
Hymns and psalms
Luke 6–10: 120, 141, 142
1 Peter: 71–76, 84–85, 95–96, 156–57, 192–93, 259–60, 279–80
Hyper–preterism
Luke 18–24: 244–45
Hypercarbia
Luke 18–24: 380
Hyperpreterism
Luke 11–17: 151, 152
Hypocrites/hypocrisy
Matthew 1–7: 63–64, 164, 351–60, 361–70, 400–401
Matthew 8–15: 68, 176, 448, 455
Matthew 16–23: 126
Mark 1–8: 62, 64, 119, 137, 214, 215, 347

Mark 9–16: 174, 176–82, 312
Luke 1–5: 319
Luke 6–10: 115–16, 165, 172, 201, 292
Luke 11–17: 96, 112–13, 201–3
Acts 1–12: 152–53
Galatians: 199–201
Ephesians: 264, 336, 347
1 Peter: 98
2 Peter & Jude: 67, 173–75, 187
avoiding
Luke 11–17: 116–25
characteristics of
Matthew 8–15: 461
evidence and
Luke 11–17: 176
exposure of
Luke 11–17: 117
of false religionists
Luke 11–17: 95–96
of false teachers
Luke 18–24: 132–33, 165–66
in Israel's history
Luke 11–17: 114
of Israel's religion
Luke 18–24: 106
of Judas Iscariot
Luke 18–24: 290
New Testament instances of
Luke 11–17: 115
Pharisees and
Luke 11–17: 96, 131, 257–65
religious
Titus: 93
Revelation 1–11: 136
of religious leaders
Luke 18–24: 18, 399
remedy for
Luke 18–24: 104, 115–16
of young ruler
Luke 18–24: 38
Hypostatic union
John 1–11: 37–38

"I Am His, and He Is Mine"
Colossians & Philemon: 129
I AM statements
Mark 1–8: 225
John 1–11: 14, 86, 184, 348–49
John 12–21: 77, 102, 262, 308
Iconium
1 Peter: 257
Identification with Christ
Hebrews: 58–60
Idolatry
Mark 9–16: 60, 81
Luke 1–5: 74, 75, 143, 205
Luke 11–17: 133
Luke 18–24: 225–27
Acts 1–12: 212–13
Acts 13–28: 71, 139, 183
2 Corinthians: 247, 250–54
Ephesians: 283
Revelation 1–11: 273
ancient
Romans 1–8: 94
modern forms of
Romans 1–8: 95
origin of
Romans 1–8: 90
self–worship and
Romans 1–8: 92
service of Satan
Romans 1–8: 92
Idols
Matthew 16–23: 106
Mark 1–8: 367, 375
John 12–21: 138
Idumea
Mark 9–16: 349
"If" (Rudyard Kipling)
Philippians: 281–82
Ignatius
Luke 1–5: 55, 226
Luke 18–24: 212
John 12–21: 169
on Bishop Onesimus
Colossians & Philemon: 231–32
commendation of the Ephesian church by
Revelation 1–11: 60
Ignorance
1 Peter: 150–51
spiritual
Matthew 24–28: 163
Romans 1–8: 183
1 Corinthians: 71
Illness. *see* Disease
Illumination
1 Corinthians: 63–65
in Christ
1 Peter: 127–34
divine
Matthew 16–23: 15, 22, 36
work of the Holy Spirit
Romans 1–8: 431, 433
Illustrations, of apostates
2 Peter & Jude: 169–82
Image, God's
Colossians & Philemon: 45
Hebrews: 311
1 Peter: 152–53
in man
Matthew 16–23: 26
Imaginations and lusts
1 Peter: 73–76
Immaturity, spiritual
Matthew 16–23: 12
Ephesians: 45
Immediately
Mark 1–8: 5, 33, 40, 52
Immersion
Matthew 1–7: 79
See also Baptism
Imminency
James: 256
Revelation 12–22: 291–92
Immorality
2 Corinthians: 436
2 Peter & Jude: 113, 165–67, 172–73
sexual
Romans 1–8: 103, 108, 320
See also Lust

Immortality
Luke 6–10: 350
Imparted righteousness
Matthew 16–23: 312
Impartiality
divine
Matthew 8–15: 82
Romans 1–8: 136
Romans 9–16: 198
of God
Matthew 16–23: 208
human
Romans 1–8: 135
Impatience
Matthew 24–28: 193
Impediment
Mark 1–8: 378
Import taxes
Luke 18–24: 134
Imprecatory psalms
Romans 1–8: 478
1 & 2 Thessalonians: 236–37
Imprisonment
Luke 6–10: 145, 146
Romans 9–16: 224
Impulsiveness
Matthew 24–28: 193, 213
Mark 9–16: 334–35
Impurity
2 Corinthians: 436
Imputation
1 Peter: 78–79
Imputed righteousness
Matthew 16–23: 312
In His (Christ's) name
Luke 18–24: 444–45
Inability, absolute
2 Peter & Jude: 74
Incarnation
Matthew 1–7: 13–14
John 1–11: 13–15, 39, 257–60
Ephesians: 139
Hebrews: 28, 119–20
of Christ
John 1–11: 40, 44–46
2 Corinthians: 19
Philippians: 118, 123
1 Timothy: 32
1–3 John: 8, 17, 158, 191–92
Revelation 12–22: 11, 108
denial of
1–3 John: 8, 158
God's glory in
Romans 1–8: 84
Holy Spirit and
Romans 1–8: 415
importance of
1–3 John: 17, 191–92
Incense
Luke 1–5: 26, 29
Incentives
1 Peter: 193–94
for salvation
1 Corinthians: 424–27
for sanctification
1 Corinthians: 429–30
for service
1 Corinthians: 427–28
Inclusiveness
Luke 6–10: 118
Luke 11–17: 73
Inclusivism
Luke 1–5: 337
in first century A.D.
1–3 John: 1, 2
modern
1–3 John: 2, 13–14, 201
as skepticism
1–3 John: 13–14
Income tax
Mark 1–8: 114
Luke 18–24: 71, 134
Incommunicable attributes
Mark 9–16: 211
Luke 18–24: 156
Incomplete healings
Mark 1–8: 409
Indebtedness, principle of
Colossians & Philemon: 226–27
Indecision
Matthew 8–15: 157
Indifference
Matthew 8–15: 262
1 Corinthians: 472
spiritual
Matthew 16–23: 128, 132
Ephesians: 336, 340
Indignation
righteous
1 Corinthians: 345–46
Individualism
1 Corinthians: 318–19
Individuality, eternal
Romans 1–8: 492
Indulgences
Luke 11–17: 202
Luke 18–24: 170–71
Indwelling (of the Holy Spirit)
John 12–21: 115, 116, 178
Romans 1–8: 421
Inequities/injustices
Mark 9–16: 136
Inerrancy of the Bible
Romans 9–16: 41
Titus: 46
Infant(s). *see* Babies and infants
Infant baptism
Romans 1–8: 150, 253
Infant sacrifices
Mark 9–16: 48
Infidelity
Galatians: 185
Influence
Christian
Matthew 1–7: 235–47
harmful
Matthew 16–23: 105
leaven as symbol of
Matthew 16–23: 13
selfish use of
Matthew 16–23: 235

spiritual
Matthew 8–15: 368–75
Inheritance
believers'
Matthew 1–7: 174–75
Ephesians: 27–36
eternal
1 Peter: 29–38
heavenly
John 12–21: 110–11
spiritual
Colossians & Philemon: 37–40, 131–32
Inheritance laws
Jewish
Romans 1–8: 443
Roman
Romans 1–8: 443
Initiative
Matthew 8–15: 138, 162
Luke 6–10: 28–29
Injustice
Matthew 16–23: 373
Mark 9–16: 96–98, 269, 322
Luke 18–24: 3–8, 54, 313, 333
Inner circle of apostles
Mark 9–16: 4, 105
See also James; John; Peter
Inner discipline
1 Peter: 137–39
Inner man
outer man vs.
2 Corinthians: 154
Inner rooms
Luke 11–17: 117–18
Innocence
Mark 9–16: 354, 361
Inquisition
Luke 18–24: 213
John 12–21: 170
Romans 9–16: 88
Insecurity, spiritual
Romans 1–8: 146
Inspiration
1 Corinthians: 62–63
Hebrews: 5, 87, 173
of Bible
Luke 1–5: 14–15
John 12–21: 120, 200–201, 207
Titus: 46
Instantaneous healing
Mark 9–16: 117
Luke 18–24: 63
***Institutes of the Christian Religion* (John Calvin)**
Romans 9–16: 159
Institutions
1 Peter: 148–49
Insubordination
2 Peter & Jude: 173–75
spiritual
Matthew 24–28: 212
Insults
1 Peter: 190
Insurrection
Mark 9–16: 175, 347, 352
Luke 18–24: 131, 135, 313, 345
Integrity
1 Peter: 150–51
concern and
2 Corinthians: 186–88
devotion and
2 Corinthians: 188–89
forgiveness and (*see* Forgiveness)
gratitude and
2 Corinthians: 189–92
lack of
Matthew 16–23: 358–60
obedience
2 Corinthians: 475–77
overview of
2 Corinthians: 181–86, 473–77
personal
Romans 9–16: 335
recognition and
2 Corinthians: 343–44
reconciliation and (*see* Reconciliation)
reverence and
2 Corinthians: 186
righteousness and
2 Corinthians: 193–94
sanctification and
2 Corinthians: 473–80
sorrow and
2 Corinthians: 269–70
spiritual
Matthew 16–23: 126
Philippians: 85
spiritual war and (*see* Spiritual war)
stewardship and (*see* Stewardship)
truth and
2 Corinthians: 188–89
See also Obedience
Intellect, saving faith and
Romans 1–8: 206
Intellectualism
1 Corinthians: 89
Titus: 129
Intercession
Luke 18–24: 295, 455
of Christ
John 12–21: 242–43
Christ's continual
Romans 1–8: 279
of the Holy Spirit
John 12–21: 272–73
Interest, charging
Romans 9–16: 245
Intermarriage with pagan women
Mark 9–16: 52–53, 59
Internal peace
2 Peter & Jude: 132–35
Interpretation
2 Peter & Jude: 65–66
allegorical
Galatians: 122
Intimidation, spiritual
Colossians & Philemon: 115–24
Intoxication
1 Peter: 280
Inverted priorities
Matthew 16–23: 383

"Invictus" (Henley)
Luke 11–17: 19–20
James: 234
Invincibility
2 Corinthians: 142–43
Ireland
Luke 18–24: 89
Irenaeus
Mark 1–8: 3
Mark 9–16: 410
Luke 1–5: 2
John 1–11: 2–4, 8–9
2 Corinthians: 5
1 Peter: 6
1–3 John: 3, 6
on apostolic authorship of Revelation
Revelation 1–11: 4
on the date of Revelation
Revelation 1–11: 8
on the number 666
Revelation 12–22: 64
Irony
John 12–21: 342, 343, 351
Irrelevant issues
Mark 1–8: 275–77
Irreverence
2 Peter & Jude: 173–75
Isaac
Mark 9–16: 64, 102
Luke 1–5: 54, 59, 109, 196
Luke 6–10: 21, 143
Luke 18–24: 50, 262
John 1–11: 42, 194, 206, 360
2 Corinthians: 16, 19, 272, 393
Hebrews: 335, 339–41
as picture of Christ
Romans 1–8: 505
Isaiah
Mark 1–8: 18, 298
Mark 9–16: 168
Luke 1–5: 42, 43, 185, 210–11, 270
Luke 6–10: 21, 143–44, 213, 263–64, 271
Luke 11–17: 246, 342
Luke 18–24: 124
John 12–21: 34, 53
2 Corinthians: 17, 20, 21, 74, 90, 103, 112, 114, 139, 154, 162, 191, 199, 200, 205, 213, 215, 225, 249, 254, 257, 378, 395, 433, 446, 465, 478, 488
1 Peter: 1–2, 20–21, 52–53, 75, 92–93, 122, 167–80, 262, 274–75
2 Peter & Jude: 11, 23, 48, 57, 82, 116–17
1–3 John: 38, 144
Iscariot. *see* Judas Iscariot
Ishmael
Luke 1–5: 108
Ishtar (Ashtoreth)
Luke 1–5: 61
Isis
Matthew 8–15: 348
Islam
Luke 1–5: 328
Luke 6–10: 132
Luke 11–17: 244
Luke 18–24: 150, 213
John 12–21: 12, 170, 189, 191–92
Romans 1–8: 336
Isolated areas
Mark 1–8: 92, 93, 94
Isolation
Luke 6–10: 102
of Jesus
Mark 9–16: 317
Israel
Matthew 1–7: 7–8
Luke 6–10: 177, 179
John 1–11: 152–53
John 12–21: 53, 54, 56, 143, 144, 406
Hebrews: 89, 98, 104, 165–66
1–3 John: 96
ancient, and God's law
Romans 1–8: 357
anti–Semitism and
Luke 11–17: 243–44
apostasy of
Revelation 1–11: 130
believing remnant in
Luke 1–5: 175
calling and blessing of
Romans 1–8: 167
chosen people of God
Romans 9–16: 1
the church and
Luke 18–24: 125
corporate accountability of
Romans 1–8: 293
covenant theology and
Luke 11–17: 247
covenants and
Luke 1–5: 96, 106–8, 120
Romans 9–16: 14
discipline, divine
Romans 9–16: 5
disobedience of
Luke 11–17: 240–43
divine judgment on
Mark 1–8: 199
Mark 9–16: 246, 258
failure of
Romans 9–16: 13
flight of during the Tribulation
Revelation 12–22: 29–30, 32
future of
Luke 11–17: 154–55, 190
future redemption of
Matthew 16–23: 403
as God's chosen nation
Revelation 12–22: 5
God's compassion for
Luke 11–17: 237–41, 245
God's covenants with
Romans 9–16: 14
God's judgments on
Mark 9–16: 169
God's mediation through
Luke 11–17: 400
as God's people
1 Timothy: 216
God's plan for
Matthew 16–23: 400
God's promises to
Revelation 12–22: 4

God's protection of
Revelation 1–11: 296
Revelation 12–22: 32
God's providential care of
Acts 13–28: 19–21
God's purpose for
Ephesians: 68
history of
Mark 9–16: 52
hope of
Acts 13–28: 370–71
hypocrisy and
Luke 11–17: 114
judgment of
Romans 1–8: 134
judgment on
Luke 18–24: 97–99, 117, 125, 186
law and
Luke 1–5: 115
leprosy and
Luke 1–5: 313
major feasts in
Mark 9–16: 268
messianic expectations of
Mark 1–8: 190–91
Mark 9–16: 205–6
mission of
Acts 1–12: 250–51
modern
Matthew 24–28: 33
Luke 1–5: 119
nation/messiah
Romans 9–16: 18
national salvation of
Romans 1–8: 171
1948 national rebirth
Luke 18–24: 246–47
northern kingdom of
Mark 9–16: 60, 169
not forsaken by God
Romans 9–16: 2–3
opposition to the gospel
Acts 13–28: 31, 117, 276–77, 319
preserved but unblessed
Matthew 16–23: 280
privileges of
Romans 9–16: 12
prophecy and
Luke 1–5: 69–72, 96
rebellion of
Luke 18–24: 130
rejection by God not final
Acts 13–28: 375
rejection of Christ
Mark 9–16: 96
Acts 13–28: 23
remnant of
Luke 11–17: 218
remnant to be saved
Romans 9–16: 6
replacement theology and
Luke 1–5: 126
restoration of
Romans 9–16: 107, 118
revival in end times
Romans 9–16: 111
revolt against Rome (A.D. 66–70)
Acts 13–28: 316, 327
during Roman Empire
Luke 1–5: 97, 171, 200
Roman occupation of
Luke 18–24: 71, 78–79
salvation of
Luke 11–17: 410–11
Luke 18–24: 194–95
1 & 2 Thessalonians: 66
Revelation 1–11: 214–15, 219, 223
Revelation 12–22: 12, 34
salvation offered first to
Mark 1–8: 362, 363, 368
Acts 13–28: 36
Satan's persecution of
Revelation 12–22: 4–5, 6, 8–10, 11–12, 27–29
scattering of
Matthew 24–28: 160
at second coming
Luke 18–24: 126–27
state of, modern
Romans 9–16: 18, 21, 46, 81
supreme court of
Mark 9–16: 321, 330
temporarily replaced by church as God's chosen
Titus: 6
in the tribulation
Luke 18–24: 127, 203
true believers and
Luke 1–5: 129, 134
and the twelve apostles
Mark 1–8: 166
twelve tribes of
Acts 13–28: 333
unfaithfulness of
Matthew 16–23: 402
unique privilege of
Matthew 16–23: 401
as a vineyard
Mark 9–16: 165–68
as the wife of the Lord
Revelation 12–22: 4
winters in
Mark 9–16: 247
See also Jewish people

Isthmian Games
2 Corinthians: 3
Philippians: 242

"It Is Well with My Soul"
Acts 1–12: 118

Ithamar
1 Peter: 108

Ituraea
Mark 1–8: 300

Jacob
Mark 9–16: 64, 102
Luke 1–5: 42, 69
Luke 6–10: 21
Luke 18–24: 2
John 1–11: 73, 137, 141–46, 153–54, 206, 212, 360
2 Corinthians: 19, 54–56, 272, 282, 377, 393, 404

Hebrews: 341–42
Jacob (Jesus' grandfather)
Luke 1–5: 246–47
Jacob's well
John 1–11: 142, 153–54
Jailer at Philippi
1–3 John: 243
Jairus
Mark 1–8: 255, 256, 258, 263–65
Luke 6–10: 230–32, 235
James (apostle)
Mark 1–8: 60, 161, 169
Luke 18–24: 273, 302, 303
2 Peter & Jude: 60–62
1–3 John: 5, 6, 58, 137, 255
James (brother of Jesus; "the Just")
Mark 1–8: 179, 263, 277
Luke 18–24: 192
James: 10, 11
1 Peter: 8, 139, 271
2 Peter & Jude: 142, 149
James (brother of John)
Mark 9–16: 103, 104, 105, 106, 107
Luke 1–5: 195, 303, 304, 308–9
Luke 6–10: 26
ambition
Luke 6–10: 43
choosing of
Luke 6–10: 40
importance of
Luke 6–10: 16–18, 39
martyrdom of
Luke 6–10: 98
occupation
Luke 6–10: 41, 47
personality
Luke 6–10: 42, 313
at transfiguration
Luke 6–10: 282–83, 286
James (son of Alphaeus; James the Less)
Mark 1–8: 161, 169, 171–72
Mark 9–16: 105, 382
Luke 1–5: 226
Luke 6–10: 16, 17, 18, 69
James (son of Zebedee [apostle])
Mark 1–8: 51, 170
John 12–21: 166, 188, 274, 275
Jannaeus, Alexander
Luke 18–24: 378
Japan, earthquakes
Luke 18–24: 204
Jastrow, Robert
Romans 1–8: 79–80
Jealousy
Mark 9–16: 353
2 Corinthians: 435
danger of
Matthew 16–23: 212
Jeconiah (Jehoiachin)
Luke 1–5: 247
John 1–11: 138
Jeeves, Malcolm
2 Timothy: 110
Jefferson, Charles
on importance of pastoral oversight
Acts 13–28: 227–28
Jefferson, Thomas
Romans 1–8: 15
Jehoiada
2 Corinthians: 114
Jehoiakim
Luke 11–17: 231
Jehoshaphat
Luke 18–24: 4
Jehovah (Yahweh; YHWH)
Matthew 16–23: 96, 137, 198, 305, 347, 348
Mark 1–8: 19, 225
John 1–11: 14, 184, 348
John 12–21: 262
Romans 1–8: 414
Spirit of
Romans 1–8: 414
Jehovah–jireh
Mark 1–8: 313
Jehovah's Witnesses
Luke 1–5: 328
Luke 6–10: 132
Luke 18–24: 150
John 1–11: 18, 348
1–3 John: 158
Jehu
Luke 6–10: 42
Jephthah
2 Corinthians: 114
Hebrews: 366
Jeremiah
Mark 1–8: 299
Mark 9–16: 168
Luke 1–5: 37–38
Luke 11–17: 342–43
Luke 18–24: 124
Romans 9–16: 10
2 Corinthians: 12, 26, 370
Ephesians: 35, 126
1 Timothy: 59
1 Peter: 32, 101, 145, 265–66
2 Peter & Jude: 64–65
divine training
2 Timothy: 52
Jericho
Mark 1–8: 29
Mark 9–16: 113, 114, 123
Luke 6–10: 170, 311, 356
Luke 18–24: 59, 69–70, 90, 92, 94
Hebrews: 361–63
Jericho Springs
Luke 18–24: 69
Jeroboam
Luke 6–10: 74
John 12–21: 73
Jerome
Mark 1–8: 308
Mark 9–16: 410
John 1–11: 323
2 Peter & Jude: 9
Jerusalem
Mark 1–8: 180, 312, 341
Mark 9–16: 114, 127, 131, 299, 310
Luke 6–10: 42, 57, 87, 179, 309–10, 312, 324, 356
Luke 11–17: 176, 239, 243, 251
Hebrews: 175–76

Antichrist forces and
Luke 18–24: 242
Antiochus IV and
Luke 18–24: 226
ark of the covenant and
John 12–21: 21
armies and
Luke 18–24: 223, 227, 228
church
1 Peter: 253
destruction of
Matthew 8–15: 313
Matthew 16–23: 308, 395
Matthew 24–28: 252
Luke 18–24: 99, 124, 134–35, 223, 282
1 Corinthians: 382
earthquake
Luke 18–24: 205
history of
Matthew 16–23: 38
holocaust
Romans 9–16: 46, 210
Jesus' entry into
Luke 18–24: 93
New Jerusalem
Luke 6–10: 241
John 1–11: 41
John 12–21: 100–101
2 Corinthians: 414
Passion Week crowds
Luke 18–24: 101–2
Passover crowds in
John 12–21: 14
passover in
Luke 1–5: 266
Paul's imprisonment in
John 12–21: 167
recapture of
Luke 18–24: 95
renovation of
Luke 18–24: 181
Roman destruction of
Luke 1–5: 107, 219, 244
John 12–21: 56–57, 406
at second coming
Luke 18–24: 220–21
temple and
Luke 1–5: 219, 244, 267
as throne of God
1 Peter: 74

Jerusalem Council
Luke 18–24: 192
John 1–11: 42
Romans 1–8: 184, 313, 366, 503
Romans 9–16: 129
2 Corinthians: 43
Galatians: 35–43, 56, 67, 75, 133
2 Timothy: 72
Titus: x, 59, 163
James: 5, 11
1 Peter: 5, 21–22
2 Peter & Jude: 4, 22, 135
Revelation 1–11: 89

Jeshua
John 1–11: 93

Jesse
Luke 1–5: 98
John 1–11: 137

Jesus Christ
Mark 1–8: 15, 35, 36, 56
Luke 6–10: 262
abiding of Christians in
1–3 John: 110–13, 125–26
accessibility of
Mark 1–8: 254–57
accusations against
Matthew 24–28: 235
Adam, antithetical analogy with
Romans 1–8: 291
admiring from distance
Matthew 8–15: 101
as advocate or defense attorney
1–3 John: 44–46, 206
affection for
1 Peter: 122–23
agony of
Luke 18–24: 306
anger of
Mark 1–8: 156–57
anguish before the cross
John 12–21: 38–39
anointment of
Hebrews: 35
Antichrist and
1–3 John: 96, 97, 100
on antichrists
1–3 John: 97
arrest of
Mark 9–16: 309–16
Luke 18–24: 313–17
James: 26
ascension of
Luke 18–24: 450, 452–55
Acts 1–12: 22
Philippians: 140
1 Peter: 236, 267
atonement of
2 Peter & Jude: 17–18, 73–76
Revelation 1–11: 172, 232
Revelation 12–22: 86, 253, 269–70
atoning sacrifice of
Romans 1–8: 302
attempts on life of
Luke 11–17: 225–27
attitude of
1 Peter: 224–26
attributes of
Luke 18–24: 237, 238
as Author of salvation
Hebrews: 66–67
authority delegated to apostles and believers
Mark 9–16: 159–60
authority of (*See also* Authority)
Mark 1–8: 61, 98
Mark 9–16: 152–54
Luke 1–5: 229, 281, 282, 287, 296
John 1–11: 15–20
2 Corinthians: 449–57, 470
Colossians & Philemon: 50, 103, 112–13
authority over Satan/demons
Mark 1–8: 41–46, 53, 57–59, 250

authority over sin
Mark 1–8: 46–49, 53, 105
authority over sinners
Mark 1–8: 49–54
authority to forgive sins
Mark 1–8: 98
baptism of
Mark 1–8: 28, 33, 38
1–3 John: 192–93, 195
being of
Hebrews: 16
believed on in the world
1 Timothy: 142
as believers' High Priest
Philippians: 141
Revelation 1–11: 44–45
betrayal/arrest of
John 12–21: 303–12, 315
birth of
Luke 18–24: 251–52
1 Peter: 1, 40, 58, 82
blood of
John 1–11: 260–63
2 Corinthians: 31, 88, 98, 107, 440
Colossians & Philemon: 62–64
1 Peter: 23–25, 76–82
1–3 John: 36, 193–94
blood sacrifice of
1 Peter: 23–25, 76–82
Body of
Ephesians: xi, 5–16, 151–62
as Bread of Life
1–3 John: 103–4
as Bread of Life, appropriation of
John 1–11: 255–64
as Bread of Life, responses to
John 1–11: 265–74
as Bread of Life, true Bread from Heaven
John 1–11: 239–54
burial of
Mark 9–16: 385–94
Luke 18–24: 396, 398
care for widows
1 Timothy: 194
certainties regarding
1–3 John: 13–20
character of
Hebrews: 43
as Chief Shepherd (See also Shepherd(s))
1 Peter: 173–74, 261–71
as the Christ
Mark 1–8: 4–5
church of
2 Peter & Jude: 1
claims of
John 1–11: 181–92
as comforter
2 Corinthians: 18–20
coming of
2 Peter & Jude: 58–61
as commander–in–chief
2 Corinthians: 70
commandments of
2 Peter & Jude: 117
compassion of
Matthew 1–7: 136
Matthew 16–23: 271
Mark 1–8: 90, 265–68, 385–87
Luke 6–10: 89–90
Luke 11–17: 235–37, 260, 388
1 Peter: 127–34
confession of, as God incarnate
1–3 John: 157–58
confession of sins and
1–3 John: 41
confirmations of deity
Matthew 16–23: 63
confirming signs
Matthew 1–7: 126–30
and conflict/opposition
Luke 11–17: 80, 176, 194--203, 206, 305
confrontations of
John 1–11: 321–30, 375–86
continual intercession of
Romans 1–8: 279
control of own destiny
Matthew 16–23: 220, 258, 269, 273–74
coronation of
Matthew 16–23: 259
Luke 18–24: 89–90
Revelation 1–11: 309
as Creator
Matthew 16–23: 26–27
Colossians & Philemon: 47–50
Hebrews: 13–15
crisis behavior of
Mark 1–8: 262–65
crucifixion of (*see* Crucifixion)
day of
2 Corinthians: 37–38, 168
death of (*see* Death of Jesus)
as deity, claims of
Matthew 16–23: 23
John 1–11: 181–92
as deity, displays of
John 1–11: 85–96
as deity, reactions to
John 1–11: 299–308
as deity, verification of
John 1–11: 285–97
as deity, witnesses to
John 1–11: 203–16
deity of
Matthew 24–28: 232
Mark 1–8: 148, 224, 225
Mark 9–16: 209–12
Luke 6–10: 92, 132, 133, 139
Luke 18–24: 149, 151, 155–57
John 12–21: 104, 143, 267–68
Philippians: 123, 125
Colossians & Philemon: 2, 43–54, 103
Hebrews: 14, 26–28, 30, 33–34, 52
1–3 John: 157–58, 190, 210
Revelation 1–11: 3, 50, 51, 68–69, 96, 119
demons and
Luke 1–5: 280–88
demon's attestation to deity of
Mark 1–8: 64, 67
and disciples
Luke 18–24: 48, 49, 52, 55–56
John 1–11: 227–38

1 Peter: 4–9, 41–42, 88, 97, 108, 127, 235–36
disciples' belief in deity of
Mark 1–8: 416
disciples of, true vs. false
John 1–11: 227–38
disloyalty to
2 Corinthians: 355–56
divine attributes of
Philippians: 127
divine nature of
2 Peter & Jude: 30–31
divine power of
2 Peter & Jude: 26–28
divine timetable and
John 1–11: 275–84
as divine Word
John 1–11: 13–24
divinity of
Matthew 1–7: 121–30
Matthew 8–15: 273
Matthew 16–23: 344
dominion with
1 Peter: 119–26, 288
earthly rule of
Revelation 12–22: 11
election by (See also Election by Christ)
1 Peter: 123–25
equality with the Father
1 & 2 Thessalonians: 14, 87, 225, 289, 313
1–3 John: 219–20
eternity of
Hebrews: 35, 36
exaltation of
Acts 1–12: 67–68
1 Corinthians: 20
Hebrews: 19–20, 65, 208
Revelation 1–11: 18, 170
Revelation 12–22: 11, 214
example of
Philippians: 119, 121–22, 129–30, 138–39
1 & 2 Thessalonians: 83
Hebrews: 378, 450
1–3 John: 59, 193
excellencies of
1 Peter: 133–34
face of (*see* Face of Jesus Christ)
faith in
1–3 John: 147–48
as faithful and true One
2 Peter & Jude: 117
faithfulness of
Hebrews: 80
false accusations against
Matthew 24–28: 235
false praise of
Matthew 16–23: 20, 344
false vs. true disciples of
John 1–11: 227–38
the Father and
Luke 6–10: 344–47
fellow sufferers with
2 Corinthians: 15, 23–25
fickleness about
Matthew 8–15: 101
finished work of
Romans 1–8: 280
Ephesians: 42
Hebrews: 240–41
first coming of
Matthew 1–7: 14, 69
Luke 11–17: 413
and forgiveness
2 Corinthians: 54
2 Peter & Jude: 24
1–3 John: 34–35
full divinity of
Galatians: 108
genealogies of
Luke 1–5: 45, 244–50
gift of
2 Corinthians: 294–95
gifts to His church
Ephesians: 133–49
glorification of
John 12–21: 88, 241–42
2 Corinthians: 168
glory of
Mark 9–16: 3, 4, 5, 13
Luke 6–10: 280, 281, 283
as God
2 Peter & Jude: 23, 26–27, 29–30
as God incarnate
1–3 John: 157–58
as God–man
2 Corinthians: 19, 43, 97, 214
1–3 John: 16, 233
God's plan for
Luke 18–24: 48, 49
as Good Shepherd
John 1–11: 421–36
2 Corinthians: 338
2 Peter & Jude: 51, 96, 208–9
gospel of
1 Peter: 80, 249
gospel of John and
John 1–11: vii–viii, 1–12
as great human teacher
Mark 1–8: 175
as Great Shepherd
2 Corinthians: 82
on hatred by the world
1–3 John: 134
as head of the church
2 Corinthians: 440–41
healing
Matthew 1–7: 126–30
Mark 1–8: 73–75
healing ministry characteristics
Mark 9–16: 117–19
heirship of
Hebrews: 11–13
hell, teaching on
Luke 11–17: 356–57
High Priest for God's elect
1 Timothy: 68
high priestly prayer (*see* High Priestly Prayer)
historical impact of
Luke 1–5: 104
historicity of
Romans 1–8: 294

honoring/confessing
Luke 11–17: 119–22
human religious authority and
Matthew 16–23: 286
humanity of
Matthew 8–15: 376
Mark 1–8: 229
Mark 9–16: 210
Luke 18–24: 153–55, 157
Philippians: 130
1 & 2 Thessalonians: 14
as humanly unordained
Matthew 16–23: 285
humanness of
Matthew 8–15: 33
Matthew 16–23: 276, 349
humiliation of
Matthew 16–23: 244
Mark 1–8: 45, 192
Hebrews: 64–65
and humility
Matthew 8–15: 376
Mark 9–16: 102–3
John 12–21: 59–69
1 Corinthians: 106
Philippians: 120
1–3 John: 255
I AM statements
John 12–21: 77, 102, 262, 308
identification of
John 1–11: 309–20
identity of
Luke 6–10: 247–48, 257–64
illegal nature of trial
John 12–21: 320–21
illumination in
1 Peter: 127–34
image of
2 Corinthians: 117, 124
immutability of
Hebrews: 36
impartiality of
James: 98
imperial sovereignty of
Mark 1–8: 27–28
imputed righteousness by
Romans 1–8: 182–83
as incarnate Word, glory of
John 1–11: 37–46
as incarnate Word, responses to
John 1–11: 25–35
incarnation of
John 1–11: 40, 44–46
2 Corinthians: 19
Philippians: 118, 123
1 Timothy: 32
1–3 John: 8, 17, 158, 191–92
Revelation 12–22: 11, 108
indifference to
Matthew 8–15: 46
intercession of
Hebrews: 210
1–3 John: 46
interrogation at trial
John 12–21: 328–31
and interruptions
Mark 1–8: 257–62
invitation by
John 12–21: 50–52, 61
Jewish leaders' accusations at trial of
John 12–21: 326–28
and John the Baptist
John 1–11: 47–58, 121–33
as judge
Matthew 24–28: 113
Philippians: 142
Revelation 1–11: 83, 97, 102, 103, 114
Revelation 12–22: 249
judgment, place of
Matthew 24–28: 115
judgment declarations
Luke 11–17: 101, 102, 106, 108
judgment of the wicked by
Revelation 12–22: 215
judgment seat of
2 Corinthians: 176–79
as King
Matthew 1–7: ix–x
Matthew 24–28: 113
Mark 1–8: 13–19
Luke 18–24: 346, 363
John 12–21: 17–18, 329, 330, 331, 343, 352–53
kingdom of
Luke 1–5: 49–50
2 Corinthians: 243–44, 288, 429
1 Peter: 131, 147–48, 152, 237–38
knowledge of
2 Peter & Jude: 43–45
as Lamb of God
Luke 18–24: 196, 267, 273
life events, control of
John 12–21: 14, 63, 304, 306
life of
Acts 1–12: 59–62
as light
1–3 John: 23, 24, 62
as Light of the world
John 1–11: 331–39
as Living Water
John 1–11: 135–50
as Lord
Mark 1–8: 187, 188
Luke 1–5: 158–60
as Lord and Master
2 Peter & Jude: 23–25, 72–76, 159–63
as Lord of the Sabbath
Mark 1–8: 137–38
Luke 6–10: 6
and Lord's Supper
1 Peter: 24
lordship of
Matthew 1–7: 137, 415, 477–80
Matthew 16–23: 194
Matthew 24–28: 340
Romans 9–16: 16, 74
Ephesians: 38, 52
Philippians: 147–49
love, manifestation of God's
1–3 John: 167

love, perfect model of
1–3 John: 131
love, teaching on
1–3 John: 61–62, 64
love for the unredeemed by
Revelation 1–11: 138
majesty of
Ephesians: 48
meaning of name
Mark 1–8: 15
as mediator
1 Timothy: 71
as Messiah (See also Messiah)
Mark 1–8: 412
John 1–11: 58–74, 92, 136–40, 153, 163–64, 261–63, 300, 470
John 12–21: 11–13
2 Corinthians: 289, 464
1 Peter: 53–56, 82–83, 105–6, 120–21, 123, 125–26, 129, 167, 170, 254, 270–71, 281–82
1–3 John: 177, 188–89
messiahship claims of
Matthew 16–23: 23
messianic credentials
Matthew 8–15: 48, 190
as Messianic King
1–3 John: 188–89
messianic predictions, fulfilling of
Romans 1–8: 14
mind of
1 Peter: 240–41
ministry of
2 Corinthians: 220–21
2 Peter & Jude: 207–14
miracles of
Luke 1–5: 291–97
John 12–21: 13, 106
miracles of, blind eyes opened
John 1–11: 387–96
miracles of, first
John 1–11: 75–84
miracles of, loaves and fishes
John 1–11: 217–26
miracles of, raising and resurrection of Lazarus (*See also* Lazarus)
John 1–11: 449–76
miracles of, unbelief and
John 1–11: 397–408
modern critics and
Luke 18–24: 45–46
Mosaic law, embodiment of
Romans 1–8: 406
name of (*see* Name of Christ)
naming of
Luke 1–5: 48, 166–68
nature of atonement
1 Timothy: 71–72
of Nazareth
Mark 1–8: 64
New Covenant and (*see* New Covenant) and obedience
Hebrews: 66, 252–53
1–3 John: 59, 193
Old Testament prophecies of
Mark 1–8: 18, 19
Luke 18–24: 46, 47, 50–52
Acts 13–28: 21–22
1–3 John: 189–90
and Olivet Discourse
1 Peter: 17–18
1–3 John: 97, 232
omnipotence of
Revelation 1–11: 119
omniscience of
Matthew 24–28: 72
Mark 1–8: 329
Mark 9–16: 125–26
Revelation 1–11: 59, 111
as the Only Begotten Son
John 1–11: 116–17
as only Savior
Ephesians: 52
parables of
1 Peter: 39, 61–62, 261–62
2 Peter & Jude: 179
patience of
1 Timothy: 33
Paul's teachings about
2 Corinthians: 2, 20–27, 81–108, 141–58, 226–30, 353, 370–87, 443–66, 474
payment for sin
Matthew 1–7: 192–93
perfect humility and sacrifice of
1–3 John: 65–66, 131
perfect priesthood of
Romans 1–8: 509
perfection and innocence of
Matthew 24–28: 233–34
perfection of
Hebrews: 125, 202–3
persecution of
John 1–11: 169–80
personal fellowship with
1 Peter: 46–47
personal relationship to
1–3 John: 59
Peter and
2 Peter & Jude: 2–3
Peter's testimony to deity of
Mark 1–8: 411–13
Pilate's panic at trial of
John 12–21: 340–42
Pilate's proposals at trial of
John 12–21: 336–40
Pilate's questioning of
John 12–21: 328–31
before Pontius Pilate
1 Timothy: 272
popular appeal of
Mark 1–8: 161–63, 177, 324, 339–40
popularity of
Luke 6–10: 86–87
Luke 18–24: 109, 120, 130
possession by
1 Peter: 127–34
poverty of
2 Corinthians: 287–95
power of
Mark 1–8: 65–68, 176, 182, 183
Luke 1–5: 291–97

Luke 6–10: 88–89, 206, 207, 228, 234, 345–46
2 Corinthians: 86
2 Peter & Jude: 26–28
power over disease and death
Mark 1–8: 253, 254, 260, 262–66, 334, 377
power over Satan and demons
Matthew 8–15: 39
Mark 1–8: 65–67, 239, 240, 246
power over storms
Mark 1–8: 334
and prayer
Mark 1–8: 78–79
Luke 11–17: 2–3
Luke 18–24: 2, 302–7
1 & 2 Thessalonians: 186
2 Peter & Jude: 37–38, 152–53, 208–9
and preaching
Matthew 1–7: 124–26
Mark 1–8: 80–81, 84, 227
Luke 1–5: 281–85, 297, 304
preeminence of
Colossians & Philemon: 43–53
preexistence of
John 1–11: 1–2, 13–14
1 Timothy: 32
as presenter of saints
2 Peter & Jude: 211–13
priesthood of (*see* Priesthood of Christ)
proclaimed among the nations
1 Timothy: 142
proclamation of
1 Peter: 133–34
promises to believers
John 12–21: 111–12
proofs of deity
Matthew 8–15: 436–45
proper view of
1 Corinthians: 93
in prophecy
Luke 6–10: 85
propitiation for sin
1–3 John: 46–50, 82, 124, 192
radiance of
Hebrews: 15–16
reactions to claims of
John 1–11: 299–308
reconciliation of
2 Corinthians: 199–208, 211–13
as Redeemer
1 Peter: 71–85
redemption, focal point of
1–3 John: 188–89
redemption through blood of (*See also* Redemption)
Ephesians: 17–26
redemptive mission of
Luke 18–24: 68, 69, 173–75
reign of
Hebrews: 36–37
rejection of
Matthew 1–7: x, 168–69
Matthew 8–15: 19–20
Mark 1–8: 165
Luke 18–24: 53
John 1–11: 437–48
Acts 13–28: 23
Romans 9–16: 3, 19
Hebrews: 13, 19, 92, 136, 148–49, 257, 279–80
rejection of claims of
John 1–11: 375–86
responses to
Matthew 8–15: 78
resurrection of (*see* Resurrection)
return of
Romans 1–8: 85
1 Timothy: 273
1–3 John: 110
Revelation 1–11: 23–24
revealed in the flesh
1 Timothy: 140
revelation and
Hebrews: 6, 10
as revelation of God's glory
Mark 9–16: 3, 4, 5
rewards of service to
John 12–21: 29–30
riches of
2 Corinthians: 289–91
righteousness of
2 Peter & Jude: 22–23
roles of
1 Peter: 165–66
sacrifice, sufficiency of
Romans 1–8: 217
sacrifice of
Hebrews: xvii–xviii, 18–19, 125, 230
and sadness
Mark 9–16: 294
salvation and (*See* Salvation)
as Savior
Luke 1–5: 152–54, 159–60, 168
2 Peter & Jude: 18–31, 34–35, 38–41, 205–14
as Savior, descriptions of
John 1–11: 59–74
as Savior, responses to
John 1–11: 109–20
as Savior, to the world
John 1–11: 151–60
as Savior and Lord
Titus: 114
scope of ministry
Luke 6–10: 178–84
seating of
Hebrews: 206–8
second coming of (*See* Second coming, Christ's)
security in (*see* Security in Christ)
seen by angels
1 Timothy: 141
self–giving death
Matthew 24–28: 272
self–imposed limitations
Matthew 24–28: 129
Sermon on the Mount
2 Peter & Jude: 186–87
as servant
Acts 1–12: 106–7
shared sufferings of
2 Corinthians: 24–25

as Shepherd–Ruler
Matthew 1–7: 33–34
siblings of
Mark 1–8: 178–79, 277
silence of
Mark 9–16: 326, 327, 348
Luke 18–24: 336, 350, 355
sin, teaching on
1–3 John: 26
sinlessness of
John 12–21: 253–54
Romans 1–8: 407
Hebrews: 113
1–3 John: 125
sins, taking away
1–3 John: 41, 124–25
as Son of David
Mark 9–16: 115–16, 127, 207–9
Luke 18–24: 60–61, 152–53
as Son of God
Mark 1–8: 19, 36, 56, 136, 160, 224, 412
Mark 9–16: 207, 227, 301, 310, 326, 417
Luke 1–5: 189, 194–96, 290, 302
Luke 18–24: 440
John 1–11: 38, 41–43, 72–74, 109–10, 162, 185–91, 193–98, 281, 311, 464–65
2 Corinthians: 18, 43, 71, 150
2 Peter & Jude: 34–35, 42, 55, 60–61
as Son of Man
Matthew 16–23: 54
Mark 1–8: 105, 146, 433
Mark 9–16: 96, 109, 256
Luke 1–5: 290
Luke 6–10: 166, 260, 263, 264, 295
Luke 11–17: 86, 123, 161, 412, 416
Luke 18–24: 236, 259–60, 338–39
John 1–11: 72–74, 86, 99, 113–17, 183, 198–201, 311, 341–42, 409–13
John 12–21: 27
Acts 1–12: 222–23
1 Peter: 254, 269
sonship of
Matthew 1–7: 80–82
Hebrews: 26–29
sovereignty of
Luke 18–24: 81–82
Romans 1–8: 18
Romans 9–16: 281
1 & 2 Thessalonians: 14
Revelation 1–11: 119
Spirit of
2 Corinthians: 27–45, 82, 99, 102–7, 116–24, 224
as spiritual King
Mark 1–8: 321
as stumbling block
1 Peter: 122–23
submitting to authority of
Mark 1–8: 56
subordination of
Hebrews: 36
as substitute for sinners
Luke 18–24: 298
suffering for
Romans 1–8: 448
suffering for God, perfect example of
Romans 1–8: 450
suffering of (See also Suffering)
Mark 9–16: 96–98, 106
Luke 11–17: 414
Luke 18–24: 53–55
2 Corinthians: 24–25
Hebrews: 124
1 Peter: 165–74, 205–21, 251–54, 266
2 Peter & Jude: 25
as Suffering Slave
Mark 1–8: 42
sufficiency of
Ephesians: 41
Colossians & Philemon: 7, 9, 91, 103–4
supernatural power of
Luke 18–24: 58, 62–64, 157
supremacy of
1 Peter: 219–20
as surety of the New Covenant
Hebrews: 197–98
as sustainer
Hebrews: 16–18
sympathy of
Hebrews: 70–72, 111–13, 123–24
taken up in glory
1 Timothy: 142
teaching of disciples by
Mark 1–8: 405, 406
teachings of
2 Corinthians: 50–54, 81–117, 155–56, 222–36, 335–37, 409–65
1 Peter: 17–18, 23–34, 69–75, 95, 108–11, 131–32, 149–53, 188–91, 208–16, 238–39, 238, 252, 265–70
2 Peter & Jude: 15, 63–65, 69–79, 153–55, 186–87, 193–204
teachings of, children of Abraham vs. children of Satan
John 1–11: 363–73
teachings of, life's ultimate question
John 1–11: 309–20
teachings of, new birth
John 1–11: 97–107
teachings of, sin
John 1–11: 341–50
teachings of, spiritual sight vs. spiritual blindness
John 1–11: 409–19
teachings of, truth
John 1–11: 351–61
teachings of, two resurrections
John 1–11: 193–202
temple clearing of
Mark 9–16: 135–39
temptation of
Matthew 24–28: 171
Luke 1–5: 251–61
John 1–11: 281
1 Timothy: 50
Hebrews: 112–13
James: 46, 48
testimony to
Luke 1–5: 233–35, 240–41
as theme of Paul's preaching
1 Timothy: 139

titles of
John 1–11: 14, 25–26, 34–35, 37–46, 47–48, 55, 102, 112–13, 116–17, 162, 183–91, 193–98, 286, 354, 422–24, 450–51
Revelation 1–11: 2, 17, 105, 118, 133, 166, 167, 171, 240, 279
Revelation 12–22: 112–13, 218, 221, 306, 307 (*See also* Name of Christ)
Transfiguration of
Mark 9–16: 2–8, 13–15
1 Peter: 252, 266
Revelation 1–11: 33, 47, 50, 301, 314
trial before Annas/Caiaphas
John 12–21: 315–17
trial of
Mark 9–16: 326, 328, 329, 352–54, 358–59
Luke 18–24: 323–25, 336, 337
in the Trinity
1–3 John: 162–65
triumph over enemies
Hebrews: 255–56
triumphal entry of
John 12–21: 9, 15–18, 50, 97, 119
Revelation 1–11: 226
as true God
1–3 John: 209–10
true knowledge of
2 Peter & Jude: 28–30, 33–46
as true Messiah
John 12–21: 11–12
as true vine
John 12–21: 142–51
true vs. false disciples of
John 1–11: 227–38
as ultimate mediator
Luke 11–17: 400
and unbelief, miracle investigations
John 1–11: 397–408
and unbelief, responses to
John 1–11: 161–68
unbelief of His brothers
James: 10
union with
1 & 2 Thessalonians: 13–14, 224–25
1 Peter: 103–17
Upper Room Discourse of
1 Peter: 18, 41, 110–11, 114–15
verification of claims of
John 1–11: 285–97
victory over Satan by
James: 205
vindicated in the Spirit
1 Timothy: 140
as vineyard owner's son
Luke 18–24: 124
virgin birth of
Luke 1–5: 54–56, 57–58
visible displays of deity of
Mark 1–8: 160, 225–26
walking in the same manner as
1–3 John: 59–60
washing the disciples' feet
Luke 11–17: 41–42
and widows
1 Timothy: 201–3
as the Word
2 Corinthians: 488
and Word of Life
1–3 John: 16
work of
Acts 1–12: 10
worship of
Hebrews: 29–30, 31–32
wounds of
1 Peter: 172–73
See also God
Jesus Christ Superstar
John 1–11: 182
Jesus Justus
Luke 1–5: 11
Jesus Seminar
John 1–11: 76, 86–87, 182
Jethro
1–3 John: 242
Jew, origin of name
Romans 1–8: 148
Jewish–Arab animosity
Galatians: 125
Jewish calendar
Matthew 24–28: 139
Jewish councils, local
Mark 9–16: 320–21
See also Sanhedrin
Jewish culture (first century)
and regulations
1 Timothy: 197
relief of widows
1 Timothy: 194
Jewish division of night
Matthew 24–28: 162
Jewish eschatology
Luke 18–24: 178–83
Jewish feasts
Mark 9–16: 268, 322
Luke 1–5: 191
Jewish house construction
Mark 1–8: 101
Jewish injustices/inequities
Mark 9–16: 136, 223
Jewish leaders
Luke 18–24: 119–20, 410
extrabiblical regulations of
Luke 11–17: 198, 259
hostility/opposition to Jesus
Luke 11–17: 80–81, 176, 194, 206–7
murder of Jesus and
Luke 11–17: 226–27
See also Essenes; Pharisees; Scribes and Pharisees; Zealots
Jewish leaders, duplicity of
Matthew 24–28: 235
Jewish people
Luke 11–17: 227, 232, 233, 393–94
Jewish people/Jews
Abraham and
Luke 1–5: 221–22
advantages of
Romans 1–8: 167
calling, unique divine
Romans 1–8: 148

Christ, rejection of
Romans 9–16: 19
Christians' love for
Romans 9–16: 109
Christ's claims and
John 12–21: 52, 56
and Christ's death
John 12–21: 334–35
at Christ's trial
John 12–21: 326–32
circumcision of
Luke 1–5: 89
definition of
John 1–11: 50
deportations of
Romans 9–16: 21
of the Diaspora
Luke 1–5: 267
Gentiles and
Luke 1–5: 209
John 12–21: 20–21
God's future plans for
Galatians: 75
heritage, trust in
Romans 9–16: 3
history of, tragic
Romans 1–8: 163–66
hostility toward
Luke 18–24: 269
kingdom theology and
Luke 1–5: 136
leaders' hypocrisy
John 12–21: 54, 326
legalism of
Romans 1–8: 120, 366
legalistic
Galatians: 77
Paul and
John 12–21: 166–67
persecution of
Matthew 16–23: 395
Pilate and
John 12–21: 336–43
pride of
Romans 1–8: 149
resurrection and
John 12–21: 216–17
reverence for Scripture
Romans 1–8: 204
salvation and
Luke 1–5: 96, 106–7
See also Israel; Judaism
Jewish religionists
1–3 John: 165, 189
Jewish religious leaders
hatred of Jesus
Mark 9–16: 164, 169, 174, 187, 206, 311
hypocrisy of
Mark 9–16: 174, 176–82
and Pilate
Mark 9–16: 393
Jewish resurrection beliefs
Mark 9–16: 184–85
Jewish revolt (A.D. 66–70)
Revelation 1–11: 293
Jewish tradition
Romans 9–16: 54
Jewish trials
Mark 9–16: 322, 325
Jewish writings, extrabiblical
Matthew 24–28: 3
Jewish zealots
Romans 9–16: 210
Jews
Luke 6–10: 126, 147, 295, 311
Jezebel
Mark 1–8: 298, 307
Luke 1–5: 231, 275, 276
Luke 6–10: 54
Luke 18–24: 351
2 Corinthians: 139, 438
Revelation 12–22: 4
Joab
1–3 John: 254
Joanna
Luke 6–10: 183
Luke 18–24: 412
Joash
Luke 6–10: 74
Job
Mark 9–16: 68, 69
Luke 6–10: 99, 213, 271
Luke 11–17: 129–30, 180, 363
Luke 18–24: 6
2 Corinthians: 12–14, 107–19, 149, 183–86, 272, 400–401, 443
Ephesians: 361
Hebrews: 388–89
1 Peter: 44, 95, 249
1–3 John: 86, 243
integrity toward God
Titus: 26
Joel
Luke 6–10: 144
John (apostle)
Mark 1–8: 19, 40, 51, 60, 161, 170, 263
Mark 9–16: 104–7, 235, 285, 383, 399
Luke 1–5: 70, 195, 225, 294, 303
Luke 6–10: 39
John 12–21: 275, 334
1 Peter: 17–19, 54–55, 125, 236, 264, 287
2 Peter & Jude: 37, 60, 62, 106, 110, 117, 130–31
1–3 John: 5, 114
background of
Luke 6–10: 47–48
as beloved disciple
John 12–21: 318, 405
characteristics of
Luke 6–10: 47, 313
choosing of
Luke 6–10: 40
commitment to truth
Luke 6–10: 48
as eyewitness
John 12–21: 394, 405
1–3 John: 18
in Gethsemane
Luke 18–24: 302, 303
importance
Luke 6–10: 16–18, 42

at Jesus' tomb
John 12–21: 368, 369
life, summary of
1–3 John: 6–7
at Lord's Supper
Luke 18–24: 290
Mary's care entrusted to
John 12–21: 355
ministry location of
1–3 John: 2, 6
occupation
Luke 6–10: 26, 41
Papias on
1–3 John: 5
Passover preparations
Luke 18–24: 273
persecution of
John 12–21: 169
Peter and
Luke 6–10: 36
prayers of
Luke 18–24: 3
preeminent place, request for
1–3 John: 255
as presbyter
1–3 John: 5–6, 215–16, 244
temperament of
1–3 John: 6–7
"the apostle of love"
1–3 John: 63
at tomb
Luke 18–24: 409, 410, 414
at transfiguration
Luke 6–10: 282, 286

John (gospel of)
Mark 1–8: 6
authorship of
John 1–11: 3–9
background and historical perspectives of
John 1–11: vii–viii, 1–12
date and place of writing of
John 1–11: 9
purposes of
John 1–11: 9–10

1 John
author, authority of writer
1–3 John: 4–5, 6
author, early church testimony regarding
1–3 John: 3
author, eyewitness to Christ's life claims
1–3 John: 4, 5
author, gospel of John, similarities to
1–3 John: 3–4
author, "John the Elder" as
1–3 John: 5, 6
date
1–3 John: 7
destination
1–3 John: 10, 72
as personal and pastoral
1–3 John: 9, 10
place of writing
1–3 John: 7
purpose
1–3 John: 9, 72, 120, 122, 201–2
recipients of
1–3 John: 10

2 John
author
1–3 John: 212, 216
date
1–3 John: 212
destination
1–3 John: 212, 215–17
occasion of
1–3 John: 211
place of writing
1–3 John: 212
purpose
1–3 John: 211, 215
readers
1–3 John: 212

3 John
author
1–3 John: 240
date
1–3 John: 240
occasion of
1–3 John: 239
overview
1–3 John: 260
place of writing
1–3 John: 240
purpose
1–3 John: 239, 241

John Chrysostom
Mark 1–8: 210
Luke 1–5: 226

John Hyrcanus
Luke 6–10: 312–13

John Mark
Mark 1–8: 1, 2
Acts 1–12: 328
1–3 John: 246
See also Mark (apostle)

John the Baptist
Matthew 1–7: 49–58, 103–4
Mark 9–16: 18, 19, 102, 157, 349
Luke 6–10: 40, 47, 105, 163
Luke 11–17: 4, 107, 219, 228, 229, 349
Luke 18–24: 115, 116, 151, 263, 349, 366
John 12–21: 13, 74, 86, 105, 148
Acts 13–28: 22–23, 30, 159, 162, 164, 165, 216, 252, 327
2 Corinthians: 20, 202, 432
Hebrews: 350
1 Peter: 140
2 Peter & Jude: 22
1–3 John: 6, 192–93
Revelation 1–11: 28, 56
Antipas's execution of
Luke 6–10: 149, 247
baptism of
Mark 1–8: 20, 21, 25, 38, 127
connections with Jesus Christ
John 1–11: 121, 124–33
death
Mark 1–8: 307–10
disciples
Mark 1–8: 126–27, 129

disciples of
Luke 1–5: 338–39
and Elijah
Mark 1–8: 23–24
as forerunner
Luke 1–5: 21–22, 25, 38, 66, 71, 92, 117
greatness of
Luke 6–10: 152–57
Herod Antipas and
Luke 1–5: 202, 231–32
Herod Antipas's fear of
Mark 1–8: 303–5
and Jesus' identity
Mark 1–8: 415–16
message of
Luke 1–5: 205–10
as Messiah's herald
Mark 1–8: 17–18, 191
ministry of
Luke 6–10: 165
and ministry of Jesus
Mark 1–8: 47
naming of
Luke 1–5: 89–91
and Old Testament prophets
Mark 1–8: 16, 17, 18, 285
personal character of
Luke 1–5: 35–38
physical appearance
Mark 1–8: 23, 24–25
preaching of
Mark 1–8: 20, 22, 25, 287, 303–4
Luke 1–5: 39–40, 86–87, 214, 228–30, 232
questioning of Christ
Luke 6–10: 145–48
on repentance
Luke 6–10: 181
testimony of
John 1–11: 47–58

John the Elder
John 1–11: 7

Johnson, Paul
Titus: 147

Johnston, Jon
2 Timothy: 166

Johnstone, Robert
on meekness
James: 169–70

Jonah
Mark 1–8: 363, 400
Luke 6–10: 21, 212
Luke 11–17: 85–86, 87
Luke 18–24: 2
John 12–21: 20–21, 204

Jonathan
Luke 6–10: 38, 39

Jones, Jim
Luke 11–17: 255

Jones, Peter
Titus: 80

Jonestown incident
Luke 11–17: 255

Jordan River
Mark 1–8: 22, 23, 29, 228, 303
Luke 1–5: 204–5, 265, 276, 302
Luke 6–10: 152, 162, 208
Luke 18–24: 59, 70, 187, 366
John 12–21: 12

Jordan Valley
Mark 1–8: 229
Luke 6–10: 208

Joseph (brother of James, Son of Alphaeus)
Mark 9–16: 105
Luke 6–10: 69

Joseph (brother of Jesus)
John 1–11: 280–81

Joseph (husband of Mary)
Matthew 1–7: 16–18, 21–22
Mark 1–8: 271, 276, 277
Mark 9–16: 60, 208, 387
Luke 1–5: 45, 49, 142, 146–48, 162–63, 166, 171, 183, 189, 192, 246–48
Luke 6–10: 144, 203
Luke 18–24: 60, 153, 266
John 1–11: 55, 70, 71, 77, 78, 138–39, 280, 433
John 12–21: 355
Galatians: 168

Joseph (patriarch)
Matthew 1–7: 172
Mark 9–16: 386–87
Luke 6–10: 143
2 Corinthians: 54–56, 282
Hebrews: 342
Revelation 12–22: 5
honoring of parents
1 Timothy: 199
parallels with Christ
Acts 1–12: 205

Joseph (son of Jacob)
John 1–11: 142

Joseph of Arimathea
Mark 9–16: 207, 389, 390, 391, 392, 398
Luke 6–10: 99
Luke 18–24: 400, 401, 402, 414, 415
John 1–11: 107, 287
John 12–21: 8, 317, 318, 363, 365–67

Josephus
Matthew 8–15: 103, 281, 420
Mark 9–16: 114, 346
Luke 1–5: 11, 201, 231, 265, 318
Luke 11–17: 243, 256
Luke 18–24: 69, 70, 356, 368
John 1–11: 100, 214, 325, 344
John 12–21: 12, 325
Romans 1–8: 157, 164
Galatians: 54
James: 88
on Ananias the high priest
Acts 13–28: 281
on the Beautiful Gate of the Temple
Acts 1–12: 99
on famine in Israel
Acts 1–12: 316
on first–century revolt in Palestine
Acts 13–28: 263
on Herod's speech
Acts 1–12: 327
on Jewish sects
Colossians & Philemon: 100
on Jews' right to execute violators of the Temple
Acts 13–28: 259

on the martyrdom of James
Acts 1–12: 4
on the Pharisees
Acts 13–28: 333
on the Scythians
Colossians & Philemon: 152
on Theudas's revolt
Acts 1–12: 172
Joshua
Mark 1–8: 15
Luke 1–5: 116, 246
Luke 6–10: 21
John 1–11: 132, 204, 399, 430
2 Corinthians: 114, 272, 354, 384, 404, 415
2 Peter & Jude: 18, 174–75
Josiah (king)
Mark 9–16: 48
2 Corinthians: 377
2 Timothy: 156
Joy
Luke 1–5: 158
Luke 6–10: 98, 192, 338, 339, 342, 343
Luke 11–17: 7–8, 292–301, 306
John 12–21: 151, 216–19, 280
Hebrews: 77
1 Peter: 39–48
2 Peter & Jude: 212–13
1–3 John: 19–20, 109, 236–37
biblical theology of
Philippians: 10–11
Christian
Romans 1–8: 287–88
1 & 2 Thessalonians: 25, 184, 185
definition of
James: 21
hindrances to
Philippians: 32–35
of Jesus
James: 22
of Paul
James: 22
Paul's discouragement
2 Corinthians: 66–68
Paul's encouragement
2 Corinthians: 68–70
restoration of
2 Corinthians: 57–58, 63–75, 241, 278
true
Galatians: 64
Joyce, William ("Lord Haw Haw")
Luke 6–10: 74
John 12–21: 72
Jubilees, Book of
Romans 1–8: 233, 248
Judah
Luke 1–5: 42, 58, 66, 67, 119
Luke 6–10: 142
John 1–11: 137
1–3 John: 38
Judah, Kingdom of
Mark 9–16: 169
people of
1–3 John: 26
Judah the Prince (rabbi)
Romans 1–8: 357
Judaism
Mark 9–16: 226
Luke 1–5: 319, 341
Luke 6–10: 93, 126, 127
Luke 11–17: 194, 197
Luke 18–24: 73, 103, 104
Acts 13–28: 156
Romans 1–8: 226
Hebrews: xi–xii, 247–48
Christianity and
Luke 6–10: 118
fasting in
Mark 1–8: 128
Jesus as threat to
Mark 1–8: 125
and lineage
Matthew 16–23: 347
lordship over believers
Matthew 16–23: 194
Messianic misconceptions in
Luke 6–10: 146
messianic theology
Luke 18–24: 49, 56, 200–201
national
Luke 6–10: 230
omnipotence
Matthew 16–23: 349
omnipresence
Matthew 16–23: 349
omniscience
Matthew 16–23: 349
Paul's position in
Luke 6–10: 270
and the Pharisees
Mark 1–8: 99
physical suffering
Matthew 16–23: 225
pride and
Luke 6–10: 300, 302
return in glory
Matthew 16–23: 64
rituals/traditions of
Mark 1–8: 29, 343, 344
Sabbath regulations of
Luke 6–10: 3, 4
and salvation
Mark 1–8: 131, 132, 133
self–righteous
Matthew 16–23: 37
servanthood
Matthew 16–23: 244
sovereignty
Matthew 16–23: 194
submission to human government
Matthew 16–23: 87
suffering and death ordained by God
Matthew 16–23: 223
temptation to avoid cross
Matthew 16–23: 41
unity with
Matthew 16–23: 103
and works–righteousness
Mark 1–8: 149
Judaizers
Matthew 16–23: 361
Acts 13–28: 63, 64, 67, 68, 250–51

Romans 1–8: 174, 202, 249, 262
Romans 9–16: 276
2 Corinthians: 106
Galatians: x, 13–17, 35, 47–60, 56–57, 72–79, 82, 96, 119, 126, 128, 144, 188, 197–201, 208
Titus: x, 3, 21, 59, 161, 163
Hebrews: 189
characteristics of
Galatians: 138–42
Judaizing heresy
Ephesians: 70
Judas
apocryphal accounts of
Matthew 24–28: 182
Judas (Jude). *see* Jude (apostle)
Judas Barsabbas
2 Peter & Jude: 149
Judas Iscariot
Mark 1–8: 161, 169, 172
Luke 1–5: 195, 261
Luke 6–10: 14, 16, 36
Luke 11–17: 129, 168, 333
Luke 18–24: 271
John 1–11: 5–6, 60, 139, 267, 273–74, 342
2 Corinthians: 272, 351–52, 411
1 Timothy: 53
1 Peter: 47, 279–80
2 Peter & Jude: 2, 71, 142, 149
as anti–hero
Luke 18–24: 280
betrayal by
Mark 9–16: 96, 286–88, 309–10, 312
betrayal of Christ
Luke 6–10: 18, 74, 79–82, 144
betrayal of Jesus
John 12–21: 14, 67–68, 71–82, 306, 307
Caiaphas and
Luke 18–24: 312
culpability of
Mark 9–16: 288
death of
Mark 9–16: 313
Luke 18–24: 344
Acts 1–12: 31–33
disillusionment
Luke 6–10: 78–80, 184
hypocrisy of
Luke 18–24: 53, 290
John 12–21: 6–8, 74–75
lessons from life of
Luke 6–10: 81–82
and Mary's anointing
Mark 9–16: 274
Matthias replacing
Luke 6–10: 16, 36, 241
motives
Luke 6–10: 76–78
name
Luke 6–10: 75–76
non–biblical writings on
Luke 18–24: 311–12
Satan and
Luke 18–24: 269–70, 291
John 12–21: 64, 80–82
Satanic influence on
Mark 9–16: 277
significance of
John 12–21: 82, 152
suicide of
Mark 9–16: 313
Acts 1–12: 31–33
Judas Maccabeus
Mark 9–16: 209
Luke 18–24: 154
Judas of Damascus
2 Peter & Jude: 149
Judas of Galilee
Luke 6–10: 70
Luke 18–24: 135
Judas the Son of James (Thaddeus) *see* Thaddeus
Judas the Zealot
Mark 9–16: 179
Jude (apostle)
Mark 1–8: 179, 277
John 12–21: 117
Jude, teachings and writings of
on apostates and apostate times
2 Peter & Jude: 157–204
on coming judgments
2 Peter & Jude: 183–92
on contention
2 Peter & Jude: 147–56
introduction to
2 Peter & Jude: 139–46
on saints' guarantees
2 Peter & Jude: 205–14
on survival strategies
2 Peter & Jude: 193–204
on warnings
2 Peter & Jude: 157–68
Judea
Mark 1–8: 22, 23, 300, 312
Mark 9–16: 53, 114, 349
Luke 1–5: 265, 266, 297, 320
Luke 6–10: 133, 309, 310, 324
Luke 18–24: 355, 378
Judean desert
Luke 1–5: 253, 254
Judge, God as perfect
Romans 1–8: 173
Judges
Luke 18–24: 3–8, 331, 332
Judging by God's Word
Matthew 16–23: 34, 138
Judging others
1 Corinthians: 87–90, 132
Judgment
Mark 1–8: 198, 199
Luke 1–5: 216–17
Luke 6–10: 84, 112, 120, 147–48, 165, 332–35
John 1–11: 27, 117–19, 163, 181–92, 199–200, 203–16, 267, 276–77, 285–86, 331–40, 416
John 12–21: 51, 56, 197–98
2 Corinthians: 12, 14, 51, 372, 457, 467–68
1 Peter: 37–38, 108, 123–32, 216–17, 230–39, 250–56, 264

according to deeds
Matthew 16–23: 34, 57
and the ancient world
2 Peter & Jude: 87–88
on apostates
2 Peter & Jude: 183–92
assurance of
2 Peter & Jude: 123–25
on Babylon
Luke 18–24: 232
by believers
Mark 9–16: 405
of believers
Romans 9–16: 260
believers and
Romans 1–8: 128
certainties of
Hebrews: 277–78
2 Peter & Jude: 188–91
Christ's declarations of
Luke 11–17: 101, 102, 106, 108–9
Christ's prediction of
Luke 18–24: 178
in Christ's second coming
Mark 9–16: 257
coming ones
2 Peter & Jude: 183–92
day of
Matthew 16–23: 52
2 Peter & Jude: 115, 120–21
1–3 John: 170–71
Day of the Lord vs. Day of God
2 Peter & Jude: 120–34
delay in
Luke 18–24: 381
deliverance from
Romans 1–8: 286
divine
Romans 1–8: 126, 127, 128, 132, 286
Colossians & Philemon: 141–42
on false teachers
2 Peter & Jude: 81–94
final
Romans 1–8: 126, 132
Hebrews: 140–41, 410, 418
final, of unbelievers
Romans 9–16: 40
of the flood
Hebrews: 322–23
God's
Matthew 1–7: 72
Matthew 8–15: 114, 377
Matthew 16–23: 34, 57, 391
John 12–21: 42
Romans 1–8: 71, 173
1 & 2 Thessalonians: 240–42
Revelation 12–22: 84, 87, 108–11, 113–14, 120–24, 137, 143, 175–76
at Golgotha
Mark 9–16: 376
Great White Throne Judgment
2 Peter & Jude: 92–93, 185–86
harvest as symbol of
Matthew 24–28: 62
inevitability of
Matthew 16–23: 391
Luke 11–17: 187–88
inevitability of God's
Matthew 16–23: 391
on Israel
Mark 1–8: 198–99
Luke 18–24: 97–99, 117, 125, 186
Israel's destruction as
Mark 9–16: 128, 169, 229
on Israel's religious leaders
Mark 9–16: 220–21, 330
of Jerusalem's destruction
Luke 18–24: 99, 371–72
Jesus' authority in
Luke 18–24: 112, 128
in the Law
Hebrews: 46–47
Old Testament predictions of
Luke 18–24: 231–34
patterns of
2 Peter & Jude: 91–93
precedent for
2 Peter & Jude: 84
on pride
Luke 11–17: 375–76
promise of
2 Peter & Jude: 83–84
as punishment for sin
Luke 11–17: 369
reality of
Luke 11–17: 82
for rejecting the gospel
Mark 1–8: 292–93, 356, 434
of Satan
Luke 11–17: 155
second coming and
Luke 11–17: 420
self–assessment and
Luke 11–17: 178
as sickness/disability
Mark 1–8: 163–64, 376
substitution and
Hebrews: 242
temporal and eternal
Matthew 24–28: 111
time of
Matthew 24–28: 114
at the tribulation
Luke 18–24: 220
unbelief and
Luke 11–17: 274–75, 419–20
works and
Romans 1–8: 127
See also God, as judge; Jesus Christ, as judge
Judgmental attitude
Matthew 1–7: 295–96
Judicial forgiveness
Luke 11–17: 39, 40
Judson, Adoniram
Philippians: 77
Julius Caesar
Mark 9–16: 408
Luke 1–5: 143
Junius
2 Corinthians: 409
Jurisprudence, Old Testament
Matthew 24–28: 198

Justice
Matthew 1–7: 192
Mark 1–8: 96–97
Luke 18–24: 3, 5–7
divine
Romans 1–8: 219, 297
2 Peter & Jude: 34–35, 82
of God
Mark 9–16: 269–70
human systems of
Romans 1–8: 217
for martyrs
1 Corinthians: 21
taking into one's own hands
Matthew 24–28: 190
Justification
Luke 11–17: 347
Luke 18–24: 13, 21, 75
Ephesians: 365
1 Peter: 37–38
2 Peter & Jude: 25–26, 205–14
1–3 John: 43–48, 124
of believers
Romans 9–16: 2, 148
by faith
Galatians: 55
Titus: 5
faith and
Romans 1–8: x, 132, 215
glorification and
Romans 1–8: 442
power of
Romans 1–8: 258
reconciliation and
Romans 1–8: 274
results of
Romans 1–8: 415
sanctification and
Romans 1–8: 318
Romans 9–16: 257
self
Romans 1–8: 109
Justifying faith, elements of
Galatians: 79
Justin Martyr
Mark 1–8: 3
Mark 9–16: 168
Luke 1–5: 2
Luke 18–24: 212
John 1–11: 4, 284, 304, 367–68
John 12–21: 170
Romans 1–8: 112
Romans 9–16: 235
1 Timothy: 176
2 Peter & Jude: 6–7
1–3 John: 2–3, 8
on apostolic authorship of Revelation
Revelation 1–11: 3
Justus
2 Corinthians: 411
Justus, Jesus
Colossians & Philemon: 196, 230
Juvenal (Roman poet)
1 Timothy: 80
Kaiser, Walter C., Jr.
Luke 18–24: 200
Titus: 13
on interpreting prophecy literally
Revelation 12–22: 232
Kant, Immanuel
2 Peter & Jude: 56
Karma
Romans 1–8: 95
Kee, Howard C.
Luke 1–5: 11–12
Keil, Johann K. E.
Ephesians: 231
Keller, Helen
Romans 1–8: 77
Keller, W. Phillip
John 1–11: 428
1 Peter: 261
Kelly, Howard
Matthew 8–15: 214
Kelly, J. N. D.
1 Timothy: 16, 291
2 Peter & Jude: 216
Kelvin, Lord
Matthew 8–15: 368
Kent, Duchess of
Luke 18–24: 88
Kent, Homer A., Jr.
John 1–11: 128, 156, 481, 488
1 Timothy: 127
on addressees of Jerusalem Council letter
Acts 13–28: 72
on the authenticity of miracle workers
Acts 1–12: 133
on the death of Terah (Abraham's father)
Acts 1–12: 203–4
Kerioth
Luke 6–10: 75
Luke 18–24: 271
John 12–21: 73
Kersa, Israel. *See* Gerasa
Khayyam, Omar
"The Rubaiyat"
Luke 11–17: 28–29
Khersa. *See* Gerasa
Kidron Valley
Mark 9–16: 228, 229, 242
Luke 18–24: 175, 176, 177, 300
John 12–21: 238, 305
Kierkegaard, Søren
2 Peter & Jude: 56
Kilpatrick, William K.
Romans 9–16: 159
Kim Ung-Yong
Luke 1–5: 188–89
Kindness
Luke 6–10: 109
Colossians & Philemon: 155–56
2 Peter & Jude: 49–50
King, Guy H.
on Christlikeness
Colossians & Philemon: 160–61
King of Israel
John 1–11: 72–73
King of Kings
John 1–11: 276

King of the Jews inscription
Luke 18–24: 383
King of the North
Matthew 24–28: 19
King of the South
Matthew 24–28: 19
Kingdom
Luke 18–24: 13, 24, 27, 43, 79, 80
Christ's earthly
Luke 1–5: 100–101
Christ's eternal
Matthew 8–15: 88
of Jesus Christ
Luke 1–5: 49–50
Jesus' previews of
Matthew 8–15: 31
the mediatorial
Matthew 8–15: 351
messianic
Luke 1–5: 100–101, 136
millennial
Luke 1–5: 99, 110–11, 129, 137, 211
mysteries of
Matthew 8–15: 105
present vs. future
Colossians & Philemon: 41–42, 57–58, 118
universal
Matthew 8–15: 351
Kingdom, spiritual
Mark 1–8: 48
Luke 11–17: 399, 400, 404, 412
See also Kingdom of God
Kingdom of Christ. *see* Jesus Christ, kingdom of
Kingdom of God
Matthew 1–7: 54–56, 379–81
Mark 1–8: 48, 49, 198, 317
Mark 9–16: 3, 7, 16, 82–85
Luke 1–5: 290, 297, 302
John 1–11: 14, 49, 80, 99, 102–3, 183–84, 241
Acts 1–12: 15, 19, 118ff.
Acts 13–28: 173, 372
2 Peter & Jude: 26, 45, 93, 112–13, 132, 158, 196
Revelation 12–22: 229
aspects of
Luke 11–17: 24–26, 64, 139
as Christ's primary theme
Mark 1–8: 317
Luke 11–17: 205–6
Christ's teachings on
Luke 6–10: 96, 182
cultural morality and
Luke 11–17: 72
definition of
James: 109
dimensions of
Mark 1–8: 48, 49
entering
Luke 11–17: 199–200
external power of
Luke 11–17: 208–12
forms of
Luke 6–10: 157–58
future form of
Luke 11–17: 23
internal influence of
Luke 11–17: 212–13
as kingdom of heaven
Luke 6–10: 181
love of
Luke 6–10: 103–9
mysteries of
Luke 6–10: 190
mystery of
Mark 1–8: 198
Ephesians: x
nearness of
Luke 6–10: 332
Paul's ministry and
Luke 11–17: 404–5
proclaiming
Luke 6–10: 180–81, 242, 252
questioned
Luke 11–17: 401
seeking
Luke 11–17: 144–45
small beginnings of
Luke 11–17: 207
as spiritual
Luke 11–17: 403–5
at the transfiguration
Luke 6–10: 282
Kingdom of heaven. *see* Kingdom of God
Kingdoms
Mark 1–8: 182
Luke 6–10: 324
Kings
Luke 11–17: 397
Kingship (of Jesus)
John 12–21: 17–18, 329, 330, 331, 343, 352–53
Kinsman–redeemer
Ephesians: 20
Kipling, Rudyard
2 Timothy: 195
Kissing
Luke 6–10: 173, 174
Kistemaker, Simon J.
2 Corinthians: 492
2 Peter & Jude: 216
on agora
Acts 13–28: 103
on authorship of "we passages"
Acts 1–12: 3
on the dating of Acts
Acts 1–12: 4
on Gaza Road
Acts 1–12: 253
on Jacob's purchase of a tomb in Shechem
Acts 1–12: 207
on meaning of Elymas
Acts 13–28: 9
Kittelson, James M.
Luke 18–24: 170
2 Corinthians: 146–47
Kitts, David B.
on gaps in the fossil record
Acts 13–28: 136
Kivengere, Festo
Matthew 8–15: 226

Knowledge
2 Peter & Jude: 28–30, 33–46
of Christian truth
Acts 1–12: 11
of God
John 12–21: 301, 302
1–3 John: 55–56, 75–77, 165
godly
1 Corinthians: 17–18
Colossians & Philemon: 28–29, 32–33, 150, 214
practical
Ephesians: 216
spiritual
Romans 1–8: 332
Knox, John
John 1–11: 240
Acts 13–28: 211
Romans 9–16: 12
1 Timothy: 19, 75
2 Timothy: 60
James: 71, 150
call to the ministry
1 Timothy: 44
Koivisto, Rex A.
on Stephen's mention of Shechem
Acts 1–12: 207
Korah
2 Corinthians: 12, 454
1 Peter: 108
2 Peter & Jude: 145, 176, 178–79
1–3 John: 248
Köstenberger, Andreas J.
John 1–11: 486, 488
John 12–21: 8, 39, 318, 329, 342–43, 349, 389, 402
Kruger, Michael J.
2 Peter & Jude: 8, 11, 216
Kruse, Colin G.
John 1–11: 243, 488
John 12–21: 7, 147
2 Corinthians: 30–31, 239, 292, 366, 492
1 Peter: 202–4
Kubeibeh
Luke 18–24: 420
Kursi. *See* Gerasa

Laban
1–3 John: 242
Labor relations
Ephesians: 321–29
Labors
2 Corinthians: 388
Ladd, George Eldon
on the Day of the Lord
1 & 2 Thessalonians: 145
Lake, Kirsopp
John 12–21: 375
Lake Gennesaret. *see* Sea of Galilee
Lake of fire
Mark 1–8: 64, 240, 244
Mark 9–16: 47, 232, 257
Luke 18–24: 196, 203
John 12–21: 42, 139
See also Hell
Lake Tiberias. *see* Sea of Galilee (Sea of Chinnereth, Sea of Tiberius)
Lamb of God
Mark 9–16: 279
Luke 18–24: 196, 267, 273
John 1–11: 47–48, 55–57, 63–69
Lambs
Mark 9–16: 284, 286
Luke 6–10: 329
Luke 18–24: 91, 93, 110, 273, 279
sacrificial
Matthew 24–28: 133
Lamech
1–3 John: 252
Lamenting
Luke 18–24: 370, 371
Lamps
Mark 1–8: 213
Luke 6–10: 199
Luke 11–17: 159
Land taxes
Mark 1–8: 114
Luke 18–24: 71, 134
Lane, William
Mark 1–8: 20
Mark 9–16: 410
Laney, J. Carl
2 Corinthians: 446
Laodicea
1–3 John: 2, 186
Laodicea, church at
Ephesians: 336
Laodicea, Council of
2 Peter & Jude: 9, 141
Last days
Acts 1–12: 53
Hebrews: 6, 10
1 Peter: 82–83, 237–38
2 Peter & Jude: 112
Pentecost and
Matthew 16–23: 59
The Last hour
1–3 John: 95–96
The Last Supper
Mark 9–16: 36
Luke 18–24: 274
John 12–21: 62
See also Lord's Supper
***The Late Great Planet Earth* (Lindsey)**
Luke 18–24: 246
Latimer, Hugh
Matthew 8–15: 222
Luke 1–5: 227
John 12–21: 189
1 Timothy: 97
Laughter, ungodly
Titus: 74
Law
Luke 1–5: 206, 319
Luke 6–10: 106, 271–72, 317, 352–56
Luke 11–17: 104, 351
Luke 18–24: 38–39, 134
1 Peter: 24–25, 67–69, 95, 108–9, 126, 167, 224–25, 242
ceremonial
Matthew 1–7: 257–59

Mark 1–8: 341, 342, 345, 376
conscience and
1–3 John: 142–43
and covenants (*see* Covenant(s))
of God
1–3 John: 45, 141
God's gospel and
Matthew 16–23: 193
God's gospel and purpose of
Matthew 16–23: 191
and grace
Matthew 8–15: 70
Jesus' fulfillment of
Matthew 1–7: 256–59
Jewish ceremonial
Ephesians: 77
Jewish view of
James: 114
judicial
Matthew 1–7: 257
moral
Matthew 1–7: 256–57, 272–73
Old Testament
Matthew 1–7: 249–82
Mark 1–8: 90, 120–21, 155, 156
1–3 John: 229
proper use of
1 Timothy: 21
purpose of
Galatians: 57, 87
righteousness vs.
2 Corinthians: 100–103
sin incompatible with God's
1–3 John: 122–24, 206
soul and conscience and
2 Corinthians: 30–31
as supreme commandment
1–3 John: 61–62
tablets of stone vs. tablets of human hearts
2 Corinthians: 82–83
Ten Commandments on love
1–3 John: 229–30
See also Mosaic law

Law of God
2 Peter & Jude: 35–36, 42, 65–66, 185–86, 189
Christian life and
Romans 1–8: 364
conviction of sin by
Romans 1–8: 366
freedom from
Romans 1–8: 363
human impossibility of fulfilling
Romans 1–8: 203, 249, 367
Jesus embodiment of
Romans 1–8: 406
purpose of
Romans 1–8: 256, 367, 374–75
redemption and
Romans 1–8: 308
salvation and
Romans 1–8: 60, 204, 228, 257, 357
spiritual ally of believers
Romans 1–8: 381

Law of Moses. *see* Mosaic law

Lawlessness
Luke 11–17: 21
2 Corinthians: 248–49
2 Peter & Jude: 28, 88–91
1–3 John: 122, 123, 124

Lawrence, D. H.
Revelation 1–11: 187

Lawyers
Luke 6–10: 156, 352, 353, 359
Luke 11–17: 108
See also Scribes

Laying on of hands
Hebrews: 140

Layman's Prayer Revival
1–3 John: 139

Lazarus (in parable)
Luke 11–17: 359–65, 367

Lazarus (of Bethany)
Mark 1–8: 253, 262
Mark 9–16: 115, 273, 294
Luke 6–10: 67–68, 139, 171
Luke 11–17: 371
Luke 18–24: 310
John 12–21: 3, 9–10, 15, 23
2 Peter & Jude: 186
1–3 John: 243
background of
John 1–11: 5–10, 113, 195, 382
Jesus' arrival and
John 1–11: 459–68
raising of, descriptions of
John 1–11: 469–76
raising of, reactions to
John 1–11: 477–86
sickness for God's glory
John 1–11: 449–58

"Lead Me to Calvary"
Mark 9–16: 129

Leaders
Christian, servanthood of
Matthew 16–23: 368
church, commending
Titus: 166
godly
Titus: 23
parental
Titus: 25
spiritual (*see* Spiritual leaders leadership)

Leadership
Luke 6–10: 23–24, 28–30, 45, 57
biblical principles of
Acts 13–28: 356
church
1 Corinthians: 28–30
Galatians: 176, 179
Ephesians: 154, 298
difficulties in
Acts 13–28: 344
godly
1 Corinthians: 484–85
importance of
Acts 13–28: 220–21
pastoral
2 Timothy: 36
qualifications for
Hebrews: 180

qualities of
2 Timothy: 128
respect for
1 Corinthians: 90–91, 484
transition
Luke 18–24: 125–26
world's view of
Acts 13–28: 343–44
See also Ministry; Spiritual leaders/leadership
Leading of Spirit
1 Corinthians: 468–69
Leah
John 1–11: 388
Learning
Ephesians: 168
Leaven
Matthew 24–28: 140
Mark 1–8: 403, 404
Luke 11–17: 212–13
symbolisms of
Matthew 8–15: 373
Lebanon
Mark 1–8: 365, 374
Luke 6–10: 87
Lebbaeus
Luke 6–10: 71
Lee, Robert E.
2 Corinthians: 323
Lee, Witness
Romans 1–8: 349
Legacy statements, Peter
2 Peter & Jude: 47–54
See also Peter, teachings and writings of
Legalism
Matthew 8–15: 71, 290, 337
Mark 1–8: 111, 121, 132, 149
Luke 6–10: 2–6
Luke 11–17: 321
Luke 18–24: 14, 84, 163
1 Corinthians: 189, 246
Galatians: 39, 58, 61, 68, 128, 138, 145, 152, 200
Ephesians: 42, 352
Colossians & Philemon: 8, 116–19
Hebrews: 76
bondage of
Galatians: 118
in church
Romans 1–8: 202, 262, 412
destructiveness of
Galatians: 15
Jewish
Matthew 1–7: 285–87
Romans 1–8: 120, 166, 174, 366
Titus: 65
See also Self–righteousness
Legalistic religion
Luke 1–5: 200, 205–6, 217–18, 341–42
Legends
Jewish
Matthew 8–15: 327
mother–god
Titus: 80
Legion
Mark 1–8: 245, 247
Luke 6–10: 222
Leighton, Robert
1 Peter: 136
Lending/borrowing
Luke 6–10: 106, 108
Romans 9–16: 245, 246
Lenski, R. C. H.
Matthew 8–15: 23
Luke 1–5: 248–49
John 1–11: 63–64, 92, 103, 348–49, 464, 488
John 12–21: 194, 268, 283
2 Corinthians: 6, 35, 436, 492
2 Peter & Jude: 77–78, 216
on abundance of gods in Athens
Acts 13–28: 129
on Christ's emptying Himself
Philippians: 126
on futility of adding works to salvation
Acts 13–28: 64
on God's providential control of Satan
1 & 2 Thessalonians: 72
on "John the Elder"
Revelation 1–11: 6
on joy as the theme of Philippians
Philippians: 3
on the new man
Colossians & Philemon: 148–49
on Nicolas and the Nicolaitans
Acts 1–12: 184
on slaves
1 Timothy: 232
on wickedness of Corinth
Acts 13–28: 146
Leo XIII (pope)
Luke 1–5: 46
Leonidas I (king of Sparta)
Luke 6–10: 37, 73
John 12–21: 72
Leper healing miracle
Mark 9–16: 273
Luke 1–5: 277, 293, 314–16
description of leprosy
Mark 1–8: 86–89
effect on Jesus' ministry
Mark 1–8: 85–86, 92–93
and Mosaic law
Mark 1–8: 90–92
See also Leprosy (Hansen's disease)
Lepidus
Luke 1–5: 143
Leprosy (Hansen's disease)
Mark 1–8: 86–89, 91
Luke 1–5: 312–14, 313
Luke 11–17: 389–91
John 1–11: 388–89
characteristics of
Matthew 8–15: 5
See also Leper healing miracle
Lesbianism
Titus: 81
Letters of commendation
2 Corinthians: 80–84
Letters to the seven churches
1–3 John: 2, 184–86
Leukodermia
Mark 1–8: 87

Levi (tax collector)
Luke 18–24: 72
See also Matthew (apostle)
Levirate marriage
Matthew 16–23: 330
Mark 9–16: 188–89
Luke 18–24: 144, 145
Levites
Luke 1–5: 170–71
Luke 6–10: 357
John 1–11: 49–54, 100
Levites' tithe
Romans 9–16: 231
Levitical priesthood. *see* Priests and priesthood (Levitical)
Leviticus
Hebrews: ix
Lewis, C. S.
Mark 1–8: 174, 175
Luke 1–5: 279–80
Luke 6–10: 216
Luke 11–17: 356
John 1–11: 287
1 Timothy: 26
2 Timothy: 72
on demons
Revelation 12–22: 13–14
on Hume's denial of miracles
Acts 1–12: 60
on the Incarnation
Philippians: 117–18
Mere Christianity
Luke 11–17: 60
on Satan and demons
Acts 1–12: 234
Lewis, Sinclair
Acts 1–12: 319
Romans 1–8: 350
Galatians: 185
Liberalism
Galatians: 4, 11
and the cross
Galatians: 205
Liberalism (theological)
Luke 1–5: 300–301
Ephesians: 42
2 Peter & Jude: 55–57
Liberation Theology
John 1–11: 182
Libertarianism
Galatians: 149
Libertinism
Romans 1–8: 315
Galatians: 16, 145
Liberty
Christian
Romans 9–16: 288
false Christian
Galatians: 146
flaunting
Matthew 16–23: 107, 115
perverted view of
Romans 1–8: 324
License
1 Corinthians: 189
Galatians: 39
Licentiousness
2 Peter & Jude: 161
Licinius
Luke 11–17: 197
Luke 18–24: 212, 213
Lictors
Luke 18–24: 379
Liddell, George
1 Timothy: 94
Lies
biblical illustrations of
James: 159
and conscience
1–3 John: 142
Life
Luke 11–17: 133
abundant
Romans 9–16: 138
after death (*See also* Eternal life)
Luke 18–24: 140
boastful pride of
1–3 John: 87–90, 92
Book of
1–3 John: 185
Christian, and God's law
Romans 1–8: 364
deeper
Romans 1–8: 425
eternal
2 Peter & Jude: 201
1–3 John: 135, 136, 197–98
experiences
Luke 6–10: 30
uncertainties of
1–3 John: 200
Word of
1–3 John: 14–20
Life's ultimate question, Jesus' teaching of
John 1–11: 309–20
Lifespan
Luke 11–17: 141–42
Lifestyle, believer's
Romans 1–8: 316, 343
Light
Mark 1–8: 213, 215, 396
Mark 9–16: 3
Luke 1–5: 122–23, 156, 272
Luke 6–10: 199, 200
Luke 11–17: 87–91, 159
and darkness
John 12–21: 50–51, 55, 88
2 Corinthians: 249
1–3 John: 24, 28, 29, 62, 64–68
in eternity
1–3 John: 66
God as
1–3 John: 23–25
living in
Ephesians: 205–14
truth of God, representing
1–3 John: 24, 25
as virtue and moral conduct
1–3 John: 24–25
walking in and sanctification
1–3 John: 36–37

Lightfoot, J. B.
Romans 9–16: 367
Galatians: 38
on apostolic use of the Greek language
1 & 2 Thessalonians: 298
on the authorship of Philippians
Philippians: 5
on being led astray
Colossians & Philemon: 91
on Caesar's household
Philippians: 317
on followers of John the Baptist in Asia Minor
Acts 13–28: 165
on *kakia*
Colossians & Philemon: 144
on Paul's persuasion of Philemon
Colossians & Philemon: 229
on philosophy in Colossians
Colossians & Philemon: 100
on *plērōma*
Colossians & Philemon: 52
on runaway slaves
Colossians & Philemon: 204
Lights, Feast of (Feast of the Dedication)
Matthew 24–28: 139
John 1–11: 5, 437–40
Like–mindedness
2 Corinthians: 484–85
Lindsey, Hal
Luke 18–24: 246
Linnemann, Eta
Luke 1–5: 3
Lippmann, Walter
on limited perfection
Colossians & Philemon: 80–81
Listening
Mark 9–16: 334
with authenticity
Luke 6–10: 200–201
with evangelical purpose
Luke 6–10: 199–200
with obedience
Luke 6–10: 202–4
with productivity
Luke 6–10: 201–2
value of
Luke 6–10: 197–98
Literal interpretation of prophecy
Luke 18–24: 200
Literature
Hebrews: 290–91
Living
Christian
Matthew 1–7: 137, 235–47
Romans 1–8: 226, 315, 332, 348
godly
1 Peter: 135–41
productive
Romans 9–16: 180
right
Galatians: x
supernatural
Romans 9–16: 182, 191
Living stones
1 Peter: 104–7, 121–23
Livingstone, David
Romans 1–8: 273
Romans 9–16: 146
Ephesians: 127
Livy
Luke 1–5: 144
Lloyd–Jones, D. Martyn
Mark 9–16: 405
John 1–11: 240
Romans 1–8: 88, 324, 327, 350, 442, 457
Ephesians: 125, 372, 383
1 Peter: 162
on anti–intellectualism
1 & 2 Thessalonians: 198–99
on the flesh
Colossians & Philemon: 149
on God's power in the believer's life
Philippians: 304–5
on the importance of thinking in the Christian life
Philippians: 287–88
on living by feelings
Philippians: 35
on repentance
Revelation 1–11: 140
on self discipline in the Christian life
Philippians: 292–93
on seriousness of preaching
1 Timothy: 19
Loan sharking
Luke 18–24: 71
Loans
Luke 6–10: 108
Loaves and fishes, miracle of
Mark 1–8: 319
John 1–11: 217–26
Lockyer, Herbert
Matthew 8–15: 162
Locusts
Mark 1–8: 24
Lodging, Passover week
Luke 18–24: 102
Lollards
Luke 1–5: 227
London, England
Luke 18–24: 88
Loneliness
Colossians & Philemon: 164
of old age
Titus: 78
Longenecker, Richard N.
John 1–11: 86–87
on Asiarchs
Acts 13–28: 187
on Ethiopian eunuch
Acts 1–12: 260
on Jewish contempt for Hellenists
Acts 1–12: 178
on Luke's historical accuracy
Acts 13–28: 152
on Stephen's speech to the Sanhedrin
Acts 1–12: 202
Longevity
Matthew 1–7: 423
Lord
Luke 18–24: 62

being ashamed of
Romans 1–8: 50
Christ as
Titus: 114
Lord Jesus Christ. *see* Jesus Christ
Lord of Glory
John 1–11: 14
Lord of lords
John 1–11: 276
Lord of the harvest
Luke 6–10: 328
Lord of the Sabbath
Mark 1–8: 136, 137, 138, 146, 151
John 1–11: 14
The Lord's Day (Sunday)
Mark 1–8: 141
Mark 9–16: 398
and Sabbath
Matthew 8–15: 287
The Lord's Prayer
John 12–21: 244
James: 48
2 Peter & Jude: 37
God's person and
Luke 11–17: 11–18
God's promises in
Luke 11–17: 49–58
God's provision and
Luke 11–17: 31–48
God's purpose and
Luke 11–17: 19–30
as model prayer
Luke 11–17: 1–8
See also Prayer
Lord's Supper (Communion; Eucharist)
Mark 9–16: 278, 279, 281, 284, 289, 290, 398
Luke 18–24: 210, 213, 265, 279, 281
John 1–11: 1
John 12–21: 38, 68, 168
Acts 1–12: 84–85
Romans 1–8: 250
Romans 9–16: 272
2 Corinthians: 65, 96, 234, 412, 487
Philippians: 19
1 Peter: 24
2 Peter & Jude: 100–101, 133
true symbolism of
Romans 1–8: 253
Lordship
Christ's (*see* Jesus Christ, lordship of)
God's sovereign
Romans 1–8: 212
partial
Romans 9–16: 86
Lordship salvation
Titus: 114
The lost
burden for
2 Corinthians: 194–96
fate of
Acts 13–28: 93
love for
Matthew 8–15: 165
Lostness
man's
Matthew 8–15: 112
marks of
Matthew 24–28: 126
spiritual
Romans 1–8: 140, 198
Lot
Luke 11–17: 416, 417, 418
Luke 18–24: 254
2 Peter & Jude: 81, 90–91, 150, 165–67
1–3 John: 242
Lot's wife
Luke 11–17: 418
1–3 John: 88
Love
Matthew 1–7: 191, 337–50, 441–48
1 Timothy: 18
2 Peter & Jude: 42
affection and
2 Corinthians: 236
affirmation of
2 Corinthians: 58–59
as apostolic attribute
2 Corinthians: 48
as apostolic mark
2 Corinthians: 368–69
attitude of
1 Peter: 289–90
believers and
1–3 John: 128, 168–69, 229
benevolence without
1 Corinthians: 335
biblical
1 & 2 Thessalonians: 117–19
of the brethren
1 Peter: 47–48, 88–93, 102, 152–53, 289–90
brotherly
Hebrews: 422–25
1–3 John: 63, 171
of centurion
Luke 6–10: 125–127
Christ as manifestation of
1–3 John: 64–66, 230
Christian, essential characteristic of
1–3 John: 130–31, 165
in contemporary society
John 12–21: 60
debt of
Colossians & Philemon: 226–27
definition of
2 Corinthians: 58–59
in discipleship
Mark 9–16: 42–45
as distinguishing apostolic mark
2 Corinthians: 368–69
divine, modern emphasis on
Romans 1–8: 373
emotion and
Colossians & Philemon: 18–19, 88–89, 169
emotional love
Titus: 83
for enemies
Luke 6–10: 102–3

evangelism and
Romans 9–16: 12
and faith
Ephesians: 40
1–3 John: 148
false
Matthew 16–23: 132, 160
fatherly
1 Corinthians: 115
for fellow believers
Colossians & Philemon: 18–19, 83–93, 157
fellowship and
2 Corinthians: 236–37
fervent
1 Peter: 90–91
forgiveness and (See also Forgiveness)
2 Corinthians: 238–39
"fruit of the Spirit"
1–3 John: 230
fulfillment of law
Matthew 16–23: 342
genuine
Matthew 8–15: 151
giving and
2 Corinthians: 286
of God
Mark 9–16: 196, 201, 203, 275
Luke 6–10: 45
Romans 1–8: 223, 373, 483
Romans 9–16: 100
Philippians: 166–67
1 & 2 Thessalonians: 20, 287
Hebrews: 154–57, 392
1–3 John: 180–81, 244
godly
Romans 9–16: 248
Titus: 75, 165
God's
John 12–21: 92–94, 226–27, 353–55
Galatians: 148
1 Peter: 87–93, 249
God's attributes and
1–3 John: 115
God's perfect
1–3 John: 81, 164, 167, 171
of God's Word
1 Peter: 95–102
holiness and
Matthew 16–23: 129
honesty and
2 Corinthians: 235–36
and hope
1–3 John: 114–18
human
Romans 1–8: 483
and humility (See also Humility)
Mark 9–16: 36
John 12–21: 59–69
2 Corinthians: 238
importance of
Philippians: 24
Jesus' supreme example of
John 12–21: 61, 309–10
John (apostle) and
Luke 6–10: 46, 47
John's commitment to
Luke 6–10: 50–52
joy and
2 Corinthians: 241
as kingdom love
Luke 6–10: 103–9
loss of first
Matthew 16–23: 47
Ephesians: 333
loyalty and (*see* Loyalty)
manifestation in believers
1–3 John: 66, 130, 165, 166, 170
marital
Matthew 16–23: 174
Colossians & Philemon: 168–69
as mark of salvation
1–3 John: 62, 67
martyrdom without
1 Corinthians: 335
mutual
John 12–21: 91
1 Peter: 241–42
for neighbor
Mark 9–16: 203
new commandment for
1–3 John: 64–66, 229–31
and obedience
Matthew 16–23: 340
John 12–21: 84, 400–401
Romans 1–8: 483
1–3 John: 181–82
old commandment for
1–3 John: 63–64, 131
in Old Testament Pentateuch
1–3 John: 63, 229
for one's spouse
Colossians & Philemon: 168–69
overview of
2 Corinthians: 233–35
parental
Matthew 16–23: 75, 102, 184
perfect
1–3 John: 81, 164–72, 167, 171
practical
Acts 1–12: 148–49
Titus: 83
praise and
2 Corinthians: 240
prosperity and (*see* Prosperity)
purity and
2 Corinthians: 237–38
reasons for
1 Peter: 91–93
reasons for God's
1–3 John: 166
righteous
Romans 9–16: 249
romantic
Ephesians: 199
sacrificial service and
1–3 John: 65–66, 68, 135–36, 165, 168
saving faith and
Matthew 16–23: 340
of self
Romans 1–8: 418, 424
Hebrews: 425

self–denying
Luke 6–10: 353–54, 358
self–sacrificing
John 12–21: 60, 61, 86, 89
Ephesians: 296, 299, 305
selfless
Romans 1–8: 225
sincere
1 Peter: 90
for strangers
Hebrews: 426–27
supernatural
1 Peter: 87–93
supremacy of
1–3 John: 61, 62
Trinitarian origin of
1–3 John: 164–72
trust and
2 Corinthians: 239–40
truth and
Matthew 8–15: 152
1–3 John: 217–18, 228, 244
type hated by God
1–3 John: 79–82
walking in
Ephesians: 193–203
worldly
Ephesians: 199, 297, 300
and worship
Mark 9–16: 275
Love feasts
2 Peter & Jude: 180
Loving concern, in witnessing
Galatians: 191
Loyalty
1 Peter: 288–89
disloyalty vs.
2 Corinthians: 354–60
love and
2 Corinthians: 239
overview of
2 Corinthians: 351–54
sorrow and (*see* Sorrow)
Loyalty, divided
Matthew 8–15: 26
Lucian
Luke 1–5: 12
Romans 1–8: 90
Lucifer. *see* Satan
Lucius
Luke 18–24: 369
Luke
Luke 1–5: 1–2, 10–11, 145
Colossians & Philemon: 197–98, 230
1 Peter: 98
Luke (gospel of)
Mark 1–8: 6
authorship of
Luke 1–5: 2–3
date of writing
Luke 1–5: 3–4
eyewitness testimony in
Luke 1–5: 14
inspiration/inerrancy of
Luke 1–5: 14–15
as logical/systematic
Luke 1–5: 15, 16
outline of
Luke 1–5: 5–8
purpose/themes of
Luke 1–5: 4–5
salvation/redemption emphasis in
Luke 1–5: 13, 15–16
Lust
Matthew 1–7: 303–4
Ephesians: 300
Colossians & Philemon: 138–41
2 Peter & Jude: 31, 113
Lusts and imaginations
1 Peter: 73–76
Luther, Martin
Matthew 8–15: 119, 232, 274
Luke 1–5: 141, 288
Luke 6–10: 32, 316
Luke 11–17: 202
Luke 18–24: 16, 171, 214, 387
John 1–11: 240
John 12–21: 188, 226, 268, 310
Acts 1–12: 217–18
Romans 1–8: ix–x, 150, 215, 402, 478
Romans 9–16: 38–39, 182
2 Corinthians: 146–47
Galatians: ix, 56
Ephesians: 103, 258, 344, 372
2 Timothy: 33, 60
1 Peter: 199
1–3 John: 214–15
Revelation 1–11: 122
"A Mighty Fortress Is Our God"
Colossians & Philemon: 31
bold prayer regarding a dying friend
Colossians & Philemon: 181
conversion of
1 Timothy: 26
on good works
Colossians & Philemon: 17
on good works as a mark of genuine faith
1 Timothy: 8
on James
James: 1, 136
rebuke to mystics
Colossians & Philemon: 122
on sacredness of work
1 Timothy: 228
Lydia
2 Corinthians: 131
and Thyatiran church
Revelation 1–11: 97
Lyell, Charles
Luke 11–17: 409
2 Peter & Jude: 114
Lying
Matthew 1–7: 319–20
Mark 1–8: 62
Mark 9–16: 182, 326, 328, 333
Colossians & Philemon: 145
Hebrews: 160, 162
pervasiveness of
James: 263
Lying prophets
John 1–11: 427

Lysanias
Luke 1–5: 202–3
Luke 6–10: 247
Lystra
John 12–21: 47, 166
Lystra church
1 Peter: 75

MacArthur, Douglas
Matthew 8–15: 251
MacArthur, John
Luke 1–5: 55, 91, 99–100
John 1–11: 91, 115–16, 186, 199, 230, 336, 356, 427, 445, 488
John 12–21: 13, 53, 80, 104, 262, 318, 354, 355
2 Corinthians: 126, 142, 266, 283, 362, 403–5, 420, 433, 468, 479
1 Peter: 211, 239, 243
2 Peter & Jude: 21, 42, 44, 61, 65, 108, 111–12, 119, 151, 154, 164, 197, 216
The Murder of Jesus
Luke 11–17: 233, 234
A Tale of Two Sons
Luke 11–17: 322
Why Government Can't Save You
Luke 11–17: 70
McAuliffe, Anthony (American general)
Luke 6–10: 38
Maccabean Revolt
Acts 13–28: 316
Maccabeus
John 1–11: 440
McCheyne, Robert Murray
Romans 1–8: 375
2 Corinthians: 40, 86
Colossians & Philemon: 126
advice to aspiring young minister
Revelation 12–22: 77
on personal holiness
Acts 1–12: 13, 160
McClain, Alva
Matthew 8–15: 349
MacClaren, Ian (Scottish preacher)
1 Timothy: 209
McConnell, D. R.
2 Corinthians: 312
MacDonald, William
Matthew 8–15: 26
McDowell, Josh
John 1–11: 88, 137
John 12–21: 204
McGrath, Alister
John 1–11: 243, 279–80, 487
Machaerus
Matthew 8–15: 240
Luke 6–10: 145
Machen, J. Gresham
2 Peter & Jude: 56
on the Holy Spirit's use of evidences in conversion
Philippians: 287
MacLaren, Alexander
1 Peter: 136
McLean, Daniel
Matthew 8–15: 148
McPherson, Aimee Semple
Ephesians: 277
McPherson, James
2 Corinthians: 323
McQuilkin, Robertson
1 Peter: 191–92
McShane, Albert
2 Corinthians: 379–80, 492
Madness
Mark 1–8: 243
Magadan region
Mark 1–8: 390, 398
Magdala
Mark 1–8: 390
Luke 6–10: 183
Magi (wise men)
Matthew 1–7: 26–30, 34–37
Luke 1–5: 171
Acts 1–12: 240
Acts 13–28: 8
Magic
Acts 1–12: 240
Romans 1–8: 251
Magistrates
Luke 18–24: 332
Magnificat
Luke 1–5: 73–83, 77, 79, 94
Magog
Matthew 24–28: 35
Maimonides
Luke 6–10: 103
Majestic Glory
2 Peter & Jude: 60–61
Majesties, angelic
2 Peter & Jude: 97–99, 174–75
Malachi
Luke 1–5: 20–21, 200
Luke 6–10: 155, 156
2 Corinthians: 377–78
1 Peter: 51, 108, 113, 250
2 Peter & Jude: 91–92, 116
1–3 John: 26
Malaria
Galatians: 116
Malchus
Mark 9–16: 313
Luke 18–24: 315, 316, 327
John 12–21: 311, 315, 317
Male chauvinism
Titus: 79
Malice
1 Peter: 97–98
Malta
Luke 1–5: 294
Acts 13–28: 359–60
Malthace
Luke 1–5: 230
Man
Hebrews: 52–60
deceitfulness of
Romans 1–8: 188
fallenness of
Romans 1–8: 87, 88, 192, 292, 294
Ephesians: 52, 57

peacelessness of
Romans 1–8: 191
rebelliousness of
Romans 1–8: 184
religions of
Romans 1–8: 89, 185, 198, 216
religiosity of
Romans 1–8: 89
self–centeredness of
Romans 1–8: 2
sinfulness of
Romans 1–8: 98, 182, 395
spiritual deadness of
Romans 1–8: 188
supreme purpose of
Romans 9–16: 125

Man-made gods
Romans 1–8: 216

Man of God
example of failure
1 Timothy: 267–68
faithfulness of
1 Timothy: 266
fleeing from sin
1 Timothy: 261
pursuit of spiritual virtue
1 Timothy: 262
and spiritual warfare
1 Timothy: 264–65
use of phrase
1 Timothy: 259

Man of lawlessness
Luke 11–17: 21
Luke 18–24: 187–88
See also Antichrist

Man of peace
Luke 6–10: 331

Man with withered hand
Mark 1–8: 152–57

Manaen
Luke 6–10: 183

Manasseh
Mark 9–16: 48
Luke 11–17: 231
Luke 18–24: 2
John 1–11: 224
2 Corinthians: 251–52, 377

Manasseh, Prayer of
Romans 1–8: 233

Mandatory exile
Mark 1–8: 87

Manger
Luke 1–5: 141, 149

Maniple
John 12–21: 307

Manipulation, dangers of
Matthew 16–23: 239

Manna
Luke 6–10: 143
John 1–11: 224–25, 243

Manoah
Luke 6–10: 213, 271
John 1–11: 212

Manoah's wife
Luke 1–5: 54

Mantey, Julius, R.
John 1–11: 18
on meaning of eis
Acts 1–12: 74–75

Manton, Thomas
Romans 9–16: 269
James: 20

Marathon
2 Timothy: 196

Marcion
Luke 1–5: 2
John 1–11: 4
1–3 John: 236

Marcus Aurelius
Luke 18–24: 212

Mariamne
Luke 1–5: 22

Mariolatry
Luke 1–5: 46–47

Marital commitment
Matthew 16–23: 174

Marital love, true
Matthew 16–23: 173–74

Mark (apostle)
Mark 1–8: 1, 2, 4
Luke 1–5: 11
Luke 18–24: 368
Acts 1–12: 328
Colossians & Philemon: 195, 230
1 Peter: 240, 290
1–3 John: 246

Mark (gospel of)
Luke 1–5: 3
abrupt ending of
Mark 9–16: 416–18
author
Mark 1–8: 2–3
date of writing
Mark 1–8: 3
intended audience
Mark 1–8: 4
longer ending of
Mark 9–16: 410–18
origin of Mark 16:9–20
Mark 9–16: 412–16
outline
Mark 1–8: 7–9
Peter's influence on
Mark 1–8: 2, 3
purpose of
Mark 1–8: 1, 4–5
Mark 9–16: 417
and synoptic problem
Mark 1–8: 5–6

Mark Antony
Mark 1–8: 308
Luke 1–5: 22, 143–44
Luke 18–24: 78

Mark of the beast
Revelation 12–22: 62–63, 91, 125, 180

Market place
Luke 6–10: 164

Marriage
Matthew 1–7: 16, 311
Mark 9–16: 52–61, 188–89, 191–92
Luke 1–5: 44–45, 148

Luke 18–24: 144, 145, 146
Ephesians: 135, 271–319
Hebrews: 429–31
adultery and
Matthew 16–23: 166
ancient Jewish
Matthew 24–28: 84
ceremony in biblical times
Revelation 12–22: 201
devotedness in
Titus: 83
family and God–ordained
Titus: 79
keys for successful
Matthew 16–23: 162
levirate
Matthew 16–23: 330
Mark 9–16: 188–89
Luke 18–24: 144, 145
principles for
Colossians & Philemon: 166–70
See also Divorce
Mars Hill
Luke 18–24: 407
1–3 John: 226
Marsh, John
on the cyclical view of history
1 & 2 Thessalonians: 140
Marshall, I. Howard
Luke 1–5: 142, 147, 161, 300
John 1–11: 76
on laying on of hands
Acts 13–28: 165
on meaning of kata mesēmbrian
Acts 1–12: 253
on the resurrection of believers
1 & 2 Thessalonians: 128
Marshall, James
1–3 John: 151–52
Martha (Mary's sister)
Mark 1–8: 262
Mark 9–16: 273
Luke 6–10: 139, 184
Luke 18–24: 310
John 1–11: 3, 287, 336, 449–76, 480
John 12–21: 3–4, 10
2 Corinthians: 292
1 Peter: 34
1–3 John: 213, 243
Martin, Ralph P.
2 Corinthians: 492
on Christ's obedience
Philippians: 133
Martyn, Henry
Matthew 8–15: 225
Luke 18–24: 427
Acts 13–28: 130
Romans 1–8: 73, 212
Romans 9–16: 190
Philippians: 137
1 Timothy: 75
Martyrdom
Matthew 1–7: 228–30
Luke 6–10: 41, 43, 69, 98
John 12–21: 170, 188–89
See also Persecution
Martyrdom for Christ
Matthew 8–15: 223, 226
Martyrs
Mark 1–8: 308
Mark 9–16: 235, 239, 249
Luke 1–5: 225–27
Luke 18–24: 212, 213, 214
1 Peter: 2–3, 143–44, 253–54
See also Persecution
Martyr's Hymn
2 Timothy: 53
Marx, Karl
Luke 18–24: 219
on religion
Revelation 12–22: 156
Marxism
Romans 1–8: 190
Mary (mother of James and Joseph)
Mark 1–8: 171
Mark 9–16: 382
Luke 6–10: 69
Luke 18–24: 412
Mary (mother of Jesus)
Matthew 1–7: 4–5, 15
Mark 1–8: 178, 185, 271, 276–78
Mark 9–16: 60, 105, 208, 382, 387, 398
Luke 1–5: 246
Luke 6–10: 144, 183, 202, 203
Luke 18–24: 60, 61, 153, 266, 440
John 1–11: 38, 48–49, 75–84, 138–39, 280–81, 324–25, 433
John 12–21: 226, 318, 354, 355
Acts 1–12: 29–30
2 Corinthians: 97
1 Peter: 198
1–3 John: 6
Elizabeth and
Luke 1–5: 37, 67–72, 87
escape to Egypt and
Luke 1–5: 189
genealogy and
Luke 1–5: 45, 98
Jesus' conception and
Luke 1–5: 37, 43, 56–62
Jesus in the temple and
Luke 1–5: 191–96
Magnificat and
Luke 1–5: 4, 73–83, 94
in Roman Catholicism
Mark 1–8: 277
Luke 1–5: 46–47, 60–62, 71–72, 149, 167, 171
sacrifice for sin of
Luke 1–5: 171
shepherds and
Luke 1–5: 162–63
suffering of
Luke 1–5: 182–84, 197
Mary (mother of John Mark)
Mark 9–16: 382
Acts 1–12: 324
Mary (sister of Martha)
Mark 1–8: 262
Mark 9–16: 273, 274, 275, 382
Luke 6–10: 171, 184
Luke 18–24: 310

John 1–11: 453–55, 459–67, 472–75, 479–80
John 12–21: 1–8, 10, 74
2 Corinthians: 292
1–3 John: 213–14, 243
Mary (wife of Clopas)
John 12–21: 355
Mary Magdalene
Mark 9–16: 105, 382, 399, 403, 404, 411
Luke 6–10: 173, 183
Luke 18–24: 409, 412, 433, 435
John 1–11: 3, 6, 330
John 12–21: 355, 368, 377–79
Mary of Rome
Mark 9–16: 382
Mary Tudor ("Bloody Mary")
Luke 1–5: 227
Masada
Luke 1–5: 23
Mass, Roman Catholic
Romans 1–8: 250
Materialism
Matthew 1–7: 143–44, 407–15, 417–18
Matthew 8–15: 177, 360, 385
Luke 11–17: 131, 134, 135
Ephesians: 56, 348
2 Timothy: 111
Titus: 136
2 Peter & Jude: 56–58
freedom from
1 Timothy: 254
See also Greed
Mather, Cotton
1 Timothy: 98–99
Matheson, George
Romans 1–8: 517–18
Mattathias
John 1–11: 439
Matthew (apostle)
Mark 1–8: 115
Luke 1–5: 226, 245, 282, 329–32
Luke 6–10: 14, 16–18, 65–66, 71, 166, 170
John 12–21: 188, 274–75
1 Peter: 8, 172–73
1–3 John: 5
banquet at house of
Mark 1–8: 117, 118
calling of
Mark 1–8: 161
Jesus' invitation to
Mark 1–8: 125
as tax collector
Mark 1–8: 60, 113, 114, 171
Matthew (gospel of)
Mark 1–8: 6
Matthias
Mark 1–8: 169
Luke 6–10: 16, 36, 241
John 12–21: 231, 274
2 Corinthians: 411
Maturity
1 Corinthians: 474–75
Hebrews: 134
spiritual
Matthew 16–23: 12
Galatians: 177
Colossians & Philemon: 80–81, 92–93
Mauling
Luke 6–10: 291
Maurois, Andre
Ephesians: 25
Mayhue, Richard L.
on Christ's confrontation of the Ephesian church
Revelation 1–11: 63–64
on the pointlessness of a posttribulational Rapture
Revelation 12–22: 213
Mayor, Joseph
2 Peter & Jude: 10
Meals
Luke 1–5: 332
sharing of
Mark 1–8: 117, 118
Meaning, ultimate
1 Corinthians: 39–40
Mediatorial kingdom, Christ's
Matthew 8–15: 351
Mediators
Hebrews: 211–12
Meditation on God's Word
Romans 1–8: 426
Mediterranean Sea
Luke 1–5: 269
Luke 6–10: 87, 208
Mediums
Matthew 24–28: 2
Medo–Persians
Matthew 1–7: 27
Meekness
Matthew 1–7: 170–76
Romans 9–16: 158
Ephesians: 124
2 Peter & Jude: 49–50
faith and
Matthew 16–23: 97
Jesus'
Matthew 8–15: 299
as mark of salvation
Matthew 24–28: 123
Meeter, John E.
2 Peter & Jude: 8
Megiddo
Mark 9–16: 232
Luke 18–24: 203, 227
Meier, Paul
Ephesians: 316
Melanchthon, Philipp
Ephesians: 223
Melchizedek
Matthew 16–23: 38
Mark 9–16: 209
Luke 6–10: 142
Luke 18–24: 154
Ephesians: 7
1 Peter: 126
1–3 John: 242
Abraham and
Hebrews: 179–80
origin of
Hebrews: 177
priesthood of
Hebrews: 123, 174–78

superiority of
Hebrews: 179–81
theories of
Hebrews: 173
as type of Christ
Hebrews: 172
Melito (second–century bishop of Sardis)
Revelation 1–11: 109
Melville, Andrew
2 Timothy: 60
Menahem
Luke 6–10: 74
John 12–21: 73
Mental illness
Ephesians: 171
Merchants in the temple
Luke 18–24: 105, 268–69
Mercilessness
Matthew 1–7: 193
Matthew 8–15: 191
Mercy
Matthew 1–7: 187–97
Luke 1–5: 105, 120–21, 308–9, 333
Luke 6–10: 9, 109, 307
Luke 18–24: 61
2 Corinthians: 56–57
1 Peter: 31–32, 132–33
2 Peter & Jude: 201, 203–4
1–3 John: 219
definition
Luke 6–10: 308
God's
Romans 1–8: 115
Romans 9–16: 141
inclusiveness of
Luke 6–10: 311–14
Jesus' demonstration of
Mark 1–8: 122
as Jesus' mission
Luke 6–10: 310
and justice of God
Mark 1–8: 96–97
kindness and
Luke 6–10: 9, 109
thankfulness for God's
Romans 1–8: 123
value of
Luke 6–10: 307
Mercy Seat
Romans 1–8: 209
1–3 John: 46, 47
***Mere Christianity* (Lewis)**
Mark 1–8: 174
Luke 11–17: 60
Merit and grace
1 Corinthians: 13–14
Meshech
Matthew 24–28: 35
Mesopotamia
Luke 1–5: 105
Messenger (forerunner of Messiah)
Luke 1–5: 21
Messengers/heralds
Mark 1–8: 16–19, 25
Mark 9–16: 17
Messiah
Matthew 1–7: 168–69
Mark 1–8: 19, 35, 412
Mark 9–16: 230
Luke 1–5: 214, 222–23
Luke 6–10: 142–46, 152
Luke 18–24: 180, 187
John 1–11: 58–72, 92, 136–40, 153, 163–64, 261–63, 300, 470
John 12–21: 11–13, 16, 205, 237
1 Peter: 53–56, 82–83, 105–6, 120–29, 167–70, 254, 270, 281–82
1–3 John: 177, 188–89
Christ as true
Luke 6–10: 258, 262, 263
John 12–21: 11–12
doubts regarding
Luke 6–10: 144–46, 153, 157, 163
false expectations of
Matthew 24–28: 261
Jesus' claim to Messiahship
Matthew 16–23: 23
Jesus' qualifications for Messiahship
Matthew 8–15: 2, 48, 190–93
Jewish misconceptions of
Matthew 8–15: 243
Jewish view of
Acts 13–28: 120
messianic kingdom of
Luke 6–10: 148
misconceptions of
Matthew 16–23: 21, 27, 53, 261, 274, 276, 304, 345
Old Testament predictions of
Matthew 8–15: 90
Matthew 24–28: 232
predictions regarding
Luke 6–10: 155
rejection of
Romans 9–16: 3
Satan's kingdom and
Luke 6–10: 340
See also Jesus Christ
***Messiah* (Handel)**
Luke 6–10: 280
Messiahs, self–styled
Romans 1–8: 41
Messianic King
Mark 1–8: 53, 56, 77, 136, 190–91
Messianic kingdom
Luke 11–17: 207, 209–13
Luke 18–24: 292, 297
Old Testament predictions of
Matthew 8–15: 48
Messianic prophecies
Luke 18–24: 46, 47, 94, 95–96
Jesus' fulfilling of
Romans 1–8: 14
Messianic Psalms
Mark 9–16: 209, 217
Messianic soliloquies
John 1–11: 302
Metamorphosis
Mark 9–16: 5
Methods, secondary importance of
Matthew 8–15: 131

Metzger, Bruce M.
John 1–11: 323
Meyer, F. B.
on believers being lights in the world
Philippians: 186
on believers' knowledge of Christ
Philippians: 236
on God's completion of believers' salvation
Philippians: 30
on Paul's evangelism of the Praetorian Guard
Philippians: 62
on Paul's Roman imprisonment
Philippians: 296–97
Meyer, H. A. W.
John 1–11: 19
Meyers, David
2 Timothy: 110
Mezuzahs
Romans 1–8: 370
Micah
Luke 1–5: 147
Luke 6–10: 144
Luke 11–17: 210
2 Corinthians: 19–20, 50, 200, 216, 290, 309, 376, 424
Micaiah (prophet)
Mark 1–8: 298
Mark 9–16: 168
Luke 18–24: 124
John 1–11: 376
Michael
Luke 1–5: 29
Michael (archangel)
Luke 6–10: 132, 283
Luke 18–24: 150
2 Corinthians: 357
2 Peter & Jude: 98–99, 145, 169–70, 173–75
Revelation 12–22: 17
Michaels, J. Ramsey
John 1–11: 488
Middle Ages
Luke 18–24: 213
Middle Eastern culture
Luke 18–24: 5
Midianites
Luke 1–5: 64, 65
Midrash
Matthew 8–15: 2
Luke 6–10: 163
Midrash Rabbath
Acts 1–12: 122
Mieir, Audrey
2 Timothy: 85
"A Mighty Fortress Is Our God"
1 Timothy: 41
Revelation 12–22: 23
Mighty God
John 1–11: 14, 86
Milk of the Word
1 Peter: 98–100
Mill, John Stuart
Luke 1–5: 188
Millennial kingdom
Matthew 16–23: 204
Mark 1–8: 48–49, 221, 381, 382, 410
Luke 1–5: 50, 99, 110–11, 128, 129, 137, 211
Luke 6–10: 148, 241
Luke 11–17: 23–24, 26–27
Romans 9–16: 40, 110, 111, 129
1 Corinthians: 138
Titus: 119
Hebrews: 52, 59, 145
Revelation 1–11: 105, 172, 214, 277, 311
establishment of
Luke 18–24: 80, 192
Passover celebration
Luke 18–24: 281
rebirth of the earth
Luke 18–24: 43
Satan's imprisonment
Luke 18–24: 196
See also Kingdom; Kingdom of God; Millennium
Millennium
Matthew 1–7: 138, 144
Matthew 8–15: 351
Matthew 16–23: 204
Mark 9–16: 122, 181, 250, 254
John 1–11: 21, 194, 199–200
John 12–21: 42, 139
1 Corinthians: 138, 419–21
James: 196
2 Peter & Jude: 124
Revelation 12–22: 131
literal
Matthew 24–28: 118
names of
Revelation 12–22: 228
Old Testament references to
Revelation 12–22: 229
prophecies of to be interpreted literally
Revelation 12–22: 231–33
salvation in
Revelation 12–22: 73
Mills, Sanford C.
Romans 9–16: 56
Minas
Luke 18–24: 82, 83, 85
Mind
Mark 9–16: 201
importance of guarding
James: 53
Mind of Christ
1 Peter: 240–41
Ministering
Mark 1–8: 46
Ministers. *see* Pastors and ministers
Ministry
Luke 6–10: 167, 230
assistance in
Colossians & Philemon: 69–93, 189–99
and authoritative preaching
1 Timothy: 170
avoidance of false teaching
1 Timothy: 162
biblical basis of
1 Timothy: 175
call to
Acts 13–28: 6, 337
Ephesians: 94
1 Timothy: 43

commitment to Scripture study
1 Timothy: 161
and devotion to work
1 Timothy: 180
discouragement in
Acts 13–28: 144
equality of
1 Corinthians: 74–75
and excellent service
1 Timothy: 158
faithful
2 Timothy: 26
false views of
Titus: 23
flexibility of
1 Corinthians: 462–63
as fulfilled calling
1 Timothy: 178
God as object of
Acts 13–28: 5
God–blessed
Romans 9–16: 154
and hard work
1 Timothy: 166
hardship of assistance in
Colossians & Philemon: 74–76, 81–82
joy of assistance in
Colossians & Philemon: 73–74
partners in
Titus: 15
Paul's pattern of
Titus: 21
and perseverance
1 Timothy: 181
and personal godliness
1 Timothy: 163
perverted
1 Corinthians: 98–99
preaching and teaching
Titus: 44
priorities of
Acts 13–28: 5, 172, 197, 210, 217, 222, 228–29
proper focus of
Acts 1–12: 179–81
requirements for
Acts 1–12: 181–82
scope of assistance in
Colossians & Philemon: 76–77
and spiritual growth
1 Timothy: 180
and spiritual virtue
1 Timothy: 172
successful
Romans 9–16: 341
thoroughness in
1 Corinthians: 463–65
vision
1 Corinthians: 460–61
warning as essential element
1 Timothy: 159

Miracles
Luke 11–17: 388
Luke 18–24: 57–58, 95, 108, 109, 396–97
John 12–21: 13, 52, 106
Acts 1–12: 60–61, 86–87, 95–96
2 Corinthians: 414–17
Hebrews: 49–50, 145
in all four gospels
Mark 1–8: 312
birth of John the Baptist as
Luke 1–5: 21, 30
boy possessed by demon
Luke 6–10: 290–94
calming the storm
Luke 6–10: 209–10, 212, 213
compassion shown in
Mark 1–8: 267–68
as demonstrations of deity
Mark 1–8: 225–26
by the disciples
Mark 1–8: 288
evidencing kingdom inauguration
Luke 6–10: 148
and faith
Mark 1–8: 280
feeding of five thousand
Luke 6–10: 57, 250–55
of healing
Mark 1–8: 163
Luke 1–5: 291–95, 320–25
Luke 11–17: 387–95
Jesus' divine power and
Luke 1–5: 291–97
number of
Luke 6–10: 250, 338–39
public nature of
Mark 1–8: 162
purpose of
Matthew 8–15: 3, 296
Revelation 1–11: 302
reality of
Luke 1–5: 275, 291–93, 296–97
See also Healing(s); *specific miracles by name*

Miraculous conception
Luke 1–5: 68

Miriam
Luke 1–5: 185
2 Corinthians: 454
1–3 John: 253

Mishnah
Matthew 8–15: 2, 461
Matthew 24–28: 4–5
Mark 1–8: 115, 342
Mark 9–16: 218
Luke 1–5: 319
John 1–11: 100
Ephesians: 236, 284

Missionaries
Luke 6–10: 40–41, 58, 225
necessary asceticism of certain
Colossians & Philemon: 123

Mistletoe
Luke 1–5: 140–41

Mitchell, Curtis C.
John 12–21: 235

Mithraism
Luke 1–5: 140

Mnason
1–3 John: 243

Moab
James: 33

Mockers/mockery
Mark 9–16: 350, 358–62, 368, 369, 378
Luke 11–17: 408–9
2 Peter & Jude: 111–12
Modalism
Luke 1–5: 235
1–3 John: 163
Modernism
John 1–11: 353
Romans 1–8: 88
Modesty
1 Peter: 179–81
Mohammed
Romans 1–8: 336
Galatians: 204
Mohler, Albert
Luke 11–17: 70
Molech
Mark 9–16: 48
Monarchies
Luke 11–17: 397
Monasticism. *see* Asceticism
Money
Mark 9–16: 137, 274, 276
Luke 6–10: 244, 245, 329
danger of loving
Acts 13–28: 102–3, 230
danger signs of love of
1 Timothy: 249–50
effects of love of
1 Timothy: 255
illustrations of love of
1 Timothy: 257
love of
Mark 1–8: 204
Luke 11–17: 129, 130, 340, 344–45
Acts 13–28: 102–3, 230
1 Timothy: 249, 250, 255, 257
management of
Luke 11–17: 333–37
nature of love of
1 Timothy: 250
obtaining
Luke 11–17: 332–33
proper views of
1 Timothy: 247–50
wealth and
Luke 11–17: 129
Money changers/changing
Mark 1–8: 398
Mark 9–16: 137
Luke 18–24: 105, 106, 334
John 1–11: 89–92
Monsell, John
Ephesians: 351
Montanism
2 Peter & Jude: 10
Revelation 1–11: 103
Montgomery, Sir Bernard L.
1 Timothy: 101
Montgomery, John Warwick
John 12–21: 204
2 Timothy: 104
Moo, Douglas J.
John 1–11: 2, 487
2 Peter & Jude: 215
on forgery in the early church
1 Timothy: xiv
on pseudonymity
1 Timothy: xiii
Moody, D. L.
Matthew 8–15: 86
Romans 1–8: 22, 186
Moral compromise
Titus: 20
Moral excellence
2 Peter & Jude: 40–42
Moral folly
Mark 1–8: 358
Moral freedom
Titus: 136
Moral law
Ephesians: 77
Hebrews: 188
Moral perversity, spiritual darkness and
Romans 1–8: 86
Moral relativism
Titus: 136
Moral righteousness
Romans 1–8: 86
Moralism
Matthew 8–15: 334
Luke 11–17: 69–74, 76, 77
See also Legalism
Morality
Luke 11–17: 83, 84
human
Romans 1–8: 221, 291
Moralization
Titus: 139
Mordecai
Luke 6–10: 74
1–3 John: 254
More, Sir Thomas
Luke 18–24: 219
forgiving attitude of
Colossians & Philemon: 225–26
Morgan, G. Campbell
Matthew 8–15: 111
Acts 13–28: 125
Morison, Frank
1 Timothy: 26
Mormon, Book of
Galatians: 204
Mormonism
Luke 1–5: 328
Luke 6–10: 132
2 Timothy: 153
Mormons
Luke 18–24: 149–50
on Christ's deity
1–3 John: 158
Morning star
2 Peter & Jude: 64
Morris, Henry M.
Luke 1–5: 252
John 12–21: 202
2 Peter & Jude: 88
on angelic warfare
Revelation 12–22: 16
on the death of every living thing in the oceans
Revelation 12–22: 141

on the earthquake in Revelation
Revelation 1–11: 205
on the earth's unstable crust
Revelation 1–11: 206
on equality of all believers in heaven
Revelation 12–22: 206
on the first six world empires
Revelation 12–22: 170
on the four corners of the earth
Revelation 1–11: 216
on the phenomena associated with the first trumpet
Revelation 1–11: 246
on prophecies of Babylon's destruction
Revelation 12–22: 167–68
on the shape of the New Jerusalem
Revelation 12–22: 281
on the song of the 144,000
Revelation 12–22: 76
on topographical changes during the Tribulation
Revelation 12–22: 153

Morris, Leon
Luke 1–5: 147–48, 156, 203, 246
Luke 11–17: 104–5
John 1–11: 2, 5–6, 19, 52, 129, 177, 214, 237, 243, 322, 335, 339, 354–55, 394, 473, 475, 487
John 12–21: 10, 18, 54, 76, 133, 239, 249–50, 279, 316, 326, 351
2 Peter & Jude: 215
on assurance
1 & 2 Thessalonians: 22–23
on forgery in the early church
1 Timothy: xiv
on grace
1 & 2 Thessalonians: 216
on the judgment of the wicked
1 & 2 Thessalonians: 245
on the meaning of "vessel"
1 & 2 Thessalonians: 106–7
on Paul's strong desire to return to Thessalonica
1 & 2 Thessalonians: 71
on pseudonymity
1 Timothy: xiii
on similarities between Revelation and John's other writings
Revelation 1–11: 7
on suffering
1 & 2 Thessalonians: 229–30

Morsel (at Last Supper)
John 12–21: 80

Morton, Dr. Jean Sloat
on being "eaten by worms"
Acts 1–12: 327–28

Mosaic Covenant
Mark 9–16: 291
Luke 1–5: 95, 113–14, 118, 119, 121
John 1–11: 123–24
2 Corinthians: 88–91, 97–98, 108–10

Mosaic law
Mark 9–16: 6, 79, 80, 81, 187, 189, 198, 199, 321, 322
Luke 1–5: 166, 167, 231, 313, 318
Luke 6–10: 106, 317, 352–53
Luke 18–24: 114, 143, 144, 145, 442
John 1–11: 45–46, 321–22
Acts 1–12: 212ff.
2 Corinthians: 87–91, 97–98, 464–65
Hebrews: 411–13
on contagious skin diseases
Mark 1–8: 90, 91
on fasting
Mark 1–8: 128
Jewish interpretation of
Ephesians: 236
Pharisees' adherence to
Mark 1–8: 149, 346
symbolic nature of
Mark 1–8: 352, 353

Moses
Matthew 1–7: 172–73, 181
Mark 1–8: 298
Mark 9–16: 6–7, 15, 102, 198, 200–201
Luke 1–5: 30, 42, 64–65, 68, 74, 89, 94, 115–16, 155
Luke 6–10: 55, 213
Luke 11–17: 15, 104, 245
Luke 18–24: 2, 160, 442
John 1–11: 45, 48, 52, 60–61, 70, 112–14, 123–24, 132, 152, 178, 212–16, 224–25, 244, 268, 294–95, 342–48, 357, 376, 398–99, 405, 424
John 12–21: 204
2 Corinthians: 93, 97–98, 101–3 105, 108–14, 274, 281, 282, 316–17, 334, 377, 415–16, 454, 461, 462, 464, 465
Ephesians: 125
1 Timothy: 58
1 Peter: 23–24, 43, 44, 51, 67–68, 72, 76, 77, 108–13, 144
2 Peter & Jude: 18, 22, 68, 98–99, 103, 121, 163–64, 169, 172–75, 178
1–3 John: 23, 57, 144, 242, 253
assertiveness of
Luke 6–10: 53–54
assistants to
Colossians & Philemon: 190–91
Christ's transfiguration and
Luke 6–10: 283–86
Egyptian heritage of
Hebrews: 349–51
faith of
Hebrews: 287, 347
faithfulness of
Hebrews: 79–83
fear and
Hebrews: 355–57
as foreshadow of Christ
Matthew 16–23: 67
God's glory and
Luke 6–10: 280
greatness of
Hebrews: 74
Jesus Christ and
Hebrews: 353
love for Israel
Romans 9–16: 12
Messianic predictions of
Luke 6–10: 142, 143
obedience of
Hebrews: 352

parallels with Christ
Acts 1–12: 211
qualifications
Luke 6–10: 14, 21, 45, 63
as type of an apostle
Hebrews: 78
upbringing of
Hebrews: 347–48
Most High God
Mark 1–8: 244
Mother–god legends
Titus: 80
Motherhood, dignity of
Ephesians: 276, 285, 287
Motivation
for faithfulness
2 Timothy: 55
of other believers
2 Timothy: 3
for service
2 Timothy: 129
Motives, Christian
1 Corinthians: 83
Mott, John R.
1 Timothy: 101
Motyer, J. A.
on attentiveness in Bible reading
James: 70
on controlling the tongue
James: 153
on hoarding
James: 244
Moule, Bishop C. G. Handley
Romans 1–8: 322, 324
on Christ's emptying Himself
Philippians: 126
Mounce, Robert H.
on the judgment of the lost
Revelation 12–22: 92
Mt. Gerizim
Luke 1–5: 202
Luke 6–10: 42, 312, 313
Luke 18–24: 363
Mt. Hermon
Mark 1–8: 228, 414
Mark 9–16: 4–5
Luke 1–5: 302
Mt. Sinai
Mark 9–16: 379
1 Peter: 23–24, 130
1–3 John: 23
Mount of Olives
Mark 9–16: 124, 227, 242, 295, 296, 404
John 1–11: 321–24
John 12–21: 81, 171, 306
Acts 1–12: 28
Bethany and
Luke 18–24: 452
seclusion of
Luke 18–24: 269, 288, 310
at second coming
Luke 18–24: 220–21, 249
Mount of Transfiguration
Luke 1–5: 49, 156–57
Mountains
Mark 9–16: 145
Mourners
Mark 1–8: 263, 264
Mourning
Luke 18–24: 370, 371, 377
sinful
Matthew 1–7: 154–55
spiritual
Matthew 1–7: 153–65
Mozambique
Mark 1–8: 229
Luke 6–10: 208
Mozart, Wolfgang Amadeus
Luke 1–5: 188
Muhammad
1–3 John: 94
Muhammed Ali
Luke 1–5: 33
Muir, John
Romans 1–8: 455
Mulberry trees
Luke 11–17: 384–85
Multiplication (of ministry)
Luke 6–10: 179, 182
Multitude. *see* Crowd(s)
Munck, Johannes
on the dating of Acts
Acts 1–12: 4
Munger, Robert
Ephesians: 107
Münzer, Thomas
mystical followers of
Colossians & Philemon: 122
Muratorian Canon
John 1–11: 4
2 Corinthians: 5
2 Peter & Jude: 13, 141
1–3 John: 3
Murder
Matthew 1–7: 289–98
Mark 1–8: 357
Luke 11–17: 43
1–3 John: 132–35
commonness of
Romans 1–8: 190
***The Murder of Jesus* (John MacArthur)**
Luke 11–17: 233, 234
Murray, John
Romans 1–8: 148, 239, 305, 324, 371
Romans 9–16: 114, 185
1 Timothy: 70
2 Peter & Jude: 17–18, 29
Music
Luke 1–5: 93–94, 141
Ephesians: 257, 261
Hebrews: 290
emotions and
Colossians & Philemon: 160
hymns and psalms
Luke 6–10: 120, 141–42
1 Peter: 95–96, 156, 192–93, 259–60, 279–80
Musicians
Mark 1–8: 263, 264
Muslim countries, hostility to Christianity in
John 12–21: 189

Muslims
Matthew 8–15: 111
See also Islam
Mussolini, Benito
1–3 John: 94
Mustard seeds
Mark 1–8: 219, 220
Mark 9–16: 30
Luke 11–17: 208–9, 211, 384
Mutual caring (of believers)
Mark 9–16: 86
Mutual love
1 Peter: 241–42
"My Savior First of All"
Revelation 12–22: 267
Mycobacterium leprae
Luke 1–5: 313
See also Leprosy (Hansen's disease)
Myconius, Friedrich
recovery after Luther's prayer
Colossians & Philemon: 181–82
Myrrh
Mark 9–16: 364
Mystery
Mark 1–8: 197, 198, 214
Luke 6–10: 158, 190
John 12–21: 161–62
biblical definition of
Revelation 1–11: 286
divine
Colossians & Philemon: 78–79, 183
kingdom
Matthew 8–15: 105
Mark 1–8: 198
Luke 6–10: 190
Ephesians: x
Mystery religions
Matthew 8–15: 348
1 Corinthians: 278–80
Ephesians: 232
1 & 2 Thessalonians: 37
2 Peter & Jude: 59
Mystical experience
Ephesians: 42, 46
Mysticism
Matthew 16–23: 307
John 1–11: 88–89
Colossians & Philemon: 119–22
2 Timothy: 104
1 Peter: 274
Eastern
Romans 1–8: 268
Titus: 80
Mythology
pagan
Ephesians: 233
Persian
Titus: 80
Myths
2 Peter & Jude: 58

Naaman
Luke 1–5: 276
Nabatea
Luke 18–24: 349
Nadab
Luke 1–5: 30, 74
Luke 6–10: 74
1 Peter: 108, 112–13
Nahum
Mark 1–8: 60
John 12–21: 47
Nain
Luke 6–10: 133, 134, 135, 326
Nakedness
Mark 1–8: 242–43
Luke 6–10: 220
Luke 18–24: 383
Name of Christ
Acts 1–12: 104
2 Corinthians: 156, 483
Colossians & Philemon: 160
1 Peter: 252–53
meaning
Mark 1–8: 15
names and titles
John 1–11: 14, 25–26, 34–35, 37–38, 55–86, 92, 98–99, 102, 127, 162–64, 183, 193, 276, 286, 353, 422–24, 450–51
Revelation 1–11: 2, 17, 105, 118, 133, 166, 167, 171, 240, 279
Revelation 12–22: 112–13, 218, 221, 306, 307
Name of God
Matthew 1–7: 377–79
Luke 11–17: 16–18
John 12–21: 261–62
covenant name of (*See also* Yahweh)
Matthew 16–23: 137
and evangelism
1–3 John: 247, 248
Names
Hebrews: 27
Naming of children
Luke 1–5: 89–91, 166–68
Nanna, moon god
Romans 1–8: 235
Naphtali
John 1–11: 332
Napoleon Bonaparte
Ephesians: 222
2 Timothy: 187
1–3 John: 94
Nard
Mark 9–16: 274
John 12–21: 4–5
Narrow gate
Luke 6–10: 269
Nathan (David's son)
Luke 1–5: 246, 247
John 1–11: 138
Nathan (prophet)
Mark 9–16: 58, 59, 69
Luke 1–5: 98
Luke 18–24: 29
1–3 John: 254
Nathanael. *see* Bartholomew (Nathanael)
National resurrection (of Israel)
Mark 9–16: 184–85
Nationalism, Jewish
Galatians: 74

Natural man, depravity of
Romans 1–8: 88, 192
Natural man, spiritual bankruptcy of
Matthew 16–23: 149
Natural phenomena comparisons
2 Peter & Jude: 179–82
Natural resources
Luke 11–17: 34–36
Natural revelation
Romans 1–8: 85, 137
Hebrews: 199
Naturalism
John 12–21: 222
2 Peter & Jude: 56
Nazarenes
Matthew 1–7: 47–48
John 1–11: 34
Nazareth
Matthew 1–7: 47–48
Mark 1–8: 28, 64, 178, 179, 270–81
Mark 9–16: 115
Luke 1–5: 44, 142, 146, 189, 200, 264, 269, 276
Luke 6–10: 60, 126, 177, 240, 250
Luke 11–17: 226
Luke 18–24: 267
John 12–21: 14, 352–53
Nazi Holocaust
Romans 1–8: 165
Nazirite purification
Romans 1–8: 357
Nazirite vow
Luke 6–10: 154, 165
Acts 13–28: 158–60, 252–53
Ephesians: 239
Titus: 38
Nazirites
Mark 1–8: 24
Luke 1–5: 37
Nazis
Romans 1–8: 190
Neale, John Mason
1 Peter: 122
Nebuchadnezzar
Matthew 1–7: 178
Luke 1–5: 82
John 1–11: 276
Romans 1–8: 93
2 Corinthians: 378, 479
1–3 John: 254–55
Needham, David C.
Romans 1–8: 335
Needs
Luke 11–17: 14, 32–36, 48
concern for other's
Matthew 16–23: 120
Neglect
Colossians & Philemon: 172
Hebrews: 275
Nehemiah
John 1–11: 144, 430
2 Corinthians: vii, 50, 110, 114, 177, 204, 272, 385, 416
Neighbor
Matthew 1–7: 337–50
Mark 9–16: 203
Luke 6–10: 356–58
Neil, W.
on first–century religious cults
1 & 2 Thessalonians: 33
Neill, Stephen
2 Corinthians: 172
Neo–orthodoxy
Ephesians: 42
and theologians
John 1–11: 182
Nephilim
1 Peter: 214–15
Nero
Matthew 8–15: 224
Mark 1–8: 3
Luke 1–5: 3
Luke 11–17: 197
Luke 18–24: 211
John 12–21: 167, 169
Acts 13–28: 145, 303, 311, 315, 346, 372
2 Timothy: ix–x
1 Peter: 3, 6, 248
2 Peter & Jude: 4, 14
1–3 John: 94
persecution of Christians by
Revelation 1–11: 39
Nettles, Tom J.
2 Peter & Jude: 56–57
New Age philosophy
Titus: 81, 146
1 Peter: 274
New birth
1 Peter: 91–92, 129
cause of continual faith
1–3 John: 177
Holy Spirit and
1–3 John: 128
results of
1–3 John: 19, 133, 136, 158
seed of is imperishable
1–3 John: 127
See also Regeneration
New commandment
John 12–21: 89–90
1–3 John: 64–66, 229–31
New Covenant
Mark 1–8: 168
Mark 9–16: 289, 379
Luke 1–5: 95, 97, 117–23, 129–30
Luke 6–10: 18, 21, 348
Luke 11–17: 369
Luke 18–24: 278, 282, 284, 390
John 1–11: 121–34
John 12–21: 381, 382
Acts 13–28: 156
characteristics of
Hebrews: 228–31
Christ–centered nature of
2 Corinthians: 111–13
clarity of
2 Corinthians: 108–11
completion of salvation and
Hebrews: 369
Gentiles and
Hebrews: 213–14

Holy Spirit and
2 Corinthians: 113–16
hope of
2 Corinthians: 107–8
life–giving aspects of
2 Corinthians: 98–99
message of
2 Corinthians: 87–92
moral law and
Hebrews: 188
overview of
2 Corinthians: 93–98, 105–7
permanency of
2 Corinthians: 103–4
purpose of
Hebrews: 230
rejection of
2 Corinthians: 110–11
righteousness and
2 Corinthians: 100–103
superiority of
Hebrews: 186–87, 212–17
transformational aspects of
2 Corinthians: 116–17
New heaven and earth
Luke 18–24: 250
New Jerusalem
Luke 6–10: 241
John 1–11: 41
John 12–21: 100–101
2 Corinthians: 414
New man *vs.* old man
Colossians & Philemon: 147–61
New nature
Ephesians: 164
New self
Ephesians: 183, 191
New Testament
Luke 1–5: 1, 280, 284
Luke 6–10: 84, 85, 241, 243
John 12–21: 200, 204, 283
Newborns, abandoned
Titus: 77
Newton, John
Matthew 8–15: 71
Acts 1–12: 263
Romans 1–8: 311
Galatians: 111
Ephesians: 356
1 Timothy: 26
Nicanor's Gate
Luke 18–24: 104
Nicholas, Saint
Luke 1–5: 141
Nicodemus
Matthew 1–7: 201
Mark 1–8: 256, 354, 399
Mark 9–16: 207, 392, 398
Luke 6–10: 99, 180
Luke 18–24: 409, 414, 415, 432
John 1–11: 1, 74, 94–114, 119, 125, 130, 140, 150, 211, 287, 309–10, 319–26, 382, 399, 485
John 12–21: 8, 317, 366, 367
2 Corinthians: 115
1 Peter: 92
2 Peter & Jude: 201–2
Nicoll, W. Robertson
John 1–11: 129
Nieder, John
on forgiveness
Colossians & Philemon: 209
Nietzsche, Friedrich W.
Acts 1–12: 319
2 Peter & Jude: 56
philosophical despair
Colossians & Philemon: 96
Nightingale, Florence
Matthew 8–15: 214
Nimrod
1–3 John: 252–53
Ninety–Five Theses
Luke 6–10: 316
Luke 18–24: 171
Nineveh
Luke 11–17: 85, 87
Luke 18–24: 175
John 12–21: 20
Romans 9–16: 80
1 Peter: 52
Nirvana
Romans 1–8: 137
Nix, William E.
2 Peter & Jude: 56
Noadiah
Luke 1–5: 185
Noah
Mark 9–16: 64
Luke 6–10: 20, 84
Luke 11–17: 416, 417
Luke 18–24: 254, 258, 262
John 12–21: 47
Hebrews: 288, 318–24
1 Peter: 211–12, 216–17
2 Peter & Jude: 69, 81–90, 114, 118–20, 150, 160, 162
Noahic covenant
Luke 1–5: 95, 113
John 1–11: 123
Noah's ark
Luke 6–10: 143
Hebrews: 319–20
Noble ambition
definition of
2 Corinthians: 172
devotion and
2 Corinthians: 174–75
goals of
2 Corinthians: 173–74
motives of
2 Corinthians: 175–79
overview of
2 Corinthians: 171–73
of Paul
2 Corinthians: 173–79
Nolte, Dorothy Law
Colossians & Philemon: 173
Nonrational philosophy
Hebrews: 290–91
Nonresistance
Matthew 1–7: 331

Northern kingdom
Luke 1–5: 119
Nuclear forces, divine manipulation of
Colossians & Philemon: 49–50
Numerology
Galatians: 122
Greek
Titus: 64
Jewish
Titus: 63

"O to Be Like Thee"
Colossians & Philemon: 92
Oaths
Matthew 1–7: 319–26
Mark 1–8: 307–8
Hebrews: 167–68, 196
taking of
Revelation 1–11: 284
Obadiah
2 Corinthians: 378
Obedience
Matthew 1–7: 119–20, 139, 195, 271–72, 477–80, 483–84
Matthew 8–15: 11, 185
Mark 9–16: 49, 181, 182, 201, 405
Luke 1–5: 60, 62, 115, 116, 128, 135, 166
Luke 6–10: 119, 198, 203, 204, 275, 289
Luke 11–17: 16, 128, 182, 240, 247
2 Corinthians: 475–77
Ephesians: 117–21, 125, 152–61, 174, 178, 207–12, 246–51, 283–85, 288, 303, 333, 338, 343, 347, 358, 363, 364, 370, 380
1 Timothy: 8
Hebrews: 125, 301–2
1 Peter: 22–23, 66–68, 89–90, 112–13
apostles' teaching on
1–3 John: 182–83
blessings from
John 12–21: 395
Acts 13–28: 358–59
of Christ
Mark 1–8: 32, 33
Christ as role model for
1–3 John: 59, 193
Christian
Matthew 16–23: 47, 50, 193
Romans 9–16: 241
Ephesians: 108, 116
Christ's teaching on
1–3 John: 182–84
commandments and
1–3 John: 55–60, 68, 146–47
condition of answered prayer
1–3 John: 145–46
cross–bearing and
Matthew 16–23: 234
and dependence
Ephesians: 363
in discipleship
Mark 1–8: 428–29
disobedience (*see* Disobedience)
and faith
Mark 1–8: 91
faith and
John 12–21: 111, 159, 263–64
Romans 1–8: 346
Colossians & Philemon: 17
in families
Colossians & Philemon: 170–71
forgiveness and (*see* Forgiveness)
and fruit–bearing
Mark 1–8: 206, 213
godly
Galatians: 68
Holy Spirit and
1–3 John: 56
importance of obeying God
Acts 13–28: 337
indicator of salvation
1–3 John: 57, 60, 207
love, reflective of
1–3 John: 57, 123, 146, 181, 231
love and
Matthew 16–23: 341
John 12–21: 117–18, 146
Romans 1–8: 483
mandate of Scripture
1–3 John: 220
as mark of saving faith
Acts 1–12: 297
overview of
2 Corinthians: 444, 473–77
in proclaiming the gospel
Mark 1–8: 294–95
reconciliation and (*see* Reconciliation)
salvation, proof of
1–3 John: 182–83, 259
salvation and
Romans 1–8: 24, 226, 307, 347
salvation results in, result of
John 12–21: 160
sorrow and
2 Corinthians: 269–70
spiritual war and (*see* Spiritual war)
stewardship and (*see* Stewardship)
test of believer's genuineness
1–3 John: 68
willing
Romans 1–8: 426, 431
See also Integrity
Objectivism, scientific
Romans 1–8: 268
Obligation
human
1 Corinthians: 12
privilege vs.
2 Corinthians: 283–84
Obstacles, spiritual
Luke 11–17: 377–78
Occult/Occultism
Romans 1–8: 95, 168
Galatians: 11
Ephesians: 232, 261, 343
See also Cults
Octavia
Luke 1–5: 143
Offerings, bloodless
Hebrews: 122
Oholiab
2 Corinthians: 114

Old age, loneliness and
Titus: 78
Old Covenant
Mark 1–8: 139
Mark 9–16: 289, 379
Luke 18–24: 278, 282, 284
John 1–11: 122–23
abandonment of
Hebrews: 137
characteristics of
Hebrews: 220–27
conditional nature of
Hebrews: 215
foundational nature of
Hebrews: 129
goodness of
Hebrews: 197
limitations of
Hebrews: 198
obsolescence of
Hebrews: 216–17, 253
purpose of
Hebrews: 248
Old garments
Mark 1–8: 132
Old London Confession
2 Peter & Jude: 38
Old nature
Ephesians: 164
Old self
Ephesians: 186, 191, 253
believers still clothed in
Romans 1–8: 412
Old Testament
Luke 1–5: 174–75
Luke 6–10: 66, 84, 85, 157–58
John 12–21: 35, 200, 233–34, 283, 347–52
amillennialism and
Luke 1–5: 127
Christ's sufferings predicted
Luke 18–24: 46, 47, 50–52
on demons
Luke 1–5: 280
diversity of
Hebrews: 3–4
exaltation of God's Word in
Romans 1–8: 356
foundational nature of
Hebrews: 129, 133
history
Mark 9–16: 167
law/requirements
Mark 1–8: 90, 120–21, 155, 156
Mary (Jesus' mother) and
Luke 1–5: 73, 77
messianic interpretation
Luke 18–24: 442
nation of Israel and
Luke 1–5: 146–47
Pharisaic ignorance of
Mark 1–8: 143
prayers
Luke 11–17: 2, 5–6
predictions
Mark 9–16: 93–94
progressive revelation in
Hebrews: 4–5
promises of
Mark 1–8: 18, 231–32
prophecy
Mark 1–8: 18, 19
Luke 1–5: 174–75
Luke 18–24: 123, 124, 174–75, 316, 400
Acts 13–28: 21–22
prophets (*See also* Prophets)
Mark 1–8: 16, 17, 18, 285
Mark 9–16: 168
purpose of
Hebrews: 1–2
Sabbath
Mark 1–8: 141
sacrificial system
Mark 9–16: 378
salvation in
Hebrews: 234–35
James: 136, 139–40
teaching on Resurrection
Acts 13–28: 371
understanding
Luke 18–24: 441–42
Older men, confrontation with
1 Timothy: 186
Older women, confrontation with
1 Timothy: 189
Olin, John C.
2 Corinthians: 466
Olive tree, cultivation
Romans 9–16: 114
Olivet (Mount of Olives)
Luke 18–24: 93, 176
Olivet Discourse
Matthew 24–28: 1, 13, 16
Mark 9–16: 227, 230, 245–50, 264
Luke 6–10: 165
Luke 18–24: 175, 200, 224, 252
John 1–11: 241–42, 321–30
John 12–21: 174
1 & 2 Thessalonians: 146–48
1 Timothy: 14
1 Peter: 17–18
1–3 John: 97, 232
Omnipotence
Luke 1–5: 305–6
of Christ
Revelation 1–11: 119
of God
Revelation 1–11: 156, 157, 315
Judaism and
Matthew 16–23: 349
Omniscience
Mark 9–16: 125–26
Luke 1–5: 304–5
Luke 18–24: 53, 92–93, 97
of Christ
Matthew 24–28: 72
Mark 1–8: 329
divine
Romans 1–8: 494
of God
Mark 1–8: 328–29
Romans 1–8: 494

1 & 2 Thessalonians: 40
Judaism and
Matthew 16–23: 349
Omri
John 1–11: 141
Onan
Mark 9–16: 189
Luke 18–24: 145
144,000 Jews
Mark 9–16: 257
Romans 9–16: 102, 111, 128
One world religion
Luke 18–24: 227
Oneness theology
1–3 John: 163
Onesimus
Luke 6–10: 175
Colossians & Philemon: 193–94, 201–35
Open door concept
2 Corinthians: 67–68
Open Theism
Luke 6–10: 134
Opet (hippopotamus–goddess)
Romans 1–8: 94
Ophois (wolf–god)
Romans 1–8: 94
Opportunity
Ephesians: 221
reaction to
Matthew 24–28: 101
responsibility for
Matthew 24–28: 102
for salvation, lost
Matthew 24–28: 92
spiritual
Matthew 24–28: 96
Opposition. *see* Persecution
Ordinances, Christian
1 Corinthians: 266
Ordinary men
Mark 1–8: 172, 284–85
Ordination
rabbinical
Matthew 16–23: 285
of women
Titus: 81
Organic diseases
Mark 9–16: 118
healings
Luke 18–24: 63–64
Origen
Mark 1–8: 3
Mark 9–16: 376, 411
Luke 1–5: 2, 140
John 1–11: 4
2 Peter & Jude: 6, 9, 141
1–3 John: 3
voluntary castration of
Colossians & Philemon: 136
Original sin
Luke 18–24: 28
Origins
Hebrews: 293–94
Orr, James
on careful thinking as the distinctive mark of Christianity
Philippians: 286
Orthodoxism
2 Timothy: 104
Orthodoxy
Romans 1–8: 155
loveless
Ephesians: 333
and salvation
Titus: 116
Orthopraxy
Romans 1–8: 155
Osiris
Matthew 8–15: 348
Ostentation
Matthew 16–23: 366
Luke 11–17: 101–2
Ostracism, discipline and
Matthew 16–23: 134
Ott, Ludwig
Luke 1–5: 46
John 1–11: 259–60
Ottley, Robert L.
Romans 9–16: 207
"Our Great Savior"
Mark 1–8: 236
Outcasts
Luke 6–10: 232
Outer man *vs.* inner man
2 Corinthians: 154
Overcomers
Matthew 24–28: 28
believers victorious over Satan
1–3 John: 174–75
Christians as
1–3 John: 174–75, 179
death overcome by believers
1–3 John: 175
faith in the truth
1–3 John: 177–78
gifts promised to
1–3 John: 184–86
love for God and others
1–3 John: 180–81
mark of
1–3 John: 180
obedience to the Word
1–3 John: 181–86
promises to
Revelation 1–11: 141
Overconfidence
Mark 9–16: 298, 333–35
spiritual
Luke 18–24: 322, 323, 327
Overprotection
Colossians & Philemon: 171–72
Overseer
1 Peter: 263, 267–70
as pastor, elder
Titus: 21, 35
Ovid
Luke 1–5: 144
Acts 13–28: 50

Owen, John
Mark 9–16: 46
Luke 1–5: 114
Luke 6–10: 195–96
John 1–11: 240
John 12–21: 100
Romans 1–8: 150, 425
Romans 9–16: 178
2 Corinthians: 40
1 Timothy: 263
2 Peter & Jude: 96–97
on Christ's glory
Colossians & Philemon: 52–53
on ministers' relationship to God
Acts 13–28: 222
on prayer
1 & 2 Thessalonians: 260
Owens, Virginia Stem
on earnest prayer
Colossians & Philemon: 180–81

p52, p66, and p75 (papyrus fragments)
John 1–11: 4–5, 9
Packer, J. I.
John 1–11: 243, 279–80, 487
Ephesians: 12
Titus: 127, 130
2 Peter & Jude: 75
on divine sovereignty and human responsibility
Acts 13–28: 37
Pagan gods
1 Corinthians: 279–80, 466
nature of
Romans 1–8: 216
Pagan intermarriage
Mark 9–16: 52–53, 59
Pagan rites
1 Corinthians: 331, 376
Paganism
Matthew 1–7: 12, 14, 27, 204, 296, 341–42, 368–69, 390, 399, 425–26
Ephesians: 71, 74, 166, 224, 232–33, 246, 334
1 Peter: 75, 277–79
Pain, refinement by
Matthew 16–23: 43
Pain warning system
Mark 1–8: 88
Palestine
Luke 6–10: 164
Luke 18–24: 182, 349
Palm branches
Mark 9–16: 127
Luke 18–24: 95
John 12–21: 15–16
Palm Sunday
Matthew 16–23: 257
Luke 18–24: 93
Pan (Greek deity)
Mark 1–8: 414
Paneas
Mark 1–8: 414
Panion
Luke 6–10: 259
Pantheism, rationalistic
2 Peter & Jude: 56
Papacy, false claims of
Matthew 16–23: 28
Papias of Hieropolis
Mark 1–8: 2–3
John 1–11: 7
Acts 13–28: 240
1–3 John: 5–6
Parables
Luke 6–10: 114, 163, 187, 188, 270, 357–58
Luke 11–17: 189, 261, 293, 294
2 Peter & Jude: 179
as divine judgment for unbelief
Mark 1–8: 182, 214
of faithful steward
James: 236
of fig tree
Luke 18–24: 243, 247
James: 25
of hidden treasure
James: 122
of landowner
James: 99
of pearl of great price
James: 122
of Pharisee and publican (tax collector)
Luke 18–24: 14–21
1–3 John: 30–31
purpose of
Matthew 24–28: 60
Mark 1–8: 193, 194, 197–99
Luke 18–24: 78
of rich fool
James: 232
on second coming
Luke 18–24: 191
of sower
James: 15, 67, 121
the talents
Luke 18–24: 80–81
ten minas
Luke 18–24: 79–85
the vineyard
Luke 18–24: 120–28
of wedding feast
James: 99
of wise and evil servants
James: 180
of wise and foolish virgins
James: 177
Parables of Christ
1 Peter: 39–40, 61–62, 250, 261–62
Paraclete. *see* Holy Spirit
Paradox
Galatians: 153
Ephesians: 9, 12, 32
Paralysis
Mark 1–8: 101
Paralytic
forgiveness of
Mark 1–8: 102, 103, 105, 107
healing of
Mark 1–8: 101–3, 113
Luke 1–5: 320–25
Pardon. *see* Forgiveness

Parents
Mark 1–8: 345–46
Mark 9–16: 64, 66, 71
Luke 18–24: 23–26, 29, 31
example of
Matthew 16–23: 183
principles for
Colossians & Philemon: 171–73
sacrificing for children
Ephesians: 307–19
teaching of children
Matthew 16–23: 182
Parthians
Matthew 1–7: 28, 31
Luke 1–5: 22
Partiality, evil of
Matthew 16–23: 115
Passion Week
Luke 6–10: 261, 324
John 1–11: 2, 91, 241–42, 322–23, 377
chronology of
Matthew 16–23: 257, 266, 275, 284
crowds
Luke 18–24: 101, 102
Passivity, spiritual
Ephesians: 363
Passover
Mark 9–16: 285–86
Luke 1–5: 191–93, 237, 266
Luke 6–10: 57, 79, 255, 310
John 1–11: 5, 51, 64, 85–92, 95–96, 219–21, 278–84, 300–302, 485–86
John 12–21: 2, 5, 62, 63, 326
Hebrews: 357
1 Peter: 71–73
2 Peter & Jude: 48, 163
and Feast of Unleavened Bread
Mark 9–16: 268
Luke 18–24: 265
lamb sacrifices
Luke 18–24: 91, 93
length of
Luke 18–24: 278
lodging for
Luke 18–24: 102
and the Lord's Supper
Mark 9–16: 279, 398
in millennial kingdom
Luke 18–24: 281
the old and the new
Mark 9–16: 284
stages in
Luke 18–24: 280
as time to kill Jesus
Mark 9–16: 272
Passover lambs
Mark 9–16: 124, 125, 279, 280, 388
Luke 18–24: 91, 93, 273, 274
Passover meal
Matthew 24–28: 141
Luke 18–24: 274
Romans 1–8: 253
1 Corinthians: 271
1–3 John: 35
Passover supper
preparation
Luke 18–24: 273–74
Passover Week
Mark 9–16: 122, 242
Pastor (overseer, elder)
as above reproach
1 Timothy: 102
with believing children
1 Timothy: 117
bishop, elder
Titus: 21, 35
disqualification by adultery
Titus: 28
divine calling
Titus: 49
example of
Titus: 25
good public reputation
1 Timothy: 119
as hospitable
1 Timothy: 107
and money
1 Timothy: 111
moral and spiritual character
Titus: 25
and moral purity
1 Timothy: 104
as not pugnacious
1 Timothy: 111
as one–woman man
1 Timothy: 104
preacher
Titus: 25
as prudent
1 Timothy: 106
as respectable
1 Timothy: 107
sexual purity of
Titus: 27
shepherd
Titus: 24
spiritual authority of
Titus: 125
as spiritually mature
1 Timothy: 118
as target of Satan
1 Timothy: 103
as teacher
1 Timothy: 108
as temperate
1 Timothy: 105
and wine
1 Timothy: 110
See also Eldership
Pastoral Epistles
authorship of
1 Timothy: x
importance of
1 Timothy: ix
trustworthy statements of
1 Timothy: 32
Pastors and ministers
Romans 9–16: 337
1 Peter: 263

attributes of (See also Apostolic attributes)
2 Corinthians: 39–48
competence of
2 Corinthians: 327–31
concerns of
2 Corinthians: 419–30 (see Concern, pastoral)
confidence in calling of
2 Corinthians: 84–86
disheartened
2 Corinthians: 63–75
evaluation of
1 Corinthians: 95–96, 100–103
fatigue, burnout
Ephesians: 118
God's evaluation of
1 Corinthians: 102
humility of
2 Corinthians: 86–87
joy, restoration of
2 Corinthians: 57–58, 63–75, 241, 278
New Covenant message of (*See also* New Covenant)
2 Corinthians: 87–91
overview of
2 Corinthians: 77–78
recognition of (*see* Recognition, men of God)
reputation of
2 Corinthians: 79–81
requirements of
1 Corinthians: 99–100
self–evaluation
1 Corinthians: 101
sorrowful (see Sorrow)
transformation ministries of
2 Corinthians: 81–84
See also Spiritual leaders/leadership
Patience
Hebrews: 330–31
2 Peter & Jude: 122, 133–34
of God
John 12–21: 45–49, 47
product of faith
Matthew 16–23: 79
See also Endurance; Humility
Patmore, Coventry
"The Toys"
Colossians & Philemon: 215–16
Patmos, island of
Luke 6–10: 51
Luke 18–24: 212
John 12–21: 166, 169, 182
1–3 John: 6
Paton, John
Ephesians: 358
Patria potestas
1 Peter: 176–77
Patriarchs
John 12–21: 205
Patterns, judgments
2 Peter & Jude: 91–93
Patton, General George
Luke 6–10: 38
Paul
Mark 1–8: 1, 2
Mark 9–16: 79, 80, 235, 236, 370–71
Luke 1–5: 1, 13, 37, 226, 294, 295
Luke 6–10: 144
Luke 11–17: 195–96, 404–5
John 1–11: 14, 22–23, 26, 30, 34, 35, 41, 42, 45, 60–61, 72, 107, 113, 122, 153–55, 166, 178, 191–96, 201, 207–12, 224, 250, 262–68, 277, 293, 302–8
John 12–21: 169, 188
1 Peter: 2–3, 5–6, 9, 18, 63–76, 180–89, 198–200, 251–58, 283–88
on adversity and suffering
1–3 John: 108–9
alleged conflict with James
James: 125
Antichrist, prediction of
1–3 John: 97–98
as apostle
2 Corinthians: 17, 32, 79–91, 383–96
apostolic authority of (See also Authority)
Romans 1–8: 6
2 Corinthians: 449–57
1 Timothy: 5
assistants of
Colossians & Philemon: 189–99
on brotherly love
1–3 John: 63
calculation and timing of
2 Corinthians: 331
call to the ministry
1 & 2 Thessalonians: 39
character of
Acts 13–28: 246, 361
and church at Ephesus
1 Timothy: 92
compassion of
2 Corinthians: 323–25
competence of
2 Corinthians: 327–31
concern for the lost
1 Timothy: 60
conversion of
Acts 1–12: 268–70
Acts 13–28: 262ff., 333ff.
Philippians: 226
Colossians & Philemon: 70–72
1 Timothy: 3, 26
conviction before salvation
Romans 1–8: 369
courage of
Luke 6–10: 54–55
2 Corinthians: 326–27
credentials of (*See also* Apostolic credentials)
2 Corinthians: 383–96
on death
1–3 John: 109–10
on Demas's defection
1–3 John: 80–81
description of
1 Timothy: 3
desertion by followers
1–3 John: 79–80
discouragement of
2 Corinthians: 66–68
on Epaphroditus
1–3 John: 135

eschatological teachings
Luke 18–24: 10
example of
Philippians: 191
1 & 2 Thessalonians: 23, 24, 51, 168–69, 305
on false teachers
1–3 John: 8, 21
family of
Acts 13–28: 293
final imprisonment
2 Timothy: 58
on financial compensation
1–3 John: 248
on Gentiles
John 12–21: 20, 22
gospel preaching of
1 & 2 Thessalonians: 294
as herald of the gospel
1 Timothy: 74
on hope
1–3 John: 106, 107
illness of
Acts 13–28: 16
imprisonment of
2 Corinthians: 151–52, 388
Titus: ix, 167
on Israel's restoration
John 12–21: 25
at Jerusalem council
Luke 18–24: 192
Jewish opposition to
Acts 13–28: 212
on leadership
1 Timothy: 92
life of
1 Timothy: 3
love for church
Colossians & Philemon: 83–94
love for fellow believers
1 & 2 Thessalonians: 69, 76–77
love for unsaved Jews
Romans 9–16: 8
and Lydia
1–3 John: 243
martyrdom of
Luke 18–24: 212
and ministry
Luke 6–10: 182
2 Corinthians: 228
1 & 2 Thessalonians: 40
Titus: 21
on the ministry
Colossians & Philemon: 69–82
ministry after first Roman imprisonment
Acts 13–28: 368
missionary journey
Titus: ix
noble ambition of (*See also* Noble ambition)
2 Corinthians: 173–79
opposition to
1 & 2 Thessalonians: 5, 6, 24, 32–33, 35–36, 61
patience of
Titus: 62
persecution of
Matthew 16–23: 391
John 12–21: 166–67, 192–93
2 Corinthians: 159–70
personal background of
Acts 1–12: 264–65
philosophy of ministry
Acts 13–28: 81, 210, 332, 337
physical appearance of
Acts 13–28: 47, 330
prayers of
Luke 18–24: 2
Philippians: 39
1 & 2 Thessalonians: 86, 253, 293, 312
preaching of
Acts 13–28: 15
qualifications of
2 Corinthians: 409–14
release from first Roman imprisonment
Acts 13–28: 376
religious credentials of
Luke 6–10: 11, 270, 298
resurrection teachings
Luke 18–24: 407–8
and riot at Ephesus
1–3 John: 210, 259
on roles of men and women
1 Timothy: 85
Roman imprisonment of
Philippians: 17–18, 57, 60
sanctification and transformation of
1–3 John: 91–92
and Sanhedrin
John 12–21: 321
Acts 13–28: 334
self–assessment of
Luke 6–10: 21, 32, 45–46
"severe letter" of
2 Corinthians: 6–7, 30, 66, 300, 322, 337–41, 433
soul and conscience of
2 Corinthians: 33–38
on the Spirit's witness
1–3 John: 54
stoning of at Lystra
Acts 13–28: 53–54
during storm
Luke 6–10: 212
suffering of (See also Suffering)
Luke 6–10: 99
2 Corinthians: 95, 386–91, 397–406
Colossians & Philemon: 75–76
1 & 2 Thessalonians: 12
and support of elders
1 Timothy: 218
teachings and writings of
2 Peter & Jude: 4, 13, 23–25, 79, 85, 93, 98, 112, 129, 172, 184–85, 194, 207–8
transformation of
Acts 1–12: 274
travel of as suffering
1–3 John: 241–42
willingness to die for the cause of Christ
Philippians: 76
and women
Acts 13–28: 92

See also Saul of Tarsus
Pax Romana
Matthew 16–23: 319
Acts 13–28: 303
Galatians: 107
Peace
Matthew 1–7: 209–18
Luke 1–5: 123, 160–61
Luke 6–10: 330–31
Luke 11–17: 169
Luke 18–24: 96, 98
Hebrews: 404–5
2 Peter & Jude: 24, 132
1–3 John: 219
believer's
Romans 1–8: 224, 275
conscience and
John 12–21: 129
defined
John 12–21: 122–23
experiential
John 12–21: 124–25, 128
godly
Galatians: 52
source of
John 12–21: 125
spiritual
Colossians & Philemon: 158
universal
Romans 9–16: 111
world's
John 12–21: 126
Peace with God
Matthew 16–23: 262
Romans 1–8: 418
Peacelessness, man's natural
Romans 1–8: 191
Peacemaking
Matthew 1–7: 209–18
Pearcey, Nancy
John 12–21: 222
Pearl Harbor, illustration on forgiveness from the attack on
Colossians & Philemon: 232–35
Pedophilia
Luke 6–10: 125
Pekah
Luke 6–10: 74
John 12–21: 73
Pekahiah
Luke 6–10: 74
Pelagianism
Mark 9–16: 67
John 1–11: 247
Peloponnesian War
Luke 6–10: 73
Penance. *see* Asceticism
Penitence
Mark 1–8: 367
See also Repentance
Penitent thief
Luke 18–24: 385–88
Penn, William
Matthew 8–15: 252
Pentateuch
Luke 18–24: 143, 147, 442
2 Timothy: 146
Pentecost
Mark 1–8: 26, 168
Mark 9–16: 149, 159, 269
Luke 1–5: 70, 179–80, 191
Luke 6–10: 240
Luke 18–24: 117–18, 265, 384, 443
John 1–11: 200, 240–41, 266–67, 315
John 12–21: 13, 115, 206, 215, 218, 229, 289
Acts 1–12: 39–40
James: 11
1 Peter: 9–10
2 Peter & Jude: 23–24, 171
1–3 John: 94
last days and
Matthew 16–23: 59
the people (at Calvary)
Luke 18–24: 382
People
Mark 1–8: 414–15
People of the Land
Luke 11–17: 294–95
People's Temple
Luke 11–17: 255
Peraea
Luke 18–24: 70
Perception, spiritual
Matthew 8–15: 158
Perea
Mark 1–8: 300
Mark 9–16: 53, 54, 76, 92, 113
Luke 6–10: 145, 247, 310, 311, 324, 362
Luke 11–17: 227, 228, 231
Perfect love. *see* Love
Perfection
Luke 11–17: 383
2 Corinthians: 405–6, 481–86
Hebrews: 185–86, 256
1 Peter: 172–73
divine
Romans 1–8: 60
in righteousness
Romans 9–16: 148
sinless
Titus: 23, 42, 115
spiritual
Matthew 1–7: 205, 349–50
Perfectionism
Philippians: 243
Perfume
Luke 6–10: 173
Pergamum
Ephesians: 334
1–3 John: 2, 184
Pericles
John 12–21: 72
Perishable *vs.* imperishable seeds
1 Peter: 92–93
Perjury
Mark 9–16: 321
Perpetua and Felicitas, martyrdom of
Colossians & Philemon: 153
Perpetual sacrifice dogma
Hebrews: 241

Perpetual virginity doctrine
Mark 1–8: 277
Perplexity, in the tribulation
Luke 18–24: 234
Persecution
Matthew 1–7: 219–33, 346–47
Matthew 8–15: 226, 230
Mark 1–8: 278, 279, 298, 300
Mark 9–16: 234–39
Luke 1–5: 225–27
Luke 6–10: 98, 329
Luke 11–17: 195–97
John 12–21: 165–71, 174, 178, 188–95
Acts 1–12: 127ff., 165–66, 230ff.
Romans 1–8: 36, 281
1 Corinthians: 179, 335, 450
Galatians: 115, 128, 142, 211
Ephesians: 224
Hebrews: xi, xix, 274, 281, 382–84
1 Peter: 39–48, 166, 189–91, 223–32, 248–60
1–3 John: 134–35
of Christians
Matthew 24–28: 41
of early church
Matthew 8–15: 222
early church experience of
Acts 13–28: 180–81
economic factors in
Luke 18–24: 211
inevitability of
Acts 13–28: 55
of Jesus Christ
John 1–11: 169–80
Jewish
Luke 18–24: 208–9
of Jews
Matthew 16–23: 395
of Paul
Matthew 16–23: 391
promised to believers
Matthew 16–23: 232
Roman
Luke 18–24: 209–13
during the tribulation
Luke 18–24: 230
See also Church, persecution of; Martyrdom; Suffering
Perseverance
Luke 6–10: 192, 195
Luke 18–24: 259–60
Acts 13–28: 33–34, 55
Romans 1–8: 513
2 Corinthians: 421–22
1 & 2 Thessalonians: 19
Hebrews: 83, 93–94, 110
2 Peter & Jude: 41–42, 206–14
Revelation 1–11: 122, 126
of the saints
Hebrews: 66–67, 273
and truth
1–3 John: 103–4
See also Endurance; Eternal security
Persia
Mark 9–16: 364, 387
Luke 6–10: 134–35
Persian Empire
1–3 John: 254
Persian mythology
Titus: 80
Persians
Luke 18–24: 377–78
Persistence
Mark 1–8: 367, 374
Luke 18–24: 6–8
faith and
Matthew 16–23: 97
spiritual
Ephesians: 343
Persistent faith
Matthew 8–15: 471
Personal accountability
Mark 9–16: 66
Personal holiness
1 Peter: 240–41
Personal resurrection
Mark 9–16: 184, 185
Perspective
God's
Ephesians: 31, 87
human
Ephesians: 32
Perversion
2 Peter & Jude: 106–8
sexual
Romans 1–8: 105
Ephesians: 56
spiritual
Matthew 16–23: 77
Pessimism
Matthew 8–15: 162
Luke 6–10: 68
world
Colossians & Philemon: 3
Pétain, Henri
Luke 6–10: 74
John 12–21: 72
Peter
Mark 1–8: 50, 51, 72, 169, 325
Mark 9–16: 303
Luke 6–10: 25, 26, 27, 39, 40, 77, 171, 213
Luke 11–17: 29, 30, 41, 195, 197
Luke 18–24: 295
John 1–11: 2–3, 6–9, 23, 28–29, 41, 52, 59–74, 86, 89, 127–28, 287, 293, 389, 423
John 12–21: 21, 79–80, 334, 401–6
2 Peter & Jude: 19
amillennialism and
Luke 1–5: 133
calling of
Mark 1–8: 40, 50, 161
in Christ's inner circle
Mark 1–8: 263
Christ's washing of feet and
1–3 John: 36
on defending hope
1–3 John: 108
denial of Jesus by
Mark 9–16: 298, 324, 332–39
Luke 18–24: 322–28
John 12–21: 92–93, 317–19, 321–22

Eusebius on
1–3 John: 5
faith of
Mark 1–8: 325, 331, 411–13
Mark 9–16: 2, 146
Luke 6–10: 132, 248, 262
fishing on Sea of Galilee
Mark 1–8: 60
Luke 1–5: 304–6
John 12–21: 390–93
foot washing and
John 12–21: 66–67
God's presence, fear of
1–3 John: 144
gospel proclamation by
Mark 9–16: 128, 340
healing miracle of
Luke 1–5: 294
healing of mother–in–law
Mark 1–8: 73–74
Luke 1–5: 291
hospitality and
1–3 John: 243
impetuousness of
Mark 9–16: 13, 149, 313–14
impulsiveness of
Luke 18–24: 321
inner circle of the Twelve and
1–3 John: 6
at Jesus' arrest
Luke 18–24: 315, 316
John 12–21: 39, 311
Jesus' purpose for
Luke 1–5: 303–9
at Jesus' tomb
John 12–21: 368–69
as leader
Mark 1–8: 169
Luke 6–10: 24, 28–30, 33, 36
life experiences of
Luke 6–10: 30–33, 56, 251
Mark and
Mark 1–8: 2, 4
martyrdom of
Luke 1–5: 225
Luke 18–24: 212, 296
naming of
Luke 6–10: 25–28, 40
occupation
Luke 6–10: 47
at Pentecost
Luke 18–24: 443–44
John 12–21: 13
persecution of
Mark 9–16: 236
John 12–21: 165–66, 169, 188, 403–4
personality traits
Matthew 24–28: 191
and pride
Mark 9–16: 297–98
primary position of
Luke 6–10: 16–18, 25, 41, 42, 55
residence of
Mark 1–8: 72–73, 315
as the rock
Mark 1–8: 170
as Satan's instrument
Mark 1–8: 420–21
saving faith of
Luke 18–24: 295–96
sermons of
Mark 1–8: 2, 168
Silvanus, commendation of
1–3 John: 246–47
spiritual struggles of
1 Timothy: 52
at the tomb
Luke 18–24: 409, 412, 414
during transfiguration
Luke 6–10: 281–86
virtues of
Luke 6–10: 33–36
Peter, James, and John
Mark 9–16: 3–5, 13, 14, 299, 302–3
Peter, teachings and writings of
on anticipation
2 Peter & Jude: 127–46
on believers' faith
2 Peter & Jude: 17–46
on creatures born to be killed
2 Peter & Jude: 95–108
on divine judgments
2 Peter & Jude: 81–94
on false teachers and teachings
2 Peter & Jude: 67–95
introduction to
2 Peter & Jude: 1–16
on second coming
2 Peter & Jude: 109–25, 127–38
on sure Word
2 Peter & Jude: 55–66
Peter's mother–in–law
Luke 6–10: 184
Petitionary prayer
Matthew 1–7: 389, 443–44
Pfeiffer, Charles F.
2 Corinthians: 3, 492
on Aphrodite worship
Acts 13–28: 8
on population of Corinth
Acts 13–28: 145–46
Pharaoh
Mark 1–8: 398, 399
Luke 6–10: 190
John 1–11: 60
Pharisees
Matthew 1–7: 60–61, 63–64, 134, 168, 205, 215, 276–79, 340–43
Matthew 16–23: 3
Mark 1–8: 398, 400
Luke 1–5: 166, 318–19, 332–34, 339
Luke 6–10: 43, 70, 270
Luke 11–17: 256–57, 295, 300
John 12–21: 22–24, 62, 223, 224
Romans 1–8: 8, 154
2 Corinthians: 99, 103, 126, 182, 195, 283, 469
1 Peter: 75, 88–89
2 Peter & Jude: 69–70, 195, 201–2
1–3 John: 123, 165
Christ's condemnation of
Luke 6–10: 117, 162

description of
Matthew 16–23: 327
and divorce
Mark 9–16: 53–54, 57–59
evil influence of
Luke 11–17: 102
extrabiblical traditions of
Luke 11–17: 98, 101
false religionism of
Luke 11–17: 99, 100, 103–10, 255, 343–44
as false teachers
Mark 1–8: 136, 166
hard–heartedness
Mark 1–8: 85
hatred of Jesus
Luke 18–24: 97, 131, 162, 269
healing on the Sabbath and
Luke 11–17: 257–60
and the Herodians
Mark 1–8: 157–58
Mark 9–16: 175
hostility toward Jesus
Mark 1–8: 153, 165, 202, 271, 279
Luke 6–10: 7, 10, 15
Luke 11–17: 80, 227, 345–46
hypocrisy and
Luke 11–17: 96, 131, 257–65
Jesus' dining with
Luke 6–10: 171–76
Jesus' indictment of
Luke 11–17: 300
John the Baptist's response to
Mark 1–8: 31
in Judaism
Luke 6–10: 230
kinds of
Matthew 16–23: 356
legalism/ritualism and
Luke 6–10: 2
legalistic Judaism of
Mark 1–8: 153, 341
lifestyle
Mark 1–8: 24
moralism and
Luke 11–17: 71, 73
origin of
Matthew 16–23: 356
Luke 11–17: 97
outcasts and
Luke 11–17: 363
parable of Pharisee and publican
Luke 18–24: 14–21
1–3 John: 30–31
philosophy
Mark 1–8: 99–100
and Prodigal Son parable
Luke 11–17: 325–29
and the resurrection
Mark 9–16: 186
Luke 18–24: 143
and Sabbath regulations
Luke 6–10: 3, 5–7
self–righteousness
Luke 18–24: 16–19
a sign and
Luke 11–17: 81
social reciprocity and
Luke 11–17: 263
spiritual blindness of
Luke 6–10: 114
theology of
Luke 11–17: 256
See also Scribes and Pharisees

Philadelphia
1–3 John: 2, 185

Philemon
Luke 6–10: 175
Luke 18–24: 2–3
Colossians & Philemon: 193–94, 201–35
1 Peter: 159

Philemon, Paul's letter to
2 Corinthians: 27, 227, 237, 307, 475

Philetus
Luke 18–24: 162, 245

Philip (apostle)
Mark 1–8: 161, 169, 171, 315
Mark 9–16: 138
Luke 1–5: 225–26, 265, 294
Luke 6–10: 40–41, 56–59, 251
Luke 18–24: 442
John 1–11: 2–3, 69–72, 77, 222–24
John 12–21: 25–26, 104–5, 188, 274, 275
2 Corinthians: 142
1–3 John: 5
choosing of
Luke 6–10: 16, 56
at feeding of five thousand
Luke 6–10: 40
ministry of
Luke 6–10: 59, 61
personality
Luke 6–10: 55, 57
priority of
Luke 6–10: 18, 56
in upper room
Luke 6–10: 58

Philip (evangelist)
Luke 6–10: 58, 59, 314
1–3 John: 243

Philip, daughters of
Luke 1–5: 185

Philip of Macedon
Acts 13–28: 117

Philip the Tetrarch (Herodian ruler)
Mark 1–8: 300, 304, 414
Mark 9–16: 349
Luke 1–5: 22, 202, 230, 231
Luke 6–10: 56, 145, 259
Luke 11–17: 228

Philippi
Luke 6–10: 54, 99
Luke 18–24: 211
John 12–21: 166, 168

Philippian church
1 Peter: 6, 100–101, 275
founding of
Philippians: 19–20, 272

Philistines
Luke 6–10: 38, 39

Phillips, J. B.
Romans 1–8: 348
Romans 9–16: 149, 329

Phillips, John
on the 144,000
Revelation 12–22: 72
on the Battle of Armageddon
Revelation 12–22: 225
on demons from the abyss
Revelation 1–11: 258
on the final false prophet
Revelation 12–22: 57
on God's protection of Israel
Revelation 12–22: 27
on Jesus Christ as a Man of war
Revelation 12–22: 216
on the judgment of unbelievers
Revelation 12–22: 251
on locust plagues
Revelation 1–11: 259
on the loyalty to Christ of the 144,000
Revelation 12–22: 78
on the pearl gates of the New Jerusalem
Revelation 12–22: 283
on the red tide
Revelation 12–22: 141
on Richard the Lionhearted's return to England
Revelation 1–11: 35
on Satan's wrath
Revelation 12–22: 23
on the songs of Moses and the Lamb
Revelation 12–22: 130
on the wealth of Antichrist's kingdom
Revelation 12–22: 188
Philo of Alexandria
Mark 9–16: 346
Luke 18–24: 180
1 Timothy: 80
James: 47
Philosophical agnosticism
2 Peter & Jude: 56–58
Philosophical dualism
Romans 1–8: 386
2 Corinthians: 166
Philosophical speculations
Romans 1–8: 87
Philosophical–theological systems
Ephesians: 42
Philosophy
Matthew 16–23: 25, 307
1 Corinthians: 36, 90
Ephesians: 42, 217
Colossians & Philemon: 7, 95–104
Greek
Romans 1–8: 54
human
Matthew 8–15: 273
Galatians: 11, 105
Phinehas
Luke 1–5: 113
Phoebe
2 Corinthians: 480
1–3 John: 246
Phoenicia
Mark 1–8: 365
Luke 6–10: 87
Phygelus
2 Corinthians: 151
1–3 John: 80
Phylacteries
Romans 1–8: 370
Physical needs
Luke 11–17: 32–34, 36
Physical resurrection. *see* Resurrection; Second coming
Physical torment
Mark 1–8: 243
Physical *vs.* spiritual strength
2 Corinthians: 152–54
Physicians
Luke 1–5: 12–13
Picirilli, Robert E.
2 Peter & Jude: 8, 216
Pierced One
John 1–11: 14
Piercing of Christ's side
Mark 9–16: 388, 389
Pietism
Galatians: 157
Philippians: 152–53
Piety, counterfeit
Matthew 16–23: 130
Pigs
Luke 6–10: 222, 223, 246, 247
Pilate. *see* Pontius Pilate
Pilate Stone
Mark 9–16: 346
Pilgrim's Progress
Romans 1–8: 372
Pillars and stones (living)
1 Peter: 104–7, 121–23
Pink, Arthur W.
John 12–21: 46–47
Romans 1–8: 240, 277
2 Corinthians: 469
1 Peter: 13–14, 160–61
on divine wrath
Colossians & Philemon: 141
on prayer
1 & 2 Thessalonians: 86
Pinnock, Clark
Luke 1–5: 337
1–3 John: 225
Pious forgeries
2 Peter & Jude: 1–2, 12–13
Piper, John
Luke 11–17: 122
2 Corinthians: 375–76
Titus: 47
Pisidian Antioch
Luke 18–24: 407, 444
Pitman, Michael
on evidence of design in nature
Acts 13–28: 133
Pits of darkness
2 Peter & Jude: 84–86
Pius IX (pope)
Luke 1–5: 46
Pius X (pope)
Luke 1–5: 46, 47
Places of honor
Mark 9–16: 106
Luke 6–10: 43
Luke 11–17: 262, 263
Luke 18–24: 165

Plagues
Luke 18–24: 205, 230
1 Peter: 77
Plain of Bethsaida
Mark 1–8: 326
Plain of Esdraelon
Luke 18–24: 203
Plain of Megiddo
Mark 9–16: 232
Plan, God's sovereign
Matthew 16–23: 37, 220
Planck, Max
on order in the universe
Colossians & Philemon: 48
Plato
Luke 18–24: 219
1–3 John: 8
Pleading
2 Corinthians: 223–25
Pliny the Elder (Roman historian)
Ephesians: 236
1 Timothy: 80
Pliny the Younger (governor of Bythinia)
Matthew 8–15: 228
Luke 18–24: 211, 212
John 12–21: 168, 169
Romans 1–8: 14
Revelation 1–11: 38
Plummer, Alfred
Mark 9–16: 168
Luke 18–24: 123
Plutarch
Luke 1–5: 12
Pods
Luke 11–17: 311
Polhill, John B.
on ancient magicians
Acts 13–28: 175
on association of meteorites with Artemis worship
Acts 13–28: 189
on connection of Acts 14:3 to 14:1–2
Acts 13–28: 45
on conversion of Sergius Paulus
Acts 13–28: 11
on divination in Greco–Roman culture
Acts 13–28: 96
on Ethiopia
Acts 1–12: 254
on Ethiopian eunuch
Acts 1–12: 254
on first–century Jewish nationalism
Acts 13–28: 251
on meaning of spermologos
Acts 13–28: 131
on Pharisees becoming Christians
Acts 13–28: 65
on Prochorus
Acts 1–12: 183–84
on Sadducees' opposition to the apostles
Acts 1–12: 130
Politarchs (Thessalonian magistrates)
1 & 2 Thessalonians: 4
Political revolution
Mark 1–8: 324, 325
Romans 9–16: 211
Titus: 98
Political revolutionaries
Luke 18–24: 131, 133
Politicism
2 Timothy: 104
Politicized faith
Titus: 138
Politics
Mark 9–16: 175–76
Poll taxes
Mark 1–8: 114
Mark 9–16: 178–79
Luke 18–24: 71, 134
Polybius
Luke 1–5: 11
Luke 6–10: 124
Polycarp
Luke 1–5: 226
Luke 6–10: 51
Luke 18–24: 214
John 1–11: 3, 8
John 12–21: 188
2 Corinthians: 5
2 Peter & Jude: 12
1–3 John: 3, 7, 236
Revelation 1–11: 72–76, 120
Polycrates
John 12–21: 318
Pompeii's destruction
Luke 11–17: 186
Pompey (Roman general)
Mark 1–8: 366
Luke 1–5: 22
Pontius Pilate
Mark 1–8: 300, 309
Luke 1–5: 201–2, 204
Luke 6–10: 122, 248, 295
Luke 11–17: 184–85, 227
John 1–11: 2, 26–27, 310–11, 358
2 Corinthians: 214, 447
1–3 John: 213
assenting to crucifixion
Luke 18–24: 363
authority of
Luke 18–24: 341
and burial of Jesus
John 12–21: 366
Christ's Roman trial with
Mark 9–16: 352–54
cross inscription of
Luke 18–24: 383
death of
Mark 9–16: 352
end of life
Luke 18–24: 363
fearfulness of upheaval
John 12–21: 340–42
Herod Antipas and
Mark 9–16: 360
Luke 18–24: 350–51
in historical records
Luke 18–24: 355–56
inscription on cross
John 12–21: 352–53

interrogation of Jesus
John 12–21: 328–31
Jewish intimidation of
Luke 18–24: 269, 345–48
Jewish leaders, proposals to
John 12–21: 336–40
life history of
John 12–21: 327
political position of
Mark 9–16: 351, 361
political stability of
Luke 18–24: 356–57
pressure on
Luke 18–24: 360–61
responsibilities of
Mark 9–16: 345–46
sentencing of Jesus
John 12–21: 342–43
See also Trial of Jesus
Pontus church
1 Peter: 15–16
Pony Express
1 & 2 Thessalonians: 260–61
Pool of Siloam, miracle of
John 1–11: 387–96
The Poor
Luke 1–5: 270–71, 274
Luke 18–24: 169, 170
Poor/poor in spirit
Luke 6–10: 95, 96, 271–73
Pope
Luke 1–5: 227
Pope, Alexander
Romans 9–16: 186
on vice
Philippians: 52
Pope, claimed infallibility
Galatians: 52
Pornography
Ephesians: 171, 273
Titus: 146
child
Romans 1–8: 103
Portico of Solomon
John 1–11: 440
Portraits, false teachers
2 Peter & Jude: 67–80
Positional righteousness
Romans 1–8: 411
Possessions
Mark 9–16: 75, 77
Luke 6–10: 267, 268
1 Corinthians: 91
material
Matthew 1–7: 335, 409–10, 418
trust in
Matthew 16–23: 198
Postmillennialism
Luke 1–5: 50
Luke 18–24: 201
Postmodern relativism
2 Peter & Jude: 56
Postmodernism
Luke 1–5: 335–36
John 1–11: 353
John 12–21: 103, 180, 222, 331
1 Peter: 274
2 Peter & Jude: 183–84
1–3 John: 213
Posttribulational Rapture, arguments against
1 & 2 Thessalonians: 128–30, 137–38
Potential/actual view (of salvation)
1 Timothy: 167
Potter's Field
Luke 18–24: 271
Poverty
Mark 9–16: 223
Luke 11–17: 32–33
gift of Jesus Christ and
2 Corinthians: 294–95
of Jesus Christ
2 Corinthians: 291–94
material
Matthew 1–7: 409
overview of
2 Corinthians: 287–89
riches of Jesus Christ and
2 Corinthians: 289–91
See also Giving
Power
Luke 6–10: 88, 137–38, 206, 207, 243
apostolic
2 Corinthians: 414–17
divine
Mark 9–16: 190, 297
Luke 6–10: 137–38
Romans 9–16: 18
2 Peter & Jude: 26–28
overview of
2 Corinthians: 405–6
See also Strength
Power of God
Mark 9–16: 190, 297, 328
Luke 1–5: 91–92
Luke 6–10: 206–13
Acts 13–28: 49
Romans 1–8: 53
1 Timothy: 271
1 Peter: 36–37, 259–60
Revelation 12–22: 99–100
over Satan
John 12–21: 87, 281–82
sovereignty and
Romans 9–16: 18
Power of Jesus
Mark 1–8: 65–68, 176, 182, 183
Luke 1–5: 291–97
Luke 6–10: 87–90, 206, 207, 228, 234, 345–46
2 Corinthians: 86
2 Peter & Jude: 26–27
and miracles
Luke 1–5: 291–97
over disease and death
Mark 1–8: 253, 254, 260, 262–66, 334, 377
over Satan and demons
Matthew 8–15: 39–46
Mark 1–8: 65–67, 239, 240, 246
over storms
Mark 1–8: 334
supernatural
Luke 18–24: 58, 61–64, 157

Practical faithfulness
Romans 1–8: 24
Practical knowledge
Ephesians: 216
Practical purity
2 Peter & Jude: 132–33
Practical righteousness
Romans 1–8: 411
Ephesians: 353
Practice
2 Peter & Jude: 45
Praetorium
Mark 9–16: 346, 360
Luke 18–24: 274
John 12–21: 62, 325–26
Pragmatism
Colossians & Philemon: 2
2 Timothy: 104
Praise
Matthew 1–7: 354, 356
Mark 9–16: 276
Luke 1–5: 93–95, 164
Luke 18–24: 64, 65
2 Corinthians: 240
Hebrews: 443
1 Peter: 26–27, 45–46, 115–16, 122, 288
continual
2 Peter & Jude: 137–38
See also Worship
Prayer
Matthew 8–15: 116, 122
Luke 1–5: 185, 237–38, 317
Luke 6–10: 15, 105, 259, 328
John 12–21: 163, 219
Acts 1–12: 85, 271, 285
Romans 1–8: 39, 225, 426
2 Corinthians: 401–2
Galatians: 180
Ephesians: 153, 375–85
Hebrews: 448–49
1 Peter: 52, 68–69, 74–75, 101, 117, 193–94, 240–41
2 Peter & Jude: 37–38, 152–53, 200–204, 208–9
1–3 John: 145–46, 203–6
Revelation 1–11: 195, 241
asking in
Mark 9–16: 146–47
attitude for
Luke 11–17: 6–8
boldness in
Luke 11–17: 53–55, 58
Ephesians: 103
Colossians & Philemon: 179–83
for Christ's return
Luke 18–24: 3, 7–8
comfort in
2 Corinthians: 27–28
components of
Mark 9–16: 142–49
at crucifixion
Mark 9–16: 375, 378
effectiveness in
Luke 11–17: 30
and faith
Mark 9–16: 145–46
false religions and
Luke 11–17: 9–10
and forgiveness
Mark 9–16: 148–49
in Gethsemane
Mark 9–16: 301–4
God–dishonoring
Luke 18–24: 166
God's glory and
Luke 11–17: 10–11
and God's sovereignty
1 & 2 Thessalonians: 255–56
for government leaders
Mark 9–16: 181
importance of
Luke 11–17: 1–2, 8
Acts 13–28: 229
Philippians: 38–39
1 & 2 Thessalonians: 187–88
"in Jesus' Name"
John 12–21: 107–8, 225–26
as intercession
John 12–21: 242–43, 272–73
intercessory
Luke 18–24: 295
Jesus and
Mark 1–8: 78–79, 327, 328
Luke 18–24: 2, 301–7
John 12–21: 235–36
in Judaism
Mark 1–8: 128
New Testament
Luke 11–17: 2–3
Luke 18–24: 2–3
John 12–21: 235–36
obedience and
2 Corinthians: 476–77
Old Testament
Luke 11–17: 2, 5–6
Luke 18–24: 1–2
John 12–21: 233–34
Passover
Luke 18–24: 280
persistent
Mark 9–16: 30
Colossians & Philemon: 179–80
petitionary
Matthew 1–7: 389, 443–44
Pharisaic
Luke 18–24: 19
postures for
Mark 9–16: 148
Luke 18–24: 17, 303
Ephesians: 101
power of
Matthew 24–28: 169
prosperity and
2 Corinthians: 319
public
Matthew 1–7: 366
purpose of
Matthew 1–7: 164, 347, 361–98, 404
reverent
Colossians & Philemon: 180–81
ritualistic
Matthew 1–7: 362–63

by the scribes
Mark 9–16: 219–20
secret
Matthew 1–7: 366–67
for spiritual growth
Colossians & Philemon: 25–42
struggle in
Romans 9–16: 351
temple as house of
Mark 9–16: 138
thankful
Colossians & Philemon: 35–37, 182–83
traditional/customary
Luke 11–17: 4
and trusting God
Mark 9–16: 144–45
unceasing
Colossians & Philemon: 27
See also High Priestly prayer; The Lord's Prayer
Prayerlessness
Matthew 24–28: 168, 213
Pre–Flood world
2 Peter & Jude: 119–20
Preachers
accountability of
2 Timothy: 170
expository
Titus: 12, 49
faithful
Romans 1–8: 371
godly
Revelation 1–11: 290–92
in nineteenth century
1 Timothy: 178
pastor
Titus: 25
teaching
Titus: 44
worldly
Titus: 47
Preaching
Matthew 1–7: 108–9, 136
Mark 9–16: 230
Luke 6–10: 180, 181, 242
Luke 18–24: 108
Colossians & Philemon: 76, 79–80
1–3 John: 224–27
authoritative
Titus: 131
Christ's emphasis on
Mark 1–8: 54, 80–81, 84, 227
content of
Acts 1–12: 50–51
danger of deemphasizing
Acts 13–28: 195–98
by the disciples
Mark 1–8: 167, 286
expository
2 Timothy: 174
importance of
Acts 1–12: 48–50, 83
of Jesus
Luke 1–5: 281–85, 297, 304
of John the Baptist
Mark 1–8: 22, 25
Luke 1–5: 39–40, 86–87, 214, 228–30, 232
priority of
1 Corinthians: 32–33, 55
purpose of
Mark 1–8: 47, 48
relational
2 Timothy: 125
on repentance
Mark 1–8: 287
significance of
Acts 13–28: 15
true
1 Corinthians: 56
Preceptive will of God
Luke 11–17: 28
Preciousness
1 Peter: 123
Predestination
2 Timothy: 61, 82
Titus: 31
Hebrews: 103
of believers
Matthew 24–28: 122
damnation and
Romans 1–8: 498
double
Titus: 111
man's view of
Romans 9–16: 30
mystery of
Romans 9–16: 37
See also Election
Predictions. *see* Prophecy
Preeminence, God's
Ephesians: 32
Preevangelism
1 Corinthians: 212
Prejudice
Matthew 8–15: 147, 149, 151, 159
Luke 6–10: 60
Acts 1–12: 289–91
Galatians: 51, 100
destruction of (*see* Unity)
Prejudice against Christ
Matthew 8–15: 308
Premarital sex
Mark 9–16: 55
Premillennialism
2 Peter & Jude: 10
Premiums
2 Peter & Jude: 102–3
Preparation
1 Peter: 64–65
Preparedness
Luke 11–17: 157–65
spiritual
Matthew 24–28: 87
Ephesians: 345–73
Presence, God's, with believers
Matthew 16–23: 139
Present deliverance
1 Peter: 48
Prestige
Hebrews: 349–51
Presumption
Matthew 1–7: 68, 163

religious
Matthew 16–23: 39
spiritual
Ephesians: 342
Pretension, religious
Matthew 16–23: 387
Preterism
Luke 11–17: 151–52
Pretribulational Rapture, arguments in favor of
1 & 2 Thessalonians: 124, 125, 135–37, 268
Priceless treasure in clay pots
2 Corinthians: 137–48
Pride (arrogance)
Matthew 1–7: 146–47, 162–63, 170, 364, 385–86
Matthew 24–28: 214
Mark 1–8: 358
Luke 1–5: 79, 80
Luke 6–10: 298–305
Luke 11–17: 264, 265, 375–76
Luke 18–24: 132
Acts 1–12: 241–42
Romans 9–16: 158
1 Corinthians: 89, 106–9, 342–43
2 Corinthians: 369–70, 435
Galatians: 181
2 Timothy: 110
James: 230
1 Peter: 124–25, 278
2 Peter & Jude: 190
1–3 John: 87–90
biblical examples of
1–3 John: 251–56
boastful pride of life
1–3 John: 87–90
consequences of
Mark 9–16: 100
deflection of
2 Corinthians: 53–56
of the disciples
Mark 9–16: 33, 298
and God's rejection of the proud
Matthew 16–23: 290
illustrations of
Mark 9–16: 101
intellectual
Ephesians: 168
Jewish
Romans 1–8: 149
and love
Mark 9–16: 36
overview of
2 Corinthians: 369–70
religious
Matthew 16–23: 6, 94, 119, 273
Galatians: 196
as root of all sin
Titus: 35
Satan's method of attack, as
1–3 John: 89–90
of the scribes
Mark 9–16: 219–20
and self–esteem
Mark 9–16: 32
and self–gratification
Mark 9–16: 103
spiritual
Matthew 8–15: 270
Mark 9–16: 37
Ephesians: 69, 121, 267, 377
the supreme sin
Matthew 16–23: 230
and true honor
Mark 9–16: 37
of unbelief
Matthew 16–23: 273
Priesthood of Christ
appointment to
Hebrews: 123
eternality of
Hebrews: 181, 196
function of
Hebrews: 79, 168–69, 209–10
order of
Hebrews: 190
peace and
Hebrews: 176–78
perfection of
Romans 1–8: 509
Hebrews: 109–10
permanence of
Hebrews: 198–99
qualification for
Hebrews: 191
sanctuary of
Hebrews: 229
superiority of
Hebrews: 118
universality of
Hebrews: 175
Priestly covenant
Luke 1–5: 95, 113
John 1–11: 123–24
Priests and priesthood
Mark 1–8: 91, 145
Luke 1–5: 23–24, 26
Luke 6–10: 5, 143, 263, 264, 357
Luke 11–17: 391–92
Hebrews: 110–11
of believers
John 12–21: 226–27
chief (*see* Chief priests)
Christ's perfect (*See also* Priesthood of Christ)
Romans 1–8: 509
holy
1 Peter: 107–13
Jewish
Matthew 16–23: 224
royal
1 Peter: 125–26
Priests and priesthood (Levitical)
John 1–11: 50–54
Day of Atonement and
Hebrews: 109
function of
Hebrews: 5, 117–18
imperfection of
Hebrews: 185–86
impermanence of
Hebrews: 181
ineffectiveness of
Hebrews: 255

lineage of
Hebrews: 190
necessity of
Hebrews: 172
qualifications for
Hebrews: 119–21, 174, 191
Priorities, inverted
Matthew 16–23: 383
Priscilla and Aquila
2 Corinthians: 4
1 Timothy: 87
1–3 John: 243, 246
Prisoners
Luke 18–24: 334, 358, 359
Privilege(s)
2 Corinthians: 129–33, 221–23, 283–84
spiritual (*see* Spiritual privileges)
***The Problem of Pain* (Lewis)**
Mark 1–8: 174
Proclaiming
Luke 6–10: 180, 181, 199, 242
Proclamation of Christ
1 Peter: 127–34
Procrastination
Matthew 1–7: 163
Procurement, divine
2 Peter & Jude: 26, 28–30
Prodigal
Luke 11–17: 307
Prodigal Son parable
Luke 6–10: 308
Luke 11–17: 305–28
2 Peter & Jude: 134
Profession of faith
Luke 11–17: 124
Professional mourners
Luke 18–24: 370, 371, 377
Progress, spiritual
2 Peter & Jude: 136
Progressive creationism
Romans 1–8: 88
Progressive healings
Luke 18–24: 62–63
Progressive revelation
Hebrews: 4–5
Promise(s)
Luke 1–5: 174
divine
2 Peter & Jude: 26, 30–31
God's
Matthew 1–7: 442–44
Ephesians: 28, 359
God's conditional
Romans 9–16: 120
God's unconditional
Romans 1–8: 171
human
Ephesians: 28
Promise and fulfillment
Hebrews: 4, 10, 212
Promised honor
1 Peter: 44–46
Promised Land
John 1–11: 114–17, 204, 398–400
1 Peter: 34–35
Prophecy(ies)
Matthew 1–7: 24, 41–43, 45, 47–48, 52–53
Luke 6–10: 77, 152, 153, 281
John 12–21: 8, 24, 34–35, 279, 364
2 Peter & Jude: 9, 61–66, 135–36, 171–72, 187–90
of coming Messiah
Luke 1–5: 42–43
confirmation of
Luke 1–5: 63–72
false
Titus: 58
2 Peter & Jude: 103–4
filling of the Spirit and
Luke 1–5: 69
fulfillment of (*see* Prophecy fulfillment)
of future Davidic kingdom
Luke 1–5: 99, 100
gift of
1 Timothy: 43
interpretation of
Luke 18–24: 200
of Israel's future
Luke 11–17: 247
John the Baptist
Luke 1–5: 210–11
literal interpretation of
Luke 18–24: 200
Revelation 12–22: 293
of Messiah's earthly kingdom
Luke 11–17: 209–12
messianic
Luke 18–24: 46, 47
near and distant aspects of
Matthew 16–23: 60
New Testament definition of
Revelation 1–11: 298
Old Testament and
Mark 1–8: 18, 19
Luke 1–5: 174–75
Luke 18–24: 123, 124, 174–75, 316, 400
Acts 13–28: 21–22
predictive
Matthew 8–15: 174
of second coming
Luke 11–17: 153–54, 409–10
of the seventy weeks
Luke 18–24: 91
of Zacharias
Luke 1–5: 96
Prophecy fulfillment
Matthew 16–23: 221–22
Christ's birth in Bethlehem
Mark 9–16: 387
Christ's burial with rich man
Mark 9–16: 391
Daniel's seventy weeks
Mark 9–16: 126
Judas's betrayal of Christ
Mark 9–16: 277
of substitutionary death
Mark 9–16: 127
of Suffering Servant
Mark 9–16: 230
Prophetesses
Luke 1–5: 185

Prophets
Matthew 1–7: 459–72
Mark 9–16: 92, 168, 171, 174, 255
Luke 1–5: 25, 31, 39, 40
Luke 11–17: 106, 107, 230–32, 239–40
Luke 18–24: 422, 442
John 1–11: 17, 28–31, 51–58, 83, 86, 105, 132–47, 154, 189, 194–95, 205–9, 292, 376, 402–4, 426–30, 484
Hebrews: 5
1 Peter: 1–2, 20, 51–55, 75, 89, 101, 113, 120, 132, 140–46, 167, 172, 179, 250, 262, 265, 274–75
2 Peter & Jude: 116–17
call to obedience by
Mark 1–8: 338–39
Elijah and John the Baptist as
Mark 1–8: 18, 23–24
Luke 6–10: 156
false
Matthew 8–15: 191
Matthew 24–28: 36
Luke 6–10: 100, 284
Romans 1–8: 7, 155, 186, 344
Revelation 12–22: 56, 59
Jewish tradition on
Luke 6–10: 146
John the Baptist and
Luke 6–10: 145, 152–55
mistreatment of
Mark 1–8: 298, 299
Moses on
Luke 6–10: 139
New Testament
Acts 13–28: 239–40
1 Timothy: 43
Propitiation
Luke 18–24: 20
Hebrews: 239–40
Jesus Christ as
1–3 John: 46–50, 82, 124, 192
Jesus' coming and
1–3 John: 124
Jewish believers and
1–3 John: 49
in Old Testament
1–3 John: 46–49
relation of to sin
1–3 John: 47–48, 167, 192
See also Salvation
Proselytism, Jewish
Matthew 16–23: 379, 380
Prosperity
generosity and
2 Corinthians: 315–17
gift of Jesus Christ and
2 Corinthians: 319–20
glorification and
2 Corinthians: 317–18
grace and
2 Corinthians: 319
love and
2 Corinthians: 314–15
overview of
2 Corinthians: 311–14
prayer and
2 Corinthians: 319
spiritual
Romans 9–16: 348
See also Giving
Prosperity gospel
Mark 9–16: 129
Luke 1–5: 260
Luke 11–17: 9–10, 32
1 & 2 Thessalonians: 252
2 Timothy: 51, 56
Prosperity of the wicked
Hebrews: 351–52
Prostitutes
Luke 6–10: 14, 172
Protected inheritances
1 Peter: 41–42
Protection
2 Corinthians: 225–30
spiritual
John 12–21: 276–82
Protestant Reformation
John 12–21: 188
Romans 1–8: 215
Scottish
2 Timothy: 60
Proud, God's rejection of the
Matthew 16–23: 290
See also Pride (arrogance)
Proven faith
1 Peter: 42–44
Proverbs
Luke 6–10: 114
Proverbs (book of), regarding purity
1 Timothy: 190
Providence
Mark 9–16: 386–87
Luke 6–10: 134–35
Luke 11–17: 140–41
Luke 18–24: 397–98
Romans 9–16: 342
Philippians: 298
divine
Romans 9–16: 342
God's gracious
Romans 1–8: 122
illustrations of
Matthew 24–28: 290
Provision. *see* God, provision by
Pruning
John 12–21: 147, 148
Psalms
Luke 18–24: 442
and hymns
1 Peter: 84–85, 95–96, 192–93, 259–60, 279–80
imprecatory
Romans 1–8: 478
Pseudo–Christians
2 Peter & Jude: 72, 98
Pseudo–conversions
John 1–11: 98
Pseudo–messiahs
Luke 18–24: 187, 230
John 1–11: 137, 214
John 12–21: 11–12

Pseudo-spirituality
John 1–11: 100
Pseudonymous works
2 Peter & Jude: 1–2, 12–13
Psoriasis
Mark 1–8: 87
Psychology
1 Corinthians: 38
Ephesians: 22, 105
danger to the church from
1 & 2 Thessalonians: 191
secular
Romans 9–16: 159, 328
2 Timothy: 109
Psychotherapy
Romans 1–8: 369
Ptolemaeus
John 1–11: 4
Publicans. *see* Tax collectors
Publius
John 1–11: 388–89
1–3 John: 243
Publius's father
Luke 1–5: 294
Punishment
Luke 6–10: 327, 333, 334
Luke 18–24: 85, 332, 358, 389
2 Corinthians: 56–57
capital
Romans 9–16: 226
corporal
Romans 9–16: 221
deterrent to crime
Romans 9–16: 222
eternal
1–3 John: 44, 91
impartial
Romans 9–16: 222
swift
Romans 9–16: 222
Pure conscience
1 Peter: 202–3
Purgatory
Luke 18–24: 388
Acts 1–12: 225
Colossians & Philemon: 76
Purification
Luke 1–5: 169
2 Corinthians: 125–28
1 Peter: 89–90, 256–57
2 Peter & Jude: 43–45
Purim, Feast of
Matthew 24–28: 139
Puritans/Puritanism
John 1–11: 240
Romans 1–8: 304
2 Peter & Jude: 96–97
1–3 John: 54
Purity
Matthew 1–7: 16, 204–7, 245–46
Mark 9–16: 46–48
2 Corinthians: 237–38, 266–67
church discipline and
Matthew 16–23: 131, 147
of God
Romans 1–8: 173
spiritual
Matthew 16–23: 124
Purple dye
Luke 11–17: 360
Purpose, man's
Matthew 16–23: 26
Purpose *(hina)* clauses, Greek
Titus: 78

Q document
Mark 1–8: 6
Quakers
Romans 9–16: 224
Quaternion
Mark 9–16: 366
Queen of Heaven
Luke 1–5: 61, 62
Revelation 12–22: 159
Queen of Sheba
Luke 11–17: 86–87
Luke 18–24: 175
John 12–21: 204
***Quelle* (source)**
Mark 1–8: 6
Questionable practices
1 Corinthians: 188–97
Questions
Annas's at trial
Luke 18–24: 334, 336, 337
countering with
Luke 18–24: 37, 115, 152, 162
incriminating
Luke 18–24: 150
by Sadducees
Luke 18–24: 144, 148
Quietism
Galatians: 153
Philippians: 152
Quirinius
Luke 1–5: 145
Luke 6–10: 70
Quisling, Vidkun
Luke 6–10: 74
John 12–21: 72
2 Corinthians: 351
Qumran
Luke 1–5: 204–5
John 12–21: 203

Raba, Rabbi
Romans 1–8: 357
Rabbi
Luke 18–24: 164–65, 413
John 12–21: 379
Rabbinic rules/restrictions
on caring for parents
Mark 1–8: 345–46
on caring for the sick
Mark 1–8: 153
on hand washing
Mark 1–8: 343
hypocrisy of
Mark 1–8: 344, 347
on the Sabbath
Mark 1–8: 139–40, 143, 150–51

Rabbinic tradition
Matthew 16–23: 3
Romans 1–8: 12, 139, 169, 271, 366, 369, 371
Romans 9–16: 19, 69
Galatians: 23, 47, 54, 144
Titus: 126
Rabbinical writings
Romans 1–8: 12, 233
Rabbis
Mark 1–8: 61
Mark 9–16: 197, 199, 219
Luke 6–10: 172, 183
Luke 11–17: 101, 103, 131, 279
ancient
Galatians: 76
in ancient Israel
Romans 9–16: 54
importance of in Jewish culture
James: 146–47
ordination of
Matthew 16–23: 285
Rabboni
Mark 9–16: 117
Rachel
Luke 1–5: 25
John 1–11: 388
Racism
Galatians: 50
Rahab
Luke 6–10: 14
Hebrews: 363–64
Raising the dead
Mark 9–16: 115, 119
Luke 1–5: 293, 294
Ramsay, Sir William M.
Luke 1–5: 144, 145
on conversion of Sergius Paulus's daughter
Acts 13–28: 11
on the earthquake at Philadelphia
Revelation 1–11: 121
on guilds at Thyatira
Revelation 1–11: 98
on historical reliability of Acts
Acts 1–12: 5
on Mediterranean sea travel
Acts 13–28: 236
on Paulus inscription
Acts 13–28: 9
on poisonous snakes
Acts 13–28: 362
on the politarchs' taking a pledge
1 & 2 Thessalonians: 6
on the site of Pergamum
Revelation 1–11: 84
on treason against the emperors
1 & 2 Thessalonians: 5–6
The Rapture of the church
Matthew 24–28: 15, 23, 55, 65
Mark 9–16: 257
Luke 11–17: 153, 156–57, 410, 417
Luke 18–24: 192, 228
John 1–11: 195, 200
John 12–21: 101–2
1 Corinthians: 365, 418, 443
2 Corinthians: 162, 166, 395
2 Timothy: 169, 171
Titus: 119
Hebrews: 154, 314–15
1 Peter: 235–37
2 Peter & Jude: 135
1–3 John: 113
Revelation 1–11: 124–25, 145, 296
Revelation 12–22: 17, 51, 212–13
imminence of
1 & 2 Thessalonians: 131–32
posttribulational view
Luke 18–24: 248
pretribulational view
Luke 18–24: 247
Rasputin
Romans 1–8: 314
Rationalism
John 1–11: 256
2 Timothy: 104
Hebrews: 289–90
Rationalistic pantheism
2 Peter & Jude: 56
Rationalizing sin
Romans 1–8: 174
Ravens
Luke 11–17: 140–41
Razis (Jewish elder)
Luke 18–24: 141
Readiness
Matthew 24–28: 76
Luke 11–17: 157–65
Reaping
Mark 1–8: 142, 144
Reason, reliance on human
Matthew 16–23: 42
Rebekah
Luke 1–5: 69
Rebellion
Luke 11–17: 20, 21, 240–41, 309–11
Luke 18–24: 90, 130, 345, 365, 378
final
Matthew 24–28: 117
of Korah
2 Peter & Jude: 178–79
political
Titus: 98
of Satan
2 Peter & Jude: 97–98
Rebelliousness
Luke 6–10: 198
against God
Matthew 8–15: 309
Rebirth
John 1–11: 97–108
Rebuke
Mark 1–8: 420–21
Mark 9–16: 65, 66
of disciples by Christ
Luke 18–24: 26–27
of sinning believers
Matthew 16–23: 127
Reciprocity, social
Luke 11–17: 272–73, 363, 373
Recognition, men of God
by compassion
2 Corinthians: 341–42

by humility (See also Humility)
2 Corinthians: 344–50
by impact on church
2 Corinthians: 340
by integrity (*see* Integrity; Obedience)
overview of
2 Corinthians: 333–38
by relationship to Jesus Christ
2 Corinthians: 338–40
Reconciliation
Luke 11–17: 392–93
John 12–21: 133
Ephesians: 58
among believers
Matthew 1–7: 297–98
definition of
2 Corinthians: 200–201
divine
Colossians & Philemon: 55–67
forgiveness and
2 Corinthians: 201–6
with God (*see* Salvation)
God's will and
2 Corinthians: 199–201
and justification
Romans 1–8: 274
obedience and
2 Corinthians: 206–8
overview of
2 Corinthians: 197–98
Red Sea
Mark 1–8: 229
Redaction criticism
Matthew 8–15: 214
Redeemer
John 1–11: 14
Redemption
Mark 1–8: 77–78
Luke 1–5: 51, 96, 97
Luke 11–17: 24–26, 339
Luke 18–24: 173–75, 238, 286, 422–23
Ephesians: 17–26
Colossians & Philemon: 41–42
2 Peter & Jude: 18, 205–14
Revelation 1–11: 172
atonement and
1 Peter: 80–83
chain of
Mark 9–16: 239
Christ's blood sacrifice for
1 Peter: 76–83
definition of
1 Peter: 71–72
description of
1 Peter: 71–85, 266
the Father's plan of
Mark 9–16: 268–70, 280, 344
God's plan of
Matthew 1–7: 112–13
Matthew 8–15: 187
and Judas's betrayal
Mark 9–16: 277
law and
Romans 1–8: 308
need for
1 Peter: 83–84
Passover and
1 Peter: 71–73
plan
Luke 6–10: 83–84
price of
Luke 1–5: 170–71
principles of
Matthew 16–23: 222
See also Salvation
Redemptive history
Matthew 16–23: 26
Romans 9–16: 259
Redemptive kingdom
Luke 11–17: 24–26
See also Kingdom of God
Reductionism
Mark 9–16: 199
theological
Titus: 116
Rees, Paul
on Christ's example
Philippians: 119
on Christ's humbling Himself
Philippians: 132
Reformation
Luke 11–17: 202
Luke 18–24: 16, 171
John 1–11: 240
Ephesians: 258
danger of
Matthew 8–15: 335–38
self–
Romans 1–8: 98, 222, 351
See also Protestant Reformation
Reformed theology
Luke 1–5: 125, 126
2 Peter & Jude: 17
Reformers
Luke 1–5: 227
Romans 1–8: 304
2 Peter & Jude: 56–57
Regeneration
Mark 1–8: 25–26, 116, 218
Luke 1–5: 266
Luke 11–17: 77
John 1–11: 97–108
John 12–21: 196
James: 58ff., 60, 62, 108, 145
1 Peter: 32–34, 91–92, 129
2 Peter & Jude: 205–14
1–3 John: 158
cause of continual faith
1–3 John: 177
divine marks of
Romans 1–8: 364
Holy Spirit and
1–3 John: 128
results of
1–3 John: 19, 133, 136, 158
seed of is imperishable
1–3 John: 127
Regression
Hebrews: 133
spiritual
Matthew 8–15: 177

Regulations
Luke 6–10: 3–6
Rehoboam
Mark 9–16: 75
Reign, believers with Christ
Matthew 16–23: 204
Rejection
1 Peter: 105–6
2 Peter & Jude: 173–75
of God, consequences of
Romans 1–8: 102
of God, ways of
Romans 1–8: 82
by Israel
Mark 9–16: 96
of Jesus (*see* Jesus, rejection of)
Rejoicing
Matthew 1–7: 231–33
Luke 6–10: 339, 342
Luke 11–17: 317
See also Joy
Relational forgiveness
Luke 11–17: 41, 42
Relationships, broken
Colossians & Philemon: 2–3, 138–41, 163–64
Relative human goodness
Romans 1–8: 144
Relativism
Matthew 1–7: 249–51
Mark 1–8: 124, 134
John 1–11: 353
John 12–21: 103, 180, 222, 331
Colossians & Philemon: 2, 28
Hebrews: 290–91
modern
1–3 John: 14, 238
moral
Titus: 136
Relevancy, false
Titus: 46
Relevant preaching
Titus: 5
Reliability
2 Corinthians: 43–44
Religion
Luke 6–10: 118
Luke 18–24: 12, 227
Hebrews: 2, 306
absolute truth and
Luke 1–5: 335–37
basis of human
Matthew 16–23: 192, 201
as cover for sin
Galatians: 200
false (*see* False religion)
forms of
Galatians: 194
history of
Romans 1–8: 216
of Jewish people
Luke 1–5: 200
man–made
Matthew 8–15: 273, 280, 453
Romans 1–8: 89, 185
Ephesians: 42
ritualistic/legalistic
Luke 1–5: 205–6, 217–18, 341–42
trust in
Romans 1–8: 250
variations of
Luke 1–5: 327–28
Religiosity, man's natural
Romans 1–8: 89, 181
Religious corruption
Luke 18–24: 103–6
Religious credentials
Luke 18–24: 18–19
Religious deceivers
Luke 18–24: 202
See also False teachers
Religious freedom
2 Timothy: 59
Religious leaders
animosity toward Jesus
Luke 18–24: 90, 120, 131, 162, 269
hypocrisy of
Luke 18–24: 399
Jesus' temple assault and
Luke 18–24: 103
rejection of Jesus
Luke 18–24: 130, 158
sins motivating
Luke 18–24: 130–37
See also Jewish religious leaders; Pharisees; Sadducees; Scribes
Religious security, false
Romans 1–8: 151
Religious superficiality
Romans 1–8: 155
Religious tolerance
Mark 9–16: 216
Religious tradition
Hebrews: 275–76
Remaining
John 12–21: 114–15, 117, 142, 146–50
Remarriage
Matthew 1–7: 307–18
Matthew 16–23: 167, 170, 171
1 Corinthians: 163, 165
1 Timothy: 212
Remnant, God's believing
Galatians: 47
Remorse
Mark 9–16: 339
Luke 6–10: 80–81
of Judas Iscariot
Luke 18–24: 343
Render
Mark 9–16: 180
Repentance
Matthew 1–7: 53–54, 65–69, 109, 192, 212, 402–3, 453–54
Matthew 8–15: 11, 181, 274
Mark 1–8: 367
Mark 9–16: 85, 136, 339, 340
Luke 6–10: 97, 156, 181, 272, 299
Luke 18–24: 34, 343, 373, 443–44
John 12–21: 183–85, 198
Acts 1–12: 73, 113–16
Acts 13–28: 216–17, 337
1 Corinthians: 130

Ephesians: 174
Colossians & Philemon: 16
1 & 2 Thessalonians: 27
Hebrews: 138–39
1–3 John: 36–41, 198
Revelation 1–11: 89, 114, 139
believers' preaching of
Luke 1–5: 40
confession and
Romans 1–8: 268
contrition and
Matthew 16–23: 149
conversion and
Matthew 16–23: 98
elements involved in
Luke 11–17: 188, 220, 350
ethnic heritage and
Luke 1–5: 221–22
evidence of
Mark 1–8: 21, 22
faith and
Matthew 16–23: 96
and forgiveness
Matthew 24–28: 219
God's patience and
Luke 11–17: 183
good works and
Luke 1–5: 218–19
John the Baptist's call for
Mark 1–8: 20, 287, 303–4
and the kingdom of God
Mark 1–8: 48
necessity of
Matthew 16–23: 189
Luke 11–17: 219
Galatians: 93
overview of
2 Corinthians: 38, 431–33
Pharisees/Sadducees and
Luke 1–5: 117–18
preaching of
Matthew 8–15: 58
prompted by God
Matthew 16–23: 203
responsibility and
Luke 11–17: 219, 284–85
salvation and
Matthew 16–23: 193
Luke 1–5: 208–10
Luke 11–17: 224, 369
Romans 1–8: 186, 223, 224, 240, 354
self–righteousness and
Luke 1–5: 333–34
sin and
Luke 11–17: 313
sorrow and (*see* Sorrow)
through gospel preaching
Mark 1–8: 80–81, 287
true
Matthew 8–15: 469
Matthew 16–23: 48
Luke 1–5: 214–15, 222–23
unrepentant sin and
2 Corinthians: 433–38
Replacement theology
Luke 1–5: 126, 132, 135
Reproach
Hebrews: 353–55
Reproduction, spiritual
2 Timothy: 42
Reproving the wrongdoing
2 Timothy: 158
Reputation
2 Corinthians: 79–81
Resistance
1 Peter: 285–86
Resources
believers'
Ephesians: 37–49
divine
2 Timothy: 17
natural
Luke 11–17: 34–36
Respect
1 Peter: 178
Respecters of persons
Romans 1–8: 47
Response
Hebrews: 40–41
Responsibilities (husbands and wives)
1 Peter: 176–83
Responsibility
Christian
1 Corinthians: 82–84
human
Luke 18–24: 302
John 12–21: 257, 258, 259, 260
spiritual
Matthew 24–28: 98, 100
Rest
Hebrews: 96–97, 101–2, 104
Restoration
of disciplined believers
Matthew 16–23: 136
of the earth
Matthew 16–23: 204
spiritual
Mark 1–8: 85
Resurrection
Luke 11–17: 86, 151–52, 268, 269
Luke 18–24: 245, 436–37
John 1–11: 193–202, 449–76
Acts 1–12: 64–67, 303
Acts 13–28: 24–25, 120, 328, 334
2 Corinthians: 147, 193–94, 207, 315
Philippians: 140
1 & 2 Thessalonians: 28, 128
Hebrews: 29, 140, 191
1 Peter: 5, 34, 83–85, 92, 208–19
2 Peter & Jude: 19–20, 34–35
Revelation 1–11: 51, 69
angels' testimony to
Mark 9–16: 400–402
appearances, summary of
John 12–21: 376–77
Christ's appearances after
Luke 18–24: 415
core truths
Luke 18–24: 408
and the cross
Mark 9–16: 12, 13

denial of
Luke 18–24: 415, 430, 431
disciples and
John 12–21: 380–86
disciples' thinking on
Mark 9–16: 2, 3, 13–17
eyewitnesses
Mark 9–16: 402–5
false explanations of
Matthew 24–28: 318
false reactions to
Matthew 24–28: 306
hope in
Matthew 24–28: 304
human beliefs in
Luke 18–24: 140
importance of
Mark 9–16: 12
Luke 18–24: 406–8
Jewish people and
Luke 18–24: 141
Jewish views on
Matthew 16–23: 328
Old Testament revelations of
Luke 18–24: 55, 142
personal
Mark 9–16: 184, 185
Pharisees' belief
Luke 18–24: 143
and power over death
John 12–21: 368–69
Sadducees and
Mark 9–16: 185–92
Luke 18–24: 142–43
salvation and
John 12–21: 373
securing hope
1–3 John: 108
significance of
Matthew 24–28: 305
theories denying
John 12–21: 373–76
Thomas and
John 12–21: 383–86
See also Second coming
Resurrection of judgment. *see* Unbelievers, judgment of
Resurrections
Luke 6–10: 238
Retribution
Matthew 1–7: 329–30
for Christ's enemies
Luke 18–24: 85
God's
1 Corinthians: 21
Return of Christ. *see* second coming, Christ's
Revelation (book of)
Luke 18–24: 183
John 12–21: 201, 207
blessings promised to those who read it
Revelation 1–11: 22
emphasis on the future
Revelation 1–11: 19
theme of
Revelation 1–11: 311
unbelievers' inability to understand
Revelation 1–11: 19
Revelation (concept)
Matthew 8–15: 272
John 12–21: 205–10, 222
1 Corinthians: 62
Hebrews: 2–5, 7
compromising
Romans 1–8: 88
general
Acts 13–28: 360–62
1–3 John: 2, 184–86, 227, 228
men's rejection of
Matthew 16–23: 392
natural
Romans 1–8: 85, 137
Hebrews: 199
progressive
Hebrews: 4–5
redemptive
Romans 1–8: 237
special
Matthew 1–7: 403
2 Timothy: 153
Hebrews: 199
Revenge. *see* Vengeance
Reverence
Matthew 8–15: 222, 470
2 Corinthians: 186, 428–29
Revolt, Jews against Rome
Matthew 16–23: 395
Revolt threat
Mark 9–16: 123, 271
Revolution
American
Romans 9–16: 206
French
Ephesians: 282
political
Mark 1–8: 324, 325
Romans 9–16: 211
Titus: 98
Revolutionaries
Luke 18–24: 131, 133
Reward
Mark 9–16: 86
1 Corinthians: 78–79, 102
Hebrews: 380–81
of believers
Luke 18–24: 85
Ephesians: 353
1–3 John: 234–35
Revelation 1–11: 319
Revelation 12–22: 104–5
divine
Matthew 1–7: 151, 161–62, 174–75, 183–84, 196–97, 207–8, 229, 231, 269–72, 367
heavenly
Matthew 16–23: 57
spiritual
Matthew 24–28: 107
worldly
Matthew 1–7: 354, 356
Reymond, Robert L.
John 1–11: 19

Reynolds, Edward
Luke 18–24: 322
Reynolds, H. R.
John 12–21: 273
Rich man (in parable)
Luke 11–17: 359–68
Rich young ruler
Luke 11–17: 128, 147, 285
Luke 18–24: 34–41
Richardson, Cyril C.
Colossians & Philemon: 232
Riches. *see* Wealth
Riddles
Mark 1–8: 221
See also Parables
Ridicule and mocking
Matthew 16–23: 116
2 Peter & Jude: 111–13
Ridley, Nicholas
Luke 1–5: 227
1 Peter: 3
Right and wrong, natural awareness of
Romans 1–8: 142, 368
Right doctrine, righteous living and
Titus: 71
Right hand of God
Hebrews: 19–20
1 Peter: 219–20
Right responses
1 Peter: 189–91
Righteous living undergirds truth
Titus: 56
Righteousness
Mark 9–16: 79, 80
Luke 1–5: 47, 166, 167, 176–77, 206, 237
Luke 11–17: 347, 370
Luke 18–24: 16, 21, 401
John 12–21: 197
2 Corinthians: 100–103
Hebrews: 34, 324
1 Peter: 92, 169–73, 200, 206, 224, 234, 239, 250
2 Peter & Jude: 22–23, 50–51, 87–88, 90–91, 107
as believers reflecting God's holiness
1–3 John: 113–14
encouragement in
Matthew 16–23: 108
external/false
Matthew 1–7: 134–35, 352–54
as gift of grace
Mark 1–8: 32, 33, 112, 122
God's law as standard of
Romans 1–8: 113, 200, 370
hatred of by the ungodly
1–3 John: 133
and hope
1–3 John: 113–14
hope and
2 Corinthians: 216–17
imparted
Matthew 16–23: 312
Romans 1–8: 182, 267
imperfection of human
Romans 1–8: 66
imputed
Matthew 16–23: 312
Ephesians: 352
integrity and (*see* Integrity)
internal/true (*see* Heart)
lawlessness vs.
2 Corinthians: 248–49
perfection in
Romans 9–16: 148
personal
Acts 1–12: 190–91
positional
Romans 1–8: 411
practical
Romans 1–8: 411
Ephesians: 353
practicing
1–3 John: 124, 126
and salvation
Romans 1–8: 411
1–3 John: 140, 144, 171, 207
of the scribes and Pharisees
Mark 1–8: 119
true
Mark 1–8: 150, 348, 354
truth and
1–3 John: 24–25
works and (*See also* Works–righteousness)
Romans 1–8: 112, 129, 221, 247, 270, 351, 420
worldwide
Romans 9–16: 111
See also Holiness; Self–righteousness; Works–righteousness
Rights
Matthew 1–7: 327–36
Ephesians: 276, 312, 314
Rings
Luke 11–17: 316, 317
Rites, pagan
1 Corinthians: 331, 466
Ritschl, Albrecht
2 Peter & Jude: 56
Ritual
Luke 1–5: 135–36, 217–18, 341–42
Hebrews: 76
Ritualism
Matthew 8–15: 68, 71, 453
Luke 6–10: 2–6
Galatians: 51, 197
Titus: 65
See also Tradition
Ritualistic Christianity
Romans 1–8: 89
Road to Emmaus
Mark 9–16: 404
Roads
Mark 1–8: 180, 195
Robbers
Mark 9–16: 315, 366, 369, 370
Luke 18–24: 108
Robertson, A. T.
Matthew 8–15: 420
Luke 1–5: 145
John 1–11: 18
2 Corinthians: 65, 96, 492

on meaning of aleiphō
James: 277
on meaning of aphelotēs
Acts 1–12: 89
on meaning of eis
Acts 1–12: 14, 75
on meaning of leitourgeō
Acts 13–28: 5
on meaning of logios
Acts 13–28: 161
on meaning of thērion
Acts 13–28: 362
Robertson, F. W.
Ephesians: 184
Robes
Luke 11–17: 316, 317
Luke 18–24: 164, 361, 379
Robinson, George Wade
1 Peter: 130–31
Robinson, Robert
Matthew 8–15: 142
Rock (Simon Peter)
Luke 6–10: 25, 26, 27
See also Peter; Peter, teachings and writings of
Rock music
Ephesians: 257, 261
Rocky/stony ground
Mark 1–8: 195, 202, 303
Luke 6–10: 189, 192
Rogers, Carl
Ephesians: 292
2 Timothy: 109
Rogers, George
Romans 1–8: 74
Role of women, God–ordained
Titus: 79
Roman army
John 12–21: 56–57, 307, 315, 351, 364
Roman Catholicism/Roman Catholic Church
Mark 9–16: 290
Luke 11–17: 197, 202
Luke 18–24: 170, 213, 283, 388
John 1–11: 259–62, 353
John 12–21: 170, 188, 226, 354, 382
Romans 1–8: 250, 504
Galatians: 4, 52
Hebrews: 241
1–3 John: 40, 52–53, 121–22
dogma of
Romans 1–8: 250
immaculate conception and
Luke 1–5: 171
Mary and
Luke 1–5: 46–47, 60–62, 71–72, 167
reformers and
Luke 1–5: 227
replacement theology in
Luke 1–5: 135–36
salvation and
Luke 1–5: 328
Roman centurion
Mark 1–8: 270
1–3 John: 194
Roman cohorts
Matthew 24–28: 183
Mark 9–16: 310, 323, 347
Luke 6–10: 124
Roman crucifixion
Mark 1–8: 427
Roman Empire
Luke 1–5: 142–46, 200
end–time revival of
Revelation 12–22: 42
homosexuality in
Titus: 82
slavery in
Romans 1–8: 5
Titus: 96
Roman legions
Mark 9–16: 314
Roman occupation
Luke 18–24: 71, 78–79
Roman soldiers
Luke 1–5: 220–21
Luke 11–17: 233
Luke 18–24: 367, 392, 431
Christ's clothing divided by
Mark 9–16: 365–66
converted
Luke 18–24: 385, 392
Jesus' death verified by
Luke 18–24: 399, 400
at Jesus' tomb
Mark 9–16: 399
mockery by
Mark 9–16: 358–62
Luke 18–24: 361, 382–83
piercing of Christ's side by
Mark 9–16: 388
Romans (people)
Luke 18–24: 131, 134–36, 378
antagonistic to church
Luke 11–17: 196–97
destruction of Israel by
Mark 9–16: 128, 179
and insurrection
Mark 9–16: 175
and taxation
Mark 9–16: 178–82
Romans, Paul's letter to
2 Corinthians: 71, 198, 428, 480
Rome
Mark 1–8: 3
Luke 1–5: 4, 22, 226
Luke 6–10: 263
Luke 18–24: 211, 212, 226, 368
John 12–21: 166–70, 325
church at
1 Peter: 227–28, 247–48
history of
1 Peter: 158–60, 247–48, 289–90
Jewish revolt against
Matthew 16–23: 395
Roof, removing
Mark 1–8: 101–2
Roosevelt, Theodore
Romans 9–16: 179
2 Timothy: 191
Roosters
Mark 9–16: 298, 337, 339
Rose, Francis
2 Timothy: 53

Rosenberger, Donald A.
Colossians & Philemon: 232–35
Rosenkowitz sextuplets
Luke 1–5: 53
Rosenthal, A. M.
John 12–21: 189
Rosscup, J. E.
John 12–21: 12
Rossetti, Christina
Matthew 8–15: 147
Royal messengers/heralds
Mark 1–8: 16–19
Royal priesthood
1 Peter: 125–26
"The Rubaiyat" (Khayam)
Luke 11–17: 28–29
Rufinus
2 Peter & Jude: 9
Rufus
Mark 1–8: 4
Mark 9–16: 363
Luke 18–24: 368, 369
Rulers
Luke 18–24: 367, 382
Rulers of the synagogue
Matthew 1–7: 123–24
Rupprecht, A.
on slavery
Colossians & Philemon: 205–6
Russell, Bertrand
Hebrews: 292–93, 420
on the purposelessness of the evolutionary view of history
1 & 2 Thessalonians: 140
Russia
Matthew 24–28: 19
Luke 11–17: 244
alliance with Arab nations
Matthew 24–28: 35
Ruth
Mark 9–16: 189
Luke 6–10: 143
Luke 18–24: 145
2 Corinthians: 239, 272
Ryle, J. C.
John 12–21: 131
1 Peter: 245–46

Sabbath
Mark 9–16: 388, 398
Luke 1–5: 155, 268–69
Luke 11–17: 197–98, 201–3, 257–60
Luke 18–24: 226, 399
John 1–11: 14, 169–80, 300, 400–401
John 12–21: 363, 367
Colossians & Philemon: 118–19
Hebrews: 101
Christians and
Matthew 16–23: 24
Acts 13–28: 202–3
for church age believers
Mark 1–8: 140–41
God's purpose for
Mark 1–8: 145–46
Jesus Lord of
Luke 6–10: 6
Jewish regulations
Matthew 8–15: 282
and the Lord's Day
Matthew 8–15: 287
observance of
Mark 1–8: 137
rabbinic rules for
Mark 1–8: 139–40, 143, 150–51, 153
Luke 6–10: 3–5, 7–9
regulations
Luke 6–10: 3–6
synagogue attendance
Mark 1–8: 60
work prohibitions
Mark 1–8: 75
Sabellianism
Luke 1–5: 235
1–3 John: 163
Sabethai Zedi
John 12–21: 12
Sacerdotalism
Titus: 65
Sacramentalism
Romans 1–8: 250
2 Timothy: 104
Titus: 65, 66
Sacraments
John 12–21: 132
Eucharist
Romans 1–8: 250
Roman Catholic
Romans 1–8: 251
Sacredness of God. *see* God
Sacrifice
Mark 1–8: 37
Mark 9–16: 48–49, 93
Luke 1–5: 104, 107–8, 171
Luke 6–10: 142–43
animal
Ephesians: 21
atoning, Christ's
Romans 1–8: 302
blood and
Hebrews: 230–38
of Christ
Hebrews: xvii–xviii, 252–57
end of
Hebrews: 110
external nature of
Hebrews: 250–51
in giving
2 Corinthians: 280
ineffectiveness of
Hebrews: xvi–xvii, 186–87, 246–47
Jewish
Matthew 1–7: 257–58
Jewish, end of
Romans 1–8: 276
necessity of
Hebrews: 172
overview of
2 Corinthians: 144–45
pastoral concern and
2 Corinthians: 424–27
of praise
Hebrews: 443

purpose of
Hebrews: 235, 248
repetition of
Hebrews: 109, 122, 249
sufficiency of Christ's
Romans 1–8: 217
temporary nature of
Hebrews: 176
See also Atonement; Propitiation
Sacrificial lambs
Matthew 24–28: 133
Sacrificial service
Titus: 83
Sacrificial system
Christ's death and
Luke 18–24: 49, 50, 262
divine judgment and
Luke 18–24: 279
justification and
Luke 18–24: 13
necessity of
Luke 18–24: 424
Sacrilege
Matthew 1–7: 437–39
Romans 1–8: 156
2 Peter & Jude: 72–76
Sacrilegious separation
2 Corinthians: 250–54
Sadducees
Matthew 1–7: 62–64, 134, 263
Mark 9–16: 185–92, 271
Luke 1–5: 166, 318–19
Luke 6–10: 70
Luke 11–17: 80, 96, 97, 255, 256
John 1–11: 53, 100, 325–26, 376, 482–84
John 12–21: 24, 63, 166, 223, 224
Acts 1–12: 128–29
1 Corinthians: 423–24
2 Corinthians: 435
James: 110
2 Peter & Jude: 195
agents of Satan
Mark 1–8: 202
description of
Matthew 16–23: 3, 327
John the Baptist's response to
Mark 1–8: 31
lifestyle
Mark 1–8: 24
motivations of
Luke 18–24: 131, 268
and Pharisees
Mark 1–8: 271, 279, 398, 400
reaction to Christ
Matthew 16–23: 327
rejection of Jesus
Mark 1–8: 165
resurrection and
Luke 18–24: 142–48
Sadness
Mark 9–16: 294, 300
Sado–masochistic sex
Romans 1–8: 106
Safford, Truman Henry
Luke 1–5: 188
Sailhamer, John H.
Mark 9–16: 56
St. James's Palace (London, UK)
Luke 18–24: 89
St. Peter's Basilica
Luke 18–24: 170
Saint Bartholomew's Day Massacre
Luke 18–24: 213
John 12–21: 170
Saints
Mark 9–16: 257
1 Corinthians: 6–7, 10–12
Roman Catholic teaching on
Philippians: 14, 309–10
suffering of
Matthew 24–28: 24
See also Believer(s)
Saints' expectation
Luke 18–24: 196–97
Saints' guarantees
2 Peter & Jude: 205–14
Saliva
Mark 1–8: 377, 408
Salome
Mark 1–8: 306
Mark 9–16: 105, 382
Luke 1–5: 231–32
Luke 6–10: 47
John 1–11: 7–8
John 12–21: 318, 354–55
1–3 John: 6
Salt
Mark 9–16: 48, 49
Luke 11–17: 288
Salt and fire
Mark 9–16: 48
Salt and light
Luke 11–17: 72–73
Salt of the earth
Mark 9–16: 49
Salutations
1–3 John: 219
Salvation
Matthew 1–7: 182
John 12–21: 246–48, 255, 269, 287, 288
2 Corinthians: 31, 45
2 Peter & Jude: 18–31, 38–41, 155–56, 205–14
accompaniments of
Hebrews: 152–53
and acknowledging Jesus as Lord
1–3 John: 198
Arminian position on
1–3 John: 140, 141
aspects of
1 & 2 Thessalonians: 163
assurance of
Matthew 1–7: 232–33, 475
Acts 13–28: 34
Romans 1–8: 223, 429, 438
Ephesians: 364
1 & 2 Thessalonians: 159–60
1–3 John: 52–60, 140, 141, 142
barriers to
Matthew 8–15: 53
Matthew 16–23: 198

Romans 9–16: 4
basis of
Romans 1–8: 267
1 & 2 Thessalonians: 15
for believers only
1–3 John: 202, 210
believers' perfect love and
1–3 John: 171
believers' responses to
1 Peter: 61–70
benefits of
Hebrews: 108
biblical invitation to
Revelation 12–22: 305
blessings of
Luke 6–10: 186
of children
Mark 9–16: 64–70
Luke 18–24: 23–31
Christ's authority to give
Luke 18–24: 112
Christ's perspective of
Luke 11–17: 67, 216–24
Christ's teaching on
Luke 11–17: 67, 216–24
cleansed conscience as a gift of
1–3 John: 143
commitment to gospel of
Luke 11–17: 339
completeness of
Hebrews: 200–201
completion of
Romans 1–8: 419, 442
Colossians & Philemon: 106–9
confession and
Matthew 16–23: 193
conviction and
Matthew 16–23: 193
and the cross
Mark 1–8: 418–20
description of
1 Peter: 89–90, 100–102, 250
divine election and
Romans 9–16: 24, 32
divine plan of
Titus: 11, 14, 159
divine provision of
Romans 1–8: 207
divinely initiated
Matthew 16–23: 216
doctrine of
Luke 1–5: 16
Romans 1–8: 231
doubt of
Romans 1–8: 430
earning
Matthew 16–23: 202
elect or "chosen" and
1–3 John: 217
elements of
Romans 1–8: 494
equality of
Matthew 16–23: 213, 310
evidence of
Matthew 16–23: 190, 278, 299, 312
Matthew 24–28: 122
Romans 1–8: 130, 347, 454
Romans 9–16: 243
1 & 2 Thessalonians: 17
and external acts
Mark 1–8: 354
and faith (*See also* Faith)
Mark 1–8: 261
Luke 18–24: 64
1–3 John: 120–22, 227
by faith
Luke 6–10: 176
by faith alone
Acts 13–28: 108
false doctrines of
Galatians: 11
false evidence of
Matthew 16–23: 190
false means of
Romans 1–8: 21
false proofs of
Philippians: 212–15
false standards for
Romans 1–8: 128
false views of
Acts 1–12: 69–71, 243–44
four stages of
Galatians: 7
Free Grace view
1–3 John: 140, 141
general revelation and
1–3 John: 227, 228
for Gentiles
Luke 1–5: 180–82
genuineness of
Philippians: 209–12
global extent of
Luke 18–24: 221, 445–47
God's
Matthew 16–23: 262, 282, 311
Luke 1–5: 13, 153
Luke 18–24: 61
Romans 1–8: 26, 27, 126, 212, 228, 357
1 Timothy: 69
1–3 John: 39, 107, 158, 164–65
God's covenants and
1–3 John: 39
God's glory in
Romans 1–8: 27
God's gracious offer of
Romans 1–8: 126
God's mercy and
Luke 18–24: 61
God's perfect love in
1–3 John: 164–65
as God's redemptive plan
Luke 1–5: 13, 153
God's saving plan and purpose
1–3 John: 107, 158
God's terms for
Matthew 16–23: 262, 311
good works and
Luke 18–24: 12, 14, 37
gospel needed for
1–3 John: 227
grace and
Mark 1–8: 112, 426

1 Corinthians: 11
1–3 John: 227
greatness of
1 Peter: 49–59
hope and
Luke 11–17: 371
humility and
Luke 11–17: 264, 265
importance to God
Romans 1–8: 26
invitation to
Mark 9–16: 153, 263
of Israel
Mark 1–8: 362–63, 368
Luke 11–17: 410–11
Luke 18–24: 194–95
Jesus as the only way to
1–3 John: 210
joy
1 Peter: 39–48
and Judaism
Mark 1–8: 131, 132, 133
as kingdom banquet
Luke 11–17: 273
knowing Jesus Christ in
1–3 John: 55, 56, 187, 198, 210
the law and
Luke 18–24: 38–39
law and God's
Romans 1–8: 228, 357
light of
Luke 1–5: 122
lordship
Titus: 114
loss of
Hebrews: 146–47
loss of (impossible)
1 & 2 Thessalonians: 286
Titus: 108
love as evidence of
1 & 2 Thessalonians: 17
marks of genuine
Ephesians: 38
message of
Mark 1–8: 12, 110, 200
missed opportunities for
Luke 11–17: 221
Acts 13–28: 301–2
natural theology and
1–3 John: 224
neglect of
Hebrews: 41–43
new birth and
1–3 John: 127–28, 133
New Covenant and
Luke 1–5: 120, 129–30
Luke 11–17: 369
no–lordship view
1–3 John: 140, 141
obedience and
Luke 6–10: 119, 289
Romans 1–8: 24, 347
of Old Testament saints
Hebrews: 234–35
opportunity for
Matthew 24–28: 92
permanence of
Luke 18–24: 215–17
power of
Romans 1–8: 220
practical effects of
Romans 1–8: 312
prayers
Mark 9–16: 75
primary purpose of
Romans 1–8: 214
progress of
Colossians & Philemon: 150
propitiation and
1–3 John: 46–50, 124
purchased by the blood of Christ
Revelation 12–22: 308
purpose of
Romans 1–8: 214
Ephesians: 59
reconciliation in
Luke 11–17: 392–93
redemption by Jesus Christ
1–3 John: 55–56, 187–89, 198, 210
redemptive kingdom and
Luke 11–17: 24–26
Reformed view
1–3 John: 140
refusal to accept
Luke 11–17: 250–51
regenerative work of
Mark 1–8: 25–26
repentance and
Matthew 16–23: 193
Mark 9–16: 85
Luke 1–5: 208–10
Luke 11–17: 224, 369
Romans 1–8: 354
righteousness as proof of
1–3 John: 140, 144, 171, 207
roadblocks to
Luke 11–17: 147–48
sanctification and
1–3 John: 125–26, 164
Scripture and
Romans 1–8: 270
1–3 John: 218, 227
self–denial and
Mark 1–8: 425–27
self–effort and
Matthew 16–23: 201
sin and
Mark 1–8: 317
Luke 6–10: 195–96, 234
sovereign work of God
Titus: 150
sovereignty of God in
Acts 1–12: 252, 267
Acts 13–28: 38, 94
spiritual
Luke 1–5: 154
submission and
Luke 18–24: 34
supreme focus of God's
Romans 1–8: 212
tasting of
Hebrews: 143–44

tests of, certainty of sin
1–3 John: 25–31
tests of, confession
1–3 John: 37–41
tests of, forgiveness of sins
1–3 John: 33–36
tests of, overview of
1–3 John: 42, 122
transformation
Luke 6–10: 223
transformation by
Romans 1–8: 318, 361
transformation of
Colossians & Philemon: 148–49
triumph of suffering and
1 Peter: 205–21
true
Romans 1–8: 113, 348
of the two blind men
Mark 9–16: 117
universalism and
1–3 John: 225
view of Jesus and
1–3 John: 187
wealth/riches and
Luke 18–24: 41, 42
which cannot be broken
Romans 1–8: 304
"wider mercy" view and
1–3 John: 225
works and
Hebrews: 154
worldwide
Romans 9–16: 111
See also Saving faith
Salvation Army
social reforms of
Colossians & Philemon: 166
Salvation message
Luke 11–17: 71
Salvation truth
Luke 11–17: 95
Salvation wisdom
Luke 6–10: 167
Samaria
Mark 1–8: 23, 300
Mark 9–16: 92, 349
Luke 1–5: 265
Luke 6–10: 133, 311, 312
Luke 18–24: 372
Samaritan woman
Luke 1–5: 266
Luke 6–10: 133, 170
John 1–11: 1–2, 28, 139–40, 142–60, 323, 414
Samaritans
Luke 1–5: 202
Luke 6–10: 42, 47, 179, 242, 311–12, 357–58
Luke 11–17: 392, 393
Luke 18–24: 363
John 12–21: 150, 327
Acts 1–12: 233
Samenow, Stanton
Ephesians: 167
Samson
Luke 1–5: 54
Luke 6–10: 38, 39
2 Corinthians: 114
Hebrews: 365–66
Revelation 1–11: 112
Samson's parents
1–3 John: 242
Samuel
Mark 1–8: 298
Mark 9–16: 46
Luke 1–5: 75
John 1–11: 17
1 Timothy: 58
Hebrews: 366
1 Peter: 156–57
San Jacinto, Battle of
Luke 6–10: 38
Sanctification
Matthew 1–7: 183
Luke 1–5: 177
Luke 6–10: 299
Luke 11–17: 161
John 12–21: 282, 283, 284
Ephesians: 226, 365
2 Timothy: 82, 142
Titus: 115
Hebrews: 67–68, 254, 263, 405–6
1 Peter: 21–22, 200–201
1–3 John: 29, 36–37, 117–18, 124–25
affection and
2 Corinthians: 481–82, 486–87
authenticity and (*See also* Authenticity)
2 Corinthians: 459–72
authority and (*see* Authority)
of believers
Romans 9–16: 143, 255–57
benediction and
2 Corinthians: 481–82, 487–89
definition of
1 & 2 Thessalonians: 93–94, 202
disciple and (*see* Discipline)
divine
Romans 1–8: 409, 433
elements of
1 & 2 Thessalonians: 202–3
and justification
Romans 1–8: 318
obedience and integrity and (*see* Integrity; Obedience)
perfection and
2 Corinthians: 481–86
principles regarding
1 & 2 Thessalonians: 208–10
repentance and (*see* Repentance)
source of
1 & 2 Thessalonians: 204
See also Holiness; Maturity
Sanctuary
Luke 18–24: 344
Sandals
Luke 11–17: 316
Sanders, J. Oswald
2 Corinthians: 172
1 Timothy: 166, 220

Sangster, Will
1 Timothy: 99
Sanhedrin
Mark 1–8: 270
Mark 9–16: 321, 322
Luke 1–5: 318
Luke 6–10: 80
Luke 11–17: 195
Luke 18–24: 330
John 1–11: 101, 103, 195, 288, 307, 320, 326, 482–83, 485
John 12–21: 3, 24, 321, 324, 325
Acts 1–12: 132, 167–68, 194ff., 219ff.
Acts 13–28: 278–79
Romans 9–16: 282
1 Corinthians: 3
2 Corinthians: 31, 43, 85, 326
Hebrews: 207
1 Peter: 2, 7
abuse of Jesus
Luke 18–24: 338, 350
attempts to trap Jesus
Mark 9–16: 204
corruption in
Mark 9–16: 321, 322
false witnesses and
Luke 18–24: 324–25
Jewish Supreme Court
Mark 9–16: 311
legal violations of
Luke 18–24: 332–33, 335, 336
local councils of
Mark 9–16: 320–21
local courts
Luke 18–24: 330
Pontius Pilate and
Luke 18–24: 345
and Roman government
Mark 9–16: 271, 346
Sadducees in
Mark 9–16: 186
Sadducees power in
Luke 18–24: 143
trial procedure of
Matthew 24–28: 199
Santa Anna, Antonio Lopez de
Luke 6–10: 38
Santa Claus
Luke 1–5: 141
Santayana, George
2 Peter & Jude: 176
Sapphira
Luke 6–10: 36, 320
Luke 11–17: 114, 129, 333
2 Corinthians: 442
1–3 John: 205
Sarah
Luke 1–5: 54, 59, 106, 108–9
Luke 6–10: 20, 144
John 1–11: 388
2 Corinthians: 16, 139
Hebrews: 332–33
Sardis
1–3 John: 2, 185
Sardis, church at
Ephesians: 335
Sartre, Jean–Paul
Acts 13–28: 18
philosophical despair of
Colossians & Philemon: 96–97
Satan
Matthew 1–7: 85–86, 90–91, 96–97, 177, 290–91
Mark 1–8: 44, 46
Mark 9–16: 257, 276, 277, 301, 304
Luke 1–5: 255, 257
Luke 6–10: 31, 191, 218, 283
Luke 18–24: 150
John 1–11: 23–24, 83, 110–11, 157, 182, 273, 334–35, 347, 354, 363–76, 379, 416, 444
Romans 1–8: 136
2 Corinthians: 41, 51–53, 61, 70–71, 105–6, 132, 183, 225, 228, 230, 234, 244, 250, 293, 329, 334–38, 356, 362–63, 371–73, 384, 400
Galatians: 10–17, 62, 185
Ephesians: 30, 49, 55, 97, 103, 121–22, 138, 159, 169, 182, 193, 199, 219, 231, 233–34, 246–54, 262, 282, 292–95, 355, 359, 370–71
1 Timothy: 14, 145
Hebrews: 69–70, 252, 255, 296, 347
1 Peter: 77, 79, 151, 209–15, 240, 257, 280–84
2 Peter & Jude: 2, 68, 82, 85, 96–102, 108, 110, 139–40, 157–65, 174–75, 185–86, 196, 204
as accuser
2 Timothy: 115
accuses God's people
Revelation 12–22: 14, 19
Adam and Eve and deceit of
1–3 John: 252
agents of
Mark 1–8: 64, 201–2
Luke 11–17: 66
allurements of
Romans 1–8: 398
antichrists, energizer of
1–3 John: 94, 96
the ascension and
Luke 18–24: 455
attacks on the church
1 Timothy: 39
attacks Jesus Christ
Revelation 12–22: 10
authority over
Colossians & Philemon: 50, 103, 112–13
as Beelzebul
Luke 11–17: 62
believer's battle with
Romans 1–8: 332
believers' opposing of
Matthew 24–28: 176
believers' victory over
Romans 1–8: 428
1–3 John: 174–75
Revelation 12–22: 22
binding of
Revelation 12–22: 235–36

causes believers to doubt their salvation
James: 13
children of
Romans 1–8: 273, 296
Ephesians: 182, 207
children of, children of God and
1–3 John: 128
children of, eternal life of
1–3 John: 135, 136
children of, hatred of God's children
1–3 John: 131, 133–35
children of, indifference of toward God's children
1–3 John: 131, 135–37
children of, murdering God's children
1–3 John: 131, 132–33
children of, as unsaved sinners
1–3 John: 126
and Christ's power
Mark 1–8: 162, 271, 399
Christ's power over
Matthew 8–15: 39, 310
Mark 1–8: 238, 239, 240
Luke 6–10: 88–89, 142, 218, 340
Luke 11–17: 218
and Christ's redemptive work
1 Timothy: 38
Christ's victory over
James: 205
counterfeit conversions, tactic of
1–3 John: 140
counterfeiting of saving faith
James: 7
cross's effect on
Romans 1–8: 215
darkness and
Luke 18–24: 389
1–3 John: 62, 126, 132
deceitfulness of
Romans 1–8: 247, 303
Philippians: 52
1–3 John: 89–90, 214
Revelation 12–22: 14, 20, 54, 60, 156–57, 246
defeat of
1 Corinthians: 20–21
1–3 John: 175
Revelation 1–11: 52, 168, 256–57
Revelation 12–22: 2, 15, 18
demonic forces and
Luke 1–5: 280–81
destruction of
Luke 11–17: 411
as the devil
James: 205
1–3 John: 126
and distortion of woman's role
1 Timothy: 78
emissaries of
Luke 6–10: 112, 113
Luke 18–24: 159, 162
1–3 John: 232, 236, 237
in Eve's temptation
Mark 1–8: 270
as "evil one"
James: 235
fall of
Romans 1–8: 1
1 Timothy: 37
and false wisdom
James: 173
fearing
Luke 11–17: 118–19
final destruction of
Luke 18–24: 196
God's enmity to at`the fall
1–3 John: 188–89
God's power over
John 12–21: 87, 281–82
and God's sovereign purpose
1–3 John: 99
hell prepared for
James: 157
hope as defense against
1–3 John: 108
idolatry as service of
Romans 1–8: 92
inability to reclaim saints
1–3 John: 207
influence of
Matthew 16–23: 41
Jesus' confrontation with
Luke 11–17: 194
Jesus' identity and
Luke 6–10: 221, 258
and Jesus' miracles
Mark 1–8: 84, 181
Jesus' triumph over
Luke 18–24: 294, 295
and Jewish exiles
James: 159
and Job
James: 260
Judas Iscariot and
Luke 6–10: 80
Luke 18–24: 269–70, 291
John 12–21: 64, 80–81
judgment of
Luke 11–17: 155
John 12–21: 42, 139, 198
Revelation 1–11: 32
methods of
Luke 6–10: 75
millennium and
Luke 1–5: 50, 286
names and titles of
Luke 11–17: 62
Ephesians: 339
James: 235
Revelation 1–11: 310
Revelation 12–22: 6–7, 19–20, 235
nature and power of
Matthew 8–15: 308
opposition to God's kingdom
1 & 2 Thessalonians: 71, 80, 264–65
opposition to God's plan
1–3 John: 94, 126
opposition to truth
Luke 11–17: 95
origin/destiny of
Luke 1–5: 280

and persecution
1 Timothy: 67
persecution of God's people by
Revelation 12–22: 8
personal existence
Ephesians: 338
power of
Romans 1–8: 92
powerlessness of
Luke 11–17: 67
present activity of
Revelation 12–22: 16
and pride
1 Timothy: 118
Revelation 12–22: 1
protection from
Luke 6–10: 341–42
rebellion of
Acts 13–28: 291
Revelation 12–22: 2, 8
resisting
Ephesians: 342
ruler of evil world system
James: 193
and salvation message
Mark 1–8: 201–2
self–deception of
Matthew 8–15: 43
as serpent
Luke 1–5: 217
and slander
James: 220
strategy for attacking the truth
1–3 John: 153, 155, 210, 214
tactics of
Romans 1–8: 270
temporary freedom of
Matthew 24–28: 24
temporary rule of
Luke 18–24: 195–96
temptation and
Matthew 16–23: 41
Mark 1–8: 42–46
Luke 18–24: 300, 301
1–3 John: 90
temptation of believers
James: 50
temptation of Jesus
Luke 1–5: 252–61
threefold temptations of
1–3 John: 90
during tribulation
Luke 18–24: 220
Trojan horse stratagem of
1–3 John: 155
unbelievers as subjects of
James: 58
war against God
Revelation 1–11: 77–78, 162, 254–55
wilderness temptation
Mark 1–8: 42–46
woman with sickness and
Luke 11–17: 200–201
and woman's role
1 Timothy: 78
works of
1–3 John: 126, 140, 210
world, control of
John 12–21: 139, 171
world system of (See also World system, present (satanic))
Ephesians: 49, 309
worship and
Luke 1–5: 74
worship of
Matthew 1–7: 95–98
See also Demons; Hell
Satisfaction
Mark 1–8: 387, 389
spiritual
Matthew 1–7: 183–84
See also Self–satisfaction
Saucy, Robert L.
1 Timothy: 83, 84
Sauer, Erich
Luke 18–24: 436
Titus: 107
on divine reconciliation
Colossians & Philemon: 58–59
Saul (king)
Matthew 1–7: 203
Mark 1–8: 144, 145
Luke 6–10: 38
Romans 9–16: 10
2 Corinthians: 114
1 Timothy: 53
1 Peter: 156–57
Saul of Tarsus
Luke 1–5: 75
Luke 6–10: 170
Luke 11–17: 195
John 1–11: 101, 326
John 12–21: 166
See also Paul
Saving faith
Matthew 1–7: 280–82, 487–89
Mark 1–8: 68, 180, 186, 198, 210, 348, 424
Mark 9–16: 238, 332, 340, 405
Luke 11–17: 220
Luke 18–24: 216–17, 295–96, 328
Philippians: 155–56
Colossians & Philemon: 15–17, 66
Hebrews: 262
and commitment to Jesus as Lord
1–3 John: 178–79
doctrine regarding
1–3 John: 120–22
elements of
Luke 6–10: 289–90
elements needed for
1–3 John: 147
emotions and
Romans 1–8: 206
evidence of
Romans 1–8: 222, 223
of Gaius
1–3 John: 247
of Gentiles
Luke 6–10: 129
God's granting through grace
1–3 John: 169, 227

good works and
1 & 2 Thessalonians: 258–59
as hold on eternal life
1–3 John: 197
human will and
Romans 1–8: 205
indicators of
Luke 6–10: 192
intellect and
Romans 1–8: 206
and love
Matthew 16–23: 340
love and obedience as product of
1–3 John: 181
nature of
1 Timothy: 50
obedience and
Luke 6–10: 119, 275
1 & 2 Thessalonians: 15–16
of Peter
Luke 18–24: 295–96
Satan's counterfeiting of
James: 7
self–denial and
Luke 6–10: 321
will and
Romans 1–8: 205
See also Faith
Saving gospel
Luke 11–17: 70–72
Savior
Luke 1–5: 152–54, 158–59, 168, 229
Christ as
Titus: 114
Scapegoat
Hebrews: 225–26
Scarborough, John
Luke 1–5: 12
Scattering of Israel
Matthew 24–28: 160
Sceva
Luke 1–5: 284
Schaeffer, Francis A.
Luke 1–5: 337
John 1–11: 352
John 12–21: 90, 91
Acts 13–28: 18
Hebrews: 289–90
1 Peter: 195–96, 274
on alienation
Colossians & Philemon: 164
on church unity
Colossians & Philemon: 88
on the meaning of the term Christian
Revelation 1–11: 53
on the meaninglessness of the naturalistic view of man
1 & 2 Thessalonians: 141
on philosophical queries
Colossians & Philemon: 96–97, 101
Schlatter, Adolf
on ancient philosophy
Colossians & Philemon: 100
Schleiermacher, Friedrich
2 Peter & Jude: 56
Schools, scribal
Titus: 126
Schreiner, Thomas R.
John 12–21: 250
2 Peter & Jude: 13, 140, 216
Schürer, Emil
Mark 9–16: 95
Luke 1–5: 131
Luke 18–24: 49
Schweitzer, Albert
Luke 1–5: 300
Science
Galatians: 183
God and
Colossians & Philemon: 1, 47–50, 57
Scientific discoveries
Luke 1–5: 103–4
Scientific method
Hebrews: 307
Scientific objectivism
Romans 1–8: 268
Scientism
Matthew 16–23: 307
Scoffers
Luke 11–17: 408–9
Scofield, C. I.
Matthew 8–15: 416
Scott, Thomas
Romans 1–8: 384
Scottish Reformation
2 Timothy: 60
Scourging
Mark 9–16: 354, 360, 364
Luke 18–24: 358, 359, 361, 379
John 12–21: 337–38
***The Screwtape Letters* (Lewis)**
Mark 1–8: 174
Scribes and Pharisees
Matthew 1–7: 33, 205, 276, 340–43
Mark 1–8: 61, 62, 100, 180–81, 342
Mark 9–16: 156, 197, 218, 220, 270, 311
Luke 1–5: 319–20
Luke 6–10: 43, 318
Luke 11–17: 103, 104, 257, 258
Romans 1–8: 154
1–3 John: 255
at Christ's arrest
Luke 18–24: 313
Christ's condemnation of
Luke 6–10: 114, 162, 179
Luke 18–24: 163–67
at crucifixion
Luke 18–24: 367
as false teachers
Mark 1–8: 136, 166
functions of
Luke 6–10: 317
hostility of to Christ
Luke 6–10: 2, 7, 10
hostility toward Jesus
Mark 1–8: 153, 165
hypocrisy of
Luke 18–24: 164–66
influence of
Romans 9–16: 55

Jesus' denunciations of
Luke 11–17: 71, 114, 115
legalistic Judaism of
Mark 1–8: 153, 341
motivations of
Luke 18–24: 114, 131, 268–69
opposition to Jesus
Luke 11–17: 81–82, 305
origin of
Matthew 16–23: 355
the prophets and
Luke 11–17: 106
religious/political dominance
Luke 18–24: 163
self–righteousness of
Luke 11–17: 109, 320–22
See also Pharisees
Scripture
Matthew 1–7: 254–55
Mark 1–8: 5, 200, 342–43, 345, 406
Mark 9–16: 190, 192, 288
Luke 6–10: 83, 84, 85, 93
applying
Ephesians: 153, 372
authority of
Matthew 1–7: 249–82, 264–65
Ephesians: 279, 287, 347, 369, 373
Titus: 127
authorship, divine
Ephesians: 368
benefits of
1 & 2 Thessalonians: 58, 198
commitment to
Titus: 10
comparing with Scripture
Romans 1–8: 323
completion of
1 Corinthians: 364
denouncing
Romans 1–8: 121
essential character of
1 & 2 Thessalonians: 198
honoring
1 Corinthians: 88
importance of
1 Timothy: 239, 288
importance of in believers' lives
Acts 1–12: 83, 257
inerrancy of
Romans 9–16: 41
Galatians: 4
interpretation
Luke 18–24: 200
interpretation, allegorical
Titus: 64
Jewish reverence for
Romans 1–8: 204
knowing
Colossians & Philemon: 28–30, 150, 159–60
loving
Colossians & Philemon: 32
obedience to
1 & 2 Thessalonians: 98
permanence of
Matthew 1–7: 261–66
pertinence of
Matthew 1–7: 267–73
power of
Ephesians: 367
preeminence of
Matthew 1–7: 249–59
public reading of
1 Timothy: 176
purpose of
Matthew 1–7: 275–82, 482–83
role of in salvation
Acts 1–12: 255
the source of spiritual growth
1 & 2 Thessalonians: 89
study of
Matthew 1–7: 164
superficial study of
Romans 1–8: 121
supremacy of
1 & 2 Thessalonians: 196
theorizing about
1 Timothy: 242
twisting of
Romans 1–8: 232
understanding
Luke 18–24: 418–19, 423–27, 442
Colossians & Philemon: 89–92
See also The Bible; Word of God
Scrolls
Luke 1–5: 268, 270
Sea of Galilee (Sea of Chinnereth, Sea of Tiberius)
Matthew 1–7: 115
Mark 1–8: 50, 228
Luke 1–5: 269, 302, 316
Luke 6–10: 15, 183, 208
John 1–11: 220
John 12–21: 390–93
and Bethsaida
Mark 1–8: 326
calming of storm on
Luke 6–10: 207, 210–13, 218–19, 229
description
Luke 6–10: 208
fishing exports of
Mark 1–8: 72
fishing occupations on
Luke 6–10: 41, 47, 210
geography of
Mark 1–8: 23, 50, 228–29
and Jesus' teaching
Mark 1–8: 161
and Jordan River
Mark 1–8: 29
Sea waves, wild
2 Peter & Jude: 180
Seal, divine
Romans 1–8: 252
Seal judgments
Luke 18–24: 220
Sealing
2 Corinthians: 45
Second Abrahamic Covenant
Romans 9–16: 131
Second birth
John 1–11: 97–108

Second blessing
1 Corinthians: 313–14
Galatians: 66
Ephesians: 46
Second coming, Christ's
Matthew 24–28: 14, 112
Mark 9–16: 242, 252, 262–63
Luke 1–5: 136, 157
John 12–21: 102
Acts 1–12: 20, 23, 40
Romans 1–8: 126, 445
Romans 9–16: 40, 120, 261
1 Corinthians: 19–22, 77–78, 365, 418, 473
2 Corinthians: 394
1 & 2 Thessalonians: 18, 28, 73, 74, 91, 116, 231–32
Hebrews: 31–32, 37, 242
James: 253
1 Peter: 37–38, 63–64, 82–83, 235–38
2 Peter & Jude: 12, 57–61, 109–46
Revelation 12–22: 108, 149, 211–12, 302
anticipation for
Luke 18–24: 253–56, 258
believers and
Luke 18–24: 197
believers' desire for
Luke 11–17: 412–13
Christ's predictions of
Luke 18–24: 190
the church and
Luke 11–17: 410, 417
date setting for
Mark 9–16: 262
Luke 11–17: 153, 157
denial of
Luke 18–24: 186
denying
Luke 11–17: 151–52, 153
divisiveness of
Luke 11–17: 419–20
doctrine of
Luke 11–17: 150–51
eternal implications of
Mark 9–16: 242
evangelism and
Luke 18–24: 258–59
events surrounding
Luke 11–17: 409
Israel and
Luke 18–24: 127
Jerusalem in
Luke 18–24: 220–21
judgment and
Luke 11–17: 420
modern signs of
Matthew 16–23: 6
necessity of
Luke 11–17: 409–11
praying for
Luke 11–17: 26, 27
Luke 18–24: 7–8
preterism and
Luke 11–17: 151–52
prophecies of
Luke 11–17: 153–54, 409–10
the rapture and
Luke 18–24: 192–93, 249
readiness for
Luke 11–17: 157–65
reasons for
Luke 11–17: 153–56
revelation at the
Colossians & Philemon: 132–33
signs of
Luke 18–24: 230, 242
spiritual separation and
Luke 18–24: 255–58
timing of
Luke 11–17: 413–18
truth of
Luke 18–24: 242
unexpectedness of
Mark 9–16: 252, 262–63
Luke 18–24: 252–55
See also Judgment; Millennial kingdom; Millennium; Resurrection; Tribulation, the Great
The Second death
James: 287–88
Second Law of Thermodynamics
Colossians & Philemon: 57
Second Triumvirate
Luke 1–5: 143
Secrecy
2 Peter & Jude: 71–72
Secret societies
Matthew 8–15: 220
Secret things
Mark 1–8: 214
Sectarianism
Luke 6–10: 50
Security
of believers
1 Corinthians: 399
doubt of
Romans 1–8: 278
eternal (*see* Eternal security)
false
Matthew 16–23: 376
Matthew 24–28: 106
Romans 1–8: 115, 139, 150, 151
longing for
Romans 1–8: 146
Security in Christ
description of
1 Peter: 119–22, 195–204
devotion and
1 Peter: 200–201
faith and
1 Peter: 201–2
pure conscience and
1 Peter: 202–3
suffering and
1 Peter: 197–200
zealousness and
1 Peter: 196–97
Sedation of those crucified
Luke 18–24: 379
Seder
John 1–11: 51
The seed
Mark 1–8: 216, 217, 218

1 Peter: 92–93
Seek and save the lost
Luke 18–24: 75
Seeking God
Mark 9–16: 74–76
Seel, John
Titus: 138
Seers
Matthew 24–28: 2
Seiss, Joseph
on the Battle of Armageddon
Revelation 12–22: 223
on the brilliant light emanating from the New Jerusalem
Revelation 12–22: 285
concern to accurately interpret Scripture
Revelation 12–22: 311
Self
dying to (*See also* Old self)
Ephesians: 76, 109, 112, 251, 267, 299
flaunting
Matthew 16–23: 363
new, in Christ
Romans 1–8: 318
old, believers still clothed in
Romans 1–8: 412
serving
Matthew 1–7: 90–93
Self-absorption
Titus: 130
Self-acceptance
Matthew 16–23: 130
Ephesians: 6
Self-accusation
Luke 18–24: 331
Self-actualization
Titus: 81
Self-assessment
Luke 11–17: 178
Self-centeredness
Matthew 1–7: 148, 279, 448, 453
1 Corinthians: 72
2 Corinthians: 424–27
Ephesians: 200, 272, 276, 367, 383
Titus: 101, 131
as man's nature
Romans 1–8: 2
Self-cleansing
Matthew 8–15: 336
Self-concern
Matthew 1–7: 189
Matthew 16–23: 341
Self-condemnation
Luke 18–24: 339
believers'
Ephesians: 23
Self-confidence
Matthew 1–7: 86
Matthew 8–15: 140
Matthew 24–28: 168, 179, 212, 216
Mark 9–16: 298, 333–35
1 Corinthians: 227, 475
Self-control
Luke 6–10: 34
1 Corinthians: 214–16
Ephesians: 125, 200, 276, 363
Titus: 92
1 Peter: 280
2 Peter & Jude: 41
Self-deception
Matthew 1–7: 239, 473–89
Luke 18–24: 38
1 Corinthians: 218
2 Corinthians: 461
See also Deception
Self-defense
Matthew 1–7: 171–72
Luke 6–10: 105
Self-denial
Matthew 1–7: 301, 305, 336
Matthew 8–15: 253
Matthew 16–23: 47, 56, 97, 162
Mark 1–8: 425–27
Mark 9–16: 103
Luke 6–10: 265, 269–74, 276, 318, 319, 321
Luke 11–17: 25, 219, 278, 281, 284, 350
John 12–21: 398
Romans 9–16: 157
1 Corinthians: 211–13
Ephesians: 42
Colossians & Philemon: 8, 75–76, 122–24, 136–37
1 Peter: 239
Self-discipline
Romans 9–16: 180, 201
Ephesians: 220, 350, 362
Philippians: 114
2 Timothy: 194
Self-esteem
Matthew 16–23: 130, 230
Mark 9–16: 32
Romans 9–16: 158, 236
Titus: 81
Self-evaluation
1 Corinthians: 87–90
Self-exaltation
Matthew 16–23: 368
Galatians: 200
Self-examination
Matthew 1–7: 475–76
Romans 1–8: 423
Romans 9–16: 158
Self-expression
Ephesians: 261
Titus: 136
Self-flattery
Romans 1–8: 188
Self-fulfillment
Matthew 16–23: 230
Galatians: 185
2 Timothy: 109
Titus: 81
Self-giving
Matthew 16–23: 162, 234
Ephesians: 200, 283
Self-glorification
Matthew 16–23: 230, 366
Romans 1–8: 130
Ephesians: 256, 283
Self-gratification
Ephesians: 200

Self-image
Romans 9–16: 252
improvement
Galatians: 11
positive
2 Timothy: 109
Self-improvement
Ephesians: 6
Self-indulgence
Matthew 8–15: 253
Matthew 16–23: 126, 385
Self-interest
Matthew 1–7: 327–28
Matthew 16–23: 152, 201
Matthew 24–28: 188
Romans 1–8: 221
Ephesians: 56
Titus: 35
Self-justification
Matthew 1–7: 293, 430
Matthew 8–15: 411
Ephesians: 183
Self-knowledge
Titus: 81
Self-love
Matthew 8–15: 482
Luke 6–10: 266
Romans 1–8: 221, 418, 424
Romans 9–16: 159
2 Timothy: 19
Hebrews: 425
James: 112
danger of
Matthew 16–23: 233
Self-mutilation
Romans 1–8: 249
Self-prejudice
Luke 18–24: 331
Self-projection
Titus: 130
Self-promotion
Matthew 16–23: 230
Mark 9–16: 103, 104–8
Self-realization
Titus: 81
Self-reformation
Luke 11–17: 76
Romans 1–8: 98, 222, 351
Self-reliance
Matthew 16–23: 48
Ephesians: 217, 347
Titus: 130
Self-renunciation
Galatians: 79
Self-righteousness
Matthew 1–7: 134–35, 182, 277–78, 292–93, 352–54, 435–36
Matthew 8–15: 64, 66, 334, 335
Matthew 16–23: 136
Mark 1–8: 111, 112, 126, 151, 339
Mark 9–16: 80
Luke 1–5: 217–18, 276, 328, 334, 337
Luke 6–10: 99, 100, 115, 179, 261
Luke 11–17: 84, 101, 320–22, 326–27, 348
Luke 18–24: 14–19, 21, 132
Romans 1–8: 114, 117
Romans 9–16: 50
Ephesians: 185, 196, 264, 336, 352
worthlessness of
Galatians: 95
Self-sacrifice
Matthew 8–15: 141, 214, 230, 233
Romans 9–16: 146, 156, 249
Ephesians: 40, 108, 198
virtue of
Matthew 16–23: 245
Self-satisfaction
Matthew 8–15: 482
Matthew 16–23: 114, 192, 288, 361
Romans 1–8: 2, 425
1 Corinthians: 109, 128
Ephesians: 6, 159, 224, 336, 377–78
Titus: 130
Self-sufficiency
Matthew 24–28: 214
Ephesians: 216
Self-surrender
Romans 9–16: 139, 157
Self-trust
Matthew 24–28: 219
Ephesians: 174
dangers of
Matthew 16–23: 199, 237
Self-will
Matthew 16–23: 152, 311
1 Corinthians: 24
Ephesians: 170, 200
2 Timothy: 15
Titus: 35
2 Peter & Jude: 95–108
as essence of all sin
Romans 1–8: 101
Self-worship
idolatry of
Romans 1–8: 92
Self-worth
Ephesians: 6
2 Timothy: 108
Selfishness
Ephesians: 76, 272, 293, 295, 298
of the rich
Mark 9–16: 84
self–deception of
Matthew 16–23: 213
Selfism
Matthew 16–23: 45–46, 230
Romans 1–8: 211, 213
Romans 9–16: 138
Selfless giving
Romans 1–8: 42
Selflessness
Matthew 16–23: 369
1 Corinthians: 344–45
Ephesians: 40, 108, 134
Selwyn, E. G.
1 Peter: 6–7
Semi–Pelagianism
Mark 9–16: 67
John 1–11: 247
Sempangi, Kefa
Ephesians: 224, 225

Seneca
Romans 1–8: 112, 178
Ephesians: 316
Sennacherib
John 1–11: 276–77
Sensationalism
Matthew 1–7: 93–94
Sensitivity
2 Corinthians: 46–48
Colossians & Philemon: 187
Sensuality
2 Corinthians: 436–37
2 Peter & Jude: 76–77
Sentimentalism
2 Peter & Jude: 155
Separation
2 Timothy: 89
Hebrews: 440–42
believers vs. unbelievers and
2 Corinthians: 250
Christian
1 Corinthians: 129
Ephesians: 166
disobedient
2 Corinthians: 254–55
harmony and
2 Corinthians: 249–50
irrational
2 Corinthians: 247–50
light vs. darkness and
2 Corinthians: 249
overview of
2 Corinthians: 243–47
righteousness vs. lawlessness and
2 Corinthians: 248–49
sacrilegious
2 Corinthians: 250–54
ungrateful
2 Corinthians: 257–58
unprofitable
2 Corinthians: 255–56
from the world
Romans 1–8: 225
from worldliness
Luke 18–24: 255
Separatism, Jewish
Galatians: 54
Sepphoris
Luke 1–5: 269
Luke 18–24: 349
Septuagint
John 1–11: 348
Hebrews: 26, 53
Sermon on the Mount
Mark 1–8: 213, 293, 426
Mark 9–16: 80, 146, 148
Luke 1–5: 206, 217, 339
Luke 6–10: 86, 94, 117–18, 123
John 1–11: 241
John 12–21: 90, 106, 127–28
2 Corinthians: 52, 450–51
Hebrews: 188
James: 2, 120
1 Peter: 153, 189–91
2 Peter & Jude: 186–87
central theme of
Romans 1–8: 370
Serpent
2 Peter & Jude: 83–84
Serpent in the wilderness
Luke 6–10: 143
Servant girl
Mark 9–16: 337
Luke 18–24: 326
Servant of the Lord
Mark 1–8: 93
Servant songs
John 1–11: 302
Servanthood
1 Corinthians: 96–97
Christian leaders and
Matthew 16–23: 368
Jesus'
Matthew 16–23: 244
virtue of
Matthew 16–23: 240
Servants
Mark 9–16: 109
slaves vs.
John 1–11: 80
Service
Hebrews: 156
calling to Christian
Galatians: 29
Christian
1 Corinthians: 84
heavenly
Matthew 24–28: 104
motives for, false
Romans 1–8: 32
sacrificial
Titus: 83
selfless
Romans 9–16: 157
spiritual
Romans 1–8: 34
1 Peter: 242–45
willing
Romans 1–8: 40
See also Ministry
Serving faith
Matthew 24–28: 97
Seven churches of Revelation
1–3 John: 2, 184–86
Seven deadly sins
James: 217
Seven sons of Sceva
Mark 1–8: 65
Seven year tribulation
Mark 9–16: 252, 257
See also Tribulation, the Great
Seventh trumpet
Revelation 12–22: 2–3, 15
The seventy
Mark 1–8: 285
Luke 6–10: 243, 324–25, 329–32, 335, 339–41
Seventy weeks, chronology of
Matthew 24–28: 34

"Severe letter"
2 Corinthians: 6–7, 66, 300, 322, 337–38, 433
Sex
biblical view of
1 & 2 Thessalonians: 103–13
gratuitous
Titus: 146
illicit
Ephesians: 56
marital
Matthew 1–7: 301–2
sado–masochistic
Romans 1–8: 106
in Thessalonica
1 & 2 Thessalonians: 102
worldly view of
1 & 2 Thessalonians: 102
Sex education
Titus: 146
Sexism
Titus: 79
Sextus Julius Africanus
Luke 1–5: 140
Sexual behavior, deviant
Titus: 137
Sexual freedom
Titus: 81
Sexual immorality
Romans 1–8: 103, 104, 320
Ephesians: 272, 359
Sexual perversion
Romans 1–8: 105
Ephesians: 293–94
Sexual purity
Matthew 1–7: 16
Ephesians: 300
Hebrews: 430–31
of pastor
Titus: 27
Sexual sin
Matthew 1–7: 299–302, 317
Mark 1–8: 242–43, 357
1 Corinthians: 141–52, 223–24
See also Lust
Shaftesbury, Lord
social reforms of
Colossians & Philemon: 166
Shakespeare
Romans 1–8: 290
Ephesians: 23, 26, 222
Shaking the dust off
Luke 6–10: 246
Shallum
Luke 6–10: 74
John 12–21: 73
Shalom
John 12–21: 122
Shame
Mark 1–8: 243, 432–34
Mark 9–16: 368
Luke 6–10: 277
Luke 18–24: 5, 383
1 Peter: 204, 255–56
hidden
2 Corinthians: 125–28
Shamefulness
Luke 11–17: 311–13, 318–22
Shamelessness
Luke 11–17: 307–11, 316–18
Shea, Nina
John 12–21: 189
Shealtiel
Luke 1–5: 249
Sheba
Luke 6–10: 74
John 12–21: 73
Sheba, Queen of
Matthew 8–15: 331
Shechinah. *see* Shekinah glory
Shedd, William G. T.
1 Timothy: 72, 73
Sheep
Mark 1–8: 154, 317, 428
Luke 11–17: 296–98
Sheep and goat judgment
James: 128
Revelation 12–22: 219, 225, 233
Shekinah glory
Matthew 1–7: 29
Matthew 24–28: 54
Romans 9–16: 13, 256
1 Corinthians: 220
2 Corinthians: 101–2
James: 97
1 Peter: 253
Revelation 1–11: 233
The Shema
Matthew 16–23: 338
Mark 9–16: 200, 201
Romans 1–8: 370
James: 131
Sheol
John 1–11: 60
Ephesians: 139
Shepherd(s)
Luke 1–5: 155–58, 160–64
Luke 11–17: 206, 294, 296–99, 402
definition of
1 Peter: 262
of flocks
1 Peter: 266–67
guardians vs.
1 Peter: 173–74
Jesus Christ as
Matthew 1–7: 33–34
John 1–11: 421–35
2 Corinthians: 82, 338
1 Peter: 173–74, 261–71
2 Peter & Jude: 51, 96, 208–9
methods for
1 Peter: 267–70
parables of
1 Peter: 261–62
pastors as
Titus: 24
roles and qualifications for
1 Peter: 261–66
suffering and
1 Peter: 173–74
Shepherd of Hermas
1 Peter: 6

Sherwin-White, A. N.
on Paul's appeal to Caesar
Acts 13–28: 340
on penalties in Roman law for frivolous prosecution
Acts 13–28: 372
on Roman law against false accusers
Acts 13–28: 308
Shibtah
Mark 1–8: 343
Shinners, L. H.
Luke 11–17: 208–9
Shirley, James
Romans 1–8: 290
Shofar
John 1–11: 312
Shunammite woman
1–3 John: 242
Shunem
Luke 6–10: 133
Sicarii (Assassins) (first–century anti–Roman terrorists)
Acts 13–28: 263, 303
Sickness
Mark 1–8: 77
Luke 1–5: 295
spiritual
Mark 1–8: 120
See also Disease
Sidis, William James
Luke 1–5: 188
Sidon
Mark 1–8: 312, 315, 365
Luke 6–10: 87, 250, 252, 259, 334
Sifting
Mark 1–8: 143
Sight
Luke 11–17: 88–91
to the blind
Luke 18–24: 62
Sign language
Mark 1–8: 377
Signs
Mark 1–8: 399, 400
Mark 9–16: 252–53, 255
Luke 1–5: 64–66
Luke 11–17: 81, 84–86, 371, 403–5, 418
Hebrews: 360
birth pangs metaphor
Mark 9–16: 230, 232, 233, 234, 243
confirming
Matthew 1–7: 126–30
divine
Romans 1–8: 252
second coming
Luke 18–24: 207, 232, 242, 247, 252
Signs, wonders, and miracles
2 Corinthians: 414–17
Revelation 1–11: 305
See also Miracles
Silas
Mark 1–8: 1
Luke 6–10: 99, 144
John 1–11: 413–14
1 Peter: 289
2 Peter & Jude: 11, 149
background of
Acts 13–28: 82–83
Silence
Luke 6–10: 237–38, 286
1 Peter: 150–51
of Christ
Mark 9–16: 326, 327, 348
Luke 18–24: 336, 350, 355
mandatory
Mark 1–8: 267, 379, 380, 417
Siloam
pool miracle
Luke 11–17: 187
John 1–11: 387–96
tower in
Luke 11–17: 187
Silva, Moises
on the Roman origin of Philippians
Philippians: 6
Silvanius (Silas)
2 Corinthians: 4, 43–44
Silvanus
1 Peter: 289
Simeon
Anna and
Luke 1–5: 186
character of
Luke 1–5: 176–77
Luke 6–10: 61
Holy Spirit and
Luke 1–5: 179–80
prediction of
Luke 1–5: 182–84
proclamation of
Luke 1–5: 158, 180–82
Luke 6–10: 258
testimony of
Luke 1–5: 175
theology of
Luke 1–5: 111, 177–79
Simon. *see* Peter
Simon (father of Judas Iscariot)
2 Peter & Jude: 2
Simon (half–brother of Jesus)
2 Peter & Jude: 2
Simon Bar Cochba
Luke 18–24: 187
John 1–11: 214
John 12–21: 12
Simon Bar–Jonah. *see* Peter
Simon Barjona
Luke 6–10: 25
Simon Iscariot
Luke 6–10: 75, 171
John 1–11: 273
John 12–21: 73
Simon Magus
Luke 6–10: 36
2 Peter & Jude: 140
Simon of Cyrene
Mark 9–16: 363
Luke 18–24: 368–69
John 1–11: 66
Acts 13–28: 4
2 Peter & Jude: 2

Simon of Cyrene's wife
Luke 18–24: 368, 369
Simon Peter. *see* Peter
Simon the leper
Mark 9–16: 273
Luke 6–10: 171
Luke 18–24: 93
John 1–11: 66
John 12–21: 3, 6
2 Peter & Jude: 2
1–3 John: 243
Simon the Maccabee
John 12–21: 16
Simon the magician
Luke 6–10: 171
John 1–11: 267
2 Peter & Jude: 2
Simon the Pharisee
Luke 6–10: 171–76, 183
2 Peter & Jude: 2
1–3 John: 243
Simon the tanner
Luke 6–10: 25, 171
2 Peter & Jude: 2
1–3 John: 243
Simon the Zealot
Mark 1–8: 161, 169, 172
Mark 9–16: 179
Luke 1–5: 226
Luke 6–10: 16–18, 25, 70–71, 171
John 1–11: 66
John 12–21: 188
2 Peter & Jude: 2
Simon's mother-in-law
Luke 1–5: 291
Simpson, A. B.
Romans 9–16: 178
Simpson, George Gaylord
on man's origin
1 & 2 Thessalonians: 141
Simpson, Sir James
Matthew 8–15: 81
Sin
Luke 6–10: 84, 85, 127–28, 156, 355
John 12–21: 175, 190, 196–98, 346–47, 361, 382
1 Peter: 50–51, 71–79, 97–98, 131–34, 139–44, 148, 185–94, 206–8, 239, 244–49, 256
2 Peter & Jude: 33–35, 84–86, 89, 95–108, 123, 133, 152–53, 164, 210–11
accountability for
Matthew 16–23: 311
acknowledging
Matthew 1–7: 136, 157–61, 192, 212, 239, 276, 393–94
acknowledgment of
Matthew 16–23: 149
atonement for
Hebrews: 121
avenues used to incite, boastful pride of life
1–3 John: 87–90, 92
avenues used to incite, lust of the eyes
1–3 John: 87–90, 92
avenues used to incite, lust of the flesh
1–3 John: 87–90, 92
awareness of
Matthew 16–23: 69
believer's hatred of
Romans 1–8: 223, 381, 388
believer's personal responsibility for
1–3 John: 121, 122
besetting power of
Titus: 72
byproducts of
Romans 1–8: 1
certainty of
1–3 John: 25–28
characteristics of
1–3 John: 85–86
children and
Luke 18–24: 27–31
Christians' incompatibility with
1–3 John: 119–28, 206–7
Christ's authority over effects of
Mark 1–8: 70
Christ's death for
Luke 18–24: 267, 304, 305
cleansing from
Ephesians: 299
1–3 John: 36–37, 144
confession of
Matthew 8–15: 66
Mark 1–8: 22
Luke 11–17: 39
Romans 1–8: 219, 426
Titus: 42
1–3 John: 36, 37–41
conflict with
Romans 1–8: 332, 369, 400
confronting
Matthew 1–7: 196, 212–13, 216, 221, 242–43, 431–32
Mark 1–8: 304, 305
conquering
1–3 John: 36, 41–42
consequences of
Romans 1–8: 396
contentment in
Matthew 16–23: 4
conviction of
Acts 1–12: 72
Acts 13–28: 335
Romans 1–8: 222, 366
danger from
Romans 1–8: 425
dealing with
Colossians & Philemon: 135–46
death to
Romans 1–8: 335
debt for paid on Calvary
Romans 1–8: 363
delusion of
1 Corinthians: 283
Demas's spiritual harlotry
1–3 John: 81
denial of
1–3 John: 25–30
denial of by those in deception
1–3 John: 29–30
denial of by those walking in darkness
1–3 John: 28–29

denial of by those who defame God
1–3 John: 30–31
depravity, human
1–3 John: 29, 85, 128, 227
destructive effects of
Romans 1–8: 290, 341
dishonors God
Romans 1–8: 157
divine hatred of
Matthew 16–23: 270
doctrine regarding
1–3 John: 120–22
effects on man
Hebrews: 55–57
enslavement to
Ephesians: 18
enslaving nature of
Matthew 16–23: 245
excusing
1 Corinthians: 146
of false teachers
Luke 18–24: 167
forgiveness of
Mark 1–8: 96, 97, 107, 126
Luke 11–17: 39–41, 236
Luke 18–24: 112, 443–44
Acts 13–28: 26, 336
freedom from bondage to
Romans 1–8: 334
futility of
Ephesians: 56
against God
Luke 11–17: 381
God's forgiveness of
Luke 11–17: 39–41, 236
God's warnings to sinners
1–3 John: 166
guilt producing
Romans 1–8: 2
hatred of
Hebrews: 34
hidden
Romans 1–8: 425
hindrance of
Hebrews: 377
Holy Spirit's conviction of
Romans 1–8: 417
hopelessness of
Romans 1–8: 3
incalculable debt of
Matthew 16–23: 148
incompatibility with Law of God
1–3 John: 122–24, 206
incompatibility with ministry of Holy Spirit
1–3 John: 126–28, 206
incompatibility with work of Christ
1–3 John: 124–26, 206
internal source of
Mark 1–8: 350, 352
Jesus as propitiation for
1–3 John: 46–50
Jesus as Savior and
Luke 1–5: 159
Jesus Christ and
Hebrews: 112–13
judgment for
Luke 11–17: 369
law of
Luke 1–5: 115
as lawlessness
1–3 John: 85, 122–23
leading believers into
Mark 9–16: 42–45
leading to death
1–3 John: 205–6
leading others out of
Luke 11–17: 379
leprosy and
Mark 1–8: 89
love of
Matthew 1–7: 162
man's denial of
Romans 1–8: 179
man's innate
Matthew 8–15: 58
meaninglessness of
Romans 1–8: 2
motivations for
Luke 18–24: 130–37
New covenant and
Luke 1–5: 120
New Testament words for
Luke 11–17: 38
one who practices is of the devil
1–3 John: 124, 126
open
Titus: xi
origin of
Romans 1–8: 294–95
original
1–3 John: 86–87
passing pleasures of
Hebrews: 351
perfectionists and
1–3 John: 121
personal responsibility and
1–3 John: 120–22
pervasiveness of
Matthew 1–7: 211–12, 238–39, 392
pride and
Titus: 35
1–3 John: 87–90, 251–56
punishment for
Hebrews: 46–48
purification of
Hebrews: 18–19
radical dealing with
Mark 9–16: 46–48
rationalizing of
Romans 1–8: 174
reality of
Ephesians: 22
recognition of
Luke 1–5: 307, 308
redefinitions and minimizing of
1–3 John: 26–28
remnant of in believers
Romans 1–8: 382
repentance and
Luke 1–5: 215
Luke 11–17: 313

revealed, aroused, condemned by law
Romans 1–8: 374
and salvation
Mark 1–8: 317
Luke 18–24: 68, 436
scriptural characterization of
Romans 1–8: 340
self–righteousness and
Luke 1–5: 333–34
self–will and
Romans 1–8: 101
selfishness and
Luke 11–17: 368
sensitivity to
Matthew 1–7: 102–3
separation from
Hebrews: 328–29
sexual (*See also* Lust)
Mark 1–8: 242–43, 357
1 Corinthians: 141–52
sickness and death and
Mark 1–8: 89, 252, 376
sinlessness of Jesus and
Luke 1–5: 58, 253
slavery to
Romans 1–8: 434
sorrow for
Romans 1–8: 224
sovereign lordship and
Luke 18–24: 40
spiritual bondage and
Luke 1–5: 271–72
temptation and
Luke 1–5: 252–53
Luke 11–17: 46–48
tolerance of
Matthew 16–23: 106
toleration of
1 Corinthians: 123–24
Ephesians: 334
tragedy of
Romans 1–8: 200
unbridled
Matthew 24–28: 28
unconfessed
1 Corinthians: 124, 130
Ephesians: 353
unconverted sinners and
1–3 John: 206
universal nature of
Luke 11–17: 37
universal transmission from Adam
Romans 1–8: 295
universality of
Mark 9–16: 67, 332, 405
unpardonable
Mark 1–8: 184, 185
the unpardonable
Luke 11–17: 62
unregenerate slaves to
Romans 1–8: 346
unrepentant
Luke 11–17: 311
Romans 1–8: 174
2 Corinthians: 433–38
venial and mortal
1–3 John: 121–22
victory over
Romans 1–8: 427
willful
Romans 1–8: 316
See also Forgiveness
Sin nature. *see* The Flesh
Sinai
Mark 9–16: 379
1 Peter: 23–24, 130
Sinaiticus (Greek New Testament manuscript)
Mark 9–16: 410
Sincere love
1 Peter: 90
Sincerity
2 Corinthians: 33–34
of heart
Hebrews: 262
spiritual
Matthew 8–15: 65
Sinful solicitation
Mark 9–16: 44–45
Sinfulness
man's innate and universal
Romans 1–8: 98, 395
sense of
Luke 18–24: 387
Singing
Luke 1–5: 93–94, 141
See also Music
Singlemindedness
Matthew 1–7: 413–15
Singleness
1 Corinthians: 153–59, 162–64
gift of
Titus: 78
successful
Matthew 16–23: 175
Sinless perfection
Titus: 23, 42, 115
Sinlessness
Mark 9–16: 174, 212
of Jesus
John 12–21: 253–54
Sinners
Mark 1–8: 58, 121
Mark 9–16: 67, 81, 85, 115, 119
Luke 6–10: 107, 108, 156, 166–67, 172
condemnation of
Romans 1–8: 396
God's love for
Romans 1–8: 305
Sinterklaas
Luke 1–5: 141
Sirach, Wisdom of
Romans 1–8: 233
Sire, James W.
Luke 11–17: 14
2 Corinthians: 330
Sistine Chapel
Luke 18–24: 170
Situation ethics
Galatians: 52, 146
Six-Day War (1967)
Romans 9–16: 18

Skepticism
Luke 1–5: 336
Luke 6–10: 58, 66, 68, 144, 281
2 Peter & Jude: 56
1–3 John: 14, 238
See also Doubt
The Skull (site of the crucifixion)
Luke 18–24: 366, 378
Sky splitting open
Mark 1–8: 34
Slander
Matthew 1–7: 294–95
Mark 1–8: 358
Colossians & Philemon: 144
1 Peter: 98, 204
Slaves and slavery
Mark 9–16: 109
Luke 6–10: 125
Luke 11–17: 386
Luke 18–24: 80, 122
John 12–21: 160–61, 168
1 Corinthians: 174
Ephesians: 323
1 Timothy: 229, 230
1 Peter: 147, 151–52, 158–59, 161
ancient
Matthew 8–15: 12
Christianity and
Colossians & Philemon: 152–53, 174–75, 201–35
in Roman Empire
Romans 1–8: 5
Titus: 96
slave revolts
Luke 18–24: 210
Sleep
Mark 1–8: 264, 265
Luke 6–10: 208, 236, 284
soul
Romans 1–8: 72
Slothfulness
Romans 9–16: 190
Smith, Alan Radcliffe
on evidence of design in nature
Acts 13–28: 133
Smith, D. M.
John 12–21: 318
Smith, Hannah Whitall
Galatians: 153
Ephesians: 362
Philippians: 152
Smith, James E.
John 12–21: 204
on Luke's account of Paul's shipwreck
Acts 13–28: 353
Smith, Joseph
Galatians: 204
Smith, M. A.
John 12–21: 169
on Christian unity
Colossians & Philemon: 153
Smith, Wilbur M.
1 Peter: 135–36
Smyrna
Luke 1–5: 226
John 12–21: 188
1–3 John: 2, 184
church at
1 Peter: 283
Snake handling
Mark 9–16: 412
Snatching
2 Peter & Jude: 202–3
Socci, Antonio
John 12–21: 170
Social behavior, forced
Titus: 138
Social Christianity
Romans 9–16: 208
Social evils, gospel and
Matthew 16–23: 267, 373
Social reciprocity
Luke 11–17: 263, 272–73, 336
Social reform, evangelical
Colossians & Philemon: 164–66
Social stigma
Luke 11–17: 389
Societal morality
Luke 11–17: 69–72
Socrates
John 1–11: 48
John 12–21: 72
Sodom and Gomorrah
Luke 6–10: 334
Luke 11–17: 416, 417
Luke 18–24: 175, 254
John 1–11: 267
John 12–21: 205
Titus: 83
1 Peter: 211, 215
2 Peter & Jude: 81, 84, 88, 89, 91, 160, 162, 165, 166, 171
Sodomy. *See also* Homosexuality
Romans 1–8: 105
The soil
Mark 1–8: 195–96, 200, 207
Luke 6–10: 188–96, 319
Sola scriptura
2 Timothy: 77
Soldiers
Luke 1–5: 220–21
Luke 11–17: 233
Luke 18–24: 367, 392, 431
Christ's clothing divided by
Mark 9–16: 365–66
converted
Luke 18–24: 385, 392
Jesus' death verified by
Luke 18–24: 399, 400
at Jesus' tomb
Mark 9–16: 399
mockery by
Mark 9–16: 358–62
mocking of Jesus
Luke 18–24: 361, 382–83
piercing of Christ's side by
Mark 9–16: 388
"The Solid Rock"
Luke 6–10: 142
Solomon
Matthew 1–7: 143
Mark 1–8: 338

Mark 9–16: 67, 126, 138
Luke 1–5: 20, 98, 100, 247
Luke 11–17: 86–87
Luke 18–24: 60, 107, 286
John 1–11: 48, 137–38, 291, 342, 366, 418, 430, 460
John 12–21: 204
2 Corinthians: 38, 153, 183, 251–52, 255–56, 272, 352, 408
2 Peter & Jude: 139
1–3 John: 86

Solomon's temple
Mark 1–8: 60
1 Timothy: 283

Son of David
Mark 1–8: 367
Mark 9–16: 115, 127, 207–9
Luke 18–24: 60–61, 152–53
John 1–11: 26

Son of God
Mark 1–8: 19, 36, 56, 136, 160, 224, 412
Mark 9–16: 207, 227, 301, 310, 326, 417
Luke 1–5: 189, 194–96, 290, 302
Luke 18–24: 440
John 1–11: 38, 41–43, 72–74, 109, 162, 185–91, 193, 281, 311, 464–65

Son of Man
Mark 1–8: 105, 146, 433
Mark 9–16: 96, 109, 256
Luke 1–5: 290
Luke 6–10: 166, 260, 263, 264, 295
Luke 11–17: 86, 123, 161, 412, 416
Luke 18–24: 236, 259–60, 338–39
John 1–11: 72–74, 86, 99, 113–17, 183, 198, 311, 341, 409–13
John 12–21: 27
Acts 1–12: 222–23
1 Peter: 254, 269–70
Old Testament predictions of
Matthew 16–23: 54

Son of Mary
Mark 1–8: 276

Son of the Most High God
Mark 1–8: 244

Sons
Luke 6–10: 134, 135, 290, 291

Sons of Abraham
Luke 18–24: 74, 75

Sons of Sceva
Luke 6–10: 304

Sons of the resurrection
Luke 18–24: 146–47

Sons of Thunder
Mark 1–8: 52, 170
Mark 9–16: 104
Luke 6–10: 42, 313
John 1–11: 8
1–3 John: 6–7

Sons of Zebedee
Mark 9–16: 104, 105

Sons of Zebedee, mother of
1–3 John: 255

Sophistry
Ephesians: 217

Sophocles
2 Peter & Jude: 39–40

Sordid gains
1 Peter: 269

Sorrow
Matthew 1–7: 66, 402
Luke 18–24: 300, 303, 306, 343, 371
godly
Romans 1–8: 224, 431
loyalty and
2 Corinthians: 263–64
obedience and (*see* Obedience)
overview of
2 Corinthians: 53–54, 259–63
purity and
2 Corinthians: 266–67
repentance and
2 Corinthians: 264–66
spirituality and
2 Corinthians: 268
trust
2 Corinthians: 270
unity and
2 Corinthians: 268–69

Soteriology
2 Timothy: 22

Soul
Mark 1–8: 359, 430, 431
Mark 9–16: 201

Soul and conscience
overview of
2 Corinthians: 29–33
of Paul
2 Corinthians: 33–38
See also Conscience

Soul sleep
Acts 1–12: 225
Romans 1–8: 72
1 Corinthians: 408, 413
Philippians: 79
1 & 2 Thessalonians: 125–26

Source, substance and sufficiency of believers' faith
2 Peter & Jude: 17–32

Southern kingdom
Luke 1–5: 119

Sovereign will
Luke 11–17: 28

Sovereignty
Matthew 8–15: 175
Mark 1–8: 56, 59
Luke 6–10: 327, 344–47
Luke 18–24: 34, 40–42, 81–82, 302, 455
Christ's
Matthew 16–23: 194
divine
Romans 9–16: 32, 37, 281

Sovereignty of God
Matthew 8–15: 121–22, 156
Luke 1–5: 59–60
Luke 11–17: 22–24, 28, 51–52, 234, 398–99
John 12–21: 257, 258, 259, 264, 335, 341
Acts 13–28: 138–39
Romans 1–8: 78, 212, 431
Romans 9–16: 37, 129
Galatians: 7, 28
Ephesians: 11
Colossians & Philemon: 153–55

1 & 2 Thessalonians: 141, 254
1 Timothy: 73, 275
Hebrews: 165, 167
James: 59, 61
1 Peter: 19–21, 51, 130–31, 147–48, 200–201
Revelation 1–11: 78, 146, 270, 282, 285, 315
absolute
Matthew 24–28: 288
election and
Romans 9–16: 24, 57
foreknowledge and
Romans 9–16: 99
grace and
Romans 9–16: 32
human responsibility and
Romans 9–16: 49
man's faith and
Matthew 16–23: 282
plan of
Matthew 16–23: 220
power and
Romans 9–16: 18
in salvation
Acts 1–12: 252, 267
Acts 13–28: 38, 94

Soviet Union
John 12–21: 295–96

Sowers
Luke 6–10: 190

Sowing
Mark 1–8: 195

Spafford, H. G.
Romans 1–8: 308

Sparta
Luke 6–10: 73

Speaking in tongues
Acts 1–12: 42–43, 245, 305

Special grace
1–3 John: 115

Special revelation
Matthew 1–7: 403
2 Timothy: 153
Hebrews: 199

Speech
genuineness of faith revealed by
James: 144
godly
Colossians & Philemon: 177–88
ungodly
Colossians & Philemon: 144–45

Speech impediments
Mark 1–8: 376

Spices
Mark 9–16: 398

Spinoza, Benedict de
2 Peter & Jude: 56

The Spirit
being filled with
Ephesians: 245–69
Holy (*see* Holy Spirit)

Spirit–controlled behavior
Romans 1–8: 428

Spirit of God. *see* Holy Spirit

Spirit of truth
John 1–11: 353, 358
See also Holy Spirit

Spiritists
Luke 18–24: 150

Spirits, testing the
command to
1–3 John: 154
as evaluation of error
1–3 John: 152–54
guidelines for
1–3 John: 156–60
reason for
1–3 John: 154–56

Spiritual adultery
Mark 9–16: 60

Spiritual arrogance
Ephesians: 377

Spiritual authority
2 Timothy: 2
false
Matthew 16–23: 357

Spiritual bankruptcy of natural man
Matthew 16–23: 149

Spiritual barrenness
Matthew 16–23: 278

Spiritual birth
John 1–11: 97–108

Spiritual blindness
Matthew 16–23: 3, 252
Matthew 24–28: 73, 77, 184
Mark 1–8: 396, 397, 399, 401, 409, 410
Luke 11–17: 81, 89
Romans 9–16: 104

Spiritual boldness
Romans 1–8: 48

Spiritual brats
Luke 6–10: 161, 162, 164–67

Spiritual callousness
Matthew 16–23: 153

Spiritual cleansing
John 12–21: 67, 68

Spiritual commitment
Galatians: 51
2 Timothy: 11

Spiritual complacency
Ephesians: 343

Spiritual compromise
Matthew 24–28: 213

Spiritual condition and suffering
2 Corinthians: 399–400

Spiritual contamination
Matthew 16–23: 386

Spiritual conviction
Matthew 8–15: 251

Spiritual danger, avoiding
Matthew 16–23: 110

Spiritual danger within the church
Titus: 57

Spiritual darkness
Matthew 24–28: 184
Luke 1–5: 20–21, 122, 272
John 1–11: 23–24
Romans 1–8: 86
1 & 2 Thessalonians: 156–57

Spiritual death
Romans 1–8: 188, 417
1–3 John: 133, 207
Spiritual defection
Galatians: 61
Spiritual deficiency
Luke 6–10: 96
Spiritual depression
Matthew 16–23: 63
Spiritual devotion
Galatians: 60
Spiritual discernment
Romans 1–8: 116
Ephesians: 343
Titus: 51
Spiritual discipline
1 Timothy: 164
Spiritual dullness
Hebrews: 130–32
Spiritual duties
description of
1 Peter: 233–34
incentives for
1 Peter: 234–38
instructions for
1 Peter: 239–44
intentions of
1 Peter: 245–46
mutual love
1 Peter: 241–42
personal holiness
1 Peter: 240–41
spiritual service
1 Peter: 242–45
Spiritual families
Mark 1–8: 186, 187, 188, 192
Spiritual famine
Matthew 1–7: 179–80
Spiritual fellowship
Titus: 165
Spiritual fickleness
Galatians: 118
Spiritual food
Mark 1–8: 321, 322
Spiritual fruitfulness
Matthew 24–28: 108
Colossians & Philemon: 31–32
Spiritual fruitlessness
Romans 1–8: 364
Spiritual gifts
Acts 13–28: 43–44
Romans 9–16: 162–63
1 Corinthians: 18–19
Ephesians: 136
Hebrews: 49–50, 81, 156
1 Peter: 242–45
discontentment with
1 Corinthians: 314–16
diverse
Romans 9–16: 154
grace
Romans 9–16: 131
identifying
Romans 9–16: 162
purpose of
1 Corinthians: 297
use of
Romans 9–16: 162–63
Spiritual growth
Romans 1–8: 226, 325
1 Corinthians: 72
Philippians: 243, 250
Colossians & Philemon: 32–33
1 Peter: 100–101
assurance regarding
1–3 John: 72–77
forgiveness and
1–3 John: 73
grace and
1–3 John: 70–71
holiness as goal of
1–3 John: 70
misconceptions regarding
1–3 John: 70–72
overview of
1–3 John: 69–70
stages of
1–3 John: 69–77
Spiritual hardness
Romans 1–8: 120
Spiritual harlotry
John 1–11: 203–16
Revelation 12–22: 165
Spiritual harm
Matthew 16–23: 121
Spiritual harvests
Mark 1–8: 218
Spiritual health
2 Timothy: 108
Spiritual houses
1 Peter: 107–13
Spiritual ignorance
Matthew 24–28: 163
Romans 1–8: 183
1 Corinthians: 71
Spiritual immaturity
Matthew 16–23: 12
Ephesians: 45
Spiritual indifference
Matthew 16–23: 128, 132
Ephesians: 336, 340, 350
Spiritual influence
Matthew 8–15: 368–75
Spiritual inheritance
Colossians & Philemon: 37–40, 131–32
Spiritual insecurity
Romans 1–8: 146
Spiritual insubordination
Matthew 24–28: 212
Spiritual integrity
Philippians: 85
Spiritual intimidation
Colossians & Philemon: 115–24
Spiritual kingdom
Mark 1–8: 48
Luke 11–17: 399, 400, 404, 412
See also Kingdom of God
Spiritual knowledge
Romans 1–8: 332
Spiritual leaders/leadership
1 Timothy: 91
Titus: 94, 168

accountability of
Galatians: 53
character of
1 & 2 Thessalonians: 49
characteristics of
Matthew 16–23: 366
checklist of qualifications
1 Timothy: 92
compelling desire for
1 Timothy: 95
in the family
1 Timothy: 116
financial support of
1 & 2 Thessalonians: 172
honor of
Matthew 16–23: 372
importance of
1 Timothy: 93
influence as goal
1 Timothy: 114
qualifications for
1 Timothy: 92
responsibilities of
1 & 2 Thessalonians: 32
teaching of the Word by
1 & 2 Thessalonians: 170–71
and temptations
1 Timothy: 120
titles of
1 & 2 Thessalonians: 167
Spiritual lostness
man's innate
Romans 1–8: 198
reasons for
Romans 1–8: 140–42
Spiritual maturity
Matthew 16–23: 12
Galatians: 177
Colossians & Philemon: 80–81, 92–93, 105–13
Spiritual obstacles
Luke 11–17: 377–78
Spiritual overconfidence
Luke 18–24: 322, 323, 327
Spiritual passivity
Ephesians: 363
Spiritual peace
Colossians & Philemon: 158
Spiritual perception
Matthew 8–15: 158
Spiritual perfection
Matthew 1–7: 205, 349–50
Spiritual persistence
Ephesians: 343
Spiritual perversion
Matthew 16–23: 77
Spiritual preparedness
Matthew 24–28: 87
Ephesians: 345–73
Spiritual presumption
Ephesians: 342
Spiritual pride. *see* Pride, spiritual
Spiritual privileges
access to God
1 Peter: 103–17
affection for Christ
1 Peter: 119–26
compassion from Christ
1 Peter: 127–34
dominion with Christ
1 Peter: 119–26
election by Christ
1 Peter: 119–26
illumination in Christ
1 Peter: 127–34
possession by Christ
1 Peter: 127–34
proclamation of Christ
1 Peter: 127–34
security in Christ
1 Peter: 119–26
separation to Christ
1 Peter: 127–34
union with Christ
1 Peter: 103–17
Spiritual progress
2 Peter & Jude: 136
Spiritual prosperity
Romans 9–16: 348
Spiritual protection
John 12–21: 276–82
Spiritual regression
Matthew 8–15: 177
Spiritual reproduction
2 Timothy: 42
process of
1 Timothy: 1
Spiritual responsibility
Matthew 24–28: 98, 100
Spiritual restoration
Mark 1–8: 85
Spiritual reward
Matthew 24–28: 107
Spiritual satisfaction
Matthew 1–7: 183–84
Spiritual security
Romans 1–8: 148
Spiritual service
1 Peter: 242–45
Spiritual sickness
Mark 1–8: 120
Spiritual sight *vs.* spiritual blindness, Jesus' teachings of
John 1–11: 409–20
Spiritual sincerity
Matthew 8–15: 65
Spiritual strength
Colossians & Philemon: 33
Spiritual subjectivism
1 Peter: 274
Spiritual superficiality
Matthew 16–23: 126
Spiritual testing
Ephesians: 153
Spiritual thinking, attributes of
description of
1 Peter: 273–76
faithfulness
1 Peter: 288–89
fortitude
1 Peter: 285–86

hope
1 Peter: 286–88
humility
1 Peter: 277–79
love
1 Peter: 289–90
praise and worship
1 Peter: 288
self–control
1 Peter: 280
submission
1 Peter: 276–77
trust
1 Peter: 279–80
vigilance
1 Peter: 280–85
Spiritual transference
Colossians & Philemon: 40–42
Spiritual truth
Luke 11–17: 108, 110
Spiritual understanding
Colossians & Philemon: 89–92
Spiritual unity
Romans 9–16: 166
Colossians & Philemon: 87–89, 152–53
Titus: 165
Spiritual unproductiveness
Matthew 24–28: 108
Spiritual victory
Colossians & Philemon: 112–13
Spiritual warfare
Luke 11–17: 73
Acts 1–12: 234
Acts 13–28: 168–72
Ephesians: 331–73
1 Timothy: 36, 40
2 Timothy: 122, 192
Titus: 137
compassion and
2 Corinthians: 323–25
competence and
2 Corinthians: 327–31
courage and
2 Corinthians: 326–27
definition of
2 Corinthians: 328
fortresses and
2 Corinthians: 328–30
overview of
2 Corinthians: 321–23
timing and
2 Corinthians: 331
Spiritual weakness
2 Timothy: 36
Spiritual wealth
Matthew 16–23: 200
Spiritual zeal
Matthew 8–15: 150
Spirituality
1 Corinthians: 70, 72
Ephesians: 298
lack of
Matthew 16–23: 363
and sorrow
2 Corinthians: 268
true
Galatians: 177, 181
See also Holiness; Sanctification
Spouses (unsaved)
1 Peter: 175–83
Spretnak, Charlene
Titus: 82
Spring, Gardiner
on legalism
Colossians & Philemon: 117
on love for God
James: 43
on pastors' need of prayer
1 & 2 Thessalonians: 212, 214
Springs
Mark 9–16: 113–14
Sproul, R. C.
Luke 11–17: 28
John 12–21: 207
Spurgeon, Charles H.
Matthew 8–15: 388, 453, 469
Mark 1–8: 33–34, 53–54, 124, 233
Mark 9–16: 305
John 1–11: 240, 245–46, 415
John 12–21: 48, 272
2 Corinthians: 63–64, 205, 234, 404–5
1 Timothy: 58, 163
2 Timothy: 26, 176
Titus: 43, 87
Hebrews: 323, 432
James: 211
2 Peter & Jude: 75, 213
on discouragement in the ministry
Acts 13–28: 144
and the "Down–Grade Controversy"
Acts 13–28: 192
on importance of study of God
Acts 13–28: 128
on knowledge of Scripture
Acts 1–12: 14
on the name "Jesus"
Acts 1–12: 108
on not trifling with sin
Colossians & Philemon: 142–43
on the pastor's prayer life
1 & 2 Thessalonians: 86
on two men in a boat
Colossians & Philemon: 17
Stadia
Mark 1–8: 330
Staff (walking stick)
Luke 6–10: 244
Stalin, Joseph
Luke 6–10: 103
Luke 11–17: 244
Standards
Luke 6–10: 23–24
1 Peter: 191–93
Standards of living, divine
Matthew 1–7: 138–39
Stars, wandering
2 Peter & Jude: 181–82
Status
Luke 11–17: 101
Steadfastness
2 Peter & Jude: 136

Stealing
Mark 1–8: 357
Stein, Robert H.
Luke 1–5: 2
Stephanas and his household
1–3 John: 246
Stephen
Mark 1–8: 270
Mark 9–16: 236
Luke 1–5: 226, 294
Luke 6–10: 98
Luke 11–17: 195
Luke 18–24: 442
John 1–11: 52, 376
John 12–21: 47–48, 166, 188, 334
2 Corinthians: 417
1 Timothy: 60
1 Peter: 2, 143–44, 253–54
parallels with Christ
Acts 1–12: 226
Stewards
1 Peter: 244–45
Stewardship
Matthew 24–28: 99
Luke 11–17: 334–40
accountability and
2 Corinthians: 304–7
biblical giving model and (*see* Giving)
commitment and
2 Corinthians: 300–301
covetousness vs.
2 Corinthians: 309–10
divine
Colossians & Philemon: 72
as examples
2 Corinthians: 308–9
as expression of love
2 Corinthians: 307–8
faithfulness and
2 Corinthians: 300–301
integrity and
2 Corinthians: 297–310
overview of
2 Corinthians: 297–99
submission and
2 Corinthians: 304
voluntary giving and
2 Corinthians: 299–300
Stigma
2 Peter & Jude: 77–78
Stoics
Acts 13–28: 18, 131
Hebrews: 112
Stokes, G. T.
Acts 13–28: 225
Stolen body (theft hypothesis)
Luke 18–24: 403, 404, 414
Stone, Samuel
Ephesians: 367
Stonehouse, Ned B.
1 Timothy: 70
Stones and pillars (living)
1 Peter: 104–7, 121–23
Stoning
Mark 9–16: 321–22, 347
Luke 11–17: 239
Stony/rocky soil
Mark 1–8: 195, 202–3
Stories
Luke 1–5: 9
Luke 11–17: 306–7
See also Parables
Storms
Mark 1–8: 328, 329, 332
Luke 6–10: 205–13, 218–19, 229
Stott, John R. W.
Romans 1–8: 212
Galatians: 27, 101, 111, 120, 188
1 Timothy: 20, 113, 177
Titus: 50
on lukewarm churches
Revelation 1–11: 137
Strangers and aliens
1 Peter: 15–16, 137
Strength
Mark 9–16: 201
spiritual
Colossians & Philemon: 33
spiritual vs. physical
2 Corinthians: 125, 152–54
Strobel, Lee
Luke 1–5: 44, 301
Struggles
Hebrews: 361
Stubbornness
Luke 18–24: 136–37
Studd, C. T.
1 Timothy: 258
Stumbling
John 12–21: 190–91
Stumbling blocks
Luke 11–17: 377–78
John 1–11: 338
1 Peter: 123–24
Subjectivism
2 Timothy: 104
1 Peter: 274
spiritual
1 Peter: 274
Submission
Matthew 8–15: 277
Luke 6–10: 33–34
Luke 18–24: 34, 304, 305
2 Corinthians: 285, 304, 392–94
Hebrews: 444–45
application of
1 Peter: 152–53
attitude of
1 Peter: 151–52
authority and
Colossians & Philemon: 166–75
believer's
Galatians: 157
Christ's demand of
Matthew 16–23: 194
to civil authority
1 Peter: 143–53
command for
1 Peter: 145–46
definition of
1 Peter: 145

extent of
1 Peter: 148–49
key to witnessing
Matthew 16–23: 91
to Lord
Matthew 8–15: 140
mandate for
1 Peter: 158–60
motives for
1 Peter: 147–48, 160–63
reasons for
1 Peter: 150–51
spiritual thinking and
1 Peter: 276–77
in the workplace
1 Peter: 155–63

Submissiveness
1 Peter: 177–78

Subsequence. *see* Holy Spirit, baptism with

Substitution
Hebrews: 63–64
divine (*see* Atonement)

Substitutionary atonement
Mark 9–16: 109, 383–84
Luke 11–17: 40
Luke 18–24: 283, 284
Romans 1–8: 118, 209, 274, 291, 309, 399
Galatians: 5, 46, 65, 198
Titus: 155

Suetonius (Roman historian)
Acts 13–28: 147
Revelation 1–11: 38
on famine in Israel
Acts 1–12: 316

Suffering (affliction)
Mark 1–8: 163–64, 261
Luke 6–10: 99
Luke 11–17: 180, 181, 414
Luke 18–24: 28–29, 292
2 Corinthians: 22–26, 386–91
Ephesians: 153
Hebrews: 124, 367–68, 384–85
of believers
Mark 9–16: 235–38
benefits of
Colossians & Philemon: 74–76
blessing of
Titus: 3
for Christ
Matthew 16–23: 50, 241
Romans 1–8: 281, 447, 448, 450
1 Corinthians: 111
of Christ
Matthew 16–23: 226
Mark 9–16: 96–98, 106
Luke 11–17: 414
2 Corinthians: 24–25
Hebrews: 124
1 Peter: 165–74, 205–21, 251–54, 266
2 Peter & Jude: 25
of Christians
Romans 1–8: 511
1 & 2 Thessalonians: 247
of demon–possessed boy
Mark 9–16: 25–28
demonic affliction
Matthew 16–23: 75
endurance of
Titus: 10
entrusting to God
1 Peter: 258–60
evaluation of
1 Peter: 254–58
expectations of
1 Peter: 248–50
exultation in
1 Peter: 251–54
grace and
2 Corinthians: 402–5
humility and
2 Corinthians: 400–401
of Job
Mark 9–16: 68–69
kinds of Jesus'
Matthew 16–23: 226
overview of
2 Corinthians: 397–98
perfection and
2 Corinthians: 405–6
prayer and
2 Corinthians: 401–2
refinement by
Matthew 16–23: 43
spiritual condition and
2 Corinthians: 399–400
submission and
1 Peter: 160–63
triumph of
1 Peter: 205–21
unjust
1 Peter: 223–32

The Suffering Servant
Mark 1–8: 13, 42

Sufficiency
of Christ (*see* Jesus Christ)
of Christians (*see* Maturity)
of God's grace
Titus: 112

Suicide, reasons for committing
Matthew 24–28: 222

Sunday
Mark 1–8: 141
church meets on
Luke 18–24: 409

Sunday, Billy
Matthew 8–15: 150
1 Timothy: 26

Superficial religion
Romans 1–8: 36, 155

Superficiality, spiritual
Matthew 16–23: 126

Supernatural, modern belief in
Romans 1–8: 268

Supernatural experiences
2 Corinthians: 394–96

Supernatural living
Romans 9–16: 182, 191

Supernatural love
1 Peter: 87–93

Supernatural power
Mark 9–16: 212

Luke 18–24: 56, 62–64, 157, 347, 448
Supersessionism
Luke 1–5: 126, 132
Supplication
Matthew 1–7: 389
Supremacy of Christ
1 Peter: 219–20
Sure Word
2 Peter & Jude: 55–66
The Surrendered life
Ephesians: 362
Susanna
Luke 6–10: 183
Sutherland, Duchess of
Luke 18–24: 89
Swete, Henry Barclay
on apostolic authorship of Revelation
Revelation 1–11: 7
Swift destruction
2 Peter & Jude: 76
Swine
Luke 6–10: 222, 229, 246, 247
Luke 11–17: 311
Swoon theory (of resurrection)
Luke 18–24: 431
John 12–21: 374
Sycamore trees
Luke 18–24: 72
Sychar
Luke 18–24: 174
1–3 John: 243
Symbolism
Luke 11–17: 98, 99
of Passover meal
Matthew 24–28: 141
Symbols
Mark 1–8: 295, 352, 353
Sympathy
Luke 6–10: 326
2 Corinthians: 391–92
Hebrews: 121, 427–28
lack of
Matthew 16–23: 361
See also Compassion
Synagogues
Matthew 1–7: 123–24
Mark 1–8: 60, 61, 71, 255
Luke 1–5: 267–69, 273, 277, 314
Luke 6–10: 6, 7, 126–27, 180, 230
Luke 11–17: 198–200
Acts 1–12: 192
development of
Matthew 8–15: 103
Galatians: 107
liturgy of
Acts 13–28: 17
Paul preaches in
Acts 13–28: 17
rulers of the
Matthew 1–7: 123–24
worship in
Matthew 8–15: 104
Syncretism, religious. *see* Inclusivism
Synoptic Gospels
John 1–11: 1–10, 91, 322–23, 453
2 Peter & Jude: 49
Synoptic Problem
Mark 1–8: 5–6
Syria
Mark 1–8: 229, 366
Luke 1–5: 145
Luke 6–10: 208
Syrophoenician woman
Mark 9–16: 208
Luke 6–10: 179
John 1–11: 167
daughter of
Mark 1–8: 366–72

Tabernacles
Mark 9–16: 7
Hebrews: 211, 221–23, 228
Tabernacles, Feast of. *see* Feast of Tabernacles (Booths)
Tacitus (Roman historian)
Matthew 24–28: 8
Mark 9–16: 346, 408
Luke 18–24: 211
John 12–21: 169
Romans 1–8: 14
2 Timothy: x
Revelation 1–11: 38
on famine in Israel
Acts 1–12: 316
Tada, Joni Eareckson
Ephesians: 266
"Take My Life, and Let It Be"
1 & 2 Thessalonians: 183
***A Tale of Two Sons* (John MacArthur)**
Luke 11–17: 322
Talitha
Mark 1–8: 266
Talking, incessant
Matthew 8–15: 315
Talleyrand
2 Timothy: 187
Talmud
Matthew 8–15: 2, 85, 281, 383, 452, 461
Matthew 24–28: 299
Mark 1–8: 87, 115, 258, 342, 343
Mark 9–16: 184
Luke 1–5: 319
Luke 6–10: 3, 103
John 1–11: 100–101
Romans 9–16: 54
Ephesians: 236
Titus: 64
Tammuz
2 Corinthians: 253
Tartarus
1 Peter: 211
Revelation 1–11: 257
Tasker, R. V. G.
John 1–11: 64, 270, 488
2 Corinthians: 492
on pseudepigraphy
James: 4
Tassels
Mark 1–8: 259
Luke 18–24: 164
Tatian
Luke 1–5: 2

John 1–11: 4
Tax/taxation
Mark 1–8: 114, 190
Mark 9–16: 178–82
Luke 1–5: 143, 144, 237, 244, 330
Luke 18–24: 71, 134, 136, 345
duty to pay
Matthew 16–23: 86, 321
half–shekel
Romans 9–16: 232
Roman
Matthew 1–7: x–xi
temple
Matthew 16–23: 86
Romans 9–16: 233
Tax booths
Mark 1–8: 115
Tax collectors
Matthew 1–7: xi
Mark 1–8: 113–16, 117, 125
Luke 1–5: 220, 307, 329–33
Luke 6–10: 65, 166
Luke 18–24: 17, 18, 19, 71, 72
parable of Pharisee and publican
Luke 18–24: 14–21
1–3 John: 30–31
Taylor, George Lansing
Matthew 8–15: 96
Taylor, J. Hudson
Romans 1–8: 213
concern for the lost
Acts 13–28: 79
Taylor, Richard Shelley
Romans 9–16: 180
Taylor, William
2 Timothy: 174, 175
Teachableness
Matthew 16–23: 15
Teachers
Mark 9–16: 177, 188
Luke 6–10: 115, 235
Christian
Romans 1–8: 114
false (*see* False teachers)
Jewish
Luke 1–5: 193, 267
Teachers of the law. *see* Lawyers; Scribes
Teaching
Matthew 1–7: 138–39
Luke 6–10: 88
Luke 18–24: 108, 113, 133
Colossians & Philemon: 79–80, 159–60
Hebrews: 40–41, 130–31
Christian
1 Corinthians: 118
false
1 Corinthians: 304
parental
Matthew 16–23: 182
and preaching
Titus: 44
repetition in
Matthew 8–15: 214
Teachings of Christ. *see* Jesus Christ, teachings of
Tearing of clothes
Mark 1–8: 263
Technology. *see* Science
Televangelists
Mark 1–8: 74
Temperance
Luke 1–5: 35, 37
Temple
Matthew 1–7: 93, 102
Luke 1–5: 180, 203–4, 244, 259–60, 267
Luke 6–10: 312, 313
Luke 11–17: 195, 199, 226, 242, 243
John 12–21: 14–15, 56–57, 316
Ephesians: 75, 262
Antiochus IV and
Luke 18–24: 226, 227
architecture and construction of
Mark 9–16: 228
Christ's assault on
Luke 18–24: 103, 106, 112, 113
as Christ's body
Luke 18–24: 120
Christ's clearing of
Mark 9–16: 136–39
Christ's curse on
Mark 9–16: 132, 135, 136
at crucifixion
Luke 18–24: 390
description of
Matthew 24–28: 8
Luke 18–24: 104, 176–77
destruction of
Matthew 8–15: 313
Matthew 24–28: 252
Romans 9–16: 46
1 Corinthians: 382
Hebrews: x, xii, xix, 91, 110, 178, 192, 217, 268
heavenly
Revelation 1–11: 146, 232
history of
Acts 1–12: 214
legal proceedings in
Luke 18–24: 333
millennial
Romans 9–16: 120, 122
merchants' abuses in
Luke 18–24: 105
policies/operations
Mark 1–8: 398
Roman destruction of
Mark 9–16: 169, 229
Luke 18–24: 108, 177
sacrifices, end of
Romans 1–8: 276
in Scripture
Revelation 1–11: 294
tax
Romans 9–16: 233
tearing of temple curtain
Mark 9–16: 291, 378–79
treasury
Mark 9–16: 351
Tribulation
Revelation 1–11: 293–94

true purpose of
Matthew 16–23: 270
Temple, William
Luke 1–5: 300
Temple of Artemis
Ephesians: 165
Temporal desperation
Luke 11–17: 220–21
Temporal *vs.* eternal endurance
2 Corinthians: 157–58
Temporary faith
1–3 John: 178
Temptation
Matthew 1–7: 83–99, 304–5, 395–96
Mark 1–8: 42–46
Luke 6–10: 192
Luke 11–17: 46–48
Luke 18–24: 300–303
2 Corinthians: 38
Ephesians: 359
Hebrews: 70–72, 112, 275
1 Peter: 281
of believers
James: 50, 51
believer's battle with
Romans 1–8: 335
believers' defense against
1 & 2 Thessalonians: 161–62
blame for
James: 54
Christ's
Matthew 16–23: 41
in Gethsemane
Mark 9–16: 300–301, 304
God's lack of responsibility for
James: 46
leading others into
Mark 9–16: 44, 45
process of
James: 52
resisting
Matthew 16–23: 110
response to
Romans 1–8: 479
source of
Romans 1–8: 101
Ten Commandments
Matthew 8–15: 281, 284
Mark 1–8: 357
Luke 1–5: 74, 115
John 1–11: 16–17
Romans 1–8: 91
2 Corinthians: 50–51, 83–84, 100
Hebrews: 188
James: 223
Ten minas, parable of
Luke 18–24: 82–85
Ten spies
Mark 1–8: 270
Tenney, Merrill C.
John 1–11: 481, 488
John 12–21: 209
Galatians: ix, 12
on the Nicolaitans
Revelation 1–11: 61
Tennyson, Alfred Lord
Romans 1–8: 393
Tent cities
Luke 18–24: 102
Teresh (Persian official)
Luke 6–10: 74
John 12–21: 73
Terracotta lamps
Mark 1–8: 213
Terrorism
2 Peter & Jude: 169–70
Tertullian
Mark 9–16: 376
Luke 1–5: 2
Luke 18–24: 211, 213–14
John 1–11: 4
John 12–21: 168
Acts 1–12: 127, 229
Romans 1–8: 77
Romans 9–16: 214, 236
2 Corinthians: 5
1 Timothy: xiv, 64
1 Peter: 6
2 Peter & Jude: 13
1–3 John: 3
on apostolic authorship of Revelation
Revelation 1–11: 4
on persecution of Christians
Revelation 1–11: 39
on the Scythians
Colossians & Philemon: 152
Testimony
Mark 9–16: 326
contradictory
Luke 18–24: 333
deathbed
Matthew 16–23: 10, 16
false
Luke 18–24: 335
harming
Ephesians: 243
Testimony of God
confirmed by blood
1–3 John: 193–94
confirmed by Spirit
1–3 John: 193, 195–96
confirmed by water
1–3 John: 192–93
New Testament as witness to God's Son
1–3 John: 190
particulars of
1–3 John: 191–97
promise and warning of
1–3 John: 198
purpose of
1–3 John: 196
Testing God
Matthew 1–7: 184–85
Tests
of assurance
1–3 John: 55–60
of believers
1–3 John: 128, 168–69, 229
of confession
1–3 John: 37–41

divine
Matthew 16–23: 42
of faith
2 Corinthians: 10–18
of forgiveness of sins
1–3 John: 33–36
of obedience
1–3 John: 68
of salvation
1–3 John: 30, 33–36
of sin, certainty of
1–3 John: 25–31
of the spirits
1–3 John: 154
spiritual
Ephesians: 153
See also Trials
Tetragrammaton
John 1–11: 348
Tetrarch
Luke 6–10: 247
Tetzel, Johann
Luke 11–17: 202
Luke 18–24: 170
Texas
Luke 6–10: 38
Textual analysis/criticism
Mark 9–16: 409–12
Thaddeus (Judas the Son of James)
Mark 1–8: 161, 169, 172
Luke 1–5: 226
Luke 6–10: 16, 18, 71–72
John 12–21: 188, 275
Thankfulness. *see* Gratitude
Thayer, Joseph Henry
1 Timothy: xiii
Theft
Mark 1–8: 357
Luke 6–10: 106
Theft hypothesis
Luke 18–24: 403, 404, 414
Theistic evolution
Romans 1–8: 88
Theme of book
Hebrews: xv–xvi, 128
Theocracy
Luke 1–5: 171
Theodicy
Romans 9–16: 133
Theodosius I (Roman emperor)
Luke 11–17: 243
Romans 1–8: 164
1 & 2 Thessalonians: 4
Theological–philosophical systems
Ephesians: 42
Theology
Luke 11–17: 247, 248, 256
covenant
Romans 1–8: 151, 171
Romans 9–16: 92
orthodox
Romans 1–8: 155
Theophilus
Luke 1–5: 1
2 Peter & Jude: 141
Theophilus of Antioch
John 1–11: 3–4
1 Timothy: 64
Theos Epiphanes
Mark 9–16: 244
Theosophy
Ephesians: 277
Thermodynamics, Second Law of
Colossians & Philemon: 57
Thermopylae, Battle of
Luke 6–10: 37
John 12–21: 72
Thessalonian believers
1–3 John: 97, 98, 107
Thessalonian church
1 Peter: 22–23, 63, 255
humility of
1 & 2 Thessalonians: 228
persecution of
1 & 2 Thessalonians: 25, 60, 223
sacrificial giving of
1 & 2 Thessalonians: 26
Thessalonica
John 12–21: 166
1–3 John: 80
Theudas (messianic claimant)
Luke 18–24: 187
John 12–21: 12
Thiessen, Henry C.
John 12–21: 36
Thieves
on cross
Luke 18–24: 383–88
Thieves at cross
Mark 9–16: 369, 370, 381, 387
See also Robbers
Thinking (spiritual)
1 Peter: 273–90
This generation
Mark 9–16: 259
Thomas (Didymus)
Mark 1–8: 161, 169, 171
Luke 1–5: 226
Luke 6–10: 16, 18, 66–69, 132, 248
Luke 18–24: 414, 435
John 1–11: 4, 6, 14, 28, 71, 287, 456–57
John 12–21: 188, 274, 275, 383–86
2 Corinthians: 488
2 Peter & Jude: 41, 141
1–3 John: 5
Thomas (gospel of)
John 1–11: 4
Thomas, I. D. E.
John 1–11: 394
2 Corinthians: 40
Thomas, Robert L.
Luke 1–5: 3, 247, 296, 301
Luke 11–17: 356
John 1–11: 7
John 12–21: 63, 207–8, 315
2 Peter & Jude: 143
on the absence of the sea in heaven
Revelation 12–22: 264
on Antichrist's destruction
1 & 2 Thessalonians: 281

on the apparent contradiction between the first and fifth trumpets
Revelation 1–11: 246
on the closing of the canon of Scripture
Revelation 12–22: 310
on differences between second coming and Rapture passages
1 & 2 Thessalonians: 131
on the last half of the Tribulation
Revelation 1–11: 231
on the literalness of the numbers in Revelation
Revelation 12–22: 230–31
on the meaning of the term Israel
Revelation 1–11: 219
on the number 666
Revelation 12–22: 64
on the phrase "angels of the seven churches"
Revelation 1–11: 47
on public reading of Revelation
Revelation 1–11: 23
on Roman wills
Revelation 1–11: 163
on Sardis's capture
Revelation 1–11: 110–11
on similarities between Revelation and John's other writings
Revelation 1–11: 7
on Tribulation martyrs
Revelation 1–11: 197
on the various lists of the twelve tribes
Revelation 1–11: 220
Thomas, W. H. Griffith
on the lordship of Christ
Philippians: 149
Thomas, Watson
Matthew 8–15: 111
Thompson, J. A.
John 12–21: 203
Thompson, Robert Herbert
Matthew 8–15: 386
Thompson, Thomas
on forgiveness
Colossians & Philemon: 209
Thorns
Mark 1–8: 196, 203–4
Luke 6–10: 189, 193–94
"Thou Art Coming, O My Saviour"
Luke 11–17: 21
Threshing
Mark 1–8: 143
Throne of God
1 Peter: 74
2 Peter & Jude: 92–93, 154, 185–86
Throne of grace
Hebrews: 114–15
Thucydides
Mark 9–16: 408
Luke 1–5: 11
Thyatira
1–3 John: 2, 184–85
church at
Ephesians: 334
Tiberius (city)
Mark 1–8: 50, 229, 301
Luke 1–5: 230
Luke 6–10: 208
Luke 11–17: 228
Tiberius (sea). *see* Sea of Galilee (Sea of Chinnereth, Sea of Tiberius)
Tiberius Caesar Augustus
Mark 1–8: 228, 301
Mark 9–16: 180, 345, 351
Luke 1–5: 144, 201–2
Luke 18–24: 349, 355, 356, 357, 363
John 12–21: 327
Tiglath–pileser
Luke 1–5: 146
Timaeus
Mark 9–16: 115
Time, value of
2 Timothy: 196
Times of the Gentiles
Luke 18–24: 224
Timetable, divine
John 1–11: 275–84
Timothy
Luke 1–5: 37, 295
Luke 6–10: 55, 182, 243
Luke 18–24: 162
John 1–11: 277, 353, 364–65, 414
John 12–21: 188
Hebrews: 454
1 Peter: 162, 237, 249, 263
2 Peter & Jude: 11, 70, 140, 151, 158, 196
1–3 John: 80, 214, 245, 248
an example in conduct
1 Timothy: 173
an example in faithfulness
1 Timothy: 175
an example in love
1 Timothy: 174
an example in purity
1 Timothy: 175
an example in speech
1 Timothy: 173
background of
Acts 13–28: 83–84
circumcision of
Acts 13–28: 84
Galatians: 38
conversion of
1 Timothy: 7
health of
1 Timothy: 225
hometown of
Acts 13–28: 48
life of
1 Timothy: 6
martyrdom of
1 Timothy: 11
with Paul and Silas
Acts 13–28: 84
summary of exhortations to
1 Timothy: 289
youthfulness of
1 Timothy: 172, 179
Tithes/tithing
Luke 18–24: 18, 19
1 Corinthians: 454–55
Hebrews: 179
Christians and
Matthew 16–23: 384

Romans 9–16: 233
festival
Romans 9–16: 232
Levite's
Romans 9–16: 231
triennial
Romans 9–16: 232
Titius Justus
1–3 John: 243
Titles
Luke 18–24: 164, 180
Titus
Luke 1–5: 3
Romans 9–16: 46
1 Peter: 76, 235, 263
2 Peter & Jude: 11, 129
1–3 John: 107
authority, designated
Titus: 2
commitment of
Titus: x
Paul's trust in
Titus: 15
Titus Vespasian
Mark 9–16: 229
Romans 1–8: 164
Today
Hebrews: 88, 103
Toga virilis
Galatians: 97
Tokyo Rose (Iva Ikuko Toguri D'Aquino)
Luke 6–10: 74
John 12–21: 72
Tolerance
Mark 9–16: 216
Luke 6–10: 162
false
Matthew 16–23: 374
Toll collectors
Mark 1–8: 115
Tomb
Luke 18–24: 402, 408
Tomb (rolling stone)
John 12–21: 366, 367, 368, 378
Tomb of Christ
Mark 9–16: 392, 400
Tongue
Ephesians: 187
unchecked
Titus: 54
See also Speech
Tongues, speaking in
Acts 1–12: 42–43, 245, 305
Topheth
Mark 9–16: 48
Toplady, Augustus
Romans 1–8: 328
Torah
Luke 6–10: 302
Romans 1–8: 357
Galatians: 23
Torment
Luke 11–17: 365, 366
See also Hell
Torrey, R. A.
on the lordship of Christ
Philippians: 149
Total depravity
Luke 11–17: 56–57
Toussaint, Stanley
Matthew 8–15: 342
Tower of Babel
Revelation 12–22: 157, 175
Tower of Maecenas
1 Peter: 248
Towns, Elmer
John 1–11: 488
"The Toys" (Coventry Patmore)
Colossians & Philemon: 215–16
Tozer, A. W.
Luke 1–5: 121
Luke 11–17: 18, 50
Acts 13–28: 95, 106
Romans 1–8: 94, 205
1 Timothy: 269
on believers' thoughts of God
Philippians: 274
on God's forgiveness of sinners
1 & 2 Thessalonians: 247
on the lordship of Christ
Philippians: 149
on the low view of God in the church
Philippians: 279
on unworthy thoughts of God
Philippians: 313
Trachonitis
Mark 1–8: 300
Tradition
Matthew 8–15: 453
Mark 1–8: 342, 343, 344, 346, 347
Luke 11–17: 4
excessive emphasis on
Colossians & Philemon: 8, 101, 106–9, 116–19
Jewish
Matthew 1–7: 147–48, 200, 252, 254, 284–87, 292, 296–97, 309, 311, 320–21, 323, 330, 340–43, 355
Matthew 8–15: 281, 458
Romans 9–16: 19, 54, 69
rabbinic
Matthew 16–23: 3, 337
Romans 1–8: 12, 139, 169, 271, 366, 369
Titus: 59, 126
Training
Luke 6–10: 182, 184, 329
Traitors
Luke 6–10: 73–75
Luke 18–24: 311
John 12–21: 72–73
Trajan (Roman Emperor)
Mark 9–16: 107
Luke 18–24: 211, 212
John 12–21: 168, 169
Romans 1–8: 14
1 Peter: 7
1–3 John: 6
Trans-dispensationalism
1–3 John: 224

Transcendence
Luke 1–5: 265–66
2 Corinthians: 277–78
Transference, spiritual
Colossians & Philemon: 40–42
The Transfiguration
Mark 9–16: 2–8, 13–15
Luke 1–5: 49, 57, 308
Luke 6–10: 47, 50, 281
John 12–21: 181, 205, 224
Hebrews: 189
2 Peter & Jude: 4, 60–61
1–3 John: 23, 144
date of
Matthew 16–23: 66
Mount of
Matthew 16–23: 62
Transformation
Luke 18–24: 74, 75, 141–42
1 Peter: 185–94, 228–30
ministries of
2 Corinthians: 81–84
New Covenant and
2 Corinthians: 116–17
See also Face of Jesus Christ
Transport taxes
Luke 18–24: 134
Transubstantiation
Mark 9–16: 290
1 Corinthians: 238
Trapp, John
on universality of sorrow
James: 34
Treasure, heavenly
Matthew 1–7: 407–15
Treasure in clay pots
2 Corinthians: 137–48
Treasure in heaven
Luke 11–17: 135, 139
Treasury
Luke 18–24: 169
Treasury (temple)
Mark 9–16: 222
Trench, G. C.
Romans 9–16: 150
Trench, Richard C.
Matthew 8–15: 93
2 Corinthians: 128, 178, 492
Galatians: 169
2 Timothy: 158
Titus: 144
on *aleiphō*
James: 277
on the meaning of *hupomonē*
Revelation 1–11: 59
on the meaning of *ptocheia*
Revelation 1–11: 76
on *phaulos*
James: 176
Trent, Council of
Romans 1–8: 250
2 Corinthians: 466
1–3 John: 53
Trial of Jesus
Luke 18–24: 323–25, 336, 337
accusation (by Jewish leaders)
John 12–21: 326–28
before Annas/Caiaphas
John 12–21: 315–17
illegal nature of
John 12–21: 320–21
interrogation
John 12–21: 328–31
panic of Pilate
John 12–21: 340–42
proposals of Pilate
John 12–21: 336–40
questioning of Jesus by Pilate
John 12–21: 328–31
Trials
Mark 9–16: 322, 325
Luke 6–10: 192, 193
Luke 11–17: 46, 48, 124, 181, 182, 383, 391
1 Peter: 247–60
inevitability of
Philippians: 56
James: 24
purpose of
1 Timothy: 48
James: 17ff.
See also Suffering; Tests
Tribes of Israel
1 Peter: 108–10
Tribulation
Mark 9–16: 8, 95
Luke 1–5: 107, 280, 286
John 12–21: 42, 150
1 Corinthians: 418
Hebrews: 12, 35–36
2 Peter & Jude: 18, 35–36, 130–31, 171–72, 185–86
Revelation 1–11: 177, 180, 191, 203, 214, 230, 231, 266
battles in
Luke 18–24: 202–3
evangelism
Luke 18–24: 127
famine
Luke 18–24: 206
fires
Luke 18–24: 207
in Jewish eschatology
Luke 18–24: 178–82
judgments
Luke 18–24: 220
the rapture and
Luke 18–24: 247–49
seven–year
Titus: 119
ungodliness during
Matthew 24–28: 74
worldwide revival
Luke 18–24: 221
Tribulation, the Great
Matthew 8–15: 350
Matthew 24–28: 36
Mark 9–16: 248–50, 252–55
Luke 11–17: 153, 156, 157
Luke 18–24: 224, 227, 230
Romans 9–16: 111, 118
James: 174

1 Peter: 283
Revelation 12–22: 3, 4, 69, 96
chronology of
Matthew 24–28: 114
Tribulation period
Mark 9–16: 236, 238
Tribunes
Luke 6–10: 124
"Trilemma"
Mark 1–8: 174
The Trinity
Matthew 1–7: 74, 80–82, 91
Mark 1–8: 36, 38
Luke 1–5: 234–35
Luke 11–17: 121
John 1–11: 15
Romans 1–8: 17, 414
Galatians: 3, 108
1–3 John: 162–72
doctrine of
2 Corinthians: 487–88
and plan of salvation
Titus: 14
Triumph
2 Corinthians: 70–71
over temptation
Luke 18–24: 303, 306, 307
Triumphal entry
Matthew 16–23: 257
John 12–21: 9, 15–18, 50, 97, 119
adoration in
Luke 18–24: 94–96
Daniel's prophecy of
Luke 18–24: 91
Pharisees condemned during
Luke 18–24: 97–99
preparation for
Luke 18–24: 92–94
Trophimus
Luke 1–5: 295
Luke 6–10: 243
2 Corinthians: 305
Trotter, Mel
Acts 1–12: 263
True apostles
2 Corinthians: 364–73
True believers
Mark 1–8: 203, 205, 217, 334
True disciples, false disciples *vs.*
John 1–11: 227–38, 269–70
True God
John 1–11: 14
True knowledge
2 Peter & Jude: 28–30, 33–46
True religion
2 Peter & Jude: 42
True worship
2 Peter & Jude: 42
Trumpet judgment, fifth
Matthew 24–28: 74
Trust
Mark 1–8: 233–34, 235
Luke 6–10: 128, 129
2 Corinthians: 239–40, 270
Hebrews: 159–60
1 Peter: 279–80
forgiveness and
Matthew 16–23: 157
obedience and
Romans 1–8: 24
obstacles to
Romans 1–8: 264
parental
Matthew 16–23: 184
See also Faith
"Trust and Obey"
Acts 1–12: 190
Trust in God
Mark 9–16: 22, 144, 145
Trusting God
Acts 1–12: 189, 323
Truth
Matthew 1–7: 320, 324–26
Mark 1–8: 5–6, 124, 213, 215, 321
Mark 9–16: 175, 177, 178, 261
Luke 6–10: 45, 305
Luke 18–24: 188–89, 330, 347, 386
John 12–21: 102, 114, 119, 160–62, 206–10, 331
2 Corinthians: 188–89, 357–60, 367–82, 477
Hebrews: 162
1 Peter: 89–90, 92, 95, 275
2 Peter & Jude: 82–83, 139–40
absolute
Luke 1–5: 335–37
Luke 11–17: 60, 343
anointing of Christians and
1–3 John: 102–3
attacks on
1–3 John: 15
avoidance of false doctrine
1 Timothy: 292
believers' upholding of
1 Timothy: 137
biblical absolute regarding
1–3 John: 200–201
blessing believers
1–3 John: 219–20
Christian perseverance and
1–3 John: 103–4
Christians' guarding of
1–3 John: 174
Christian's knowledge of biblical
1–3 John: 75–77, 142, 143–44, 160
Christ's application of
Luke 11–17: 273
church as steward of
1–3 John: 214–15
control of believers
1–3 John: 220–21
doctrinal
1–3 John: 14, 75, 153
embodiment in the gospel
1–3 John: 217
and error
1–3 John: 155
false teachers and
Luke 11–17: 353, 413
1–3 John: 58, 152–53, 155
foundational
1–3 John: 159

of God's promises
Luke 1–5: 87–88
governing the exercise of love
1–3 John: 217–18
guarding of
1 Timothy: 291, 293
1–3 John: 235–37
indwelling believers
1–3 John: 218–19
Jesus as source of
Luke 1–5: 301–3
Jesus' proclamation of
Luke 6–10: 2–3
John's commitment to
Luke 6–10: 46–48
learning
1–3 John: 237–38
living in
1–3 John: 215–20
loss of doctrinal certainty and
1–3 John: 14
and love
Matthew 8–15: 152
love and
1–3 John: 217–18, 228, 244
loyalty of Christians to
1–3 John: 231–35
Mary (Martha's sister) and
1–3 John: 213–14
mercy and
Luke 6–10: 307–8
moral
Titus: 46
obedience to and joy
1–3 John: 237–38
perversion of
Matthew 16–23: 381
practical use of God's
Romans 1–8: 304
receiving of
Luke 11–17: 346, 372
rejecting evidence of
Matthew 16–23: 5
righteousness and
1–3 John: 24–25
sabotaging of by Satan
1–3 John: 155
salvation and
Luke 11–17: 95
1–3 John: 218
seeking after
Matthew 8–15: 152
spiritual
Luke 11–17: 95, 108, 110, 304
Titus: 46
spiritual young men and
1–3 John: 75
as theme of 3 John
1–3 John: 241
transmission of God's
1 Corinthians: 62–65
uncompromising
Matthew 8–15: 152
undergirded by righteous living
Titus: 56
uniting believers
1–3 John: 215–18
walking in
1–3 John: 220, 246, 247
of the Word, abiding in believers
1–3 John: 219
Word of God as source of
1–3 John: 159–60
worship and
Luke 1–5: 76–77

Trypho
John 1–11: 284, 304, 367

Tsar Alexander II
Luke 11–17: 244

Tubal
Matthew 24–28: 35

Tuberculoid leprosy
Mark 1–8: 87

Turkey
Luke 1–5: 226

Turretin, Francis
2 Peter & Jude: 56

Twain, Mark
Acts 1–12: 289

Twelve apostles
Mark 1–8: 166–72, 312, 314, 315, 340
Mark 9–16: 92, 277, 284
Luke 6–10: 47, 162, 241
Luke 18–24: 48, 270, 271, 272, 274
John 1–11: 1–7, 63–74, 221–38, 272–79, 287, 336–37
John 12–21: 3, 20, 65–69, 73–80, 166, 231
2 Corinthians: 17, 358, 385, 387, 407–17
1 Peter: 4–9, 57–59
2 Peter & Jude: 2–3, 50–53
call of
Matthew 1–7: 114–20
choosing
Luke 6–10: 15–17, 46
commitment
Luke 6–10: 64
importance
Luke 6–10: 18–21
preaching
Luke 6–10: 240, 247
pride of
Matthew 16–23: 232
sending
Luke 6–10: 17–18
training
Luke 6–10: 182, 184, 297
weaknesses
Luke 6–10: 19–21, 24, 182
See also Apostles; Disciples

Twelve legions of angels
Mark 9–16: 314

Twelve tribes of Israel
John 1–11: 224
2 Peter & Jude: 18

Twenty-four elders, identification of
Revelation 1–11: 148–50

The two thieves
Mark 9–16: 387, 388
Luke 18–24: 383–88

Tychicus
2 Corinthians: 305

Colossians & Philemon: 192–93, 230
Tyndale, William
John 12–21: 189
Romans 1–8: x
Ephesians: 373
1 Timothy: 161
1 Peter: 3
Type, biblical
Matthew 1–7: 42–43
Typology
Hebrews: 171–72, 210–11
Tyre
Mark 1–8: 312, 315, 365, 374
Luke 6–10: 87, 250, 252, 259, 334
Tyrian purple dye
Luke 11–17: 360
***Tzaraath* (leprosy)**
Mark 1–8: 86
See also Leprosy (Hansen's disease)

Ultra-Calvinism
Romans 9–16: 84
Unbelief
Matthew 1–7: 12–13
Mark 1–8: 203, 270, 277, 278–81, 344
Mark 9–16: 200, 226, 270, 330, 355
Luke 11–17: 274–75, 368, 418–20
John 12–21: 55–57
1 Corinthians: 45–47
Hebrews: 89–90, 92, 94, 377
arrogance of
Matthew 16–23: 273
blindness of
Matthew 16–23: 273
characteristics of
Matthew 8–15: 408–14
determined
Matthew 8–15: 103
hardness of
Matthew 16–23: 263–64, 286, 288, 300, 378, 390
as miracle
John 1–11: 397–408
no excuse for
Romans 1–8: 82
responses to
John 1–11: 161–68
willful
Matthew 16–23: 5, 77
Unbelievers
Luke 1–5: 280, 294, 295
Luke 6–10: 105, 107, 108, 144
blasphemy of
Revelation 12–22: 303
characteristics of
Romans 1–8: 362
culpability of
1 & 2 Thessalonians: 243
enemies of God
Romans 1–8: 273
excluded from heaven
Revelation 12–22: 272–73
hell as destiny of
Romans 1–8: 397
judgment of
1 & 2 Thessalonians: 163
Revelation 12–22: 251
separation from (*see* Separation)
as slaves to sin
Romans 1–8: 346
spiritual blindness of
1 & 2 Thessalonians: 22, 283
See also Believer(s), false
Uncertainties of life
1–3 John: 200
Uncials, Greek
Galatians: 194–95
Unclean spirits
Mark 1–8: 240–48
Mark 9–16: 29
Luke 1–5: 283
Luke 6–10: 220
Luke 11–17: 75–76
See also Demon possession; Demons
Uncleanness
Luke 1–5: 169, 171
ceremonial
Matthew 8–15: 80
Unction, extreme
Titus: 129
Undefiled status
1 Peter: 35
Understanding, spiritual
Colossians & Philemon: 89–92
Understanding and consideration
1 Peter: 181
Understanding Scripture
Luke 18–24: 418–19, 423–27
Unforgivable sin
John 12–21: 175
Unforgiveness
Matthew 16–23: 152, 154
Ungodliness
2 Peter & Jude: 88
and false teaching
Titus: 8
Ungodly persons
2 Peter & Jude: 161
Ungrateful separation
2 Corinthians: 257–58
Unholiness
Ephesians: 353
Uniformitarianism
Matthew 24–28: 81
Luke 11–17: 409
Luke 18–24: 186
2 Peter & Jude: 113–15, 118–19
Union with Christ
Galatians: 59
1 & 2 Thessalonians: 13–14, 224–25
1 Peter: 103–17
United Kingdom
Luke 18–24: 89
United Pentecostal Church
Luke 1–5: 235
Unity
2 Corinthians: 268–69
with Christ
Matthew 16–23: 103
church
Titus: 165

in decisions
1 Corinthians: 29–30
in doctrine
1 Corinthians: 25–30
faith and
John 12–21: 287–88
false
Galatians: 17
features of
John 12–21: 290–92
forgiveness and
Matthew 16–23: 143
Jesus' request for
John 12–21: 289–90
marks of
John 12–21: 286
result of
John 12–21: 277–78, 292–93
spiritual
John 12–21: 285
Romans 9–16: 166
1 Corinthians: 31–32
Colossians & Philemon: 87–89, 152–53
Titus: 165
in standards
1 Corinthians: 29
Unity School of Christianity
Ephesians: 277
Universal kingdom
Luke 11–17: 24, 399–401
See also Kingdom of God
Universal peace
Romans 9–16: 111
Universalism
Matthew 16–23: 130
Romans 1–8: 69, 72, 307
1 Timothy: 70, 167
Titus: 109
1–3 John: 225
error of
Colossians & Philemon: 59–60
The Universe
creation of (See also Creation)
Hebrews: 14
sustenance of
Hebrews: 16–17
Unjust suffering
1 Peter: 223–32
Unleavened bread
Mark 9–16: 268, 286, 289
Luke 18–24: 274
Unleavened Bread, Feast of
Mark 9–16: 268
Luke 18–24: 265, 278
John 1–11: 89
Unlimited forgiveness
Luke 11–17: 43, 44
Unnoticed persons
2 Peter & Jude: 158–59
Unpardonable sin
Mark 1–8: 184, 185
Luke 11–17: 62
Unpreparedness
Matthew 24–28: 193
Unproductiveness, spiritual
Matthew 24–28: 108
Unprofitable separation
2 Corinthians: 255–56
Unreasoning animals
2 Peter & Jude: 99
The Unregenerate
Luke 11–17: 144
Unrepentance
Matthew 16–23: 135
1 Corinthians: 130
The Unrepentant
1–3 John: 49–50
Unrepentant sin
2 Corinthians: 433–38
Unrighteousness, man's natural
Romans 1–8: 182, 343
Unsaved
condemnation of
Matthew 24–28: 125
mind, description of
Philippians: 286
spiritual death of
Romans 1–8: 417
spouses
1 Peter: 175–83
Unselfishness
Matthew 8–15: 192
Ephesians: 201
Unworthiness, man's
Matthew 8–15: 91
Upper Room
Luke 6–10: 58, 201, 245
John 12–21: 5, 50, 65–69, 74–80, 97, 238
2 Corinthians: 422, 470
1–3 John: 66, 134, 167
location of
Acts 1–12: 28
1 Peter: 110
Upper Room Discourse
Titus: 48
1 Peter: 18, 41
Ur of the Chaldeans
Luke 1–5: 105–7
Romans 1–8: 235
Urban II (pope)
Luke 11–17: 243
Urgency
2 Peter & Jude: 48–49
Uriah
Mark 1–8: 298
Urim and Thummim
Revelation 1–11: 91
Utopia
Luke 18–24: 219
Utterances of God
1 Peter: 245
Uzzah
Luke 1–5: 75
1 Peter: 108
Uzziah
Matthew 1–7: 173
Luke 1–5: 314
John 1–11: 451
1–3 John: 254

Valerius Gratus
Luke 1–5: 203

John 1–11: 483
John 12–21: 316, 317
Valley of dry bones vision
Mark 9–16: 184
Values, Christian
2 Corinthians: 285–86
Vanity
2 Peter & Jude: 105–6
Varro
Romans 1–8: 90
Vaticanus (Greek New Testament manuscript)
Mark 9–16: 410
Vedder, Henry Clay
John 12–21: 188
Veil of the temple
Mark 9–16: 291, 378–79
Luke 18–24: 390
Velikovsky, Immanuel
Luke 18–24: 231
Vengeance
Matthew 1–7: 329–30
Matthew 16–23: 152
Luke 1–5: 274
Luke 6–10: 103, 104, 106
Ephesians: 127, 195
Colossians & Philemon: 207–8, 219
Days of
Luke 18–24: 223
God's (*see* God, vengeance of)
personal
Revelation 1–11: 189
See also Forgiveness
Venning, Ralph
2 Corinthians: 210
on sin
James: 225–26
Venomous serpents
Mark 9–16: 412
Verbal abuse. *see* Mockers/mockery
Verification of Jesus Christ's claims
John 1–11: 285–98
Vespasian, Titus
Romans 1–8: 164
Via Maris
Mark 1–8: 60
Victoria (queen of England), coronation of
Luke 18–24: 88–89
Victors, Christians as
1–3 John: 174–75, 179
See also Overcomers
Victory, spiritual
Colossians & Philemon: 112–13
Victory over Satan
Romans 1–8: 428
James: 205
1–3 John: 174–75
Revelation 12–22: 22
Vigilance
Mark 9–16: 303
Hebrews: 406–8
1 Peter: 280–85
Vikings, death beliefs of
Luke 18–24: 140
Vincent, Marvin R.
2 Timothy: 182
on the meaning of iris
Revelation 1–11: 280
on meaning of radiourgias
Acts 13–28: 10
on slavery
Colossians & Philemon: 204–6
Vindication, God's, of believers
Matthew 8–15: 219–21
Vine, W. E.
John 12–21: 159
2 Peter & Jude: 59, 71–72, 216
on meaning of anaskeuazō
Acts 13–28: 72
on obedience
Colossians & Philemon: 17
on prautēs
James: 75
Vine/vineyards
Mark 9–16: 165–67
John 12–21: 141–53
Vineyard owner
Luke 18–24: 121–23
Vineyard owner's son
Luke 18–24: 124
Vins, Georgi
Romans 9–16: 213
Virgil
Luke 1–5: 144
Virgin birth
Matthew 1–7: 11–22
Luke 1–5: 54–58
Hebrews: 28, 296
Virginity
Luke 6–10: 202
Virgins
Luke 1–5: 44, 45, 48
Virtues
2 Peter & Jude: 40–42
Visions
Ephesians: 42
Visitation
1 Peter: 140–41
Vitiligo
Mark 1–8: 87
Vocation
Romans 1–8: 20
Voluntary giving
2 Corinthians: 281–83, 299–300
von Harnack, Adolf
2 Peter & Jude: 56
von Schlegel, Katharina
2 Corinthians: 28
Vos, Howard F.
John 12–21: 167
2 Corinthians: 3, 492
on Aphrodite worship
Acts 13–28: 8
on population of Corinth
Acts 13–28: 145
Votive gifts
Luke 18–24: 177
Vows. *see* Oaths
Vultures
Luke 11–17: 420

Walk, the Christian
Ephesians: 115–31, 193–227
Colossians & Philemon: 30–31, 92–93
Walker, Edward
John 12–21: 188
Walking
in darkness
1–3 John: 28–29
in same manner as Christ
1–3 John: 60
in the truth
1–3 John: 101, 220, 246, 247
Walking in the Spirit
Hebrews: 312
Walking on water, miracle of
Mark 1–8: 329–31
John 1–11: 230–34
Wallace, Daniel B.
John 1–11: 488
2 Peter & Jude: 4–5, 216
Wallace, Lew
1 Timothy: 26
Walter, Tony
on need–centered Christianity
Philippians: 252–53
Walvoord, John F.
John 12–21: 131–32
on futurist interpretation of Revelation
Revelation 1–11: 10–11
Wandering stars metaphor
2 Peter & Jude: 181–82
Wannamaker, John
Matthew 8–15: 483
Warfare, spiritual
Luke 11–17: 73
Acts 1–12: 234
Acts 13–28: 168–72
Ephesians: 331–73
1 Timothy: 36, 40
2 Timothy: 122, 192
Titus: 137
compassion and
2 Corinthians: 323–25
competence and
2 Corinthians: 327–31
courage and
2 Corinthians: 326–27
definition of
2 Corinthians: 328
fortresses and
2 Corinthians: 328–30
overview of
2 Corinthians: 321–23
timing and
2 Corinthians: 331
Warfield, Benjamin B.
Matthew 8–15: 106
Luke 18–24: 30
2 Peter & Jude: 56, 217
Warner, Charles Dudley
Mark 9–16: 175
Warning
Hebrews: 41, 86, 128–29, 146, 270
Warnings to apostates. *see* Apostates and apostate times
Wars
Luke 18–24: 202, 230
Washing the disciples' feet
Luke 11–17: 41–42
Washings
Hebrews: 139–40
Watchfulness. *see* Alertness
Water baptism
Romans 1–8: 21, 320
Water into wine miracle
Luke 1–5: 36–37
Waterless clouds metaphor
2 Peter & Jude: 180
Watson, Thomas
Luke 6–10: 272–73
Luke 11–17: 5
John 12–21: 233
Romans 1–8: 74, 100, 380, 478
1 Peter: 71, 204
on the false peace of the unregenerate
1 & 2 Thessalonians: 314
on the incompatibility of peace and sin
1 & 2 Thessalonians: 315
on sanctification
1 & 2 Thessalonians: 203
Watts, Isaac
Matthew 8–15: 37
Romans 1–8: 220
2 Corinthians: 471
The Way
John 12–21: 103, 104
Weak faith
Mark 9–16: 146
Weakness, spiritual
2 Timothy: 36
Weaknesses
Luke 6–10: 19–21
2 Corinthians: 399–400
Wealth
Matthew 1–7: 407–15
Mark 9–16: 77, 81–84, 87, 137, 223
Luke 6–10: 99, 267, 320
Luke 11–17: 32–33, 128, 129, 339, 340, 357–61, 367
Luke 18–24: 40, 41, 42, 169, 334
Hebrews: 354–55, 433
content to wait for dividends
1 Timothy: 285
danger of uncertainty of
1 Timothy: 282
dangers of
Matthew 8–15: 24
to meet others' needs
1 Timothy: 283
must avoid conceit
1 Timothy: 281
spiritual
Matthew 16–23: 200
and stewardship
1 Timothy: 280
Webb, R. A.
Mark 9–16: 68
Luke 18–24: 28
Wedding in Cana, miracle of
John 1–11: 75–83

Weddings
Mark 1–8: 129–31
Luke 1–5: 266, 340
Luke 6–10: 164, 166
Luke 11–17: 262
Weeds
Luke 6–10: 189
Weeping
Luke 18–24: 371
Weldon, John
Ephesians: 342
Wellhausen, Julius
2 Peter & Jude: 56
Wenger, J. C.
on evangelical social reform
Colossians & Philemon: 165
Wenham, John
on the imprecatory Psalms
1 & 2 Thessalonians: 237
Wesley, Charles
Luke 1–5: 272
Luke 6–10: 141, 142
John 1–11: 17–18, 40, 361, 380
John 12–21: 129
Romans 1–8: 288
James: 69
Wesley, John
Luke 18–24: 427
John 1–11: 240
Romans 1–8: x, 207
Galatians: 105
Ephesians: 368
2 Timothy: 62
Titus: 73
on social reform
Colossians & Philemon: 165
Wesley, Susanna
Ephesians: 319
on self–control
Philippians: 49
Westcott, B. F.
John 1–11: 5, 42, 323, 488
John 12–21: 304
Western Allies
Luke 6–10: 37–38
Western confederacy
Matthew 24–28: 35
Westminster Abbey
Luke 18–24: 88
Westminster Confession of Faith
John 12–21: 285
James: 29
1–3 John: 53, 104
Revelation 1–11: 79
Westminster Shorter Catechism
Romans 1–8: 83
Romans 9–16: 124
"What a Friend We Have in Jesus"
James: 275
Wheat
Luke 18–24: 295
and tares
Hebrews: 152, 153
Whitcomb, John C. Jr.
2 Peter & Jude: 88
White, Hayden V.
2 Peter & Jude: 55–56
White, John
Titus: 49
White, William Jr.
2 Peter & Jude: 217
White horse
Mark 9–16: 256
Luke 18–24: 237
Whitefield, George
John 1–11: 240
1 Timothy: 75
2 Timothy: 62
on repentance
James: 210
social reforms of
Colossians & Philemon: 165
Whitney, Donald S.
2 Corinthians: 122
on the Pony Express
1 & 2 Thessalonians: 260–61
Whole world, meaning of
1–3 John: 48–49
***Why Government Can't Save You* (John MacArthur)**
Luke 11–17: 70
Wicked, prosperity of
Romans 1–8: 64
Wickedness
Luke 11–17: 82, 83
Luke 18–24: 220
Widow of Nain
Luke 6–10: 184
Widow of Nain's son
Mark 1–8: 253
Widow of Zarephath
1 Timothy: 200
Widows
Mark 9–16: 221–23
Luke 1–5: 275, 276, 277
Luke 18–24: 3, 5–7
Ephesians: 286
church's responsibility to care for
Acts 1–12: 284
criteria for church support
1 Timothy: 198
duties of older ones
1 Timothy: 206
plan for younger ones
1 Timothy: 210–14
responsibility of church toward
1 Timothy: 196
Wiersbe, Warren W.
Ephesians: 41
on great nineteenth–century preachers
Acts 13–28: 14
on values
James: 23–24
The wife's desire
Mark 9–16: 56, 57
Wilberforce, William
slavery reforms of
Colossians & Philemon: 166
Wild honey
Mark 1–8: 24

Wild sea waves metaphor
2 Peter & Jude: 181
Wilde, Oscar
Romans 1–8: 350
Galatians: 185
Wilderness
Mark 1–8: 20
Luke 1–5: 204–5, 207, 252, 254
Luke 6–10: 153–54, 165
temptation
Mark 1–8: 41–46
Wilderness of Judea
Matthew 1–7: 87
Wildfires
Luke 18–24: 206–7
Will, God's
Matthew 1–7: 381–86, 403–4
Luke 1–5: 257, 260–61
Luke 11–17: 27–30
Luke 18–24: 303–5
Acts 13–28: 6
1 Peter: 226–28
Decretive
Luke 11–17: 28
hidden
Luke 11–17: 28
knowing
Colossians & Philemon: 28–30
Preceptive
Luke 11–17: 28
and reconciliation
2 Corinthians: 199–201
sovereign
Galatians: 6–7, 28
Will, human
Matthew 1–7: 383–84, 450–52, 474–75, 488–89
Galatians: 153
Ephesians: 11
Christian's
Romans 1–8: 338
and saving faith
Romans 1–8: 205
Will of disposition (God's)
Luke 11–17: 28
Williams, David J.
on length of Saul's reign
Acts 13–28: 20
on Philippi's legal status
Acts 13–28: 91
on receiving the Holy Spirit at salvation
Acts 13–28: 164
on wickedness of Corinth
Acts 13–28: 146
Williams, Ted
2 Timothy: 194
Wilson, Geoffrey
Romans 9–16: 71
Wilson, T. E.
on sleep as a metaphor for death
1 & 2 Thessalonians: 127
Wine
Mark 9–16: 285, 286, 291
Luke 1–5: 36–37, 266
Luke 18–24: 280, 383
kinds of ancient
Ephesians: 235
Wine from water miracle
John 1–11: 75–83
Wineskins
Mark 1–8: 133
Winnowing
Mark 1–8: 143
Wisdom
Mark 1–8: 274
Luke 1–5: 190
godly
1 Corinthians: 40–47, 50, 52–54, 60–65
Colossians & Philemon: 29–30
human
Matthew 8–15: 270
1 Corinthians: 36, 88
limitations of human
Matthew 16–23: 42
walking in
Ephesians: 215–27
worldly
Matthew 16–23: 6
Wisdom of Sirach
Romans 1–8: 233
Wise men (Magi)
Matthew 1–7: 26–30, 34–37
Luke 1–5: 171
Acts 1–12: 240
Acts 13–28: 8
Wishart, George
John 12–21: 189
Witherington, Ben, III
John 12–21: 238
Witness (testimony)
1 Corinthians: 15–16, 54
of Christians
John 12–21: 181–82, 189, 284
courageous
2 Timothy: 10
Witness of God. *see* Testimony of God
Witnesses
Mark 9–16: 321, 322, 324
Luke 1–5: 165, 166
2 Corinthians: 446–47
false
Luke 18–24: 324–25, 330, 336, 337, 343
gospel proclamation and
Luke 18–24: 447
Herod and Pilate as
Luke 18–24: 351
to incarnation of Jesus Christ
John 1–11: 44–46
to Jesus Christ as deity
John 1–11: 203–16
Jewish law rules for
Luke 18–24: 330, 331, 332
two
Romans 9–16: 119, 121–22
Witnessing
Romans 1–8: 147, 213
and loving concern
Galatians: 191–92
personal
Matthew 8–15: 156, 165

Wives
Ephesians: 279–89
abused
Romans 1–8: 191
principles for
Colossians & Philemon: 166–68
responsibilities of
1 Peter: 176–81
unsaved spouses
1 Peter: 175–83
See also Marriage
Wives and husbands, responsibilities of
1 Peter: 176–83
Woe (declaration of judgment)
Luke 11–17: 101, 102, 106, 108
Woman caught in adultery
John 1–11: 325–30
Woman with bleeding
Mark 1–8: 258–62
Luke 6–10: 232–33
Women
Mark 1–8: 366
Luke 1–5: 169, 192
Luke 6–10: 183, 184
appearance of
1 Timothy: 79
and childbearing
1 Timothy: 89
conduct of
1 Timothy: 78
and the deacons
1 Timothy: 130
equality and role of
1 Timothy: 85
and evangelical feminism
1 Timothy: 77
and exercise of authority
1 Timothy: 86
and Fall
1 Timothy: 88
God's design for
Titus: 83
and hair styles
1 Timothy: 79
kinds of good works
1 Timothy: 208
low esteem by first–century Jews
1 Timothy: 83
and the mission field
1 Timothy: 87
ordination of
Titus: 81
proper attitudes of
1 Timothy: 81
and remarriage
1 Timothy: 212
role in church
1 Timothy: 74, 77
status under Mosaic law
1 Timothy: 83
status under New Testament
1 Timothy: 84
and submissiveness
1 Timothy: 85
as teachers
1 Timothy: 82
testimony of
1 Timothy: 82
testimony to the resurrection of
Luke 18–24: 420
as witnesses
Luke 18–24: 331, 408–13
Women, men and
Colossians & Philemon: 166–70
Women's liberation
Acts 13–28: 90
Ephesians: 339
See also Feminism
Wonder–workers
Luke 1–5: 12
Wonders, signs, and miracles
2 Corinthians: 414–17
Word
John 12–21: 148
Word, God's inerrant
Romans 9–16: 41
Word, Jesus Christ as divine
John 1–11: 13–24
incarnate, glory of
John 1–11: 37–46
incarnate, responses to
John 1–11: 25–35
Word Faith movement
Luke 11–17: 9–10, 32
See also Prosperity gospel
Word of God
Mark 1–8: 200, 342
Luke 6–10: 83
Luke 18–24: 250
Hebrews: 105, 144–45, 389
1 Peter: 95–102
2 Peter & Jude: 2, 36, 56–57, 61–66, 82, 99–109, 111, 117–18, 120, 172, 184
Believers' defense against error
1–3 John: 155
Christian living and
Romans 1–8: 304, 348
communicable
1–3 John: 17–18
exaltation in Old Testament
Romans 1–8: 356
historical
1–3 John: 16–17
honoring
1 Corinthians: 88
joyful
1–3 John: 19–20
meditating on
Romans 1–8: 426
obedience of believers to
1–3 John: 123–24
person and work of Jesus
1–3 John: 16
relational
1–3 John: 18–19
test of spiritual ideologies
1–3 John: 159–60
truth of
1–3 John: 220–21
unchangeable
1–3 John: 14, 15
See also The Bible; Scripture

Word of Truth
Luke 11–17: vii
Words of Christ
Mark 9–16: 260, 261
John 12–21: 150
Work
Mark 1–8: 139–40, 153
Christian view of
1 & 2 Thessalonians: 302–3
employers and employees
Ephesians: 321–29
1 Timothy: 231, 233
Greek view of
1 & 2 Thessalonians: 120, 300
Jewish view of
1 & 2 Thessalonians: 300
principles of conduct
1 Timothy: 234
relations at
Colossians & Philemon: 174–75
theology of
1 Timothy: 227
Workers
destructive
1 Corinthians: 86
worthless
1 Corinthians: 85
Works
Matthew 24–28: 122
Hebrews: 154, 285–86, 302, 317–18, 444
divinely provided
Matthew 16–23: 57
evidence of salvation
Matthew 16–23: 57
and faith
Galatians: 45–60
faith and
Romans 1–8: 26, 129, 132, 140
of the flesh (*see* The Flesh)
and grace
Romans 1–8: 315
1 Corinthians: 12–13, 84–86
judgment by
Romans 1–8: 127
and salvation
Titus: 118
of salvation
1 Corinthians: 14, 82–85
trust in
Romans 1–8: 112, 129, 221, 247, 270, 351, 420
Works–righteousness
Matthew 1–7: 62, 277–78, 281, 451–52
Mark 1–8: 110, 133, 137, 156
Mark 9–16: 71, 77, 238
Luke 1–5: 328, 342
Luke 11–17: 346
Luke 18–24: 17, 25, 388
Romans 9–16: 2
Galatians: 12, 67, 200
Ephesians: 55
Titus: 65, 118
basis of human religion
Matthew 16–23: 201
futility of
Matthew 16–23: 192, 202
See also Self–righteousness
The World
John 1–11: 115–16
believers and
John 12–21: 171–76, 180, 262–63, 281
1–3 John: 82–92, 175–77
blindness to truth of
John 12–21: 114
Christ's redemption of
John 12–21: 228
corrupted by sin
Matthew 24–28: 274
definition of
1 Timothy: 32
James: 92, 193
as demonic ideologies and enterprises
1–3 John: 83
God's control of
John 12–21: 238, 239
God's judgment on
John 12–21: 42
natural deterioration of
Romans 1–8: 456
not fearing
Matthew 8–15: 218
as passing away
1–3 John: 90–92
peace/turmoil of
John 12–21: 126
Satan's influence on
1–3 John: 209
self–destruction of
1–3 John: 90–91
separation from
Romans 1–8: 225
sinful characteristics of
1–3 John: 85–90, 175
as spiritual system of evil
1–3 John: 82–83, 175–76
system, present
Romans 1–8: 447
victory over by Christians
1–3 John: 175–77
war against kingdom of God
1–3 John: 83
what it does
1–3 John: 85–90
World system, present (satanic)
Galatians: 6
Ephesians: 49, 74, 309
overcomers of
1–3 John: 175–76
World War I
Luke 11–17: 152
World War II
Luke 6–10: 37–38
Luke 11–17: 152
Worldliness
Matthew 1–7: 158–59, 226
Matthew 8–15: 360
Mark 1–8: 204
Romans 1–8: 316, 513
Romans 9–16: 150
1 Corinthians: 68
Ephesians: 334, 348, 367
Hebrews: 328–29

Revelation 1–11: 81–82
rejecting
Colossians & Philemon: 125–34
Worldly ambition
Matthew 16–23: 236
Worldly influence
Matthew 8–15: 243
Worldwide Church of God
Galatians: 204
Worldwide righteousness
Romans 9–16: 111
Worry (anxiety)
Matthew 1–7: 91–92, 417–27
Luke 11–17: 138–39
Luke 18–24: 256–57
absence of
Luke 11–17: 140
divine preference and
Luke 11–17: 142–43
God's provision and
Luke 11–17: 140–41
God's sovereignty and
Luke 11–17: 142
salvation and
Luke 11–17: 147–48
Worship
Matthew 1–7: 35–36, 296–98
Mark 1–8: 332, 333, 338, 339, 344, 391
Mark 9–16: 273, 275
Luke 11–17: 45, 382
Luke 18–24: 157
2 Corinthians: 284
Revelation 1–11: 155–59, 228–29
Revelation 12–22: 75, 76, 296
of angels
1 Corinthians: 235
attitude of
Luke 1–5: 78–81
of Christ
Hebrews: 29–32
components of
Luke 1–5: 76–77
of demons
1 Corinthians: 236
of emperor
Romans 1–8: 9
false
1 Corinthians: 234–36
freedom of
Romans 9–16: 208
genuine
Matthew 24–28: 135
of God
Revelation 1–11: 155
Revelation 12–22: 75, 76, 296
God's presence in
Matthew 16–23: 139
Holy Spirit and
Luke 1–5: 76
hypocritical
Matthew 8–15: 448
idolatry and
Luke 1–5: 74, 75
limitations of
Hebrews: 226–27
location of
Hebrews: 221–23
motive of
Luke 1–5: 81–83
objects of
Luke 1–5: 81, 164, 259, 307
of pagan goddess
Titus: 82
and praise
1 Peter: 26–27, 45–46, 115–16, 122, 288
self–
Romans 1–8: 92
services of
Hebrews: 224–26
true
Romans 9–16: 138
value of
Hebrews: 220–21
Wounds of Christ
1 Peter: 172–73
Wrath. *see* Anger; Judgment
Wrath of God
Mark 9–16: 302, 358
Luke 11–17: 74
1 & 2 Thessalonians: 29, 65–66, 163
Hebrews: 278, 418
1 Peter: 73, 77, 171
Revelation 12–22: 91
believers and
Revelation 12–22: 238
characteristics of
Romans 1–8: 62, 76, 201
false teaching about
Romans 1–8: 72
manifestations of
Romans 1–8: 65, 100
nature of
Romans 1–8: 66, 201
neglect of
Romans 1–8: 373
New Testament and
Romans 1–8: 61
Old Testament and
Romans 1–8: 61
present forms of
Romans 1–8: 100
reasons for deserving
Romans 1–8: 76
revelation of
Romans 1–8: 64
Wuest, Kenneth S.
Romans 1–8: 320, 363
Romans 9–16: 149
on meaning of apostellō
1 Timothy: 4
Wycliffe, John
Luke 1–5: 226–27
1 Timothy: 98

Xavier, Francis
Romans 9–16: 349
Xenophon
Luke 6–10: 73
John 12–21: 72

Yahweh (Jehovah; YHWH)
Matthew 16–23: 96, 137, 198, 305, 347, 348
Mark 1–8: 19, 225
John 1–11: 14, 184, 348
John 12–21: 262
Romans 1–8: 414
Spirit of
Romans 1–8: 414
Yam Kinneret (Sea of Galilee)
Mark 1–8: 228
Luke 6–10: 208
Yamauchi, Edwin M.
on gold refining at Sardis
Revelation 1–11: 109
on Zeus's altar at Pergamum
Revelation 1–11: 86
Yancey, Phil
Matthew 8–15: 83
YMCA, YWCA, social reforms of
Colossians & Philemon: 166
Yochelson, Samuel
Ephesians: 167
Yom Kippur
Ephesians: 22
Hebrews: 110, 247
See also Day of Atonement
Young, Edward J.
Luke 1–5: 55–56
Young man from Nain
Luke 6–10: 131–39
Young ruler
Luke 18–24: 38
Younger men, confrontation with
1 Timothy: 188
Younger women, confrontation with
1 Timothy: 189

Zaccheus
Luke 6–10: 166, 170
Luke 11–17: 128
John 1–11: 64, 287, 479
1–3 John: 243
salvation for
Luke 18–24: 68–72, 90
transformation of
Luke 18–24: 74–75
Zacharias
Mark 1–8: 30
Luke 6–10: 144, 258
John 1–11: 29, 48–49, 124, 411, 466
2 Corinthians: 110
divine punishment of
Luke 1–5: 28–29, 86
naming of John the Baptist
Luke 1–5: 90
prophecy of
Luke 1–5: 39–40
response of to angel
Luke 1–5: 27–29
righteousness of
Luke 1–5: 23–25, 31
temple service of
Luke 1–5: 26
Zacharias (John the Baptist's father)
Luke 18–24: 440, 443
Zacharias's Song of Salvation (Benedictus)
Abrahamic covenant and
Luke 1–5: 105–11
Davidic covenant and
Luke 1–5: 97–101
New covenant and
Luke 1–5: 117–23, 131
See also Covenant(s)
Zarephath
John 1–11: 388
Zeal
discipline and
Matthew 16–23: 131
evangelistic
Matthew 1–7: 113
spiritual
Matthew 8–15: 150
Zealots
Matthew 1–7: 134, 168
Mark 9–16: 186
Luke 1–5: 166, 318–19
Luke 6–10: 70, 103
Luke 11–17: 96, 255, 256
Luke 18–24: 102
John 1–11: 100, 325–26
John 12–21: 24
description of
Matthew 16–23: 328
Jewish
Romans 9–16: 210
Zealousness
1 Peter: 196–97
Zebedee
Mark 1–8: 52
Mark 9–16: 382
Luke 6–10: 41, 47
John 1–11: 6
1–3 John: 6
Zebi, Shabbethai (false messiah)
Luke 18–24: 187
Zebulun
John 1–11: 320, 332
Zechariah
Mark 9–16: 168, 388–89
Luke 6–10: 144
John 1–11: 93, 423, 427
2 Corinthians: 20, 98, 114, 325, 392, 408, 423
2 Peter & Jude: 70, 174–75
1–3 John: 97
Zechariah (prophet)
Luke 1–5: 27
Luke 11–17: 108, 211, 231
Luke 18–24: 124, 271
Zechariah son of Jehoiada
Mark 1–8: 298
Zedi, Sabethai
John 12–21: 12
Zeitgeist
Romans 9–16: 150
Zephaniah
Luke 11–17: 292–93
2 Corinthians: 241
Zerubbabel
Matthew 24–28: 20
Luke 1–5: 249

John 1–11: 93
Zeruiah
1 Peter: 157
Zeus
Mark 1–8: 374
Luke 18–24: 227
John 1–11: 439
1–3 John: 2, 242
Zeus idol
Mark 9–16: 244, 245
Zimri
Luke 6–10: 74
John 12–21: 73
Zinzendorf, Nicholaus
Romans 1–8: 57, 507
Zion
Hebrews: 413–14
1 Peter: 121
Zionism
Romans 1–8: 165
Zipporah
Luke 1–5: 89
Zoroastrianism
1 Timothy: 36
Zwingli, Ulrich
Romans 1–8: 150

The MacArthur New Testament Commentary series includes:

Matthew 1–7
Matthew 8–15
Matthew 16–23
Matthew 24–28
Mark 1–8
Mark 9–16
Luke 1–5
Luke 6–10
Luke 11–17
Luke 18–24
John 1–11
John 12–21
Acts 1–12
Acts 13–28
Romans 1–8
Romans 9–16
First Corinthians
Second Corinthians
Galatians
Ephesians
Philippians
Colossians & Philemon
First & Second Thessalonians
First Timothy
Second Timothy
Titus
Hebrews
James
First Peter
Second Peter & Jude
First–Third John
Revelation 1–11
Revelation 12–22